BLOOD AND WAR
AT MY DOORSTEP

BLOOD AND WAR AT MY DOORSTEP

North Carolina Civilians in the War Between the States

Volume I

October 2013

BRENDA CHAMBERS MCKEAN

Brenda McKean

To order additional copies of this book, contact:
Xlibris Corporation
1-888-795-4274
www.Xlibris.com
Orders@Xlibris.com
72312

Dedication

.

This book is dedicated to my late parents—
Faye Reynolds Chambers and Burl A. Chambers of Tennessee.
"They would have been proud."

CONTENTS

ILLUSTRATIONS

ACKNOWLEDGMENTS

I would like to thank all my friends and family who encouraged me to write this book and who stood by me through the end. Accolades go to my two sons, Bernie and Ryan McKean, who helped with computer glitches. Special thanks go to friends and acquaintances who loaned the use of letters, pictures, and material in alphabetical order: P. Ailliot of the CWRT France; George C. Allen; Joel Bailey; Byrd S. Barnes; Carol Banz; Byron Beale; Jennifer Bower Bean; Doris Beck; Tom Belton; Merlin Berry; Glenda Biggerstaff; Greg Biggs; Betsie Bloomer; Jennifer B. Bower; Robert Brewer, Jr.; Myrtle Bridges; Bill Briedenstine; Scott Buie; E.M. Bullard; Judy Bunch; Virginia O. Busby; Victoria Bynum; Susan Carpenter-Smith; Nadean Carter; Kent Cash, Allen Cochran; Bob Cooke; Ron A. Cook; Robert N. Cook, Jr.; Peter Cooper; Joel Craig; Tony Crumbley; Patti Daniels; Robert Doares; Ernie Dollar; Judge Robert Eades; Peter and Karen Edwards; Jean Eno, Greg Fields; Lila Ford; Jennifer Fore; Jack Fisherman; Freeman sisters and brother; Franklin Fussell; Julie H. Ganis; Lynn Gantz; Julie Garrison; Randall Garrison; Jodie Gee; Jason Goodnite; Betty Green; Tim Griggs; Ned Gulley; Belinda S. Guerette; Mary Hadley; Rachael Hake; Frances Hanes; Mary Rinck Harbinson; Edward Harding; Michael Hardy; Bill Harris, Elizabeth Harris; Derrick Hartshorn; Dr. Hubert B. Haywood, Jr.; Charles L. Heath; Louise Heun; Scott Holmes; Michael Honey; Gary Hunt; Don and Sue Humphrey; John Humphrey; Greg and Linda Humphries; Earl Ijames; Mary C. and Gertrude Jenkins; Sherri Jester; Clint Johnson; Stacy Jones; Ann Kalata; John L. Kimbrough; Sally Koestler; Denna Larson; Rebecca G. Lasley; Tommy F. Lee; Martha Marble; Betty Marsicek; Greg Mast; Kent McCoury; David McGee; John B. McGowan; Louise McKlveen; John McManus; Virginia Mescher; Sandi Miles; Scott Mingus; Bob Maffitt; Betty Monteith; Claude Moore; Kate Moore; Faye Moran; Dr. Charles Muse; Jane Nardy; Jean Newell; Brenda Normandin; Dan O'Connell; Josephine Osborne; the Page Family of Morrisville; Roy Parker; Barbara Parsons; Guy Potts; Guy Rabb; Clayta Richards; Dave Robinson; Barbara Breece Roesch; Aimee Russell; Stephen Schaufter; Patricia Schiro; Barbara Schmidt; Thomas Schroeder; Russell Scott; Lamont Sible, Jr.; Charles Silver; Elizabeth H. Smith; Tommy Smith; Skip Smith; Walt Smith; Professor Charles T. Smith; Amy Snyder; Emma Sommnerville; Jeff Stepp; Jim Taylor; Jerome Tew; Bernhard Thuersam; Brock Townsend; Clem Trotter; Scott Troutman; Jan Tyler; Ron Vinson; T.C. Wagstaff; Mary Warshaw; Charles J. Whisnant; Shirlet Whisnant; Dr. Mary Wilson; Thad Wiseman; Jennifer Wisener; Windflash.com; Pam Wood; Richard B. Wood; Kenneth Wooster; Kent Wrench; Maury York; the Tar Heel Civilians; the 26th NCT Re-activated along with the Soldiers' Benevolent Society; and three anonymous donors of material.

Without the help of the Person County Library, I would have floundered. Interlibrary loan was a God-send. Thanks also to the staff at UNC, Wilson Library; Duke University Manuscripts Department; the North Carolina Department of Archives and History; UNC Wilmington; the Joyner Library at East Carolina University; UNCA, Special Collections; Friends Historical Collections at Guilford College; Appalachian State University; Salem University; Historic Jamestown Society; N.C. State Library; Camp Chase Gazette Magazine; Virginia Military Institute Archives; Western Carolina University—Hunter Library; Wake Forest University; East Tennessee State University; The University of Georgia; The Museum of the Cape Fear in Fayetteville; Museum of the Albemarle; Bentonville State Historic Site; the Bennett Place State Historic Site and the Averasboro Battleground Commission; Carteret County Historical Society; Lower Cape Fear Historical Society; Molly Averitt at St. Mary's School, North and South Carolina Division of the United Daughters of the Confederacy; and local libraries throughout the state.

INTRODUCTION

Delving into North Carolina's history on women during the War of Northern Aggression, I noticed that something was missing—the story of the civilians left at home during the conflict. Very little information has been published on this topic. Wanting to alleviate the matter, a trip to the state archives turned up nothing on organizations such as the Soldiers' Relief Society or Ladies' Aid Society. Instead, the files contained information on organizations postwar. One can get a glimpse of these women from books by Mary Elizabeth Massey, Kathleen Smith, or Drew F. Smith.

The book *North Carolina Women of the Confederacy*, published in 1929 by Lucy Anderson, left me thirsting for more. The small book of one-hundred-plus pages was not documented. I wanted dates, places, and details. I thought it was time to correct the situation; however, there is so much information available now that it would take me two lifetimes to record everything I thought was necessary. This book tells only a part.

At first, I was only going to write about North Carolina Confederate women; but in doing the research, I found that I could not leave out other women (and men) regardless of their allegiance. I tried to stay away from pure military matters since so much has been written about it, but the constant involvement with the military and militia was intertwined with the civilians. Interaction with the local forces led me to include their stories. I tried to avoid politics, but again, those instances popped up.

There is a chapter on slaves and free blacks. These unfortunate people were involved in many different ways with the war, and I found out that some Negroes did not have it as bad as modern scholars would have us to believe. The twenty-first-century populace does not understand the bond between those blacks and whites. Those who were treated well give positive memories. Those abused tell horrendous stories. Both sides need to be recorded.

Patriotic times spawn music and poetry. I have included a few written by North Carolina civilians.

Whenever possible, I used the person's name and location for genealogical purposes. Communities and individuals donated articles for the war effort. Newspaper editors printed the names and articles of these women in their papers. This was entirely new for the Victorian times. In the past, the only time a lady's name appeared in the newspaper was to announce her engagement, wedding, or death. In wartimes, the name was printed along with the article the person donated to encourage other women to see what their peers had done so as to foster patriotic fever; however, this was not the only reason. These newspapers have helped the genealogists tracing the female line.

This book is not solely on Southern people. When Northern people of both sexes interacted with North Carolinians and it was a good story, I included it. I could not leave out information left by Northern soldiers as they controlled the eastern part of the state. When Yankee troops entered the mountains from Tennessee, another chapter was written on their forays, skirmishes, and involvement with the civilians.

The names of towns in North Carolina are used without the comma, then NC. All towns from out of state are marked as such. Assume the name of the town to be in North Carolina if there is no state following it. The town of Washington in this book is the one from North Carolina. Washington DC is entered as Washington City, the way it was during the wartimes.

The English language utilized throughout this period was a tad different than what we use today. For instance, "the cars" refer to railroad cars; "go flying or flying around" refer to someone dating or "sparking." "Skedaddled" means to run away. "Shirker" is a soldier who tries to get out of duty for different reasons—such as the one who would insist on staying in the hospital long past his time. "Defense" was spelled "defence" at times in both newspapers and letters. Some words used then are not recognized on the computer. Many letters used the ampersand either by itself or with the small letter c next to it as in "&c" instead of "etc."

Politically correct phrases will not be used in this book. Those names didn't exist in the nineteenth century and would look out of place in this text. The N-word is used in its context. Personally, I would never use the word and don't condone it; but in historical writings, it was commonly used and was not necessarily condescending.

North Carolinians would spell cities differently such as New Bern, Newbern, New Berne, Goldsborough, Goldsboro, Tarborough, Tarboro, etc. At other times, the writer would spell a person's name differently in the same letter. The use of capital letters and punctuation was misused quite frequently. Victorian newspapers printed too many words and commas, and they misused capital letters. In the poorly educated writers, sentences ran together without using a period or comma, making the letters hard to read. Most of the common folk spelled phonetically which was hard to decipher. Letters in this book are kept as pure as possible unless they cannot be read easily. For those most difficult, I have rewritten it to better understand, and it will be indicated when this happens. Minimum change was desired. I did add some words in brackets for clarity when I thought the writer left it out.

Federal officers will be identified by preceding their name with "Federal" or "Union" except for General Grant, General Burnside, and General Sherman. All Confederate officers are assumed to be such by the simple way of saying Col., Gen. Lee, Major, etc. To make it easier for research, an appendix and index are used to list names of women, free blacks, and others for genealogical purposes.

Famous women such as Rose Greenhow, Mrs. Mary Custis Lee, Mrs. Anna Jackson, Varina Davis, Belle Boyd, and Harriet Jacobs will not be discussed in length because so much has been written about them even though they have a North Carolina connection. Several Northern women are mentioned because of their interaction with the locals.

I want to bring the war to your door, the way the civilians had to deal with it, in their own words; hence, you will read again and again about people's homes being burned, crops and livestock destroyed, murders, revenge killings, homes used as hospitals, devastation, etc. I was surprised to learn of so many murders. It took away the romantic, flowery legend of the war. The beginning of the war was the romantic part with flags given to young officers, speeches, farewells, and promises made to defend to the last the fair maidens and mothers at home. After a year had gone by, reality set in caused by shortages due to the blockade. Young men were dying of disease and injuries. Military news and death notices appeared daily in the newspapers while civilians sat in the taverns, reading aloud. Poorer women gathered at the post office, awaiting the posting of the latest announcements to see if their loved one was alive or dead. Tears flowed in rivulets. Slaves in town on errands took the formidable news back to the plantations. As the war progressed, the tone of letters to the soldiers changed. No longer were they full of enthusiasm for the "cause," but instead, the letters contained doubt as to whether the state should not talk about peace instead. Governor Vance insisted that the state furnish accoutrements and foodstuffs to its troops, putting a heavy burden on the women to fill in the gaps left by state contractors. However, not *all* people felt this way. There were many who never doubted for one minute that the South would fall. I am in no way belittling the sacrifice of the North Carolina civilians in this great tragedy.

I found many heroes, and I found some despicable scalawags. Too many people died unnecessarily in this war; that's why their story should be told.

I apologize to the readers whose ancestors are not mentioned. There just wasn't enough time to include everybody. I apologize to the readers whose ancestors may have been shady characters. Such is history. I apologize to the readers for insisting upon naming people, places, and dates. That was important to me because the war covered four years, and each one was different.

This book will be the most comprehensive work on North Carolina women to date. Please read both volumes for the complete research. I would also like to encourage the readers to help with the preservation of historic sites and to record the history of their families for future generations.

It aught never to be that the past is the parent of the present.
—John C. Calhoun, 1848

CHAPTER ONE
Fanatics and Fire-eaters

The war is on everyone's lips.

North Carolinians were divided in sentiment over whether to secede or stay in the old Union. W. W. Holden, editor of the *Raleigh Standard*, said to "watch and wait" after Abraham Lincoln won the election.[1] Reaction of the Northern people to John Brown's raid led to a renewal of patriotism in the South. Several counties had formed militia units before the South seceded.[2] As early as July 1860, a meeting held in Goldsboro to petition the legislature to organize the militia came about after hearing rumors of South Carolina's impending secession. Goldsboro, a railroad hub, was the layover place for members of the Charleston Secession Convention that summer of 1860.

Writing about the assembly later, Council Wooten wrote that a lawyer from Wayne County, Mr. E. A. Thompson, "uttered one remark that I will never forget." In speaking of the election of Lincoln, he said it would be a disgrace for the South to submit to him. He declared, "I am no fire-eater but I can swallow hot coals of fire as palatable as I can disgrace . . ."[3]

Throughout the state, people voiced different feelings. Caroline Eliza Clitherall penned in her diary on November 6, 1860: "The Presidential Election, in favor of Lincoln, has created great excitement . . . has not Our heavenly Father told us to call upon him that our faith may not fail us."[4] A man from Rockingham County was quoted as saying, "If Lincoln is elected, I do not consider that my property is worth one cent."[5]

"Dr. John Bellamy at his own expense purchased all the tar barrels procurable in Wilmington . . . and headed a great torchlight procession celebrating the event" of South Carolina's secession that December 1860.[6] Older citizens in Wilmington appeared devoted to the Union. The city was divided until Mr. George Davis returned from the failed peace conference in Washington City and spoke to the congregation at Thalian Hall. He said the news brought profound silence.[7] Before the formal secession, citizens thought that the Northern fanatics living in the state might attempt to reenforce the forts along the coast. A "committee of safety" quickly formed to call for volunteers to enlist for service. John Hedrick was elected leader, and this was the group of men that overtook Fort Caswell and Fort Johnson at the mouth of the Cape Fear River on January 10.[8] The *Richmond Daily Dispatch* reported that "the Secession flag, with fifteen stars, was raised here [Wilmington] today by a large and enthusiastic gathering of people. A second meeting was held tonight at the theatre, which was densely crowded. The secession feeling is increasing daily."[9] A similar militia group developed near Morehead City to take Fort Macon. In writing his memories, James Sprunt recalled:

> Men too old for service in the field formed a cavalry company . . . for home defense, and one company of quite elderly gentlemen was known as the "Horse-and-Buggy Company" and though they did not drill, they held themselves in readiness . . . . These men did assist in the equipment of companies sent to the field, and many of them aided and supported, during the whole of the war, families of men in the service.[10]

Persons with Union flavors in Rutherford and Polk counties held meetings after Christmas and said, "It would be unwise and suicidal to the best interests of North Carolina to secede from the Union for any cause now existing." At least six highland counties in December and January met to denounce their neighbors who were in favor of secession.[11] John W. Stockard recalled that Judge Thomas Ruffin, at a barbeque on the plantation, held up his white handkerchief and told those assembled there that his handkerchief could hold *all* the blood "that is to be spilled in this War" as an inducement to volunteer. Stockard, along with other young men, immediately signed up to fight. The Stockard family did not own slaves. Stockard's kin said he was making a mistake.[12]

One woman said she intended to leave the state if North Carolina seceded, but she later relented. "We have some fears that this Union will be dissolved. South Carolina has seceded, the states are making every preparation for War [.] Next Friday is the day set aside for prayer and fasting by President Buchanan, that God would save us from Civil War and blood guiltiness," said Mary Bethall, mother of several sons of military age, who was in agony about future events.[13]

In Halifax County at Looking Glass Plantation, Catherine Edmondston started a diary, writing on January 9 about their trip to Charleston. She and her husband, Patrick, had witnessed the shelling of Fort Moultrie by a Federal steamer. She called it the *Star of the West* sent to reenforce U.S. Major Robert Anderson at Fort Sumter. Catherine, a vehement secessionist, said that President James Buchanan had lied about reenforcing the fort. Mrs. Edmondston and her family were at opposite ends concerning secession as were other North Carolinians. Her sister Fanny and her mother were against it. Fanny replied, "This glorious Union, broken up for the sake of a few negroes! Rather let them go than destroy the Union. This is to me treason against liberty."

Catherine answered, "In the first place, it is not a few negroes. It is the country, for I should like to know who could live here were they freed?" A few days later, she would write, "It gets almost painful to go to Father's we differ so widely. Mother and Susan [another sister] do go on so about the 'flag' [U.S.]." Her father was upset with the South Carolinians for seceding. Susan would not relent until late May when she came around and asked her sister if she could help them sew uniforms.[14]

Sallie Lenoir, after hearing of Lincoln's election, stated, "I dread the dark future. If the South would only keep cool and try him first I think we need not fear much but I cannot hope that."

Thomas I. Lenoir, her brother-in-law, from Haywood County said, "This aggressive policy of the Black Republicans will sometime, if they do not now, drive us from a Union once so dear but now so little respected."[15]

One North Carolinian who had grown tired of all the secession talk quipped, "For God's sake! Let South Carolina nullify, revolute, secede, and be *damned!*"[16] The editor of the *Raleigh Register* gave his opinion:

> If we do not prevent the Yankees from getting possession of our country, our church edifices, will be of little use to us, as their pulpits will be occupied by puritanical, crop-eared Yankee Abolition parsons, who will teach blasphemy through their noses and compel us to pay for it.[17]

A judge from Martin County felt strong emotions:

> How any Southerner, not deprived of his manhood, and spirit of freedom, can be willing to submit to the insolent foe who demands our subjugation at his feet, with his heel in our faces, the confiscation of all our property, with the ignominious and debased condition of becoming the slaves of slaves—is to me distressingly painful and amazing![18]

Jonathan Worth, a former Quaker, said, "The voice of reason is silenced. Furious passion and thirst for blood consume the air. Nobody is allowed to retain or assert his reason."[19] Some had given up trying to convert their neighbors.

Goldsboro's militia petitioned town officials for money to gather equipment during the beginning of January 1861. The state had sent them rifles without ammunition. Volunteers stepped forward and began training. In April, farmers and citizens crowded the telegraph office, spilling out into the streets, waiting for news about the firing on Fort Sumter, South

Carolina. Since New Bern had no telegraph, people there chartered a train to Goldsboro to seek this information.[20]

Diarist Elizabeth Wiggins from Halifax County wrote on January 15, 1861: "What will become of our poor distracted country?"[21] She had every reason to be concerned. Before the war was over, Elizabeth would have seven sons to join in the fray. Two were killed. The youngest son, Eugene, ran away from his boarding school and joined the army at fourteen. He was reported to be a wounded veteran at age fifteen.

North Carolina sent five delegates to the Washington Peace Conference in February 1861. Edmondston commented that she "would not have such a Peace as they are negotiating, rather patching up."[22] At Montgomery, Alabama, representatives met on February 4 to set up rules for a new government of the Confederate States. In Washington City, those Southern men holding offices in Congress or the military had a decision to make—whether to choose the North or the South filled them with anxiety as never before. Many sought their homelands. Asa Biggs from Martin County chose to go home:

Williamston, N. C., April 23 1861.

To Abraham Lincoln,
President of the United States.
    Sir:—I hereby resign my office of District Judge of the United States for the District of North Carolina, being unwilling longer to hold a commission in a Government which has degenerated into a military despotism. I subscribe myself yet a friend of constitutional liberty.
    Asa Biggs[23]

Emotions intermingled with vexation and jubilation. While some thought it to be an "air of uncertainty," young men saw it with a sense of excitement. The residents of Bertie County sought a "wait and see" attitude before the state decided to hold a convention for secession; others had a depressing attitude of "impending doom" from the start. Of those who kept diaries, girls stated that they would have a "normal life no longer."[24] Sallie Person shared her thoughts with a friend:

Some predict "civil war" is inevitable while others say there will be a peaceful cession of the Southern States from the Union. At all events there is bound to be some step taken & let come what [,] well sooner the better. Such a state of affairs should not exist.[25]

Rumors from the North told of President Lincoln's move to garrison Federal troops at the forts along the coast. Previously mentioned, the local militia, who captured the forts along the beach, was ordered by Governor John Ellis to return the garrisons back to the United States. He felt the impetuous men had jumped the gun. North Carolinians had not yet decided to hold a convention for secession.[26] "Lincoln believed—that a majority of the citizens in each Southern state except South Carolina were still loyal to the Union . . ." He thought they would assist his troops to squash the rebellion.[27] This was why he wrote to each Southern state asking for seventy-five thousand troops to put down the rebellious South Carolinians.

Men who had been pro-Union until Lincoln's call then turned secessionists. President Lincoln's letters to the states calling for troops actually unified the Southern people. Taking up her pen, Catherine Edmondston wrote, "Never was known such excitement as was caused by Mr. Lincoln's proclamation. The whole South flew to arms!"[28] Immediately, Southern states began to leave the Union. Civilians in the Piedmont expressed their views too:

Whereas, we, the people of the counties of Wayne and Duplin, have seen a proclamation from the black republican president, Abraham Lincoln, calling for seventy-five thousand men . . . for the purpose of subjugating our

Southern brethren of the Confederate States, who are asking nothing but for their rights to be respected and their institutions let alone, the interest of North Carolina being identified with the said Confederate States, we . . . deem it highly necessary to express our views to the world, irrespective of former party ties; therefore

Resolved, That the example of our patriotic forefathers is too plainly set before us to be unmindful of our duty. We know the cause of the Confederate States to be the supreme interest of North Carolina; therefore, we pledge our fortunes, our lives, and our most scared honors in the maintenance of the said cause.

Resolved, That, for the aid and furtherance of said cause and the defense of our homes and our rights, we will form a military company for the purpose of drilling that we may be the better prepared to defend our homes and our country.

Resolved, That we call upon all good citizens to sustain us and give us their aid for the support of our company.

Resolved, That the manly and patriotic courage of His Excellency, John W. Ellis, in ordering our forts taken and held by troops of this State, and his independent denial of troops to Abe Lincoln to sustain him in his diabolical policy, meets the entire approbation of this company and this community.[29]

In Bladen County, Elizabeth Robeson inscribed in her diary on March 1:

How the fate of the nation may be determined is for wise men to say, but we should put our trust in Him . . . . We should invoke his blessing on us as a nation to avert the impending calamity and not put our trust in a set of feeble men.[30]

She was the sixty-three-year-old widow of Samuel Robeson and had nine children, all of whom died while very young, except for four sons. Two of her sons served in the Confederate Army. R. H. Wills of Plymouth, in a letter to his father on March 1, replied, "I understand that some (or at least one) of the Union men are now secessionists. I listened to a secession argument this morning." Writing his brother on April 18, he said his feelings for the Union "are poor indeed."[31] A resident near Asheville sent a letter to the editor of a newspaper with his comments concerning secession:

As far as we know the sentiment of the people of this section . . . are in favor of a perpetual non-intercourse with the North. If they had their choice they would never again buy a dollar's worth of goods in any Northern state . . . . If this be so, and it is, is not the Union already virtually dissolved? Why continue it any longer, if we can only remain in it with arms in our hands.[32]

The scholar Boykin confirmed that "as the Civil War approached, four distinct groups were perceptible in North Carolina. To the extreme right and the extreme left were the ardent pro-slavery, pro-southern, and pro-secessionist faction, and the ardent pro-Unionist. In the center was the more moderate pro-slavery and pro-southern faction, which loved North Carolina and the South but which was nonetheless anti-secessionist. The fourth was formed of neutrals."[33] In Buncombe County, secessionist David Coleman wound up almost tarred and feathered for his views when he went into Madison County to see who held his beliefs.[34]

North Carolina began preparing for war while citizens were arguing for or against secession. Simultaneous meetings were held throughout different sections of the state and counties both for and against a convention to leave the Union. When the votes were counted that February 28, the majority had voted not to secede. Failure of the peace conference to Washington City and the election of Lincoln as president caused some folks to change their mind in favor of separating.[35] President Lincoln's blockade of Virginia's and North Carolina's ports at the end of April persuaded the borderline voters. The second vote passed, and the state seceded on May 20, 1861.

> With brave hearts they bade us good-bye,
> With never a quiver of the love-filled eye,
> To hastily seek sweet privacy and cry
> The tears their heroes must not descry.[36]

Elizabeth Wiggins wrote:

> I heard this evening that Fort Sumter had been taken, God be merciful to erring humanity. What trials there is in for hearts at home God only knows. God have mercy on erring creatures. This breaking up of families is so trying . . . with little hope we shall never see each others faces in the flesh again.

In early April, her sons left for military duty. On April 26, she said, "I am called upon to part with Alfred [only son left at home] this morning, not knowing if we shall ever meet again." Seven would serve before war's end.

The same day, Elizabeth Robeson said, "The whole topic of conversation was about the distressing state of the country. I am heart sick. I know not what to do."

R. N. Lenoir recorded in a letter on April 12 to his Aunt Sade, "I have hoped and believed that we would be allowed to depart in peace from the old Union, but so many are desponding [sic] and the news every day seems to be against peace . . ."[37]

In another part of the state, Sallie Person echoed, "What a dreadful time it is to think that the people of the United States is about to be in war with each other. It will be brother against brother."[38]

One unhappy person, Mr. William L. Robinson of Taylors Bridge, sent his resignation to the governor with these words:

> I hereby resign my office as one of the JUSTICES of Peace for Sampson County. As for my reason's for doing, JUSTICE is hard to obtain & PEACE seems to have fled the land.[39]

On April 15, Governor John Ellis wired Captain Craton to take possession of Fort Macon and Fort Caswell since the war had started, but North Carolina had not yet seceded. About this time, a famous correspondent with the *London Times* was passing through Goldsboro. William Howard Russell jotted down what he saw:

> . . . the wave of Secession tide struck us in full career. The station, the hotels, the streets through which the rail ran was filled with an excited mob, all carrying arms, with signs here and there of a desire to get up some kind of uniform—flushed faces, wild eyes, screaming mouths, hurrahing for "Jeff Davis" and "the Southern Confederacy," so that the yells overpowered the discordant bands which were busy with "*Dixie Land.*" Here was true revolutionary furor in full sway. The men hectored, swore, cheered, and slapped each other on the backs; the women in their best, waved handkerchiefs and flung down garlands from windows. All was noise, dust, and patriotism.[40]

One student at the Goldsboro Female College, Mary Hinton Carraway, inscribed in her diary the importance of April 13: "The ball is opened. War has commenced . . . . Oh the horror of civil war. The gentlemen of Goldsboro are collecting funds to provision Fort Macon ere they take possession . . ." Four thousand dollars was quickly raised. Two days later, she would pen:

> . . . father came in . . . and offered to take me to Goldsboro to see the military off for Beaufort. We arrived there about two . . . the volunteers left amid the cheering of the crowd . . . the waving of handkerchiefs and good wishes of the Ladies. One Anderson Deans came near being hanged for some treasonable remark concerning Jeff Davis but owing to Mrs. Richard Washington his life was saved. Everything in the greatest excitement . . .

Ms. Carraway said that her cousin Martha Best told her that the speeches were made, that bells tolled, and that Lincoln was hung in effigy. Her cousin also related that the unionists were turning into secessionists, and the ladies were meeting to sew mattresses while the young women at the college had started a silk flag.[41]

The *Carolina Watchman*, a Salisbury newspaper, printed on April 23, 1861:

> . . . how emotionally wrenching women would find the experience ahead of them but it laid out a theme that would be echoed throughout the mountains in the months to come.
>
> The millions of weeping mothers, wives, and sisters, and the millions of prayers going up from hearts burdened with grief, will not restrain the voluntary human offerings which are to be made in defense of our rights and honors, but rather increase them, and nerve them for conflict.

Mary Ann Hill sent this letter to her son, Joshua:

> It gives me comfort this far to see that you have acted like an honourable gentleman for your Country, are even willing to die in defense of it. But Oh! How near and dear are you to my weeping heart. I will try to keep my eyes dry long enough to write . . .[42]

In the piedmont, women like Mrs. Frances Timberlake must have been looking to the future when she decided to write the governor:

> I seat myself to drop you a few lines to beg you to let Francis B. Timberlake off [.] I am a widow and living in a house buy my self and you will do me a great favor if you will let him off [.] I beg you with all the Semethy [sympathy] that is in my Power [.] I wosh to do right if I knew how [.] I hope that you will have compassion on me [.] I am gitting old and I have bin left a widow and have rase my children and have see a great trouble [.] I hope dear Sir that you will have compassion on me and let him off [.] Please direct your letter to Roxboro[*43]

Elizabeth Flowers of Fayetteville mailed this letter to Governor Ellis in June:

> . . . my husband enlisted and forced a son of mine that is only fifteen years . . . . This boy has been delicate in health and is now verry weak, he is hardly able to shoulder a muskit, I am doubtful of his being able to stand the fatigue . . . I am a poor woman . . . low in health myself, I wish . . . to beg you . . .

---

*   On the back of this letter are the following instructions from Ellis to his secretary: "Speak kindly to her and say her son will not be long absent. That all must fight our battles."

to discharge my little Son James Everit Flowers . . . . Sir if you was to see him I think you would discharge him. Your unknown friend.[*44]

In April of 1861, the adjutant general called for thirty thousand volunteers by order of Governor Ellis. The General Assembly passed the resolution. North Carolina had not yet seceded at this point. After Governor Ellis received the letter from Lincoln requesting North Carolina to send troops, those without any doubt of loyalty chose the Confederacy while those who were reluctant changed their minds, going with the secessionists. The governor wrote Lincoln the now famous lines, "You can get no troops from North Carolina."[45] He then sent word to the militia to retake Fort Caswell, Fort Johnson, Fort Macon, the Arsenal in Fayetteville, and the Charlotte Mint. In addition, he had the lens removed from the lighthouses. Numerous folks attributed Lincoln's act as drawing the state together. "Abe's proclamation in a twinkle, Stirred up the blood of Rip Van Winkle" posted the newspaper.[46]

Before secession, Rocky Mount citizens raised a large lone star flag while fifteen cannons fired.[47] The county of Rockingham voted to support families of soldiers and gave twenty-five thousand dollars to outfit the volunteers.[48] The *Weekly State Journal* reported that the flag of the Confederacy was run up on the state capitol.[49] A small contingent of Union men planned to raise the U. S. flag at the old Alamance Regulator Battleground. Letters were sent to certain individuals to ask them to attend.[50]

Patriotic individuals were sporting secession badges on their lapels or their bonnets. Described as folded blue ribbons, some badges were red, white, and blue ribbons. Others wore a flower posy called a Southern badge, which consisted of a cluster of hyacinths and arborvitae tied with red/white/blue ribbons.[51] Other men preferred a rosette of pinecones. Both men and women wore the blue cockades during secession in Rockingham County.[52] Schoolgirls at the Wesleyan Female College placed small paper Confederate flags in their hair and around their throats.[53] Carrie Fries, a teacher at Salem Academy, told of a student who wore an apron colored like the Confederate flag, only her apron had twelve yellow stars in a circle. "She works for thee soldiers in every spare moment she has."[54] Kate Curtis, a student at St. Mary's School, observed three secession flags hanging on the gate to the school in Raleigh.[55]

At the Select Boarding and Day School in Hillsborough, student Harriet Cobb, along with her friends, raised a Confederate flag over the courthouse. "The Nash and Kollock girls sang their songs with fervor . . ."[56]

Annie Darden was making a quilt. She said, "I have finished all the squares for my quilt. I think I shall call it a disunion quilt as it will be made different from any I ever saw."[57]

W. S. Ashe of Branchville wrote to Governor Ellis on April 24, 1861, to tell him that "the boys are eager for a foray."[58] The proclivity to sign up for the military turned into a feeding frenzy. Young men of all colors began volunteering with gusto. None expected the war to last more than three months. Some voiced fear that the war would be over before they had a chance to fight. Both blacks and whites wanted to sign up. The Salem *People's Press* told of fifteen freemen of color that left Salisbury to go to Wilmington to offer their services to the state. Each man wore a hat with a small notice tucked in the hatband that read, "We will die for the South." These Negroes from Hillsborough called themselves the Orange Blacks.[**60]

At Cape Hatteras, L. D. Starke also wrote to the governor, "To-day one hundred and forty free negro laborers arrived, and were immediately put to work throwing up sand."[61]

T. J. Minns of Fayetteville, while in New Bern, wrote Governor Ellis: "Fifteen or twenty negroes came forward and volunteered their services as laborers or in defense of the city."[62]

Ellen Mitchell of Rutherford gave a speech to the departing new recruits:

---

*   Both were in the Third Regiment and killed at Gettysburg.
**   Hillsborough was in Orange County.

> We should never leave the Union on account of South Carolina. We should not follow the example of such a domineering State. If we have to leave the Union, we should not be dragged out by a State whose citizens consider themselves our superiors in every respect. They would want to lead us continually, and we could not get along in peace with them five years. For example think how they shaved North Carolina money, when it was really as good as their own; and yet we are her sister State, and called by the same name. The ladies feel proud of the Sunny South, proud of the Old North State, but prouder still of this glorious mountain county whose sons, at the first sound of the tocsin of war, have rushed to the standard of our insulted country . . .[63]

Hundreds of college students left school to join with other young men from the community. Judge Asa Biggs contended:

> In April 1861 my son William, then about 18 years old, and in his Junior year, was at school at the University of North Carolina at Chapel Hill. Before the secession of the State, he applied to me for permission to join a company who proposed to tender its services to Prest. Davis. I declined to give my consent, advising him to apply himself diligently to his studies, as he might soon be deprived of any further educational advantages, a matter of vast importance to him. The students however became so much excited, that college exercises were partially suspended, and he ventured to visit home. He reached there in the morning . . . when we were engaged in forming the volunteer companies in the County. He remained in the house but a few minutes, and asked my permission to attach himself to one of the companies, which I promptly granted.

William was "elected 3d Lieut. of Capt. Lamb's company of 12 months Volunteers, called the Roanoke Guards, and started with that company to Cape Hatteras on 20th May. It is remarkable, they carried no guns, no intrenching tools, and for weeks were stationed on the bald sea beach without any means of defence. In August 1861, the garrison at Fort Hatteras were captured by the enemy, carried as prisoners to New York, and from thence to Fort Warren in Boston harbor, and were kept for 8 months before they were exchanged."[64] Perhaps these same young men were the ones described by the enemy as having on civilian clothes, not uniforms.

When Louis Leon joined the Charlotte Grays that boarded the train for Raleigh in April, he said that at every station, the ladies met them with flowers and good wishes. As the troops trained in the Garysburg and Weldon areas, women provided food to them as long as the food held out.[65] Leon's description of Camp Ellis: "Lo and behold! Horse stables with straw for bedding is what we got. I know we all thought it a disgrace for us to sleep in such places with our fine uniforms—not even a washstand, or any place to hang our clothes on. They didn't even give us a looking-glass." That was written April 25, 1861.[66] North Carolina at this point was still a part of the United States.

Captain Richard P. Paddison recalled that when the war first broke, his comrades went on the train to Wilmington. They objected when told they had to sleep in the Negro jail overnight. A judge paid for accommodations elsewhere, and the young men "had a hot time in the old town that night." The next morning, the crew ended up at Fort Johnston.[67] A sixteen-year-old recruit recalled:

> From Statesville to Wilmington the wildest and most intense enthusiasm greeted us at every point. The waving of handkerchiefs, the smiles of ladies, the throwing of bouquets and the continuous cheering made the scene a grand ovation all along the route, and was well calculated to inspire us with unbounded enthusiasm.[68]

Five days before the state's secession, "the young volunteers met at the courthouse which was then in the center of the square at Albemarle. Uniforms had been made, using the sewing machine of Mr. McCain . . . . It was said that this was the only sewing machine in the county at that time. Dressed in their uniforms and with two fifes and a drum, they marched from the courthouse to the Marshall Hotel on the square. Louisa T. Hearne appeared on the balcony . . . and sang . . . *The Old North State* . . . . The people cheered and threw their hats into the air as the soldiers started their 30 mile walk to Salisbury. Since Bob Carter was the first volunteer, he was chosen to carry the flag to Salisbury. They left on the night train . . . to Raleigh where they went in training at Camp Ellis."[69]

After South Carolina troops captured Fort Sumter, Mrs. Edmondston wrote in her diary, "We are really at War!" At home, young men were inspired to join companies for the conflict. On May 13, in her diary, Elizabeth Robeson inscribed:

> A long day to be remembered by me and many other sorrowing mothers. Our sons have left us, we know not when (if ever) they will return. We can only commend or commit them to the care of our Heavenly Father . . . . Not that I would not want them to fight for their country but I sincerely hope that with Divine assistance all grievances may be settled without any bloodshed.

That same day, Mary Bethall recounted in her diary:

> All day after my dear son Willie left my soul was over whelmed with sorrow, my heart seems almost to bled. The thought of a bloody war is awful to contemplate.

Mrs. Ruben Jones of Robeson County said to her husband, "I know how to live as the widow of a brave man, but I do not know how to live as the wife of a coward." All *eleven* of her sons volunteered within a week.

In Gaston County, Mrs. McLean told her son, "God knows I need you but your state now needs you worse than I do."

Aunt Abby House, the colorful personality of Franklin County, said of her nephews:

> I can tell you that not a man of my family would I let stay at home in peace if he was able to tote a musket. I said to them, boys all 'er you go along to the field whar you belongs, and if any of you gits sick or is wounded, you may depend on your old Aunt Abby to nuss and to tend you. For so help me God if one of you gits down and I cant git to you no other way, I'll foot it to your bedsides; and if any one of you dies or gets killed, I promise to bring you home and bury you with yor kin.[70]

Kemp Plummer Battle, among the citizens gathered on the capitol square for the results of the secession convention, said that Congressman Zebulon Vance (later governor) began a speech, "Fellow citizens, I died last night a Union man. I am resurrected today a Secession man."[71] It was a festive day filled with excitement as Colonel Stephen Ramseur's artillery fired a one hundred gun salute. Women were waving their handkerchiefs as the crowd cheered.

David Whiting, though a boy of eight at the time, remembered it well. He said the cannon's booms broke all of the windows downtown. Throughout town, all the church bells were tolling as he held his ears.*[72] Down East, the Wilmington Horse Artillery

---

* A funny incident happened at this event. See chapter 23.

fired a salute when the state seceded.[73] One man wrote to his daughter: "Yesterday, all was quiet, peace, and happiness; today, terror, excitement and confusion."[74]

Jubilation continued throughout the state. In Chatham County, the Beavers brothers rushed into church with the good news of secession. It broke up the service, and the congregation didn't take it lightly. James and George Beavers were excommunicated from Mount Pisgah Baptist Church for their rowdiness. The young men in the congregation joined up with the Cedar Fork Rifles.[75] In a letter to her sweetheart in Richmond, Cornelia McGimsey from Burke County, wrote: "You said that every body was alive with excitement in Richmond [,] so they are here, some are almost frantic, I never hear anything but war mentioned . . ."[76]

A cousin of the Mangums in a letter dated May 29 told of how good the boys looked in their uniforms. "My friends up here have all volunteered," she said.[77]

"The Volunteers marched in church with their uniforms. It was a solemn sight to see my neighbors' children prepared for battle, sitting in the church of God, perhaps for the last time, to hear the gospel preached . . . ," wrote Annie Darden.[78]

The Lenoir sisters said that they had been busy sewing for the soldiers and did not think that "this time last year of our making military suits." They continued:

> Bro' John [Tillinghast] got home last week, the Seminary broke up for they were kept in such an excited state that study was almost impossible there. Fayetteville has never seen such a May day before . . . men tearing themselves from their wives and children . . . presenting them with some elegant flowers from the ladies as a last token of the farm . . . . Isn't it sad to think how many such partings are taking place all over our land . . .[79]

Melinda Ray, a neighbor of the above family, inscribed in her diary:

> August 12, 1861, Ma & sister & Mrs. Tillinghast's people have been busy all day making coats for the cavalry. They are getting up a box and subscriptions to send to the hospital at Yorktown. All the girls are in a mighty humor of knitting socks for the soldiers.[80]

In Fayetteville, Louis Tillinghast sent a letter to his kin, Mame:

> I consider myself now fully posted in regard to all preparations necessary for a military company . . . uniforms . . . haversacks, canteens, tents & all. The ladies have been exceedingly busy sewing for the companies here . . . We have had a trying and crying time yesterday when the Lafayette Light Infantry left for Raleigh, destined for Washington citty [sic] . . . . Judge Shepard made a short address to them as they stood drawn up on the [shore] . . . . I never saw such a shaking of hands—so many goodbyes & God bless you's to be said . . . the band was playing . . . tears streamed from the eyes of men and soldiers as well as the women and children as they waved their last adieus . . . . There are two ladies in town whose husbands are in the northern Army . . . one sends to his wife saying how much he . . . missed her, but says they are coming down here to cut all our throats as soon as possible, determined to bring the South to its knees if it takes twenty years. She folds up the letter and writes on the back "I want no more of such love neither do I send anymore of mine."[81]

Mary Brown of Davidson wrote a poem, which was widely carried in the newspapers, on May 4, 1861:

NORTH CAROLINA A CALL TO ARMS

Ye sons of Carolina awake from your dreaming,
The minions of Lincoln upon us are streaming,
I wait not for argument call or permission,
To meet at the onset this treacherous invasion,
Defend the Old North State forever.

O think of the maidens, the wives and the mothers,
Fly ye to the rescue sons, husbands, and brothers,
And sink in oblivion all purity and sections,
Your hearthstones are looking to you for protection
Defend, Defend the Old North State forever.

Their name stands the foremost in liberties story,
Round the flag of the South. Oh in thousands now rally,
For the hours departed when freeman may sully,
Your all is at stake then go forth and God speed you,
Onward to victory and glory.[82]

A very similar poem was published anonymously by a person signing the name of Luola in a book about North Carolina songs in 1861. For that and some missing verses from the above poem, see the appendix, chapter 1, #A.

With poems such as these read by the young women to the enthusiastic recruits, how could a man refuse to join? "Male hesitation in the face of such preeminent danger was unthinkable," penned a citizen.[83] The act of volunteering was a personal matter, but when neighbors joined up and a man didn't follow, everyone looked at him with a suspicious eye. Was he of unionist flavor? Was he a coward? Didn't he love the South? Surely if he did, he would sign up. These attitudes spilled over to the wife. Friends in the community gossiped at sewing circles and quilting bees. What was wrong with her husband? Why hadn't he gone yet? Is he a Black Republican? Doesn't he care enough to protect his family from the Northern rogues? A man's honor was at stake here. The reputation of a soldier was as important as virtue was to a woman. The home became a battleground. Discord prevailed.

After bearing up to these idle gossipers, the wife began to question her husband's motives for staying home. She then began encouraging her husband to enter the military. Soon, he would leave due to pressure to please her. If he were killed or to die from disease or injury, she would carry a tremendous burden of guilt. This situation became real for the following couple. Controversy abounded in Ashe County when North Carolina chose secession. William M. Norman volunteered in May. He said peer pressure was heavy to join. Shirkers were frowned upon, but how is a man to feed his family if he is away? "A great many young men who had nothing to hinder them from volunteering failed to act the part of the soldier," he later recalled. "Their cowardice and toryish principles, talked of in every crowd, caused Letitia [his wife] to reconsider and began to think that, if I was to get a substitute or back out, it would affect my standing as well as hers, for she knew a great many would accuse her of providing recreant to my duty."[84]

Perhaps the next lady felt guilty. From Pittsboro, she confessed to her husband, who had volunteered:

I hope you will not think me too forward in telling you for I think you ought to know what I have to hear, and it is this: that I persuaded [?] you off to war. I did not deny it; I was too stout. I only said I don't care if I did, for I much rather you was there doing your duty than to be walking about like the husbands of those that has such talk . . . . I know when you and Jan(?) Thomas was going to muster, you both asked my advice, and I told you both that if I was a man, I would volunteer, and I think that is as much as I ever said about it. I have never been ashamed to tell where you was, and I don't think I ever will be, unless there is a great chance.[85]

Women would be shunned by their community if their husbands, sons, or fathers held back. Young men would be shunned too. Twenty-one-year-old Laura Norwood declared that unless a man served, she and her girlfriends would not marry one who did not join.[86] Some married women were jealous that other married women in the community had not sent their husbands to serve. Mary Bell, in Macon County, said she hoped a draft would come and get their husbands.[87] Other ladies were afraid they would be left unprotected with Union sentiment so strong in their area.

Joseph S. Lipe Agreement
Lipe Family Papers. Southern Historical Collection, Wilson Library, UNC-CH

In Iredell County, when Joseph Lipe decided to enlist, he wrote down a contract with his neighbors. He asked them to "aid Margaret and the children." His neighbors also promised to aid his family in their farming operations.[88] Those who chose to stay home fought ridicule to the point of newspaper announcements:

> **Home Guard** Rumor is busy, and I hear that some are trying to form a band in this city under the above title. Will you be kind enough to inform the energetic ones who are engaged in this movement, that we desire no such company. Tell them to go where they are needed. The Father of the fatherless and Husband of the widow will protect us, while for their safety this prayer shall hang on our lips. "Thous who colorist the raven's wing burnish the swords of our precious friends, and shield them in the thickest fight." A Lady[89]

Other men felt it would be a disgrace to stay home when their beloved southland was being invaded. Richard T. Daugherty wrote on July 10, "My Great Father fout in the revolution to gain our freedom. I shall fite through to perfect it or die. Victory or death is my aim . . . . I resign, to stay would be a dishonor to my ancestors, who fought for freedom of speech and honorable council between leadership and the public."[90]

Another recruit voiced: "I hope Mother is not much pestered about my leaving for I hate leaving bad enough any how; I hope she will become reconciled, for it is my duty to go to war, and do the best I can."[91]

Other men chose a wife instead of the army, thinking that would save them from volunteering. "Polly McCall . . . stopped her lover from going to war . . ." by marrying him.[92] That may have worked at first, but would not continue.

Women of North Carolina were also quick to show support for their state. Most chose the "feminine" way of sewing flags and uniforms while others preferred the scandalous position of Home Guard soldiers as noted in the *Winston Sentinel*:

> Application has been made at this office to know whether there are any means, public or private, by which ladies can get hold of sufficient number of light arms, such as repeaters or small rifles, suitable for the use of females. Some thirty to forty of the patriotic ladies in one of the two adjoining counties have formed themselves into companies and determined, if possible, to secure arms, and in the event of a necessity, defend their homes and fight for the cause of liberty.[93]

Numerous ladies of Murfreesboro were learning to shoot, and some had become "quite skilled in the use of fire arms."[94] In Halifax, Mrs. Edmondston recorded in her diary on June 1: "He is teaching me to shoot. What more significant fact of change in our country, when a husband gives his wife a parting present of a pistol." Two weeks later, she would write:

> The women many of them wept, sobbed, nay even shrieked aloud, but I had no tears to shed then [on men departing for camp]. The sentiment of exulted patriotism which filled my heart found no echo in lamentations, no vent in tears.[95]

That would come later.

Everyone had the war fever. Women wrote the governor requesting positions as nurses. A Mrs. Stevenson of Charlotte beseeched Governor Ellis on May 7, 1861:

> Excuse the liberty I have taken in addressen you I will state my business I am desirous of going to wait on the sick and wounded if ther should be so unfortunate

as to be any [.] I hafe a Brother in the Charlotte Grays and that makes me more ancious to go because he is young [.] I have a Cousin a middle age lady that offer her servesses to go if you accept of us [.] please let me know how long befor we could start as I am very uneasy about my brother, please keep this privat.

On the back of this letter are the following instructions from the governor to his secretary: "Thank her for her services. I will accept them as soon as needed but not at this time."[96]

Ms. N. H. Whitfield of Enfield wrote the newspaper in July requesting an appointment as a nurse for the soldiers, and she asked that the government authorize "sisters of mercy" (non-Catholic) for that purpose.[97] Numerous ladies of all ages came forward to serve as nurses.

Local bands performed for the crowds as young recruits were gathering to leave. The gaiety was infectious. "A group of Asheville women . . . serenaded the volunteers with a rendition of *Dixie*." Afterwards, "the orderly sergeant put the women through the drill paces."[98] Even schoolboys drilled with wooden rifles, tin swords, and sticks in the streets of Wilmington. In the piedmont section of the state, young girls of Caswell County sang this song for the Locust Hill Home Guard in June as they were preparing to leave. It goes to the tune of "Dixie" and reflects the high feeling of the ones staying at home:

> Here I am in the land of cotton
> The flag once honored is forgotten
> Look away, look away, look away Dixieland
> On every evening, every morning
> To save our land—the oppressor scorning
> Look away, look away, look away Dixieland
>
> CHORUS
> Hurray , hurray
> In Dixie Land I'll take my stand
> To live and die in Dixie
> Away, away, away down south in Dixie
> Away, away, away down south in Dixie
>
> I suppose you've heard the awful news
> Of "Old Abe" and his kangaroos
> Fight away, fight away, fight away Dixie Land
> His Myrmidons they would suppress us
> With war and bloodshed they'd distress us
> Fight away, etc.*[99]

Governor John Ellis did not live long after the state seceded. He died July 7, 1861, of consumption at a Virginia springs. Colonel Ramseur's battery fired every half hour from sunrise to sunset in honor of his service to the state. Former speaker of the Senate Henry T. Clark filled the position as the next governor. After the state made the decision to leave the Union, former governor Charles Manly made this statement: "All are unanimous. Even those who were loudest in denouncing secession are now hottest & loudest the other way."[100]

John Gilmer, previously a Union man, turned for the Confederacy after the state seceded. He said, "We are all one now."[101] But were we really one? Hordes did not feel that way.

---

*   For the remaining verses, see the appendix.

After secession rumors began to fly. Young girls away at school feared that with the absence of men gone to war, male slaves would be free to molest white women. The girls at the Glenn Anna Female Seminary were especially frightened. Some women feared a slave uprising while other females felt secure that their slaves would protect them from harm.[102] Perhaps this was due to how the women had treated their servants. Other schoolgirls feared the presence of the enemy so near their school. Ms. Josie MacRae wrote her father about the Federals, who were at New Bern, although far from St. Mary's in Raleigh:

> St. Mary's Hall
> March 16th/62
>
> My dear Papa,
> I suppose you have heard that the Yankees have taken Newbern and burned the bridge, and are expected to come in on Goldsboro today. It is reported that [CS] Gen. Branch behaved disgracefully, how much of it is true I dont know. The girls are terribly frightened. Dr. Smedes has told us to hold ourselves in readiness to leave at any moment. Poor Dr. Smedes is very much distressed, he says that if his school is broken up, he is a ruined man.
> It is terrible, only think how near they are to us, and they say that Wilmington will certainly be the next place of attack. Let us put our trust in God, for what is the use of having a God, unless we trust in Him. Write to me immediately, and tell me what to do. We may be unnecessarily alarmed, but if what we have heard is true, I am sure we are not. Write soon and tell me what you think about it.
> With much love for yourself and Rob.
> I am your affectionate daughter   Josie[103]

Throughout that spring and summer, recruits continued to be honored and adorned with attention upon leaving. "On June 1st, the people of . . . Wake County and a part of Chatham County gathered at Morrisville to give a sendoff to the company . . . called the North Carolina Grays. Captain York, then in command of the company, drilled the soldiers before the crowd. On behalf of the young women of the community, Miss Fanny Lyons presented a flag to the company."*[104] In Duplin County, the recruits boarded a train at Faison to go to Smithville. Area farmers furnished provisions to soldiers in camp while they drilled.[105] Ladies of Murfreesboro gave a bouquet to each soldier leaving for camp. "Mrs. Carter, 'an original secessionist' and her daughters were busy making clothes for the soldiers."[106] Annie Darden said the ladies were "fretting because the volunteers have orders to leave next week, and they are afraid they can't get the uniforms ready in time." Annie went to Mrs. Winborn's home to sew on the uniforms, saying, "We have three suits to make." The next day, she had made two more pairs of pants; after three days, the two ladies had made three uniforms.[107] When the Hertford County volunteers departed on June 12 amid tears and waving handkerchiefs, they had the attention of two girls' schools who rivaled over the volunteers, much to their satisfaction.[108]

While waiting for the train to depart from Salisbury, a recruit said that two little girls carried water to them. A citizens of Huntsville gave Captain Spears's company of volunteers and Captain C. L. Cook's men a sit-down dinner before they left for the front.[109] Jesse Person in a letter to his sister in Texas wrote on June 21:

> They [new recruits] will be ready to march as soon as they can get their uniforms, which is [sic] being made by the ladies of Louisburg & the County. Tempie, Mart, Mother & Mrs. Burwell are in the house busily sewing for them.

---

* See chapter 2 for the speech.

Louisburg is perfectly deserted. All the youth of the town have gone to war or in other words those that were old enough and the unmarried.[110]

Chocowinity was bustling with activity at the same time. The newly enlisted left after being presented with a beautiful bouquet and speech from Ms. Martha M. Fowle. When the Pee Dee Guards left Richmond County in June, they marched to the Old Hundred Depot and boarded the cars for Wilmington, but got only as far as Laurinburg. They encamped for the night. "Some lady friends come out to welcome the arrival of the soldiers . . . . The night was exciting, 'lively, and agreeable,'" replied Henry C. Wall. (This is the Victorian way of saying the men and women probably had sex).[111] Other soldiers mentioned hot times away from home.

———————

Soldiers already in the field wrote home about their experiences. Lewis Warlick wrote his sweetheart about his regiment's arrival in Richmond three days after North Carolina had seceded:

I have to laugh at part of our company when they get into a city. They look at every thing and in every direction and their fingers pointed at every curiosity, which their eyes may behold; it shows at once they never traveled a great ways from their native place.[112]

With the influx of soldiers, politicians, and civilians seeking jobs, the capital of the Confederacy must have been the biggest city a number of new recruits had visited. Another soldier forged his views:

Richmond Va
Nov. 16th 1861
My Dear wife   I can not tell when we shall get to Manassas on the account that we can not get our baggage a long on the cars [.] it is the hardest matter in the world to get freight to go on to its destination . . .

Upchurch and cohorts were unable to get their possessions at the station and went on to Richmond. He described the large town and what he saw:

the people seams kind here but I have to pay a high price for the kindness. I receive only $2.50 for day night and lodging . . . . I went to the soldiers theaton [theater?] and saw a goodeal this morning[.] me & a young soldier from Orang took a strole in town[.] went to . . . one of several market houses which made me open my eyes to see so much & so many things[.] the house is some 3 hundred yards long . . . started a gain went to a grist mill where I saw 13 wheat mill running & several still and a host of other things[.] the greatest was the monument to Geo Washington on a large horse away up in the air . . . . went to the paper mill saw them making paper[.] Richmond is a great place for any body to see that has never seen no more than I had. You may gow out look all around and see buildings 2 or 3 miles every way[.] Just over the river there is Manchester[.] there is buildings here 10 storis high[.] I am in the American hotel 5 story . . . . I.S. Upchurch[113]

Captain Charles Blacknall from Granville County said in a letter written to his brother on May 27:

...camp life is more pleasant than you think.... All the little inconveniences of cooking, etc, drinking champagne out of TIN CUPS and eating half-cooked food is not so annoying as you may suppose.[114]

Just think how the times would change! John Sutton with the Sixteenth Infantry wrote to his father from Asheville on May 26:

> it is with great pleasure that James, Silas, and myself are all well at present. We will leave this place on Thursday for Raleigh. We have got orders to start North .... The boys are all in good heart and want to git in a fight .... The Jackson Company have taken the praise of being the best Company that ever was in Asheville, and the ladies think more of ours than we do of ourselves. We was respectfully invited by the ladies to a concert in Asheville .... we formed in ranks and marched to the place where it was to be. The ladies formed themselves and sung the tune of Dixie Land. The Jackson boys will never run from Yankee cannon, sword, nor gun. So I remain your true son until death. John Sutton   ·
> Give my best respect to all my friends—especially the girls. John Sutton
> Since I have sign my name, I heard we would have to go to Virginia to form a regiment of mountain boys to swipe Yankees. We are glad to hear the news—hip hip hip hurrah hurrah hurrah. John Sutton[115]

Dr. Thomas Fanning Wood described "the almost vacation-like atmosphere of the early days in the army and the juvenile attitude of most of the soldiers. He observed how any rank and file scoffed at discipline . . . men perceived it as a manly challenge to disobey orders."[116]

Another saw it as the opposite:

> this June the 26th day of 1861
> Dear Cousin
> I take the opportunity of writing to you. as for my health I am not very well. in fact there [is] none of us but what has been aleden [ailing] some way or other, though we have good water up here, though the place appear to be not healthy [,] I think it is owing to the quantity of persons [.] there is a great many up here and see a thousands pass on the cars. our head quarters is with in 30 steps of the railroad where we can see them every day by numbers. I hope those few lines may find you well and the family and also the neighbors. I want to see you all very bad but I do not no when we ever shall see each other a gain. remember my respects to them all. tell Joseph and Elizabeth howdy for me and the rest of the family for my love to ward [toward] you all is more than I can express at the present for you 'er all of you are a family of folks of my relation. I peticular respected you. there is not a family but that I loved, but the time has come on when I fear that we shall not see each other again. I am now at Garisberg [Garysburg], Northamton County, N.C., but I expect that we shall leave hear before many days but I do not no where we shall go. Yet it is talked that we shall go on the course. But I soon as think that we shall go to Verginia as not. Our guns and tent canvass came in this morning. We are making preperrations to meet Old Abe and his band. As for my part I want to do one—one or the other—fight or go home. it is a very strict time up here. negroes up with you nows [knows] nothing about strictness to what we are. We are all cooks and washers. A greener set you never saw and awkward. I think that we are improveing in the course of a year or two we shal be so that

we can cook and wash so well that if ever get home a gain we can do very well without a wife but I want to see those girls so bad I do not no what to do. there comes some uphere some evenings to see us on dress parade but that is all. I have spoke to one sence I have ben up here and she was about Eighty years of age. I will come to a cose at this time tho I have a plenty to say yet, but will stop a while. I want you to write to me if you pleas and all that will tho I cannot tell where I shall be by that time. profily [possibly] I may be here or may be gone.

Your truly and Obedient cousin
Francis M. Pollock [117]

James S. Beavers, in writing to his brother from Camp Alamance on July 2, 1861, said that the camp of instruction turned out to be very strict:

> . . . we are not lowd to go to the Shops without a permit and we are not lawd to miss a drill without a furlo sickness permit [.] we are under tite rules [.] you don't know haw tite they are [.] I wish I coud see you and then I coud tell you what I thought of campt life [.] it is very tite rules and confinen [.] we have got our fun[d]s [.] we have returned our muskets and got rifle muskets [.] they look much better but I haven't tride them [.] we haveent got any close [clothes] since we have bin up here [.] some of us have got shoes [.] we haveent got but fifteen dollars apeace since we volunteerd[.] Tom is well except his arm where he was vactiannated[.] Ive bein vactionnated twice and now my arm is very sore [.] we have meat and bread and coffey and sometimes molasses and some times other things when we pay for them our selves[.] there are sevel here to day from cedarfork[.] Mr. Lo Mr Lewter Mr Larence and severl more [.] some went down yesterday [.] there is a rite smart of sickness in this campt [.] we are crowded in our tent [.] there is six of us and our guns and bedding and cloathing[,] satchels &c[.] Isham I wish you would come up here [,] you and pappy or John [.] it looks like some of you might come to see us . . . I wish I coud see the Girls about home[.] if I could come to old Chatham I would hug them as hard as ever I did for when I was down there before I hugged them and they hughed so good[.] I want to hug them again [.] I don't know the Girls up here and if I did I could not have the chance to be with them [.] there is some mity pruty ones up here and some ugly one mity ugly[118]

Another Beavers brother offered insight into his cravings for food and drink from home:

> State of Va. Aug the 24 1861
> Dear Brother
> I should be glad to here from you all again [.] I should be glad to be there with you [,] eat water millions with you[,] an drink cidar. I should be glad if you would com an bring som cidar an whiskey[.] I rather hav cider than any thing you cood bring . . . . I hav been so sick that I cood not write . . . I wish you cood be with us a while to see how we fair. Miss York has ben here about a week[,] she tends to us all like a mother[.] I want to no where you hav made any cider or not . . . if you have I should like to have som of it for I hant drunk a drop this year. Mr. H Mulkalon an Ms Wm A. Barbee and Mr Wm. Batchelor leves here on the 28 of Aug[.] I want som cider worse than any thing in the world[.] it looks like you mite com for expence would only be $15 dollars an if I was there I would give twenty to com[.] . . . I hant had a bit of water million this year[.] I crave cider an water million more than any thing in the world[.] Tell diley I should to see him very well. I should like to help you eat peches . . . Be sure an

bring me som cider an peches [.] box them up in a strong box so that they may keep good. Direct your letters to monases junction N.C. State trops 6 infentry company 1 in care of capt R.W. York

Your affectionit Br.
G.T. Beavers[119]

Lewis L. Swindell wrote his grandmother that his company was building a battery at Swan Quarter. "I am staying home tonight for the first since I volunteered. I like soldering very well so far."[120]

Captain Alfred Belo communicated to Carrie Fries, "Carrie I assure you that it is magnificently grand to hear the continued rattle of musketry, the clash of bayonets, the shouts of exultation rending the air when any point is attained, mingled with the booming field pieces . . ."[121]

That spring, Private W. P. McCullin in Camp Beauregard, Warren County, sent a letter to Ms. Bettie Kornegay: "Very frequently ladys come here from different parts of the State to see us and to hear the butiful Music in our Camp."[122]

Captain Robert F. Webb wrote to Martha (Pattie) Mangum from Camp Alamance Shops on June 30: "I don't dare to think of home and the little ones [.] it is terrible to be torn from home and family but more terrible will our vengeance be upon those who have caused it . . ."

Again, in June, William P. Mangum said in a letter to his sister, Martha, that his unit had to lay over in Durhams (station) for two to three weeks because Raleigh couldn't accommodate more troops. The soldiers had to sleep on the floor of his quarters. They ran out of food. Stacked up at the depot were boxes of provisions donated to troops, and the recruits probably got into those. Willie, in camp at Company Shops in July, had not yet left for the front. He penned his comments to his sister again:

> A great many ladies are visiting the camp everyday. A great many were up from Hillsboro the other day to see the review. I hope that when ever or where ever we go that we shall perform our duty like men and give no reason for our friends at home to be ashamed of us. No one knows how much they think of home and those at home until time and absence and the uncertainty of life reveals it to them.

After his company left, they settled in Winchester, Virginia, where he wrote this letter to Martha on July 17: "We all suffered much from fatigue and want of food and the bad weather. But soldiers must become accustomed to privations."[123]

In Rutherford County, Ellen Mitchell gave a speech to the departing young volunteers at the beginning of the conflict:

> The ladies feel proud of the Old North State, but prouder still of this glorious mountain county whose sons, at the first sound of the tocsin of war, have rushed to the standard of our insulted country . . .

The Mitchell family was nonslaveholders.[124] Elizabeth Wiggins signed off her diary July 24 with these words:

> Cousin Pattie and Bettie went down to Enfield with Octa [her son] to take the train for Chapel Hill. Colonel Fishers corps was on the train. The girls did not return until near night, such excitement & such quantities of troops, that pass daily over the road from the south to Virginia.[125]

While in church, Annie Darden made this comment: "I felt very sad to look around at the vacant seats of many who have gone, perhaps never to return to their homes and their church again."[126]

Early that spring, North Carolina residents who were Northern-born began to feel uneasy in their surroundings. Local citizens reacted to Northern-born visitors in their area accusing them of abolishable measures.[127] The native North Carolinians grew suspicious of these neighbors. What were their allegiances? Whose side would they support? What were their motives? Maybe they were spies. To quieten antislavery views before secession, the dissenters were often banished from the state.[128] Author Mark Neely has suggested, "The Alien Enemies Act of the Confederate States of America, approved 8 August 1861, proclaimed 'all natives, citizens, denizens or subjects of the hostile nation or government, being males of fourteen years of age and upward, who shall be within the Confederate States and not citizens thereof . . . are liable to be apprehended, restrained or secured and removed as alien enemies." These people were given forty days' notice to leave the Confederacy or be declared an alien enemy. If they didn't depart the South, they were hunted up and arrested. Those such men expelled, who then returned to the South, were labeled as spies or prisoners of war. Noteworthy is the fact that this law *did not* apply to true foreign-born men. Real foreign men had to carry papers stating such was the case.[129]

William King Covell of Rhode Island was living in Wilmington at the onset of war. He went back to Rhode Island because he decided it was not safe to live there any longer. Charles Duffy at Catherine Lake, Onslow County, wrote to the governor requesting a pass for a Northern-born teacher residing with the family. She wished to return to Vermont. For some unknown reason, it was denied.[130] Mary Armstrong was the white nanny for the Pettigrew family. She returned to the North when the war started. Hugh Downing, a Northern-born resident, petitioned Governor Ellis for a pass to return to Pennsylvania. Mr. W. H. Twichell, living in Smithfield at the time, was held in jail because he was from Connecticut. Neighbors petitioned the governor to release him. Two alien enemies from the Green Swamp Land Company near Brunswick County tried to carry on their lumber business with their Northern partners but had to leave.[131] A Northern-born man named King had taught his Negro janitor to read and write. A mob of angry neighbors sent him and his wife on a northbound train. A Northern female teacher fled with them.[132]

A person had to be very careful what he said and to whom it was directed. In the mountains, businessman James Gentry made this remark: "A man is in great danger to express Northern preferences here now."[133]

Dr. William Hooper refused to allow the students of Chowan Female Institute to fly the Confederate flag over the school. He was bombarded by secessionists seeking his hide, so he resigned.[134]

Down in Beaufort, Eli Swanner voiced his anti-Southern views and was arrested twice.[135] Thomas Dougan snorted, "Secessionists are rascals and traitors and would be whipped." He was instantly arrested and charged a one thousand dollar fine.[136]

One Christian woman questioned whether her neighbor, a Jewish woman, collected provisions with the intention of passing them only to Northern or Southern Jewish soldiers.[137]

The uncertain times brought out feelings of hostility toward known Northern sympathizers. These people feared for their lives with good reason. There were casualties before the state seceded. Differences of opinion leading to violence occurred during secession in Madison County. In Marshall, the pro-Confederate sheriff was killed; and in Hendersonville, an arsonist set fire to several homes. Despite this, volunteers continued to step out of the woods.[138] Catherine Edmondston reported that a man from Weldon was hung due to his suspected abolitionist views.[139]

Emily Tillinghast's aunt Huske didn't care who heard her opinion about the war. Mrs. Huske said:

> . . . she would like Lincoln to be taken to hell and ridden around by the
> evil spirits till he was scared [sic] out of his wits, and moreover she would like

to be there at the time and see the ceremony performed; she thought Satan superior to Lincoln in bravery and courage, they being equal in other things.

Emily replied, "I think Lincoln is of too contemptible a nature and too great a fool for people to hate as some do, as for myself he is too insignificant for people to be angry with."[140]

A teenager, a neighbor of the Tillinghasts', added, "I don't know how we Southerners ever stayed in the Union as long as we did with them."[141] Women remained safe with their opinions until Federal occupation Down East. Those opposed to the North, whether by actions or words, frequently found themselves banished from their towns or state.

Researcher Mark Neely found that "there was never a moment in Confederate States history when pro-Union opinion could be held without fear of government restraint . . . such opinions were more dangerous near the borders and . . . active military fronts than in the interior, but nowhere were dissenting beliefs secure." Around 13 percent of civilian arrests were about political opinion. At first, citizens were held without records, being kept of the military government's accusations towards them, length of stay, etc.[142] Most of North Carolina's political prisoners found themselves inmates in Salisbury Prison, but some ended up in Norfolk.* Thomas Kennedy, a family man with four children, expressed his antisecession and antislavery views in front of the wrong person and was arrested. He spent time at Salisbury. A Confederate officer impersonating a Northern man caught him. Other North Carolinians imprisoned were Amariah B. Allen, Jesse W. Davis, and Edward B. Hopkins. Hopkins told authorities he had to take the oath to the U.S. or starve. Authorities believed him, so he was released. Most of these types of people arrested were of the poorer class. From Chowan County, Jeptha A. Ward became an inmate when he said he did not believe in conscription or emancipating the Negro.

Quaker Calvin G. Perkins of Kinston made salt in New Bern. When under occupation by the enemy, he claimed neutrality. Later, he was arrested by Southern men. Other religious men in prison were Ison Wood and James Sinclair. Political prisoners included W. C. Loftin of Craven County and Michael Tighlman and John Medlin Sr. of Union County. Medlin owned fifty slaves but was sent to prison for harboring his son, a Confederate deserter. "Confederate interrogators . . . wanted to know about the prisoners prior political affiliations . . . during the war being a 'Union man' had a sinister meaning."[143]

Newspapers of the period printed military notices for all to see. This article appeared in the *Tarboro Mercury* on May 22 two days after secession:

AN ACT TO DEFINE AND PUNISH TREASON AGAINST THE STATE OF NORTH CAROLINA

SECTION ONE: Be it enacted by the general assembly of North Carolina . . . . That treason shall consist only in levying war against the state, or in adhering to its enemies, giving them aid and comfort; or in establishing, without the authority of the General Assembly, any government within its limits separate from the existing government; or in holding or executing in such usurped government any office, or professing allegiance or fidelity thereto, or assisting in the execution of the laws under color of authority from such treason, if provided by the testimony of two witnesses to the same overt act, or by confession in open court, shall be punished with death.

SECTION TWO: Be it further enacted— That if any free person; knowing of any such treason, shall not . . . give information . . . to the Government of the state,

---

*   Discussed in chapter 4. Two hundred records of dissenters were located by Neely. He was unable to find records for the piedmont and mountain counties.

or to some conservator of the peace, such person, shall be punished by the fine and imprisonment at the discretion of the court.

SECTION THREE: Be it further enacted—That if any free person devise or conspire with a slave to rebel or to make insurrection in this state, or with any person to induce a slave to rebel or make insurrection such person shall upon conviction suffer death, whether such rebellion or insurrection be made or not.

SECTION FOUR: Be it further enacted—That this act shall be in force from and after its ratification.

An additional session to the state convention held in November of 1861 had this message presented by Mr. Raynor:

AN ORDINANCE TO DEFINE AND PUNISH SEDITION

Be it ordained &c., That if any person in this state shall attempt to convey intelligence to the enemies of the Confederate States, or shall maliciously and advisedly endeavor to incite the people to resist the government of this state or the Confederate States, or persuade them to return to their connection with the United States, or maliciously and advisedly terrify and discourage the people from enlisting into the service of this state or of the Confederate States, or shall stir up or incite tumults, disorders or insurrections in this state, or dispose the people to favor the enemy, every such person thereof legally convicted by the evidence of two or more credible witnesses, or other sufficient testimony, shall be adjudged guilty of a high misdemeanor, and shall be fined and imprisoned at the discretion of the court, and shall enter into recognizance with good security, in such sum as the court may deem proper, to be of the peace and good behavior toward all people in the state for three years thereafter.[144]

At the beginning of the conflict, men began seizing free Negroes to serve them in the field. In Wilkes County, a free black man killed a white man who was trying to force him to go as a body servant. Senator Jonathan Worth, with Quaker connections, "did all he could to save the negroes. One new recruit seized a free negro, Henry Stith, who had been working for Worth . . ." The senator also wrote to the adjutant general several times about others taking freemen.[145]

"There are no negroes here with the exception of one of William Parishes a boy a free negro with Mr. Webb and one with another mess," said Willie Mangum to his sister, Martha.[146]

The Yankees have been "tampering with the negroes & fisherman who in that region are mere nomads owing allegiance to Neptune & Bores only selling their service to the highest bidder," wrote Mrs. Edmondston on July 8, 1861, before the Federal forces landed on the Outer Banks in August.

Other soldiers paid Negroes to work for them in camp. Major William Morris inscribed a letter to his wife in 1862: "We have a free boy hired at $12 pr Month to cook & wash for us."[147]

North Carolina had a large Quaker population confined mostly in the piedmont counties of Randolph, Forsyth, and Rowan. "The Quakers of North Carolina have memorialized the state Convention to release them from bearing arms, on the grounds that they cannot consciously do it. They say the whole of Friends of the Confederate States does not exceed ten thousand," printed the *Milton Chronicle*. There were Quakers in Rich Square, Hertford County, Perquimans, Wayne, and Edgecombe County.[148] The state also had a large percentage of Moravians in the Piedmont. "Moravians also felt an attachment to their brethren in Pennsylvania." Most of Forsyth's eleven thousand citizens had no slaves; however, some of the Moravians did own slaves.

When the state seceded, young Moravian men volunteered while ladies in the community sewed their uniforms. "A June 19 decision by the Provinzial Aeltesten Conferenz [PAC] amended the wording of prayers and litany of the church to reflect the new Confederate government . . ."[149] With doubts cast aside, the Moravians now supported the South.

Other denominations found themselves in turmoil. The Northern and Southern Presbyterians split prewar, possibly over slavery. The Southern Presbyterians called themselves the United Synod of the South. This organization "did not deny that slavery was an issue in the dissolution of the General Assembly, but they maintained that the attempt by some to make it the principle cause was false and that it had but little or no influence in the decision to divide."[150] The Presbyterian churches in North Carolina voted to separate from the national group. In an October meeting held in Johnston County, the following minutes were read:

> We regard the action of the Assembly [Johnston County] in adopting a series of resolutions requiring us to sustain, unhold [sic uphold], and encourage the Federal Government, as unconstitutional, oppressive, and schismatic.[151]

Different denominations split. "Out of the great Baptist Church came the UNION Baptists . . ." The Methodists parted also.[152] With secession, the Southern dioceses broke with the National Church to form a separate Protestant Episcopal Church in the South.[153]

The first battle of the war took place at Bethel Church, eastern Virginia, in June. The Southern soldiers were victorious. North Carolina troops were engaged, and the first soldier killed hailed from the state, hence the title First at Bethel. The second much larger battle, consisting of several thousand troops, occurred at Manassas, Virginia, in July with the routing of the Union Army. As casualties began pouring home, Judge B. F. Moore stated, "Civil War can be glorious news to none but demons or thoughtless fools, or maddened men."[154]

"To talk of war and to fight are different," quoted Catherine Edmondston. She said, "We are really at war."

At Pittsboro, P. H. Scovell wrote on August 13, discussing "our victory at Manassas" and said, "I think it is enough to convince those fanatics that the idea of subjugation is an impossibility, but it seems not."[155]

"Almost every family has sent one some two and three —sad hearts are many about here, for if they should escape being killed I fear most of our young men will be ruined, camp life is not all conducive[sic] to religion or morality," quipped R. N. Lenoir in Wilkes County.[156]

A young girl wrote her cousin:

> I was sorry to hear that cousin Flinn was wounded. I hope he will get well. We heard that Mr. John Murchison was killed and Mr. Sandy Elliot, son of Mr. John Elliott. What distressing times we have. I do hope that we will hear better news before long for I know that our cause is just for we have the Bible on our side. And the Yankees cannot subdue us I dont believe.[157]

After the wounded had been cared for and the dead buried, recruiting was back in full swing. The victory for the Confederacy at Manassas encouraged hordes to volunteer. It was common for young men to volunteer in companies nearest their home. Yet there were those men who still held back. Ladies were known to make the best recruiting officers. One teenager threatened to put a petticoat on her friend if he did not volunteer. The *Raleigh*

Standard printed an article "about young ladies in Wake County ignoring, snubbing, and labeling as cowards men who did not volunteer."[158]

As the recruits were getting settled in camp, they wrote home to anxious relatives wanting to know about their health and activities while parents wrote to their sons not to yield to temptation. In a conversation with her aunt Mary discussing Rebecca's four sons in the military, Rebecca P. Davis of Warren County said she was aware of the demoralizing effect of camp life, but told her aunt that "the boys had nothing to fear but bullets, that my boys had fixed principles."

"Habits formed, principles fixed, and nothing to fear," quoted Aunt Mary.[159]

J. A. Strikeleather joined at age sixteen. He remembered the first few days of camp life. He said that the soldiers wasted as much food at the beginning of the war as they consumed during the fourth year. Strikeleather said that one of the unwritten rules among the soldiers was that when two men got in a fight in camp, they were never to be separated until one or the other called out "Enough!" After a few months' service, fighting amongst themselves cooled.[160]

John W. Mercer of Supply sent this letter to his son Oliver E. Mercer of the Twentieth North Carolina Troops: "Carefully avoid the influence of bad company and bad examples and devote your leisure to useful study."[161]

A few weeks after Thomas Setzer's company arrived at a COI (camp of instruction), he described to his relatives the sinful activities taking place around him:

> I hav bin in and at meny plases, but this is the god dams plase that I ever seen—Som sings, Som gets drunk, Som Curses, Som plays cards and all sorts of devilment that white men coulda think of.[162]

Because of this atmosphere, it was not a suitable place for ladies to be present. Dr. John Alexander had another opinion concerning the visitation of females in the camp:

> I never want to see you here . . . if you value your modesty I beg you not to come . . . I think the place for a soldier's wife, during his absence is at home.[163]

Young Ed Wills, after he joined the Junior Reserves, wrote his mother about camp life in Weldon:

> I think this is one of the most low life company ever was [,] nothing but the lower class of the country except two or three. Nothing but swaring all the time or something just as bad. I don't want you to come down here unless you go over to Mr. Samuels house because the men has no more respet for a lady than if she was a hog [.] they will say any thing in the world that comes to hand.[164]

However, it was not at all unusual to see women in camp. The wives of the officers visited frequently. Most stayed with friends or rented a room in the nearest town. When ladies with families in tow visited the soldiers on the Outer Banks, it was called the ladies' invasion. Even before the war, persons rented homes from the islanders to escape the swampy-type weather. "Captain B. F. Hanks put his steamer in service making regularly scheduled voyages to haul all the parcels and people awaiting passage" to the island.

Martha A. Fowle wrote all her female friends the exciting things that happened while visiting the soldiers at Hatteras.[165]

"Among the few bright occasions for the men were the arrivals of the river boats bringing their wives, children, and sweethearts for visits that were all too brief," wrote one soldier.[166]

Another recruit stationed at Harrellsville commented on the girls who had come to hear their band music: "Ladies used to come in the evening at dress parade to see us."[167]

Paul Barringer, as a small boy, traveled by train going with his father, General Rufus Barringer, to Camp Beauregard near Ridgeway. While his father was attending to his duties, Paul rode around in an ambulance and amused himself. His father's body servant helped watch over the boy, and both slept in tents. Paul stayed with his father for several months. While there, General Barringer's wife, Eugenia Morrison, and a relative visited him, staying not in camp, but with a family in Warrenton.[168]

Octavius A. Wiggins, Thirty-seventh NCT, was stationed near Wilmington at the beginning of the war. He sent a letter to his family in Halifax that read:

> Our camp life around Wilmington was a most enjoyable and easy one. Almost every man in the company had his body servant to attend his personal wants and his horse, his trunk full of fine clothes from home; and the city offered many attractions to be beaux rather than soldiers.[169]

Also stationed at the beach was R. P. Crawford from Jackson County. In the fall, he wrote his cousin about the conditions in camp:

> Dear Cosen Wm Eastis
> I and all of the Redgment is in camp & near the see cost not more than 2 hundred yards from the Beach . . . . you can see all the steam boats and steam ships running all the time . . . . you may stand on the beach and look as far as your Eye can see and it is nothing but one world of water . . . . We have see Breeses which is as helthy as they are up whare you live. The water that we have is the very worst of water Such as you never Drank in your life the wigeltails is as thick as Bees in gum . . . . That is all the fault I can find . . . . I can wright Ten thousand things But I have Rote six or seven letters to day and you must excuse me . . .[170]

Troops leaving the mountain counties at the end of the summer failed to get the same enthusiasm from townsfolk as earlier units had. At Camp Davis in New Hanover County, Thomas Garrison on October 8 recorded this letter to his parents, brothers, and sisters:

> wee had a fine old time after wee got to the Rail Road. wee came here in double quick time. The depots was crowded with girls. They threw Apples & flowers in the Cars by hand fulls and waved their Handkerchiefs to us to cheer us onward in this holy cause. The people were very kind to us in places. Some places they were not so kind. I suppose the cause of this was that Volunteers seem like an old thing to them. They have seen so many of them their love is all extinguished towards them. Your affectionate Son & Brother TM Garrison[171]

A soldier stationed within six miles of Fort Macon wrote the editor of the *Spirit of the Age*, a Raleigh newspaper, about conditions on post:

> Our quarters here are not as comfortable as what we are accustomed to [,] situated as it is along the coast in a deep sand, with wells about as deep as molasses hogsheads; we are very much annoyed too in sultry weather by mosquitoes and sand flies which become so numerous as almost to fill the atmosphere as nightfall approaches. And when we would rest from the toils of the day,
> "Again the gaunt mosquito comes,
> That brigand of the night,
> With all his starving family,
> To put our dreams to flight."

The soldier signing the letter with the initials JEM went on to say: "But it remains for us to speak of the kindness shown to us by the ladies of New Bern. We had often heard of that place. The whole regiment on arriving there were kindly treated by them . . . delicacies in abundance were served by their own fair hands to the soldiers as they sat in the cars. May God bless them & reward them abundantly."[172]

John Alexander Muse enlisted in October 1861 and left Carthage on the way to Jonesboro where he and his comrades boarded the train for Fayetteville. At Fayetteville, the group took a steamer for Wilmington. He related, "We used our pistols between Kelly's Cove and Wilmington shooting ducks, which was plentiful, and furnished nice practice for us." Before the unit left town, each was presented with a bowie knife and pistol. "The knives were made by a blacksmith from Carthage from old files and scrap iron . . ." Upon the arrival in Wilmington, his company took the train to Goldsboro, where they partook of another large meal hosted by the citizens.[173]

John A. Young, an officer in the Fourth Regiment, took pride in his new job to outfit his comrades. His dairy read:

> After the regiment had gone into camp it became a matter of much interest to equip it with good and useful material. This duty was assigned to me by Col. Anderson and I succeeded in uniforming it in the best military goods made at the Rock Island Mills, and our cartridge boxes and accoutrements were made by S. M. Howell (?) of Charlotte. Our uniforms and accoutrements were of the very best, and so superior as to cause the attention and special notice in the Richmond Papers. No Regiment sent into service of the Confederate States better fitted out in all its appointments, including arms, than the 4th No. C. State Troops.[174]

Families separated with kinfolk living out of state were likely to feel greater anxiety due to long periods between letters. Elizabeth Wiggins had a daughter in Texas and had not heard anything from her in four weeks. She penned this in her diary: "I feel very unhappy about them if the blockade keeps up I fear I shall have to do a long time without hearing."[175]

In another instance, Mary B. Clarke, a native North Carolinian, was living in Texas when her husband enlisted. Instead of living there without help with the children, they decided to move back to North Carolina where both had relatives.

Many North Carolinians had sons and daughters in northern schools. Usually, the parents made sure the daughters returned home. It was much easier to accomplish this in 1861. The second year of the war proved to a greater degree vexing. Officers on both sides grew suspicious of people requesting passes to travel across the lines. Occasionally, a son would choose to remain in the North. He would be watched with suspicion by residents there and vice versa. Charles Bahnson from Salem was in school in Philadelphia training to be a jeweler when the war commenced. He wrote to his father:

> I am getting awfully disgusted with the North, a person dare not go on any prominent street, and speak in favor of the South. Several have been very nearly killed for uttering their sentiments . . . . A Vigilance Committee will be formed, & all Southerners warned to leave; they also say that they know the names of all Southerners in town . . .[176]

That August, he was still in town. Bahnson chose to go home almost too late, for the communications between North and South were rapidly closing down. He learned that Nashville, Tennessee, was supposedly the only route open. From Philadelphia, he traveled via train to Cincinnati, took a boat to Louisville, Kentucky, then the stage to Nashville. In Nashville, he boarded another train on its way to Chattanooga. From Chattanooga, the train carried him North to Bristol. From Bristol, he took the stage to Wytheville, Virginia, thence to Mount Airy, and finally to Salem.[177] He joined the army in the fall of 1861 in the Second Battalion (Twenty-first). When writing home for supplies in December, young Bahnson requested "a quilt or blanket, chalk, Neat's Foot Oil, a dozen panes of glass, a wash pan, two buckets, shoe leather, two dozen clay pipes, a pillow slip, and some red flannel in addition to some 'eatables.'" He wrote, "This is a hungry country . . ."[178]

Margaret Walker Weber, a graduate from St. Mary's School as it was known during the war, mused about her difficulties. She became a teacher and several years later married. At the time of the hostilities, Mrs. Weber was living in Nashville, Tennessee, but went to visit her relatives in Alabama. These are her words:

> When Carleton was one year old I went to Alabama to visit my mother and sister. My husband promised to come after me; but I had gone only two weeks when Fort Donaldson fell and Nashville was taken. My husband being a Union man and my people intensely Southern, the exigencies of war detained him in Nashville and prevented my returning, he obtained a passport from General Thomas, requiring officers and soldiers of the Northern Army to aid me in every way to reach Nashville in safety, but this passport was never received; consequently my children and I remained in the Southland until peace was declared. My brother came to Alabama for me, intending to provide a home in these troublous times; but, on arriving with him in Raleigh, I went with my children and nurses to St. Mary's School, and there taught two years. The generosity and loving attention of my dear sister, Mrs. Hale, provided me with every comfort at this time and during the remainder of the war.
>
> My dear Mother returned to North Carolina with us; and, after a few days illness, she died . . . . My step-daughter, Mary, joined me at St. Mary's and taught there . . . . My step-son, Frederick, joined the Southern army when he was sixteen years old, and was a brave soldier throughout the war, the last months he was a prisoner at Camp Chase.
>
> You will find among my papers, "Reminiscences of the War," which I wrote at the request of Bishop Quintard for his book which he intended to publish. In that paper you will see the difficulties and troubles which be-set us on our way to Nashville soon after peace was declared. I had put into a bag to be worn on my person, a small stock of jewels and heirlooms which I then posessed [sic] (the best I had given to a missionary), such was my grief and distraction that I left this bag in a trunk, and on reaching Fortress Monroe, I discovered that the soldiers on Roanoke Island had rifled the trunks, and taken these treasures and everything else of value. The horror of my situation, with my two little boys, is not to be depicted, not knowing if my husband was alive, as communication during the war was cut off.
>
> In Baltimore I had the happiness of hearing from my husband, who sent money for the journey home. I went first to Washington; President Davis had just been incarcerated; and knowing President Johnson, I went to the White House with my two little boys and made bold to plead with him for Davis' life.
>
> My husband, by appointment, met us in Louisville; and when little Carl was told this was his "Papa" (he had not seen him for four years), he excitedly told him of my pleading with President Johnson for the life of Davis, and his rebuff; My husband exclaimed, "My God! I have just gotten home, and for this, tomorrow you may be in the penitentiary."

Her husband, Johannes Heinrich David Christian Frederick Weber, a music professor, died in 1878. Mrs. Weber lived into the twentieth century.[179]

Written from Hamilton on September 5, 1861, the Reverend R. H. Wills sent a letter to his father, Rev. William H. Wills, of Brinkleyville. He wrote that a friend had a daughter in school up North when the war commenced. He had now brought her home. Wills said:

He managed to get her here by taking a Yankee lady with him [North] and dressing in uniform and going as a recruiting officer. They suspected him once or twice but did not take him up. He says he learned their [U.S.] plans which first was to rush into Virginia and arm all the Negroes that would receive [illegible] and failing in that, to winter in North Carolina and arm the Negroes here.[180]

Susan Becton, a graduate of St. Mary's School, became a teacher far from her roots. When the hostilities started, Becton was teaching in Paradise, Lancaster County, Pennsylvania. The Southern girl wrote to a friend in North Carolina, describing her loneliness and alienation. She apparently stayed there:

Paradise, Lancaster Co. Penn
Dec. 14, 1862

My Dear Jane,

I learned last week that the letter sent you some time since, has been unavoidably detained; I cannot hope now that it will ever reach you, and so endeavor to replace it by another and briefer . . . . I am alone in a strange land. But no arrow tells these complacent Pennsylvanians, who so far from seeing anything singular in the name of the village, have bestowed the same upon a township, and linked to it the equally happy titles of Eden Hall (the village Seminary) and All Saints Church. Congratulate me . . . on having exchanged the rattle snakes and pine trees of old Carolina (her only productions, one of our teachers coolly informed me) for such bliss, at least *in name*. I have left the refinement and intellectual pleasures of the Hall behind and am now seeing a new phase in life. And true, democratic life it is; one in which every body labours; the men earning their bread by hard toil, and their wives, alternately mistress & maid, performing with their own hands, the drudgery, which, with us, devolves upon slaves. At first I was rather pleased with this; in the evening I met men, who had worked all day in the field, and they appeared intelligent, educated gentlemen—I saw a lady step from the parlour to the kitchen, and perform her duties with equal ease and facility in each—but six months familiarity banished the illusion. The nobility and elevating influences of labour are lost in the daily, hourly strife with petty cares and means; men become narrow-minded and pernicious; women sink beneath the double burden of natural and assumed duties—Care for the body usurps care for the mind and the tone of society is inevitably lowered. Of course I speak only of this part of the state—of other parts, I only know that the same fanaticism rife here, prevails there—You will think I do not like Penn—No, my dear, I do not. Next to North Carolina, New Jersey holds a place in my affections. And because circumstances exclude me equally from both, is my longings for the former doubled. There are times indeed when my whole soul arises in arms against the iron hand of necessity, pressing so cruelly upon me—but it is soon past—God has been very merciful in raising up friends for me and everywhere smoothing my path with loving kindness . . . . Eighteen months have passed since I heard from home; your letters have been among the most sadly missed . . . .

Lovingly,
Susan G. Becton[181]

After the men left for war, hundreds of women changed their residence. Some went to live with parents, some with kin while other women chose to stay on their property. Northern-born women married to Southern men usually stayed in the South, but continued to correspond with their relatives when possible. For a while, boats carrying the flag of truce from Fortress Monroe, Virginia, would deliver mail and packages.

You could tell by the letters written that many men had not been separated from their wives before. Sentiments expressed in their letters would bring a person to tears. Joseph J. White, a member of the Twenty-sixth North Carolina Troops, had not been in the army but a few months when he yearned for his wife. He wrote frequent letters urging her to come visit him in camp. Senura White of Chatham County in September answered one of his letters:

> I don't recon you are sceared any worse than some of them are sceared so bad tha don't know which end is up [.] I am in hopes that some of them will have to go if tha cant fite . . . . you must wright to me evry chance you have [.] it is all tha satisfaction that I see in this life [.] You don't know how lonesome I am . . .

In his letter written on "September 27th from Camp Bergwyn Boges [sic] Bank," he asked her for rags to clean his rifle, tobacco, ink, pens, and envelopes. Three days later, he wrote his father and asked him to send two sheepskins sewn together. In October, he again begged her to come for a visit:

> Senura there has been several ladies in camp with there fathers and brothers and relations since we have been on Boge Island. Merit Rossons wife stayed in camp with us last night she wil stay down two weeks I guess maby longer than that [.] there has been two ladyies down here from Montgomery Co to see there folks. Senura for Gods sake come never mind the cost. I would give my hole years wages to get to see you and Willie [son].[182]

Determined to convince her, he went on to say it would only cost eight dollars for a round-trip from Chatham. He told her not to make any more cakes because the sugar cost too much. Joseph asked her to make him a shirt because those drawn from the quartermaster were much too short, "just about to the waist." He wanted her to make him some brown jeans cloth, pants, and a coat. By November, Senura still had not made the three-hundred-mile journey to the coast. He wrote on November 6 and said "not to be afraid to come, that it was safe there. Colonel Vance's wife was here last night." He reported that he had made arrangements for them to stay in Morehead City if he could get a furlough. If not, then she would have to stay in camp. Apparently, his wife and parents did get to visit for a few days because her next letter to him told of their safe arrival back home.

In Iredell County, Margaret Lipe sent a letter to her husband, Joseph, that fall, enclosing a few lines written by their daughter, Martha Jane: "Pap I want you to come home. I would rather see you than eat my supper . . ." Margaret said that she would send him his clothes "and some dish-cloths . . . to keep if you should get a wound." In the same letter, his son Milas, wrote that he had enclosed a little bottle of pills in with the clothes "for you if you feel unwell. Take 4–5 before supper."[183]

In camp at Fayetteville, Virginia, Colonel Francis Parker of the Thirtieth NCT wrote to his wife, Sallie, living in Halifax. He stated that they were "so busy in camp the day passes quickly and sometimes they forget what day it is." He begged forgiveness from his wife because he had forgotten what his daughter, Hattie, looked like; and he wanted her to send him a "likeness" (picture). He said "not to send any more clothes at present except 1-2 pair of socks." He wanted her to send him a list of the Negroes' shoe sizes so he could get them at Lincoln County (West Virginia?) at the shoe factory. Parker wrote:

> There was a great error committed in recruiting so extensively and promiscuously. We have men in our company who have never been of any benefit whatever to us, or to the Confederacy. You spoke of sending me a box of eatables, do not do so; the freight is worth more than the contents of the

box, unless it should have bacon or something of that kind for generally boxes are so long getting here, that all the contents are spoiled.[184]

Soldiers complained to kin at home for not writing enough. Joseph White wanted mail so bad that he said he would "be glad to here from a dog if he was a good one." Joseph told Senura White he always filled up the page even if the contents were not interesting. He also said for her to write more pages and tell him about the crops and stock.[185]

W. W. Lenoir wrote to his cousin Walt on October 2, alluding to the Yankees: "I would a thousand times rather fight them than live with them."[186]

Charles Blacknall in camp wrote to Jinnie that he sent circulars to brother George to hand them to the ladies "to get them to raise us all the articles they could for the winter." George was in winter camp in Union Mills, Virginia.[187]

A volunteer stationed near York sent his thoughts to a Raleigh newspaper:

For the Register.
Fifth Regiment N.C. Volunteers

Curtis' Lane, Nov. 14th, 1861.

Mr. Editor:—We are now at this *delightful* retreat for the second time. It is about ten miles below Yorktown, and a little over a mile from the noted Bethel. When we were here before, we spent five or six days *charmingly*, being exposed to pelting rains and the chilling winds of October. We took up our quarters under some old sheds made of pine tops, that had for some time been used by all the hogs of the neighborhood as a retreat, and on our routing them, they left behind, to our very great annoyance, any number of fleas, that feasted themselves on the beef-fed flesh of our mortal bodies. Poor fellows! how we scratched, and rolled, and sometimes said ugly words about these naughty and ill bred fleas.—But we should not blame them. They were only patterning after the most of the bipeds of this Peninsula, who are always on the *qui vive* to make themselves fat off the poor soldiers. We should not blame the fleas, then—we *do not* blame them, and therefore ask their pardon for any insinuations to that effect.

Withal, we had a jolly time of it. We were soaking wet sometimes, but then, again, (as a worthy Sergeant of ours once said, when asked if he is'nt [sic] *dry* enough to take a drink,) we were "as *dry* as a shuck blown by the strongest north winds over the highest peak of the Appenine Mountains." We were literally dry inwardly and outwardly, for not a wee drop of *spirits* had we, except a few (a *very* few) "*spirits* of just men made perfect." These *spirits* sometimes light their lamps, and after supplying their quart pots, deliberately put them over their lamps, and thus *cruelly* shut out the *bright* light of their *holy* lives. But these blessed churchmen may do this in humble imitation of Devereux valet Desmarais, who said "one ought to get drunk sometimes, because the next morning one is sure to be thoughtful; and, moreover, the practical philosopher ought to indulge every emotion, in order to judge how that emotion would affect another."

But to our jolly time,—and a *jolly* time had we. The morning after our arrival, we rose at the tap of the drum, and when we came to look about for something to eat (for we soldiers *eat* sometimes,) lo! and behold! not a mouthful could be found. A turnip-patch was near by, and we had a *delicate* little breakfast of this elegant and very degestible [sic] (raw) vegetable. An epicure could not have got such a breakfast in Paris, the great city of victuals and pretty women. About noon we got some beef (oh! glorious and blessed beef!) how we love it! how we love it! for, to tell the truth, it is a very great *rarity* with us (?) We have been forced to eat turkeys, canvass-back ducks, *fried* chicken, and such gross and heavy food (?) [note: question marks in original]

Well, to our dinner. The bill of fare was beef and bread (sorter india rubber bread, a capital good article to make trace chains of.) We did'nt have a bit of salt, "not a grain, sir." The beef was fresh, *very* fresh. (*Very* fresh beef, you know, would be spoilt, ruined, by the application of the least particle of salt, and besides, to eat the smallest quantity of salt might give a poor soldier the scurvy, and then, why, the d___l would be to pay, for he might die, and nobody would know he was dead.)

We had a fire to cook by, and a rousing, cheerful fire it was, too. At a little before 12 we gathered around, every fellow with his long sharpened stick, with a piece of beef (God bless the beef!) stuck on the end. Every fellow toasted for himself—some preferred it rare, some well done.—(There was no orders from Head Quarters, Fore quarters, or Hind Quarters, to eat this blessed beef in a raw state, and so we ate it as we pleased, or rather, as we could.) Our bread! well, we cooked it. *Cooked* it, did I say? Yes, we *cooked* it! Some in spontoons (those long handled shovels, we always ever remember to bring along, to exercise ourselves in the elegant art of ditching) others—well, I dont know how they made out!

Dinner was over, and to ditching we went, and you never saw dirt fly so. We did a heap of work that day, and our children, and children's children, will never die contented until they visit Curtis' Lane to see the great breast-works their good old daddies threw them up with their own hands.—The Yankees aint coming to Curtis' Lane, sure. They are too smart for that. Why, sir! we'd destroy 'em to a man. The "sleepy fifth" gets up *every* morning before breakfast, and the Yankees (we are told) have got wind of it. They aint coming, sir!

In the evening of the first day, we had supper. Bill of fare—Beef (no salt) and *bread*. Although we had none of the *delicacies* of our breakfast on our tea table, yet we made out between the beef, fleas, rain and cold, to worry through the night, and get up next morning ready for another attack upon the beef (no salt) and bread.

The first day and the last were pretty much the same. We left one Thursday morning about 3 o'clock. No *long roll* was beat. We were ordered to leave as quickly as possible. We did so almost in breathless silence. Who would have made a fuss, when *they* said the Yankees were in great numbers, just over the branch? We went up to Grafton Church, 3 miles from Yorktown, and staid there till the 31st October, when we left again, and came down here o' purpose to have a fight (so *they* said.) We aint had a fight yet, but we've gathered more corn, and hauled it up, from down below Bethel; than ever you saw, and we would be glad to have our friends with us at the great husking frolic.

As to having a fight here, I don't dream of such a thing, unless we go down to Newport News.—I think we could get accommodated there. (We wont go there *this* week.) How long we'll stay here nobody knows, and I reckon nobody cares. It seems that we will have to worry through the winter in our almost worn out tents, or else let the winter worry us through our few short days.

Really, it seems to me, that we are sufficiently *human* to have winter quarters. Why not? Cannot something be said or done by North Carolina for us. Can she offer no inducement, no prayer, in our behalf. This is the first winter of this terrible civil war. It may last as long as the siege of Troy. If so, and we have no winter quarters provided for us, how can the Government expect us to volunteer our services in her defence any more. "Tis bad policy to freeze men to death in the winter, when it can be avoided, with a hope that they'll thaw again, and be as good as new in the spring."

If anything, therefore, can be done for us, by or through North Carolina, in the way of providing us winter quarters, let it be done without delay. The nights are cold now, and it is quite reasonable to suppose that winter nights will be a *little* colder.

Our regiment is almost itself again. The men generally are sober, quiet, well-behaved; sometimes hungry, and *mostly* at work, such as ditching, cutting down trees, &c. Some of us would like to have a little fight, by way of variety.—More anon.

Your Friend,

Aminadab. [188]

Another soldier sent his daughter a letter describing his feelings and camp routine:

My dear daughters affectionate and most welcome letter of the 12th is received this evening . . . . The vaccine virus that you used has been introduced into the arms of several persons and has taken finally. Moses was vaccinated on the 16th inst and it did not affect him until he came to camp, more than a fortnight—So long a time I never heard, or read before—For a few days after reaching camp, he was very lively. Walked up and down streets between encampments of different companies, the observed of all, quite a hero regarded with especial regard as the Col's body servant—I read your letter to him, in which you charged to take good care of his master, at which he had a significant—"hem" as much to say that his master had to take good care of him and such indeed has been the case. For last week, it became necessary for me to communicate with Gen'l Roberson & Gen'l D. H. Hill . . . as my presence was required at camp. I sent to Col Cahoon, unfortunately his horses ran away and he was thrown violently to the earth, escaping narrowly with his life, so there was no alternative; I went. Moses was my escort. We returned to camp between midnight and day having ridden on horseback nearly 70 miles. You may suppose that I was somewhat fatigued, but the next day, or rather 3 hours after, when I arose I felt bright as a lark, but my valet keeled over fairly, and went to bed, a very sick man: for 48 hours, the surgeon regarded his case as critical: meanwhile I watched & nursed him attentively: hence his significant "hem" when I read your monition "to take good care of his master." He has now reported for duty however and has gone out and attended to Fanny's [horse] wants. I hear him now laughing in his own peculiar nervous manner. In consequence of his indisposition we have no washing done this week, and the clothes he washed last week are not ironed. I have just put on a collar, and although white and clean, this is not so smooth as you have seen, but quite comfortable.

All my acquaintances are surprised at my being in the army. And none are surprised more than myself. In the still hours of night, when no sound is heard save the tread of the one sentinel as he paces his beaten path, I often lie sleepless on my camp cot and think, is it possible? Can this [be] myself? Once so peaceful, almost a preacher—Splendid with all the appretenances of war in a military camp, sleeping soldiers all around me, my daily vocation to learn and teach the dreadful art of killing men, away from my home, on the hard fare of camp life, not infrequently sleeping in the open air leading a life entirely at variance with all my former habits—Can this be me? Well the deed is done, The Rubican is passed and my course is onward, no lingering regrets must impede my course.

Perhaps you would like to know how my daily labors are arranged—Well at day break, the bugle sounds Reveille, when all arise, the general stir among the soldiers, excites horses, chickens, dogs and for about an hour there is general hubbub, and at 7 a.m. the bugle sounds Stable call, at 8 a.m. we are called to breakfast, at 9 a.m. the Guard is mounted—At 10 a.m. the whole regiment is ordered out to drill—at 12 p.m. bugle sounds Stable call, dinner at 12 1/2 p.m.—Regiment drills begin at 2 p.m. At 5 p.m. soldiers wash & prepare for formal dress parade—this is the event of the day. Stable call—or horses fed—at 6 p.m. Supper at 7 p.m.—At 8 p.m. the Retreat is sounded and at 9 p.m. the curfew sounds—or in military language—"Lights Out" and all retire.

As to the location of the camp, my own habitation, my messmates, daily fare etc. I must defer writing until my next letter. Remember me affectionately to my dear sister & all the family & write again to

Yr. Affectionate Father

S.J. Wheeler to Miss Kate Wheeler[189]

When the volunteers' time was up and they started for home, townsfolk welcomed them with open arms and much ado. A teenager from Fayetteville left this in her diary:

November 16: We have been kept in constant excitement for the last two days looking for the LaFayette & Independent Companies. The banks of the Cape Fear were crowded . . . . we got down to the markethouse the soldiers were up there the town bell was ringing & tar barrels were burning and the markethouse had been decorated by the ladies. There was "Welcome Heroes of Bethel" in large letters lighted with gas which looked very pretty. Speeches were made.[190]

On December 25, 1861, Mary Bethall took time to record this in her diary:

This is Christmas day, a beautiful day, but very cold, how different this Christmas from last, now that our Country is filled with armies to defend our country from the Northern army, many bloody battles have been fought, hundreds have been killed on both sides, and a great many soldiers have died in the camp from disease and want of attention while sick, it is sad to contemplate, perhaps the Lord is chastising his church, I believe he permits it for our good.

B. Armstrong Thomasson from Yadkin County was exempt from service because he filled the job of teacher, farmer, and minister. It is possible that he could have been conscripted later in the war, but he died in 1862 helping his neighbors. Mr. Thomasson kept a diary and mentioned Christmas early in the war:

December 24, 1861

Christmas passed off with much noise. A good many of the rowdies whose delight it was to disturb the peace and quietude of our neighborhood on former occasions like this are now in the army. The scarcity of powder will account for the little shooting.*[191]

Lieutenant Alonzo E. Bell, captured at Hatteras in August, inscribed in his diary while a prisoner of war on Governors Island, New York:

Tuesday, Dec. 24, 1861

Weather cold, ground frozen. It begins to look a little like Christmas. A great many packages were brought today: apples, raisin and eggs cakes, etc. for to make a Christmas dinner for the men. But what difference in Christmas here and Christmas at home! For my part I feel very indifferent about the matter so far as eating is concerned. But suppose we had as well be merry as sad.

Wednesday, Dec. 25, 1861

---

*   In some communities in North Carolina, the shooting off of black powder muskets and firecrackers is still practiced today.

Christmas Day. And I would say Merry Christmas to all! But who could say that when he was a prisoner in the hands of the enemies?

Today thousands of religious devotees will assemble and chant forth pealing anthems and praise to the most high and yet the whole country is convulsed in the throws of a revolution in which brother is engaged against brother, father against son, friend against friend. What a strange anomaly is man? What an inconsistency?

The steamer brought a great many presents in the shape of turkeys, oyster cakes, and etc. The generosity of kind friendly ladies to the prisoners. Christmas was kept up among the prisoners in the same manner as at home. Many of our men actually got intoxicated. The officers were up early in the morning stirring eggnog.

Our boys have had a merry day of it. Singing, fiddling, sliding on the ice, etc. were resorted to—all seemed merry as a "marriage bell." The Yankees looked on in astonishment when he saw our table set for dinner. He had eaten but one piece of bread during the day and he thought it strange he said that our fellows could have Lager enough to get drunk on when he could not even get a drink. They are very surprised at the feeling existing shown between our officers and men. They see there is a vast difference in our treatment of them and that of the Federals. Our boys frequently talk with them and have a great deal of sport with them. We had a fine dinner. The bill of fare consisting of turkey, beef, butter, coffee, biscuits, mince pie, cakes, wine, etc. A great deal of this was sent to us by a young lady of N. Jersey. We call her "Little Jersey."

The officers were so pleased with the dinner that they gave 3 cheers for "Little Jersey." All seemed in high glee. But for the life of me I could not feel like Christmas. I was too, too, far from my loved ones.[192]

Prisoners of war from both sides early in the conflict did not suffer the hardships as those inmates in 1864–1865.

Christmas for noncoms found a simpler celebration. Stationed at Goldsboro the second year, a veteran replied: "This is certainly a hard Christmas for us—bitter cold, raining and snowing all the time, and we have no tents. The only shelter we have is a blanket spread over a few poles and gather leaves and put them in that shelter for a bed."[193] A soldier's letter written on Christmas Day from Drewry's Bluff, Virginia, told his parents how uneventful it was for the soldier:

I wish you all a Happy Christmas & a Merry New Year; & sincerely hope you all enjoyed the commencement of these Holidays more than I have. It has been extremely dull here, nothing at all to remind one that this is Christmas Day, the day for which many of us had made elegant & splendid plans, & all have been disappointed, nothing was done.[194]

For Christmas the following year, Charles Bahnson found himself stationed near Orange Court House, Virginia. "One thing that adds to the unpleasantness of this Christmas is that we have nothing good to eat; now I do not mean our fare is so much worse than usual, but we miss the messes of ribs, back bones, souce[sic], puddings and sausages, besides many other things . . ." In a letter written November 25, 1863, Charles Bahnson told his father that he probably could not get a furlough for Christmas. "I would like very much to be there to assist in putting up the Christmas Tree, for I might be able to put one up a little differently to what they generally are in Salem . . ."[195] A North Carolina cavalryman reflected his thoughts one Christmas Day in 1864:

Dec 25 Christmas Sunday—Last Christmas I was at home a schoolboy enjoying my two week vacation. Now how different, I am a soldierboy suffering the prevations [*sic*] and enduring the toil of a long march of twenty five to thirty miles. I hope that when Christmas '65 comes around all soldiers will be at their homes enjoying the peace with [which?] they so long have been fighting for.[196]

Christmas affected the girls as well. A cousin wrote:

Christmas passed away very bad, indeed, with me. It brought forth many sad remembrances of the past which only created discontent. I have been to two quilting parties since Christmas [,] at one of them there were one man, and two boys, at the other there were five gentlemen two of whom were furloughed soldiers, there were some 15-20 lads. I wish you could see them for they are enough to make any person call for the camphor bottle.[197]

Citizens, in a further show of support to the new Confederacy, denounced northern-made goods. Ladies in Asheville and throughout the state urged their friends to shun northern-produced commodities. The manufacture of homemade goods, slow at the beginning of the hostilities, then burst with activity. It is discussed in later chapters.

Advertisements in the newspapers called for volunteers. Many responded that spring; however, by fall, volunteers enlistments slowed. Governor Clark then issued a proclamation in the newspaper encouraging men to reenlist and others to step forward and volunteer. Captain Joseph W. Latta placed this advertisement:

NOTICE: Fifty able bodied men to complete a company of twelve months volunteers now in service to be placed as a guard at the State Prison in Salisbury and also along the line of the North Carolina Railroad as a protection to the bridges. Apply to Thomas Webb, Hillsborough or address me at the Company's Shops.[198]

If North Carolinians could only see into the future, they would never believe that the war would affect each and every citizen no matter the color. Their stories follow.

CHAPTER TWO

Making Flags

North Carolina women did not wait for the state to secede before they began making flags. With patriotic fever high as the men in the neighborhood formed companies and practiced drill, it was assumed that the state would also leave the Union and the men would need flags. Research gives evidence of several flag controversies as to whom actually sewed the first. It appears that the glory may go to the ladies of Washington. "The first flag displayed in little Washington was made at the home of Sam Waters, by Mrs. S.B. Waters, Mrs. Claudia Benbury, Miss Jeanette McDonald, and Miss Sarah Williams, and was flung to the breezes from the window over the door of the court house on the occasion of a speech in favor of the doctrine of State's Rights, and secession, delivered by William Rodman, and replied by David Carter, in the fall of 1860."[1]

Confederate General W. A. Smith told postwar that the First Secession flag was presented on February 1, 1861, by a group of fiery secessionists from Anson County who made a flag of calico, with two large stars at the head marked South Carolina and Mississippi, "the first two states severing their relations with Washington [DC]." From these stars led stripes of alternating red, white, and blue. In the lower corner at the tail end was another star of like proportions, half turned down and marked NC, representing North Carolina—faint and drooping, hanging her head in dishonor, shame, and disgrace. In large letters at the top of the flag was the word "secession." Underneath was this motto Resistance to Oppression Is in Obedience to God.[2] Research revealed that these "fiery secessionists" were four men: T. A. Wadell, J. B. Wadell, W. A. Threadgill, and J. M. Wright. Ms. Kate Smith and Winnie Wilkins pinned silk rosettes on the flag makers. The flag was hung in the night, and immediately upon dawn, residents of Ansonville objected. Later that night, two men climbed the pole and cut the flag down. The original makers of the first flag were not staunched in their efforts. In the morning, Mrs. Garrett and the young ladies in the town stitched another larger flag showing more stars. It carried the same motto. This was hoisted that afternoon. Some in the village refused to walk under the flag. This flag was later presented to Governor John Ellis by Anson County soldiers.[3]

Professor Gilliam, a teacher at the Carolina Female College, was at first against secession; but he softened up, changed his mind, then gave a speech under the second secession flag condemning the North for its "aggressions against the South, and their repudiation of the States' rights, for their contempt for the Constitution . . ." A picket was posted to guard this flag until the town cooled off. The flag at the college was raised twice. The one on top of a store was cut down and then replaced.[4]

However, another claim to the first flag of Washington was from the needles of Mrs. F. C. Roberts and Ms. Manly, who presented it to the guardians of Fort Macon in April of 1861. The Old State Flag pictured a rattlesnake entwined around a pine tree, and the flag was so big they had to stretch it out the full length of the room in the Masonic Hall to sew it.[5] This flag was sometimes referred to as the Pine Tree. Later on, Fort Macon received and flew the garrison flag similar to the Stars and Bars. Susan P. Roberson, with her sisters, made this flag by ripping up the United States flag and restructuring it .[6]

James A. Graham, stationed at Fort Macon, wrote to his mother on May 8, 1861:

> Some ladies came over from Morehead City the other day and brought us a Southern Confederate flag. We hoisted it and fired a salute of nine guns.

Perhaps this was the same flag sewn by the Roberson sisters.[7]

In May 1861, eleven girls representing the eleven Southern states that seceded stood on a porch in Washington as Ms. Clara Hoyt presented a flag to the Washington Grays. Spirits were high as the band played when the young men marched to the wharf, followed by the citizens—some crying, most waving their hankies, and others throwing flowers over them. These recruits were stationed at Portsmouth, which was a resort town prewar. The wives of the officers moved there; and many, many young girls followed, chaperoned by the older women. All stayed there until the capture of Fort Hatteras in February 1862.[8]

A flag presentation from the ladies of Washington to the Jeff Davis Rifles, captained by J. R. Corner, on June 21, 1861, was featured in the newspaper:

Dear Sir:
It is our pleasant duty to present you and your gallant company with the accompanying flag. The ladies of Washington have made it for you. With every stitch has been woven [,] thought of the gallant men who are so soon to risk their lives in our defense, perchance some silent tears have spoken of feelings too deep for utterance, but think not, our tears flow from any cowardly wish to withdraw those we love from this glorious contest. Not so, our hearts may be wrung with sorrow but the ladies of Washington, believing that their cause is a righteous one, and trusting in God for his aid and protection, would urge you on, by every call of honor or duty, by every tender tie, by your duty to God and to your country, by your love for your mothers, wives, and children, to protect our homes and our rights. We do not say, "Protect our flag, let it not be disgraced:" we have no fear for that; in giving it to you, we know that it will be preserved with honor, and we look forward with pleasure to (we hope) the not too far distant day, when you will return to us, and we only claim the privilege of wreathing it with laurels which we know you will win for it.
And now in bidding you farewell, we would pray that The Lord of Hosts be "round about you as a wall of fire, and shield your heads in the day of battle."

On behalf of the ladies of Washington—Mrs. T. H. B. Myers, Ms. Annie C. Hoyt, and Ms. M. M. Fowle—this particular flag was made from the satin wedding gown of Mrs. Myers.[9]

When Rufus Barringer joined the army, local ladies from Cabarrus County presented his unit with a flag on May 18, 1861.[10] Ladies in Gaston County made flags from their dresses for the Gaston Blues and the Watauga Minute Men.[11]

Some people say that it was Orren Randolph Smith who supposedly designed the first Confederate flag. He had asked Ms. Rebecca Murphy of Franklin County to sew it for him. She cut the cloth twelve inches by fifteen inches from flour sacks. He designed seven stars because only seven states had seceded by February 1861. This little model he sent to the Confederate Congress at Montgomery, Alabama, and it was adopted on March 4, 1861. Mr. Smith bought additional fabric and asked Ms. Murphy, again, to make a larger flag of the same kind. She completed it on March 17, 1861. Rebecca's sister, Sarah Ann, refused to help stitch the flag because she held unionist sympathies.[12]

O. R. Smith said, "Whether the flag committee accepted my model or not, I was determined that one of my flags should be floating in the breeze." Henry Lucas, a free black man, cut the pole; and Smith's flag was raised over the courthouse in Louisburg. Unfurled, it flew until Sherman's forces cut it down. A third flag was assembled from Smith's design. The ladies of the community made a flag for the Franklin Rifles and presented it to the company. It was a silk flag with heavy silver fringe, carrying the words: Our Lives to Liberty, Our Souls to God, Franklin Rifles. Presented by the Ladies of Louisburg, North Carolina, April 27th, 1861.[13]

The flag dispute arose in 1904 when the magazine Lost Cause printed an article that the Frenchman Peleg Harrison and German immigrant Nicola Marschall claimed credit. Major Smith's daughter disputed this, and the flag controversy was on. "Orren R. Smith's claim to have designed the Stars and Bars was investigated by a committee of the United Confederate Veterans in 1912 and upheld against other claimants."[14]

The flag controversy continues, but research has shown the last word as to who was first. The first Confederate flag was hoisted March 4, 1861, in Montgomery, Alabama. "William Porcher Miles, head of the Committee on Flag and Seal of the Provisional Confederate Congress in Montgomery, Alabama, detailed the selection of the First National flag via the committee." Neither Major Smith nor Nicola Marschall's design was the first according to researcher Greg Biggs. He said official documents in the Library of Congress show "Smith's claim states that it was after Ft. Sumter that he got the ideal for the flag." Marschall purportedly gave his design to a lady who took it to the governor of Alabama "to be presented to Miles." Mr. Biggs further states that in the National Archives, the names of the two men do not appear in the records. According to Porcher Miles, this committee designed the flag that was accepted.[15]

In April of 1861, the embroidery class at Wayne Female College assembled a silk flag. Class members Ms. Corinne Dortch, Mrs. Thomas Slocumb, and Mrs. Broadhurst used these words on the flag: Goldsboro Rifles, Victory or Death. The college closed in 1862 and was then converted into a hospital.[16] A Confederate flag was constructed by the ladies of Littleton for the Roanoke Minute Men, Company A, Fourteenth North Carolina Troops. Before the Oak City Guards left Raleigh for the seat of war, they were presented a flag on June 1, 1861, stitched by Mrs. F. L. Wilson, and handed over through her husband, who delivered a very appropriate poem as the young recruits were leaving for Virginia. Another gala send-off was in progress at the same time in Morrisville. Ms. Fanny Lyon gave a speech while presenting a flag to the Cedar Fork Rifles. Rev. A. D. Blackwood gave each recruit a Bible.[17]

Other ladies who made flags for different units were the students of St. Mary's, who sewed the flag for the Ellis Light Artillery.[18] Ms. H. Weatherspoon wrote a short note to the *Raleigh Standard*, which said that the local ladies had formed an aid society and presented a flag to former professor R. W. York, who was captain of the volunteers.[19] In Charlotte, the Hornets Nests Riflemen were bestowed a beautiful flag. The last paragraph of Ms. Sadler's speech to the departing troops went as follows:

> The prayers, the hopes, the hearts of our ladies go with you. We feel success will crown our banner. We have no room for fears. To God and our community we devote you.

Also in Charlotte, a hand-painted flag was presented to the Charlotte Grays by Ms. Hattie Howell. Her speech was short and sweet: "Captain Ross, I present to you this flag for the Charlotte Grays, knowing that whatever happens it will never, while a man of you lives, be lowered in disgrace."

After the usual words of thanks, Captain Ross explained:

> . . . we promise you, in the name of the Charlotte Grays will never see it dishonored. We may die in its defense, but dishonored it shall never be.[20]

On May 8, 1861, the following beautiful and inspiring address was delivered at Charlotte by Ms. Ann E. Wilson on presenting a flag of the Confederate States to the cadets of the Military Institute before they left for the military encampments near this city:

> I have been commissioned by the young ladies of Charlotte to present to you this beautiful ensign, the FLAG OF OUR COUNTRY. Here upon the revered soil of Mecklenburg we commit to you, not simply the fabric of which this banner is made, nor only the hopes and wishes of its donors, but we commit to your keeping, the dearest cause we have, the cause of JUSTICE AND HUMANITY.
>
> For the good of your country, you have shown a laudable desire to leave your Institution of learning and many pleasant associations which you have

formed here, and go in the defence of our rights, and whilst many a tear of friendship will flow, and many a bright hope be crushed, yet we bid you "God speed" in this great work, and may the God of BATTLES, and the God of NATIONS, and the God of JUSTICE protect and defend you.

The South has been called upon for her jewels, and like Cornelia, the mother of Gracchi, she presents her sons. Already this flag with its bright galaxy of seven stars, whose luster has been increased by an eighth, Virginia, and the reflection of a ninth, North Carolina, is waving in triumph over Sumter, and unfolding its pure and unsullied folds to the boys of the entire south. In this cause and under this flag, you will take into battle, and recollect, that wherever you may be, you have our kindest wishes, our sympathies and our prayers,

Let me say, now, in bidding you adieu, that we know to whom we have confided this sacred trust, and we have the highest assurance, that when the "thunder of war" shall be heard no more, and the glad tidings of peace shall spread over our land, we shall welcome the return of this banner with honor and victory perched upon its folds, or it will become the winding sheet of the brave hearts and strong arms, which have borne it to the battle field.

> "Go forth then ye brave where glory awaits you,
> The voice of your country exultant, now greets you;
> The good and the true with favor regard you,
> And the smiles of the fair with blessings reward you."[21]

"May 15, 1861, made flag for the homeguards at Ringwood," wrote Mrs. Elizabeth S. Wiggins of Halifax County in her diary. She was fifty-seven years old and would later have seven sons serving in the war.

Catherine Edmondston penned in her diary:

> . . . tomorrow the ladies of Scotland Neck present to the Scotland Neck Mounted Riflemen a flag. The Edgecombe Guards, the Enfield Blues, the Halifax Light Infantry are coming and they gave a grand ball to the ladies. The flag is a beautiful one of blue silk with heavy bullion fringe & tassels. One side is the coat of arms of North Carolina surrounded by gold stars, one for each state; on the other a wreath of corn in the silk & ripe ear, cotton in blossom & bole, & wheat encircling the words Scotland Neck Mounted Riflemen—organized Nov 30th, 1859, & on the ribbon which ties the wreath the words, "Pro aris et focis." The staff represents a corn stalk surmounted by a battle axe—peace and war juxtaposition![22]

Young women of Henderson County "presented the young men with a beautiful flag, white with fifteen blue stars, emblematic of the Southern States, radiating from the center, forming one large star. On the reverse side is worked in blue and white 'To the Henderson Guards, follow your banner to victory or death.'"[23] The ladies of Asheville donated a flag they had made to the troops known as the Watauga Rangers. Young and old alike took food and treats to the training camp.[24] At the Confederate Armory in Asheville, a flag was raised and flew continually until the Federal Army burned the complex in April 1865. Upon the flag were these words: "Of liberty born of a patriot's dream, Of a storm-cradled nation that fell."[25] Caldwell County ladies constructed a flag, as did the young women of Lenoir County and the women of Hendersonville. In Shelby, ladies sewed a flag, and Ms. Julia Durham was chosen to render the speech.[*26]

---

*   See the appendix for the complete speech.

Over the courthouse in Jefferson flew a flag constructed by townswomen. Amid fanfare the Yadkin Grays Eagles were presented a silk flag on June 17, 1861. Ms. Louise M. Glen, Mrs. Mary Lilley Conelly, Ms. Fannie Conelly, Ms. Elizabeth Glen, and Ms. E. S. Conrad are credited for the construction. This particular flag, fashioned from the donors' dresses, was embroidered with the words "We scorn the sorid lust of pelf, and serve our country for herself." The captain of the Eagles finished his acceptance speech with the words, "When this cruel war is over, Miss Lou, this flag untarnished shall be returned to you."[27]

The *Raleigh Standard* printed word for word the presentation from the ladies of Morrisville to the North Carolina Grays on June 5, 1861:

> Captain York drilled the men, had a dress parade, and much singing, Miss Fanny Lyon stepped forward and presented the Cedar Fork Rifles with a flag the ladies had made:
>
> "Gentlemen, I have been commissioned by the young ladies of Cedar Fork, to present to the brave sons of this vicinity, this beautiful ensign. Indeed it charms me that I have the pleasure of presenting to this, I must say beautiful and brave men of North Carolina.
>
> This ensign showing to the world the eagerness of the young ladies in assisting their brothers, and attached friends, in defence of their country. We can help only by our prayers—we regret very much that we cannot help them more.
>
> For the good of your country, you have shown laudable desire to leave your institution of learning, various occupations, and the many pleasant associations which you have formed here, and go to the distant part of the country, to aid in the defence of our rights, and while many a tear of friendship, of sympathy, shall flow for the brave and noble sons of this company, we promise you our kindest wishes, our sympathies and our prayers. Be of good cheer! Do not fall, or be crushed in the hands of despair. I have one dear brother—with all the timidity due my sex, I am ready to offer him up in defence of our country's rights and honor, not with grief, but thanking God that I have one brother to offer. May he, and this noble company, prove to be faithful, intelligent and chivalrous sons of the south.
>
> When the direful contest is over, and the patriotic husband, brothers, and friends return, the ladies of Cedar Fork will meet you with tears of joy, the smile of welcome, the bosom of delight, and the embraces of pure and unsullied affection.
>
> In behalf of our society, I now present to the North Carolina Grays, this beautiful flag. We bid you all God's speed.

The speech of acceptance was made by one of the officers of the company, Lieutenant Malcus Williamson Page. "Afterwards the ladies of Cary served a meal to the crowd. That afternoon Reverend A.D. Blackwood preached a sermon and gave a bible to the military company."[28]

The Eleventh Regimental flag, sewn by the women of Windsor, though torn and patched, succeeded through the war and was secretly burned at Appomattox. Captain Edward Outlaw was able to cut a small square from the flag before destroying it. Mrs. Patrick Henry Winston, Ms. Webb, and the Mses. Outlaw are credited with constructing this flag.[29]

The Ellis Flying Artillery marched to the St. Mary's campus to receive their flag constructed by the students. Not to be outdone, students of the Salem Female College completed a flag for the Forsyth Rifles commanded by Alfred Belo. Forming up on the square in town, the men listened to the Rev. George Bahnson as he prayed for their safety and to resist "temptations of a soldier's life."[30]

Forsyth County's flag, "made for Co. I . . . was sewn by Misses Bettie and Laura Lemly, Nellie Belo, Carrie and Mary Fries [sister of John Fries]. It was made of red, white, & blue silk and embroidered in large letters with yellow silk, on the white side, with the words 'Liberty or Death.' A second flag was made by the same young ladies. They could not get any more silk like the first [,] so used white silk for the whole flag, embroidering it in blue silk . . . both of these flags were presented to the Forsyth Rifles."*31 A third flag was constructed for Company G, Captain W. Wheeler's men, based on the first national pattern sewn by Lavinia Boner, Laura and Bettie Lemly, Kate Kremer, and Addie Shober. About forty wagons left Salem with the new recruits bound for Danville, Virginia.

H. W. Barrow, member of the Twenty-First Regiment, said, "The ladies of Danville say we have . . . the best looking flag in camp . . ."32

Skirts that women wore in the mid-nineteenth century enveloped a wire hoop. It took a minimum of five yards to cover the bell shape of the hoop. It is no wonder that these skirts contained enough fabric to make flags, and they were used for that purpose. It also makes for a romantic story to tell future grandchildren. In Lenoir County, Ms. Lina Caison made a flag from a dress belonging to Ms. Annie Rankin. In another reference, Ms. Annie Rankin was given credit for making the flag. This flag was blue with the North Carolina coat of arms painted by Annie's sister. On July 31, 1861, in Hickory, Ms. Norwood presented this flag to Captain Rankin of the Twenty-sixth Regiment, Company F. They were known afterwards as the Hibriten Guards. Little girls wearing white dresses with blue sashes took part in the presentation ceremony representing the thirteen seceded states.33 Another flag of the Twenty-sixth Regiment came from the needles of several mothers and sisters of the Waxhaw Guards. Mrs. Anna Cureton Stevens presented the flag on July 4, 1861, to Company B.34 The Buncombe Rifles carried a flag made from the silk dresses of Mses. Anna and Lillie Woodfin, Mses. Fanny and Annie Patton, Mary Gaines, and Kate Smith of Asheville.35

Other students recorded who executed flags were the girls from the Chowan Institute, presenting theirs to the Hertford Light Infantry. In Greensboro, the students of Edgeworth School and Mary Morehead spoke these words upon presenting the flag to departing troops:

> In the name of my subjects, fair donors of Edgeworth, I present this banner to the Guilford Greys. Fain would I have it a "Banner of peace" and have inscribed upon its folds, "Peace on earth good will to men;" for our womanly natures shrink from the horrors of war and bloodshed. But we have placed . . . upon it "the oak"—fit emblem of the firm heroic spirits over which it is to float. Strength, energy, and decision mark the character of the sons of Guilford, whose noble sires have taught their sons to know but one fear—the fear of doing wrong . . .
>
> Proudly in days past have the banners of our country waved o'er yon battlefield, where our fathers fought for freedom from a tyrant's power. This their motto—"Union in Strength," and we their daughters would have this our banner unfurled, only in some noble cause, and quiveringly through our soft Southern breezes echo forth the same glorious theme, Union!, Union!

Henry Gorrell collected the flag and made his acceptance speech:

> In time of war or in time of peace, in prosperity or in adversity we would have you remember the Guilford Grays; for be assured your memories will ever be cherished by them. And we would have you remember that we are all in favor of union—union of states, union of hearts, union of hands, union now and forever, one and inseparable.36

In Tarboro, Mrs. Anna McNair sewed a flag, and Ms. Cornelia Crenshaw gave it to the Edgecombe Guards. The Arsenal's U. S. flag in Fayetteville was removed and replaced with

---

* Note: an article in the NCHR said it was Company I instead of Company D. Perhaps this was the second flag made.

the state flag. The Stars and Stripes was given to the town women, who converted it into a Confederate flag "when the Stars and Bars had been settled upon." The ladies of Fayetteville stitched a flag for the First Regiment. "To commemorate the fight [Bethel, Virginia], the legislature adopted a resolution calling for a special flag for the First Regiment." The ladies of Fayetteville drew the assignment to make it. The regiment was near Yorktown, Virginia, when the flag was finished, so John Baker Jr. carried it to the camp and presented it to the troops.[37]

At Floral College in Robeson County, the Highland Boys received a flag in July of 1861, then boarded the train and left Shoe Heel (presently Maxton) to the tears of the females. Sergeant L. J. Hoyle, of the Southern Stars from Lincoln County, received a flag from the fair hands of a gentler sex. The recruits left for Raleigh and stayed in the basement of the Baptist church until continuing on to camp.

Ladies of Wadesborough sewed a silk flag, and it was painted by Lemuel Beeman. They marched to Cheraw (South Carolina) and took the train to Florence, South Carolina, which went to Wilmington, then into the Raleigh training camps.[38] Recruits from Carthage, after an all-day celebration, took the train to a distant camp. In addition, the day they left, they were given a large meal by townsfolk; and each member of the company was presented with a small silk flag by Mrs. Eliza Short. On one side of the flag appeared these words:

> Our cause is just, Our duty we know.
> In God we trust, To battle we go.

The other side of the flag read:

> We are sending our boys, Our best and bravest,
> Oh, God protect them, Thou who savest.[39]

The Sixth North Carolina State Troops ensign came from a ladies' blue shawl. Ms. Christine Fisher stitched the flag for her brother, which he took with him to Manassas. It featured the state seal with the words "Do or Die" on one side, and the reverse read "May 20th, 1775." Unfortunately, he was killed. Other girls in Salisbury stitched a flag for the Rowan Artillery.[40] Ladies from Stokes County made a flag for the Brown Mountain Boys.

Mrs. Robert Ransom alone constructed the flag carried by the First NC Cavalry. "She requested that the flag never be surrendered, and after the fall of Appomattox, one of the men wrote, they never surrendered it but sunk it in the river." Other known women acting alone in sewing flags are Ms. Rachale McIver, who gave a flag to the Twentieth NCT, and Mrs. W. T. Sutherlin, whose husband's company became the Milton Blues. On that silk flag appeared the words "On to Victory."[41] It is believed that Mary B. Clarke made the flag for her husband's regiment, the Fourteenth.[42]

"While the North Carolina Assembly was struggling to prevent having a flag on the capitol, a Raleigh newspaper reported on April 24, that the flag of the Confederate States of America had been run up on the capitol . . ."[43] It must be remembered that many of the congressmen at this point were of Union sympathies. Some thought a United States flag was more appropriate. The U.S. flag was rejected, and at the first secession, convention members voted to have a state flag. William Browne, a local artist, designed this flag. The secession flag is similar to the present North Carolina state flag.

Women continued to construct flags as needed. Silk, although a very strong fiber, did not stand up to the heat and weather; so it was not unusual for them to make another. Wool bunting became the fabric of choice. At the end of the war, ladies in Wilmington made the second national Confederate flag, which flew over Fort Fisher from December 1864 to January 1865. Some North Carolina regiments carried three flags: the battle flag, a regimental flag, and sometimes a company flag.[44] The story of flag makers is not complete, but this gives the reader some examples.

The Stars and Bars are furled, but loved the same,
And through the bloody stains we love the name
Of Stars and Stripes, for which we fight today,
The old flag is not lost, but laid away,
So do not say, FORGET!

Anonymous[45]

This picture of the Thirty-seventh Regiment flag was sent to me by Dan O'Connell of Hagerstown, Maryland. He said that it was picked up after Antietam on the Otto farm near Burnside's Bridge. "The 37th was with A. P. Hill on September 17, 1862 and come from Harpers Ferry to Sharpsburg 17 miles in 8 hours then took on the Union late in the day."

The 61st Regiment NCV
N.C. Division of Archives & History, Photographic Archives

CHAPTER THREE

Benevolent Scavengers and Patriotic Exhaustion

Confederate President Jefferson Davis was known to have said, "The domestic labors of the women contributed much to supply the wants of our defenders in the field and their faith in our cause shone a guiding star undimmed by the darkest clouds of war."[1]

When the hostilities began, both governments soon realized that they would need outside help to assist with the vast numbers of men requiring supplies. The South did not have a central organization such as the North's Sanitary Commission. Instead, small groups popped up like mushrooms throughout North Carolina and other Southern states. Heavier populated cities had more members who usually met in a central location such as a courthouse, city hall, or large buildings. In Raleigh, women met in the "state house" (capitol building), with their sewing machines. The names of these benevolent groups vary. In Raleigh, they were known as the Baptist, Episcopal, and Presbyterian Sick Soldiers Relief Society; the Christ Church Sick Soldiers Society; Ladies' Soldier Aid Society of the Methodist Church; Baptist Sick Soldiers Relief Society; and the Wake Female Aid Society.[2] Ladies from Washington named their group the Military Sewing Society.[3]

Large amounts of money was circulated at the beginning of the conflict for war supplies. Lenoir residents raised four thousand dollars in one day, then later donated ten thousand dollars. Cumberland County citizens subscribed forty-one thousand dollars. The *Richmond Dispatch* printed a notice that men in Charlotte donated a large sum of money:

> Old Mecklenburg has appropriated $50,000 to defray the expenses of her soldiers, and private though wealthy gentlemen of this place, say they will increase the amount as soon as it is needed.[4]

Research indicates that the earliest date for group donations occurred April 19, 1861, by the citizens of Warrenton. In a letter to Governor Ellis from William A. Johnston, he says, "Three thousand five hundred dollars was raised at a meeting . . . here last night for the Warren Guards." At first, the Bertie County residents donated four thousand dollars, then after hearing of Lincoln's letter to Governor Ellis, pledged ten thousand dollars more for the troops, with part of the money going to assist families of soldiers.[5]

Women on all economic levels participated in the endeavor to supply the soldiers whatever their needs. Citing passages from author King, "There was little distinction in class, a common safety making all neighbors, the richer and the poorer sharing alike in them."[6] A female told the story of a Mrs. Arnett in the local paper, and she challenged other women to follow her example:

> I noticed in the Observer [Fayetteville] . . . among the contributions of blankets, that Mrs. Arnett gave two blankets and two quilts. Mrs. Arnett is dependent on her daily labor for a living—her husband and three brothers are in the army, all of whom she influenced to enter into the service of her country—so different from a great many wives and sisters, who insist on their husbands and brothers remaining at home. I was pleased to see this contribution published which was liberal throughout, as I intended to give all the blankets I had but after seeing Mrs. Arnett's contribution, I shall not make mine until I see if I can't buy some more. In addition to what she has already done, she wishes to knit one dozen pair of socks, if she can procure wool. Stir up, you wealthy, or you will be outdone in liberality by the poor of our country. Mrs. Arnett shall never want [for] a friend.   Signed ESPER[8]

It was not unusual for black people and children to voluntarily donate money, socks, or their time to help with the war effort. One black servant, a driver, reportedly went to his master and insisted that he accept his savings of one hundred dollars to help equip the volunteers. In Charlotte, colored ladies donated twenty-five dollars. Afterwards, another donation came from the members of the colored Methodist church, amounting to $13.75.[9]

A Young Ladies Knitting Society, comprising girls ages ten to thirteen, was begun in Fayetteville. If the girls did not finish one pair every two weeks, they were fined ten cents. Two boys were in this club. Not to be outdone, younger children were in the Juvenile Knitting Society. Both boys and girls knitted socks and scarves called neck comforts. The receiver of a pair of socks made from this group sent this message: "The members of the third company Battalion, Washington Artillery of New Orleans, embrace this opportunity of tendering to the 'Young Ladies' Knitting Society' of Fayetteville, N.C., their thanks for the recent present of sixty-five pair of socks."[10]

> For all the socks the maids have made,
> Our thanks for all the brave,
> And honored be your pious trade,
> The soldiers sole to save.[11]

A member of this society, Melinda Ray, wrote in her journal on November 20, 1862:

> The young ladies have a knitting society which meets every thur & we school girls every Sat. evening. The club has knitted 85 pairs of socks since they began in November.

Another children's knitting club developed in Raleigh. A child's name and sometimes a slave's name were printed in the newspaper, along with the article they had donated. Little girls were still knitting socks, and women gathered items to go in a box as late as March 1865, one month before the war ended.[12]

The need for socks was so great that it was socially acceptable to knit while the minister was preaching. Women could be seen knitting as they were *walking* in town. "Everybody was knitting 'socks for the soldier,'" wrote Catherine Edmondston. She continued, "Ladies & children, all seemed absorbed in it. Ladies took their knitting in the carriages as they rode out & knit in the intervals and indeed DURING their visit. Children left their play & voluntarily sat for hours steadily occupied."[13]

C.S. General James Gordon said of women, "That every click of the knitting needle was a prayer and many a stitch was dimmed with tears."[14]

Mrs. Margaret DeMill wrote to C.S. Captain Thomas Sparrow on April 23 that a Military Working Society had been formed by the ladies of Washington for the purpose of making military clothing, picking lint, making bandages for the soldiers, and to "aid them in any other suitable manner." Ms. M. M. Hoyt, president of the society, sent ten mattresses and military clothing to Captain Sparrow on May 22.[15] Ladies of Lincolnton formed a society and were given cloth to sew into uniforms. By April 29, nearly all the men were equipped.[16]

The *Raleigh Standard* printed a letter addressed to Mr. William Holden, editor:

> Dear Sir—I send you an account of the organization of a Society of Ladies at our place, the objects of which are: 1st to present the company of volunteers . . . a flag; and 2nd—to administer to the comforts, and relieve the wants of the same, and to keep up a regular correspondence. This, we think, is movement in the right direction, as it must be consoling to the volunteers to know, while undergoing the fatigues of campaign, that their mothers, wives, sisters, and sweethearts, are using their best efforts to render their conditions as pleasant as possible . . .[17]

Editors of newspapers took it upon their own to place notices encouraging women to organize committees for the troops. In the late summer of 1861, the local newspaper in Salem published notices calling for a Ladies Relief Association to make blankets and socks for its volunteers.[18] A few days later, the *Standard* published remarks from Ms. E. F. "Lizzie" Weatherspoon, with the Cedar Fork Academy:

> I wish to explain the objects of this society, known by the name of the CEDAR FORKS SOLDIERS' RELIEF SOCIETY. The objects are simply these: that we wish to do something about the defence of our country, and that our desire is to render the burdens of those whose duty it is, to take a more active part in the defence of the same, as light as possible. We sincerely hope this society may prove a great blessing to this community. We wish to render this company as comfortable, as cheerful, and as pleasant as our feeble abilities will allow. We can do something—we can furnish some one of the company with a garment, or perhaps something in the way of nourishment, once a month at least.
>
> While they are compelled to leave the old homestead and their loved ones at home, can we not speak one word of consolation to their poor sorrowing hearts? Can we be of any relief at all? Mothers, have your sons volunteered in the defence of the rights of their own country? If they have, they have shown themselves worthy patriots, and they also deserve our most affectionate sympathy. Will you now show the love you have for them and your country, by uniting with us in their behalf?
>
> Wives, where are your husbands? Have they forsaken you and their dear children for the purpose of preserving their once peaceful and happy homes? Have they offered their lives as a sacrifice to their beloved country? If they have, grieve not on account of their absence! Their wives, mothers, sisters, and sweethearts, are using their best efforts to render their condition as pleasant as possible. I trust that a similar movement may soon be made in every community, and with great success. The following is the organization: Mrs. L.F. York, President; two Vice Presidents: Mrs. M.A. Barbee and Ms. M.H. Lowe; Ms. R.J. Weatherspoon, Sec; Ms. E.F. Weatherspoon, Treas. With a long list of names of members who obligate to make monthly contributions to the objects of the association, ladies, let us hear from you.[19]

Ms. Laura Norwood of Lenoir kept a diary in which she listed the work done for three volunteer companies the first three months of the war. She does not mention how many of the women were in the sewing group, but the ones present did a tremendous amount of needlework in a short period. The Lenoir ladies made for Captain Jones's company, which left Lenoir on June 3, ten pairs of pants, one hundred haversacks and straps, one hundred knapsacks and straps, a flag, a quantity of lint and roller bandages, and three days' provisions. A notation on the page of the diary read, "This company furnished with tents." For Captain Rankin's company, which left on July 31, the society had made twenty pairs of pants (twelve pairs made by the Valley Ladies), ninety fatigue jackets, eighty haversacks with straps, twelve mattresses, a flag, lint, testaments, and three days' provisions. Another note at the bottom of the page said, "This company also had fifty blankets given them." For Captain White's company, which departed two weeks later, he received ten mattresses and "some shirts." It is not known if the ladies became exhausted, if their supplies were unattainable, or that another benevolent group supplied him.[20]

Other ladies did not sit and wait on the state to furnish fabric for tents and uniforms. Mrs. Edmondston scribbled in her diary: "Brought home another tent on which my forces [slaves] are busily engaged. The Cloth for these Uniforms & Tents is purchased by individual subscription, not waiting for the State to equip its men . . ."[21]

People belonging to aid societies wore many different hats. Some families chose to make uniforms and socks. Women who didn't feel they could construct a coat could have sewn the simpler hospital shirts or hospital slippers. Males donated money and/or food. If a person didn't have any of the above, they could donate their time in nursing or by taking part in bazaars or tableaux; plus this gave the public something for their money, and it was fun.

A local newspaper published an article about the principal of the Institute for the Deaf, Dumb, and Blind, Mr. W. J. Palmer:

> . . . has tendered to the Governor the services of all the pupils in that Institution—the boys to make cartridges, etc. and the girls to do any sewing that may be required. We learn from Mr. P. that it is with difficulty he can restrain some of the Deaf and Dumb boys and young men from quitting the Institution in order to volunteer in defence of their country, so anxious are they to fight the Yankees.[22]

Students from the various schools wanted to be involved in the war effort. Girls at St. Mary's Female College were very anxious to help. Having made a flag, they began sewing for the volunteers. Soon, 176 mattresses and 118 towels were ready for shipment. The girls petitioned and received a two-and-a-half-day vacation from their studies, but after making all of the above, they declared it was no holiday. Next they knitted socks and gloves, then made shirts and uniforms. The volunteers repaid the favor by serenading the girls.[23] Other Wake County students at Ms. Partridge's school made and gave items to area hospitals.[24] One schoolgirl in Fayetteville wrote that the girls went wild: "No use was it to mention books to them; it was their plain duty to sew for the soldiers, though, I much fear some of the work might have been criticised by particular persons. There were dress parade suits and fatigue suits to be made, and under clothing suitable for camp life—tents, haversacks, canteens to be covered, etc . . . ."[25]

Children of all ages helped with the war effort in any way they could. Many wrote poems and placed them in pockets of soldiers' shirts or tucked them between hospital clothing. Young children helped with packing small bags of food for the aid societies. They ran errands for the different clubs. Some rolled bandages; others carried water and fresh straw to medical buildings. Mrs. Lucy Robertson remembered that she and the children in Hillsborough turned table and bed linens into lint for the hospitals.[26] Children carried flowers and reading material to the sick. The soldiers loved interacting with the young folks.

The *Richmond Examiner* accused Forsyth County of disloyalty. A rebuttal was published in the *People's Press*, listing all the donations and benevolent work the citizens of Salem and Winston had carried out.[27] The Piedmont Moravian community involved with charity received this note of thanks: "We thank all the people of the county [Forsyth], ' . . . not forgetting to give special credit to the Trustees of Salem Female Academy for the very liberal donation of one thousand dollars to the Central Committee.'"[28] A Young Ladies' Relief Association formed in Salem, along with a group of older women from both Salem and Winston, who spent weeks in making clothing for the volunteers.[29] A number of ladies formed a relief society, five of whom volunteered as nurses, going to Manassas. This was the rebuttal printed in the *Press*:

> Several gentlemen with their ladies accompanied them, and after administering to the wants of the sick in Virginia for about two months, with good results . . . returned home. Does this look like there was any secret organization in this community to give aid and comfort to our enemies, or in any way opposing the Southern Confederacy?

That particular area of the state was known for Union sympathies. People in counties surrounding the Quaker Belt were curious to know what their neighbors were doing to support the war.[30] Other Salem women worked for the troops. Carrie Fries, owner of a sewing machine, penned in her diary June 23:

I go to church, Mother and Mollie attend to the baking, and when I get back they are making Captain Miller's blankets. Mother cuts out a uniform coat for Doctor [Shaffner] . . . I sew on the machine all afternoon. Mollie moulded [*sic*] bullets this afternoon and mother cut out [uniforms].[31]

Another Raleigh newspaper, the *Christian Advocate*, got into the act that spring:

PROVISIONS FOR THE TROOPS

The forces now in the field must be for sometime mainly dependent for support upon voluntary contributions. ALL barrels or packages of flour, cornmeal, bacon, lard, butter, or anything else which the soldier may . . . need, should be delivered at the nearest depot . . . secured and directed . . . and they will be transported free of charge. Let it be directed to the commandant of Fort Caswell or Fort Macon, as the donors prefer. We suggest . . . that the provisions designed for the Raleigh soldiers . . . be directed to Capt. R. S. Tucker, QM, Raleigh.

Mrs. Edmondston said the one thing that struck her throughout the whole progress of the summer was "the universality & the eagerness with which the women entered into the struggle! They worked as many of them had never worked before, steadily & faithfully, to supply the soldiers with clothing and the hospitals with comforts of various kinds. Everything must be given to them, every thing done for them. The ladies all over the country had formed themselves into hospital associations & were at work on quilted comfortables, shirts, drawers, etc. for the sick & wounded. The hearts of the whole population was fired—& could Lincoln & Seward have seen with what unanimity & self abnegation they acted [,] they must have been shaken . . ."[32]

A soldier from the mountains had nothing but good comments for the benevolence of the community:

Camp Martin Feby 17th 1862
. . . The people are very kind to us & they bring into camp to sell chickens, turkeys, egg, butter, pies, cakes, potatoes, cabbage & apples. They sell them at very moderate prices. The ladys have a soldiers aid society here & have some clothing on hand that they had not sent off. They called on me & other officers to know if we had any very needy men that had not a change of clothing . . . they distributed in proportion to our wants. They say they will have enough to supply our wants by Friday. This is Southernism in true Dixie & if every body had such host our soldiers would be well provided for . . .[33]

The ladies of Franklin County in obedience to the call of Governor Clark held a meeting at Plank Chapel, Hayesville district, on Wednesday, August 28, and organized a society by electing a president, Mrs. Feraby A. Stote. Williamston ladies called their group the Soldiers' Relief Society.[34] Citizens from Moore County took layers of canvas or thick cloth and sewed them together for cartridge belts and boxes. The items were then varnished.[35] The Rockingham Soldiers Aid Society constructed uniforms distributed by county agents to the women to be made up, and in the breast pockets of the coats, they placed small testaments or prayer books. Young girls cut up their merino dresses to make shirts for the recruits; blankets formed from carpets were lined with oilcloth.[36] Even before the state seceded, the Ladies Aid Society of New Bern headed by Ms. Annie Daves made three hundred mattresses for the defenders of Fort Macon.[37]

In the 1860 census, Wilmington is listed as the largest city in North Carolina with over nine thousand inhabitants. It was a port city and railroad hub. Women would call on

Confederate General William Whiting, commander of Wilmington forces, for tasks to assist the soldiers. He must have been overwhelmed with requests because he wrote C.S. General Beauregard, "I have started the ladies of Wilmington making cartridge belts and sand bags, and that keeps their little hearts quiet and happy."[38]

Many organizations were fortunate enough to meet every day to gather provisions for the soldiers. Daily meetings were a tremendous sacrifice, and it is not known how long these women kept up the pace. In Wilmington, Mrs. Armand DeRossett, president of the Soldiers' Aid Society, said, "The ladies would daily gather at the City Hall and ply their busy needles or machines, with never a sigh of weariness."* Her assistants were Mrs. Alfred Martin, Mrs. Mary Sanders, the wife of Major Stevenson, Mrs. Alfred DeRossett, and the German women of the city. The theater, Thalian Hall, was filled in the mornings and afternoons with these energized patriotic women. The ladies made uniforms, haversacks, socks, and powder bags for the large columbiads and filled sandbags used on the fortifications at Fort Fisher. Other ladies rolled cartridges and covered canteens. Mrs. DeRossett had a room fitted out in her house to receive and store supplies they had made and collected for the troops. "Never were the spiritual needs of the soldiers neglected. Bibles, prayer books, and hymn books were distributed." Society members would go every Sunday to Fort Fisher to have devotions with the military. The women also nursed the sick and wounded at the fort. Dr. Armand DeRossett, a physician at the fort, was assisted by his wife.[39] Patients from Virginia's hospitals were sent into Wilmington's port, where they were temporarily cared for by the society afterwards traveling by train into the Deep South.[40]

The women of Greensboro voted to meet every day at a central location downtown. Some brought their sewing machines, others their knitting, and the remainder brought articles to work on.[41] Greensboro ladies met all trains, "even in the small hours of the night, to hand out refreshments to weary troops . . ."[42]

Mrs. J. Henry Smith of Greensboro said of the ladies: "Every piece of old linen was scraped and cherished, bandages made, carpets taken up; and all blankets, clothing, food, and whatever could be given up for the comfort of the boys were sent to the camps."[43]

The aid societies formed their own rules whether to charge dues or to commit a certain amount to be finished and ready for shipment by the week or month. The rules were very flexible. Some groups chose to meet three times a week. Catherine Edmondston wrote in her diary on January 31 that her sisters had sewing machines and had spent three days each week at the society room sewing since last September "and show no signs of flagging. Susan Raynor carried me into the Ladies Soldiers' Aid Society, the same one to whom I gave my wool mattress in the fall to be knit into socks. We found a dozen ladies all hard at work on hospital shirts & drawers."[44]

Mrs. M. A. Obsorne of Charlotte's Soldier's Aid Society reported about three meetings held each week; each Wednesday was used exclusively for sewing, "the ladies plying their needles, not in embroidery, but making uniforms, drawers, overcoats, shirts, haversacks, gloves, comforts, bed-ticks, pillows, and socks." Each member of this society had to pay twenty-five cents per month to belong, and if they didn't come to the meetings, they were fined. "The first year our organization made 301 garments of which 207 was sent to the Montgomery Hospital in Virginia for the use of the North Carolina soldiers there; nine comforts went to the Charlotte Hospital; nine pairs of socks went to the wives & sisters of soldiers who passed them to their kin; they also report having on hand eighty-two garments, fifty-seven pairs of socks, & eight pairs of woolen gloves." This group had sixty-five members

---

*   Vice President, Mrs. Parthenia Barnes; for Secretary, Mrs. Minerva Overton; for Treasurer, Mrs. Elizabeth O'Brien—Executive Committee: Ms. Promelia Gill, Ms. Martha Best, Ms. Pattie E. Huller, Ms. Fannie Hays, Ms. Mariah Ellington, Ms. Angelia Stone, Ms. Bettie Smith, and Mrs. Lucy Hight.

at the beginning of the war. They claimed to have enough fabric on hand to last through the war (later proven false). These ladies sewed garments for the troops until the Confederate government took over furnishing uniforms in 1862. In addition, they gave fabric to indigent soldiers' wives to be cut and sewn for the military. Charlotte's aid society dispersed money and goods donated by other people for the use of the soldiers' families.[45]

Mentioned earlier, the Sick Soldiers Relief Society of Raleigh decided to meet three days each week for four hours a day. "The amount of work accomplished by this society since its organization was as follows: shirts—140; drawers—98; sheets—44; towels—183; pillow cases—64; pillow ticks—33; comforts—2; and pillows—24." This group sent other items to the surgeon general's office. "The donations to the Society has been as follows: Mrs. G.W. Mordecai—24 shirts, 24 prs. drawers, 30 bottles Catawba brandy, tomato catsup, 6 prs. socks; Miss Pettigrew—24 flannel bands; Mrs. John Deveraux—12 prs. cotton socks; Mrs. F.G. Haywood—2 comforts; Miss Ellen Mordecai—6 prs. drawers; W. Mahler—a stencil plate; Mrs. Flowers of Wilmington—one barrel rice flour; Miss Maggie M—a pin cushion; Miss Nellie (?) Deveraux—a Mexico book; Mrs. Colten—6 sheets, 3 spreads; Mrs. J.H. Bryan—4 prs. socks; Mrs. R. Tucker—5 bottles wine, 1 bag rice, bottle Catawba wine; Miss T. Love and Miss Ellen M—22 prs. socks; Mrs. Walker Anderson—2 prs. drawers and 2 blankets."[46] Wake County women, both white and free black, took up space in the capitol and area churches and constructed in a couple of months' time three thousand uniform jackets, two hundred pantaloons (pants), four hundred shirts, two hundred haversacks, six hundred towels, and fifteen hundred mattresses.[47]

When the cars brought a load of soldiers passing through Hillsborough, the students of the Nash and Kollock School ran to the depot and shared baskets of food when available. They had the help of Lisbon Berry, a young Negro. At the beginning of the war, Sally Nash, co-principal of the Nash and Kollock Female Boarding School, wrote that they got very excited every time they heard the whistle of the train because "we are kept in a constant state of excitement. I hear the whistle of the cars now, and can scarcely go on with my letter until I know whether they bring any intelligence [news about the war]. We have formed a Soldiers' Aid Society, and are to meet once a week to prepare necessities and comfort for our wounded soldiers." Mrs. William Graham, wife of the ex-governor, served as president.[48]

Hillsborough had a very active aid society. The ladies were "issued permanent passes from the head of the North Carolina Railroad to give them access to all trains on the main line."[49] Mrs. William Cameron devised a plan to "go down to Morrisville on the [eastbound] train . . . feeding the men on board, then getting off at Morrisville with baskets, papers, etc., going into the waiting room and there making the divisions into separate bundles, and on her way back to Hillsboro giving the packages to the men on board. The conductors would tell us how eagerly the men would inquire when they would reach this town." Mrs. Lucy Robertson said as a child, she helped her mother with feeding the sick and wounded passing through Hillsborough. The young folks scrapped lint from bed linens for hospital supplies.[50]

Other cities on the rail line saw benevolent groups meeting the trains. Potatoes, onions, and wheat bread were passed out to traveling soldiers at the depot in Charlotte.[51] The Wilmington Soldiers' Aid Society mentioned earlier placed several long tables laden with food at the main depot for the soldiers. Much of the food had been contributed by the owners of blockade-runners. Louise Medway of Wilmington said the Soldiers' Aid Society assisted six to eight thousand soldiers per month with meals or whatever they needed.[52] The *Greensboro Patriot* printed information on the sewing societies, which met the troop trains as canteen workers doled out food or sustained them with nursing assistance if needed. When the trains came, "it was a signal to broil bacon, bake corn bread, set out milk . . . buttermilk, and sorghum."[53] In Raleigh, another railroad hub, "it was common . . . for us to go to church and for the pastor to announce that several cars of wounded soldiers would be in that day; there would be an intermission for all to leave who desired to prepare food and comforts for them," quoted Mrs. Jonathan McGee Heck.[54] Mary Carraway said the ladies in her neighborhood around Goldsboro met to make much needed mattresses for the soldiers.

Gray's Chapel Soldiers' Relief Society in the fall formed up in Rutherford County.[*] Mrs. D. A. Davis, president of the Rowan County Soldiers' Aid Society, announced that they would collect provisions for the military of that county.[55] In Duplin County, ladies met in the Franklin Institute to sew items for the volunteers. The *Fayetteville Observer* printed this notice September 16, 1861:

> The Ladies in the vicinity of Zion Church met in the Temperance Hall . . . . for the purpose of . . . forming an association called the "Zion Ladies Aid Society" to obtain money, clothing, provisions and everything that will make the gallant soldiers who have gone to fight in the defence of their country, comfortable during the coming winter season.[**]

The *Observer* had this notice in the same edition:

> In accordance with announcements previously made, a large number of Ladies assembled at Laurel Hill Church, Richmond County . . . . for the purpose of forming a Society to provide suitable clothing for our volunteers . . . .

Reverend McPherson explained the object of the meeting, after which he read and explained a constitution that he had prepared and which was immediately subscribed by thirty ladies. The following officers were elected, viz, Mrs. Mary Ann Patterson, president; Mrs. Effie Gilchrist, vice president; Ms. Jane E. McPherson, treasurer.

Recorded below is a typical list of donations found in period newspapers. It catalogues the person's name, servants, or children and the item donated. It is from the Ladies Aid Society of the Little's Mill area of Richmond County:[***]

Mrs. M.E. Austin . . . gloves, socks, shirt, red pepper.
Family of N.T. Bowden . . . $4; a bed comforter, pair of drawers, shirt, pants, and quilt.
Ms. Cornelia Bowden . . . gloves, pillow slips, and socks.
Reddick Bowden . . . $3
Master Thomas O. Bowden . . . one lot of slippery elm bark.[****]
Family of W.F. Brookshire . . . socks, shirt, drawers, & $5.
Mrs. John F. Ledbetter . . . quilt, pillow & slip, socks.
Homer LeGrand . . . $4
Mrs. William LeGrand . . . socks.
Family of John P. Little . . . wool pants, other clothing, & $10.
Ms. Lizzie Little . . . socks.
Ms. Sallie Little . . . socks.
Mrs. E. Little . . . socks.
Family of B.F. Little . . . cotton mattress, pillow slips, towels, bandages, [knit?] jackets, 6 pair merino gloves, one gross buttons, 4 testaments, one cake mutton suet, ½ gal. honey, one lot slippery elm bark, $6 worth of woolen cloth, and $23.

---

[*]   The president was Mrs. R. G. Twitty, with Ms. M. A. Miller as vice president and Ms. M. Littlejohn as the assistant secretary.
[**]   The society was organized by the election of the following officers, viz, Ms. Harriet M. Gaines, president; Ms. M. Fannie Wooley, vice president; Ms. M. A. Pemberton, secretary; Ms. M. F. Christian, treasurer; Ms. Fannie Barringer, Ms. M. A. Christian, Ms. E. Oliver, Mrs. E. Deberry—Committee of Reception Treas.
[***] In the appendix are several lists of other comparable donations.
[****] Chewed to treat diarrhea and to allay thirst

Mrs. M.B. McRae . . . socks, drawers, red pepper, and a cotton mattress.

Ms. Julia A. McRae . . . wool gloves.

Mrs. C.A. Patterson . . . linen blanket, shirts, wool pants, pair wool gloves, pillow, 4 pairs socks, dressing gown, bandages and old linen, one paper of sage, one lb. candles.

Fanny, **a servant** of Mrs. C.A. Patterson . . . one lot of sage.

Mrs. L.S. Powell . . . linen blanket, pillows and cases, towels, pair of sheets, one bundle linen, lot of sage and mustard, and one dozen phials.

R.J. Powell . . . $2

Miss Julia Powell . . . socks, neck comfort.

Hattie, **a servant** of Mrs. L.S. Powell . . . linen blanket, a roll of bandages, pair gloves.

Mrs. E.J. Robinson . . . linen blankets, shirt, pillows, 2 pillow cases, towel, 4 pair socks soap, red pepper, sage, pair of drawers, bundle of old linen, 2 lung protectors, mattress tick, and a pair of gloves.

William P. Stanback . . . $1

Mrs. E. & Mrs. P.N. Stanback . . . cotton mattress, 8 sheets, 6 pillows, 5 pillow slips, linen blanket, drawers, 8 Confederate jackets, 8 pr pants,2 towels, 13 pr socks, 2 pr gloves, comfort, overcoat, shirt, 2.5 yards of sheeting, bottle & box of mustard, corn starch, bottle & box of boiled flour, bottle of blackberry wine, and honey.

The Little's Mill Society was not the only organized effort of this nature in the county. Other groups formed to give support were the Laurinburg Soldiers' Aid Society, Laurel Hill Soldiers' Aid Society, and the Rockingham Ladies' Society.[56]

In early summer, citizens were thinking about equipping the troops for winter. This notice appeared in the *Iredell Express* in mid-July:

BLANKETS FOR THE SOLDIERS

There is a certainty that the supply of blankets in the Southern cities and towns is exhausted, and now is the time to be casting about to furnish our brave volunteers with this indispensable article when cold weather shall set in. How shall it be done? We answer, in this way: Every family in the south, the wealthy especially, have more or less blankets; let these be appropriated by sale or donation for the soldiers, and families supply themselves with comforters, which can be made of cotton and any kind of thin material, for which there is abundance of time till cold weather. The "Comforter" is an admirable covering, nothing can be better, and the south supplies the very article of which to manufacture them to any extent, and any little girl can put them together, the cost being ¼ that of blankets. But the blanket is better suited for the use of the soldier, because when wet [,] it is not so heavy and can be dried much easier.

Let families in the South attend to this important matter in due time, for we know of no other method by which blankets can be procured.[57]

Also in mid-July, the *Fayetteville Observer* published:

In all our state exchange, we find acknowledgements of blankets and socks received by the sheriff; and in several of them various donations to the Ladies' Aid Associations. There are signs of very liberal if not an altogether adequate provision for our brave soldiers from these sources. (This proved to be untrue—much more was needed.) We are pleased to learn that every body has sent, or is preparing to send socks, blankets, and other articles of clothing to our brave soldiers. Our ladies will not allow our . . . men . . . to suffer for such things as long as they can knit and sew —they can send socks, and make shirts as well as their mothers, and they will be glad to do it. The men will buy the cloth for jackets, pants, shirts, & etc., and the women and girls will make them.[58]

Officers began to write newspapers addressing the ladies as to what was needed for winter use. They requested heavy homespun wool clothing, flannel shirts, quilts, blankets, socks, and shoes. Captain Oscar Rand said that overcoat material was being shipped out to homes by the quartermaster. Some people received compensation for their donations.[59]

Catherine Murchison, wife of Duncan Murchison and owner of a cotton mill in Manchester, mailed a letter to her daughter Janie M. Fairley, wife of Rev. David Fairley, in which she mentioned that her other daughter, May, and another lady came to cut out shirts for the reverend's company:

> Mr. Williams had a letter from David this week appealing to the Patriotic people of Cumberland for clothing for his company, that they had <u>never</u> received <u>any</u> thing except from the officers. The letter was sent to Mrs. Myrover and the Society is busy sewing for them, and they will get off as large a box on Monday's boat . . . May [,] Kate, with the assistance of the Factory women, and Sister Elira's will make twenty-one flannel shirts, and I want them to make a <u>comfortable</u> for David·in addition by <u>one o'clock</u> tomorrow. David represents the men in a suffering condition for the want of clothing & covering to protect them <u>from</u> the cold. Your Pa has contributed cloth for shirts for some of them, and all will continue to work till their present wants are supplied. Jane has had a letter from John saying, that their men were dying for the want of covering, and have sent out an order for materials for making <u>eight</u> comforts.[*][60]

By the fall of the first year of war, recruits sent letters home requesting winter clothing and blankets. W. O. Ruddock at Culpeper, Virginia, asked his uncle to send him clothes: "I am needing some clothes badly . . . . One thing I will need very bad that is a pair of gloves. I cannot handle my musket without it . . . . Another is a pair of boots. Shoes will not be of much service in snow knee deep . . . . There cant be anything got here . . ."[61]

Numerous other benevolent associations were created over the winter in the first year of the conflict. Those soldiers without overcoats or thick socks must have felt the sting of frostbite tremendously. Authorities contacted the editors of local newspapers to request winter equipage:

Notice to the ladies of Orange County
> I am requested by the governor of your state to call upon you to furnish for the soldiers in the army woolen socks and blankets for their comfort and protection during the approaching winter. Each donor will please accompany her gift by her name. Come then to the relief, furnish them with those necessary articles to relieve suffering. R.M. Jones, Sheriff[62]

One Winchester, Virginia, woman described members of the Thirty-seventh North Carolina Regiment passing through the town as "destitute, many without shoes, all without overcoats or gloves, although the weather was freezing. Their poor hands looked so red and cold holding their muskets in the bitter wind."[63] Many a wife or mother hated to think that this could be their husband or son marching along in the frigid weather without the proper clothing.

Facing the winter of 1862 caught military authorities short on clothing, blankets, and shoes. Officers appealed to the public for help. Even the governor, formerly a soldier himself, asked the public for assistance. His proclamation appeared in the *Raleigh Standard* and was picked up by other newspapers:

---

*   David Fairley was pastor of Longstreet and China Groove Presbyterian Church and chaplain of the Twenty-seventh NC State Troops. The letter was written December 14, 1861.

PROCLAMATION FROM GOV. VANCE
To the People of North Carolina

Raleigh, October 15, 1862

After a most strenuous exertions on the part of its officers, the State finds it impossible to clothe and shoe soldiers without again appealing to that overflowing fountain of generous charity—the private contributions of our people.

The rigors of winter are approaching, our soldiers are already suffering, and must suffer more if our sympathies are not practical and active. The Quarter Master's Department is laboring faithfully to provide for them but, owing to speculation and extortion, will fall short. The deficiency must be supplied by the people. We shall have an active winter campaign, and how can our troops, if ragged, cold, and barefoot, contend with the splendidly equipped columns of the enemy?

The articles most needed, and which the State finds it most difficult to supply are shoes, socks, and blankets, though drawers, shirts, and pants would be gladly received. If every farmer who has hides tanning would agree to spare one pair of shoes, and if every mother in North Carolina would knit one strong pair of either thick cotton or wool socks for the army, they would be abundantly supplied. A great lot of blankets also might yet be spared from private use, and thousands could be made from carpets upon our parlor floors. With good warm houses and cotton bed clothing, we can certainly get through the winter much better than the soldiers can with all the blankets we can give them.

The Colonels of the Militia Regiments throughout the State are hereby appointed agents for the purpose and collection of all such articles as can be spared by our people, who, through their respective Captains, are ordered immediately to canvass every county and visit every citizen in the beats for their purpose. A liberal price will be paid for everything where the owner feels that he or she is not able to donate it; and active agents will immediately forward them to our suffering regiments. Expenses will be allowed the officers engaged in this duty, and transportation furnished the Colonels or their agents to bring articles to Raleigh.

And my countrymen and women, if you have anything to spare for the soldier, in his name I appeal to you for it. Do not let the speculator have it, though he may offer you enormous prices; spurn him from your door and say to him, that our brave defenders have need for it and shall have it without passing through his greedy fingers. Do not place yourselves among the extortioners—they are the vilest and most cowardly of all our country's enemies, and when this war is ended and the people come to view the matter in its proper light you will find that the most detested Tories are more respected than they. When they tempt you with higher prices than the State offers, just think for a moment of the soldier and what he is doing for you. Remember when you sit down by the bright and glowing fire, that the soldier is sitting upon the cold earth; in the wind which is whistling so fearfully over your roof, only making you feel the more comfortable because it harms you not, he is shivering in darkness on the dangerous out-post, or shuddering through the dreary hours of his watch. Remember that when you come forth in the morning well fed and warmly clad, leading your family toward the spot where the blessed music of the Sabbath-bells tells you of the peaceful worship of the God of Peace, the soldier is going forth at the same moment, perhaps, half fed, after a night of shivering and suffering to where the roar of artillery and shout of battle announce that he is to die, that your peace and safety may be preserved. Oh, remember these things generous and patriotic people of North Carolina, and give freely of your perishable goods to those who are giving all that mortal man can give for your safety and your rights. Z.B. Vance

What a speech! After that, who wouldn't contribute? Zeb would make a good emcee for public television requesting donations.[64] Captain J. A. Maultsby wrote from Whiteville that "no blankets are to be had & but few quilts. Our county people gave so liberally last year, that they have nothing to give or sell and cards & cotton yarns are so high that they can not make anything. I cannot get leather or shoes for the rogues have taken off nearly all the leather of which there was not enough for home consumption before—I have just issued notices that 50 cts a pair will be paid for wool & 33 1/3 cts a pair for cotton socks—Shall I recall it or continue? Good jeans sell for $4 a yard—"[65]

In the highlands, women formed the Soldiers' Aid Society of Burke County.[*] They met once a week at the same house to cut cloth for uniforms. In addition, the ladies solicited for money and cloth. When all was finished, they packed the boxes for specific units. Ms. Cornelia McGimsey wrote her future husband that the aid society had packed up forty shirts, eleven towels, one hundred pairs of socks, and thirty-one pairs of drawers.[66] Other ladies of Burke County's Mountain Grove Church formed a group to assist in the needs of the military. "The official members of this Society are as follows: Miss Lizzie M. Parks, Pres't; Miss Laura J. Avery, Sec'y; Miss Susan A. Moore, Assistant." The first box sent contained eighty pairs of socks, thirty drawers, nineteen shirts, thirty blankets, and two pairs of pants. The second contained twenty-three pairs of socks, ten pairs of drawers, five pairs of pants, four pillow ticks, and one vest. The Potecasi Soldiers' Aid Society of Northampton County sent to the military the following items: twenty-eight blankets, 128 pairs of socks, nineteen shirts, forty-two pairs of drawers, four pillow ticks, five pairs of pants, and one vest. Fifty women had worked on the first box shipped. The second box sent contained the work of fifteen women and one child. The cloth for the clothes that were made was bought with the money given to the society for the benefit of the volunteers.[67]

Officers were quick to place an article in the newspaper requesting articles and thanking the ladies for their donations:

> **To the citizens of NC:** please carry provisions such as chickens, eggs, butter, and vegetables to me along with hospital clothing.—Wm J. Hoke, Col. 38th Regt NCT[68]

> **Mr. Editor—**I take pleasure in informing the "Ladies of the Mountain Grove Soldiers' Aid Society" through this newspaper that on Jan 3rd[62], I received the boxes of blankets and clothing presented to my company through their noble and generous efforts. I indeed feel thankful on my part, while I know that my company manifests the same feeling toward the Ladies of their native state and county.   Capt. E. J. Kirksey, 11th Regt NCT.[69]

Captain F. W. Johnstone wrote a note of thanks to others in the community, namely, Mrs. F. W. Johnstone—who had sent fifty-one flannel shirts of which seventeen were made by the ladies of East Fork, fifteen were made by the ladies of Davidson's River, and eighteen were made by Mrs. F. W. Johnstone. Recognition also went to Ms. M. P. Johnstone, who sent twenty-eight pairs of socks; Mrs. T. D. Jerry, who sent ten pairs of socks; and Rev. J. S. Hanckel, who sent five pairs of socks. Captain James Reilly, while in Centerville, Virginia, wrote a note of thanks to the secretary of the Ladies Aid Society of Salisbury, which was published in the *Carolina Watchman*:

> It is with the kindest feelings of respect, to the Society you represent, I pen this note acknowledging the receipt of the box . . . received in good order, and the private packages delivered to the owners . . .

---

[*]   This could be separate from the Mountain Grove Church.

The same edition of the *Watchman* carried a similar message of thanks from Captain F. M. Y. McNeely to Ms. Beard representing Salisbury. He said that the box arrived when most needed. Other notices of thanks from officers are shown:

> Camp Hill, Dec 16, 1861, Mr. Britton
> Dear Sir, allow me through your column to thank the Ladies Soldiers Aid Society of Charlotte for the valuable contributions of clothing made to my company; they were of the right kind and came in time of need. T. H. Brem, Capt., Co C, 10th NCST

Another officer answered in the *Asheville News* May 15, 1862:

> In behalf of my company, I return sincere thanks for the following contributions: to the Soldiers' Aid Association, Hillsborough, for 20 blankets; the Soldiers' Aid Association of Chapel Hill for 13 pairs of pants . . . The wants of my company are now pretty well supplied. Joseph Webb, 27th NCT, Orange Guards.

> Allow me through this column to acknowledge on behalf of the Buncombe Rangers, Co G, the receipt of a box of clothing presented by a few ladies of Asheville—40 shirts, 40 drawers, 40 prs. socks, gloves, and other articles. Camp Ransom HQ, First NC Cavalry (no name listed)[70]

C.S. Captain John H. Kinyoun, Twenty-eighth NCT, reported that for a one-month period, citizens from Yadkin contributed these items: beans, chickens, honey, whiskey, cordials, custards, mutton, pork, bacon, loaves of bread, biscuits, cucumbers, pickles, potatoes, squash, beets, onions, radishes, cabbages, milk, vinegar, cornmeal, cider, brandy, sugar cakes, fruit pies, molasses, sugar, and lots of dried wood. These perishable items would have to have been carried by wagon. If sent by rail, they would have spoiled. Lieutenant W. R. Chesson, stationed in Kinston, wrote out a receipt for these provisions in June 1862 as donated by citizens: fresh beef, salt beef, pork, bacon, lard, sugar, flour, hard bread, cornmeal, beans, rice, rye, vinegar, candles, soap, salt, molasses, krout [*sic*], sheep shears, chickens (none at this report), scoops of hay, boxes of meal, butcher knives, empty boxes, empty barrels, and a pair of scales.[71]

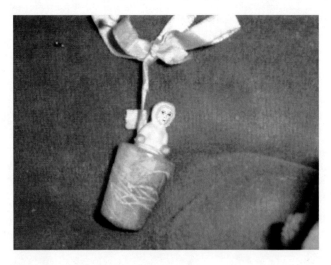

Frozen Charlotte in wax thimble sold at a bazaar to raise money for the war effort. Anonymous donor

Women in Hickory unraveled their carpets to reuse the yarn into socks for the military. Other groups cut their carpets into blankets, lining it with flannel. The Soldiers Aid Society of Statesville bought two bolts of fabric to be cut into soldiers' shirts. The *Raleigh Register* said a military committee from Robeson County acknowledged the following donations for the Robeson troops: "Mrs. Judge French, cash of $10; Willie R. French, $10; Beverly Tucker French, $10; Miss Molly J. French, $5; Miss Berta S. French, $5; Mrs. Captain Condary Goden, 100 pairs of socks; Mrs. Berry Goden, 100 pairs of socks; Mrs. Thomas A Norment, 6 pairs of socks and 2 blankets."[72]

The ladies of Little Coharie District, Sampson County, met at Bethel Church in the vicinity of Owenville for the purpose of organizing the Bethel Soldiers' Aid Society. Dr. D. R. Parker explained the purpose of the group and the members elected.* Thomas A. Norment, chairman of the Presbyterian Military Committee, said that Reverend Culbreth was called upon to address the society, and fifteen dollars was collected from men in the audience. In Sampson County, women established a group called the Lisbon Ladies' Aid Society to assist the soldiers. In Johnston County, the ladies of the Strickland District formed a Soldiers Relief Society early that first winter.[73]

"The ladies of Thyatira and vicinity wishing to aid in providing clothing and other necessaries for the comfort of our soldiers, who are now engaged in the defence of our country, organized themselves into a society called the Thyatira Soldiers Aid Society . . ."** In four months' time, the members shipped the following: three mattresses, nineteen pillows, thirteen sheets, nineteen blankets, four comforts, one counterpane, twenty-four pillowcases, fifty-four towels, sixty-one cotton shirts, thirty-two flannel shirts, eight pairs of flannel drawers, three pairs of cotton drawers, one pair of woolen pants, sixteen pairs of gloves, 156 pairs of woolen socks, three boxes of lint, sixty bandages, one double wrapper, two jars of apple jelly, three gallons of blackberry wine, three gallons of brandy, two sacks of dried fruit, 120 pounds of soap, sage, hops, red pepper, etc., along with six boxes of provisions, four Bibles, seven testaments, two prayer books, tracts, and other small books. Sixty-two dollars was contributed.[74]

While aid societies in larger towns were being organized, ladies remaining at home, seized with patriotic ardor as well, may not have had the opportunity to get into town as frequently as others. Poorer classes had no means to get to town, so they labored at home or at the local church. Various women held meetings in their homes for the purpose of making accoutrements. The wife of a wealthy planter, Catherine Edmondston penned in her diary:

> . . . hard at work in the Piazza & through the open window could hear their [slaves] comments on the "War" & the "**Cloth house**" they were making for their Master to sleep under.

She went on to say "brought home another tent on which my forces are busily engaged. The Cloth for these Uniforms & Tents is purchased by individual subscription, not waiting for the State to equip its men, & this thing is going on all over the whole South. Thousands of Ladies who never worked before are hard at work on coarse sewing all over our whole country."

---

* Mrs. T. N. Culbreth, president; Mrs. M. White and Mrs. B. Parker, vice presidents; Ms. Maggie A. Owen, secretary; and Ms. Sallie Williams, treasurer. The president appointed the following committee for their contributions to the society, viz, Mrs. John W. Matthews, Mrs. John Culbreth, Mrs. W. F. Culbreth, Mrs. John R. Fisher, Mrs. F. Cooper, Mrs. John T. Fort, Mrs. W. G. Fowler, Mrs. T. Sessoms, Ms. Virginia A. Owen, Ms. Mary J. Owen, and Ms. Martha L. Culbreth.

** Elected were the following officers: Mrs. J. C. McConnaughey, president; Ms. S. J. Sloan, Ms. H. Houck, and J. Lowrance, vice presidents; Mrs. J. K. Graham, secretary; and Ms. Lydia Lowrance, treasurer.

Catherine wanted to sew her husband's uniform instead of trusting the job to her slaves. Another diarist, Elizabeth Robeson, signed off the evening of May 10: "Mary Allen, Amelia Allen, and Betsy Devane and myself busily engaged in making mattresses, flannel shirts, etc . . . for the volunteers." They went to a friend's house to sew soldiers' pants. Later that year, she and a neighbor went to Maysville to a friend's home where the women met to cut out and distribute soldiers' shirts, etc.[75]

James L. McKee of Yanceyville wrote his sister Ada Aveline Jarrett of Cherokee, Valleytown, the first of June, "Our whole community, that is the females, drop their own work and go to work for the Volunteers and make them uniform shirts . . . etc."[76]

Fifteen-year-old Emily Tillinghast of Fayetteville kept a journal and wrote that in July (1861), her mother's home was the central location for the ladies of the neighborhood to meet for the sewing society. "I worked on some coats, but found it very warm work, so I wasn't sorry that there was not enough work for me to be employed all day." The women had made uniforms for two companies who left earlier. By mid-August, they had thirteen more coats to make before the third company left Fayetteville for the front. "I don't believe the ladies show as much zeal in behalf of this company as they did when the Lafayette, and Independent [infantry] went away but I suppose some think they have done their part in the sewing line." It is believed that other women had the same feelings but did not admit to it.[77]

Julia Lenoir wrote her grandmother that fall: "We have been working a good deal for the soldiers, I believe the homeguard [the ladies left behind] have supplied . . . clothing for the winter . . ." She mentioned that the women kept asking the agents for more work, but "they don't send any now. Cousin Lizzie has been working very hard lately [.] they have a great many overcoats to make, and a great many gloves and socks to knit. We made some shirts, and knit some gloves, socks, and comforters for their box."

Early next year, Laura, in Lenoir, sent a letter to her uncle Walt:

> Now that our soldiers have received some clothes I hope I have a little time to read and study [she had received an offer to teach]. Some of the folks around here were much concerned because men complained of the size of their pants we sent. They were too large and the soldiers did not like them, and the people said if they were so particular and (tasty), let them go without. One said to me, "I think we might as well let the Society fall through any how, for we got no thanks for what we have done!"

She said they were tired and wanted to give up.

When a box was received in camp, most captains, as mentioned earlier, sent a personal letter of gratitude to the organization; or they would send it to the local newspaper for all to see. Apparently, these girls never saw the letter if there was one.[78] Not all women during the time were handy with the needle. One girl wrote her sister's sweetheart about sewing for the soldiers:

> Neal has told you about our clothing we gave to send to the volunteers [.] I will tell you about a pair of drawers made in Powelltown under one of Hattie Averys apprentices, they are about one and a half yards long in the seat, and are cut eight cornered before and large enough in the waist for Dunn Kincaid, the seams are filled in ridges about the size of a halter and nothing under the sun to keep them over the hips. I'll bet the man that gets them will curse sight.[79]

The troops were not forgotten during Christmas. The state government tried to include different victuals than the ordinary food distributed to the soldiers. The first of December, eight hundred boxes were forwarded. For their Christmas dinner, four hundred boxes were shipped. "Christmas boxes have been pouring in . . ." wrote a soldier. "They came just in time for the men had gone three days without beef or pork."[80] Individuals either shipped

Christmas goodies, or it was hand carried to the camps. Apparently, this Wilmington soldier wanted to make sure his comrades were not overlooked during the holidays. He placed a notice in the local newspaper:

> The ladies intend to give us a Christmas Dinner at the Depot on Saturday, the day before Christmas. Let every person give liberally that can. Let them be grateful for the safety of the city. Charity has saved the city perhaps. We believe the Lord of Hosts is with us; the God of Jacob is our refuge. Signed S.T.[81]

The predominate religion in the South in 1860 was Baptist and Methodist. Second came the Presbyterians, then the Episcopalians. North Carolina had ten Catholic churches and no synagogues, although there were Jewish people and soldiers living in the state.[*] Other denominations included a few Lutherans, German Reformists, Moravians, Quakers, and Christians. Ministers at the beginning were just as active as the ladies in requesting donations for provisions and money for the printing of religious tracts and testaments. In the annual session of the Beulah Baptist Association held with the church at Friendship, Stokes County, the representatives had this notice printed for their members:

> Our soldiers, now far from their pious parents, and sin-restraining sisters, need bibles, books, and tracts to fortify them against the alluring snares with which Satan always surrounds the military camp.[82]

In a letter to the editor of the *Spirit of the Age*, a Raleigh newspaper, from local ministers appeared this appeal:

> Let no man think of moneymaking until every battlefield is whitened with the bones of our sensual, brutal and depraved invaders. Every thought about gain and self must now yield to the wants of our brave soldiery.
> We earnestly conjure all who are not in active military service to prepare for the winter campaign. All our energies must be directed to providing sufficient warm and comfortable clothing for our soldiers. The soldier is subject to so much exposure, that he will need his winter clothing by October. Besides the lectures of Reverend Dr. Reid, through "whose instrumentality handsome contributions were procured for the relief and comfort of the sick soldiers of the Southern Army, during the past week . . . the Ladies gave a concert for this humane and patriotic purpose."[83]

Army colportage was considered essential by ministers and families, the means to fight vice in the military. At the North Carolina Baptist State Convention, Chairman R. B. Jones reported:

> Colportage has long since been deemed an official means of disseminating religious truths. The morals of these men must be cared for, or society will suffer an irreparable loss, however brilliant may be their victories. Army colportage is one of the most effective means of counteracting the demoralizing inferences of the camp.[84]

When the Henderson Guards left for the front, the Reverend George Parks, pastor of the Hendersonville Presbyterian Church, gave each soldier a Bible contributed by the ladies of the church. Church members made their uniforms, shirts, knapsacks, and tents.[85] Thirty-eight dollars was taken up by Baptist elder B. B. Williams for the distribution of the

---

[*]   Northampton, Chowan, Beaufort, Alamance, Cumberland, Montgomery, Wake, and Craven Counties

Biblical Recorder for the soldiers. Buckhorn Church collected twenty-four dollars for army colportage. Another church gave sixty-four dollars after a sermon by elder R. B. Jones.[86] The *Church Intelligencer*—published in Raleigh by the Reverend Thomas S. W. Mott—when available, ended up in the soldiers' camp. Throughout the state, church members did not want the recruit to leave without some form of religious booklet. Pre-secession, army colportage was gathered to distribute to the volunteers.

Five Episcopal churches got together and contributed money to purchase five bales of cotton, which were sent to England to defray the cost of printing the *Confederate Book of Common Prayer*. The book was printed in England and shipped back via the blockade. This particular book became known as The *"Cotton" Book of Common Prayer*.[87] In September 1861, the *Spirit of the Age* showed who had given Bibles and testaments donated by Rives Chapel "Milton" Friends ($50), Winston ($8), Lexington Female Tract Society ($2), Ladies from Chapel Hill ($24), Richmond County ($19), Windsor ($13), Salem Tract Society ($125), Salem Church ($66), Paw Creek Church near Charlotte ($24), Salisbury Female Tract Society ($16), Rocky River Church ($17), Ladies at New Bern ($109), Greenville ($11), the Soldiers Friend in Clemmonsville ($4), Bethesda Church in Caswell County ($8), Chatham County of Bear Creek, ($31), Henderson ($50), Sardis and Sharon Church near Charlotte ($20), and Lenoir County ($75).[88]

The move to get army colportage actually took hold in the second and third years of the war. The period 1864–1865 found difficulty due to shortage of paper and money.* The *Raleigh Register* gives us examples of the pamphlets:

> The General Tract Agency of this city is publishing from 20,000 to 50,000 copies of each of the following excellent tracts, approved by all the pastors here: "A Mother's Parting Words to Her Soldier Boy;" "Christ In You;" "Are you ready?;" "The Life Preserver;" "Why Will Ye Die?;" "Lovest Thou Me;" and so forth. We are striving to supply our whole army with the gospel truths. Each dollar given will send out 1,000 pages, which will be carried, through the great kindness of the Express Company, to the soldiers without charge. We can print 30,000 tracks a day.* Yours truly, W. J. W. Crowder, Agent[89]

Other religious tracts published for the military included:

> "Death-Bed Repentance;" "Doers of the Word;" "Claims of the Church;" "Letters to a More Bewildered Among Many Councilors;" "A Plain Tract on Confirmation;" and "Prayers for the Sick & Troubled."[90]

One soldier of the First North Carolina Bethel Regiment said that "Come to Jesus," which was given to him while encamped, was blessed to conversion during the first month he was in Virginia and that he had committed all of it to memory.[91] Walter Clark's father was an agent for the tract society. He solicited funds to publish the tracts. Walter's mother said, "I have just given him twenty dollars of your money that you so generously gave to the cause of Christ . . ."[92]

"The years 1863 and 1864 appear to have witnessed a revival in the army . . . over one hundred thousand Confederates were converted during the war years . . ."[93]

C. C. Chaplin, chairman of the Baptist State Convention in 1862, reported that the publication of fifty thousand copies of the New Testament had been secured. In addition, they published many hymnbooks for the soldiers. "Christians in camp have been comforted and the ungodly are being reclaimed from vice." He reported that they had raised over five thousand dollars for missions and army colportage. Numerous religious groups sponsored programs for the assistance of destitute families. Southern Jewish families contributed money for the support of the Jewish soldiers' families. North Carolina Presbyterians raised funds to educate children of deceased and diseased veterans. Many church members

---

*   Believed to be thirty thousand pages, not individual copies

pledged themselves to sell necessities to the poor at reduced prices. Some planters volunteered to share their produce with the needy.[94]

Ministers left at home faced problems as they tried to staff the churches. Rev. John M. Sherwood reported: "We cannot hope to supply our feeble churches and missionary fields with the preached Word, as we would gladly do, while the war continues . . . . The wants of the army have been considered, and much has been done to supply our soldiers with the preached Word."[95]

An unsigned notice was printed in the *Confederate*, a Raleigh newspaper, encouraging women to keep writing their loved ones in military service:

> Mothers! Let your boys in the army know that you pray for them; and they will be braver soldiers and better boys. A mother's prayer is a safer shield for her boy than boomproof fortifications.[96]

A young diarist from Fayetteville inscribed on April 2, 1862:

> Gen. Beauregard is calling for all the bells to melt into cannon. A good many churches are sending in their bells. I feel so much older since last April & I don't see any chance of the war's ending. I believe it will last forever & if the men are all killed [,] I don't want to live.

Two weeks later, she added, "Our church (the Presbyterian) has offered our bell to the Confederacy I don't know whether it will be accepted . . ."[97]

Many churches gave their bell to the government to be melted down for war munitions. The First Presbyterian Church of Greensboro surrendered its bell for the cause. The Presbyterian Church of Salisbury donated its bell and asked the female members to take up the church's carpets and make them into blankets for the soldiers. The Baptist church in Raleigh gave its bell, which weighed thirteen hundred pounds. It was told it could make three six-pound cannons.[98] Lucy Anderson said that a four-gun battery was made out of the bells from the Episcopal, Presbyterian, and Baptists churches of Raleigh. St. Paul's Church in Edenton donated its bells. "It helped form the 'Edenton Bell Battery,' which was organized in the winter of 1861-1862, by Captain William Badham, Jr."[99] Three cannons cast from these bells were known as the "St. Paul," the "Fannie Roulhac," and the "Columbia."[100] The fourth cannon in the Edenton Bell Battery derived from the Chowan County Courthouse bell was called the "Edenton." The battery saw action until the last battle in the state. Some were captured, and the others are rumored to have been dumped in the Eno River.[101]

All major churches in Asheville "agreed to donate their church bells" in the spring of 1862. The *Asheville News* reported that two individuals, Mr. Blair of the Eagle Hotel and Mr. Winslow Smith of the Confederate Hotel, desired to furnish their bells too.

Other churches throughout the state relinquished theirs as well. The bells from St. Bartholomew's Church in Pittsboro, as well as the Presbyterian church, were turned over to the Confederacy. The Grace Episcopal Church of Plymouth gave its pews and gallery to be made into coffins. One church in Tarboro subscribed its bell. On April 15, 1862, churches of this city (Charlotte), reported the *Spirit of the Age*, "have all donated their church bells to the government, to be melted into cannon." An author wrote that four cannons were made from the bells of the Episcopal, Presbyterian, and Baptist churches of Hillsborough for the Orange Light Artillery.[102] In Wilmington, the bells from St. James Episcopal saw use when melted down.

Not all bells offered to the Confederacy from the state were melted down. Those bells loaded on the steamer *Alice* were captured by the enemy mid-1862. C.S. Captain Thrower had just gone up the Roanoke River to Windsor with provisions for the troops when the Federals attacked his ship. He managed to escape. The spoils included nine thousand pounds of bacon, barrels of lard, and the church bells.[103]

Caldwell County Ladies' Gunboat Fund.
S.H. Pattterson Papers. Perkins Library, Duke University.

GUNBOAT FUND

The *Daily Journal*, in December 1861, published a letter from a lady who suggested that each woman in the state contribute one dollar for a gunboat fund. "One of the women of Duplin suggested a general fund drive, and the Wilmington paper endorsed it." A couple weeks later, the *Raleigh Register* had this to say about the gunboat fund:

> Our sisters of Alabama, South Carolina, and Louisiana have set us a noble example by subscribing for the building of a Gunboat. Shall we, the ladies of North Carolina remain [illegible] to the dangers of our beloved state? While the enemy has invaded our coast, our beloved brothers, husbands, and sons are withstanding them to death. Let us at once arise in our freewill offerings. All that is precious to us in the world is now in danger. Let the ladies of each county open a subscription and send forward the amount you can to the cashier of the nearest Branch of the Cape Fear Bank.[104]

Another notice in the *Register* appeared in April:

> The fact that the Confederate government has also entered upon the business of creating a navy, and has directed the attention largely to this class of vessels, neither renders this effort unnecessarily, nor does it interpose any insuperable barrier to state or voluntary effort. The slightest reflection will be sufficient to convince all, that the present struggle calls for and will continue to call for the exertion of every energy on the part not only of the government authorities, but also of the people of the confederate states. The ladies ever foremost in good works may be said to have initiated the movement in North Carolina. We trust that they will continue to lend their valuable aid and countenance to the patriotic effort. Without claiming for Wilmington any peculiar right to take the lead or assume the control of this matter in any way, we may be permitted to allude to the deeply . . . regretted state of facts which necessarily indicates the Cape Fear River as now affording the only available locality in the state, still within control of the Confederacy, for carrying this project into practical effect. At Wilmington, at Fayetteville, or at some intervening point, the work must be done, so far as the shipbuilding is concerned. The preparation of materials and the construction of machinery can go on at any other available and convenient points.
>
> The fact that now the Cape Fear is the only unobstructed outlet to tide water which our state possesses, gives to all measures for the defense of that outlet. It is true that the Confederate government may build vessels in our waters, but these when built, do not, by any means belong exclusively or even peculiarly to our harbor, or to our defense. They may, when completed, be ordered off to any point on the whole Confederate coast, and may never return to the waters of North Carolina. We want something made by our people of the state to be used peculiarly for their own defense.
>
> Feeling the necessity of organization for the accomplishment of any workmen . . . we have urged the formation of associations and the appointment of committees . . . in every town and county . . . for the collection of funds . . . and invite co-operation of their fellow citizens. In all counties of the state, but especially in the counties of the Cape Fear section, at the same time placing the matter in the charge of the Safety Committee of the town which has constituted Messrs. O.G. Parsley, A. J. DeRosset, and William Wright, a special committee on this matter—to solicit and reserve subscriptions and to make all necessary arrangements for carrying out the object which subscribers have in view.
>
> The Committee of Safety . . . in Wilmington referred all matters connected with the construction of one or more iron clad gun-boats or floating batteries for the defense of the entrances of the Cape Fear River and the coast of North Carolina, have constituted the undersigned a special committee . . . . The means of defense indicated, whether by an iron clad gun-boat, or by an iron clad floating battery, to meet the impending exigency should be constructed as soon as . . . possible. Contributions for this purpose are earnestly solicited. Should the amount contributed not be sufficient, or should any un-foreseen contingency prevent the commencement of this work, the sums tendered will be returned to the respective donors. Signed, O.G. Parsley, A.J. DeRosset, William A. Wright, Wilmington April 9, 1862[105]

Women from all over the state established committees to collect money for the building of these iron-clads. Kate Wheeler mentioned in a letter that a young girl had donated five dollars to the gunboat fund. In the mountain counties of Caldwell, Buncombe, and Macon, a few ladies were more in tune with the gunboat subscriptions that spring than helping indigent women in their county. Mary Bell, wife of a wealthy planter, wrote to her husband,

Alfred, that some women were sponsoring a "gunboat" fund; but she thought it was too late for that, so she only contributed fifty cents. Her daughter gave twenty-five cents.[106]

This unsigned letter was found in the Samuel F. Patterson Papers:[*]

> Palmyra April 24, 1862 Mrs. Ellis Dear Madam, I have just received yours of the 18th instant. I am glad to find that a proposition for contributions to construct a Gun Boat for the defence of our good Old North State has, at last been made. I have been hoping for weeks past, that some lady more proficient than I can be, would make a move towards the accomplishment of that object. I will appoint [an] agent in that place . . . and . . . do what I can in this section of the country. The women of Caldwell have done nobly in contributions . . . . I will report the amount I may be able to collect in the Branch Bank at Morganton . . . . My post office is Patterson, Caldwell Co, NC

A. A. Scruggs in Salem wrote to Mrs. Patterson, May 12, 1863, regarding a gunboat fund:

> I have received a number of circulars (for the gunboat fund) like the enclosed requesting me to send them to the President of the "Soldiers' Aid Society" . . .
>
> I have called upon Mrs. Rankin and she informed me that the Society has some money on hand, but she does not **feel** willing to lend that without some expression from the members in the "Valley" inasmuch as they mainly contributed these funds. She requests to communicate with you as soon as possible concerning the matter.
>
> From the number of soldiers who have already been entertained in Salisbury, together with the prospect that **more** will call upon them it would seem very desirable if something **more** could be done. Mrs. Rankin thinks that—no supplies, or even delicacies could be raised here—acting however in connection with her and the Society. I will distribute these circulars and see what we can do. Please communicate with the post and Mrs. R at home at your earliest convenience. Yours truly, A.A. Scruggs[107]

Citizens of Salisbury gave money for the gunboat fund in the spring of 1862, but this money was diverted to pay for a wayside hospital, which opened in mid-July. Wayside hospitals were officially established by the Confederate Congress in September 1862, and will be discussed in chapter 4.

Adjutant General Martin wrote a note of thanks published in the *Raleigh Register* in May for the receipt of $250.70 for the North Carolina gunboat fund, in addition to $142 raised by a concert at Chapel Hill.[**] The ladies of Raleigh deposited $1,965 in the Bank of North Carolina for the gunboat fund. Some women chose to give jewelry and silver in place of money. The teachers and students of St. Mary's contributed $86 and their jewelry. A question was raised if this was a reasonable project to finish. A few women commented that maybe their money could be used for other projects such as hospital equipment or as a fund to help indigent wives of soldiers.[108]

Citizens of Martin County, on the appeal of Mrs. Sally R. Collins, contributed for the building of an iron-clad steamer the *Old North State*. Ms. Elizabeth Hyman of Williamston took it upon herself for the collection of funds and collected $140 in three to four days. It was sent to Adjutant Martin in Raleigh.[***][109] John N. Peebles wrote to the governor:

---

*   Possibly signed by S. F. Patterson
**   For a list of donors, please see the appendix.
***   Ibid.

Enclosed please find check on Bank of North Carolina for $60. a contribution by my wife & daughters & the Citizens of Kinston & Vicinity as a Gun boat fund, which project Exploded after the fall of Several of our Sea port Towns & Fort Donellson,—Not Knowing whom to send the check to, we have taken the liberty of Enclosing to you.[110]

Whether any of the money collected for the construction of gunboats was ever used, it is not known. Research indicates that part of the fund was reverted for hospital use.

The *Asheville News* informed readers that spring that a Ladies Association for the Defense of North Carolina was in operation. "Let each county set up a subscription for artillery placed on the forts." Now the citizens were asked to donate for artillery![111]

Minstrel shows were one of the most popular stage entertainments in the nineteenth century. One way to raise money for the troops and get something in return was to hold concerts and plays. In August of 1861, the Julius and Ransom's Burlesque Opera Troupe, which was an amateur group of local slaves, performed to raise money in Wilmington. It was called a contraband performance and consisted of songs, glees, and instrumental music for the relief of the sick and disabled soldiers. At times, these slaves were hired by local citizens to perform. This same group consented to do a repeat performance a year later for the unhealthy soldiers in Kinston. The Confederate Minstrels, the Ethiopians, and the Contrabands were black performers.[*][112]

Plays and tableaux (a mute scene or representation) were not confined to adults. Children were involved in this section of raising funds for the war. In Salem, the Board of Elders forbid the tableaux "since acting on a stage was contrary to church regulations."[113] The *Spirit of the Age*, a Raleigh newspaper, chronicled this in October of 1861:

Tableau Vivans— A group of young people presented a Tableaux at the Deaf and Dumb and the Blind Institution. They gave these presentations: The Confederacy, Autumn Flowers, The Game Of Chest, The Gamblers Wife, Choose Between Us, The Witch, Blue Beard, The Stolen Kiss, The Daguerreotype, The Bride, Maternal Instruction, The Stupid Lesson, Indignation, May-day Morning, Flora McFlimsey, Prayer, and The Burgler. One hundred-fifty dollars was received and then given to the Raleigh boys in camp.

For two months in the fall of 1861, approximately 130 children performed a cantata entitled *The Palace of Industry* for the benefit of the soldiers, along with the juvenile cantata, at Thalian Hall. Not to be outdone, Salisbury women of all ages performed sixty scenes from the *Bunyan Tableaux*. Girls from Shelby performed a tableau, raising $200, which was given to the hospitals, while young women in Pittsboro held a concert, which brought in $105. On the other end of the state in New Bern, ladies and children began practicing for a benefit concert for the troops.[114]

In a letter from T. Lenoir Norwood of Chapel Hill to his grandmother that fall, he wrote, "We had a great concert here for the benefit of the soldiers, & made about $125.00." There were sixteen ladies and six men involved. "I think a hundred & twenty five dollars will go a right smart way in relieving suffering of the soldiers, & if every little village will do as well, it will do a great deal of good." He was right. Throughout the state, it must have been a wonderful thing to see the patriotism evolving that fall—concerts, plays, parties, bazaars, etc. It makes one wonder when they had time to do their work.[115]

---

* These could have been the same ones or different groups.

CONCERT!

FOR THE BENEFIT OF

The Soldiers.

Greensboro Female College.
A Concert will be held in the
College Chapel
on the night of the 20th inst.,
for the benefit of our volunteers. Doors open at 6 and
a half o'clock. Exercises will
commence at 7.

Price of admission 50 cents. Children 25.

Perkins Library, Duke University

One of the most popular entertainers in the state was William Augustus "Gus" Reich from Salem.* He was a magician, comedian, ventriloquist, and musician in the Twenty-sixth North Carolina Troops Band also known as the Salem Brass Band. When his group came to town, large ads were placed in local newspapers. This ad appeared in the November 22, 1861, issue of *People's Press*:

> Mr. Wm. A. Reich will exhibit Magic Mysteries, consisting of humorous and amusing illusions, for the benefit of the Ladies Relief Association, in behalf of the Forsyth Volunteers. The Salem Brass Band will be present.

---

*   Also known as Gus Rich. Augustus "Gus" Lewis Hauser was another member of the Twenty-sixth NCT band. In 1862, while home on furlough, Gus Hauser died at the age of twenty-one. Fellow band members played at his funeral.[116]

All those wishing to enjoy themselves . . . and at the same time contribute their mite for the relief of our brave volunteers, will avail themselves of this rare opportunity.

––––––––––––––

Rich's Magic Mysteries/Numerous Amusing Illusions!/Grand Soirées Magique/The eye deceived—the ear amused and the mind astonished/Dixie Magic/Illustrating the philosophy of science/Its deceptive character, and immense power of modification! Admission twenty-five cents.[117]

Appearances of the Twenty-sixth's Brass Band along with Gus continued throughout the war as these next newspaper ads confirm:

September 11, 1862, The *Daily Journal* (Wilmington):
Captain's Mickey's Band attached to the 26th Regiment NCT will give a concert tonight, at the Theatre, for the benefit of the sick and wounded soldiers of our army. Thalian Hall will be filled with citizens hoping to get a glimpse of Gus Rich, the Southern magician and member of the band. Tickets fifty cents.

People's Press on October 24, 1862:

The Friends of the 26th Regiment Band will be pleased to learn that the series of concerts recently given by them, "assisted by Gus Rich" in his inimitable deceptive feats, were very successful.

They performed in Raleigh, Wilmington, Goldsboro, and Petersburg, Virginia. A donation of over $250 was collected, a portion of the proceeds were donated to the North Carolina Hospital at Petersburg. In May 1863, the Twenty-sixth NCT Band performed in Greensboro, with the proceeds distributed to the various hospitals. Gus Rich amused the crowd with his magic.[118]

REICH'S MAGIC MYSTERIES.

NUMEROUS AMUSING ILLUSIONS! AND EVERYTHING TRANSFORMED!

Wm. A. REICH of this place, will perform for the benefit of the

Ladies' Relief Association.

IN BEHALF OF THE

FORSYTH VOLUNTEERS,

AT THE

TOWN HALL,

Friday Night, Nov. 29th,

INTRODUCING

GRAND SOIREES MAGIQUE!

The Eye Deceived—The Ear Amused and the Mind Astonished.

DIXIE MAGIC!

Illustrating the philosophy of SCIENCE its deceptive character, and immense power of modification.

ASSISTED BY THE

Salem Brass Band!

who have kindly consented to contribute to the interest of the occasion.

COME EARLY FOR SEATS.

The *Raleigh Register* and the *Spirit of the Age* had a small paragraph showing funds raised by tableaux and their sponsors. Little information was given.

Tableau and Pantomimes Performed
This reporter spent Christmas night at the School for the Deaf-Dumb-Blind. It was a comedy. Proceeds of the TABLEAU under the direction of Mrs. Judge Saunders raised $137.50.

Ladies from the eastern portion of Wilkes County sent Adjutant General Martin $286 derived from a concert.[119]

Even though Frank Johnson was eighty years old when the war broke, he helped "the cause" by playing for recruiting officers. "One of the officers later recalled that the band's music threw the recruits into a 'paroxysms of revelry, during which patriotism was at fever heat . . .'" Before they knew what was going on, the men had signed their names. Frank Johnson was a slave who hired his time from his master to play for soirées, balls, and parties. His six sons were equally talented and performed with their father. At Jones and Shocco Springs in Granville County, they stood on a platform outside when the weather was nice, or they played in the ballroom of the hotels. Their band was quite famous.[120]

Blind Tom, another talented Negro musician who helped raise money for the troops, born to slave parents from Columbus, Georgia, was what is known today as an autistic savant. His real name was Thomas G. Wiggins or Thomas Bethune, his owner's name. Tom's mother was a house servant. At the age of four, Tom once discreetly went into the parlor to play the piano. He had been listening to the owner's daughter practice and wanted to try it himself. Ms. Bethune had tutored under a prominent New York composer. When his talent was discovered, the daughter gave him lessons so that within four years' time, he went on tour in the large cities of Georgia.[121] He is mentioned as being in Fayetteville in the spring of 1862 by a member of the Tillinghast family:

> Blind Tom . . . . has performed several nights to a crowded house; he can play anything he hears any one play, no matter how hard, he plays Thalburgs Home, Carnival of Venice, Norma, and other pieces from celebrated operas, also a piece of his own called the Battle of Manassas which is represented as being "perfectly splendid" by the girls and a great many jigs with variations, he can play two tunes . . . one with one hand and one with the other and sing a third and he can stand with his back to the piano and play very well [.] besides his musical talents he is gifted with an extraordinary memory that he can repeat one of Douglases speeches perfectly, I never heard of anything so wonderful in all my life, the "Duke" actually condescended to play with him the other night . . . . he took the treble & Tom the base then they reversed.[122]

The *Fayetteville Observer* noted on May 19, 1862:

> The blind negro Tom has been performing here to a crowded house. He performs many pieces of his own conception—one, his *"Battle of Manassas"* may be called picturesque and sublime, a true conception of unaided, blind musical genius. This poor blind boy is cursed with but little of human nature; he seems to be an unconscious agent acting as he is acted on, and his mind a vacant receptacle where Nature's stores her jewels to recall them at her pleasure.[123]

Mary "Mollie" Hinton Carraway, a teacher, said that in Goldsboro during the conflict, Blind Tom gave a concert at which she attended. "He played one tune with his right hand, another with his left, and sang the third tune. After completing the concert he would invite any one from the audience who would like to do so, to try it." Ms. Mollie tried it successfully. It is possible that Blind Tom played in gratis for benevolent causes as other bands were known to have done.*[124] Blind Tom played in other Southern states as well.

Colin Shaw, chaplain of the Fifty-first NCT with his troops on Long Island, South Carolina, thanked merchants Fulton and Price for three hundred dollars gained via proceeds of an entertainment given by the ladies of Duplin County for the benefit of the soldiers in C.S. General Clingman's brigade.[125]

In June of 1864, professional actors and actresses performed at Thalian Hall for the Soldiers' Aid Society, raising $1275.** Other professionals in Wilmington were the Katie Estelle Company and one troupe called Bates and Jenkins. Other distinguished musicians were the Sloman family who achieved notoriety with frequent shows in Raleigh and the Confederate Minstrels. This newspaper ad shows that bands raised funds for different reasons:

> A parlor entertainment will be given on Saturday night by the 27th Infantry Band [a rival of the 26th], Cooke's Brigade, in this city for the purpose of raising funds to procure school books, as the General commanding intends to establish schools this winter for those who wish to be instructed in the English branches and writing. Contributions of money and school books earnestly solicited.[126]

Wartime teens in Wilmington presented a series of tableaux to raise money for disabled soldiers.

Ordinary citizens overcame their shyness to step upon the stage. In the past, female actresses were disdained. They wore makeup and revealing costumes. Heaven forbid if father's little daughter painted and powdered her face like those harlots! That would never do; however, these ladies did perform in the name of charity for the soldiers. The drama club of Greensboro Female College gave benefits for military purposes. Costumes were designed from curtains and drapery. (Does this sound like *Gone with the Wind*?) They also held dances.[127] One way the citizens of Salem earned money to supply the troops was by having bazaars, performances, and tableaux.

One unique way the Wadesborough Aid Society raised funds was to go from town to town with a traveling magic lantern show. The magic lantern was the precursor of the modern slide projector. Only the wealthy could afford to own a magic lantern. This must have been equally entertaining to both adults and children alike.[128]

In the last few weeks before General Sherman occupied Raleigh, Monsieur Latelot of the Burlesque Troupe and his performers executed another benefit. He had a notice placed in the newspaper for all to read:

> To Dr. J.M. Pelot, in charge of the Episcopal Church Hospital: "I have the honor to turn over to you for the benefit of your hospital $500 being the proceeds of an entertainment given in this city by those who delight to do everything to ameliorate the condition of the suffering soldiers." Very respectfully yours . . .[129]

---

*   Research has shown that Tom played "Dixie" with one hand and "Yankee Doodle" with the other and, at the same time, sang "The Girl I Left Behind"—all popular tunes during the war.

**   Thalian Hall has been refurbished and is still in operation. During the war, it held performances every night, including holidays. The only time it closed was during the yellow fever epidemic. Six tableaux vivants on July 11, 1864, charmed the crowd in Wilmington: "Famine," "Dead Drummer Boy," "The Duel," "Soldier's Return," "Marble Heart," and "Sic Semper Tyrannis." On Christmas Eve of 1864, the public went to see the North Carolina Ethiopians.

Men unable to stand the rigors of military life pitched in for the war effort. Certain millers asked lower prices for grinding the corn of military wives. Likewise, a few farmers or merchants reduced the cost of goods sold to these women. Men ineligible for military service headed committees such as the Safety Committee, which functioned like benevolent societies with a few similar duties of the militia. Soldiers' wives were assisted by neighbors to plant/harvest the crops or to make shoes or bury their dead. Those who had wagons helped civilians with transportation. They were indispensable for carrying provisions to the troops. Men assisted the ladies in organizing bazaars, concerts, and entertainments. They willingly gave food to destitute families. In Fayetteville "Dr. McDuffie, having learned that there was great need of shoes and socks in Captain Mallet's and Sinclair's Companies, took a boy and a bag . . . and obtained by short walk through one or two of our streets, eighty-five pairs of shoes, two-hundred pairs of socks, and eighty dollars in cash, besides shirting, blankets, and handkerchiefs."[130]

Notices were placed in the local paper to announce when authorities would be in town to collect items for the soldiers. The following is a good example:

> **TO THE FRIENDS OF THE ARMY** Editors of the *Bulletin*:
> Mr. John Terrell and myself have permission for ten days to visit Charlotte for the purpose of collecting provisions for the sick and wounded soldiers from North Carolina in Richmond.[131]

Another ad in the *Bulletin*:

> **TO THE CITIZENS OF MECKLENBURG:** The people of Mecklenburg County are most earnestly requested to send to Charlotte meat, sugar, meal, and all kinds of vegetables to be prepared here for the large number of our wounded soldiers who are arriving daily & need food already prepared for them on their arrival. Any contributions for this purpose will be forthwith appreciated to the use of our wounded soldiers. S.A. Harris(?), Mayor[131]

> **APRIL 14, 1862** The ladies of Mecklenburg and all others interested in the soldiers now sick in the hospital at Kinston, North Carolina are hereby informed that any contributions of hospital furniture or articles necessary for the use of the sick, will be most thankfully received by the undersigned, who is now in Charlotte for the purpose of procuring necessities for sick soldiers. Articles may be left in the store of Messrs Brown, Stitt & Co, to be packed for immediate transport. J.B.F. Boone (?) Quartermaster, Co. H.[132]

Mr. Raynor in Wake County had a room fitted out to store articles collected from the Ladies of the Soldiers' Relief Society. The items they gathered—which included dried fruit, rice, blackberry wine, soap, hominy, pickles, hams, coffee, tea, sugar, lint, bandages, cotton rags, pieces of oilcloth, castile soap, and empty vials—were sent to the hospitals in Richmond.

William Graham wrote, "some of the citizens of Charlotte have contributed two barrels of molasses to my company, and the men are faring finely now." Messrs. Buie, McNeill, and company sent two barrels of apples to the troops at Fort Caswell. The soldiers made pies and apple dumplings from it.

J. B. McNeil in a letter to his cousin Mollie said that "we can beat you gals up in Robeson all to pieces making 'nick nacks' and fineries . . ."[133] W. H. Wyatt, a druggist from Salisbury, declared that he would give free medicine to soldiers' families with a doctor's certificate of need. Kenneth Rayner contributed his pay of forty-five dollars received from his "convention duties" to be used for the families of volunteers from Hertford County.[134]

Upper-class families had the means to furnish their sons provisions, as well as their friends. Paul Cameron, owner of 650 slaves, contributed clothes to the volunteers of Orange County. "To the needy and destitute, who included the soldiers, wives, and families, he had made large donations."[135] At Bonarva, on Lake Phelps, the mistress of the plantation had her servants to "sew for the defenders." In one day, they made fifteen pairs of drawers that she had cut out that morning. Carey Pettigrew donated several blankets her servants had made. Eng and Chang Bunker, the Siamese twins in Buncombe County, intermittently sent provisions to their sons and fellow prisoners at Camp Chase, Ohio.

The Wiggins family from Halifax County prepared clothing and food for their son Eugene who had gone into camp before April 5, 1861. Mr. Wiggins carried him a box containing clothing, cakes, fruit, and a writing box. Another son Alfred was going to Raleigh to seek a surgeon's position. Mrs. Wiggins noted in her diary that her husband had bought her a sewing machine, which cost $46.50. She attempted several times to use it but could not sew on it. She suspected the machine was faulty. "I fear we have been imposed on, as we cannot get it to work." A cousin who had used one before was helping her. Mrs. Wiggins had a very frustrating spring trying to get the machine to work. She continued to make clothes, sheets, blankets, caps, and oilcloth capes (ponchos) for her sons and their friends. On June 19, she wrote that "cousin Mary Harrison's appropriation by the commissioners is given to her . . ." (This probably meant that she had contracted to sew uniforms for the state.) It wasn't until the end of July that she was able to use the sewing machine. Mrs. Wiggins immediately made her sons drawers and shirts. Son Alfred, in a camp seven miles below Wilmington, received a welcome box from home containing three pound cakes, gingersnaps, sugar biscuits, plain biscuits, iced cakes, and some letters. To prevent spoilage, it was hand carried that July 4. Then four days later Wiggins was up before daybreak, packing more provisions for the boys. This box contained five cartons of butter, blackberry jam, honey, pickles, six fried chickens, bacon, and two hams. Sam Pitts took this box along with a box for Blake Pullen. Ms. Polly Johnson got Blake's fiddle and box of eatables ready for Sam. Elizabeth Wiggins provided her sons with three more boxes of provisions in August. Mr. Wiggins carried one box early in the month, along with a gallon of scuppernong wine. The end of August, the whole family went to his camp carrying two more boxes—one with food, the other filled with chickens. They stayed at the North Carolina Hotel in Wilmington. While there, they viewed the soldiers' dress parade. The young people went swimming while her husband went boating. She said it took twelve hours by train to get back home to Halifax County.[136]

Walter Clark was fortunate to have family who sent him boxes continuously. With the constant movement of armed forces, except in the winter months, boxes from home seldom reached their intended person. Those sent by rail were subject to be "off-loaded" at some depot if military shipments took precedence. When this happened and the donor had sent perishable food, you know the result. Mrs. Clark wrote her son that a friend was to deliver his next box. She said, "The Express refused to take it on account of its weight. I ventured to put a roast turkey in . . . the weather being very (cold) thought it would keep . . ." Mrs. Clark sent these articles to Walter—ink, a lamp, shoes, vegetables, money, fruits, meat, socks, suit, a Bible, honey, sugar, butter, raw hams, bucket of lard, cakes, tinplates and cups, slippery elm bark as medicine, tableware, books, gloves, crackers, light bread, eggs, a Beauregard, and neck scarf. Clark had requested some rhubarb pills and rhubarb syrup, which his aunt sent.[137] Most recruits were not as fortunate to receive so much from home.

Catherine Edmondston mentioned earlier, was another individual who worked tirelessly for the war effort. She led a privileged life, was barren, and put her slaves to assist her in this endeavor. Throughout the fall of 1862, she oversaw the servants to make candles and spin thread. She sent boxes of candles, bacon, and six pairs of drawers for the soldiers that time. To the quartermaster in Raleigh she sent twelve yards of cloth, six pairs of homespun drawers, a woolen fatigue shirt, two pairs of socks, and a blanket. She confided to her diary of making wooden-sole shoes for the slaves and their continuing to spin, weave, and make candles all winter.[138]

In Greensboro the former governor Morehead, also a merchant, contributed several hundred dollars to the Ladies Soldiers' Aid Society. The populace dealing with him made a comment to the effect that if he would only lower his prices, it would benefit the poor even more. John T. Battle of Edgecombe contributed a barrel of sorghum syrup to be distributed to the families of soldiers who needed it. Michael Kelly gave four boxes of coffee manufactured by himself valued at $16.75. Near Wilmington, a man contributed a stand of pine trees worth fifty dollars to be used as lumber.

Ms. Harriet McIntosh received a letter from her aunt Elmina on January 15, 1865, saying that she heard from her sons and that they got the box sent for New Year's Eve dinner. "They got about as much loaf bread as would make six biscuits, six small bites of turkey, and the shoulder of a sheep with all the meat cut for dinner." The box was hand carried.[139]

In Rockingham County "tables were spread on the old Dillard porch and adjacent buildings and supplies of vegetables, meats, and nick-knacks, with great quantities of buttermilk, were placed on these tables; while our noble women, young and old, gave them [soldiers] a hearty welcome from six in the morning until nine at night" as the men were passing through.[140] Salem residents continued to help supply the defenders. Long lengths of cloth could be seen hanging on the fences where persons would paint it, thereby rendering it waterproof, turning it into "oilcloth."[141]

After giving generously to the soldiers, North Carolina residents dug into their pockets to help the citizens of Washington after it was sacked and burned by the Federal Army. A fund was started to help the destitute. Persons in Wilmington raised nearly three thousand dollars for the benefit of the Washington inhabitants. Members of the Presbyterian church in Salisbury took up a collection of one hundred dollars, sending it to the residents of Charleston after General Sherman burned it. The Mocksville Girls' School on December 19, 1861, held a tableau and raised thirty-two dollars for the benefit of the First Maryland Confederate Regiment after a visit and solicitation from a former North Carolina woman married to the colonel of the regiment.[142]

In addition to volunteer benevolent societies on a local level, the counties appropriated different amounts to fund the troops and their families. In Caswell County, a called court for May 25, 1861, decided "it was unanimously determined by the Court that at the regular July term 1861 . . . a tax shall be levied to raise the funds to re-imburse the sum of five thousand dollars which has already been laid out in the equipment of volunteers or which has been borrowed by divers citizens for that purpose and also to equip such volunteers as are now enrolled . . . in the county and also to support the indigent families of volunteers." In the July 1861 session of that court, politicians appointed three men "to aid and provide for the families of such soldiers as have volunteered to serve in the War against Abe Lincoln's scoundrels." Caswell County levied thirty-five cents on one hundred dollars of land to be collected for soldiers' wives, as well as thirty cents on every one hundred dollars' worth of slaves for county purposes, thirty cents on one hundred dollars' worth of capital, and seventy-five cents on each white and free black poll. Three thousand dollars was set aside for the soldiers' wives.[143] This was only the beginning of taxation. More to come.

"Local justices were to establish rules for the division and distribution of state aid, and they had the option of taking their county's relief in cash or provisions." Eventually the programs failed, so they had to seek assistance from the state government wherein they sought aid from the central Confederate government.[144]

State government agencies commandeered cotton and woolen mills for state use. A bill was passed in Congress to "exempt sewing machines from execution." This meant that the ladies could keep their machines for home use.* Government contractors traveled the state, passing out cloth to women at home who chose to sew for profit. This act helped supplement poorer families.

---

*   By the end of the war, there were sixty-three thousand Singer and Wheeler models of sewing machines in use. "The shirt that took fourteen hours to make by hand now took one hour by machine."[145]

Weldon Edwards was appointed by the state to oversee needs of the poor. Money was appropriated to buy provisions for soldiers' wives. Purchasing agents were appointed by courts to find and secure food for families of soldiers and also the poor. County commissioners were appointed for Relief of Indigent Soldiers' Families.[146] A relief agent was appointed in each of the eighty-six counties in the state.

Guilford County decided to give each soldier's wife twenty dollars a month and for each child, they were to receive an extra ten dollars. Wake County voted to give each soldier's wife one-half a bushel of cornmeal and five pounds of bacon. Each child got one peck of cornmeal. One woman in Cumberland County said that the relief they received was as good as before the war. Relief agents tried to secure cotton/wool cards and salt for these women.[147] In Onslow County, an all-male committee was picked to serve the ten different districts there. They purchased and stored food to be later distributed to soldiers' wives. Cotton cards/combs were also supplied to dependent families.[148] The Disbursing and Safety Committee of Pitt County collected both voluntary and court-appropriated funds to equip the soldiers and look after their families. In Fayetteville, the Cumberland Supply Association grew from the need to provide the destitute soldiers' families.[149]

The following order gives evidence of the red tape involved in collecting and distributing provisions to the soldiers:

GENERAL ORDER #9
EXECUTIVE DEPARTMENT ADJUTANT GENERAL OFFICE [Militia]
Raleigh, October 25, 1862:

I. The Colonel of the Militia Regiments in the state will immediately direct the Captains to call without delay on every family within their districts for the purpose of purchasing and collecting such articles of clothing (blankets, jeans, linseys, leather, shoes, socks, and carpets) as may be sold or given for the army in the field.

II. The Captains will keep a list of the articles and money, and the name of the person from whom purchased or received, and the price. The Colonels will bring their lists and the articles with as little delay as possible to the Quartermaster of this city, when funds will be given to pay for them.

III. All donations for individuals or companies will be reserved for them, if the names and companies are given and the articles will be sent to them by the Quartermaster at Raleigh, in charge of specific messengers. Those many donations may be assured that the articles will be given to the parties for whom they intended them.

IV. Each company will send to this office a list of the shoemakers, tanners, cloth-manufacturers in his regiment, with the probable amount [of] each manufactures. Pay particular attention to the purchase of shoes and leather, see that none go into the hands of speculators, and seize for the use of the soldiers any of these articles going out of the state, or in the hands of speculators for that purpose.

V. The expenses of the officers engaged on this duty and the transportation of the articles will be paid, and any officer who neglects or fails to comply with this order will be court-martialed and reduced to the ranks.

By Order of Governor Vance[150]

The Colonels of the Militia right through the state are hereby appointed agents for the purpose of collecting of all such articles as can be spared by our people, who, through their respective captains are ordered immediately to canvass every county and visit every citizen in their beats for this purpose. A liberal price will be paid for everything where the owner feels that he or she is not able to donate it; and active agents will immediately forward them to our regiments. Expenses will be allowed the officers engaged in this duty; and transportation furnished the Colonels or their agents to bring the articles to Raleigh.[150]

Apparently, the soldiers didn't always receive their boxes. Captain Houck responded to Governor Vance's appeal of October 15 and went throughout Rowan County. He submitted the same concern from the citizens about their packages not getting through to a particular company. He suggested that an agent visit every family and get the proper information about the soldier written down, along with a list of what they were sending. (Note: there was no reply to Captain Houck's suggestion.)[151] There probably were black market sales prompting a citizen to write the governor:

> Stocksville Nov. 10th 1862
> One good efficient man can turn out and get more clothing than all the commissioned Militia officers in the State. The people have not got confidence in those little Militia officers and the 'Aaid Societies' in this part of the state are doing but little good, as they cannot agree among themselves who to sen their goods to, I know men who are willing to contribute 25-50 and some $100. but they want to give it to a responcible authorized agent of the State. This is the true state of affairs in my section . . . what we need is Some Sistim and the right Kind of agents . . . our ladies bless them are ready and willing to make the garments for nothing if they had the cloth or make the cloth & Garments if they had the raw material . . . ther has ben so much clothing lost that the people are not willing to trust it to every one. R.V. Blackstock[152]

Written in the edges of the general order no. 9 was the cost of the soldiers' clothing from an officer:

> Shoes . . . $6.08 according to quality, heavy preferred; Pants . . . $6.09 according to quality, heavy preferred; clothe $2.03, according to quality, heavy preferred. Money may be expended in payment for articles and the articles marked in the list . . . PAID[153]

Citizens continued to donate their time and provisions to the hospitals or a doctor. Dr. Ed Warren from Tyrrell County was appointed surgeon general of North Carolina. In addition to his other duties as a doctor, he organized monthly shipments of provisions donated from citizens. When smallpox occurred in central North Carolina, Dr. Warren supervised the inoculation of seventy thousand civilians.

Author Crawford noted, "The needs of individual community continued to outstrip the capacity of the state and local government to meet them . . . . Areas such as western North Carolina were particularly vulnerable to the loss of artisonal labor, men where skills as with blacksmiths, millers, carpenters, tanners, and shoemakers could not be dispensed with or readily imported."[154]

"On 10 February 1863, the General Assembly, in a statewide measure, allocated Ashe County $22, 500.50 for the relief of soldier's families . . ." Other counties collected similar amounts, and this was constantly increased due to inflation. In 1865, the state had spent more than six million dollars for aid alone.[155]

James Sprunt in writing his memories told, "The Confederate Government used to send some queer agents abroad at the expense of the people. A Mrs. Grinnell was sent out by the surgeon general—so she stated—to get bandages, etc. which nobody else . . . but Mrs. Grinnell could get." Grinnell, an upper-class Englishwoman, claimed to be the daughter of a baronet.[156]

Other charitable groups evolved throughout the war. An early well-known organization put this notice in the *Spirit of the Age* in September 1861:

TO THE FRIENDS OF THE SICK AND WOUNDED SOLDIERS OF NORTH CAROLINA

The undersigned having been duly organized as an Army Committee of the Young Men's Christian Association of Raleigh, for the purpose of soliciting and forwarding contributions of all kinds suitable for the afflicted in the hospital at Petersburg, or the Army Committee at Richmond, for the sick in the city, as may be designed by the donors.

They would respectfully and earnestly request the citizens of Wake County; and of the counties on the line of the Rail Roads connecting at Raleigh to forward as rapidly as possible, such contributions as they can spare of money, arrow root, sage, wines, jellies, corn starch, red pepper, smoked beef and tongues, soap, blankets, socks, shirts, sheets, dried fruit, rice, old linen, and any other article which a sick man, far from home and friends, and destitute of every thing necessary to his comfort, may need.

By arrangements secured, all the expenses of forwarding will be saved to the donors, and all contributions, with list of the same, sent to P.F. Pescud, Chairman of the Army Committee, Raleigh, will be prompt, forwarded as directed, and acknowledged through our city papers. And all packages sent to our care will be forwarded immediately, without further expense. P.F. PESCUD, J.M. TOWLES[157]

The response to this appeal pleased Mr. Pescud and his committee. They received and forwarded to W. P. Munford of the Army Committee at Richmond, Virginia, the following articles and cash, contributed in just a few weeks time: Ms. E. C. Boddie, five dollars; Ms. Mary Stronach, two dollars; Mrs. Joseph Fowler, two sheets, a lot of towels, and pillowcases; Mrs. Joseph Cook, five dollars; Mrs. Larkin Smith, a bed quilt, two pairs of socks, and lot of sage; Ms. Nannie P. Jones (a child), one bottle of strawberry wine; Mrs. E. T. Jones, a flannel shirt and three pairs of flannel drawers; Mrs. P. H. Mangum, two woolen blankets; Mrs. Needham Price, five dollars, four woolen blankets, four sheets, twelve pillows, eighteen pillowcases, six towels, a flannel shirt, six pairs of drawers, twenty-five pairs of socks, a bag of sage, a bag of red pepper, one bushel of dried apples, twenty-four pounds of soap, four bottles of blackberry wine, three bottles of strawberry wine, one jar of blackberry jelly, and one jar of apple jelly; Mrs. E. A. Nixon, four blankets, six bottles of blackberry wine, one package of black tea, one package of castile soap, four bottles of mustard, a bag of sage, three vests, a bottle of camphor, seven pillowcases, and six pairs of socks; Mrs. John Primrose, a loaf of sugar, tea, and coffee; Ms. Helen Litchford, a package of sugar and ground coffee; Mrs. B. F. Moore, two bottles of domestic wine; Mrs. G. B. Bagwell, one box of soap, a lot of loaf bread, rice cakes, preserves, pickles, sugar, coffee, and old linens; Mrs. E. C. Fisher, four bottles of very superb wine and one hundred dollars in cash, received at the lecture of Reverend Dr. Read.[158]

The Young Men's Christian Association of Raleigh have for several weeks past taken upon themselves the self-imposed duty of looking after the sick soldiers who may reach this city on their way to or from home. And in this way they have performed many a friendly office by conducting the stricken invalid to the neat little hospital near the depot, and seeing his wants kindly attended to. We have known the poor manner borne from the cars, too far gone to pursue his journey, and in few hours his eyes closed . . . . And we have seen the weary one refreshed and strengthened, so that in a day or two he was able to hurry forward to meet the embrace of wife and children . . . . They need more of the young men of our city to engage with them in this and other philanthropic works. Will not our noble young fellow-citizens come to their assistance?

Another goodly work they have undertaken—and that is to look after boxes and other packages, designed for soldiers in distant camps. The friends of soldiers sending things of this kind to loved ones in the camp and hospitals, if they will mark them to the "care of the Y. M.'s Christian Association, Raleigh" will insure their safe and speedy transmission to the place of destination.[159]

Besides the Ladies' Aid Societies in North Carolina, other benevolent organizations chose to sponsor a specific thing. When a soldier, either diseased or wounded, entered the hospital, he was bereft of belongings. The hospital furnished him drawers, a gown, and sometimes slippers. When he was discharged, he was furnished with a coat, shirt, pants, socks, shoes, and drawers if the hospital linen closet had the items. A portion of these articles were furnished by the state and the others by donations. When people donated money, it was used in any method the surgeon saw fit, whether for food, medicine, equipment, etc. The Cumberland Hospital Association formed early, led by Mrs. John C. Smith as vice president; it contributed fifty dollars, with the money going to purchase fifty pairs of woolen socks made by soldiers' families at twenty-five cents a pair. "It was decided to send $50 each to our companies at Ship Point, for hospital expenses, to expend $30 for chloride of lime and medicines desired by Dr. Graham. It was also determined to extend aid to all the companies from Cumberland and Harnett [Counties]." This group decided to have weekly sewing meetings at the seminary for the purpose of making warm clothing for sick and invalid soldiers, with a fund being appropriated for the purchase of flannel, etc. The Young Ladies' Seminary reverted to a hospital. "Each ward or floor was presided over by four ladies who attended to their wants giving medicine, nourishment, etc . . . After Sherman's memorable visit to Fayetteville, a Marine Hospital was established." Local women brought them meals. The ladies established a committee to rotate turns with the meals each day. Younger women carried flowers, brought delicacies, or sung for the troops. Mrs. Annie K. Kyle was the head nurse.[160]

The Raleigh Ambulance Committee did not begin operation until the last two years of the war. They solicited goods like other organizations:

> Raleigh Ambulance Company . . . a few more volunteers are needed to complete the organization of this committee . . . also lint, bandages, and delicacies for the sick and wounded.[161]

Mr. P. F. Pescud was on this committee too.

In 1863, the Raleigh Mutual Relief and Charitable Association was formed to sustain the poor. They asked for wood, food, and money specifically.[162] The Cumberland County War Association grew out of the desire to assist local needy families, and it operated similarly to the Raleigh charity.[163] In that same year, people established an agency to aid the poor of Rowan County. They collected money to buy provisions for families of soldiers. With this, they also bought wood and shoes.

The orphans were not overlooked. The Reverend Dr. Deems journeyed over the state to collect funds for a school. He had raised eighty-five thousand dollars by mid-1863. Delegates to the State Baptist Convention agreed in 1864 to pay tuition for children of soldiers already in school. Mrs. Agnes Patrick taught at the orphans' school without being paid. She had forty students, which included destitute children of soldiers. By the middle of 1864, North Carolina had raised five hundred thousand dollars for the education of orphans.

The secretary of the orphan fund, Charles Deems, called for a meeting at the institution for the Deaf, Dumb, and Blind School in Raleigh. He said that "those who cannot be present should send proxies. A full attendance is desired for important business. The committee of the Grand Lodge of Masons for St. John's College are respectfully invited to be present."[164]

Masons James Wright and C. S. Winstead received a pass to travel to Petersburg and Richmond to "look after our wounded soldiers and do anything necessary for their relief and comfort and carry such things as may be provided for them by our people . . ."[165]

People throughout the world sided with the plight of the Confederates. Ladies from Havana sent boxes of lint and funds to assist the Confederacy.[166] A bazaar was held in Liverpool in October of 1864 to assist the Southern Prisoners' Relief Fund. It would provide relief such as food, clothing, and blankets to Southern men held in Northern prisons. The fund also would donate to wounded Southern men, either in hospitals or on their journey to and from camp. The bazaar would be similar to the U.S. Sanitary Commission fairs, which took place all over the North. Among the notables attending were James Mason (of the Mason-Sliddell affair) and John Laird, the famous local shipbuilder. Some former officers from the CSS *Alabama* attended.

Inside the gas-lit building—decorated with Confederate, French, and British flags, along with large pictures of Confederate statesmen—were found twelve divided stalls, each represented by people from each Southern state, along with Kentucky. Mrs. James Spence staffed the North Carolina booth. On display at the bazaar was an artfully designed large silver piece. It featured the outline of the Atlantic coastline with cannons and a Clydebuilt steamer at anchor. The piece was made for the Anglo-Confederate Trading Company as a gift to Colonel Lamb, commander of Fort Fisher.

Contributions came from Canada, Europe, India, and the Confederacy, totaling upwards of twenty thousand pounds sterling. "The Liverpool *Daily Courier* pronounced the Bazaar 'a triumphant success,' and the Index left its readers in no doubt that the credits should go to James Spence, 'whose indefatigable exertions for weeks in advance wrought out such harmonious results in the arrangements . . .'"

A committee called the Southern Independence Association of London, run by Lord Wharncliffe, was unable to get permission from the U.S. Secretary of War, William Seward, to deliver the funds to the prisoners. Accounts are foggy as to where the money was then used. It was believed that part of the funds went to assist former Southern prisoners of war and to wounded soldiers who had gone to Great Britain.[167]

Throughout the war, North Carolina's citizens sent boxes of provisions to its military. The boxes may not have been as full as in the beginning, but nevertheless, they found something to give. Always appreciated however puny, the troops loved the boxes from home. The war was almost over when this notice from Lane's brigade appeared in the newspaper:

> The North Carolina soldiers receive a great deal of boxes constantly . . .
> a large number of potatoes, onions, and kraut has been sent to our soldiers
> during the winter by our government.[168]

Sam Walkup described what was in his barrel from home, which arrived on January 1, 1865 as three balls of butter, sausage, pound cake, sweet cakes, opossum, backbones, and a broken jug of molasses.[169] "During three months in 1864, it was reported that $325,000 worth of supplies [aid to soldiers] was sent from North Carolina through the Post Office in Richmond."[170] Local women had not given up and were still knitting socks as shown in this announcement: "The knitting club will meet March eight at the residence of Mrs. L. Bryan . . ." Little girls still knitted socks, and women gathered items to go in a soldier's box as late as March 1865. The war would be over in a month.[171] A benefit for the soldiers' relief took place in Raleigh on March 27, after the fall of Bentonville.

Caroline Fries wrote her fiancé, Dr. J. F. Shaffer:

> You spoke of the bravery of the women of the South. I think their hardest struggle is after the excitement of preparation is over, they are lett [sic] to await the future as best they can.[172]

Caroline was right. The women had been sewing and knitting frantically to get the soldiers ready; flags had been made, tearful good-byes said, and now many were left alone to wonder about the safety of their loved ones.

After the ladies had gathered all that they had made and collected, it was time to ship the goods to the camps or to the hospitals as the need might have been. In order to make it easier for the folks left at home, the *State Journal* printed guidelines for its subscribers:

TO HELP CITIZENS:
A box 24" X 16⅛" X 8" deep . . . holds one peck
A box 24" X 16" X 22" deep . . . holds one barrel
A box 16" X 16⅛" X 8" deep . . . holds one bushel[173]

The women of North Carolina had indeed worked themselves into patriotic exhaustion. In a mid-war recognition of their efforts, the general assembly passed this resolution:

> December 9, 1863, Equal to our appreciation of the valor and patriotism of our troops in the field is our admiration of the self-sacrificing and noble devotion of the women of our country in encouraging the soldiers on the way to the field of duty and of danger; in their untiring efforts to supply them with every comfort which their ingenuity can invent, and their indefatigable ministrations at the couch of the suffering, whether it be by disease or by wounds received in the defense of their country. This devotion to the cause of independence for which we are struggling is alike sustaining to the soldier on duty and the patriot at home and inspire all with that energy which enables us to work with confidence to its successful termination and in a Confederate Government established upon an equitable basis and entitled to the highest possible position among the nations of the earth.[174]

North Carolinians continued to contribute money and provisions throughout the war years as the supply of commodities decreased. Very little money was circulated. Barter was the order of the day.

The following lines were found in a bundle of socks, sent by a lively old lady, in Amherst, New Hampshire, to the U.S. hospital in Philadelphia. It could be said of the Confederacy as well:

KNITTING THE SOCKS

By the fireside, cosily seated,
With spectacles riding her nose,
The lively old lady is knitting
A wonderful pair of Hose.
She pities the shivering soldier,
Who is out in the pelting storm;
And busily plies her needles,
To keep him hearty and warm.

Her eyes are reading the embers,
But her heart is off to the War,
For she knows what those brave fellows
Are gallantly fighting for.
Her fingers as well as her fancy,
Are cheering them on their way;
Who under the good old banner,
Are saving their Country to-day.

She ponders how in her childhood,
Her Grandmother used to tell—
The story of barefoot soldiers,
Who fought so long and well.
And the men of the Revolution
Are nearer to her than us;
And that, perhaps, is the reason
Why she is toiling thus.

So prithee, proud owner of muscle,
Or purse-proud owner of stocks,
Don't sneer at the labors of woman,
Or smile at her bundle of socks.
Her heart may be larger and braver
Than his who is tallest of all,
The work of her hand as important,
As cash that buys powder and ball.

And now, while beginning "to narrow,"
She thinks of the Maryland mud,
And wonders if ever the stocking
Will wade to the ankle in blood.
And now she is "shaping the heel;"
And now she is ready "to bind;"
And hopes if the soldier is wounded,
It will never be from behind.

Ye men who are fighting our battles,
Away from the comforts of life,
Who thot'fully muse by your campfires,
On sweetheart, or sister, or wife, —
Just think of their elders a little,
And pray for the grandmothers too,
Who, patiently sitting in corners,
Are knitting the stockings for you. [175]

She cannot shoulder a musket,
Nor ride with Cavalry crew,
But nevertheless she is ready
To work for the boys who do.
And yet in "Official Dispatches,"
That come from the Army or Fleet,
Her feats may have never a notice,
Though ever so mighty the feet!

And thus while her quiet performance
Is being recorded in rhyme,
The tools in her tremulous fingers
Are running a race with time.
Strange that four needles can form
A perfect triangular bound;
And equally strange that their antics
Result in perfecting the round.

And now she is "raising the instep,"
Now "narrowing off at the toe,"
And prays that this end of the worsted
May never be turned to the foe.
She "gathers" the last of the stitches
As if a new laurel were won;
And placing the ball in the basket,
Announces the stocking as "done."

Catherine Edmondston said, "Congress has passed a vote of thanks to the women of the South—'for their ardent & cheerful patriotism;' and well do they deserve, for they have indeed done nobly & upheld the hands & strengthened the hearts of the soldiers."[176]

CHAPTER FOUR

Gearing Up . . . "Yankees, Look Out, We Are Coming!"*

In the aforementioned chapters, you have read about secession, making flags, uniforms, and the recruits leaving for camp. Now that North Carolina had officially left the old Union, it was time to get serious about generating the infrastructure to carry on war. The formation of different arms of the military will not be discussed because there are several good books solely on this.

Because North Carolina held out the longest, seceded states contacted Governor Ellis before the state's secession, asking the state to furnish them with men, muskets, percussion caps, and accoutrements. Ellis told the secretary of war in Richmond that he had sent 9,500 rifles and couldn't send any more. North Carolina continued to send supplies to other states for a few months, creating a shortage of supplies for its own troops. These items were soon needed by North Carolina. On June 19, 1861, Samuel Person, department of quartermaster general, replied to the request of General Walker Gwynn in New Bern that they had no blankets and tents for the soldiers at Oregon Inlet because all had been sent to Virginia.[1] The state purchased part of its military supplies from Norfolk.

Hundreds of men petitioned the governor for positions, mostly as officers. Ostentatious men bombarded the governor, requesting commissions; but most wanted a high rank, such as captain. Patriotic individuals "tendered their services" as guards in their own locale.[2]

Jurisdiction over the forts in North Carolina—as well as the lighthouses, beacons, the future Charlotte Mint, the Arsenal in Fayetteville, and two marine hospitals—was turned over to the central Confederacy in June 1861.[3]

Briefly mentioned earlier, comrades challenged their known Northern-born neighbors to ascertain their allegiance. Accused individuals were served a notice to appear in court. Most failed to do so, and their property was sequestered and sold with the money or property going to the Confederate States government. Sequestration was a transaction whereby the Confederate government took possession of property located within the Confederacy that belonged to citizens of the United States. If you were a Southern citizen who owned property in the North or owed money to a Northern company, the Confederate government would file a garnishment proceeding, and you had to pay the Confederate government that amount.

Before April 1861, ships belonging to the seceded states lying in New York harbors found themselves sequestered. The schooners *Ben* and *Hickman* from Wilmington lay in port for three days in April, along with two more from Plymouth, the *Resolution* and the *Gale*.** Since North Carolina would not secede until one month later, it is probable that their cargo was safe.[4] Uncertainty caused Adjutant W. Andrews to write Governor Clark:

> HQ, Camp Hatteras to his Excellency Henry T. Clark:
> Governor Since my last [,] the privateer steamer Ariner has brought into port as a prize the schooner Pricilla[?], of Baltimore, from Curacoa, with six hundred bushels of salt. I had some doubt as to the legality of the prize, but

---

*   Quote by a North Carolina recruit.

**   Author Jim McNeil indicated that the *Uncle Ben* was on her way to reenforce Fort Sumter when gale force winds blew her near the Cape Fear River, where she was captured by its citizens and turned over to the Confederacy.[5]

having seen that Baltimore vessels, laden with coffee, had been seized in the mouth of the Chesapeake and sent to New York as prizes, I ordered her up to New Bern to-day. The Winslow has a large brig at the bar laden with sugar and molasses, and the Gordon has two schooners coming over the bar now.

The Mariner has taken a schooner into Ocracoke, and is now in pursuit of another. These will be fully reported as soon as the captains report to me. I am doing all I can to prevent the news of captures spreading, but so long as the crews are sent up to New Bern immediately, it cannot be prevented. Your dispatch through the Adjutant General's office of the 27th instant is received.

The directions of Captain Barron, with regard to Hatteras Light-House, will be followed. You did not direct me what to do in regard to the coffee. I am trying to save the copper on the bark, Linwood, and will await your orders how to dispose of it. I suppose it is needed to make percussion caps. Yours very respectfully, W.S.G. Andrews, Major Commanding Fort Hatteras and Dependencies.[6]

The prizes taken by sequestration was governed by a law dating back to 1800. One was called "An Act for the Better Government of the Navy of the United States, known by sailors as the 'Rocks and Shoals.' Because the new Confederacy did not own any ships, it issued 'Letters of Marque and Reprisal' to privateers authorizing them to capture naval vessels near southern ports. These privateers after paying a fee according to the size of their ship and crew could then capture northern merchant vessels. Once the contents of the cargo was sold, the profits would be kept by the owner and crew. An added bonus included '20 percent of the value of any captured United States Navy ships.'"[7]

"The Letter of Marque Act of May 6, 1861, set aside five percent of all privateer prize money to the government for a privateersman's pension fund. The remaining ninety-five percent went to the ship's owners and crew, usually on a contracted scale of shares."[8]

President Davis permitted the practice of privateering when he first took office. After Lincoln imposed the blockade on Southern ports, Davis, according to author Flannery, "upped the stakes and added enticements to Southern vessels' seizure of enemy cargoes by reducing by one-third the normal duties on captured goods and granting 5 percent on all such 'good and lawful prizes of war.'"[9]

In the beginning, the goal of the Confederates was to disrupt United States commerce. Privateers and the Confederate Navy captured Northern vessels on their way to Southern ports. Local pilots built log towers to site ships passing by. These pilots then steamed out to "offer" to guide ships through the inlet, as well as to seize Northern ships going to the Southern islands, much like the pirates of old. Numerous ships seized in this way affected the insurance industry of Northern merchants, prompting them to complain to President Lincoln to stop it.[10] A ship owned by New York merchants appeared in the news:

Capture of the Steamtug Uncle Ben at Wilmington, N.C. by Secessionists:
The seizure of the steamtug Uncle Ben happened on the 20th of April, when she was lying at anchor at Wilmington, North Carolina. She was commanded by Captain W.H. Dare . . . . In the afternoon of that day the vessel was boarded and captured by a body of armed Secessionists and the captain and pilot were imprisoned as spies. They were kept in confinement eleven days, but were released by the interposition of the Cape Fear Flying Artillery. Fortunately the Alba, a New York vessel, was at Wilmington at the time . . . and brought them safely to New York. The tug is now in the hands of her captors, and will most probably be used for the purpose of the Southern Confederacy.

The tug was owned by New York merchants.[11] Another Northern daily told its readers:

The following vessels are ashore in the vicinity of Ocracoke and Hatteras: the schooner Stephen Duncan, from Mobile, with cotton bound for New York; the schooner Alice Webb with an assorted cargo from New York, bound for the South; the brig, Black Squall, from Cuba, with a cargo of sugar . . . a schooner is ashore on Hatteras shoal, name unknown, crew supposed to be lost; probably War Eagle, from Port au Prince for Philadelphia, reported by the steamer Keystone State—by telegraph.[12]

The following appeared in Frank Leslie's *Illustrated Newspaper*:

Southern Ordinance of Privateering

As the President of the United States had rejected all overtures for a peaceful solution of the disagreement between the two Governments, and had called for seventy-five thousand men to coerce the South, he had accepted the alternative. He also announced that he has made an alliance, offensive and defensive, with Virginia. He also informs the Southern States that the following States had refused to comply with President Lincoln's call for men, viz., Arkansas, Missouri, Tennessee, North Carolina, Maryland, Kentucky and most probably Delaware; also the Territories of Arizona and New Mexico and the Indian Territories south of Kansas. He therefore resolves to use the whole force, naval and military, against the aforesaid Lincoln and the United States.

Jefferson Davis therefore invites all persons who may wish to become privateers to apply to him for letters of marque, requiring two responsible sureties for the due fulfillment of the conditions.[13]

The newspaper said that most remarkable section of the article was this:

Section 10. That a bounty shall be paid by the Confederate States of $20 for each person on board any armed ship or vessel belonging to the United States, at the commencement of an engagement, which shall be burnt, sunk, or destroyed by any vessel commissioned as aforesaid, which shall be of equal or inferior force, the same to be divided as in other cases of prize money—and a bounty of $25 shall be paid to the owners, officers, and crew of the private armed vessels, commissioned as aforesaid for each and every prisoner by them captured and brought into port, and delivered to an agent authorized to receive them, in any part of the Confederate States; and the Secretary of the Treasury, is hereby authorized to pay or cause to be paid to the owners, officers and crews of such private armed vessels, commissioned as aforesaid, or their agent, the bounties herein provided.[14]

"A major incentive for individuals to enlist in the navy was the promise of 'prize money,' . . . a share of the money value of a captured ship and its cargo." After capture, the captain filed a claim in the navy's court for disbursement. It was important to do this quickly because the ship may be carrying cargo that would spoil. The *Transit* and *Hannah Balch* were two ships captured early by Confederates, afterwards the *Herbert Manton*.[15] Another section provided that the captain of the privateer shall keep an exact journal of all his prizes, number of guns, and men found on board.

To impound a ship, you must have proof it was carrying military supplies. The crew of a North Carolina ship, *Winslow*, captured a Northern vessel, *Transit*, then advertised it and the ship's contents to be sold in the *Daily Progress*, New Bern, and other Southern newspapers. "One half of the net proceeds were paid to the officers and crew of the Winslow." The remainder was split among the state, attorneys, court costs, etc.[16] The *Winslow* and its crew were so prosperous in capturing commercial vessels that Northern merchants became outraged and demanded that Lincoln do something to stop the pirates as they called them.[17]

North Carolina's two other ships, the *Raleigh* and the *Beaufort*, subverted many more ships carrying sugar and coffee.[18] One captain of a captured Northern ship, while on parole in New Bern, told of seeing more than twenty-four "pirated" ships in port being unloaded of its cargo.[19]

After secession, until the end of August 1861, seven more ships were sequestered with the contents sold. Money from the sale, after being divided up, was deposited in a bank in the district where the trial was held, where it was then transferred to Confederate treasury in Richmond.[20] Sequestration cases tied up the courts in Goldsboro most of September 1861.[21] The following rules regarding sequestration appeared in the November 1861 Confederate Court Records:

> 1st. On the first day of each and every month commencing from the first day of March . . . Receivers shall file with the Clerk of Court a true and perfect account of matters in his hands or under his control under the Sequestration Act and make and state a just and true account of all matters connected within each estate of an alien enemy of which he is a receiver.
>
> 2nd. All monies which may be received by any receiver shall be deposited by him immediately after thereof in the Bank of North Carolina or Bank of the Cape Fear or . . . one of the branches of said bank reserving only what is proper to meet necessary expenditorys in the administration of the fund, an account whereof as the separate amount received and from whosoever he shall render in his monthly return.
>
> Ordered that a copy of these rules be furnished by the clerk to each receiver of the district. Jno. S. Cantrell, Clerk

After the Federals got a foothold on the eastern shores, the courts from that area were moved to the interior. This court was held in Salisbury in June 1862, although the persons listed were from the Pamlico District Court. Examples of articles seized from the "aliens" are listed with location and description as is:

John Sherman . . . property sold
Robert Gadd . . . a mine
H.W. Ross . . . household goods, furniture, crockery, clothing
H. Morgan . . . perishable property, boxes of patent medicine
A.J. Fulchman . . . blacksmith tools
Mr. Price . . . blacksmith and carpenter tools, mining tools
W. Richards . . . same as above plus household furniture, lumber, rope, chains, an iron safe
R.P. Hames . . . portable grist mill
R.W. Allison . . . one trunk with contents
William K. Covell . . . property
James Cassidy . . . dredge boat and machinery
Thomas P. Hunt . . . property and one slave named Jacob
Wellington D. Murphey . . . bonds, slaves named Sally, with two children; Margaret; Alice; Ami; Mary and children, also an infant, [August 30, 1861]
George A. Newell . . . carriages
William H. Cullem . . . clocks, fur skins, and a box containing Yankee writing
F.J. Robinson . . . a storehouse and a lot in Clinton
Frazier & Robinson . . . a store containing hats, drygoods, harness
Amos T. Johnson and Amos Johnson . . . contents of store plus a wagon, turpentine hooks, a turpentine still, 50 acres of land in Johnston County, a chest and trunk with contents, and $7.*[22]

---

*   See the appendix for a complete list.

Southern citizens had to pay their debts with interest owed to Northern companies. The debts ran from a few dollars to hundreds. L. B. and R. Bryan of Rutherford County owed John Ford of Philadelphia $217. The court condemned and confiscated that amount from the Bryans; then it was turned over to the Confederacy. Case no. 552 in the Pamlico District in August 1861 revealed Huldah Robbins had a garnishment. Robbins was left $7.20 by her husband, James E. Robbins, deemed as an alien enemy, which had to be turned over to the courts. Apparently, he had fled the home.[23]

The government was still seizing property the second year of the war. This advertisement appeared in the *Hillsborough Recorder* in July 1862:

> **SEQUESTRATION NOTICE:** The undersigned, appointed Receiver under the Sequestration Act, for the county of Orange, Wake, Cumberland, and Harnett, hereby, gives notice to all persons having any lands, tenements or hereditaments, goods or chattels rights or credits, or any interest therein, of or for any alien enemy of the Confederate States of America, speedily to inform me of the same, and to render an account thereof, and so far as practicable, to put the same in my possession, under the penalty of the law for non-compliance.
>
> I also notify each and every citizen of the Confederate States speedily to give information to me of any and all lands, tenements, and hereditaments, goods and chattels, rights, and credits within said counties. I will attend the different counties in a few days for the purpose of receiving, of which time due notice will be given. G.H. Wilder

An agent for Mr. DuBrutz Cutlar's Sequestration Office proclaimed that Dr. John Bellamy owed several thousand dollars to Northern businesses who had shipped him supplies during the construction of his large home just before the war. As ordered, Dr. Bellamy had to pay the Confederate government his condemned debts. After the war, he was billed from those Northern merchants and had to pay again.[24]

Property and Southern vessels in Northern territory were likewise seized and held for auction. The same newspaper printed this notice:

> **CONDEMNATION OF A NORTH CAROLINA VESSEL AT NEW YORK . . .** United States vs the Mary McRae:
>
> This is the first decision on a seizure made under the act of July 1, 1861, on the ground that the vessel was owned in whole or part by parties residing in the rebel states. The judge condemned three-fourths of the vessel owned in Wilmington, North Carolina & released one-fourth owned by a New York owner. The loyal owner made a claim against the Southern shares for a rateable proportion of the advances made by him on account of the vessel. The judge overruled this claim, deciding that the forfeiture was superior to all liens & equities, and the remedy of the loyal part owner (if any) must be had upon application to the Secretary of the Treasury.[25]

Senator John W. Thomas went to New York in August 1861 to collect debts owed to several North Carolina citizens for a percentage of the debt. Apparently, something irregular happened because he was criticized in the local newspaper. The *Fayetteville Observer* reported the incident and accused him of being unlawful.

Citizens along the coast began holding Yankee vessels loaded with North Carolina products.[26] Disloyal North Carolina residents weren't the only persons with property sequestered. The government took what they needed from loyal residents. Ships were seized from nine private individuals around Roanoke Island to be sunk in an attempt to slow or stop the enemy from using the shipping channels.[27] The *Winslow, Ellis, Raleigh*, and *Beaufort* were former riverboats turned into the North Carolina Navy.[28] Jonathan Worth had one of his businesses, the North Carolina Transportation & Mining Company, seized. The following two cases show examples of the court proceedings:

Confederate States of America by John Manning, Jr.

vs

Jonathan Worth

This cause coming on to be heard it is ordered, adjudged and decreed by the court that the land belonging to North Carolina Transportation & Mining company be sequestered to the use of the Confederate States of America and that the same be sold by Jno Manning, Jr., Receiver at the Court House door in the Town of Asheboro for cash after advertisement for three weeks in the Fayetteville Observer and that he report his proceedings to the next Term of Court.

The Same

vs

Mooring and Coble

This cause coming on to be heard and it appearing to the satisfaction of the court that Manning & Coble, copartners having under the same and style of Mooring & Coble are indebted to the Codingtons of New York, who is an alien enemy, in the sum of one hundred dollars August 3rd, 1861.

It is ordered, adjudged and decreed by the court that the said Codington is an alien enemy and that the said sum of one hundred dollars with interest therein from August 3rd, 1861, is sequestered to the use of the Confederate States of America and that Jno. Manning, Jr. Receiver, receive the same of Mooring & Coble.

That execution issue for the costs in this case to be taxed by the Clerk and deducted out of the principle sum due, and that this cause be retained for further directions.[29]

––––––––––––––––––––––––––––––––

Free black men and slaves worked next to soldiers all along the Outer Banks, constructing forts starting in May 1861. Fort Oregon on the Outer Banks was rumored to be built by fifteen hundred free Negroes. L. D. Starke reported to Governor Ellis that one hundred-forty free Negroes had arrived and were immediately put to work constructing Fort Hatteras.[30] Many blacks had volunteered to work on fortifications and received payment. Slaves were used if the commander could not get enough of the free black men. Mr. J. N. Floyd of Edenton in June 1861 wrote to Governor Ellis:

—please confer with Genl. Gwynn and let him advise me what price I shall offer for slave hands & free Negroes, the free Negroes however have nearly all been taken from this county and are now on Beacon Island.[31]

Slaves, free Negroes, and Indians, along with recruits, were put to work building dirt fortifications around larger cities in the eastern part of the state.

In the second year of the war, shortages of manpower appeared; therefore, authorities advertised in the various newspapers around the state. Confederate General Lawrence O' Bryan Branch placed an ad in the *Raleigh Register* for free Negroes to work on fortifications. The response was so poor that he advertised again the next month.

WANTED 500 NEGROES TO WORK ON FORTIFICATIONS:

They will be furnished transportation, quarters, subsistence, and will be paid ten dollars per month. They are necessary to the public defence and I appeal to you. The soldiers are now at work, and have been for weeks. I wish to take

the spade from them and give them their muskets. Citizens now at home must furnish laborers to take the spade. Axes, spades, and grubbing hoes should be brought.
Address your letters to: LOB Branch, Brig. Gen., Confederate Head Quarters, District Of Pamlico.[32]

When the shortage for workers became acute, authorities were permitted to "impress" slaves and free Negroes. This meant the government could legally come and remove the said men for military purposes. Planters with a large number of slaves were contacted first. Rebecca Davis wrote her son, Burwell, that the impressment agents had been there to get slaves to work on forts:

> Joe [a slave] has gone to Weldon to work on fortifications and we have had two pressed this week but they pay us for them . . . the agent insisted that Mr. Davis send one since he didn't send any last time he came around.[33]

Catherine Edmondston with her husband lived in close proximity to where another fort was to be constructed in Martin County. She wrote in her diary in March 1862 that they had an order "for one fourth our men hands to work on entrenchments for Colonel Leventhorpe's regiment at Hamilton." The Edmondstons owned eighty slaves. In the fall of that year, Edmondston's brother went down to Hamilton with a gang of free Negroes "whom he called 'Falstaff's ragged regiment,' to report to the engineer in command."[34] One hundred slaves built Fort Branch known as Rainbow Banks below Hamilton on the Roanoke River. When warned that the Federals were approaching, authorities removed the slaves.[35]
Lumbee Indians from Robeson County were conscripted to work on the construction of embankments around Wilmington, as well as Fort Fisher below the town.[36] The Indians objected when forced to work alongside the bondsmen. The Lumbees said it made them feel like slaves as they considered themselves above slave status. Some Indians ran away to the swamps.[37] Colonel Charles Lamb hired five hundred Negroes to build Fort Fisher. An advertisement in the *Wilmington Daily Journal* requested "three hundred slaves to work on the defenses. They will be paid $28 a month with rations, clothing, and medical attention. Overseers also needed and paid $100." This was an excellent salary if you consider the private soldier was only earning eleven dollars a month.[38] John James agreed to send two of his slaves to help fortify Fort Fisher.[39]
Another wealthy slave owner, Elizabeth Robeson, said, "Some men came after the hands to work on the fort." Robeson sent a slave named Rage.[40] In March of the second year of war, citizens wrote to the governor to raise a company of free mulattoes because their spirit was so high to join the ranks. "They say they are willing to raise arms against our Yankee foe and guard the coast."[41]

North Carolinians had only a few industries at the onset of secession. Only 3,689 small manufacturing plants existed.[42] Out of a population of 992,622 in 1860, 14,217 men were employed outside the home.[43] The number of workers for wrought iron was listed as 125; cast iron workers, 59; tailors, 12; cobblers, 176; tanners, 93; and pharmacists, one.[44] There were seven woolen mills and thirty-nine cotton mills in operation when Fort Sumter was fired upon.
Western North Carolina had more than a dozen iron-making forges prewar. These were located in Ashe, Watauga, and Cherokee counties.[45] Indians had first discovered and used the old Cranberry iron mine. Cranberry produced tools for the new Confederacy.[46] Iron was manufactured on Heltan Creek in Ashe County, which supplied iron for the war to make gun barrels. An iron factory in Salisbury made Parrott shells and horseshoes.[47] The Davidson River Iron Works—operated by Charles Moore, James W. Patton, George

Shuford, and Thomas Miller of Henderson County—was impressed by the Confederate government.[48]

Rogers Magnetic Ore Deposits were shipped down the Dan River to a furnace at Danbury's to the Moratock Forge.[49] Lincolnton was considered an iron center with many foundries where the Vesuvius Furnace was located. Endor IronWorks, near Sanford, consisted of a large smelting furnace, which produced iron throughout the war years. It is still standing, but in a sad state of repair. John Calvin ran an iron furnace in Harnett County near Buckhorn. "Most of it went up the Deep River by steamer to the Western Railroad terminus at McIvers Station near the Egypt Coal Mine . . ."[50] In Guilford County could be found the North State Iron Manufacturing Company. An iron foundry was established in Clarendon. The New Market Foundry in Randolph County made ploughs, straw cutters, threshing machines, corn-shellers, and farm equipment. It was water powered.[51] Wilmington had an ironworks. The Novelty Iron Works advertised in Raleigh that they manufactured steam engines, saw and gristmills parts, plows, and iron railings.[52] A copperas mine existed in Rutherford County. Among the many contributions from Kinston was a foundry. Clover Garden had a nitre and mining department.[53]

Charcoal was needed to make the transition from ore to iron. One cord of wood equaled thirty-three bushels of charcoal. A total of 165 bushels are needed to make one ton of iron. One bushel of charcoal equaled twenty pounds.[54]

Schoolchildren showed their patriotism by collecting old pieces of iron, mainly damaged iron pots, kettles, or scrap iron. These were used for war munitions and plating for the iron-clads.[55] A diarist wrote, "A man stayed here & took off all the old castings, scrap iron &c. to make cannon balls of in Asheville. He got near a 1000 lbs."[56] Adjutant W. S. Ashe bought old scrap iron, either cast or wrought for the state. Cast iron paid one to one and one-half cents while wrought iron brought four cents.[57]

The Cape Fear and Deep River Navigation Company was organized in 1849 to improve the river to get steamships farther into the interior of the state. It went from the lower Cape Fear River to Moore County (Deep River) at Hancock's Mill, a total of ninety-eight miles. It handled twenty-three locks along the way and was capable of passing vessels one hundred by twenty feet. The company raised funds for operations by charging a toll. It also owned and rented ships. The business used locks and dams to get ships over the rapids and shallow obstacles. This system was called the Slack Water System. In 1860, steamboats went up the Deep River as far as Egypt. Originally, the company was to carry produce from the area to the sea. The state bought the company in 1859 when creditors forced a sale. It took boats four days to go from Wilmington to Fayetteville, a distance of one hundred miles by water. The town of Buckhorn contained rapids, as did Smileys, Pullen, Gulf, and Endor where the ironworks were in operation. The coal mines were located in Egypt, Cumnock, and Farmersville. Boats carried coal, in addition to tar, rosin, timber, lumber, and turpentine. Lockkeepers were probably exempt from military service.

Completed in 1860, the Fayetteville and Western Railroad came to within nine miles of Egypt. Coal was hauled by mule for this distance to the depot.[58] The quality of coal from the Egypt Mine was considered inferior to that from Pennsylvania, but was used anyway by steamships and blockade-runners as a last resort. Egypt's coal produced more smoke, making it easier for the U.S. Navy to spot and chase the South's ships. The LaGrange Coal Mine employed eight miners, carpenters, boatmen, and an engineer. A good portion of the coal went to the Southern hospitals.

The Dismal Swamp

The Dismal Swamp Land Company, started in the late 1770s, owned its slaves but used hired slaves, as well as free black men, to work the wood and keep it open.[59] Confines of the Dismal Swamp included parts of Virginia, Gates, Pasquotank, Camden, and Currituck counties. Lake Drummond lies on the Virginia side near the center of the swamp. It is a lake of eighteen to twenty miles in circumference.[60] The swamp encompassed about 210,000 acres during the war, but was double the size in past centuries.[61] The tinted brown water in the swamp contained tannic acid from the cypress, gum, and juniper trees, thereby prohibiting bacteria growth, making it perfect for sailors to carry on board as drinking water. The canal through the swamp connected Norfolk harbor with Pasquotank River. The D. S. Land Company's canal connected the lake with the Nansemond River near Suffolk, Virginia.[62]

The swamp was a haven for runaways, deserters, and outlaws. Only those who lived and worked nearby knew how to find their way in its confines.[63] Confederate soldiers fleeing after the fall of Elizabeth City in February 1862 burned the CSS *Appomattox* because it was too large to go through the canal, the width of the canal being seven to ten feet. Other canals gave competition to the Dismal Swamp Canal because they were wider. During wartimes, "the Dismal Swamp Land Company suspended its activity in the swamp. Most of the mules went to the Confederacy, and a lot that were left got lost in the war," said researcher Bland Simpson. After this, the activity around the Dismal Swamp Canal was mostly guerilla warfare, bridge burning, and ambushing people. After the war, the company was in ruins. County agent Willis Riddick wrote of the losses in May 1865 of more than ten thousand dollars, including damage or destruction to bridges, skiffs, buildings, timber, etc.[64]

The Albemarle and Chesapeake Canal opened in 1859. Its locks could float larger ships than the Dismal Canal. It linked New Bern and Washington to the Norfolk area.[65] The Roanoke River Canal was built prewar to bypass the rapids near Weldon. Both the Blue and the Gray used the canal during the war to move supplies between Norfolk and the eastern piedmont.

Not long after secession, the Confederate Navy Yard located in Norfolk, Virginia, transferred to Charlotte where iron projectiles, naval ordinance and equipment, shafts, etc., were produced. The plant employed hundreds of workers. Numerous factories complained to the government about the lack of workers and mechanics during wartime. In May 1864, it was reported in Charlotte that "a number of our most important tools [steam hammer] are idle a large portion of the time for want of mechanics to work them . . ."[66] Most workers had been conscripted.

Four cities in the Southern states—Asheville, Tallahassee, Richmond, and Fayetteville—built the principle output of guns. Rifles were made by private businesses in Asheville until the Confederacy took over the business in the fall of 1862.* In the latter part of 1861, Colonel R. A. Pulliam, Mr. Ephriam Clayton, and Dr. George Whitson of Asheville turned out about three hundred rifles that year.[67] The armory was only operational for twenty-six months; they had made approximately nine hundred rifles during that span. Two hundred men were employed while in operation.[68] Ben Sloan, commander of the armory in Asheville, wanted to make sure that his employees and their families had enough to eat. He made contracts with local farmers to prepay their crop. When that did not bring in sufficient produce, he contracted with out-of-state farmers. Transporting these goods to Asheville became a big stumbling block. After the factory closed, the machinery was dismantled and hauled away. The buildings were then converted into a stockade to hold Federal prisoners. Union cavalrymen burned the stockade on their raid near the end of the conflict.[69]

Three major things were needed for the gun factory: iron for the barrels, hardwood for the stocks, and copper for the mountings. Three things caused production to slow down: unskilled workmen, a poorly motivated workforce, and the lack of transportation necessary to move needed commodities.[70] The armory foreman earned $5.15 per day while unskilled workers made $1 per day. They worked an eleven-to twelve-hour shift. On Saturday, they could make time and a half, whereas on Sunday, employees would double their salary. A man with a wagon and a four-horse team received eight dollars a day to haul supplies. The company hired slaves to overcome staff shortages. The white workers resented their presence.[71]

The Arsenal in Fayetteville was a small operation until the machinery was moved from the Arsenal at Harpers Ferry, West Virginia, after the skirmish with John Brown's failed takeover. The Arsenal made four hundred guns per month, including repairs. Some pistols were produced along with sabre bayonets. When U.S. General Sherman crossed the state lines from South Carolina, the machinery was dismantled and moved by train to Chatham County. It was later captured and moved to Raleigh.[72].

Approximately fifty to eighty women worked at the Arsenal, rolling and filling cartridges. On July 15, 1861, it reported that fifty to sixty white women and girls worked there and that "various operations were going on, such as molding balls, rifling muskets, etc."[73] "Those women who were used in office work received special treatment in lieu of adequate money compensation. Pay was given in the form of black apalco [sic] [alpaca] cloth," which was normally used in the making of large gunpowder bags. The women used this fabric to make dresses due to the shortage of cloth. In eight months' time, in 1864, the women had made nine hundred thousand cartridges.[74] Ms. Alice Campbell, Ms. Stedman, Ms. Taylor, and Ms. M. E. Ellison worked as clerks or copyists.[75] Victorian society frowned upon women working outside of their sphere. This must have weighed heavily upon Ms. Ellison for she wrote a letter explaining why she chose to do so.**

The Arsenal employed an enormous amount of workers who lived nearby and depended on the factory to sustain them. At times, the employees were paid in victuals

---

*   In a letter from Colonel W. R. Young, with the 108th Militia, to Governor Vance on November 13, 1862, are mentioned children workers, ages twelve to seventeen, at the Confederate Armory.

**   Ms. Ellison's letter appears in the appendix.

instead of money. Colonel Frederick Childs, to supplement the operatives with food, started a farm near Fayetteville, as well as fisheries up the Black River down to Wilmington—not merely for food, but for the oil. Laborers for these enterprises were old men and Negroes.[76] On September 17, 1862, Melinda Ray inscribed in her diary that Major John C. Booth, commander of the arsenal, had died. She described the funeral through town. Men wore crepe armbands, and the pallbearers had crepe streamers from their hats. Employees both black and white were in the funeral procession.

Immigrants Charles and Fenner Kuester erected a gun shop in Raleigh where they converted the old flintlock muskets into percussion rifles. The company also made percussion caps and "small implements of war."[77] Paper for cartridge rolling and gunpowder was taken to the Deaf, Dumb, and Blind School in Raleigh whereby the students made and packaged the cartridges.

Around the state, smaller gun factories developed partially due to need, but partially due to the worker being declared exempt from military service. The hated Conscript Act of 1862 encouraged skilled gunsmiths to increase production by enlarging their business or to start a new business. Constructing guns at home was preferable to marching. A man may have only made a few rifles before the war, which was not considered a business. In order to get an exemption, he would have to enlarge the business or report for duty. Most small companies had a contract to turn out a certain number of rifles per month to stay exempt, making it desirable for all concerned.

The piedmont area of the state seemed to have a concentration of these artisans. Opened on October 21, 1861, the Mendenhall & Jones Company made about fifty guns a month with a force of seventy-five craftsmen. In March 1862, they took a contract to produce twenty-five hundred at twenty dollars each. Another contract was awarded seven months later to turn out eighty-five rifles per month, "or else forfeit the sum of $5 on each gun lacking to fill out that number. The state is to pay us $30 instead of the $20 . . . ," said Mendenhall.[78] The Henry C. Lamb & Company of Jamestown made less than three hundred rifles a year. Gunsmiths H. C. Lamb & Company, Mendenhall, Jones & Gardner, and the Clapp, Gates & Company constructed four thousand firearms during the conflict.[79]

The Gilliam & Miller Company operated in High Point. Clapp, Gates & Company in 1863 made guns at the Alamance Armory, formerly called the Cedar Hill Foundry, in Guilford County.[80] Earle Cooley, of the firm of Arnold-Cooley Gunsmiths, operated in Wadesboro during wartime. Their company had a contract with the Confederate government for the manufacturing of firearms, swords, etc. Authorities wanted to make sure certain employees met the qualifications for exemption, so Mr. Cooley had to make an oath of truth that the laborers in question, Peter Swink and Hiram B. Braswell, did indeed work for him.*[81] At the Confederate Arsenal in Asheville, Colonel R. W. Pulliam had to write out a list of the specific duty and age of each employee for the conscript board. In an 1862 roster of his employees, two are listed as age fourteen, and one is twelve years old.[82]

Others factories were not free from suspicion. Conscript officers contacted businessmen to enforce the rules for hiring men as shown in the next letter:**

Office Iron District, N. Carolina
Salisbury April 2, 1864

Messrs Clapp, Gates, & Company
Newton, NC
Gent:
    Orders have been issued from the bureau in Richmond that all contracts should be detailed. I have therefore to request that you at once inform me of

---

*   "Sworn to subscribed before me a Justice of the Peace of said county this 9th day of July, 1862 John Robinson, J.P."

**   Read more on this in chapter 10.

the status of each member of your firm, embracing age; rest; occupation, how exempted heretofore, whether by reason of having furnished a substitute or otherwise, and any other particulars.

Very Respectfully,

Your obedient Servant,

A.G. Brenizer, Capt. Act[83]

Other gunsmiths included J. W. Howlett, who made rifles in Greensboro, and the Garrett family, T. and F. and E. T. Garrett. The J. and F. Garrett & Company, also of Greensboro, made sewing machines, switching in the latter part of 1863 to carbines.[84] Jere H. Tarpley of Greensboro turned out muskets. Julius Holtzscheiter Down East made rifles.[85] In Richmond County, a master gunsmith, John Buchanan, had just retired from his business before the war. Murdock Morrison, a friend, apprenticed with him and continued to turn out the famous Buchanan rifle. Morrison enlarged the business. When rumors of the approach of Sherman's army reached his ears, he dismantled the equipment and threw all in the Richmond Mill Pond. Murdock hid on an island in the small lake. His guns and machinery were never found nor was Morrison; however, the enemy burned his shop and home.[86] The Confederacy could not produce rifles fast enough; hence, boxes upon boxes of the Enfield rifle was shipped from England via blockade-runners.

To further supplement the supply of arms, Adjutant General James Martin requested the militia to be on the lookout for guns to purchase or for those owning guns that belong to the state. Martin wanted the militia to report if there were any materials used in the manufacturing of gunpowder in the county, especially saltpeter.[87] Early in the second year of the war, Martin called for the sheriffs in each county "to collect all public arms within their respective commands." The sheriff was to report the number collected back to him.[88] The Confederacy needed all the weapons they could scrounge up. When one woman refused to comply, the sheriff had to show her the letter from the captain of the militia before she would give up her weapon. It read:

> **To the People of North Carolina:** At the request of President Davis I have undertaken to collect all arms from the citizens of our state. I have been entrusted with authority to borrow, purchase, or if necessary to impress them. None but a craven or disloyal citizen will refuse to comply.
>
> W.S. Ashe, April 4, 1862[89]

Civilians were given thirteen to twenty dollars each for a good rifle or musket and thirteen to thirty-eight dollars for double-barrel shotguns. Many chose to keep their guns.

To be used, guns needed percussion caps, gunpowder, and lead balls. The lead mined in Wake County was not the quality to make ammunition, but its graphite found use in artillery and mechanical and naval objects.[90] Mosby Hall, a private residence in Littleton, contained a lead roof. The wealthy owners donated the lead to the state to be made into bullets.[91] Percussion caps were manufactured in Raleigh and Tarboro while thousands were brought in through the blockade.

North Carolina was the fifth-largest producer of gunpowder in the Confederacy.[92] The firm of Waterhouse & Bowes produced gunpowder and percussion caps in Raleigh. The first year, two thousand pounds of powder was made. In the third year, the mill "provided . . . more than half a million dollars worth of powder" to the Confederacy.[93] On Crabtree Creek in Raleigh, a powder mill was established. Another originated in Charlotte at the navy yard. Both plants had explosions more than once, injuring and killing several employees. "We regret to learn that the powder mill located fourteen miles from Charlotte was blown up Saturday . . . and killed five men . . . and all that was in it," reported the *Weekly News*.[94] A second Charlotte explosion was noted in the *Augusta Daily Constitutionalist* a year later in which a white man and two mulattoes died. Several more suffered wounds. Laborers worked shoeless due to fact that boots contained nails, which could cause a spark, resulting in an explosion. Much gunpowder was purchased abroad and shipped by blockade-runners.

REBEL GUNPOWDER.

[*From the Selma (Ala.) Sentinel of Oct.* 1, 1863.]

" The Ladies of Selma are respectfully requested to preserve all their chamber ley collected about their premises, for the purpose of making ' Nitre.' Wagons, with barrels, will be sent around for it by the subscriber.

[Signed,]   JOHN HARROLSON,
Agent of Nitre and Mining Bureau.

John Harrolson ! John Harrolson !
    You are a funny creature ;
You've given to this cruel war
    A new and curious feature.
You'd have us think while ev'ry man
    Is bound to be a fighter,
The women, (bless the pretty dears,)
    Should be put to making nitre.

John Harrolson ! John Harrolson !
    How could you get the notion
To send your barrels 'round the town
    To gather up the lotion.
We think the girls do work enough
    In making love and kissing.
But you'll now put the pretty dears
    To patriotic pissing !

John Harrolson ! John Harrolson !
    Could you not invent a meter,
Or some less immodest mode
    Of making our salt-petre?
The thing, it is so queer, you know—
    Gunpowder, like the crankey—
That when a lady lifts her shift
    She shoots a bloody Yankee.

John Harrolson ! John Harrolson !
    Whate're was your intention,
You've made another contraband
    Of things we hate to mention.
What good will all our fighting do,
    If Yanks search Venus' mountains,
And confiscate and carry off
    These Southern nitre fountains !

Gunpowder contains three-fourths saltpeter or nitre. Nitre was extracted from bat excrement. Common livestock's urine, which was heavily saturated with ammonia and nitre, became the second choice of use to make the powder. Legend has it that human urine was collected during the war. A wagon came around and collected the stale urine whence it was taken to a central location.[*] The urine was collected in vats, washed with water, then treated with carbonate of potash. Potash created nitric acid by introducing oxygen into the solution. The water was boiled down, like salt brine. This left crystals of potassium nitrate—saltpeter. Add a little charcoal with sulfur, and the result is gunpowder.[95] To make charcoal, you had to burn a great deal of wood. Nitre for gunpowder was often dug from old smokehouses and barns.

Kenansville was known for producing swords for the Confederacy. In 1861, Louis Froelich opened a sword factory in Wilmington, moving it to Kenansville after the yellow fever struck in 1862. It was destroyed July 4, 1863, by Colonel George W. Lewis of the Federal Army in a raid. Froelich rebuilt the company, which continued to operate until March of 1864. The company turned out over 800 gross military buttons, 300 sabre belts, 300 knapsacks, 18 sets of surgical instruments, 3,700 lance spears, 2,700 officers' sabres, 6,500 sabre bayonets, 11,700 cavalry sabres, 600 navy cutlasses, 800 artillery sabres, and 1,700 sets of infantry accoutrements.[96]

Raleigh was engaged in hammering out swords also. "A local Negro blacksmith in Dr. Fabius Haywood's employ, manufactured the prototype for a ten-foot lance . . ." These were called pikes, but they saw very little use. Another gunsmith in Raleigh made percussion caps, and a factory in town produced bayonets. A paper mill North of Raleigh turned out the paper necessary for the cartridges.[97]

On Queen Street in Kinston, a bakery produced hardtack, tough unleavened crackers. At first, Confederate soldiers were detailed to work in the bakery. "They were often seen standing in a huge trough, barefooted and with their trousers rolled to their knees," wrote author Powell. "They used common garden hoes to work up the dough."

Prewar Wadesborough ran a large tanning business. The Washington family of Kinston owned a large tannery and produced soldiers' shoes during the war.[98] Kinston also produced iron and made shovels, plows, and carriages.[99] Tarboro produced waterproof cloth, oilcloth, Confederate caps, soap, cottonseed oil, and candles for the government.[100]

Around 80 percent of the Southern cotton supply was sent to Great Britain in the ten years before the war.[101] In 1860, England bought almost two million bales of cotton from the South. King Cotton provided four to five million jobs in Great Britain.[102] When the South seceded, they at first withheld cotton from England. At the time, England had a stockpile of bales. After two years, the British felt the pinch and began laying off its workers, shutting down the smaller mills. Called the "cotton famine" in England, 40 percent of their workers lost their jobs.[103]

Antebellum North Carolina had thirty-nine cotton mills, almost forty-two thousand spindles, and eight hundred looms, which employed 1,764 wage earners. These mills consumed 11,100 bales of cotton per year.[104] Of the seven woolen mills in the state, Rock Island in Cumberland County and the one in Salem were the largest. E. M. Holt's Alamance County Mill in 1830 was the first cotton mill to start with raw cotton, going all the way through the process to finished cloth.[**][105] Holt's cotton mill was the first to produce plaid and colored cottons South of the Potomac River.[106] Cotton sold at three cents a pound in the state and could be sold for one dollar a pound outside its boundaries.[107] Another reference listed a pound of cotton at twelve cents in 1860, then rising to one $1.42 near the end of the war.[108] The onset of war "stimulated a major conversion of the textile industry from yarn spinning to the manufacture of material for the war effort . . ."[109] Author Woods stated, "A substantial portion of the state purchased cotton was consigned to Saxapahawee Factory, in Alamance County, run by John Newlan & Sons."

---

[*]   This supposedly took place in Alabama and a poem was written about the job.
[**]   The military artist Mort Kunstler painted a picture of the Alamance Mill.

After the cotton was made into yarn and cloth, the cloth was "delivered to the Quarter Master for the use of the army, and the yarn was exchanged in Virginia for leather . . ."[110] On Cane Creek, Alamance County, the Clover Orchard Manufacturing Company operated.[111] In 1864, a cotton-batting factory opened up in Charlotte.[112]

Holt's Alamance Cotton Mill
N.C. Division of Archives & History, Photographic Archives.

Young women, girls, and boys dominated the workforce of the nineteenth-century textile mills, particularly after 1860, when the introduction of the new continuous spinning technology known as ring frames replaced an intermittent process using a device called spinning mule. Ring spinning was easier to operate. Adult white males were usually the supervisors or machinists and were exempt from military service.[113] In viewing company ledgers, the ages of the women were not listed, only the hours they worked with a twelve-hour day being the usual. Many names recorded gave only a first initial, then the last name. Perhaps these could have been children. Several members with the same last name worked these factories. In Forsyth County, people lived in company houses while the women and older girls worked in the mills. Richard Gwyn's cotton mill in Elkin employed sixty females, and Mr. Curtis in Franklinville employed several females.[114] "A group of women in Salisbury—some of whom were working at pitifully small wages in government clothing shops, were unable to procure food for themselves & their children at prices they could pay."*[115] Cumberland County employed the greatest amount of females in the cotton mills of all the counties.[116]

Cedar Falls Manufacturing Company, located on the Deep River in Randolph County, became the leading supplier of cloth for shirts and underwear for soldiers.[117] A total of 133 male workers there were exempt, primarily due to the efforts of Congressman Jonathan Worth, a former Quaker.[118] Below is an account of the number of employees for the war years:

CEDAR FALLS MANUFACTURING, Cedar Falls, North Carolina

	FEMALES	MALES
April 1861	57	22
April 1862	59	27
April 1863	57	28
April 1864	60	25
April 1865	<60	<20

---

*   I have not found any specific buildings or shops listed as "government clothing shops" because most women worked out of their homes.

The workers stopped temporarily on April 27, 1864, to "take down some horse thieves." Workmen caught twelve thieves and twenty horses. During the last six months of the war, the company stepped up production, working more than a twelve-hour day. On January 10, 1865, a flood destroyed some buildings and bridges at the factory.[119] Cedar Falls had a contract with the state to make fifty thousand shirts and drawers for the military. According to author Richard Goff, "The official uniform of the regular army was to consist of a semi-annual issue of one blue flannel shirt, four pair of grey flannel [wool] trousers, three pair of red flannel undershirts, four pair of cotton drawers, three pair of wool stockings, two pair of boots, one blanket, one leather stock, and one cap." Total cost was $26.95.[120] Multiply this with the 125,000 soldiers from North Carolina who fought, and one can see why women at home were needed to help supply their kin in the army.

Local raw cotton was bartered for use by the Rocky Mount Mill in Nash County. The standard of exchange prewar consisted of one yard of a three-yard sheeting for a pound of raw cotton, which was one-third of a pound made into cloth, for one pound in the raw state. This mill was the oldest in the state.[121] Families bartered with the mills for yarn or thread. Cornelia Henry in Asheville said she "exchanged my coarse wool for thread, got 4 1/3 bunches for 13 lbs. wool."[122]

James Smith Battle, another large slave owner, owned around twenty thousand acres. His son, William S. Battle, became owner of the Rocky Mount Mill at James's death. The mill could boast of two thousand spindles doing both spinning and weaving. Other buildings owned by Battle included a sawmill, gristmill, cotton gin, and two warehouses. Federal cavalrymen burned the entire village on July 20, 1863.[123]

Fries Woolen Mill at Salem
N.C. Division of Archives & History, Photographic Archives.

The Salem Manufacturing Company was owned by Francis Fries and his brother, Henry, who had a mechanical carding machine for wool.[124] The Salem "jeans" worn by slaves prewar called Negro clothing was a durable cotton/wool blend. His mill ran twenty-four hours a day. After his father's death, John W. Fries, age seventeen, took over running the mill with his uncle. "Supplies were frequently sent from Salem to the men in camp by wagons from the mills . . . during the war."[125] As the demand for products escalated, the Fries brothers used up their supply; and they tried to get more wool from Texas, Memphis, and Charleston. At the time, railroad authorities said they could only transport goods for the military. Henry Fries's partner wrote Governor Henry Clark on November 18, 1861, that if he did not interfere with these rules regarding the transport of raw materials and supplies by the railroad, the people and soldiers from North Carolina would soon suffer the consequences.[126] "The Fries mill smuggled wool through the Union lines to make Confederate uniforms. When agents seized the wool because the import duty had not been paid, the mill was unable to replace it." Therefore, they couldn't fill their contract.[127] Governor Vance intervened.

The shortage of raw wool was an ongoing headache that grew worse. Mr. D. Curtis of the Franklinville mill wrote his friend Lieutenant Gray: "We are very busy in our factories in these days and the govt. wants our goods for the soldiers . . . cotton goods are in great demand now [.] we cannot fill one half the orders . . . that come to us for goods."[128] Cotton mills found in Lincoln County were the Buena Vista Manufacturing Company and the Lincolnton Cotton Factory. The Rockingham mill was known as the Richmond Manufacturing Company. The Concord Steam Cotton Factory produced during the war twenty-six thousand yards of cotton goods and nine thousand pounds of cotton yarn. Most of the other mills were powered by water. In Iredell County, the Eagle Cotton Mill was burned in April 1865 by U.S. General Stoneman's raiders as was Patterson's Cotton Factory in Caldwell County and Buena Vista. The Mountain Island Mill, in Gaston County, formerly a cotton mill, reverted to a woolen mill in the war years. It employed mostly slaves instead of the usual women and children as before.[129] Two other mills operated in Gaston County—the Woodlawn Cotton Mill, known as the Old Pinhook Mill, and Stowe's Mill.[130] The Yadkin Manufacturing Company in 1861 turned out kersey, jeans (fabric), and sheeting. The Alspaugh Cotton Mill in Alexander County, established prewar, sold yarn to the locals, which "they carded, spun and wove into cloth . . . the unit for selling yarn was bunches which usually sold for $1.00 per bunch."* Some workers received yarn instead of a salary for work done. Merchants traded molasses, coffee (if available), oil, lumber, and the use of their wagons for hauling products. Cotton bunches sold by merchants cost $1.10, giving them a ten-cent profit. The Alspaugh Mill probably closed in 1861–1862.[131] Rhett's Mill in Flat Rock produced wool for uniforms.

The Fayetteville area could boast of several cotton mills in operation during the war, but all were burned when General W. T. Sherman occupied the city. The Rockfish Manufacturing Company "for its time" was the largest mill South of Petersburg, Virginia. It employed 150 people. The Phoenix Manufacturing Company, the Cross Creek Cotton Mill, the Union Cotton Mill, the Little River Factory, and the Beaver Creek Company set up operations around Fayetteville. Duncan Murchison owned both the Little River Factory ten miles from Fayetteville and one in Manchester.[132] Later on in the war, a cotton card/comb factory was established.

"The governor declared in November, 1861, 'that our state is in absolute want of cotton goods, especially domestic clothes for the use of our volunteers.' An appeal was sent out by Governor Henry Clark addressed to 'The Proprietors of Cotton Factories in N.C.,' asking them to break contracts with private buyers and to sell to the government at prices equally remunerative."[133] John Devereux Jr., chief quartermaster for North Carolina, had agents to roam the state and other Southern states for goods. He had them to make contracts with factories and private individuals to produce articles for the military. James G. Martin, adjutant general, "bought almost the entire output of the state's forty-seven cotton and woolen mills."[134] The state agreed to compensate the mill owners a 75 percent profit. Martin, like Devereux, sent agents to other states to buy the raw materials.[135] Because of this act, that left the civilians in a bind for cloth. Women of all ages and servants on the plantation retrieved their looms and spinning wheels from storage and began the production of fabric for home use. However, all females did not know how to go about the

---

*   Five pounds of factory cloth equals one bunch, which can be made into fifteen yards. A hank was
        840 yards of cotton thread, which weighed one pound. One pound of yarn cost seventy-five cents
        to one dollar and would make four pairs of socks. [136A]

home manufacture of cloth, so they were forced to buy high-priced fabric when available. Even if they did know how to weave, the women may not have had access to wool or cotton yarn, which was always in short supply. Perhaps they had not planted any cotton or raised sheep that year. This made the civilians depend on the output from the mills, which created further shortages.

The majority of soldiers' uniforms were of wool; however, research has indicated that some may have been made of cotton. A Northern newspaper reported in December of 1861:

> The clothing of the "secesh" taken in the recent battle at Drainsville [Virginia] proves that the enemy are, indeed, intense sufferers for want of Quartermaster's stores. Thus, three—fourths of their coats are of cotton cloth—not woollen—lined in some instances with a heavier cotton cloth, or padded with cotton. The coats of the South Carolina troops engaged were colored by being dyed with tobacco juice.[136]

Other businessmen around the state joined in manufacturing cloth, for it was a lucrative enterprise. The Leaksville Cotton Factory, owned by former governor John M. Morehead, furnished blankets and tents for the troops. This mill—first a cotton mill, then converted to a woolen mill in 1860—employed twenty-five men and eighty women.[137] Citizens took their raw cotton to trade for thread at the Patterson mill on the Yadkin River.[138] In Flat Rock, Rhett's Mill produced cloth for military coats. The woolen mill located near Camp Fisher in High Point produced cloth for uniforms.[139] One man described the situation of women requesting cloth and yarn in a letter written midwar:

> They are generally rushed there for cotton and cloth. Such a mess as they have there daily . . . such pulling and hauling, growling, grumbling, and even cursing you hardly ever herd . . . its impossible to supply half that for yarn and cloth and it's a scuffle who shall have it . . . the company are abused at round rates, and threatened with mobs and burning and etc. because they cannot after running night and day supply all that come for yarn and cloth.[140]

Merchant David Worth owned a dry goods store and mill in Creston. His wife, Elizabeth, trained slaves to fashion cloth into clothing for men and boys, then sold them in his store in the Three Top Creek area.[141]

Much of the cloth manufactured for uniforms was sold to official agents in Raleigh. The cloth was cut by expert tailors and then given to women to be made into garments. Some of the material was delivered to various towns in the state and distributed. Either sewn by individuals or aid societies, the uniforms were picked up when finished and returned to a warehouse. In this way, a very large number of poorer women were able to support their families.[*][142] The state agent would either give the woman the fabric to make uniforms or money to purchase fabric. She could choose to make her own fabric or buy it from others. In addition, tailors contracted with the state to make uniforms. "On a larger scale contracts were let to men and materials requisitioned from the mills for garments to be made by poor or destitute women."[**][143]

---

*   A letter to Governor Vance from a woman with a government contract said she got fifty cents for each pair of lined pants and seventy-five cents for a coat. A list of prices for articles the militia was to purchase for state use included woolen socks, forty to sixty cents each pair; cotton socks, thirty to fifty cents a pair; shoes, five dollars a pair; country jeans (homespun cloth), two to four dollars a yard; blankets, three to six dollars each; and quilts, two to five dollars each.[144]

**   In Charlotte, Young, Wriston & Orr contracted with the government to make uniforms, as well as Hughes & Best in Salem and Howard & Beard in Salisbury.[145]

"By law of September 20, 1861, the legislature agreed to receive commutation money from the Confederate government and to assume the obligation of clothing and shoeing her own troops. The state agreed also to sell all her surplus supplies to the Confederacy if all Confederate agents would be withdrawn from the state and leave the field to North Carolina."[146] Richmond assumed responsibility for clothing all Confederate forces in October 1862. The authorities in Richmond would repay North Carolina fifty dollars a year per soldier for their part in supplying the military.[147] The total amount was never fully repaid, which incensed Governor Vance and the State Treasurer, Jonathan Worth.

To increase the supply of uniforms, this ad appeared in the January 9, 1862, issue of the *Charlotte Daily Bulletin*, from the quartermaster's office:

> . . . any person or persons who may be desirous of taking contracts for making military clothes for the army of North Carolina can obtain terms, etc on application to this office. Goods will be issued, to any responsible parties in quantities sufficient to clothe single companies which can be made up in their own neighborhoods, and the money will be paid to the parties receiving the goods, at the return of the manufactured articles. Parties may furnish the cloth, which will be paid for by the state.
> J. Devereux, AQM

In another newspaper, Captain A. Myers, AQM, asked for jeans and linsey fabric. He claimed to be paying with cash.[148] Officers couldn't wait on the state to furnish supplies. The *Raleigh Standard* featured this ad:

> **TO EDITOR of the STANDARD:**
> Head Quarters 26th Regiment, Kinston, March 17, 1862
> Will you please announce to the good people of the State, that my regiment is here in a most destitute condition. Any persons that will send a coarse cotton shirt, drawers, or socks will be doing us a great kindness, as it will be weeks before the State can supply us.[149]

The *Standard* asked other papers to copy Vance's request for help from the people. The *Fayetteville Observer* also appealed for aid for the troops and copied this letter:

> In F there was collected a total of sixty-four shirts, ninety-eight pairs of socks, forty yards of carpeting, three pairs of pants, one coat, some tobacco, and $98.70 in cash for one company alone.

Kemp Plummer Battle gave to Sheriff High of Wake County $114, which was applied to the purchase of clothing for Vance's regiment and for the Wake County destitute at Kinston.[150] Stationed in a camp near Winchester, Virginia, Colonel Walkup wrote the governor of the shortages of blankets, shoes, medicine, clothing, and cooking utensils. He stated that one-half of his regiment was absent from duty because of lack of the above in addition to despair and disease:

> I mention these things to show that our destitution is no fault of the Regiment. It was—the fault of the misfortune of the C.S. government in not furnishing us with sufficient means of transportation [for supplies from home]. But what I do insist on now is that North Carolina—exert herself—to supply these just wants—& save them from the extreme sufferings [of the]—now rapidly approaching—winter. What we most pressingly need now is our full supply of BLANKETS, of SHOES & of PANTS & SOCKS.[151]

In 1864, the hard-pressed Confederate government made a determined effort to wrest control of the factories from the state. On September 19 of that year, Governor Vance wrote to the Secretary of War, Seddon, charging that Quartermaster General A. R. Lawson was "trying to force the mill owners to break their contracts with North Carolina by threatening to withdraw labor details." Vance named these men "necessary state employees" under the Supplementary Conscription Act of May 1863. "The loophole that he exploited was supposed to have been enacted to protect state administration, legislators, and law-enforcement officials from the draft." The governor stretched this to include industrial workers. The only way the Confederate Congress could get these recruits was to change the law.[152]

"By the summer and early fall of 1861, the North Carolina Quartermaster Office was poised to purchase cheaper and more durable wool bunting state flags, probably because of the high cost and low durability of silk, as well as the uncertainty of a reliable future supply. In addition, the state apparently had a least some bunting already on hand for military use. On September 9, 1861, the quartermaster general noted that 'Bunting is probably the only material accessible out of which flags can be made for this when it shall be determined to furnish them.' A few days later, on September 20, a letter went to Lieutenant Colonel Samuel J. Person, acting quartermaster general, stating that a supply of bunting was being sent for flag use."[153]

Two women took a government contract to make wool bunting regimental flags for the quartermaster, Mrs. Henry W. Miller and Frances Johnson Devereux Miller. "Although most of the flags they produced are clearly identified on invoices as regimental flags, the 'Millers' also fabricated 'smaller flags,' guidons, hundreds of knapsacks and canteen straps, and one large state flag for Camp Mangum," according to Tom Belton, curator at the Museum of History, Raleigh.

The state continued to seek contacts for other articles of clothing such as hats, tinware, and leather goods. Messrs. Kerner and Gentry had a government contract to make one thousand pair of shoes for the troops.[154] H. W. Ayer, a state agent, made a list of the manufacturing companies for the government listing products, cost, sale price, amounts, employees, etc. Ayer said there were several small shoemaking businesses. He noted that J. Shelly & Son of Thomasville made shoes, and they employed twenty-five workers of which one was a female. One person could make one and one-half pairs a day. Cedar Falls and Franklinville cotton factories in Randolph County employed 106 workers with eighty-two females. Of the articles made for the war, sheeting and cotton yarn topped the list; but they also made osnaburg fabric (for drawers), salt sacks, grain sacks, and post office twine. Ayer stated that he thought this company's charges were above the price permitted by the government.[155]

A newspaper reported, "The 'Goldsboro Rifles' having procured a complete set of Dies of the State Arms, are prepared to furnish Buttons for all the North Carolina Military Companies, at 33 per cent less than they can be purchased elsewhere, all applications must be made to the Captain."[156] "As with uniforms and other military goods, civilians made both bunting state flags and flagstaffs under North Carolina quartermaster contracts for state purchase. The only person identified in North Carolina who produced flagstaffs was N.S. Harp of Raleigh. He furnished staff poles in two sizes, at one dollar and three dollars respectively. The smaller flagstaffs were likely intended for flank markers or cavalry guidons, and the larger ones for regimental state flags. Before the war, Harp had manufactured spokes, rims, and shafts for buggies and wagons; after the war, he operated the Raleigh Coach Works. He probably found it easy to move from turning spokes and shafts to manufacturing flagstaffs."[157]

Drums and fifes were manufactured in Asheville, percussion caps in Raleigh, and crackers in a Kinston bakery.[158] A stocking factory in Wilmington employed one hundred women. "The ladies would carry machine knitted upper and lower parts of a stocking home with them to sew together, returning the finished product to the mill."[159] North Carolina produced thousands of yards of material for clothing, and just as much merchandise arrived through the blockade at Wilmington. In Limerick, Ireland, the Peter Tait & Company made uniforms for the South. The uniforms were shipped aboard the blockade-runner *Evelyn* to Wilmington.[160] For a list of goods brought in by blockade-runners, see the appendix.

Besides what the state made for its own troops, Governor Vance sent to General Longstreet the winter of 1863 fourteen thousand uniforms. At the end of the war, the state had a surplus of ninety-two thousand uniforms, blankets, and leather.[161] From the first of October 1864 to December 31, the state of North Carolina delivered to the central government at Richmond the following articles of which $1,203,144.30 was reimbursed to the state:

Jackets	32,482	pants	11,556
Shirts	39,060	drawers	19,212
Blankets	17,946	hats	1346
Shoes	13,184	prs. socks	22,169
Lbs. leather	2102	haversacks	2500 [162]

Persons raising their own sheep for the wool told of dogs running loose and killing their sheep. The wool was too precious to let this happen. On July 31, 1864, an Asheville resident killed a neighbor's dog because the dog was killing his sheep.[163]

MEDICAL DEPARTMENT

The state had two so-called hospitals before the war, but not for ordinary people. A small marine hospital for seamen was found in Wilmington and Portsmouth. The Moravians had established a sick house in Salem in the eighteenth century for their members. One reference found a physician in Wilmington treating Negroes at the Negro Hospital in 1859. While not called a hospital, the state mental institute known as Dix Hill opened in 1858 in Raleigh to house epileptic people, drug addicts, mental patients, and alcoholics. The state at once began gathering hospital equipage and assigning medical officers.

Dr. Charles E. Johnson opened the first military hospital in Raleigh in May 1861 known as the Fair Grounds Hospital.[164] Large buildings were revamped for hospital use to hold from two hundred to four hundred patients. The Guion Hotel in the capital city converted to a hospital. Pettigrew Hospital in Raleigh, built in 1864, was the only new building constructed in Raleigh as a hospital.[165] It would hold up to 588 beds. Hospital no. 4 in Wilmington, previously known as the Seaman's Hospital, opened early.[166] It was considered the largest and best equipped in the state. The Convalescent Hospital in Washington admitted its patients in 1863.[167]

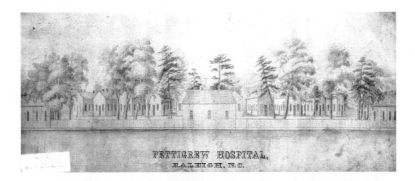

PETTIGREW HOSPITAL,
RALEIGH. N.C.

Pettigrew Hospital
N.C. Division of Archives & History, Photographic Archives.

Women began making and storing hospital supplies such as bandages and clothing before hospitals were established for the soldiers. The last chapter discussed all their efforts. Chapter 7 will go into detail concerning nurses. Newspapers encouraged those left at home to economize so that troops in the field could be supplied.

At the beginning of the war, convalescing soldiers became the nurses if they were able to stand the rigors of medical work. Apparently, they were not attune to sanitary conditions because people visiting the areas commented on the filthy conditions present in these buildings. Everyone knew a woman's touch would clean up the place, and their tender care would enhance the surroundings. The next letter made such a suggestion. It is from N. H. Whitaker, Enfield, to Governor John Ellis and was written July 1, 1861:

> No doubt you will be surprised at receiving a missive from such a source, but I hope the MOTIVE will excuse the liberty which I take in addressing a letter to Gov. Ellis.
>
> Doctors Bellamy and Hunter reached home last night after a visit of several days at York Town [Virginia.], and their account—of the sick and suffering, is indeed sad, is sickening to contemplate— There are nearly 200 N. Carolinians alone, now in the hospital, who are suffering for the want of proper attention.
>
> The floors of the hospital, (the sick men say) have not been swept for weeks; and the dirty bandages which have been taken from their wounded limbs are thrown aside near the bed, rendering the rooms so offensive it is disagreeable to go in them—if these poor soldiers are not better cared for many more will fall victims to NEGLECT—perhaps this humble effort of mine for the comfort and relief of the sons of Carolina—may never be noticed, but it costs ME little to make the effort which MAY result in good.
>
> Will you not authorize ladies of your state to endeavor to get OTHERS to enlist as "sisters of mercy" for the relief of the sick at York—and other places. All the compensation which I ask, is a free passport—both in procuring volunteers and in reaching our—destination. Do you think such a move on my part unmaidenly, or indelicate? Gov. Ellis will please excuse a want of Parliamentary etiquette with which this letter is penned, attribute it rather to ignorance, than a want of respect.*[168]

Dr. Edward Warren, a North Carolinian stationed in Virginia, informed the governor that he must do more to assist the troops there. His letter is as follows:

Staunton October 11th, 1862
> There are at least 3000 soldiers in the Hospital here & of the number at least ¼ are North Carolinians. Dirty, naked, without shoes, hats, or socks, wounded in everything possible manner, utterly dispirited & entirely indifferent to everything they present a picture of wretchedness & misery which no thing or pen can describe. They are arriving at the rate of one thousand a day from the Army in trains which consume a whole week in making the journey, [hungry and suffering] . . . the condition of these poor unfortunates is enough to wring tears from hearts of stone . . . I have visited all the hospitals & hunted up our soldiers in every ward—assuring them that their Governor remembered them in their suffering . . . and resolved that they should not be . . . neglected.[169]

Medical department authorities developed several medical facilities known as general hospitals throughout the state. These were given numbers instead of names. By the end of

-----

*   Note: Evidence shows this to be written by a female.

the war, fourteen general military hospitals and seven wayside hospitals were identified.*[170] Every general hospital had a surgeon in charge and one medical officer or a contract surgeon to care for seventy to eighty ill soldiers. Usually, the ratio was much greater.[171] Wayside hospitals were located next to the railroad depots (or in the depots) for convenience in towns such as Tarboro, Greensboro, Salisbury, Charlotte, Kittrell, Fayetteville, High Point, Wilson, Weldon, and Goldsboro. These wayside stations were equipped with refreshments and clean bandages/bedding, etc. The small wayside institutions served an important role and were invaluable for saving lives. There were instances when the sick or wounded soldier could not tolerate the lengthy trip home or a transfer to another hospital. Women would meet these trains and remove the patient to the nearby temporary hospital or to their homes. In 1862, the Confederate government took over these and the larger general hospitals. Schools, colleges, hotels, churches, warehouses, barns, sheds, and private homes caught the overflow of the wounded, especially after battles. All vacant houses in Washington were used as hospitals to house sick soldiers early in the conflict.[172] Dr. John Gallagher converted a building near the bridge in Washington for medical use. Approximately six hundred soldiers were sick at one time there. In Kinston, a long line of tents was erected near the Neuse River to house smallpox victims, but two local houses were needed as well. The Methodist Episcopal Church reverted to a hospital, as was Nichols Store.[173]

The above-mentioned hospitals were different from a field hospital, which was located about one mile behind the battlefront. It moved with the changing of battle lines. Mostly these consisted of tents, but private homes would be commandeered for this purpose. Dr. Thomas F. Wood described in a letter home to his folks a division hospital that was also made up of tents:

June 10, 1864
Rode's Division Hospital, Cold Harbor
    Our hospital is in an apple orchard. Let me give you a description of a Hospital Camp—Each Brigade has a hospital wagon and each Div. one for transporting stoves, cooking utensils, tents, etc. Each tent is marked the same as that of the Brigade, and laid out in regular order. One large tent fly is located centrally as a tent for operations . . . . The wounded are placed in these tents, and are operated on in such order that suit the case of the patient.[174]

Despite additional facilities, which could lower the ratio of patients to attendants, problems continued to arise. Found among the papers of Dr. E. B. Haywood was a newspaper clipping in which an anonymous person had written to the *Daily Confederate*. The letter was addressed to Dr. Gorman, proprietor of the Wayside Hospital in Raleigh:

    Editor of newspaper: at the request of many soldiers I would respectfully invite the attention of the proper authorities to the condition of the Wayside Hospital in Raleigh.
    In the first place, the building which I understand was originally a grog shop is totally unadapted to the purpose for which it is employed; being too small for the accommodations of one hall, and frequently one-fourth of those who apply for admittance. The whole number of beds is only 15, and of these several are destitute of coverlets while the rest have only one apiece, which are dirty and ragged at that.
    I submit the [*illegible*] whether some better provision cannot be made for the comfort of our soldiers traveling to and fro from their commands? After being worn down by hardships and disease, or maimed with honorable

wounds; received in the heroic discharge of their duties as patriots, I think they may justly claim a rest to shelter their weary heads, and comfortable beds upon which to rest their wore-torn limbs.

North Carolina has in most respects well provided for the comforts and welfare of her gallant defenders, and I make this appeal hoping that it may not be allowed to pass without the attention which I think it merits. Signed TANK Kittrells' Springs, January 1, 1865[175]

At first, the established hospitals filled up with diseased men, not those with battle wounds. It was found that soldiers with rural backgrounds had very little immunity to communicable diseases, such as measles, smallpox, mumps, etc., in comparison with urban men. Complications from measles can lead to pneumonia, encephalitis, convulsions, and otitis media (ear infections). In November 1861, 115 soldiers, all members of the Thirty-fifth Regiment, were hospitalized in Raleigh for twenty-seven days due to rubeola. Two men died from the measles, and two succumbed to pneumonia.[176] John Young's diary told that during their stay at Camp Hill, Virginia, the summer of the first year of war, his unit caught the measles. Thirty-five were immediately hospitalized and treated by Dr. McKenzie of Rowan County, a private in the regiment. The ladies in Richmond nursed the men, taking some from the overloaded hospitals into their homes. Young continued:

The measles continue to prevail in our Camp, and the Typhoid fever seems also making its appearance. Our Sick list in daily averaging from 170 to 200 and to add to our trouble, we have had constant rains for near a week. But for the indefatigable exertions of Dr. King and his assistant, the thin shelters of our Tent Hospitals, the Damp Ground, with but little straw and the humid atmosphere would Cause the mortality [rate] to be fearful. Thus far, however, we have lost but Eight men (August 19th) since the organization of the Regiment, and Three of them Corpses in our Hospital today.[177]

A lady in Hyde County wrote her mother in October that her neighbors had all contracted the measles. "They got them from the soldiers that came down from up country."[178] It is possible that relatives visiting their sick kindred could contract disease. Mrs. Henry said, "Old Mr. Parker died yesterday morning. He has been to see his son in the 60th Reg. & came home sick. Tom Parker died whilst he was there." She then told of another neighbor: "G. W. Candler & his son Charlie are both dead. They both died sometime in July in Va. near Richmond. He had gone to see his son & took sick & died."[179] Both nurses and doctors had died while doing their duty in the hospitals.

Although the germ theory was unknown during this period in history, doctors did know to keep patients infected with smallpox, mumps, measles, and typhoid separate from regular hospital inmates. The smallpox vaccination had been developed in the Revolutionary War decade and was used to inoculate the soldier when supplies were available; however, in the South, the vaccine and other drugs were in constant short supply. At the camp of instruction in Raleigh the fall of 1861, John Muse related that he received a vaccination for smallpox, and "I thought I was going to lose my arm, it was so sore. The next vaccination was for measles and mumps.* I had the measles and was carried to the hospital which was a log hut." When he was able to sit up, his uncle came and carried him home to recover.[180]

There was always a need for smallpox vaccinations. Medical officers could not keep up with the demand. Soldiers were vaccinated upon entry into service. Sick troops had to be vaccinated upon admission to hospitals. Inmates in prison were vaccinated. When Henry Bahnson received his vaccination for smallpox at Cape Lookout, Maryland, he developed osteomyelitis. Surgeons surgically removed the infected bone of the right arm, rendering it

---

*   Muse is incorrect here. The measles/mumps vaccine was not available until the twentieth century.

useless, but saving his life.[181] George Lee told his mother, "I was vaccinated last week and my arm is now very sore. I am excused from duty on account of it."[182] When James Elliott's unit guarded Federal prisoners on the way to Andersonville Prison, he said the prisoners were infected with smallpox, and two of his friends caught it from them.[183] Perhaps they did not get vaccinated, or their scab was ineffective.

When smallpox occurred in central North Carolina, Dr. Ed Warren, surgeon general of the State, supervised the inoculation of seventy thousand civilians.*[184] Walter Clark, encamped at Winchester, Virginia, in October 1862, wrote his father that "most of the soldiers are vaccinated . . . say nothing of this as it might prevent men at home from joining their regiments . . . or produce a panic . . ." Walter advised his father to vaccinate all the children and their Negroes.[185] In a letter to Walter Clark from his mother, she commented, "Your Uncle Ed has just vaccinated me and three of the children & one of the servants (from a scab he got in Enfield) . . ."[186]

The shortage of scabs used to vaccinate people caused drastic measures. Doctors were to collect the scabs from patients, but also children in the neighborhood. To increase the supply of scabs, children of both races were vaccinated. In 1865, the medical officers were "authorized to pay private physicians five dollars for each reliable scab . . ."[187]

Dr. Charles E. Johnson, who located his hospital at the fairgrounds in Raleigh, was appointed the first surgeon general.[188] When the war commenced, North Carolina officials passed a bill for "approximately $300,000 for the relief of our sick and wounded soldiers." This amount was separate from and in addition to funds set aside by the Confederacy for the care of sick and wounded troops. The "hospital fund" assigned to hospitals was supposed to cover the purchase of food for the staff and patients "not obtainable through government channels." In addition, doctors could purchase articles "for the subsistence or comfort of the sick." Dr. Johnson asked North Carolina women to volunteer as nurses for the North Carolina hospital in Petersburg, Virginia. Ms. M. L. Pettigrew answered the call. There were six hospitals in Richmond where North Carolina soldiers were carried, but only one of these was staffed by a North Carolina doctor, Dr. E. Burke Haywood. Dr. Haywood stayed until 1864 when he returned to the state to take charge of the Pettigrew Hospital in Raleigh.[189]

Ever diligent, the *Raleigh Register* placed this notice:

> P.P. Pescud, medical purveyor of North Carolina, requests that all persons living near the railroads please contact him if you can accommodate the sick and wounded soldiers. If you live within the Yankee lines, report to the North Carolina Hospital at Petersburg or Raleigh for treatment or protection. The Soldiers' Aid Society in North Carolina please forward to me the supplies gathered for the soldiers.[190]

As wayside hospitals were gearing up, this appeal appeared in a local newspaper:

ROWAN WAY-SIDE HOSPITAL, Salisbury

> This hospital has been established one month, and during that period it has given accommodations to 134 soldiers. Of this number 87 were wounded and 47 sick. This hospital was established, and has been kept in operation, mainly, by the liberality of the citizens of Salisbury, for the comfort and accommodation of sick and wounded soldiers from different parts of our state. In order to keep it in operation, it is necessary to have means, and it is believed that, if proper exertions are made, it need not be trammeled in its charitable operations for the want of funds;—and when we consider the obligations under which we lie to the sick and wounded of our army, we think

---

*   Dr. Ed Warren was a volunteer doctor in New Bern, March 1862, then served as state surgeon general for the rest of the war.

we can confidently expect to receive from those who remain at home, their cheerful and efficient co-operation in the way of money and provisions. For this purpose we have taken the liberty of appointing you an agent in your county to raise and forward to the chairman, Major James C. Smith, any money or provisions which may be contributed by your section.

Should any citizen of your county get sick or wounded and reach this their friends may be satisfied that they will be attended to in a proper manner. It is hoped that you will attend to this appeal at your earliest possible convenience as the expenses of the hospital are great, and as there is scarcely a family that cannot spare something for the sick and wounded, "we trust the spirit of patriotism which burns in every Southern heart, will prompt them to immediate exertion in this manner." Jas C. Smyth, Chairman[191]

Another notice was posted by Mr. P. P. Pescud:

Wayside Hospital, Greensborough . . . . By orders from Dr. Edward Warren, Surgeon General for the state of North Carolina . . . I have opened a Wayside Hospital in the town of Greensborough, where all sick and wounded solders traveling can find a resting place. J.N. Neagle, assistant surgeon will be in charge. [June 18, 62][192]

On a day in March 1862, the mayor of Raleigh was notified that the medical department would need St. Mary's Female School as a medical facility. Dr. Aldert Smedes, president of the school, became distraught and agitated. The school must remain open for students, he felt. Dr. Smedes contacted the authorities and got the order changed. The government turned instead to the unfinished Peace College building in town.[193] Although incomplete with no glass in the windows, that didn't stop the doctors from using it. Workers hung sheets over the open spaces. The college contained three floors and eventually held three hundred beds. Dr. Charles Johnson called for women to come forward to staff the hospital.

Kittrell Springs Resort reverted to a wayside hospital from 1862 to 1865. The hotel was owned by the three Blacknall brothers—George W., Charles C., and Thomas H. The complex had rooms to house six hundred to eight hundred guests at a time. The resort consisted of several hotels, a bowling alley, a billiard room, a spa, and a dance floor. It was frequented by the elite and Confederate officers throughout the war. The Kittrell Hospital lost just under seventy patients who passed away from pneumonia, typhoid, chronic diarrhea, and battle wounds. Twenty-one hundred were treated in a ten-month period. Most of those that died from pneumonia and typhoid were only sixteen to eighteen years of age. Sixteen of the fifty-four causalities at Kittrell were members of the Junior Reserves.[194]

The High Point Wayside Hospital, established in September of 1862, treated a total of 5,795 men. Some soldiers were stranded, some were hungry, some were in need of medicine, and some were picked up at the railroad station.[195] The North Carolina Military Institute of Charlotte was reverted to a wayside hospital. Dr. Gregory, in charge there, placed a notice in the *North Carolina Whig* calling upon ladies to send butter, chickens, eggs, and potatoes.

The following is a summary of the different buildings used as hospitals around the state although inconclusive. Wayne Female College became a hospital and was used until the Federal takeover when it was converted to a U.S. hospital. Formerly the Barden Hotel, it was four stories tall.[196] The Griswold Hotel and the seminary in Goldsboro were revamped for medical purposes for Federal soldiers after the Battle of Bentonville. The Queen Street United Methodist Church in Kinston took in sick and wounded soldiers during and after the war. Kinston could boast of three hospitals, including a long line of tents for smallpox victims.[197] Two physicians in Kinston saw their homes commandeered for hospitals. Dr. A. R. Miller's home became the Confederate; and Dr. John Cobb's house, the U.S., as was John Jackson's III.[198] In Washington, a Convalescent Hospital opened in 1863, and the Mount Tirzah Hospital of the Confederacy had beds ready for occupancy in 1865. The Young Ladies Seminary on

Hay Street in Fayetteville was renovated for hospital use. It was three stories high with four female volunteer nurses on each ward.[199] Near the end of the war, Sarah A. Tillinghast, in Fayetteville, wrote her aunt that authorities had taken the high school and flour warehouse, thereby converting it into a place for the sick and wounded from Wilmington.[200] A hospital established in Salem the third year grew out of the former post office, and beds were set up in the town hall. A rotating schedule composed of married ladies was felt sufficient to nurse the sick without fatigue if a two-woman team worked one week at a time.[201] A lady said there were two hospitals in Asheville, "gen vance has one, the other the ladies hospital."[202]

Raleigh, being a hub and home base for the government, appeared to be a city of sick and wounded men. The Guion Hotel, the Peace Institute building, the Bank of New Bern building, First Baptist Church, and Dr. Fabius Haywood's office were used to house the afflicted, along with all the other military medical buildings and wayside hospitals. That is probably why a newspaper gave its citizens this advice:

> To correct the offensive odor of wounds, mix one hundred parts of calcined plaster of paris and two parts of coal tar. Rub together. Sprinkle on the wound twice daily.[203]

In the mountains besides the government hospitals, Dr. V. W. Cooper ran a small hospital in Madison County housing forty-two patients.[204] The Confederate hospital in Asheville was located on South Public Square. Originally, the Wilson Female Seminary, the military hospital in Wilson, was managed by Dr. S. S. Satchwell. One reference cited fifteen new buildings being built in Salisbury in 1864 to be used for medical purposes.[205] The McCullock Castle in Jamestown served temporarily as a hospital.[206]

Hospitals, no matter the size, could not run without its ancillary personnel. Besides male or female nurses, people such as woodcutters, laundresses, bakers, cooks, and orderlies, etc., were employed. Free blacks and slaves found employment throughout the war in these medical fields. Regulations stipulated that there was to be one laundress for every twenty patients, but this was not possible.[207] Their salary was better than the common soldier as cited in this newspaper article:

THE CONGRESS OF THE CONFEDERATE STATES OF AMERICA DO ENACT ON May 1, 1861:
> . . . Sec 2: That the pay hereafter to be allowed to all laundresses in hospitals or other places, in the service of the Confederate States, shall be twenty-five dollars per month, with rations and quarters, instead of pay now allowed by law.[208]

The cost allowed for feeding each soldier was raised from $1 to $1.50 in 1863 after surgeons complained that it wasn't sufficient. The Southern soldiers' diet, known as the 3-M/2-H—molasses, meat, meal (corn), and hogs and hominy—which dominated the fare most of the time, caused untold illness. If the trooper was lucky to get boxes from home, fruits and vegetables could save his health.[209]

Dr. E. Burke Haywood of Raleigh left very good records of his service to the Confederacy. He, as were other officers, was transferred to different places as needed. As the surgeon in charge of hospital no. 7, Raleigh, he left us a fifteen-month summary of his duties beginning in May of 1861:

Taken Sick	Sent to Gen. Hosp.	Returned to Duty	Furloughed	Discharge	Deserted	Died	%
4,731	44	4,228	241	16	32	170	3

The figures for January 1863 to January 1864:

1,351	25	945	295	6	39	41	4

Dr. Haywood made regular reports to the surgeon general:

> Sir: I believe that there has been received in this hospital more very sick men than any other in this state, on account of its having been the receiving hospital for a large camp of instruction which at one time contained between five and six thousand soldiers. Camps of instructions have a much higher rate of mortality than any other camp. E. Burke Haywood, Surg. in charge[210]

In July, he made four requests and received four thousand dollars for hospital supplies. For the first part of October, the hospital ministered to 223 patients cared for by fifty-four attendants, both male and female. Rations were basically the same as before with the addition of fish, vinegar, and tobacco.

In a letter written to Surgeon General Peter Hines, March 20, 1864, Dr. Haywood told him that he thought that his hospital needed two ward masters because of the size and separated wards (hospital no. 7). He reported that the nurses needed constant supervision, and the ward master was a militia officer. He said they had two laundresses. Three months later in his report to Dr. Hines, he wrote that he had two stewards, two assistant surgeons, two acting surgeons, one ward master, two matrons, and sixteen Negroes as cooks, nurses, and washerwomen (June 28, 1964).

Dr. Haywood seemed to prefer male nurses, but for whatever reason, it is unclear. In mid-1862, he listed an advertisement for male nurses in the *Raleigh Register*:

> Wanted to hire 15 intelligent nurses for the North Carolina General Military Hospital at Raleigh. Middle-aged men preferred.
> Also two washerwomen. Apply to E. Burke Haywood.[211]

The previous January, his ad said, "WANTED: one matron, one assistant matron, and one good nurse for the General Military Hospital at Raleigh." In May of 1862, "Dr. E. Burke Haywood, called on Father Thomas Quigley, to find out how he could get three Sisters of Mercy to aid him in nursing the sick. He promised them a large room in a house, where, he said, they would be free from all intrusion and from insult, since the place was guarded by military law and there was a chaplain there." None were available to go.[212]

Once the soldier had recovered, if able, he was sent back to camp sometimes after a short furlough. Convalescing soldiers made poorer nurses and were less qualified, so they became indifferent and careless nurses since they knew they would eventually be returned to the ranks. Frustrated surgeons grew burdened under the circumstances. Dr. Haywood must have felt that he was constantly training men to help with hospital duties. He petitioned the surgeon general of the Confederate States, Samuel Moore, to keep the same seven conscripts he had mentored because they made better nurses:

> They are intelligent, well trained and faithful nurses. Their good nursing has saved many a valuable life during the war. I believe these men will do ten times more service for the Confederacy as nurses than as soldiers. Nurses who are detained on account of permanent disability know that they are not liable to be returned to the field and therefore do not exert themselves to please. They are generally worse and discontented at being detailed and put to nursing in hospitals after being disabled by wounds, instead of being furloughed or discharged. Such will [,] nor can [,] make good nurses. A nurse who is liable to be returned to duty . . . for disobedience or neglect of duty, is much more easily managed and ten times as efficient. A disabled man cannot lift the sick, carry out the beds, scour the floor or set up at night or do many other things which are necessary in a well conducted hospital. I think it hard, that the Medical Department should have to give up its skilled employees. The Medical Department, I am proud to say is the best disciplined one in the

service. I have complied with the order, and given up my best ward-masters and nurses . . . . Col. Mallett is perfectly willing that I should have them.[213]

The problem of detailed soldiers, whether by illness or injury, for hospital duty plagued other surgeons as well. Surgeon General Moore felt the necessity to contact the War Department to help alleviate some of the problems concerning poor nursing care:

> By recent instructions, the Superintendent of Conscription has (on the authority of the War Department) directed that all disabled men detailed from the Army of Northern Virginia, should be returned for such duty as they may be able to perform in the field.
> Objections cannot reasonably be made to this, provided the men not found equal to any duty in the field be returned to the same hospital from which they have been taken. But by Circular No. 35* . . . from the Bureau of Conscription, generals of reserves are directed . . . to organize for certain local service "all men found for light duty and not otherwise assigned and actually employed," which deprives the Medical Department of the' opportunity to replace with conscripts found for light duty the detailed men relieved in the manner above stated, or to fill the requirements arising from time to time for hospital attendants. The hospitals cannot be properly conducted without a liberal allowance of white male attendants, and it is recommended that Circular No. 35 . . . from the Bureau of Conscription, be modified so as to permit either conscripts found for light duty, or reserves over forty-five years of age, be assigned as hospital attendants.[214]

Dr. Haywood continued to request nurses for hospital work in January 1865: "I have great need at present of white nurses [male]." He stated that five of his best nurses were ordered back to their commands.[215]

With a constant shortage of supplies and staff, conditions in the medical facilities continued to deteriorate, prompting General P. T. Beauregard to write the editor of a newspaper alerting folks and hoping the situation could be remedied:

> John M. Otley, Assistant Adjutant General, Raleigh, March 21,[1865]
> To Brig. Gen. B. T. Johnson at Salisbury
>
> Much suffering among the sick and wounded soldiers for want of hospital accommodations is reported at your post. Have necessary arrangements made to relieve their wants and suffering. By Command of Gen. Beauregard.[216]

Leonidas Torrence wrote his father that he was in a hospital in Charlottesville, Virginia, not as a patient, but as a nurse. Torrence said he had been sent there to nurse T. L. McGuire, F. M. Beatie, and T. H. Johnston. While carrying out hospital duty, Torrence caught typhoid pneumonia. In other letters home, he asked his mother to send him winter clothing, boots, and the recipe for making pills "to cure the chills." The following spring, Torrence was still working at Delavan hospital but became ill again with the same illness. Apparently, he recovered enough to continue as a nurse through April 1862.[217] Torrence must have been a terrific nurse to have stayed in one place for so long.

Henry Bahnson probably wished he had the services of Torrence. Sick with the fever and confined to a hospital in Lynchburg, Virginia, Bahnson of Salem recalled with displeasure at his treatment:

---

*   General Orders: soldiers either sick or wounded and likely to remain unfit for military duty for sixty days were furloughed *most of the time*.

The doctors left at night, and a man was detailed as night nurse for the hundred or more patients on one floor of the big factory [tobacco], but he and his companions on the other floor drank and played cards or slept . . . and I never saw one give the least attention to a sick man after ten o'clock. Cries for help or water, oaths and threats, were wasted on deaf ears. They would rouse up about daylight and go around to forcibly straighten bodies of poor wretches who had died neglected during the night, and make up tales to tell at the doctor's visit in the morning.[218]

Walter Lenoir with a fresh leg amputation described his ordeal of a wagon ride without springs, which many failed to have: "Every little jolt of the wagon caused 'a pang which felt as if my stump was thrust into liquid fire, and was as fierce as that awful pang which first announced that my leg was broken.'" He wrote his brothers that when in the hospital recovering from his amputation, it was impossible to sleep mainly because he had sit halfway up for the stump to drain properly. He called this his "sleep famine" period of recovery. Walter's younger brother, Rufus, decided to go to Virginia to bring him home. At the time, Confederate officials in central Virginia were turning away civilians from using the railways. Rufus took a circular route traveling North and West through East Tennessee into Virginia, then along the Blue Ridge Mountains. As he approached Middleburg, he was turned back due to smallpox in the area. At this point, Rufus talked with soldiers who knew all about the affair, so he decided to go home and return for his brother in a few weeks. Another brother then traveled to Middleburg and retrieved the wounded Walter.[219]

Another soldier left his experience for readers after he was wounded in the thigh at Gaines' Mill, Virginia. George Washington Cochran with the Thirty-seventh NCT said that helpers placed cedar brush to cushion the bottom of the wagon as they started to the hospital miles away:

> It was a ten mile trip in the darkness and every pebble a wheel hit caused pain to the sufferers; gullies, rocks, stumps brought forth groans, wails and entreaties from every wagon in the train, to all of which I contributed my fair share . . . a wagon turned over in front of mine filled with maimed soldiers. Cries, groans, and bitter curses, supplemented by the finest efforts of our gifted quartermaster who uttered eloquent and lurid profanity, filled the air . . . . But the worst was yet to come. The long street over which we must travel upon reaching Richmond was paved with round river rocks and when we entered it, it was a continuous series of bounces. I was in so much pain that I could not refrain from crying out . . . . That awful ride will forever stand out in my memory as a hellish nightmare beyond the range of any man's imagination.

After a few days' time, Cochran's father came to take him back to Catawba County on the train. Cochran continued:

> There were no accommodations on the trains for wounded soldiers. I could not sit on a seat owing to the nearness of the wound to my hip; I could not have two seats owing to the crowded cars, so the only way I could rest was to lie down between the seat and stretch my legs across the isle, which I did, and nearly everyone who passed, it seemed to me, took particular pains to strike my foot so that it would jar my wounded leg. It was a very weary trip and when I got home I fainted every time I rose to walk on my crutches.[220]

His mother nursed him back to health, which took two months to heal, but the severed muscle prolonged recovery. Cochran said he returned to duty three months later. George had a twin brother, Marion.

A North Carolina doctor described his frustrations in practicing medicine to his father in Wayne County:

White Sulfur Springs, Dec 4th 1863(?)

My dear Pa;

Having to go to Lewisburg on yesterday on business; I enquired at the office and found two letters from you . . . . The cause of the delay was in consequence of your direction being directed to Floyd's Brigade, they . . . sent to Raleigh C.H.___Head Quarters and from there resent to me . . . . I informed you of my new Quarters on my arrival and the bad impression that it first made on me is not extremely erased . . . . it is an excellent place for the pursuit of Knowledge and by close application to Hospital duty; it becomes an excellent school.

There is nothing to revert the mind from the proper channel here, your daily routine is the first thing thought of in the morning and the last at night and were a physician disposed to be somewhat idle, he could find nothing for amusement. I do not want to create a false impression in your mind by having you think that I am reading very closely, but I would have you know that I have very few hours to throw away and have done more mental and physical labor than ever before. My hospital is full to repletion all the time, having from one hundred and twenty five to fifty patients to see every day. Our diseased are mostly of a Typhoid character and at the present we have to contend with epidemis [sic] Enysipelas [sic Erysipelas], which is very fatal. The least scratch any one received has the tendency to emerge into an enysipelas inflammation.

Our Surgeon and two assistants are now suffering and it creates some little anxiety where ever there is an abrasion of the skin. I am inclined to the belief . . . that it is as much owing to the contaminated atmosphere of hospitals as any thing else, probably more, and for that reason I have been trying to be cautious using disinfectants daily. I was comfortably situated in Lewisburg, having an excellent room, intelligent room mate and every thing tended to establish contentment and satisfaction and it was not until I was ordered to white Sulphur [Springs] that the inconveniences and privations of Western Virginia presented themselves to view . . .

It is bleak and . . . unusual section of country and perfectly useless only for summer scenery . . . . In two days the number of inmates have decreased some two hundred.

In consequence of such demolition, there will be no telling where they will order me next, most likely though to be Richmond to stand my examination, which I shall respectfully refuse. Your suggestion about seeing the Surgeon General, relative to my position, does not fully meet my approbation. I am willing to act as others in the premisis [sic], provided, there is not an order current of prejudice against me to contend with. From what I learn, the medical Faculty submits a Candidate to a strictly practical examination and have one or two witnesses.

I have never heard of them deviating from such a course. There are many . . . a majority of assistant Surgeons who will not stand. The reason is that while they may feel their competency and ability, to practice medicine and also understand the theory of Surgery . . . they argue that their future destiny is in the hands of these five men if they choose to ask them questions on the minutiae of medicine and surgery which they can not answer, they are thrown, and their future reputation ruined to a certain degree. I had much rather resign, attend another course of lectures and then present my self before the board for a permanent commission.

I feel no embarassment [*sic*] at all in practicing without a diploma, for the reason that my knowledge of the practice of medicine is not inferior to those who have their diplomas as [to] my mortality [rate] this will prove during my stay in the hospital.

I have given you my views and would rather lie dormant until I hear from the board. Some think that they will not examine those who have their commissions. I rest under no such fancied security . . . I am plain in dress, having bought only one suit, for $60 which I have to wear every day. My shoe bill is the worst of all. I cut through them over these weeks in two or three weeks, the cash from 6.50 to $10 a pair . . . . I am in excellent health. Dr. Somers is now prostrated from an attack of cont'd (?) Fever. More than likely I will be ordered to Red Sulphur [Springs] in a week . . . it will be impossible for me to get a furlough to go home Christmas, unless for good . . .

Your Son
Windal T. R[obinson][221]

At the beginning of the struggle for independence, the question of medicine was third in importance behind first, arms and ammunition; second, clothing and shoes; then medicine. Four drugs were needed at all times during the conflict: quinine, opium, and the two anesthetics ether and chloroform. Another reference listed rhubarb as a fifth need.[222] Home manufacturing, local companies, and blockade running were the only sources of supply during the war years, except for those captured from the enemy. Almost all of the morphine used for pain relief came through the blockade. Citizens were told to plant poppies for personal medicinal use, or if their crop was large enough, it could be sold to the government. Opium came from Turkey and the Far East via blockade-runners.[223]

Medical supplies were always inadequate in the South both for the military and civilian population once the war commenced. The War Department was compelled to depend entirely upon purchasing agents and contracts awarded to individuals for a supply of hospital furniture, bedding, and drugs, except those that ran the blockade. Many times, these contracts never lived up to their potential, or they may have been broken. Dr. S. P. Moore, surgeon general, wanted to use detailed soldiers to fill the void; and he asked that they be permanently exempted to work for the medical department. He said:

> These employees of the laboratories, purveying depots and distilleries, are in a great measure expert chemists, druggists and distillers and men of professional skill, whose services are absolutely indispensable for the manufacture of medicines, hospital furniture and alcohol stimulants.[224]

Doctors preferred to use alcohol for ill soldiers as a stimulant. They claimed it helped with fatigue and exposure as well as lifting their "spirits," that alcohol "is frequently required to relieve temporary debility of the system." Alcohol found use too as a solvent to be mixed with other chemicals.[225] As the war progressed, residents made whiskey for profit instead of using the grain to feed the hungry, which caused an uproar. Newspapers from the time period allude to this.* At the start of the conflict, medical officers received the alcohol from private distributors. "The contract price for whiskey ranged from $1.50 to $3.50 per gallon whereas that for alcohol stood near $3.25 for the same amount. Purveyors were allowed to use grain instead of money to contract for whiskey; but in doing so, they were directed to make certain that the government received all the whiskey made from the grain furnished."[226]

---

*   See chapter 8.

The surgeon general of North Carolina felt that the quality of the distilleries was inferior. The medical department requested the state form their own distilleries so it could be controlled better. The state did exactly that, setting up a distillery in Salisbury. Different grains were used, such as barley, rye, wheat, and corn. Surgeon Moore said of the Salisbury distillery that it used one hundred bushels of rye/wheat, one thousand bushels of corn, and sixty bushels of rye *each* month. This produced two hundred to five hundred gallons of liquor per day.[227]

Governor Vance was known to butt heads with Confederate officials in Richmond, and the success of the state distillery caught the eye of these officials. They claimed that the distillery belonged to the Confederacy, not merely to North Carolina. The following letter from Dr. S. P. Moore, medical director to the Secretary of War, James Seddon, pointed to the controversy:

> [T]he Medical Department has no contract for alcoholic stimulants in the State of North Carolina. The distillery at Salisbury referred to by Governor Vance is owned by the Medical Department and is engaged in the manufacture of whiskey and alcohol for the sole use of the sick and wounded of the Army. This distillery was purchased by this department for the purpose of dispensing with the system of contracting for alcoholic stimulants, as it has been found that a large quality of whiskey manufactured by contractors is of an inferior quality, and their contracts were not in other respects faithfully complied with. It is also believed that a large quantity of the whiskey made by contractors has been sold to private parties when it should have been delivered to the Government . . . .
>
> The Attorney-General has decided that the Confederate Government has the express power to support armies; that any means may be used which are necessary and proper to obtain supplies for that support . . . . In conclusion I would state that it is absolutely necessary for the comfort and welfare of the sick . . . that the Government distillery at Salisbury should not be interfered with or the supply of grain cut off.[228]

A similar letter from Moore to the central government stated:

> For the supply of alcoholic stimulants, the [Medical] Department has been until recently dependent upon contracts with individuals. It was ascertained that this mode of supply was susceptible of gross fraud, for although expressly forbidden by the terms of the contract, but frequently manufactured so indifferent and spurious an article that the Department was obliged to reject it, thus leaving large quantities of whiskey in their hands, which they readily disposed of at prices largely in advance of Government rates. At the suggestion of this bureau, Congress . . . granted authority to the Surgeon-General to establish distilleries . . . . Accordingly they have been established at Salisbury . . . Columbia, South Carolina, Macon, Georgia, and . . . in Alabama . . .
>
> A large portion of the grain consumed by these distilleries is rendered useless for other purposes, being damaged in transportation or from insecure storage, and turned over by the Quartermasters to this Department. Thousands of bushels of grain are thus saved to the Government and made available for army purposes . . .[229]

Governor Vance saw more letters coming from authorities in Richmond. E. W. John, the top-ranking Confederate medical purveyor, wrote:

Purveyor's Office Richmond Va. October 3rd. 1862

I have the honor to represent that a large amount of Alcoholic stimulants are indispensable in the treatment of the sick & wounded of the Army, and that the duty of providing the said stimulates is devolved upon this department. Of the required amount according to an estimate made in this office, a considerable portion has been contracted for, but still remains a large quantity to be provided.

I therefore respectfully request that authority be granted to this Department, to contract for the manufacture & delivery of as much Whiskey & Alcohol as may be required, for the Army . . . for Medical and Hospital purposes . . . and parties contracting for [distillation and] delivery . . . be exempt from the . . . order, prohibiting the distillation of grain . . .[230]

Vance replied to Mr. John that perhaps brandy could be used in its place. "The Convention, on February 21,1862, had adapted an ordinance which prohibited the distillation of spirituous liquors from grains, the prohibition to last until January 1,1863." It levied a tax of thirty cents a gallon on all spirituous liquors manufactured in North Carolina out of corn, wheat, rye, and oats up to April 15,1862. "It prohibited manufacture after April 15 and levied appropriate penalties for violation; it also provided for a tax of one dollar a gallon on liquor manufactured elsewhere but sold in North Carolina after March 1, 1862."[231]

Vance on his lecture to the legislature November 17, 1862, told of his desire to continue the prohibition of distilling grain for alcohol. He wanted to use fruits instead of grain. "Should even the supply for the army fail, it cannot be doubted that it is much better for the soldier to go without spirits than that his wife and child should be without bread."[232]

Citing passages from author Flannery, the law could annul any outstanding contract, and Southern states "could legislate away any national need, no matter how pressing."[233] Dr. Thomas F. Wood said at first that ten gallons of whiskey was issued to each regiment, then as shortages appeared, five gallons or less, which was supposed to be used by the sick in the hospitals.[234]

Drugs were manufactured in Charlotte and Lincolnton, and larger cities had pharmacies, but their stock was soon depleted. The deficiency appeared by the middle of the second year of the war. Dr. A. S. Piggott ran the lab in Lincolnton. Workers, either old men or young boys, made tinctures and extracts from the "indigenous crude drugs sent to them."* Capture of the enemy's supply trains and blockade-runner auctions helped to restore a part of the inventory.[235] A physician from Smithville said he never had problems getting quinine because he could salvage it from grounded blockade-runners. The need for quinine was so great that any effort was used to smuggle it between the lines. "Small packages were placed in letters which the Adams Express Company would guarantee for the sum of two dollars to deliver to the post office authorities at some point in the Confederacy. Officers speculating in it, buying and selling until this created a scandal almost as equal to that of speculating in cotton, and it was finally stopped by a strong proclamation."[236]

Surgeons in Virginia sent their attendants and convalescing patients to the countryside to collect herbs used in medicine, or they would have medical purveyors place ads in newspapers calling for citizens to comb the woods and fields. Some purveyors doled out poppy seed for ladies to plant. When mature, the bulb was sliced causing a liquid to ooze out. Once hardened, people collected the result and sold it to the purveyor.[237] These would

---

*   The lab was located on the Catawba River with machines powered by the river. "Local towns and surrounding villages serving as collection points, residents recalled large wagonloads of medicines coming into and out of the . . . lab; they also recalled a large poppy and sorghum field proximate to the facility."

be used at home *and* sold to the military. It was another way for the indigent soldier's wife to make a little money. A typical advertisement would read:

> The *Statesville Express* says that Lt. Col. John A. Young of the 4th Regiment, North Carolina State Troops, urges the importance of furnishing the army at Manassas with a large supply of dogwood bark as a substitute for quinine . . . dogwood bark, steeped in water or spirits is the best remedy for chills and fever we ever saw.[238]

or

> M. Howard, medical purveyor & surgeon of Charlotte makes application for roots, herbs, bark, and etc. collected for the medical purveyor's office. Will refund freight if accepted. We no longer want: red cedar, juniper tops, sarsaparilla roots, popular, white oak, willow, slippery elm bark, and poke root.[239]

Just two weeks earlier, Howard had requested these herbs, which he would pay from twenty cents to one dollar to the bearer: dogwood bark, blackberry root, Indian tobacco, sienna, fleabane, barberry leaves, wild ginger, wintergreen, skunk cabbage roots, snake root, wild cherry bark, etc. Sassafras pith and red pepper and hops brought more than one dollar.

Amongst the scarcest items needed in the medical field were bottles, vials, corks, paper, and twine. Medical purveyors called for old champagne, wine, or castor oil bottles to recycle paying as much as one dollar or more per dozen. Druggists used every kind and shape of glass bottles they could get. "Some of the drug stores obtained old life preservers from abandoned river boats . . . ," which were cut up and used for corks. If he couldn't obtain corks, corn-cobs stoppered the bottles. Others tried to make corks from tupelo trees.[240] Other hospital supplies that needed frequent change and were scarce in number were the stuffing for the mattresses. Blood and bodily fluids that soaked through caused health concerns, as well as unpleasant odors. Rags, cotton, straw, oak leaves, pine needles, Spanish moss, and wood shavings or sawdust filled the void.[241]

Soldiers confined in close quarters during the wintertime complained of getting the itch, a common occurrence of epidemic proportion. "The routine treatment in the South was a sulfur, arsenic, or alkaline bath, but the difficulty of procuring the ingredients for such baths prompted physicians to turn to various other treatments for relief." Poke root baths followed with soap suds helped some if the treatment began early when symptoms appeared. If the skin became inflamed, then the poke root baths burned the skin, so it was substituted for a mixture of slippery elm or broom straw used three or more times a day. Another treatment was to use ointments made from the sweet gum tree or elder bark.[242]

When short on quinine, the doctors applied an external application of bandages soaked with turpentine to the lower chest. Those at the Pettigrew Hospital gave the victim a dose of opium tincture mixed with a solution of ammonia before the expected chills.[243] Dr. Haywood treated malaria patients by slathering turpentine over the body. Dr. Walter Loehr has said that gray mass (Spanish moss) and lamb's ear served as substitute bandages. Apparently, the citizens responded very well to the surgeon's call. The next notice indicates that herbs were used by military surgeons:

STANDARD SUPPLY TABLE OF THE INDIGENOUS REMEDIES FOR THE FIELD SERVICE AND THE SICK IN GENERAL HOSPITALS, 1863
Surgeon General's Office, Richmond, VA, March 1, 1863, by S.P. Moore, Surgeon General Confederate States of America:
> The articles of this supply table are intended as adjuncts to, or substitutes for those of the original Supply Table of the Regulations for the Medical Department. When the articles of the original supply cannot be procured from the Purveyors, or when they are deficient in quantity, Medical Officers

are instructed to make requisition for such indigenous preparations from the following table as will supply the deficiencies.*[244]

A newspaper article appearing in the *Raleigh Register* asked farmers and citizens to collect indigenous medicinal plants. The types of plant and their use were listed:

Butterfly weed . . . use as an expectorant; a diaphoretic
Blood root . . . . an emetic; expectorant
Snake root . . . . for rheumatism; a tonic; a stimulant
Wild ginger . . . a tonic; a diaphoretic
Sweet flag . . . . A stimulant and tonic; for GI cramping and flatulence
Queens root . . . . for a chronic hepatic condition; for syphilis; for scrofula
Queens delight . . . same as above
Carolina pink . . . the most powerful enthelmiutics [dewormer]
Poke . . . . an emetic; slight narcotic value; a cathartic; good for rheumatism and
      syphilis; ointment for the itch
Water pepper or smart weed . . . used to rid of bedbugs. Stuff the plant in cracks and
      corners of the room or make a decoction and use as a wash
Elderberry leaves . . . to rid the home of roaches, ants, and sometimes the fly. Lay on
      shelves.[245]

The medical purveyors of the South were divided into districts, with Charlotte designated as district no. 2. Dr. Ed Warren headed up the field purveyor office in Goldsboro. "Medical purveyors controlled the laboratories, employed pharmacists and chemists to analyze and produce medicines," noted author Carol Green. The medical purveyor's job consisted of procuring the drugs and to keep a supply on hand at the depot or a warehouse.** Drug shortages made this a difficult undertaking.[246] He more so received and used items sent by the aid societies. When these ran short, he would place an ad in the newspapers. Food was requested along with clothing, bedding, linens, books, straw, wood, soap, candles, toilet articles, etc.:

> Vegetables and fruit are needed for the hospitals around Richmond. They will be collected in Greensboro and Raleigh. Also requested are eggs, butter, chickens, and clothing.[247]

When items could not be donated, the purveyor was permitted to purchase these articles at lower prices:

> From the office of Surgeon General in Raleigh: Wanted the following articles are required by the sick and wounded soldiers: shoes, hats, coats, socks, pants, leather, shoe thread, shoe-making lasts, drawers, buttons, cloth, flannel, potatoes, brandy, butter, & eggs. Ed Warren[248]

> On the 28th instant, the Medical Purveyor will be prepared to purchase: corn, barley, & lard for which market prices will be paid. Rice, coffee, sugar, salt, cotton yard and cloth will be given in part payment when desired.
> J.T. Johnson, Surgeon and Medical Purveyor[249]

---

*   Sixty-four plants are listed. For an addition list, see the appendix.
**   For a list of medical quantities for one year for one thousand troops, see the appendix.

Mr. R. B. Saunders of Chapel Hill opened a lab for manufacturing medicine. Blue mass was the chief output.[*250] Mr. Meares owned a pharmacy in Wilmington but was not able to produce large quantities of medicine. He could procure drugs from the blockade-runners. The central government oversaw the supply of medicine to both the military and civilian population.[251]

Among other supplies of hospital equipment in short supply were tin buckets, basins, furniture, dishes, and tableware. The tin roof on the courthouse in Ashe County was removed for war purposes.[252] North Carolina potters, primarily in Moore and Randolph counties, made storage crocks and cups, as well as hospital tableware, for the Southern Army. Potters were exempt from military service. This reproduced cup made by the Bolick Family Pottery is a copy of an original in the North Carolina Museum of History collection. Other items needed by inmates and personnel included chamber pots, hospital clothing, sheets and pillowcases, mattresses, spittoons, spitboxes, eating utensils, soap, candles, and stoves. The surgeon's assistants had to keep an inventory of equipment in his wards.

Hospital Cup

The only town in Brunswick County, Smithville, was frequented by prosperous clientele as a resort area before wartimes. The area was inhabited by rice farmers, turpentine farmers, and boat pilots.[253] Town buildings became temporary hospitals soon after troops were stationed at nearby forts. Duncan Buie, a soldier, was smitten with the location. Buie wrote a letter to his friend from the hospital saying that it was a perfect place to convalesce because of the quietness, floral beauty, live oaks, ocean/river view, and "an occasional glance at the gentler sex as they pass and a good old mama to contribute to our wants . . ."[254]

Unfortunately, not all hospitals held such an idealistic setting as Smithville. Mentioned earlier, buildings of all types were seized to be converted into medical facilities. One soldier wrote home that he was situated in a horse stall at the fairgrounds. Hospitals were unhealthy places. Sanitation was inferior to present-day standards due to ignorance of the germ theory and lack of proper supplies. Soldiers with wounds took months to heal instead of days. If antibiotics were available then, the healing of wounds would have been totally different. Odors wafting through the wards were described in writings of the period. A. F. Morrison with the Seventh Regiment, stationed in Virginia, wrote to his sister:

---

*   A mixture of chalk, mercury, and honey used for bowel complaints

. . . I was really glad to get away from the hospital as soon as I was able to return to my regiment for there is so many bad wounded and it smelt so bad that I could hardly stand to eat my dinner in the ward.[255]

When he was riding in a railroad car with wounded soldiers, Kemp P. Battle described the odor as "air charged with the smell of half-putrid blood."[256] A lady traveling at the end of the war said the odor lingering in the cars from hauling the wounded would overpower a person. Female nurses and visitors were known to faint at the noxious odors drifting throughout the wards. Tin buckets became bedpans and sat at the foot of the bed waiting to be emptied. Overflowing spit buckets turned the weak constitution upside down.

––––––––––––––––

Medical director Peter Hines wrote Dr. Haywood, who was then in charge of the Pettigrew Military Hospital in Raleigh, a letter about all the women in the hospitals:

The Ladies Relief Society has been of benefit and added to the comfort of the sick and wounded of this hospital more by the cheering influence of their visits, gently ways, and sympathetic attentions than by any articles of food they may have furnished.[257]

Whenever possible, women flocked to the hospitals when news reached them of their ailing relative. So many in fact that they became a burden to personnel. Weary patients encouraged their visits—anything to relieve the monotony of convalescing. These women got in the way of the nursing staff but were probably appreciated when the patient load became too much for them. In general hospital no. 8 in Raleigh, a soldier mentioned this to his betrothed so that she would come to see him.[258] These female visitors could be overbearing and bossy to the point of exasperation. Apparently, Dr. Haywood was considering limiting the visits by the ladies' relief societies, prompting him to write to Dr. Hines. Haywood also suggested that they hire a "diet matron" from the group who was a good cook. Her duties would include the need to abide by the army rules and regulations of the facility, which some women found hard to do.[259]

Medical officers were attune to discharging veterans back to their regiment as soon as possible. A strict record was necessary to keep up with the sick or wounded, their injuries, and their progress made toward rehabilitation. Officers sent letters or came in person to learn the improvement of its troops, more so during the last two years of war when manpower was so depleted. Surgeon General Peter Hines sent a special letter to Dr. W. Holt, warning him that the inspectors were on their way to his hospital in December 1864 to examine patients and see if they could be returned to duty. He urged Holt to discharge those type patients quickly. In Dr. Holt's reply to Hines, he wrote that he had returned four men to duty but one, Private W. D. Weaver, from the Tenth Regiment (artillery), who was "subjected to the influence of chloroform and found to be an accomplished malingerer" and was still there. He wrote, "There is perfect mobility in all his joints and no shortening of the leg." Apparently, Dr. Holt passed inspection, for they complimented him on the neatness of his wards and proficiency of his assistants; they praised him for returning soldiers to active duty:

The small percent of men found fit for field service (less at this hospital than any other) may be mentioned as one fact to show how conscientiously the medical officers of this hospital have discharged their duty.[260]

Most men who had recovered from illness were anxious to return to military duty. However, there were those who lingered around feigning sickness to keep from going back to the front. These men—called hospital rats, shirkers, or malingerers—found all sorts of excuses to stay. Mentioned earlier, it did take longer to heal without antibiotics, prompting the patients to spend months recovering. To help pass the time, the men were issued passes to enter town where some got into mischief. Residents living near hospitals complained to the provost about missing fruits and vegetables and damage to their gardens. Peter Hines sent a notice to Captain S. B. Waters that he wanted Waters to arrest all sick or convalescing soldiers in the city without a pass. "Complaints have been made of the conduct of soldiers in visiting gardens, orchards, and other property of the citizens . . . ."[261] These same soldiers could have gone to the saloons.

Apparently, it was enough of a problem that Dr. S. S. Satchwell in charge of the military hospital in Wilson suggested to the governor that he do something about it:

> . . . Major Holmes issued a special order to me to confiscate all liquor here belonging to those who retail the same &c. I have executed this order . . . if you will recommend in your Message the passage of a law forbidding the sale of liquor in the vicinity of Confederate Military Hospitals in this state . . . Detached hospitals especially like this need such a protection from the State . . .[262]

Guards placed at the hospitals to keep order also watched for deserters. Dr. Haywood, then at hospital no. 7, sent a notice to Colonel Evans, Fifth North Carolina Cavalry, at Louisburg, that Private William Hampton (McRae's Battery) was placed in the guardhouse but escaped by cutting through the floor. "I suppose he will endeavor to reach the Battery as he expressed a desire to go there," said Haywood. Hampton must have been afraid that they would make him a nurse and keep him there. He deserted *back* to his unit.[263]

Another duty of the surgeon was to detail a person to accompany the sick trooper home when he was well enough to travel. Confederate Congress passed a law whereby the sick passenger had a reserved seat on the train, but this was not always followed.[264]

Averasboro and Bentonville had fallen to Sherman's forces, and the wounded were taken to the interior of the state for treatment, many as far away as Charlotte. This advertisement appeared March 27, 1865, in the *Raleigh Conservative*:

> **WANTED:** one hundred fifty negro men, females and boys for nurses, cooks, waiters, and washerwomen in the hospital of this state. Apply to me at Raleigh. P.E. Hines, Surgeon and Medical Director OR to Surgeon J.G. Broadnax, Wake Forest; Surgeon W.H. Moore, Greensboro; Surgeon W.A. Hall, High Point; Surgeon S. Barncle, Thomasville; Surgeon J.W. Hall, Salisbury; and Surgeon R. Gibbon, Charlotte.

Private citizens took the wounded in their homes to help with the overflow. After Fort Fisher and Wilmington had been overrun by enemy troops, Joseph C. Shepard, the doctor at Fort Fisher, was captured, subsequently released, then traveled to Greensboro. He chose the Presbyterian church for a temporary hospital in anticipation of the upcoming battles with General Sherman's forces who had recently entered the state.[265]

The following is the last entry in Dr. Haywood's ledger as U.S. General Sherman's troops entered Raleigh. He listed the price paid for supplies sent to Pettigrew Hospital. April 7 was the last day listed in the ledger:

> April, 1865: Nails—$5 for 20 pounds; Geese—$12.50 each; butter—$7 for 8 pounds; potatoes $20 bushel; eggs—$3.50 per dozen; chickens—$6.25 each; Milk—$2.25-$3 a gallon; buttermilk—$1.50; corn $25 a bushel.[266]

Dr. Peter Hines tried to staff and equip a hospital when Sherman entered the state in 1865. He said that it was very difficult to procure straw for beds and lumber to construct hospital buildings. Despite all the criticism and problems that erupted due to shortages, North Carolinians could be proud of the sacrifice its citizens made to help the invalid and wounded soldiers.

Most people are aware of the term "sawbones" used to indicate a surgeon. Will George Thomas wrote his friend, a new physician, Thomas Fanning Wood his opinion about being too quick to amputate:

The dexterous use of the knife, let me remind you, is not the most important of its teachings; but whether an operation should be performed, and when and how and where is of equal importance, requiring much thought and decision. I am sure the knife has been used too often by military surgeons. I am aware of the obstacles which must be removed before a clear, satisfactory decision of mind can be reached in these important points. The confusion incident to battle, the urgent importunities of each wounded man to be attended to first, the gravity of the wounded, and the shrieks of the dying are well calculated to disturb that causes investigation and close though, that a solitary care in private matters affords; but the life and limb of each unfortunate soldier claims this at the hands of the surgeon. It is for him to determine whether it is not better to act deliberately and safely for one, and then save him, than to attempt to render relief to two, and endanger the lives of both. In these causes, preventing that composure of mind and feeling, which is necessary for clear and concise thought, may be attributed, perhaps, more than to incompetency, many of the operations, which might have been left, with better results to conservative surgery.

Decision of character is as necessary to the surgeon on the battlefield as to the General in command; for many lives hang upon the proper exercise of it by both of them. Nothing can supply its place. All the tenderness of a woman, all the care of the dearest friend, fail to answer in the stead of this all important and rarely exercise trait. It gives character to him who always exhibits it, and he only is successful whose practice shows the steady control of its influence.

I can not then, urge upon you too much the importance of a constant cultivation of decision of character [illegible] will see the facts before you, all that is favorable, and all that is unfavorable to an operation, and the proper way, time and place to perform it, and never for a moment allow yourself to hesitate after that. New facts, and before seen changes may arise to alter the soundest human conclusions, and give rise to another occasion for the exercise of decision, still the importance, the indispensable necessity for its exercise remains. Each unwavering decision enables you to exercise it with more care and satisfaction the next time, until it becomes your ordinary habit.

The study of chemistry, whether you follow it as a specialty or not is of the vastest importance, and I can not commend too highly your determination to learn it minutely and practically.[267]

Of interest to medical personnel is the following from the *Richmond Enquirer*:

NOVEL SURGICAL OPERATION—We were permitted to examine, a day or two since, the subject of quite a novel surgical operation performed, a few days after the battles around Richmond, by Dr. J. C. Clarke, Surgeon in charge of the 3d Alabama Hospital, in this city. J. W. Wacaster, a member of the First North Carolina Cavalry, received a severe gunshot wound through the ankle. By an ingenious and skillfully performed operation, the foot was removed, leaving the heel with half its bone, which was drawn around and applied to the end of the leg bones, previously sawed off. The heel has now become firmly attached in its new positions, thus making the limb almost as long as the opposite one and avoiding the necessity of either crutch or artificial leg. We are informed that this operation was first devised by an eminent Russian surgeon named Pizogoff.[268]

The entire medical corps of the Confederacy consisted of less than three thousand. The majority of the workload fell to the medical purveyor and hospital stewards to collect the medicine, compound the chemicals, and distribute it to the proper place albeit the camps, hospitals, or cities. Hospital stewards held the rank of sergeant.[269]

When a soldier died, the chief surgeon wrote a note to the auditor of the medical board in Richmond listing the cause of death with a list of the soldier's belongings.[270] The surgeon general's office in Raleigh proposed to establish a factory, April 27, 1864, for making artificial limbs. A notice read:

> Privates and non-commissioned 'men will be furnished gratuitously. Commissioned officers will be charged the actual cost. Disabled soldiers are requested to correspond, giving name, regiment, and rank, locality of amputation, and the precise measurement of the remaining member.[271]

SALT FACTORIES

Salt was the number one item desired, but lost to the civilians and the quartermaster general's top priority. "The government . . . . required that meat be salted more heavily than it would have been salted for use by civilians . . ." probably because it had to be stored and shipped. Without salt, residents could not preserve their meat for future use. Prewar, the South had purchased most of its salt supply from Europe and the West Indies.[272] In the United States, three states were manufacturing salt—New York, Arkansas, and an area in western Virginia. Another reference listed salt made in eastern Kentucky, southwest Alabama, northern Louisiana, Georgia, and southern Mississippi. The Kanawha Valley in western Virginia was overrun by Federal forces early in the war. The salt factory in northern Louisiana was destroyed by the enemy midwar.[273]

North Carolina businessmen saw salt production as lucrative commerce to pursue. Salt manufacturing was the second-largest source of income in the state next to the shipping industry. Very quickly, salt-evaporation factories spread along the coast. Approximately one hundred private companies were registered for the war period. The state entered the salt-making business in January 1862, building salt factories at Morehead City, Currituck Sound, and Wilmington.[274] Those working in Morehead City/New Bern area quit business or moved their factories farther South along the coastline when U.S. General Burnside took over the area in 1862. Two private companies operated for a short period in Smithville.[275] Milton Worth, brother of Jonathan, was the State Salt Commissioner. Each county was appointed a salt commissioner. One salt agent was assigned to each tax district. North Carolina had a contract with the salt mines in southwest Virginia at Saltville.[276] This particular factory remained open until it was shut down by the Federal Army in December of 1864.

Congress passed legislation regarding salt. In the May 1862 term in Caldwell County, "a majority of the magistrate being present, it is ordered by the court that Joseph Corpening be appointed as agent to proceed immediately to the salt works, in Virginia and ascertain upon what time a sufficient supply of salt, say 3500 bushels, can be procured for the individual use of the people of Caldwell County and that if they are satisfied, the said agent be authorized to make contract for the same . . . in no case, nor under any circumstance shall it be sold to any person not a citizen of this county nor for a greater sum than the actual cost including expenses of delivery" (State of North Carolina, Caldwell County, Court of Pleas and Quarter Sessions).[277] At the special term in Wilkes County, May 5, 1862, the court ordered E. M. Welborn to "procure from the state agent five hundred pounds of salt to be delivered to the railroad at Statesville, which said Welborn was to distribute among the citizens of Wilkes County in quantities of one to fifty pounds at cost. He was to have two and one half percent for the faithful discharge of his duties."[278] The two previous court orders were typical in each county. The commercial standard for salt was fifty-six pounds to a bushel. The agent was to dole out one-half a bushel to each head of the household.

Older men were hired by the state to help distribute salt and supplies to citizens. Oftentimes, this was the sheriff's duty. Mountain residents voiced complaints that they were often overlooked for government subsidies and felt like those living nearer the coast or piedmont got first choice. Their concerns were real. Wagon transports and the breakdown of the rail system compounded the problem of distribution.

Saltville in southwest Virginia was extremely busy serving mountain residents from three states. Citizens wrote of the traffic jams with wagons and horses everywhere.[279] Locals could make decent money hiring out their wagon teams; or if preferred, the person could take his wages in salt, then resell it at a profit. Mr. N. W. Woodfin, North Carolina's Salt Commissioner at Saltville, employed slaves and paid their owners twenty dollars a month. He said his worst problem was feeding the workers; so he set up a barter system—salt for grain, salt for meat, salt for cloth, etc. Woodfin also persuaded the farmers to stagger killing time for hogs.[280] An anxious citizen wrote the governor expressing his opinion:

> I will inform you of our suffering condishion in ashe [Ashe County] for the want of sault the salt that we are getting from Mr. Woodfin is comparative nothing to our wants We have a large surplus of hogs in ashe if we could get salt to save them & thare is thousands of bushels at Saltville Va & we cant get it & we the Citisons of ashe has com to the conclusion to go & take it by force if the oners of it wont let us have it for a fare price . . . they have nuf salt at the works at this time to salt all the hogs in the confederacy.[281]

Citizens complained in the newspapers about the distribution of salt, prompting local editors to vilify authorities:

> **THAT SALT**—can anyone tell us where the salt is that the authorities of this State have been promising the people for the last eighteen months? And where is the salt our County Court has been pretending to provide for the last 12 months? We have yet to see the first parcel. The people of Halifax county, Virginia, get salt at five cents per pound, while we, on this side of the line, pay fifty cents a pound and can't get it at that.[282]

In 1863, the North Carolina legislature passed a law that taxed salt above a certain production. It also passed restrictions on speculation and profiteering. No one was allowed to have profits above 75 percent of the actual cost.[283] It was also "ordered by the court that the salt purchase of county agents shall not be sold to anyone that is able to go to the salt lick for salt, and that the applicants for the salt shall bring a certificate from the district agent before the county agent be authorized to let them have salt. It was further ordered that the salt purchased by the county agent be intended for the wives of soldiers in the Confederacy or the poor & indigent persons of the county."[284] Just imagine the paperwork that the poor soldier's wife had to go through to obtain salt for her family.

"The North Carolina Works at Saltville produced about 100,000 bushels in its peak year . . ."[285] Milton Worth, salt commissioner, told congressmen that he had provided "twenty-one thousand bushels of salt to seventy-five counties, at an average cost to the counties of $3.50 a bushel" for the first year of the war.[286]

Salt Works near Morehead City
N.C. Division of Archives & History, Photographic Archives

The State Saltworks at Currituck and Morehead were closed early in 1862 when the Federals came ashore. The USN came ashore several times and destroyed the saltworks at Swansboro, Jacksonville, New Topsail Inlet, and the New River Inlet. The sailors would capture and burn schooners and other vessels as well. Some businessmen lost all their equipment during these raids. Others were able to move their evaporating pans to Masonboro Sound under Confederate control. The saltworks were reestablished at Smithville, Lockwood Folly, and Supply (a real name for the town). "The State Salt Works near Wilmington produced between 60,000 and 70,000 bushels during it's peak year."[287] Milton Worth reported that the State Saltworks in Wilmington made eighty-five thousand pounds daily and employed two hundred seventy men.[288] All saltworkers were exempt from military duty; however, most of the employees were slaves, free Negroes, and Quakers. The Quakers were exempt from military duty *if* they showed a statement of membership in the Society of Friends *or* if they had paid a fine of one hundred dollars. If unable to pay, these men were sent to the State Saltworks or to the hospital as nurses.[289] Commissioner Worth, plagued with desertion of saltworker employees, kept up a continuous rhetoric with Governor Vance over the situation.

To better understand the production of salt, some trivia is included:

A bushel of salt could be extracted from fifty to sixty gallons of water from local wells on the sound. This small enterprise was developed by the ordinary citizen. One fourth a pound of salt would be processed from one gallon of water.

An average salt pan held two hundred fifty gallons of sea water.

It takes two bushels (one hundred pounds) of salt to cure one thousand pounds of pork.

It takes one and a quarter bushels of salt to cure five hundred pounds of beef.

One hundred twenty cords of wood were needed to make eight hundred bushels salt.

One thousand pounds of sea water would boil down to twenty-seven pounds of salt.

One bushel of salt is equal to fifty pounds.

A "SACK" of salt is about three bushels or one hundred fifty pounds.
Salt sold in 1861 at four dollars a bushel. Mid-war it sold for twelve, at the end
it cost seventy-five dollars a bushel.[290]

Windmills pumped water from the sound along wooden troughs to the salt pans. One salt factory near the interior of Wilmington had its seawater shipped in barrels to the factory. Solar evaporation was attempted but found to take more time to make salt because it could only be worked on bright, sunny days. The government calculated that the salt ration would be one and a half pounds per soldier per month and one pound to each citizen.[291] The State Saltworks ran twenty-four hours per day, seven days a week, but had to be shut down when the yellow fever scourge hit Wilmington in 1862.

In 1862, the cost of an average bushel of salt was $3.50 to $4. State Salt agents advertised in local newspapers when salt was available for sale. The price fluctuated almost daily according to production and distribution.

Citizens tried to make their own salt. A lady near Wilmington made a few bushels for her family's use by boiling seawater. Her extra was distributed to needy soldiers' dependents. A private salt businessman, Thomas F. Wood, made salt on Masonboro Sound. Those far away from the coast attempted to extract salt from the dirt floor of their smokehouses. Southrons took the fresh-killed hams, salted them down to deter insects, then hung the hams up to smoke in a small log building.[*] A desperate mountain family dug up the dirt to extract the salt where they had urinated or tossed the contents of their chamber pots daily. North Carolinians would barter for salt. Rebecca Davis in June 1864 told her son, "I think I can swap my wool in Louisburg very easily . . . as to that salt . . . if we whip the yanks we can get salt, and if they whip us, we shall have nothing to salt . . ."[292]

Salt was used in the tanning industries, the third-neediest commodity. Salt was utilized in drying fish too.

Employees making salt along the coast were not free from danger even though they were within Confederate lines. S. S. Biddle Jr. wrote to his sister:

> The Federal steamers lying off the coast near Fort Caswell fired upon the men making salt. When the men are not boiling, they go fishing. The gunners apparently did not damage anything but sent the salt boilers on a stampede like Bull Run. They did not even wait to take their pots and kettles, but left everything, salt, tents, provisions, etc.[293]

USN Lieutenant William Cushing more than once landed his crew along the Topsail Sound for the purpose of destroying the multiple salt factories there. At first, he had no pilot, but he later captured three Negro pilots near the Wilmington area. After the capture, it was easier for him to enter the sounds undetected to land troops for raids. Captured prisoners enabled Cushing to locate other works to destroy.[294]

Two hundred men labored at the State Saltworks at Masonboro.[295] C.S. General William Whiting, commander at Wilmington, long suspected that some of these men collaborated with the enemy and were disloyal. General Whiting declared that the enemy's destruction and raids upon the saltworks were not worth the effort of making salt in that area. He demanded of Vance to move them or close the works altogether. Milton Worth and the general argued regularly over the saltworks. Worth didn't know whom to answer to—the military or Governor Vance. He chose to follow Vance's directives. Worth later resigned; and his brother, David Worth, took charge.

In the late fall of 1862, Whiting and Worth were at it again. Whiting ordered 150 men from the saltworks to be transferred to his command to work on fortifications at Fort Fisher.[296] With that many workers gone, the production dropped dramatically. The governor

---

[*]   To learn how to extract salt from dirt and fish barrels, see the appendix.

intervened in favor of the saltworkers, they were returned, and the manufacturing resumed. The U.S. Navy landed in April 1864 and set the factory on fire, doing great damage. Bombs blew up the steam machinery, but the evaporating pans were not harmed.[297] Two men, John Orrell and J. H. Puckett, led the enemy to the State Saltworks, where they destroyed everything and captured 160 men.* The saltworkers, who escaped to enemy ships, reported that the saltworks were poorly defended; and it would be easy for them to overrun the facilities. One of these escapees said he could pilot them into Masonboro Sound to find the saltworks, "provided we would take off the people employed there, as they would be conscripted into the rebel army if the works were destroyed."[298]

Whiting took no time to notify the War Department that his suspicions came true. He wanted the saltworks moved. General Whiting insisted that Governor Vance move the State Saltworks closer to Fort Fisher because of the frequent desertions. He warned the governor that the saltworkers tended to be disloyal, and some had turned to spying. Whiting felt like the Quakers should be in the army, not making salt.

The summer of 1864 saw letters written by state officials, General Whiting, and the central government crossing back and forth in regards to the saltworks. Whiting wrote to the War Secretary, Seddon, in Richmond about his problems with Governor Vance. Vance, too, had written the war secretary, proposing to keep the saltworks open with a strong guard. J. A. Seddon replied to Whiting, asking him if that would solve the solution. General Whiting answered:

> I will endeavor to avoid all conflict with State. The guard Governor Vance proposes will be welcome if composed of better material than his salt workers.

General Whiting continued his disagreement with the governor. He wrote in July 1864:

> I have at length positive information that at least two thirds of the Conscripts at the State Salt works, belong to the treasonable organization called "H.O.A." [Heroes of America] Their mode of communicating with the Enemy has been ascertained . . . . I recommend strongly that the whole force be turned over to the Conscript Camp for distribution in the Army and their places be supplied by free negro or slave labor. As I am still pursuing my investigations into this traitorous association and hope to be able to detect some in overt act, you will see the reason for making this letter personal and confidential.[299]

The governor informed David Worth, salt commissioner, of his correspondence with the war secretary and Whiting. He asked Worth to move the works nearer to Fort Fisher. Mr. Worth replied that it was impracticable because it would take two to three months and forty thousand dollars to move. Nothing changed except the addition of one company of soldiers sent to guard the saltworks in place of the two that the general had requested.

The quarrel between Vance and Whiting continued into the fall. In September, the governor wrote:

> . . . you infer that I did you injustice in expressing a want of confidence in your command of Wilmington, . . . I solicited the President to send you to Wilmington . . . . Only one thing has ever occurred to impair the . . . confidence which you inspire . . . . and that is a very general impression that you drank too much . . . . general, you have tried me sorely on more than one occasion. Citizens have been shot down wantonly in the streets by your patrols; my trains have been frequently seized; my boats seized; and the salt-works stopped . . . you have no idea of the complaints made to me.[300]

---

* Another reference named John Sears and John Wheeler as accomplices.

Vance went on to say that he believed Whiting was the man for the defense of the coast and that despite the hurtful rumors invoked upon himself, he still had confidence in the general.

The State Saltworks shut down in November 1864 due to constant enemy forays nearby. It was suggested that the business be moved to South Carolina or Lockwoods Folly in Brunswick County. The U.S. North Atlantic Blockade Squadron built up its number of warships soon afterwards and shelled Fort Fisher in December. In February of 1865, salt was selling at seventy-five dollars a bushel.

———————————————————————————————

Postal workers were in a dilemma when war broke out. As the Confederacy was establishing laws, the employees of the old government didn't know what would happen to their jobs. Postmaster James Corpening didn't wait to see the future. He wrote the U.S. postmaster:

> Post Office . . . . Copenhagen, Caldwell Co. May 31, 1861:
>
> Sir the post master general of the Confederate States having determined to assume the entire control of the post office and mail, within the jurisdiction of on the first of June, 1861, I hereby resign my commission as post master at this office [.] my account for the present time qts [quarters] to this date will be forwarded to the department in a few days and the balance due to the United States will be paid as heretofore to the contractor on route number 5232 and the recpt will be duly forwarded to your department. Respectfully
> To—William M Blair, Post Master General of US from James Corpening Postmaster

Afterwards, Corpening wrote to James Reagan, postmaster general of the newly established Confederacy, for instructions at Richmond. He was then able to post an answer:

> **Notice**: June 1, 1861 On and after the first day of June, 1861, US Postage stamps will not be taken in payment for postage on a letter. The postage which must be paid in cash [,] will be on each letter weighing one-half ounce or less, [and] is five cents or less for any distance less than five hundred miles and ten cents for any distance over five hundred miles in the Confederate States by order of Honl. James H. Regan, Post Master General of the Confederate States.
> Joseph Corpening, Post Master at Copenhagen, North Carolina[301]

Many post offices had been established in the railroad depot buildings. Postmaster General Reagan called for a convention with VIP railroad officials during the organization of the Confederate nation.[302] The delivery of mail varied in North Carolina. Newspapers would post the names of individuals who had failed to pick up their accumulating mail. Mail came once or twice a week by horse or stage in Caldwell County. Mail in the Lincolnton area was announced with the stagecoach driver blowing his brass horn. His route went from Charlotte to Lincolnton.[303] In his request for amnesty after the war, William E. Martin of Wilkes County said that he was a mail carrier from Hamptonville, thence by Oak Level to Ausburnville, Lovelace, and finally to Wilkesboro, which was a course of twenty-nine miles and back. The route was repeated once a week.[304] Cornelia Henry at Sulfur Springs received mail twice a week. When her husband, the postmaster, was away with the militia or on business, Cornelia filled his shoes. In Pitt County, "mail was often brought or carried by a boatman, as most planters lived by the river. Official letters were required to be forwarded from plantation to plantation, and so on to the destination, a severe penalty being prescribed for anyone who caused delay," noted author King.[305]

Cynthia Parker of Sparta temporarily carried the mail "abandoned by a cowardly courier . . ." after skirmishing with bushwhackers.[306]

"Only unmarried or widowed women would have been eligible," recorded Gregory Field, "to serve as postmasters because only single women could be legally bonded." The post office advertised in the *Daily Journal*, a Wilmington newspaper, near the close of the war for two female clerks.[307] Postmasters earned about two hundred dollars annually. Carriers made less than a few hundred dollars.[308]

Postmasters and mail carriers drew an exemption from military duty. A great number from the mountainous region applied for this position to avoid serving, and their letters for amnesty after the war gave the reasons for doing so. The majority claimed to be Union men. Giles Williams, postmaster at the Brooklin post office on his plantation twenty miles from the Raft Swamp Post Office, Robeson County, claimed to have been pressed into serving as the postmaster by the Confederate government. After the war, he sought a pardon from President Andrew Johnson claiming to be a Union man. It is not known if the pardon was granted; however, his son Dr. Warren Williams, postmaster of the Raft Swamp Post Office, was pardoned. Dr. Williams owned slaves and bought a substitute for a while to keep out of the army. But conscription officers came knocking at his door when he failed to pay the bounty to the substitute. Dr. Williams did receive his pardon and continued acting as postmaster until the end of 1866.*[309]

The first stamp of the Confederate States of America was the five-cent green stamp lithographed in Richmond. Second came a ten-cent red stamp. The third was a two-cent stamp for drop letters and newspapers. When no stamps were available to buy, persons signed their names on the upper-right-hand corner of the envelope. This practice was known as "franking."[310] The person was expected to pay the postmaster the price of the needed postage. Thousands of letters were hand carried by friends during wartime, especially if it contained money. There were complaints of mail carriers stealing and opening the mail. To add further confusion, the *Spirit of the Age* printed this notice:

> The Express Company cannot carry letters in the US except they be enclosed in a US stamped envelope, nor in the Confederate States except in a Confederate stamped envelope. Therefore, to send letters North by Express, first get the US stamped envelope, then have this stamped PAID by the post office here, and your letter will go to its destination, both by the post being collected in advance and the Express Company then taking the letter in its charge for delivery, relieving the post office department of all further trouble. [June 12, 1861]

The *Raleigh Register* carried an ad on January 22, 1862, from the post office department, which read:

> The first delivery of postage stamps by the contractors was made on the 15th of Oct. last, and since that date only 1,430,700 stamps have been received all of which have been issued to post offices near which large bodies of troops have been situated, with a view to their special accommodations.

Major G. W. F. Harper made his own stamps after waiting all spring and summer for the new issues. Sixty post offices in the South were given permission to issue their own

---

*   On an interesting note, Dr. Williams's account books reveal that the one-room post office held groceries and that he traded with the Lumbee Indians. He probably treated patients in there as well.

stamps. The town of Lenoir was chosen. Major Harper whittled a stamp pattern out of holly wood for the use of the post offices there.[311] Postmaster Willis F. Riddell invented his own adhesive stamp for use before he could get Confederate stamps.[312]

"Provisionals" or "locals" was a term used by the postmasters who contracted with local printers to prepare wooden-graved or lithographed substitutes for stamps. Some postmasters used a prepaid envelope. They would "prepare in advance envelopes with postage paid markings on them," noted Tony Crumbly.

The same company that was printing stamps was also printing money. President Davis sent an agent to England. There the De la Rue Company printed millions of stamps for the South. They sent electrotype plates back to the South via blockade-runners.[313]

Author Dietz recalled, "The Prisoners of War [POW] and the Flag of Truce covers [envelopes] represent the only officially recognized postal intercourse between the warring sections. Letters sent abroad were usually placed in charge of the captain of the blockade-runner, addressed, but not franked [stamped]. On arrival in a foreign port, the skipper would either deliver in person, or frank them with stamps of that country . . ."[314] It was July of 1865 before the U.S. Federal Post Office would reopen in the South.

This Northern newspaper told how to pass a letter through the lines:

Daily Republican Advocate—Batavia NY, July 26-1861

POSTAGE TO SECEDED STATES:
The Adams Express Company gives notice that they will forward letters to the Confederate States when the following directions are observed:

Enclose each letter in a U.S. GOVERNMENT ENVELOPE—an ordinary envelope with a stamp affixed WILL NOT ANSWER. The Company will forward AND DELIVER at any point where it has an office, or will mail as near as possible to the point of address, paying Confederate postage, for a fee of 25 cents.

The rate here given is for letters not exceeding 1/2 oz. being charged 3 cents by U.S. Government; and 25 cents by the Express Company.
H.B. Ferren, Agt.[315]

The *Record*, a Richmond newspaper, printed this article for those wishing to send letters North:

CORRESPONDENCE BY FLAG OF TRUCE:

Those desiring to communicate with prisoners or friends within the federal lines will do well to study the rigid requirements set forth below, which we copy . . . as issued by the federal authorities. In order to secure the transmission of letters across the lines, the following rules must be complied with:

1. No letters must exceed one page of a letter sheet, or relate to any other than purely domestic matters.
2. Every letter must be signed with the writer's name in full.
3. All letters must be sent with five cents postage enclosed, if to go to Richmond, and ten cents if beyond.
4. All letters must be enclosed to the commanding general of the department of Virginia, at Fortress Monroe. No letter sent to any other address will be forwarded.
5. All letters sent to Fortress Monroe without a strict compliance with these rules, except for prisoners of war, will be transmitted to the dead letter office.

The same identical rules will be applied by Gen. Winder to all letters sent from the South to Fortress Monroe for parties in the United States. Parties who wish to correspond, should cut out and preserve this notice, as failure to comply with it in one single particular, will consign their correspondence to oblivion. All letters to go North should be directed to "Maj. Gen. J. H. Winder, commanding Department of Henrico, Richmond, Virginia," and should be endorsed "Flag of truce."[316]

POW letter author's collection

SALISBURY PRISON

Salisbury Prison was first a cotton mill, a boy's academy, a meat-packing plant, then, lastly, converted into a prison. It was conveniently located beside the railroad tracks belonging to the North Carolina Railroad line. The cotton factory had been formerly owned by Maxwell Chambers. The state purchased the building from him to be turned into a prison when the war started. Originally, the prison was to be used for Confederate convicts, prisoners of war, and treasonable persons. In 1862, the exchange of prisoners helped to keep down the number of inmates. It wasn't until the fall of 1864 that the prison became overcrowded due to an order handed down from U.S. General Grant that forbade the exchange.

Salisbury was the base for the commissary and military depot for the Fifth District. A bustling town, two railroads converged, making the city more active than towns of the same size. A lady writing after the war said that the town did not want the prison. "No one was detailed to guard the prisoners and the townsfolk had to volunteer for this disagreeable duty" at times.[317] She was partially wrong, for young soldiers became guards. The Reverend Dr. Braxton Craven, president of Trinity College near High Point, in December the first year of the conflict trained his students for military duty. These students did guard duty around the state before becoming the prison guards at Salisbury. Sometimes these students didn't have ammunition, and for one night, the inmates were not guarded at all. In 1864, there were only fifteen hundred guards defending the prison of eight thousand inmates.[318]

David McRaven, a guard in the Senior Reserves, served at Salisbury. In a letter dated October 17, he told his wife, "There are 9 thousand yankies and three hundred Confederate prisoners here to guard . . . . we have to be on guard 24 hours together and some times an alarm is given and we have to get Out of our blankets and go and stand all night [.]"[319]

Early in the struggle, men thought that the duty of a prison guard was degrading; but later, this image changed, and men were eager for the job especially after conscription. This advertisement appeared in the newspaper:

NOTICE . . . 50 able bodied men to complete a company of 12 Months volunteers now in service to be placed as a guard at the State Prison in Salisbury and also along the line of the NC RR as a protection to the bridges. Apply to Thomas Webb, Hillsborough or address me at the Company's Shops Joseph W. Latta, Capt.[320]

Dr. J. W. Hall, in charge of the prison hospital, had assistance from Dr. Richard O. Curry, from Tennessee, who arrived in August 1864. He stated that there were only eight hundred prisoners at the beginning, which consisted of Confederate criminals, Yankee deserters, and political dissenters. Salisbury Prison held the most Union-loyal inmates of all Southern prisons. Members of the Heroes of America and the Union League, a secret antisecessionist society active in the state, were confined there.* It held men from Tennessee and Virginia as well. A Northern war correspondent sent to the prison said that there were five hundred inmates when he arrived. Of those, he related that one hundred fifty were Southern unionists, Yankee deserters, convicts, fifty Northern men, and twenty-three U.S. soldiers.[321]

In addition to the nine wells within the prison walls, prisoners could get water from a creek. A water patrol comprising ten to twenty inmates went out every day, guarded of course.[322] An inmate recalled after the war that "I had the good fortune to go out with the water squad to-day and succeeded in trading a finger ring for three sweet potatoes, which I ate raw. I also cut two brass buttons from my blouse for which I got the half of a sweet potato pie."[323]

"In the early part of the war, some prisoners were even paroled and allowed to work in town," according to author Brown.[324] Captured Federal soldiers near Fort Fisher found themselves on the way to Salisbury Prison. One wrote that they had "free range, on parole, of the garrison yard . . . were comfortably lodged; furnished with fuel 'ad libitum.' Our rations, though insufficient and of a very poor quality of bread and bacon mainly, were the same as those served out to their own men. There was no restraint upon purchasing outside, and our treatment throughout by all the officers of the garrison was, I feel bound in justice to say, entirely courteous and considerate."[325] This would be true before the prison became crowded. A. D. Richardson recalled that resident Luke Blackmer lent the inmates books from his library. Richardson said that while he was there, "in one instance only was the hard labor imposed." The remainder of the time was spent in boredom. Richardson related that once the prison overfilled in the fall of 1864, the shortage of food became so critical that some inmates went without rations for twenty-four to forty-eight hours.[326]

Members of the Fifth Massachusetts Volunteers were captured at New Orleans in February 1862 and ended up at Salisbury. Somehow, a woman's dress was smuggled in, and the prisoners put on a drama. The wearer "played his feminine part so well that Confederate officers drew their swords and rushed towards the performers demanding to know how that woman got there." When these prisoners were released, they traveled by rail to Tarboro, got in a scow, and went down the Tar River to Washington, which was under Federal control at the time.[327]

Union men were offered the oath to join the Confederacy, and many did, or they could remain neutral and work for the government. Several Irishmen "galvanized" and became Confederate soldiers. A few received pay from Confederate authorities to work as joiners, harness makers, gunsmiths, mechanics, tailors, cobblers, and blacksmiths. "One of the major needs of the hospital was lumber . . . but [U.S.] Kirk's raid of a few weeks earlier had virtually destroyed the saw mill." Some inmates found work making wooden bowls. Citizens exchanged food and tobacco for prison-made trinkets. Closer to the end of the war, Confederate authorities denied the privilege of exchanging trinkets for food.[328]

During the spring and summer of 1864, the prisoners were allowed visitors. "Well dressed women would come now and then, and from the guard's platform look down on

---

*   See chapter 11 for more on the HOA.

our suffering as if we were some kind of beasts," recalled one inmate. H. S. Chamberlain wrote that in Salisbury, where she lived during the war, alarms were constant and were raised by evil men in town who committed crimes and blamed them on the prisoners "so that by this means there would be no investigation."[329] This murder of a civilian could have been perpetrated by either a prisoner or townsman:

> We learn from the Salisbury Watchman that Mr. James Horah was killed in that town on the night of the 31st of July. His throat was cut from ear to ear while walking through the street about 12 o'clock at night. The murderer is unknown. The Mayor of Salisbury and the brothers of the deceased offer a reward of four thousand dollars for the detection of the perpetrators of this horrid crime.[330]

The people of Salisbury were suffering from the lack of provisions too, and that was blamed on the prison. They got up a petition and sent it to the Confederate Secretary of War, Seddon. It read:

Please remove one half of the prisoners because:
1.   The prison is too small and cramped. Conditions go against "comfort and health of the prisoners."
2.   There is a shortage of water and wood.
3.   There is also a shortage of food.[331]

The secretary did not comply with their request.

The town council of Salisbury passed a liquor curfew to help control disturbances. None was to be sold to soldiers after eight in the evening until seven in the morning. The law changed so that the merchants could not buy more than a barrel. Eventually, they could not purchase a gallon.

Prisoners on both sides found themselves exchanged until the spring of 1863, which kept the prison population down. When the influx of prisoners overcrowded the prison in October 1864, conditions changed for the worse. "Hospital conditions, like all other areas of prison needs, were adequate until the great avalanche of prisoners began to arrive . . . ," noted author Brown. Stench from the prison blew into town. Citizens feared smallpox, and the town council ordered all civilians to be vaccinated. Several residents refused. The doctors "prohibited members of the garrison from coming into town . . . . surgeons were instructed when practicable to vaccinate young children within the vicinity of the hospital in order to keep a sufficient supply of fresh vaccine on hand."[332]

Residents in both the county and prison lockups competed for the food supply early in the last year of the war. That January, the court appointed a person who collected food for indigent soldiers' families for Rowan County. This agent reported that he had been unsuccessful in finding enough food for the 750 needy families, including 1,063 children under the age of ten. "The court then authorized him to make efforts to purchase Confederate tithe corn and wheat for the relief of the poor." The yield for wheat and corn in 1864 proved to be much less than before. A "bread riot" occurred in the city.* Dr. Curry sent out special agents to purchase food for his prison patients. They had to pay the full price, which was greatly inflated. "In August, Curry agents were prohibited from such purchases because it worked a hardship on the Commissary Department." This was later rescinded.[333]

The "walking sick" lined up each morning for their medicine. A. D. Richardson—a Northern citizen, war correspondent, and prisoner at Salisbury—helped with recording the names of inmates; he also assisted in the prison hospital.[334] President Lincoln labeled medicine a contraband of war from the beginning. The only way for the Southern people to

---

*   See chapter 9 for more.

get medicine was through the blockade, capture of the enemy's supply, home manufacture (herbs), and a few pharmaceutical companies. This created a shortage of medicine felt by all. Other shortages included clothing. Dr. Currey ordered the inmates working in the hospital to remove all the clothes and shoes from the dead before burial due to an extreme shortage, which were reissued to the threadbare prisoners. The local aid society donated blankets and socks when available. The benevolent Mrs. Sarah Johnston had a son in Confederate service, but that did not stop her from bringing food and provisions to the prisoners. Dr. Curry wanted to place the hospital outside the walls, but was denied. Diseases most prevalent within the prison walls were pneumonia, diarrhea, typhoid, and hospital gangrene. Author Brown's research indicates that from October 1864 to February 1865, "it was owing more to the lack of shelter and of clothing than lack of food that Federal prisoners died here."[335]

Salisbury inmates playing town ball.
Courtesy of Winkflash.com

Prison guard McRaven wrote his wife: "The yankies are Dyeing pretty fast 7 or 8 in a night . . ."[336] The estimated number of deaths per day from October 1864 to February was twenty-seven. In all, nearly twelve thousand men died in the prison. Dr. Curry died of meningitis, probably contracted from a patient, one month before the war ended.

A Northern prisoner gave a compelling account of his incarceration:

> . . . the "dead wagon" made its daily tour of the grounds, halting at the "Dead House" to load the bodies lying there, and then passing out the south gate to the grave yard, or trenches, which are about 250 yards south west of the prison . . . . The dead are gathered up during the forenoon, brought to the "dead house" and piled up against the end like sacks of grain, counted by a sergeant who registers the number in a book kept for that purpose . . . . I went out with the water squad . . . through the kindness of the gray-beard guards . . . while they were unloading the dead, and hardened as we were to the sights of suffering and acts of inhumane treatment among the living, the scenes at the grave yard were such as made the blood almost run cold in our veins. There were twelve or fifteen corpse piled on the wagon, laied [sic] in like hogs, and entirely destitute of covering . . . . Two men stood on the wagon and each taking hold of a foot and a hand of a corpse, would give it a swing or two and then heave it head long into the trench . . . .[337]

When the prison was inspected in December 1864, the War Department deemed it an unfit place and said it should be moved to South Carolina. The lack of sufficient guards must have played heavily upon the decision also.[338] War Secretary Seddon ordered them to look at an area near Killian's Mill, halfway between Charlotte and Columbia, South Carolina. On February 17, 1865, Columbia fell; and the exchange of prisoners was once more revived. Confederate troops began to remove Federal prisoners to Wilmington and New Bern since those places were under United States control. Nearly all of the prisoners left by February of 1865, except many civilian dissenters. The greater invalid convicts were sent via trains to Richmond to be released; and the others walked or were sent to Greensboro, a distance of fifty miles, to catch the train to Wilmington. The released prisoners on their way to Greensboro were allowed to "straggle over the country . . . where many harassed the locals for food or alcohol."[339] When the prisoners arrived in Wilmington, a Union band played for them as the men broke down emotionally. A doctor was assigned to keep the freedmen from eating too much. Numerous local citizens brought food to the depot for the former inmates.

In June 1864, U.S. Colonel Kirk raided Morganton. With Federal forces that close, some prisoners chose to escape. Salisbury residents W. G. Crawford, Tandy Kiser, and Duncan McPherson were known to have aided escapees after the prison was established. Duncan McPherson once considered killing President Davis.[340] Five months later, a large prison break took place. The citizens' worst nightmare occurred, which involved the townspeople and Junior Reserves to quell the hostilities because most of the older soldiers had been recalled to the front. David Livingstone's son, Robert, was one of the men who died during the breakout attempt.[341] He took the assumed name of Rupert Vincent while an inmate. The next month, A. D. Richardson and Junius Browne, *New York Tribune* correspondents, escaped, fleeing to the mountains. They both had worked as hospital attendants. Federal officers planned an escape October 15, 1864, but one of their own told authorities. Another breakout schemed for the twentieth failed for the same reason. On October 20, all officers transferred to the prison in Danville, Virginia.[342]

As the number of inmates swelled again, Salisbury residents in January 1865 said that there were more than a three-to-one ratio. U.S. General George Stoneman tramped to Salisbury to destroy the vast amount of government warehouses there. They held more than usual because Vance had ordered the storehouses in Raleigh emptied and removed prior to the arrival of General Sherman. Stoneman destroyed the arsenal, distillery, foundry, government warehouses, and the Nitre and Mining Bureau. After the capture of Salisbury, the prison was used by the enemy to house Confederate captives.[343]

Dr. Charles Carroll Gray, transferred to Salisbury Prison from the prison in Columbia, South Carolina in June 1864, kept a diary while incarcerated:

> We are hard up for food; very little that is eatable, no money to buy with.
> I find that I am getting as thin as a race horse in the running season. Am called "Bones" (without the "Saw").
> June 6 Quite a sensation this morning when the Capts. drew lots to determine which two of them should be held as hostages for the two Confederates held as guerrillas by Fremont somewhere & threatened with death.

Upon hearing the rest of his comrades would be exchanged very soon, he added, "Nothing of the sort is capable of inciting us to any enthusiasm after our experience." He said he liked being in the open air, baseball playing was frequent, and everyone played cards; but there was not enough reading material. Once he was so hungry that when night came, he took a large dose of opium "to silence my clamorous stomach." He took doses at other times to help him sleep but maintained it was for chronic diarrhea and weakness. Gray said he wanted to walk around the grounds to enjoy the outside but was too weak.

He mentioned many men suffered with scurvy. Dr. Gray said officers got drunk frequently. Letters would arrive for prisoners almost daily.

More from his diary notation on June 22 revealed a plot by the citizen prisoners to escape. "They had sunk a shaft under the southwest house" nearest the outside palisade. The prisoners dug a tunnel about seventy-five feet long to the outside. "The work was progressing at the rate of about six feet in twenty-four hours," when someone ratted.

> June 23—Poor old Mrs. Johnston still comes to the gate frequently with something for the prisoners to eat. Being undoubtedly loyal to the S.C. [Southern Confederacy] and having a son at its service, she is of course above suspicion.
>
> June 28—Major Godwin [prison commander] forbid the playing of Yankee Doodle and Star Spangled Banner on July 4th.
>
> June 29—Another attempted prison break by the civilian prisoners occurred. They took a slab [stone] from the inner wall and ran for the palisade during a rain storm. Lightning flashed showing their deeds and they were again captured.[344]

Dr. Gray said the Confederate Medical Department was useless. Hospital supplies were zero. "No medicine furnished worth mentioning." Gray was discharged for exchange July 24, 1864. Another inmate, Lieutenant John Lafler with the Eighty-fifth New York, recorded his experiences. He estimated the town to be about two thousand inhabitants. "It had suffered badly from the war . . . . the townspeople were openly friendly to the Union people."[345]

The garrison population was constantly being enlarged by recruits, black and white, from the local area. Many of the blacks were escaped slaves who wanted to join Federal forces. The writer said thirty men a day came to the prison.

Most Union prisoners were permitted to keep their personal belongings, which they could use to trade for food or services. Lieutenant John Lafler escaped from different prisons in Georgia and South Carolina in 1864, but he was usually captured. He, along with other prisoners, was taken by train to Charlotte in February of 1865. The men bribed a guard with a five-dollar greenback and soon escaped, planning to go to New Bern, which was under Federal control. Outside of Rockingham, they found a canoe and crossed the Pulec [sic] Pacolet River (?). It took the escapees three weeks to get from Charlotte to New Bern.[346]

————————————

Charles Hover was captured at Cedar Creek and sent to Salisbury Prison. He said that in December, the inmates decided to overrun the guards, but the rout ended in failure. Sixty men were wounded and twenty killed in the fracas. The men spent most of their time talking about getting exchanged. One of the guards told him it was the fault of (General) Grant for not exchanging prisoners.

The inmates killed rats and mice for food. Once, a pet dog disappeared and fed four men. The excess meat was sold. Hover reported many inmates dying every day, and the numbers increased as the war dragged along. Only the ones with the strongest will to survive could tolerate the horrendous conditions. Prisoners were offered the chance to join the Southern Army. Many chose this route in escape of prison life. Some would bribe the guards for a chance to run away. When the inmates learned that Sherman's army was marching toward the state, their hopes revived. Around February to March, told they were to be exchanged, the Northern men couldn't believe it. They had been disappointed frequently with those tales. As the date for freedom came nearer, the prisoners who could would walk along the railroad tracks in a northwardly direction. When a train came along, a few were able to catch a ride. The goal was to get to Goldsboro where they would be exchanged. It took four days to make the trip. Around five thousand inmates, both black and white, left Salisbury Prison on their way to Greensboro under guard.[347] The group rested a spell and were fed. The next day, they arrived at Stony Point near Wilmington[348]

S. S. Boggs, with the Twenty-first Illinois Infantry, was in several Southern prisons, but lastly in Florence, South Carolina. He wrote that in February 1865, those who were healthy enough started from the Florence prison for Goldsboro. Boggs, being a member of the hospital crew, stayed with the sickest placed under a shed. The guards asked the hospital workers that if they would take an oath not to go beyond the stockade, they would remove the guards. A train took these invalid men on the trip to Wilmington. Several died along the way. Just outside the city, the train, with its flag of truce flying, ran into Union pickets. The patients were unloaded, camps set up, and fires started for boiling coffee. The surgeons cautioned the skeleton-like men to eat light meals slowly. The next morning, those who could took a bar of soap to the nearby creek to bathe. A few of the former prison hospital workers had the energy to walk the mile into town. At the sight of "Old Glory," Boggs said, "we are in God's country at last."[349]

Another Union soldier and prisoner there, William Crossley, left his remembrances:

> March 13, 1862: arrived at Salisbury Prison.
> April 20th: They let the boys out of the factory into the large yard, one floor a day now, & some of them they are having to bury alive, up to their chins. Doubtless many of you have seen or heard of "deadheads," but here was the other kind, a droll well as somber spectacle. A dozen or more live and human heads, sticking up just above the ground; just heads and nothing more. A queer looking crop, and how it would have pleased some of the ladies of the Confederacy to have gotten into that lot with a lawn mower or a tennis racquet. So much for scurvy.
> May 23rd: left the prison and traveled through Raleigh, Goldsboro, Tarboro. Got on a boat to Washington City.[350]

After Salisbury Prison was emptied of inmates, it became a storage facility for Southern supplies. Richmond and Columbus, South Carolina, had sent their military stock there to prevent its falling into the enemy's hands. When U.S. General Stoneman entered the city, they skirmished with a force composed of armed citizens, the Home Guard, the Reserves, detailed factory workers, and some three hundred former Union prisoners.[351]

FINANCES

Around 80 percent of the Southern cotton supply was sent to Great Britain in the ten years before the war. In 1860, England bought almost two million dollars' worth of cotton bales from the South.[352] "The operation of market forces usually produces a drastic reordering of economic life," noted author Ralph Andreano. "Even within a controlled situation, war-time conditions and responses can restructure an entire economy in a relatively short time period." The quick demand for uniforms and munitions caused a spur of activity never before seen in the United States or the Confederate States. There were very few factories in the South to make these supplies. Many commodities were imported or shipped from the North prewar.[353] The South was ready to explode with industry. Author Thomas Cochran found, "Immigration to a nation essentially short on labor was unquestionably a stimulant to economic growth."[354] Only 15 percent of the immigrants, mostly Irish and Germans, lived in the South.

In the early 1800s, the U.S. exports were dominated by cotton as much as 60 percent. When the South seceded, they at first withheld cotton from England. At the time, England had a stockpile of bales. After two years, the British felt the pinch and began laying off its workers, shutting down the smaller mills. Called the "cotton famine" in England, 40 percent of their workers lost their jobs.[355] England furnished the South so much of its war materials that they made a better profit in wartimes than when at peace. The Confederacy passed state and national laws to restrict the exportation of cotton. "They urged planters to withhold their crops from the market, limit the acreage, and . . . burn quantities as a patriotic duty . . ."[356]

North Carolina was already in debt before the war started. "Two weeks after Lincoln was elected the state owed over ten million dollars, most of which was for railroad bonds and investments in other internal improvements. There were three ways of raising money for the state— by printing notes, by taxation, or by borrowing. On May 11, the legislature appropriated five million dollars to be used during the next two years. The treasurer had to raise this by issuing treasury notes or borrowing money from the banks in the state in return for six per cent bonds on which interest would be paid annually. In case the banks refused to lend money to the state, the treasurer could issue notes up to the five million dollar maximum; if the banks were willing to make loans on the specified terms, the treasurer was to alternate issues of notes and loans from the banks. The banks had suspended specie payments in November, 1860, and the law promised that no bank which loaned money to the state would be required to resume specie payments until the state paid back what it borrowed under the terms of this basic defense act."[357] "The Convention had postponed the issuing of treasury notes authorized by the General Assembly until March 1, 1862. Meanwhile, it had permitted the treasurer to borrow three million dollars from the banks, less the amount already loaned under the act passed by the assembly in Extra Session," wrote Boykin.[358] North Carolina had state banks in Wilmington, Elizabeth City, Charlotte, Raleigh, and Tarboro. They would borrow from other banks as well.

After the state seceded, Congress was busy making and adjusting new laws. They voted to increase the taxes on land, then to tax slaves. "It subjected all free males between the ages of twenty-one and forty-five . . . to a capitation tax equal to the tax on land worth three hundred dollars and declared that both lands and slaves should be taxed according to their value . . . . the value of the slaves had to be determined by the legislature on the basis of age, sex, and other personal characteristics." A poll tax on each slave earned $1.20 for the government's coffers. In midwar, the state placed another tax on the owners of 5 percent each time a slave was traded.[359] A special tax of five cents on every one hundred dollars of valuation was levied for the support of the wives and children of soldiers of the war.[360]

Jonathan Worth, chairman of the finance committee, wanted to tax livestock and other items. The western representatives of the state strongly objected, saying they would rather issue bonds to pay the state's war costs than raise taxes. Worth preferred treasury notes. Again, the committees disagreed. In September 1861, the legislature authorized the state to print a million dollars' worth of notes.[361]

The government's finances at the being of the war came from money snatched from Federal customs house located in the South with a pledge of a five-hundred-thousand-dollar loan from Alabama. The central Confederate government then decided to increase their funds by offering "loans" for sale or bonds. In early February, the first bonds totaling fifteen million dollars went on sale. "On March 16, the Secretary of the Treasury Christopher G. Memminger announced that the first $5 million portion of the loan would be sold on April 17. That news was enthusiastically received by the public, and the loan was heavily oversubscribed within nine days. The balance was placed with equal ease during the next several months. While the loan provided the government with short-term operating capital, it also had the unintended consequence of draining a great deal of the individually held currency out of the hands of the banks to pay for the bonds."[362]

People began to hoard their gold and silver coins with the war only a few months old. Persons did not trust the paper money and bonds being offered, which prompted newspaper editors to make comments:

MONIES OF METAL AND PROMISES OF PAPER from the *Charlotte Bulletin*:
    The gradually increasing differences in the marketable value of gold and silver, compared with paper monies of every description, throughout the South and West may be explained with out reference to exertion upon the part of any one—"to force a peace or to depreciate the value of Confederate

notes"—according to an idea suggested by [*illegible*] In consequence of the complete suspension of coinage, at all Southern mints, with simultaneous interruption of foreign commerce, gold and silver have been horded [sic] by banks and private individuals. Such valuables daily diminish among us, by smuggling to the North; because certain articles of urgent necessity, expensive drugs, for instance, can only be obtained by means of gold. Coin is demanded in the West for purchases of meat for Commissaries' stores, as well as for arms and ammunition in Europe. On the contrary, the uses of paper money are limited in extent by our own borders; while the amount in state or Confederate notes and bonds has largely increased, by imperative necessity, to carry on the war. There is plenty of paper money everywhere among us, with an obviously diminished supply of gold and silver coins. Larger sums in paper money must consequently be paid for in gold and silver by a common law of trade, as we are entirely cut off from foreign coins, in exchange for produce. During a period of 15 years, the product of gold from Southern mines approached the sum of $18,000,000 . . . .

By simplification and management in the details of expense, a charge of 5% upon the value of deposits of bullion, would met the cost of fabrication into coins, without any other appropriations by the government.[363]

"The money spent by the Confederate government to purchase war supplies came largely from the printing press [paper money]; tax collections and bond sales raised relatively small amounts. As the ratio of money to goods available increased, prices rose," creating inflation, the steepest rise since the eighteenth century.[364] For the remaining months in the first year, state officials authorized additional treasury notes and bonds and the borrowing from banks. Six individual men loaned the state money for war purposes.[365]

"Next to bonds and treasury notes, the state's largest source of income during the war period was a series of bank loans that began in May, 1861, and continued through February, 1863," exclaimed author Richard Zuber.[366] "The sources from which the largest amounts of revenue were derived under the tax laws of 1862-63 were slaves, land, solvent debts due, and liquor dealers; these were followed in order by taxes on dividends and profits from manufacturing companies, brandy, money on hand, and town property." When the coast was overtaken by the Federals, tax collectors faced trouble with collections. "Some slaveowners were subjected to double taxes on their slaves when they moved from eastern counties to avoid losing their slaves to the enemy." Congress passed a resolution that sheriffs could only collect the tax in the county where the owners "maintained a legal residence."[367]

By 1862, the central Confederate government owed North Carolina about six million dollars from a contract it had made with the governor to furnish uniforms, horses, and supplies for the Confederacy. Jonathan Worth, as state treasurer, tried to collect the debt. By mid-1863, Richmond had repaid the state four million dollars. The central government continued to purchase clothing from North Carolina. For two months beginning in 1864, "the state supplied over seven hundred thousand dollars worth of clothing to its troops . . ." When Worth tired to collect the rest of the debt, "the Quartermaster General decided that he would reduce the amount of North Carolina's claim by one-third."[368] Worth vehemently opposed this measure but had no power to change it.

"For thirty-one months starting in October of 1861 . . . the general price index of the Confederacy rose . . . ten per cent a month." Some businesses refused to sell their produce "for currency alone" in early 1862. This became the order of most businesses in 1863.[369] In December 1861, one dollar in gold equaled $1.20 in Confederate treasury notes. By midwar, the price sky-rocketed to $9.70. Another reference proved that $1 in gold equaled $1.25.

By March 1865, the same gold coin brought $60-$70. A captured Union soldier passing through North Carolina on his route to Libby Prison in Richmond said:

> On my way here, in North Carolina, I bought another poor thin rag of a blanket, and paid $20 for it; that was at Weldon. Cigars were 50 cents apiece.. and whiskey $2 a drink. Am glad I use neither. Confed. Money was worth $5 to $10 for $1 of Uncle Sam's money.[370]

"Both state and Confederate currency depreciated at about the same rate until late in 1862, when the state money began to be considered more valuable; the highest premium for which it could be sold, in terms of Confederate money, came early in 1864, when the premium reached 150%," stated Zuber.[371] "On February 17, 1864, the Confederate Congress enacted a currency reform. All existing notes except small notes were to be exchanged for currency at the ratio of three for two by April 1, 1864," wrote Eugene Lerner, another author.[372] The following is the official form letter sent to banks:

TREASURY DEPARTMENT, C.S.A., RICHMOND, MARCH 14ᵀᴴ, 1864

The President and Directors of
the Bank of _____

GENTLEMEN:

Under the recent act of Congress to reduce the currency, it is provided that if any Bank of Deposit shall give its Depositors the 4 per cent Bonds authorized by the Act in exchange for their deposits, and specify the same on the Bonds by some distinctive mark or token to be agreed upon with the Secretary of the Treasury, then the said Depositors shall be entitled to receive the amount of said Bonds in Treasury Notes, bearing no interest and outstanding at the passage of the act, provided the said Bonds are presented before the privilege of funding the said notes at par shall cease.

By the first section of the act the privilege of funding will cease on the 1st of April, 1864, east of the Mississippi, and on the 1st of July, west of the Mississippi. It is obviously impracticable to furnish the Bonds before the 1st of April, and therefore, to give any effect to the provision of the Act; the certificates issued by the Depositaries must be substituted for the Bonds. The Bonds being required by the Act to be registered, the certificates must be conformed thereto and must be assigned in the Form usually required for Registered Bonds. By writing the words "for Deposits" over the signature of the officer of the Bank, who shall assign the certificate, a sufficient token can be established, and I propose that course to the Banks.

There is another matter in which I respectfully ask your concurrence. It certainly will be a great object gained to adjust prices and business operations as speedily as possibly to the new currency, which will be issued after the 1st of April. The Banks have the power to promote this object most effectually by accepting deposits in the old currency payable in the new. If for every three dollars so deposited, the Banks will give credit on their books for two dollars payable in new issues, the old currency would be rated accordingly in all transactions, and prices everywhere would have relation to the new currency. It would also follow that so much of the business of the country as can be transacted by checks on Banks would be carried on as heretofore without actual delivery of money, and so much time would be gained for the preparation of the new issues. It is true that the Banks will thus encounter the risk of not being supplied with new notes, in as much as it is obvious that the means of supply are not adequate to the pressure which will suddenly be thrown upon the Treasury. This pressure will be relieved by the immediate issue of certificates and five hundred dollar notes, and by the further issue of all denominations as speedily as possible.

I respectfully submit the matter for your consideration, and request that your Bank will at its earliest convenience issue an advertisement to the effect, that it will accept deposits of all currency, except one hundred dollar notes, payable in the new issues at the rate of two dollars of new for three of old.

Very respectfully, your o'bt servant, *Secretary of Treasury.*[373]

Confederate Congress "authorized a new issue of notes . . . to be printed in unlimited quantities . . . one billion dollars was eventually printed. All earlier notes were to be retired after being funded into bonds. Certain dates were set for certain value notes. Unbonded notes were to be taxed at 33% upon exchange . . ."[374]

Mentioned briefly, soon, North Carolina's notes were worth more than Confederate notes. "Like all people who live through prolonged and rapid price rises, southerners came to realize that the only way to avoid the tax on holding money was to reduce their cash holdings."[375] Citizens scrambled to spend their money before it depreciated, which drove prices up. Soldiers writing home to their wives expressed an urgency to exchange their currency before the date of expiration occurred and to get the help of a relative or neighbor if they didn't know how to do it. A. W. Bell sent this letter to his wife:

> Camp Dog River 6 miles south west of Mobile Ala   Feby 25th 1864
> My Dear Wife
> I would send you 8 or ten hundred dollars but the old issue has to be funded by first April or it looses 33 ¼ cents in the [?] so I will post pone drawing until I can get the new issue which will be in April I reckon . . .[376]

Author's Collection

As both Confederate notes and state notes continued to depreciate, everyone began to barter. Some businesses chose to pay their workers part money and part produce or goods. This happened to the employees at the Arsenal in Fayetteville and to another woman working as a clerk for a captain. Newspapers constantly advertised businesses that traded goods for their products. Many women took jobs away from home because it was considered patriotic. "The wages of the unskilled workers in the South . . . rose more than those of skilled workers already in the labor force," stated one article.[377]

Because less cotton was grown during the war, planters didn't need all their slaves to take care of the crop; therefore, they "hired out" these men and sometimes women to supplement their falling income. Slaves were very well paid during the conflict, with most of their wages returned to the planter. Another author has suggested, "There was a shortage in agricultural capital, a reduced area under cultivation, diminished agricultural production, depreciated land value, stifled industry, demoralized commerce, totally inadequate banking and currency facilities with a correspondingly high rate of interest."[378]

Businesses grew quickly if it was the type that catered to supplying the military. "On Thursday . . . our town [Wilmington] was full to overflowing with the merchants and speculators, Jews and Gentiles, men from East and West, North and South, who came to attend the advertised auction sale of goods."[379] "Cargoes landed in the Confederate States were usually paid for with Confederate currency. The blockaders then changed this into gold at an enormous discount, thereby producing a perceptible depreciation in the status of money."[380] Civilians bringing in goods to sell had to get a pass. "When applying for a passport, they have to produce somebody who knows them, as a voucher, a thing not always easy to do."[381]

It wasn't long before businessmen refused to take Confederate bills. They wanted gold instead, or they would take the old issue for greatly reduced exchange. Middle—and lower-income persons could not trade like this. To add fuel to the fire, bills from one state would not pass in another except at a discounted rate. In a December 1862 letter, Wyatt G. Jordan, overseer to Jonathan Worth, notified him of those problems:

> . . . I cannot engage any pork without paying gold [,] $8 per hundred in gold is all the way I can get it(.) I engaged 5 or 6 hun'ds at $20 before I rote you for myself but cannot get any more (.) Confederate money will not pass at all here (.) Men are offering 35 to 90$ in confederate money for pork but cannot get it nor could not for $50 in confederate money. Pleas send salt soon as we ought to kill the hogs soon (.) Send it to Graham (.) We will take a load of flour and get it but I do not know whether to take condefer. Money.[382]

Sisters wrote to each other March 1, 1864, that "everything high the confederate money that has been plentiful has almost played out here."[383]

Agents working in the capacity of impressment officers were hated as much as speculators. The public cried foul to high prices, writing their congressmen and the Confederate government. In response, officials enacted a price control, which was constantly changed. It was difficult for the businessman to keep abreast of the fluctuating prices.* "The controls the South imposed were ad hoc measures designed to placate an outraged citizenry," states author Andreano.[384]

Counterfeiting flourished during the war. A business in Philadelphia advertised the sale of counterfeit Confederate notes. This is why the color and design of the notes needed to be changed frequently. Author David Norris has stated, "There were so many new kinds of Confederate currency circulating in North Carolina that neither the public, nor apparently the counterfeiters, could keep up with them." A batch of fake North Carolina three-dollar bills showed up, even though the state had no three-dollar bills in use at the time. As early

---

*   See the appendix for examples.

as December 1861, the *Richmond Daily Dispatch* reported the appearance of a counterfeit ten-dollar note drawn on the Bank of the Cape Fear. The bills turned up in Charleston the end of the first year of war. Some fifty-cent shinplasters were counterfeit. The *Greensborough Patriot* posted this notice January 22, 1863:

> We received by a late mail from the North West part of this State, two bills, purporting to be three dollar Treasury Notes of this State, which are the most glaring counterfeit we have ever seen. They are wretchedly printed on bluish bad paper . . .

"Counterfeiters didn't . . . need presses or engraved plates . . ." Norris commentated that "some counterfeiters did good quality work; the *Weekly Register* of Raleigh noted in 1862 of a new counterfeit, 'the paper . . . . is whiter, stiffer, and better than the original.'"[385] Another business from the North advertised the sale of one hundred fake twenty-dollar bills for fifty cents. An engraver, Samuel Upham from Philadelphia, printed bogus notes; but in the margin, he marked them as facsimiles along with his address. It is believed that Upham printed about fifteen million counterfeit notes. The Confederacy made it a capital offense to counterfeit, punishable by death.[386] The government put out a contract on Upham for ten thousand dollars. A Negro man named Andrew, slave of William White, was charged with passing a counterfeit silver dollar on Isaac Jacobs according to newspapers.[387]

People hoarded their coins, leaving fewer in circulation, which led to the printing of fractional currency. A Northern magazine commented on the lack of coins:

> The system of shinplasters is becoming very general in the seceded States, owing to the scarcity of money. Gov. Ellis, of North Carolina, declared in a recent official message that gold and silver were not to be had in that State.
>
> Farmers are obliged to take these worthless shinplasters in exchange for their produce. Secession, however, is so excellent a remedy for them, for all their past suffering under the Federal government, that they feel willing to part with their corn, beef, and bacon, for anything that will promote secession, and the peculiar blessings that follow in its train.[388]

It was difficult for the mints to produce more coins. Author W. Buck Yearns said, "In 1863 Congress tried to stem inflation by forced funding. On March 23 it ordered a gradual reduction of the interest rate of bonds into which notes could be funded; after a certain date they would be acceptable only for government dues. In the same act, however, Congress authorized Memminger to issue fifty million notes a month. Meanwhile the rapid inflation made bonds an increasingly poor investment."[389]

Some businessmen did all they could to extract money from individuals during the conflict. Soldier James Beavers stationed at Camp Alamance in Burlington wrote his brother in July, the first year of the war, "We caint get money changed up here without giving fifteen or twenty per cent . . . if you can come bring me some one dollar bills or some silver or both."[390] "Gold is quoted by the Richmond Examiner at twenty-two hundred per cent premium and silver at nineteen hundred. One hundred dollars in gold will buy twenty-two hundred dollars of Confederate seven per cent Bonds. Bakers have increased the amount of bread from fifty cents to one dollar and at the same time decreased in bulk and weight to about one-half the former size. If the price of flour went up in Richmond, then it increased everywhere else. True of all commodities and money."[391]

Prices of gold for the Confederacy money compiled by B.F. Brady, Exchange Broker and Banker, Wilmington, 1865:

Date:	Year	%	
July 15-Nov. 15	1861	10	
Nov. 15-Dec. 31	1861	20	
Jan. 1-Feb. 15	1862	25	
Feb. 15-Apr. 15	1862	60	
Apr. 15-June 1	1862	80	
June 1-Aug. 1	1862	2.00	for one
Aug. 1-Oct. 15	1862	2.50	" "
Oct. 15—Dec. 31	1862	3.00	" "
Jan. 1-Mar. 1	1863	3.00	" "
Mar. 1—June 1	1863	5.00	" "
June 1-July 1	1863	7.00	" "
July1-Aug.1	1863	15.00	" "
Aug. 1-Sept. 1	1863	14.00	" "
Sept. 1-Nov. 15	1863	15.00	" "
Nov. 15-Dec. 31	1863	20.00	" "
Jan. 1-Mar. 1	1864	21.00	" "
Mar. 1-Sept. 15	1864	20.00	" "
Sept. 15-Dec. 15	1864	26.00	" "
Dec.15-Dec. 31	1864	50.00	" "
Jan. 1	1865	60.00	" "
Jan. 15	1865	65.00	" "
Feb. 1	1865	50.00	" "
Feb. 15	1865	45.00	" "
Mar. 1	1865	60.00	" "
Mar. 15	1865	60.00	" "
Apr. 1	1865	70.00	" "
Apr. 15	1865	100.00	" " [392]

According to scholar Neely, "The paper money with which the Richmond government funded the war in large part was not required by law to be taken in payment for debts."[393] A sum of $37,702,109 was spent for military purposes during the four years of the war. The sum does not include amounts spent by separate counties for the relief of the widows and children of soldiers and for the distress among the old, infirm, and civil dependents. Neither do they include the very large amounts arising from blockade business carried on by means of blockade steamers.[394]

The Confederacy shut down all navigation beacons on the coast in the spring of 1861. Fort Macon soldiers cut down trees and blew up the Bodie Lighthouse to get a clean sweep of the surrounding area just before the enemy arrived.[395] Confederate authorities wanted the upper lighthouses destroyed to keep the enemy from using them. Lens from both Cape Lookout and Bogue Banks turned up in Raleigh found by the occupying enemy at war's end. The Cape Hatteras Lighthouse Fresnel lens had been dismantled for safekeeping. It remained dark for one year. Federal authorities desperately wanted the Hatteras Lighthouse lens replaced, so they threatened the local people. "I propose holding the authorities responsible for the return of the lens before I promise protection to the inhabitants . . . . I shall, if possible, ascertain the guilty parties and take all the property I can find . . . ," wrote Union officer L. M. Goldsborough. These people could not help Goldsborough, for the Hatteras lens had already been removed and taken to Tarboro, thence to a plantation and hidden in Granville County.* The Union commanders had another installed in 1862.[396]

In the end of 1864, two attempts were struck to destroy other state lighthouses, "partially in retaliation against the traitorous keepers who were working for the Union." A party of Southern sympathizers sailed the Core Sound in April 1864 to the Cape Lookout Lighthouse for the purpose of destroying it. Emeline Pigott, a local girl, took part in the clandestine activity. Attempts to blow up the lighthouse failed, but it did damage it slightly.[397] Loyal men took the lens from the Ocracoke Lighthouse, but by 1864, the Federals had the light established again. The lighthouse beamed the way into Ocracoke Inlet, which led to Albemarle Sound, New Bern, Edenton, and Elizabeth City.

Lighthouse boats were stationed along the sounds and river inlets to guide ships at night. The Frying Pan lighthouse was destroyed by fire. Confederate forces would fool the U.S. blockade squadron by hanging false light signals near Bald Head. Both the Gray and Blue used false signal lights to engage the enemy. Both sides sunk ships to block river routes to make navigation harder. It was the duty of the keeper to clean the lens every day. While under Southern control, the keeper had difficulty procuring oil for it.

Starting with practically nothing in the way of equipment to fight a war, the Confederacy quickly started up business with Great Britain. An import/export company, John Fraser & Company, owned five ships, which regularly ran between Liverpool, England, and Charleston, South Carolina. Other well-known importer/exporters included the firm of Trenholm brothers in New York and the Fraser, Trenholm & Company in Liverpool. Once the hostilities began, George Trenholm closed his New York office and reopened it in Nassau and Bermuda. These businesses owned several fleets of blockade-runners. Other smaller firms would own one or two ships.

Confederate officials sent one-half million dollars to Fraser, Trenholm & Company early in the war to set up operations for trade in Liverpool. The firm was to "accept deposits of specie sent overseas by the government, handle the purchasing agents' letters of credit abroad, arrange the shipping of purchased supplies, and to act as an overall clearing agent for the shipment and disbursement of cotton in Europe . . . for their services, John Fraser was permitted to charge a 1.5 percent commission on orders it handled for the government . . . . the Trenholm firm earned fees for transporting government cargoes on their ships and they were free to continue transacting business for their own account."[399]

Punch Magazine
Look, here boys, I don't care twopence for your noise, but if you throw stones at my window, I must thrash you both.

JOHN BULL'S NEUTRALITY.

---

* It was hidden on the plantation of Dr. David Tayloe and not found until 2002.[398]

Though Queen Victoria chose to stay out of the fight, she, on May 15, 1861, issued the Queen's Proclamation of Neutrality act.[400] This law did not stand as merchants continued to do business with the South.

Blockade-runners carried all types of goods, but the first ship to carry mostly military equipment was the *Bermuda*. Captain William G. Crenshaw, a Virginian and owner of woolen mills, saw the profits to be made in blockade-running; he started an import/export business. He established a company with Alexander Collie in London. An "arrangement between the partners and the Confederate government was that the government would pay three-fourths the costs of building new transport ships, with Collie and Crenshaw paying the remainder. Half the cargo space aboard the new ships was to be allocated to the War Department, one-fourth to the Navy Department, with Collie and Crenshaw having the remaining fourth for their personal use."[401]

The Confederate government and some states sent different buying agents to England to purchase military supplies, causing stiff competition especially because the U.S. had done the same. After floundering around for months, Congress appointed Colin J. McRae as head agent. He did a tremendous job expediting the orders and saving the government money. McRae felt that the import/export business should be under the full control of the government. Furthermore, he said the government should buy up all the cotton and tobacco to control prices. It wasn't until early in 1864 that the central government took his advice. A law was passed giving Congress the authority to stop shipment of cotton and luxury items on private ships unless they had prior approval. One-half of all cargo either imported or exported would be filled with government materials. The Confederate Ordinance Department used their own ships, the *R. E. Lee*, *Eugenie Merrimac*, and the *Columbia* to transport guns and cannons.[402]

After all this, the government decided to buy more not-for-profit vessels. It ordered fourteen steamships to be made in July 1864, but they could not be built quickly enough before the war ended. More than one hundred blockade-runners were built in Britain from 1862 to 1864.[403]

The Bahamas "afforded neutral waters to within fifty miles of the American coast," making it the ideal place to load and unload its cargo. British blockade-runners left England flying the British flag with papers designating a neutral port to unload. When a ship entered or tried to leave a blockaded port, it was immediately labeled as a hostile vessel. "The blockading force is entitled to treat such a ship in all respects as an enemy, and to use any means recognised in civilised warfare to drive off, capture, or destroy her. A crew so captured may be treated as POW, and their vessel carried into the captor's port where after condemnation by an Admiralty court she becomes his prize. Nor is any resistance to capture permitted, and a single blow or shot in his defence turns the blockade-runner into a pirate." The Northern Navy stopped ships because the "*Doctrine of Continuous Voyage*, a legalism accepted in United States prize courts, that said simply stopping at a neutral port in midvoyage did not eliminate the illegality of the entire voyage. Henceforth, the British flag no longer guaranteed immunity for the shipping of Confederate supplies." British ships arrived in Nassau, unloaded their cargo at the John Fraser & Company, reloaded their vessel with cotton, and sailed for home while their stored cargo was reloaded onto a ship going to Southern ports.[*] A British sailor when captured was held only long enough at the "Prize trials," then released where he usually returned to Bermuda or Nassau.[404]

Many British runners took an alias when blockade-running. The captain of the *Don* called himself Mr. Roberts while his real name was Hobert Pasha. Sir William Nathan Hewett, a British officer, changed his name to Sam Ridge while captaining the *Condor*.[405]

Crew members totaled one hundred men for the typical blockade-runner with a minimum of three cannons.[**] Crewman soon became wealthy for the pay was issued in gold.

---

[*]   Nassau was two days shorter a trip than Bermuda.

[**]   Other research proved that the runners would never have been outfitted with cannon.

For a round-trip, the captain earned $5,000; the chief engineer and pilot made $2,500; the third officer drew $750, and seamen $250.[406] Another reference showed a pilot earning 700 to 800 pounds sterling per round-trip. With ordinary seamen, 50 to 60 pounds sterling was the norm.[407]

After a discussion with Adjutant James Martin, Governor Vance believed the state could do better furnishing provisions for its troops if he had his own blockade-runners. He convinced Congress of the profitably of those vessels. The state "purchased a ¼ interest in three . . . vessels which assisted in taking out cotton & bringing in supplies for both soldiers & the people." North Carolina was the only Southern state with its own blockade-runners.

Nonessential luxuries brought in via blockade-runners grew proliferate when the ships should have brought in needed supplies. Confederate Congress took notice of the goods imported and the money it was making for North Carolina. This brought President Davis and Congress to pass laws in February 1864 prohibiting the importation of luxuries. "Privately owned vessels were required to carry half of their outgoing and incoming cargoes on Confederate government accounts," they said.[408] Governor Vance showed his disproval at Davis's rules:

GOVERNOR'S MESSAGE
The Honorable, the General Assembly of North-Carolina:

Since your last adjournment, various and important changes in the situation of our affairs have occurred, and many of them require legislative action at your hands.

The late act of Congress conferring power on the President of the Confederate States, to impose regulations and restrictions on commerce has given rise to such a system, on the part of the Confederate authorities, as will effectually exclude this State from importing any further supplies for the army or people. The port of Wilmington is now more effectually blockaded from within than without. The terms imposed upon ship owners, being such that a heavy loss is incurred by every voyage—and notwithstanding the said act provides, "That nothing in this act shall be construed to prohibit the Confederate States, or any of them, from importing any of the articles herein enumerated on their own account,"—yet this is so construed by the government, as to compel the States to submit to the same terms as are imposed on private parties; and clearances are refused and the guns of the fortifications brought to bear upon our own vessels to compel a compliance.

Private parties importing supplies for the government, by contract, for enormous profits, are not taxed by these regulations; yet the State of North-Carolina, importing almost solely the same articles for the same purpose, is compelled to submit to them. I deem it inconsistent with the public interests to refer more particularly to our blockade running transactions and the loss which the State will suffer on both ships and supplies on hand, if these regulations continue in force. When this is considered with the farther fact, as I hold it, that the general government has no right to seize one-half, or any part of, the interest of a sovereign State in the vessels employed in importing her supplies (this being the terms, to which we are called upon to submit), or to impose such regulations as will destroy instead of regulating commerce, it becomes your province to demand a repeal or modification of the act, and I respectfully and earnestly recommend that you do so. And in case Congress should decline to repeal or modify the act, I respectfully ask for directions as to what I shall do with the ships and supplies on hand. A detailed statement of these supplies together with an account as accurate as can be, without vouchers for expenditures abroad not yet received, is herewith submitted—together with the report of Mr. John White, our special Commissioner to Europe. In reference to this gentlemen, it is due to him that I should say, that I have every reason to be pleased with the skill and fidelity with which he performed the duties of his difficult mission. A report of the operations of our other Commissioner, Col. D. K. McRae, necessarily incomplete, is also submitted, and will, I believe, be found equally satisfactory, and creditable to him as Commissioner. In this connection I respectfully ask for the appointment of a committee to investigate all matters appertaining to the blockade-running of the State, to be appointed at an early day, so as to report to your present session if possible. No appropriation has been made by your honorable body to pay the current expenses of the vessels engaged in running the blockade, and none will be necessary, for these expenses can be paid by selling bills, drawn on our agent in England, as being incurred in Wilmington chiefly for the expenses connected with the loading and unloading vessels, compressing cotton, &c., and they can be discharged in currency. I would suggest that you authorize the Treasurer to purchase these bills out of any money in the Treasury, and thus keep the sterling exchange in the Treasury—which otherwise would have to be put on the general market, and be lost to the State.

Being convinced from experience that the legitimate business of my office, now four-fold greater than formerly, is sufficient to tax all my energies of mind and body, and that I cannot do justice to the interest of the State in a business so complicated as many of the transactions, which are carried on at such a distance, I respectfully recommend that a commission of one or more gentlemen, skilled in such business be appointed to conduct the future operations of the State, in importing supplies, whether for the purpose of continuing the operations or winding up the business.[409]

North Carolina not only confiscated vessels, but made their own. Beery's Shipyard in Wilmington constructed the iron-clad CSS *North Carolina*, and Cassidy's Shipyard there built the iron-clad CSS *Raleigh*. These companies repaired boats too. The CSS *Raleigh* steamed up the mouth of the Cape Fear River on duty to protect the area but ran around and sank. The CSS *Neuse* was constructed at Whitehall. The CSS *Appomattox* was a renovated ship.

The South did not have the resources of the U.S. Navy. North Carolina had problems procuring iron for its iron-clads. Iron was in short supply at this time, and the contractors "borrowed" iron from the little-used railroad tracks. The Atlantic & North Carolina Railroad furnished some engines for the ships from old locomotives. Captain James Cook had men going from farm to farm to collect scrap iron from citizens. People would donate broken pieces of cast iron farm implements or leaky pots. Part of the railroad rails on unused routes was removed for the gunboats. For his effort, Captain Cook earned the moniker Iron Monger. The tracks from New Bern to Kinston were taken up to keep the enemy at bay.

A contract was given to nineteen-year-old Gilbert Elliott to build the iron-clad CSS *Albemarle*. With nothing to start with, he started moving supplies and constructing a sawmill in a cornfield by the Roanoke River, several miles above Plymouth. The CSS *Albemarle* was hurriedly built to help Confederate General Hoke in his raid to retake Plymouth.

The CSS *Albemarle*'s life was short-lived unfortunately because she had done a great of damage to the U.S. Navy in the area. The navy had orders to destroy the ship whatever the cost. U.S. Commander Flusser had lost his life trying to sink her. In one battle, the *Albemarle* had its smokestack shot to pieces. The machinist told Captain Cook the engines had stopped because the fire wouldn't draw, causing the coal to die down. Captain Cook told him to burn the bacon and lard stored on board, which he did. They were able to get up enough steam to leave the U.S. Navy in its wake and escape.

U.S. Lieutenant Cushing, a longtime friend and student of Flusser, vowed revenge on the crew of the *Albemarle*. He asked for and received permission to be transferred to Plymouth to blow up the *Albemarle*. In a daring mission, he and his small crew placed a torpedo under the iron-clad and blew a hole in the front. Cushing almost lost his life in the explosion. He jumped in the river and swam with the current until he was a safe distance away, then climbed upon the bank into the weeds and hid from his pursuers. He made his way safely back to the Federal lines.

At Whitehall, now called Seven Springs, construction of the gunboat CSS *Neuse* began in 1862. Engines from the Atlantic and North Carolina Railroad found a new use in the making of the ram. It was floated unfinished down to Kinston where iron plates added bulk to the sides. Still not completed by March 1865, when Federal forces were near, the commanders did not want it to fall in the enemy's hands; so they burned the ship and sank it in the Neuse River.[410]

John Devereux Jr. at one time managed the state's blockade-running business. "About 84 percent of the 2,054 recorded attempts to run the blockade into ports along the North and South Carolina coasts from April 1861 to February 1865 were successful." The *Hattie* ran the blockade sixty times many times in daylight.[411] For more information on blockade-running, see chapter 16.

Prewar, the South had eleven different gauges of railroad tracks. The standard gauge was 4 feet 8½ inches. Cars couldn't transfer from state to state. This proved a hindrance to the Confederacy. Rails and cars literally wore out due to severe use of transporting troops and heavy equipment.[412] Rules were established permitting the soldier a passage for two cents a mile. Military freight was charged at "half the regular local rates." The railroads were to get paid in bonds or treasury notes.[413]

North Carolina had a series of good railroads established before the war. The Wilmington, Charlotte, and Rutherford Railroad was started in 1855. By 1861, 103 miles of track composed the line.[414] This rail went through Laurenburg and Rockingham. The line from Wilmington to Florence, South Carolina, called the Wilmington and Manchester Railroad was 161 miles long. In 1856, a person could board a train known as the North Carolina Railroad, built with state aid, in Charlotte and travel ninety-five miles through Greensboro and Raleigh to Goldsboro. There he would change cars for the line known as the Atlantic and North Carolina Railroad and proceed to New Bern or Morehead City. Or he would change trains in Goldsboro and travel on the Wilmington and Weldon Railroad to Wilmington. Running North of Raleigh to Warren County and Weldon, then Petersburg, a distance of eighty-six miles, the line was named the Raleigh and Gaston Railroad. From Greensboro to Danville, Virginia, the Piedmont Railroad, finished during the war years was the line that President Davis took from Danville on his escape South. The Western North Carolina Railroad went from Salisbury to within five miles of Morganton, a distance of eighty-four miles. No line was laid to Asheville. Charlotte had one line through Lincoln County called the Wilmington, Charlotte, and Rutherfordton Railroad; the other line from Charlotte to Statesville was named the North Carolina Railroad. A short track from Fayetteville to the Egypt Coal Mine was called Western Railroad. You could travel from Wilmington to Black Rock, then Lumberton, on to Gilopolis, then Laurenburg. The Wilmington and Weldon Railroad ran 161 miles from Wilmington to Weldon. It was known as Lee's lifeline in the latter part of the war, shipping him army goods brought in by blockade-runners.

No. of stations	Distance from Weldon	Dis. bet'w Stns.	NAMES OF STATIONS.	Arrives		Leaves		Time between Sta.	Time at Stations.	REMARKS.
				HOURS.	MINUT'S.	HOURS.	MINUT'S.			
25			Weldon, P. M.			8	45			Terminus
24	8	8	Halifax,........	9	08	9	10	23	2	R. S.
23½	12	4	Ruggles, ...	9	22	9	23	12	1	
23	19	7	Enfield, ...	9	42	9	46	19	4	P.No.3.
22½	25	6	Whitaker,......	10	04	10	05	18	1	Flag.
22	29	4	Battleboro',....	10	17	10	18	12	1	R. S.
21	37	8	Rocky Mount,...	10	39	10	41	21	2	R. S.
20	46	9	Joyner,........	11	05	11	06	24	1	W.& W.
19	54	8	Wilson,........	11	29	11	31	23	2	R. S.
18	60	6	Black Creek, ...	11	48	11	49	17	1	Flag.
17	67	7	Nahunta, A. M.	12	08	12	09	19	1	Flag.
16	70	3	Pikeville,......	12	18	12	19	9	1	Flag.
15	76	8	Goldsboro',.....	12	43	12	48	24	5	Ch. Eng.
14	83	6	Everittsville, ...	1	06	1	07	18	1	Flag.
13	86	3	Dudley, ...	1	16	1	18	9	2	Flag.
			Milton,........							Flag.
12	91	5	Mount Olive,...	1	33	1	34	15	1	Flag.
11	98	7	Faison,........	1	55	1	56	21	1	Flag.
10½	102	4	Bowden,.......	2	08	2	12	12	4	W.& W.
10	106	4	Warsaw,......	2	24	2	25	12	1	R. S.
9	113	7	Magnolia, ...	2	46	2	47	21	1	R. S.
8½	120	5	Rose Hill,.....	3	02	3	03	15	1	W.& W.
8	123	5	Teachey, ...	3	18	3	20	15	2	P. No.1
7	128	5	Leesburg,.......	3	34	3	35	14	1	Flag.
6	132	4	So. Washington,	3	46	3	47	11	1	Flag.
5	139	7	Burgaw,.......	4	06	4	10	19	4	W.& W.
			Asheton, ...							Flag.*
4	147	8	Rocky Point,...	4	30	4	31	20	1	Flag.
3	150	3	Marlboro',.....	4	40	4	41	9	1	Flag.
2	152	2	North East,....	4	47	4	48	6	1	Flag.
1	162	9	Wilmington, †..	5	10			22	1	Terminus

*16½ mile Station.

☞ Wood and Water to be taken only at the places marked, if it can be avoided.

†Take Breakfast.

Wilmington Daily Journal train schedule for the W&W RR

Before the war, there was a forty-mile gap in the railroad between Greensboro and Danville, Virginia. Governor Vance was at first leery of completing this line. He felt that it would take business away from the Wilmington and Weldon Railroad. Necessity changed that. With the Federal takeover of Wilmington in 1865, this rail line proved to be a great help to continue to supply General Lee's army for the next four months. During the later part of the war, when the tracks were torn up by Butler's cavalry between Richmond and Raleigh, people had to take a detour through Danville to get back to Wilmington. One man said it took him three days to get from Richmond to Wilmington using this route.[415] North Carolina had twenty-three engines in 1861. More would be needed, but where could they get them?

Catherine Edmondston jotted down in her journal a good description of the railroads on her trip from Petersburg to Weldon:

> . . . five long trains loaded with soldiers and their equipage on their way to the Peninsula . . . . Cobb Legion . . . on one, a full Battery on another, and a sixth was loaded with what may be called the sinews of War, viz, "provisions." The men on the open cars were most picturesquely huddled, some in groups, some singly, under any temporary shelter they could rig up, the corner of a tent, the body of a baggage wagon, whilst their baggage in its diversity & arrangement was really artistic. Cooking utensils, camp furniture, trunks, muskets, stools, baggage wagons, cannon, tents, caissons, beds, blankets, and wheels and men thrown together at random would have delighted the heart . . .[416]

Most railroads ran two daily passenger trains. One was totally passenger, and the other was mixed with freight cars. Sometimes the train did not go all the way to the depot ending miles from the station. The *Concord Flag* had a comment from a disgruntled passenger, which read: "At Concord the engineer frequently overshot the station, forcing ladies to walk in the mud while boarding the train."[417] People had to walk or hire wagons to get into town. The *Raleigh Register* criticized officials because there was no Raleigh depot for the North Carolina Railroad and no platform for passengers to wait upon, just mud.[418] The Wilmington, Charlotte, and Rutherford Rail Road ended five miles from the depot at Wilmington. Passengers had to disembark and catch the steamer into the city.

Frequent breakdowns and military interruptions caused the schedule to change too often for passengers' patience. Chaplain Betts wrote that he could find "no seats on the train from Durham to Weldon. Takes 34 hours to go from Chapel Hill to Richmond."[419]

Author Trelease noted, "The *Concord Flag* declared in May 1862 that 'the present condition of the North Carolina Railroad is absolutely frightful. Crashes, smashes up, collisions, broken axles, running off the track, and accidents of every . . . description, are of such frequent occurrences that they are scarcely noticed . . ."[420] Several members of the Thirty-seventh Regiment were injured when the engine and cars of the Wilmington and Weldon Railroad jumped the tracks.[421] In 1863, a railroad accident occurred between Tarboro and Rocky Mount. Equipment and men were thrown together, wounding twenty who were sent to the hospital in Tarboro.

One soldier mentioned a train wreck involving three engines near Goldsboro. One of the trains was going backward to pick up troops from a recent battle when it wrecked. Luckily, no one was injured. His company had to help clear the damaged cars and engines to open the line again.[422] Soldier T. W. Setser, a cousin to W. A. Setser, Esq., wrote about a train wreck involving troops on the way to Virginia on May 21, 1863: "We air in Virginia. we lefte North Carolina for Fredericksburg, but the trains run together and that thodes [throwed] be hine the time." Several were killed in this incident.[423] Near Huntersville the Raleigh and Gaston Railroad wrecked causing four deaths and injuring fifteen.[424]

D. K. McRae, editor of the *Daily Confederate*, was especially vehement with the railroads. He wrote in 1864, "God save the country if its destiny in any wise depends on proper and conscientious performance of duty by Railroad corporations." The North

Carolina Railroad could boast of only one passenger killed in an accident during the war years. But a collision North of Charlotte occurred, injuring soldiers from Georgia and South Carolina. "A subscription of $120 was raised in Charlotte to aid the injured soldiers," noted Trelease.[425] A diarist from Fayetteville mentioned a train wreck, although she failed to name the company. On May 7, 1863, she wrote of passengers pushing the railroad cars with the engine behind. Apparently, they didn't see the cattle on the tracks, and the train ran over the cows and killed them. The cars turned over, but no one was killed. A Negro man needed a leg amputation from his injuries.[426] The installation of the telegraph greatly reduced these problems.

North Carolina's railroads soon wore out due to overloads and failure to keep up repairs. Governor Vance wrote to A. C. Myers, quartermaster for the Confederacy, for help to relieve the state's rail problems. Improved rail service was necessary to get needed supplies to soldiers and the public.

> The season is now far advanced and the condition of every class of our people will be truly deplorable, unless salt is brought to them. Independent of that, the supply for the Army, will be seriously diminished. A large amount of pork is now awaiting for salt, to be packed, and unless it is received very soon, an immense loss will ensue, which in the end will be a Serious public calamity.[427]

Mail and newspapers were carried by train, and when the railroad failed for whatever reason, people involved with the mails became irate. Thomas F. Wood recorded his opinion:

> The railroads were badly out of repair. The cars were worn and dilapidated so that one could hardly go from one place to another without getting vermin on them. Freight to the Army always took precedence, and it was only by special favor that a package could get through. Should it be favored with shipment it ran through another risk of being lost at the warehouse and at the Army end . . . being robbed. Frequently packages were opened and robbed, but as the blame could not be charged upon any one person, but . . . the wagon driver . . . the guard . . . or the railroad agent.[428]

Other complaints directed at railroad officials included the type of merchandise it shipped. When urban residents in Charlotte and Raleigh had to do without gaslights due to the lack of rosin to fire the gasworks, they blamed railroad personnel. Food and liquor seemed to be the common item shipped via the freight trains. These cars were frequently vandalized and robbed.

Military authorities "borrowed from Peter to pay Paul" by using as much iron as possible from less-used rails along the lines. These tracks would be dismantled and melted down for the ironclad gunboats. Seventeen miles of the unused iron rails between New Bern and Kinston was removed and sold to the Confederate Navy.[429]

Use of the railroads during wartime doubled and tripled in some instances. Wood was burned as fuel, and logs were needed as crossties. There was plenty of wood nearby, but a shortage of laborers to cut it. Woodcutters furnished logs to urban dwellers in larger cities and to the hospitals, so they were always busy. Railroad businessmen hired free Negroes and slaves, paying owners from sixty to two hundred dollars each per year for their use.[430]

The railroads decided to ship soldiers' care boxes free of charge in the beginning of the struggle. At times, Confederate officers impressed trains, causing mail and supplies to be delayed. They would also suspend civilians from using the trains. Sick soldiers took their seats in the regular passenger cars. Travelers would at times complain of the odor of the infected, sick men. The Wilmington-Weldon Railroad fitted up a few hospital cars for the severely ill men. Occasionally, free blacks and slaves sold provisions to the passengers. At Durham Station, travelers could dine there.[431]

The Adam Express Company had both a Northern and Southern branch. When the war began, the Southern office was sold, and it became the Southern Express. The Confederate government "made the Southern Express the official custodian of all funds being transferred from place to place. Its agents were exempt from conscription," according to Trelease.[432] The Southern Express also built the telegraph lines in North Carolina.[433]

The railroads had three classes of passengers. Paul Barringer recalled that the first class "went anywhere at will; the second class were more restricted and in an emergency, the males might be called upon to help throw wood on the tender when speed was urgent; the third class were seated well forward, and when the engineer gave a peculiar whistle, THEY also may be called out to push."[434] Citizens wishing to travel had to have a pass. Guards placed at every railroad, the stageline, etc., checked passes and asked questions, no matter the social standing of the traveler. Several incensed travelers said it made them feel like a slave showing their pass. This precipitated many delays.[435] The railroads transported 5 percent of our soldiers in 1860–1861, which increased to 65 percent in 1864–1865. Soldiers paid a lesser fare than civilians, so the railroads didn't take in as much money. The public became angered as the war progressed due to constantly rising passage rates. The *Raleigh Daily Confederate* posted this note: "It is difficult not to view rate increases as a form of extortion when one sees the paper profits of railroads escalating simultaneously."[436] The busiest stations on the line were Charlotte, Greensboro, and Raleigh, with Goldsboro next.

A soldier said the trains were so slow that traveling from the coast of South Carolina to Goldsboro took four days on four different railroads for soldiers in the Twenty-fifth Regiment to reach home.[437] A Confederate nurse traveling from Richmond to South Carolina said that in Raleigh, "we change cars again . . . & miserable work again getting from one car to the other, just one puddle after another . . ." It took the train five hours to go from Weldon to Raleigh, then another twelve to Charlotte. She said they had "rye" coffee at the hotel in Charlotte. On the way back to the front, the nurse traveled through Wilmington on a sleeping car. She said she didn't get any sleep though for all the noise from the soldiers and refugees. The yellow fever quarantine had been lifted, and folks flocked back into the city.[444]

A civilian described his very frustrating train trip from Richmond passing through North Carolina on his way to Columbia, South Carolina:

A Glimpse of Dixie

Crowded is not the word which will express the conditions of the cars—*scrowged* is better—except that slang doesn't look well in print. People filled the gangways and platforms—hanging on to the latter in the most determined manner, to the great danger of projecting trees and water-stations.

Wounded soldiers had their wounds pushed and rubbed against, and indiscriminate well people had their toes mashed and their general comfort very much disturbed . . . .

At the Weldon depot there was a tremendous jam. Wounded soldiers had a bad time again—so had every body. Passport was *vised* again by bayonet—that is, he tore off a piece of it; and after a great deal of fuss, and no supper, we were off to Weldon . . . . I got a very good place to stand up in [on the train], near a water-cooler which had long since ceased to perform the cooling process . . . which had leaked all over the floor.

I would state here that I like babies . . . but I *do not like* fifteen babies hungry, dissatisfied babies who cry without ceasing—shut up in a railroad car with me . . . I learned . . . that these fifteen infants . . . were returning from a visit to their . . . . [fathers] . . . who were in the army . . . . after a good deal of fussing amongst the mothers, the babies disappeared . . . under the maternal shawls, and became unaccountably quiet.

I waited patiently for some body to get out, for I was getting tired holding up the side of the car . . .

Several people who were standing got off; and finally, he took their seat, sat down, and soon was asleep. He said a Negro selling "possum 'n' bred" for fifty cents woke him up. He refused the meal. The writer continued:

But my Confederate companions bought and consumed freely; and I became very much entertained at the trading, and the professed knowledge of our varied currency exhibited by the institution, even to the probable sticking qualities of a poststamp. If the verdict on the latter form of currency was, "Dis wont stick, Sah!" . . . there was no trade . . . but my attention was diverted from abstruse mathematics by the strikingly original position by an old lady—I was obliged to keep an apple in my mouth, to conceal a disrespectful grin at the old lady's expense . . . The old lady in question monopolized a whole seat for the purpose of making herself comfortable. [Could this have been Aunt Abby?]

We passed Gareysburg, with its fine groves of splendid oaks, and deserted camps, in which the dismantled bowers looked like so many Sioux graves, and soon checked up to cross the bridge over the Roanoke. This river looked so grand—though it is not very wide—under the glorious moonlight, that I stepped out on the platform . . . I feel proud of our Confederate rivers, which unfortunately, are so accommodating to Yankee gunboats.

The guard at the end of the bridge looked so cold, with his musket barrel glistening frigidly in the moonlight, that I went in to the stove from sheer sympathy with him.

"Weldon," some body sang out. I looked, and perceived that we were somewhat in a depot, and taking the conductor's word, that it was Weldon, I descended, and pulling an instinct which never deserts me, I went in search of something to eat. I found it, and have nothing to say about it except, that it cost one dollar. We tarried here, almost long enough for our beards to grow . . . At any rate, we staid until it was next day . . . . every body was mad except those who were asleep on the floor of the hotel office. Some consoled themselves at the bar, but the majority smoked hard, and expressed themselves in violent terms about the delay.

We were off at last, and when day broke, we saw the spires of Raleigh. The Old North State has reason to be proud of the public buildings of its Capitol. The State House did not please me altogether, architecturally considered, but it stands embowered amidst grand oak trees, and it is massive, if not very graceful. A copy, in bronze, of Houdon's Washington, stands in front of the Capitol. Some of the churches which front on the grounds, or square, are very handsome, and have a more metropolitan look than many of those in larger cities than Raleigh.

Gov. Vance has cause to be proud of at least one of his fellow citizens. Not being very much occupied I thought that I would smoke. I asked a young man of whom I purchased the cigars, if they were good. "Oh! Yes, first rate, sir . . . made in Greensboro." I am glad that N. Carolinians are so fortunate as to have a town where they make a reasonable cigar, and a citizen honest enough to say that they were made there instead of . . . . Havana.

We passed Greensboro going South, and it was the first place where food was served to the soldier on the train gratis. I contented myself with looking at the fair dispensers of this hospitality, and ate further on, at the Company Shops, where, in a neat hotel, I actually got more for a dollar than I could eat.

I think these trains must travel on the "festina lente" I observed as much to a breaksman, and he remarked that there was no danger to be apprehended, unless a bull should catch up with and attack the train.

We waited about on the road for nothing in particular that I could see. Sometimes the engine positively refused to go up a steep grade, and would leave the train standing out in the woods, and water.

We connected with the hotel omnibuses at Charlotte—the train to Columbia had gone about twenty minutes earlier . . . . we all had to bundle out and scramble in the mud for omnibuses—[it had rained hard]—and some of the crippled soldiers came near being badly hurt. We didn't get any great deal for our money in Charlotte—but where can you get a great deal for it now-a-day? It seems to be a very pretty place. The private residences, some of them, are handsome, and so are the churches.

I only had time to sketch the water-works in Charlotte which are quite extensive of their kind. We were off again at eight o'clock, with a further accession to our crowd.

The author went on to tell of the rest of the story of his trip. He signed his name anonymously as Stozanboz.[439] For more on the condition of the railroads, read Sarah Smiley's journal, chapter 21.

CHAPTER FIVE

Fleeing and Federal Occupation Down East
"Massa runs one way and dey de other."*

OUTER BANKS

Outer Banks residents called "bankers" and other coastal people fished only enough for themselves, with a little to spare to barter for corn and vegetables from the mainland. Only once or twice a year did they trade salted fish for basics such as sugar, coffee, or flour. Around the Hatteras Inlet grew many trees, figs, and grapes. A few residents grew vegetables for their own families.[1] Women of all races worked beside their kin on the Outer Banks, gathering and shucking shellfish, cleaning and preserving the catch. The commercial fishing industry, small at best, kept to North Carolina and some Virginia cities with a few exports. The Southern tip of Hatteras fell on August 29, 1861. One of the islands is described by a Union soldier, J. W. Denny, when his unit landed on Bodie Island, as "Several hundred people . . . scattered along this bar, who get a living . . . by fishing, gathering oysters, picking up a [ship] wreck now and then, and doing a little piloting."[2]

Union Private Henry Clapp defined the poorer inhabitants of eastern North Carolina "as looking pale, sallow, and low in intelligence and energy. The women either dipped snuff or ate clay."[3] The occupying forces of Hatteras depicted the people as ignorant, with few schools. Another soldier said that the inhabitants "knew little about the political questions that were agitating other people and for the sake of being let alone they would have joined either side."[4] A third Union trooper said that he found Hatteras to be the "most desolate of creation."[5]

Before any Union expedition had occurred at Hatteras, General Ben Butler received word, probably through spies, that Southern troops were fortifying the Outer Banks.[6] After secession, authorities gathered up free blacks and slaves and had them construct forts along the Outer Banks. These were poorly manned by North Carolina troops with inferior equipment. Early in the conflict, C.S. General D. H. Hill notified Richmond that:

> Roanoke Island is the key of one-third of North Carolina, and whose occupancy by the enemy would enable him to reach the great railroad from Richmond to New Orleans. Four additional regiments are absolutely indispensable to the protection of this island . . . . I would most earnestly call the attention of the honorable Secretary of War to this island . . . . The towns of Elizabeth City, Edenton, Plymouth, and Williamston will all be taken should Roanoke be captured or passed.[7]

Governor Henry Clark echoed his opinion. He also wrote officials that "if the Federals controlled the sounds inside the Outer Banks, Norfolk with its navy yard and commanding position was doomed to fall." Both men asked for more troops to defend the sandy banks. Congress failed to act. The United States Navy sent heavily armed ships totaling 148 guns to subdue Fort Clark, equipped with eighteen guns, and Fort Hatteras on the Outer Banks at the end of August 1861. The pitiable-equipped forts were no match. Within just a few hours, Confederate Colonel William Martin surrendered. He said:

---

*   Quote by a Contraband near New Bern.[8]

Such a bombardment is not on record in the annals of war. Not less than three thousand shells were fired by the enemy during the three hours. As many as twenty-eight in one minute were known to fall within and about the fort [Hatteras].

Nearby homes were totally destroyed.[9] When these forts fell, Southern troops pulled back from the bulwarks on Ocracoke and Oregon Inlet. The commander of Fort Morgan felt it was useless to fight in face of such odds, so he had his men retreat. "The Nags Head Hotel was headquarters for C.S. General Wise during the battle of Roanoke Island. He burned it before his troops evacuated the banks . . ."[10] Fort Granville (circa 1753) was torched by its own men after the fall of Ocracoke.

The *Lewisburg Chronicle*, a Pennsylvania newspaper, printed that U.S. General Ben Butler had three objectives. First was to consolidate the forces at Hatteras, take Roanoke Island, and then overthrow New Bern, Beaufort Harbor, and Fort Macon. General Butler had at his fingertips nineteen gunboats. His men used explosives to clear the rivers of sunken ships and debris the Southerners had used to prevent the enemy from advancing. Federal soldiers easily stormed over Roanoke Island, and the Southern troops surrendered on February 7, 1862. In a matter of days, Elizabeth City, South Mills, Edenton, and Winton toppled like dominoes. Not far behind went Morehead City, Carolina City, Beaufort, Newport, and New Bern on March 14, 1862, and Fort Macon on April 25, 1862.

As the Northern troops attempted to embark at Hatteras Island, two nor' easterners blew them around for two weeks. Nearly one hundred ships attempted to land that January 1862 in the choppy swirling waves. Much equipment was lost as both troops and horses drowned. By the end of the month, only sixty vessels survived the rough landing.[11] A soldier said of his experience:

Hatteras Inlet January 23rd 1862

Dear Mother,

Well Sunday we still remained at anchor. We had just passed through a dangerous storm for as all the ballast had been thrown overboard the ship was very light and the wind blew very hard and it was the opinion of the sailors that this vessal would draw her anchor and drift on to the breaks . . . . In the morning when I got up I found the storm had passed over and it was very pleasant. You would little have thought it was Sunday . . . . The "boys" were all around the deck and rigging. In an hour if you had gone below you would have found some of them playing (Bluff) a game at cards for money. Some shaking dice and so on. So passed the day . . . . I could see the breaks of three vessals were in sight [.] all three belonged to our fleet. We were glad to be in high and along side of the vessals [.] we could see two forts and nearly 100 ships of different sizes. We thought our sailing was over. There we lay, nothing happening until last night when it began to blow. Yesterday the ship that lay aside of us drifted up against us and did a little damage. Last night at 12 o'clock I woke up and every little while [,] something would strik the ship and she would shake. I asked the boys what was the matter. The mail is going now so I cannot write anymore. Am well

Arthur W. Palmer Drummer,
Co E 8th CV General Burnsides Expedition Annapolis, Maryland[12]

The guns of Fort Bartow were too small a caliber to reach the gunboats at sea. Dr. Lorenzo Traver, a Union soldier, maintained that eight rebel gunboats were in Albemarle Sound in February 1862 while others proclaim that six to nine fought.[13] Rebel Colonel H. M. Shaw with the Eighth North Carolina State Troops manned the forts while small gunboats under the command of Commodore Lynch, North Carolina's little mosquito fleet, patrolled the sound.

Hatteras fell with little resistance. Federal Admiral David Porter, speaking on the fall of Fort Hatteras, said:

> ... the moral effect ... was very great, as it gave us a foothold on Southern soil .... It was a death blow to blockade running in that vicinity, and ultimately proved one of the most important events of the war.[14]

He was right. The Confederacy failed to oust the enemy from North Carolina in this area, and soon, Northern soldiers would take over and hold this section until the surrender in 1865. The "foot-hold" would grow to gigantic proportions. Roanoke Island had been crucial to the safety of the Dismal Swamp Canal and the back door to Norfolk, Virginia. After the island surrendered, Confederate forces left the town.

A correspondent wrote that after the capture of Hatteras, people came forward subscribing to the oath of allegiance to the United States. Perhaps the islanders thought their property would be protected if they took the oath. Some may have seen it as an economic opportunity. Neither worked. Federal raiders showed no partiality. The first enemy troops who managed to land plundered local inhabitants on Hatteras Island. They stole women's clothing and accessories.

ROANOKE ISLAND

Some people of Roanoke Island "were rather indifferent about the outcome of the war [surrendering of the forts on Hatteras] and just wanted to be left alone."[15] A Northern soldier agreed with other's opinions that:

> The inhabitants of whom there are about 500 are . . . a hard looking set of "critters," who all profess to be good union men, and are flocking to the Gen headquarters to give in their adhesion to the government, some come on horseback, others on carts, and the rest on foot, their horses are quite small, and with the exception of the Artillery horses I have not seen a single strap of LEATHER harness not even a collar, the harness is all rope, the harness wood, which must hurt the horses in drawing their cargo.[16]

Another of the invaders said they traded greenbacks to prisoners for Confederate money. He reported that most of the homes were deserted on the island. His force found one house open, which they visited. The owner told him that three hundred people lived on the island, which was about twelve miles long and six miles wide. Only two stores and two churches stood on the island. The old man complained about the Georgia soldiers stationed near him who robbed him of his potatoes and killed his cow. The residents were said to be fishermen; a few farmed sweet potatoes, Irish potatoes, and cabbage, which they took to Elizabeth City to sell.

U.S. Colonel Rush Hawkins, commander of the New York Volunteers, came on August 30, the first year of the conflict. In a letter to his superior, he asked for instructions:

> Sir: during the afternoon of the 30th, a delegation of this island waited upon me and placed in my hands a paper, a copy of which is here enclosed .... In answer to this communication I requested that as many of citizens as could should meet me the next day for the purpose of arranging terms by which they might be permitted to remain here. Thirty* people showed up. On my

---

*   250 took the oath later.

part I have agreed verbally to give them all the necessary protection against the vigilance committee."[17]

Hawkins included the notice sent to him from the civilians:

> Dear Sir: We, the citizens of Cape Hatteras, do ask of your honor that you will allow us to return to our homes and property and protect us in the same as natural citizens, as we have never taken up arms against your government nor has it been our wish to do so. We did not help by our votes to get North Carolina out of the Union. Believing that your clemency will not allow you to treat us as rebels, who have always been loyal citizens, we do earnestly request for the sake of our women and children that you will comply with our wishes, as we seek protection from your honor.
>
> Yours very respectfully, Citizens of Hatteras. [17A]

State of North Carolina, Hyde County

> We, the undersigned, do solemnly swear that we will true allegiance bear to the United States of North America; that we will not take up arms against said government or hold any communication with its enemies' in any way whatever, and that we will give to the commandant at Fort Clark any information we may obtain or receive of the approach of the enemy; and in case we are called upon we will assist the commandant of said fort in his defense thereof against any and all the enemies of the said United States of North America, and we will always under any and all circumstances support the Constitution of the United States. [17B]

Colonel Hawkins said of the North Carolina people: "In the South, even to breathe one word in favor of the Old Government, or to do a single act which might wake a suspicion that one was not committed body and soul for the success of the rebel cause might bring the inflection of every kind of fiendish insult and outrage."[18] Hawkins asked for more troops to be transferred to the area. "I fear that if I am superseded the promises I have made will not be carried out," he said. Colonel Hawkins continued to use the Black Dispatch (Negro spies) for information on North Carolinians.[19] "I am informed by some of these people that Union meetings have been held in several of the counties bordering on the Pamlico Sound . . . ," wrote Hawkins to Major General John Wool at Fortress Monroe.[20]

It was thirty-five miles from Roanoke Island to Elizabeth City. Hawkins said his forces did not loot Elizabeth City as accused but they agreed to go ashore and help put out the fires started by fleeing citizens and soldiers.[21] A citizen reported that pillaging by the officers and men of the Twentieth Regiment, NY Volunteers occurred not long after their arrival.[22]

The next long letter from a Union soldier stationed on Roanoke Island renders a good prospective of the daily life in the army, along with interaction with the natives, black and white:

Roanoke Island, NC June 4th, 1862

---

* The vigilance committee to which he referred was the Confederate Partisan Rangers. The Rangers served as Home Guards and scouted the countryside on alert for treasonous men. Thomas Speller Sr. of Bertie County was arrested.[23] They apprehended a Mr. Dribble and his brother of New Bern. The "Yankee born" brothers were suspected of complicity to the enemy. They were sent to Salisbury Prison, along with two Federal soldiers accused of stealing two pianos and other articles in New Bern.[24]

My Dear Mother,

. . . my whole pay is only $20.00 per month & I have had [*illegible*] use for a little money all the time since I started. Our living at times is miserable & we would actually suffer, some of the daintiest of us at least, if it were not for the occasional opportunities we have to purchase a few eggs, fish, etc . . . . The money [bounty] is my honest due as I am not indebted to New Hampshire for anything never having received my bounty money, a cent of pay of any kind for enlisting, not even my uniform.

I was quite sick for a week or ten days but after all had a good opportunity to rest. I went to a private house as soon as I was taken. Jo went with me & took the best of care of me. I staid there 3 weeks which was longer than absolutely necessary but as I had a good bed & good living I staid as long as I could well keep from duty. I am perfectly well now as good as new except that I have lost 22 lbs. of my boasted 175 & do not feel so bouyant & elastic as I did when I came on this Island . . . . I have been & still am doing all the duties of an Asst. Surgeon . . . . It only pays me 7 dollars more a month than an ordinary soldier but I have a tent by myself, have more liberty to go & come & am treated with as much respect as tho I had my commission in my pocket . . . . I know that my reputation in this Regiment as a Physician is all a young man could desire . . .

Speaking of the niggers. What disposition do you Northerners intend making of them? We haven't a great many of them compared to the other stations on this coast but if you can find any occupation for 741 of them in Gilmanton or vicinity I think Genl. Burnside would be glad to accomodate [*sic*] you. We have got that number on this Island under our "protection" which means that we feed clothe & shelter them & in return receive—the approval of our conscience. What bosh this is. This welcoming these black rascals simpley [*sic*] because it will annoy those whom we suppose are our enemies. I say "suppose" because all the niggers unite in swearing that "massa one damned rebel." Of course nig knows. If he don't who does. While I was away from camp, I went one day over to the mainland with Capt. Baum a native with whom I boarded. After we got there he found he had to go off two or three miles. I was too weak to go as far & promising to be back in an hour or two [,] he left. I didn't like the idea of being left alone but getting tired of lounging on the beach [,] I overhauled my revolvers & started towards the "interior." After going thro the woods a quarter of a mile or so keeping a bright lookout not for "secesh" but for "ye pesky sarpints" I came to a plantation on which rice, cotton, corn, potatoes & flax were growing finely. I strolled on 40 or 50 rods & came suddenly on a farm house almost hidden in a grove of Mulberry & peach trees, the peaches by the way being as large as an English Walnut. In the dooryard playing on the grass were five of the longest heeled, brightest, & blackest specimens of humanity I ever saw. Ten black diamonds in pearl settings could hot have flashed more brilliantly than their eyes did when I opened the gate. One look & they were off like a flock of partridges. I went round to the leeward door which I knew would be open & found an old lady busily spinning. As I was quite pale & tired & had on a clean shirt & white collar I suppose I did not look quite so dangerous that day as I generally do. Anyway the old lady bid me good evening (it was just after dinner) invited me in, handed me a rocking chair, asked me "had I been sick" & sent "Venus," about 7 years old & as black as the ace of spades to tell the Capt, that there was a stranger in the house. The old man soon came hobbling in & greeted me cordially, offered me a glass of their native wine which they make in large quantities on these banks, produced pipes after which we had a pleasant chat for an hour. The old man was quite intelligent for these regions, had been in all the principal cities north & seemed quite conversant with the habits & opinions of Northern men. Had served in the last war in which he lost an eye & had a bayonet thrust thro his thigh crippling him for life. Was a "Union man" as long to use his own language "as there was use in being Union in North Carolina." He reckoned there wasnt much Union feeling in the State. About the niggers he said. "You folks haven't acted wisely about our slaves. I know you don't want to liberate all the niggers cos you wouldn't know what to do with them but I can't make my folks beleive [sic] so for our niggers do run away & you take care of them. You don't come over & take them but you encourage them to do so by feeding & clothing them. The other day because a few white men undertook to stop a gang of slaves from 'stealing one of their schooners & running away & got into a fight in which 4 or 5 niggers were killed. On the testimony of those who escaped you send up an armed force & arrest these men & threaten to hang them for murder. The people of N.C. will never be good Union men until some other course is taken about their slaves.'"

I thought the old man's views were sensible & after another glass of wine I returned to the boat the old man accompanying me & urging me to repeat the visit. I have given you a lengthy account of this trip & our conversation that you might form an idea of the opinions of the people in this neighboorhood. [sic] I have had a good opportunity to ascertain the views of these men on Hatteras as well as here & I can safely say I haven't seen but three Union men on both islands & they were all spies in our employ & to be trusted just as far as one could sling a bull by the tail & no farther. Some other time I'll tell you a conversation I had with an officer whom we arrested at Elizabeth City. He was taken prisoner when we took this island and released on parole. We found him in the corner of the street watching our troops. A nigger told the Col. that he was a recruiting officer. He was made prisoner & brought down here & after six weeks confinement was discharged for want of proof that he had violated his parole.

With much love your aff son, Con[*25]

———————

Soon, five U.S. ships were in the Albemarle Sound battling with North Carolina's five little ships called the Mosquito Fleet. The first capture by the state's navy of the Federal ship, *Fanny*, netted one thousand overcoats, one thousand dress coats, one thousand pairs of shoes, and one thousand pairs of pants.[26] Another steamer commanded by Captain Jester overtook a Federal ship with 150 arms, fifteen dollars, blankets, overcoats, and forty-eight prisoners.[27] Victory was short-lived. The Federal Navy overpowered the sound, thus opened the first naval battle of the Civil War. The Confederates had captured one U.S. vessel, but ultimately, the state ended up with all its ships disabled.

Tories (Union sympathizers), afraid of Confederate forces, traveled with Federal troops in the famous race down Hatteras Island, now known as the Chicamacomico Races. It began on October 1, 1861, on the Northern end of the island at Rodanthe, the first town below Oregon Inlet. Roanoke Island was about fifty miles from Hatteras. Chased by Confederate troops, Union soldiers fled to the Southern end of Hatteras. Fleeing with the Federal Army were civilians of all ages who professed Union sympathies. The group had not taken any water along. High temperature and thirst overpowered many, causing them to drop from heat exhaustion. That evening, the throng reached the lighthouse, a distance of more than

————————

[*]   Con C. Badger was first a nurse with the New Hampshire Sixth Infantry, Company I. He mustered on January 31, 1862, at Hatteras and was later promoted to assistant surgeon on March 1, 1862. He remained on the Outer Banks as a contract surgeon's assistant on detached duty until August 11, when he mustered out.

twenty miles. For unknown reasons, the Confederates chose not to capture the Yankee troops and civilians at that time. Instead, they awaited reenforcements. Mistake! It was the Federal soldiers who were reenforced that night. In the morning, the race was reversed, with the Southern Army on the run up the island. One U.S. soldier described the Union flight down the island:

> . . . they were joined by dozens of the island's villagers, who looked to the Union troops for protection. Mothers carrying their babes, fathers leading along the boys, grandfathers and grandmothers . . . straggling along from homes they had left behind. Relying on our protection, they had been our friends, but in an evil hour we had been compelled to leave them.[28]

Portsmouth had been represented as one of North Carolina's many resort towns before the insurrection. People with means frequented the area in good weather. The Albemarle Sound area was also considered a retreat for the affluent. Fine homes and hotels dotted the rivers and inlets into the sound. Elizabeth City could boast of a one-half-mile long wharf to handle the large steamers. It was of importance to the shipping industry in the same manner as Beaufort.[29] The Dismal Swamp Canal connected Elizabeth City to Norfolk, Virginia.

A North Carolina soldier, Sergeant John Wheeler, stationed at Portsmouth, wrote his mother in June before the enemy arrived:

My dear Mother

I eagerly embrace the first opportunity of writing you. Yesterday evening we arrived safely and with the exception of a delay mentioned in Hertford's communication to the "Express" we had not a single accident to happen to us. The news you will also learn in that letter; I suppose to employ this letter giving you private news. You must excuse the defects of this as I am constantly on duty and the few intervening moments are much confused by the conversation of the officers just now commenced dining.

Rest assured last Wednesday I will long be remembered by our company with gratitude to Murfreesboro. I scarcely believe memory when she tells me of those few weeks.

Having finished dinner I shall continue my letter. We had crabs, bluefish, spots, and mullets besides ham for dinner. Our table was made of plank unplaned set on legs of unhewn timber. Our utensils of tin made up our soldierly table quipments. But Oh! The water such stuff I never attempted to drink! Out of our tin drinking cups we strain it through our lips. Our cake today we saved for hard times which we expect at most any time. Our company is of good cheer and their only solicitude is sympathy with the feelings of those at home. We are very well situated. Better by far than we expected. Portsmouth has about 500 inhabitants. Joshua Taylor is dead and his family removed. All this region is called Ocracoke. Most of the troops are on this; the fort is on Beacon Island. We are ready. Goodbye.

Your son John

Send by Dr. Poole
1 mattress or at least a case for one
3 silk handkerchiefs
1 piece of sponge 1 inch thick 2 square
Other necessaries or luxuries as you chose especially plenty of applejack
Direct to me Portsmouth via Washington care of Capt Sharp Hert'f'd Inf.[30]

Unfortunately, John Wheeler died three weeks later from typhoid fever.

Portsmouth citizens "had very keen financial interest in the maintenance of slavery, if not the Confederacy. With the abandonment of the fort on Beacon Island, the entire city of Portsmouth was evacuated for the duration of the war by the entire population, save one poor woman. She, too, earnestly desired to go, but while others were fleeing, she was compelled to remain, according to tradition, she was too fat to get through the door. However, when everyone returned after the war she stated that she had been very courteously treated by the Yankees."[31] "The Portsmouthers did not abandon their homes for the preservation of slavery . . . . They left because of . . . panic. They fled in whatever boats were left . . ."[32] A noted writer described, "The most sorrowful sight of all was the Islanders leaving their homes from fear of the enemy. They could be seen in groups fleeing for dear life . . ."[33] The refugees feared for their life and preferred to travel with others but would flee alone if necessary.

Headlines in a Raleigh newspaper read:

> Robbers from North Carolina sack citizens and soldiers' belongings, Washington County and down east. With the capture of Hatteras, the inhabitants of Portsmouth fled. Many·in their haste having left all. A large portion of the baggage, clothing, money, & etc. of the regiment together with some arms, were left. The enemy did not and has not up to this time taken possession of Beacon Island . . . . Vandals . . . from Brant and Hog Islands and Hunting Quarters, on and near our water of Core Sound, went to the Fort and to Portsmouth and took clothing, stores, trunks, mattresses, and every thing upon which the scoundrels could lay their thieving hands on and carried them off. They broke open some of the trunks and took out the money, in one officer's trunk $150 in gold. They entered the poor citizens' houses and took feather beds, cooking utensils, ladies dressing, etc. There were 75 of them. They were armed. They were bold; swore they would have what they wanted, as it was war times . . . here is a foe in our mist, secret, malignant, and ever ready to take advantage of any disaster to eat us up.[34]

It was common practice in warfare for soldiers to destroy equipment that could not be carried off when the enemy overran them. When the Federals landed, newspapers advised citizens to burn their homes to keep it out of the enemies' hands. After the North Carolina's Mosquito Fleet had been disabled, the countryside panicked, and a few civilians of Elizabeth City set fire to two city blocks when word of the approaching enemy reached them.[35] W. W. Holden, editor of the *Raleigh Standard*, told his readers that he was against the practice of burning. Citing passages from diarist Catherine Edmondston that a Mr. Fearing of Elizabeth City, "after starting his wife & children to a place of safety, remained behind to fire his dwelling. As he left his own door he was shot [by the enemy] . . ."[36]

Confederate soldiers fleeing there after the fall of Elizabeth City in February 1862 set fire to the CSS *Appomattox* because it was too large by a few inches to go through the canal. Other canals gave competition to the Dismal Swamp Canal. After this, the activity around the Dismal Swamp Canal was mostly guerilla warfare, bridge burning, and ambushing people. Postwar, the canal and company were in ruins.[37]

Officers commentated on seeing the city's people fleeing and crowding up the roads with all types of carts and baggage. The roads both South and West were flooded with refugees who fled in all directions, especially to the interior of the state, to Oxford and Chapel Hill.[38] Arthur Jones is credited with saving the court records, carrying them off in a wagon to a barn in Parkville, where they were secreted until the close of the conflict.

Once the inhabitants of Elizabeth City heard that Roanoke Island had capitulated, terror seized them. What were they to do now? Those antisecessionists decided to stay while the opposite threw their valuables in any type of conveyance to flee before the gunboats arrived. A local man explained it as utter chaos:

> All the people of the town were on the road, most of them afoot, shoe-tops deep in mud and slush, muddy, bedraggled, unhappy, wretched. They were looking for an asylum of safety among country friends. We met scores of our town friends, forlorn and miserable. We asked for others, and they told us the town was on fire and deserted . . .[39]

E. M. Forbes, rector of the Christ Episcopal Church, wanted to surrender the city formally so the enemy wouldn't destroy the town. Sheriff Pool managed to move some of the records from the courthouse before it burned.[40] Once occupied by the enemy, citizens of Elizabeth City had four days to take the oath, "or they will take all property and be prisoners" printed the *Raleigh Register*. Soon, depredations began. Monroe Whedley lost all his chinaware, poultry, and hogs to foragers. Rev. Shadrack Warrell of Gatesville had a large cargo of corn stolen.[41]

Several families returned after the Union occupation. Of those who did, a teenager at that time recalled the disorder in a letter to her nephew postwar:

> . . . most of the homes were unoccupied, so your father selected the old home opposite the Marlins . . . . Every day or so, troops would come pass thr' the town, sometimes camp for the night, sometimes pass right on. Finally a detachment of troops, New York men and well behaved gentlemen—or well disciplined troops . . . were quartered in the Marlin home just in front of us and a Massachusetts detachment in the old Grandy home. Every woman in the town had to go there for a pass if she wanted to leave the town, and take the oath of neutrality—your mother and I took it there.
> Most likely your father took the oath of allegiance there or probably he was compelled to do so one night when he was arrested but released the next day.
> Am very sure your father's sympathies were with the South after his state seceded tho like many other fine men of the state he may have been a Union man before that time. Never did he ask those officers to his home or associate with them in a friendly way tho in some way Capt. Kent must have befriended him . . .
> As you say it was often a matter of life and death with the people living within the Yankee lines. They had no choice but were compelled to take the oath tho' we consoled ourselves by cofiding [sic] to our friend that we did it with an oriental reservation. Your father had a family to support, he could engage in no kind of business without their permission and there was nothing for him across the lines . . .[42]

Some citizens chose to join Federal forces, others tried to remain neutral, and still others became guerillas. Raids came at night, the military visiting the homes the next day. Retaliations on both sides killed many. Confederate soldiers visiting their families in the occupied area were at times found and hanged by unknown sources.[43] Federal raids continued in subsequent years.

This rebellious attitude of the "down-easterners" did not come as a surprise to the conquerors. The upper coastal regions on North Carolina were thick with antisecessionists. President Lincoln had written to U.S. General Winfield Scott on September 16, 1861, in which he asked that officers be appointed to go to Fort Hatteras to recruit loyalists.[44] Governor Henry Clark got wind of the throngs of North Carolina men taking the oath of allegiance Down East. He wrote the Secretary of War, Benjamin in Richmond that the men were probably "under duress." In a reply to Clark, Benjamin wrote September 27, "that anyone known to have sworn the Oath of Allegiance to the U.S. should be indicted for treason."[45]

North Carolinians who had waited to see the outcome of recent battles hurriedly packed their valuables to run to the interior of the state. Some families chose to flee to Suffolk, Virginia. It was their choice to run or not. Author Drew Faust has suggested that "a woman with the option to become a refugee was in some ways like a conscripted man able to hire a substitute."[46]

THE SOUTHERN REFUGEE
What sudden ill the world await,
From my dear residence I roam;
I must deplore the bitter fate,
To straggle from my native home.

The verdant willow droops her head,
And seems to bid fare thee well;
The flowers with the tears their fragrance shed,
Alas! Their parting tale to tell.

'Tis like the loss of Paradise,
Or Eden's garden left in gloom,
Where grief affords us no device;
Such as thy lot, my native home.

I never, never shall forget
My sad departure far away,
Until the sun of life is set,
And leaves behind no beam of day.

How can I from my seat remove
And leave my ever devoted home,
And the dear garden which I love,
The beauty of my native home?

Alas! Sequestered, set aside,
It is a mournful tale to tell;
'Tis like a lone deserted bride
That bade her bridegroom fare thee well.

I trust I soon shall dry the tear
And leave forever hence to roam,
Far from a residence so dear,
The place of beauty—my native home.[47]

That poem written by the black poet George M. Horton sums up the plight of civilians upon hearing of the enemy landing near their town. All wars create refugees, and North Carolinians were no different. Residents both black and white became refugees. Most well-to-do families took their slaves and fled to the piedmont area. To transport slaves out of harm's way, a person would need to take their tools, teams, and enough meat hauled in wagons over rough roads, which would be near impossible in the winter. Lower-income citizens did not have the means to leave.

Several parents whose homes were on the coast decided to leave their daughters at schools located in the interior of the state during the encroachment of the enemy as they fled. Mrs. G. W. Capehart and family in Bertie County left their home known as Scotch Hall to escape the enemy. Not wanting to completely abandon the place, Mrs. Capehart left the grounds to a caretaker by the name of Smith. One day, Mrs. Smith saw blue-coated soldiers with torches in their hands surrounding the house. Smith told them the family could not leave due to a sick child who could not be moved. The soldiers left but returned later and burned the Capehart fish house. The home was near the Albemarle Sound.[48] Mrs. Edmondston recorded in her journal that she was baking bread to carry to the refugees staying at her father's plantation. They were probably fleeing from Elizabeth City or Edenton. Edmondston said that they brought the news of the arrest of Mr. James C. Johnston who had been threatened with death because he refused to take the oath of allegiance to the United States. Seventy-year-old Johnston replied, "If you do, you cannot cheat me out of much of life." He became a prisoner in his own home.[49]

Numerous citizens Down East abandoned their homes because of roving bands of bandits, whether from the occupying forces or local individuals. Usually, their homes were destroyed. This situation caused a resident, John Pool, to write the governor:

> Some of the leading farmers and citizens of Bertie County had a consultation . . . in Winsor—for the purpose of making a representation to your Excellency in regard to the condition of affairs in this County, and to ask for some executive action on their behalf. This county is almost entirely surrounded by waters of the Albemarle Sound & the Roanoke & Chowan Rivers—all of which are navigable to the largest of the enemy's steamers. The gun boats of the enemy are traversing these waters almost daily. There is not a Confederate soldier here, and not the least show of protection extended to the citizens. They are at the complete mercy of the enemy. The greater part of the able bodied men of the county have volunteered. Some have been taken out by the Conscript law—& the attempted execution of that law has drove many—to the enemy at Plymouth. The loyal citizens have more to dread from these deserters than from the regular army. By the Census of 1860, it appears that there are 8000 slaves in this County, & only 6000 whites . . . . It is with great difficulty that the few men left here, unsupported—are able to guard the avenues of escape & keep up efficient police regulations.
>
> If the Slave holders, being men of means, fly, upon approach of danger, & leave poorer classes who are unable to move, & the families of soldiers in the Army, exposed not only to the enemy, but to the gangs of run away slaves, it will produce—a feeling much to be dreaded.[50]

Slave owners thought they had the solution for runaways. A man wrote: "All the boats and canoes are sunk about here to keep the negroes from getting them to run away in. Though none is gone from about here yet. I hope when the Yankeys come here they will not stay long."[51] This may have stopped some, but a determined runaway would find his own route.

Those who chose to stay, no matter their allegiance, faced danger each day.[52] A diarist penned of a neighbor:

> . . . they have been driven from their homes by the advance of the enemy and are now seeking an asylum, a shelter for their heads . . . 19 whites of all ages plus their 70 Negroes, all homeless & houseless.[53]

With that number of persons needing shelter, a person could see why it would be difficult to take the entire group in as guests. While John Shute was serving in the Southern Army, his father put the family in a horse-drawn wagon and left the city, but not before he had burned his house to keep the enemy from getting it.[54]

Once owners left, abandoned homes became a treasure ripe for the picking. Whether by the Union soldiers or homegrown thieves, property was then stolen, damaged, or burned. On occasion, the pillaging was carried out by ex-slaves or Loyalist men with a grudge.[55] After a base camp was constructed, enemy soldiers went on foraging treks. Adjutant G. Winsor said:

> You might paste the order against foraging on each man's back, and still you would find them going through every house, even the quarters of the negroes, and if they left anything to eat, or did not change the water in their canteens for applejack, they would not be human.[56]

Federal General George McClellan ordered General Ambrose Burnside during his occupation of eastern North Carolina to "use great caution in regard to proclamations," to say as little as possible about "politics or the Negro," and to "merely state the true issue for which we are fighting is the preservation of the Union & upholding the laws of the Gen'l Govt, & stating that all who conduct themselves properly will as far as possible be protected in their persons & property." Burnside had this notice published in the newspaper:

PROCLAMATION—TO THE CITIZENS OF NORTH CAROLINA

The mission of our joint communications, not to invade any of your rights, but to assert the authority of the United States, and thus to close with you the desolating war brought upon your State by comparatively a few bad men in your midst.

Influenced infinitely by the worst passions of human nature than by any show of elevated reason, they are still urging you astray, to gratify their unholy purposes.

They impose upon your credulity by telling you of wicked and even diabolical intentions on our part,—of our desire to destroy your freedom, demolish your property, liberate your slaves, injure your women, and such like enormities, all of which, we assure you, is not only ridiculous, but utterly and willfully false.

We are Christians as well as yourselves, and we profess to know full well, and to feel profoundly the sacred obligations of the character.

No apprehensions need to be entertained that the demands of humanity or justice will be disregarded.

We shall inflict no injury unless forced to do so by your own acts, and upon this you may confidently rely.

Those men are your worst enemies. They, in truth, have drawn you into your present condition, and are the real disturbers of your peace, and the happiness of your firesides.

We invite you in the name of the Constitution, and in that of virtuous loyalty and civilization, to separate yourselves at once from their malign influence, to return to your allegiance, and not compel us to resort further to the force under our control.

The Government asks only that its authority may be recognized; and, we repeat, in no manner or way does it desire to interfere with your laws constitutionally established, your property of any sort, or your usages in any respect.

A.E. Burnside,
Brig. Gen. commanding Dep't. N.C.
J. C. Rowan,
Commanding Naval Forces in Albemarle and Pamlico Sounds.[57]

TO THE PEOPLE
OF EASTERN
NORTH CAROLINA.

The Government of the United States, by Major-General Burnside, in command of the Department of North Carolina, has authorized the raising of a regiment in the Eastern part of this State, which regiment will be under the protection of the United States, and commanded by a United States Officer We, the undersigned, having full authority so to do, invite the citizens of this and the neighboring counties to assist us in the enterprise.

All who are willing to enlist under the "Old Flag," will be paid, clothed, and fed by the United States.

The Line Officers will be chosen by the men of the respective companies. The Colonel, Lieutenant Colonel, Major, and Adjutant, will be appointed by the United States.

It is to be understood that this regiment is intended for the protection of loyal citizens, by bringing them together under military discipline, and will not be called upon to leave the State. Those able to bear arms, who stand aloof from this movement, cannot expect that the Government will protect those who make no effort to aid themselves.

EDWARD E. POTTER, CAPT. U. S. A.

COL. COMMANDING 1st REG N. C. V.

JOHN R. RESSVESS,

ACTING LIEUT. COL. 1st REG. N. C. V.

Washington, Beaufort Co., North Carolina,

May 1st, 1862.

General Burnside's Proclamation
Perkins Library, Duke University

Burnside instructed his corps to "support the constitution and the laws, to put down rebellion, and to protect the persons and property of the loyal and peaceable citizens of the state. While on the march, he stipulated, 'all unnecessary injury to houses, barns, fences, and other property will be carefully avoided, and in all cases the laws of civilized warfare will be strictly observed.'"

Citing passages from author Mark Grimsley, "Within four days of his proclamation . . . a Union brigade from Burnside's command burned an entire village to the ground."[58]

A lady recorded in her journal: "The inhabitants of Edenton were leaving panic stricken to avoid the alternative of the oath of Allegiance to the U.S. or a residence in fort Warren [Boston]. The Gun Boats came up to Edenton & issued Burnside's proclamation . . ."[59]

In early December 1861, U.S. General Edward Wild marched his troops from Norfolk, Virginia, into South Mills. His target was the Camden County Courthouse. General Wild was after traitors hiding in the swamps. Most of all settlements discovered on his march were burned and confiscated, innocent men were hanged, and women were taken as hostages.[60] He and his men now had a reputation for brutal violence. The locals feared and hated him. Wild bragged about his conquests to superiors:

> At a public meeting in Elizabeth City 523 citizens of the county signed a petition asking the state government and Gov. Vance to withdraw the Partisan Rangers so that [Gen.] Butler would not send Wild back.[61]

The great exodus of white citizens began while slaves escaped to Union forces. February 21,1862, "Today there were quite a number of Contrabands arrived from the main land who represent the Rebels very much scared and clearing out as fast as possible . . . ," wrote a Northern soldier.[62] As the months passed and more servants ran away, a lady said:

> We have to depend almost entirely upon ourselves for the negroes do not half work and they are just as good as free in this section. I have done more hard work this year than I ever thought I could do and do it with more ease than any negroe you can find but goodness knows I don't like hard work AT ALL; but I must work or STARVE.[63]

1854 students of Wesleyan Female Institute.
UNC Collection Photographic Archives

This scenario repeated itself throughout the eastern counties. Hundreds of Negroes escaped or ran amok, disobeying their masters. Pillaging took place by the Negroes on innocent persons.[64]

Once safe under the protection of the invaders, it was not always the idealistic place made out to be. The previous woman received a letter from her friend informing that:

> Some refugees from Carteret and Beaufort stopped with us and told us all the news—it seems the Negroes are willing to be free but they do not want to fight; they are like the Onslow Secessionists—they want the war continued but they keep at a respectable distance from the battlefield. The Yankee had a draft in Newbern some four-five weeks ago and the Negroes became so unmanageable in consequence of it that the Yankees shot eighty-ninety of them before they would submit, they have no idea of fighting for THEIR liberty.[65]

Students of Chowan Female Institute in Murfreesboro were sent away when General Burnside took Roanoke Island. Wesleyan Female College closed with the news of an enemy landing and did not reopen until postwar.[66] Pandemonium spread as rumors were flying about. John Moore recalled that citizens met each day at various churches to pray. The inhabitants of Murfreesboro quickly packed and left, throwing their trunks in various conveyances. Kate Wheeler wrote on February 19 that the town was packed and ready to flee if the enemy came near. Instead, the town, churches, and schools filled with Confederate soldiers. "The Baptist Church was converted into a hospital . . ." On February 26, her mother dug up the valuables she had hidden from the Yankees. The commander of these troops wrote that the white population "have been so long neglected that they are perfectly demoralized." The young ladies in town welcomed the soldiers who frequently visited and entertained the girls.[67]

John W. Graham wrote to his father about the conditions Down East in Camden and Pasquotank, where it was sparsely populated by both blacks and whites:

> You meet very few Negroes, and not a great many white people. The large majority of them are still true to the South, and freely gave what they could to the soldiers, and what they did sell was very cheap . . . bacon—$1 lb.; 2 hams for $10.00; 7 dozen eggs at 25c, & "RATIFICATION" money as the Confederate money is called.[68]

Edenton was next in line to conquer. With no Confederate troops in sight, Mr. Norcum, a Union sympathizer, gave up the city to the Federals. Originally a town of thirty-eight hundred people, when the enemy arrived in Beaufort in 1862, only five hundred old folks and children remained in town.[69] During occupation, a Union soldier said, "It is a pleasant place [Edenton], only it looks lonely and deserted. Yet quite a number of people were there. Saw a number of pretty girls."[70] Aurora in Beaufort County held many refugees, fugitives, slaves, Indians, and free Negroes.[71] The countryside of Gates County was described by a Confederate soldier as being rich with grain and livestock. The citizens owning Negroes had fled with them.

Residents Down East continued to flee the enemy throughout 1862. The CSS *Appomattox* carried refugees out of harm's way. The Federal Army sought to take the Dismal Swamp Canal to break the Confederates' supply line from southeast Virginia. With the approach of the enemy, the CSS *Appomattox* tried to escape through the canal but was a couple of inches too wide. The captain burned the ship rather than let it fall to the Federals.

As the Union command traveled inward from the coast, the flight of civilians continued. Most female refugees rarely returned to their homes until after the war; however, other families returned when they were told the area was free of the enemy. A soldier bore further testimony to his mother:

Some of the ladies determined to remain at home, but the Yankees commenced throwing shells & for fear of having their houses burnt over their heads, had to leave, one lady had to take up 2 sick children (with diphtheria) & go into the woods or any where she could, & it was during that snow. Many of the people took their carpets & made tents of them & run their families & Negroes into the woods [describes Hamilton].[72]

Later in the war, this soldier told of other refugees: "We marched 25 miles, until . . . we got within ten miles of Plymouth when we met the fugitives from the town which had been evacuated two hours before."[73]

At the New Bern railhead, it was utter chaos as panicked women tried to get their belongings on the train. Mrs. F. C. Roberts's husband was in the Confederate service. As the town of New Bern got word that the enemy was advancing, Mr. Roberts took a pistol to his wife and said, "Don't fall into the enemy's hands, use this if they come tonight, on the children, and on yourself; tomorrow, it they don't come you must leave town." She sat up all night with the pistol at her side. The wounded and dead were brought into town and laid on her lawn. The next day, the Methodist church was turned into a hospital. She sent nourishment to the patients, then went to the depot with her children and nanny. Roberts revealed that there was complete disorder at the station with panicked women trying to get out of town. Mrs. Roberts ended up in Hillsborough. In one month, she returned to her home because the enemy did not show. She and a Ms. Manly began sewing a flag for Fort Macon.[74].

Mary N. Bryan, a citizen of New Bern, almost waited too late to leave. She had prepared a hot meal and sat down to eat when the Federal troops came ashore. Leaving everything on the table, she barely caught the last train leaving the city. Tradition said the soldiers came in and enjoyed her supper. The family had a year's supply of meat in the smokehouse, which was stolen.[75] Countless New Bern persons took refuge in Kinston, Goldsboro, Raleigh, and Hillsborough during the conflict. Thomas Burgwyn's family moved to Raleigh as refugees. Leonidas Polk's family became refugees living in different states including North Carolina. Mrs. Frances Devereux Polk, her children, Fanny and Hamilton, refugeed in Raleigh and Asheville. The Rodman family traveled to Greensboro as refugees.

Mrs. Edmondston's husband, a member of the militia in Hertford County, discussed with her how pitiful it was to see the fright of the inhabitants (near Hamilton). "The roads are crowded with refugees in vehicles of every description, endeavoring to move what of their property they can to save it from the grasp of the invaders," she wrote.[76] A. F. Harrington penned a letter to his brother, J. M., back home in Harnett County that the people fleeing the area (Onslow) helped carry the soldiers' equipment on their carts.[77] The piedmont area was considered a safe haven from the invaders. A public meeting was held in Yanceyville to invite the families that had been evacuated from Washington to receive their hospitalities.[78]

That spring, the *Raleigh Register* told its subscribers:

> The city [Raleigh] is crowded with refugees from Virginia, and different parts of the state. On Thursday last several ladies were compelled to sleep on the floor of the parlor at the Yarborough House and one party of ladies were obliged to sit up the whole night for the want of beds.[79]

Mrs. Mary Bryan went first to Greensboro, then Lexington before settling in Wake County. She was able to have a garden at the last place and a cow. Mrs. Bryan's elderly mother also accompanied them, along with their slaves. All the women knitted socks for the military, and she said they sent off a box every day. Like other Southern women, they cut up carpets for blankets.[80]

Only young boys and old men remained at home, which seemed to be the norm in all Southern states by midwar. The South was described as a land devoid of men. Citizens from other cities fled to what they considered a safe area throughout the war.[81] James Cameron and family from Wilmington refugeed in Anson County. Lillie V. Archbell, author of *Carolina and the Southern Cross*, was eleven when the foes came to Kinston. She was a refugee from New Bern.[82] A family from Charleston, South Carolina, refugeed at Davidson.[83] Other families from Norfolk and Petersburg took refuge in Chapel Hill later in the war.

"The rich and poor met together. Charity was more freely dispensed, pride of station was forgotten" in most situations, wrote Cornelia P. Spencer.[84] This may have been true regarding the donation of time and materials for the military; but when it came to refugees, traveling, and housing, this was not always the case. The war caused different levels of society to mix. Paul Escott has said, "The war aggravated class conflicts, [and] propagated bitter social dissension . . ."[85]

UNION SENTIMENT DOWN EAST*

Once the Union Army and Navy infiltrated eastern North Carolina, towns along the rivers and sounds became vulnerable for the taking. Only six channels could be approached by steamers—Beaufort, Ocracoke, Hatteras, Oregon, and two in Cape Fear.[86] Hatteras Inlet was deepest and most important as far as location. "This inlet offered the safest and most reliable escape from the . . . sea."[87]

Union troops left remembrances of the inhabitants:

> April 20, 1862— Among the white people about here, are very few who would be ranked among the first or even second class. Nearly all of them are what is called the poor white trash or clay eaters. The women dip snuff and chew plug tobacco.
>
> April 1863—The natives for miles around come in droves [to] take the oath, get their amnesty papers and order for salt, and after being cautioned not to be found breaking their allegiance they go away happy. There are probably some honest men among them who would like to do about right if they dared to, but the whole thing looks ludicrous, for there is evidently not one in 100 for the hope of obtaining a little salt. The boys call it the salt oath.[88]

U.S. Colonel Rush Hawkins on the Outer Banks said, "Within ten days after the landing nearly all the male adults had taken the oath of allegiance."[89] U.S. Commodore Rowen told Lieutenant Quackenbush to go easy on the populace of Bertie County:

> Say to the people . . . their safety depends on their neutrality and good conduct. Promise nothing in the way of protection . . . keep your people [sailors] in hand, that they neither scatter nor do violence to private property.

Rowen also ordered him to "seize and destroy public property . . ."[90]

This part of the state, because of strong Union sympathy, became an unsafe place to live. It seemed that neighbors turned on one another due to their allegiances. Vandalism, robbery, and bushwhacking took hold. Deserters, men avoiding conscription, and Tories formed in bands to wreak havoc on Southern families. The locals called this gang Buffaloes. About seventeen miles above Edenton on the Chowan River sat Wingfield Plantation, home of Richard Dillard.[91] The Buffaloes selected to make this as their home base. A soldier with the Forty-ninth NCT described the Buffaloes his unit was to hunt down:

---

*   For more information on this see chapter 11.

Negro Life on the Trent River
N.C. Department of Archives & History, Photographic Division

There was a class of men in Bertie County known as buffaloes. They were similar to the Tories in the Revolution, only they were not armed like the Tories were. They were simply spies for the enemy. Whenever our troops made a move in that country they ran from one house to another until they carried the news to the enemy at Plymouth, however, [we] broke up their headquarters, and they were now hiding about in the swamps. Company I was detailed and sent down among them, with orders to shoot every one we could find without halting him. Of course we disobeyed that order, for it too barbarous to shoot a man without halting him.[92]

He pointed out that the better class of citizens wanted them to capture the Buffaloes because those with Southern sentiments had problems keeping their provisions out of the hands of the Tories. Another description of Buffaloes follows:

. . . the term Buffalo becoming a generic name for those who avoided Confederate service and Civilian Buffaloes can be divided into two classes . . .

the first—and worst—were those who refused military service on either side, hid out in the woods and swamps, and preyed on the inhabitants of isolated farms and homesteads. They were bushwhackers, thieves, and scoundrels who enjoyed living wild. The second and larger class were the non-violent fiscal Buffaloes. They traded between the lines under Union permits, or sold their services to the Northerners after Federal troops occupied parts of the state.[93]

In order to protect themselves, secesh citizens composed their own local defense, which was not strong enough to face regular military. Some called them a guerilla band. The Perquimans Partisan Rangers were formed primarily as Home Guards to protect Southern loyalists. "The rangers contributed to the ongoing civil strife that characterized the Albemarle during the war . . . rangers harassed Federal forces, prevented slaves from crossing Union lines, plundered, terrified, and murdered Union citizens." This force only operated a year.[94]

Dr. G. C. Moore in Mulberry Grove informed his brother-in-law of the struggle with Buffaloes:

> We are kept constantly in a state of apprehension, either by a Yankee advance or a night visit of the Buffaloes. The provisions laid up for a years supply of the family are in constant jeopardy. The visits of robbery to those having provisions and other valuables in this county are al most a nightly occurrence. They come to one of my nearest neighbors on Friday night last and took off a cart load of bacon, clothing, and other valuables. How soon they may rouse me from my chamber & demand my keys, God only knows, but every morning when I awake and find everything safe, I feel that I am under new and special obligations to my divine protector . . . . When my neighbor's wife (for he is in the army) was despoiled of at least half of her living, the State had 1000 men between her and the Yankee line (the Chowan River). But these robbers are living in our midst, they know where the troops are stationed, and easily avoid their pickets. They are deserters or fugitive conscripts, outlying in our swamps or pocoson. Dr. Weaver [his son-in-law] has been robbed of about 400 pounds of his meat, which was probably carried off by a band of these fellows. They did not arouse him from his sleep, but made forcible entrance to his smoke house & helped themselves. Are we to be subjected to this condition of things for much longer? Those in the Yankee lines beyond the river are much better off at present than we are. They are not, robbed, nor are they in constant apprehension of disturbances but I hope as Gov. Vance has at last sent down a force sufficient to drive the Yankees from Colerain, he will keep a part of it . . . here until he has also driven beyond the river these robbers.[95]

The eastern area was perfect for illegal trading, as the Dismal Swamp hid guerillas, Negro runaways, and deserters. Concerned citizens met and approved a resolution by the Union General Ed Wild, who "promised sanctuary from the universal 'panic and distress' that had been visited upon Perquimans if the country would renounce blockade running and petition Gov. Vance to disband the Perquiman Rangers."[96]

Hatteras residents sent a letter to U.S. Commander Rush Hawkins to ask for protection and return of their property because they had been loyal citizens, not secessionists. Hawkins ordered his men to shoot any soldier caught looting these civilians. This act swayed the loyal subjects to take the oath to the United States.[97]

After capture and occupation by the enemy, Hatteras residents could no longer get basic provisions such as flour, sugar, and salt from the mainland. That fall, conditions worsened. Residents needed a leader. To remedy the situation, a meeting held in November proclaimed Methodist minister Marble Nash Taylor as Provisional Governor. The new governor went to New York City to ask for assistance for the loyal bankers. By the end of November, approximately eight thousand dollars had been collected, along with food, which was shipped by steamer to the Outer Banks.[98] When things had calmed down on Hatteras, the inhabitants with Union sentiment who had remained on the islands carried on business as usual.

President Lincoln, in hopes of bringing the "rebel" states back into the Union, began appointing military governors to those seceded states with strong anti-secession views. Taylor was told to hold a congressional election. Elected was Charles H. Foster, but Congress refused to recognize him. Instead, Lincoln appointed Edward Stanly, formerly from the state, as provisional governor and Foster as captain to recruit North Carolinians into the Federal Army. It was hoped this appointment would bring the state back into the Union and reestablish Federal authority. Stanly toured towns in the eastern part of the state to encourage them to return to the Union. He held frequent meetings with General Burnside in New Bern, then under Federal control. An officer recorded in his diary: "A salute of 16 guns was fired from Fort Totten in honor of the arrival of the Honorable Edwin Staton [sic], the appointed governor of this state . . ."[99]   .

A Northern soldier wrote:

> Governor Stanly established his own standard for determining the loyalty of residents in eastern North Carolina. In some cases, he allowed citizens to take an oath of neutrality instead of the prescribed oath of allegiance to the Federal government. He gave citizens "protections" against the interference of Union military authorities and issued permits for the transfer of goods through Union lines.[100]

Stanly threatened the confiscation of owners' vessels that carried slaves away from New Bern. Provisional Governor Stanly "had restored slaves to loyal masters, for almost all the inhabitants of New Bern had gone away and he wished to reassure them that if they should return, they would be well treated . . ." Other times, when slave owners took the oath to the Union, he had their slaves restored to them.[101] To illustrate, Nicholas Bray and his wife went to New Bern to find their escaped property. Bray was looking for two sisters—found one, but not the other. The escapees' friends hid her until Bray grew tired and left. Townsmen were incensed that Stanly would allow such an abominable thing to happen. The colored people had just grown secure in their new "city" when they had to start hiding again. Stanly issued passes for these planters to come into town to look for their runaway property.[102]

In another similar case, Stanly reported to U.S. authorities that armed soldiers and Negroes "visited the premises of a Mrs. Page . . . and carried away Several negroes, and a parcel of bedding & other furniture: that they were very insolent in their conduct and threatened to have the town shelled if they were interfered with." He said the Negroes were led by Matthew, a slave belonging to James C. Johnston. Mr. Stanly asked the general to protect the residents from such outrages.[103]

The newly appointed governor's executive powers came under question by Northern congressmen. Stanly had a friend who had been jailed for his secessionist beliefs released. Stanly could be labeled as a unionist, but not as an abolitionist. It is interesting to note that his brother, Alfred, became a Confederate supporter. Edward Stanly tried to please the secessionists, the disloyal residents, and the Union military. One can imagine the pressure he was up against. He was regarded with hatred, suspicion, and contempt as a traitor to his state.[104] Military officials frequently questioned the sincerity of the citizens who "enjoyed the governor's favor."[105]

Mentioned earlier, the partisan rangers continued to roam the eastern counties, committing depredations on those loyal to the old Union after occupation. Five men wrote a lengthy letter to Governor Stanly:

TO THE COMMANDER IN CHIEF AT NEWBERNE

Dear Sir,

We the Under Signed Loyal Citizens have been robd and ruined by the rebels & consequently have been compeled to flee from Our homes & firesides. We have taken Reffuge within the Federal lines and many have left all that is near & dear to us in Hyde and we dare not go there to see Our Wives & children as there being a company of Gurrillas Stationed in the County who Stile themselves Rangers but they are Steam Roling all the Loyal Citizens (that) they can (lay) thare hands on & many of the citizens of Hyde County have Volunteered in the Federal Army with the promis that the County should be protected but the promise has not been fulfilled. The Loyal Volunteers have been kept at Washington, N.C. & are now stationed at Bearn [New Bern], N.C. whare they remain in Inglorious inactivity, anxious to go to Hyde County to avenge themselves (on) thare enemies and the Enemies of the best Government ever established on Earth. By Refering to a map go and See the Location of Said County. the Soil is more fertile than any in N.C. and furnishes more Supplies to the Confederacy than any 4 County within the limit of Said State. Thare are ¼ Million Bushels of Corn in Hyde County at this Present time wheat and pork in abundance & many Other necessaries of life all of which the Rebels for the past 12 months have been wagoning out to the Enemies of the United States unmolested—back by a band of Rebels & that within a few miles of the federal lines. Courts are held in Said County. Thare members are Elected to the Legislature of No. Carolina & they are acting as independent as if they were 1000 miles from the federal lines. we the Undersigned therefore humbly pray the Authorities in this Department to assist us in driving the miscreants from Our fertile County, we pray you to furnish us with [*illegible*] North Carolina troops, arms & ammunition the County can easily be garrisoned & the proper place will be near Rosebay Bridge & the County once Subdued can be easily kept in Subjection by throwing up fortifications & when the works are completed thare will be no need of the regulars. thare would be a Sufficient Quantity of Loyaliusts & deserters to hold the County without being any expense to our government & be able to furnish the Markets at Newbern & Beaufort with abundant means of life & the Surrounding Country. we therefore Submit this to your considerations Humbly praying you to Assist us.

Sylvester McGowan
Wm. B. Tooley
Redmond Tooley
John G. (his mark) Sadler
Jesse H. Jones?[106]

The governor's reply:

Edward Stanly
Military Governor of the State of North Carolina
In the United States of America
To
Sylvester McGowan, Gent.

By virtue of the authority conferred on me to enlist Independent Volunteer Companies of loyal citizens, to Serve within the State or their respective counties and districts during the present rebellion, I do hereby authorize and empower you to form a company, of good and loyal citizens, to act as a home guard in the County of Hyde, and to aid the government of the United States in its efforts to provide the means of maintaining peace and Security to the loyal inhabitants of the State of North Carolina, until they shall be able to establish a civil government.

The Said company will be organized, officered, armed, equipped, and paid, while in actual Service and Subsisted as other Volunteers.

A company consists of Sixty four men.

If they Muster and Keep together the United States will pay them, and furnish clothing, subsistence, and every thing usually furnished to Volunteers.

If they met only occasionally, they will have furnished to them rations and arms. When Sixty four men shall be Enlisted, and elect a captain and other officers, I will give them commissions.

When you enlist twenty men, they will be furnished arms and ammunition.

You will enlist only good and fine citizens of the United States, whose loyalty is unquestioned.

Your chief duty will be, to protect loyal and peaceable citizens, in the exercise of their rights and privileges, Secured to them by the Constitution of the United States, and to arrest all traitors, who are giving aid and comfort to the Rebellion now existing, and especially to Secure loyal people from being arrested, and dragged from their homes, without the benefit of trial, having violated no law, and not knowing who their accusers are.

You have authority to see, that all men who have given aid or comfort to the enemy, and who refuse to subscribe the oath of allegiance, be deprived of their arms.

You will not permit any prisoner to be punished in any way, only using such restraint as is necessary to prevent escape.

You will take special care to prevent all pillaging, and destruction of, or injury to property.

If any man is taken prisoner, whose previous good character justifies you in relying upon his keeping his promise, and will subscribe the oath of allegiance, you are authorized to discharge him.

Particular instructions will be given you when requested.
New Berne, Nov. 18th, 1862   [signed] Edw. Stanly
                                                    Military Governor of North Carolina[107]

Mr. Stanly wrote Lincoln that "the Emancipation Proclamation had destroyed all hopes for success of his [Stanly] conciliatory policy in North Carolina." He felt the proclamation "would only prolong the war . . ."[108] Lincoln ordered Stanly to hold an election for the Thirty-Seventh Congress. The election was only open to white men who had resided in North Carolina for more than a year. Jennings Pigott, his secretary, won the election.[109] "After a year of disillusionment and thwarted efforts, during which time he [Stanly] accomplished nothing," he resigned January 15, 1863, went to Washington City, receiving a cool reception there, then returned to California, where he lived prior to his appointment.[110] Having served less than a year, his short term was over.

THE EFFECTS OF THE PROCLAMATION—FREED NEGROES COMING INTO OUR LINES AT NEWBERN, NORTH CAROLINA.—[SEE PAGE 319.]

Freed Negroes coming into our lines at New Bern, 1863
N. C. Division of Archives & History, Photographic Archives.

General A. E. Burnside, stationed in New Bern, wrote on March 21, 1862, to Secretary of War Stanton that "the city is overrun with fugitives from surrounding towns . . ."[111] The influx of runaways and white unionists overpowered the infrastructure set up by the Federals. When slaves learned that the U.S. army was in control of the Outer Banks, the sounds, and New Bern, they left the plantations in record number. By late spring, about one thousand congregated on the island. Finding the road to freedom, a multitude of ex-slaves strained the resources on the islands. General Burnside chose not to return the runaways back to their owners. He declared them "contraband," a term that stuck with the runaways throughout the war. Contrabands continued to pour in, along with indigent whites, so many that the numbers overtaxed the general. Burnside appointed missionary Vincent Colyer as the "superintendent of the poor" in February 1862.[112] Colyer had been working in the hospitals of Washington City with the YMCA. Mr. Colyer was sent to New Bern after occupation, and Rev. Horace James took his place at Hatteras. Ed Stanly arrived a few weeks after Colyer.

Although General Ben Butler promised not to influence the slaves, his men conscripted fifteen to twenty enslaved men without the owner's permission to be used as guides and boatmen.[113] Butler said to use runaways as workers because he didn't have the authority to arm and train them the summer of 1862.

More slaves ran to the occupied area after the Emancipation Proclamation in January 1863. U.S. Secretary of War Stanton then said to start recruiting blacks. In August 1863, the recruiting business was in full swing. None came forward until okayed by Abraham Galloway, an octoroon.[*][114] Galloway had great influence over his peers. When the Northern army tried to recruit blacks in occupied New Bern and Roanoke, he would not let them enlist until certain provisions were passed. The Negroes were to get the same pay as those in the Massachusetts regiment, their families provided for, and their children taught to read; and if captured, they were to be treated as prisoners of war. Federal authorities agreed, and then hundreds signed up.[115]

---

*   Octoroon, a person who is one-eight Negro. Research has shown that Galloway had a Negro mother and a white father, making him a mulatto.

Freedmen as Union scouts
N.C. Division of Archives & History, Photographic Division.

Negroes in occupied New Bern
N.C. Division of Archives & History, Photographic Division

Virtually, every able-bodied black man could find employment with the army. The old and disabled were out of luck. A New Jersey private wrote in his diary that they went to a meeting where the speaker was an octoroon named Galloway who was in the detective service of General Butler and that Confederate authorities had offered ten thousand dollars' reward for his capture. Galloway would be considered today as a civil rights leader. William H. Singleton left the plantation to seek freedom. He went to the Federals, offered his services, and recruited and trained black men as soldiers.

By mid-1863, living conditions for the runaways had grown so acute around New Bern that Roanoke Island was chosen as the site to erect a village for the freedman and their families. But how could this be done without implements—without saws, hammers, and agricultural tools? Federal soldiers initially helped; then after another trip North to solicit aid from benevolent people of New York and New England who opened their wallets, Rev. James came home with almost nine thousand dollars.[116]

Missionary Colyer told that he employed hundreds of former bondsmen in building fortifications at eight dollars a month. They were to receive a clothing allowance one time. He estimated that ten thousand refugees swarmed to the area, of which approximately twenty-five hundred men were physically able to work. These men also worked on Roanoke Island, and the whole eventually ended up at New Bern. He further stated the men built Fort Totten at New Bern, Fort Burnside on Roanoke Island, and another fort in Washington. Three hundred black men served as crewman on forty steamers; others loaded and unloaded cargo. The U.S. quartermasters, commissary, and ordinance offices employed the black refugees. The newly freed men built the railroad bridge across the Trent River, other bridges in the area, and the docks at Roanoke Island and elsewhere, "upwards of fifty volunteers . . . were kept constantly employed on . . . duty of spies, scouts, and guides." These scouts were considered invaluable to U.S. forces. These brave souls would travel between thirty and three hundred miles into the interior of the state to cities such as Kinston, Goldsboro, Swansboro, Tarboro, Trenton, and Onslow. In some instances, Colyer armed the scouts. A colored man named Charley made frequent trips inland to gather information on the rebels. Two free Negroes from Onslow County went to Colyer. They had hidden in the swamps for more than a year to escape conscription. If they had not bathed their feet in turpentine, the hounds would have caught them. Those caught would be hung or shot on the spot. One scout was killed; others known to Southern men ended up missing.[117] A Northern soldier wrote, "About 20 Counterband [sic] arrived hear from little Washington, N.C. & gave information to the effect that the Rebels was fortifying themselves very strong in the vicinity of Washington and that they ware going to make a desperate stand . . ."[118] The Confederacy sought the use of Negroes to spy on the Federals too.

Women were employed as maids, cooks, laundry workers, and seamstresses. Those working in the hospitals earned four dollars a month with one food ration and one clothing allowance. Black Aunt Charlotte, employed by the Federals as a cook to the sick, also cooked for Union officers in New Bern, earning six dollars a month. She was highly thought of and was mentioned by soldiers writing home to their families in the North. Charlotte's owners fled their large home, which the Sanitary Commission transposed into a hospital. Charlotte "managed the other Negroes on the plantation as if her mistress had been there."[119]

When the refugees arrived in the New Bern area, they crowded into every available empty building including deserted homes of the white residents. Speaking of contrabands just outside of New Bern, a Northern soldier described them as wearing rough hats and living in log cabins with a stick and clay chimneys. He said:

> Many of the able-bodied among them have found opportunity to labor
> in the Government employ, yet the conditions of life among them are such
> as to touch one's heart, for the helpless creatures are "as sheep having no
> Shepard," and in that passing hour was born the resolve to do something to
> make their freedom indeed a boon to these freedmen.[120]

Soon, schools opened taught by Northern women. Eighteen hundred penniless white people sought out Dr. Colyer for provisions. Colyer had work for the refugees, offering to the whites twelve dollars a month compared with eight dollars given to black men.[121]

No one could describe the plight of the refugees in New Bern and Roanoke Island better than Horace James:

New York, June 27, 1863

To the Public:

Four days ago, I was ordered by major-General Foster, commanding the 18th army corps, to proceed northward as far as this city and Boston, to collect materials and implements for colonizing the families of colored soldiers upon Roanoke Island.

It might have been done through other agencies, but not so quickly. Time is an object with us, that we may save a portion of the present season for crops and gardens, and gather together within a few days, the resources which might not have been secured by correspondence alone, in as many months. This is my apology to the public, if one were necessary, for being here.

The exigency now existing in the department of North Carolina, is this: We hold possession of several important places along the coast, the principal of which are *Beaufort, Newbern, Washington, Plymouth, Roanoke Island,* and *Hatteras Inlet.* At all these points we have troops, and from them our lines extend back some distance into the country. Within these lines dwell large numbers of loyal colored people, and but few whites. Eight thousand negroes reside at Newbern, and at all the other points named several thousands more. It is among these people that Gen. E. A. Wild is now enlisting his African brigade. One regiment is already full, and another is well advanced. As the work goes on, it becomes a question of more and more interest what shall be done with the families of these colored soldiers? How shall we dispose of the aged and infirm, the women and the children, the youth not old enough to enlist in the regiment? In the absence of the able-bodied men to whom they would naturally look for protection and support, it is evident that the government, or benevolent individuals and agencies co-operating with the government, must make temporary provision for them, locate them in places of safety, and teach them, in their ignorance, how to live and support themselves.

The remedy proposed to meet this unique state of things, is to colonize these freed people, not by deportation out of the country, but by giving them facilities for living in it; not by removing them north, where they are not wanted, and could not be happy; nor even by transporting them beyond the limits of their own State; but by giving them land, and implements wherewith to subdue and till it, thus stimulating their exertions by making them proprietors of the soil, and by directing their labor into such channels as promise to be remunerative and self-supporting.

The location decided upon in which to commence this work, in North Carolina, is Roanoke Island. Its insular position favors this design, making it, like the islands around Hilton Head, in South Carolina, comparatively safe against attack, and free from fear of depredation. It is an island ten or twelve miles long, by four or five miles in breadth, well wooded, having an abundance of good water, a tolerably productive soil, a sufficient amount of cleared land for the commencement of operations, and surrounded by waters abounding in delicious fish.

The time in which to do this work, is the present. It is desirable not to lose a single day. Two months earlier, had circumstances favored, would have been better. That there may be no longer delay in setting the project on foot, and commencing to give it a practical development, an appeal is hereby made to all the friends of the NEW SOCIAL ORDER IN THE SOUTH, and in particular to those who believe that the solution of the negro question is the turning point of the war, for prompt and efficient help in the prosecution of our designs.

The materials required are the same which any colony, designed to be agricultural and mechanical, must need at the start, viz: boards and shingles, and a steam-engine, to saw our own lumber, and grind our own corn after the first few months, cross-cut saws, and hand-saws, crow-bars, shovels, picks, and spades, hoes, axes, hammers and nails, two or three sets of carpenters' tools, with extra augurs, squares, and gimlets; butt-hinges, screws, and latches; an assortment of garden seeds, padlocks, and door-locks, oil-stones and grindstones, bush scythes, water buckets, baking kettles and covers, tin plates, cups, spoons, pans, basins, knives, forks, files and rasps, coopering and soldering tools, glass and putty, fish-hooks, lines, and lead, and twine for seines, a pair of platform scales, and counter scales, and a quantity of tin, and sheet iron, and tools to work with it. All these we need this moment. And as the government has few supplies of this sort in the department of North Carolina, and of many of the kinds none at all, we are compelled to appeal to chartable organizations, and patriotic individuals, to furnish them.

To clothe and educate these people we need quantities of clothing of all descriptions, particularly for women and children, with shoes of large sizes; primers and first reading books, primary arithmetics and geographies, with slates, pencils, and stationery of all sorts.

To present this subject personally to all interested in it, during the few days of my sojourn at the North, is simply impossible. Will not the ready good sense, and eager philanthropy of thousands of warm-hearted men and women respond to this appeal immediately, and place at my control within a few days all we need and ask for?

To fight the country's battles, is our *first grand* duty. *To lay new foundations* for a just and prosperous peace throughout the recreant South, is our *second*. For some time to come the two processes must be carried on *together*. Let us fight with our right hand, and civilize with our left, till the courage, the enterprise, and the ideas of the North have swept away barbarism and treason of the South, and made of this country ONE GOODLY AND FREE LAND.

Send contributions in cash, clothing, shoes, instruments, and supplies of every kind needed, to the undersigned at *No. 1 Mercer Street, New York* (rooms of the National Freedman's Relief Association.)

Horace James,
Supt. Of Blacks for the Dept of N. Carolina[122]

His second letter:

Roanoke Island, Sept 5, 1863

Having just finished a two days inspection of matters here, I am happy to report progress in regard to our operations. The colony is fairly on its feet.

There are from eleven to twelve hundred negroes now on the Island. They have come here from Plymouth, Elizabeth City, Newbern, and from the country around these and other points. For the present they are living in close quarters, too much huddled together in barracks, formerly occupied by soldiers. But a large tract of well-wooded land has been laid off in streets running at right angles, and upon these streets lots of nearly an acre (40,000 ft.) have been assigned to the various families desiring them. We have already staked out the outlines of an African village of grand proportions. It would gratify our friends at the north could they see the energy and zeal with which the freedmen enter upon the work of clearing up their little acre of land, by cutting the timber upon it, and preparing it for their rude log-house. They are so animated by the prospect of a homestead of their own, and the little comforts of a freehold, that they labor, every spare moment by night as well as by day, and are as happy as larks in their toil. Let the unbeliever declare that the negro does not desire his freedom, and has no wish to secure the privilege of owning personal property, and real estate. The axes which I sent on a month ago and which are now ringing merrily in the green woods of Roanoke give the lie direct to all their reasonings, and falsify all the assertions. So do the singing voices of these happy men and women, who now really believe that they have powerful friends, and ask nothing more than a decent chance to make themselves wholly independent of government aid, and be thrifty, wealthy citizens.

Well were it if our steam engine were even now ready to saw out the boards for the dwellings. But it cannot be got to work for months yet, and meanwhile these people must be contented with ruder structures for the present winter. They are contented, and more than this, and are developing an energy and vitality which is highly encouraging. We can already see the smiling cottages of virtuous and industrious people clustering along the streets which the woodman's axe has opened through these before unbroken forests, and which will be the future glory of this noted island. I am surprised to find it so healthy here. Of the troops garrisoning the three forts only sixteen are ill enough to be off duty, and only one is dangerously sick. The breezes are strong and pure from the sea, and our teachers can begin here as soon as they can get transportation hither. On the whole island smiles, the prospects are bright, the work advances.

We are beginning in the very wilderness, to lay the foundations of a new empire, but the results when carried out to their proper results no mortal mind can foresee. We sow in faith, and expect to reap in joy.

I shall next address you from Newbern, between which place and this my communications will be frequent for a while.

Yours truly, H.J.[123]

Reverend Colyer was soon overwhelmed with the runaways. He said many came in rags; and in order to quickly clothe them, they were issued captured Confederate uniforms and soldiers' brogans, which had been left as the Confederates fled. He put out the word up North as did Reverend James that food, medicine, clothing, garden tools, books, and home furnishings would be needed for the contrabands. Soon, shipload after shipload of provisions steamed for North Carolina.

Destitute white persons went to live near Federally controlled New Bern. On the outskirts of town, a white slave owner lived in a shanty with two to three colored women. He abused the women and was sent flying at the end of a bayonet. In another story, a Union woman related to her servant, Juno, that she could no longer afford to care for her own children, much less her slaves. Her rebel-loving husband had refused to make a coffin for Juno's child. This infuriated the mistress, who proceeded to construct the small coffin herself. The mistress gave the slave a basket of eggs and told her to seek out the bluecoats in New Bern. When Burnside's men trampled inland to her farm, the mistress of this plantation left with the army.[124]

One of Colyer's jobs was to gather five thousand men for labor. He had only employed twenty-five hundred by July of 1862. The Negro men received eight dollars a month, clothes, and one food ration. The freedmen were scheduled to build forts at first. As their numbers increased, the Negroes loaded and reloaded cargo for the quartermaster, commissary, and ordinance departments. They became carpenters, blacksmiths, coopers, bridge builders, ship joiners, and makers of cots for the hospitals.[125]

The Reverend Means took over in July 1862 after Colyer left; then Rev. Horace James had charge of the freedmen. The African Methodist Church, the Baptist Church, and the Methodist Church admitted the colored as members in New Bern. On Roanoke Island, black people built their own church from discarded quartermaster boxes and pine trees. They built their own log cabins. Deserted homes had new tenants and were revamped for use by the military. Also on Roanoke Island, the home of Dr. Ashby was taken as a Union medical facility.[126] At the Roanoke colony, assistant superintendent Streeter, under Rev. James, forced the young sons of the freedmen to go to work in New Bern, much to their mothers' dismay.[127]

Northern missionaries grew frustrated when their black pupils did not embrace their religious principles no matter how eager they were to learn. At one time, Union officials changed the schools into hospitals, which further hindered their education.[128]

In his quest to please both sides, Governor Stanly also asked Vincent Colyer to close the colored schools that had been established in New Bern so as "not to harm the Union cause," according to an influential woman. Stanly said he ordered the closure due to the "negro schools as being contrary to the Statute Law . . ."[129] Colyer immediately closed the school. The schools, built by freedmen, had made tremendous progress in educating all ages of Negroes along with the whites. Soldiers had volunteered as teachers until Northern teachers had the opportunity to come South. When word of these last two orders reached Northern ears, enraged people demanded Stanly's hide as they accused him of having Southern sympathies. He soon resigned in January 1863, after Lincoln's proclamation.[130]

"Federal authorities seldom hesitated to impress workers when it was impossible or inconvenient to obtain them by other means. Many black men became military laborers at gunpoint." When officers tried to impress black workers in Virginia and eastern North Carolina to work around the capitol at Washington City, they balked. "The frustrated quartermasters therefore sought permission to recruit laborers by 'forcible persuasion . . .'"[131] Freedmen living at the Roanoke Island colony were forced to work on the Dutch Gap Canal in Virginia. They complained of being treated worse by their saviors than when in slavery. Most importantly, these impressed men did not get paid for their work. Further, the freedmen told of white Union soldiers stealing from their gardens. They relayed to authorities that when Horace James was gone, his subordinates allowed white families to steal the black man's rations.[132]

After two years of being yanked around working here and there with the promise of being paid, the black refugees on Roanoke Island grew disgusted. They had a friend construct a letter to President Lincoln in which they asked him for help:

> . . . last fall a large number of we men was conscript and sent up to the front and all of them never return Some got Kill Some died and When they taken them they treated us mean and our owners ever did and they taken us just like we had been dum beast. Those head men have done every thing to us that our masters have done except by and Sell us and now they are Trying to Starve the women and children to death by cutting off they ration.[133]

The writer went on to say that they had done everything in their power to lessen their dependency on the government. They were willing to work and needed the salary.

The other letter to Stanton and Lincoln was written the same day. The authors stated they had written General Butler and others about the starving condition of the refugees, and the situation had not improved. These colored people were especially angry at the camp's military superintendent, Captain Horace James, and his assistant, Holland Streeter, with good reason. The letter to General Butler written on November 20, 1863, was signed by seventeen men (spelling not corrected):

> the undersigned Colored Citizens of the town of Beaufort in behalf of the Colored population of this Community in view of the manner in which their Brotheren on oppressed by the military authurities in this Vicenity

Respectfuley pitision you are at the Head of this military Department for a redress of grievunces

Your politiness [petitioners] disire to make known to you that they and there brothern to the President of the United States are undiscriminatly impressed by the authorities to labor upon the Public woorks without compensation that in Consequence of this System of fource labor they Have no means of paying Rents and otherwise Providing for their families

Your pitisioners disire futher to Express ther Entire Willingness to Contribute to the Cause of the union in anyway consistant with there cause as Freeman and the Rights of their families

Anything that can Be don By You to relieve us from the Burden which wee are nou Labooring will be Highly appricated By Your Pitistior

And your pititioners Will Ever pray

Yours Respectfully Soforth[134]

This petition did not receive an answer. A third letter was drafted to the president in which these same individuals asked Lincoln if the Reverend James had the right to take away their young sons from school and force them to work in New Bern without the parents' consent. Boys age fourteen and over were made to work for their rations, but Reverend James had taken boys as young as twelve. Another complaint was how the white soldiers behaved in church. They threw firecrackers among the groups of women to scare them. When the colored minister asked the white soldiers to cease, they threatened him with a pistol to his head. The freedmen had friends write letters to both General Butler and Horace James about their unsatisfactory conditions to no avail. "Here is men . . . working for the last three years and has not been paid for it . . . ," they complained.[135]

The colony on Roanoke Island grew despite their troubles. Northern teachers moved to the island and set up schools for the freedmen and illiterate whites. When January 1865 rolled around, Reverend James revealed that 591 houses had been built for 3,091 contrabands; however, the contraband city was short-lived due to the return of property to their rightful owners after the fighting ceased.[136] By 1867, the majority of the former slaves and poor whites had deserted the island for good.

"The Chowan River became the unofficial demarcation line between Confederate and Union controlled territories. The counties east of the river—Chowan, Perquimans, Pasquotank, and Currituck—came under Federal domination, while the counties to the west, including Bertie, Gates, and Northampton, remained under Confederate influence." It was illegal for citizens along the river to trade or pass goods to folks living on the other bank of the river.[137] Smaller boats of the enemy traveled the rivers. Guides were needed to navigate the inlets and rivers as Tories and ex-slaves filled these positions. A diarist wrote that a boat traveled the Albemarle Sound, not under military rule, but crewed by pirates who docked to "help themselves to whatever they desire. Unmolested by any military authority whatever, they rob, plunder, and arrest by wholesale." Her brother informed her that "the people are *true* & this company of Union men which they boast so of raising in Chowan & Gates [counties] is composed of the offscouring of the people & foreigners, people who can neither read or write & who never had a decent suit of clothes until they gave it to them, poor ignorant wretches who cannot resist a fine uniform and the choice of the horses in the country & liberty to help themselves without check to their rich neighbors belongings."[138]

Two black men sailed across Pamlico Sound to warn the Federal Navy that the Bodie Lighthouse had been torn down. Navy officers had planned on using it for guidance through Oregon Inlet for their own ships. A local turncoat harbor pilot took over the USS *Cambridge* when it returned to Beaufort for refueling.[139] U.S. troops came upon the home of James R. Gist, who "claimed to be a Union man, yet his loyalty was thought to be that selfish kind that could easily be turned rebelward in the fortunes of war appeared to lean in that direction." Later, his home was used as a hospital for the enemy.[140]

Company I of the Forty-ninth Regiment was ordered to hunt down the Buffaloes and shoot to kill. In searching for these men, they came upon a house full of women. A member told, "They said they didn't know where the men were, and didn't know anything about the shooting [of a warning]. They told this like they were in good practice; we soon found out it as no use to depend on them for information." In one neighborhood, Company I captured a young boy and strung him up to get information. The boy changed his mind and told them what he knew. One captured Buffalo said the men hiding would move around continually. Another man who said his name was White surrendered and said he belonged to the Thirty-second Regiment.[141] A citizen in Perquimans lost his life. Mr. Frank Newby answered his door to face villains with their faces blackened. They shot Mr. Newby's son dead, then trounced the father. Horrified at the calamity, Mrs. Newby fainted. The miscreants proceeded to help themselves to their property, and as they left, they carried off a hundred Negroes.[142]

Carolina Campbell, a.k.a. Mrs. George Van Slyck, a Unionist from Elizabeth City, was charged for trading with the Southerners near Currituck Sound. Her husband wrote the occupying authorities in 1863 that under orders from General Ben Butler, their money and belongings were confiscated. The couple was sent to jail for nine days, then released and told that it was "all a mistake." Federal officials said of Mrs. Van Slyck: "She gave enough intelligence to Union authorities to retain their support, while selling enough goods to Confederate supporters to guarantee their good will and protection." Upon release, they asked that their money and possessions be returned. It was not. Mrs. Campbell operated a drygoods store. Her husband took the case to the Judge Advocate General Holt. Van Slyck testified the store was sixty miles from the enemy lines and that it was impossible for his wife to trade with the enemy. Witnesses at the trial, perhaps "secessionist guerillas," had it in for his wife who was rumored to be of Union sentiment. The witnesses had said that Mrs. Campbell would pass along information to Federal forces in the area. Another witness, U.S. Major J. L. Stackpole, told the court that Campbell's store was very close to the Federal lines and that she traded with both sides. The case was dismissed, and her money and belongings supposedly returned.[143] Sylvester McCowan had seventy-five bushels of corn in the barn. Confederate soldiers stole some of his chickens and hogs, burned up one thousand cypress rails worth fifty dollars, and tore down his outbuildings, using it for their fires.[144]

Stephen Barton Jr., brother of Clara Barton, the famous nurse, owned a mill on the Chowan River. Stephen had a factory that made plow handles and wood products. In 1861, he closed the business except for minimal workers and restricted business. Several employees moved North, along with his wife and children. Suspicious local citizens ordered him to leave the state. Barton was assaulted but vowed to stick it out for the war. Determined to remain neutral and keep the business open, he and his neighbors tried to help the poor by trading cotton with the United States. Barton had a pass from Federal officers permitting him to exchange this cotton for bacon and other much-needed provisions. In 1864, Barton was arrested for this and sent to jail in Norfolk whereby he became sick. His sister, near the Richmond area, influenced General Butler to rescue him, which he did. After Stephen's death, the family tried to recover his business and farmlands. U.S. troops burned his village.[145]

George Schroeder offered insight into the situation Down East in a letter to his son in the Seventeenth NCT:

> The citizens of Newbern put fire in some Turpentine and it caught some houses and burnt part of the town. We are looking for the Yankeys here every day. The people in Washington is putting their turpentine in vessels and carrying them above the bridge and setting them on fire. I heard three was burned last night. Beaufort County is given to the Yankeys. Marshe's negroes has all run away and gone to the Yankeys but 3. lot Evetts Beachmon's and some few others from South Creek. It is said that the mail will not come to Blounts Creek no more . . . .[146]

A letter was captured from a steamer in the Albemarle Sound from (Augustus S.) Montgomery of Washington City to General Foster in New Bern "proposing a general Negro insurrection, and destruction of all railroad bridges, etc., in the South." Governor Vance sent it to Jefferson Davis, who in turn sent it to General Lee, who advised Vance not to publish it in the newspapers for fear of a generalized panic.[147]

Ms. Carroll, a Union girl Down East, laid to paper a poem:
> The secesh girls looks mighty loansum
> Walking the road in there homemade homespun
> The Union girls dont look sad
> Walking the road in there Yankee plad.[148]

Many citizens of New Bern proclaimed their secesh views while others kept them under cover. Federal authorities grew tired of their insolence and tauntings, prompting extreme measures such as being exiled. A Southern soldier wrote that his company had to march to Cove Creek west of New Bern to pick up a large group of refugees from New Bern, which "the Yankees had brought out and emptied on the ground. They stayed out all night in the rain [a downpour]—had been there several days. We got what four wagons could bring and left the others to wait until we could hire some private wagons to send for them. There were seventy-nine of them — mostly women and children, wives of soldiers in our army."[149]

TAKEOVER OF TOWNS

After the capture of the major towns along the Albemarle Sound, the Federals focused on those located on the Pamlico Sound. Beaufort fell in March 1862, followed by Havelock Station, Carolina City, Morehead, and then New Bern.

BEAUFORT

Three thousand people lived in Beaufort in antebellum times. When Federal troops entered Beaufort and garrisoned the town, everyone had to obtain a pass to move about, and they had to take the oath of allegiance to the United States. James Rumley wrote that "very few citizens do this willingly. Some are compelled by their situation to do it. Persons from the country, who come to town, not knowing the regulations exist here, are not allowed to return to their home without a pass . . . most of them regard the oath under such circumstances as compulsory and not binding . . ." He continued, "Most of the citizens, feeling their utter abhorrence of either oath, keep within the limits of the town . . ." Many with secession beliefs left town before occupation. The *New York Herald* printed that most people welcomed the Yankees. "Invitations to partake of the hospitality of some of the leading citizens of Beaufort have been freely extended to our officers, and other evidences of kindness have been made apparent on every side."[150] The Balance and Fulcher families on Hatteras invited Federal soldiers to their homes where their daughters entertained the men. Other girls did not hesitate to mingle with the troops.[151] In February of 1865, the Hammond Hospital building, according to a New Jersey soldier, held balls "for the 'shoulder straps' with women wearing bright colored dresses." The following evening, a ball was opened for refugees.[152] Another grand ball took place the next month. Shorter-than-normal courtships took place during the war.

A Ms. Bell of Carteret County married a Union soldier after six weeks of dating. Young Southern ladies attended dress parades, concerts, parties, and dances despite what the community thought. A Pennsylvania officer wrote, "Had dinner with Mr. Neal who lived near the lighthouse . . . . We had quite a lovely time as the ladies were very lively & all came off very well."[153]

Sister M.M. Joseph, Sisters of Mercy, Beaufort, N.C.

Beaufort was described by a Northern woman visiting the city as a "shabby 'fishing village, a decayed Marblehead.'"[154] The three-story Atlantic Hotel with its five hundred beds stood on thick pilings at the waterfront. It was considered the largest resort hotel Down East. Under Federal occupation in 1862, it became the Hammond Hospital.[155] At first, conditions were reported to be unsanitary and dreadful. As the news reached U.S. Secretary of War Stanton, he referred the problems to the Sisters of Mercy from New York City. They, in turn, hastily sent several nuns to straighten up the hospital. Upon arriving at the medical facility, the nuns discovered that they would need far more supplies than what greeted them. They went right to work caring for the sick and wounded, as well as performing janitorial duties. Notifying their friends in the North about the scant hospital equipment, the nuns received donations by the boatload. These nuns stayed about a year, then went back North, replaced by recuperating soldiers, volunteer civilians, and the U.S. Sanitary Commission workers. Other research has shown that it was General Burnside who requested the nuns. Prior to the Sisters of Mercy's trip to Beaufort, they insisted upon a set of arrangements before they would go. "They required that a chaplain was to be appointed, paid, and maintained; private apartments allotted to the use of the sisters and provisions, medicine, and utensils supplied for the patients and themselves." When the nine nuns of the Sisters of Mercy debarked the ship at Beaufort, they caused quite a stir. Some locals had never seen nuns before, dressed in their black garb. They figured them to be widows coming for their husbands' bodies; others thought the nuns were Freemasons.[156]

In wartime, the U.S. government employed black women as nurses and cooks. These women received a salary of ten dollars a month. Aunt Clarissy became chief cook for the Hammond Hospital. Other former slaves found hard work at the facility. Chloe and Ellen took care of the laundry, along with the assistance of other runaways. Negro men hauled water, chopped wood, emptied bedpans, and helped with kitchen and laundry duties. In addition, the wives of Northern officers came South once the state was under Federal control. They filled their time caring for the patients. An ill Union soldier commented, "It does a sick soldier more good to have a lady visit him than all the medicine he can take."[157] Other houses in the neighborhood were commandeered as hospitals, offices, and soldiers' quarters. Rev. John Jones's home and Dr. Josiah Davis's home converted to medical facilities. The Easton home found use as both a hospital and prison. Joseph Hackburn's house and the Odd Fellows Lodge filled with the sick and wounded. Even these homes didn't have enough beds for all the afflicted. The Mansfield Hospital in Morehead City took in the overflow.[158]

The occupying army at times went to black church services or boarded with Negro families while others showed their racist views.[159] Beaufort officials established Union Town to house black refugees. Twenty-five hundred runaway refugees comprised the town in 1864, which expanded to about thirty-two hundred by the end of the war.[160]

When the Confederates attempted to retake Beaufort, a Yankee soldier said, "The Doctors wife & all the other Northern women were sent across the channel to Fort Macon . . ."[161] Beaufort and Fort Macon were cut off from their Southern comrades. Next the enemy took Carolina City, where the railhead ended. "Landing at Morehead, we went directly to the general hospital, a range of buildings once used as an academy," wrote one Northern soldier.[162]

Beaufort became an important refueling station for the Union Navy. The city was under Federal control throughout the conflict.

Northern teachers in occupied New Bern
UNC Photographic Archives

NEW BERN

New Bern sits at the confluence of the Neuse and Trent Rivers, which flow into the Pamlico Sound. A harbor town, it is about forty miles from Morehead at the Beaufort Inlet where the North Carolina Railroad ended. Several fine homes and churches lined the tree-shaded streets. It was the hometown of the first royal governor of North Carolina, William Tyron. The gaslit city was the second-largest town at the beginning of the war with 8,795 white and 10,476 blacks. During the early days, the Masonic Lodge found use as an arsenal. "Young women volunteered their services in making cartridges there . . . ," as well as other war supplies. Both women and children were practicing for a benefit concert for the troops. Everyone wanted to contribute. A newspaper reported that black people contributed two thousand pounds of scrap metal to be melted down and cast into cannonballs.[163] After Federal occupation, the building converted to hospital use. Coffins were made there too. Postwar, the lodge received a cash claim for damages during occupation.[164]

Citizens had heard that the enemy controlled the Outer Banks. And the scramble began. Two sisters with secessionist feelings left their Union-loving brother, Mr. Graham, alone as they fled. Confederate Private Joshua Hill wrote that "the citizens of Newbern put fire in some Turpentine and it caught some houses and burnt part of the town. We are looking for the Yankeys here every day."[165] Perhaps this was the fire that burnt two hotels. Rhode Island soldiers were able to extinguish the fires. Whether perpetrated by civilians, blacks, or soldiers, a Union soldier said, "Nine tenth of the depredations on the 14th, after the enemy & citizens fled from the town, were committed by the negroes, before our troops reached the city . . . . Gen. Foster . . . established a system of guard and police—"[166] Retreating Confederate soldiers did burn government warehouses and the seven-hundred-foot Trent River Bridge.

The occupying forces left a mountain of notes, giving the reader an excellent picture of the situation. "In houses and general appearance, Newbern does not compare favorably with any place of like size in our part of the world." He continued:

> Most of the white inhabitants have left the city, and with them went the majority of able-bodied black men. The whites who remained were obliged to take the oath of allegiance. There are lots of "contrabands" around; from sunrise to sunset they are in the camp with almost everything in the eating line: gingerbread, pies, oysters, plenty of cookies, sweet potatoes, fried fish, etc.[167]

Private Albert Mann said, "The city was one vast [camp?] with but a few white citizens. A few enterprising citizens remained and did a thriving business."[168]

Another Massachusetts soldier had a negative opinion about women there:

> There were few intelligent women. Most of the females were so coarse and unfeminine in habits, as to degrade their sex. The leaded eye, sallow skin, swaggering gait and uncouth slang were too much for the Northern man, and made him devoutly thankful he descended from a nobler lineage. A lady's evening call (they never speak of afternoon) would be incomplete without snuff, and to omit to offer it to a caller was unpardonable. After the seating of the guests, the hostess was expected to pass saucers, twigs, and a bladder of snuff, with which the visitors regaled themselves during the call. Some were so addicted to the habit of snuff-dipping, as to indulge in it upon the streets, regardless of their disgusting appearance . . .[169]

Perhaps most of the upper-class women had fled before occupation.

Private Charles Leonard said, "A family of aged maiden ladies who fled when the city was taken, left behind them quite a fine library of old English books, most of them being Queen Anne's or earlier dates, 1714 . . . . General Foster took Mrs. Smallwood's house."[170] The enemy evicted Rev. William R. Wetmore from the Church of Christ.[171] Another soldier wrote that "Mrs. Moore at Newbern served delicious meals to the Union troops. She was a secesh woman and would not give in. Old black 'Gatsy' sold sweet potatoes, pies, and cakes to the soldiers. The camps were full of peddlers, black and white."[172]

In the city, Ms. Mary Attmore was kept as a hostage by the invaders so the Southern troops would not shell the town. She was choked by ruffians trying to extract information on the whereabouts of her valuables. Attmore admonished the ruffians for digging up graves looking for jewelry on the corpses. They put down their shovels and left.[173] The enemy was known to desecrate graves of Southern people. Undisciplined troops broke open the grave of former governor Nash, demolished the vault, carried off the bricks, and took the casket away, leaving only bones. They probably used the coffin to send their dead comrade North.[174] Connecticut soldiers reportedly dug up the grave of former governor David Spaight to reuse his metal coffin to ship their comrade's body northward. When Federal officers learned of this, they forced the accused to re-inter the body in its original condition. Others did remove the body of Mr. Richard Donnell's mother from her casket and replaced it with that of one of their officers to be shipped to New York.[175]

More of a soldier's life is depicted in the next letter:

In Camp, Newbern, N.C. Dec 26th, 1862

Dear Mother,

Day before yesterday the great box of Dec 7th arrived together with a vast number of others for the regiment and company . . . . To begin with—I was carried away by a splendid pair of gloves which seems to me almost too nice to wear, and the delightful stockings . . . . The paper and pens, too were peculiarly acceptable—and the ink . . . .

All of the reading matter too came in the nick of time. And the goodies, they were every way perfect. The pies were in a perfect state of preservation and have excited a "furore" of enthusiasm among our mess—boys who have tasted them . . . . One can of milk was used last night at our Christmas dinner of which I will speak to you presently.

The other articles are as yet intact in their savoriness and sweetness—Oh I forgot we ate the figs yesterday, and Willie's nuts at our Christmas dinner . . . . We spent Christmas as follows. After getting up at the usual hour I took an elaborate wash and adorned myself with my gayest apparel, then breakfasted . . . on salt fish and potatoes (government but really good) coffee with plenty of "consolidated" and buttered hardtack. I mean toast for we had soft bread yesterday—mince pie well warmed and figs. (And that reminds me that we have bought, two large stoves which head [sic—heat] up our barracks splendidly. The open fire place was pretty to jook [sic—look] and the fire in it every poetical and suggestive, (chiefly of the artic regions, but it did not give out heat enough to warm a polar-bear) And I forgot to say that Christmas Eve and Christmas night, Hopkinson read Dicken's charm "Christmas Carol" in the barracks to a delighted audiance [sic]of the company. Day before yesterday . . . Balch of Co. F . . . had a barrel of fine northern apples and gave two to every man in F.) After breakfast . . . wended my way to the Sanitary Rooms, where I spent the morning in chat paper-reading & letter writing. I wrote three letters . . . . At about twelve, we four . . . discussed a couple of bottles of ale with crackers and Dutch cheese . . . .

Then we wended our way to the barracks got our party . . . got together and wandered down to the abode of Mary Ann, a famous cook, who had arranged to provide our great dinner. A party from Company G. had dined before us and the preparations were so much delayed in consequence that we did not begin our diner [sic] till 4 ½ P.M. The bill of fare consisted of oyesters [sic] for soup—roast ducks and chickens, with one turkey for entrees, and for vegatables (prepared to be astonished) potatoes, squash, cabbage, onions and beets. Cranberry sauce also—one plate and apple-sauce in abundance. The Plum pudding (very good) with excellent cold sauce; (and finally nuts, shellbarks, almonds, pecans, and filberts) and raisens[sic] . . . . Then we had a few toasts—and sentiments . . .

Yr's affectionally
Henry. H.A.C.[176]

A private with the Twenty-first Massachusetts Volunteers informed his parents of a skirmish at Washington. He said too that the canal to Norfolk was open, that the railroad bridge across the Trent River had been rebuilt, and that he was sending them money. His June 1862 letter revealed the problem typical of the season:

> We have had some pretty warm weather here but I think I shall stand it as well as the rebels. The flies and mosquitoes are very thick here. The latter are very large and are true Secesh. Even cold steel will not frighten them. You can judge something of the enormity of their size by the following: I was on guard duty and sat my gun by a tree for a minute. When I took it, the bayonet was gone and looking up I saw a mosquito picking his teeth with it. There is a great many poisonous snakes such as the copperhead, moccasins, king snakes and bullheads and many of these have been killed when we were on picket . . .[177]

Under Federal occupation, Northern citizens flocked to the area to set up businesses, to teach, and to mission to the needy. All available buildings and houses found use. It wasn't long before Northern merchandise stocked the shelves in town. Union officers profited from the occupation by exporting goods and pocketing the sales.[178] It was illegal to trade with the enemy, though a clandestine operation continued as contraband supplies poured into the interior of the state.[179]

A soldier recalled that "trade in naval stores was suspended until the navy filled its wants, except families in need could sell one barrel of turpentine or tar every two weeks. A fee of five percent of the sworn invoice value of goods shipped was imposed. Imports also were subject to a duty of five percent of value. Only the collector of customs at Beaufort could grant permits, though local special agents were appointed to assist him and were stationed in New Bern, Plymouth, and Washington. One exception from the import duty was sutlers supplying goods to Union regiments."*[180] Apparently, the Federals controlled prices with merchants during occupation. A barber complained that he would have to go out of business with the prices they imposed upon him. Shaves were fifteen cents, haircuts twenty-five cents, and shampoos thirty cents. A Northern trooper said that there was an established fee for every pass and permit, even a permit to buy a coffin.

Union soldiers visited residents, ate with them, worshipped with them, and bought provisions from them. Many recruits took their meals with Aunt Rachel, paying her $5.50 a month for washing and cooking. Rachel had the reputation as the best cook in town. In one Thanksgiving service, also attending was the Benevolent, Friendship, and Perries Chapel Society, composed of colored people, which was organized in 1854. An observer described the society as wearing blue circlets around their necks and brightly colored clothes. A couple of drummers led the procession.[181]

Continuing his tour of duty, a private gave insight into the everyday occurrences in the city. Merchants were fined for overcharging people. One offense was five dollars; another was charged six dollars. A black man was fined ten dollars for fighting. He reported that a certain captain was going to send a Mrs. Leecraft out of the lines if she refused to take the oath. A local woman proclaimed that U.S. General Foster's wife, "taking two orderlies with her, broke into the Masonic Temple at New Bern. The rich velvet carpet woven with Masonic emblems, was ripped from the floor and together with the jewels and other treasures was transferred to her possession."[182]

A person fired a shot into the New Bern Provost Office in town. When captured, he claimed to be a Unionist. He retorted he was forced into the Southern Army and did garrison duty at Fort Macon, then deserted. It seemed the man did not know which side to support.

---

*   Sutlers—merchants who followed the army; a few were assigned to units.

Southerners did not celebrate Independence Day, but the occupying forces did. July 4, 1862, the First Rhode Island Battery celebrated the event by ringing bells in New Bern, having a parade, and firing a thirty-four-gun salute at noon and at 6 p.m. Tar barrels were burned at night. The Northern troops enjoyed a fine dinner with whiskey punch. Going to church and going to a parade were about the only entertainment left for the inhabitants of New Bern while under martial law and Federal control.[183] Men would make their own entertainment. Garrisoned soldiers and sailors made reverie in camp and town, prompting an officer to write: "Slept very little last night on account of the men who ware drunk bawling around the shelter like a lot of mad men."[184]

When he arrived, a Pennsylvania soldier wrote home:

> Fresh fish are abundant here now. This is the fishing season & the North Carolina coast has long been celebrated for its fisheries. We can get Herring, shad, Perch, trout & a number of other kinds & the supply is so abundant that they are very cheap & form a great addition to the army ration.[185]

When the Forty-fifth Regiment Massachusetts Volunteer Militia swept the woods around New Bern for dissenters and guerillas, they told that many of those killed and captured wore citizens' clothes. "When they saw a considerable body of our men approaching, they were unionists, neutrals, or 'know nothings,' as they chose." Most captured held passes of neutrality from Edward Stanly, provisional governor.[186]

In an incident worth mentioning, the Twenty-fifth Massachusetts Regiment near New Bern marched to join up with their comrades to storm a small Confederate outpost in the Gum Swamp area. "As the northern troops approached Batchelder's Creek at the entrance to the swampland, a mysterious electric wind came up from nowhere and split the regiment right down the middle. When the devil wind was gone, two hodgepodge piles of terrified soldiers were hiding in ditches on either side of the dirt road. The officers quickly reassembled their men, but as soon as the regiment took it first step forward, the electrifying wind rose again, wreaking havoc. An official report described the encounter to superiors who attributed the phenomenon to flocks of owls . . ."[187]

When the prisoners passed through New Bern, some were recognized as those who were previously in the city with a trading permit from Governor Stanly. "One prisoner was marched through the city with a woman's skirt on, and on his back a placard with the words, 'guerilla caught dressed in woman's clothes, with a protection in his pocket from Governor Stanley.' The cavalryman asserted that he had a commission from Jeff Davis in the other pocket."[188]

The Federal Army and Navy made New Bern their base of operations, which continued under their control throughout the war. Before regular hospitals could be established to treat the thousands of soldiers, authorities put wounded men in Negro shanties. Homes were commandeered as medical buildings. The Stanly house served as General Burnside's headquarters, later converting to a hospital. A small house on the property owned by the former governor was remodeled into housing for the Sisters of Mercy who had come from New York. Mother Augustine and Mother Madeline tended the sick.[189] Other homes transposed into medical facilities included the George Dixon house. Surgeon George Otis said that the Harrison home turned into a field hospital. Otis used four homes in New Bern as his hospital located near the fairgrounds. The first summer of occupation typhomalarial fevers ran rampant. Otis claimed to give every man a tablespoon of whiskey mixed with one grain of quinine each morning to prevent disease. The Confederate prisoners did not have this luxury. It was, in many instances, in short supply for them.[190]

Male and female members of the U.S. Sanitary Commission arrived to find the base lacking in supplies to treat their patients. Announcements to their Northern friends who shipped supplies South added to their larder. The commission requested that men dig them a deep well for the sick.[191]

A tragedy occurred at Batchelder's Creek where the Federal Army had constructed three torpedoes. The torpedoes held two hundred pounds of powder each and were sitting on a railroad flatcar. Union soldiers rolled the kegs down a gangplank. When the barrels hit each other, the powder exploded, killing thirty soldiers and wounding seventeen. Nearby ten civilians and contrabands also died, and twenty-three were wounded. It was told the remains of the victims were scattered for one-half a mile. The explosion was heard twenty miles away.[192]

New Yorker Henry White signed up as a Methodist Episcopal chaplain in a Rhode Island unit. He was captured in May 1864 at Croatan Station a few miles from New Bern carrying mail and religious tracts to the forts. Reverend White, along with sixteen hundred of his comrades, upon capture marched from there to Kinston, then Goldsboro to reach the Wilmington and Weldon Railroad to Wilmington. From Wilmington, they traveled to the prison in Andersonville, Georgia. The reverend wrote a series of letters about his experience to the *Zion's Herald* in the fall of 1864. Only those concerning North Carolina will be used here.

In letter no. 3 written on November 16, 1864, White said that when the officers surrendered their small fort East of New Bern, they asked for certain provisions to be honored such as their personal property to be respected. This was not done. "This they violated by creeping up and rushing to the quarters of the officers and men and stealing whatever they could get hold of . . . nor was the plunder confined to the privates; line and staff officers and surgeons all went in together. Two white men were taken with us to Kinston and put in jail." He said that the blacks in the camp ran to the swamps.[193]

Dissenting sides as mentioned earlier dealt with the invasion in their own way. Some folks welcomed the enemy's presence. When the Forty-fifth Regiment MVM left New Bern in April of 1863, loyal citizens sent them a delightful note of thanks:

New Bern, North Carolina
April 25, 1863
Colonel C.R. Codman, Officers and men of the 45th Massachusetts Volunteer Militia
Gentlemen:
    Having learned with regret that your regiment is about to retire from duty of guarding the city, I beg leave on behalf of all loyal citizens, myself, my family, and other families here, to render you our sincere thanks for the efficiency & courtesy with which you have discharged your duties.
    It has seldom been our lot to see a body of soldiers, so uniformly civil & comparatively free from the vice of profanity, & so prompt in restraining those, who, by any violence, would attempt to disturb our streets.
    Accept gentlemen, out thanks for past kindness, & wishes for your future welfare.

W.H. Doherty, A.M. Principal of
New Berne Academy[194]

YELLOW FEVER IN NEW BERN

Yellow fever raged in New Bern the fall of 1864. In tracing down the culprit, it was rumored that the first victim, a stevedore at the harbor, wore clothing sent there from a benevolent society in New York City. Authorities believed the clothing was contaminated purposely to spread disease. A Dr. Blackburn in New York City had the clothes brought from Cuba to the city for the purpose of distributing it to the poor, which, in turn, was shipped to New Bern. Whether the story is true or not, there were instances that the Confederacy had thought of similar ideas.

Some who fled the town went to Fortress Monroe, Virginia. Businesses closed mid-October; the city was deserted. Even the mail was stopped during the outbreak. Once it was determined that the outbreak was truly yellow fever, Federal officers did not permit the residents to leave. Mrs. F. C. Roberts had two sisters stricken with the fever at the same time. Unable to care for their family, the small children ate uncooked ham and raw potatoes until the mothers could get back their strength. Most of the Southern folks had fled the city prior to the arrival of the enemy except those with Northern sympathies, so there were not as many North Carolinians affected. She related that "all day and night the death carts passed along the streets."

Union soldiers succumbed to the fever as well. The Dead Corps went around to pick up the bodies. About twenty to twenty-five died each day. Thirteen hundred people died, mostly soldiers and their families who had moved to the area along with physicians. Workers threw lime on the ground and streets, which gave the appearance of snow.

When the fever struck military members of the Fifteenth Connecticut, they were ordered to go beyond the railroad tracks between New Bern and Morehead City where most soon recovered. Ordered to replace the unit were the First Regiment North Carolina Colored Volunteers. Apparently, the First Regiment Colored Troops did okay. "The colored people seemed to be proof against its attacks," recalled a white soldier. He continued, "At night we were ordered to keep bonfires burning on all the principle street corners . . ." Scarcely a person would be seen on the street after nightfall, but a lonely guard walking his beat. Mostly poor refugees died from the fever. The fever spread to Beaufort. Orders came in early November to open up all homes and buildings the first night a frost appeared to ventilate them.[195]

North Carolina's troops tried to take back the town twice during the war. In March 1863, poor whites and citizens waited on the wharf to leave. Two U.S. gunboats came up the river and ended the fight in their victory.

FORT MACON

It was known that residents in Beaufort stood on the second-story porches of homes to watch the shelling of Fort Macon. "At sunrise on April 25, 1862 it is said that Charity Hatchel [the name later evolved to Hatsell] along with her sixteen year old daughter Julia, stood with Emeline Pigott, a Confederate spy, on the south end of her upper porch to watch the shelling of Ft. Macon. She had relatives in the fort."[196]

At Fort Macon, seven were killed and twenty wounded to oust the Confederates as eleven hundred shells pummeled the fort. After the surrender, Union officers turned the fort into a prison.

A teenage drummer from Connecticut wrote home his experiences that spring:

> On the Banks
> April 27, 1862
>
> Dear Mother,
>
> When I wrote you last I was in Beaufort. Since then our Company has moved over to the Banks (a strip of sand on which Fort Macon is situated). The Encampment is about 5—miles from the fort and by going to the beach one can see the fort in the distance. Yesterday Fort Macon surrenderred to Gen. Burnside . . . . Last Thursday the fleet came in sight. We were at Beaufort and we expected the bombardment would commence but the day was spent in Flags of Truce. We had orders to pack knap sacks and get ready to move

at night. After dark we got aboard a flat and some darkies piloted us over to Carolina City, about— six miles. As we neared the wharf Whisss—came a ball right over our heads. We heard no challenge of the guard. He was probably frightened and discharged his piece at us. Me I layded and stacked arms and "the orders" were to lay down by the guns. The wind was blowing "right smart." I went off a little way and found the remains of an old shed. Under it I lay and coughed away almost incessantly. About 5 o'clock in the morning we "fell in" and marched to the wharf. Got on a flat and started for the Banks. As we started the batteries and Gun boats commenced to bombard the Fort, now most out of sight. We arrived at the Banks about 8 o'clock. The company went to work and put up their tents and brought up their baggage. The rest of the regiment was up on duty. The [illegible] it being their day for duty. I went up within about a mile and watched the engagement. It was grand. They kept at it until about 5 o'clock when a flag of truce came from the Fort for conditions for a surrender. So all firing was stopped at 8 o'clock. The 5th Battallion R.I. relieved our Regiment. They stood [under(?)] fire all day and no man of them were injured. 2 of the Zauves were wounded and one killed. next morning at 9 the Fort surrendered to Gen. Burnside and the U[nion] troops marched in.

[A later notation]
 The [illegible] is in camp in a miserable situation. Nothing but sand—sand—sand. Our clothes, shoes, hair, knapsack and food are full of it. On one side is the ocean, on the other a series of swamps, not a vestige of good wood. Nothing but low scrubs-scrawny unhealthy things. 3/4 of the Regiment are sick, unfit for duty. Col. is sick. Our Maj. is wounded, our Lt. Col. has resigned, our senior Capt. is at home wounded, our 2nd Captain is at Morehead City, our 3rd Captain-M.B. Sink commands the regiment. There are 7 companies in Camp. Neither of them have a Capt. fit for duty except Co. E. Of the other Companies 2/3 are sick . . . . There are many of Co. E men sick at New Bern . . .

> From your aff son,
> Arthur W. Palmer
> Drummer Go E 8th CV Gen. Burnsides Div Beaufort, N.C.[197]

Another letter sent North:

In camp opposite Newbern N.C. Tuesday May 6th 1862
Dear Mother
 You see by the top of the letter that our regiment has moved from Bog[ue] Banks (down near Fort Macon). We are now encamped in sight of Newbern on the opposite side of the river. We left Bog Bank on last Thursday and crossed over to Carolina City. Here we spent the night embarked . . . . After crossing we marched down the beach about a mile. "Stacked arms" and worked for our huts . . . . By the operation before dark our Battalion had got their huts all put up . . . . The other 6 companies were to come on the Wheelbarrow [.] Saturday night the other companies came up . . . . The Regiment is all together over again, but how long we shall remain so I do not know. I am satisfied with the camp. Hope we shall have alittle rest. I am well and strong. I went over to Newbern yesterday and enjoyed myself much . . . .

> Your aff. son
> Arthur W. Palmer
> Drummer Co. E Con V
> Gen. Burnside Division[198]

When the Northern soldiers took over Fort Macon, every person left except for the Wade family. Soldiers visited the Wade household and saw the girls as snuff dippers with dirty hair.[199] Soldiers had no problems getting help from the black population. One Union soldier recalled a black named Cuff who would row over the bay at Fort Macon and take any soldier to Beaufort. "We had many visitors from the army, often accompanied by ladies . . ." Captains of the blockade ships came too.

Growing tired of their same old rations, soldiers left the fort to explore. In Carolina City, where the Twenty-seventh Massachusetts was stationed, a farmer had a large watermelon patch and would not sell any to the soldiers. That did not deter the young men. One night, the field was raided, bringing the farmer, his dog, and shotgun outside to check his melons. The raiders shot his dog and the lantern the old man was carrying. He retreated back inside. The next morning, the farmer went to camp to try to find the culprits. Officers understood his plight and allowed him to search for evidence, rinds, etc. He climbed off his horse and looked intently. While doing this, someone stole his horse, and he had to walk home empty-handed.[200] In another instance, soldiers on picket duty stole a black pig and ate it. The owner went to Fort Macon for restitution. The thieves had to pay him for it.[201]

North Carolina men who had joined the Federal Army pulled duty at Fort Macon, Morehead City, Beaufort, and Newport, thereby allaying their fears of capture by the Confederates.[202]

RAIDS

A diarist set down these words: "What a life is ours, kept on tenter [sic] hooks of anxiety by these miserable Yankees. Scarce do we recover from one raid before we are threatened with another."[203] The spring of 1862 saw the enemy leaving their base camps to make their presence known in the area. The Confederates were aware of this movement. They insisted that those living within the area East of the Wilmington and Weldon Railroad remove their cotton or burn it to keep it out of the enemy's reach. Tarboro citizens met in March to discuss options of the enemy's arrival. They had been told to remove all their naval items and tobacco as well. They first asked Confederate officers for an extension on the deadline, then decided to destroy by fire the aforemenioned articles.[204]

General Burnside was called to Virginia after the Seven Days Battles, so General John G. Foster replaced him late in 1862. General Ed Potter was chief of staff for Foster in 1863. Foster left New Bern with ten thousand troops in an attempt to break up the Wilmington and Weldon Railroad, to destroy gunboats, and to burn important bridges. The Federals used pitch from damaged pine trees to start fires along their march. Citizens fled before them. Confederate forces felled trees along the roads to obstruct the marchers. They skirmished with the enemy all the way into the interior.

Pollocksville was known as a guerilla nest. As they marched down the streets, Union soldiers found several deserted houses, and they helped themselves to booty. Again the Southern Army cut down trees along the road to Trenton to block them, which was quickly removed. Described by the enemy as very dirty and dilapidated, Trenton offered no resistance. One recorded that he saw a whipping post and stocks downtown. Federal cavalrymen on the way to Onslow Court House burned the bridge. A long line of bonded Negroes followed his army. A colored man there said, "He wanted his freedom, but he wanted to go 'Clar,' meaning that he wanted to take his whole family with him, 4 of his children were at home, but he had 5 still in slavery."[205] After skirmishing, the Simon Foscue plantation became a temporary hospital for enemy soldiers.

The battle of South Mills began in April, the intention being to blow up the locks. Union troops failed in this and retreated. The smaller Confederate brigade left the area. The next month, after capturing Norfolk, the Federal Army took control of the canal and started shipping their equipment and supplies South. U.S. General Edward Wild and his forces came through the canal with the intention to apprehend roving bands of deserters and secessionists who ran to the Dismal Swamp. These swamp rats came out at different times to attack the Northern vessels or marching troops, then fled back to their cover. General Wild burned houses in his path, along with the Camden Courthouse. His men took innocent men and women as their prisoners.[206]

C.S. Colonel James Hinton, in charge of the troops around the Chowan River, wrote Governor Vance, who in turn passed the information to Judge Robert Ould in Richmond. Hinton told him of U.S. General Wild, in charge of black soldiers in the area. Vance's letter:

> I beg call your attention to the conditions of the troops of this State on the Chowan river under the command of Col. Hinton. As you will see by the letters from a Yankee General by the name of Wild, which Col. H. will show you, they refuse to treat them as prisoners of War, although regularly commissioned by law. They have murdered several soldiers, and have arrested two respectable ladies whom they keep handcuffed as hostages for two negro soldiers and declare their purpose to hang them in case the negroes are hung. I must ask you to see if some arrangement cannot be made to include these troops within the cartel of exchange and repress if possible this horrible, cowardly and damnable disposition on the part of enemy to put women in irons as hostages for negro soldiers! Such men as this Wild are a disgrace to the manhood of the age, not being able to capture soldiers they war upon defenceless women! Great God! What an outrage. There is no reason why those men are not entitled to be treated as prisoners of war. If it is not done and these outrages upon defenceless females continue, I shall retaliate upon Yankee soldiers to the full extent of my ability, and let the consequences rest with the damnable barbarians who begun it.[207]

Even General Burnside commented on Wild's actions as extreme:

> Wild took the most stringent measures, burning the property of some of the officers of guerrilla parties, and seizing the wives and families of others as hostages for some of his negroes that were captured, and appears to have done his work with great thoroughness, but perhaps with too much stringency.[208]

The *Richmond Daily Dispatch* informed its readers of a raid into Elizabeth City mid-war:

Negro Troops in Elizabeth City:
> The last northern news confirms the reports . . . of the presence of two regiments of Yankee negro troops with white officers . . . . that the treatment to which the white people of that unfortunate area are subjected is heartrending . . . the negroes compel white women of delicacy and refinement to cook and wash for them. In one instance we have heard of a body of these negroes entering a private house and demanding dinner, which they insisted should be cooked by the Lady of the house. Whilst engaged in preparing the food for her negro guests, the scoundrels indulged in the most loathsome ribaldry, one of them with his foot throwing the lady's clothes over her back and shoulders, whilst the rest sent up loud peals of laughter. These statements are upon authority . . . and surely enough to stir the blood of those who would go back to a fellowship with a nation of whites who can only permit this, but encourage it.[209]

The enemy stealing fence rails for firewood.
UNC Photographic Archives

The Abbott House in South Mills reverted to hospital use after the skirmish. U.S. cavalrymen captured a suspicious Jewish man, Falk Odenheim, in the woods around South Mills in September 1863. He was attempting to escape through the lines. Falk was carrying twelve thousand dollars in gold, Confederate notes, along with a number of watches. The next month, the Yankees captured near Ship Landing Timothy Douglass, a citizen of Pasquotank County, who had in his possession two leather hides. They destroyed his boat. Other guerillas were seen in the neighborhood. A Union soldier reported that C. S. Captain Hughes "had a guerilla band uniformed, near Indiantown . . ."[210]

Of their raids into the interior of the state, a Northern soldier said:

> . . . we are indebted to the rail fences of Secessia. They give us comfortable fires, hot coffee, and sometimes shelter itself. I can hardly conceive how we could live without them. Perhaps we are equally indebted to the pigs and potatoes of the country, for soldiers certainly never could march ten days upon hard tack and coffee alone.[211]

These incursions prompted local residents to write the authorities to inform them of conditions. They felt they had been abandoned by their own troops. Conditions at home grew worse:

Kinston N.C. Oct. 13th 1862
Sir, though an entire stranger to me, I deem it not improper to address you on a subject of so great importance, to the inhabitants of Eastern Carolina, which part of the state has been so sadly neglected.

In regard to this matter, let me beseech you, to apply those who have it in their power to send us aid, and let those Blood Thirsty Demons (The Yankees) be driven to their Rendezvous, so that the present inhabitants of this part of the state, may hence forth be free from molestation. A very small portion comparatively speaking of our OWN BRAVE CAROLINA BOYS will prevent them from repeating their previous outrages. In the name of God send forces and let them be repulsed in their DIABOLICAL efforts They spare neither woman or children; they are alike liable to their insults.

Families who are left almost destitute whose Husbands, Fathers & Sons have gone to shed their blood for their Country's rights, who have not the means by which to move are left without protection, and are compelled to bear the insults of those unrelenting Tryants . . .

Surely if the higher authority were aware of the cruelties and outrages that have been manifested towards the daughters of Carolina, they would send resistance to avert the impending evil without delay, and the only means by which this can be done, is to send sufficient forces to keep the enemy in New Berne.

Wives daughters & Sisters of Comp A 40, Regt[212]

A lady left her home near Jacksonville to refugee at the home of Colonel Amis of Young's Crossroad in Granville County. Mrs. Mary Scott received a letter from her friend Sarah Murrill of Plum Hill:

A Yankee gunboat landed at Jacksonville at the old bridge, troops poured out and they sacked every house except two. They sacked the post office and jail—took all the arms, clothes, some slaves, and took Dave Marshall, an old man. I have one homespun dress and another in the tub . . . . We are all the time in a dread.[213]

Two months later, Sarah notified Mrs. Scott about a Yankee cavalry raid of about six hundred who came from New Bern. She reported that they didn't do as much damage as before but did take bacon, horses, etc.:

I cannot tell how people are going to live every thing is so high . . . . We have more cavalry down here than can be fed much longer, corn is $10 a barrel, pork 25 cents per pound, and flour $40 a bushel—we shall have a famine, and perhaps the worst will come, but I hope the poor will not suffer; how they are to be fed is a mystery to me, I do hope a way will be provided for all.[214]

Another neighbor wrote Scott, telling her about the home situation:

The Yankees came to your & my house, took dresses, broke all locks, . . . they make a practice of breaking out all the window glasses and all the furniture where ever they find a house deserted . . .[215]

He suggested she get someone to live in it. Disenchanted individuals within the war lines changed. They were growing indifferent to death. When the Northern forces rode off New Bern to raid nearby towns, along the way, a soldier observed "one dead rebel stretched upon a piazza as we passed a house . . . and marveled at the stolid indifference of two or three white women who sat near the corpse and gazed at us as though nothing unusual had happened."[216]

By December 1862, most residents heard rumors of the enemy's advance from New Bern. Apparently, the news didn't reach Mount Olive. At an important stop on the Wilmington and Weldon Railroad, the stationmaster was completely surprised when New York cavalrymen stormed the station. They cut the telegraph wires, destroyed track, and arrested those waiting for the train. Mail was stolen or destroyed. Afterwards, they rode seven miles in the direction of Wilmington and burned a bridge. A correspondent wrote that the riders skirmished with Southern soldiers near the area. He reported the Confederates to have brought down a large cannon on the Merrimac Railroad car, which enfiladed the woods, but the cavalrymen had already left.[217]

The Wilmington and Weldon Railroad ran through Warsaw and near Kenansville. In July of 1863, U.S. General Foster's men raided Kenansville, burning the depot along with the telegraph office, barrels of rosin, turpentine, gunpowder, and the mail. A Northern newspaper reported "two miles of railroad at Warsaw, with culverts and telegraph for five miles or more, was destroyed at Kenansville."[218] The cavalry left to go back to Trenton, followed by prisoners, captured stock, and Negroes composing one hundred men with three hundred women and children.[219]

Another expedition to destroy Southern property went through Hyde County in 1863. Union troops with cavalry and artillery support steamed up the river in two ships and unloaded. Captain C. Richardson reported that there was a delay due to the want of a good pilot for both. He further stated in his report that the Negroes had torn up much of the road to delay their advance. A resident, Henry Cradle, with a letter of protection from provisional governor Stanly, had ordered the blacks to cut trees and destroy the road. Mr. Cradle was subsequently arrested. Guerillas, sometimes as many as eighty, skirmished with the invaders around Lake Mattamuskeet. Captain Richardson brought in his artillery and dispersed the men harassing him. Many from both sides were wounded and killed. When Richardson learned that about 250 to 300 guerillas had gathered and lay in ambush outside of Swan Quarter, he decided to fall back to the steamer.

Other Federal units told of guerillas who constantly fired on their men. When caught, the troops were disposed to show them little mercy. "They dressed in citizen's clothes, and shot our men in cold blood, whenever opportunity offered. When they saw a considerable body of our men approaching, they were unionist, neutrals, or 'know-nothings,' as they chose. One scouting party went up as far as Matrimeskut [sic] in Hyde County. The day they arrived there, they had a skirmish with a band of guerillas, and it is said killed ten of them. The captain of the guerilla band sent a challenge to the officer of the scouting party to fight him the next day, giving him the choice of place. The Union officer replied that he should fight him whenever and wherever he found him."[220]

A naval party landed at Pitch Landing on the Chowan River in December 1864. Crew from the USS *Chicopee* learned that the landing held a Confederate government warehouse stocked with cotton and army supplies. Commodore A. D. Harrell said they carried off "85 bales of cotton, a quantity of yarn, together with 7 prisoners and 52 contrabands." They destroyed "75 barrels of beef, 7,000 pounds of tobacco, 5 barrels of molasses, 100 boxes adamantine candles . . . 75 sacks of salt, 1,000 pounds of coffee, 10 barrels crushed sugar, 300 pairs of cotton cards, 2000 blocks of cotton yarn, 45 sets army harness, 31 mules, 6 horses, 10 army wagons, 250 grain sacks, 4,000 pounds of bacon; also a quantity of peas, beans, leather, shoes, boots, clothing, etc . . . ." Two days later, Harrell wrote that he failed to include other items demolished—875 sacks of salt and Confederate money/bonds. He said that they burned the bridge and killed one rebel.[221]

In possibly the same raid, Federal troops arrested civilians in Hertford. In two homes, they entered the bedroom of two different ladies who had recently given birth and taunted them. Their husbands were taken to prison at Point Lookout. A man from Elizabeth City, known to be a guerilla, one Addison White, proposed to join the band; but Federal soldiers captured him. When he refused to take the oath, they used him for target practice. His body days later was sent home to his wife. Other older men in the area faced Negro soldiers who burst into their homes firing pistols. James Skinner explained they had been led there by former runaway slaves.[222]

Citizens, whether male or female, faced jail or prison for questionable minor infractions. Mrs. Edmondston recorded in her diary that two Negro women broke into a dairy house owned by Mrs. Wright of Camden County, drank up all the milk, subsequently got violently sick, then died. Yankee troops accused Wright of poisoning the women. They tied her up, threw the lady in a cart, and took her to prison in Norfolk. At trial, Wright told them the women had eaten fish, oysters, and everything else before consuming the milk. She stayed in prison. As the Yankee detachment worked its way to Norfolk with Mrs. Wright, a group of guerillas and civilians skirmished with the force, shooting some and taking Negroes as prisoners. The enemy learned that local militia guided by Lieutenant Munden attacked this band. They went to Munden's home, found Mrs. Munden, tied her up, and took her to jail in Elizabeth City. Guarded by two black soldiers at all times, she suffered through the indignities. Yankees went to Windsor and carried off noncombatants, the cashier of the bank, a "leading" merchant, and the Episcopal minister.

In a Herford raid, plantation owners related the insolence of slaves, some rushing into the house to steal clothing and furnishings from the masters. A lady was slapped in the face by one, cursed at by another. Yankees shelled the town but did little damage.

Additionally, Mrs. Edmondston proclaimed a story of Mrs. Charles Wood, whose servant girl had run away but returned with Negro soldiers to take what she wanted from the missus's closets.[223]

WINTON

Winton is found about forty miles up the Chowan River from Edenton. The enemy saw it as a way to reach the back door to Norfolk. Southern forces dug in there didn't have enough men and equipment to properly defend the area, which grew an abundance of food for the military. Confederate officers commandeered the few homes and buildings in the tiny hamlet. As with other towns bursting with military activity, its people feared an attack might be imminent. Very soon, a Union gunboat plied the river. Actually, eight vessels steamed up the river unbeknown to the Confederate colonel, who planned a ruse to capture a ship. His plan consisted of getting a female to signal the ship that it was safe to dock; then his troops could overpower those who came ashore. Colonel Williams had "hired a thirty year old mulatto woman named Martha Keen . . ." As one of the ships, *Delaware*, piloted by a local man named Nassa Williams, steered near the dock, Rush Hawkins on board noticed a flash of light in the trees, indicating manned rifles. He hollered to the pilot to change course and retreat. The hidden rebels opened fire on the gunboat. When out of range of the rifles, the gunboat opened fire with their cannon. The Southern boys skedaddled, and neither side had anyone killed, though some were wounded.[224]

The following day, the townsfolk heard the Yanks were coming back. The Confederates knew they were no match for the Union Navy, so they departed along with the civilians. Taking whatever they could carry, the panicked citizens fled. Mrs. John Anderson, a wealthy widow, had some of her slaves hide her piano in the woods by burying it. She did not want to leave her stately home, but was forced by her son to get on a cart with her valuables. The majority of inhabitants left town, except for a Negro woman who had recently given birth, a few blacks, and a very old woman. Soon, a gunboat shelled the town; but when no fire was returned, it stopped. Union troops then took possession of the city.

A Northern soldier writing home described the destruction of Winton:

> Court houses, churches, beautifully furnished dwellings with velvet carpets, pianos, etc., all shared the same fate, and you may be sure we gave it a pretty good ransacking while the flames were doing their work.

U.S. Colonel Hawkins first fired the buildings and courthouse, which were filled with supplies for Southern troops. Then other homes containing war munitions blazed up. He made a search and found Martha Keen, the woman who had betrayed them. The historian Parramore explained it: "The wily wife of a brickmason, her safety hinging on her reply, rose superbly to the occasion by explaining to a sympathetic Hawkins that she was the slave of one of the rebel officers and drawing out that 'Dey said dat dey wan't going' to let anybody lib at all, but was goin' to kill ebery one of 'em." Citizens whose homes flamed up—Mrs. Anderson, Mrs. Halsey, Mr. Northcott, and Dr. Shields—recalled the enemy broke furniture, slit feather beds, killed their stock, and stole their clothing and valuables. One brave soul went aboard a gunboat seeking the commander and demanded his clothes be returned. When they could not be found, the officer said he would see that he would be paid for them, which never happened.[225]

HAMILTON-WILLIAMSTON

When the Northern soldiers entered Williamston, they found no one—black or white. The enemy confiscated local produce and filled up on apple brandy. After foraging, they left for Hamilton the next morning. The tiny hamlet of Hamilton flourished on the banks of the Roanoke River. The *Spirit of the Age* printed that eight Yankee gunboats came up the river without the slightest notice and opened fire upon the town. One infant was killed.[226] A mad scramble ensued as citizens threw their belongings in carts and wagons to flee. But before leaving, some community members filled their wells with rubbish, then cut the ropes, and, at the same time, hid their apple brandy, which was later found.[227] A bluecoat said *that* was the reason they burned the deserted town. He reported fifteen houses set afire in Hamilton and two in Williamston. They found that the Southern army had withdrawn from the fort on Rainbow Banks about a mile East of town. Soldiers from the gunboat did find a local physician in Hamilton, who was kidnapped, to treat the wounded on board.[228] The Federals reported that the roads there were strewn with furniture and apparel. The object of the Union forces was to march to Tarboro to destroy a rebel gunboat. Words leaked back to these officers that a large rebel force was in and around Tarboro, so they retreated. On their way back to New Bern, the enemy burned the jail, stocks, and whipping post in Williamston and occupied the courthouse, damaging deeds, wills, and other important papers.[229] The enemy returned to Williamston and Hamilton a few days later. Writing in her journal, Mrs. Edmondston recorded that they arrested the magistrates and held them responsible for the earlier skirmish.[230] Mrs. Kinchin Taylor in the fall of 1862 described in detail the raiders at her home, "The Zouaves swarmed in like Devils, yelling, whooping, & screaming."

Her brother said, "Her negro servant, Ness, drew a knife & took his station by her telling them that he would kill the first man who laid a finger upon her. They sacked the house, threw everything out of it, breaking every thing that could break & chopping the furniture to pieces! They built a fire out of doors, cut up the corn crop & threw it on it, killed all the fattening Hogs, sheep, cattle, & cows & threw them also into it. They took her carriage & every horse on the premises, telling her that they would have burned the house but that she was in it. She went herself on foot to head quarters, saw General Foster, the officer in command, & requested that her horses might be returned to her. He looked & spoke so cross that she feared him, but his Aid, to his praise be it spoken, Capt George Anderson of Boston interceded & obtained one horse for her. Her carriage was also returned with the harness cut to bits. He (Capt. A), when he saw the desolation & destruction wrought in her house, actually wept! His tears did him credit."[231]

Subsequently, Mr. John Williams lost by fire his (cotton) gin, screw, and all his cotton and leather. The burning continued at General J. R. Stubbs's farm of Halifax as his outbuildings and barn caught fire. His stock was either killed or carried off with his victuals, as the Negroes followed their deliverers.[232] At Indian Ridge, Currituck County, James B. Morgan notified his son, Patrick, a cadet at Virginia Military Institute:

> Your Uncle James has again been driven from his home by the shelling of his premises, and together with his family is now residing with us. The enemy occasionally makes raids upon us & plunder & destroy our property. A few weeks ago they came over to Indian Town & burned all the buildings on Dr. Marchant's place . . . together with the academy, & plundered several citizens taking horses, carts, (..groes)[Negroes], salt, &c. They have since removed from Shiloh & have made their headquarters at E. City.

The Diphtheria has been very prevalent this winter. I believe I wrote you of the death of two of Mr. Baxter's children. Now I inform you of the death of Shaw of the same horrible disease. It was a heart rendering scene to witness the distress of the family. All of us have had sore throats & your Ma has been doctoring for diphtheria, all are . . . better now, Lillie & Ida going to school & Jodie playing about the house.

There are so many changes. I received a letter from Mr. Lassiter . . . since then I learn he has sold out & removed. You must neglect no possible chance of letting us hear from you . . .[233]

Two weeks later, the father wrote his son again:

We have just heard that the guerillas had attacked the enemy in Pasquotank killing [Tim] Cox & probably some others. We hear that the Capt. Commanding in E. City has ordered all the people white & black to report to him, & it is said he intends to compel them to take up arms. The whole country is in a perfect ferment. The people are growing desperate & the inhuman conduct of our enemies seems to be driving every man capable of bearing arms into the bushes or into the army . . .[234]

As the war progressed, the pillaging continued. Citing passages from other letters, Mr. J. B. Morgan offered insight to his son:

The Yanks have been making frequent raids among us for the last three weeks, one a week at least. Saturday night they carried off one of my mules, but I was fortunate enough to recover him . . .

He continued, "We have felt a great deal of anxiety about you . . ."

Rumors reached Mr. Morgan that several high-ranking Confederate generals had been killed. He replied, "But should it be true, God will raise up others to fill their place. He will not suffer our enemies to succeed in this unjust, cruel & unholy war."[235] In October of 1864, Mr. Morgan told his son about the enemy in a letter:

We have had a good long respite from the raiders, not having been troubled with any since you left. They have passed on the Indian Town Road once since, but none came up the road. I have never seen so dry a season. I do not know how I shall manage to house my crop as there is no laborers to be had.[236]

A number of towns invaded in the 1862 reconnaissance fell victim again. On one raid in July 1863, Foster's subordinates stole $6300 and the horse from relief agent George Greene, who had earmarked the money for the poorer classes. When the enemy arrived at Greenville, they reported that the town was empty of Confederates, except for a few convalescing soldiers in the hospital. Local citizens told of the pillagers stealing $8300 from two physicians. Females did not escape unscathed. They recalled the enemy soldiers took their breastpins, watches, and earrings. The commissary stores and government warehouses went up in flames. Soldiers looted the saloons and barrooms.

Superior Court Judge George Howard sent a letter to his wife, stating:

I am as busy as a bee [sic] preparing for the coming of the Yankees. I believe they will certainly be here this Fall, probably this summer . . . . And I am attempting to so arrange matters that the family can all leave in case of an emergency. Mother is very nervous about affairs and Alice is terribly frightened—all her boasted courage has oozed out of her fingers' ends.[237]

After the Greenville conflict, cavalrymen rode through Falkland and Sparta. The Third NY Cavalry dashed into Rocky Mount, firing their guns, scattering the inhabitants. Several soldiers and citizens were captured, along with a train. The conductor was relieved of his clothes in addition to $1000 in gold. Destruction continued. The depot, an engine, its cars, a water tank, the telegraph office, and warehouses caught fire. The raiders burned the railroad bridge over the Tar River. About one mile North of the depot lay the Rocky Mount Mills, where the cavalry headed next. It too went up in flames. Also incinerated were the flour mill and great quantities of hardtack. About five thousand bales of cotton belonging to private individuals went up in flames. Resident William Pope had his personal belongings, including his toothbrushes and children's clothing, filched along with $20,000. Another wealthy citizen reported the loss of his stables, barns, buggy, and $70,000. Mr. Parker placed a reward for the return of his stolen horses in the newspaper. Thirty-seven commissary wagons containing various supplies stood loaded, ready for distribution, fell into enemy's hands and went up in smoke—a big loss to the state.[238]

Leaving Rocky Mount, the New York cavalry rode to Tarboro, burning cotton bales, cotton gins, and wagons along their path. The troops rushed into Tarboro firing their pistols just like at Rocky Mount. A resident said the takeover only lasted a few minutes. Here, they burned the depot and cars, which held a large stockpile of medicine and cotton. Most important of all was the incineration of a partially built ironclad gunboat. The author has stated that the destruction of the gunboat ended further attempts to build any more in the Tar River—Pamlico Sound area.[239]

An interesting article found in the *State Journal* during that time noted that after Tarboro resident Michael Cohn's gristmill was incinerated, he followed the enemy back to New Bern to ask for reparations. They refused. The miller was exempt from military service, and when his lifeline was destroyed, it left him eligible for conscription. This he would not have. Cohn decided to pass on information of the construction of gunboats on the Roanoke and Tar Rivers. He later signed up with the enemy in the quartermaster's department. Usually, the Union army did not plunder homes of Confederate Freemasons, but they did steal the jewels and artifacts/regalia belonging to the Tarboro Masonic Lodge. It was many years after the war before some of the items were returned to Tarboro.

At Otter Creek Bridge, Confederate Colonel Claiborne shelled the woods to dislodge the Union raiders. A Mrs. Drake rode through the skirmish to warn the Southern men that the Yankees had escaped. Those Federal men separated from their company got captured.

Hundreds of contrabands had followed Colonel Potter's troops from Tarboro. Approximately three hundred contrabands and one hundred Confederate prisoners returned to New Bern with Colonel Potter. Daniel's Schoolhouse became a temporary hospital after the brief fight with the Federals. Union General Potter's men, after skirmishing with Confederate cavalry near Otter Creek, had the help of a Negro to find a way to escape. Some militiamen fired on the enemy there, and the cavalry went back that night and burned their houses.

Potter's raid wreaked havoc on North Carolina's railroad, shipping, and cotton industries Down East. They did a great amount of damage in that short time. The *Governor Morehead* and the *Colonel Hill*, ships docked on the Tar River, "ended Confederate steamboat traffic for the remainder of the war."[240]

When the Federals left Tarboro, they continued burning government property such as artillery caissons, warehouses, the jail, and market houses. Private establishments were not safe. A gunsmith named Julius Holtzscheiter stood helpless as his shop went up in flames. The steam-powered gristmill and a blacksmith shop were destroyed. At private homes, the looters stole jewelry, money, and valuables. Mrs. Clark, wife of the former governor, and another young lady fled to their kitchen as the raiders went through their home, taking what they desired, busting up trunks and chest of drawers. Clark's wine cellar yielded many fine bottles of brandy and wine. Soldiers threw junk into the well and carried off food.

GREENVILLE

Enemy forces from the above raid left more details for the reader. Their entrance came as a complete surprise. A cavalryman told that:

> We found no enemy in force, but unoccupied earth works, forts, and rifle pits, extending around the town . . . . We bivouacked two or three hours at the corners of the street, in the yards and vacant places in town and fed our hungry and jaded horses . . . . The authorities . . . gave us a carte blanche and the freedom of the town, which we freely used, making ourselves intimate with the interior arrangements of stores, public buildings, dwelling houses, iron safes, money drawers and every other place where a single article contraband of war could possible be secreted. The result was the capture of a large quantity of fire arms and equipage, some $50,000 in secesh and North Carolina money, besides a few thousand dollars in gold and silver . . . . We broke open the jail . . . set at liberty 25 negroes; some of whom had been confined over two years . . .[241]

Woodbury said their crime was for aiding some slaves to escape. The raiders commented on the rich farmland in the area but said that at some places, the fields were not cultivated due to the lack of men and exit of their slaves. Another New York cavalryman left his thoughts:

> Greenville is a very nice-looking and pleasantly situated little village. Its chief and about the only productions, are very pretty ladies, who were much admired by us all. Ladies are somewhat of a rarity down here, but secession was stamped on every feature of the birds, esp. when we demanded the keys to the smokehouse, and took out the many nice hams, honey, and etc., and the numerous stores which were opened and the contents destroyed as we liked. All this led them to feel delightful towards the Yankees; but it couldn't be helped.[242]

After the Federals advanced into Greenville, the mayor surrendered the city. Negro soldiers pulled their artillery through the town and when leaving tried to persuade the local slaves to go with them. Those bondsmen refused at that time. Withdrawing, the Federal troops took with them ten civilians. On their way to Washington, these men were held a few days, then released.

C.S. Colonel N. M. Hammond, the tithe agent in Pitt County, had on hand a large supply of provisions, which became known to the Union soldiers nearby. Usually, the stockpile was guarded by Confederate forces; but at this particular time, it was not. Colonel Hammond was awakened one night by a cavalry squad wanting sustenance for their horses. He told them to go to the barn and help themselves. Shots were heard in the distance. The Northern soldiers were told that Confederate troops were in the vicinity, so the Federals left without taking the tithe stockpile.[243]

Some churches in Pitt County ended up in flames because they had stored provisions for the Southern forces, Red Banks and the Black Jack Church among them. In a skirmish near Scuffletown (Greene County) and Contentnea Creek, Confederate soldiers had placed a brass cannon on the back of a mule and fired into approaching enemy troops. Little damage was done except for scattering the masses of Negroes that had taken up the march along with the bluecoats. Women and children dropped their carts loaded with furniture, clothing, food, and fowls. A general melee ensued. Panicked people fled in every direction. Several black babies and children had been hastily abandoned by their mothers in the pandemonium. The rebels captured many horses and Negroes while other soldiers pursued the Federals who continued to vandalize neighborhoods.[244] Mrs. Peyton Atkinson complained in a letter to the governor:

Governor Vance,

I beg of you to read this, as I know your kind heart will not accuse me of presumption in writing to you. My own feelings and the entreaties of our citizens prompt me to the act. We come humble, imploring our noble governor to send help to rescue us from these Yankee wretches. You may have seen an outline of their deeds, but you know not the deep, black outrages committed by them. In Greenville they destroyed, it is thought, three hundred thousand dollars worth of property, robbed citizens of everything, valuables, such as watches, jewelry, silver and money . . .

Believe me, there was not one man there at the time of the invasion, any soldiers, between Tarboro and Greenville, except a few sick ones at Greenville and one of our plantations, which is headquarters for Major Kennedy, who belongs to Col Griffin's regiment. In all of this fighting, Major Kennedy and his men did the effectual work, but he no longer comes to his quarters than Gen. Martin orders him away to where it is believed no enemy is advancing. At the time of this raid, he was ordered to Hamilton and not a man capable of service was anywhere when the federals advanced. These Yankees destroyed the bridge at Greenville, proceeded to Tarboro unmolested, except only a few shots from helpless citizens. On their route from Greenville to Tarboro, they stole all the horses they could get, robbed persons of all their money, watches, brandy, silver, arms, pushed into homes at midnight, bursting open doors into ladies' bedrooms whilst they were in bed, tied citizens and locked them up in gin houses, destroyed everything belonging to the government in Tarboro.

After the fight at Tarboro, you think the wretches did not go the hotel and dine? You know they destroyed the factory and other property at the Falls of Tar River. I can't begin to tell you in a letter of their deeds. This is a rich portion of the state you know and our crops promise an abundant harvest, notwithstanding heavy rains, but if we are left exposed in this way, we can do nothing for the state or Confederacy.

Now allow me to invite the sentiments of the community. It is believed that General Martin is in colleague with Gen Potter. Do you know they married sisters? General Martin's headquarters is Kinston and I am told that Mrs. Martin goes to New Bern just when she pleases. Men who were in this fight say every Yankee could have been captured at Swift Creek bridge, if Gen. Martin would of let them remain there, but he ordered them away about half of an hour before the Yankees came to loot and just gave them passage. The citizens are holding meetings to send to the authorities to remove old Martin. Governor Vance, we call on you. Oh in the name of God do something for us. Examine into this matter; come down here to see the good people who elected you, who will support you through life and death. We call on our governor for help. Don't allow us, while Carolina's noble sons have responded to the call of troops, to be trodden down so.[245]

Mrs. Atkinson said, "Many a lady & her helpless little children slept in the woods with the Green grass for their beds & the Canopy of Heaven for their shelter."

KINSTON-GOLDSBORO

A non-slaveholding soldier from the mountains stationed at Goldsboro in the winter of 1862 shared his opinion with his parents about the countryside in the flatlands:

Goldsborough

Dear Friends and relations, I can inform you all that Goldsborough is the nicest place I ever saw in my life. The cars run here from Raleigh and from

Richmond and from Weldon and from Newbern and from Wilmington, and the telegraph also from several places. We can get the news from Richmond in Virginias here in ten minutes and we can get papers, that is printed in Richmond in the morning here by two o'clock. If you was here three hours you would see more than you ever saw before . . . G.J. Huntley[246]

A letter mailed home in February read: "There is lots of women and children moving up here from Wilmington and New Bern to get out of the way of the Yankees."[247] A letter a few days later revealed: "As we came down today there were strings of ladies along the roads every mile or two and they cheered us as long as we could see them." He was in route from Goldsboro to Halifax. "At every town we passed they would wave their handkerchiefs at every window. I saw a good deal coming down from Goldsboro to this place, which is about 80 miles distant. We passed through the heart of the turpentine section and I saw the most swamps I ever saw before in my life. Swamps some times on both sides of the railroad for a mile or more and black gums and sweet gums [trees] as thick as you ever saw. Cane and the whole earth covered with water as far as your eyes could see appearing to be about knee deep and the cane as thick as it could stand and as high as your head . . . I will just say that the Eastern portion of North Carolina is a power-ful scenery to a mountain boy . . . . I can inform you that the people is scared hear about the Yankies."[248]

A month passed; and Lieutenant Huntley, marching through Martin County, claimed, "Most of the richest and best farms in this section is deserted by the owners. There is lots of cotton here just lying about, doing no body no good. Some of the people is hauling their cotton into the woods and hiding it to keep the Yankies from getting it."[249]

Retreating Southern troops, according to a Northern soldier who followed, said that "the rebels had stripped the houses of most of the moveable furniture and of all eatables . . . . desolation and starvation reigned.[250] When Federal General John Foster left New Bern for Kinston, his men pillaged the area of animals and goods. Southern troops put up a good battle to protect the town. Outside of Kinston, Foster overtook the home of Mrs. Williams, commandeered her home for a hospital, and forced her to leave. Mrs. Williams's daughter lay dying with typhoid. She vehemently objected, but it was of no use. The critically ill daughter was carried to a neighbor where she soon passed away.[251] The Caswell Street Methodist Church, which had burned just before the war, was under construction when the war commenced; it found use as a hospital.[252]

A Northern soldier in describing the inhabitants of Kinston in 1865 painted a bleak picture:

> In the little dilapidated city of Kinston, desolation and starvation reigned. The women and children who alone remained all looked care-worn and hungry. Many of the poorer class came rambling through the Union camp, begging bread of the soldiers . . . the women . . . expressed much surprise at the gentlemanly appearance and demeanor of the northern troops. But three white men were found left in Kinston, and they were Union men who had hidden themselves from rebel rule. All the rest had been carried off, either voluntarily or involuntarily, by the rebels.[253]

After four years of war, how could it look otherwise? Union Chaplin Henry White, taken as a prisoner, described the desolation of the land, homes, and abandoned plantations he saw as they marched to Kinston. Fields lay barren, uncultivated. The woods crawled with stragglers in the tall, large pines and swamps. Captured rebel soldiers came back to their lines carrying bags of food from foraging on the neighbors. White repeated what he saw of the disciple of the Southern troops. He said it was poor indeed, but talking to them, the officers said they would fight when necessary. "If they are absent two or three days no notice was taken of it, they told us, but if a fight came on and they were not present, they were severely punished. Plenty of negroes were in the army in Confederate uniform with muskets in their hands. When asked if the negroes were not soldiers, they said they were servants to planter's sons, and when on a march carried their arms." When the prisoners reached Pollocksville, the Southern soldiers wanted to trade with the prisoners any article they carried. Reverend White, all along the trek, talked to both soldiers and civilians. A cavalryman told him that horses cost between three and five thousand dollars. If your horse was killed in battle, it was replaced free. A plain gold ring cost twenty-five dollars and a gold watch, fifteen hundred to two thousand dollars. A silver watch went cheaper, from two hundred to eight hundred dollars. After marching forty miles, the prisoners arrived in Kinston.[254]

In his next letter, he depicted Kinston in an unfavorable light. He with friends asked an officer to go to a nearby home to bathe, and surprisingly, the wish was granted. He observed:

> The carpets were gone, and everything bore marks of the great convulsion that we were more and more to see. There were but few negroes about. Nearly all had gone to the Yanks. There were no men about fit for military service. Ladies were plenty, pretty, and saucy; they understood and made us feel that we are prisoners of war . . . . As the trains passed through town, Confederate soldiers called on these ladies . . . . In the presence of ladies they would scorn to notice or speak to us. Long and mournful was the tale they told of the trials and privations the war had brought; and from what I know myself, I guess some of them have . . . crowed a little. No conversation runs long with these people before "nigger, nigger," is thrust into the theme . . .
>
> Before the war there might have been from one to two thousand inhabitants but it is in the region of raids from our forces, some have gone further inland. Small boats can come up the Neuse River to this point and above.[255]

Eighteen miles up from Kinston lay Whitehall, also known as Seven Springs. The Federal Army sought out the area to destroy the CSS *Neuse*,[*] an iron-clad, rumored to be under construction there. The engines were borrowed from the locomotives belonging to the Atlantic and North Carolina Railroad. The *Neuse* was to be used in a combined land and naval attack against New Bern. The gunboat saw no action and got stuck on a sandbar, and Confederate troops burned it rather than letting it fall in the hands of the enemy.[256]

U.S. gunboats steamed up the Neuse River to within two miles of Kinston. Confederate troops were aware of the advance and would at times shoot at the boats. Smaller boats could turn around and go to safety, but the *Ocean Wave* was too large to turn around in the river and had to reverse its engines to retreat. It was told that the rebs followed this boat for twenty miles using small arms fire. Men on board claimed to have found spent bullets "dipped in verdigris, to poison the wounds they inflicted, and others had copper wire attached for the same purpose."[257]

A Northern correspondent composed his report: "Besides destroying the bridge at Whitehall, the rebels destroyed two gunboats constructing at that point, and thereby saved us the trouble of the operation. A few miles beyond Whitehall, we bivouacked for the night and the next day pressed on to Everttsville . . . where we had the happiness of destroying a long tressel-work bridge on the railroad connecting Goldsborough with Wilmington."[258] Actually, only one gunboat was demolished. In describing the battle to take Kinston, a veteran in the Forty-fourth Massachusetts Regiment recollected that his unit "passed through the streets upon our first entrance and found many bales of cotton piled up and set on fire. The Kinston rebels no doubt thought we were dying to get possession

---

[*]   The remains of the ship is preserved and now a state historic site.

of their precious staple. Near the depot a great pile of corn was also on fire . . . a few Union people we found here . . . one lady hospitably entertained some of the officers, and afforded interesting information of the enemy's hopes and discomfiture. They confidently expected to hold the place, but left with great precipitancy, strewing the way with clothing, equipment, guns, etc."[259]

In talking with captured Confederate prisoners after the battle, the Southrons related that they had thrown the bodies of their comrades into the river to conceal the number of dead.[260] Old Abe's soldiers pictured rebels captured on the road to Kinston as "dressed in butternut homespun, wearing headgear of all sorts and conditions. They were first-class soldiers, though, brave, resolute, and reliable, as we soon had occasion to know."[261]

One of the bluecoats commented that during the battle, C.S. General Nathan Evans showed a flag of truce and requested a place of safety for the women and children, "as he intended to return the fire from his artillery. Our artillery ceased firing, and the women and children that could be found, were conducted to a place of safety . . ."[262] Union soldier Hubbard reported the death of a Mrs. Phillips, shot dead by Confederate troops in Kinston. No reason was given. Civilians were caught in the cross fire.[263] Union causalities from the fight were carried to C.S. Colonel G. H. Whitfield's home near Seven Springs.

According to a Massachusetts soldier after the battle of Whitehall, his comrade swam to the burning bridge, picked up a torch, and attempted to fire the two partially constructed iron-clads there. The Confederates shot at him but missed. Union artillery destroyed one iron-clad. Troops marched on to Goldsboro to cut telegraph lines and to destroy the railroad and the bridge over the Neuse.[264] It only took railroad employees a few weeks to rebuild the important bridge.

Captured Northern troops were taken to the fairgrounds in Goldsboro. The overflow ended up in the courthouse whereby citizens sympathetic to the Union cause cared for them. Ladies attended their wounds and gave them breakfast of bean soup, coffee, and corn bread. Some secesh girls in Goldsboro, standing on their balcony porches, reviled and insulted the bleeding men.

Seventy-eight miles of railroad separated Goldsboro and Weldon where these Northern prisoners were sent on the way to Richmond. They debarked at Weldon and marched to a church that had a stove, which was welcomed by the prisoners because it had been so cold in the boxcars. Here they exchanged greenbacks for vittles with interested parties.[265]

On the U.S. raid back to New Bern from Goldsboro, a soldier said of foraging, "In our need, we must have left many a household with nothing of their winter's supply of bacon and sweet potatoes. Upon what they were to live during the weeks of winter we asked not. They were our enemies and we were hungry. Such is war . . ." General Otis commented "that probably there was not left alive a chicken nor an unburned fence rail between Newbern and Goldsboro within half a mile of the line of march." Five hundred or more slaves accompanied the enemy back to New Bern.[266]

Goldsboro residents saw their first bluecoats the winter of 1862. Union General John G. Foster's troops left New Bern on his trek into the heart of the state. It was reported the line was five miles long, including all branches of the military with 150 wagons. Waynesborough, near Goldsboro, had started to decline prewar. Only a few warehouses remained, which were burned by enemy. The town never flourished after that. A Northern minister mentioned earlier and taken prisoner described the area as he passed through. Reverend White, along with sixteen hundred of his comrades, upon capture marched from there to Kinston, then Goldsboro to reach the Wilmington and Weldon Railroad to Wilmington. From Wilmington, they traveled to the prison in Andersonville, Georgia. The reverend wrote a series of letters about his experience to the Zion's Herald in the fall of 1864. Only those concerning North Carolina will be used here.

Letter no. 6 recounted the scenes in Goldsboro. Reverend White talked with the Baptist Reverend Dill from South Carolina who believed that God sent the slaves to the South to be elevated. "He said they could not educate them [slaves] above a certain point, and that the policy of course prevented their employment in the higher department of industry."

White told of the filthy jail located near the courthouse, which also contained inmates, especially elderly men, some wealthy, who were political prisoners. Negroes came around selling pies. Civilians would try to get a glimpse of the bluecoats. He said, "The young boys that came to see us were an uncombed and ragged crowd, saucy and bold. The women showed the prevalence of caste. Some dressed richly, but most were dressed in the most untidy manner. Many of them had a stick protruding from the mouth several inches. These persons were chewing snuff."* White continued, "The negroes were all about, and did not seem to me to be so very much below the common whites that were to be seen on the cars and at all the places we visited. This is a small town of no special importance, aside from its connection with the railway intercept. There are a few good buildings. The Atlantic and North Carolina and the Wilmington and Weldon Railroad cross each other at this place."[267]

During the battle to take the Goldsboro Bridge, people in New Bern heard the sounds of battle. The Federals mingling with the few white women left in town said they "were anxious for the war to end and living under a reign of terror, and that they had more to fear from the rebels than the Union troops. The retreating rebels had stripped the houses of most of their movable furniture and of all eatables."[268]

The reader is fortunate to learn of the conditions of one raid from New Bern to Goldsboro by a Union soldier who signed his name with "George." Spelling is not corrected:

New Bern Jan. 8 1863
Dear Aunt Maria,

I have long been trying to write to you but my time has been so ccupied that it has been very difficult for me to commence, but I have seized this moment and my aunt shall have a letter from her nephew. No doubt you have heard of me, viz. uncle George every time he has written; he has written everything of note that has taken place in Newbern; but uncle George did not go on the expedition; so I have the start of him here, and write from experience what he was not permitted to witness.

In our first expedition it was not my fortune to see the rebel army what little there were that run from us. But this time we have met the rebel horde, been under the fire of his heavy guns, and come off victorious in the combat. From the time we left Newbern we had the post of honor, in guarding a supply train of over 200 wagons as far as Kinston; and a greater part of the time we were 6 or 8 miles in the rear of the main army. (by we I mean that 5th reg.) liable at any time to be attacked by guerillas.

During the battle at Kinston . . . we were halted 6 miles in the rear . . . but alas our quiet was disturbed about noon, by the booming of artillery at K . . . . At eve our colonel was officially informed that the rebels had been put to flight, and in retreating over the bridge fired it behind them, so that our boys could not follow them; but our cavalry was to close upon their heels; the rebel in his haste to fire the bridge got some turpentine on his clothes which ignited and he was burned to death. The cavalry quickly put out the fire and charged the rebels terribly; trampling them down beneath the hoofs of the horses. 400 prisoners were captured ten heavy cannon, and military stores in abundance. We lost in this battle 120 killed & wounded.

---

*   He described how the women made the snuff brush: "A stick of some kind is taken, perhaps six inches long, and pounded, or chewed till it becomes splinted like a broom. This they roll in the snuff till it is full, when they place it between the cheek and the teeth, and suck it with great apparent relish."

The next morning before we resumed the march we had a breakfast that did us a "heap of good" we had coffee, and we confiscated corned pork, sweet-potatoes, &c from a sesesh house in the neighborhood; & it was a dainty meal in comparison with hard crackers that we are fed with on marches. About noon and before we were aware of it we came upon the hospital where the wounded of yesterday's battle were quartered; a little beyond this we entered the woods where the battle commenced the boys left the ranks, and scoured the woods for bullets &c for relics; trees were scathed by bullets, and slivered by cannon-balls, rebel blankets were found saturated with blood, and cartridge boxes laid scattered in all directions.

The rebels contested the ground inch by inch, until they arrived in front of Kinston where they made a stand; here the battle lasted two or three hours, when the rebels were forced to retreat in the manner above described. Here we passed the baggage train and rejoined our brigade in advance, while some other reg't was doomed to occupy our late position. We marched this day 23 miles, and tonight I feel tired enough to turn in to rest, but I shall feel better in the morning if I sit up a while, I have wandered some 500 yards from camp to a fire in the woods where some half dozen men are cooking poultry they foraged on the march there is no place on the march where so much comfort is taken as at night after a day's weary march, as around a camp-fire; there the events of the day are rehearsed, "jokes pass round, & merry chat," until the small hours of night, steal upon us unawares and then we never have a campfire without we have something to cook by it.

The troops have coffee and hard crackers served them by the government, but we have the privele of forageing what ever we can find, so we have a good supper usually. The nights this time of the year are very cold; contrasting strongly with the daytime, when the sun pours down his hot rays with as little sympathy for the human race as regards their comfort as on a day in june. The next morning . . . before we broke camp . . . we could hear the cannonading at Whitehall; we marched leisurely along for 2 hours, when we halted about a mile from the scene of action, capped our guns &c, and were ordered forward. We all expected to be thrown into action. But we were not however permitted to fire a gun, we filed around a hill in front of the enemies fire, we kept on toward Goldsboro leaving some to finish the work nearly completed (of whiping the rebels) . . . . Truly the farther we advanced the more we see of war.

The next day . . . about noon we came upon the railroad at Everettsville about 6 miles this side of Goldsboro; the sight of several rebel reg'ts in an open field called forth a salutation from our artillery in advance. The troops halted in the road, and presently General Foster rode through the lines to the front accompanied by his staff; they were immensely cheered as they passed. Several batteries of artillery followed them, thundering along the road at double-quick. The rebels had taken refuge in the woods where they were well fortified; their position was ascertained, the batteries formed inline of battle, and we were ordered forward to support them. The artillery poured shell & shot into the woods at a fearful rate; the 5th reg't was formed in the woods along the line of railroad, where the shrub-oaks were so thick that we could scarcely move.

The rebels after a short time were driven from the woods and in full retreat toward Goldsboro. The 3rd Mass reg't was ordered to destroy the railroad. The first thing they done was to burn the railroad bridge and a "mill that stood by it." They tore up 4 miles of rails, piling them upon the sleepers and then setting the sleepers on fire, in this way the rails were warped so as to render them useless for future use. This done we filed out of the woods into an open field where the other reg'ts had been formed in line of battle. Three cheers were proposed, and given for the accomplishment of the expidition; which was to break the railroad communication between Richmond and Charleston.

Prepar was nearly completed for our return to Newburn which we heard the rebels cheering in the woods where they had retreated but a short time before: it seems that they in their retreat were reinforced by more rebels, and turned back to assail us; but we were soon ready for them, our lines were formed, and Belger's Battery was ordered to the front, and the 5th ordered to support it. On came the rebels charging on us at double-quick yelling like demons. We were ordered to fix bayonets; while we were doing this Capt Belger had sighted one of his own guns and gave the order fire.

We waited a few moments to see the result. Oh! It was a splended shot; the shell burst in their midst, scattering them like frightened sheep but many of them never lived to run; many of them lost their limbs, many were knocked sever-al feet in the air, and fall to the ground: many a traitor was seen to "grin in the pangs of death and bit the ground." Our artillery by this time was pouring shell and shot into the rebel ranks at a rapid rate. While we were directing our fire at the rebels in this open space some rebels on our left opened on us with artillery: the first discharge was grape shot which ploughed up the grounds ten feet in front [of] us throwing the sand in our faces. The 5th reg't was then ordered to lay flat on the ground.

The rebels finding that their shot fell a little short elevated their guns a little, and if we had been standing would have cut our ranks terribly; but the most of them passed over us. One of my company was struck in the hip by a spent grape-shot which caused quite a bruise, he secured the ball and has it now in his possession as a relic . . . . Capt Belger after he fired his gun, and had given some orders to his men, he went to the rear, as he was passing our company he inquired what reg't this was? The fifth mass was replied, very good said he, and for god's sake! Don't let them capture my battery! For two hours we laid flat on the cold ground shivering with the cold, and rebel shot and shell flying above, around, beneath us; everywhere we could see them striking in the ground or cutting off the tops of the trees.

It pained me to hear the profanity on the battled field: the "powder monkies" as they are called, were quarreling continually as to which had carried the most cartridges, each ascerting that they had carried 3 to the others two. Just before the close of the battle these cartridges had got low & there were none at hand. But those in the baggage train, far in the rear, in consequence of this, the gunners did not fire as rapidly as usual, in order to make them last longer: Capt Belger noticing this came to the front and inquired the cause: the reply was that the powder was nearly exausted; never mind about that said Belger, load and fire as fast as you can; and make every shot tell.

What shall we do when the powder is gone? Inquired the gunner. Load and fire h _ _ l & d _ _ nation at them replied Belger; and then went to the rear to order forward ammunition. The battle did not last more than half an hour after this. The rebels could not stand the shower that was cutting them down, like grass, and they retreated once more in haste toward Goldsboro, leaving us victor of the field.

During the battle, the rebels destroyed the dam to the mill, letting the water fill the valley in our rear; through this we had to wade with the water up to my waist. You can imagine what our feelings were on this occasion; it was a cold winter's day, we had been laying on the cold ground, shivering for two hours; to make the scene more gloomy and dismal, darkness was fast throwing her mantle over the battle field; here we stood on the edge of the flood, dreading to take the step.

The stream was full of floating timber and rail fences; the current was very strong as much as I could do to stand on my feet. After we had gained the opposite bank our col made his appearance climbing up the bank, during the battle our field and staff officers sent their horses to the rear so they with the men had to wade; one of the men asked the col if he had to go into the water? Yes boys he said I had to polly-wog it with you.

The Major got beyond his depth and had to swim the stream. After crossing and everything was ready to start I was detailed as one to report to the chaplain at the hospital. The ambulances had gone on in advance with the wounded, but by some mistake two were left behind at the hospital, and these we were to carry by hand until we could be relieved.

This is the saddest experience of a soldier's life, to take care of the wounded. In a battle we can see our companions fall on our right hand and on our left, and the excitement of the conflict will not permit us to notice it. But when the combat is over, and it becomes necessary to bury the dead and look after the wounded it is then the sensitive heart feels sad and mourns over the wreck that war has made.

I entered the house, and at the door as I entered lay a man that had been killed. I went into the room on the right of the entry first; there was a faint fire burning on the hearth, that cast a flickering light around the room which was relieved of fur-nature with the exceptions of a few chairs and a table that stood in the middle of the room on which the wounded had their wounds dressed, as they were brought in from the battle field. The table and the floor around it was covered with blood. A large pile of cotton-wool was in one corner of the room used to dress the wounds. In the room on the left laid the two wounded men on a table [illegible] The other on the floor. Both shot through the head. It was some time before we could find anything suitable to carry them on, and then we had to take a form bench as the best thing we could find. Gently we raised the wounded man, worked his rubber blanket under him, and lowered him on the bench: we placed a gun under each end of the bench so that four could carry him, while two walked beside him to steady him on the bench.

By this time the troops were two miles in the advance and we were in the rear of everything but a few cavalry who were acting as rear guard we had carried him about a mile and a half when he died. We were ordered to leave him by the roadside. We learned afterward that he was buried by the rear guard. Poor fellow, none of his friends, (but a cousin who was with us) knows his last resting place: he sleeps beneath the tall pines . . . far from his native home; if I was an artist I could draw a touching picture of a soldier's grave.

I hastened forward and rejoined my reg't. That night we encamped on the same ground that we did the night before. Our march to Newbern was made in quick time without any disaster. Now I have written you a good long letter Aunt Maria and I want one from you in answer. We are all well, enjoying good health which is the greatest blessing we can receive from Our Heavenly Father.

From you affectionate nephew
George[269]

Louis Leon entered in his diary that he and friends went to an area where the Kinston battle occurred. "The Yankees are poorly buried, as we saw several heads, hands, and feet sticking out of the ground where the rain had washed the dirt off them."[270] Most of the time in letters sent home, the writer would spare the reader the gory details of war unless the reader happened to be a male.

In the second attempt to capture Kinston in the six months of war, Dr. Cobb's home at Wyse Fork reverted to a temporary hospital for the enemy. Cobb's home filled with wounded soldiers who found shelter on the piazza as it began to rain. In the attic are scribbled the names of some patients housed there. Wounded Blue and Gray alike took refuge in an old storehouse in town. Confederate surgeons performed amputations in the nasty dimly lit warehouse. All the wounded were loaded onto a boxcar for the trip to Goldsboro. One Union soldier said the train started and stopped twenty times before it arrived, causing the afflicted tremendous pain and suffering. In Goldsboro, about one hundred wounded Federal soldiers ended up in another old warehouse awaiting the trains to take them to Salisbury Prison. They did stop at High Point, ending up in the Masonic Hall. A Federal trooper said that Confederate Dr. B. F. Smallwood and his wife cared for the prisoners. This prisoner, Henry C. Baldwin, who had acted as a nurse to his comrades became sick himself. He had nothing but good comments about Dr. Smallwood.[271]

After the Wyse Fork battle, the Federals rebuilt the railroad from New Bern to Goldsboro,* which helped re-supply Sherman's troops before his march to Raleigh. Thousands upon thousands of Sherman's army then occupied Goldsboro and denuded the countryside of all its produce and animals. Foraging was necessary until Sherman could get his provisions moved from New Bern. Soldiers confiscated fresh mounts and killed all the old worn-out stock, throwing the carcasses in the Neuse River, which dammed up the river many days. A number of residents came out in force to accept the occupiers. As the band played amid a cheering crowd of civilians and soldiers, the lofty American flag went up over the courthouse roof. News of Lee's surrender reached Kinston three days after his surrender at Appomattox.[272]

Post the Battle of Bentonville, the column of U.S. General Cox was met by the mayor of Goldsboro, Honorable I. H. Privett. The next day, General Schofield's forces arrived. Upon entrance to the town, a bluecoat said, "Goldsboro is an insignificant hamlet, not important enough even to be noticed in a general gazetteer. It is but a little more than a railroad station."[273] It may not have been seen as significant as other eastern towns he had passed through, but it was of critical importance to the Confederacy because of its railroad junction. Goldsboro was one of the few remaining rail lines open to feed General Lee's troops in Virginia.

Confederate A. F. Harrington wrote his brother about his march in Onslow County in 1862. He said the troops were so tired that refugees helped carry their equipment:

> . . . our knapsacks was hald a part of the way Bye the People on the way with carts they ware Mty accommodating in the County The People is amoving off down here in a hurry. We met Mrs Sanders a moving away She told us how the Yankeys served her thare was 100 of them went to her House or Cavelry she was in the kitchen when they come & the Captain Raised up in his stirrups & Shucked his sword over her & told her to go in the House like She would tell her niger then made her give up her keys & then took her juelry one gole watch Rings Bed close Sugar & coffee & money 7 mules & 7 horses wagon & Carts Carriages 6 negro men One of them is now here in jail he Come back to a mans house to Bye him a Bugy & the Pickets got him & Brought him her today He was her driver He Sayed it was easer to ride in a Bugy than a cart John I never was so sorry for a women in my life She was a crying when She was a talking . . .[274]

Union troops got as far as Jacksonville from New Bern on a trek to storm Wilmington in conjunction with the naval bombardment. The enemy had possession of the *Raleigh*

Progress and learned of Confederate General D. H. Hill's intent to storm the bridge at Goldsboro in 1863.[275]

In 1864, a skirmish occurred at the Dismal Swamp Canal. The next day, Southern troops marched to Suffolk, Virginia, and found the town garrisoned by colored troops. William Day of the Forty-ninth Regiment wrote, "An old Negro servant belonging to the doctor had an axe in his hand to kill every Nigger he could find, but I don't know whether the old fellow killed any or not." U.S. General Wild with Colonel Draper and regiments of colored troops began a foray via the canal into Camden County. A correspondent with the *New York Times* accompanied the regiment, reminding its readers that at the Ferebee Plantation, fourteen slaves encompassing men, women, and children left with their saviors. Continuing the trek, at Dr. McIntosh's place, soldiers and slaves cleaned out his office of drugs and instruments, along with provisions from the farm. Union troops fought near Shiloh Church and Sandy Hook. The reporter noted that they fought the Sixty-sixth North Carolina Volunteers and the "state defenders militia." This group took potshots at General Wild's regulars near Elizabeth City. The militia captured a colored soldier in Wild's brigade. Wild called this group of defenders "guerillas."[276]

As the Federal troops continued their march, at each homestead, slaves followed the army, increasing the numbers to thousands. It slowed the expedition as did the swampy terrain. Unfortunate for the "home defenders," in one camp, the enemy found their muster roll book as the militia fled the scene. General Wild marched his force to the home of each name on the muster roll and burned that person's house. In Pasquotank, Daniel Bright, a guerilla, according to Wild, was hung. By the end of the raid, the war correspondent reported that two to three thousand slaves tagged along with them. The Federals captured fifty saddle horses, one hundred rifles with accoutrements, three hundred fifty oxen, horses, and mules; with four camps destroyed. They destroyed thousands of bushels of corn. Besides taking fourteen Southern soldiers as prisoners, four hostages, thirteen killed and wounded guerillas, the march concluded with little deaths for the enemy. The countryside felt totally demoralized.

A war correspondent with the above raid described how Elizabeth City had been altered by war:

> I was surprised to see how its appearance had been changed . . . three years ago it was a busy, beautiful city, noted for the number of stores and manufactories, the extent of its trade, for its enterprise . . . . Now most of the dwellings were deserted, the stores closed, the streets overgrown with grass, its elegant edifices reduced to heaps of ruins by vandal Georgian troops, the doors of the bank standing open, and a sepulchral silence brooded over the place.[277]

The *Times* failed to tell the story and removal of women by the enemy to Norfolk. A Southern version of the raid, published on January 6, 1864, by the *Richmond Whig* copied from a Raleigh paper is given:

The Recent Expedition of the Enemy to Elizabeth City, N.C.

> The Raleigh State Journal gives the following account of the proceedings of the negro brigade which recently visited Elizabeth City, under command of a white negro named "Wilde:" The expedition was commanded by Brigadier General Wilde, and consisted of two regiments of negroes, one of which was commanded by Ex Governor Todd, of Ohio. They landed at Elizabeth City on Friday, 18th inst., and spent some eight days before they returned, during which they destroyed ten buildings in the counties of Pasquotank, Camden and Currituck, and outraged and plundered the people in the most heartless manner. Whilst in Elizabeth City, the officers were all quartered with the most respectable families, indiscriminately (the commissioned officers being white,

the non-commissioned black,) and did not pay a dollar for anything they received. In most cases they compelled the white ladies to cook and wash for them. Reporting at Wilde's headquarters daily they were questioned to know if they had been treated as "gentleman," and particularly if any of the male members of the families were quartered on talked secession doctrine.

On the streets the ladies of the place were jostled by the negro troops and had to permit them to walk by their side and converse with them, on pain of arrest and punishment for insulting "United States Troops!" Any information laid by a negro against man or woman was received as conclusive evidence and brought swift punishment upon the alleged offender. The negro ran riot during the Yankee stay in the Albemarle country.

The commands of Capt. J. T. Elliott, 66th N. C. troops, and of Capt. Sandlin, came up with these villains twice and succeeded in killing some forty to fifty of them and wounding many more. They fled like wild deer on being fired upon and were shot as they ran.—A bright mulatto was captured and mistaken for a white man and sent as a prisoner to Richmond, by Capt. Elliott. On learning this, Gen. Wilde seized three ladies, one a relative of Capt. Elliott, and *ironed them* and took them off, notifying Capt. E. that if his negro soldier was hanged he would hang the ladies. Capt. E. replied that he would do his duty unawed by the General's threat.

With these helpless women a number of men were also captured. All of them were kept confined in the garret story of a house in Elizabeth City—in one room—the women being made to cook for the men, and this for several days.

One of Col. J. R. Griffin's men, 62d Georgia cavalry, was captured, and on the bare statement of a negro was *hanged* by Gen. Wilde as a *guerrilla*. This murder was ordered and witnessed by Wilde. On the Yankee retreat he was taken, with the other prisoners as far as Hinton's cross roads, and there in the presence of the women and the negro troops, he was hanged from a cross beam of an old house, where his remains were found forty-four hours afterwards by his Colonel and buried with military honors.

The unfortunate man's name was Daniel Bright, Co. I, 62d Georgia cavalry. Colonel Griffin, after overcoming many obstacles, traveled sixty miles to come upon these murderers and thieves, but hearing of his approach they fled.

We have not space to narrate the many heartless cases of cruelty perpetrated by these fiends. One or two cases will suffice as examples. They entered the house occupied by the wife of Captain Elliott's Quartermaster. As the poor woman sat at the fire she saw them deliberately cut a hole in the middle of the floor and build a fire therein to consume her house over her. She asked them if they could do that. They replied they could and would. "Then burn," was the lady's patriotic response, "and I'll be the stronger Confederate than ever." A little before daylight the woman's husband returned, and found his wife and four children huddled together in the corner of a fence in sight of the ashes of their late home!

In one other case they fired a residence without giving any notice to the sleeping inhabitants, who were saved from death only by the timely waking up of a faithful slave.

We have strung these incidents together without regard to their legitimate connection and from memory. Of their general accuracy, our readers may have no doubt, for the facts were received by us in person from Colonel Griffin and Captain Elliott. The part taken by these officers in the matter gave them full opportunity for knowing all the facts. Captain Elliott and Captain Sandlin hung upon the heels of the scoundrels for many miles, and killed and wounded and captured as many of them as their own commands consisted of Col. Griffin, in consequence of circumstances we [do] not feel at liberty to mention, did not succeed in coming up with them, or there would have been a very different result. The Colonel avows his determination to have Yankee blood for that of poor Bright, and he will keep his word.

The *Richmond Whig* edition of January 4, 1864, printed that U.S. General Wild took two Elizabeth City ladies, Mrs. Weeks and Mrs. Munden, handcuffed them, and, under Negro guards, took them to Norfolk's prison. A person reported seeing one lady bleeding at the wrist. No reason was given as to their capture, but it could be due to their not taking the oath of allegiance to the United States. These two could also have been a part of the "three" ladies taken prisoner mentioned above.

WASHINGTON

In 1860, the population of Washington, twenty-five hundred, dwindled to about eight hundred as people fled in front of U.S. forces in early March 1862. With the enemies' approach, civilians had taken their belongings to the wharves in hopes of escaping. There was no railroad to help carry them away as in other places. An important bridge across Blounts Creek near Washington found the Southern Army removing the planks to stall the approaching Union troops. A trooper wrote his father:

> The people in Washington is putting their turpentine in vessels and carrying them above the bridge and setting them on fire. I heard three was burned last night. Beaufort County is given to the Yankeys. Marshe's negroes has all run away and gone to the Yankeys but 3 lost Evetts Beachmon's and some few others from South Creek. It is said that the mail will not come to Blounts Creek no more . . .[278]

Washington was thirty to forty miles away by land and 150 miles by water from New Bern. Rodman's Point was across the river from Washington. Both Blounts Creek and Hill's Point, Confederate strongholds, were found on the south side of the Pamlico River near Washington.

With New Bern overthrown, Federal officers knew their next marching orders would be to take the surrounding towns. A land force of about five thousand men with twenty-six pieces of artillery left for Washington on November 2, 1862. Simultaneously, naval gunboats steamed up the Pamlico River to Washington where they found the town evacuated except for some citizens. The Confederate Army offered no resistance this time. The band played jaunty tunes as the troops marched to the courthouse and raised the American flag. Certain men with Northern loyalties went aboard a gunboat and had dinner with the officers.[279]

In Washington early on, Union officers let civilians leave with their belongings. This was modified later whereby the residents could only take the clothes on their back. "Though the freed negroes who had collected in the town were given better food than the inhabitants could procure, bands of these Negroes roamed the streets at night, pillaging, and stealing." The besieged citizens, when expressing their patriotic enthusiasm, caught the ire of their occupiers. It was forbidden to sing Southern songs even in their own parlors, or they would be arrested. No letters could be sent or received, except through military headquarters, and these would be opened.[280]

Citizens wrote President Davis to let the North Carolina troops in Virginia return home to protect them. They accused Davis of ignoring the situation. Runaway slaves poured into the town with a sigh of relief. They had made it to freedom, but the situation was not all that rosy. An officer reported that they distributed rations to about two to three hundred contrabands. "When they become too numerous, they were passed along to Roanoke Island . . . . once a month there was a visitation of from seventy-five to one hundred beggared Falstaff's famous recruits, carrying away their rations in the arms of old coats, pant legs, etc. As payment, we received the pleasing knowledge that their men-folk were in the rebel army trying to kill us, while we fed the starving families."[281]

Once captured, the Episcopal Church saw use as barracks. This sign was found nailed to a tree in Washington in April 1863:

> YANKEES—We leave you, not because we cant take Washington but because it is not worth the taking. Besides the man who lives here must be amphibious. We leave you a few bursted guns a few stray solid shot and a man and a brother, rescued from the waves to which he was consigned in a fray with his equals. We compliment the plucky little garrison of the town and also salute the pilot of the "ESCORT". Yours, Company K, Thirty-second North Carolina S.T.

The words "man" and "brother" referred to the body of a brave Negro who jumped into the water and shoved off a grounded boat, thus saving the lives of several men.[282]

When the Federals entered the city, soldiers spoke of citizens waving their handkerchiefs, and one brazen individual flew the U.S. flag. A number of pro-unionist residents wished the bluecoats would "protect them from the rebels."[283] The U.S. provost marshal demanded that citizens take the oath of allegiance. U.S. General Potter insisted that the locals take the oath. He issued this order:

> Office of the Provost Marshal, Washington, N.C. April 18, 1863
> In pursuance of the foregoing "Gen Order," all persons residing within our lines are required to call . . . at this office . . . to give satisfactory evidence of their loyalty to the United States government. All persons not conforming to this order must remove within five days beyond the federal lines.
> Capt. W.A. Walker, Provost Marshal[284]

Apparently, most were holding back, which prompted a newspaper notice:

> The attention of the Provost Marshal has been called to the fact, that many persons are residents within the lines at Washington and under the protection of the United States forces, who have not taken and subscribed to the Oath & Parole required by General Order # 49, Dept. of Virginia & North Carolina.
> The terms of the order require that NO PERSON can have any protection, favor, passport or privilege, or have any money paid them, who does not take and subscribe to the Oath & Parole. Notice is therefore given TO ALL PERSONS of the years of discretion MALE AND FEMALE that one weeks time from this date will be allowed for the purpose of taking the Oath & Parole.
> T.J. Hoskinson, Capt and P.M.[285]

Mrs. Thomas Sparrow refused to take the oath, so she was forced into exile. Her story follows:

> A proclamation was issued to the effect that every Southerner over twelve years of age must take the oath . . . or leave town within ten days. The order was sent to every Southern home, and consternation and dismay to all hearts. Many of our people could not go away. All they had was in our little town, and they had no means and nowhere to go when they left . . . . Those who stayed took the oath with the mental reservation that they did not mean it. That an oath under such compulsory circumstances was not binding, and they all disregarded it at the first opportunity . . . . So we prepared to leave our home with no idea where we would go or what would become of us . . . . Every night

after it was dark, my mother and her children had been engaged in carrying to the neighbors who were going to stay . . . such things as we most valued and could carry ourselves. My parents had never owned but three slaves and the only one remaining with us was a poor crippled girl . . . . No negroes were allowed to go with their owners . . . . My mother left her provisions to his girl and left her in the care of some negroes who lived near us . . .

Sparrow said everyone was crying. She continued:

The soldiers stood around the porch jeering and laughing in evident enjoyment of the scene. As we went out, they went in and nothing of what we left . . . did we ever see again. It was the same case at all the homes of all the other refugees.

The ambulance carried us a mile from town, and there, with many other families of loyal friends, we were left to fare as best we could . . . . It was a pitiful sight to see a family here and there all over the lawn sitting on their trunks and wondering what would become of them. The situation soon became known through the surrounding county, and farmers who could, came, or sent, for the refugees, and during the day all found shelter.[286]

Mrs. Sparrow and her six children walked seven miles to a friend who took them in. While there, two of her children broke out with the measles.

––––––––––––

A local physician, Dr. Gallagher, stayed in Washington during Union occupation, attending to the sick and wounded. The Grice mansion became a Union hospital after soldiers clashed.

During the Battle of Blounts Creek, Mrs. Jewell and the children left because the Northern invaders wanted her home as a first aid station. Every sheet, pillow slip, towel, napkin, quilt, bedcover, and tablecloth found were used as bandages. Nearby Mr. William Adams's farm was temporarily used to treat the wounded on the Confederate side. Walter Ruff lived on the land where the skirmish occurred.[287]

––––––––––––

Washington changed hands back and forth during the war. C.S. General Hill in March 1863 sought to recapture the town. Confederate forces turned back gunboats and land troops. They captured large quantities of grain and provisions stolen by the Federals. Before the battle, General Hill demanded that General Foster release loyal women and children left in the town. Foster refused, prompting the general to reply that he would take no quarter unless they were released. The noncombatants then left.[288]

Artillery duels destroyed a lot of the area. Local women cared for the wounded in their homes after the battles. In October of 1863, Union troops retook Washington. In the spring of 1864, Confederate soldiers returned with a vengeance, pushing all Federals out of the city; but the enemy had time to pillage the city and burn several buildings. Much plundering was done when the U.S. forces left. The bluecoats cut up the town's fire hoses, then set the town on fire. A good deal of the city went up in flames.[289] Northern forces burned the Catholic and Presbyterian churches.

During the bombardment, a woman described the sensation of such a siege in this way:

It seemed as if a score of spinning wheels were running upon the roof of the house, and claps of thunder constantly bursting in my ears . . . . The citizens for the most part lived in holes dug from the cellars, and retired there on the least alarm, so that few casualties occurred among them.[290]

PLYMOUTH

Plymouth, located on the Roanoke River as it empties into the Albemarle Sound, played an important part as a port city. The rich sandy bottomland nearby sustained valuable food crops for the Confederacy. Thick pine forests provided a natural resource for the naval industry as did cypress trees. Boatloads of shingles were shipped to other ports, helping the economy prewar. A great majority of these workers held anti-secession beliefs. About five thousand white men joined the Union Army and Navy. During the conflict, thousands of tons of agricultural products were shipped North to feed General Lee's Army of Virginia, of which consisted of many North Carolina regiments. It became a target for early capture by old Abe's army and navy. A few poor whites from Washington County hightailed it to Roanoke Island after the Battle of Hatteras. After Union occupation soldiers assured them of their safety, they returned home.[291] In a Union Soldier's account, he noted that "contrabands arrive here from 'up country' by steamers, well loaded, on an average of once a fortnight. They are then sent to the colored colony on Roanoke [Island]." One free colored woman had her own bakery business and sold items to the enemy.[292]

Stationed at Plymouth, a Northern soldier's first impression of the city is recorded in his journal, keeping in mind that he didn't arrive until 1864:

> The town consisted of a few tumble-down houses that had escaped the flames, two or three brick stores and houses, and the rest a medley of negro shanties . . . in which the surrounding country abounded, and a number of rude frame buildings, made for government use, from material sawed at the steam mill which government possessed by confiscation. The place was a general rendezvous for fugitive negroes, who come into our lines by families, while escaping from conscription or persecution . . . . Schools had been established for the young and middle-aged colored population . . . . The whole place had a Rip Van Winkle look.[293]

Sergeant Goss said the town was guarded by five forts, and he found two companies of loyal North Carolina soldiers drilling alongside the regulars. Most citizens of Plymouth had no slaves, so it didn't seem to bother them as much when the Federals overtook the city. One U.S. officer wrote, "The hearts of the people of North Carolina are not with the rebels; the woods and swamps are full of refugees fleeing from the terror of conscription."[294] In other reflections, Sergeant Goss indicated, "Let me record the fact that many of the pretended Union men and women of the town were suddenly developed into exultant Secesh and shouted their defiance as we passed through the place after capture—the same who a few days before, were glad to draw government rations and accept of like favors."[295] A letter mailed North reported, "There are not over eight hundred troops here now, & a considerable part of them are N. Carolinians, & how much they can be depended [on] we do not yet know."[296]

A diarist documented that the enemy in 1862, with Negroes, "had taken shelter in the Custom House, a brick building, which they had pierced for musquetry & from which they fired upon our men. [C.S.] Capt Moore turned his attention upon it & in a few shot nearly battered it down over their heads. The loss of life was terrible . . . . About fifty negroes were captured . . . . Many negroes were killed."[297] Several escaped slaves turned soldiers took part in the Battle of Plymouth. A mulatto named Titus Hardy was mistaken for a white and sent to Andersonville Prison with other enemy soldiers while other ex-slaves were returned to their masters. A portion of men with Union views, as well as Federal soldiers, said that Plymouth was another Fort Pillow Massacre. Confederate newspapers decried "this was not true." Witnesses say otherwise. Both sides denied it even occurred.[298]

U.S. Commander S. C. Rowan related to Plymouth officials that U.S. soldiers had no intention of pillaging its citizens once they took charge of the town. While near Plymouth, Union officers sought shelter from the icy weather at a plantation. "The women members of the household were implacable rebels, and were incessant in their nagging all of the officers. At first Col. Peirson had given orders that the belongings of the place . . . should be unmolested. For a considerable time he endured the vulperations of the women, till at last he could endure their tongue-lashing no longer," and let his men kill their poultry.[229]

When Roanoke Island fell to the enemy, Charles Pettigrew, with his seven-month-pregnant wife, Carey, and five children—left Washington County for the interior of the state. Traveling with them were his sister and five servants. The first day of travel took them to Williamston, a forty-mile journey. At this point, he had to return home to protect his property. The women were without a white male to accompany them, unheard of during peacetime. The entourage continued for another 130 miles to Raleigh. After the birth of her daughter, Mrs. Pettigrew went to South Carolina to stay with relatives. George Patterson, a friend and minister, kept Captain Pettigrew informed of the business on the plantation. At Bonarva, their home, Pettigrew lost several slaves to the enemy; and those who stayed were reported as insolent and failed to make a good crop.[300]

With the influx of the U.S. Army into the state, the Pettigrews realized that class conflict in their neighborhood had mushroomed. The yeomen farmers and lower-income classes, known as swampers, threatened their wealthier secesh neighbors. Mrs. Pettigrew said she "saw a clique who supported 'the Yankees because they assert, [that] they are the poor man's friend & wld [would] only take from the rich . . . . Low whites were not to be trusted at all . . . they wld betray or murder any gentleman."[301] Guerrilla bands with both persuasions terrorized folks in Washington County. One Buffalo, a rebel deserter named John Fairless, formed a gang who severely alarmed the countryside.[302] Among the prisoners captured by Confederate troops at Plymouth were twenty-two Buffaloes, formally of the state, who were executed in February 1864. Other Buffaloes' fate was similar. They were marched up the riverside to Hamilton. "Compassionate southern women gave these prisoners water along the way. Six of these men were hung near the Spring Green Church."[303]

U.S. gunboats anchored at Plymouth while it was under Federal occupation. The enemy would take smaller boats up the river to load and unload foraged provisions from the countryside. The Yankees went on a foraging trip from Plymouth to Harrellsville in Hertford County. Being short of wagons, they destroyed over 150,000 pounds of pork and large amounts of salt and sugar. They did manage to haul away huge quantities of provisions from the residents. U.S. Sergeant Merrill described just one foraging trip as "a half-mile of cattle, sheep, hogs, carts, Negroes, furniture, etc . . . and nine guerilla prisoners." Most of the furniture came from the Collins and Pettigrew families, large slave owners.[304]

Rev. George Patterson communicated to the Pettigrews the enemy's raid to Bonarva and next to Somerset, the Josiah Collins property—both the largest planters in the county:

> On Monday July 21st 1862, about 10:00 P.M, Capt Woodward a Federal officer with Twelve of his men came to Somerset Place. As soon as I could dress myself, I went out and met the Captain, who introduced himself, & assured me that I should not be annoyed in any way, & that none of the servants or the property on the Plantation should be troubled.
>
> He then said he wished to examine the house to see if there were any arms, or ammunition; I showed him into the office where we found one Gun which he did not take; after this, I carried him into the Parlour, Library, & Dining Room, and offered to take him up stairs which he said was unnecessary, as my word that there were neither arms nor ammunition was sufficient. I

remarked that I had two bags of shot in my room which I was using as weights to press my sermons, & asked him if he wished to see them, he said that he did not.

After this conversation & search, I sent Alick Millin [?] over to Mr. Chas. L. Pettigrew's to let him know that the Federals were here; the boy, however, was stopped by one of the Federal Soldiers, who was acting as a guard on the Bridge near the house, & brought back to the Capt, but at my request was allowed by him to carry my message over to Mr. P. I then went down to the overseer's house in company with Capt Woodward, and a soldier, to let Mrs. Spruill know, (the overseer being absent in Plymouth on business concerning the Mill, which had been made a public Mill by the order of Capt Flusser, a Federal officer,) that she should not be troubled in any way. When I arrived there, I found that the house was guarded by soldiers, but as we returned the Capt kindly took away the guard from the overseer's house, & brought them up to the Collins' residence, where they remained all night, sleeping, when not on guard, by my permission, on the lower Kitchen Piazza. Mr. John Giles, who came in with the Yankees, also staid with the soldiers on the Piazza, as I had previously told Capt Woodward that I could not allow either his men, or Mr. Giles, to enter our house for any purpose whatsoever; So they did not go into the House or the Colony. Having reached the house, the Capt & I sat down in the Dining-room, when he informed me that he had orders from his Government to take away a lot of Corn & Wheat; I asked him if the U.S. Government intended to pay for the grain, he said no, but that it was to be taken to Plymouth, to be distributed among the poor. We then conversed about the War, I asked him when he tho't it would end? He said before a great while, & then enquired of me when I tho't there would be peace?—I told him I was in his power, &, therefore, perhaps it would be better for me to be silent, he replied, "Oh! No, when do you think it will end?-" I answered there would be peace, either when the Federal Government gave up, or in the next case, when every man, woman, & child in the Confederacy had been killed. We sat and talked until about 12 M. when we parted for the night. I had the room usually known as "Miss Alethea's" prepared for the Capt, to which he retired.

On the morning of Tuesday, July 22nd, about ½ past 4, I went down to the Mill, where I found the Captain; & two of his men acting as guard. While there the Capt was either talking to me, or attending to the business then on hand. The Overseer returned from Plymouth this morning, and was able to in person to attend to the business; As the Yankee Capt had told me the night previous that our hands were to prepare the grain & get it ready, & to put it on board the Yankee Schooner, they remained in by my orders, & were all busily engaged when I reached the Mill. There being Corn and Wheat enough in the Mill to satisfy the orders of the robbers, it was as speedily put on board the Flat as possible, and carried down to the Schooner by our force. Altho' Capt Woodward had assured me that the Federal Government did not wish our Negroes, that they were not allowed to go within their lines, & that our servants should not be carried off in his vessel, still, I tho't it best, & was strengthened in my belief by the advice of my friend, Mr Pettigrew, to go down to the Scuppernong river with the Capt, his men, and our people, & see for myself that our Negroes neither ran away, nor were carried away. I remained either on board the Schooner, or in the neighborhood until the vessel was loaded, & all our servants were on their way back to the Lake.

The whole am't of grain taken by the Yankees is as follows—which is the statement given to me by the overseer—to wit.—

Corn—1.080 bushels[*]
Wheat—.238   " "

Whilst we were at the Mill, a man by the name of Durham Lassiter, came into the Lake, & took away with Capt Woodward's permission, & from the lot of corn which the Capt had already forcibly taken from us Two (2.) barrels of corn. Also another man by the name of John Ainsley carried off Two hundred (200.) pounds of Flour which he paid for.

Mr. Chas. L. Pettigrew came over to Somerset Place, & went down to the Mill, where he met with Capt Woodward, & had some conversation with him on the subjects of the day.

I am happy to say that all our servants behaved with great propriety. None were carried away by the Yankees, & not one of them so far as I could learn was at all desirous to run away. The Capt treated me kindly, & regretted to me that he had been sent on such an unpleasant mission. I replied that it was most unpleasant to me, &, that I hoped the like would not occur again.

While the Yankees were here, I gave orders that breakfast should be prepared in the Wash-house for the men, The Capt, however, I of course invited to eat with me in the house. I endeavored to treat him politely, tho' not cordially while he was at the Lake; & when I went on board of his vessel, he showed me marked kindness.

On our way down to the River, Geo. B. Davenport desired to ride with us as far as Danl S. Phelp's house, in order that he might have a private conversation with the Capt; What Mr. Davenport said to the Capt, I, of course, do not know. So we were delayed at the Mill until 11 O'clock A.M., & as it would be quite late before it could be put on board the Schooner, &, as we had no provisions with us, the Capt & I accepted an invitation to eat dinner with Mr Davenport. Mr D, was evidently very much alarmed, but did nothing so far as I know against our Government.

When I parted from the Capt, he thanked me for the kindness he had recd, & said that he would mention it to his superior officers. I replied that I trusted he would only speak of it, as an assurance that Mr. Pettigrew and myself were as likely to speak the truth as the "Buffalo Yankees," for we were gentlemen, &, that if any reports were circulated against us, I hoped we might be allowed an opportunity of speaking for ourselves.

Whilst I was on board the Federal Schooner, Mr John Giles apologized to me for the taking away of our Corn & Wheat, and said that he did all he could to prevent it. He also regretted the War and its consequences upon us & the people of our neighborhood. I asked him if Mr Lassiter had paid for the Corn which he had taken; he said no! that Mr L., was a poor man & unable to work. I remember nothing else in regard to this visit of the Yankees to our Plantation, that is worthy of record.

Second Visit of the Yankees to Somerset Place

Lake Scuppernong.—
July 27th 1862

On Sunday July 27th, Capt Woodward with about Thirty of his men, Mr Giles, & a young man by the name of William Alexander, a resident of Tyrrell County, who had been bro't here under guard, & against his will, for what

---

[*]   Probable a transcribe error. Believed to be 1,080 bushels and 238 bushels.

cause I know not, paid a 2nd to this plantation, for the purpose of pressing Twelve (12.) horses into the Federal service, to be used in this County in case the Yankees were attacked by the Confederate Cavalry.

That morning Mr C. L. Pettigrew, and Geo. C. Newbury who had come here on an errand from his father, were sitting with me in my room, when we were all surprised by the painful news, that "the Yankees is here." I went out immediately, & found two soldiers stationed as a guard on the Bridge near the house; I asked them where their officer was?—learning that he was down at the Mill, I went there at once, & found him in company with Geo. W. Spruill, our overseer, & John Giles, examining our horses. Capt W., after saluting me told me his business, & showed me his order to take Twelve horses, which order is now in the possession of the overseer. The Capt regretted the cause of his visiting us a 2nd time, & said that it was not his fault; I begged him to leave us some horses, particularly our Carriage horses, & Conrad, as the last named was a favorite horse which belonged to a deceased member of our family; but it was all in vain, the Capt feared that he would be compelled to take such horses as would be of use to his Government. I think, however, that he would have left us these horses just named, & I am almost sure that he would not have taken Conrad, had it not been for Giles, who seemed most anxious to take those that were most valued by the family.

When Capt Woodward had examined & selected our horses, & found only Seven (7.) that suited his purposes, he went over to Bonarva [the Pettigrew Plantation], & took Five (5.) horses belonging to Mr Pettigrew, which were carried down to our Mill by Mr P.'s servants, & after dinner the whole Twelve (12.) were taken away by the Federals. I asked Capt W., & the Master's Mate, a man by the name of Williams, to dine with me, at the same time I had dinner provided in the Wash house for the soldiers; Mr Giles ate at the overseer's house. Just before dinner Mr Pettigrew came over to see the Capt at his request; it could have been Easily perceived by any person with two grains of sense, that the visit of the Yankees was not at all relished by Mr P., & in a proper manner, he showed them very plainly that it was not, at the same time remarking, that no Government could prosper which took away the property of the people against all law & order, &, that whilst he did not blame Capt W., for obeying the orders of his Superior Officers, yet he did very much blame any Government that resorted to any such means to establish itself. After some conversation neither very agreeable, nor of much importance, the Yankees left us, & we returned to the Colony in no very pleasant frame of mind.

The soldiers, so far as I know, during this visit behaved very well; tho' from what I can learn they talked to some of our servants about freedom, & asked some of them if they would not like to go away with them, where they could work, & receive wages for their work.

I am sorry to say that Fred Elsy [Fred Littlejohn] did not behave properly; I ordered him to remain in the garden, in order that he might take care of the fruit, & report to me if the soldiers stole any; instead of remaining where I had placed him, & where he belonged, he went down to the Mill, &, as William Penny said was the 1st to bridle the horses for the Yankees. It is my opinion that he should be severely punished, not only for his disobedience, but also because he was very impudent to me when I remonstrated with him about his conduct. He has since apologized to me for his misconduct, & as I then hoped, sincerely, but his conduct afterwards has been extremely wicked, & tho' I forgave him freely for his 1st offense, yet now I fear he is worthy of punishment.

It is due Mr Collins overseer, Geo. W. Spruill to say, that before, during, & since the two visits of the Yankees to this plantation, he has behaved with great propriety, & is I believe & hope true to the Southern Confederacy.

This is a copy of my 1ˢᵗ rough ~~draft~~ description of the Yankee's two visits here.—Reverend George Patterson, Minister, Somerset Place.

On August 4, 1862, U.S. Lieutenant Flusser made an official report that referenced Woodward's activities at Somerset:

I seized some days since, in accordance with the wishes of the Governor, 1,100 bushels of corn, and 240 bushels of wheat on the farm of Josiah Collins, a wealthy secessionist absentee. I turned over the grain to the superintendent of the poor at Plymouth for distribution. At the request of Capt. Hammell . . . I sent the *Shawsheen* to Scuppernong River, where Capt. Woodward seized twelve horses for the use of a mounted picket from the farms of Josiah Collins and Charles Pettigrew. The horses and grain were both seized before we had seen the President's proclamation concerning the confiscation act. Lt. Cmdr. Charles W. Flusser.[305]

In another incident, two rebel prisoners told of finding articles such as salt and spun cotton stolen by the enemy. They were able to trade it for food.[312] A number of citizens didn't mind trading with the bluecoats.

The occupiers had heard from informers that the state was building an iron-clad up the Roanoke River. Construction of the gunboat commenced around Edward's Ferry in a cornfield. Local timber made up the gunboat. Gilbert Elliott was in charge. Much of the credit for saving time during construction of the CSS *Albemarle* can be attributed to Peter E. Smith, who invented the modern version of the twist drill. This supposedly enabled a man to drill the hole in the iron in just four minutes rather than the twenty it took previously. Iron pieces gathered from scrap and unused railroad tracks covered the outside. Peter Smith also helped build it on his father's land.[306]

In March 1864, a carpenter turned deserter from the building team of the *Albemarle* fled to Plymouth and "reported guns on board and the craft ready to sail." This deserter also said a large land force accompanied them, and they were ready to move on to Plymouth. Captain Cook, skipper of the CSS *Albemarle*, was called into action *before* the iron-clad was finished because the attack was to coincide with a land invasion led by General Hoke. The workers were still putting on the iron plates as she streamed down the Roanoke River. The CSS *Albemarle* burned bacon in its furnaces to get up steam on the way to Plymouth. A successful raid, one gunboat was sunk and three disabled as the rest reversed engines and steamed off. The town was once again under Southern control. The *Albemarle* steamed back up the river for repairs. Confederates held control for six and one-half months. Six months later, the *Albemarle* once again went downriver to Plymouth. This time, she was not so successful. U.S. Lt. William Cushing carried out a plan to torpedo the iron-clad, which was instigated one dark night on October 27, 1864. The *Albemarle* sank, and Cushing barely escaped with his life. After the engagement, the Northern soldiers governed the town again.

In anticipation of imminent Battle of Plymouth, women, children, as well as the wives of *loyal* North Carolinians were put on board the *Massasoit* bound for Roanoke Island. Sergeant Goss noted that during the battle to retake Plymouth, rebel gunboats came down the river and, with a combined river and land force, overtook the city. Near the river, both blacks and whites who did not manage to escape dodged cannonballs. He revealed that Margaret Leonard, the wife of a private in his unit, was inside making coffee when a ball passed through the building "taking with it one of her dresses, which hung on a nail . . . . Another carried away the front legs of the cooking stove . . . . Goss went through a long and severe imprisonment at Andersonville, Macon, and Castle Thunder, Richmond."[307] Amanda Speller from Bertie County, a former slave, lost her life in the battle.[308]

A story persists within the Latham family who lived near the river. A cannonball came through the window of the basement where family members and neighbors had taken refuge. One brave soul picked it up and hurled it back through the same window. Grace Episcopal Church was damaged when Federal gunboats shelled Plymouth. When occupied by enemy troops, the inside of the church was sacked and destroyed. The Methodist church became a temporary hospital as was the Armistead home.

Once captured by the Confederates at Plymouth, hundreds of prisoners under guard marched out of town. "Crowds of women and children lined the roadside, apparently eager to get even a glimpse of the '—Yankees,' of whom they had heard Such fearful things, but we marked what seemed to us a look of surprise, as they surveyed what was unquestionably a set of decent respectable looking fellows."[309] One local woman said, "What did you'uns come down here to fight we'uns for?"[310] From Plymouth, the prisoners advanced to Williamston , whose inhabitants came out in droves to see the throngs of prisoners passing through on their way to Tarboro. The postmaster there said he would forward their letters North if they desired. In Hamilton, again, the crowds came to stare. The Thirty-fifth NCT guarding the prisoners allowed the public to trade with the enemy as they rested. Robert Kellogg said of his captors that the North Carolina regiment treated them well. When these same prisoners passed through Tarboro, they recalled that townspeople lined up on the side of the road to gawk at the Yankees. A secesh woman with several children in tow made the remake to a guard, "Where are their 'horns'?" She had always heard that Yankees had horns and "was surprised to see we had none." As the line halted, the men bartered for food. They said that Tarboro was "the prettiest place we had seen in the South." From there, the entourage went to Goldsboro to catch the boxcars to Wilmington and on to a prison in the Deep South. Soldier Kellogg said that Confederate officers stopped the bartering in Goldsboro because "there was a law making it a crime for a Southerner to possess or attempt to pass them [greenbacks] . . . ," but everyone ignored the law. The prisoners had Confederate money obtained from a raid in Elizabeth City from the Farmers Bank. They had stolen a large amount of unsigned certificates of deposit, later signing them, which was used to buy food when they were captured.[311]

CHAPTER SIX

Roll of Honor

This honor is given to those individuals during wartime who went above and beyond the call to help persons less fortunate than themselves. It may have been a monetary gift, a portion of their harvest, or just their time.

My favorite person from North Carolina who heads this list is Ms. Abigail House of Franklinton, otherwise known as Aunt Abby. One could officially call her an old spinster. Born around 1797, she couldn't remember when. Her sweetheart left for the War of 1812. When news reached her that he had fallen sick in Norfolk, Virginia, she walked all the way there—a distance of 160 miles—to nurse him. But it was too late for he had died before her arrival.

The Federal Census of 1860 listed Abby as sixty-three years old. Unmarried, she cared for several nephews throughout this period. Her sister, Nancy House Dickerson, reared a large family next door. Stubborn, hardheaded, ferocious, turbulent, unmanageable—these words were used to describe her. Some people called her a rough woman in her talk and actions. Aunt Abby dressed in simple homespun with patches, wore a black shawl, smoked a corncob pipe, and carried two canes—one for walking and one to "emphasize her wishes."[1] When she got an idea to go somewhere or had a mission involving the troops, nothing could stop her. She vowed when the war started to watch after her nephews, tend to them if they became sick or wounded, and bring their bodies home for burial if they died while in service. This "angel of the battlefield" made numerous trips to Virginia on her mission. Aunt Abby was known to have carried mail and provisions through the lines.[2]

Abigail "Aunt Abby" House
Courtesy T.H. Pearce

The Raleigh and Gaston Railroad ran close to her farm of three hundred acres.[3] It mattered not if she had ticket money when she boarded. The conductor always asked her, but most of the time, he left empty-handed. Aunt Abby was on a mission for the "boys" and couldn't be bothered with such formalities. Her money could be better spent for the troops. Many times, she "hoofed" it to Petersburg, as she liked to tell.

"She would walk through the trenches during the bombardment of Petersburg with great coolness, frequently going under heavy fire to carry water to the wounded."[4] "On one occasion she was reported to have searched the battlefield around Fredericksburg for twelve days before locating the body of one of her nephews . . ." Aunt Abby also cared for other soldiers from Franklin County and men from other Southern states. When she was at home, she met the trains in either direction, putting the soldiers' needs first. Residents said she would "impress" food and clothing for these troops. "On one occasion, station master, Isham Cheatham, recorded that he and a group of friends had prepared a stew and just as they were about to have a feast, Abby appeared, took charge of the pot . . . and marched off with it, saying that there were those who were sick and needed it more."[5]

A Mr. Minga found out that his son had been wounded and was a POW at the Seven Pines battle. He was unable to procure a pass to reach his son. Aunt Abby was on the premises, and he told her of his plight. She replied, "You jest wait right here and let me see what I kin do." Mr. Minga waited several hours, then saw Aunt Abby approaching in the distance with two Yankee litter bearers. She was able to get a pass, find the boy, and persuade the enemy to release him to her care.[6]

Aunt Abby is frequently mentioned in North Carolina soldiers' correspondence. In a letter dated July 15, 1863, Ben Freeman with the Forty-fourth Regiment, camped at Orange Courthouse, Virginia, stated, "Aunt Aby left here yesterday morning."[7] That was a far piece from North Carolina for an elderly woman to be traveling alone. Freeman sent another letter from the Orange Courthouse campsite on February 9, 1864: "Aunt Aby House is here and she has been here three to four days." Freeman wrote a long letter, dated September 24, 1864, to his parents later that fall, in which he spoke of her again: "Aunt Aby House is here and has been here for the last fornight trying to get a detail for Marcillus Dickerson [nephew] to stay at the hospital at Kithel [Kittrell Springs, NC]."[8]

The Reverend Dr. R. H. Whitaker described her as follows:

> She was a turbulent woman; fond of contentions and law suits, and that she was able to stand her ground in the court house, on the courthouse grounds, or anywhere else, and that no man could beat her in swearing. In one battle in Virginia, she was seen in an exposed place holding the reins of a horse. Some said, "Old woman, you'd better get out of here before one of those shells tears you all to pieces." She replied, "I aint gwine a step. I told Colonel . . . I'd hold his horse til he came back out of the fight, and I'll do it, shells or no shells."[9]

Abby was a constant visitor to the governor's office and General Robert E. Lee in camp. Aunt Abby was with Lee's army when it surrendered, according to Reverend Whitaker. When asked about it:

> She said they told her that she must wave her handkerchief to let the Yankees know that she was willing to surrender, too.
>
> "Did you wave it?" Reverend Whitaker asked her.
>
> "Not much, I shook it so, a time or two, and then I stuck my hand behind me. Then I shook it again, and put it behind me. I never was so mad in all my life as I was when one of them Yankees came along and sed to me,
>
> 'Old woman, you needn't mind about shaking that rag any more, we don't care whether you surrender or not.'"

I said, "Drat your mean soul, if I had a gun I'd shoot you off that horse and leave you here for the buzzards to pick. He didn't say another word but rode off . . ."[10]

When Aunt Abby arrived at Raleigh from Greensboro, after the surrender, the city, of course, was in the hands of the Yankees; and as she was getting off the car at the depot, a Yankee soldier, seeing an old woman hobbling out, went to help her down. She raised her stick as he approached her and said with an oath that shocked him, "Don't you come any nigher, if you don't want your head cracked. No d__d Yankee shall touch me."[11]

The U.S. officers made their headquarters in Governor Vance's old office in the State Capitol. Abby went to see them about her stolen horse. She stood in the doorway and stared at the men, then replied, "Yes, here's where gentlemen used to sit, but now it's a den of thieves."[12]

Aunt Abby "footed it down to Greensboro when she heard that President Davis was on his way and she 'cooked the last mouthful 'o vittles Jeff Davis eat in North Carolina . . .'"* according to her story. It was told that he answered, "Goodbye, Aunt Abby. You are true grit, but it is just what I expected of you."[13] A historic marker for Aunt Abby in Franklinville reads:

Patriotic, she had been a well-behaved camp follower as self-appointed nurse, 1st aid counselor, and scolder of all soldiers.[14]

Miss Mary Ann Buie, Soldiers' Friend
Courtesy of the South Carolina Division UDC

---

*   Editor's note: This may be stretching it a bit. I'm sure he ate in Charlotte on his flight to Georgia. Aunt Abby died on November 23, 1881.

Mary Ann Buie was known as the "soldier's friend" or the "soldier's comforter" by the public. One acquaintance called her the "very empress of benevolent scavengers." She devoted most of her life for charitable causes. Daughter of J. R. Buie of Richmond County, Ms. Buie attended Flora College and became a teacher for eight years in South Carolina and Georgia prior to the secession. Perhaps she was conniving for a position when she wrote this letter to Governor Vance:

> Edgefield Court House, S.C. Sept 21,1862
> To His Excellency Gov. Vance of N. Carolina:
>
> In the first place I must introduce myself to you and in the second place congratulate you, that the people of noble N. Carolina have been true to their trust in the election of Governor Vance a tried and true patriot, a military man and statesman in this bout of national birth. 1st/ I am Miss M.A. Buie a native of the "Good Old North State." I have been professionally engaged—teaching school in this state (S.C.) and in Augusta Geo. [GA] for the last eight years, I have written for the press several years, wrote for amusement. The public have known me as "Viola Carolina"[,] "Justice"[,] "Ind-pendent Carolina" &c. I was pleasantly situated and I may add profitably, as I was principal of a female school receiving a total salary of $800 for ten mo. for a yr. I have a very high position in Society as I came to this section very highly recommended from N. C. by the very first from my section Richmond Co. N. Carolina and the Pres. of the college where I graduated, Floral Co.[college]. The [*illegible*] much interested in my educated [*sic*] as he was a first cousin of my father, J.R. Buie who has many relations in Fayetteville, N.C., I have been teaching for the most refined and wealthy in this state and Geo. [GA] and with much success and satisfaction to parents and pupils. I have the respect and confidence of the first citizens in this section and have been introduced to many distinguished persons & yes, I know Gov. Brown of Geo. personally as I was at the Atlanta Springs at the same time he had the Trout House there for the Executive Department. I presume you heard of the suspension of schools in this section—not one in twenty have continued. I am very fond of history and have studied the best of Authors. Historians have paid a beautiful tribute to women's patriotism since war, cruel war; disturbed the peace and happiness of man and when disgrace and dishonor threatened a nation and the men had to defend their rights or fight out a quarrel, woman has wielded a powerful influence and in the accomplishment of much which gave success to the efforts of the soldiers in all ages. When the startling realities of this terrible Revolution burst forth in all its fury and desolation and devastation threatened us on every side and the whole country was in confusion and terror. The very . . . . [next page missing][15]

Apparently, her letter of introduction was enough for the governor to permit her to collect provisions for the soldiers. In Wilmington, she placed a notice in the newspaper requesting hospital articles, money, clothing, lint, or anything else to benefit the sick and wounded. NEGLECT HAS KILLED MORE THAN BULLETS, read the headline. The following day, Buie reported that 160 dollars had been collected. Later, she turned over to Rev. Colin Shaw money for the Tar Heel soldiers on Sullivan's Island, South Carolina, part of the Immortal Six Hundred. She then concentrated on helping the sick troops located in North Carolina and Virginia.

Somehow, Ms. Buie obtained a permit to collect goods from blockade-runners and pick out delicacies for the hospital inmates. It was told that Mary Ann became critical of anyone who refused her when soliciting for donations. She kept butting heads with one particular owner named Colonel W. G. Crenshaw of Richmond. Apparently, he was stingy with his gifts. Buie told him that she wished he would lose his ship, which actually happened a few days later. Colonel Crenshaw refused to give her a donation after that. He accused Ms. Buie of putting a hex on him because the colonel lost four ships in three months. She requested from "officers of ships landing [,] articles through her 'permit' to inform her when they are landed as she has 'legal' authority to collect and land such delicacies from ships."[16]

A notice appeared in the paper written by Ms. Buie who said she was in Augusta, Georgia, when she heard of the yellow fever epidemic in Wilmington, which occurred in 1862. Buie collected three thousand dollars there from its citizens and sent it to Wilmington. She said General Beauregard also sent money to the Wilmington people.[17] Another article appeared the following year:

SS Cronstadt, Fort Anderson. Cape Fear River, July 16, 1863:

The owners of the SS Cronstadt will [illegible] to Miss Buie. They have read with emotions her appeal inserted in the Wilmington papers on behalf of the wounded soldiers suffering in our hospitals. They regret exceedingly that at present, cargo aboard the Cronstadt remains [illegible] calculated for use by the sick. They have now received a cask of limes which they gladly give to the perusal of Miss Buie, hoping that to some slight degree, they may be instruments in alleviating the suffering of so many men in agony for so sacred a cause.

The Cronstadt is intended to run between Wilmington and Nassau, and her owners beg that Miss Buie will do them a favor to consider the steamer quite at her disposition for any quantity of Hospital requisites, free of any charge of freight.[18]

For two months in June and July 1864, Mary Ann collected the following:

Seventy-two pounds of coffee, four bottles of wine, four bottles of brandy, and one pound of tea, which were sent to the hospital in Wilson; coffee, french brandy, wine, and tamarinds, which were shipped to Winder Hospital in Richmond, and fifty dollars went to hospital no. 4 in the city. To the North Carolina Hospital in Petersburg was shipped 150 bags of sugar, a bottle of honey, forty-eight quarts of ale, seventy-six yards of shirting for bandages, forty-two pounds of loaf sugar, one-half pound of tea, six bottles of brandy (for General Beauregard), four bottles of ale, thirty-eight dollars, one bottle of pickles, forty dollars in Confederate notes, and five dollars in silver. Hospital no. 4 in Wilmington also received fifty dollars, one case of gin, along with two pounds of tea, one and one-half dozen nutmegs, pineapples, black pepper, fifty bottles of French brandy, eighteen bottles of wine, twelve bottles of ale, one pound of soda, two bottles of port, eight gallons of molasses, forty-five yards of linen duck cloth, and 136 pounds of coffee.*

Two gallons of brandy and a sack of coffee went to the hospital no. 5 in Wilmington. Coffee, tea, and liquor continued to be requested by the surgeons. Ms. Buie sent to the Wilson Hospital a sack of coffee, a gallon of French brandy, a bottle of wine, limes, soap, and linen. She gave one thousand dollars to the wayside hospital in Columbia, South Carolina.

---

*   Hospital no. 4 was at the corner of Dock and Front Streets; the wayside hospital was at Front and Red Cross, and the Naval Hospital was on Chestnut between Water and Front Streets. Another hospital was at the city garrison.

"During 1864 there were at least two Relief Associations and five hospitals in Wilmington . . . the Soldier's Aid Society and the Wilmington Relief Association."[19] It is probable that she worked independently from them.

A note in the newspaper from Mary Buie thanked the captain of the *Annie* for kindly donating the following items for the volunteers: limes and two bottles of brandy. She thanked Mrs. Thomas Roberts for two bottles of wine, three cakes of soap, a pack of old linen, four yards of bandages, two packages of cornstarch, and one hundred dollars. Jervey and Mueller of Nassau contributed eighty pounds sterling. She expressed thanks to Mr. Shackleford for two bottles of french brandy, Mr. Salinas for fifty dollars, and Howell and Harriss for a deduction of $1280 and a large lot of coffee. Ms. Ann Smith gave ten dollars for the Winder Hospital. Captain Coxetter gave ten cases of gin. Mr. Donnelly donated four hundred dollars on a lot of coffee for the Georgia soldiers, and J. W. Murray of the CSS *Alice* donated limes. She especially gave praise to the Express Company for carrying the articles for free.[20]

Ms. Buie kept the governor informed of her charitable work:

October 11,1864:
Gov. Vance, I have the honor of informing you that I have succeeded in accomplishing much . . . since I saw you. Mr. Wm Collie has just given me tea & coffee which I am dividing to different hospitals in the state. Mr. Stringer of Mr. Collie's firm has just returned from Halifax & he says if the authorities will permit him to land his delicacies that he will give me some wines & brandies for the sick & wounded of this state. I expect to sail the next dark night. I shall visit England & Scotland . . . . Randolph & lady will go on the same ship with me. If you will procure permission for Mr. Collie & Stringer to land unmolested their donations [,] many poor soldiers will be benefited. Mr. Collie has given me a letter of introduction to his brother Alex Collie of London. They are very liberal to our cause. I know them well. I do not understand how the Confederate agents manage affairs. The men of this state are better cared for than those of any other state. I have just returned from Richmond. I have evidence of the fact you will cause your name immortal in all time to come for your kindness to your brave men has not an equal in the Confederacy. I am truly sorry you lost the Advance. I hope you may be more successful with your next ship but the Advance did great service. The late laws not permitting delicacies to land & seizing all such articles has put many poor fellows in their graves. I must close by thanking you for your letter. Respectfully, M.A. Buie, Soldiers Friend[21]

Buie continued to advertise when and where she would be collecting for the troops:

For Our Soldiers at Charleston
Miss M.A. Buie, a native of the State and district, but for some years past resident in Augusta Ga., and Edgefield, S.C., where since the commencement of the war has distinguished herself by her devoted and untiring exertions to contribute to the health and comfort of our soldiers, is now here endeavoring to raise a fund for the North Carolinians taking part in the defence of Charleston, who may be wounded or become sick while so engaged. Many things are needed by the sick and wounded besides what the public authorities can give, or their own limited means procure. On calling upon some of our citizens yesterday Miss Buie was pleased to find that many responded liberally and cheerfully. In due time all moneys received will be duly acknowledged through the papers and the amount faithfully transmitted to Charleston. Miss Buie will remain a few days longer at the City Hotel where she can be found.[22]

Just before the first battle of Fort Fisher, ten soldiers there sent the following letter to:

Miss M.A. Buie, Soldiers' Friend, Wayside Hospital #5,
Wilmington, Fort Fisher, December 16th, 1864

Dear Miss Buie: We enclose you herewith $135, being the proceeds of a concert given tonight at this place, for the purpose of aiding you to give the sick soldiers at Wilmington a Christmas dinner.

Wishing it were more, we remain your hearty well wishers.[23]

Ms. Buie was mentioned as egotistical by James Ryder Randall:

> Her vanity has swollen into the ultra prodigious and sublime. Her mouth widens to gulp down upon her for compliments of interested wags who have designs upon her for blockade brandy and sardines. Still she has been of stupendous value in making the extortioners disgorge and I regard her as the very empress of benevolent scavengers. Miss Buie's motives appeared to be composed of equal parts of patriotism and matrimony . . .[24]

People that knew her said she was a smart businesswoman and made money speculating, but she was too ugly to get a sweetheart. One caller said she gave him one hundred dollars, a pound of coffee, and some towels so that he could no longer criticize her. Another said that her "gifts were accompanied with 'egotism and trumpet blowing.'"[25] Nevertheless, Buie accomplished a great deal for the Confederacy.

There is no date on the next letter to the governor, but it was probably written after the war and appeared in a newspaper:

Gov. Vance

You will pardon me for asking this favor of you. I have not been remunerated for my services by the Government nor do I ask it. As I am going to a strange place I would like to have some cotton shipped out for my benefit. I have to buy the cotton & pay high for it but when it is shipped it will enable me to do much service. I have not done any thing for myself . . . Jany 1861 The South Carolinians have been very kind to me and made some money but I have given the soldiers the greater part of it. If I was a favorite of the President he would perhaps do as much for me as he has done for other ladies leaving this country. I go out as [a] Volunteer to aid the cause by my affects to those sympathizing with us in the other lands. You know I have succeeded in S.C. & Geo. before I came to N.C. In every other place I have been treated with much more civility & kindness than in my own state. The editors mayors &c. in the other cities all have been very kind to me. I feel that I have not received justice in this state for my success with out the aid of ladies or Editors. I have a set of silver presented [to me]. I have written many notices of you in the Geo. & SC papers in a few words praised you for clothing the soldiers or taking care of their families. Your name is familiar all over the land & in Europe [as] the Patriot & Soldier. Please write to me immediately [.] I have collected more than any one else in the Confederacy & sent it direct where needed daily all over the land—1/2 million and . . . my donations sent to the army. All the letters I have are from true southerners feeling . . . Respectfully, Mary Ann Buie, Soldiers Friend[26]

After the bombardment of Fort Fisher in 1864, a refugee from the bombing sent a note of thanks published in the newspaper to Ms. Buie for helping them get food and lodging when no one else would help. They reported that Buie paid for it from her own pockets.

Following the war, Mary Ann continued to do benevolent work. She raised funds for orphans of Confederate soldiers.[27] "She moved her school from Edgefield in 1870. Her 'hook' to attract students was by advertising that she was the 'soldier's friend.' Buie accepted her paying students and provided a few scholarships for Confederate orphans. When she did not meet with success, she moved to Aiken in 1872."[28] Buie died on October 9, 1878, and is buried in Aiken, South Carolina.

Mrs. Armand DeRossett of Wilmington worked untiringly throughout the war. Her home was turned into a storage facility for boxes of supplies for the hospitals and aid stations. The editor of the local newspaper felt she went above the call of duty in her ministrations to the needy:

> Once before we have felt it duty as well as a pleasure, to bear testimony to the great and useful, and patriotic efforts of this association of ladies, but we never fully realized the spirit of the Association, or the energy of its most efficient President, Mrs. deRosset, before the close of last week, when on the occurrences of an emergency at a late hour [it was Christmas Day], she, with some other ladies casting aside every other consideration, most gallantly—turned out, with all they had . . . to minister to the comfort of the soldiers. Such instances of active unobtrusive working, usefulness are worth the whole volumes of puffs or pretension.[29]

Businessmen helped the war effort in different ways. One company chose to ship soldiers' boxes for free. This advertisement appeared in the last year, showing that the troops were not forgotten:

> All boxes for soldiers or prisoners of war from North Carolina delivered to the following named persons will be promptly forwarded free of charge: Sprague Brothers—Salisbury; Dr. R.F. Sumney—Asheville; Dr. W.A. Collet—Morganton; Dr. J.W. Allison—Statesville; Dr. J.L. Neagle—Greensboro; Mr. A. Hagen—Charlotte; Mr. Edward Hege—Salem; Capt. J.N. McDowell—Raleigh; Joseph A. Worth—Fayetteville; E. Murray & Co.—Wilmington; Mr. E.L. Bond—Tarboro; Mr. J.A. Askew—Colerain; F.L. Roberts—Murfreesboro. The boxes should be sent roped, properly marked and delivered in time for my special messenger who leaves Raleigh on the first day of every month.
>
> Ed Warren, Surgeon General, N.C.[30]

Alexander Collie, owner of several blockade-runners and the president of the London Shipping Company, gave permission for his agent in Wilmington to make a gift of twenty thousand dollars to Governor Vance "to be distributed among those who are suffering from the present state of things in your country."[31] The gift came just in time for Christmas. W. A. Thompson of Hillsborough volunteered to take boxes to Kirkland's and Clingman's brigades.[32] In the postwar letters to President Andrew Johnson requesting amnesty, several gentlemen said they had given aid to needy families during the conflict, namely James Gwyn of Wilkes County, S. F. Patterson of Caldwell County, and Robert C. Pearson of Burke County.[33]

Elias A. Vogler, president of the Board of Sustenance of Forsyth County, received a letter from Captain R. W. Wharton with the Twenty-first Regiment in October 1862 to ask for a pair of shoes and two pairs of socks for *each* man in his company. He wrote that the articles mentioned should be brought to a certain drop-off in Salem on November 5. (Editor's note: that was a tall order for only one month's notice because a company consisted of one hundred men.)[34] Mr. Vogler—a member of the Central Committee, a relief organization—packed and forwarded two to three hundred boxes of goods to the volunteers in the first few months of the conflict. The committee paid the freight due, as well as expenses for the women who went to nurse the soldiers.[35]

In November 1862, $41,355 was subscribed for poor soldiers' families from Cumberland County. Likewise, the residents of Caldwell County collected four thousand dollars.

John Peebles sent a sixty-dollar check to Governor Vance, which his family and citizens of Kinston had collected for a gunboat fund, but "which project Exploded after the fall of Several of our Sea port Towns & fort Dollenson, the money was returned to my wife." He wanted the governor to disperse the funds to a needy agency for shoes and clothing for the soldiers.[36]

Charles Deems—a Methodist minister, journalist, professor, and college president— "could not bear arms during the war, but he did work unceasingly for the Confederate Cause," noted author Sutherland. "He raised money to care for the war's homeless, destitute, and bereaved. Rev. Deems attempted to establish a college in the state for the orphans of southern soldiers. By 1864, he had secured pledges of $100,000 which ultimately failed because of the war." Deems had been a Union man and a slaveholder but "was not sorry to see slavery abolished."[37] When Dr. Deems gave a speech in Tarboro about the war and orphan fund, he collected about forty dollars in one evening.

In Wilmington, J. L. Prichard, pastor of the First Baptist Church, daily visited troops stationed around the city, taking with him pamphlets, magazines, and provisions. Prichard situated himself at the depots where he would hand out testaments and religious tracts. He cared for sick soldiers in his home and shared meals with other troops.[38] In June 1862, he procured a boxcar, loaded it with provisions, and set out on his way to Richmond with the intent of donating the contents to the sick in the hospitals. He inscribed in his diary:

> At almost every station additions were made to the load. I wish you could have seen the quantity at Warsaw, Faison's, Mt. Olive, and other places. Another car would have been almost filled. All things went on smoothly till we reached Weldon, where the conductor on the Petersburg road refused to take my car. I entreated him but it was useless, and there was no alternative but to submit. My car was rolled out from under the shed . . . it was 3 am . . .

The reverend took his overcoat, lay down in the car, and tried to sleep; but the coops of chickens made such a racket that it was impossible for him to do so. "Soon the Petersburg train came in and the conductor said he would take my car. At Petersburg, I delivered the packages for that place, and reaching Richmond at 9 p.m., had to see the car unloaded." The next day, the government sent out wagons and hauled them to the hospitals. After his death, the reverend was remembered and praised by soldiers alike for his untiring benevolence.[39] Prichard also worked until he dropped when the yellow fever spread in Wilmington, catching the disease, ultimately dying.

"Throughout the war Delphina Mendenhall contributed both money and influence to assist Quaker men imprisoned for refusing to fight . . ." Mary W. Smith's husband converted his church, the First Presbyterian Church, into a hospital in Greensboro.[40] The Jewish ladies of Charlotte turned in $150 to be used for the sick and wounded.[41] Reverend DeSchweinitz, principal of Salem Female Academy, frequently rode through the neighborhood and countryside seeking donations of food for his students. An employee exempted from military service due to his age of forty-one, Augustus Fogle, helped the reverend gather supplies. He also was the bodyguard to the students during the conflict.[42] In Raleigh, Rev. Aldert Smedes went out of his way to procure provisions for St. Mary's students and the refugees who occupied his school.

"Elder Dodson gave his salary to objects of benevolence, home, & foreign missions, education and the poor," printed the *Raleigh Register*. Father Tom Murphy, pastor of St. Thomas Church, Wilmington, was a hero to the residents during the yellow fever outbreak in 1862. Approximately three thousand people were left in the city for unknown reasons as the others fled to nearby counties. Succeeding him was Rev. James Corcoran, who conducted the funeral of Rose Greenhow, a famous Confederate spy.*[43] Reverend Brent, chaplain of the Twenty-eighth Regiment, traveled the countryside "to solicit aid for the purpose of buying & distributing tracts for our soldiers . . . ," wrote Elle Andrews.[44]

Others around the state contributed simpler things instead of money. James F. Kornegay would give fifty bales of cotton. An anonymous donor from Wilmington donated five hundred dollars for the war effort.[45] Mr. Joseph A. Bitting, a merchant of Germanton, assisted poorer families in need during wartime.[46] Donations were solicited from the countryside. November 10, 1864, W. L. Barker, a hospital steward at Pettigrew Hospital, recorded items collected: 182 chickens, 229 pounds of dried fruit, eight and one-half dozen eggs, twelve pounds of tallow, and one-half bushel of corn were brought to the hospital by Mr. Galloway.[47] Levi Cox worked thirty-two days cutting wheat for neighbors before the Home Guard threatened him because he was working away from his mill (Spoon Mill area).[48]

Wealthier North Carolinians dug deep in their pockets for the cause. Paul Cameron, planter, contributed clothes to the volunteers of Orange County. Author Jean Anderson said of Cameron, "To the needy and destitute, who included the soldiers, the wives, and families, he had made large donations." Cameron owned three plantations cared for by nine hundred slaves. His plantations encompassed several thousand acres in the piedmont area.[49] "Mr. Cameron has sent meat and meal and by contributions with the state we will be supplied with flour, meat, sugar, and coffee . . ."[50] Paul Cameron wrote to Martha Mangum, a neighbor, on July 31, 1861, from Hillsboro that he would have the town hearse at the station in Hillsboro to pick up her son's body.[51] Mr. A. H. Van Bokkelen provided sustenance to every wife and child of a soldier serving in his son's company.[52]

As the war was closing, the governor called for citizens to help with the food shortage for soldiers. Mr. James Davis of Mecklenburg County responded by agreeing to feed one hundred soldiers for six months.[53] Patrick Edmondston and his wife, of Halifax, shared their provisions with soldiers and the poorer classes. Mrs. Edmondston penned in her diary:

> A poor woman came here yesterday, she wanted some things for her husband, as he was going to start to the army on Thursday, he is a soldier. I had the pleasure of giving her something for him. I sent him a Testament to read, sent him word to put his trust in God. I gave her some advice, and exhorted her to seek religion . . . I have had a good deal of company, over one hundred soldiers have stopped here to get something to eat, they were on their way from the army.

When the blockade was declared, her father "had on hand a quality of salt which he had bought . . . for agricultural purposes. This he instantly stopped & reserved it. The poorer classes throughout the country, those people who had from 3-8 or 10 hogs . . . & who had been in the habit of supplying themselves from the neighboring merchants with the few bushels they needed, were terribly ground and imposed upon with speculators, who in some instances had the face to ask 25 and $28 a sack." Her father "gave notice that he would distribute in parcels not exceeding 5 bu, all he could spare & as money was scarce, he would take his payment in SOCKS which he intended to bestow upon the government. He collected four pairs of socks per bushel which came to about eighty cents."[54] Mrs.

---

*   She died on September 30, 1864, and is buried in Oakdale Cemetery in Wilmington.

Edmondston sent to the North Carolina hospitals in Richmond all the old linen, cotton, wine and, cordials that she could spare for several months in the summer of 1862.[55]

When Catherine went to visit a poor neighbor, she felt somewhat guilty that her home was so luxurious compared with the leaky hovel they were in. Her husband decided to build the neighbor a better cabin.[56] She wrote in the diary that they had planted a larger crop of Irish potatoes than usual for the army. Mrs. Edmondston traded eight hundred bushels of salt for knitted socks from her neighbors. She hired a destitute girl as her spinner.[57]

Whether they gave the full amount or collected from a group, the next gentlemen are credited in the newspaper with giving large amounts of money to a particular regiment:

> John Fleming, $1,7000 to the 13th N.C. troops.
> J.H. Lindsey, $1,327 to the 12th Regiment.
> Dr. McDaniel, $2,500 to the 4th and 11th Regiments.
> R.B. Pascall and W. D. Tyson, $5,000 to the 5th and 26th Regiments.
> William Peel and others, $400 to the 2nd Regiment.
> M.D. Smith, $1,100 to the 11th Regiment.
> May Warren, $6000 to the 4th Regiment.
> S.H. Hand, $1,300 to the 11th Regiment.
> Samuel P. Hill, $500 in money to the 6th Regiment.
> M.C. Winston, $200 to the 5th State troops.[58]

Major James Boggan and Ben K. Pond, Esq., from Anson County traveled to Virginia with six thousand pounds of clothing for the volunteers.[59]

Jonathan Worth wore many hats. A lawyer, politician, businessman, slave owner, and Quaker, though excommunicated when he married outside the church, he was successful in keeping some Quaker men out of military service on the front line by employing them in his cotton factory, as overseers, and finding them jobs in the salt factories. Worth saw to it that the wives of these Quaker men working away from home were cared for in the way of provisions.[60]

Elizabeth Ann McNair, twice a widow, owned a huge home named Argyle, with thirty slaves in Robeson. She took in two families of her relations during the war years. Being a giving person, she took in weakened Confederate soldiers.[61] In Colerain, Mrs. Annie Ellison, alone, traveled by horseback throughout her county soliciting clothing for the boys in gray.[62]

Planters and neighbors in Washington County, Josiah Collins and J. J. Pettigrew financed a company of volunteers. Both had hundreds of slaves that worked the land raising food for the armies. Collins died in Hillsborough in 1863. Josiah Pender bought uniforms for his own militia regiment. The owner of the Rock Island Woolen Mill on the Catawba River furnished wool for soldiers' uniforms. John G. Young stated his father "gave each man a suit of gray . . . and a cap." His unit consisted of eleven hundred men of the Fourth Regiment. Later in the war, Governor Vance asked the elder Young to resign his commission because he could do his duty better by staying with the factory.[63] A newspaper reported that the Messrs. Young, Winston, and Orr Manufacturers from the Rock Island Factory gave one hundred fifty dollars to the sick at a Richmond hospital.[64] "The *People's Press* reported . . . . the Messrs. Fries have presented the two volunteer companies formed in this place and vicinity, numbering about 100, the material, and the ladies of Salem are busily engaged in the Temperance and Odd Fellow Halls, in making up the Uniforms and preparing other supplies, thus contributing to the defence of the state."[65] Another mill owner chose to assist the soldiers' widows by seeing to it that they got first choice when the yarn was doled out. General W. H. Neal had only five hundred spindles at his mill in Mecklenburg County.[66]

Eng and Chang Bunker, the Siamese twins living in Wilkes County, owned twelve hundred acres farmed by fifteen slaves. They bought bonds for the war effort and sent provisions to the soldiers and prisoners."[67] Duplin County farmers furnished provisions to soldiers in camp while they drilled early in the war. The recruits boarded the train at Faison and traveled to Smithville. Ladies met in the Franklin Institute to sew items for the volunteers.[68]

Mr. O. G. Parsley, president of the Commercial Bank, Wilmington, supplied an entire company called the Cape Fear Rifleman out of his own pocket.[69] He also helped the families of the soldiers in his son's unit. During the war, a Mr. Davis, a bank manager, knitted socks for the soldiers as good as any woman. Captain Robert M. McIntire from Rocky Point raised a cavalry company, donating twelve horses, many saddles, and several sabres.[70] Levin Meginney opened a private school for boys in New Hanover County. Since he was partially disabled, he was not eligible to fight; therefore, he helped outfit one of the first gunboats in Wilmington.[71] Other notable men from Wilmington, Dr. John Bellamy and additional large slave owners let the Confederate government "borrow" their slaves to erect defenses and did not accept compensation because they felt it their duty.[72]

Other people upon hearing of the sick or destitute went right to work. Mary Bethall was just such a person to assist the downtrodden. "There has been a great deal of sickness in my neighborhood [Rockingham County]. I have been visiting the sick, and I carry them something nice to eat, lightbread and rice."[73] December 6, 1861, she wrote that female neighbors visited the sick at New Bern. "Mrs. William Smith and F. Benson's wife was there."[74] Women visiting the hospitals were known to bring home remedies to sick patients. Perhaps they used spirits of turpentine for the bellyache as told by the James family.[75]

When one hundred Confederate prisoners escaped from a ship called the *Maple Leaf* South of Fortress Monroe, women near Elizabeth City sheltered them and sent provisions and conveyances. They were carried by river thence to the railroad.[76]

As mentioned before, illnesses took longer to recuperate unlike today. Two ill soldiers at different locations chose to bide their time with gardening. Burwell Davis was at Peace Hospital in Raleigh, recovering from a wound. While there, he started a vegetable garden for the hospital.[77] On the coast, a soldier created a garden for family and friends while he was mending.

An advertisement appeared in the *Daily Confederate* for provisions needed for three hundred new patients at general hospital no. 1 located at Kittrell Springs. Articles requested were milk, butter, eggs, fowls, old linen rags, vegetables, fruit, pickles, and cakes; but the nurses would take anything. Mrs. Elliot, a refugee living in Oxford, sent an entire wagonload of food.[78] Mrs. M. A. Harris of Henderson wrote she and her neighbor in Granville County asked the Richmond authorities for one hundred or more sick and wounded men to nurse back to health. Some families took four, some two, others more. These soldiers enjoyed the cool country-fresh milk and butter, recovering much faster.[79] Mrs. W. F. Askew took in the sick soldiers from Camp Mangum in Raleigh. Every week, she took a basket of provisions out to them. "She obtained from the commissary department a large quantity of remnants from suits made there for the soldiers, paying $25 Confederate money to have a two horse load hauled to her home; and out of these scraps she made more than a hundred suits by combining different colors. She and the other ladies gave their own blankets to the volunteers."[80] Jake James was granted semi-permanent leave of military duties to help out on the farm because his produce continually fed the army. They had enough food and clothing during the war for both black and white. He also gave to needy families in the neighborhood.[81] A minister from Jonesville Academy agreed to educate the children of soldiers for free.

---

*   The twins had sons who fought for the Thirty-seventh Virginia Cavalry. Christopher, son of Chang, was imprisoned at Camp Chase, Ohio. The family sent him boxes of provisions and money. Stephen was the son of Eng. Eng and Chang married sisters, Addie and Sally Yates. Sally had eleven children, Addie ten. Chang spent three days with his wife, then they switched, so that Eng could have three days with his.

One would think that during wartime, agencies would work together for the common good. However, such was not always the case. There seemed to be a fierce competition in the piedmont. In this instance, it was the soldier and his family who won. One county called the other disloyal. An article in the *Salem Press* read:

> This "disloyal" county, through the Central Committee, has expended for our 5 volunteer companies the sum of $11,287.47; assistance to volunteer's families, in mostly payments to subcommittees, $2,213.32. For the above figures we are indebted to Mr. Vogler, of the Central Committee, who also informed us that he packed and forwarded from his house alone, in the way of contributions, and etc., between two and three hundred boxes in all; paid freights for such as did not go free, amounting to $251; expenses incurred by nurses, having free transportation tickets, $200.75. Also, about 200 pairs of homemade socks, 119 blankets and quilts were handed in for general distribution, besides numerous bundles and boxes, contents not enumerated but far exceeding the other in variety and amount.

Other contributions included shirts, gloves, drawers, etc.[82]

Sarah Tillinghast and the women of Fayetteville cooked for C.S. General Hardee's Army, along with sewing and mending for them. Sally Hawthorne, age seven, and her sisters handed out sandwiches to the retreating Confederate troops near the Arsenal.[83] A newspaper announced that "the widow Marshall . . . sent to Mr. E. Hutchison, 25 bushels of meal for distribution among the Volunteers' families." Other persons in Union County who contributed wheat or meal included Tom Robinson, James A. Leak, John Little, J. C. Bennett, and John Knotts. Alex Misenheimer and his brother owned a gristmill and sold wheat at a cheaper rate to soldiers' families. Mr. James Dunn would only sell his corn to the soldiers' wives.[84]

"William Lea, Esq, has been selling fine beef at 25 cents a pound and refused to receive more, while every body else exacted more than double, & cried because they couldn't get more!" wrote the editor of a newspaper.[85] The *Milton Chronicle* published other acts of benevolence: H. A. Dowd, adjutant quartermaster, advertised that he had a shipment of cotton and wool cards to be sold only to soldiers' families at twenty-two dollars and sixty cents each.[86] The newspaper continued: "Samuel Good is selling flour at ten dollars a barrel to soldiers' families where it is selling elsewhere at $60-100 in Rockingham." William Paylor of Person County sold wheat to soldiers' families at one dollar, twenty-five cents a bushel and corn at six dollars a barrel. The distillers were offering twenty dollars a barrel for corn to make alcohol, but Mr. Paylor refused to sell his to the distillers.[87] Merchant Samuel Fels did not gouge his customers in Yanceyville.[88] In Robeson County, one miller told soldiers' wives he would grind their corn for free. The *Raleigh Standard* printed that "Dr. Wesley Heartsfield of Wake County sells bacon at fifty cents per pound to the indigent families of soldiers and corn at three dollars per bushel . . ."[89] The same newspaper told of Mr. William T. Rogers, part owner of a grinding mill, who would sell corn to volunteers' wives at one dollar a bushel when he could have charged two dollars. He also offered to grind corn for free for volunteers' wives if the owners of the corn would sell to him at reasonable prices.[90] A Haywood County man refused three dollars per bushel of corn so that he could sell to soldiers' wives for less than one dollar. In Stanly County, a man sold flour at ten dollars per bushel to soldiers' families' instead of the usual thirty dollars he charged other customers. "Mr. William Parles of Wilkes County is selling corn to soldiers' families @ 50cents a bushel. He will not sell any to distilleries at any price. He was offered $1.25 a bushel from the Distillers," wrote a person to the newspaper.[91] This was news to brag about. Newspapers throughout the state gave attention to the farmers who sold produce to soldiers' wives or the indigent at reduced prices.

Men at home also pitched in for the war effort. Near Wilmington, elderly men formed a home defense group commonly referred to as the Horse and Buggy Company. "Though they did not drill, they held themselves in readiness to do what they could when called upon." The seniors gave through their pockets by equipping the recruits and aiding soldiers' wives.[92] Cobblers not conscripted made shoes; others who had wagons helped the civilians with transportation. There were few wagons left in the community, many being impressed for the military. A Salem man helped poor women and children in his neighborhood. It was reported that President Braxton Craven of Trinity College assumed the responsibility of providing thirty to forty families with corn. Mr. Allen Wooten, of Kinston, made ink and soap in huge quantities for the army free of charge.[93]

Another news article appeared:

> We take pleasure in stating that one of our leading citizens has deposited with me, D. Byerly, 1000 lbs of sugar for sale to the wives and families of soldiers whether of low circumstances, at a low price, 30 cents lb. Apply to D. Byerly[94]

These merchants were not following the norm, which was to sell everything at inflated prices. They kept several families from starving by their benevolence. Messrs. Young, Winston, and Orr, manufacturers with the Rock Island Factory in Charlotte sold wool and jeans cloth to army quartermasters at the usual price "with only the difference of the advance of the raw wool . . ."[95]

Luke Blackner, a Salisbury resident, bought provisions for inmates, at times having to smuggle it in the prison. He would also hide escapees in his basement.[96] Mrs. Sloan Johnston visited the Salisbury Prison daily. She was called "the prison mother." Mrs. Mary Wrenn and daughter, Betty, ran a hospital in Salisbury. They sold their jewelry, silver, and clothing to raise money to supply it. Near the community of Round Knob, the wives of seven Irishmen employed on the unfinished railroad to the mountains walked eighteen miles every week or two to Asheville to ask for help for destitute families in their area. Mrs. Nicholas Woodfin let the women use a room to rest and collect provisions before starting back.*[97]

Down East, citizens continued their benevolence. In Tyrell County, Mary Cahoon Dillon Ambrose had an auction at her home to raise money for the troops. Federal troops passing by became curious of the crowd. Mary "met them at the gate and pleaded, Please do not interrupt the funeral we're having." The squad traveled on. She was able to raise five thousand dollars. Mrs. Ambrose sewed the money in her clothing and proceeded to Tarboro. Stopped again by the enemy pickets, she told them she was on her way to visit her sick grandmother in Tarboro. These soldiers let her pass.[98]

With the war in progress, many women were left alone and needed protection from roving bands of lawless men. William Baker of the Twenty-sixth Regiment got drunk one night and "attempted to force his way into a house occupied by two frightened women. A neighbor responded to the women's request for help." Baker pulled a knife and was shot in the stomach by their rescuer.[99]

The *Greensboro Patriot* would not give the name of the next heroine but used her as an example for others to follow suit:

> **Socks for the Soldier**—We learn that a young lady of this county, a few days since, took a horse and rode a half day, soliciting socks for the soldiers, and succeeded in procuring twenty-five pair in her first half-day's trip. We are not authorized to give the name of the young lady. There are, we doubt not,

---

*   Round Mountain is in Polk County northwest of Tryon. I-26 passes through Howard Gap between Round Mountain and Miller Mountain. The rail line goes through Saluda Gap. Howard Gap is located between Warrior Mountain and Tryon Peak. The route that the women walked is actually about thirty miles instead of eighteen.

hundreds of other ladies in the county willing to engage in the same patriotic work, and who would meet with equal success.

Vina Cury, a free black, helped fifteen slaves escape bondage. The Mendenhall family in Forsyth County assisted slaves to leave the state. So one can see that North Carolinians helped their fellow beings in many different ways throughout the conflict.

The roll of honor should include those families who had multiple sons enlisted in the military. Former Confederate General D. H. Hill repeated the line uttered by Mrs. Reuben Jones, of Robeson, who had eleven sons to volunteer within a week, "I cannot hold you when your country calls you . . . ."[100] In Alamance, Lucy F. Simpson's eleven sons fought.[101] Mrs. Fannie Autry Tolar, of Cumberland County, had a husband and nine sons in the army, along with a son-in-law and a fifteen-year-old grandson. The Stephen Lee family of Buncombe saw eight sons leave for war. John Wright and his eight brothers fought in Twentieth Regiment.[102] Janie Smith, in Averasboro, had eight brothers in service. The Bunch family of Person County contributed eight sons.[103]

The widow Polly Ray of the Longstreet community in Cumberland County had seven sons, ages sixteen through thirty, in the military. Unfortunately, *all* seven died in the war.[104] Polly's neighbor Mrs. Charity Boyles had six of her seven sons to die.[105] One can just imagine the sorrow in that community. Mason and Elizabeth Wiggins had given seven sons.[106] Seven Hicks boys from the Faison community served in the war.[107] The Robert Collins family of Oconaluftee had seven sons who fought, with only one killed.[108]

Other families include Mrs. Eliza L. DeRosset, who had six sons serving.[109] Miranda Sutton's husband served, along with their six sons. Her husband and two sons died.[110] The Horne family, of Johnston County, saw six sons leave for the army. Mr. and Mrs. Thomas Tatham in the mountains had six sons to take up arms.[111] Young Bennett, a herb doctor from Haywood County, had six sons in the Confederacy; but only three returned home.[112] In Burke County, the Thomas Clayton family sent six sons to take up arms.[113] The Thomas Morgan family in Granville had all six of their sons killed, as did the Thomas Carlton family of five sons. In Charlotte, Mrs. William White saw six sons to take up arms.[114]

Mrs. William Graham had five sons who fought.[115] When questioned by a minister "whether she were not terribly anxious about the safety of her sons . . . she said, 'No, I would not have it otherwise. My only prayer is that if any of them are to be taken, it may be those who are ready to go.'"[116] Harriet Stephenson had five sons to fight.[117]

Mrs. Margaret Burwell managed to keep the Charlotte Female Institute open the entire war. She also took in young female refugees. Burwell had five sons in the military.[118] Kitty Daughtry, of Sampson County, saw five sons leave for military service.[119] In Ashe County, only three of the five sons in the Barker family returned after the war.[120] Mrs. Oran Palmer lost four sons at Gettysburg.[121] Another family, the L. D. Bennetts, with five sons volunteering, lived in Anson County.[122]

Research indicates that these are not, by far, the entire list of multiple soldiers in one family. Put yourself in Polly Ray's shoes—to be a widow with a home full of children, with seven volunteering for the army, and not one returning.

CHAPTER SEVEN

Nurses, Female Soldiers, Spies, Smugglers, and Soiled Doves

In order to understand the Southern woman in wartime, one must explain a background of her circumstances. A patriarchal society dominated the old South. Women knew their place in society, which centered around the home sphere. Ladies were trained to believe that a woman's service must be channeled primarily through the home rather than any outside projects. A girl's desire in life was to marry and bear children. Her life rotated around her husband, children, and home. Females were taught from an early age to subdue their carnal desires.* They must be morally pure and set the example.[1] A clergyman speaking at the commencement of a female college talked about the "physical, mental and moral culture necessary to produce a female character worthy of the name of Southern matron." In summary "a wealthy Southern girl was educated not to support herself but rather to better serve her family for, 'A woman's occupation and her mission is to have a home other than her father's and knit with dearer ties.'"[2]

Young Southern women training for their future household responsibilities carried the basic assumptions of slavery as a social system. A planter's daughter's duty previous to the conflict consisted of caring for her room and clothing, although this can be debated, gathering and arranging flowers, helping to make preserves, reading, shopping, visiting, drying flowers, dressing the hair, and writing letters.[3]

Responsibility decreed that an unmarried woman live with relatives, devoting all her energies toward promoting their happiness, whether or not this brought personal satisfaction. "The single woman embroiders the clothe of other people's children."[4] Women were to be charitable to the downtrodden "by personal contact rather than organized philanthropy."[5] Society discouraged women from developing many of the characteristics typical of Northern women such as clubs, voluntary associations, factory work, or popular movements (temperance and abolitionists).[6] Any deviation from this brought stares and hushed talk from her peers. Heaven forbid if the single woman expressed a desire to work outside the home or follow the call in nursing! Such behavior was just unsuitable for young ladies.

Citing passages from author Catherine Clinton, "Women's personal identification included all the tensions that resulted from subordinate and dependent status in society as well as in the households that anchored it. Women were bound to each other in the household, not in sisterhood, but by their specific and different relations to its master. White women rarely challenged the 'master' directly. Ladies knew whom they should and should not greet in public places and observed rules in the matter of calls. There were fashionable calls and sociable calls of friendship. The conventions that defined the lady included a strong emphasis on purity, chastity, in the single girl and decorum in married women."[7] The above comments referred to an upper-class woman and an upper-middle-class female.

In a previous chapter, women working at factories was briefly mentioned. These females would more likely have been in the lower-class strata, and they were not defined as "ladies." That is why Ms. Ellison, alluded to earlier, felt the need to write a letter explaining why she had to go to work at the Arsenal. Southern women believed that disorderly

---

* The reading of novels by young women, which covered all types of females, horrified their parents and was forbidden in many households. It was considered racy for their time period.

manners, the type picked up by working in a factory, testified to disorderly character, with which they were loath to be associated with.[8]

Southern ladies drew the social line between themselves and other white women whom they perceived as their inferiors. The war caused different levels of society to mix, much to their consternation. They abhorred women in superfluous dress. They disliked women, "who proved incapable of keeping disorder of their personal lives hidden from public view," noted Clinton.[9] "Belonging or nor belonging lay at the heart of the matter. Some emphasized breeding, some manners, some character, but all agreed on fundamentals. To be welcome in their circle, a woman must be a lady. A middling town woman (country girl) and yeomen were not ladies." Clinton described lower-income girls as one having coarse manners, voices too loud, and lacking culture. It was felt at the time that men and women working in the same building would lead to sexual promiscuity. The lower-class females who had to work were considered of freer social inhibitions.[10]

The yeoman's house was small, somewhere between the size of a paltry farmer's home and a slave's cabin. Some had a window, and others did not. Many had pine floors; a portion did not. The yeoman's family worked alongside him in the fields, raising just enough to feed the family or, in better times, enough to trade for basic supplies not grown. Rarely did a yeoman farmer own a slave. If prosperous, he may have had enough money to hire a part-time slave. This class of person did not have enough time to make social calls or to belong to an organization. Labor filled the entire day.

Unfortunately, for modern historians, most lower-income persons left little written information about their lifestyle. After the war, J. R. Dennett, a Harvard graduate hired by a Northern newspaper to travel the Southern states, passed through North Carolina. He interviewed people of all walks of life, including former slaves. Dennett chronicled an excellent description of these lower-income individuals. "Many log cabins have crude furniture and rush bottom chairs. Overhead hang skeins of brown or blue yarn. Most have spinning wheels. The women dip snuff or take tobacco in some form—chew or smoke a pipe. Their dresses are faded and clay colored." He described the women unfavorably, as barefoot, with locks of tangled hair, dirty, with snuff stains in the corners of their mouth, and wearing a man's hat:

> Several hundred farmers distill peach and apple brandy for themselves,
> promising not to sell it to soldiers. In the home of a miller near Lexington are
> 29 dresses hanging from pegs and covering the walls. There are two big piles
> of counterpanes and quilts in the room.[*][11]

Upper-class families, because they owned slaves, had the leisure to visit. Author Clinton reported that upper-class individuals made calls of condescension to lower classes. "Her charitable gestures were as important to her role as a lady as was her embodiment of fashion.[12] Fashion reflected class position. Extravagance defied it. Ladies (once married) no matter how young, became superfluous in dress. As dress, it represented standing in the world. As a way of life it represented a continuing of those brief years as belles that they were expected to put behind them upon marriage."[13] Due to war and the blockade, the fashions changed considerably and will be discussed in a later chapter.

Southern society decreed that women were not to travel alone. It was not considered safe. This grew more so during the war when thousands of men were on the road. A woman would get a friend of the family, a minister, or a relative to escort her. However, there were

---

*   A miller during this time period would probably have been included in the middle class. Still, twenty-nine dresses was a great amount for even an upper-class lady. Perhaps the miller had many daughters.

times when this was impossible. The simple, laid-back lifestyle of the Southern woman came to a halt. Now the world had become a dangerous place.

When the war began, men in close proximity dropped like flies with disease. Overwhelmed surgeons called out for help from the ladies, sparking vehement outbursts in families. There was much discouragement among the elite that proper women did not pursue work outside the woman's sphere, and certainly anything as crude as nursing was downright unthinkable! To see men half-undressed and to wash them, that was just unacceptable for their delicate constitution! To nurse male relatives was one thing, but to care for a male stranger was unthinkable. This was one reason that Dorthea Dix, Superintendent of the U.S. Army nurses in the North, would only accept older women with the "motherly" look. However, many young women did volunteer to assist these poor helpless soldiers. In the South, women of all ages volunteered their time as nurses. In North Carolina, some served locally; others left the state to serve in the hospitals in Virginia. Patriotic duty called regardless if the tongues wagged.

Before the state had officially seceded, women stepped forth to volunteer their time in making hospital shirts and drawers, as well as nursing. The following letter, dated April 28, to Governor Ellis is from a group of unmarried girls from Greene County:

> To his Excellency John W. Ellis, Governor of North Carolina:
> We the undersigned, hereby tender our services to the state as nurses, or in any other capacity in which we can aid brave Volunteers. We are willing and ready to take the field with them and there minister to the wants of the wounded. Hoping that your Excellency will accept our tender, we have the honor to be, Your Excellent Obedient Servants: Sarah Corinne Hunnicutt, Annie E. Williams, Kate J. Randolph, Emma F. Williams.[14]

Mrs. Stevenson of Charlotte, possibly a lower—to mid-income-situated woman, presented herself as a volunteer nurse in a letter to Governor Ellis.[15]

Women prewar were loath to have their names in the newspaper. In the Victorian era, etiquette dominated how ladies were supposed to act concerning involvement with strangers especially men. She would not have written a male without prior introduction. Wartime exigencies dismissed it. The next letter to Governor Ellis was obviously written by a female, but she did not sign her name:

> Will you not authorize ladies of your state to endeavor to get OTHERS to enlist as "sisters of mercy" [non-Catholic] for the relief of the sick at York—and other places. All the compensation which I ask, is a free passport—both in procuring volunteers and in reaching our—destination. Do you think such a move on my part unmaidenly, or indelicate? Gov Ellis will please excuse a want of Parlimentary etiquette with which this letter is penned, attribute it rather to ignorance, than a want of respect . . .[16]

A woman with grandchildren said she would accompany the First Regiment as a nurse. Ms. N. H. Whitfield, of Enfield, wrote to the newspaper on July 1, 1861, requesting an appointment as a nurse for the soldiers and asked that the governor appoint women as nurses.[17] Fourteen men and women from Salem went to Manassas to assist sick soldiers that September.

Hospital scene drawing
N.C. Division of Archives & History, Photographic Archives

Mentioned earlier, the first nurses were convalescing soldiers. William Octavus Ruddock, with the Twenty-third Regiment, survived the war and left the next two letters, describing his detail as a nurse after he himself was a patient:

Culpeper, C.H. Oct. (1861)
Dear Uncle,

As I have a chance of sending a letter direct I will write you a few lines to let you know that I have got able to be put on duty in this ward as a nurse which is worsting me right smart. I said I had got able that is a mistake. I could not walk half a mile without resting I don't think. The regular nurses have all left this ward and the sick must be attended to. There are men half more able than I and I expect would have take the place instead but it was the request of my friends for me to do it. They not being willing to take medicine from just anybody and three of them was very low and one [S. Conner Little] of which I am sorry to say accompanies this letter to be placed in his native land . . . . The other two men are improving fast. There is seven of our men here now but none very sick. My time of service is from twelve at night til eight in the morning which is the hardest tour but I had to take the tour of the last man that left. He only went home for a time. He is sick but I hope he will return shortly. If he does not someone else must be got. I can't stand it. I am afraid it will give me Pneumonia and that would [be] rather bad after having the measles, chronic Dysentery and Typhoid Fever. All of them I think were bad cases but a man should not judge himself. I must have a good constitution or I never would have come through but I thought it was pea time for me a long time. There was a while that I was not conscious of anything but it was the will of God for me to stay a little while longer. I looked for Esq. Burch yesterday . . . . I hope he will get here today. I am needing some clothes badly. I understand by a letter from Frank Blythe that he started or would start last Monday. I received your letter a few days ago stating that you would send some of them by him. You spoke of an overcoat that you were having made . . . . One thing that I will need very bad that is a pair of warm gloves. I cannot handle my musket without it.

[It] would freeze my hands. Another is a good pair of boots. Shoes will not be of much service in snow knee deep. The citizens tell me the snow is 22 inches deep at times. I will need an undercoat but I am putting you to financially too much trouble but if you have one made have it regular military with brass buttons. I will need one or two pair of socks. They can be had without much trouble. There can't be anything got here. Accept my thanks for what you have done for me . . . . My hands have been sore with poison. They are near about well now. Give my best love to all the family and all the county.

Truly Yours Respectfully,

W.O. Ruddock

PS. Have the legs of the boots long so as to come over my pants. We are expecting a fight every day. I do wish I was able to join in it. I would soon be able if they did not impose on me here. I won't stand it but a day or two long . . .

Lynchburg, Va. April 28, 1863

Dear Uncle,

Your very kind letter was received a few days ago. Also your letter to the surgeon has been received. But do not know as yet what effect it will have toward getting a discharge. I hope it will have the desired effect. The surgeon of this hospital is a very strict old cod from Edenton, N.C. known as Dr. Warren. He has not been in charge of this hospital but a short time. He has never examined me consequently does not know my case. He told me yesterday he had received a letter from you but had been otherwise engaged and neglected to enquire for and examine me. I don't know whether that was a plan to get off or not, anyhow he promised to examine me and see what he could do. I told him I did not think I would be able to stand the service that I thought I had tried it sufficiently to know that my constitution was too weak . . . .

In your letter to me you spoke of writing to Capt. and Colonel Johnston. I think you could have more influence with them than with Warren. If I fail to get a discharge or furlough here I will go to my regiment and try there and I think with the aid of Colonel Johnston I think I will be successful. If I were able to stand it I would do so cheerfully but I am not able and do not wish to be enduring the hardships of the army when I can do nothing for my country . . . . Now if I could get a situation in Charlotte a situation as Assistant Quartermaster or Commissary it would be much better but I would have to have a discharge or certificate of disability even to take the situation. I think it would be easily gotten to take a situation in the C.S. My health is tolerable but have not much strength . . . . I will let you know when I am examined and the result. I sent you a paper the other day containing an address which contains a great many facts concerning the war . . . . I read home papers with a great deal of interest. Give my respects to all my friends. I will close asking you to write as soon as convenient.

Yours Respectfully,

Wm. O. Ruddock[18]

———————

After battles, the number of wounded outpaced the workers. Surgeons began to ask for women to volunteer. The medical department placed ads in newspapers:

To the Ladies: Those ladies who are willing to devote a part of their time to nursing sick soldiers belonging to the companies stationed at the Marine Hospital, are respectfully requested to hand their names to the undersigned . . .[19]

Ministers from the pulpit called out for women to donate supplies and their time to assist in the hospitals. Female nurses stepped in to freshen up the hospital and keep it clean. While some surgeons thought the ladies were interfering in their space, others felt them a godsend. Confederate Congress passed a law in September of 1862 defining the duties and compensation for female nurses:

> The report presents many valuable and interesting statistical facts, showing the superiority of female nurses as compared with males. Mr. Semmes reported that "where males have charge [of hospitals], the mortality averages ten per cent; where females manage, it is only five per cent."
>
> There be allowed to each hospital with rations and suitable places of lodging the following matrons in chief, at a salary not to exceed $40. per month . . . . whose duties shall be to exercise a superintendence over the entire domestic economy of the hospital, to take charge of such delicacies as may be provided for the sick; to apportion them out as required; to see that food or diet properly prepared, and all such other duties as may be necessary.
>
> Assistant matrons [there should be two] shall superintend the laundry, to take charge of the clothing of the sick, the bedding of the hospital, to see that they are kept clean and neat. Their salary is not to exceed $35 per month. Surgeons in charge are authorized to employ such other nurses, either male or female, and pay them not to exceed $25 per month. Cooks are to receive $25 a month.[20]

Two ward matrons were the usual. Other duties consisted of doling out medicines, helping with bedside treatments, whitewashing the wards, and controlling the whiskey ration. Due to mismanagement while under the control of the surgeons, in 1862, Congress ordered the ward matrons to be in charge of the liquor cabinet. They further stated that females were the first choice for ward masters. If a male was chosen, he must be free from military service. The surgeon of the hospital could detail a soldier who was designated as "skillful and competent." He had the chance to be permanently assigned if he was good. He could also be dismissed by the surgeon for neglect and inattention. So it was settled. Women now had an official place in the hospital with amenities. However, some women chose not to receive any compensation.[21] Black men and women, both free and slave, found employment in the wards.

Dr. T. F. Wood stated, "Many ladies wanted to imitate Florence Nightingale, but . . . had not prepared themselves by study or practice in the art of nursing, and who having some success at home nursing a single patient, were greatly at sea when they undertook to look after numbers of rough soldiers, with few of the appliances at home." He went on to say: "There was a matron in the hospital a sister of Dr. Robert Gibbon of Charlotte, who had left her home to minister to the sick. She had a good deal of zeal . . . but little knowledge of her duties . . ."[22]

That fall of 1861, the North Carolina Hospital opened in Petersburg, Virginia, supervised by Dr. Peter Hines. Working with him as assistant surgeons were Dr. Henry Hines and Dr. F. M. Anderson. Mrs. C. G. Kennedy, of Wilmington, served as chief matron, with Mrs. Mary A. Beasley, of Tyrrell County, and Ms. Mary Pettigrew, sister of General Pettigrew, as her assistants.[23] Mrs. Beasley served for four years and gained the moniker Mother Beasley. Ms. Pettigrew was known as the Florence Nightingale of the South.[24] Mrs. Eliza Kremer, a teacher and president of the Ladies Relief Association of Salem, went with a group of women (Lizetta Stewart, L. Shaub, Laura Vogler, and Margaret Clewell) to a hospital in Culpeper, Virginia, to help with the wounded.[25]

In July, the first year of war, several ladies from Mecklenburg County left their homes to nurse the sick in Yorktown, Virginia, taking with them wagonloads of supplies. They only stayed until September, though doctors asked for more women from North Carolina to come and help with the fourteen hundred causalities from their state.[26] Annie Eliza Johns traveled to Danville to nurse the sick and wounded. Ms. Kay Gibbon, mentioned before, working in Yorktown, Virginia, had a notice posted in the *Weekly Catawba Journal* asking for provisions while the patient census was down:

> Many of the hospitals are suspended for the purpose of ventilation and cleansing in preparation, perhaps for the spring battles; also to get clear of all the vestiges of the still lingering small pox.

A wayside hospital across from the Spotswood Hotel in Richmond requested fresh vegetables for the sick soldiers. The article went on to say that Ms. Gibbon had permission to visit Charlotte for ten days to collect food and hospital supplies "as may be furnished for the use of this hospital . . ."[27] It was common practice for Virginia hospitals to request articles from other states. At Chimborazo Hospital in Richmond, Phoebe Pember, head matron, had to dismiss a North Carolina woman who failed to do her nursing job. Nursing was "a job [that] was unfit for self-respecting women . . ." No explanation was given why she was discharged.[28] Mary Eliza Gore served as a nurse in a Richmond hospital until she contracted a disease and died. Her husband had served with the Sampson Grays, Twentieth Regiment, and died as well.[29]

Though not as large as other battles in the state, Kinston, New Bern, Plymouth, Washington, and other cities Down East had casualties that overtaxed their small hospitals. The New Bern Methodist Church was turned into a hospital. Mrs. F. C. Roberts first sent nourishment to the patients, then went to the depot with her children and nanny in preparation to flee the city before the enemy appeared. Mrs. Elizabeth Carraway Harland studied medicine with her father. He treated Confederate prisoners ill with yellow fever when it broke out in New Bern in 1864.[30] While the outbreak did not claim the number of casualties as the epidemic in Wilmington two years before, it was significant to make a Charleston newspaper:

> The *Goldsboro Journal* learns upon good authority that yellow fever is prevailing at Newbern. The number of deaths daily is said to be from twenty to forty, and the number increases.
>
> This is certainly a large mortality for a place like Newbern, unless indeed there be a goodly number of Yankee traders or runaway negroes, all of which classes would make good food for fever and we trust that a respectable number of them may be devoured by Bronze John.[31]

Mrs. Alex Taylor also nursed yellow fever patients. Taylor frequented the prison, carrying provisions to the Southrons. "She was a prison angel, secretly clothing and feeding the destitute sufferers."[32]

Young women in Goldsboro assisted the older ladies at the hospital. Ms. Patsy Blount took three soldiers in her own home to nurse them back to health. She fed many more every night. Ms. Fanny Owens of Goldsboro converted a few rooms in her home as a substitute hospital.[33] Mary "Ms. May" H. Carraway Parker worked at the hospital. Her home was near the Wilmington and Weldon Railroad.[34]

Fatima Worth, of Fayetteville, grew on twenty-six acres of her farmland poppies for the sick and wounded in her home, which was a temporary medical facility. Though a frail woman on crutches, Mrs. Annie K. Kyle gave her time as a chief matron in the hospital when the Southern veterans started their leave of Fayetteville before Sherman's troops entered the city. She, along with her uncle, Dr. Kyle, gathered all the food they could for the patients. Mrs. Kyle and other ladies cooked for days to feed the soldiers. After the skirmish at the Longstreet community, the hospital needed her more, so Mrs. Kyle tended the wounded. The next morning, when she returned to the hospital, all but two of the wounded were gone, the others having left during the night.[35]

Another Fayetteville resident, Alice Campbell, helped with the sick. Federal officers commandeered her home in 1865. She asked one officer if she might take some things to the one hundred Confederate prisoners rounded up behind her house. Surprisingly, he consented. Mrs. Campbell passed out many pairs of socks, hats, and gloves that the knitting society had made. Alice had been president of the knitting society. She described the scene:

> They took all the horses in town that they could not take away with them
> and put them in an enclosure on Cool Springs Street, and shot them; so they
> left hundreds of dead horses lying there, there being no way to get rid of them.
> They were burned, and you may try to imagine the odor . . .[36]

In Wilmington, Dr. and Mrs. Armand J. (Eliza L.) DeRosset treated the defenders at Fort Fisher. Other local women who assisted at the fort were the wife of Major Stevenson and her sister, Mary F. Saunders. Ms. Mary Ann Buie, another Wilmington citizen, known as the "soldier's comforter," collected food and money for hospital use for soldiers in North Carolina and Petersburg, Virginia.

Mrs. Mary A. Wrenn, of Rowan County, took the position of chief matron of the immense hospital in Salisbury. With her daughter Betty, "they sold their silver, jewelry, and clothing . . . . to buy food for the patients." Sarah Johnston worked untiringly as a nurse there too. She had a son in the Confederate Navy stationed on the CSS *Albemarle*. She also took fresh food to the prisoners. Local civilians would often visit the prisoners, bringing them food and sometimes buying or trading their trinkets before conditions became worse in 1864.[37]

Once the students left the North Carolina Military Institute in Charlotte, the building was converted into a hospital. A Mrs. Wilkes took charge of the nursing department and was called the Godmother of Charlotte Hospitals.[38] Greensboro and Highpoint were on the main rail line, making them good locations for wayside hospitals. One woman stands out in her effort to get things rolling in this capacity. Mary Watson Smith, wife of Rev. Jacob H. Smith, nursed the sick and wounded, fed the troops, and persuaded local women to do the same. Other women involved included Mrs. Montgomery, who oversaw the Wayside Hospital, and Mrs. Jesse McCallum, who offered her services to the sick at the old garrison. Ruth Worth Porter, a physician, stayed in Greensboro and helped the community as well as the soldiers.[39] Once the Piedmont Railroad had been completed from Danville, Virginia, to Greensboro in 1864, the Piedmont became General Lee's lifeline. This meant much greater activity with troop movements. Canteen workers met those trains.

Edgeworth Female Seminary, the courthouse, and the Presbyterian church were used as hospitals in Greensboro after casualties came in from the Battle of Bentonville. A lady wrote in her reminiscences that she left the church that night and returned the next morning to find the dead laid in a semicircle around the pulpit. The town was divided into districts, and the female residents of each neighborhood would feed the men nearest them. "Children would beg to go with their parents when they attended the sick and wounded." Boys would talk with the soldiers, and girls would bring flowers. Of the 234 patients in the church who died, only four were identified. "The benevolent objects of our church were allowed to be suspended . . . ," during wartime, said one woman.[40]

High Point had a general military hospital as well as a wayside hospital staffed by women. The High Point Female Seminary gave a concert, a "soireé musicale," for the soldiers there and sang an original song called "Camp Fisher."[41] Ladies opened their homes to offset the crowding upon the arrival of the wounded from Bentonville. The wayside hospital, formerly the old Barbee Hotel, treated over five thousand troops during the war. Only fifty of those died. Twenty-year-old Ms. Laura Wesson was passing through High Point and became sympathetic to the plight of ill soldiers lying around. She stayed and assisted medical personnel, treating smallpox victims, unfortunately contracting it herself. Poor Laura died within three months of her arrival. Another nurse, an unknown Quaker lady, helped with the smallpox victims in the "pest house," located on the outskirts of town. She had recently been vaccinated and used part of her own scab to vaccinate local children.[42] Laura C. Vogler cooked at the Blantyre Wayside Hospital, which was near her home. She would not turn away any soldier who needed assistance. Other Salem ladies—Lizetta Stewart, Ms. L. Shaub, Ms. Margaret Clewell, Ms. Mary Elizabeth Clewell, and Mrs. Eliza Kremer—gave their time during the war as nurses.[43]

For three years, life went on as usual at Kittrell Springs. Parties and balls continued until 1864 when the wounded came and the resort was converted for hospital use. In June 1864, it was commandeered as general hospital no. 1. Mrs. Sarah Elliot, a refugee from Elizabeth City, settled in Oxford and cared for the patients at Kittrell. By June 28, three hundred sick veterans settled in as patients, with many of these the Junior Reserves.[44] Mrs. Elliot was the mother of Gilbert Elliot who constructed the CSS *Albemarle*.

The historian Crawford argues that "families negotiated . . . personal crises [such as soldiers absences or death] with varying degrees of success. . . . The strength and effectiveness of kin and neighborhood support system were a key determinant of household's prospect of survival."[45] Women wanted their ill relative under their own care. A mother, Jane Hanes, of Davie County, was truly fortunate enough to be able to travel to Virginia to retrieve her dying son, Spencer. He was nursed back to health at home and lived through the war.[46] A Greene County mother went to Richmond four times during the war to nurse her sons, pick up their bodies, and return home.[47]

One anonymous patient wrote that the ladies visited every week and brought provisions. Soldiers loved to have visitors as noted in chapter 4; however, it taxed the patience of hospital workers:

> . . . a suggestion to those who come here on errands of Mercy. I think it is not deemed desirable that large numbers of ladies should visit the wards at the same time. This often produces in very sick patients unusual excitement which often results in injury . . .[48]

That statement was probably written by a female nurse. Medical personnel did complain from time to time about the number of visitors in the wards. Medical personnel felt that these long-staying kinfolk got in their way. Victorian women dressed in the big hoopskirts, and there was very little space between the cots. At times, the soldier's wife would "camp out" next to his bed, staying for days. You also had family members who sneaked home remedies to the patient. A Greene County mother went to Richmond to nurse her son sick with typhoid. She had carried a coop of live chickens with her to make broth. She actually made the trip four times. When her other son, Jim, was killed at Chancellorsville, she went to retrieve the body but could not find it.[49] Mrs. Cooper, of Asheville, traveled to Georgia to retrieve her thrice-wounded son, Dr. V. W. Cooper, following the Battle of Marietta. After twenty days of healing, they were able to make the trip home.[50] Without antibiotics, unknown at that period, it took months for wounds to heal. In hospital no. 8 in Raleigh, a soldier mentioned his boredom to his betrothed so that she would come to see him.[51]

Sophia A, Partridge, originally from New York, lived in Louisburg. A woman of many talents, she ran the Select School for Young Ladies in Raleigh. The school stayed opened during the war. Martha and Caroline Jordan and Mrs. John Bobbitt assisted at the school. Partridge nursed the wounded and organized her students and other ladies to help out at the hospitals.*[52]

The small city of Weldon on the rail line between Wilmington and Petersburg exploded with troops. It became a training camp for the new recruits. The Reverend John Garlick and his wife, along with neighborhood ladies, attended to ill soldiers in Garysburg. The

---

*   She was also a painter, having her works illustrated in the *Orator*, a monthly paper published by Thomas J. Lemay. Her work called *A Wreath from the Woods of Carolina* was published in 1859.

United Methodist Church, converted to a hospital, became refuge to the troops passing on their way to and from the Virginia front.[53] Mrs. Ida Wilkins and Mrs. Hamlin Allen nursed ill soldiers in their homes. In Granville County, several ladies contacted Richmond authorities to let them nurse one hundred or more sick or convalescing troops. Richmond complied. Some women took into their home four, some two, and others more.[54]

Annie Johns in Rockingham County volunteered her services at a hospital in Danville, Virginia. Johns collected books, magazines, milk, fresh vegetables, sugar, and feather pillows from her neighbors for hospital use when available. Mrs. Johns became the assistant matron in charge of clothing at the former tobacco warehouse converted to the hospital. She revealed that her first paycheck of thirty-five dollars went to purchase pictures for the hospital walls to brighten up the quarters. The nurses planted tomato plants in window boxes. Running short on supplies, she had soap made to wash the bedding and hospital clothes.

Once when she and her cohorts complained about the way ill soldiers from Richmond were sent to Danville (in a boxcar without heat), the newspapers picked up the story. Afterwards, she said it was not repeated. Most surgeons had been programmed to return the invalid back to his regiment or to do detail work such as to be hospital assistant, to drive wagons, etc. Mrs. Johns discovered a recovering soldier with a leg amputation acting as a nurse. The female nurses argued that such patients should be furloughed to recover at home. They believed the soldier would mend faster at home.

Mrs. Johns repeated the complaints of other matrons in dealing with the soldiers' wives and mothers who came for a visit and stayed—for days!

> Late one afternoon, during a pouring rain. There came a knock at the door leading to our rooms. On opening the door I found several women, with two babies, who had walked twenty and thirty miles that day, to take the train the next morning to visit their husband in camp. A woman in my neighborhood said she could not get along without talking to Mr. ___, her husband. As to whether he expressed the same desire to her talk, I did not understand.

Visitors got in the way of the hospital workers. In another incident, Annie Johns said:

> One day an order was received from the Government, which surprised me much, though on further experience of the subject I confess that I understand it better. It was that all alcoholic liquors used for the sick soldiers should be taken out of the hands of the hospital stewards and surgeons, and put in those of the matrons. It was a responsibility which I did not in the least desire, but there was no help for it . . . She also said one patient died from a medical overdose.

Though she failed to mention the year, Johns admitted that the former tobacco warehouse turned hospital converted to a prison. She continued to visit the ill inmates whenever possible and carried them food. "The feeling between the Confederates and federal prisoners seemed to be that of entire cordiality. I have known Confederate soldiers as they passed through Danville to take the provisions from their own haversacks and give them to federal prisoners on their way to Salisbury [prison]." Mrs. Johns concluded, "A soldier, even the most common, was to us an embodiment of chivalry, and rarely did we have occasion to look upon him in any other light." She was unafraid to work among the hundreds of men while nursing the enemy prisoners. Nurses on both sides echoed these sentiments.[55]

The rainy month of March 1865 was no different except that this particular spring, Harnett County inhabitants viewed thousands upon thousands of the blue-coated enemy marching across their fields. Confederate General Johnston sought to stop or delay General Sherman's march. He chose to take a stand first at Averasboro, then a week later at Bentonville. Three wealthy Smith brothers around Averasboro had their homes commandeered as hospitals. Family members were drawn in to assist the wounded on both sides. Four miles North at Averasboro, the Confederates left some of the grievously wounded men to the mercy of the townspeople. Teenager Janie Smith and her family rolled bandages and brought food to the sick and wounded soldiers. Every barn and shed was filled with wounded men. Amputations were performed under the cedar trees, using tables that had been carried from the house. The blood lay in puddles in the grove; the groans of the dying and the complaints of those undergoing amputation were horrible, as told by Janie. Neill Stewart's home in Averasboro also took in wounded men. An Arkansas soldier was cared for by the McClellan family but died, so he was buried in the family cemetery. Other wounded Southern casualties from the battle were carried across the Cape Fear River to be cared for by families there. Those that died were buried at Bunnlevel.[56]

Near the little village of Bentonville, in Johnston County, the Harper house served as a hospital for both armies.* The Harpers and their children, along with neighbors, nursed the wounded during the spring of March 1865 and into early summer. One neighbor, Penny L. Autrey, and her fifteen-year-old brother volunteered to help the Harpers. Mrs. Joab Lee went to Mrs. Harper and offered her aid with the fifty wounded men left behind.[57] Perhaps the ladies had to use this formula to help with the odors in the homes occupied by convalescing veterans: "To correct the offensive odors of war wounds, mix 100 parts of calcined plaster of Paris and 2 parts of coal tar. Rub together. Sprinkle on the wound twice daily."[58]

After the battles of Averasboro and Bentonville, towns located along the rail line, where the wayside hospitals had developed, began to overflow. Most available buildings, private homes, and churches saw an influx of the wounded. This was especially true of the piedmont section of the state, including Charlotte. Other women who served as nurses were Jane Wilkes and Sallie Chapman Gordon Law.

The Episcopal church in Raleigh became a temporary hospital where Mary N. Bryan assisted with the sick. Church pews became beds for many unfortunate men.[59] Also used as a medical facility, the Guion Hotel filled with the wounded. Residents opened their doors for the sick. It was as if a tide of mangled soldiers had swept over the area, with each new wave bringing more and more men needing help, pushing them further and further away from the enemy. "About six hospitals have been taken charge of by the ladies, who tend the sick and spare no pains. Miss Patsy Blount took three into her house and usually has about six soldiers to eat with her. The men were sick with measles, and typhoid fever," reported an article in *Carolina and the Southern Cross.*[60]

At Pettigrew Hospital in Raleigh, Mrs. Mary Saddler worked at the site for six months, leaving on March 31, 1865. Mrs. Mary E. Roberts and a Ms. Skinner were ward matrons at this large facility run by Dr. E. Burke Haywood.[61]

When the wounded from both sides were placed together in a hospital, most patients or nurses did not mind; however, a woman working in a Union hospital in eastern North Carolina "was so incensed at the prospect of treating the enemy's wounds that she had all the Confederate wounded removed from her ward."[62] A Northern soldier serving in the occupied territory near New Bern summed up the way men felt about female nurses:

> . . . as to helping the soldiers, there is nothing so much wanted in the hospitals as the service of ladies, using that noun in its broadest sense; intelligent refined, judicious, whole-hearted women are needed as the soldiers protectors and friends in the hospitals against the avarice and heartlessness and injustice to which the sick and wounded are often exposed. This, their incidental work, is of a most valuable service.[63]

---

*   For a good description for both battles, see chapters 19 and 22.

The following North Carolina women outstepped the bounds of the female sphere of domesticity. They chose to risk their lives in service for the Confederacy and their state. Whether by smuggling goods and food or acting as spies, most felt a patriotic duty to help in some way.

Women of the state followed the current fashion of wearing the enormous hoopskirt. The fashion made an ideal vessel for smuggling. Underneath the hoop, the girl wore several petticoats. These petticoats would have numerous small pockets sewn in, waiting to be filled with contraband. President Lincoln had declared medicine a "contraband of war," and he put a blockade upon the Southern people, making it very difficult to obtain drugs. Medicine such as morphine, opium, and quinine seemed to be the most needed and desired. Mail hidden in the pockets was lightweight and easy to conceal. Larger objects such as shoes or pistols could be tied with strings to their waists. Metal objects were wrapped in padded cloth to keep them from "clanging" together. Clever girls secreted innumerable articles under these skirts. The wife of Dr. Miller of Kinston was Northern-born. She was traveling South on the steamer *Mississippi* carrying Massachusetts soldiers to North Carolina. She said she was loyal to the North; however, a search of her trunk yielded a large quantity of quinine. Later, the Federal officers went to her home and burned Miller's cotton and other things.[64]

Preparing pockets for smuggling

Military officials never dreamed that those delicate creatures would attempt to interfere with war issues, which was another reason females did so well. The women may be suspected, though at first they were not searched. This changed after frustrated Union authorities attempted to locate the source of the covert activity, which embarrassed them. The official would locate a black woman to examine the suspected lady and her clothing.

Civilian operatives arrested were mostly classified as spies. "When a military man was captured, it became very important to him to be classified as a 'scout' and not a 'spy.'" Scouts were given prison sentences while spies were either shot or hung.

The wearing of the uniform did not necessarily prevent a man from being classified as a spy according to the "Rules of Land Warfare:"

> The fact of being in the enemy's lines dressed as a civilian or wearing
> the enemies uniform is presumed to constitute a spy, but it is possible

to rebut this presumption by proof of no intention to obtain military information . . .[65]

A Southern soldier wearing civilian clothing in Federal territory could be hanged as a spy; however, if the same man were arrested wearing a Confederate uniform, he would be treated as a prisoner of war. Women civilians were known to keep a Confederate uniform for agents they may assist. For her to be found with the uniform was dangerous, and she would have to have a good explanation for Federal authorities or be arrested.[66] Federal officers would rather expel Confederate females suspected of disloyalty than deal with them.

Once Federal troops occupied the New Bern/Beaufort area, espionage commenced. U.S. General Foster's officers were baffled as to how the Southern army knew their plans. How was the mail getting through? There must have been a leak. That leak was due to local teens and ladies. Ms. Abigail Hart kept Northern soldiers as houseguests in order to learn their secrets.[67] Sixteen-year-old Sidneth Ann Canady was captured as a spy during the Union occupation of Newport.[68] Susan P. Longest wore a petticoat with many pockets in which to smuggle food, medicine, supplies, and letters to soldiers stationed at Russell's Creek.[69] Susan, known for her fiery temper, once threw her bucket of water, along with the bucket into the face of a Federal officer. It took the intervention of the mayor and friends to release her from custody.[70]

Twenty-five-year-old Emeline Pigott, of Harlowe Township, early on helped with the sick and wounded soldiers. Near Morehead City, wrote author Wilson, "she had fisherman meet Northern vessels, ostensibly to sell them fish, but really to find out about tonnage of each cargo and what port they were going to next. She passed this information on to military and civilian authorities." Emeline witnessed the battle and capture of New Bern.[71] More is known on Ms. Pigott, vice president of the Soldier's Aid Society of Morehead City. "She loved Private Stokes MacRae. Pigott would refuse to attend officer's balls because privates were not allowed at those functions. She made Stokes a tiny silk Confederate flag that he carried with him." Unfortunately, Private MacRae died at Gettysburg. Emeline continued to nurse soldiers in her father's home. She also helped in the hospitals in New Bern until the Union army arrived. Ms. Pigott stayed with the sick and wounded as the town was being evacuated by train. Soon, her patients were transferred to Kinston. She continued to assist the sick at Kinston until those soldiers were removed to Concord. Again, she traveled with them. "At Concord Emeline befriended a Mrs. Brent, the widow of a chaplain from the Federal army. Together they 'worked their way through the Federal lines' and returned to Morehead City."

Emeline Pigott, Confederate Spy
N.C. Division of Archives & History, Photographic Archives

Emeline Pigott's Buggy

"With the aid of her brother-in-law, Rufus Bell, Emeline ran a regular blockade service certain days in the weeks. Mail was distributed under logs in the woods, and to a well known tree, food, clothing and quinine were carried, and by means of special signals the men were notified." She entertained Federal officers who commandeered their home while Rufus carried food to Southern troops nearby.

"In Beaufort there were many strangers, who were profiting by the war conditions, among them were two northerners, with their help she was able to take through the lines to the southern boys such articles of food, clothing, and medicines as she could conceal beneath her 'hoop skirt.' One day there dropped from these two northern men some very valuable information, <u>as she thought</u> to the Southern cause and she succeeded in persuading them to give it to her in writing. With this information hid next to her heart, and her hoop skirt loaded, she started with Rufus Bell on her regular rounds. This day, however, they didn't pass the lines so easily, they had already been suspicioned, so were arrested by the Yankees and sent to jail in Beaufort. Mr. Bell was searched first, finding no writing of suspicious nature on his person, he was released. The order was then given to search Miss Emeline; a negro woman was delegated to do the job, but she didn't succeed, Miss Emeline protesting, told her if she came near she would 'shoot to kill,' that she was used to a negro maid, but if they would send a white woman whom she knew she would not object to being searched." This was just a feigning excuse to delay the search so she would have time to destroy the note.

"While the officers were securing someone to do the searching, Emeline chewed the memorandum of information and swallowed it," also tearing up the mail in small pieces. "When the searching party came back and found the scattered bits of mail they were very angry, but proceeded with the search and found concealed under the famous 'hoop skirt' almost everything from a fine tooth comb to a suit of clothes."*

She was then ordered to prison at New Bern (on Edenton and Pollock Streets), but was permitted to spend the night with her parents.** By urgent request, her cousin, Mrs. L. W. Pigott, was allowed to go to prison with her the next day.

"Miss Emeline was in prison one month, during which time the people of Newbern were exceedingly kind to her, especially the little Taylor boys who carried her food every day. Day after day she was brought from prison for the trial, but for some reason the trial was never held. She would most assuredly have been killed as a spy if the trial had taken place. During her stay in prison she was subjected to all kinds of embarrassments and indignities as well as exposure to conditions over which she had no effort to correct the almost unbearable conditions of the jail.

---

*   Keep reading for the list of articles secreted under her skirt.

**   The "prison" referred to was actually the Jones House, the town jail during Union occupation.

"One night an attempt was made to kill her and her cousin by pouring chloroform through a broken panel in the door. Her cousin was asleep, but Miss Emeline was wide awake; as soon as the fumes reached her she realized the situation immediately . . . and they began to devise some means to avoid the deadly effects of the chloroform. Fortunately a window pane was broken and from this source fresh air was breathed by first one and [then] the other until the strength of the chloroform died away sufficiently to enable them to escape death. In the meantime a guard on duty from the outside came near enough that they could relate the circumstances, so he rendered necessary assistance and the situation was relieved.

"Immediately after the attempt to destroy her life, the two men whom she had met at Beaufort and volunteered what she thought was information she could rely upon, but which proved to be an intrigue to trap her, were sent for, and came to the jail. She said to them 'If I die here, you'll die also,' they knew of course what she meant, so these two imposters at once set about to have her released, which was done without delay, and she returned . . . home. The Federals watched her closely after that. Every night her home was searched for contraband. Emeline was never arrested again."[72]

Once when Pigott was arrested in the last few months of the war, a Union officer wrote this in his diary:

> Questioned by the mayor, the young lady declared she had no contraband goods about her person. But on being searched by two women a number of articles were found beneath her hoops. She wore two pairs of Pants and a pair of boots. She is now in confinement. The provost arrested a number of Beaufort citizens disorderly and some drunk at Lowenberg's store. I suppose that this has something to do with the case of Miss Pigott.
>
> This afternoon a rebel deserter now in the 1st North Carolina Volunteers discovered the form of a pair of shoes bulging out of a lady's dress. Afterwards the mayor had the lady brought to the office where she was examined by Aunt Ednay [black]. The lady was . . . much opposed to this move but had to submit. Aunt Ednay found a number of articles put in sacks under the hoops. When she first had a permit made out these articles were not mentioned in it, but afterward when she found that she was suspected she got Wilson [a clerk in the office of the Provost Marshall] to put them down. I think she meant to smuggle.[73]

Jail where Emeline Pigott was held, New Bern
UNC Collection of Photographic Archives

The *Old North State*, a paper published in occupied Beaufort, reported on February 18, 1865, an article on Ms. Pigott:

> She blustered about high toned Southern ladies as though they could do nothing wrong . . . the following stock in trade was found concealed under her clothes: 1 pair of fine boots; 2 pair of pants; 1 shirt; 1 naval cap; 1 dozen linen pocket handkerchiefs; 1 dozen linen collars; 50 skeins of sewing silk; a lot of spool cotton and needles; tooth brushes; hair combs; 2 pocket knives; one razor; 4-5 pounds of assorted candy; dressing pins; several pairs gloves; also several letters addressed to rebels denouncing the federals . . . and giving information about supposed movement of federal troops. It is one of the most important arrests that has been made.

Remember this is only *one* time she was caught. Think of all that Southern women smuggled under their skirts! Emeline wrote in a diary:

> January 29, 1865 Lieut. General Grant has touched at this point from sea on his way somewhere with his staff.
>
> Jan 25th, 65 Lient Gen Grant in town today came over from Morehead with his staff. A [*illegible*] is no doubt fast for the capture of Wilmington.
>
> March 1st, 65 Over twenty thousand it is estimated have arrived within a week. Many of them are from Schermans army south.*
>
> February, 1865 Troops are arriving at Morehead City from the north and the general belief is that a march into the interior of our state, from Morehead City or Newbern is designed. Preparations are being made today for the track of a rail road as the army advances. A thousand work-men have arrived at Morehead City within a few days, for the purpose of working on the road. Others are already at Newbern.
>
> Feb 8th—On leaving Beaufort I was arrested on suspicion of being engaged in carrying Confederate mail to Confederate soldiers, [and] mailing Confederate spic [specie] and blockad[e] runner. Thes[e] charges I do deny [.] The two out fits that I had [on] was for two Confederate officers in the Confederate army [.] I did it to accommodate an old gentleman friend who sent them to his two sons in the Confederate army [.] I never knew exactly what I had. Or how much, I often met the Confederate scouts as I often carried the scouts their meals in the roads [.] they had places to hide[.] some times Yankees would be in the house while the Confederates were both fed from the same table. [ed. Note: but not at the same time] On one occasion we had quite a large crowd of citizens of Beaufort who were true to the south who . . . . [diary ends][74]

Once Emeline was arrested, a "large, prominent store in Beaufort was closed as it was said to be in complicity with Miss Pigott."[75] Emeline Pigott died in 1919 and is buried in Morehead City.

---

*   Out of sequence in her notes

arnoldus vanderhorst
1 2 3 4 5 6 7 8 9 10 11 12 13 14 15 16 17 18 '9

a b c d e f g h i j k l m n o p q
1 20 21 6 13 22 23 15 24 25 26 5 27 3 16 28 2;
10 12 11 4

r s t u v w x y z
2/3 8/11 19 7 9/17 30 31/32 33

I me or mine. *write* = 0   Double letter a ll ·5·5·=·5·2
You your yours   „ = 1'   write thus l²
he him his   „ = 2'   Numerals a 48– (48)
We us ours   „ = 3'
They their theirs „ = 4·
Who whom whose   „ = 5''
that _ _ _ _   „ = 6'
which _ _ _   „ = 7
that _ _ _ _   „ = 8
the _ _ _ _ _   „ = 9 .

N.C. Confederate Cipher Code
T.H. Holmes Family Papers, Perkins Library, Duke University

A female rider from New Bern delivered a note to a North Carolina citizen and told him to ride with haste to headquarters in Trenton. The note was completely blank. Confederate Colonel Stephen Pool took the note to a friend's home while the lady of the house heated an iron. He then took a hot iron and ironed the blank paper whereby words appeared reporting the movements and strength of Federal General Foster's army in New Bern. Confederate officers reacted to the news, and Southern troops were sent to block him. That night rider was most likely Emeline Pigott or Mary Frances Chadwick.[76]

In the end of 1864, two attempts were struck to destroy other North Carolina lighthouses, "partially in retaliation against the traitorous keepers who were working for the Union." A party of Southern sympathizers sailed the Core Sound in April of 1864 to the Cape Lookout Lighthouse. Emeline Pigott was the lookout. Attempts to blow up the lighthouse failed, but it did damage it slightly.[77]

Parents used their children to observe the enemy because children would not be suspected. After New Bern fell to the enemy Mr. W. H. Marshall "managed to communicate with Capt. Tolson of Whitford's regiment, and by the aid of a lady from Swift Creek, J.H. Hunter, and Capt. Broughton carried on a secret correspondence with Confederate officials in Kinston . . ."* Marshall sent his twelve-year-old son to Havelock to "learn how many of the enemy were there." The boy went to the camp on the pretense of selling lemonade and cigars. He learned which regiments were there, the number of guns and cannons, the number of tents and men, etc. This was relayed to Kinston.[78]

Another woman used her children in espionage. "Mrs. Elizabeth C. Howland of New Bern wrote down specifications of Yankee forts under construction." She was able to send messages rolled up inside a hambone. The children would present the guard with flowers, and he would let them pass without being searched. Mrs. Howland had studied medicine with her father and helped treat the Southern patients when yellow fever occurred in New Bern.[79]

A northern-born lady married to a physician in the Confederate Army, after being harassed by Southern sympathizers, decided early in 1861 to visit her parents in Vermont. Mrs. Dellia Miller left Kinston with her small daughter for the trip North. The daughter caught diphtheria while there. Mrs. Miller decided to return home without her. She later

---

*   Perhaps this was Mary Frances Chadwick.

traveled back to Vermont to pick up her child. In order to help pay for the trip, Miller had hidden tobacco in her trunks. On her return home in February 1865, she managed to secrete twenty-five dollars worth of needles, a scarce commodity in the South. This trip for home became very difficult, much more so than before. An officer told her she would have to wait until the army finished its expedition, unless she wanted to go on the gunboat with them. Mrs. Miller chose the latter, and up the river they went, firing the guns. She asked the captain to please aim the guns away from the towns because they would be firing on the women and children. He complied.[80]

Mrs. Taylor Alexander had "deep pockets" in her petticoat with which she hid the mail for Confederate soldiers. She had permission to go freely about New Bern once occupied by the Northern army. Taylor visited the prison often smuggling mail and provisions to her rebel friends. Federal officers could not find the source as to who was distributing it.[81] Suspicioned, the officers questioned the lady, but all was denied. Mrs. Alexander was called the prison mother.[82]

Some civilians chose to stay at home while under occupation. One citizen, Mrs. Thomas (Anne) Sparrow, remained at her home with her two children. Because her husband served in the Southern army, she was accused of sending her husband information on troop activity. The Federal commander labeled her the Rebel Mailbag. Her children "considered it a grand title." She and the children were exiled into the country occupied by Confederates.[83] Nancy White, the daughter of a suspected guerilla, was accosted and exiled to Virginia as a prisoner.[84]

Other ladies involved in espionage were Mrs. Julia Lewis, who kept Northern officers in her home to learn important information for the South.[85] Mrs. Ann Meekins ran the blockade into New Bern to ascertain for General Lee the exact strength of the Federal forces before Fort Fisher was attacked. Disguised as a countrywoman with a bale of cotton to sell, she made the rounds, got the information needed, and safely went back through the lines.[86] Mary L. Ambrose, of Tyrrell County, with a Negro boy as her only companion, penetrated the Union lines on horseback with five hundred dollars in cash strapped about her waist. She succeeded in delivering the money to the Confederate lines near Tarboro.[87] Another possible spy could have been a Mrs. Grinnell. James Sprunt, in writing his memories, told, "The Confederate Government used to send some queer agents abroad at the expense of the people. A Mrs. Grinnell was sent out by the surgeon general—so she stated—to get bandages, etc. which nobody else . . . but Mrs. Grinnell could get." Grinnell was an upper-class Englishwoman claiming to be the daughter of a baronet.[88]

"The procedure of Carteret County agents in sending information to the Confederates was as follows: messages and reports were secreted through Union-held territory to Newbern, where another agent was met. He [or she] would somehow smuggle them out."[89] A secret correspondence was carried on for thirteen months until U.S. General Foster exiled forty families from New Bern out of the Federal lines.[90]

A letter was captured from a steamer in the Albemarle Sound from Augustus S. Montgomery of Washington City to General Foster of New Bern "proposing a general Negro insurrection, and destruction of all railroad bridges, etc., in the South." Governor Vance sent it to President Davis, who in turn sent it to General Lee. General Lee advised the governor not to publish it in the newspapers for fear of a generalized panic.[91]

Union officials in eastern North Carolina expected the Confederates to try to destroy the lighthouses. They had already removed the lights from Hatteras. Near the Hook of the Cape (Lookout Bay), two Federal steamers laid to watch activities in the area and guard upon invasion by the locals. The Southern forces had plans to destroy both the old and newer Cape Lookout lighthouses. Confederate soldiers made a feign attack on New Bern in early February 1864 to draw attention from their main goal, which was to blow up the lighthouses. It could not have been accomplished without the help of Confederate spies Josiah Bell and twenty-two-year-old Ms. Mary Francis Chadwick. Confederate Colonel

Whitford was her contact person in New Bern. She took the papers he gave her, hid them in secret pockets sewn inside her hoopskirt, and returned to Beaufort to allay suspicion. Chadwick then left and met Mr. Bell. Since the lighthouses were in enemy territory and this was to be carried out by a land force, extreme caution was necessary, for there were many Union sympathizers in the area. It was important to get reliable guides and boatmen. The clandestine foray took place over several days, and the perpetrators were never apprehended.[92]

Little is known about the "French lady" spy or the "French woman" from North Carolina rumored to have knowledge about the plot to assassinate President Lincoln. Sarah Antoinette "Nettie" Gilbert Slater—perceived as a petite, attractive, demure Northern-born lady—had moved with her father and three brothers to North Carolina.[93] All the brothers joined in Confederate service.[*] She married Rowan Slater, working in New Bern as a traveling dance instructor. After he went into military service, she left the state on her way to Richmond. There she secured a pass to move North to live with family. Sarah's sister and mother lived in New York. Confederate Secretary of War Seddon recruited her to act as a courier between Canada and Richmond probably because she spoke French. If caught, Nettie could always speak French and pretend she knew very little English.

For her safety, the French lady was accompanied on her trips by Confederate agents, passing through Maryland, Washington City, and New York. Mrs. Slater frequently visited Mary Surratt's home in Maryland. Sarah, or Nettie as she was known, used different aliases: Kate Brown, Mrs. Howell, Sarah Slater, Mrs. Olivet, Olivia Floyd, and Kate Thompson. Mrs. Slater totaled three missions transporting money and dispatches between Richmond, New York City, St. Albans, Vermont and Canada during her short career. On one of her forays, she carried dispatches and ciphers to Montreal relating to the St. Albans Confederate raiders. Slater delivered the papers and was to return to Richmond immediately. Apparently, the lady met John Surratt in New York, and he accompanied her to the Surratt house.[94]

She knew John Surratt, who saw that she traveled her route safely. She also met John Wilkes Booth in Washington in early April. On April 1, 1865, both Slater and John Surratt left Richmond on their way to New York thence on to Canada. It was known they carried a great deal of money.[95] Since it was near the war's end, Slater was to relay Confederate money stashed in Canada to England.

On April 4, 1865, Sarah Slater went to New York City, then vanished. Even her family never heard from her again. It was speculated that she had dispatch money and may have known of the plot to kill President Lincoln, so she left the country for parts unknown. She was never seen again.[**] Near Morehead City, a ciphered message, believed to be a hoax because it was too easy to decipher, was found on April 15, 1865. This message was introduced into the court records when Lincoln's assassins were tried.[96]

Could the next newspaper article be about the famous spy?

A Maryland Heroine

The Richmond correspondent of the Nashville *Union and American* communicates the following interesting paragraph about a Southern heroine

---

[*]   Confederate Lieutenant Eugene Gilbert was court-martialed for persuading fellow soldiers to desert. His two brothers deserted to the Union side in New Bern.

[**]   Postwar, an anonymous person sent a letter to a northern newspaper with information on Mrs. Slater. Booth's accomplices mentioned her to Federal investigators. She was brought in and questioned in May 1865, never jailed, then disappeared forever.[97] George Atzerodt stated, "She knew all about the affair"—meaning plans to assassinate President Lincoln.

now in Richmond: "Among the notabilities of the city, there is a Maryland heroine, young, pretty, wonderfully intelligent and accomplished, who preserves the strictest incognito, and is known even to her most intimate acquaintances only as Mademoiselle Nina. Small in person, almost fragile, she has nevertheless the courage of a lioness. Her whole soul is bent on the liberation of Maryland, and were her deeds, tending to this consummation, to be known, she could rank among the most famous women of history. Alone, unaided, by routes known only to herself she passes through the Confederate and Yankee lines, carrying hope to the oppressed and bringing material comforts for the free but exile[d] sons of her native land." [98]

Three Confederate men with a North Carolina connection were thought to have been involved in covert activities during wartime. Josiah Bell is mentioned earlier. Sally Hawthorne's half brother, Micheaux Waterbury ("my mother's older son by her first marriage"), had remained in the South and was in complete sympathy with the cause. Hawthorne wrote, "For a time he had charge of the telegraph office in Fayetteville and trained several young men . . . to do the work while he was waiting for orders. He was under General D.H. Hill and became a scout, a wild, reckless one, virtually a spy, for he had never lost his Northern accent. Whenever specific information was wanted, he would go through the lines, wearing a Federal uniform he had procured, get the information needed and hurry back to his chief with it. Most of his work was in southern Virginia, but sometimes he went over the state line, and then he would ride his horse almost to death in order to get home . . . . Our darling brother grew more and more daring as if the need grew greater to find out the secrets of the other side, til at last he was listed as a dangerous spy and a price put on his capture, dead or alive. He was captured and sent to Point Lookout, but escaped."[99]

"The Confederacy . . . employed pseudo-deserters to plant misinformation on the enemy."[100] Jacob Thompson, born in Person County, worked for Confederate authorities as head of the Secret Service, although it was called the Safety Committee, commanded by General John Winder.[101] Congress provisioned the department with one million dollars for their budget. Thompson was formally the U.S. secretary of the interior from 1857 to 1861. Isaac Applewhite, formerly a captain in the Confederate Army, was arrested on the charge of being a rebel spy.

Another scout, Franklin Foy, lived near New Bern; and his mother said the bluecoats placed a reward for his capture. The Federals set a trap for him, surrounding Mrs. Foy's home, and they forced her and the grandchildren inside. The troops stayed three days, all the while refusing food and water to the prisoners. Faithful slaves slipped them nourishment. The ruse failed, so they left empty-handed.[102]

SUSPICIOUS CHARACTER: These were the headlines featured in the Richmond Whig on November 12, 1864. "Miss Mary Jane Bayne, a young woman of fascinating appearance, was committed to Castle Thunder this morning as a suspicious character. She claims to be a native of North Carolina, but says that for a year . . . she has possessed as her paramour a certain Yankee lieutenant, who sojourned in Knoxville, Tennessee." Was Bayne a spy?

Two famous women from the South, Rose O'Neal Greenhow and Belle Boyd, noted as the Siren of the Shenandoah, passed through North Carolina. So much has been written on these spies that only their connection with the state will be mentioned. Carrying dispatches, Belle Boyd left Wilmington for England in May 1864. Soon, her ship was overtaken by the enemy, but not before Boyd burnt her dispatches in the vessel's furnace. After the ship was seized, navy men removed her to the USS Connecticut, where it was diverted to Hampton Roads, Virginia, then under Federal control.[103] A vessel subsequently took her to Boston, where she was later released.[104]

Rose O'Neal Greenhow went to Wilmington to take a blockade-runner to England for personal reasons, but she was also known to be carrying dispatches for the Confederacy. On her return trip via the *Condor*, it was chased by the Union Navy. The *Condor* ran upon a bar during a storm and began to sink. Greenhow insisted upon being put ashore in a small boat. Over the captain's objections, she had a crew row her ashore. The small rowboat capsized, drowning all aboard except one person. There were two reasons she may have drowned, one being that she wore many layers of petticoats and the other being that she had on a money belt laden with gold coins. Her body washed up near Fort Fisher.*

The role of a woman masquerading as a soldier was certainly an uncommon sight during the nineteenth century; however, there remains evidence of such women. Approximately four hundred documented cases of females disguised as male soldiers appeared in various records. From a total of three million participants, this number appears small. It is believed that hundreds of females enlisted for whatever reason, and their gender was never discovered. When a female posing as a soldier was revealed, she was usually dismissed.

The most well-known female soldier from North Carolina was Malinda Pritchard Blalock of Alexander County. The second and third most notable Amazons from the state were Bill Thompson (a.k.a. Lucy Matilda) and Mollie Bean. What is known of these women will be told. Other female soldiers included a few found in North Carolina newspapers, but with no North Carolina connection.

Twenty-two-year-old Sarah Malinda Blalock came from a pro-Union family. Why she, her husband, and her brother joined the Confederate forces is unclear; for neither served very long. Malinda was described as a "good-looking boy," weighing about one hundred-thirty pounds and standing five feet four inches tall. It was told they were in camp near the beach one time when the other soldiers went in swimming, but Malinda remained on the beach.[105] A few weeks after joining, her husband, Keith, who held Union sympathies, was determined to leave. He rolled in poison ivy, causing huge blisters to appear. The surgeon gave him a permanent discharge. Malinda, posing as "Samuel," who had passed as her husband's younger brother, revealed to officers her sex; so she was then dismissed.[106] "Sam" only served one month. Malinda and Keith lived in Watauga County and enlisted March 1862 while her brother enlisted in the Caldwell Rough and Ready Guards.[107] After leaving Confederate service, the Blalock family became outlaws in the mountains, raiding and burning the homes of the secesh. After being wounded in the shoulder, Malinda cut down her number of forays. She was wounded at Carroll Moore's farm in the Globe community, where the Tory band had gone to rob Mr. Moore. Later in the year, the Blalocks ambushed the community again and were repulsed. During one of his plundering on loyal families, Keith was shot in the eye and lost his vision but was able to continue with his depredations throughout the war.[108]

Assistant Surgeon Underwood of the Twenty-sixth Regiment said of Mrs. Blalock, "Her disguise was never penetrated. She drilled and did the duties of a soldier as any other member of the company, and was very adapt at learning the manual and drill."[109]

Some Wilkes County women formed a group that joined with deserters and unionists in organized raiding parties. "They attacked pro-Confederate families and took supplies." Females acted as lookouts, signaling with a horn when the enemy approached. A few females became guides. Some gave either food or shelter to deserters. Perhaps Malinda Blalock was in this group.[110] The *Milton Chronicle* published an account about soldiers from Kinston discussing the female Amazon named Blaylow. The paper had misspelled her name. Malinda "Sam" Blalock died on March 9, 1901.

Lucy Matilda Thompson, alias Private Bill Thompson, was part Waccamaw Indian. Her six-foot, 165-pound physique resembled a man especially after she trimmed her hair short.

---

* For more information on this, see chapter 16.

Her reason for joining Confederate service was that she did not want to be left behind after her husband, Bryant Gauss, volunteered. Gauss received a wound and was transferred to a hospital in Scottsville, Virginia, whereas Lucy traveled there to take care of him. It was here she became pregnant. After her husband died of his wounds, Lucy took his remains back home to Bladen County. Apparently, wanting to avenge his death, Lucy joined the Eighteenth Regiment in mid-1863. The Amazon left active service for a few months to give birth to a daughter. When she returned to the regiment, a great-granddaughter related that Lucy was wounded more than once, requiring a steel plate to be placed in her head. Perhaps her sexuality was discovered then, perhaps not. After the war, Gauss moved to Georgia and married a Union veteran, apparently keeping secret from him her earlier life. The family had six children.* When the female veteran took sick in her elder years and thinking she was not long for this world, she revealed her past to her minister. Lucy Thompson Gauss Kenney lived another eleven years.[111]

Lucy M. Thompson Gauss Kenny a.k.a. Pvt. Bill Thompson
The South's Last Boys in Gray

"A young woman named Mollie Bean, dressed in male attire was on Friday night sent to this city on the charge of being a suspicious character. It appeared that she had been serving in the 47th North Carolina regiment for two years; and during that time had been wounded twice. She was committed to Castle Thunder," reported the *Richmond Sentinel*.[112] Another Richmond newspaper, the *Daily Dispatch*, added a little more information on Bean: "She hails from North Carolina and once before was an inmate of the prison for the same offence."[113] Mention is made of a female soldier from Macon County in 1862 named Mrs.

---

*   The last child was born when Lucy was sixty-nine years old, according to her family. The twins were born when she was fifty-five in 1868, a daughter in 1873, another daughter in 1876, a son in 1879, and another son in 1881. These are confirmed by descendants but believed to be wrong. Perhaps the descendants read the bible dates wrong. Census records show otherwise.

McLane, but research failed to find a first name or any other information.[114] The *Charlotte Times* recorded "a lady dressed in the uniform of a Captain passed through the city via train. She said she was from Mississippi and had been in several battles."[115] Enslaved, John Jackson, living in Wilmington during the war, told of seeing the Georgia Zouaves passing through. "They had all ladies as officers." Louisiana Zouaves with their vivandieres traveled through Wilmington.* Perhaps it was the vivandieres he saw.

"A handsome youth apparently twenty years of age, dressed in a neat artillery uniform, endeavored on Saturday to become a member of Company E, Palmetto Sharpshooters, Capt Conkling; but an unfortunate fact connected with military statue of the dashing lad, coming to light, 'he was destined to disappointment.' The necessary medical exam of the lungs developed the fact that the bosom was entirely too full for a man, and the enthusiastic applicant was put under arrest and sent to Castle Godwin, where it was immediately ascertained that 'Miss Margaret Underwood' who had but recently been discharged from that prison on parole, was the identical young man, rigged as a soldier. It seems that she had come into our lines from Washington and being suspected as a spy, was placed in durance.

"After her parole, she fell in love with a young sharpshooter and endeavored by the above means to accompany him to the war. She was retained in custody." This had been reported in the *Whig*, but it had been copied from the *Richmond Enquirer* issue of February 18, 1862.[116]

The *Memphis Avalanche* on September 12, 1861, wrote: "One of the Louisiana companies in the battle of Manassas lost its captain. The company then unanimously selected the wife of the deceased captain to fill his place, and the lady, in uniform, passed thru the city yesterday, on her way to assume command of her company."[117]

A Washington correspondent of the *New York Post* related the following: "A horseman clad in a sort of cavalry costume with heavy overcoat& slouched hat had been noticed for some time dashing about the city in rather a suspicious manner. At last the authorities felt themselves warranted in arresting him, and accordingly, one morning when trotting down Penn. Ave, he found himself suddenly surrounded by a file of soldiers, and was carried off to prison. But the funniest part was soon to come. The investigation that followed resulted not only in the discovery of certain papers but also the fact the cavalier was a woman. How long she had been at the game it is impossible to guess."[118]

A North Carolina soldier, Louis Leon, kept a diary throughout the war. After he was captured and sent to Point Lookout Prison in Maryland, he mentioned a female prisoner there. She had been in an artillery unit. Leon was released on July 25, 1864.[119]

Previously mentioned, the first months of the war saw women volunteering their services in one way or the other. The following girls seemed determined to fight. It is not known if any donned the soldier's uniform, but they did feel they needed to learn how to fire a gun. "The ladies in the area of Murfreesboro were practicing to use the pistol. Many women were learning to shoot and 'some had become quite skilled in the use of firearms,'" noted a bystander.[120] "There was a regiment passed here a few days ago [in which] one of the soldiers told me that the Ladies in his naborhood had formed themselves in to Companys and were drilling and said they would guard the young men that would not volunteer."[121] The *Winston Sentinel* reported that women wanted to place an ad to procure pistols and guns for their newly formed group of vigilantes.[122]

Walter Clark's mother said, "Nature has denied us the right & strength to join in battle but our hearts & prayers are there ever . . ."[123]

---

*   Females traveling with the troops dressed partially in trousers of soldiers and sometimes carried weapons. Usually, the girls served more in a nursing capacity.

Very little information has been found on fallen women during the war years in North Carolina. Polite society may have talked on such matters in private, but they seldom left any record. This section includes mixed marriages, rape, and rowdy women. "Fallen angels" was a nineteenth-century euphemism for prostitutes as were "public women," "soiled doves," "abandoned women," "easy women," and "fancy girls."

Women of New Bern sent this petition to Governor Vance on August 11, 1863:

> We pray your excellency to consider that in absence of all protection, the female portion of this community may be subjected to a system of outrage that may be justly denominated the harrow of harrows more terrible to the contemplation of the virtuous maiden and matron than death.[124]

Their fears came true in some neighborhoods. Neither white nor black were immune. Rev. George Patterson near Lake Scuppernong said that when U.S. Captain Woodward visited Somerset Plantation to impress wheat and corn, one of his men raped a Negro girl:

> I am sorry to say, that tho' Capt W., did his best, I am sure, to prevent any disorder among his men, yet one of them went into the Cook House & shamefully ravished our Sv't Lovey, threatening her that she should be shot, if she resisted or made any noise; he also drove away some servants who went to her assistance by threats. The Capt promised me that the man should be severely punished for his disgraceful misconduct.[125]

Federal soldiers made forays into the eastern counties and didn't always act in a professional manner. A daughter of John Vann was molested by the raiders.[126] Twenty-two-year-old Private James Preble, member of the Twelfth New York Cavalry, Company K, was executed by a firing squad on March 31, 1865, in Goldsboro, for attempted rape of Mrs. Rebecca Drake, age twenty-three, and Ms. Louise Jane Bedard, her seventeen-year-old cousin, and for the rape of Ms. Letitia Craft, her aunt, age fifty-eight, near Kinston.[127] A Northern newspaper reported than James was "about six feet in height and his appearance in no way gave indication of the brutality . . . His grave was dug in the square formed by his comrades."[128] U.S. General Rossier's men attempted a rape on a forty-five-year-old servant named Nancy while robbing her house Down East.[129] In another incident, Federal soldiers roughed up black people. One Zouave committed "violence on an old Negro woman" who was ninety years old at the time.[130]

Confederate General D. H. Hill wrote a letter to U.S. General J. G. Foster, whose men had been causing havoc in the eastern part of the state, that his men were out of control. Hill wrote, "With such a hint to your thieves it is not wonderful that your raid was characterized by rapine, pillage, arson, and murder."[131] In his wartime reminiscences, J. M. Hollowell wrote of a similar incident near Goldsboro that involved Negro soldiers:

> A gentleman . . . who was a member of those scouting parties told me . . . of an outrage, committed only a few miles from Goldsboro . . . . that a white sergeant with six negro soldiers, went to the home of unprotected women and commit a crime; they were caught on the premises by Frank Coley and a squad of his men; the negroes were promptly shot dead in the yard, and the white sergeant, who begged piteously for his worthless life, was strung up by his heels to a tree, and his throat cut from ear to ear.[132]

A free black named Wesley McDaniel was accused of raping Mary Boyd in Montgomery County. White friends of Wesley got him off, for he was believed to be innocent.[133] An Orange County slave named Elias was accused of raping Martha Burton. His owner, Christopher Stevens, "sought a reprieve from the court on condition that Elias enlist in the army."[134]

Early in the conflict, a slave named Oscar found himself on trial for the attempted rape of Mrs. Bryant of Concord. The jury found him innocent, but an angry mob took the accused out of jail and hung him.[135]

Private Alfred Catlett, age twenty, originally a farmer from Richmond and member of the first heavy artillery, U.S. Colored Troops, Company E; Pvt. Alexander Colwell, age twenty-six, a farmer from North Carolina and member of the same unit; Pvt. Charles Turner, age eighteen, a farmer from Charleston, South Carolina, member of the same unit; and Pvt. Jackson Washington, Company K, age twenty-two, a farmer from North Carolina: all four were shot at Asheville on May 5, 1865, for the gang rape of "a young white girl."[136] Residents of Alleghany County chased away a group of Confederate cavalrymen who were raping a woman.[137] Mr. Tyre York informed Governor Vance on May 5, 1864, that "some 5 or 6 of them undertook to rape a very nice decent white woman and some of her neighbors heard her scream and immediately went to her assistance . . ." York said it was soldiers from General Morgan's command.[138] Four Negroes raped a woman at Fort Macon.[139]

Thomas Settle, from Wentworth, wrote Governor Vance on July 16, 1863, that five men were in the Rockingham County jail. "Two are slaves charged with the rape of a white woman. Things there should be a court of Oyer and Terminer for their trail," he said.[140] In Asheville, "Rumor says that J.L. Henry's negro Bob was hung yesterday. I hope it may be true for he certainly deserves death. He committed rape on an old woman some three years ago & effected his escape," said Mrs. Henry.[141] Cornelia Henry also reported a rape at the end of the war: "The yanks brought one Regiment of nigs to town when they first came but they are gone long ago. They killed five whites in town for ravishing a young lady . . ."[142]

In North Carolina, a black man named John Allen, beaten and bleeding from the head, rushed into a Union camp, begging for help. An officer heard the row and came out of his tent to investigate the matter. He heard Allen explain that soldiers had beaten him and his wife and was attempting to rape her. A short distance from Allen's house, soldiers arrested an Illinois corporal named A. C. Warner. During the trial, Allen was introduced like a witness, but the judge advocate objected that "this witness had not sufficient intelligence to comprehend the nature of the oath;" judges concurred without questioning Allen, and the court dismissed the nature of the oath against Warner! This took place Down East.[143]

The *Charlotte Daily Bulletin* featured an advertisement on September 13, 1861, for a reward for the capture of two runaway felons:

> $400 reward—broke jail in Alexander County—Frank Sherill and a man that says his name is Andrews. Said Sherill was confined on a charge of rape and Andrews for stealing a horse. $400 reward for both delivered to Taylorsville, N.C. Sherill is a 24 year old, about five foot ten/eleven, fair skin, spare in make, has brown-yellow eyes, and his front teeth are out. Andrews is 43-44, stout build, five foot ten, and dark skin with brown eyes. He passes himself off as a school teacher. J.C. Smith, Sheriff, Alexander County.

Alfred Locke, a free black man, was tried by the military court at Salisbury for assault, battery, and rape. Roseann Hendrick testified that during the night, he broke down the door of Mrs. Mary Sloan's house, jerked Mrs. Sloan out of bed, and beat her. "He got her chock down & just went to ravishing her." President Lincoln approved the sentence of hanging, but he escaped before execution. Another version to the story said he knocked on the door and claimed to be a Yankee to gain entrance. At trial, one witness claimed that black men had gone there before during the night.[144]

Dr. J. W. Jamison, assistant surgeon of the U.S. Navy, in the spring of 1863 in North Carolina, made indecent proposals and attempted rape to Ms. Margaret Harrell. He was arrested, but punishment is unknown. Federal officials in the occupied section of North Carolina could not stop the depredations committed upon local women. The next letter explained it:

Headquarters District of Wilmington, April 1, 1865
U.S. Lieut. Col. J.A. Campbell,
Dept. of North Carolina

The country over which I am obliged to exercise more or less control extends on radii of from ten to forty miles. The authority of the government is weakened and brought into contempt by the impurity with which stragglers, deserters from either army, marauders, bummers, and strolling vagabonds, Negroes and whites, commit outrages upon the inhabitants . . . to say nothing of insults and plundering, there have been three cases of rape and one of murder, to say nothing of rumors of others . . . Jos. R. Hawley, Brig-Gen, Commanding[145]

This telegram to Colonel Campbell, assistant adjutant general in Goldsboro, was sent by D. N. Couch, major general, in Moseley Hall on March 28, 1865: "Women are ravished and robbed by stragglers all over the country."[146] A woman reported that one of U.S. General Rossier's men attempted a rape on her servant, age forty-five, and they robbed her house.[147] The *Official Records* recorded another rape mid-war Down East:

Expedition from Portsmouth, Va. To Jackson, N.C. Report of Major Sam Wetherell: Left bivouac at 8 A.M., the regiment in the rear, Capt. Loomis commanded the rear guard. August 3, 1863—Private James Currance, Company A, First NY Mounted Rifles, was brought to him by the caterer of my mess, Dennis Riley, Co. D who, with one or two others, caught Currance in the act of committing a rape upon an old woman, sixty years of age. While Captain Loomis was securing him, he shot at one of the men who was detailed to tie him.[148]

What drives a woman to prostitution? Scholars have written many books on the subject. Research has shown that poverty drove many to it during the war years. Some prostitutes seemed to do well. The latest fashions from Europe were found on prostitutes because they could afford the high prices. This is probably why some troops called them "fancy women."[149] Prostitutes set up business near army camps. In Kinston, the well-known red-light district flourished at Sugar Hill. Wilmington men and sailors frequented Whiskey Lil's Tavern for their sexual needs in the Dry Pond area.

A senior reservist wrote his wife that "about 750 ol mean women resided in Salisbury." He was referring possibly to prostitutes, but it is hard to believe that there would have been that many in the small town.[150] Another soldier on duty there told of how wicked the city was: "I see so much of it daily both men & women are very Corrupt indeed."[151] In Wilkes County, Fort Hamby was known to harbor "rough women." A woman from Huntersville wrote her soldier husband about the disreputable females in Charlotte:

. . . I heard that _____ ____ had taken up with one of them bad wemon in Charlotte and was doing no good [.] dont you forget your self and go among them filthy weaman [.] I have more confidence in you than that . . . .[152]

For keeping a bawdy house in Wilmington, Ann W. Barcliff went to court on December 20, 1861. Agnes, alias Mary Grant, appeared before the judge in April 1862 "for keeping a disorderly house." Julia Barber, alias Julia Cruise/Cruse, was arrested in March 1862 "for keeping a bawdy house," as was Abby Clennahan/McClenny/McClennan. All women resided in Wilmington.[153] A house of "ill-fame" is mentioned in the *Raleigh Register*, August 6, 1862. The article listed the house as being the place where two soldiers involved in a fracas were killed. Soldier Albert Thompson wrote his wife, Cate, that he had "seen so much of the badness of man and woman that I am worse than ever on the thoughts of the like." He said that two women visited a soldier in the guardhouse and sat on his lap; then later, the man's wife arrived.[154]

During the fall of 1863, at Petersburg, Virginia, "about two weeks ago there was a female come from Petersburg and stopped about two hundred yards from our camp [55th NCT]. Several of the boys went up and had lots of fun with her. It was about drill time and one of the boys missed drill and they put him on double duty."[155] From the *Richmond Enquirer* comes this report: "Prostitutes like buzzards and vultures, were simply a part of the army's entourage." Mollie and Mary Bean of North Carolina posed as Confederate soldiers, assuming aliases of Tom Parker and Bob Morgan, and worked the ranks for two years before they were charged with "aiding in the demoralization of General Early's veterans." The two women were put on trial, found guilty, and sentenced to terms in military prisons.[156]

Other North Carolina soldiers were involved with disreputable Petersburg women as shown in this letter: H. D. Cameron stationed at Sexton Mills, Virginia wrote to his friend, John M. Harrington on February 24, 1863, about his experience with the fallen angels of Petersburg. He said three girls cost him eleven dollars, a month's pay for a private. "John . . . I [*illegible*] got some with me twice from the same girl." He said it is "some better than the widow [*illegible*]. John I expect you give them old Hoars fits in Raleigh. They come nigh getting all of your subsistances I guess." Cameron continued: "John the scarcest thing about here is cunt the d_md negroes will not give a fellow a bite. I have not got but three tasts since I have been in Va. and . . . I got that from two fine looking women . . ." Cameron had been drinking and apparently got into trouble Christmas Day. He wrote, "I got on a spree . . . and I did things that I regret verry much this morning." At the end of the letter he said, "I am done drinking I think forever."[157]

Plymouth had its share of lewd women. After the takeover by the Federals, Dr. William M. Smith of New York was called to examine a very sick young woman known to be a whore. He described the house (squalid poverty) as wretched and filthy. The stench was overpowering. The woman's sister left to get provisions. The one remaining had a fever and was very sick. Dr. Smith sent his aide for medicine. About a week later, he again was requested to call on the sick prostitute as she had grown worse. She had been unable to take food or drink for over five days. The U.S. Commissary Department had given her rations, but she was unable to partake of them. He took pity on the women, loaned them his cook, and sent over medicine from the hospital. The next day, the provost marshal accompanied the doctor to the prostitute's house. Two women were brought along to help, one a colored maid and the other a nurse. They cleaned up the hovel, gave the sick woman clean clothing and bed linens, and a nutritious meal. The girl died two days later. The remaining sister, age sixteen, begged the doctor to help "get her straight." She told the doctor they had turned to prostitution in desperation after their invalid mother passed away last Christmas. Her only brother was in Salisbury Prison due to his Union sympathies. Dr. Smith told her to stay with his colored cook until he could find the girl a family. The government furnished her sustenance.

Dr. Smith reported that U.S. Colonel Belknap "keeps company with abandoned women." He also said that the colonel had been sexually harassing his colored cook for a long time. The doctor treated Capt. Seneca Allen for venereal warts known as syphilitic vegetations while in Plymouth.[158]

At Rodman's Point on the Pamlico River, U.S. ships fired heavy shells into that area. Rodman's plantation was totally demolished. A Union soldier said one of his cohorts visited a well-known house of ill repute there.[159] In Kinston, U.S. General Foster allowed prostitutes to stay to boost the morale of his men. Local polite society refused these fallen angels admittance to the city, so they had to camp at the edge of town near the end of Heritage Street.[160]

"The *Tarboro Mercury* of Wednesday, says, last Friday afternoon, an officer in the Confederacy was shot by a young lady on the front of a hotel in Goldsboro. The beautiful but desperate girl (and she is said to be really beautiful) approached within 4 ft. of the officer and firing a Colt's repeater, the ball passed through his left shoulder. She was accompanied by her little sister at the time. Rumor tells us that the unfortunate affair is the result of disreputable conduct on the part of both the officer and the girl. The wounded soldier will recover, while the law will endeavor to teach the girl to be more quiet in her promenade."[161]

A refugee living in Washington during wartime recalled as an adult the lewd women she saw:

> Across the street from us . . . was a small house occupied after the town was garrisoned by a class of women whom I blush to name. they sat on the porch day and night, and always some soldiers were with them. So offensive was the proximity that we kept the windows closed next to them and passed the street by another way. But at sight of any of us in the yard or garden they would sing loudly, "Hang Capt. S . . . on a sour apple tree."[162]

Families who fled their neighborhood were exposed to the riffraff one sees on the road. Mothers tried to protect their young children from interaction with unsavory persons. A family fleeing from New Bern ended up in Warrenton. She said that they were exhausted trying to get lodging. "Where else to go we are perfectly at a loss. There are some characters here that would afford you a constant fun of entertainment I am sure. There are four ladies in the house beautiful enough to make the reputation of a trite, much less one house. They are refugees!"[163]

When the bewildered refugees left New Bern for Kinston, a perfect disarray ensued. Intermixed were soldiers, blacks, whites, and children of all ages. One observer recalled:

> Amid this rabble was an ambulance driven by a young man of Newbern laden with a number of women of shamefully immoral character, who were amusing themselves laughing at and taunting honorable and virtuous ladies, whose tears and wailings for help were heard on all sides.[164]

Nancy Richardson wrote to Governor Vance from Eagle Rock, on November 1, 1864, that "there were 'easy wimin' in her neighborhood who expected to live off the public funds and who sold their 'meet' in order to get money with which to have their spinning done. They never did work neither do thay now. Their men never kept them up as mutch as thay get now."*[165] A mid-upper-class gentleman on a visit to Richmond said of the ladies he saw there: "There are a great many ladies on the streets and very gaudy. I don't know how many thousand I saw yesterday of the F.F. V's., some are very fond of their persons and are grinning & tittering as though the world was on a pleasure trip." His wife described a woman in Asheville she did not like as being "a very fast woman, disgusting in my eyes."[166]

A Northern soldier mentioned marching into Kinston near the end of the conflict and seeing the whorehouses. "Houses containing certain classes of women were surrounded by large gangs which had to be continually dispersed. Three poor women were given shelter in the guard house. The 'prison room' was filled with civilians, negroes, rebel deserters and soldiers."[167] Another Federal soldier stationed near New Bern said that he and his friend left the port to visit Mr. Neal, a local resident. "On our return home we had quite a time as the ladies was very lively & all Came off very well."[168]

Willie Couch of Orange County said that when he returned from the war, his wife had been transformed into a "lewd woman and common prostitute," who had given birth to another man's child. Two other veterans from Orange County complained that their wives were no longer virtuous. Elizabeth Bowling, Nancy Jane Wells, and Emma Couch were

---

*   This story can be interpreted two ways—these could be low-class women who were lazy and got government aid like today, or they could be prostitutes.

common prostitutes. Sophia Anderson was known as a "notorious" prostitute. Mrs. Micajah Lancaster and Agnes Belvin sold their bodies for sex.[169]

Dr. R. Blacknall of Durham had his home commandeered by U.S. General Kilpatrick and General L. G. Estes the last month of the war. Both men were accompanied by women dressed as soldiers and one pregnant mulatto. Dr. Blacknall wrote that they were of dissolute character. "The privacy of my family was not respected by them, neither was the wardrobe of my two daughters, they appropriating their dresses and underclothing." The lewd women rode about town "dressed in their indecency."[170]

Prostitutes were not all confined to towns. Just as the war ended, a soldier told his friend Dick Paddison of his voyage from Wilmington to Charleston. He said that because of the weather, they got no farther than Smithville:

> The girls were the dirtiest things on board, and attracted much attention by their singular appearance, they were however of service to me also, for by their means, I was able to get in the lady's cabin, and that part of the boat where only men, who had lady acquaintances were admitted. They were all sea sick, as the sea was very rough. Sarah . . . is rather a good hearted girl, and disposed to do any service, she is requested, and no mock modesty about her . . .[171]

While prostitution was considered the lowest of the low, white women with black children raised the eyebrows as well. White people feared the mixing of the races known as miscegenation. A diarist wrote, "The greatest piece of scandal now going on is, that one of our soldiers' wives has had a black baby and murdered and buried it a few days ago. There was an inquest held over the child last Wednesday."[172] After the war, a black man named Anthony Ransome told that his mother was the daughter of a white woman. His father was a cobbler in Hertford County.[173] A former slave, Adora Rienshaw, said that her father was the baby of a white woman in an abusive marriage. His father was the coachman for the family. No names or location were given.[174]

Divorces increased during and after the conflict due to unfaithful wives. In some instances, babies were born even though the wife's husband had not been home in more than a year.[175] "Last Sunday we went to several houses on the main land and in one found a family . . . . good-looking white girl bout twenty . . . with a nigger baby . . . She said it was hers but the father of it was not here."[176]

Prostitution plagued the towns that sported military bases either for the North or South. A newspaper article from Richmond sums it up:

> *An Example Made.*—It has been well known for some time past that cyprians, resident and accumulated since the removal of the seat of Government to this place, as well as loose males of the most abandoned character from other parts of the Confederacy, have been disporting themselves extensively on the sidewalks and in hacks, open carriages, &c, in the streets of Richmond, to the amazement of sober-sided citizens compelled to smell the odors which they exude, and witness the imprudence and familiar vulgarity of many of the shame faced of the prostitutes of both sexes. Smirks and smiles, winks, and, when occasion served, remarks not of a choice kind, in a loud voice, denoted the character of the female occupants of open carriages, gotten up in humble imitation of the powers that be. The mayor, in answer to many complaints, having determined to enforce the vagrant law, has caused one lewd character—a female—to be taken up for obtruding herself in an obnoxious attitude before decent people. It is to be hoped that she will not be the only example.[177]

Thievery was very common during the war, filling up the jails. It was sad to think that these desperate women would be among these inmates. Poverty was likely the inducement. In Orange County, Mary Canaday was known locally as a thief.[178] In Rocky Mount, two women got in a fight. The younger woman had stolen a petticoat from an older woman, and she was made to take it off while fifty men watched with interest.[179] Mrs. Mary E. Barnes's name appears a few times in criminal records in New Hanover County. She was arrested for gambling with Negroes. Facing the judge, she refused to give her name and was fined fifty dollars extra in addition to her other fine. In the spring of 1862, Barnes got in an altercation with Sarah Eileef. They both used "abusive language," and Sarah beat up Mary. Eileef paid one hundred dollars in fines. Women were arrested for drunkenness. Members of a brass band mentioned being in Wilkesboro playing for Governor Vance's reelection tour. One said, "We saw something new under the sun, for us, in Wilkesboro, to-wit, viz.: women going into the grog shop to drink whiskey with the men."[180]

True stories of fallen women in the Victorian period are difficult to find. That is why this article is short.

CHAPTER EIGHT

Taxes, Impressments, Inflation, Shortages, and Poverty

IMPRESSMENTS AND TAXES

As early as 1861 the Confederacy began to impress foodstuffs; however, planters donated food to the soldiers without coercion.[1] "Impressment by its very nature was supposed to be an emergency measure . . . ," noted author Scarboro.[2] "On 23 May 1861 the [Ashe] county court, meeting in extra session, appropriated $2000 for the benefit of volunteers and their families. The money would be raised by adding ten per cent to the aggregate county tax and by a loan from the bank . . . ."[3] This was a typical scenario in other counties as well, with different counties donating various amounts. Shortly, the politicians realized that it could not meet the quickly rising requirements needed to carry on a war. Legislators would have to pass resolutions to increase their budgets.

The first passage of the Tax-in-Kind alleviated most of the problems of supplying food to the poor and for military use.[4] The state received from each farm one-tenth of all meat and produce. The tithing bureau had agents in each neighborhood, with an agent over them in each county.[5] Colonel N. M. Hammond of Pitt County said he collected so much that a squad of soldiers was needed to guard it.[6] Colonel Thomas Amis, commissary officer, lived in Lumberton. "Nearly every plantation grew wheat & rice," he said. Food was in abundance. Goods subject to the tax were corn, rice, buckwheat, beans, peas, Irish potatoes, sugar, molasses, cotton, peanuts, and fodder.[7] J. W. Hunt, tithe and commissary agent for Person County, collected tons of food and horse feed and stored it in the old tobacco factory in Roxboro. His workers loaded up wagons and hauled the goods to the soldiers. They also carried mail back and forth for the troops.[8]

Courtesy of an anonymous donor

Another receipt:

Person Co. N.C. March 5th 1863 Received of Mr. David Vanhook under order of impressment from Secretary of War, (427 lbs) four hundred and twenty seven pounds of bacon, to be paid for at government prices (less the cost of transportation for (22) twenty two miles at four cents per hundred per mile) by Maj. Thos S. Knox at Danville Va, who will also give a certificate of impressment, if desired, by which further compensation may be obtained if the matter is regulated by Congress

M. Spragins Agt

For Major Thos S. Knox—A.C.S.—C.S.A.

Early on, the Confederate government in Richmond expected the countryside to help with the war effort:

Confed'te States of America,
Quar's Master Gen's Department,
Richmond. November, 1861.

Circular—The following additional instructions, in reference to impressments of private property for military purposes, are issued for the information and guidance of officers and agents of this Department:

1. An officer appointing agents to make impressments will, in all cases, furnish to such agents written evidence of their authority to act; and agents, whenever required by parties interested, will exhibit the orders or authority under which they are acting.

2. Agents who make impressments will, in all cases, give to the owner of the property impressed, or his agent, a certificate to the character and value thereof; and they will, moreover, return to the officer of this Department, from whom they derive their authority, a statement of all property impressed by them, with the value of the owners. An abstract of these statements will be forwarded to this office by the officer to whom they are returned.

3. Impressments must not be resorted to except when absolutely demanded by the public necessities, and their burden must be apportioned among the community, so far as any be possible, equally and impartially, having due regard to the means and ability of owners of property.

4. When teams and owner property, including slave teamsters are impressed into the service of the Confederate State since owners thereof may be compensated by officers of the Quartermaster's Department, at the usual rates of hire.

5. When the owners of any property impressed into the public service, slaves accepted, are willing to relinquish the same to the Government, the officer of the Quartermaster's Department may pay the fair appraised value thereof, and take up the property in their return, to be accounted for as other public property.

6. When private property has been duty impressed by order of the commanding officer and it shall appear by satisfactory evidence to have been expended in the public service, officers of the Quartermaster's

Department may pay the fair appraised value thereof although the property
may not have been regularly received and issued by any Quartermaster.

A. C. Myeen.

Acting Quartermaster General[9]

The people grumbled and replied "that no deduction is allowed them in the act for the corn used in fattening their pork. They contend that they should not be subject to the tithe on the corn, inasmuch as they pay it by a tithe on the pork, and if they are required to pay a tithe on the corn upon which the pork is fattened, as well as a tithe of the pork, that they virtually pay a double tax on the corn." One reason for a tax-in-kind, which turned out to be a tithe-in-kind, involved the Secretary of the Treasury, Memminger. Memminger said that "it was, doubtless intended as a substitute for direct tax on lands and slaves, and to avoid the constitutional objection to such a tax until the census is taken."[10]

Susan Staton's tithe bill receipt
Frances M. Manning Papers, Joyner Library, ECU

As the new year of 1862 rolled around, Sophia Corpening paid $17.20 in tax for the poor, county, and a railroad tax. "By December of 1862, the General Assembly was beginning to express resentment over some Confederate government policies. Bills were passed prohibiting shipments of certain products out of state, calling for Confederate troops to guard the Carolina coast, and supporting Gov. Vance's increasing resistance to the Confederate government." These problems persisted for the next two years as well, only growing worse.[11] In 1863, the rules got tougher. Senate Bill no. 2 (called A Bill to Regulate the Price of All Articles Produced, Manufactured, or Sold in This State), enacted by the General Assembly, told that it was unlawful to anyone producing, manufacturing, or selling any article listed in the published schedule of prices fixed by commissioners of North Carolina or selling unless the authorities be authorized to increase the fixed prices to an amount greater than 25 percent. Three commissioners would be appointed to make out a schedule in their county of the fixed prices with the list posted at the county courthouse door. Section no. 3 of the bill punished persons for selling above the fixed prices "the full amount for which the article was sold above the fixed price . . ."

Section no. 4: "In case any person . . . having a surplus on hand, or more than is actually necessary for the support of himself and family refuse to sell the same," the court had the power to press the surplus. Section no. 5: Persons were not allowed to export certain articles out of the state without punishment.[12]

In addition, counties increased taxes to supplement their coffers for the poor. The "county courts raided other funds to obtain money for poor relief . . . . education had to give way to alleviating hunger."[13] A special tax of five cents on one hundred dollars of valuation was levied for the support of the soldiers' families in Wilkes County.[14]

The process of assessing taxes was complicated. Those collecting the tax wrote authorities to try to clear the confusion. The next letter gives a good example:

> Morganton, Nov 28th 1863
> Joseph Coperning Esqr & J. Harper
>   Dear Sirs I have Received Instructions from the Commissioner of Taxes deciding that corn Cut and Cured is long forage [,] So you will assess taxes as well as fodder[.] you are directed to assess the grain at the value for which it it [sic] would sell in the neighborhood where they were produced without any Regard to the value Set by the State or Confederate Government [.] I have received only the two Cards and cannot Send you one I wish you to make Distilling account for all the Bandy they may make of whatever kind of fruit it may be made [.] those who Should have Registered and have not done So to assess a double tax [.] I find we are going to be put to the line and squar[?]
>   I have a quantity of Blanks I will send you as soon as possible but only 100 of No. 7 [.] I have written for more and a Receipt Book for Mr. Clark [.] if you have assessed Crops by the rule of the State or Confederate Government you are required to reassess them by the marketable value where they are produced [.] you will See in the Instructions I Sent you by mail last week that Cows & Calves have to be valued [.] you are to judge what number of animals necessary for the Cultivation of the farm and all others must be valued at what they would bring in Confederate Notes &tc. I am required to send a Scedule [sic] of the prices assessed to the State Collection at an early day.
>   I have Honor to be with much Respect your humble Servant
>   TA Dorsey[15]

It wasn't long before citizens had to give over the use of their wagons, teams, slaves, and leather for military purposes. Scarboro continued, "Second only to conscription as a source of discontent in the Confederacy was the impressments of agricultural supplies and private property by the army. With the epoch of the new confederation, slaves and free blacks were impressed to build breastworks and forts much to the vexation of the owners."

The enslaved and free black men were used in different capacities throughout the war by state officials. Slaves found themselves driving wagons for army use. Walter Clark wrote to his mother that "Gov. Vance has ordered out 1/5 of the hands in five counties to work on the fortifications . . ."[16] Will Rodman writing from Washington in the fall of 1861 to his uncle, General W. A. Blount, said:

> Col. McMillan "requests me to send hands from the south side of the river to work on the fort and throw up entrenchments" [sic] . . . . He is determined if hands are not furnished more liberally to seize them . . . He seized Miss Fanny Owen's rooms in the Long Row for a hospital, and drove her off "at the point of the . . . bayonet."[17]

Catherine Edmondston, owner of around eighty slaves, was peeved that state authorities found it necessary to "borrow" her wagon teams and drivers. Citing passages from her diary:

> Early in the morning the overseer sent me a requisition from the Qr. Mster of the 34th regt. calling for all our team & wagons to move the baggage & equipage of the regt. down from the railroad to Hamilton.[18]

One month later, the army was back impressing slaves to work on breastworks. "They got an order 'for one fourth our men hands to work on entrenchments for Col. Leventhorpe's regiment at Hamilton . . . ,'" she said.[19] That summer, she was irate that the impressment officers came calling again, this time,

> to furnish Negroes to work on defences near Petersburg. It is most rash . . . . oppressive & unequal. There are Negroes enough on James River whom their owners would be glad to employ . . . Negroes whom they fear will go over to them [Yankees]. Why not take them and leave these here in this peaceful country . . . . To remove forty hands now [from her and her father's] is to destroy it.[20]

Later that fall, her brother went to down to Hamilton with a gang of free Negroes, "whom he called 'Falstaff's ragged regt,' to report to the engineer in command."[21] Elizabeth Robeson penned in her diary on September 17, 1862, that "some men came after the hands to work on the fort [Fisher]." The next day, she sent Rage, a slave, to the fort.

Into the first year of the conflict, this advertisement appeared:

> **To the People of North Carolina:** At the request of President Davis I have undertaken to collect all arms from the citizens of our state. I have been entrusted with authority to borrow, purchase, or if necessary to impress them. None but a craven or disloyal citizen will refuse to comply. W.S. Ashe

Civilians were given thirteen to twenty dollars each for a good rifle or musket and thirteen to thirty-eight dollars for double-barrel shotguns. Ashe also bought old scrap iron, either cast or wrought. Cast iron paid one to one and one-half cents and wrought iron, four cents.[22] Another ad had this to announce:

> **General Order #9:**
> I visit every family to get shoes, blankets, & clothing. I will procure if you cannot donate. You can give money if you don't have any stuff. We want the goods in preference to the money.
> Joseph Pinnix, Col. Cmdg, 47th Regt, N.C. Militia[23]

North Carolina's citizens began to grow fatigued with the constant requisitions from their resources as early as 1862. How could they continue to give to the military? They were already seeing shortages of supplies to feed their own. Julia C. Jones of Bethania described "a train of army wagons that descended upon the community, loading up corn, wheat, bacon, and eggs. 'They got 3 sacks of hay from us,'" she wrote. They also took corn.[24] A lady in Asheville reported that for the tithes in the fall of 1863, she "paid 60 bu of tithe corn & one load of hay."[25] Near the end of the hostilities a Confederate artillery unit in Hillsborough wiped out the entire county of forage. Residents of the communities described the cavalry as a swam of locusts.

"In April 1863, the Confederate government passed a law empowering the central government to claim one tenth of most kinds of farm produce throughout the South." Additional personnel had to be hired to carry out this plan.[*] Further research revealed "there was a tax of eight percent on all agricultural products in hand on July first, 1863, on

----

[*] A total of 1,440 appraisers and 2,965 agents worked throughout the Southern states. They collected over five million dollars in just five months. The three top states providing the most crops were North Carolina, Georgia, and Alabama.

salt, wine, and liquors, and one percent on all moneys and credits." In addition to that tax was imposed "a ten percent on all trade in flour, bacon, corn, oats, and dry goods during 1863 . . ."[26]

The historian deRoulac Hamilton noted that "a tax-in-kind, by which each farmer, after reserving fifty bushels of sweet and fifty bushels of Irish potatoes, twenty bushels of peas or beans, one-hundred bushels of corn or fifty bushels of wheat out of his crop of 1863, had to deliver [at a depot within eight miles] out of the remainder of his produce for that year, ten percent of all wheat, corn, oats, rye, buckwheat, rice, sweet and Irish potatoes, hay, fodder, sugar, molasses, cotton, wool, tobacco, peas, beans, and peanuts; and ten percent of all meat killed between April 24, 1863 and March 1, 1864."* One can see how confusing it would be for the farmer's wife to keep up with the newest rules because county officials constantly changed them.

Farmers weren't the only ones taxed. Other taxes included "an occupation tax ranging from fifty dollars to two-hundred dollars and from two and one-half percent to twenty percent of their gross sales was levied on bankers, auctioneers, brokers, druggists, butchers, fakirs, liquor dealers, merchants, pawnbrokers, lawyers, physicians, photographers, brewers and distillers; hotels paid from thirty dollars to five-hundred dollars, and theatres five-hundred dollars."[27]

The distribution of food was another problem. Sometimes poor families received script or certificates in place of money similar to food stamps that people get today. The agents tried to be fair. These commissioners also received a small honorarium for their work. Concerned about impressments of foodstuffs for the poor, agents wrote to the president for his attention to this matter.[28]

"Confederate regulations allowed a county to purchase back only what it would have contributed to the tax-in-kind . . . Confederate documents make clear that the government's basic intention was not to reduce the size of overall tax-in-kind collections but to allow minor redistributions of them in accord with local circumstances."[29]

Person County court records disclose:

> It is ordered by the court that Alex Walker commissioner be authorized to use so much of the money in his hands to buy corn to pay for provisions already furnished soldiers' families. It is also noted that he loan corn in his possession to the needy persons of the county by their making affidavit in writing that they need the same for their own use and that they will return after harvest next, one bushel of good wheat for every bushel of corn they receive.[30]

In another case, the officials of Sampson County wrote the secretary of war and the secretary of the treasury on November 1863. They said that crops had done poorly, many hogs died, and the men had been conscripted, leaving few to labor. They wanted to "permit the tithes of Sampson County to be collected and sold to the county at government prices for the relief of our suffering poor."[31] When 1864 rolled around, Person County officials passed a motion: "It is ordered that a tax of three-fourths of one percent be laid for county purposes and one-forth of one percent be laid for the poor tax and one dollar and eight cents poll tax for county purposes."[32] Frustrated with the rules, J. M. Sneed in a letter to a friend had enough:

> I understand they are coming round in a few days to press what little Brandy I made after paying all the law required me to pay to distill [.] now they are going to take it from me and allow me little or nothing for it [.] I think

---

*   Each farmer had to give 10 percent of his residue and 10 percent of his bacon to agents after keeping one hundred bushels of corn or one hundred-fifty of wheat.

it is verry hard indeed and they are now impressing horses in Orange and will be at it I expect in Person this week. I expect they will get one from me this way [.] they are pressing in Orange but I hope not as I have none to spair[33]

At a later time, this same person wrote: "I am looking for the pressmaster along every day pressing Horses [.] I don't expect any thing but what they will take Mike [his animal] when they do come [.] if they do I am broke [.] I shant be able to Haul fire wood this winter [.] Uncle Billie has taken Luce [mule] to his house to Keep them from pressing any of yours but I fear it will do no good [.]"[34]

To help combat shortages, Governor Vance imposed an embargo on the exportation of provisions; speculators were punished by fines, and he made up a committee to fix prices and forbid the distillation of grain because the corn was needed for the destitute.[35] In the fall of 1862, Governor Vance announced his proclamation:

> Whereas, in order to stop, if possible, the wicked system of speculation which is blighting the land & prevent the production of famine in the midst of plenty, the Legislature . . . have authorized me to lay an embargo upon the exportation from the State of certain articles of prime necessity, except to certain persons and for certain purposes.[36]

Items on the embargo list included salt, bacon, pork, flour, cornmeal, shoes, leather, beef, hides, potatoes, cotton cloth, yarn, and woolen cloth. The following persons were to be exempted from the proclamation: all quartermasters and commissary agents of the central and state government, agents of every county, and all persons who took the oath that the articles purchased were for their own private use and not for resale. "The exception is to extend to salt made by non residents on the sea coast and in their own works and to cargoes entering any of our ports from abroad." If caught breaking the law, that person would have the goods confiscated and turned over to the state.[37] Unfortunately, the proclamation only lasted one month and had to be extended several times. The information trickled down to the county level:

> It also appearing to the court that the effect of recent issues to the enrolling officer of this county . . . [is] to communicate to the farmers, by which the farmers are restricted to sell their surplus provisions to none except the government or to soldiers' families . . . or those authorizing the impressments of all the wheat for more than government prices.[38]

Apparently, the proclamation was slow to reach the mountainous counties. From Flat Rock, a man wrote Vance about the militia capturing a farmer within three miles of the South Carolina border on his way to sell his produce. The writer felt the farmer was entirely ignorant of the proclamation, but the rules had to be enforced. He said that the militia "have little knowledge of what may leave the State . . ." and that none of them lived close to the roads leading out of the state.[39] Problems with impressment continued, prompting the government to make an announcement:

> The impressment of property of citizens by officers and agents of the Confederate government, harsh enough in itself, has become doubly so, by the constant disregard of the provision of the law regulating seizures. In addition to this, the flagrant outrages committed, in every part of the country, by straggling soldiers, and other persons in the Confederate service, having no shadow of authority to impress property, has become a grievance almost

intolerable. A recital of many instances of such, which have been brought to my knowledge, would shock the moral sense of the most heartless.

I have urged in vain upon the authorities of the Confederacy to check this evil, and have used every possible effort to do so myself. But it seems to grow worse, and as the supplies of our people become more scant they feel more sensibly this unjust deprivation of their property, which reduces them almost to the verge of starvation. It must be stopped, if possible, and I earnestly recommend such action on your part as you may think best calculated to aid me in remedying the evil. My correspondence with the War Department on this subject is submitted for your consideration.[40]

To make sure the residents knew where to go to pay taxes, announcements such as this helped them out:

Notice of Payers of Tax in Kind:
County Agents Office
Notice is hereby given to all persons holding Assessor' estimates of the tax in kind due by them to the Confederate States that I will be ready to receive said tax at Yanceyville, Hightowers, Hunts Depot on the 1st of October, 1864. Persons in Shady Grove, Farish's, Locust Hill and Popular Grove are required to deliver their tithes in Yanceyville; those in Andersons, Hightowers, Prospect Hill and Leasburg, at Hightowers; those in Milton and Yanceyville District at N. Hunt's; those who prefer it can deliver their wheat and rye to Major McCleish in Danville, take his receipt for the same and return it to me. All taxpayers are earnestly requested to bring forward their quota of produce immediately as the Government needs it. Persons hauling their quota will be paid six cents per mile per 100 pounds.

In case of the failure of any one to deliver the whole or any portion of the tax due by them, within one month from the date hereof, the Quartermaster is instructed to turn over the estimate of the amount in default to the district collector, who will at once proceed to collect the same, with the 500 per cent and costs additional by warrant of district, to be levied on any property belonging to the party in default.

The tax payer will be required to deliver his produce in such form and ordinary marketable condition, as may be usual in the section in which it is to be delivered.

Grain will be received the standard weight. Bags will be furnished, for the delivery of grain at this office, Hightowers or Hunts. The depot will remain open for thirty (30) days.
W.H. Holderness, QM Agent for Caswell County
September 26, 1864[41]

Notice—Confederate Tax August 11, 1864:
The Taxpayers of Orange County are hereby notified to attend at the times and places above stated nearest their respective residences, and furnish to the Assessors a correct list of the following subjects of taxation on hand, held, owned on the 17th of February, 1864: Number of acres of Land, and value in 1860; Slaves, number, sex, and value; number of Horses, Mules, Asses, Jennets, Cattle, Sheep, Goats and Hogs, value in 1860; Cotton, Wool, Tobacco, Corn, Wheat, Oats, Rye, Potatoes, Peas, Beans, &c., Flour, Meal, Sugar Molasses, Bacon, Lard, Spirituous Liquors, &c., on hand 17th February, 1864, and not necessary for family consumption in 1864; Household and Kitchen Furniture, Agricultural implements, Mechanical Tools, Musical

Instruments, Carriages, Carts, Drays, Wagons, Books, Maps, and value in 1860; Property of Corporations, Joint Stock Companies and Associations, Gold and Silver Coin, Gold Dust, and Gold and Silver Bullion; amount of all solvent Credits, Bank Bills, and all other paper issued as currency; value of money held abroad, and bills of exchange in foreign countries, and the value of all articles of primal or mixed property not enumerated above, and not exempt from taxation.

Land, Slaves, Cotton, and Tobacco purchased since the 1st day of January, 1864 must be listed at the amount paid for them.

H.M.C. Stroud, M.A. Angier, Assessors[42]

Rev. T. B. Kingsbury wrote to William A. Graham about inflation and taxation in the spring of 1864:

the taxation referred to is unjust and unequal, for no other class of persons is taxed, not only all interest, but more than the interest. If you can accomplish anything towards altering the tax bill, so as to bear less oppressively upon the class described, you will doubtless confer a substantial favor on a large number of persons in North Carolina.[43]

Diarists writing in war years frequently mention the impressment agents and paying their taxes. "January 4th, 1864 I went to Maysville to pay my cattle tax," wrote Elizabeth Robeson. A few days later, she sold some corn, pork, a horse, and farming utensils. She also hired out some of her Negroes. Widows took over the running of the farm when their sons were away in military service.

When the coast was overtaken by the Federals, tax collectors had problems collecting what was owed them. "Some slave-owners were subjected to double taxes on their slaves when they moved from eastern counties to avoid losing their slaves to the enemy." Congress passed a resolution that sheriffs could only collect tax in the county where the owners "maintained a legal residence."[44] Mary Outten wrote to friend Ike Brown on March 31, 1864, from Hillsborough where she was a refugee:

I am growing quite despondent as it regards my pecuniary affairs, the heavy taxes which have been laid upon us, is ruinous to persons in my situation. It will take nearly or quite ALL my little income to pay my taxes . . . I shall have to pay taxes on all my property in New Bern which is entirely out of my control.[45]

Continued impressment of items plagued everyone. Students relied on the staff at schools to help them through their studies, as well as to supply their basic needs:

Chapel Hill, N.C.
Thursday, Novr 23d 1864
My dear Sir,
A new panic is hereabouts. The impressment of sorghum syrup, wheat, beef, &c., is daily expected. Mr Purefoy told me that he was expecting the officer every hour at his house (to-day). He wanted to sell me syrup at $10. Govt is giving $5. Now to me this movement so early in this neighborhood will interfere with the life of the University more seriously than the conscribing of our students. For if our eating houses cannot get food for our students, even those under 17 cannot come or cannot stay here. Mr Purefoy says he is resolved that hereafter he will have nothing on and that Govt. can impress but [page torn]. He will continue to make corn but nothing else. Is there no mode of stopping this process here? With the food in the immediate neighborhood

gone & no horses for hauling in from a distance, we town-folks will be in a serious dilemma before the year is out. The officials of Govt ought to be very discreet in a work that is at all times terrific to the people.

Examples are sometimes easier to follow than precepts. So my walk to Mr Purefoy's revealed that the impressing of wood from the lands of the Trustees goes on bravely. The students that room out of the buildings are in a bad fix. Prof. Fetter says he cannot haul for them. If we (Faculty folks) cd [could] get our hauling paid in wood, there might be some relief to such folks, by making the haulers sell to our students, or by some other such regulation.

We are well. I wish I could add hopeful of getting our desires.

Yours sincerely,
Charles Phillips[46]

By the end of 1864, the tax-in-kind had vanished, forcing the Confederacy to rely on other means of feeding the army. It was then that the central government in Richmond authorized the impressments of *one-half* a family's yearly supply of meat and "**three-fourths** of all the surplus of corn in eastern counties."[47]

Southrons came to hate the government for the impressments of their property and servants. One female civilian called them the Army Worm. Another citizen said that impressment officers were "robbers." Author Escott has written that "James Seddon, Confederate Secretary of War, stated in November 1863 that the army had depended almost totally on impressments since the fall of 1862." Many complaints were heard that "tax-in-kind agents seized crops from soldiers' wives and other people so poor that they should have been exempt under law."[48]

"Prior to the passage of the **Impressment Act of March 26, 1863,** the arbitrary appropriation of supplies from the civilian population was neither regulated nor sanctioned by law."[49] Those citizens who lived near the railroads and waterways suffered more than those living in isolated rural areas. "Our best protection will be our poverty and bad roads, which will make it cheaper for them to buy grain and beef from the north west than steal them here," said W. W. Lenoir to his mother.[50]

It was not beneath men to pose as Confederate officers to steal from the civilians. John Frazier stationed at Milford Station, Virginia, wrote to his wife, Rossennah, about agents taking her cattle and food:

. . . . if any one wants to take aney you demand his authority for there
is fake pretenders going about collecting such there was one apprehended in
this state he had officers cloaths on . . .[51]

Mary F. Scott mentioned the Confederate cavalry companies in the county and said, "They have ate up nearly all the corn in the county—they press what they get now—corn sells for $15 a bushel—what the poor people will do Heaven only knows." She mentioned Mr. Ellis, her overseer: "He don't do much but drink liquor when he can get it."[52]

Speaking of impressment agents, in a letter to her son, Burwell, Rebecca Davis stated:

. . . they are fixing for a draft, it makes the ladies look rather gloomy.
I think I told you in my last letter that they had been pressing beef here, &
hands too, to go to Wilmington . . .[53]

The agent insisted that Mr. Davis send a slave since he hadn't sent any the last time he came around. In another letter, she wrote that if he wanted any meat sent to get it before "the agents come round, they are going round in Franklin now, they weigh all the meat, and leave 2 lbs to all over 12 and 1[lb] to all under, that is if they find that much, and I guess they will not get much on those terms." More of her slaves were conscripted to work on fortifications. "Joe has gone to Weldon to work on fortifications and we have had 2 pressed this week but they pay us for them . . ."[54]

From the encampment near Weldon, George Walker sent a letter home on April 13, 1864:

> I was sorry to hear that the soldiers was up there a pressing and doing so much mischief [.] I think they will have something els to do between now and June besides running over the country stealing [.]
>
> I was sorry to hear you had to pay so much tax [.] I dident think you had anything subject to taxation [.] you said you did not see how poor women could live and pay so much tax [.]

By September 18, he was in Petersburg, Virginia:

> I think it would be a good idea to sell him [steer] and evry thing els you have to spare as soon this fall and winter as you can before the cavalry comes in and presses it from you and pays confederate money for it.[55]

The *Daily Journal* showed how prices had risen by December 1864:

Hire of Labor, Teams, Wagons, and Horses

Baling long forage per 100 lbs . . . $.75; shelling & bagging of corn, sacks furnished by government, per bushel . . . $.25; hiring of two horse teams, wagon, & driver, rations furnished by owner per day . . . $12; same with gov't rations . . . $7; four horse team, wagon, driver, with owner furnishing rations . . . $20, same except government furnished rations . . . $10.50; hiring of six horses, wagon, driver, rations furnished by government . . . $23.50, same except rations furnished by owner . . . $26; hiring of laborer, rations furnished by owner per day . . . $4 and by month . . . $90, furnished by government . . . $2.50 per day and by month . . . $45; rental of horse per day . . . $2; Cotton yarn per bunch, of 5 lbs . . . $8; washed wool per lb . . . $8, unwashed . . . $6; raw cotton per lb . . . $1.

The commissioners respectfully suggest that if it be found practicable, the producer should be allowed to retain a fourth part of their surplus, to be sold at market rates, to pay for their necessary plantation supplies which they have to purchase at high market prices. They earnestly call upon the farmers to bring forward their corn now so necessary to the support of the army in the immediate front, and which alone will prevent the loss to the enemy, of all their crops, stock, Negroes, & etc. The commissioners would also recommend that the impressments should be universal and uniform, leaving out no one.

For the information of all persons concerned, we publish the following instructions, with the hope that they will be strictly obeyed.

No officer, or agent, shall impress the necessary supplies which any person may have for the consumption of himself, his family, employees, slaves, or to carry on his ordinary mechanical, manufacturing or agricultural employments.[56]

C.S. Major Reid posted this in the newspaper Christmas Day:

> I will pay for all meats and breadstuffs brought in voluntarily. If not brought in voluntarily previous to that time, the agents are instructed to impress at scheduled rates.[57]

The *Daily Conservative* advertisement, January 12, 1865:

> I respectively appeal to the farmers of Wake, Orange, and Chatham to bring in their surplus corn immediately for the support of our army. If you bring it in I won't have to impress it. Capt W.E. Pierce, QM

"The General Assembly passed two resolutions calling upon the governor to find out whether impressments then in progress were sanctioned by the government and to take steps to prevent more than the legally collected agricultural tithe from being removed from the state."[58]

Walter Clark corresponded with his mother from headquarters in Williamston that fall about General Stubbs of the militia:

> All the woman [*sic*] and the children left the town. I had to press a wagon from Genr'l Stubbs to move some torpedoes out of town . . .[59]

As the war toiled along, the poorer class grew despondent of the impressment laws and resentful of the "twenty-nigger law." Poorer women were embarrassed to ask their wealthy kinfolk or the government for assistance. These poor women had to get help writing letters to officials and the governor.[60] Also in 1863, women started criticizing government officials and even the governor himself. Bettie Horner and Margaret Guess wrote the governor, complaining that the Orange County Cotton Factory would not sell them any yarn. They said country people would be "naked and freezing by the winter."[61] Margaret Perry wrote to Zebulon Vance. She had not heard from her husband since he left for duty. "If he does not return shortly, nothing but starvation, devastation, and final ruin to his family will be the consquence . . ."[62] One poor woman wrote Governor Vance on January of 1865:

> For the sake of suffering humanity . . . . and especially the sake of suffering women and children try to stop this cruel war, here I am without one mouthful to eat for myself and five children and God only knows where I will get som thing now you know as well as you have a head that it is impossible to whip the Yankees . . . my husband has been killed, & if they all stay til they are dead what in they name of God will become of us poor women.[63]

Nancy Mangum threatened Governor Vance that if he didn't lower prices, "we wimen will write for our husbans to come . . . home and help us we cant stand it."[64] Women did that very thing. The result was increased desertions. General Lee wrote to Governor Vance of the sad letters received by the North Carolina soldiers. He said they influenced the men to desert. He asked Vance to "try to get influential citizens to 'cheer the spirits of the people.'"[65]

Two evils—"the unjust distribution of the burden of poverty and the inflation . . . were remedied . . . by state action . . ." The first evil was met by higher taxes, impressments, distribution to the poor; the second evil was met by a tax-in-kind, barter, and selling items at reasonable prices.[66] If the state government had enforced the rules on speculation, maybe prices could have been lower, enabling the poorer classes to keep from starving.

General Whiting was notorious for impressing property, even that belonging to the state. In early 1863, soldiers manning coastal defenses complained that General Whiting was starving them because he commandeered the farmers' wagons to "haul materials for fortifications, and the farmers had stopped bringing food into Wilmington to sell."[67]

The controversy mentioned earlier between Milton Worth and General Whiting continued during the winter. General Whiting "took" flatboats from the State Saltworks to haul his supplies to Fort Fisher. Then he impressed some of the workers. Frustrated, Milton resigned in July 1863. His nephew and son of Jonathan Worth took the job. The confrontation calmed down temporarily but renewed after April, when Federal soldiers burned the saltworks, capturing forty-seven workers. David Worth wrote to Governor Vance that General Whiting had "ordered" him to move the saltworks inland and that it would not be feasible. The governor ruled in favor of Worth. These flatboats in question carried the wood necessary for the boiling of saltwater. They burned sixty cords of wood every day. Whiting on October 27, 1864, closed all private saltworks. In November, he shut down the State Saltworks on Masonboro Sound; thereby, all saltworks in the state ceased working. Vance took this action to the legislature, but nothing changed.[68]

The residents of Johnston County complained to the governor that impressment agents only took articles from nonfriends as indicated by the next letter:

Boon Hill Johnston County NC.
Jan 3rd 1863—

To His Excellency Gov. Vance,
Sir,

  The people of Johnston County owe allegiance first to *North Carolina* secondly to the Confederate States, and accordingly, to my Humble judgement *protection* is due from North Carolina to her citizens even against the injustice of the Confederate authorities; but so far from the State protecting Johnston County and equalizing her among her sister Counties, the State itself seems at the present time to be almost as unjust as the would be Aristocratic and demanding Horse leeches of the Confederate Service. Not long since a man, who said he had authority from the Commander at Goldsboro, but who could not read his letters came to this his native County with an armed force to press and take our wagons & mules from us, his particular friends he passed by lightly, those whom he before had old grudge against, he robed [sic]of all they had in the way of teames [sic], and if they objected he threatened them should they not hush there complaints to take [them] and force them into Confederate Service thereby implying it was a bad place; which according to Assy Biggs is treason.* Such men appear at our homes with bayonets and demand that we feed them & give them quarters . . . in addition to this when every wagon mule is gone [,] comes the Governor with his bob tail malish [militia] demanding half of our able bodied slaves . . . slave owners must feed all the poor, and sustain the Confederate Government & Gov Vance; afterwards comes the sheriff in loud tones demanding his taxes, and the speculator demanding his profits, and after the whole set is done with us, we are left beggars . . .[69]

The author Crawford has said, "All Confederate volunteers were to be exempted from payment of the poll tax . . . ," which helped ease the family's burdens.[70] Historians have agreed that the Confederate government itself "made the conditions far worse through impressments . . ."[71] Author Escott has stated that about 40-plus percent of all white women in the state received aid during the war. "Tar Heel county governments contributed $20,000,000 to aid the needy but never did solve the problem of destitution."[72]

---

*   Asa Biggs was a district judge.

FOOD SHORTAGES AND POVERTY . . . "Beggars and Starvers"*

In the first months of the war, thousands volunteered for service while some men stayed home to finish planting for their wives. The second year of warfare, men were conscripted, which left few men to tend or harvest crops.[73] The loss of laborers added to residents' worry of getting in the crops. One farmer said that he could work a dozen or so slaves including children, but that they never could get all the work done that needed to be done. A Person County farmer writing to a friend in Guilford County stated in July 1864 that because of the decrease in labor supply, "I make only half my flour, 1/3rd of my pork. Now how far will $2000 Confederate money go towards buying 2/3rds of the supplies of the family of 14?"[74] When the largest planters Down East sent their slaves into the interior for safekeeping, not enough were left to make a sufficient crop for General Lee's army. Documentation provided by author Crawford explained: "Families negotiated such personal crises [such as soldiers absences or death] with varying degrees of success . . . the strength and effectiveness of kin and neighborhood support system were a key determinant of household's prospect of survival."[75]

In order to feed her family, Mrs. Aaron Thomas wrote there were not enough daylight hours to get all the work done. After the children were put to bed, she went out into the fields to work by moonlight.[76] The population of both whites and blacks was fewer in the high country. By late spring in the mountain counties in 1861, "wartime inflation and shortages were already being felt in the region's general stores."[77] Author Stephen Wise has stated: "As early as May, 1861, the reduction of goods in the South was beginning to have an effect on the Southern economy. The mere announcement of the blockade had a profound effect on business." Merchants in Wilmington started to sell their goods for cash instead of credit.[78] A comment was made by one man regarding shortages in July 1861: "The merchants are not selling many goods as there is not much money in the country." He continued, "Tobacco prices were way down and the farmers have planted a great deal more corn."[79]

Prices rose more quickly in some locations. "By the time of the August Love Feast, Salem residents did without their coffee and sugar cake due to high prices."[80] Ben Lawton, a bookkeeper from Wilmington, commented on August 17, 1861:

> We have no coffee or sugar here-— flour and corn are very low. But the northern people must lay aside the idea of STARVING THE SOUTH OUT. It can't be did.[81]

He was wrong. "In the early months of the war, southerners encountered shortages of primarily nails, glass, and manufactured items, but soon spread to food," noted one historian. Other goods in short supply were cotton and wool cards, which was necessary for the production of cloth.[82] Lawton may have had a reprieve that December for merchant O. G. Parsley & Company advertised that they had three thousand bags of coffee direct from Rio for sale.[83]

Hoarding and speculation became paramount to the cause of inadequate supplies. Local shortages were caused by citizens buying up supplies and hoarding them. A man from Warrenton bought out the entire contents of a store for himself.[84] Poverty by 1862 was so widespread it overpowered relief agencies. The state, charities, and Confederate government were needed to help combat starvation.

"By 1862, citizens' needs had outstripped the capacities of county governments at that time, and the scope of suffering so alarmed county officials that they created extensive new mechanisms to provide food and needed commodities."[85] "Gov. Vance and the General Assembly did all they could to alleviate food shortages by instituting a state-run program to

---

*   Quote by a North Carolina woman

sell food at cost to the families of absent soldiers, but they achieved little when it came to attempts to curb the excesses of impressments . . . . additional personnel were appointed to help county officials carry out their burgeoning duties." These agents traveled the county looking for destitute families while visiting the affluent to beg for foodstuffs or to buy them at a lower price. Agents would purchase food, salt, cards, and commodities for those who were suffering.[86]

The state government requested in the local newspapers for farmers to grow more corn and wheat rather than tobacco and cotton. The *Raleigh Register* responded with the following comment: "There is an insane greed for money that some men actually plant cotton for market instead of for the support of life."[87] Catherine Edmondston said in the spring of 1862: "We only plant 40 acres of Cotton. Last year we planted 300."[88] Large planters chose to plant more corn and wheat.

Officials in Onslow County named an all-male committee in ten districts to look after families of soldiers. They purchased and stored food to be distributed to them. Cotton cards were supplied to dependent families.[89] These agents also sought to supply the indigent families with a salt ration. Julia Tillinghast's niece wrote from Yadkin County of the food shortages in that area due to absence of the volunteers. Soon, the fields were barren. She was loath to ask her aunt for food but found it necessary.[90]

In August, citizens of Bertie County keenly felt shortages of food. Authorities ordered that pork was to be given out to needy soldiers' wives. Money was given to the wardens for the poverty-stricken.[91] "By the winter of 1862 the mountain people began to suffer from deprivations of the necessities of everyday life."[92] Scholars attribute this again to the lack of men left at home. Colonel H. H. Davidson wrote to Lieutenant Colonel William Walker about feeding the hungry of the county:

> A number have not had bread in their house for days. Send by some safe hand all the sacks [corn] you have on hand or can get from the waggoners. I understand that Mrs. Julius Young has some infirm and decrepit Negroes in her family. If so, in issuing the rations to her you will include those.[93]

"Beyond question the standard for defining poverty was rather a strict one, because county courts determined need by the number of people who were actually without enough food to maintain life. Women without children were supposed to fend for themselves," noted Escott.[94] The amount of corn and bacon distributed to families varied from county to county, and it also had to do with the victuals available at the time. On average, a woman with one child got three pecks of corn and about four pounds of bacon each month. The more children you had, the quantity increased. In Chatham County, a clerk listed amounts furnished in January 1864 for a soldier's wife and three children as "$3.21 and to one person, an amount of 20c to $1.66. Another mother and one child: received $11.15 in the form of flour, $30 worth of beef which turned out to be 20 lbs, and $20 worth of corn (one bushel)." Next month, "one mother and child received 11 lbs of Flour ($13.25), 3 gal of molasses at $36.00, and 1 ½ bu of corn which had gone up to $30.00."[95] A lady from Hillsdale informed the governor about the changes in her neighborhood:

> . . . I am only allowed $10.00 for my self and one child [.] a woman with two childrens only allowed $13.00 per month to get meat and bread with [.] grain is from $20.00 to $30.00 per bushel[,] bacon from $3.00 to $5.00 per pound . . .

She complained that there were men who had it to sell but would not. Those men sold to the factories instead of soldiers' wives. Other men who had molasses to sell would only take grain in exchange. Women felt desperate measures needed to come about. She told Vance:

> . . . I have never tried to discourage my husband any at all . . . but you think for yourself of this manner if you was in the army and was to hear your

wife and children was suffiring and could not get anything to eat [.] I think you would be very much tempted to start home . . . please fix as soon as you can . . . . they have got spun cotton out of reach [.] it is $80.00 per bunch in Greensboro that will take eight months wages a soldier gets to get one bunch of cotton . . .[96]

Agent George W. Collier kept a list of provisions he gave to destitute families. The list is of soldiers' wives in Pruetts's District. An additional list featured in the appendix shows the number of children with the mother, whether they are needy or not for a total of seventy-nine.[*]

February 25, 1864   CORN SENT TO SOLDIERS' WIVES
Mrs. R.E. Fleming..2 ½ bushels corn
Mrs. Jackson Branche ....2 ½ bu corn
Mrs. Davis Barber 2
Elizabeth Clark...1/2
Mrs. Robert Braswell 1

March 2, 1864
Mrs. S. E. Bently..2
No one is to get more than 2.5 bushels

March 30, 1864
Gave out potatoes and three cotton cards
Mrs. R.E. Fleming..1 ½ lb potatoes
Mrs. Thomas O. Setzer ....1 lb potatoes and 4 cotton cards

Some of the people who received corn got other foodstuffs too. In May, they were given peas. In August, they were given salt, usually five to ten pounds. In August, Mrs. Elizabeth Hood got a pair of cards, as did Mrs. Catherine Suddeth.[97] One lady recalled after the war that the women that lived below her would have to come to get their allowance of salt or corn at the Whiteville depot, and they would have to take it on their shoulders and carry it from ten to fifteen miles, and "my house was their stopping place. We were frightened most of the time. We would hear all kinds of rumors and were listening all the time to hear that some of our loved ones were dead."[98]

——————————

Being in the poorhouse was nothing new to certain people. Antebellum citizens were committed to helping the destitute through church contributions and with government funding. Several counties collected a certain percent of taxes from its people. These supported the poorhouse. In 1862, Dr. B. F. Mebane was appointed physician to look over the poorhouse in Orange County. The following information in 1862 would be a typical inventory for poorhouses around the state—cattle, mostly hogs, farm tools, a wagon, churns, chairs and tables, tubs and buckets, a stove, chests, bedsteads, feather beds, eating utensils, tinplates, tin pans, a coffeepot, Irish potatoes, and grain such as oats and wheat. The inventory for one year later listed approximately the same farm tools with less hogs and grain, but more cattle. Due to inadequate clothing supplies, the home was given a loom, five spinning wheels, and two pairs of cotton/wool cards. Thirty-two paupers were then boarding. There was also more "Out-Door" poor listed, meaning those *not* living at the poorhouse, probably destitute soldiers' wives.

——————————

*   See the appendix for names in Pruetts's District and Orange County poorhouse and amounts doled out to families in Chatham County in January 1864.

Of other miscellaneous expenses recorded during the November term of 1862, the court ordered payment of three dollars to A. M. Jordan for making a coffin for Abram Hood. The court passed an order to reimburse Mrs. Hopkins fifteen dollars for the care and attention to the burial of Mrs. McGee when she became sick and died. Apparently, the court reimbursed persons for business with the "Out-Door" poor too. By February 1864, the court had petitioned for five thousand dollars yearly for support of the poor in Orange County alone. In September of that year, the poor house still had its wagon but had lost the ox and had fewer cattle with six hogs.

A year later, the request for money had gone up to fifteen thousand dollars.[99] Escott goes on to say, "Officials in Orange county recorded that in 1863 there were five hundred eight women receiving aid and that in 1865 this increased to almost twenty percent of white women population."[100]

"In those heroic times the condition of need was so universal that there was no feeling of mortification because of the absence of accustomed luxuries and indeed of the merest necessaries of life. Women suffered; and save for their mourning and for their anxieties for loved ones in peril, they made no sign of discontent," replied a woman who lived the era.[101] That statement was written forty years after the conflict. Perhaps the author had forgotten the real hardships as shown in another woman's opinion. This one had lost many relatives in the war and became angry instead of despondent. Her anger was directed at gender because it only left women to pray and provide for the "defenders."[102]

Mrs. Nathaniel Phillips's husband, a soldier in Thomas's Legion, wrote to Colonel Cathey in an attempt to get grain for his family:

> I hope you will try to help me[.] I have bee in the Service nearly three years & my family has not got provisions to DO them a month & the frost & the Bushwhackers & Yankies has Ruined this County so it is impossible for them to stay here [.] Let me hear from you by first mail as what to do [.] I must do promptly Direct your letters to Valley Town North Carolina Your Best N. G. Phillips[103]

Those residents who before the war were self-supporting faced very real problems with starvation during the conflict. "The poor were no longer the infirm or the few without character or shame; they were ordinarily respectable citizens on whom the government depended for military service and loyal support."[104]

"By 1863 the threat of starvation was quite substantial in many sections of North Carolina," according to researcher Crawford.[105] A soldier stationed at Fort Holmes informed his mother late in 1864, "I am afraid that starvation will end this war yet."[106] The next writer gave a sample of the destitute condition of her family and the difficulty she had in getting her needs met. Emma A. Shoolbred of Henderson County wrote to Colonel Joseph Cathey of Haywood County on March 30, 1863:

> Flat Rock, Col. Cathey Sir: Though personally a stranger to you, I know that you are acquainted with my son, James, and am induced to apply to you in a time of difficulty [.] I have been a widow for three years, and James and his two younger brothers being in the army, in Virg., and my eldest at [illegible] I am entirely with out anyone to assist me [.] the war has greatly reduced my circumstances, and I find it hard to live. I have many small negro children besides their parents to feed, and would be glad to know if I can purchase some corn from you at reasonable price, and if you would allow me to purchase from you an ox, as I have lately lost one of mine, and understand from W [illegible] Taborn that I cannot procure one in this neighborhood. I should also be glad to know the price of wheat flour, and if I can get any from you. An early answer will oblige.

Yours respectfully, E.A. Shoolbred Flat Rock, N.C.

Please name the price of the ox corn and flour if I can obtain them from you or in your neighborhood
Emma A. Shoolbred[107]

"There is a scarcity of grain in this section of the Country [Shallowford, NC]. Our County made large appropriations to buy grain for soldier's families, and for the poor who are not able to procure it for themselves. Agents employed by the County went to South Carolina, bought large quantities of corn and peas, got it to the railroad depot and not one bushel can now be got on the railroad," said a civilian. Due to regulations, the military needs came first.[108]

In occupied territory along the coastal counties, inhabitants grew thin from lack of food. It caught the eye of a Union cavalryman. He described the scene in a letter home:

I know the truth of the reports of famine among them; day after day, men, women, and children come to our lines to get into New-Bern to buy bread, and beg to be allowed to enter the lines; the women weeping and the children crying for food; but it can not be; many of them are spies, and we can not sacrifice our cause to alleviate the suffering of a minority; but it can not last long. The men will not stand idly by and see their wives, mothers, and children dying of hunger, and their sons often times taken by force from their homes, to fill the ranks . . .[109]

Starvation did occur during the war. Nimrod J. Bell was a conductor on different Southern railroads. He worked on the Wilmington–Manchester (SC) line during the war, frequently carrying cotton to port. In 1864, he told the story of a boy and his sister who lived outside of Wilmington. When Mr. Bell's train would be sidetracked, this couple would come over and beg for food. He always "gave them all the meat, bread, potatoes, and syrup that they could carry away." These children had both a sick mother and grandmother. Their father had been killed in the war. "Some months afterwards I was passing at the same place where I usually saw the children, and a man got on my train. I asked him about the two children, and related the circumstances to him. He said the women died, and the little boy and girl starved to death. I lay over one night at a station on the Wilmington-Manchester Railroad where corn was issued out to the soldiers' wives by the Confederate government. I never saw so many carts, some pulled by horses, some by mules, some by oxen, and the drivers all women."[110] Mr. Bell had access to coffee that others found hard to obtain. He kept his family in good supply.

Mary Hinshaw lost her infant son to starvation. Emotional stress has been known to cause a decrease in mother's milk. Mary didn't have enough milk to nourish the baby, and their cow had been stolen too. She was unable to find a wet nurse.[111] In a letter written from Rebecca Davis to her soldier son, Burwell, she noted:

Your Aunt Jennie did send down to your uncle Sam two weeks ago and asked him to give her something to eat to keep her from starving. She hadn't a grain of corn in her crib, nor a mouthful of meat in her smokehouse.[112]

Mrs. Jennie Powell, a widow, said, "To beg so humbly, even from a near relative, was as great an agony as hunger hirself."[113] Poorer women were embarrassed to ask their wealthy kinfolk or the government for assistance. These unfortunate women had to get help writing letters to officials.[114] Thomas Ruffin received a letter from his friend Walter Gwyn, which told of the plight of his family: "I fear starvation, meal is $3 a bushel. I have witnessed great distress among the lower to poorer classes."[115]

"In Cherokee County, the costs were so high that many local women could not afford to purchase supplies." A Jackson County woman stated that the wives and children of Cherokee Indian soldiers were "living on weeds and the bark of trees . . . ," wrote author McKinney.[116] A common occurrence along Sherman's march through the state found residents following the army trail and picking up grains of corn the horses had spilled.[117] They were desperate.

Although the Edmondston family in Halifax was wealthy, the lady of the home said she felt humbled by the poverty around her. "Surely this war is meant to check the profusion in which we have lived & to teach the rising generation economy & the employment of their resources." Two months later, she would lament, "A dinner of four courses is . . . a rarity now-a-days."[118] In writing her friend Isaac Brown, Mary Outten told him that "the war has taught me to deny myself many things which I once thought indispensable."[119]

A teenage boy of fourteen in 1864 recollected that "cotton could no longer be gotten to market, and the fertile fields, formerly devoted to its culture, now yielded abundant crops of corn, peas, potatoes, . . . oats, and wheat."[120]

In January 1864, the Rowan County court appointed a person who collected food for indigent soldiers' families. This agent reported that he had been unsuccessful for the 750 families, including 1,163 children under the age of ten. "The court then authorized him to make efforts to purchase Confederate tithe corn and wheat for the relief of the poor."[121] "In Duplin County thirty-three per cent of adult white women were on relief . . . forty per cent were found in Cumberland County."[122] "A study of surviving records from several counties in North Carolina found that from one fifth to two fifths of the white population depended on government relief efforts for cornmeal and pork."[123]

Not all counties suffered with shortages at the same time. Shortages appeared according to your location. If a person lived near a training camp, a battleground, or along the rail lines or waterways, he would be more prone to run short on food due to soldiers stealing from him. Confederate soldiers were equally disdainful of property rights. They took what they needed, giving Confederate States promissory notes to those deemed loyal to the South. Those in the country seemed to fare better than their counterparts in the city. Their needs were different at times. In the city, a person may need firewood, housing, or a decent cheap meal, whereas the rural family had those but needed salt to preserve meat or yarn to make garments. Food shortages evolved due to poor transportation facilities causing victuals to rot alongside railroad tracks.

Writer Escott admitted, "Inequities in the war effort become such a source of strong complaint. As conditions deteriorated, yeoman families and the poor begun to suffer well in advance of the rich, and they often felt that they were making a larger contribution . . . . The poverty of the masses fed the alarming increases in class resentment, desertion, and the resistance to authority."[124] With inflation, tithes, the blockade, and shortages, yeomen farmers and the lower class of people were staring starvation in the face with some dying. The poor houses began to fill up.

Being poor had a social stigma attached. The public looked negatively on these individuals; and they had a tendency to classify them with the insane, with criminals, with the elderly, and with the handicapped. Theft of food occurred so often that it was not always reported. "Tens if not hundreds of thousands of small farmers in North Carolina fell into the frightened grip of poverty," proclaimed author Paul Escott.[125] Another view of the period may have been colored by time. "Those persons recalling events years afterward failed to mention or did not want to remember the really hard times."[126]

Women of all educational levels wrote to officials about their situation. Ladies found problems retrieving goods from state-run charity programs. Margaret Smith wrote on February 9, 1863:

We have not drawn nothing but want in three months an without help we must starv. How can our husbands suporte ther famileys at a Levin dollars

amouth when we have to give to the Speculator 2 dollars a bushel for Bred
and fifty sent a pound for our meet?* . . . now wee have Becom Beggars and
Starvers an now way to help our selves.[127]

To make it easier for families to receive their share, advertisements were inserted in
the local newspapers:

> **Notice to Soldiers' Families**: I will attend at the Court House in Raleigh
> on Wednesday and Saturday of each week, for the purpose of paying off the
> orders issued by agents for the relief of indigent families of soldiers. JD Hayes,
> County Commissioner.[128]

Perhaps the next woman had not seen the advertisement. Mrs. Louisa Reavis felt it
necessary to write the governor:

> Mr. Vance:
> Sir I will drop you a few lines to inform you that I want you if you please to
> send me a order to show to the committy so they will allow me something to
> eat [.] my chance is so bad that I Cant go myself to sea you [.] I have three small
> children and I have no person to stay with them [.] I hope you will do as well for
> me by riting as if I have to go sea you [.] my husband has bin serving 18 months
> and I have never drawed anything at all [.] I have tried the committy and they
> wont do nothing for me without leaf from you or the cort and I am without
> meat and I cant get one mouthful [.] I never wood apply to the committy as
> long as I could live without it but I have come to the place I am bownd to draw
> or suffer. I want you to send an answer by this black man if you pleas [.] I went
> to sea last Thursday but you was not at home . . . . the committys names Simon
> turner Simon Smith and Jonathan Smith [.] they try to ceep all of us from
> drawing anything [.]if you will send them a order . . . tell them how much to
> give a month [.] they will cheat me out if they can . . .[129]

Eliza Stinson recollected that the people in Fayetteville were not "subject to the horrors
of actual battle, [yet they] endured privation never before dreamed of. Those called the
poor got along as well as ever . . . as they didn't scruple to ask for help; but the suffering was
among those families who were accustomed to every comfort, and were above asking or
even receiving assistance from others, and many families of this class found great difficulties
in procuring the bare necessities of life!" She said she knew of cases where corn bread was
the only food used all day. When the town grew with refugees and workers at the Arsenal,
meat became scarce.[130] Another lady recalled: "In the summer we lived upon a vegetable
and fruit diet, but in winter, corn bread and pork formed the bulk of our living." Many times,
all the family had to eat for supper consisted of a roasted potato or a bowl of mush. To help
with storing food for winter, the family used molasses or honey "to put up fruit." Molasses
or apple pie formed the favorite sweet consumed.[131] In Fayetteville, teenager Melinda Ray
entered into her diary a comment about candy:

> Jan. 5, 1863—I had a very pleasant tho' not a very merry Christmas. I did
> not see a bit of candy. I have a little tiny piece put away & marked "candy" to
> remember how it looked, not enough to taste.

---

*   Privates made eleven dollars a month, and this was impossible to support one person, much less
     a family. There were some months in which the private was not paid at all. The situation at home
     became desperate.

Former General D. H. Hill told of a society belle who wrote him, "I had eleven ladies working in the field with me today. I have myself recently hoed 2500 hills of corn."[132] One cousin made the remark to another cousin, "This has been the good as well as the bad . . . (speaking of her healthy stout friend from all the hard labor she did on the farm)."[133] One woman found temporary work as a clerk for Captain Marsh in his office. The following month, she started a primary school and a music school in her home. Elle Andrews reported that she had to sell part of her furniture along with the house to survive. Mrs. Andrews took a job teaching at the widow Roxanne Worth McNeill's home in Fayetteville and said, "It was good company to her."[134] Elizabeth Robeson wove cloth for sale or barter. "I warped 38 yards of cloth for a friend," she said. Later in the fall, she recorded in her diary, "I warped a piece of cloth 32 yards for Miss Sally."[135] Apparently, some white women hired themselves out as domestics. This is mentioned in a letter between friends: "They will not stay over a month at a place and are not to be depended on."[136]

Women managed to earn a few coins with their ingenuity. Farm women had the usual "butter and egg" things to peddle. Sallie Blount dyed feathers and sold them. Ladies were forever trying to get new bonnets. "I don't know when ever I can have it done [a bonnet], there is no milliner at all here now but I am going to try to have it done somewhere before summer," she wrote. Parts of old bonnets were recycled. Tarboro had been a modern town prewar. One milliner claimed to have sold a bonnet and dress to Queen Victoria. Blount complained to her aunt how difficult it was to purchase goods.[137] A Mrs. Boles made ink and gave it to the soldiers passing through Wilmington. The money raised from sales helped to purchase food and cloth. "One article I remember was the English goods for gentlemen's suits cost me $75 a yard. Flannel was $40 a yard," replied Mrs. Boles.[138] A lady earned twenty-five dollars when government cattle drovers stayed overnight at her home on their way to the quartermasters. She also hired out some of her slaves. A January notation in her diary, Elizabeth Robeson said, "Our Negroes that were hired out came back last night, great rejoicing with them."[139] The North Carolina Railroad Company advertised not only for workers, but for goods needed by the workmen. Women along the line could earn money or provisions by sewing pants and shirts, doing laundry, or cooking for the hands. Of the list of goods sold to the railroad in 1863, one-half of the commodities were from women.[140]

Author Charles Bolton explained, "Women who headed landless households in the Central Piedmont regularly worked for wages outside their home to support themselves and their families."* Most of these women worked in the mills or tobacco factories. Another historian has written, "Wherever women were hired in these trades, wages fell."[141] A few women worked at the salt factories. An Asheville company employed women to make cigars.[142] "There is a family of girls here [Fayetteville] who have started a bucket-making business," wrote one Tillinghast to his brother.[143] A stocking factory, part cottage industry, employed women and girls at Wilmington. Tops and bottoms of stockings were factory made, then taken home and finished. Mrs. J. C. Wood, a supervisor, said she had to turn away eighteen women seeking employment.[144] Near the end of the conflict, the *Daily Journal* advertised for female mail clerks. This is surprising because that position was one of the most sought-after job by men trying to avoid conscription. Mrs. D. A. Hunt from Wilkes County became a postmistress.[145] A researcher said, "Child care outside the home played an equally important role in providing supplemental income for poor white households."[146]

To keep from starving, white women sought respectable jobs outside the home. Urban upper-class women turned to teaching, boarding house, music lessons, needlework, etc., to support themselves and their children while the father or husband was away in the army.

---

*   In 1860, 3 women worked in the flour mills, 1,315 in cotton mills, 10 in copper mines, 6 in gold mines, 11 in sawmills, 140 in woolen mills, 35 in paper mills, and 23 in rice mills.

Before the war, most teachers were male. Trinity College hired female teachers in 1864 and began to subscribe female students. In Raleigh, Mrs. H. W. Miller took in members of the legislature during the war to supplement her earnings.[147] Mary Bayard Clarke wrote her son, Willie, in January 1865 that she was "trying to get a permanent position in Col [Peter] Mallett's office as he has permission from the Sec of War [John Breckenridge] to employ lady clerks." She said, "If I do you are to have all I make to pay your board which will be however only $150 a month."[148] Ms. Elizabeth M. B. Hoyt of Washington, when the Federals burned her home, went to live with family. She sought a job as a clerk for Major W. E. DeMille,* head of the commissary department in Greenville. Her salary was paid in tobacco, which was exchanged for a barrel of snuff and then sold for twelve dollars.[149] Ms. Anna Johnson from Sampson County became a clerk at brigade headquarters midwar. Ms. Isabell Gill worked in the Confederate Treasury Department signing notes. With the death of her husband, E. J. Holton, Rachael Holton took charge of the *North Carolina Whig*. She felt that the news should continue during the war and worked as editor until a paper shortage closed the business in 1863.[150] People gathered cotton and linen rags and sold them to the paper factories, earning three cents a pound.[151]

In Asheville, Cornelia Henry wrote in her journal: "Mary Rollins brought home some stocking yarn she had to spin. She is busy making clothes for R.W. Candler who is commissary for four or five counties to furnish clothes . . ." for the soldiers.[152] Laura E. Lee Battle recalled her mother riding fifteen miles to Raleigh to collect fabric to sew uniforms. The commissary agent distributed "one hundred soldiers' jackets to make for our soldiers." She and Nealie (a sister) began sewing on them the next day, and so they "continued to do through the four long years . . ." Battle continued: "My poor mother, at intervals, would stop sewing to help weave the cloth for our clothes, Aunt Pallas [slave] usually finding time to spin the cotton. My task was given me every day after school, either to make a pair of linings for the sleeves of the soldiers' jackets or go to the kitchen and help Aunt Pallas spin the cotton."[153] Another Raleigh woman made uniforms from scraps. She obtained from the commissary department a large quantity of remnants from suits made there for the soldiers, paying twenty-five dollars (Confederate money) to have a two-horse load hauled to her home, and out of these scraps she made more than a hundred suits by combining different colors.[154]

Most women of the time period knew how to sew. An account paid to a seamstress in 1861 recovered a receipt for making three calico dresses, $3; one walking dress, $3.50 and another for $2.50 and one for $1; a cloak, $3.50; a jacket, $1.50; a dress, $5; nine garments trimmed for $5; and a jacket for $.75.[155] In the next letter, a woman told how much females were paid to make uniforms for the state:

> We are all soldiers wives, or mothers . . . how far will eleven dollars go in a family now when meat is from 75 to $1.00 pr. Pound, flour $50 pr bll, wood from 4 to 5$ pr load, meal b[ran]4 an 5 dollars pr bushel, eggs 50 to 60 cts pr dz . . . molasses $7[.]00 per gal . . . . we are willing & do work early & late to keep starvation which is now staring us in the face. But the Government only allows us 50 cents a pr for lined pants and 75 cents for coats and there are few of us who can make over a dollar a day and we have upon an average from three to five helpless children to support . . . . Now Sir how we ask you in the name of God are we to live?[156]

Research has found a typical letter written to the governor telling him of their situation at home. Letters of this type really pull at the heartstrings. Unfortunately, most went unanswered, so we don't know their outcome:

---

*   "No record of Beaufort County during the war would be complete without mentioning Miss Elizabeth M.B. (Aunt Bet) with her brother-in-law, Major DeMille. She had the distinction of being the first woman in North Carolina appointed to the Confederate forces."[157]

Nov The 29 1862 NC Iredell Co

Ser it is with and aking hart and tremulous hand I seat my self this morning to inform you of my condition my onkly der son volunteered and inlisted to fite for his country May the 2, 1862 he rented my farm to Mr Shearer left my self and a sister in his car he dide last april I cold not get any person to tend my farm my dorters as of delicate constitution my friends ar all in the army and the most of them ded my son en lar went with the recrutes in March and dide from the forteague of the battles around Richmon hour farms join he left six childr his name was Edson he lost his life for his country my der son lives as far as I no I received a letter from him last weak he was in the valleys in Va ner strors Burge Gen Lees army & hedy NCA troops co H car of capt Osburn he is serlj in that co hs is Fin a soalder as ever lived he fort thru the battles around Richmion and in mererland nd agrate many more The God of battle has spared his life he is a tru son as a Mother eve r rased he oud 50 od dollars when he inlisted for which I was security for my land is now advertised for sale for That det he has bin Trying to pay that deat eve r since he left it has Taken all he cold get for my serport and to alorate his own sufferings The cost and in Trust on that det now amounts to ninety dollars pleas bee so condersendin as to bar with my weak partision as nesesaty compels me to apply I have made all exsersions during This awful war to do all I cold Towards cloathing the soalders tho it is hard to get much don at that the Specurlators will prove too hard for us as we have every thing to by and so little to by with som times I am all moast reddy to giv up the struggle as Thar is no ey to pitty or hand to suath her I li in a pore neighborhood Those That can as sis The nedy will not do so tha all have exceuse some say I cold of cep't my son from going others say thars wold not have gon if it had not bin for him I had one side of bacon from the Government the summer after my son left is all I have hade I am in my 72 yer my husband served 6 months in the last wor he has binded 10 yer and I was left my son I do not no What he wold do if he nu it pleas excuse bad spelling and writing and help me if you pleas I cannot see well I old and nervus.

Jamima A. Thomas*[158]

Her son Isaac H. Thomas enlisted June 1861 in the Fourth Regiment. This poor elderly soul couldn't get any help from her neighbors. They even complained that her son took their sons with him when he volunteered. Thomas said she only got one ration of bacon since the government gave to the needy. For the readers, her letter is translated into a more readable form found in the appendix.

A soldier's account to his friend about inflation mid-war said his wife made cider from white apples:

> . . . We are getting the tenth of crops to feed on, are horses are faring well, corn is worth $20 for barrel as for wheat, there is none to sell. Bacon is worth $2 per lb butter the same, sweet potatoes $4 eggs from 50 to 75 cents per doz. Lard $2 pound chickens $1 each fish and oysters are cheap and plenty close to camp. Brandy is worth from $10-12 a quart.
> PS write to me all the news about the Union men and deserters in Wilkes Co[159]

Widows were especially hard-hit, and there were many due to the war. With the death of her husband, a lady who had lost her servant on loan from another family recalled that

---

* For a more readable version of the letter see the appendix.

friends furnished her bread, but she said she did all the rest of the work in providing for her small household.[160] Widows chose to live with family members if possible.

———————

The editor of the *Church Intelligencer* blamed ladies for bringing on the war. He said, "The ladies have brought about this war. They must have their finery, comfort and luxuries from the North." A rebuttal to this accusation was printed soon after. The authoress did not sign her name but was livid in her response. She said the minister who wrote the comment was probably Northern-born and wore northern clothes. She also said that editors of other newspapers had been busy asking the ladies to "ECONOMISE—as if we could not, would not, and did not." She went on to say:

> Gentlemen, gentlemen, ECONOMISE! Quit smoking, it injures your nerves and debilitates your purse; quit chewing, it ruins your breath your teeth and your wife's temper; no lady can abide the abominable practice. Quit wearing cravats! Of what earthly use is a piece of cloth doubled about your neck? Show your good sense by depriving fashion, and fatten your purses by saving that much money.—"What's the use of coat-tails?" Have them cut off forthwith; they're nothing but superfluous danglers in the air;—it won't take near so much cloth to make a coat minus the tail. Boots are another useless expense and waste of leather. Get you some good brogans and coarse home-knit socks to keep your feet warm and dry, then wear your pants short enough to keep the hems from being frayed . . . as for appearances, you're too sensible to care for THAT.
>
> The question is—do you really know what economy is? Do you deny yourself a box of Havanas or champagne wine? Quit hounding your wife to economize and to sew, sew, sew.
>
> Once and for all, gentlemen, let us assure you that you waste time and materials, when you get upon the subject of Ladies affairs. The only effect has been to excite contempt in the minds of the fair sex, which is inevitable when a man descends from this high position in which nature and necessity places him, to dabble in matters which do not belong to the "Lords" of creation [ministers].[161]

David Schenck, of Lincoln County, blamed the cause of shortages on editor W. W. Holden, with his peace movement, and Judge Pearson, for releasing deserters who robbed the poor. Even more significant, the fall season in 1863 found inflation rampant. Currency had lost its value. Most agreed it would be better to hire slaves at this point than buy them, but hired slaves were getting difficult to find.[162] Advertisements flooded newspapers with persons seeking to hire. Charles Pettigrew of Washington County took many of his slaves to Salisbury to work on the railroad.

———————

One researcher claimed that North Carolina's civilians suffered more than the average Southerner "due to guerilla warfare, union occupation along the coast, the state supplying its own troops, and union sympathizers."[163] No matter the reason for poverty, several historians claim that the loss of white male laborers from the home front as the main cause. A planter wrote his friend:

> If all of our efficient men are taken off, I think it questionable whether we will make more provisions than will answer our purposes, and I am certain we can't keep that order and discipline that is necessary in the neighborhood, as there is now disposition among the Negroes to be more sulky and not so

biddable. I have no overseer and can't get one . . . . In fact the Negroes are doing pretty much as they please.[164]

Brothers writing to each other mid-war discussed multiple problems:

> Angus you never saw such times. Corn is from $3 to $4 per bushel. Bacon if it could be had is worth from 75 cts to one dollar per pound. Spun thread is said to bring $10-$12 per bunch at Beaver Creek and every thing that we have to buy is extremely high. We have planted a tolerable crop this year if we can get provision to work it [illegible] the cattle are out of danger now except the old yellow cow. She is getting so she can get up by herself . . . We have very dry weather right now . . .[165]

FOOD IN SHORT SUPPLY

> The ladies down south they do not denigh,
> They usted to drink the coffey & now they drink the rye,
> The ladies in dixey, they are quite in the dark,
> They used to bye the indigo & now they bil the bark.[166]

Leonidas Torrence wrote to his mother about the high price of food a few months after the war started. He had to pay "50c for watermelon, 2cts for a rostenears [roasting ears], 25cts for a chicken the size of a partridge, 20cts a dozen eggs . . ." In six months, the price of food rose to fifty to seventy-five cents for chickens, eggs climbed fifty to sixty cents, butter seventy-five cents a pound, and milk from fifteen to twenty-five cents a quart. If only he knew the price would go much, much higher.[167] Southrons produced more for the consumption of their family members than did comparable households up North because society offered fewer opportunities for the purchase of basic foods, clothing, and commodities.[168] Home manufacturing increased during the war whenever possible so farmers could barter or sell their surplus.

The lower-income citizens of Wilmington would suffer from the lack of proper food, as the elite could pay the exorbitant prices. The mountain counties ran short of food for many reasons. The weather certainly influenced production and harvest. So did the Southern Army. Confederate troops from North Georgia and Union soldiers from East Tennessee would forage and recruit men from the western part of the state.[169] The cavalry would also harass the inhabitants and eat up their meager provisions. They brought the horses into these counties to feed and rejuvenate them, as well as to gather new mounts. These cavalrymen took horses and stock. A man from Traphill found it necessary to inform Governor Vance of their plundering:

> May 5, 1864
> . . . a detachment of Genl. Morgans command eight hundred strong passed through & . . . 50 of the best horses in . . . Wilkes . . . Surry . . . and part of Allegany County was stolen . . . in nos of cases they stole horses from the wives [of soldiers] . . . . the only horse . . . left to tend their crops . . .
> A few weeks ago Genl Longstreets army they robed the County of every yoke of oxen and cows that could go & pretending to have receipts for them that are not worth carrying . . . starvation seems to be inevitable . . . we cannot live under such treatment . . . we cannot pay such taxes . . . our tithes are a true horror . . . our horses . . . are all stolen from us. Something must be done.[170]

A citizen commented, "It requires at least 4-6 quarts of grain (corn or oats) and 6-10 pounds of forage (fodder or hay in bulk) to feed one average sized horse or mule one day."[171] One of authority said that the soldiers coerced the farmers to sell them corn much less than the market value. Governor Vance wrote to both Jefferson Davis and Seldon, secretary of war, to complain about the Confederate cavalry pasturing their starving mounts in the western counties. Vance said it threatened the countryside with famine. "When the question of starvation is narrowed down and women and children on the one side and some worthless cavalry horses on the other, I can have no difficulty in making a choice." He went on to say that if the horses weren't removed soon, he was calling out the militia.[172]

Soldiers either North or South had a way of eating everything in their path. "One member of the 30th Virginia opined that the basic trouble with the civilian population [in NC] was that 'there has been so many troops here that everything has been swept.'" C.S. General Montgomery Corse increased guards and strengthened regulations requiring passes off base.[173] Troops continually stole potatoes, hogs, chickens, etc., from the neighborhood.

Natural disasters and disease occurring during the war had a devastating effect on supply and pricing of food. A man wrote his son that an early frost came in September 1863:

> Our crops are short and the winter has been the longest ever known, having the frost the 18th of Sept., to kill all vegetables and grasses so from that time to this, cattle, stock of all kind has had to be fed.[174]

A severe drought occurred in 1863–1864, causing a food shortage. One disastrous freeze killed young piglets, lambs, and calves. The drop in temperature occurred all over the state that winter, 1864–1865. Ice was three to four inches thick on the creeks. Anna Fuller composed a letter to her friend: "Vegetation is very backwards. The buds of the forest trees are scarcely swollen. Corn is selling at $2.30 per [bushel] butter at $5 and bacon at $7-$8 lb." That was in mid-April.[175]

Friends writing to each other in the spring of 1865 said:

> The people is the latest with ther plowing I ever knowed them [.] we have had a heap of Jany weather [.] the wheat & winter Oats is badly damaged by the hard freeze [.] last winter Oats sold verry Scarce & every thing els in the way of provisions Some corn Selling at $40.00 pr bushel flower $300.00 pr Barrel [.] We have had the worst winter you ever saw I reacon for wet weather [.] We havent ploughed any scarcely but for the last three day it is beautiful weather and I hope it will remain so for some time so that what few people there is at home can fix to plant their crops[.] Wheat is looking as sorry as you ever saw it [.] I think it will be entirily too thin. it has been the worst winter I ever saw [.] we have done nothing but cut wood and make firewood[.][176]

Soldier A. M. Gray received two letters from family members about the extremely cold weather and its effect on his stock:

> Some of your sows had pigs in the sleat [.] I think about 14 in all but they are all dead but 7 and two of them look like they will die [.] some of your Sheep had little lambs but there is only one living now [.] Major said all but six of you[r] little pig[s] dide in time of that Sleat [.] thur was four lamb[s] but two is dead [.] you[r] horses is in good order [.][177]

A woman said in a letter in the fall of 1863: "Nearly all our hogs have died of the cholera—the whole community is infected with it . . ."[178]

The January flood of 1865 tore up railroad tracks in the piedmont, as well as washed away bridges, mills, and buildings. The freshet in Chatham County washed away all the bridges on the Haw River and damaged Brown's and Turner's mills. "All bridges on the Neuse River towards the east except Powell's and Battle's [Bridges] were swept away. Much fodder was ruined," noted the *Daily Conservative*, a Raleigh newspaper.[179] There were fires in Charlotte and Salisbury, in which these two natural disasters caused the price of flour and corn to skyrocket. Court records reveal action taken to alleviate the shortage:

> . . . owing to the very heavy freshet of last year and the long and severe drought of the present . . . a very small supply of grains and provisions for the use of the people are on hand . . . It is ordered that our County Commissioner . . . to use . . . all government dues of grain & provisions, but especially by grain arising from tithes or otherwise . . .[180]

Meat was difficult to buy for some individuals. Rebecca Davis said, "Dr. Mat was here a few days since . . . meat, he says doesn't aspire to, says he never could supply his family with that article . . ."[181] W. W. Lenoir wrote his brother, Rufus: "We are not in such straits for food. You say we will not have salt enough to save our meat. Meat is a luxury."[182] B. M. Kimberly in a letter to his sister said, "Beef is a rarity we seldom see, when we do get it we pay from ten to twelve cents a pound . . . Money is so very scarce here that nothing hardly would be sold if prices were any higher."[183]

Overseer Wyatt Jordan wrote his employer, Jonathan Worth, about the problems procuring meat for winter. The first letter was written in November and the second in December 1862:

> . . . I have been trying to buy pork but find no one ready to say what he will sell at (.) I could have engaged pork two weeks ago at $20 and think I can get some yet. You can send salt as soon as you can for if I buy it will be coming in sum.[184]

The supply of meat was especially short following the fall of Vicksburg because it was difficult to get the beef out of Texas. One main reason for the inadequate supply of food throughout the army was poor distribution, poor conditions of the railroads, and downright bad management.[185] Officials bought beef from the state of Florida. The shortage of meat grew so desperate in 1864 that General Lee "asked permission to trade cotton and tobacco for meat through the Northern lines. Secretary of War, Seddon, agreed, and a limited exchange was started," wrote author Stephen Wise.[186]

Boys trapped rabbits and muskrats using both the meat and selling their pelts. The population of wild animals decreased in the war. Some Wake County boys talked about the scarceness of rabbits when Sherman's troops came through. People must have grown tired of eating the same things as indicated by the following poem:

> Rabbits hot & rabbits cold,
> Rabbits young and rabbits old;
> Rabbits tender and rabbits tough—
> Thank the Lord, we had rabbits enough.[187]

Two men in Person County went hunting around Christmas: "I was a squirrel Hunting yesterday and today kill[ed] 16 yesterday and me and Harvey Roundtree killed 12 today [.]"[188]

Walter Gwyn wrote to Thomas Ruffin in 1864:

> Much suffering among the people exist . . . in Chatham county, one of the best counties in the state for provisions, a great many have not had any

meat for months. Clothing is very scarce. People known as the poorer class are almost destitute.[189]

George Walker said that he went all through the war and never had any milk or potatoes.[190] Yet Rebecca Davis wrote her son that they had a bumper crop of potatoes that year. One measured twenty inches around. She told him she had sold a bushel of dried apples for ten dollars.[191] A refugee in Hillsborough, Mary Outten, sent a letter to her friend: "I have not had a mellon in two years . . . they sell for $3 to $10 . . . which we used to get two for five cents . . . the war has taught me to deny myself many things which I once thought indispensable . . ." She told about a friend in Petersburg who reported that several people were killed there from the shelling of the town. The citizens were living in tents in the woods.[192] At least she had a roof over her head.

Citizens economized on meals. People had different solutions for combating the lack of victuals they had grown so accustomed to love in the past. Mrs. Aaron Thomas, a soldier's wife with small children, said she cut back on the amount of food during the war by serving only two meals a day. They grew accustomed to this routine. After better times, the family continued the schedule.[193] A couple from Halifax decided to cut back on desserts, having baked apples instead. A woman wrote her husband that she had to ration the family to one meal a day:

> I understand you have got your ferlow lengthend you are wise in doing so for times is a great deal worse that when you left we only get one meal a day I dont know how we may stand it [.] I will look for you to bring me a little of something to eat but remans your friend til death. Hanna Holland to ML. Holland[194]

A slaveholder thought about reducing the amount of food given to servants. She said that the army was reduced to one-fourth pound of pork per day. "We are discussing the propriety of reducing our Negro allowance in the face of it & sending the surplus to the Qr. Master." She sent off more food and tobacco to her nephews in the army. Her family sent food to other noncombatant relatives as well.[195] W. N. Tillinghast informed his sister:

> They [children] can not now get the sweet things and will not be tempted to stuff themselves. Our breakfast has lately been bread, milk, ryethy [substitute coffee], and tomatoes, or muskmelon. The latter taking the place of meat or butter.[196]

Laura C. Norwood told her brother, Walter, how she solved the food crunch. She revealed to him the formula their mother gave her on how to ration the year's supply of beef for the servants:

> Our Negroes have been doing with less than that of late, for finding that we had very inadequate supply of bacon for this year, and no prospect . . . of getting . . . any more, I have . . . allowed the men 1/3 lb of bacon a day . . . . they have plenty of peas but scarcely any milk.

She would frequently give the servants "what is left on the table after the white family have eaten." She would often weigh the meat portions out along with the leftovers to ensure they got the proper amount. "I think two pounds of salt beef is adequate to one of bacon . . ."[197] A cousin divulged to Emily Tillinghast that her aunt "had to give us soup for breakfast. Isn't that a coming down? However some people don't have that much . . . ."[198] In Davidson County, Eliza Clodfelter wrote to her cousin about neighbors suffering from lack of food.[199] Other cousins writing to each other discussed the plight of food shortages:

[There are] . . . few farmers to cultivate the soil in this section they have all gone to meet the Yankee vandals. There are a dozen or more widows in this district. I do not see what is to become of them if this war lasts long. I am afraid that the poor soldiers will perish if there are not better provisions made than are made at present. [200]

The usual diet in the piedmont was corn bread, sorghum, hominy, and peas. One young man recalled eating mostly long sweetening (sorghum), milk, corn, muffins, and hominy as his evening meals.[201] Dried peaches and apples were a luxury. Winter food for everyone consisted of onions, turnip greens, corn bread, lettuce, and pork if you were lucky to have gotten salt to cure it. "A typical 'blockade meal,'" wrote author Cochran, "consisted of milk, one wheaten biscuit, and a bit of honey." The next meal could be switched to a corn dodger and hominy.[202] Women dried fruit and vegetables to preserve them. Pumpkin, fruit, berries, persimmons, green beans, peas, beans, squash, corn, and such could then be used in the winter. "Nothing that could be dried and so made longer available was wasted," disclosed a planter's wife.[203]

Early in the war, it was easy to obtain coffee as shown in this newspaper ad from the *Hillsborough Recorder*:

3000 bags, good quality, now being landed ex-brig *Union State*, direct from Rio De Janeiro, for sale in bits of ten bags, and upwards, for cash or the equivalent. O.G. Parsley & Co. Wilmington[204]

Coffee was difficult to obtain during the war years. Families fortunate enough to have coffee beans managed to stretch it out by blending a few beans with different grains. Nobody liked the coffee substitutes of sweet potatoes, rye, parched okra seeds, acorns, barley, peanuts, or parched corn.[205] Eliza Tillinghast, of Fayetteville, wrote to her sister:

. . . I tried okra seed coffee yest.; I think it is the most awful stuff I ever tasted, worse than castor oil, salts or anything of the kind. It smells so bad that I could hardly stand pouring it out and as to drinking it that was past the corner.[206]

Of all the coffee substitutes, roasted okra seed was voted as the best. By August 1863, okra sold for seventy-five cents in Wilmington for one dozen pods.[207] Like it or not, substitute coffee was served everywhere. Hotels and hospitals served substitute "rye" coffee. The recipe included these ingredients: one-half cup peanuts, one-half cup wheat or rye, and one-half cup cow peas. Roast then grind. Take one ounce of powder to three-fourths pint of boiling water to make three full "dishes." Another recipe included two great spoonfuls or two heaping tablespoons to each pint of water.[208] "An Excellent Substitute for Coffee" appeared in the *Raleigh Register* four months after secession with the recipe, "for a family of 7-8 persons, take a pint of well toasted corn meal, and add to it as much water as an ordinary sized coffee pot will hold, and then boil it well."[209] Another recipe appeared a month later, which said to use parched ground wheat mixed with one-third part real coffee beans. When January 1862 rolled around, a Raleigh paper published prices from the blockade-runner *Hanna*:

1038 sacks of coffee 60-60 ½ c lb
29 pcs of navy and army cloth at $10, to 12 ½ a yard
100 hhds clarified and brown sugar brought at $8.115c lb.
80 reams of letter paper brought $9.105c per ream
20 carboys carbonic acid brought $1 a lb[210]

A planter wrote in January 1864:

> I am short of everything except rough food for my stock, of which I have enough, perhaps some to spare. My corn and other grain ought to do me very well till harvest, after paying my tithes. I made 1400 lbs of pork which is not enough for my folks for a year, at the rate they have been consuming bacon since I came out.
>
> If the corn fed to the hogs had not been seriously injured by the frost, I would have had some bacon to spare after paying my tithe.[211]

That same month, another person wrote that people became depressed over the high price of provisions. Pork had gone up to two dollars a pound, corn fifty dollars a barrel, and flour even higher. Perhaps they realized it could and would go higher. The meat price was as bad as in other places, but corn and flour worse. As Wilmington's speculators gathered for the weekly auctions near the end of the conflict, inflation made it almost impossible for the ordinary citizen to buy food. A quarter of lamb sold for one hundred dollars and a pound of tea for five hundred dollars.[212] Flour was selling for five hundred dollars a barrel in 1865. Wheat was fifty dollars.[213]

Imported tea was sorely missed. Mrs. Drury Lacy said in a letter to her daughter, Bessie, "I do long for a cup of tea sometimes . . ."[214] One planter's wife mixed blackberry leaves with regular tea leaves to stretch it out. Citizens made yaupon tea, dandelion tea, sassafras tea, and just about any other of kind of tea. Former bondsman Allen Parker said they made tea from the long green needles of the pine tree.[215] In Halifax County, a mistress of a large plantation grew her own tea bushes. She did not record the type of tea.

Apparently, there was no shortage of corn Down East. The problem was of moving it out of the area into other parts of the state for consumption by the military and the civilians. The newspapers published a letter written from the secretary of war to Governor Vance about soldiers running out of food in two weeks, and they must get some from North Carolina. A smart lady said, "The want is not provisions but *management*; they do not feel uneasy about *meat*. It is bread."[216]

More and more farmers planted corn, not necessarily for bread, but to sell to distilleries. The use of corn for whiskey alarmed many people. Farmers could gain a considerable amount more for selling their corn to whiskey distilleries. Sherwood White wrote his soldier son, Joseph, about his neighbors contemplating doing just that:

> They report that the neighborhood made a good corn crop . . . the people are A going to making whiskey out of it [.] there is several that speak of going instead by the hole sale and the consequnce will be corn will be scarce Before another crop can be made . . .[217]

A distillery in Salisbury used one thousand bushels of corn, sixty bushels of rye, and one hundred bushels of wheat *each month* to make whiskey.*[218] It is understandable why the public cried foul. Officials became very concerned that farmers chose to make whiskey from their corn. They felt that the grain would see better use feeding the hungry. Angry persons flooded the newspapers with their comments:

> In Wake County there are thirty distilleries. In Pitt County says a correspondent of the Wilmington Journal, there are 20 and from one point alone in that county can be seen the smoke ascending from 14 distilleries! Averaging 5 distilleries to each county in the state, which is far below the true average—we have for 87 counties 435 distilleries.

----

* Salisbury manufactured 200 to 500 gallons of both whiskey and alcohol per day.

Shall human kindness and human life be jeopardized and thousands of our fellow citizens be subjected to the acceptance of one of two alternatives—starvation and a miserable death, or that of crime by getting money out of the misery they have induced?

Will the Convention sit inactive, inert, perfectly passive, and permit this subject to pass by them unheeded, while in their power to check it? We believe not.[219]

January 29, 1862: **Whiskey Distilleries**—The rapid increase of whiskey distilleries in the state, causes much uneasiness in regard to the increase of whiskey and the decrease of bread. A correspondent of the *Petersburg Express,* from Granville [County] says: "It is truly mortifying for me to add that, from the large number of whiskey distilleries now in operation in this county (17), the prospect for bread, for the poorer classes, is becoming gloomy indeed, and unless our convention, which will meet in a few days, shall do something to rid us of these soul and body destroying institution, the people should and will rise up in defense and exterminate them. Corn, which sold readily in our market and through the county generally, two months ago, at from $2-$2.50 per barrel, can't be bought today at $3.75, and the only palpable cause or reason for it is the high price offered and being given by the distillers."[220]

A correspondent to the same paper from Wilmington said:

The great difficulty is to procure corn. I am told that there is not a bushel in town, and meal is almost as scarce. This is owing to the fact that the distilleries (whose name is legion) are buying up all the corn at $5 a barrel, and turning it into poisonous liquor. There is great indignation at this state of things, and these distilleries will have to be dealt with, or our men starve for bread.

Corn and meal are becoming scarce, and we have heard that between 20-30 whiskey distilleries are in operation in this county. We call attention of the convention and the press throughout North Carolina to the actual state of the case. We must attempt to save our food. We think that four out of five are in favor of something being done. A meeting should be held, not to denounce distillers, but to work out the solution.[221]

In Polk County, B. M. Ednery wrote to the secretary of war to "please not give permits to distillers, who were 'stilling up all the corn from Soldiers' Wives' and would 'ruin & Starve our poor people.'"[222] Objections continued to pour in to newspapers:

Whiskey Distilleries—Statesville, North Carolina:
I sincerely wish that the members of the Convention could be made fully sensible of the large increase in the number of distilleries in the state, and the absolute necessity there is for some efficient legislation, to prevent a consumption of All THE CORN, rye, barley, wheat and other grain, in the manufacture of whiskey. I say all the grain, for of a truth, it will ALL be DESTROYED in this way before mid summer, if some agency be not interposed to prevent it. In this and adjoining counties, the increased number of distilleries is prodigious, and all the grain is being bought up to manufacture into whiskey. If the farmer, who sells the corn, could receive the full benefit, the case would be less objectionable; but he does not. Corn is now selling, say, for 80 cents a bushel, which is the price here at present that the farmer gets. A bushel will make three gallons of whiskey, which is worth here $1.10

cents per gallon by the barrel; that the distiller gets. The retailer will realize, say $4 per gallon. But the consumer—what does he get? Alas! Poverty! Brags! And a drunkard's grave! Meantime, the people will be deprived of bread, and our soldiers cannot live upon whiskey rations. Something must be done to arrest the stupendous evil, and that immediately. I notice that the Convention proposes to license distilleries, and thus secure revenue to the state. In my opinion the state stands in need of no revenue derived in this way. The object should be to abate the evil, and not encourage it; at least, not impose a duty on distilled liquor, but impose a heavy tax upon any "Still," to be paid before a gallon is made. If people be allowed to go on and make whiskey, they will not, except in very few instances, make correct returns to the sheriffs. Let each "STILL" be taxed $1000, to be paid to the sheriff before a gallon is made, with a penalty of $2000 and 12 months imprisonment for violation. Then, if the distillers obtain irresponsible persons to conduct the business for them, to defeat the law, such persons will suffer by imprisonment.

I give it as my candid opinion, that is some salutary action be not taken by the Convention in this matter, corn and wheat cannot be bought next summer for $5 per bushel. PRO BONO PUBLICO[223]

"Only laws against distilling and not against sale or consumption were passed." These laws weren't passed for moral issues, but to keep the grain for the poor.[224] The people did conduct the meetings as shown in the letter from D. O. Harrington, of Harrington, North Carolina, to his brother, Sion: "We had a prohibition meeting at Dave McNeill . . . . We can't get any whiskey now down here but blockade prices—the gallon is the smallest quantities we can get."[225] City officials in Wilmington prohibited the sale of alcoholic beverages in small quantities. They requested the steamboat and railroad lines to not transport liquor to town. Other communities asked for martial law to help control the drunk soldiers.[226] They said drunkenness increased crime. One lady replied that a murder occurred in her neighborhood caused by excess drinking. In Milton, R. B. Lawrence sought to stop the sale of liquor and smuggling the same into his area.[227]

Despite prohibition forces, taverns grew numerous. With the depressed economy and inflation, owners felt they deserved to earn a living too. Those selling liquor did not always obtain a license. In the criminal court records of New Hanover County, there are sundry records of arrests for "retailing." The antique phrase "retailing" refers to those selling liquor by the glass or by "small measure" without a license. In perusal of the entire file for the years 1861–1865, these appear numerous. Most of those arrested were males; however, women were charged also. Several of those arrested were repeaters throughout the war years.*[228]

Women did indeed take a more active role in this early prohibition movement. Like Carrie Nation of the twentieth century, that spring, the *Raleigh Register* reported:

> The patriotic ladies of Newbern, North Carolina destroyed 1000 gallons of whiskey at the depot in that place . . . by knocking out the heads of the barrels & letting the poison flow to the ground.[229]

Other women took up the axe as well:

> Some twenty ladies of Statesville, North Carolina proceeded in a body to the RR of the town a few days ago, and with hatchets and hammers destroyed five to six barrels of whiskey and poured the liquor poison upon the ground, a fitting libation (says the Iredell Express) to the devil and his imps from the

---

*   For a list of those charged, see the appendix.

hands of patriotic women, whose mission, pending the war, is to go about doing good.[230]

"The actual effects of these measures is difficult to assess. S.S. Barber of Huntsville . . . complained that despite state law, the state authorities were ineffectual in controlling distilleries, that a hundred or more continued to operate in North Carolina . . . that 'as the necessities of the army are so urgent . . . the military authorities ought to take the matter in hand.'"[231] Foremost, doctors considered alcohol a needed stimulant for ill soldiers. After 1864 when the central government controlled shipments of non-government cargo, alcoholic beverages almost disappeared. Surgeons complained to government officials. Surgeon Thomas Fanning Wood recalled that army regulations allowed a thousand sick men ten gallons of whiskey a month. "No sooner did it come than the officers came boldly up and upon some pretext or other got it all, and when the real necessity arose there was none for the sick. When I was the officer in charge I after awhile declined to make the requisition for it, as I had to certify that it was 'used by the sick alone,' and this I could not do."[232]

Alcohol was made at home, or it was smuggled. In addition to making whiskey, peach or apple brandy became a household item. Because it took food out of the mouths of hungry persons and alcohol consumption considered a sin, distilling became a hot topic of discussion. Private Elroy Helsabeck said in a letter to his brother:

> I was sorry to hear that members of our circuit think more of making brandy and having it made than they do of pleasing God. It is astonishing indeed that Ministers, who have preached rightousness for years until they have grown gray in the service of God, will at last for the sake of money lay such examples before their fellow men.[233]

Despite a new resolution prohibiting the use of fruit to distill liquor, the governor tried his best to regulate the cost, but wasn't very successful. In Burke County, Governor Vance rescinded the order temporarily, which started a barrage of letters to his office protesting the use of grain for alcohol when the poor were starving.[234]

———————

Wounded Southern men left behind by the Federals after battles suffered from the lack of supplies and food. What is more, the countryside had been denuded of sustenance before the battles of Bentonville and Averasboro. Consequently, nearby residents had little to share with the sick men.[235] Mrs. James Briggs of Columbus County had her cook to trade with the enemy. She exchanged corn bread for real coffee beans. Other losses of food came from the fact that bacon and/or lard were used to fire up the gunboats in emergencies, leaving less food for soldiers and civilians. With Northern ships bearing down on blockade-runners, captains sometimes threw bacon overboard to lighten their load. Invariably, both the Blue and the Gray burned stockpiled food to keep the other side from using it, which eventually was felt by the lowly citizen when soldiers came to impress more provisions to replace what was lost.

———————

During wartime, schools felt the pinch due to shortages. Some schools folded; others survived using different resources. The Select Boarding and Day School in Hillsborough run by Misses Nash and Kollock managed to keep their school open. Payment of tuition at this time was partly made in commodities:

> Board to be paid in advance in bacon, corn or flour, delivered here at the following prices current of December 1863, viz: bacon $2.50 per pound, corn $60 per barrel, and flour $80. Each pupil is required to furnish her own towels

and table napkins, one pair sheets, one bolster case or two pillow cases, a counterpane, drinking vessel, and three dozen candles.[236]

The Salem Girls' Academy had to raise prices twice in one year to meet their needs. School officials told the parents of girls seeking admission, "We have no more beds, but if you will furnish beds we will try to take care of your daughters." Additionally, food shortages plagued the school like ordinary civilian families. "In their old age, students would recall with amusement how their principal rode a horse at the head of a herd of pigs destined for the school's table." Once, the governor gave the school a bag of sugar.[237] The school held two hundred girls. Many of those who had been students there earlier stayed during the conflict, yet other families of non-students sent their daughters there for safety. The overflow was taken in by private families.[238]

Girls' schools allowed their students to go home if it was safe for various reasons (e.g., a death in the family) as the war dragged on. In contrast, wealthier families sought out the academies to place their daughters there because to them, it was a safe place to be. As a result, this strained the schools' resources as they took in refugees.[239] Students were sometimes caught away from home when the hostilities began, and such was the case of Johanna Mack, a student at Salem. Her parents lived in the Cherokee District, Oklahoma Territory, as missionaries. Mack had lived seven years at the school and was ready to go home.[240] The PAC "considered how this girl could be provided for in view of the continuing war and the complete breakdown of communication with her parents in the Cherokee mission." A family in Salem was asked to board her, but refused. Johanna was finally placed in the sisters' house. Mack was to get her meals at the girls' boarding school. Sister Lavinia Williams enabled her to take in sewing and music students to help pay her living expenses. Later in July 1861, Sister Williams decided she could no longer support Mack, so Johanna went to live with a relative in the North. Mack returned in late 1863 to begin her career as an instructor with the girls' boarding school.[*][241]

A routine schedule ensued for the first couple of years at St. Mary's School. The girls carried on like there was no war going on, taking part in charades, tableaux, fund-raisers, and the usual classes. In 1862, when Roanoke Island, Edenton, Elizabeth City, New Bern, and Washington fell under Federal control, the director became alarmed. Dr. Smedes told the students they may have to do away with most luxuries and that they should be prepared to tough it out. They were to be ready to run in case the Yankees showed up in Raleigh. Smedes worked very diligently trying to keep the same standards as the beginning of the war. However, he too had to deal with inflation and shortages of supplies. He asked the girls to bring textbooks from home and inquired of the alumni to please donate their used books. Things had gotten so terrible in January of the last year that he resorted to bartering like so many others. Partial payment of tuition came in the form of corn, cotton, and bonds. Inflation ate up the budget Smedes had prepared for the 150 students. Meat was especially hard to obtain at decent prices as pork cost six dollars a pound and chickens ten dollars each. Turkey sold for twenty-five dollars apiece. Coffee rose from twelve dollars to one hundred dollars a pound *if* you could find it. Those who wanted white flour bad enough and had four hundred dollars, the barrel was yours.[242]

Mr. A. McDowell, chairman submitting to the *Biblical Recorder* on the Chowan Female Collegiate Institute, said, "This institution, formerly so successful and prosperous is now suffering like most others in our country from the blighting influences of war." He reported that they only had half the number of students (twenty) in past times since the fall of Roanoke (Island). By March of 1862, when the enemy came, the girls fled. After the danger passed, months later, a few girls returned; and the roll increased.[243] Fifty-six students

---

[*]   It is uncertain if Johanna ever got back to the Cherokee mission for in November 1862, Brother
       James Ward was murdered by Cherokee Indians belonging to the Federal Army. Brother Gilbert
       Bishop was taken prisoner at the time.

stayed at Davenport College in Lenoir throughout the conflict. The girls had difficulty procuring enough white fabric for their graduation dresses.[244] Sallie Southall (Cotton), at age seventeen, called her graduation in 1863 a "homespun commencement" because all graduates were dressed alike in homespun, made in the state.

William Gannaway, president of Trinity College in 1865, talked about the shortages affecting his school:

> Another serious embarrassment confronted us, and one much more difficult to overcome—the depreciated money and the scarcity of provisions . . . . This government demand [of tithes] . . . so reduced our food resources that I applied to President Davis for a limited exemption from paying the required tithes. Before I received a reply . . . Grant had captured Richmond and the Confederacy was rapidly toppling . . . . General Johnston's army . . . was moving in this direction, and in a few days the advanced division . . . arrived . . . and tents were scattered about among the trees . . . . The presence of the soldiers, the excitement of the students, the anxiety and consternation of the people, rendered further college exercise useless . . . . It was determined to close till the storm pass, peace be made, and civil order once more restored.[245]

"Relatively little devastation had attended the brief march of the armies through Moore County, but the people were without money, without prospects, almost without food. The repudiated Confederate currency could purchase nothing. Transportation was at a standstill." Those were the words of author M. W. Wellman.[246] North Carolinians reported that their own cavalry was as bad as the enemy plundering foodstuffs from their farms. Farmville and Falkland were visited by Confederate General Joe Wheeler's cavalry, when they raided horses, provisions, and property from the civilians. The Federal Army did the same.[247]

SALT SHORTAGES

"Other factors influencing the shortages of food had to do with less crops being planted, as well as the lack of salt. Even though these counties were near Saltville, Virginia, the citizens did not get a sufficient supply of it due to corrupt officials and the lack of transportation."[248] After only five months into the war, Southern newspapers began to fret over the shortage of packing salt.[249] Mentioned previously, private individuals and the state set up salt-making factories along the coast. Workers were needed to cut wood and keep the fires burning twenty-four hours continuously. Free Negro men were conscripted to work there. One colored freeman wrote Governor Vance that his family would be destitute if they made him go again:

> Laurinburg Richmond Co N.C.
> July 28th. 1863
> His Excellency the Governor
> Sir
>   If your highness will condescend to reply to my feeble Note, you will confer a great favor on me, and relieve me of my troubles . . . . there is a man living near me, who is an Agent of the State Salt-workes . . . he took all we colored men last winter to make Salt, he is now after us to make Barrels . . . comes at the dead hours of night and carries us off whenever he thinks proper, gives us one dollar and fifty Cents pr day . . . . I cannot support my family at that rate and pay the present high prices for provisions . . . . I am willing to su[b]mit to his Calls, for I am perfectly/willing/ to do for our Country whatever

the laws require of me . . . . please let me know if this Agent [has] the power
to use me as he does. Daniel Locklar[250]

The governor replied that he did not have authority. Concerns for the lack of salt
appeared throughout correspondence of the time. In Jackson County, Elizabeth Watson
wrote to her soldier husband, James, on October 29, 1861:

Dear friend and husband
        times in our county is hard for the poor class of people for every thing is
giting so deer that tha cant By hardly a naught to [*illegible*] an salt is from nine
to ten dollars a sack her and every other thing is proportion [.] thier crop is
good crops made in our county . . . money is scerce here.[251]

William Auman wrote to his friend Allen King in the fall of 1861:

        I hear some people are not going to faten no hogs this year for there
is no salt to be had . . . the scarity of salt is going to make meet vary hard to
cum . . .[252]

Two hogs could feed a family of five for the winter.[253] Joseph J. White received a
letter in November 1861 from his parents in Chatham County. It was almost hog-killing
time, and they had been unsuccessful getting salt for the kill. His father talked about
trying to get salt from Fayetteville but was unable to get any. They told Joe that some
neighbors had traveled to Saltville, Virginia, and came back empty-handed. They told him
of the wagons "that were crowded for a mile waiting their turn . . ." (a nineteenth century
traffic jam!). Three weeks later, Mr. White wrote his son, asking Joseph to try to get them
some salt. Mr. White reported that Joe's mother "cannot kill the hogs for lack of salt."[254]
        Those living in the northwest mountain counties did not have far to go to obtain salt
from Saltville, Virginia, but had problems just as well. Martha Choate informed her soldier
husband:

        I will give you a history of my trip to the lick. They hauled a load for the
government at $3.25 a hundred [pounds]. A part of it was paid in salt at the
government price. Mother put her mare and we got four bushels and 14
pounds. They brought us a bushel and half apiece at twenty three dollars per
bushel. They started to the lick again yesterday to haul for the government
and I sent my wagon and team. J.S. Choate put in with me. We get part of the
pay in salt. I don't expect to send my team anymore this winter.[255]

One woman found a fair example for saving salt: "Killed a hog this morning & salted
it by a new process. Scalded it in brine that would float a potato. The meat to stay in three
minutes & then hang & smoke till cured."[256]
        Entered into her diary, a lady recorded, "We can wear old clothes and live off the
plantation for years without suffering if we can only get salt . . ."[257] A man said it was
necessary to venture to the coast by horse and wagon to get seawater, which was boiled
down for salt. Goods along with salt were smuggled from Norfolk through the Dismal Canal,
through Perquimans, and across the Chowan River. Merchants Clark and Turlington (by
Chatterton) of Wilmington returned an answer to John H. Dalton on April 7, 1862, who
requested salt:

        Dear Sir—your favor of recent date is at hand. There is no salt in this place
except sea-salt made on our coast and that is very scarce and when to be had
sells at six dollars a bushel.[258]

Sarah A. Tillinghast told a relative that she "does not have any salt, sent darkeys to get some, couldn't . . . they say this sound salt melts . . . . three bushels in Dr. Rays store melted so that it ran out of the door on the sidewalk."[259] John Motley Morehead wrote of his trip from Goldsboro to Greensboro:

> Above, below, and around the depot, there were hundreds if not thousands of sacks of salt, lying on the ground, some piled up—others lying promiscuously around as they were tumbled out of the cars—the ditches filled with them, and the rain-water poured up against these piles of salt. Most were without protection from the rain.[260]

The price of salt fluctuated according to supply and demand. Distribution was a constant problem. Salt was nineteen dollars a bushel at Wilmington while seventy dollars in Raleigh. In Halifax County, a planter's wife told of salt selling for thirty dollars a bushel and apple brandy twenty dollars a gallon. Robert Francis said, in a letter addressed to Mrs. Mary Ann Jones, a cousin:

> Camp Gragg, near Fredicksburg, Va., January 18, 1863 . . . You say salt is $30 a bushel in Ashe, It cannot be bought here for less than $50 . . . Pills are a dollar a piece . . .[261]

At times, your location determined how quickly you received your ration of salt. Merchant J. B. Howell advertised in the *Milton Chronicle* in October 1864 that he had salt for sale at forty dollars a bushel. Salt was selling at seventy dollars a bushel in 1865.[262] The quartermaster general's top priority was to procure salt.

When salt became scarce, desperate farmers dug up the earth under their smokehouses and washed it thoroughly, then strained the water and evaporated it to recover precious pinches of salt. This salt would be colored brown, not very appetizing. This practice was common throughout the Southern states. "Mr. Henry is having the dirt dripped where the smoke house was to try to make salt of the water. It tastes salty," wrote a lady from Asheville. She continued, "I boiled down some brine after dinner, made near 4 qt. of salt. It is dark."[263] Residents in Davie County tried to develop the salt licks found on Dutchman Creek.

LEATHER AND SHOE SHORTAGES

This ad appeared in a Raleigh newspaper on January 8, 1862:

North Carolina Wooden Shoe Factory:
We take great pleasure in calling attention to the advertisement of Messars. Theims & Frapps which will be found in todays newspaper. At much expense these enterprising gentlemen have fitted up an extensive factory for the manufacturing of wooden shoes. The machinery of the factory is driven by steam, and a visitor to it can in a few minutes see all the operations from the steaming of the wood (gum & popular) out of which the shoe is made, to topping it with leather, & painting it black. These shoes are said to be lighter than brogans of the same number, and for warmth, durability, and protection against dampness, are infinitely superior to the best brogans ever made, for when the leather tops wear out, they can be re-newed at a trifling expense, over & over again, on the same bottoms. The proprietors deserve great credit for their intelligence and enterprise. They are supplying a great want, & giving employment to a large number of workmen at remunerating wages. Already they are turning out 100 pairs a day. The wooden shoes with leather tops

cost $2 per pair.[264] Theims & Frapps also made solid wooden shoes which resembled the Dutch shoe.

The ease of procuring shoes wrestled with civilians at home. The majority of the supply of leather went for military purposes. Impressment agents were known to take hides from individuals. S. B. Erwin, from Burke County, wrote to the governor that he had his tannery ready but was finding it very difficult to get hides. He wanted a government contract, hoping to get hides cheaper that way.[265] When W. B. Lovelace contacted Governor Vance, he told him that he was tanning and making shoes but, like the other fellow, had trouble getting the hides:

> . . . it is impossible to get any hides in this part of the Country [Cleveland County]. The cattle has . . . been sold and taken off . . . if I could get the hides I could make leather in from 3 to 4 months with the improved system of taning [sic] that I now have . . . and make better leather.

Lovelace relayed that his neighbors told him that in Kinston, there was a surplus of hides and that "they think the Brigade commissary has been selling of them."[266]

Citizens expressed as the second item missed the most next to salt was leather, although some would say it was coffee. In Salem, children wore wooden shoes when leather was out of reach. Many schoolchildren wore wooden-soled shoes to save the leather for soldiers' use, or they went barefoot.[267] A mountain diarists recorded: "Children and many grownups went barefoot through the winter. One pair of shoes a year was a luxury."[268]

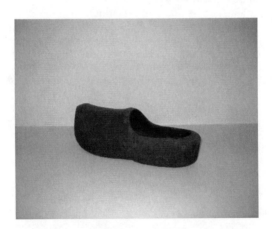

Wooden shoe made by Theims & Frapps, Raleigh
Courtesy of the Bennett Place State Historic Site

Different animal hides were used for shoes.* From the *Wadesboro Argus*: "A citizen suggested that folks use dog hides for shoe leather. We have 100,000 worthless dogs. Many kill sheep and we can't waste the wool and mutton."[269] In Franklin County, the locals used cured dog hides for shoes.[270] A. W. Bell wrote his wife, Mary, "You had better get Baldwin to make you a pair of shoes out of Buciks skin as dogskin makes nice shoes."[271] House

---

*   There is a pair of ladies' boots made from raccoon skin in the Museum of the Confederacy in Richmond, Virginia.

slippers were made from a mixture of either squirrel or rabbit fur and old tent canvas or cardboard-covered fabric.[272] Others were made from old carpets, thick fabric, and recycled leather from old books and furniture. Some homemade shoes consisted of woven straw / palmetto leaves / corn shucks types of material. These self-styled versions didn't hold up very long. One lady had a pair of leather shoes made for her son from her deceased husband's cavalry boots. The Bryan family was fortunate enough to have a shoe last, and Mary made her daughter several pairs of shoes from goat hides bound with ribbon.[273] In the spring of 1862, an Asheville woman penned in her diary that they could not get any children's shoes. By fall, she wrote: "Little Zona is perfectly barefooted. Other two kids have shoes. We have some nice goat skins to make them but don't know when I can get them made as old Presley is making for the negroes." Apparently having trouble getting shoes for herself that fall, Mrs. Henry wrote: "I have made me some cloth shoes today . . . they do not fit very well but are very easy. I put some old soles to them. They are very warm as I made them of jeans out & in."

By November that same year, Cornelia Henry said, "I made Zona & Willie some jeans shoes . . . they will not stand wet weather, neither will they last long but perhaps they will do till they get leather shoes. Some of the negroes are barefooted . . ." Either the shoes wore out quickly, or she wanted them to have second pair because she made another pair nine days later. When 1863 rolled around, still no shoes for children. She fashioned another pair of jeans shoes for herself. A week later, Henry said they finally got leather ones, and she was able to get a pair "the negroes all shod."[274]

Elizabeth Robeson must have had a hide of leather, for she inscribed in her diary that a Mr. DeVane had come to make shoes and made two pairs. Mrs. Staton of Martin County had leather hides. She paid Mr. A. O. Turner eighteen dollars for eighteen pairs of Negro shoes in November 1862. The next month, she paid Spencer Stokes three dollars for cutting out twenty-one pairs of Negro shoes. These were considered cheap prices.[275] Patrick Edmondston sent Henry, his slave, into town to try to find some leather; but Henry came home empty-handed. The leather was to be made into shoes for the house servants. Two months later, he was able to get two pairs for them at ten to eighteen dollars a pair. A month later, Mrs. Edmondston claimed to have shoed all her slaves in shoes with wooden soles.[276] A citizen said in February 1862 that shoes in his area were selling for four to five dollars a pair. Waterproof boots cost fifteen dollars.[277] A lady remembered having to pay a great deal for common shoes, ranging from two hundred to three hundred dollars; boots cost four hundred to six hundred dollars during wartimes *if* you could find them.[278] "Blockaded shoes" brought high prices.

Family members would ask for shoes in letters to their kindred in military service. Those soldiers encamped out of the state were sometimes able to get a pair or two. Captain Charles Bahnson wrote his father from Hagerstown, Maryland, on June 21, 1863: "I will try to buy some Ladies shoes . . . they are selling at old prices here . . ."[279] Jacob Hartsoe, stationed in Goldsboro, wrote his wife that he tried to get shoes there for his daughter, Laurah, but could not. He told her:

> I want you to git shoes made for her if you cant git non. I want you to git some made for her. I want you to git Dadey Wike some bodey to by you some lether as soon as you can for it will git higher and higher. By it before fall . . .[280]

The need for shoes was so great that it was one item smuggled under the large hoop dresses worn by Southern girls. Emeline Piggott was caught with shoes tied under her dress at New Bern and was arrested. In 1863, Mrs. Drury Lacy told in a letter that she had been to every store in Warrenton to look for shoes for her children, but none could be found. The Drury Lacy family had two pairs of shoes, one for every day and one for Sunday.[281]

A brother wrote to his sister that "Tom had five sides of leather stolen [from] his tan trough the other night." Hides had become a hot commodity for theft.[282]

Some ladies chose to stay home from church, embarrassed because they didn't have decent shoes to wear. A farmer wore a pair of homemade shoes into Fayetteville. He said little boys and even adults made fun of him. One person borrowed a pair of glasses to have a better look at the "so-called shoes."

Even though the supply of leather went to troops in the field, the soldiers didn't always have shoes. One Winchester, Virginia, woman described members of the Thirty-seventh North Carolina Regiment passing through the town as "destitute, many without shoes, all without overcoats or gloves, although the weather was freezing. Their poor hands looked so red and cold holding their muskets in the bitter wind."[283] A soldier wrote his father a year later: "Many of our men are barefooted, some have neither blankets, nor overcoats & some again have only one of the two articles. They suffer very much during these cold nights, especially when they go out on picket, & are not allowed fires."[284] When short of leather, soldiers were given "prepared cloth" shoes.[*][285] Others wore canvas tops with wooden bottoms.

CLOTHING AND COTTON/WOOL CARDS—"Enforced plainness of wartimes."

Northern women by the antebellum period had shed most substantive textile production. After the Napoleonic wars, importation of English cloth resumed. By 1820, the North was joining England as a regular source of cheap manufactured cloth. From 1820 to 1860, homemade-cloth production decreased. In Ohio (1850), the spinning wheel and handloom grew to be curiosities. Homespun would be conspicuous on people, but one-half of the white people in Mississippi dressed that way. By 1850, women above the rank of the smallest slaveholder did not dress in homespun, although many of their slaves did.[286] Machine-made cotton and wool fabric, spooled thread, sewing notions, and yarn stocked the merchants' shelves before the conflict. Women found it simpler to buy rather than take the time-consuming chore to make it.

One fortunate person considered herself lucky: "Several boxes of Yankee calico drifted ashore down here last week, our friends ask the moderate price of $2 a yard state money . . . . They will not take Confederate money . . ."[287] The middle class had the funds to buy manufactured cloth. These women of the sixties had grown accustomed to buying fabric. Spinning wheels and looms had gathered dust in the corner. Wealthy folks would buy their clothing in the big cities, or they would have a tailor/dressmaker take care of their needs. For this reason, numerous women grew up never having done any spinning or weaving. The war caught them off guard. Now all of a sudden, with the blockade and merchants selling off their stock, there became a frantic hunt for cloth. Women retrieved the spinning wheels from the attic, repaired the looms, and set about to make cloth again. It was at some homes that black women "taught" their mistresses and others how to spin and weave. Spinning wheels were not necessarily used 100 percent. Drop spindles found use too. If you had both, great! Drop spindles were easy to make and a favorite of the children.

Once the war had been in progress and fabric disappeared from merchants' shelves, young girls were loath to wear anything of Northern production. They felt it was their patriotic duty to buy Southern goods. Anna Fuller informed others that she " . . . even spurn the thought of ever again using anything from Yankee land."[288] Young girls considered themselves more patriotic if they wore homespun fashions, which became their "badge of sacrifice and loyalty." A very popular song written about homespun clothing called

---

*   Painted and waterproofed canvas uppers with leather bottoms, 1863

"The Homespun Dress" quickly spread throughout the South.* Similarly, homespun was also called Dixie silk. Ladies and schoolgirls in the state also wore the famous Alamance plaids. A soldier in the Twenty-third Regiment expressed his opinion about homespun to his fiancée:

> Dec. [no year]
> Henderson
>   . . . knitting socks for the soldier is not the only thing the ladies here make with their delicate fingers. It is no uncommon sight to see young ladies of the first class parade on the streets in homespun dresses, spun, woven, and made by their own hands . . . homespun is the fashion with both sexes and tinsel are [torn paper] off by the blockade . . .
>   Henry G. Turner[289]

Children were involved in the combing of wool and cotton. Wool and cotton had to be combed to remove the knots and trash imbedded in them. This was the first step needed to get the fibers ready to spin. The construction of the cards/combs was more intricate. Wood for the paddles was affluent, but the little metal teeth was difficult to obtain. Rebecca Davis told her friend, "The cards Mr. Davis bought were not put together . . . the teeth and wood were separate."[290]

Blockade-runners brought in sixty thousand complete cards during wartime.[291] The price fluctuated like other commodities. As part of his plan to assist soldiers' wives, Governor Vance wanted the combs to go to them first when they were available. The state sought to regulate the price so that soldiers' wives could acquire them and supplement their meager income. While merchants charged enormous prices for these combs, the government did control the price.

It must have seemed like manna from heaven when the impoverished women acquired these combs. "I have seen," wrote Mrs. Cornelia Spencer, "tears of thankfulness running down their cheeks of our soldiers' wives on receiving a pair of these cards by which alone they were to clothe and procure bread for themselves and their child."[292] The need for cards was so enormous that it was frequently mentioned in letters and diaries of the time. A husband in Raleigh on business told his wife: "I have tried here for cotton cards but cannot get any. I will try in Salisbury as I go back . . ."[293] This was eight months after the state seceded. Later that fall, Mrs. Edmondston said a neighbor had bought a pair of cards and four pounds of sugar in Wilmington for twelve dollars—a real bargain for the time.[294]

Newspapers carried advertisements when businesses expected to receive a shipment. One year after the state seceded, the *Milton Chronicle* printed this advertisement for cards: "Expected to receive in a few days a box of #10 cotton cards, price ten dollars. David Patterson, Merchant."[295] Two years later, the price in that small town had grown to forty dollars. In a letter dated June 9, 1863, sisters corresponding said combs were $2.25; and homespun fabric brought $2 a yard.[296] This would be considered a very cheap price because another woman paid $15 for one pair.[297] The price continued to climb, prompting a mistress to proclaim to her diary: "Sent to Mary Egerton for her pair of cards for $35 . . . fear they'll be gone before she gets a letter. If so I expect to give $50 . . ."[298] Still, the price increased. In 1865, cards were selling at seventy dollars in one place and one hundred twenty in another. Rebecca Davis drafted a letter to her son, Burwell, and mentioned she had obtained some cards because she wrote him on November 1, 1864, that she needed another pair: "There are some in town for $60."[299] Mrs. Fanny Yates, in Martin County, paid one hundred twenty-five dollars for a pair of cotton cards in March 1865.[300]

---

*   See the appendix for the words.

Most women used hand carders/combs,* but an enterprising merchant bought a steam-powered comb, which saved hours of work for those at home. Poor soldiers' wives could not afford his prices. His ad appeared in the *Hillsborough Recorder*:

> I will do wool carding by steam machinery—12.5C a pound for white wool or for 1/5 part of the wool. Mixed, if the different colors are pulled together before being brought, will be carded for 15c a lb. If not, then extra charge. Put one lb of grease to 12 lbs of wool, and you will get good work. Lemuel Wilkinson[301]

"The scarcity of cotton and wool cards became a severe hardship for Southerners during the war. In an effort to alleviate the problem the North Carolina State Convention, in March 1862, passed an ordinance authorizing a loan of ten thousand dollars to anyone who would erect buildings and construct machinery for the manufacturing of cards."[302] Mid-war, the governor attempted to buy from Georgia machinery and wire to make cotton/wool cards. Joseph Brown, Georgia's governor, wrote to Vance that although his state had bought one-half interest in the Pioneer Card Manufacturing Company, he could not sell any machinery or supplies. His state's interest had moved some machinery into the state armory buildings inside the penitentiary where they were duplicating the machinery. He said it would be unfair to the other owner and the people of Georgia to sell the machines. Governor Brown did relay to Vance that if he would send "a competent machinist" there, he could "inspect, take the dimensions and make drawings of our machines."[303] An agent was sent. Whether the state made copies is not known.

However, later that year, the *Advance* brought through the blockade five machines to make the wire teeth necessary for the combs, which were later distributed to soldiers' wives.[304]

Apparently, the state set in motion the making of these much-needed carders for everyone's use. The quartermaster posted a note in the news:

> **NOTICE:** Here is now ready to be issued from this Department to the different counties in the state, a lot of cotton and wool cards. This lot of cards will be sent to the Agents, with backs ready for tacking the cards on, and be sold at $2.60 per pair to the citizens generally; in no instance is more than one pair to be sold to a family. These cards are not intended for the families of soldiers.
>
> The Department is having a large lot backed ready for use, which will be dealt out and sold to the families of soldiers as quick as they can be made at a much less price. Agents are requested to make arrangements and send for them.
>
> H.A. Dowd, QMA[305]

The *North Carolinian*, a Fayetteville newspaper, carried this ad:

> The Fayetteville Cotton Card Manufacturing Company is now manufacturing cards superior to any run through the blockade, and at present selling for a lot less price than a single pair or by the quantity. Any person ordering six or more pairs, they will be securely packed and delivered at Wilmington. A.A. McKethan, J.A. Worth, Alex Johnson, Jr.[306]

---

* "One good carder can card one pound of cotton per day. Five pounds of cotton makes one bunch of spun thread. One bunch equals fifteen yards of cloth."[307]

No price was listed. A businessman with a physical disability that kept him from serving in the military offered to help the government dispense them:

Wilkesboro. Nov. 19/63

Dear Governor,
  I understand you have provided some Cotton and Wool Cards for distribution, amongst the Destitute, and occupying a central position & being in constant communication with the people by means of my store. I propose to you to the requests of some of those interested to <u>accept</u> the Agency for their distribution if it be agreeable to you. My service shall be free. Should you wish to ship Cards to the Co. [county] mark them to Statesville & [*illegible*] by consignee by Mail with instructions how to distribute. Some persons are supplied and need none [.] others are so trifling as to merit none as they will not use them if they get them—how will you arrange in such cases?
  Awaiting your reply
  I am as ever Most respectfully Yours   C.J. Cowles[308]

Making home-spun cloth and clothing
N.C. Division of Archives & History, Photographic Archives

  The looms came out of storage, and the process of stringing up the loom began—a tedious task if you knew how to do it, a tragedy if you didn't. What is more, you would have to get on the list and wait your turn for a knowledgeable person to come around and "harness" the loom for you. This enterprise is mentioned in letters and diaries from the time. Bettie Little expressed to a friend, Harriet McIntosh in Mecklenburg County, "I am weaving all the time. I have want of dresses for my self and sis and have along [*sic*] web to weave for Mrs. Whitley and a web of jeans for Mrs. North. When I get that all wove I am going to make a nice dress for Christmas." After Christmas, one cousin bought a pound of wool, and "now Hannah has just finished weaving nine yards of very nice black jeans cloth . . . this has been the good as well as the bad . . ." Here she was speaking of her healthy, stout friend from all the hard labor she did on the farm. Another cousin of Harriett's told her that she had "been weaving ever chance I can get and expect to be at it till spring." Violet

Ann had two new dresses by March and was getting ready to weave a calico. An aunt of Harriett's wrote, "I wish you would come over and help me spin. I have been spinning aline [sic] and bed ticking . . ."[309]

Drury Lacy said his neighbor Margaret Guin reported that a person could get two yards from one pound of wool. A mother wrote her soldier son: "I have some weaving now for you a coat & pair of pants & your Aunt Martha gave a me an overcoat that was your uncle Williams, which I am having turned & made smaller for you . . ."[310] One man was not too happy with his jeans cloth pants; a neighbor made Mr. Henry some jeans cloth. Mrs. Henry lamented, "He don't like it much because there is too much hair in the wool. It is the mixed he don't like." Apparently, the woman picked out all the fine wool and left the coarse. Henry had been weaving cloth for the plantation, along with the help of a neighbor girl and occasionally a servant. Cornelia Henry had two looms and multiple spinning wheels going during the war years. She sent a part of her wool to South Carolina to have it machine carded. Henry confessed, "Sept 8th, 1863 I warped a piece of cloth 32 yards for Miss Sally." She later remarked that she had made "15 yds of cloth from 5 lbs wool."[311]

A woman Down East said, "I have given $2 a Pound for spinning wool and had to furnish cards. I put sixteen yards of flannel in the loom . . ."[312] Malinda Plummer wove cloth to support her huge family in the war. Mrs. W. H. Polk chastised her friend Mrs. M. E. Hawkins, of Waverly, for failing to write more often. Mrs. Hawkins replied, "I have cut out and wove and spun about 600 yards cloth since last fall[.] you will overlook my not writing."[313] Julia Gwyn confessed to her uncle:

> We have kept two looms going constantly all summer and spring . . . I have not told you anything about the children yet. I know one thing about them. They are very bad and nearly all in rags, for we have been working so much for the soldiers that we have not done anything scarcely for the family.[314]

The Scarborough sisters said, "We are always busy spinning and can card and spin six cuts a day . . ."[315] Another said, "I card and spin every day & am having me a loom made. I expect to spin filling and thread, $2.50 to 5 per bunch, not 1 yard of cloth shirting [could be found] in the country . . ."[316]

Mrs. Clark reported that she paid four dollars for a paper of needles.[317] Mrs. Henry in Asheville bought a paper of needles and a spool of thread for one dollar each mid-war.[318] Elle Andrews told a friend, "I have bought nothing at all for myself to wear in nearly two years excepting having my bonnets repaired every season." That was in the spring of 1863.[319]

What came in through the blockade was not enough to keep the citizens clothed. The home manufacturing of homespun and jeans cloth flourished. Jeans cloth is not to be confused with "blue jeans" of today, as jeans cloth then was made from a blend of cotton and wool.

Planters' wives not only had to clothe themselves, but their servants too. Both participated in the chore. On the larger plantations, Negro women had been trained to spin and weave. These women did not have to go work in the fields. W. W. Lenoir sent a letter to his mother explaining that two of his servants, Maria and Delia, "have done very badly about spinning, not having spun filling enough during the year to make [a] comfortable allowance of clothing for the Negroes."[320] Mrs. Fanny Yates in Martin County hired white girls to do her sewing. It is not known whether she couldn't sew or just didn't have the time. She left a plethora of notes and receipts for her descendants. An account with Ms. Lloyd in 1861 showed a "receipt for making three calico dresses—$3; one walking dress—$3.50; another for $2.50; one for a dollar; cloak—$3.50; jacket—$1.50; dress—$5; nine garments trimmed for $5, and a jacket—75c."

When times got tough, Mrs. Yates took in boarders and hired out her slaves. As the war progressed, she hired three seamstresses who came the same day to work. Mary Jones charged $12.50 for making twelve Negro jackets in 1863. Mary Bradley's bill for sewing four jackets was five dollars. Mary Elizabeth Griffin collected $11.25 for making nine jackets. She also paid Jordan Jones $45.00 for warping, spooling, and weaving two hundred fifty yards of Negro cloth.[321]

Once the spinning was complete, a person could then start knitting. People knitted socks, neck comforts, gloves, mitts, vests, underclothes, etc., for their family and soldiers. A mistress mentioned knitting a set of undershirts for her father. "The war deprives him of his usual from Shetland."[322] Women and children knitted socks and gathered provisions as late as March 1865. About mid-war, civilians could purchase spun yarn from the factories, or they would barter for it. Elizabeth Robeson penned in her diary: "Sent some lard with Mr. Cain to trade for spun thread."[323] In 1864, Mrs. Henry said, "I sent some wool to Ham Cannon's yesterday for him to exchange for cloth or thread at the factory . . . went to Asheville today, tried to exchange a tissue dress for calico but could not . . . exchanged my coarse wool for thread, got 4 1/3 bunches for 13 lbs. wool."[324]

It was found that the suffering for cloth became so acute that certain days were set aside, on which goods might be sold to the neighbors (of the millers); and on these days, very large numbers of women would collect to buy their share. In some cases, these women walked ten to twelve miles or carried their yarn or cloth home on their backs or in wagons. These millers (cotton and wool) made a 75 percent profit, and some would sell it at a larger profit out of state, and many did.[325]

Other people had problems finding black crepe for mourning. A young lady asked her friend in Tarboro to search for her.[326] If you could not find mourning fabric, the lady would just dye a dress black or wear black ribbons on her bonnet. Dallas T. Ward, conductor at age nineteen on the Raleigh and Gaston Railroad, was part of the entourage to meet Sherman's cavalry encamped at Smithfield. He stated that he was told to find white cloth for a surrender flag. Cloth at the end of the war was very difficult to procure. He had to go from house to house to find enough for the flag. He was afraid that the small amount he retrieved would not be big enough to attract attention, drawing the enemies' fire.[327]

In Williamston, when the war began, Louisa Staton kept an account with merchant C. B. Hassell. Items cost very little compared with the end of the war. For instance, she purchased one and one-half yards of jeans cloth (homespun), one yard of bleaching (plain cotton), and one spool of cotton thread, paying just forty-five cents for all. The most expensive thing she bought from him in 1861 was a bridle bit and seven yards of cassimere with trimmings at $7.65. Six yards of calico with buttons and thread that she purchased cost ninety cents.[328] The price of fabric and shoes varied according to supply, demand, and location. By 1864, calico fabric sold for seven to ten dollars per yard, homespun ten to twenty-five dollars per yard *if* you could find it.

Women who owned sewing machines would be considered fortunate. A lady from Halifax County penned in a diary that her husband bought one for $46.50. It became a source of headaches. She had tried for several days to make it work and finally declared that the salesman must have taken advantage of her. It was days afterwards before she mastered the machine and months before she felt comfortable using it.[329] Cornelia Henry's husband in Asheville bought her a machine, and she succeeded using it right away. Six months later, she had to buy more machine needles priced eight for one dollar. Needles and spool thread would rise in price, becoming difficult to obtain later in the war. A blacksmith in Wilkes County commenced making ladies fine sewing needles, which he said were "good for cambric and linen."[330] It is possible that Mrs. Henry may not have had any problems obtaining sewing notions because she could make a dress or garment in one day's time. What had taken fourteen hours to make a shirt by hand was whittled down to one hour by sewing machine. Women in Raleigh carried their lightweight machines into the State Capitol whereby they sewed for the soldiers.

Exactly when homespun dresses for white women came into vogue is not certain; but the next letter, written in October 1861, by Charity Swindell of Hyde County provides documentation. To her mother, she claimed, "I have got me some homespun dresses, they are not pretty but they are good and strong."[331] "If you get the papers to enable you to come home you had better get plenty of clothes, shirts, coats, pants, and caps, for unless you can wear <u>homespun</u> you will not be able to get any here unless you pay enormous prices for them," said Sarah Tillinghast in a letter to her brother. She replied that clothing that has "run the blockade" carry high prices. "They [merchants] charge $2.50 per yard for calico—and we won't wear Yankee calico, so we wear homespun. Needles, thread and cloth are also very scarce and command very high prices."[332] Merchant W. N. Tillinghast sent a letter to his sister announcing he had a bolt of forty-one yards of "streaked striped" homespun at one dollar twenty cents. He said the river (Cape Fear) was down, and the boats could not come up past the jetty, which was three miles below town.

The majority of the people of the mid and western counties of North Carolina dressed chiefly in clothes of local manufacture.[333] Anna Fuller in February 1865 mentioned that she sent a "coarse pair of undergarments to her son in school because that was all that was available." Her husband went out to try to find some clothes for the family. He managed to find fabric for three people at a cost of twelve hundred dollars.[334] A betrothed young lady was described by Mrs. Edmondston as wearing "unmentionables" (underclothes) cut from bedsheets and her grandmother's fine cotton drawers.[335] This practice grew to be common.

A lady confessed, "Few students possessed more than three-four dresses." Prewar, the students at St. Mary's wore a blue-colored dress uniform. That changed due to shortages of indigo dye and fabric. Girls wore homespun or calico every day and old reworked silk dresses for Sunday.[336] General Lee's daughter, Mildred, a student at St. Mary's, followed the trend for plainness. Author Coulling explained:

> Mildred had no need of new outfits, since most of her friends dressed with wartime simplicity. Hoop skirts, if worn at all, were smaller than antebellum petticoats, and dresses were often remade from old silks, and cambrics. Many girls wove their own sunbonnets and tied their upper top shoes with string that they dyed in black ink. Because of the blockade hairpins were almost nonexistent, so most of the students used hairnets to keep their heavy chignon in place.[337]

Though the war was being fought, a wealthy man insisted his only daughter be married in high style. He went to Wilmington to purchase sugar and silk. The silk cost one hundred dollars a yard. The six bridesmaids couldn't get matching dresses, so each wore something different—from a broad flashing plaid to a modest pink-and-white pinstripe. No gloves could be found. This unusually rich wedding during wartime was rare.[338] Blockade prices from the ship *Hanna* listed in January 1862 twenty-nine pieces of navy and army cloth at ten to twelve dollars, fifty cents a yard.[339] In 1864, a lady mentioned she paid seven hundred dollars for a cloak and two hundred forty dollars for a wool dress.[340] By April 1865, calico was selling in Raleigh at thirty dollars a yard. Socks cost ten dollars a pair; wheat straw hats were twenty dollars, and country jeans cloth sold for twenty-five dollars per yard[341]

Children outgrew their clothes constantly. "Cut-down" clothes were the norm. These hand-me-downs soon turned to rags. A child could not always wait until a holiday for new clothes. Here is a letter from Santa Claus written to Reverend Lacy's granddaughter, Ms. Amy L. Dewey, on April 2, 1864:

> Noticing that your brothers and sisters were out walking the other day without you and learning from yr. Mother that you had no dress to wear and that you were a mighty good little girl and behaved mighty well about it—I

send you sixty dollars to buy you a new dress—get yr. Mamma to attend to it for you—.

Always be a good little girl and you wont be forgotten by

Yr Friend[342]

No mention was made of distributing clothing to soldiers' wives like food, but it was for the Indians in the mountains: "The widows and orphans of those [Cherokee soldiers] . . . were to be issued clothing." Each child was to receive three articles of clothing. Of the four hundred Cherokee Indians who served with Thomas's Legion, ten were killed, and nineteen died from disease.[343]

Knitters mixed all sorts of animal fur—cat, rabbit, squirrel, cow, etc.—with their cotton and wool to make it go further. Catherine Edmondston knitted a pair of gloves for her husband made from equal parts of rabbit fur and wool.[344] Slippers were made from squirrel and rabbit fur with old tent canvas.[345] In the manufacturing of blankets, rabbit fur and cotton was used instead of wool.[346] A newspaper noted that you could use cow hair mixed with cotton to make nice heavy cloth.[347]

One lady told a friend that she had the solution for prolonging a pair of socks for her soldier son so that he never ran out of socks:

When the feet get full of holes I just knit new feet to the tops, and when the tops wear out, I just knit new tops to the feet.[348]

SUBSTITUTES/CONFEDERATE MAKESHIFTS
Inveniam viam aut faciam "I will find a way or make one."

The *People's Press* ran a regular column in 1863 called Practical Hints for Hard Times, which offered readers substitutes for items that could no longer be purchased. Rabbit fur, it advised, could be used instead of wool; and feathers stuffed between two layers of cotton made a warm quilted jacket.[349] Rat skin was sometimes used in place of kid for gloves. Cornelia Henry said, "Mr. H. went to Asheville this morning, got me steel for a hoop which I have to put together . . . with cord. Will put on tape when I can get them in shape. They are very troublesome."[350] Instead of buying a hoopskirt petticoat, she could have substituted the steel springs with hoops made from grapevines or white oak splits. Wire grass, which grows abundantly Down East, was used to weave into matting and thence made into shaker bonnets with calico fronts and skirts. Palmetto leaves and dyed corn shucks plaited into bonnets and shoes were popular. Buttons whittled from pine wood or gourd into round shapes and covered with cloth adorned their garments. Persimmon seeds saw use as buttons.[351] Thorns from the Osage tree found use as pins or for fastening garments.

"During wartimes when we were unable to get gloves, they were knit from the ravellings of silk, or we made our own from sheep skins and rat skins. Ladies then wore very large hoopskirts, the hoops of which were supposed to be made of whalebone, and for which grape vines, or white oak splits were substituted. Old bonnets were cut or ripped up, and made over to conform to the then prevailing styles, while men's hats were made of cloth, or wheat straw. Felt hats were so scarce that they brought from three hundred to four hundred dollars each."[352]

One lady told of the difficulty people had to restore their wardrobe. "Many and unique were the devices that women resorted to during the war for in order to make clothes for no money could be spared for new ones," said Mrs. Forbis, ten years old at that time. She told how she made a hat from an old silk umbrella. Another time, she scalded the inside leaves of corn shucks and plaited them to made a hat; wheat and oat straw was used for the same purpose. She made a sort of matting or carpet of iris leaves or cattail leaves gathered from the swamp. "Best dresses were turned and re-turned, and then the best parts of 2-3 were used to make one. Almost all cloth had to be raised, spun, and woven at home." Two old dresses could be revised into one with different lines appearing as a new one.[353] The "turned" dresses meant that they took the dress apart and wore the inside outside. Others would turn the paneled waist part to the hem and vice versa.

Mrs. Cornelia Henry of Asheville would be considered upper-middle class. The family owned servants for both inside and outdoor work. Nevertheless, she worked alongside them. Notes in the journal proved Mrs. Henry to have been a frugal person. Her journal kept during the war years is explicit of the work she did separate from her servants. Henry said: "I began to turn my old calico dress bottom side up to make them last a little longer as calico is dear to purchase now . . . began to turn my side stripe dress upside down . . ." That was in 1861, then the next year: "I changed a dress waist. It had a draw string & I put a belt in . . . homespun dress made from 4 threads of purple [dyed with willow root] and 1 of white. Made a dress for Gus [younger son] from Willie's old one of linsey . . . knitting husband a pair of mitts double cuff." Henry made a shirt for one son from old flannel, which was softer than her homemade flannel. She had two "homespun linsey ones." Mrs. Henry cut up a blue silk shawl and trimmed her son's shirt in it, using the remainder for her daughter's sacque and another son a cloak. Never to waste anything, she recorded making one son an apron from old carriage cushions. Son Willie was in diapers: "I made 11 double napkins for Willie—one side good cloth, the other old table linnen."[354]

Individuals had to come up with uncommon usages to revamp their clothing to make it last. Women resorted to wearing *Dixie skirts*, which was a dress that used very little yardage in the skirt section being different from the voluminous dresses prewar, which could reach ten yards. Ladies wearing this type of garment were considered more patriotic and not a slave to fashion. The women took pride in their homespun dresses too. Another lady living during those times recalled that they cut off their trains, shortened their skirts, and wore linsey-woolsey as well as homespun. She said black-and-white checks grew popular. Others colors mentioned included gray/brown flannels piped with scarlet and garibaldis made from different fabrics of velvet to muslin and worn with black or plaid skirts. This would be called the "plainness of wartimes." Skirts, petticoats, and jackets were knitted. Old ragged knitted garments were unraveled, the yarn used into something else.[355]

Stains could be covered with a patch, bow, or trim. Some skirts may have been dyed a darker color to cover stubborn stains, or it would be dyed just to get the look of a new garment. For children's clothes, growth tucks were let out, and faded lines were covered with trim. Children's recycled clothing, called cutaway clothes or hand-me-downs, showed up every day and at church. Women would make dress pockets out of scrap material or inferior fabric. Elizabeth Wiggins pointed out to her son she would take his old shirts, change the pleated linen fronts, but keep the remaining portion of the garment.[356]

Fanny, a house servant of Mrs. Edmondston, was upset because her owners had to have their underclothes made out of bed sheets during wartime. She used an old piece of flannel and made them into cuffs and collars. When sewing for the soldiers, she lamented she did not have enough cloth to finish them, so she made the sleeves from a pillow cover. Catherine boasted that one woman's dress taken apart could be made into six children's dresses.[357] Rebecca Davis told her son, Burwell, that she had a couple of linen shirts on hand that she could rework with some colored muslin, making them tri-colored if he would wear them.[358]

Wartime prices varied considerably according to location and demand. Other prices here are given. A lady jotted down her prices in 1862: "Negro shoes—$10-18, ladies gaiters—$15, spool of cotton—$1, flannel—$5 yd., coarse woolen cloth—$12 yd, country homespun—$1-2 . . ."[359] Cotton was selling for twenty cents a yard in Petersburg; in Nashville (North Carolina), it was thirty cents if paid for in gold, forty-two cents if paid for in greenbacks, and fifty-five cents if paid for in Confederate money. "Needles, thread and cloth are very scarce and command very high prices," said Sarah Tillinghast. "Combs were $2.25 and homespun fabric brought $2 a yard."[360] Scissors seemed hard to find too.

In no random order, other persons listed substitutions. A mistress had her servants to make table mats from corn shucks. Other items made from corn shucks were mops, chair bottoms, stools, and house slippers. Wool was removed from old mattresses, re-carded and re-spun, and could be mixed with different fibers from discarded items. A plantation mistress told how the slaves fixed Spanish moss to use as mattress ticking: "Put the pile in the canal at low tide just enough to cover. Leave in water for 2-3 weeks until the fiber or outer covering falls off. Dry in the sun, then thrash and shake to remove dirt and dust. All that is left is the black hair."[361] Spanish moss was made into horse blankets and interwoven into bridles.

Tillinghast's advertisement used as stationery
Tillinghast Family Papers, Perkins Library, Duke University

A shortage of raw materials and workers curtailed paper production. Blank pages were torn from books and ledgers. Old letters were opened again for blank spaces/sheets; envelopes were turned inside out and reused. Persons corresponding would turn the page crosswise and continue writing. This made the letter difficult to read. Extra wallpaper made good stationery, as well as extra flyleaves from books. A girl in Fayetteville used pages from her uncle's ledger for letter-writing. Ink was made from pokeberries, oak apples, and burnt copperas. If newspapers could not be cut down on the number of pages or the size, they ceased printing altogether. In April of 1863, editor Harrington of the *Weekly News*, a handwritten newspaper near Lillington, had to go to a single sheet of news where the previous one was two pages. By September of that year, the size of a single sheet shrunk to about seven inches by eight inches; then in the spring of the next year, it ceased altogether. "By virtue of Lincoln's blockade, the size of the Chronicle has been reduced to one sheet only," wrote the editor of the *Milton Chronicle*.[362] People who never subscribed to a newspaper before were then compelled to take the Richmond dailies to read the latest war news. Others passed around newspapers to friends and neighbors until they became too ragged to read. Smaller newspaper companies keenly felt the shortage of raw materials. The *Daily Progress* had an ad that read, "This newspaper will pay 20 cents a pound for clean cotton and linen rags, delivered to this office."[363] A substitute ink recipe called for a strong decoction from the bark of the chinquapin tree.

The military ran short of paper too. Lieutenant J. A. Little wrote to Captain Baker at Camp Holmes in Raleigh that he was entirely without paper and ledgers and could not get any at Lexington in March 1864.[364] A teenager in Fayetteville, devoid of sufficient notepaper, said she was only going to write in her diary when she had something good to say.[365]

When folks were unable to get ice for their drinks, it was suggested they chew mint leaves. Seeds from the maypop plant could be utilized as a substitute lemonade. Another recipe for Confederate lemonade used sorghum, vinegar, and water. This is similar to switchel. Beer was made from maize, persimmons, sassafras, or the sweet locust. Elderberry and blackberry wine was made in most homes in the South. Citizens turned to a variety of things to use as substitute spices—rose, peach, and cherry tree leaves. Cane syrup replaced sugar. Juice from the watermelon, when available, found use as a sweetener. People robbed the bees. Sorghum and molasses were called long sweetening. *Confederate raisins* were dried peaches clipped to bits with scissors.[366]

North Carolinians turned to using natural dyes for their cloth-making experience. Federal soldiers made remarks to those at home about Southern girls wearing dull-colored clothes. Women dyed homespun cloth with maple bark and plaited wheat straw to make hats. White oak set with alum made a gray dye.[367] Aniline dyes had been invented in the 1850s, and women loved the bold colors. These were mostly given up due to the blockade, and the ladies reverted to natural substances for their dyeing. Mrs. Forbis recalled the most satisfactory dyes used were made of green walnut hulls, which gave a dirty brown color. "These colors were not beautiful but they kept the garments from showing soil; so perhaps the small boy did not object, if his big sisters did."[368] Check the appendix for more on dyeing.

Slaves were sent into the woods to collect wax myrtle berries, which were used as furniture polish or candles. It also left a pleasant scent when burned. Sycamore balls or sweet gum balls served as substitute candles. Just soak the dried balls in bacon grease overnight and burn them the next day. A cotton string in a small container of oil or grease made a light but the black smoke and odor was not very pleasant. Tallow candles almost disappeared. Beeswax and resin were mixed and burned as candles.[369]

A newspaper claimed mid-war that "nearly all of our southern cities are now supplied with gas manufacturing from pine 'Blockade Gas.'"[370] Another ad read, "On or after the first of March[1865], the price of GAS will be $80 per 1000 feet. Waterhouse & Bowes, lessees."[371]

The blockade caused severe shortages of kitchenware, glassware, and teapots. Once broken, then good-bye! There were five potters in Lincoln County, three in Randolph, and one in Moore County during the war. Potters made kitchenware for the hospitals. Dr. J. H. Faust bought one dozen cups for two dollars and sixty-seven gallon containers for forty-nine dollars. "The only time potters made any amount of tableware or 'Dirt Dishes' as they were called was during the Civil War."[372] Potters were exempt from military service. Broken windowpanes would be impossible to replace. Oiled paper patches filled the void.[373]

The following were articles made from wood during the blockade: combs, hairpins, knitting needles, buttons, belt buckles, and jewelry such as pins, rings, and bracelets. Thorns were worn in the hair and used to fasten clothing together. Buckles would be made from horn, gourds, and wood. Other ersatz jewelry were watermelon seed brooches, corn kernel pins, bone, army buttons, and fish scales that resembled mother of pearl. When there was a shortage of tobacco, men chewed rosin. Toothbrushes were made from hog bristles, or the person used homemade twig toothpicks.

Dolls sold in Columbia, South Carolina, for two thousand dollars. Most dolls were made at home, such as cloth dolls with the face painted or with nut heads. The body was stuffed with cotton or sawdust. Mothers constructed stuffed animals, and fathers carved wooden toys and made doll cribs from wood. Boys especially liked toy soldiers. Jumping jacks would be made out of wood. The Henry family of Asheville made a "check board" with a puzzle on the back for their children. Corn kernels could be used in place of lost checkers.[374]

Ladies in that period of history wore their hair long, and some women used hair pieces. As these hair pieces, or "rats" as they were called, deteriorated from constant use during the blockade, a lady used a small pillow and turned the hair over it. One female even placed a pair of satin boots in place of the pillow for her hairdo.[375]

BARTERING/BUSINESS PROPOSITIONS

Unheard of before, businesses during wartime chose to barter with individuals rather than shut down. Prices of commodities fluctuated, it seemed, like every day. The Orange Factory Cotton Mill, at one time, would only accept wool or cotton in exchange for yarn, which extreme poorer women did not have. They refused Confederate money. The mill later bartered for bacon, tallow, or lard in exchange for cotton yarn.[376] Always in short supply, mills would request raw wool from individuals. Francis Fries, owner of the Fries Woolen Mill, offered to trade cotton for corn. A father writing to his soldier son informed him that

> I hauled my butter and Mary Ann's and one tub of Martha Choate's to the factory and bartered for thread and cloth . . . they paid fifty cents per pound in cash for the balance. They gave me one bunch of thread for ten pounds of butter, one yard of cloth for a pound of butter . . . . they paid me thirty cents per pound of cheese, two dollars per bushel of chestnuts.[377]

People of Watauga cut hickory saplings, bundled them, and traveled to Saltville to trade the wood for salt. The hickory was used to make barrel hoops.[378] The food shortage became so acute one month before the war ended that the foundry in Salisbury was accepting provisions if the buyers chose to barter.[379] A publisher posted this announcement:

PROVISIONS WANTED

For the use of the hands in our office, we desire to obtain bacon, meal, potatoes, and any other article of food which can be spared. In exchange, we will give envelopes, paper, pens, ink, books, powder, caps, tobacco, shoe tacks, and many other useful goods; or will pay cash as may be preferred.

We want these necessities of like for the use of our employees only. We hope our friends will bring us what they can spare to the BULLETIN OFFICE. August 30, 1864

Notices desiring barter appeared in most all newspapers. "I will exchange fruit trees, roses, grapevines, and other nursery stock for cotton, at market prices. Thomas Carter."[380]
Near Charlotte:

BRING IN THE RAGS

This newspaper wants the rags. We want all the rags that can be bought for us and will give the highest cash price for all that may be delivered at this office, or at the Bookstore.[381]

Notice

The North Carolina Rail Road wants persons to deliver 100-200 cords of wood. This newspaper will pay 20 cents a pound for clean cotton and linen rags, delivered to this office.[382]

The *Richmond Dispatch* printed that ten-penny nails were being passed in upper North Carolina as five cents each.[383] James Wagg wrote that he had saved two to three hundred pounds of nails after fire destroyed his home.[384] George Whitfield and John Mitchell manufactured plug tobacco and peddled it to eastern counties. On their rounds, they brought back fresh fish to sell.

A lady working for the commissary department received tobacco in place of currency. Some highland families hired out slaves to be paid back not with cash, but foodstuffs. Other farmers around the state followed suit. Elizabeth Robeson inscribed in her diary that she "sent some lard with Mr. Cain to trade for spun thread."[385]

Even proprietors of boarding houses and hotels demanded food instead of money: "Our landlords will not board except for provisions, putting board and provisions both at old prices, or what will buy them, which runs board up to $150 per month, and this our patrons can't stand . . . ," quoted a member of the Lenoir family. Refugees found it difficult to find lodging due to the full capacity of hotels and available places to rent. Many were able to stay with family or friends, but a few had no choice but to rent or buy a place. Complaints about the high cost of rent are mentioned in letters. Mrs. Drury Lacy wrote to her daughter Bessie "that Mr. Wilcox raised their rent to $95 a month which was the second time that year . . . we cant do any better in Warrenton and where else to go we are perfectly at a loss."[386]

On a trip through the state, one resident recorded the prices he paid in 1863. Sam H. Walkup in a journal listed these prices in Goldsboro: "Rent for one week—twenty-one dollars; oysters—two dollars; paper—thirty-five cents; use of a hack to carry me and trunks to hotel—one dollar; washing done—ten pieces at ten cents each, pants are twenty-five cents. " He said, "Missed my connections at Weldon and had to stay over, it is a dirty horrid place to eat or sleep at, no comforts, coat—two dollars; railroad ticket to Raleigh from Weldon—five dollars." Recorded May 14: "Sent a box of fifty-two fish to our wives. It cost twenty-three to twenty-four dollars."[387] A lady had to spend the night in Raleigh while having a tooth pulled. She said the hotel bill was one hundred twenty dollars for one night. She had one tooth filled and another pulled for ninety dollars.[388]

Various hotels furnished meals on European plans only. (This was probably the continental breakfast.) "Hotel Fare: food-potatoes—$2, onions—$4, oyster soup—$3; pie—$20; roast beef—$5, chicken—$20, bread—$2, w/butter—$1 more; fish—$8, oysters—$7."[389]

Numerous churches and schools had to close because of lack of instructors. Donations to churches slowed to a trickle. Charitable civilians had less to give to the poor.[390] Churches were not exempt from inflation and money problems. In 1863, when the value of Confederate currency sunk so low, church trustees agreed to refuse it when selling land; but they did agree to accept it for church dues. They also agreed to waive dues for families of soldiers.[391] "Communion was omitted in July[1863] for lack of wine . . ."[392] Everything became scarce. "A silver dollar placed in the offering plate at Home Church in 1864 was estimated to be worth $40."[393] Ministers from Salem received donations from Northern church members. The Moravian PAC by 1864 was struggling to stay afloat. Female teachers asked for and received a raise from twenty dollars to twenty-eight dollars (for four weeks), and male instructors got a bonus. "Since the expense of all necessities still continues to mount and the paper money is steadily losing its value, if we should follow the precedent set in dealing with ministers in past wars—a grant for $125 for each member of his family [Br. Grunert,] servants excepted . . ."[394]

The quartermaster general was willing to barter with civilians. The state had plenty of factory-made cotton yarn, but they lacked wool. A notice appeared in the newspaper from H. A. Dowd, AQM, for the North Carolina army. He advertised that he was "prepared to exchange cotton yarn for wool at: one bunch of yarn for three pounds washed wool and one bunch for four pounds . . . . unwashed wool. Agents are appointed to make exchange at Oxford, Tarboro, Kinston, Catherine Lake, Concord, Rockingham, Pittsboro, Asheville, Hendersonville, Louisburg, Fayetteville, Statesville, and Colerain."[395] In the 1860 Agricultural Census, North Carolina raised just over one-half million sheep compared with over one million in Virginia. Randolph County raised the most with over eighteen thousand, and Carteret County the lowest with less than one thousand.[396] Sheep had become an important, necessary animal like the mule.

MISCELLANEOUS
HOLIDAYS, PARTIES, AND WEDDINGS

Parents wanted their children to have presents during Christmas even through wartime. It was difficult at best to find something for the little ones. Eliza Tillinghast described Christmas of 1862:

> We tried to get up a Christmas Fete by dressing the parlor with evergreens . . . . and the boys made up for the want of gifts by the VEHEMENCE of their shouting "Christmas Gift," . . . they even came upstairs at sunrise . . . to us girls . . . we rewarded Johnny with a brass button . . .

The girls later went to Dr. Long's to get a Christmas treat. Instead, they found out they had to entertain the boarders with "all kinds of plays, such as consequences and comparisons, etc . . . The treat consisted of syllabub and cracking corn bread, ginger cake and apples."[397] Another woman wrote of Christmas in 1862:

> Little cousin Johnny came over before we arose this morning to see if SC [Santa Claus] had left anything here for him. We had a little WAITER full all ready for him (sitting at the chimney corner) . . . the Negroes are all free to go where they please today & the streets are full of them.[398]

The following Christmas, she said the presents were few. Her son got a book and a piece of cake. The next year, she reported, "We had molasses on popcorn for Christmas." Her gift to her son consisted of a ball with candy in his stocking.[399]

A citizen said that striped stick candy was not available during the war. Sorghum was about the only type of candy available in the South. Candy-pullings took place if you had the right ingredients. Peanuts, popcorn, molasses cakes, ginger cakes, and fruit were placed in the stockings at the chimney. The Christmas tree usually was not cut and decorated until Christmas Eve. Some people liked to use a patriotic theme—a star on top was replaced with the Confederate First National Flag, or they attached small pictures of General Lee over the branches. Popcorn strings also trimmed the tree.

As a student in college during the Christmas holidays of 1862, sixteen-year-old Sallie Southall (Cotton) and her friends who could not go home for the holidays went AWOL to visit a fortune-teller to find out their future with boys. The Thomas children in 1862 did not see a lack of Santa's gifts but did the following year. They were told that Santa Claus had "gone to the war," so the children received cakes and coins instead of opulent gifts. In 1864, nothing was mentioned about Christmas except what a dull dreary day it was when they went to church.[400] Author Coulling described the practice of gift giving at Christmas during the war as sparse. Gifts exchanged within the family were thimbles, pins, a set of balls, ribbons for the hair, and homemade toys. The home was decorated with holly and cedar branches.[401] Cousins writing to each other felt different from the above happy holiday:

> Christmas passed away very bad, indeed, with me.[*] It brought forth many sad remembrances of the past which only created discontent. I have been to two quilting parties since Christmas [.] at one of them there were one man, and two boys, at the other there were five gentlemen two of whom were furloughed soldiers, there were some 15-20 lads. I wish you could see them for they are enough to make any person call for the camphor bottle.[402]

Santa's gifts to the children depended on how wealthy the parents were, the availability of store-bought toys, and perhaps their location. The larger cities advertised for German and French dolls and tin toys for boys. Lincoln's blockade of Southern ports cut into the supply of toys. Those without any means to buy the articles scoured their trunks for bits of ribbon, cloth, and such to make their children and slaves trinkets and toys.

Lavish tables groaning with food for parties may have been the norm prewar, but during the conflict, the food was scanty. Adults felt like the young people needed to keep up the spirits of the military. One way to do this was to have fetes, dances, and parties. These took place without the abundance of food and were considered very patriotic. Designated as "cold-water walk-arounds, starvation sociables, and tacky sociables," the attendees at the so-called parties "each came hungry and left empty."[403] The young people didn't seem to mind as long as they were together. Parties continued even as the war was ending. While thousands of both Confederate and Federal soldiers were in Greensboro during the parole process, the young ladies in town held dances at the Britton House Hotel. Always ready to have something new, girls sewed their dresses from draperies. The Sloan family of six sisters delighted the troops at their spacious home. Other ladies around town had parties for the men.[404]

One woman insisted that her friends, returning from their wedding trip, have a spectacular party. At the time, she had the means necessary to fund it. Her soldier husband was stationed in Virginia, and he had just sent her thirty-three pounds of sugar. Her menu consisted of turkey, ham, chicken salad, wafers, jellies, pound cake, silver cake, jelly cake, and syllabub.[405] Elle Andrews said that foodstuffs were not as high in Statesville as they were in other places in the state. After another wedding for friends, she served ice cream and cake for the newlyweds. The following early spring, she procured a deluge of food for an engaged couple consisting of turkey, ham, chicken salad, cakes, jellies, crackers, and coffee. It was unusual for folks to have lavish parties. Unfortunately, Elle's good fortune came to an end when her husband died, and she was forced to support her family. She lost her servant, Susan, who was on loan from another master. Friends furnished her bread, but she said she could do the rest of the cooking and housework.[406] Mrs. Andrews must have spent her resources on her friends because she replied: "I have bought nothing at all for myself to wear in nearly two years excepting having my bonnets repaired every season." A lady from Down East described a bride's cake made from dried cherries and whortleberries. They probably used sorghum as the sweetner.

Birthdays were celebrated, but not as exorbitant as in the past. One mother lamented her sparse holdings. Her daughter, Anna, had a birthday; but there were no gifts to give.[407]

---

[*]   For other people's description of Christmas see chapter 22.

Soap could be made from turpentine or powdered pine rosin with fat and lye added. Treat crushed cottonseed with lye to turn out soap. Ink could be made from oak apples and burnt copperas or pokeberries. When hemp was unavailable, folks used the innards of the sunflower stalk. Different substances found use in mattresses after the people had removed the cotton, feathers, or wool, which was given to the military. Palmetto leaves—split into shreds, boiled, and dried—made a light fluffy mattress, as did Spanish moss. Cattails fluffed up also found use in pillows and mattresses.[408]

Iron was especially needed by the military, industry, and civilians. "There was always a shortage of tools, belts, wire, and oil for the cotton/wool factories." When tools such as a plow were broken, it was difficult to get them repaired. Agencies began to request iron from the railroads. This was especially true of the Confederate Navy and their quest for iron. Governor Vance had them "robbing Peter to pay Paul" by taking away the unused rails.[409]

Wood never was insufficient, but a lack of labor to cut it and haul it to the place requested curtailed the distribution. A newspaper ad said the North Carolina Railroad "wants persons to deliver 100-200 cords of wood."[410] It seems every industry needed wood: the salt factories, ironworks, hospitals, boat builders, railroads, etc. The list goes on. Persons needed wood for heating their homes and cooking. Wood for the individual consumer rose in price. The last winter of the war, Mr. Brown wrote, "Wood is very high . . . $30 per load which is less than half a cord."[411]

With his brothers away at the war, teenager Neill Smith Blue helped keep the farm going. He "stored seed, collected abandoned livestock, cured meat, and hoarded gold coins such that after the war he quickly was able to plant crops and harvest early."[412] Other items in short supply are mentioned. In a letter to his son-in-law, Thomas, Reverend Lacy wrote on October 2, 1862, from Warrenton that he could not get any tobacco. Willis Palmer—principal of the deaf, dumb, and blind institute—replied that the students previously received their supply of broomcorn from the North, and supplies had dried up. He encouraged folks to plant broomcorn for the school.

Candles and lamp fuel grew almost unattainable during the war. In the last year of the war, Judge Battle, while in Raleigh, wrote that "although his correspondence's letter had arrived the preceding evening he had been forced to wait until morning to read it as there was not a candle in the house."[413] Tallow candles almost disappeared

Peach leaves mixed with potatoes and water found use as substitute yeast in raising bread. Cottonseed oil was used in making soap as was myrtle berries. The ooze from the plum tree made a substitute glue. A Georgia newspaper informed readers how to make potash required for making soap: "1000 lbs of oak wood burned equals 2.5 lbs of potash; 1000 lbs of corn stalks burned equals 17 lbs of potash; 1000 lbs of oak leaves burnt to ashes equals 24 lbs potash."[414]

Old ragged knitted garments were unraveled, the yarn used into something else or would be recarded, then spun. A Federal soldier commented to his Northern friends of a rope shortage in the eastern area: "I heard that thear was a scarcity of wash Lines . . ." The lines had been taken and made into horse harnesses.[415]

Paul Barringer related that as a child, he helped out at home with the war effort. "I, seven years old, worked every day for the soldiers, scraping the inspissated juice of the poppy from the bulbar ovaries that had been punctured a few days before [for pain relief]." Barringer said about fifty poppy heads yielded a mass as big as a small peanut. He reported that they scraped lint and gathered the resin from the sweet gum tree. His mother used a pokeberry root poultice on his itch. During the war, quinine sold for two hundred dollars an ounce *if* you could find it.[416] A substitute for opium is the juice from the lettuce plant.[*][417]

Citizens turned to herbs for medicinal purposes. Newspapers printed substitutes:

MEDICAL VIRTUES OF PARSLEY . . . the seeds of this indigenous plant are said to posses immense resources from which the healing art may draw in the management, and cure of the various diseases. They possess incontestable febrifuge qualities or properties and a decoction made of them may be substituted for cinchona. The active principle drawn from the seeds, which is designated under the name of "APROL" is equivalent to quinine in the treatment of intermittent fevers. The plant grows spontaneously in all the gardens of the South & its medical properties should be more fully tested by the professionals.

Wearing Collard leaves to cure headache
Courtesy of the North Carolina Museum of History

The Mercer family used cool collard leaves on the forehead for headaches. She used Dr. Gunn's medical book to help with family illnesses.[418] A lady living in the time period said, "In the pine belt they used turpentine fresh from the stills in typhoid fever most successfully."[419] Rebecca Davis told her son that some neighbors were injured, and they called for three doctors; none came until the next morning when a fourth was sent for. One lady had a tooth filled and another pulled for ninety dollars in December 1864, but someone else had a tooth pulled the last month of the war for ten dollars. Due to inflation, doctors raised their fees like everyone else. "We the undersigned physicians of Anson County are constrained by the high prices of Medicines and the Necessities of Life, to advance our charges. We will, from the 1st of January, 1863, charge 50 cents per mile—with $1.50 for prescription

---

*   Check the appendix for a long list of substitute medicine.

& Medicine—extra for Quinine, Blistering, and costly Prescriptions, and 50 cents for each additional case. And we will require half yearly settlements, in January and July."[*]

To help with deficient commodities, both readers and the editor of newspapers posted their solution for all to see:

> A neighbor of mine says SAUERKRAUT may be made from ½ turnips and ½ cabbage. Turnips alone make good kraut. She urged through our column to send this to the soldiers.[420]

How to make ink: take the bark of the chinquapin and add copperas. Another recipe: "Use gall berries (black fruit), get iron pots partly filled with water, and a good hot fire. Boil bushes for several hours."[421] The following is another receipt for ink:

> Take half an ounce of powdered dogwood bark, 2 drachmas of copperas, 2 scruples of gum Arabic, cherry tree gum, and put them into one pint of rain water; mix them together, and in a few days it will be fit for use.[422]

> To protect grain from insects . . . a gentleman reports to the *Greenville Patriot* that a few stalks of ELDER placed in a barrel of rice, wheat or other grain will effectively drive off & keep off the insects that usually attack such things. We suppose the Elder referred to the "Sambucus" or as the boys everywhere know it, "PopGun Elder."[423]

> As hops will be difficult to obtain, life-everlasting has been suggested as a substitute. Now is the time to gather it, before a hard frost . . . gather the flowers by breaking off the tops, spread them in the shade, and when dry put them in a bag. To make yeast, take a double handful and boil in a half gallon of water, strain and thicken the liquid with flour, about the consistency of batter; add a tablespoon of molasses or sugar, and a little salt. Put in a jug slightly corked, and shake it now and then. It will then be fit for use as yeast. The life-everlasting may be used as a poultice instead of hops, as an anodyne.[424]

> A correspondent sends us the following receipt for curing hams: Jersey Hams—to 80 lbs of hams or shoulders take 4 oz of brown sugar, 3 oz saltpeter, 1 pint of fine salt, thoroughly pulverize and mix. Rub hams well, particularly on the fleshy side. Make the above quantity hold out—shake off lose salt. Lay on boards for 36 hours, then add 2 quarts of fine salt and pack away. In 15-20 days it will be ready to smoke.[425]

To His Excellency
Henry T. Clark
Gov of NC
Sir: The inquiry which you made yesterday respecting the value of brine which has been employed for preserving meat is important at this time. Old brine will contain a large portion of the salt used, and may be recovered by

[*] Drs. W. C. Ramsey, H. Y. Hauze, E. F. Ashe, A. L. Jackson, W. H. Glass, C. B. Coppedge, P. T. Beemon, and J. C. and J. G. Smith[426]

boiling it. Let the brine be poured into an iron kettle, and stir in, while cold the white of several eggs. Boil the brine & skim off the dirt from the top as long as it rises. Now strain the liquid, while hot, in order to free it from a stringy sediment. Boil and skim again, if necessary, reducing the quality of brine by evaporation until a pellicle of fine salt forms upon the surface. It may now be set aside to cool while crystals of nearly pure salt will be formed. The brine should never be boiled til a dry mass is formed, as in that case, it will be impure and dark colored. By repeating the evaporation, the salt may be obtained as pure & white as table salt.

         Most truly your servant

         E. Emmons, state geologist

PS If the brine is stirred while cooling, fine salt will be formed. If it is allowed to cool at rest, a coarse salt will be deposited.[427]

       TO SAVE BACON: make a solution of salt in hot water, put pork in the hot brine. Let hams and shoulders be kept in 3 ½ minutes. Hang up and smoke. You can save 4/5 this way.[428]

       Economy in Boots: How to make three pair of boots last as long as six, and longer. The following extract is from Colonel MacErone's Seasonable Hints, which appeared in the Mechanic's Magazine, dated February 3rd, 1843. "After stating the quality of sheepskin clothing, for persons whose employment renders it necessary that they should be much outdoors, etc., he says: I treat them in the following manner—I put a pound of tallow and a half a pound of rosin into a pot on the fire, and when melted and mixed, I warm the boots and apply the hot stuff with a painter's brush until neither the sole or the upper leather will suck in any more. If it is desirable that the boots should take polish, dissolve an ounce of beeswax with an ounce of turpentine, to which add a teaspoon of lamp-black. A day or two after the boots have been treated with the tallow and resin, rub over them the wax and the turpentine, but not before the fire. Tallow or any other grease becomes rancid and rots the stitching as well as the leather, but the rosin gives it an antiseptic quality which preserves the whole. Boots or shoes should be so large to admit of wearing in them cork soles—cork is a bad conductor of heat.[429]

IMPORTANT TO FARMERS AND OTHERS: A VALUABLE METHOD OF PREPARING LEATHER:
MODE OF PREPARING LEATHER DRESSED WITH HAIR ON:

1st. If the hides are old, hard, and dry, soak them in pure water about 2-3 days.

2nd. When well soaked, or when fresh hides, flesh them thoroughly.

3rd. Prepare a pickle made of 3 lbs alum, and 5 lbs common salt to a pail of water enough to dissolve the salts for each hide; this is an average proportion. For a very large single old hide, 3 ½ pounds of alum and 8lbs of salt my be necessary; whereas for a small calf's hide, ¾ lb of alum and 2 lbs of salt may be enough.

4th. Soak the fleshed hides in this pickle solution from 8-10 days.

5th. Soak them again 2-3 days in pure water to remove the salt.

6th. When about half dry, break them with the proper currier's breaking knives.

7th. Smoke them, flesh side down, 8-10 days over hard wood (hickory or oak) smother, continuing to break, roll, grind, in succession.

8th. Boil the neatsfeet for oil, save the oil and lubricate the hides with the jelly and greasy water, breaking them all the time.

The small hides can be finished in 6-8 days. Medium sized hides in good condition, from 12-15 days. The largest and worst conditioned hides can be furnished in from 18-20 days. If you want the hair off, soak in limewater first until the hair sloughs; but then you must carefully work the limewater out, or it will eat the fiber of the leather. The leather is best with the hair on. It makes the best and most comfortable shoes. Put the hair of the upper soles inside, and of the soles—put upper sole hair out, and outer sole hair in, thus filling the soles with the best of water proofing, and make the soles the more elastic and lasting. With the hair on it is especially best for saddle covers, stirrup leathers, shabracks, traces, horse collars, caps, gloves, sentinel coats, halters, trunk covers, and every use known.[430]

WATER PROOF OVER-CLOTHES FOR SOLDIERS—We know that an incalculable amount of comfort was derived by some of our Fayetteville volunteers on the Peninsula, from a over-coat and gaiters, of the water-proof cloth spoken of in the annexed communication from a lady:—Every one must see the absolute necessity of water-proof over-coats for our soldiers; especially in winter, when their wet clothes are constantly liable to freeze to their skin. It is said that 50,000 British troops in the Crimean war, died from the effects of wet and cold. What is to hinder our brave defenders from sharing the same fate? Therefore, believing that every lady will take pleasure in devoting a few days and a few dollars to this sacred object—it is proposed that each one contribute one or more sacques or cloaks with lined hoods, ready dipped in the water-proof solution (made of alum and sugar of lead) and send them in to the Association during the present week. The case is urgent; life and death, and our own safety, are concerned in it, and every day is important. Also add to this one or more under flannels—new or old—and also ginger and pepper, and a cake of mutton suet in small coarse bags, with strings to hang up in the tents. Let everyone make up her own bundle, labeled with her own name, to be sent on as speedily as possible. This will be the most speedy way of accomplishing an object in which all are equally interested.[431]

HOW TO WATERPROOF CLOTH

Two pounds, four ounces Alum dissolved in ten gallons of water.

Dissolve same quantity of Sugar of Lead in similar manner. They form a precipitate of the sulphate of lead. The clear liquid is now withdrawn, and the cloth immersed for one hour in the solution. Remove the cloth, dry out in the shade. Wash in clear water and dry again likewise.[432]

Confederate Lemonade: use sorghum, vinegar, and water. You can substitute pomegranate instead of lemons. Stew with sugar to make a syrup. Strain out the seeds. Use one tablespoon with a glass of water.[433]

The following is a quote by Mary Mendenhall Hobbs at the close of the war: "When you have no opportunity to buy anything, your wits become active and you invent fashions adapted to the quantity of material."[434]

CHAPTER NINE

Speculation, Extortion, and Riots
"Sir hear the crys of the pore I beg you . . ."*

Dr. Thomas F. Wood wrote: "It was not long before merchants, especially Jews, were ransacking the country to pick up anything they could find to hold for higher prices. An editor of one of the newspapers said that they would bottle up air to hold for a rise if they could."[1] Peddlers, who were mostly Jewish, were issued a permit for one year.[2] Major G. W. F. Harper said that before the state seceded that "groceries of all kinds advance in price since the blockade. Coffee worth 25c."[3] Those businessmen with experience of past rising and falling of prices saw the war as an opportunity to make money. One elite family bought a large supply of provisions before the blockade was imposed by Lincoln. They ordered salt, iron, cotton bagging, rope, coffee, and sugar not to resell, but for their use on the plantation.[4]

"In December[1861] . . . the Convention took action to halt speculation in the process of trade. In an ordinance which was to be in force only 'during the present war,' unless repealed or modified by the General Assembly, the Convention made speculation a misdemeanor and ruled that whoever shall engross or get into his hands, by buying, corn or other grain, pork or beef . . . fish, salted, or smoked, cheese, coffee, sugar, tea, salt, saltpeter or other dead victuals whatever, and leather, to the intent to sell the same again at unreasonable prices, or to keep the same from market, and prevent the same from passing into the hands and use and consumption, or for sale at reasonable prices, or for charitable distribution amongst the poor and necessitous persons . . . upon conviction . . . or confession, shall be punished for a misdemeanor, and . . . required to enter into recognizance with sufficient surety for his good behavior for the space of three years, in such sum as the court may direct."[5]

"Our people suffer terribly from extortioners and speculators," penned a lady. Mrs. Edmondston said, "We must curb our wants." A couple months later, she commented, "This war has developed one bad phase of human nature, 'Extortion.' The worst thing to be dreaded by the government is that the necessities of the people, the want of SALT particularly, will force them into trading with the Yankee invaders, or rather pedlars [sic] who follow in their wake."[6]

The condition over extortion and speculation prompted persons to address both newspapers and the governor. A lady signing only her name in initials wrote the *Spirit of the Age* with this message:

Word To The Ladies
It behooves us, my sisters, daily and hourly to pour forth our prayers in behalf of our soldiers and our country. It is our peculiar privilege now. Few of the praying men are left behind. Soldiers find little time to attend to Heavenly things. The cowardly speculators who occupy their places, methinks would rather pray the evil one to continue this opportunity to grow rich on the country's necessities . . .[7]

Another woman sent a letter to the governor:

I have four little children and myself. The government allows me just $19 per month. I have to pay from $28 to $30 per barrel of corn, $1 per pound for bacon and I cannot live at such rates. I have had to pay fifty cents per pound

---

* Quote by Mrs. Lydia A. Bolton, November 5, 1862, to Governor Vance[8]

for salt all this year and the very highest prices for everything until I have paid out. My husband has been in the army 16 months. He has toiled and undergone hardships not only for me and my children but for those poor timid chicken-hearted speculators who are afraid to go themselves; then when I get out of something to eat and want to buy they would take the last cent for breadstuff enough to last me one week.[9]

Many of the letters recorded, which flooded the governor's office in November, during the second year of the conflict had to do with leather or salt, then yarn. Some merchants cooperated with the government prices for their goods while others balked. Governor Vance wrote to Francis Fries of the Fries Woolen Mill in Salem:

Suffice it to say that without the assistance of the manufacturers the State cannot clothe the troops and they must brave the severities of the coming winter naked. When men of intelligence and public spirit take such a position, we may expect suffering & ruin to overwhelm our country. There is only one remedy to arrest the evil which threatens us, and that is for the civil authorities to permit the military to put forth its strong arm and take what it wants. October 10, 1862[10]

A lady wrote the governor in November 1862:

You have appealed, to the kind-hearted ladies of North Carolina, to make up clothing, and to contribute anything they can spare, for our suffering soldiers, as the government cannot do it. Sir: The ladies of this county have done, are doing all they can with the means with which they are provided, they are still willing to do, if they could get a little help from the factories, but Sir we go there, and have to give six dollars for a bunch of cotton, to the tanyards, and give three dollars a pound for leather. Who can pay such prices for themselves and soldiers too? Now the speculators are going round, buying up all the corn for the purpose of making *liquor,* and such as this will cause making a poor soldiers family to suffer from cold, and hunger. What should this be, when it can be prevented by a few words from you, to the Honorable Legislature? In the name of the ladies, and especially the soldiers families, I beg you to set a price on things . . .[11]

In Macon County, Colonel A. L. Corpening told Vance:

. . . the women in this part say if they could get thread they woud have done a great deal more for the soldiers, but owing to speculation they Could not get any thing to work on and earnestly appeales [sic] to you to put down some of those things that we are compelled to have such as thread and wool if it is in your power . . .[12]

In the piedmont, Reverend W. W. Allen echoed the lament that many would respond to the call to help supply the troops if they could get cheaper prices on cotton and leather.[13] Apparently, speculators escaped prosecution, prompting the governor to pass another proclamation:

PROCLAMATION BY THE GOVERNOR OF NORTH CAROLINA
November 26, 1862
Whereas, in order to stop, if possible, the wicked system of speculating which is blighting the land & prevent the production of famine in the midst of plenty, the Legislature of North Carolina, by Joint Resolution thereof ratified on the 22d. day of this month (November) have authorized me to lay an embargo

upon the exportation from the State of certain articles of prime necessity, except to certain persons and for certain purposes.

Now therefore, I Zebulon B. Vance Governor of the State of North Carolina, do issue this my Proclamation, forbidding all persons, for the spare of thirty days, from the date hereof, from carrying beyond the limits of the State, any salt, bacon, pork, beef, corn meal, flour, potatoes, shoes, leather, hides, cotton cloth, and yarn and woolen cloth. The following persons are alone to be exempted from this prohibition—viz.

All Quarter Masters and Commissary Agents of the Confederate Government, and of any state of the Confederacy exhibiting proper evidence of their official character. Also all Agents of any County, district, town, or corporations of other States, who shall exhibit satisfactory proof of their authority to purchase such articles in behalf of such a town, county, districts, or corporation for public uses or distribution at cost and transportation and not for resale or profit. Also all persons who make oath before the nearest

Justice of the Peace that all the articles purchased are for his own private use and not for resale before they are removed. Also all persons, non residents, who may have bought such articles before the dates hereof. The exception is to extend to salt made by non residents on the sea coast and in their own works and to cargoes entering any part of our ports from abroad. Any of said articles that may be stopped in transit from our borders are to be confiscated to the use of the State. Until further orders the Colonels of Militia in the different counties are enjoined to see that this Proclamation is enforced.

Not intending or desiring to prevent the people of our Sister States from sharing with our own citizens whatever we can spare but to repress speculation so far as may be possible. I earnestly appeal to all good citizens to aid and sustain me in the enforcement of this proclamation for the common Good.[14]

Zebulon B. Vance, made when inagurated Governor, 1862
N.C. Division of Archives & History, Photographic Archives

Evidently, those agents who had contracts to move supplies out of the state before the proclamation took effect got caught up in the new ruling. It wasn't clear to officers about this last ruling, inciting them to flood the governor's office with questions:

N.C. Rutherford County
November the 9th 1862
J.M. Edwards

—an old gentleman of South Carolina twelve months ago sold to a taner of North Carolina 25 or 30 hids and made a verbal contract with the tanner to let him have enough leather this Fall of the same hides for his own use [.] the old gentleman came the other day and got 50 lbs of the leather and a captain of my Regiment seized it and has the leather in his possession at this time the old gentleman contends for his leather, he sold the hids & buys the leather, I wish to know if I must give the old man the leather, or take it to Raleigh. I also wish to know if it is in violation of general order No 9th sent to me by the Adjutant General for a tanner of North Carolina to sell to a person of South Carolina a side or two of leather for their own use and also if it is a violation for the ladies to exchange cloth for spun thred with the South Carolinians to get thread for their own use."[15]

November 6th, 1862:

Hearing of a little meanness & rascality in this neighborhood I came up here on yesterday, and the most important item I have to communicate is this . . . WW Long [former sheriff] has a LARGE QUANTITY of sole & upper leather on hand, for which he is asking the BLOCKADE price of $300 per sole and $350, for upper pr lb . . . . There is also in this town, two BALES of factory sheeting belonging to a Mr Gibbony of Wythville, for which he has been offered 40cts pr yard; (it cost him only 20), but he refuses to take it holding it at 75c I write these facts, so that you may know where to find the articles if you wish to press them, for the army. If you want the cloth and leather address Col. Joseph Masten 71 N.C. Militia. H.W. Ayer, Salem N.C.[16]

Colonel W. R. Young with the militia told Vance:

I can get no shoes or leather what articles I have to purches I receive donations in money to fut the bill There are some persons purchasing all the wool they can get at enormous prices & Sending it out of the State if it can be stoped there are women here that will manufacture it into jeans [cloth] if thread can be obtained.[17]

Colonel Samuel Forkner, doing his duty, questioned a man he stopped necessitating a letter to Raleigh authorities:

Mt. Airy N.C. Nov. 4th 1862

I have seized on Some 400 lbs of Leather in the hands of Elisha Banner, he Claims that it is not the object of the 4th Artic of Gen Odire No 9 of Oct 25th under which I am acting, to interfere with former contracts, I have agreed to mak no dispostition of the leather untile we herd from you

Mr Banner has made a Salt trade for which he has bought leather to Give in exchange, the object is Speculation. We have a County Contract with the Va Salt works which will suply this County if we can get it hauled with what the State works can do for us,

Were it not for Speculation many of our Soldiers Wifes & Children in this Section would have ben saved of going bare footed this Winter [.] I wish to here [sic] from you Soon on this subject, likely there may be other contracts of a like nature[18]

Banner did have a contract to exchange four hundred pounds of leather for one hundred bushels of salt. He asked the governor for a permit to show the militia it was legit. People in the mountains grew desperate, for it was time to kill the hogs, requiring salt for preservation of the meat. Six men from Burke County wrote a revealing letter to Governor Vance in December:

we the under Seigned implore your exelancy to intercede for us the citizens of Burke County with the Legislature to pass an act for the more sure prompt and cheap Supply of Salt for the County of Burk [.] Thomas G.

---

*   Colonel Edwards of the 104th Militia did receive a reply from Governor Vance that stated that the gentleman could have his leather and that the ladies could exchange their products.

Walton got in as Salt agent for the County [.] he advertised the people to come in to Morganton Thursday the 4th of December to receiv their Salt [.] the people had their hogs fat [and]ready to kill and Corn Scare but Thomas G. Walton refused to let them have more than three pounds for each member of the family—here stood Women thinly clad the wives of our Suffering Soilgers in the mud in front of Thomas G. Waltons Salt House from early in the morning til near night [,] eighteen miles from home awaiting till Thomas G. Walton could wegh out Salt for a hole County . . . he prices the salt $5 per Buishel . . .

S. C. Wilson begged the governor to pass an act and let the local people elect a salt agent. His letter was signed by James G. Lanes, Joseph S. Turner, W. F. Gibbs, Joshua Gills, and Joseph Shooke.[19]

The Reverend Braxton Craven from Trinity College also sought the advice from Vance that November:

Shoes cannot be made at $5.00 unless we have the authority to press leather. I could get some two hundred sides to morrow, but they ask even for the Government $2.25 for sole and $2.75 for upper. Your state contractors will not furnish the army, they can do much better by selling to others. There is a large amount of clandestine trade now going on. I have . . . sent a considerable amount of . . . fine carpet-blankets. Soldiers Shoes bring $10 to $18 per pair, wool socks 75 to 1.00 [,] good blankets $5.00 to $12.00. Every sort of device is practiced. Soldiers are now sending word to their friends, that they are barefooted, and urging their friends to buy and send at any price.[20]

John Dawson's letter:

The undersigned Citizens of Wilmington would respectfully represent to you Excellency that James L. Barnwell of Columbia S.C., now here, came among us bringing supplies for our sick and suffering people and tendering him own services . . . while in Wilmington purchased some lots of Salt for Sale . . . at actual cost and charges in Columbia . . . and not in any way for purposes of speculation . . . Mr. Barnwell had 300 bushels waiting to be shipped to the poor in Columbia. Mr. Dawson and the citizens of Wilmington asked the governor to waive the ruling on the embargo for this specific purpose. Governor Vance wrote that Gen. Whiting "has been instructed to ship all salt purchased previous to the prohibition." I did not intend to violate any contract with citizens of other states. [November 13, 1862] (Note: The citizen's names were not listed in this reference.)[21]

Vance called speculators "the vilest and most cowardly of your country's enemies."[22] Governor Vance imposed an embargo on the exportation of provisions, speculators were punished by fines, and he made up a committee to fix prices and forbid the distillation of grain. Some speculators were buying grain to be sold outside the state for a higher price. Bruner, editor of the *Carolina Watchman*, reported the speculators and extortioners "could do more damage to the Confederacy than . . . the unprincipled Yankees."[23] Alexander Dickson, quartermaster for Ashe County, confiscated a wagonload of cotton from James Culbert that he had recently bought from an Iredell County mill. Dickson had written to the governor that Culbert was a known speculator and was headed to East Tennessee to sell the cloth from the Eagle Mills Factory.[24] Captain Bell also wanted to hear from the governor:

Franklin, N.C.
Feby. 23rd 1863
Gov. Vance
Dear Sir,

I desire that you instruct me whether or not dried fruit can be removed from this state to the state of Georgia for the purpose of distillation. I know that it cannot be distilled in this state, as there is an express prohibition against it. Now the question with me is whether the party moving the fruit from this state to another is liable or not. I am of the opinion that the party is just as liable as if the distillation as made in the state, for the fruit was brought for the express purpose of being distilled, but when a law was enacted forbidding its distillation then in order to evade the law the fruit was moved to the state of Georgia just across the state line and then distilled. Now it is evident if this state of things is not stopped, that the law prohibiting the distillation of fruit is rendered entirely worthless, for the high prices of brandy will cause all fruit to be run out of the state and be converted into brandy and our suffering soldiers in the field will have to suffer in consequence of the evasion of a law, passed expressly for their benefit.

We have a lark in our town now, who is thus engaged. His name is H. W. Nolen, he has some two or three hundred bushels dried fruit is moving it just over the line into Georgia to be distilled. Now I ask that your Excellency will instruct me in the premises. I belong to Gen. Braggs Army 39th Reg N.C.T. was detailed to come home and enroll conscripts, acting under the authority of Gen. Pillow, but have some difficulty. My authority is disputed. Our senator from this district says there was a contract made between the Confed.Gov. and your Excellency in furnishing conscripts; that the Government of N.C. would furnish them when called on, in her own way. Of this fact I desire information. I have made the inquiry in regard to the fruit, believing it to be my duty as an officer.

The same Mr. Nolen had been and is now carrying on the shoe & boot business and it is evident from the high prices that he is charging twice the percent allowed by law. He has petitioned I understand for the appointment of Post Master in order to exempt himself from the army. He further alleges that he has a government contract and claims exemption.

The citizens have been very much enraged at his course, having completely monopolized the shoe business. He bought up all the leather he could, made it into shoes and sold them to the citizens and soldiers at high figures, they being compelled to buy. He has been speculating in brandy and in fact in everything he has been engaged in extortioning upon poor wives of soldiers in selling them shoes at astonishing rates. It does not seem right when the women of the county are doing their full duty in the cause of our independence, in providing for our brave troops, sacrificing their sons upon their country's altar, it does not look right that the Yankee Pet, should be permitted to extortion and amass a fortune off of those who are defending our rights, when the country is demanding and is entitled to his services, it should have them. I saw in a Georgia paper, where the editor was commanding the policy of your Excellency in putting into the service, those who are charging over 75 percent. This policy of yours needs no comment and if pursued, will prove a blessing to the state and I am confident that Mr. Nolen has charged much more than the percent allowed and I am in for placing him in the army it will be sanctioned by almost all who know him.

I am very Respectfully Yours
Alfred W. Bell Capt. Co. B 39 N.C.V.

The following is Vance's answer:

> I have no power to prevent his distilling the fruit in Ga. but I should be very glad if he would submit proof to the enrolling officer for the dist., of his selling shoes & leather for more than 75 percent. He can be brought up a standing on that very quick. Z.B.V.[25]

Methodist Reverend R. L. Abernethy felt the need to inform the governor of the situation in Marion:

> If it is Constitutional, and if your position as Governor of N. Carolina gives you the power to do so, in the name of God, of suffering humanity, of the cries of widows and orphans, do put down the Speculation and extortion in this portion of the state. Here in Marion, beef is being sold to the poor wives of the soldiers who get but $11 per month in the field, at the enormous price of 11 and 12 cents per pound! Leather at $4 per pound! Bacon at 40 and 50 cents per pound; Corn from the heap, at $1.50 per bushel! Salt at near 50 cents per pound! Many children of the soldiers in the Camps are nearly barefoot and naked without the possibly of getting clothes or shoes. here in Marion, Messrs Maroney and Halyburton have a large Tannery —yet one pound of leather cannot be bought—by private purchase.

When Reverend Abernethy talked with the owners, they replied, "If we sell to one man privately we must sell to others, and we will not do it."[26]

Newspapers got in the habit of condemning speculators and extortioners. The *Raleigh Register* reported, "There is an insane greed for money that some men actually plant cotton for market instead for the support of life." In a copy of the *Carolina Watchman*, the editor urged speculators to read the Bible and follow the rules.[27] The *Milton Chronicle* suggested a roll of honor and dishonor:

> **Roll of Honor and Dishonor** . . . We hear of a lot of honor being kept in our state, and we respectfully suggest the propriety of also keeping a Roll of Dishonor. In this roll we would record the name of all extortiners and speculators on the necessities of life.

The *Raleigh Standard* likewise vilified the speculators:

> . . . occasionally . . . we find some passage in history . . . that applies so directly to class of vampires now sucking out the life blood of the nation, that we cannot resist the temptation to copy it . . . even though it proves that mankind . . . has been prone to the vice which we so freely condemn. The following is an extract from Botta's, *History of American War* Vol. 2, p.212: "There sprang up a class of men who sought to make their private advantages out of the public distress. Dependence, liberty or no liberty, were all one of them, provided they could fatten on the substance of the country, while good citizens were wasting themselves in camps . . . while they were devoting to their country their time . . . estates . . . . and their very existence, these insatiable robbers were plundering . . . the public . . . and private fortunes. All private contracts became the object of their . . . gains. All army supplies enriched them . . . and the government often paid dearly for what it never obtained.[28]

The *Standard* continued:

> We have repeatedly said, that the extortion and speculation now practised[sic] in the South are doing more to hasten our subjugation than

anything else beside. Every thoughtful person in the country not involved in the high crime of beggaring the people and the government must see it. Look at the deadening, chilling effect of this speculation mania upon the large masses of the people whose sons and brothers are in the army. Everyone is melancholy and dejected, not at the ill success of our arms, but at the certain disaster which is being brought upon the country by the speculators. The worst enemies of the Confederacy are those who speculate upon salt, flour, bacon, leather, cotton and woolen goods. Many have become suddenly rich, both Jews and Gentiles, and they have no concern except to keep the war raging that they may make money.[29]

The *Southern Illustrated News* had a long column about the problem:

THE SPIRIT OF EXTORTION

Is ruling "wild and wide" throughout the Confederacy. It is prevailing everywhere, from the wholesale dealers, to the fashionable and fancy stores, and thence downward to the little shops in the by-ways and alleys.

All classes of dealers seem to be inoculated with its virus, until the disease has become both epidemic and contagious. A regular tariff of prices is as much a thing of impossibility as it[s] truth in the dispatches of Pope and McClellan. Israelites and Gentiles, by hook or by crook, manage here and there to pick up odds and ends for purposes of speculation; and it would strike one unfamiliar with the fact that the blockade has broken up the specialities [*sic*] of trade, with ludicrous wonder to see the revolution which a few months have effected in the mercantile world. You would find the dry goods man exhibiting in his window, side by side with a silk dress pattern of last year's fashion, perhaps a pair of cavalry boots or so, and a bundle of cherry pipes, flanked by a box of brown paper envelopes and ditto of adamantine candles, the result of recent purchases from some successful smuggler. Boots, shoes and hats have become articles of confectionary; and packages of pain-killers, and bottles of patent medicines, and boxes of pills, properly or improperly, we will not say, range side by side with Bologna sausages, five-shooters and breech-loading rifles. The millinery shops sell matches, and on the counters of quasi-tailors cabbages and geese are not considered articles beneath the dignity of trade and exchange.—Spools of cotton and boxes of blacking, plugs of tobacco and war songs of the South, mingle together in incongruous assortment, "black spirits and white, red spirits and *grey*"—the last much in demand.

The advent of a smuggler, (and it occurs very often,) is hailed with rapture, and the process of *skinning* becomes a subject for the ratiocinations of cels, psycologists and optionists[*sic*].

The smuggler skins the wholesale purchaser of his miscellaneous wares; he, in turn, skins the small dealer, who, in justice to *himself,* skins the buyer at his counter; until the conscience of the mercantile public becomes as bare of usurers, or the departed spirits of defunct Yankee Generals.

How long this state of things is to last, we may not say; but it is the impression of some, who claim not to be prophets nor the offspring of soothsayers, that these patriotic individuals who, notwithstanding the blockade, obtain supplies for the dear public, and who, at some risk, more trick, and five hundred per cent profit, furnish clothing, shoes, and medicines for the necessitous, will wake up some fine morning to learn that our troops, now on Northern soil, have opened, for the benefit of our suffering people many highways and thoroughfares of trade, and that their, (the vendors',) stock of miscellaneous wares, more incongruous than the motley masques of a Carnival, have fallen with more rapidity than, and with nearly the fatality, of the descent of Satan from Heaven.

And who will be sorry? Not the poor, hard-fisted, honest-hearted mechanic, whose weekly toils scarcely suffice to give the commonest and coarsest food to his wife and dear children. Not the pale, pining, serving girl, whose little weekly earnings are nearly all exhausted in the price of the candles, by whose dim, yellow light she wounds her thin fingers and strains out the brightness of her swollen, tearful eyes, and counts the quick pulses of her breaking heart. Not the subordinates in government departments, who toil over the desk until the long rows and lines of figures seem massed into black columns of contraband regiments from Kansas, with Jim Lane at their head, all photographed with a confused notion about the price of sterling and Sterling Price. Not the poor, little ragged, shoeless children, whose tender feet, mud-covered and chill, seem to court a fatal affinity, and yet wage an unequal controversy with angular brickbats and irregular curbstones. Not the sickly and suffering, who have to grin and groan, and "bear the ills that flesh is heir to," because physic they once would have [been] thrown to the dogs, is not to be had save at a cost involving the expense of breakfast, dinner, and supper. Not those who are compelled to eat bread as stale as the jokes in "Harper's Weekly." Not those whose *Attic Salt* wants seasoning with that once graced the *cellar.* Not those who have to pay as much for Lucifer matches as though they were made in Heaven. Not those who have been compelled to wear their garments till they have become threadbare as the wit of the Louisville Journal or the promise of Mr. Seward to crush out the rebellion in a given time. Not thousands of those whose hearts and pockets have been wrung by an extortion they have had to meet at ruinous expense, or suffer "pangs that the poor alone can know, the proud alone can feel."

Have we a remedy? Perhaps not. But we have a *public opinion.* And that should make itself heard through the various avenues of which it is a legitimate and respected traveler. *The Pulpit* and the *Press*—the two great levers that move the world of thought, feeling, and action, should not fail in their duty here.

Let the one, in its winged words of eloquent denunciation of wrong—let the other, as it sends forth its morning and evening messengers to the ten thousand ponderers of its thundering didactics, stir up an honest indignation at the spirit of extortion, and invoke a spirit of resistance to its encroachments.

We saw a nurse, not long since, trying to quiet a red-faced, red-haired baby. The more she tried to pacify the little imp, the more blatant he. "What makes a child cry so," we asked the despairing Ethiopian, as, in the vigorous display of muscle and lungs, the air seemed vibratory and resonant with his shrieks. "Jis cos he kin cry," was the response. So, we think, there is no legitimate reason why articles of trade should be so very extravagantly high. And in many instances, we doubt not, these venders of the necessaries of life, and its luxuries too, charge exorbitant prices, without reference to any standard or rule, "jis cos they kin."[30]

"James Zimmerman told his wife there were so many speculaters grasping and grabing at what little the poor women have to spair to get cotton and other things [that] they are helping more to whip us than the Yankes."[31]

The noted Justice Asa Biggs wrote:

Frequently . . . I have been greatly depressed in spirits, with pain and grief realizing what I did not expect to see prevail so extensively in the South—a spirit of covetousness, selfishness, extortion and avarice that induces me to suppose this cruel war is still to be prolonged, until a just and merciful God, shall humble our people more, and extirpate the distracting and fell spirit that so generally prevails. How any patriot, philanthropist, or Christian can permit himself to be absorbed in making a fortune out of the miseries of this war, is past my comprehension! How men of standing and wealth, can remain at home, accumulating their thousands and millions, at the expense, misery, and discomfort of the families of those brave and gallant soldiers, who are protecting our rights at such great sacrifices, is but another evidence of the ingratitude and depravity of poor, fallen, human nature![32]

A Federal soldier in the occupied eastern part of the state recalled his involvement with local residents. "The interested loyalty of the proprietor [Grist] was revenue-making in large amounts of Confederate currency at a great discount, and then, through some sort of connivance, he was sending the same through the lines and buying cotton, paying for it in depreciated scrip at face value. His purchase he was able to sell at immense profit."[33] By 1864, apparently, speculating continued to run rampant as indicated in this letter: "Unless speculating and extortion is put down I see no hope for the confederacy and it seems impossible to reach that cruel class of men among us[.]"[34]

Businesswoman Mrs. Holliman doubled her price of sugar when she heard that New Orleans was under enemy control.[35] Another woman made money illegally. The Widow Camel, age thirty-five, lived near the swing bridge on the Carolina Cut of the canal. When her "man" died, she made a remark: "There, G.d, d . . . n you, you won't watch me anymore." It was rumored that she had made a great deal of money buying goods at New Bern and Roanoke, then selling them across the lines.[36]

The entire cut nail supply of the South was in the hands of four to five speculators in Richmond. The price started at four dollars a keg up to ten dollars. Salt was selling at one cent to fifty cents a pound in the beginning. Bermuda businessmen grew very rich. The island had an influx of gamblers, prostitutes, Confederate agents, sailors, and speculators from several different countries.[37] Henry Trenchard, a merchant from Wilmington, whose home office was in Bermuda, advertised to Confederate merchants that he had the best-quality woolen cloth for sale or barter.[38]

Not all businessmen engaged in speculating. W. B. Lovelace, of Cleveland County, wrote to Governor Vance that he was a tanner and had about used up all his supplies. Lovelace requested the government to send him some leather. "I hope you will make an arrangement to furnish me and others who are working at government prices (instead of speculation) with good hide to tan and sell them to us at a fare price and we will make leather at a fare price and try to keep down speculation."[39] Merchant W. N. Tillinghast wrote to his brother:

I could have made a fortune by speculating but I did not think it was right. We are living very comfortably and though deprived of some things which we once thought necessary, luxuries and that we can not only DO without them but a[re] really better without them. I think our girls look prettier in homespun dresses than they ever did before.[40]

That fall, he wrote to the same brother:

I have agreed to be a partner with Mr. Alex Johnson, Jr. in the management of the "Cumberland County Supply Associates" which is an association of gentlemen who have subscribed $42,000 for the purchase of buying abroad and in our own market provisions and selling them at cost to the poor and others in town who are not able to pay exorbitant prices of market people and shopkeepers. We are to be allowed ten percent commission on our sales out of which we pay all expenses of managing the business.[41]

N. T. Perkins, a Quaker, lived in Pikeville. He said he had three hundred pounds of rosin waiting to be put aboard the train but was having trouble with the railroad company. "I have heard that such rosen is worth $9 to $10.00 pr [lb] at Morehead City . . . I would sell it for three dollars pr [lb] where it is to be paid before [illegible] or delievered . . . if I cannot do that I shall hold it for a better price . . ."[42]

A lady from Mount Gilead communicated to her brother that "Father went on a trip to Fayetteville in December . . . took flour and syrup . . . [sold the] flour for $86 a bushel, $9 for a gallon of syrup. We could have gotten more for retailing it out."[43] Peter King from Auman's Hill, Montgomery County, wrote to his soldier son, Allan, in 1862, that he had "killed 563 lbs. of pork for you—and sold it for 10c a pound." King told him that "I and Rankin went in the distillery [business] together. We cleared eight hundred dollars."[44]

A person claimed that Caswell County beat all other counties for high prices. "Preachers of high standing" told of corn being sold at Red Mountain, Orange County, of three hundred barrels at eight dollars a barrel sold for "money that will pay debts."[45]

Mrs. Staton, of Martin County, kept excellent records and gave a good example of prices mid-war. These are some notations from her ledger:

Mrs. Staton's ledger of purchases.
Frances M. Manning Papers, Joyner Library, ECU

November 3, 1862—bought 12 sacks of salt for $574.92

November 3— paid $1.50 for drayage—paid $2300.20 in full for freight for 1597 pounds of salt from Wilmington to Rocky Mount.

November 7—paid Mr. A.O. Turner $18 for 18 pairs of Negro shoes.

November 7—paid Levi Yates $76.25 to bring daughter from Edgeworth Seminary to Williamston. [A portion of the bill included medicine and music bought on the way home.]

December 3—paid Spencer Stokes $3 for cutting out twenty-one pairs of Negro shoes.

December 29—paid 50 cents to have spinning wheel repaired.

January 10, 1863—paid C.E. Barnes $5 for making a coffin and $1.25 to mend a bridle & straps.

March 1, 1863— paid Jennielle Lloyd for making clothes, $28.30—including 2 Zouave jackets—$3, silk body—$1.50, silk long basque—$5, worsted long basque—$2.50, three worsted dresses—$7.50, poplin dress—$3.50, muslin dress—$2.

March 18— $8 was paid to A. Nelson for warping and weaving cloth for the Negroes.

April 1— $180 paid to Thomas Sheppard for eighteen pairs of Negro shoes.

In January 1864, Mrs. Staton bought postage stamps—$5; paper and nails—$4.25; envelopes—$3; fifty-four pounds of beef—$27; Irish potatoes—$12; and medicine—$3.50. In July 1864, she paid one hundred dollars for one ounce of quinine, fifteen dollars for blue mass and cathartic pills, and seventy cents for stamps. In January 1865, some of her Negroes were working at the saltworks in Virginia. She paid two hundred forty dollars to Simon Daniel for expenses incurred when he went to look for them after they went missing. Stanton later heard the bondsmen had been captured by Federal soldiers.[46]

For further comparison of wartime prices, Rev. John Flintoff kept a diary:

	1861	1862	1863	1864	1865
corn	.60c bu.	$2.00	$15.00	$30.00	$50.00
wheat	$l.00 bu.	3.50	20.00	40.00	60.00
oats	.50c bu	2.00	10.00	15.00	40.00
potatoes	.50c bu	1.00	5.00	20.00	50.00
Bacon	.15c lb.	.50	5.00	7.00	10.00
Tobacco	.05c lb.	.75	1.50	1.50	6.00
Sugar	.125c	1.50	3.00		
Coffee	.165c lb.	3.00	10.00		
Iron	.06c lb	.40	1.00	2.50	5.00
Leather	.30c lb.	2.00	10.00	20.00	25.00
Calico	.125c yd.	1.50	5.00	12.00	20.00
Cows	$25 head	100.00	300		1,000.00
Paint	.25c	.75c	2.50	5.00	12.50
Horseshoes	.25c each	.50	2.50	4.00	7.50
Load of wood	1.50	2.50	10.00	2.50	[47]

Mary Otten, a refuge in Hillsboro, informed her friend Isaac on January 27, just after Fort Fisher was captured, that "the northern government can prevent much suffering and hardship by exchanging prisoners. Wood is very high ($30) which is less than ½ cord." Isaac Brown related, "Speculators will tell you there is no suffering in the Confederacy . . . . but we know better."[48]

This anonymous person wrote to a newspaper on August 30, 1864:

> A short time ago the farmer was obliged in self defense to do a bartering business in order to get what he absolutely needed in the way of clothing and other articles for his family. The manufacturers advertised that they would exchange their products only for provisions thereby making it decidedly more advantageous to the farmer to barter than sell his surplus provisions for money, knowing that Confederate money would not be taken for the articles he needed; therefore it would have been very bad policy in him to have sold all his surplus provisions (which was his income) for money, with which he could not buy a bunch of yarn, a yard of cloth or sack of salt.
>
> The farmers are not responsible for the high price of provisions, and to prove that they mean what they say, they propose to give Confederate money a SPECIE VALUE during the remainder of the war and to sell their produce accordingly, provided the manufacturers, merchants, and every class of dealers will do the same.
>
> Now, when shall this reform begin and what will be the most advisable course to pursue in order to bring it about? We propose a meeting of the farmers, manufacturers, proprietors, and dealers of this county be called and some plan adopted by which all interests may work together, harmoniously, to bring about the reduction of prices. A FARMER[49]

North Carolinians were growing very weary with the situation of inflation, speculators, and extortioners. It seemed there was no solution to the problem. Residents tried as we have just read. Walter Clark had the answer in this letter to his father: "When we begin to strip the speculators, beat drunken officers & place both in the ranks I think then we shall have a shadow of hope . . . ."[50] But could the speculators be stopped? Another citizen thought he had the answer:

> The speculators ought to be gathered up by a Regiment of detailed soldiers or the Country will be ravaged by them which are Yankees in principle if not by birth and acknowledgment. The prices of provisions are ranging at long figures at this time and as I am unfortunately a purchaser I feel the effects while paying One dollar a pound for Bacon & Lard and other things proportionally. So we will have to do as the Soldier, eat when we can get it on a limited scale . . . . H.H. Ellis[51]

Speculation doomed the poor. Frantic women asked officials to stop inflation if they could. Margaret Smith wrote on February 9, 1863:

> We have not drawn nothing but want in three months an without help we must starv. How can our husbands suporte ther familys at a Levin dollars amouth when we have to give to the Speculator 2 dollars a bushel for Bred and fifty sent a pound for our meet? . . . now wee have Becom Beggars and Starvers an now[no] way to help our selves.[52]

Due to the strain of war, speculation, extortion, impressments, lost of loved ones, etc., North Carolinians had had enough. They began to question authority. They began to resist all the rules imposed upon them. Violence and theft grew common. In 1863, this grew to a fever pitch. For the remaining years of war, frustrated civilians became numb to the violence and robberies occurring around them. No one was safe, especially those seen as "rich folk." Destitute people had the attitude that "you have what I can't buy. If you don't share, I will take what I need." So they stole from the wealthy. The Davis family of Warren County, like others, lost stock and equipment through thief very frequently. Rebecca Davis wrote in 1864: "We lose a fat sheep every week . . . we cant keep a thing . . . and I see that those who try to have things, and those who do not will soon be all even."[53] Cornelia Henry near Asheville frequently entered comments about someone stealing either a sheep, hog, or hams from them.

Soon, stealing wasn't regarded as theft by popular opinion. What makes a person act like this? Put yourself in their place. These families were starving. They were desperate. A mother will do anything she can to alleviate the cries of her hungry children. She would not have acted like this prewar. Hunger drove them to riotous behavior.

Usually known as docile, pious creatures, women resorted to disorderly conduct brought on by frantic attempts to feed their families. Starvation faced them daily. It is possible that more bread riots occurred than what was reported due to officials covering them up. In Richmond, Confederate authorities asked the newspaper editors not to print stories of the bread riots because it would be bad publicity for patriotism.[54] In North Carolina, the bread riot that received the most notoriety occurred in Salisbury; but there were many, many other documentations of desperate, famished women who overpowered merchants and took what they needed to stave off hunger. A large number of soldiers' wives armed with clubs, hatchets, and tools approached the merchants of Salisbury to buy flour. The merchants would not sell to them at government prices. The women then proceeded to chop down the doors and take the provisions. At the next store, the frightened owner *gave* the group ten barrels of flour. In all, twenty-three barrels of flour, molasses, and two sacks of salt were taken.[55] The newspapers* criticized the women, calling them thieves because some reportedly took items from a millinery store. Confederate soldiers were called out to break up the disturbance.

A leader of the "female gang" wrote to the governor explaining the reasoning behind the women's actions. She said that they offered the government price for the food, but the speculator/merchant refused.

> Salisbury, NC
> March 21st./63
> To His Excellency the Gov of the State of NC
> Dear Sir—
> Having from absolute necessity been forced into measure not at all pleasant to obtain something to eat by the cruel and unfeeling Speculators who have been gathering up at enormous prices, not only bread stuffs but every thing even down to eggs Chickens & Vegetables to carry out of our State for the purpose of Speculating upon them We feel it [now] our duty Honored and esteemed Gov to inform you truthfully of our proceedings and humbly pray to inform us whether or not we are justifiable in what we have done—and if not for Heavens Sake tell [us] how these evils are to be remedied.
> We Sir are all Soldiers Wives or Mothers our Husbands & Sons are now separated from us by this cruel War not only to defend our [humble] homes but the homes & property of the rich man and at the same time that we are grieved at this separation yet we murmur not—God bless them our hearts go with them and our prayers follow them for Heavens protection through all the trials and difficulties that may surround them, but Sir we have to live and we must live while they are gone from us and that too without much or in many cases any assistance from them for how far will eleven dollars go in a family now [when] Meat [is] from 75 to $1 pr pd flour $50 pr bll. wood from 4 to 5$ pr

---

* See the appendix for the full report.

load, meal 4an 5 dollars pr bushel, eggs 50 to 60 cts pr doz chickens $7 pr doz, molasses $7 pr gal rye 20 cts. pr qt. &, addition to that we are willing and do work early and late to keep off starvation which is now staring us in the face, but the government only allows us 50 cts a pair for lined pants and 75 cts for coats and there are few of us, who can make over a dollar a day, and we have upon an average from three to five helpless children to support and still we complain not at Government prices if we can only get bread divided among us and meat at a reasonable price but Sir many of us work day after day without a morsal of meat to strengthen us for our Labors and often times we are without bread Now Sir how We ask you in the name of God are we to live.

Laboring under all these difficulties Sir we as we have told you in the commencement of this letter were from Stern necessity compelled to go in search of food to sustain life and some forty or more respectable but poor women started out backed by many citizens to get food we took our little money with us and offered to pay Government prices for what we took but the Speculators refused us any thing or even admittance into their premises We then forced our way in and compelled them to give us something & we succeeded and twenty dollars in money, which was equally divided among us in the presence of our highly esteemed friend and Lawyer Blackmen, besides many other gentlemen of good and high standing in society. Now Sir this is all we done and necessity compelled us to do it and the reason we have addressed you Sir is that we understand that we have reported to you as plunderers of the town disturbing the peace and quiet of the community, but Sir we have honestly told you the whole proceeding and we now pray your protection or a remedy for these evils—we as much as any one deplore the necessity of such proceeding and do humbly pray you in behalf of our helpless children to so fix the prices of bread and meat that we can by our own labor gain an honest portion of that which sustains life—

To whom else can we go but to you our highly esteemed and cherished Gov to redress these evils. You were the choice of our Husbands and Sons an we too look up to you Sir with prefect confidence as being able and willing to do some thing for us—we ask not charity we only ask for fair and reasonable prices for provisions and leather for Sir many of us have been shoeless this whole winter except cloth shoes we can make for ourselves which are no protection even against the cold, in conclusion Sir we humbly beg you after carefully and prayerfully considering our letter to let us hear from you—you can address Mary C Moore Salisbury NC and that Heavens richest blessings and a long life may be your portion with your happy family is the earnest and heartfelt prayers of many Soldiers Wives[56]

"A week after the 'Salisbury food riots,' the price of flour in the region had dropped by $20 a barrel."[57] Irate and exasperated merchants complained to the governor. Vance condemned the women, answering by newspaper—"Broken laws will give you no bread, but much sorrow; and when forcible seizure have to be made to avert starvation, let it be done by your county agent . . ."[58]

———————

By 1863, women started criticizing government officials and even the governor himself. In Montgomery County, ten women marched to Sanders' mill with clubs and demanded flour.[59] Mrs. Henry mid-war said women "impressed" five hundred pounds of bacon by rioting: "Old Jim & Bill Knight got home last night with the bacon. The trash of Bent creek pressed five hundred lbs. of it. The women did it. They paid 50 per lb. for it."[60] A few poor Orange County women raided McCowan's mill, stealing flour in early 1864. Alamance

County resident Nancy Mangum rioted against the Holt Cotton Mill because neighborhood women could not buy cotton yard.[61]

When merchants, especially millers, complained to the governor about women rioters, the governor took the side of the ladies. An agent told some females that if their husband was a deserter, they could not get any yarn or sustenance. Vance said that "it was not official state policy to deny the wives of deserters access to their services, contrary to what many were told by local Confederate officials." Author Bynum revealed, "A self-styled group of women 'regulators' from Bladen County objected to giving up sons, brothers, and husbands to a war being fought for the 'big man's Negroes.'" A raid in Bladenboro encompassed five women who stole six sacks of corn and a sack of rice.[62]

FEMALE RIOT IN JOHNSTON COUNTY read the headlines in the *Greensborough Patriot* on April 16, 1863. Ten women and three men overpowered the Stephen Dement homestead and stole one hundred pounds of cotton in Granville County in the closing months of the war.[63] Several dozen women from Yancey County "broke into a government warehouse in broad daylight."[64] General J. W. McElroy of the Home Guards wrote the governor about this incident:

> A band of tories, said to be headed by Montreval Ray, numbering about seventy-five men, came from Burnsville, Yancey Co, ... surprised the guard, broke open the magazine, and took all the arms and ammunition; broke open Brayly's store and carried off the contents; attacked Captain Lyons . . . . On the day before about fifty women assembled together . . . and marched in a body to a store-house . . . and pressed about sixty bushels of Government wheat and carried it off.[65]

At Boon Hill, women assembled and implored merchants to sell them corn for one dollar instead of three dollars a bushel. Sallie Southall Cotton recalled a bread riot in Greensboro when she was a student at the female college mid-war.[66] These women took part in raids on merchants: Rebecca Davis, Nancy Bowers, and Nancy Carroll, of Orange County, at McCowan's mill early in 1864. Lucy and Sally Fuller attacked James O. Coghill at White's mill.[67] A book about Lenoir County mentioned two hundred females armed with hatchets, who created a disturbance in town demanding flour from the merchants.[68] This could possibly be the same incident that occurred in Kinston recalled in Paul Escott's book.[69] A Northern cavalryman wrote home about hungry families. He said, "Already several bread riots have occurred in this State. Women, armed with axes and knives, have gone to the government store-houses in Wilmington and taken flour by force . . ." This was mid-1863.[70] Other riots taking place in 1864 occurred in High Point. A soldier wrote his wife that his unit had been called out to guard a train carrying grain:

> Fair Bluff, NC April the 10th 1864
> Dear . . . I will inform you that I am 65 miles from Wilmington. There is twenty of us that was sent to fair Bluff to guard the train from fair Bluff to Wilmington. The reason we have this to do, the women is pressing the corn and we have to keep them from it . . . B.F. Gatton.[71]

Citizens in Ashe County considered taking Saltville, Virginia, by force if the company did not give them salt at a fair price. The leader said he could easily raise four to five hundred men. Jesse Reeves wanted to know it they would be punished if they carried out the plan. He said that "they have nuff Salt at the works to salt all the hogs in the confederacy." Salt was selling at fifty dollars a bushel.[72]

Encounters with dishonest merchants and women continued throughout the remainder of the war. One year after the Salisbury bread riot, the *Weekly Catawba Journal* informed its readers about marauding women:

We publish in another column of this day's paper a highly interesting letter from our Salisbury correspondent detailing the action and movements of the wives, mothers and daughters of soldiers who have gone from that section of the country.

It seems that the women are in need—that they are suffering from the want of bread, and inasmuch as their providers and protectors have gone to the war and are not able to supply the necessary subsistence for their families out of a soldier's pay, the women have resolved to IMPRESS what they need.

We would not encourage such proceedings on the part of women, but speculators—we mean men who buy and hold from market the necessaries of life, to extort large profits from the needy—are responsible for the beginning.

We caution those who are extortionate in their demands for bread and meat that they are provoking a storm which may sweep from them before long their worldly gins and perhaps their blood to water it will be shed. There is a point beyond which forbearance may cease to be regarded virtue by the needy families of our war worn soldiers.

A word to the wise is sufficient.[73]

Perhaps successful attempts to obtain provisions encouraged other groups to try the same tactic. In January 1865, a swarm of women toting axes and bringing wagons descended upon Jonesville. A lone official confronted the group, which scared them. They left empty-handed and went to the next town of Hamptonville, where they succeeded in getting their booty.[74] In writing to her aunt about the last two raids, Lizzie Lenoir portrayed the group as "women" in a derogatory manner who carried axes and came with wagons, intent on taking all the corn they could steal. She said, "An old drunk man scared the horses into bolting" as a guard "held them off," and they didn't get any of the corn. Some wealthier ladies looked down upon the plight of the starving poorer women who were forced into unacceptable behavior during this period in history. Lenoir blamed the debased women, though she thought they may have been "put up to it" by deserters.[75] Maybe she assumed the women had anti-secession tendencies. This unfortunate attitude poked its head up throughout the state.

When U.S. General Gillem and his troopers crossed into the state from East Tennessee, they told the Pearson family to expect plundering after the news of General Lee's surrender flew around. The next day, U.S. Colonel Kirk and his men, along with hordes of local women, robbed and vandalized the entire town of Morganton, stealing food, clothing, tableware, silver, liquor, etc.—anything else that wasn't nailed down. One soldier tried to take a piano, but it was too large to fit through the door.

Mr. John H. Pearson—owner of a gin house, sawmill, and lumber room—watched as his buildings went up in flames. The home of Mr. R. C. Pearson's, Esq., was vandalized by both the enemy's troops and the women that followed them. Every single thing in his house was either stolen or destroyed. A member of the Pearson family described the women as disloyal, dirty, ignorant, illiterate, lazy, uncultivated, traitors, and "false to their God." An old woman was among the numbers. "The very day that the Federal command under Gillem entered and occupied the town of Morganton, these women from the 'South Mountains' swarmed our streets proclaiming their 'jubilee,' and rejoicing that the Yankees had arrived, they under pretense of great devotion to the 'union cause,' claimed to be loyal people and thus these dishonest traitorous hordes . . . conspired and leagued with the Yankees, urging them on in the work of plunder, and wholesale theft . . ."[76]

Greensboro women planned a coordinated attack on the merchants of the city by hitting the merchants from the East and West at the same time.* Approximately thirty to

---

*   For a full newspaper account, see the appendix.

forty females approached from the West. Men went out to reason with the ladies. While this was taking place, twenty women invaded from the East and commenced breaking into the stores. The provost sent the eastern women to jail while the western females turned homeward.[77]

Greensboro near the end of the war was no place to be especially in April. A town formerly of eighteen hundred inhabitants grew to over ninety thousand in three months. Camp Stokes just outside of town held Confederate deserters, along with two hundred Federal prisoners. The remnants of Lee's ragtag army who had surrendered earlier passed through the city. They helped themselves to the storehouses. The commissary warehouse at McLeansville was destroyed. Officials tried to get rid of the wine and liquor stock, breaking open the casks. When the railroad cars full of ammunition exploded, barrels of molasses and whiskey burst open. Hungry women scooped up the molasses in buckets from the gutters. "Hopeless men lapped up the liquor like dogs."[78]

The surrender negotiations between C.S. General Johnston and Sherman had taken place at Mr. Bennett's farm West of Durham Station. The majority of Johnston's soldiers bivouacked in Greensboro and High Point. Over thirty thousand of Johnston's veterans were waiting for their paroles to be printed. Add thousands of Federals, and you get a volcano ready to erupt. Before the Union soldiers came, a riot by Southern troops broke out. They knew the end was near, and the hungry soldiers broke into warehouses, stealing food and blankets in the city and also Graham. Other Confederate soldiers quelled the mob.[79]

In the wild melee, plundering continued as horses and mules disappeared. Citizens stood guard over their horses and gardens. "The Confederacy had bust up," said one. Former soldiers felt that if they didn't get a piece of the stored provisions now, the enemy would. "Southern Independence had gone up and they wanted their sheer [share] in whatever was left." Men stole saddles, a bag of flour/meal, shoes, and bacon. Campfires were built on the sidewalks. The Forty-fifth NCT were called to break up the mob, which was mostly from Lee's discharged soldiers. Four men in the mob were shot. Next came the women of the town wanting to get into the state warehouses, which were stocked with over two million dollars' worth of goods, but these were to be distributed only to the soldiers.[80] The disorder continued in part when the Federals took over the city in April 1865.

CHAPTER TEN

Conscripts, Substitutes, Exemptions, Deserters

Prewar in North Carolina, a law existed whereby all white men between the ages of eighteen to forty-five had to enroll their names for the state militia. The only exception then was ministers. Once the hostilities began, officers placed advertisements in the newspapers calling for volunteers for the regular army. Many thousands of men responded that spring; however, by the fall, volunteer enlistments slowed. Governor Henry Clark then issued a proclamation that appeared in the newspaper encouraging veterans to reenlist and others to step forward and volunteer. The central Confederate government also wrote states, urging them to fill their quotas. Not being satisfied with the results, the Confederate Congress passed the Conscript Act in April 1862, taking men between the ages of eighteen to thirty-five, except certain approved exemptions, for three years' service or for the duration of the war. All troops already in service had to stay in the war. This ruling allowed men to buy substitutes.[1]

Major Peter Mallett, commander of the conscript bureau in Raleigh, established two areas for camps of instruction. The first and largest was located in the capital city, the second in Statesville. Major Mallet was responsible to the Bureau of Conscription of the Confederate War Department kept under Brigadier General John S. Preston. Mallett's battalion stayed in the state. Mallett received orders to "send all conscripts to specified brigades without individual wishes," causing great consternation. If a man did not report to officers at Camp Holmes in Raleigh that summer after the April 16 proclamation, he was considered a deserter. If the recusant volunteers had gone to Raleigh before May 17, 1862, which many did, they could have chosen their commander.[2]

The amount of work that Mallett and his two brigades had to do was overwhelming. His men were assigned to pull duty in the state alone, which was divided into districts. The district office was concerned with enrollment, exemptions, Senior Reserves, deserters, disabled soldiers on limited service, substitutions, work details, absentees, furloughs, and manpower problems.[3] "Upon arriving at home, each soldier was required to report to his local conscript officer, present his furlough document, and make his presence in the county known. When his furlough expired, the soldier had either to apply for an extension, return to his unit, or be declared absent without leave."[4] Conscript officers were called the "Conscript Hawk."

The Conscript Act changed again in September 1862, requiring men from the age of eighteen through forty-five to take up arms; however, President Davis only required men up to the age of forty to report. At this time, changes were made in the exemptions.

Author Hilderman has written that the Confederate officers were given leave to go to their state to recruit, paying bounties and giving certain privileges to the new man while bypassing the state conscription department. Officers claimed to get more volunteers this way than through the local bureau. This caused a rift among state and central authorities. It was also an outlet for dishonest men to jump from one regiment after securing the bounty, then desert and join another. The conscript law was suspended temporarily to straighten out this confusion. This problem was not resolved until January 1864.[5] By the winter of 1862–1863, the number of conscripts slowed down, causing officers to place advertisements in the newspapers. The next is typical to encourage men, playing on their sympathy and offering one hundred dollars bounty:

Recruits Wanted

Having been detailed by Maj. Gen. G. W. Smith, commanding department of N.C., I have come to Caswell county to offer the last call for volunteers.

I would say to every man who is worth calling a man, and who has a spark of patriotism burning within his bosom—who would not see his Country subjugated—his home burnt—his property stolen—the female relatives insulted and outraged—that his Country needs his services. Who then will falter? Certainly not those who are liable to be conscripted! Then come forth like a man—and volunteering receive a bounty of $100. Let it not be said that conscription had to drag you in defiance of yourself—your mother, sister, wife and Country. I shall remain in Milton about three weeks to receive recruits upon the volunteer principle, and the door will be closed and the Conscript Officer will demand you. I am directed to notify all absentees from the army, without authority, that if they will return to their respective companies or report to me prior to the 10th inst., they will be pardoned, otherwise they will be shot as deserters whenever caught.

Samuel H. Hines, 1st Lieut.
Company I, 45th Reg. N.C. Troops[6]

There were two things the enlisted soldiers hated the most: "men who refused to enlist . . . and those who supported peace movements," noted one researcher.[7] Jesse McIntosh felt the same as other volunteers. He advised friends to volunteer. Jesse wrote his sister speaking on conscription:

I suppose Mat [brother] will get the same chance ere long. Tell him if he is any relation of mine not to see his Country ruined by the Yankees. I know I ought not to advise him, as he is the oldest yet it is nothing but right that I should feel a deep interest in this family and name. For my part I think it is a disgrace to be drafted.[8]

From Mount Gilead, S. Scarbrough informed his son, Franklin, in October:

The new conscript bill will play havoc with this neighborhood—I cannot see the end of the present struggle in any way than the subjugation of the south with almost certain starvation of a great many of our women & children under the full execution of the late law we will [have] but a few old men & boys to support the county . . .[9]

Samuel Bracy wrote to his cousin Arch that the conscript officer would get Preston (a son?), and he could not get along without him. Samuel said he would have to cease blacksmithing, creating a hardship on the community of Alfordsville.[10] Similarly, concerned men asked officials about the draft. One said,

If all of our efficient men are taken off, I think it questionable whether we will make more provisions than will answer our purposes, and I am certain we can't keep that order and discipline that is necessary in the neighborhood, as there is now disposition among the Negroes to be more sulky and not so biddable. I have no overseer and can't get one. In fact the Negroes are doing pretty much as they please.[11]

M. A. Young bore further testimony about conscription and was against it because:

the state can put no force in the field that will be valuable and that we better leave it alone and let the Confederate government to manage our defenses. I am discouraged by the spirit which is manifested in this legislature . . .[12]

One citizen in a letter to the newspaper said:

> to inform Jeff Davis and his Destructives, that after they take the next draw of men from this mountain region, if they please, as an act of *great* and *special* mercy be so gracious as to call out a *few* of their exempted pets . . . to knock the women and children . . . in the head, to put them out of their misery.[13]

The Conscription Act of April 1862 caused men to fight the order. "Because of the potential for violence inherent in attempts to enforce the draft, Governor Vance adopted a policy whereby the state militia aided, and partially supplanted, the Confederate conscript officers in enrolling conscripts, a move which the governor hoped would prevent clashes between the population and Confederate forces."[14]

One woman in Randolph County swore before a justice of the peace that she and her husband never "kept a record of the ages of their children." She and her deceased husband could not read or write; but she thought that the one son conscripted, John Hancock, was over forty-six. The enrolling officer who captured him in the woods thought he was under forty-five. An investigation was necessary.[15] Some men had trouble proving their age. One conscript's name was recorded in the Bible, but the house burned down, destroying evidence.

A group of civilians wrote to Governor Henry Clark in 1862 requesting "a military appointment to help protect against 'disaffected and dangerous persons on the border.'" Most of the men had volunteered, and no one was left to plant. Overseers with less than twenty Negroes to supervise received a visit from the enrolling officer.[16] It was long before communities, emptied of men, began to worry about male protection. Mrs. Sarah Smith wrote Governor Vance that fall asking for an exemption of the only man around:

> Cypress Creek N. Carolina Dec 7th 1862 —I will endeavor to write you a few lines on this subject. I as well as 10 other families are left here with[out] any masculine protection—[I] ask you to discharge John B. Smith from the service of war—he is near 50—he is all the man in this vicinity to look for protection.[17]

Author Crawford has suggested, "The needs of individual community continued to outstrip the capacity of the state and local government to meet them . . . areas such as western North Carolina were particularly vulnerable to the loss of artisanal labor, men where skills as with blacksmiths, millers, carpenters, tanners, and shoemakers could not be dispensed with or readily imported."[18] By 1863, Governor Vance and citizens from Watauga County wrote President Davis and Secretary of State Seddon, asking that conscription be suspended from mountain counties and that a regular army be placed there to protect them.[19] William Auman wrote to Allen King:

> I tell you Allen the men is missing about here now—there is some conscripts hear yet but that is no good for they lay out & hide them selves so you cant see them no way or shape so they ar no company [military] hear nor any body else.[20]

Anti-secessionist Elisha Blackwell, of Cherokee County, worked at Saltville, Virginia, and afterwards at a local ironworks. He guided pro-Union families and/or men on their escape to Tennessee. To avoid conscription, men were elected to become a justice of the peace, sheriff, coroner, postal worker, Home Guard, tax assessor, collector of tithes, ministers, etc.[21] In his amnesty request to President Andrew Johnson, B.F. Atkins claimed to have taken the position of tax assessor to avoid military duty.[22] Soldiers stationed in New Bern wrote home about male civilians there wearing women's clothing to escape military service.[23]

Every month, newly conscripted men would be called up to see if they qualified for military service or if they would be "weeded out." An Allegany County woman expressed to her son that,

> . . . the conscript was ordered out to forty and they met at the Gap yesterday to be examined. I think if you all would come home and be examined that you could get discharged.

She said that one hundred ninety-six got discharges. She further requested him to purchase some calico and buttons if he "gets the chance."[24] Another lady revealed to her husband that his mother was so troubled about one son and made the comment that it looked like everyone's boys got to go home but her boys.

Conscription changes kept the surgeons busy as posted in the next notice:

Special Order #39, Medical Director's Office,
General Hospital Raleigh, May 28, 1864:

Hereafter hospital Medical Examining Boards will examine first all detailed soldiers and all white males subject to conscription duty in General Hospital where they hold their meetings during the first week in every month, and report, that this duty has been performed to the surgeon general through this office . . . . P.E. Hines, Surgeon and Medical Director[25]

After the last Conscript Act took effect, persons revealed their sentiment in Robeson County:

> Philadelphus N.C. April 23rd 1863
> Mr. Angus McPhail
> Dear Sir.
>   I received your letter and was glad to hear that you were still in the land and among the living and resigned to your ardorous task of soldering through the present war that has been waged against us by one certain Abe of Rail splitting fame. I hope you may live to see the end although the present presents rather a gloomy appearance of peace. Nevertheless a few weeks may bring a great change in war matters. And I think if the Confederate brave Soldiers can succeed in keeping the prowling wolves off for some 6 weeks longer from the coast that they will have to return to their dens as lean as when they ventured out at first. To day is the last call for Robeson conscripts. I presume when this levy is over the next draw will take I suppose from 45 to 65 . . . H.H. Ellis.[26]

Only 11.3 percent of people owned slaves in the western counties. "Studies of Haywood and Jackson counties have indicated that there was also a significant tenant farming group in the mountain counties." Many of the men volunteered for twelve months' service while others hesitated to join at all. "In Henderson, Madison, Polk, and Wilkes counties, mountaineers showed a distinct reluctance to volunteer for Confederate service. When the war lengthened, conscription was imposed. Internal warfare flared into the open, and regular armies marched." Author McKinney stated, "For some mountain women, the only solution to the difficulties they faced were the relocation of the family or the forced seclusion of male members. Many [secessionist] women encouraged sons and husbands to hide from conscription officials."[27] When conscript officers came calling at home, they were often unable to find the male. Occasionally, men "worked the fields, dressed as women" to fool the conscript officers. A dark-skinned man was alleged to be part Negro. Perhaps he was a Melungeon or a mulatto because there were thousands of persons with mixed blood in the South. To get a medical exemption, some men would cut off a finger or two. "Skin [was] scalded to produce sores, diseases feigned . . . Family Bible birth records were changed."[28] Men would sometimes feign illness as a lunatic.

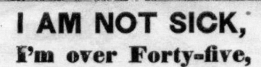

I AM NOT SICK,
I'm over Forty=five,

I will make my Wife stay at home and give the Baby Catnip Tea.

AIR.—"I wish my Wife had no crying Baby."

I'm exempt, I'm exempt, I vow and desire,
I'm exempt, I'm exempt, from the "draft" I will swear,
What, though the rebels our soil may invade,
And *wipe out* each general of pick-axe and spade?
Oh! what do I care though a million are slain;
And our starry-gemmed banner is tramped on the plain?
Oh! what do I care, who may fall or may thrive,
I'm exempt, I'm exempt, I'm o'er forty-five!

Oh! what do I care, what my neighbors may say,
That I've jumped o'er ten years in less than a day?
Oh! what do I care for my nation and laws?
I heed not her shame, I seek not applause;
But still for the Almighty Dollar I'll drive,
I'm exempt, I'm exempt, I'm o'er forty-five!

I always was healthy from heel unto nobe,
But now I have troubles as many as Job;
You may wink and may sneer, and say "it's all gas,"
That such a lame "HO'SE" with the doctors won't pass:
But I'm aches, I'm pains, from the head to the toe,
I'm exempt, I'm exempt, from the draft, you must know!

I'm free to confess that I find greater charms,
In a trip to England, than takihg up arms;
I'm off, I'm off, with the very first train,
And when the war's over I'll come back again:
You call me a sneak—I heed not your twaddle,
I'm exempt I'm exempt, I mean to skedaddle!

Many, many women wrote the governor about their home situation if their husband or father had to go to fight. Their letters would break the hardest of hearts. Martha Coletrane of Randolph County wrote such a letter:

> Dear Sir this is a greate undertaking for me as i never wrote to a man of authority before [.] necessity requires it of me as we are nonslave holders in this section of the State [.] i hope you and our legislature will look to it and have justice done [to] our people as well as the slaveholders [.] i can tel you the condition of my family and you can judg for your self what its condition woul be if my husban is called from home [.] we hav eight children and the oldest is not forteen years old and an old aged mother to support, which makes eleven in our family and without my husband we are a desolate and ruined family for extortion runs so hie here [.] we cannot support and clothe our family without the help of my husban [.] i hope you will look to the justice of this section of the state and i trust you will hold the rane [reins] in your own hands and not let the confederate congress have full sway over your State [.] i appeal to you to look to the white cultivators as strictly as congress has to the slaveholders and i think they men from 35 to 45 be hel[d] as reserves at hom to support ther families if the[y] are calld from home [.] it is bound to leave a thoasn [thousand]families in a starving condition in our country [.] we trust in god and look to you for some help for our poor children [.] so no more.[29]

EXEMPTIONS

Exemptions from military service included the physically unfit, employees of the Confederate States, judicial and executive officers of the Confederacy and state, members of Congress, state legislators, government clerks, postal workers, ferrymen on postal routes, pilots of boats and the railways, telegraph operators, ministers, ironworkers, printers and their helpers, professors and presidents of a college or academies, teachers with twenty or more students, superintendents of hospitals or asylums with their nurses and attendants, only one apothecary in each store, superintendents and employees of cotton and wool factories who were exempted by the secretary of war, and teachers at the deaf, dumb, and blind school.[30] Quakers in the beginning fell into this category.

This military notice appeared in the *Raleigh Register*:

EXEMPTIONS UNDER THE CONSCRIPTION LAW OF CONGRESS:
The following exemption bill was passed by congress and signed by the president . . . **A Bill To Be Entitled,** "An act to exempt certain persons from enrollment for service in the armies of the Confederate states."
Section 1: The congress of the Confederate States of America do enact, that all persons who shall be held to be unfit for military service under the rules to be prescribed by the Secretary of War; all in the service or employ of the Confederate States; all judicial and executive officers of the Confederate or State Government; the members of both houses of congress; and of the legislatures of the several states and their respective officers; all clerks of the officers of the state and the Confederate governments allowed by law; all engaged in carrying the mails; all ferrymen on post routes; all pilots and persons engaged in the marine service and in the actual service on the river and railroad routes of transportation; telegraphic operatives; ministers of religion in the regular discharge of ministerial duties; all engaged in working iron mines, furnaces, and foundries; all journeymen printers actually employed in printing newspapers; all presidents and professors of colleges and academies, and all teachers having as

many as twenty scholars; superintendents of public hospitals, lunatic asylums, and the regular nurses and attendants therein, and the teachers employed in the institutions for the deaf and dumb and blind; in each apothecary store now established one apothecary in good standing, who is a practical druggist; superintendents and operatives in wool and other factories, who may be exempted by the Secretary Of War, shall be, and are hereby exempted from military service in the armies of the Confederate States.[31]

Type of Exemption Before July, 1863:	Number:
Employees of state asylum	23
Apothecaries	18
Blacksmiths	588
State & county officers	282
Military cadets	15
Colliers	11
Confederate Judicial officials	1
Tax collector	2
Details	1913
Disabled men	7868
Executive action	87
Express company workers	47
Factory workers	155
Firemen	57
Harness makers	1
Militia officers	2346
Magistrates	407
Millers	668
Millwrights	123
Mail contractors & carriers	73
Miners	36
Non-combatants	196
Overseers	120
Iron workers	17
Ministers	156
Doctors	264
Paper workers	14
Policemen	34
Cobblers	651
Salt makers	627
School teachers	121
State ordinance workers	258
State agents	2
Seamen	11
Steamboat agents	1
Superintendent of gas works	2
Tanners	174
Telegraph operators	18
Wagon makers	29
Wheelwrights	13
Powder manufacturers	3
Government agents	17
Men discharged on Writs of Habeas Corpus	31
	Total: 21,558[32]

Early first exemptions included the men who supplied wood, built roads, and used slave labor on the railroad. The second wave of exemptions kept railroad machinists out of military duty. Munition workers got paid more than railroad workers.[33] Lists were kept in the enrolling officers' quarters of men exempted by occupation, disability, age, substitutes, etc. One adjutant wrote to the ironworks and the Egypt Coal Mine, seeking names of men on their payroll.[34] Conscript officers also kept a list of soldiers furloughed and those hospitalized.

Exemptions changed throughout the war according to need. The marshal, clerk, and other appointed officials had to pay a bond to the judge "for the faithful performance of their offices."[35] In confusing circumstances, in 1863, certain men in the militia who were farmers could get an exemption. The *Weekly Progress* printed:

> We are glad to learn that the government is awakening to a sense of the danger likely to follow the conscribing of farmers at this time. We learn that sixty-one farmers have recently been released from Camp Holmes and sent home to cultivate their farms . . .[36]

With all these exemptions, it's a wonder any were left to be a soldier. In May 1864, it was reported in Charlotte that "a number of our most important tools [steam hammer] are idle a large portion of the time for want of mechanics to work them . . ."[37] Most workers had been conscripted. The loss of men to conscription had a devastating effect on North Carolina's economy. Of the jobs left vacant, women could only partially work at them. The rest went unfilled.

John W. McElroy, brigadier general of the Home Guard, in writing to the governor said:

> Swarms of men liable to conscription are gone to the tories or to the Yankees. Conscription is now going on and a very tyrannical course pursued by the officers charged with the business, and men [are] conscripted and cleaned as [if] raked with a fine-toothed comb.

Governor Vance answered, "Impossible to get any man out there unless more home guards at this time is only certain Distraction to the country eventually. In fact, it seems to me, that there is a determination of the people in the country to do no more service for the cause. If something is not done immediately for this country, we will all be ruined, and the homeguards now are not to be depended on."[38]

After many inquires about the position of postal workers, the Postmaster General of the Confederacy sent this notice to Governor Vance to post:

Post Office Department Richmond October 17th. 1862
    . . . Postmasters as are appointed by the President and confirmed by the Senate, and such clerks in the large offices as are allowed by the Postmaster General, are exempt from conscription. All other postmasters and clerks in post offices are liable to conscription. But there is no intention to discontinue the post offices. They will be filled . . . with persons not liable to military duty . . .[39]

The position of postmaster, rider, or driver was to be filled with men not liable for conscription and, later on, women; but numerous anti-secession males took over this job.

This notice appeared in the *Raleigh Register* on May 31, 1862:

An Ordinance to Exempt Members of the Society of Friends from Performing Military Duty:
The members must be in good standing with the church, have to produce a regular certificate of membership and need to pay $100 to the sheriff. If they can't pay, then they are detailed to assist in the manufacturing of salt or help in the hospitals. W.N. Edwards

Research has shown that some Quakers paid several hundred dollars to stay out of the war. Jonathan Worth, a former Quaker living in Asheboro before the war, was an opponent of secession yet had many slaves to work his land and businesses. Worth's writings indicate that he was a good owner. "While he [Worth] dismissed slavery as the underlying cause of the coming conflict, he was worried about the fate of the black man of the South and said, 'If the civil war is protracted and the Northern troops sent among us they will ultimately incite insurrection. The poor Negroes will be killed.'"[40]

Worth, the state bureau of finance president, offered jobs to Quakers. They could earn twenty dollars a month as a laborer and three dollars a day per man with a team of horses. Some private manufacturers would pay six dollars a day. Nereus Mendenhall, John Crenshaw, and John Carter carried the Quakers' written stance on war to Confederate officials in Richmond. Upon return, the men told of being treated with respect and tender feeling. However, their request to exempt Quaker men from fighting was only partially granted. The requirements were that the man had to pay a five-hundred-dollar fine or be conscripted.[41] Substitutes were allowed for a short period. Two Quakers, a father and son, W. A. and J. M. Prevo, were conscripted. The father was sent to Salisbury Prison as a guard for the North Carolina Senior Reserves. The son went to the State Saltworks at Wilmington in 1864.[42] Individuals in Randolph County wrote the adjutant general's office complaining about the so-called saltworkers. Immediately, the office sent a letter to the colonel of the militia there, which read:

> There are persons in yr. co. who pretend to work at the salt works but who remain at home most of the time & when they do work, they return home with salt or brandy to speculate. If they are conscripts, arrest them & send to camp. It is regretted these reports came through private citizens rather than through the militia office.[43]

Worth, as a state officer, secured for his brother, Milton, the position as state salt commissioner. When Milton resigned mid-1863 because of constant conflicts with military authorities, Mr. Worth helped his nephew, David, to fill that position. David Worth inherited the same problems as his father. Confederate General William Whiting, commander of Fort Fisher, quarreled with him over too many "disloyal" (Quakers) men working at the saltworks. In April 1864, a small group of Federal sailors came ashore and burned some of the buildings at the works. They took forty-seven employees with them. After the raid, General Whiting insisted that Worth move the saltworks from the area. Worth felt like Whiting had no jurisdiction over him. He contacted Governor Vance, with Vance telling him to stay put. The following June, Whiting again ordered the saltworks to be moved. This time, Mr. Worth contacted William Graham, senator, from the state:

> Whether you can do anything to arrest this high-handed proceeding I know not, but I have thought it expedient to inform you of the facts.[44]

Worth then sent a letter to the secretary of war listing the facts. In addition to the above information, he confirmed that Whiting said the laborers were in contact with the enemy, and Whiting felt as if the works could be run by slaves rather than "white exempts." Furthermore, General Whiting, "would not let the flatboats which hauled wood for the salt works to cross the . . . sound."[45]

The dissention between the two did not abate immediately. Governor Vance contacted General Beauregard to counteract Whiting's orders and "threatened to ask for the removal of Whiting." Both Whiting and Vance began to rile each other's feathers. General Whiting inspected the mail leaving the Confederacy. He arrested political prisoners who were sent to either Richmond or Salisbury.[46]

T. S. Whitaker, bookseller and vendor, was arrested per order of General Whiting for selling "the fourth of July 1864 'extra' issue of Holden's *Raleigh Standard* in Camp Holmes." The general said it was a "treasonable document" because of Holden's peace movement editorials. Whitaker was exempt by his other occupation as fireman in Wilmington. Vance got Whitaker released.[47]

Things went a little smoother that summer, but in October, General Whiting closed down the salt boilers. He ordered the men to leave and take the equipment with them.[48] That same October 1864, the workers at Saltville, Virginia, closed due to conscription of men into service and Federal raids.[49] Again, Vance objected to the higher-ups in Richmond; but this time, they did not listen to him.

Jonathan Worth had the power to keep Quakers, friends, and family out of military duty; and it was all done legally. Two men from Randolph County, Abijah and Charles Mason, had been Quakers "until they married contrary to the rules of the Society."* They had been attending the Methodist Church. After the government exempted Quakers, the men decided that they were Quakers after all and paid one thousand dollars to stay out. No good says the conscription officer. Worth intervened and got them off.[50] "In June, 1863, three Quakers, Nere Cox, Seth Cox, and Eli Macon, were taken from their fields and not given time to secure enough money to pay their exemption."[51] After they arrived at Camp Holmes in Raleigh, they appealed to Worth, who was able to help them get the fifteen hundred dollars needed for exemption. John B. Crenshaw, another Quaker, made arrangements with officials to mediate the problems with conscripted Quaker men.

A Baptist minister named Jesse Buckner from Chatham County, when conscripted, refused to go to war on account of his joining the Quaker faith. The conscript board took him anyway because he was not "of the faith" before the war. Many claimed the Society of Friends after the war began to escape military service. These men carried the name of War Quakers.[52] Another petitioner claimed exemption because he was a member of the Society of Friends, but he was rejected due to the fact of being "removed" from the society before his conscription. Dunkards were also exempt but could pay five hundred dollars to stay out of service.[53] Quakers were forced to pay a five-hundred-dollar fee. Other references reveal one hundred to three hundred dollars for an exemption. Quaker Isham Cox paid this fee with the help of the Society of Friends throughout the state.[54] Thomas Hinshaw rejected the offer to pay for whatever reason, so he was conscripted. Because Hinshaw refused to carry a rifle, soldiers taunted him constantly.[55] One Society of Friends member, Solomon Frazier, was almost tortured to death by the military.[56]. Conscript and Quaker Tilghmon Vestal told his friends that he had been tortured while in camp because he declined to take up arms or do any sort of duty. Guards jabbed him repeatedly with their bayonets, but not enough to seriously hurt him.[57] A thirty-year-old Quaker named Jackson Jones was conscripted and immediately caused trouble. "He refused to answer roll call, stand in the ranks, or cooperate in any way with the war effort. As punishment, he was imprisoned, 'bucked down' [hands tied between his knees], pierced with a bayonet, refused food and water, and had one of his ears cut off. Despite this torture, his brother testified before the Claims Commission, that 'he always spoke his sentiments boldly and openly, no matter who was present,' and finally the army discharged him."[58] In the highlands, "officers found

---

*   Quaker churches lost many members by "marrying out" (someone outside of the church membership).

sixteen members [Quakers] of Forbush, Deep Creek, and Hunting Creek. These young men were taken from their home . . . Lewis Caudle was taken to the front with a gun tied to him and was made to enter battle and stand amid the contending forces; but he did not fight. When the Confederates retreated he lay down among the killed and wounded. When everyone left, he got up and walked home."[59]

Conscript officers picked up James Haydock, a Quaker; but he was allowed three days to pay the exemption, or he would be marched to Richmond. Haydock chose to go with the conscript officers. While in service, he refused to carry a gun and was tormented by his comrades. He related, "Some Quaker men had been drafted, some of whom had no objection to paying the Exemption Tax, and there avoid engaging bloodshed; but two of them did not feel free to avail themselves of this way to escape and had gone with the soldiery, though refusing to bear arms."[60] William H. Hare wrote to a comrade:

> Friends of Perquimans have been paying their military fines. Those of North Hampton, what few have not been exempt from bodily infirmity, have been attending to stock or something of that sort. Those of Contenea Quarter . . . were [,] except one, let go home with sick furloes [sic] a day or so before Newbern was take [sic] and have not been cald [sic] out since. The one that did not go had not bin heard of about a week ago. It was said he did not run and said he could not. Some think he is with the Northerners . . .[61]

Jonathan Harris had been drafted but was able to get discharged by Friends. Once back home, Harris was thinking of leaving the state for good. He wrote a letter to John Crenshaw to thank him for the passport. "I think I should have started sooner but J.E. Cox thinks of crossing the line & going over into Va. & wished me to wait for him . . ."[62] Harris was still at home a month later because he sent a letter to the same man asking him to help get four brothers released from duty.[63] He apparently did leave because an acquaintance saw him on a northbound train later that year.

Quaker Stephen Hobson, conscripted into the Fifty-third Regiment, wrote from camp at Proctor's Creek, Virginia, that he was awaiting release:

> December 28th, 1862,
> My discharge has not come to hand yet [.] our Regiment left here tu weeks ago . . . the[y] went to Goldsborough N Carolina [.] we don't know whether the[y] will come back or not [.] if not we will halve to go to them shortly I expect [.] as to George Thompsons case I canot see eny thing that can bee done while things are as they are at present [,] only send thee that paper that hee has got an see what thee can doo for him [.] So I will Sen it and iff thee can do iny thing for him do it at once if thee can for we are looking for help from home evry day . . . Simon D. Kemp Said that I should say to thee that he was looking for some one to come after him [.] I think it likely that if the[y] come thee will find it out when the[y] come. I remain thy friend
> Stephen Hobson[64]

Delphina Mendenhall wrote that "William Hockett's sons are in prison at Kinston. [They] had been kept 24 hours when last heard from, without anything to eat or drink, simply for the reason that they are 'Christians, & therefore cannot fight.' Four other young Friends are in the army, who cannot see it right to pay the $500. tax. Two of them are Nicholas Barker's sons, and one, his soninlaw."[65] H. M. Hockett, while imprisoned in Kinston, got a letter off to his wife, Rachel, on February 2, 1863:

> We missed the opportunity of sending home and are still in prison having been 3 days and nights without one morsel of sustanance [sic] either bread or water and the captain visits us twice a day [,] tells us that we will find Gen

Ransoms orders carried out for he will see us dead and buried before he will give way one particle. We however [do] not think it safe to give way to his demands having a master even Christ to whom it is our duty to yield ourselves servants to day . . . . Whatever our fate may be we feel perfectly resigned to Gods blessed will which is a duty all Christians must come unto, and we have felt that we could give up all things in this earth for his sake near and dear as they seem to us. Such has been our comfort after three days and nights of starving that we have rested many times perfectly at ease not knowing the need of any thing . . .

Having been deprived of sending you a letter [in] the last mail we now embrace the favor. We went 41/2 days without one morsel of nourishment [.] by this time it pleased the Lord to touch the hearts of [these] people and we were given one half pint of sugar and [illegible] the first night and the next morning we received bread and other victuals as we were thought able to bear it, it being 5 days we eat nothing at all. We are now recruited up and feell [sic]quite well. We have been quite well with very little exception ever since we left home. We were placed in care of captain Ro(?) Baxter of the 9th regiment co H. who is detailed at this place with his company to keep the prisoners, and who merits our grateful(?) thanks for his kindness to us. He kept us under guard for some days and then told us he should take the guard away from round us only when we had occasion to walk out of doors [.] we mus take a man with us also that we might walk where we pleased over the house. The building is a large house with 4 rooms upstairs 15 feet square and a passage of twelve feet between them [.] We have one room with privilege to go into any of the others when [illegible]. We have corn bread and meat brough to us from the bakery [,] buy our own coffee. There is a woman in one of the rooms with her husband who cooks and washes for a company of soldiers [,] her husband being one of them, who makes our coffee for us, and is very kind and sympathizing to us: in short we are treated with a great deal of sympathy by all the soldier in Battery company who think strange that we are not sent home expressing a belief that we will be in a short time . . .

We want to hear from home by next mail [.] please tell us how Ellen is getting along and all the people in general [.] we cannot write to all now but will write as opportunity is afforded. Show this letter to Jesse's family and let it suffice for us both as he does not expect to write now. I would like to know how thee was getting along with the work and how the stock were doing. I would rather the stock were all kept at present if they can be taken care of, as I think them better than any thing they can be turned into. Is Wm B. Hockett at home, has Sol. Swain got well [,] who is staying with thee. Well write me a long letter of small particulars. Do not be discouraged but look toward with an eye of faith my dearest ones and I humbly trust that better days will soon arise. Bless & kiss the children for me & tell them how I love them. Direct your letters to Kinston Lenoir Co. N.C.[66]

H. M. Hockett was able to get another letter out on April 10, 1863:

Dear wife & children

Having the chance of sending home a few lines rather unexpectedly I conclude to write though under circumstances which I fear will prove trying to thee [.] I am in pretty good health and have been quite well for me [illegible] . . . nearly ever since I left home. Jesse is not quite as well [.] he has taken cold and has quite a troublesome cough though we hope nothing serious. We were assigned to Captain Bunting's Wilmington horse artillery company stationed at Kinston and brought here last fourth day and remained in camp till this morning [.] on being required to drill, we refused; and were sent up to town one mile this s[ide] of the battery to appear before General Ran[som]. He told us that he would hear no pleas about religion as the law had made provision and he was bound to execute them. That he should put us in a room up stairs and we should not have one drop of water nor one morsel of provision neither communication with any man (unless authorities) till we agreed to go to duty or pay the $500. tax.[67]

Private William B. Hockett, conscripted into the Twenty-first Regiment, practiced his Quaker religion faithfully. The thirty-six-year-old farmer refused to carry a rifle when his comrades were in the Shenandoah Valley. Officers promptly had him arrested. Attempts had been made to get him to take up arms several times before. On the march into Pennsylvania, Colonel William Kirkland assembled a firing squad to execute him. Those chosen for the firing squad refused to pull the trigger. Other officers would have had the squad arrested, but Colonel Kirkland rescinded, and the Quaker was ordered to fall in with the wagon train.

Traveling through York County, Hockett saw the countryfolk going to church. He wrote: "Oh! How I wish I was at home to go with my dear wife to go to Centre meeting today to worship the Lord in spirit and truth. But the Lord's will be done, not mine." One evening, his reflected thoughts were set in pen: "I have spent the day in reading my Bible, and in silent waiting on the Lord. My heart is sick, seeing the roguery our men are up to; taking horses, cattle and provisions of all kind. Nothing that they see escapes their grasp, and they are thrown away because men cannot carry them." Later on, the Quaker private was allowed to leave the army and returned home to his wife and two children.[68]

John B. Crenshaw, a spokesperson for the Quakers, kept up a constant flow of letters to the secretary of war about paying the tax or releasing the Quakers. The secretary of war said that all they had to do was pay the tax, and they would be released. Crenshaw in a letter to Tilghman Vestal said that 182 Friends had paid the fine while seven refused. Crenshaw said:

> I could not advise any one to pay it against their conscience, but there are several points on which thou seems to be misinformed, first, all monies paid under the conscription act go into the common treasury, & upon Congress rests the responsibility of how it is appropriated . . . should thou change thy mind & wish to be released by paying said tax let me know & I will aid thee therein.[69]

Mr. Vestal, native born, lived in North Carolina first but moved to Tennessee and was conscripted in a unit there because he refused to pay the five-hundred-dollar fine. He was sent to the prison first at Castle Thunder then Salisbury. Vestal said that while confined, another prisoner, an Irish bully, beat him. Guards placed the Quaker in a separate room.[70] Vestal was considering staying in the army and either acting as a cook or doing something else instead of carrying a rifle. Crenshaw wrote him a long letter on October 3, 1863:

> Thy last favor was received to day. I have thought much of thy case since I last wrote thee. In reverting to the writings of early Friends in reference to the subject of war, I find that Thomas Clarkson their great historian writes of the Quakers, "They believe it unlawful for Christians to engage in the profession of arms, or indeed to bear arms under any circumstances of hostility whatever." Hence there is no such character as that of a Quaker soldier. Where he has no choice, he either submits, if he has property to distraints upon it, or if he has not, to prison. The Quakers have been charged with inconsistency in refusing military service, & yet in paying those taxes, which are expressly for the support of wars . . . Thou queries of me in reference to cooking for the

soldiers; this is a very close question, for they are our fellow men . . . yet I certainly could not cook for them as soldiers any sooner than I could clean up a soldiers camp . . . Thy friend, John B. Crenshaw.[71]

A Quaker lady told Crenshaw that other Friends would be willing to pay the tax for Vestal if he would let them.[72] Apparently, Vestal was adamant that he did not wish it. He also turned down offers to be detailed for the military. Still in prison at Salisbury in the spring of 1864, Vestal sent this letter to Mr. Crenshaw:

> . . . As for accepting a detail I think it is not advisable for me to do so. If I had felt willing to do government work I could have gone at it before I was punished and could have missed all this imprisonment; I chose rather to be punished and am not sorry that I did so . . . as far as making shoes for soldiers is consumed [sic] I am sure I could not do that . . . when details were offered to me last August I replied that if I were to do anything to assist the army I would take the gun at once and be a soldier indeed . . . I do not know what to do!—I would like to work at the potters business; and if it as a trade would exempt me I would willingly do so; but to go at it as a detailed hand working for the government, is more than I will promise to do without further consideration . . .[73]

Vestal wrote to his aunt in March:

> I send this by Jamestown that thou may see it and say to Friend Crenshaw anything that thou can, for I do not know what else to say. I have spoken my sentiments and if it is not pleasant I cant help it. I would like very much to get out of prison but if the Lord ever required anything of me, to show publicly to the people that I am truly, religiously or conscientiously opposed to war . . . and I fear that the reason I have been chastised so far is that I have not attended to the small still voice of God as I should have done . . .[74]

Vestal's aunt Judith told Friend Crenshaw that he was allowed to receive books and favors from home while incarcerated. She said he did not object to working in the prison garden occasionally but would not consent to help the prison carpenter or blacksmith.[75]

A large contingent of Quakers settled in the Holly Springs community of Randolph County. The Hinshaw brothers and the two Barker brothers suffered at the hands of the military. Once they were tied to a wagon and forced to go through rivers. They were on the march to Gettysburg. All four refused to fight. Thomas helped with the wounded. General Lee with his army retreated July 4 in a downpour. The twenty-five-mile-long wagon train moved slowly southward. Darkness fell, and the four Quakers got separated from the regiment. Exhausted, they sat down and discussed their situation. All decided to desert. Nearby they found a Quaker home. Freedom, however, was short. The grapevine told of a family caring for four "rebels." Union soldiers picked them up and sent them to the Fort Delaware Prison.

At Fort Delaware, they met another Quaker from Centre, North Carolina, William B. Hockett. The Society of Friends around Fort Delaware gathered up provisions for the Quaker prisoners. These benevolent folks managed to get the five men a pardon from President Lincoln. Secretary of War Seward wrote them a pass to move freely in the loyal states. Immediately, they set out for Indiana, seeking relatives there.[76]

The Hinshaw and Barker brothers received a reply for their request from the War Department to write home. The secretary wrote:

> August 2, 1864 You have permission to write letters to your relatives in North Carolina, on domestic matters, sending them unsealed by a Flag of Truce . . .[77]

Quaker Levi Cox was exempt because he ran the mill for the community. When wheat was ripe, on many occasions, his wife watched the mill while he helped neighbors with their crops. Once, he worked thirty-two days cutting wheat near the Spool Mill area. The Home Guard caught him away from the mill and told him that if he left again, they would shoot him as a deserter.[78] The guard came and took Thomas and his brother, Jacob Hinshaw, and two neighbors, Simeon Piggott and Nat Cox.[79]

Those Quakers who chose to run from the state had the help of benevolent neighbors. It was told that baskets of food hung in the log barn behind the school farmhouse for passing Quakers, unionists, secessionists, or bushwhackers—all alike hungry men to the Quakers.

"Six hundred people joined the Society of Friends during the war." Many others with Union sentiment joined the Heroes of America, which was a secret society.* One of the duties of this resistance group was to assist draft dodgers and deserters.[80]

The eastern Quakers settled in Rich Square, Hertford County, Perquimans, Wayne, Pasquotank, and Edgecombe County. The Quakers did take a dim view on desertion and deserters who plundered, murdered, or stole from neighbors.[81]

Captain Allen, at Salisbury Prison, encouraged recruits to join him by this enticing advertisement:

NOTICE TO NON-CONSCRIPTS:
I now have a company of non-conscripts permanently stationed at Salisbury, NC, as prison guards and will receive 25 or 30 more recruits if an early application is made to me. The company will not be removed from this place. H.P. Allen
Capt. Co. B, Prison Guards, Salisbury, N.C.[82]

———

Quaker women felt the need to go to influential persons to inquire about their sons. The mother of Elias Reek, age eighteen, said that her son tried to reach the "free states" along with Haley Sills; but both were arrested in western Virginia. They became inmates in Castle Thunder. "They get nothing but bread and water, & one of them, Sills, seems much enfeebled for want of food, both suffering for clean clothes." Another person asked to seek out Harrison M. Barton, a miller, forced to go to Richmond. The mother of Ellwood Moore didn't know whether her Quaker son was in a hospital in Virginia.[83]

Numerous women wrote to officials asking for a son or husband to come home because of hardship. "The most significant war-related cause of poverty was the army's enlistment and conscription of men . . . who were needed as laborers on many small farms," wrote Paul Escott. Citizens would write the governor to excuse certain non-related artisans such as millers so that they could remain at home. "72% of its white citizens had no slaves to do the essential work of raising food."[84]

Once the Conscription Act passed, authorities were bombarded with letters seeking exemptions. Whole communities would petition for a particular person to be pardoned from service. Women would write the governor, the president, the secretary of war, a judge, lawyer, a minister, politicians, or the man's commanding officer. Those who could not write had someone else do the job. The letters are very colorful, some are truly sad, and some threatening. Most of the requests were denied.

Sixty-year-old Harriet Stephenson, with five sons in the war, communicated to the secretary of the state, "I think I hav did enough for you for you to take sum intrust in what I so much desire of you."[85] She wanted exemption for one son to stay home and help around

———

*   This is discussed in chapter 11.

the farm. John Thompson asked to get his son, George, off because he was chronically sick:

> State of North Carolina, Alamance Co
> John Thompson Personally appears before me & makes oath that his son geo Thompson has not been able to do a days work in two years that require walking upon the account that he is subject to bad spells of rheumatism he has been so bad some times that he could not get from the bed to the fire without his crutches he has made some shoes at times when he was at the best. Sworn to before me this Oct 4th 1862. JAJ Patterson Capt, 48(?) Reg. of 12 Brig NC Militia[86]

Cass A. Marlowe sent this letter to Governor Vance on November 6, 1862:

> I take the present opportunity of dropping you a few lines to inform you that we have a cooper in the twenty sixth regiment that went as a conscript that we cant well do with out [.] he was all the man that followed this trade anywhere near in this neighborhood [.] people depended on him for all kinds of vessels in our country [.] he followed this for his trade mostly for the last six or seven years . . . people come from fifteen to twenty miles for his work [.] he is a man that insures his work to be good . . . he is a splendid shoemaker too so when he cant work at one trade he can the other [.] we would be thankful if the Said Albert Marlow to be exempted if it can be done . . . he has favored the women and children all he could in their distress at their time of need [.] since this war commenced he sent to the soldiers in the army all he could . . . Mr. Govener I will forfeit and pay fifty dollars in the Treasury for the said Albert Marlow to be discharged to come home . . . he is a very good carpenter when call on for furniture . . . I don't do this because he is my loveing companion [,] it is the request of my friends and fellow citizens in this desolate County of wilkes [.] you need not think I rote you a lye because he is my husband for that is one thing I wouldent do . . . This to, Z.B. Vance governer from Miss Cass. A. Marlowe yours respectfully.[87]

Women asked for an exemption for their son or husband. The governor was flooded with letters in the fall of 1862:

> From ELENDER GIBSON: Nov. 3rd, 1862
> State of North Carolina, Caldwell County
> this is to no of you whether ther should be any chance for me to get my Two sons Discharged or furlowed home or not [,] that is Harrison & Paton Gibsons that formerly belonged to your Regement [.] they are both sick and has ben for along time not able for Service and I am ferful they never will again [.] if you please instruct me how to get them home [.] if I had them home I cold nurse them up and maybe save their lives or Recrute them up so they wold be able for service again [.] my Boys has been in the War over fifteen Months and have don all they cold in defince of there contry [.] if you please to assist me in tryin to get them home for I am apoore widow woman Dependnt on my boys for support [.] I have don all I cold for the War I have in both Clothing and provision, and I should vary Glad if I cold get to see my son for a short time [.] I want you to answer this letter if you please and if ther is any chance you will no it in so doinge you will oblige your humble servant
> Direct your letter to Bucke Shoal P. off (post office) Caldwell Co. NC.[88]

Apparently, the governor never answered.

From LYDIA A. BOLTON: November the 5, 1862
    I set down to rite you a few lines and hope and pray to god that you will oblige me [.] I ame a pore woman with a pasel of little children and I will have to starve or go naked [.] me and my little children ef my husband is kept away from home much longer I ask you to lat him come home and burn cole for the state [.] I don't want him to come and do nothen for the confederacy but he can see to his family and burn cole and I beg you to tell him to come[.] tha don't give me but thre dollars a month and fore of us in family and I cant cloth my children [.] I have knit 40 pare of socks fo the solgers and it takes all I can earn to get bred and I beg you in the name of the lord to let him come [.] my sister en law is nearly as bad of as I ame and she wants her husban ef you can spare him [.] I hope that can serv the stat as such a burning cole as tha can thear [.] if you cud hear the crys of my little children I think you wod feel for us [.] I am pore in this world but I trust rich in heven [.] I trust in god and hope if he wil cos you to have compaahion on the pore—
    rote by James A. Bolton wife—he is at Wilmington—Joab Bolton—he is at the same place I umblr beg in the name of our father in heven to send my husband home—Sir hear the crys of the pore I beg you[89]

There was no reply listed in Governor Vance's papers.

From CHARLOTTE ROWELL:
Brunswick county NC nov 23 1862
    address to the honerfle govener frome a old widow lady that has a grat many servents and other property and has no person to attend to enny bisness at tall for me [.] I would be thankful to you if you would assist me [.] you would a assist me a grate deal if you will have John N register detailed from serves to at tend to bisness for me [.] he is the best overseer that I in my noing [.] all th men is gon from a bout her pretty much and there is nobody that I can get to pertect my servents for me [.] I can not doo with out some-boddy and I rother have him then enny one elce I no of [.] I have no boddy but myself and 2 daughters and sense he has been in servis, my property has ben goin to destruction [,] no boddy to sea to it [.] if you will have him sent home you will doo me a grate favore.[90]

The governor wrote back that he has no power to detail an overseer from the army.

From SARAH F. SMITH:
Cypress Creek N. Carolina Dec 7th 1862
    —I will endeavor to write you a few lines on this subject. I as well as 10 other families are left here with any masculine protection . . . [I] ask you to discharge John B. Smith from the service of war . . . he is near 50 . . . he is all the man in this vicinity to look for protection.[91]

This father wrote to Major Walter Clark to discharge his ill son:

January 15, 1865 Majer Clarke my dear sur I take this opportunity to inform yo that I receved a letter from Rl Wagner stating that my son LM Charles was left at the Camp near hamelton verry sick and no wone to tend to him but Wagner [.] he rote to me by his reqest for me to cum and se to him an bring him sum clothing an sumthing to eat [.] I fixet up as quick as I cud [.] it cammest raining an raind all nite an all next day [.] I started the 11 am went to Lexington [NC] thru the mud knee deep [.] tha informed me that the bac rode briges was all swep a way so I cud not go [.] I regret verry much that he was not sent to Raleigh or greensbury hospittle whar he Cud a had medical attendance an sumthing fit for a sick person to eat an & bed to keep him warm [.] if he is destitute of clothing tel [him] I can cum an bring him sum [.] I want you to help him to get a furlo and send him home as quickly as he is able to Cum an if he is not able have him sent to Raleigh hospittle petagrue [Pettigrew Hospital] No. 13 whare he was before [.] Majer I want you to anser this letter as soon as you can fale not

Martin you must take as good Care of yore self as possible an tri an git well and cum home wonst more and rite as quick as you git this letter so I will no whare you are [.] I must close for the present.[92]

Petitioners from Nash County asked the secretary of war to let their doctor remain at home. They "pointed out that they collectively had done enough to benefit the Confederacy and for that reason, they deserved their requested discharge. They claimed to have already sent one thousand men to serve in the army, and they needed a doctor to attend those who remained. In making their request, they assured the government that they acted 'without any intention or desire to injure the cause in which he is now engaged.'" [93] Twenty-nine citizens of Randolph County wrote to the Honorable T. S. Ashe to exempt their village blacksmith. "He can do the country infinitely more good by staying here than by going," they proclaimed. "Granting the exemption or discharge would promote justice and, thus, the greater interests of the Confederacy," wrote Elizabeth Adams to President Davis.[94]

Citizens from Nash, Wilson, and Johnston counties wrote similar letters to congressmen. Duncan Buie wanted an exemption due to his being the "main stay of several families." He cared for a lunatic brother. He was denied. Some letters were signed by multiple civilians. Kitty Daughtry of Sampson County wrote on June 20, 1863, to President Davis, asking if he would just "detail him for a short period." She had five sons in the army and only wanted the youngest to come home for harvesting the crops. She said both she and the government would benefit for most (crops) would go for the soldiers' needs. Five neighbors also signed the petition[95]

"Men trying to evade conscription sought work from anyone holding a state or Confederate contract, including such ordinary contracts as supplying the North Carolina Rail Road Company with lumber for sills and firewood."[96] Owners or managers of businesses would ask for exemptions for their employees. On March 19, 1863, another petition arrived with sworn testimony signed by J. P. Chesly of the LaGrange Coal Mine. It listed eight coal miners, four boatmen, two carpenters, and one engineer. All except the boatmen were excused from duty. The owner of the New Market Foundry in Randolph County, Frank Gardner, asked for D. M. Roach and William Green, his employees, to be excused from military service. The exemption was granted.[97] The New Market Foundry also made farm equipment.

The adjutant of the county wrote to the iron-works and the Egypt Coal Mine, seeking names of men on their payroll.[98] Thomas F. Cheek requested an exemption on March 26, 1863. Before entering the military, he was a supervisor and manager of a wool-carding factory. In July of 1862, he was conscripted but instead got a substitute who was thirty-six years old—but the substitute was discharged, making him liable to serve. His request was approved.

Residents from Wake County wrote James Seddon, Secretary of War, asking for the exemption of Henry Holloway, a cobbler in the Fifth Cavalry. They stated he had a family of fifteen, had a medical disease, and was the only cobbler in the community. They further stated that he made shoes at lower prices for soldiers and their spouses.[99] Others throughout the state circulated petitions, thinking more signatures might influence a positive response:

Onslow County, North Carolina August 29, 1864

We the undersigned subseribers [*sic*] citizens of the above named county and state do request that W.W. Smith be detailed for miller as he is keeping the only mill in the district or within twenty miles of this neighborhood.[100]

It was signed by thirteen people. A petition for Silas Hobson was sent to Jefferson Davis and signed by a justice of the peace from Randolph County on May 17, 1864. Hobson was in the Sixty-fourth Militia and was a cabinet and coffin maker.[101] Citizens petitioned for the exemption of W. B. Gainey because he knew how to repair cotton/wool cards on September 21, 1863. He was denied.[102]

The Confederate States of America Bureau of Conscription's Seventh District contained the counties of Anson (Wadesboro), Stanly (Albemarle), Moore (Carthage), Randolph (Asheboro), Montgomery (Troy), Chatham (Pittsboro), and Davidson (Lexington). This file, found in the Southern Historical Collection, produced several letters to officials asking for exemptions:

November 4, 1862 To His Excellency President Davis:

Whereas, we the undersigned petitioners, being female citizens of a certain district on New Hope River, Chatham County, North Carolina, live in a neighborhood containing a great many slaves,* and whereas, most of the men are already in the army, we do [feel] anxious about our personal safety. And whereas Willis A. Dameron is a bold and fearless man, a good disciplinarian of Negroes and one in whom we could put confidence as a protector; therefore we most humbly petition His Excellency, the President, to grant a Special Exemption to the said Willis Dameron for the better preservation of quiet and order in our midst. We boast not in saying that we have given up our husbands and brothers without a murmur, and have contributed to the extent of our ability to the Southern Cause. And that we would not willingly deprive the army of a single soldier but when we feel that our own safety is at stake, we are constrained to ask for <u>one</u> single exemption in our favor. We do moreover believe that the said Dameron would be of more real service to the Confederacy by remaining in our midst, than by entering the army, and that if our President knew the true condition in which we are placed, he would make the exemption, on the ground of both justice and necessity.

Praying Heavens blessing on you, and our noble cause, we subscribe ourselves your humble petitioners.[103]

From the same collection:

March 13, 1863, North Carolina, Moore County:

We the undersigned, respectfully show that Kindrick H. Hare is engaged in making stone ware, with Hardy Brown and J.D. Craven; that since Crockery ware has become so scarce in the country, there is a pressing demand for plates, cups, crocks, &c, that the necessities of the country demand that the factory be kept in operation it being the only place where such wares can be had, in this section of our country.** That said K.H. Hare and J.D. Craven are [the] only hands who attend to moulding and turning the wares that they are both now conscripted and the factory must stop unless they are detailed to

---

*   Some women could not write, so another lady wrote her name; fifty-six women signed the petition. For a complete list, please see the appendix.

**   They made hospital wares.

work at their trade; they are now supplying a large section of country with wares, and the demand is increasing daily. If they be taken away the work must stop & the country remain without such furniture as is absolutely necessary to every housekeeper. We therefore pray that K.H. Hare be detailed to follow his trade.

Respectfully submitted, A.R. McDonald, Adjutant 51st regiment and Col. W.B. Richardson, 51st NCT.

Also signed are these men: S. Bruce, Angus Currie, Alex Kelly, J. Kelly, W. D. Smith, A. H. McNeill, A. M. Branson, T. B. Tyson, and one other illegible name.[104]

Women continued to write to officials asking for a son to come home because of hardship. Miranda Sutton gave her husband and six sons for service. The husband and two sons had died. Miranda needed help to obtain sustenance. One blind woman pleaded with the governor to please not conscript her last son. All three of her other sons were already serving.[105] Martha Curtis wrote to the governor on February 13, 1863, "I has won small son that is sickly and is not able to work. All the way that I has to git my living is to keep up my farm . . ." She asked for her other son to be returned from military duty.[106] One very destitute woman from Iredell County pleaded with the governor to send her son home to help her. The lady's neighbors could have assisted her, she said, but would not; they gave her all kinds of excuses.[107]

This soldier had two excuses why he should be discharged. In a letter from H. H. Thompson, encamped near Kinston, on November 21, 1863, to James Scott, he penned:

Dear Sir, I wish you to make out a pertition for me in which you will make it appear that I would be more advantage to the government in being home fishing & oustering [oystering] for the soldiers than I would to be in service myself and also as there is several fisherman on new river which cannot get barrels to put up there fish in. I can be an advantage both ways by coopering & also by fishing and oustering. You know that I was talking to you about the same thing you will pleas make out the form stating those facts and send it to David R Henderson of Wolfpitt Dist. Onslow Co. and much ablige a friend yours respectfully—Hillary H. Thompson[108]

The next letter asked for an exemption for a friend and requested that the letter be worded in his particular style:

Wilson, N.C. Sept. 1st, 1864
Majr. R.S. Tucker
My very dear sir—
I have been so troublesome to Gov. Vance. He has always heard me with attention and treated me with kind help. I am now actually ashamed to ask anything further from him, but I have a friend—a mutual friend of ours—James L. Fowle of Washington; that I am exceedingly desirous of serving—of saving him from conscription. The great bulk of both his and his fathers estate consisted of slave property. They lost in the early part of the war all but one of their Negroes. They have been impoverished by the war, the old gentleman is very old and feeble. He is utterly unable to transact any business with the activity requisite to make a living for such a large family. James has a large family of his own and if his and all of his sisters are thrown before the old gentleman, it will present a case of hardship, that I have not seen surpassed

during this war. It will be terrible to reduce that large and most estimable family to the condition unnecessarily incident to the deprivation of its active head. In addition to this James is one of the most valuable citizens of our county—public opinioned and energetic, and the county can not spare him. He was appointed a magistrate by the last legislature, but could not qualify on account of no courts being held.

He would make a most excellent agent of the State Quarter Master's and Commissary Departments for the purchase of supplies from Beaufort, Hyde, Washington and Tyrrel counties and if once employed in any such capacity the chief's of those departments would never consent to dispense with his services.

W.H. Williard who was the Q.M. of the 14th Reg. North Carolina Militia has moved out of the state. That place is vacant. There is no commanding officer of the Home Guards or QM for Beaufort and Hyde counties (that I know of). Please do me a favor of trying to obtain some place for him that will exempt him. It is a specialty meritious case, and any effort you may make in his behalf will be only appreciated and should an opportunity ever open, he most heartily reciprocated.

If D.G.F. is in Raleigh consult with him about this matter. Ask him how it would do for the Governor to claim his exemption as a Justice of the Peace saying, "It having been certified to me that there's no acting JP now actually residing in the town of Washington, and J. L. F. having been heretofore appointed as J.P. for the county of Beaufort to supply said want and not having heretofore qualified as such, owing to no causes on his part, I do hereby certify to the recipient of his exemption as an officer necessary to the claim of exemption to close should the said Fowler neglect to qualify as justice as before said, (at the next court of P. & Q. sessions of Beaufort County) or within ten days after the commencement of the next session of the General Assembly." Ask D.G.F. to look and see when he was appointed and whether he can qualify at next court. If the time since his last appointment is to long for him to qualify now & could not the Gov. issue a new commission? He has been recommended by the General Assembly.

Yours truly,
Jno A. Handy[109]

This letter to Governor Vance from Private O. Goddin reveals the frustration poor men had against the exemption of the Twenty-Negro Law:

Please pardon the liberty which a poor soldier takes in thus addressing you as when he *Volunteered* he left a wife with four children to go to fight for his country. He cheerfully made the sacrifices thinking that the Govt. would protect his family, and keep them from starvation. In this he has been disappointed for the Govt. has made a distinction between the rich man (who had something to fight for) and the poor man who fights for that which he never will have. The [Confederacy's] exemption of the owners of 20 Negroes & the allowing of substitutes clearly proves it. Healthy and active men who have furnished substitutes are grinding the poor by speculation while their substitutes have been discharged after a month's service as being too old or as invalids. By taking too many men from their farms they have not left enough to cultivate the land thus making a scarcity of provisions . . .

Now Govr. do tell me how we poor soldiers who are fighting for the "rich mans Negro" can support our families at $11 per month? How can the poor live? I dread to see summer as I am fearful there will be much suffering now . . .

I am fearful we will have a revolution unless something is done as the majority of our soldiers are poor men with families who say they are tired of the rich mans war & poor mans fight, they wish to get to their families & fully believe some settlement could be made were it not that our authorities have made up their minds to prosecute the war regardless of all suffering . . . A mans first duty is to provide for his own household the soldiers wont be imposed much longer.[110]

The area of the state referred to as Down East and the piedmont section grew thousands of acres of corn, which fed General Lee's army. The governor would write President Davis to ask for exemptions of certain laborers. He wanted the president to let up on impressments and conscription in North Carolina so that they could help out with farm produce. He even suggested that they be furloughed long enough to get a crop out, then return to active duty.[111] The following is one instance where a farmer was exempted temporarily. Elias Carr had a plantation, Bracebridge Hall in Edgecombe County, and another in Warren County, away from the miasmas and malarial climate. He had excellent farming skills and the rich land to go with it. Carr was discharged from the army so that he could raise corn and forage for the military. During the last part of the war, he found himself a soldier again.[112]

Exemptions kept on file needed constant upkeep because the situation changed frequently. Each case was investigated, sometimes taking weeks to complete. It involved "miles" of red tape and caused enrolling officers to be ever vigilant. The following information comes from files in the Wilson Library, Chapel Hill.

To Major and Adjutant Col. Mallett:
I am informed by Henry Kisett and sons, contractors with the department for leather shoes, and lumber [,] that from some cases to them unknown [,] two of their detailed men [,] Vestal, and Stephen Kisett have been forcibly arrested by order of Lt. Little enrolling officer for the district in which they live.
The cause of the arrest I do not know. Those contractors are among the very best, and have been in charge one the tanyards belonging to the contractor now left without any person in charge.
In addition to the tan yard a steam saw mill is attached which the dept. or system [illegible] . . . with lumber to manufacture packing boxes &c.
I respectfully request (unless changes of a grave character is preferred) that they be retuned to their work.[113]

Captain Little of the Seventh District responded that they were arrested because one was a deserter and the other a recusant conscript. Both commenced their occupation after enrollment.

The following are other similar letters:

Captain,
I have the honor to report that I have strictly complied with endorsements in the case of William N. Moore; that I have instituted a full investigation, in person, in this, as I shall in all cases, even though it shall delay the return of papers.
The fact as stated by these informants are substantially true, though made by prejudiced parties. By the time Moore made his first petition for exemption his case was a pitiable one, the grounds on which it was made

were then true <u>but</u>, the petition was returned for corroboration of the facts by six reliable citizens and by that time the principle cause for exemption had been removed; to wit: his brother's orphan children were taken off his hands and bound out to other parties, except the oldest who can earn his living. Maurice Waddell his lawyer however removed the difficulty in the minds of these reliable men by telling them to testify "not to his status now but at the time the petition was written." So he was exempted. The other fact perhaps still exist: Moore is a poor man, so are many thousands of our soldiers and since the prime circumstance which induced the Secretary of War to extend clemency to him no longer exists, and as there are more pressing cases, [his] should be revoked yet [I] respt. submit the facts to yourjudgment.

W.C. Reuchs, Lieut and Enrolling Officer, Chatham County

Little's reply:

As to our informant's statements that "men get lawyers to go to the Secretary Of War with pitiful stories &c by paying them two or three hundred dollars" &c. I am unable to say but it is unfortunately true that some of our lawyers are too ready to demand and receive large fees for interesting themselves in obtaining exemption from military service.[114]

Moore returned to war in the cavalry. His petition took months to conclude. Lieutenant Reuchs, mentioned above, sent a letter on October 14, 1863, to Captain Little in Asheboro:

Rufus London was "Flying around with Pittsboro girls in citizens clothing." On being asked his cause of exemption, he produced a furlough from the firm of Williams & Co. representing him as a clerk in the Piedmont Railroad Company. Are further inquires necessary?.[115]

––––––––––––––

D. Spruill wrote the conscript board on March 3, 1864:

With fifty Negroes under my care, I withdrew from Washington County in September of 1862 and came to Randolph County and commenced following my former business of farming. Have at this time twenty-five of the above.[116]

He indicated that he was the only person outside the enemies' lines who had any control of them. Spruill's letter was witnessed and verified by eight men. T. H. Smith, contractor of a shop that made flour barrels, made application for exemptions for his workers. Smith contracted with Confederacy to make forty to fifty barrels by each employee per month.[117] In October 1863, Major Sam R. Chissman, quartermaster's office in Greensboro, said he exempted two men who made buckets.

––––––––––––––

J. P. Miller requested an exemption in May 1864. The board of investigation said he should remain at home because of his occupation and because he was too obese ("a very stout man") for field duty. Stout or not, he did have to report for detail on January 1, 1865. Another family named Miller found themselves in trouble with the conscript department. Quaker James Haydock and his wife, Frances, told the story that conscript officers had been at the mill; and because Mr. Miller would not reveal the hiding place of his three sons, "they hung him up three times almost to the point of strangulation. Josiah Barker, who owns the mill, and lives close by, hearing the screams of Miller's wife, came out and they seized him, asking him the same questions. They found one of the missing conscripts, whom they hung til dead."[118]

Many people wrote directly to President Davis, some wrote to the governor, and some wrote to the secretary of war for exemptions. Most requested a furlough or exemption for their loved one. Judge Thomas Ruffin literally received bags of mail requesting such favors. Another prominent man, Jonathan Worth, mentioned earlier and a Quaker descendant, figured among those who intervened. These men had better success convincing state officials rather than Confederate personalities. Governor Vance wrote to Davis that it was a "rich man's war and a poor man's fight after the conscript bureau passed exemption for the 20 nigger law."[119] This term pops up frequently in soldiers' letters all over the South. Historians have stated that the war caused class distinctions to emerge. The yeomen and poorer class could not afford substitutes. Others felt the need to balk because their civil liberties were infringed upon like their ancestors had before.

W. O. Ruddock, with the Twenty-third NCT, volunteered in 1861 and soon became sick. When he was well enough, the surgeons detailed him to work as a nurse while stationed in Virginia. Apparently, he never fully recovered to his prewar strength. Ruddock tried for months on end to get a medical discharge. He informed his uncle in a letter the spring of 1863 that "your letter to the surgeon has been received. But do not know as yet what effect it will have toward getting a discharge . . . . If I fail to get a discharge or furlough here I will go to my regiment and try there . . ."[120]

FREE BLACK EXEMPTIONS

Black men served in the Confederacy and were conscripted like the whites. However, they could also receive exemptions:

> You are authorized to exempt in cases, where the cultivation of a farm depends <u>entirely</u> upon the labour of one male free negro, age 18-45, provided that the employer gives oath that he cannot obtain labour elsewhere and you are satisfied of the truth of the affidavit.
> Col. BC Hopkins, 45 N.C.M. Adjutant-General's Office[121]

Giles Mebane wrote in August 1861 to Governor Clark for an exemption for Sterling and Leonidas Day, age about fourteen to fifteen. "Jerry Day, a respectable free man of colour who lives in the county of Orange has now five sons in the army, who heretofore worked with said Day & assisted in the support of his family . . . Day and his wife, aged 75 and 64, were rearing four orphaned grandchildren and needed the labor of the sons who remained at home, Leonidas and Sterling . . . a company of Volunteers under Capt Miller now being formed not far from said Day have been to look at these boys & say they will take them away . . . the family would then be unable to support themselves & become a charge on the county."[122]

There were many occurrences of white women petitioning the local board for the exemption of a free black man in their neighborhood. Rebecca A. Pierce of Randolph County wrote the enrolling officer to release from duty Boswell Bunting, age forty. Their answer:

> She is a widow with four children. She farms 260 acres and has cattle. Her aged mother lives with her.

Bunting worked for her. Mrs. Pierce sent her petition to the secretary of war on May 7, 1864. It was denied, and Bunting was conscripted.[123]

Nathan Winslow, a member of the Society of Friends, petitioned for Allen Lloyd, a free black. Lieutenant Holt of the bureau wrote that "he [Winslow] is a member of the Society of Friends and desirous of keeping every one out of service." It was not recorded if Lloyd was exempted or not. From the enrolling office in Randolph County, July 1864, Mrs. Flora Nixon from Jamestown (Society of the Friends) petitioned to oppose a free Negro going into service. She said she had five to six members of the society working for her. The officer said, "She has the means and can hire . . ." Richard Cox, the free black, was sent to camp.*[124]

Lieutenant J. A. Little was flooded with petitions to exempt free black men working for white female farmers. He wrote, "The principle feature in white persons making application for free Negroes is that they can rent their lands and get one third of the produce [.] it makes them eager to have their free negroes around them."[125]

———————

The Statesville camp of instruction, which had closed in 1862, reopened in August 1863 in Morganton.[126] By the end of 1863, changes took place among the officers staffing the conscript bureau. Each district, county, town, etc., would be run by disabled officers; lower-end jobs would be staffed by disabled noncommissioned men.[127]

On February 17, 1864, the conscript law changed to sweep up men ages seventeen to fifty, meaning that teens ages seventeen and eighteen were drafted to serve in the Junior Reserves; men ages forty-five to fifty had to pull duty in the Senior Reserves. When the teenager reached age eighteen, he would be reverted into the regular army. These new recruits stayed in the state. Other changes to the new law reduced the number of exempted positions. At this time, the use of free blacks and borrowed slaves increased to release white soldiers who had been detailed in non-combat duties.[128]

Work-related deferments were called detailed soldiers. *Detail*, a cushy job, which men desired and pursued, soon was abused. Colonel Archer Anderson's letter to General Bragg in the summer of 1864 told that one hundred men applied for detail service daily. These would be agricultural details, those of public necessity, and, lastly, as contractors and government officers.[129] Once granted, "details were good for periods from sixty days to one year . . ." Afterwards, these had to be reviewed or continued.[130] As the war ground on with the wounded figures rising and leaving the ranks, the conscript bureau assigned these men to detail work. But first, it had to be cleared with the surgeon. "Unfit for duty" written on the surgeon's certificate meant the soldier was released from regular military assignments. The soldier may not be able to go back to the lines, but he could be of use somewhere else and remain in the service.

In February 1865: "General Order # 17 abolished the Bureau of Conscription and the Camps of Instruction and restructured the medical evaluation process for conscripts. Reserve generals were given complete responsibility for all conscription enforcements within their respective states. They were to report to the secretary of war through an 'Officer of Conscription' in Richmond, who was attached to the Adjutant and Inspector General Cooper's Office. State commandants and county enrolling officers were ordered to report to their reserve generals for assignment."[131] All this came about because of General Braxton Bragg. He wanted to reform the conscription department. After the conscripts reported in Richmond, they were assigned a unit; then they received a physical. No longer could a man wait at home for his exam and orders. Exemptions and any controversy were to be settled *after* the recruit had been assigned a regiment. This placed the soldier into service much quicker than before. Back in the state, the county enrolling officer filled duties formally carried out by Colonel Mallett's battalion. His duty continued to keep a record of names of furloughed soldiers, detailed men, and exempt men.

In a twist of irony, a white man chose to take a free black man's place in the war. Richard V. Michaux of Burke County explained in his letter to President Andrew Johnson when he requested amnesty postwar. He said that he "acted as Tithe Agent for the collection of tobacco for the county of Burke which later office I accepted for the sole purpose of keeping a free man of color from working on the fortifications being entitled to the serves of one laborer as a primer of tobacco."[132]

———————

*   For a list of sixty-six petitions for free black men, see the appendix.

Union-sympathetic men were offered the oath to join the Confederacy, and many did, or they could remain neutral and work for the government. Some were paid by Confederate authorities for work as joiners, harness makers, gunsmiths, mechanics, tailors, cobblers, and blacksmiths.[133] A great deal became tax assessors, tithe collectors, or postmasters.

Nimrod J. Bell was a conductor on different Southern railroads during the war years. He often ran the line between Columbia, South Carolina, and Wilmington. This line was called the Wilmington and Manchester Railroad. The conductor was the "boss" of the line, with the engineer the "pilot." His job was to avoid collisions, keep the train in running order, and stay on schedule. Bell was exempt from serving in the military.[134]

College students were exempt if there were twenty or more students in the class. Most boys chose the military. It was difficult to keep boys age sixteen to eighteen in school. The son of Anna Fuller, Edwin, age sixteen, left school at Chapel Hill, saying he would rather be in the army than away at school.[135]

Exemptions by February of 1865: 7,885 were physically disabled; 5,589 were state officers; 400 were ministers; 5 were superintendents and doctors for the deaf, dumb, and blind; 21 were newspaper editors; 99 were newspaper employees; 31 were apothecaries; 374 were doctors; 173 were teachers; 246 were overseers and agriculturalists; 967 were railroad workers; 100 were mail contractors; 47 were drivers of postal vehicles; 342 were noncombatants; 167 were foreigners; 49 were men exempt by the War Department—totaling 16,564.[136] The *Richmond Daily Dispatch* reported information concerning the number of exempt persons in North Carolina in February 1865 as 5,121, which was the second highest of all Southern states. The number of men detailed for the Southern Express Company was eleven with eleven detailed for the telegraph company. A total of 960 were working on the railroads. Exempt mail contractors/drivers of postal coaches were listed as ninety-nine, and drivers were forty-seven. Exempt agricultural workers numbered 285, while detailed agricultural men totaled seventy-seven.

SUBSTITUTES

Men believed that those who had paid for substitutes "violated a contract and it was unconstitutional."[137] Substitutes received different amounts of money to take the place of a conscript. It was cheaper to buy a substitute earlier in the war. Person County men paid as much as two hundred to seven hundred dollars for a substitute. "On December 12, 1862 Colonel Peter Mallet received a list of names of twenty-five men who paid a total of $10,050 for the hire of substitutes." James McAden wrote on November 8, 1862, that one J.G. Franklin "succeeded in getting a substitute . . . for $1000."[138] James M. Jones paid Henry Starling fifteen hundred dollars to be his substitute. Henry received a rifle and a complete uniform. Some Statesville men paid three thousand dollars for a substitute.[139] A Harnett man could buy a substitute for four hundred dollars up until 1862, when the conscript law took effect.[140] By the next spring, the price increased as seen by this advertisement in the *Milton Chronicle*:

> Any person wanting a substitute over 45 years old can get one by applying at this office Price-$4000.[141]

The *Raleigh Standard* carried an ad that two men desired to be a substitute for twelve hundred dollars each. It is not known if anyone took up their offer. The usual going price for a substitute was from two hundred to seven hundred dollars.[142]

J. E. May, Second Regiment, encamped near Fredericksburg, Virginia, wrote to his mother:

> Ma I want you and Pa to try to get some body in Whitfords battalion to
> _____places with me. I will give fifty dollars to boot. Ma please rite to me

for I have not had a leter from home since _____ frank was home last winter
and you don't know now how glad I would be to get one. I must come to a close
for I have to rite several leters today— Your der son until death J.E. May.[143]

Apparently, he did not know how high men were paying substitutes. Silas H. Stepp in
the Seventh Cavalry wrote his wife, Eleanor, to get Ben Fortune as a substitute for him:

i rote 2 [letters] to ben to swap for mee if hee can [.] i will give my horse
to boot if i can stay amoung the mountains this summer.[144]

Stepp, unable to get a substitute, was captured in June 1864 and died in Elmira Prison
in January 1865. The wife of Captain Charles Blacknall asked him to get a substitute and
retire from the army. His reply:

If my rations are reduced to bread alone & the suffering & exposure
doubled, and the substitutes get down to ten cents a piece, I shall not employ
one, as long as others who are just as good as I am . . . .[145]

In Robeson County a soldier wrote to his brother:

. . . Dr. Williams has hired Abram Moore and Berry Godwin has hired
Wiley Sealy as substitutes. We have no more conscripts left but Oliver Rozier
and Russell and Hector McMillan and he thinks he will be exempt . . . your
affectionate brother Daniel McPhail to Angus McPhail[146]

Wilkes Morris lamented his problems securing a substitute:

Wilmington No. Ca.   April 18, 1863
Capt Geo Tait
Fort Fisher No. Ca.
Captain,
        Your communication of the 14th inst in regards to a Bounty for Mr. McPhail
at hand this morning and contents noted, I am somewhat astonished at the
Statement made by Mr. McPhail & will proceed to give you a few facts connected
with him & Myself. In the first place, on or about to 1 of Sept last I advertised
for some one over 45 yrs of age whom I might procure as a Substitute. I had
a number of Applications all of which did not suit me. Shortly afterwards Mr.
McP applied & liking his Appearance, entered into an Agreement with him.
He stated at the time that he was then a member of Capt Godwin Co A 31
N.C.T. but that his time would Expire on the 19th when if I could wait until
that time he would be pleased to go into Service for Me. The question was
asked him by Myself, if he had Served the three Months additional which was
required at that time, from all when term expired by virtue of their being under
or over age. His Answer was that he had not! A few days Afterwards an order
was received from the A&IGO ordering all persons over and under age to be
discharged at the expiration of their time for which they had engaged to serve.
Having Obtained a Copy of this order, I proceeded to Lumberton on the 27 of
Sept & had Mr. McP discharged by his Captain & had the same approved by the
General in Command (Rains). I there Saw McP & it was expressly understood
that it was my desire that he should go into the Camp of Instruction at Raleigh,
which Mr. McP agreed to, but upon the Same day I returned from Lumberton An
order was received from the Cmdg Genl of the Department (Martin) Allowing
Conscripts the priviledge of joining any Company of Heavy Artillery & Infantry
that did not Exceed one hundred men. I confirmed with the Adjutant General

at Head Quarters & his Opinion was that under this order it was not necessary for me as a Conscript to go to Raleigh, but that I could join a Company in this Disct and then could put in a Substitute. I mentioned the facts to Mr. McP who was [illegible] and Expressed a desire to join Capt. Kell's Company which was then stationed at Fort St. Phillip, As you are Aware. I applied to Capt K & he had accepted a Substitute within one month [and] could not take McP. I consequently applied to you & the matter was arranged.

Now as to the Bounty, I Expressly Stated to McP while Sitting in the passage at Head Quarters, when he asked me for the Bounty, that I would not guarantee him any Bounty, but all that I would do was to pay him $1000. His price was at first $1200—which I declined to give, & we arranged it for the $1000—I stated to McP that I would not so far as I was concerned apply for Bounty, but, if he could get it he was welcomed to it. I knew that if he went to Raleigh, he would not get any and was [uncertain whether ?] he would get any by joining your Company or not. At all events I told him I would not become responsible for it. I have Capt endeavored to give you a full History of what passed between us, & you can readily see that it would have been perfect folly in me to make McP think he would receive any Bounty after his having agreed to go to the Camp of Instruction. I did not become responsible for it, neither do I think I should pay it.

Respectfully Wilkes Morris[147]

Captain Little, the enrolling officer at Carthage, received a letter on October 19, 1863, from Lieutenant T. R. Emery:

I have made out the lists of Habeas Corpus cases, thirty-seven in no.[number] but not knowing the ages of the substitutes will post pone sending, till next mail. Major Dowd, QM wishes to detail: And[rew] Jones, Neil McIntosh, J. H. Harrington and Malcolm Blue—to haul for him. He says if not allowed Many [or Manning] wants the two first—what is to be done with John McKinnis case? You gave him [a] furlough his family is now in a terrible fix. Children all sick, wife down with rheumatism. I gave exemption till I could hear from you. What is to be done with all able bodyied men who have commissions in the Home Guard? What time, or rather when must I commence to enroll.[148]

Robert Carpenter, also from Chatham, sent a long letter home begging his father to get him a substitute:

. . . i want you to get me a Substitue if you can for ever thing i have got give all of my land 150 acres and give my horse and buggy and if that wont do give that peace of land on Buchorn 47 acres for i had rather be at home and have nothing in the world than to be her[e] and have ten Thousand Dollars i want you to attend to this if you please and i will pay for you for your trouble i had rather be at home and work for my bread daily than to be her facing the cannon balls and have fifty Thousand Dollars . . . . if that aint Anuff to get A Substitue you may go to Angiline and she will give you forty dollars and then go to uncle Elbert Patridge and tell him to pay you $160 Dollars give all the land I own and horse and buggy and two hundred . . .[149]

Carpenter said that if it didn't work to sell his land, etc., to the highest bidder and give it to his substitute. Apparently, the soldier never got someone to take his place. Dr. Thomas Fanning Wood recalled that he did not join his regiment until September 1862. He said,

My friends were expecting me, but I was not legally a soldier until I had been mustered in. There was a Jew by the name of mason Loeb who was trying to get out of the company so that he might go into some money making enterprise. He proposed that if I be enrolled on a certain day that our Capt. would be willing to sign his release, and in that event I would have his pay which had accumulated since April about $66.00. This I agreed to, and the boys were very much amused at the transaction, calling me a Jew's substitute.[150]

At the beginning of the hostilities, in Harnett County, J. Watkins hired out as a substitute for W. Gill. He remained in the army for four years and surrendered at Appomattox.[151] As the war progressed, the death toll mounted, thinning the ranks. Congress changed the age for conscription to eighteen through forty-five. Men between the ages of thirty-five to forty-five were now called up to serve. Substitutes were still legal, and the price to obtain one rose. If a substitute became disabled or was killed, the person who hired him was required to go, unless he could get another to go in his place. Dr. Richard Chambers in Robeson County bought a substitute who was sent to Fort Fisher. When the substitute's family failed to receive the bounty offered by Chambers, the soldier deserted. Conscript officers came calling for the doctor.[152] After October 1862, the second conscription act dried up all the substitutes from the first conscription. Buying substitutes was abolished by the end of December 1863.

LEGAL PROBLEMS

North Carolina had three supreme court judges and three districts. "The county courts of North Carolina were known as the Court of Pleas and Quarter Sessions." Circuit court judges held court twice a year in each county of their district.[153] From January 1863 to December 1864, the State Supreme Court handled forty-six cases, mostly on the writ of habeas corpus and military matters, mainly conscription. Citing passages from Neely's book: "The decisions of the state supreme courts were sovereign in many areas and could not be overridden. The individual justice had the power to say what the law was at least until the whole court [two other judges . . . William H. Battle and Matthias E. Manly] met for the next term. His decisions, though written alone, carried the weight and prestige of supreme court decisions . . ."[154]

The literary scholar William Robinson Jr. has noted, "The Supreme Court of North Carolina (by majority decisions) sustained the constitutionality of all provisions for compulsory military service . . ."[155] "The government's authority to raise armies was subject to various restrictions, including those which provided for the exemption of necessary state officers. State legislatures were given the power to decide which officers were needed . . . ," according to author Mitchell.[156] Mitchell continued, "The military officers were seemingly fighting a losing battle with the courts. Legal procedures caused delay even when the petitioners were remanded to the military personnel."[157] "The operation of the stay laws and the suspension of the statutes of limitation tended to reduce the number of cases," but the war brought many cases to court. Some cases were delayed until the next term, or they were moved to a different district if under hostile occupation.[158]

The chief government in Richmond never formed a supreme court, which caused diverse problems. "The failure of the Confederacy to set up a federal court of appeals in which state decisions could be reviewed was an inherent defect which contributed to the downfall of the government. The judicial interpretation given to the conscription and exemption laws by the judges of the Superior and Supreme courts in North Carolina added to the confusion, discontent, and chaos which existed in the Confederacy. The applications of the conscription and exemptions laws to individual situations resulted in constant disagreement between the military authorities and the civil courts," noted author Memory Mitchell.[159] One such case involved a minister. Samuel Curtis claimed exemption as a Baptist minister but then served as a substitute. He was arrested due to the fact that "he had given up the trade that exempted him." He sued and lost.[160] These type of cases took up the court's time and kept the male out of the army for months. Another situation is given:

> June 16, 1863 . . . . Rcd. Yours of 3 June. You assert that the state's highest court ruled that militia officers have no right to arrest deserters & thus the governor cannot expect militia officers to do the unlawful. No such decision has been made. I applied to the judges of the Supreme Court & they responded as follows. The legislature had the right to confer the power on the executive; the judges were unaware of an unpublished act in Feb 63 which gave the governor war-time rights to call out the militia for local & temporary service. This act "unquestionably confers the power upon the Governor to order out the Militia . . . and the arrest of deserters and recusant conscripts is a service of this character." Militia officers "in this time trial and danger" are to enforce the law "and the ranks of our army kept full."[161]

The statements of Judge R. M. Pearson follow:

> It concerned the case of 4 men jailed in Yadkin Co for murder; the case involved the authority of the governor to use the militia to arrest conscripts. The facts were that a "fight had taken place, between a band of recusant conscripts, and a squad of the Militia of Yadkin County who were attempting to arrest them under the order of the Governor." 2 on each side were killed. I could find no law to support the governor's authority. I consulted with Gov Vance & then with judges Battle & Manly. Mr Gilmer was a counsel for the prisoners in Salem; Mr Dobson was an associate counsel & Mr Abernathy the state's solicitor. On my way I meet [met] the sheriff of Forsythe & Capt Burnett of Stokes as stage companions; I advised Burnett to delay arresting deserters because I believed the order to arrest would be revoked in a few days, but the governor soon discovered the act authorizing him to call out the militia . . .[162]

Chief Justice of North Carolina's Supreme Court, Richmond Pearson, was "noted during the civil war years for his advocacy of the freedom of the individual as opposed to the demands and exigencies of the Confederate Government in Richmond when that authority ran low on manpower. Pearson did not hesitate to assert boldly the freedom of the person of the conscript for military service against the exactions of a desperate government and military power, as he issued writ after writ of habeas corpus in behalf of conscripted men who felt themselves aggrieved when taken to the Confederate Army against their wills."[163] Justice Pearson declared the governor had no authority to arrest deserters and that the state militia could not enforce conscription. After the Guard of Home Defense was organized in July 1863, Pearson ruled that Confederate conscription officers could not draft the Home Guard. Vance permitted Confederate officers to use the militia as a posse after Pearson's rule. Pearson's decisions were known to "undermine congressional attempts to end the privileges of purchasing substitutes." He said that:

> If the Confederate Congress could repudiate its own contracts under the war powers, it may repudiate its bonds and notes now outstanding, a renovated currency being necessary to support the army, or it may conscript all *white women* between the ages of 16 and 60 to cook and bake for the soldiers, nurse at the hospitals, or serve in the ranks as soldier, thus uprooting the foundations of society; or it may conscript the Governor, the Judges, and Legislatures of the several States, put an end to "State Rights," and erect on the ruins a "consolidated military despotism."[164]

Judge Pearson's reputation for releasing conscripts caught Jeff Davis's eye. He and his staff reviewed Pearson's decisions; and at one point, in February 1864, Pearson made the president and his assistants angry enough to arrest him.

Soldiers blamed Judge Pearson for causing desertions. In a letter from Confederate General Dorsey Pender to Major W. H. Taylor, April 1863, he wrote that a great number were deserting due to comments that appeared in the *Raleigh Standard* and rumors of Judge Pearson's decisions. General D. H. Hill drafted a letter to Governor Vance about Judge Pearson: "He is injuring the noble old state incalculably . . ."[165] Pearson declared conscription unconstitutional. The soldiers "draw the conclusion that enrolled conscripts will not be justified in resisting the law, but that those who have been held in service by law will not be arrested when they desert. I have heard . . . that the conscripts and deserters go unmolested in Yadkin County."[166]

FRAUD

The usual forwarding of requests sent this petition to Richmond's Confederate Bureau of Conscription. Assistant Adjutant C. B. Duffield answered:[167]

> April 11, 1863
> Respectfully referred to Col. Mallett for local investigation and report of facts bearing on the minds of this application. No action will be taken on this or any other petition until supported by some sworn testimony.
> The Bureau and the War Department have been some times deceived by very plausible and numerously signed petitions forwarded with favorable opinions which have afterwards been reported deceptive by the enrolling officers who originally recommended them. The general rule has been determined on to require formally authenticated evidence.
> By order of the Superintendent.[168]

Colonel Peter Mallett, commandant of conscripts in North Carolina, sent this petition back to the Bureau with a sworn testimony on May 22, 1863.

John Thompson wrote to the governor about men he knew who were not being honest about their exemption from the military: "These men pretended to make salt petre for the government but they 'don't make 12 lbs. a month.'" He knew some men who claimed to be under eighteen and over thirty-five that had lied about their age. He said he knew several men who claimed to make shoes and shoddy guns for the exemption. "There is a screw loose in the government Waggon somewhere and it ought to be examined . . . ," he stated.[169] Sergeant George Richards sent this letter to the governor's office:

> First & foremost I believe there is a collution between the Malitia Capt. & some of his favorites, with whome the most flimsey excuse is suficient to pass them over & lay them on the Shelf.
> One man by the name of John W. Rose a man of some property . . . who attempts to get out by buying an interest in a contemplated tannery . . . to avoid going into service—No mechanic himself but purely a Speculator in every sense . . .
> The next is one Marshel Broadway a very stout able young man . . . who bot out a little mail contract carried on horse-back once a week 10 or 12 miles, and he in his turn, hires another conscript one Moses Gordon . . . to ride for him . . . so this little 10 mile mail, (formerly carried by a little boy) once a week deprives the service of 2 very stout able men,

The next is one John Shute a speculator . . . who has Managed to get 2 or 3 neighbors to pretend to have him as an Overseer but realy attends to speculating & not to their business—

The next one is one John Holm, with a little sore on his leg that no one heard of before, got a certificate from a hired Physician of disability and he slips through also, The next, a pretended "Doctr" Henry Tribble who never obtained diploma or perhaps never heard a Medical lecture a man of Very limited education a near-quack, All . . . are in the little town of Monroe Union County NC.[170]

Dr. William McCanless was arrested in 1863 for hiding deserters. He also falsified papers deferring men for medical reasons.[171] An anonymous writer using only his initials wrote to Peter Mallett on October 18, 1863:

I consider it my duty to inform you of an exempt in the county of Anson [.] he has been exempt by Dr. Snowden [.] the case is a fraudulent one as all of his neighbors know he did not get any of his neighbors to sign the certificate [.] it is not every man that can get a few names to a certificate that ought to be exempt. It is time that he has a brother or two that is afflected, but he is no help to them as I and others can testify. I am a soldier and have been home and know that there is considerable dissatifaction about this case.

PS I would give my name in full but it might cause some problems if it should get out that I reported this case.[172]

You can be sure than Colonel Mallett sent a squad to investigate that report. Males from Surry County complained that suddenly men who could do their jobs alone before the war suddenly needed assistants after the conscription and exemption law was passed. To avoid service, men established drugstores claiming to be druggists, although they may have only stocked a few bottles of castor oil and even fewer bottles of pills. "In 1864 the law was changed to snare these draft dodgers by stipulating that applicants for exemption as pharmacists had to have been 'doing business as such apothecary on the tenth day of October, 1862, and had continued said business, without intermission, since that period.'"[173]

DESERTERS

An outlyer, or outlier, was a man who refused to serve in the military because of his anti-secession beliefs, religious beliefs, or antigovernment beliefs and left home to hide from authorities. Another definition goes to those men who were once in the Confederate Army, then left for whatever reason, being AWOL. Some outliers lived in caves while others wandered about from place to place with only a quilt and rifle. A lucky few avoided the draft for years. At times, these outliers joined others and roved as a band of brothers. At one time, this number swelled to five hundred outlaws. These ruffians killed others to avoid capture, or sometimes it was just to avenge the death of relative. Some men were lucky not to get caught while snubbing their nose at conscription officers. Daniel Squires and Gideon Bray were able to cultivate their farms for the entire war, hiding when the agents came around. To keep their sons out of the army, some older men bribed the agents with whiskey or money.[174]

The community looked unfavorably toward a deserter. Churches would expel members, either black or white, who fled to Union lines or if they deserted from the Confederate Army. The Mount Carmel Baptist Church took a dim view of deserters. In April 1864, the church voted John H. Renfro out of the membership for desertion. The church supported loyal soldiers by collecting money for the troops' spiritual needs. Renfro petitioned for reinstallation of his membership in October of 1865 but was rejected. The church also expelled runaway slaves. Delilah, Jack, and Bill—slaves belonging to N. J. Taylor—couldn't return to the membership.[175]

Jonathan Worth proclaimed that by mid-1862, rebel deserters, unionists, and scouts formed up; and they were ready to destroy the railroad tracks and would burn the bridges. By that December, the hunt was on for deserters. The adjutant general's office in Raleigh wrote one militia colonel to do just that. It was one of many of their jobs and the most dreaded:

> Arrest & send to Camp Holmes the following men from your county; should they have left the county, ascertain where they have gone . . . John Medlin—about 6 foot, 175-180 lbs, about 24, fair skin with light hair; Eben A. Helms—5'8", fair skin, light hair, age 22, three fingers off his left hand, about 160 lbs; Hilburn Hasley—5'6" to 5'10", 150 lbs, 22 yrs old, freckled face, light hair, round shoulders; Calvin Williams—5'10", 150 lbs, boy faced-rather down look, round shoulders, swarthy complexion, dark hair . . . These men are deserters and have used force against those attempting to arrest them. You will use every effort to arrest them.[176]

The usual rate for a captured deserter was thirty dollars. An adjutant wrote a militia officer: "When deserters are arrested and placed in jail, the Confederate States will pay the jail fees. I would prefer that they be brought to the Camp at this place, where the thirty dollars will be paid including expenses, except transportation."[177] A notice appeared in the newspaper:

> $100 Reward for the capture of John Medlin, a conscript, who deserted two months ago. The said was from Union County and is charged with the murder of Lt. Hosea Little of the 82nd Militia. He jumped the train at Company Shops and was in handcuffs. By order of Gov. Vance and John C. Winder, AAG[178]

The reward for Medlin's capture was higher than most deserters, perhaps because he had killed the officer. Further information said that Medlin left Camp Lee near Richmond. He was described as above. Medlin was later captured, tried in court, then convicted in November 1864.

Officers continued to post rewards for deserters. The *Daily Journal*, a Wilmington newspaper, read:

> The following men have deserted from here [Clarendon Iron Works]. Militia and other officers are requested to arrest them: P. Kennedy, moulder; J. Parker, machinist.[179]

From the *Greensboro Patriot*, January 8, 1863:

REWARD

I will give One Hundred Fifty dollars for the apprehension and delivery to me of the following deserters; or Thirty dollars for each one: JAMES POWERS, HOWELL BARHAM; JOHN ALRED; DANIEL CLAPP; HENRY REAVES. I will also pay the same reward for all members of my company who are not on proper furlough.

Captain J. Albert Hooper, Co. E, 22nd Regt.

From the *Daily Journal*, December 26, 1863:

NOTICE

William J. Ward is a deserter from my Company, I will pay $30 reward for his apprehension and confinement in the Military in Wilmington, N.C. He is probably in Columbus County, but lived in Bladen when enlisted.

John T. Melvin,
Capt. Commanding, Co. I
36th N.C.T.

From the *Carolina Watchman*, June 15, 1863:

A reward of thirty dollars ($30) will be paid for the arrest, and safe delivery of every deserter, from the Confederate States Army, at this post, or fifteen dollars for the arrest, and safe confinement, of any deserter, in any jail, of the different counties, so they can be secured by the Military Authorities.[180]

Deserters when caught got thirty-nine lashes, branded on the left hand with the letter *D*, or other types of punishment. Certain ones got hard labor with a ball and chain around the ankle or not. Likely, soldiers may receive prison time or a death sentence. Each deserter was handled differently. Private James King with the Fourth Regiment was executed on January 30, 1864. The provost marshal, Lieutenant Goff, informed Colonel Grimes of his last words:

After bandaging his eyes . . . I . . . asked him if he had any messages he desired to send to his relatives or friends. He replied, "I have no message. I only wish that my body may be sent to my friends, but I want to say to you, Lieutenant, though others persuaded me to do what I did, the reading of Holden's Papers has brought me to this . . ."[181]

It would be a shock to many soldiers accused of desertion when they didn't make it back to camp after their furlough had expired. Sometimes the first they had heard of it was when the provost knocked on their door. Other times, they heard it from a friend or neighbor or in the newspaper like the above. Period newspapers were full of letters to the editor defending their honor when accused of desertion. At times, it was merely a mistake. The soldier had the legal papers to prove he was not AWOL, and he explained this publicly. Reputation was at stake. To be blamed of desertion brought shame to the soldier, his family, and the community. Isabelle McDonald confessed her shame in a letter to Governor Vance:

Rushes mills, Montgomery County
Governor vance i have the impodence to rite to you a bout my son he was in the state salt works he wasent conscripted before he went nor inroled he was their a 11 months he was take[n] of[f] last june 1864 as a deserter which dont belong to our ginerations . . . nothing has greaved me more in this lif[e] then taken him of in that way we are all vance peple in this neighborhood and I hope you will do something for my son or give som directions how to get him back a gane to the salt works . . .[182]

The governor wrote across the letter with these words, "It will be impossible now to get him back to the works—We have more hands there now than are required. ZBV"

What makes a man want to desert? The reasons are many. "The war . . . fueled animosity between the classes," said one. "Laborers and workers couldn't afford substitutes to serve in the war," said another.[183] Most working men hated the "Twenty Negro Law" part of the Exemption Act. The suppression of their civil liberties caused men to revolt. Those who had volunteered felt that disloyal men conscripted into the Confederate army would choose to run the first chance they could. Some soldiers only left the ranks long enough to go home, plant or harvest the crops, then return to their units. Oftentimes, it was the wife who pleaded for her husband to come home.

When did desertion start? Different historians argue this point. In the *Raleigh Standard*, a "Wanted for Desertion" posted on January 22, 1862, appeared for twenty-three-year-old Thomas Pleasant Myers, who ran away from Camp Mangum in Raleigh on December 25, 1861. A volunteer who failed to show for his medical exam and training camp was considered a deserter. So desertions started before conscription and continued throughout the hostilities. Paul Escott proclaimed "a strong feeling against the conscript law among the uninformed part of the citizens" was the main reason men ran to the woods and became outlaws and murderers. "So hostile was public opinion that deserters 'always had many more active friends than they [the militia officers] had' and could always get timely information of every movement to arrest them and so avoid it. Now the citizens 'readily conceal the murderers and convey intelligence to them,' and loyal men feared that it would be 'exceedingly difficult' to capture them, even with a large force."[184]

A few soldiers "went home to see their families" in the fall of October 1862. Caught by the provost and sent to Camp Hanes, they wrote Governor Vance about their predicament and asked his pardon. The letter was signed by eight men:

> . . . Mr. Vance, I am absent from my command [by?] a vote [.] [We] left and I am sorry that I done so. It is the first offense I ever was guilty of and if you will pardon me and send me to my command, I never will do so no more. I come hom to see my family. I didn't come to get shed of the war. I come to provide for my family and I am here under guard at this time. I didn't lie out in the woods to escape from being taken up. I will wait for your Dispatches. Yours respectfully,
> James Rhodes, Benjamin Loveless, Drewey Green, Albert Toney, Gilford [J]Ones, Calvin [J]Ones, Thomas Camell, Henry Ramsey.[185]

As the war drew on, depredations, high taxes, and food shortages at home caused soldiers to desert. Their loyalty turned more to home after receiving alarming news from loved ones left behind. Unionists complained that the secesh people were hoarding salt from them, and it was done to punish them.[186] Perhaps the soldier felt the necessity to go home and protect his family. "Some soldiers no doubt deserted because they thought their families desperately needed them, but most of them deserted because they no longer had any faith in a losing cause," was the belief of the Eller family in Wilkes County.[187]

Private Jesse Hill with the Twenty-first Regiment said in his weekly letters home in 1864 that if the men didn't get better rations, they were going "to take a walk" in the spring. He complained of starvation, not being paid, and rough duty and said other men always talked about doing the same. The daily ration doled out in 1864 was three-fourths pound of meat, sometimes pickled beef, or fat-back, and one-fourth pound of salt. Hill relayed that he only got four crackers most of the time in place of meat. The troops rarely received coffee and sugar. Hill did go AWOL for two months but returned to his unit without severe punishment. For more of his comments, read the chapter on soldiers' letters.[188]

Cary Whitaker informed his brother:

> . . . I think the people as well as the Government ought to make extra efforts to feed and clothe the soldiers, for if our soldiers were well clothed and fed I don't believe there would be one tenth of the desertions then. If the

Yankees were fed and clothed as we are they wouldn't have an army a month, while if our army received their treatment, we would seldom have a deserter. Though I have a pretty good character for veracity at home, my friends would hardly believe me if I were to tell of the destitution and suffering I have seen in the army—when in the Valley of Va, the snow on the ground, I have seen soldiers with their pants worn off up to their hips, and nothing but an old pair of drawers on, worn out and exposing the person in many places—and still were I to go to Halifax [NC] and point out this in the most glowing colors I would hardly get a dozen pairs of pants for the very army which is now keeping the enemy from their homes and firesides . . .[189]

Public opinion regarding conscription and desertion played heavily upon those left at home and those in service. Letters to and from soldiers and their families reveal the anguish tormenting them:

North Carolina Robeson County May 24th 1863
        Dear Brother . . . We would be glad to see you come home but do not wish you to desert for the Militia officers and a company of soldiers are under orders engaged in this County hunting up deserters and conscripts . . . It is a needy time. I did not make enough [crops] by some right smart. I am about out of corn and it is hard to get but it seems that I cannot come down to see you. Though if you can see any safe chance I would be very glad of anything [money] you can spare me if you can send it by safe hands.[190]

Julia Gwyn wrote her uncle that "some women write to their husbands to leave the army and come home and that's the reason that so many of them are deserting."[191] Women at home begged their husbands to come home only to help with the harvest, or perhaps they had a dying child. As many wives encouraged their husbands to leave, other women would not stand for the dishonor of a deserter. Thomas Price, with the Fifty-sixth Regiment, Rutherford County, talked of deserting:

        Sarah, that is the one time I think you did not tell the truth. I know if you want to see me as bad as I want to see you that you would not care how I get home. I never did like the thoughts of running away, but I don't intend to stay much longer without coming home and though you don't like it, can let it alone. You don't know anything about our fare here. If you did you would not say anything about not running away, Sarah. I expect to come home while I am able and then I will tell you the news in full.[192]

Private Elroy Helsabeck didn't give a reason why some men in his company deserted in September of 1862:

        A great many are gone to the hospital and some have run away. Our company is getting small, nine run away last night, among the rest George W. Bowman and A.M. Ling out of our tent. We will have more room now and not so many to cook for.[193]

T. L. Morrison, encamped near Fredericksburg, wrote home on April 13, 1863, that men were deserting and that some were liable to get shot. "It looks like its death to stay and death to try to get home, so I will stay an doo the best I can."[194] John Futch wrote his wife, Martha, that "I would like to come home. But I do not know when I get the chance to come again. But I am going to come before long if I have to runaway to do it."[195] Desertions increased the summer of 1863, after Gettysburg.

Two sisters writing later that summer said that people were despondent over desertions. One agreed with a correspondent of the *Richmond Enquirer* "that Holden ought to be burned to death and his ashes sent to Boston and Philadelphia."*

"Something it seems to me ought certainly be done to prevent such incalculable injury as the influence of his paper is said to produce," said Emilie Tillinghast.[196] In his letters, Colonel William Lowrance said, "It is disgraceful 'pease' sentiment spoken of by the *Standard*. Some-thing should be done; every effort should be made to overhaul them, and everyone should be shot. Let us hope to check it now, for if this should pass by unnoticed, many more will soon follow."[197]

General J. J. Pettigrew sent a letter to Governor Vance regarding desertion. He said:

> A certain class of soldiers is influenced by this condition of public opinion. They are told, as you can see by the letters, that they can desert with impunity; that the militia officers will not do their duty. I write this to you because you are the only person in the State having sufficient influence . . . to reform matters.[198]

In midsummer of 1863, General Lee was notified of the thousands of absent men in the ranks. He issued an order in August granting amnesty to the soldiers if they returned to the ranks. Lee wrote the president the reason behind the order, and President Davis approved it.[199] Perhaps the next soldier took advantage of General Lee's amnesty proclamation:

> January 22, 1864, Pine level, Johnston Cty.
> Mr. Z.B. Vance, Sir,
>   I wil now Send to you by my Father for you to accomdate me so far as to send me papers that will Return me to my Regt. Without any punishment [.] I wil now State to you my name an Regiment and company H.F. Peedin Co. C 50th Regt N.C. Troops [.] when my Regt left the Eastern part of N C, an went to Georgia I was left sick at Wilson Hospital an Remaind thare one month and was to Report to my Regiment, when at the same time Being Barefooted and Badly clothed goin within sixteen miles of home I Come home after Some Shoose and clothes [.] I have bin absent without leaf 20 dais [.] I have bin Rite at home an is now a having chills Evry other day [.] Ples send me those papers to Return to my Regt.[200]

A dozen North Carolinians left one night, taking their rifles along. They were challenged near Bowling's Landing in Virginia, whereby a skirmish ensued. Two deserters were killed, others wounded, as was the arresting officer who died soon after. Ten Tar Heels from the Third Regiment were taken to Castle Thunder in Richmond.[201] All were found guilty at trial, and the order came down to return them to their regiment for the entire brigade to witness the mass execution by a firing squad. Rev. George Patterson, Third Regiment chaplain, stayed with the condemned until the appointed time.[202] Two privates, George Black and Jeremiah Blackburn, convicted deserters, were executed due to repeated desertion. Previously, Blackburn had shot off one of his fingers to keep from serving, but he was forced to work in the hospital. He made a stupid move when he forged furlough papers for himself for "1000 days."[203]

———————————

As different classes of people mixed while dealing with war contingences, the upper class were appalled at the actions of lower-class people. They seemed to blame the problems on

———————————

*   W. W. Holden, editor of the *Raleigh Standard*, had a platform as a unionist and was blamed by soldiers as well as loyal citizens as fomenting disaffection among the general public.

these type persons who had Union sympathies and owned no slaves. "The disunity and class hostility that emerged in wartime horrified North Carolina's elite. The wartime behavior of many yeomen confirmed the gentry's deepest fears about the character of the masses the mob."[204] A lady described traveling to a teaching job in Charlotte as formidable at best:

> About a dozen came up this way [via train] to Lenoir: two young snuff dipping ladies; plenty of deserters had destroyed a hotel room. Twenty-five hardened bed bugs having a supper on me in one hour and in the morning the list had increased to at least 50,000.[205]

Bandits roamed like Robin Hood, robbing the rich for the have-nots. The inner war was very difficult to put down. "Support for deserters, draft resisters, food rioters, and bandits became so substantial among the lower classes that some local leaders feared a—loss of control," wrote author Escott.[206] Another researcher has said, "Desertion takes place because desertion is encouraged . . . and though the ladies may not be willing to concede the fact, they are nevertheless responsible . . . for the desertion in the army and the dissipation in the country."[207] In many instances, "popular sympathy with war resisters was blocking the enforcement of the laws."

Whites and coloreds combined to form gangs intent on robbing the countryside. The Lowry gang from Robeson County stole from their wealthy neighbors and distributed it to the poor.* Several gangs used Fort Hamby in Wilkesboro as their base to commit depredations. It was reported that eighty-five deserters from Wilkes and adjoining counties gathered at Fort Hamby. The leaders of this gang, Wade and Lockwood, were deserters from U.S. General Stoneman's cavalry. The Wilkesboro *Journal-Patriot* reported these men to have the best army rifles.[208] Deserters near Brunswick County fled to the Green Swamp in wartime. Today it is known as Soldier Bay.[209] The Dover Swamp and the Great Dismal Swamp in the East hid both runaway slaves and men escaping conscription or those who had deserted.

About midwar, the residents still had not come to terms with the insurrection. White women left alone on the farm especially fell into this category. There were few white men in the neighborhoods, and females feared for their lives, even writing to the governor about the situation. A measure proposed to exempt overseers on white women's farms where no white male was present failed to pass. Vigilantes sprang up to protect those left at home, especially women. Women living near these areas crawling with gangs had every reason to be afraid. The South was a place without men. Most were away at the war.[210] A woman from Richmond County wrote the governor that he needed to send soldiers to protect the women from an anticipated Negro revolt since all that were left were a few old white men. She said there was not a "young white man for ten miles."[211] Federal prisoners on the march to Salisbury Prison commented on the lack of men they saw. "The women along the road . . . treated us very kindly waving their handkerchiefs to us. Men are so scarce. I counted eighteen women at three houses and not a man to be seen."[212]

Feeding a deserter or helping him in any way was illegal. Local authorities could prosecute citizens for assisting their relatives. Sixty-seven-year-old Susan Flora, a widow and Union woman, used her home to hide deserters. Sarah Bailey did also, in addition to dressing her son-in-law in female clothes when the Southern agents came around. Mrs. Louisa Stiles was another who provided aid to Union sympathizers. Rebel soldiers "put ropes round the necks of her children and threatened to lynch them if she did not stop her activities."[213] Federal raids, along with pillaging guerillas in western North Carolina, forced desperate women to write to the governor requesting protection or to send guns so that they could protect themselves:

---

*   Lowry is spelled three different ways, Lowery, and Lowrie.

Please order out the militia of Rutherford, or send ammunition and arms
to supply the ladies and we, for the name of the Old North State, will defend
their homes for them.[214]

Perhaps she had met up with George Shuttles. He had killed Mr. Ben Washburn, "an old
and respectable citizen . . . the act was unprovoked."[215] In Montgomery County a notorious
deserter and thief named Riley Cagle murdered an old man named Simmons. This time, he
was caught, tried, convicted, then shot.[216] J. F. Woodard of Alexander County met up with
deserters who killed him. The Davie County Home Guard lost a member, Mr. Glasscock, when
deserters came to his home to rob him.[217] It was necessary in some highland communities
to form a vigilante force to curtail the continuing murders and lawlessness. Men felt they
still had to retaliate previous outrages. Former soldiers made up this force.[218] Despite all
they did, the outnumbered Home Guard and local militia lost control. Many bushwhackers
were never brought to justice. Killings or retaliations were still going on the spring of 1865
after Lee's and Johnston's surrender. Washington Miller was one such person murdered in
May of 1865.[219]

Jim Taylor has said that 20 percent of deserters captured in the mountains were
from other states. One researcher piped, "Gov Vance estimated that more than 1200 men
were holed up in the Blue Ridge by the end of 1862."[220] The area between Greeneville,
Tennessee, and Shelton Laurel was commonly known as "a general resort and hiding place
for outlaws."[221] "Deserters from both armies roamed through the mountain sections, and
the people of Henderson County were frequently terrorized by men passing over what
was known as the under-ground railway. Such travel was by stealth and in a surreptitious
manner, but one route passing from Bat Cave through Hendersonville, along which men
found their way to East Tennessee and Kentucky."[222] Traphill in the north part of Wilkesboro
became known as a place where the outliers hid. Tories raised a U.S. flag over a building
there.

Confederate General W. D. Pender wrote to Major W. H. Taylor in 1863 concerning
deserters:

. . . the whole trouble lies in the fact that they believe when they get into
Nor. Car. they will not be molested, & their belief is based upon the dictum of
Judge [RM] Pearson, chief justice of the State, in a recent trial of persons who,
killed some militia officers while in the discharge of their duties.[223]

"Keith and Malinda [Blalock] knew men who even dressed in women's clothing as they
worked their land." If such a person was suspect, the Home Guard would search them.[224] In
Yadkin County, deserters killed two magistrates. Another man recorded,

Times had got so a man could scarcely pas the Mulberry road without
being robbed. Numerous houses have been plundered. A few of the
bushwhackers have been shot in Alleghany . . . I must tell you a little about our
fight with the bushwhackers in Wilkes but I suppose that David Pugh has given
you a full history as he was one that participated.[225]

He went on to tell that he was carrying the ammo, so he did not fire. "The Alleghany
boys fought like heroes." None from their group was hurt. Captain J. C. McRae in the
mountains notified his commander (Mallett) that the Ninth and Tenth districts was overrun
with Tories and deserters who robbed soldiers' wives, disarmed citizens, and constantly
pillaged the communities. He asked for the regular military to intervene. Likewise, Colonel
G. W. Lay notified authorities that he had found these rogues roaming in bands of fifty to
one hundred plus in Randolph, Catawba, Yadkin, Cherokee, and Wilkes Counties.[226] William
Henry belonged to the militia. His wife wrote in her journal about deserters near Asheville:

Eleven soldiers eat supper here. They are part of a detail from the 25th Reg. to get up deserters. I heard that a little boy named Jones was taken up today. He was carrying news. Some money, 1900$ was found in the pad of the saddle, also a letter. He was carrying news to Tenn., to Wiley & Doc Jones, both tories.[227]

C.S. General Robert Hoke was sent to the Sixth, Seventh, and Ninth Congressional districts to quell the Tories, recusant conscripts, and deserters in the summer of 1863 with about three thousand troops.[228]

"The Confederacy employed a new and controversial tactic to pry men from the hills. The Rebels rounded up the families of the men [outliers] and threw them in jail." Females and their children were put in jail without sustenance. "Then word was sent out that whenever the men decided to give themselves up, their families would be released." This ploy worked but would not be tolerated today.[229] "In the same county, the wife of Unionist Thomas S. Runnion was warned by Confederate raiders that 'if she didn't leave they would burn the house and her in it . . .'" Reversing the situation, "pro-Confederate women in Cherokee County were threatened with death by Unionists and deserters firing guns near their homes," noted author McKinney.[230]

You could not trust a woman in the mountains. Thomas Lenoir and a group of soldiers hunting deserters said that a "woman guiding them broke out in a song signaling their arrival to the waiting Tories. There were about ten of the enemy, not three, and they killed one of their pursuers and forced the others to flee for help." He did not say if the woman was punished.[231] A mountain resident wrote:

> They have terrible state of things upon the Tennessee line particularly in Watauga [County]. There is band of robbers and villains who are constantly plundering the people in the night, when resolute and prepared they succeed in driving them off, but a man is occasionally killed on either side. Some ten days go they attacked the house of Paul Farthing—his brother Young being there. They resisted and fired upon them out of the house and skirmish ensued.[232]

Thomas Farthing was shot through the heart when he chased them with a gun. "They go in bands of 12-14." The same gang robbed Mr. Evan's home of about five hundred dollars while holding his wife at bay. Norwood continued:

> The men who have heretofore avoided the fight and by coming forward at this crisis and encouraging the remaining conscripts and deserters might restore confidence [,] are increasing the difficulty by crying out for peace which means submission.[233]

Elijah F. Case was conscripted, served a while, apparently disappeared, then was found serving with the Federals.[234] About thirty-two hundred men served with the Union Army. A soldier at Camp Vance in Morganton mentioned to his father that while rounding up deserters, a man was shot dead for running from them in Rutherford County. For unknown reasons, Private Miles Dobbins, a deserter, killed Soloman Sparks in Yadkin County. Governor Vance asked the secretary of war to let another soldier who had witnessed the killing for a brief furlough so that he could be a witness at the trial.[235] When conscription officers came calling in Alamance County, Michael McPherson would not divulge where his son was hiding, so he was strung up and hanged till dead.[236]

PIEDMONT AND DOWN EAST DESERTERS

The Rockingham Ladies Society "passed a strongly worded resolution condemning a problem which had been largely accepted during the Revolutionary War but which, in 1863, had become a far more serious concern to the Confederate Army." That problem was desertion. The resolution read in part:

> Resolved, that we, the Ladies of Rockingham, do hereby pledge . . . our united efforts to induce all able men who have absented themselves from the service . . . to hasten back to their camps.
> We deeply commiserate the families of the miserable deserters, who have . . . forfeited the esteem of all good men, and heaped contumely and disgrace upon the heads of their families.[237]

A newspaper reported:

> A man dresses in women's apparel *minus* the hoop, was detected and arrested in this place [Greensboro] . . . he was traveling in company of a woman, and represented himself as a Georgian, a deserter from Virginia . . . the short skirt left exposed a huge foot, while the countenance which he disported was not so angelic as is supposed to belong to nymphs—or even our own country women . . . he was sent off [to prison].[238]

Early on, men in the eastern counties volunteered to become Partisan Rangers, which was different from the Home Guard. They were told they would only serve in certain counties in the eastern part of the state and that they would never have duty beyond North Carolina's borders. Colonel Nethercutt was in charge. Many complaints arrived at the governor's desk about these rangers. Apparently, they were committing depredations on citizens of Union sentiment. This notice was printed in the *Raleigh Register*:

> Responsible parties in North Carolina, having reported that many entering the Partisan Rangers' service or professing to enter it, with the expectation of staying about their homes and always beyond cannon shot of the enemy; notice is hereby given, that all enrolled men in the district are subject to orders from these headquarters; and that more active duty will be required of the Partisans than of other soldiers. When the orders for more active service are not promptly complied with, the Partisan companies will be disbanded and enrolled as conscripts.[239]

Randolph County, the hotbed of anti-secessionists, had fifty or more deserters avoiding conscription as early as October 1862. Four Randolph men wrote to General Holmes that they needed the help of the Senior Reserves to catch the horse-stealing outlaws. Unionist John Hedrick had the solution for deserters. He said, "The way deserters and refugees are treated is to put them in prison until they are willing to volunteer in the Union Army."[240]

Vance had sent Confederate soldiers three times to squash the rebellion in those counties. This alleviated the problems temporarily. These veterans skirmished and were able to capture one hundred raiders, killing several. In response to Vance's request for military force to squelch the roving bands of deserters and desperadoes in the mountains, General Lee sent General Robert Hoke and his troops. Even though this regiment captured about thirty-five hundred outlaws, the peaceful situation was short-lived.[241] One month before, conscript troops had to be sent to Chatham County to hunt deserters; the next month, Confederate troops sought deserters in Laurel Valley [Madison County]. In the last eight weeks of the war, General Lee sent five hundred troops to capture deserters in Chatham and Moore counties. His orders cautioned soldiers "to take no prisoners among those deserters who resist with arms . . ."[242]

While researching Down East, the word "Buffaloes" kept emerging. Historian Fred Mallison gives the best description of the phrase:

> . . . . the term Buffalo becoming a generic name for those who avoided Confederate service and Civilian Buffaloes can be divided into two classes. The first—and worst—were those who refused military service on either side, hid out in the woods and swamps, and preyed on the inhabitants of isolated farms and homesteads. They were bushwhackers, thieves, and scoundrels who enjoyed living wild. The second and larger class was the non-violent fiscal Buffaloes. They traded between the lines under Union permits, or sold their services to the Northerners after Federal troops occupied parts of the state.

Confederate troops were ordered to hunt down the Buffaloes and shoot to kill. In searching for these men, they came upon a house full of women. "They said they didn't know where the men were, and didn't know anything about the shooting [of a warning]. They told this like they were in good practice; we soon formed out it as no use to depend on them for information." In one neighborhood, Company I captured a young boy and strung him up to get information. The boy changed his mind and told them what he knew. One captured Buffalo said the men hiding would move around continually. Another man, who said his name was White, surrendered and said he belonged to the Thirty-second Regiment.[243]

One man resisting the draft hid in a hollow tree, fed by his wife for weeks; another hid out under the henhouse, where he had dug into the ground. One escaped into an abandoned mine for months, making shoes to pass the time.[244] Peter Edwards said his relative Jonathan Edwards hid from conscript officers by digging out a cave in the muddy banks of the Neuse River. When the water level was low, he commenced the work, digging out a room in the clay above the water level much like a muskrat. Seasonal rains raised the river to where the entrance couldn't be seen. Once, he was almost caught in his home. He jumped out the window and ran to the river. The soldiers shot at him and would have killed him except that he jumped behind a tree before he dived into the river.[245] In another instance, cousins writing to each other discussed the desertion problem: "Those that are at home have a trying time arround here hunting deserters [.] I think I would rather be in the army than to have to hunt those unfortunate men that are in the woods [.] they seemed determined on their own ruin or they would not stay in the woods now . . ."[246]

A newspaper gave notice of the conduct of Southern troops operating in the piedmont:

OUTRAGES BY THE MILITARY

We published in our last the resolutions introduced by Mr. McKay, of Harnett, denouncing the conduct of a squad of Confederate troops in burning a house in that County, and requesting the Governor to call out any portion of the military force of the State to prevent such wanton and lawless destruction of property . . . . It seems that this squad of soldiers required the wife of a deserter to tell where her husband was, and because she refused to do so, or, not knowing, could not tell, they set fire to her house and burnt it to the ground. We learn that Gov. Vance has very promptly and properly had these soldiers arrested, and we suppose they will be held to answer for their conduct.

In the course of the debate on the subject Dr. McCormick, of Harnett, said that the proof of this wanton destruction of property was ample, and he urged the house to take prompt action, so as to warn evil doers against such conduct. He said he was determined to insist at all hazards on the rights guaranteed to his constituents by the Bill of Rights, and to see to it . . . that those rights were not trampled on with impunity. He said he had it from good authority that preparations had been made to burn the house of another citizen of his county, thus showing a disposition to make these outrages more general.

Dr. McCormick and Mr. McKay deserve the thanks of their constituents for the firm and determined manner in which they have asserted their rights.

No citizen is disposed to obstruct or embarrass the military authorities in their efforts to arrest deserters. But nothing will justify the destruction of property, whether belonging to the innocent or the guilty. It is the business of the officers who command our troops to protect, not to harass and oppress the people. No deserter, unless in the act of resisting, should be shot without a trial; and the families of deserters ought not to be punished on account of the guilt of the deserters. But we have heard, and fear it is true, that horses have been taken from the plow, provisions seized and carried away, and even the fathers and mothers of deserters roped around the neck and hung up until life was in jeopardy, because they could not or would not tell where the deserter was.

We have heard also that these cruelties, together with the arrest of citizens on the charge of disloyalty because they had attended public meetings, have depressed and alarmed the people in many localities in the western part of this State, insomuch that they were deterred from going to the polls and exercising the right of suffrage at the late elections; while the *domestic detectives*-certain Destructives-who are regarded by certain officers as the only *true* men, and who are swift to give false information against their Conservative neighbors, went to the polls with their heads up, and voted.

We repeat, deserters must be arrested and sent to their regiments, and all proper steps to this end should be sanctioned and commended; but no military officer has a right to order the destruction of property, or the personal punishment of a citizen, or even the arrest of a citizen without civil process, or the death of a deserter without trial, unless the deserter is in a state of resistance or rebellion. *This is a government of Christian people, upheld by reason and based on LAW;* and every wanton, cruel, illegal, unconstitutional act by the military, tends to array our people against the government.

It is the interest as well as the duty of military officers to act in such a way as to make the people love, not hate the government. If they love it, they will die for it if necessary; but if they hate it, it will perish, and with it our independence.[247]

A large group of deserters hid out near Buckhorn Branch. Jake James helped to try to capture these. Deserters killed one civilian named Isaac Rochelle.[248] Other stories of deserters continue: "One of my neighbors was shot dead last night (.) He was a deserter and ran and a very low man shot him dead."[249] A tunnel was dug under a house in Davie County to the woods near Dutchman's Creek to hide men from conscription or for deserters. Abner Glasscock, the provost marshal of the Home Guard—warned not to travel to the Northern part of the county—rode there and was ambushed by unknown persons.[250] The *Fayetteville Observer* announced:

> **DARING OUTRAGE** . . . We learn that some of the armed white men with guns went yesterday to the home of the late Lt. Argus Shaw, entered, & rifled in the house while the family was absent at church after fighting off a Negro woman.[251]

In Person County, the Home Guard, when they went to hunt deserters, found themselves brawling with the women there:

> I had to go last week to Roxboro, to hunt Deserters but we caught none [.] I tell you some of the women the other side of Roxbor know how to use profane language. Maleuris[?] Webb tried his hand with them but they soon backed him out.[252]

Politicians in the South tried to direct their (citizens') anger away from the government by repeating the fear of racial equality if the North won. Equally, it was hard to maintain order within the state. Blacks and whites cavorted together to rob and terrorize people. In Randolph County, a woman complained, "Our negroes are nearly all in league with the deserters." In another instance, a refugee from Wilmington reported the same type rogue band on her trip to Fayetteville. Nearby residents formed a posse to rid the area of the marauders.[253]

J. B. Harriss, the notorious Confederate conscription officer in Robeson County, was hated by both white and Indians and "feared by all who knew him . . . . he was the 'roughest of his class, overbearing and abusive' to the Indians, and he was 'charged with being too familiar with the wives and daughters of his customers . . .'"[254] Briefly mentioned earlier, the Lowrie gang of Robeson County did not start out as deserters. Brantly Harriss, in January 1865, murdered two Lowrie brothers who had been conscripted to work on Fort Fisher's fortifications. The Lowries received a furlough and were on their way home when Harriss had them arrested as deserters. There had apparently been a feud prewar between the Harriss family and the Lowries. Harriss and others started with the two Indians on their way to Moss Neck depot. The Lowrie boys were slain before they reached the station. "A warrant was issued for Harriss' arrest and placed in the hands of Sheriff [Reuben] King on Friday." By Sunday, Harriss had been shot, most likely by the Henry B. Lowrie family.[255]

Robberies previously happened at night, and the gang attempted to hide their identity. In the winter of the last year of war, the Lowries' mob did not care if anyone recognized them. The gang plundered the farm of neighbor John McNair, who had befriended the Indians, giving them wages for work performed on his farm. Mrs. Alex Bullard, home alone with five children, found the men to bust in and pillage her home. Also robbed of their guns, wine, clothes, horses, etc., were Richard Townsend and his sister-in-law, Mrs. Jackson Townsend. The month of February 1865 was especially troubling for the citizens of Robeson. Numerous families were robbed by the gang.*[256]

As the war progressed, the ranks thinned due to the three *D*s—death, disease, and desertion; however, captured Confederate soldiers may have decided to revert to the Union rather than go to prison. Writing her parents during the war, a Northern lady who was a nurse on the *Knickerbocker* said:

> Four hundred prisoners just arrived by the railway from General Porter's command. They were nearly all North Carolinians—fine-looking men, well fed, and in good spirits. One man wanted to buy one of our tin cups; I laughed, and gave it to him. Another asked Dr. Ware to change a ten-dollar Confederate note, and expected ten of our dollars for it. Dr. Ware said: "If we beat you, what good will those notes be to you?" "Oh!" said he, "the United States Government will take them." General Van Vliet told me that a great many of these men had asked to take the oath of allegiance.[257]

Since so many of North Carolinians were in the Army of Northern Virginia, General Lee wrote personally to Governor Vance on February 24, 1865:

> Desertions are becoming very frequent and there is reason to believe that they are occasioned to considerable extent by letters written to the soldiers by their friends at home.[258]

---

*   Homes robbed belonged to Henry Bullock Jr.; Mrs. Martha Ashley and David Townsend, Esq.; Daniel Baker, McKay Sellers; William Sellers; Robert McKenzie; Mrs. Dr. Neil McNair, who had a wounded Confederate soldier recuperating at her home (both fired pistols at the raiders); Dougald McCallum, John McCallum, Robert Graham, John Purcell; and Robert Graham and his daughter. In March of 1865, the house of Joseph Thompson was rifled.

A week later, John Breckinridge, secretary of war, also wrote the governor in regard to desertion among North Carolina's troops. The very next day, Vance answered General Lee's letter:

Raleigh, March 2, 1865
General R.E. Lee:
    Dear Sir: Yours has been received, giving me the distressing intelligence of the increase of desertion from our armies. I had heard from other sources of this defection of our troops and was already too well aware that the cause of it was to be found in the general public despondency. I inaugurated a series of public meetings in this State, by my recent proclamation for the purpose of receiving public sentiment, and though many have been held and many more will be held, yet the near and triumphant approach of the enemy has so alarmed the timid and so engrossed the loyal in preparation for his coming, that I fear they will hardly have their proper effect. I have myself been so busy in trying to organize my militia and secure my vast public stores that I have only been able to address the people at two or three points. Rest assured, however, general, that I am fully alive to the importance of the crisis, and whatever man can do in my situation shall be done. I shall now order out in every county that class of the home guard not subject to duty in the field, and put them to work arresting deserters. In many counties, however, they are necessarily inefficient from the great number of the deserters and the natural fear of the destruction of their property, &c. If you could send me as many as two regiments of cavalry, by quartering them in the midst of these disaffected districts and foraging upon friends of the deserters, they could not only arrest many, but could recruit themselves and horses, restore confidence, and inspire with courage the local forces. I earnestly recommend this action, general, and think in the long run it would not weaken your army. I think our people will respond liberally to the appeal for supplies, which I have just published this morning at the instance of the Secretary of War. The first answer made to it, two hours after its appearance in the morning papers, was from a poor widow of this city, who, hard pressed to live in these distressing times, as I know she is, came yet to offer me two pieces of bacon and a barrel of meal. Such offerings, on the sacred altar of our country, hallow our cause, and I hope will secure God's blessing upon it.
                                                    Very truly, yours,
                                                    Z.B. Vance
P.S.—I send you a copy of my appeal to the people of my State. Z.B.V.[259]

Soon afterwards, Vance clamped down on deserters as seen from a newspaper item:

> NOTICE . . . . LAWLESS DESPERADOES . . . if detected in committing outrage they will be shot, Randolph County, March 1865. Posted by order of Lt. General Holmes.[260]

That fall, the Confederacy was extremely low on troop numbers. They had to "shake the bushes" so to speak to get recruits. On April 25, 1865, Lieutenant J. A. Little sent a circular to the Randolph office to have the Home Guard desist rounding up deserters and concentrate on those conscripts who failed to report to camp.[261]

"More than one half a century after the Civil War, an illiterate, though intelligent old woman, living in the back woods of Beaufort County, stated the situation as succinctly as one could. When asked what part her father took in the war, she replied, 'Pa took his gun and went at the first call. It took him ni' on to two years to find out it was a rich man's war and a po' man's fight. Then he quit and laid out till the war was over.'"[262]

CHAPTER ELEVEN

Questionable Allegiance, Unionists, and Inner Strife

To Cure Secession and its Ills,
Take Dr. Scott's last Iron pills.
Well mixed with powder of saltpeter,
Apply it to each "Fire Eater."
With Union Bitters, mix it cleaver
And treason is warned off forever.[*]

"The Alien Enemies Act of the Confederate States of America, approved 8 August 1861, proclaimed all natives, citizens, denizens or subjects of the hostile nation or government, being males of fourteen years of age and upward, who shall be within the Confederate States and not citizens thereof . . . [are] liable to be apprehended, restrained or secured and removed as alien enemies." These people were given forty days' notice to leave the Confederacy or be declared an alien enemy, who would then be hunted down and arrested (August 1861). Most of those arrested were Northern-born. If the arrested person was expelled and consequently returned to the South, he wore the label of a spy or prisoner of war. Noteworthy is the fact that this law *did not* apply to true foreign-born men. These foreigners had to carry papers stating such was the case. "Confederate interrogators . . . wanted to know about the prisoners prior political affiliations . . . during the war being a 'Union man' had a sinister meaning."[1]

Author Georgia Tatum defined *disloyal* as "applied to persons living in the Confederate States, who not only refused to support the Confederate government, but who also appeared to be actively working against it;" *disaffection*, those opposed to the Confederacy who remain passive; *unionist*, sentiment from the first and strong advocates of the Union.[2] "*Destructives*" were known to be for a dissolution of the Union. "*Conservatives*" fell in with Union sentiment. Besides staunch pro-Southern families, the state contained all those listed above. Allegiance to the other side brought terror and sometimes death to those who made their choice known. "There was never a moment in Confederate States history when pro-Union opinion could be held without fear of government restraint . . . such opinions were more dangerous near the borders and . . . active military fronts than in the interior, but nowhere were dissenting beliefs secure." A total of 13 percent of civilian arrests were about political opinion. At first, citizens were held without records being kept of the military government's accusations towards them, their length of confinement, etc.[3] For a list of political prisoners held in Salisbury Prison, please see the appendix.

The state had three geographical areas in which the inhabitants chose not to support the Confederacy. Historian William Auman revealed that there were "three underlying causes accounted for the radical anti-confederate stance taken by many people of the Randolph County area: first—social class antipathies; second—staunch Unionism; third—cultural factors." With Randolph being on the top of the list, other counties affected were Guilford, Alamance, Surry, Davie, Davidson, Chatham, Yadkin, and Forsyth. Counties partly affected were Allegany, Montgomery, Orange, Stokes, Wilkes, Moore, and Iredell. Pro-Union sentiment was especially active in the eastern counties of Pitt, Northampton, Wayne, Beaufort, Hertford, Perquimans, Pasquotank, and Sampson.[4] "A senator from Beaufort declaimed in his place the other day that if the Eastern part of the state should be over run by the enemy, that the people there would begin to calculate to which govert. they assert allegiance."[5]

---

[*]   Verse printed on a patriotic envelope in 1861

People of all races in the mid-nineteenth-century South were class conscious. You knew your standing in society, whether upper, middle, or lower class. Upper-income persons would be considered as planters, presidents of companies, judges, some lawyers, etc. Middle income would be merchants, businessmen, doctors, artisans, manufacturers, numerous farmers, and elected officials. The lower class meant lower income, not morals. These included yeomen farmers, persons without property—tenants, renters, common laborers, free blacks, and the poor. The war incited animosity between classes. Another author wrote: "The disunity and class hostility that emerged in wartime horrified North Carolina's elite. The wartime behavior of many yeomen confirmed the gentry's deepest fears about the character of the masses of the mob."[6]

It was known in the highlands that the lower class would burn out a wealthier neighbor's holdings in disputes. Obadiah Sprinkle and Milton Sparks, convicted by vigilantes, took thirty-nine lashes and had their heads shaved and served time in jail for arson. Released early due to volunteering for the military, the men deserted their first chance and continued mischief when back home.[7] Thomas Lenoir in the mountains owned slaves but hired poor whites. He managed his debts by accepting livestock as payment or by hiring day laborers to work off some of their debt.[8] Conscription and the "twenty-nigger" law drove the classes apart. The middle class and lower-income recruits couldn't afford substitutes like the upper class, which caused resentment among the lower classes. This may have caused men to think the Union side looked more attractive. "Conflict between states and the Confederacy over enforcement of such laws" caused more disaffection. The reason men opposed secession was caused by the economic differences in families.[9]

In Washington and Tyrrell Counties, the "swampers" (mainly lumbermen and shingle weavers) and the "agrarians" (proponents of land distribution) resented their more affluent planters. A lady remarked that she "saw a clique who supported 'the Yankeeys because they assert [that] they are the poor man's friend and wld [would] only take from the rich.'"[10] Author Vickie Bynum proclaimed, "A self-styled group of women 'regulators' from Bladen County objected to giving up their sons, brothers, and husbands to a war being fought for the 'big man's Negroes.'"[11] Lower-income non-slaveholders decided to join the Union Army for protection and the monthly salary.

After occupation, a soldier talked to a local resident. He informed him:

> That there were men went into the Rebel army because they would have starved at home—and that the coming of our troops was anxiously looked for by nearly all the inhabitants of the island whilst they were compelled to look smilingly at the rebels who were the cause of all their troubles.

The soldier continued, "This man was quite intelligent which is quite a wonder as the majority of the citizens that I have seen are without exception the most stupidly ignorant of any set of critters I ever saw. They know absolutely nothing but fishing and boating, the extent of their knowledge of places is Nags Head and Elizabeth City . . ."[12] Thomas Merrill described Roanoke Islanders to his father early in 1862:

> It is mighty poor country down here and the looks of things I should judge that they raise more fever and ague than anything else. The people in this section are mostly pretty poor, depending chiefly on fishing for a living. Most of them have small farms & a few slaves, but the wealthy people are few and far between. They all say that North Carolina was forced out of the Union and they all are willing to go back to the old government.[13]

A Virginia soldier on duty near Kinston pictured the inhabitants of North Carolina as follows:

> . . . a very dirty set & I think are excusably [missing word?] considering the wretched country that they inhabit. The people are rotten to the core on the

question of loyalty to the South but I believe it is from ignorance as in this part of the state they seem to be a very ignorant set, with no refinement at all. Tell Lottie not to think that all North Carolina troops are like these people.[14]

Henry J. Risley was jailed in July 1861 because "he did make use of the following language, that he would not fight for the South, and that if Lincoln would land on the coast, he would get not less than a hundred in this place." He was fined two hundred fifty dollars.[15] Reverend Van Antwerpt, an Episcopal minister in Beaufort, "had committed two grave acts of disloyalty," so said the *Goldsboro Tribune*. "He refused to open his church on President Davis's recommended Fast Day June 13, 1861, and he did not 'mention Thanksgiving Day' after the Manassas victory."[16]

Several pro-Union men left the state rather than face their adversaries. Ben Hedrick settled in Washington City to work in the Treasury Department. Secessionists in Murfreesboro ousted Northern-born Charles H. Foster, who returned when the Federal Army overran the East. The Reverend Marble Nash Taylor also left the city, accused of relaying messages to the enemy. He came back too. Foster, along with Reverend Taylor and another unionist, went on a mission to New York with Lincoln's blessing to collect money for the loyal people of eastern North Carolina in December 1861.[17] The *Fayetteville Observer* hurled a barbed retort in the news on December 5, 1861, when it was found that the reverend had gone to New York City:

> The meeting was gotten up, apparently for the benefit of a certain Rev. M.N. Taylor, whom we presume to be the half-witted Methodist preacher who deserted to the enemy after the fall of Hatteras.[18]

As alluded to in chapter 5, President Lincoln considered the secession movement as merely a slaveholders' rebellion without much strength; and he was considering a plan for the restoration of the Southern states by establishing military governments, about which those citizens who were loyal to the Union might rally and thus weaken the power of the state administration.[19] After Hatteras fell, the Lincolnites, as they were known, met and decided they were not going to live under secession; so they initiated steps to form their own government in November of 1861. In May 1862, Lincoln appointed Edward Stanly as military governor over the counties under Federal occupation. He gave Stanly the rank of brigadier general. *General Burnside was to cooperate with him.* "Stanley [sic] agreed with Lincoln in 1861-1862 that the only purpose of the war was to preserve the Union, not to disturb the . . . laws of the southern states." Stanly set up "executive officers and judicial tribunals, and was authorized to suspend the writ of habeas corpus . . ."[20]

Mrs. Emondston's brother told an eyewitness account of "the meeting of Edward Stanley [sic] and an old Negro of his father's [Stanly] when he came to North Carolina as military governor:"

> The Negro it seems was sick & in consequence Mr. Stanley went to see him. Abram, for such was his name, turned his face to the wall as his young master entered the cabin. When Stanley, holding out his hand, addressed him thus, "Well Uncle Abram I am sorry to see you laid up thus. I know you must have been sick or you would have been to see me."
>
> To which the Negro replied, "God knows Marse Ned, that I never thought to live to see the day when I should have to say I was sorry to see you. But what are you doing here?" Go over Marse Ned, go over and stand long side of your own folks. Take a glass of water & a crust of bread with them, but stand by them, & if you won't do that [,] go back, Marse Ned, where you came from! Go back! & never let it be said that your father's son turned against his own folks. [Ed Stanly's father was a secessionist][21]

A man inscribed in his diary the second year of the war: "There is much discontent it seems in No. Ca. The Raleigh Standard is doing what it can to fan the flame, excite public indignation against the authorities here . . . Feb. 19, 1862 . . . . Col Wheeler . . . . says that there is a good deal of disloyalty—and a parcel of them had the boldness to hold a meeting at [R]oxobel, Bertie Co . . . . the people are afraid to interfere with them, as they threaten to burn and destroy the property of anyone doing so."[22] The conditions Down East deteriorated to a complete shambles. It was neighbor against neighbor. After the largest planters left for the interior, local landless Tories took everything not nailed down from the plantations. Runaway blacks became squatters. After the Battle of Plymouth, these planters returned to find their homes devoid of furniture and possessions. Gardens were overgrown, tools broken, fences removed, and livestock missing.[23] In Chowan County, both Southern and Northern men roamed the counties in search of prey. A resident contended:

> There a local contingent of Confederate rangers occasionally attacked Federal troops and harassed Union sympathizers, while a notorious band, called Buffaloes—composed of Unionists, Confederate deserters, and fugitive blacks— wrought their own kind brand of lawlessness from a base of Wingfield Plantation . . . .[24]

Buffaloes were also hated like the Yankees. In Carteret County, they crossed to Cedar Island, where they stole food, livestock, and barrels of fish. Hog Island experienced the same destruction. Civilian Buffaloes actually outnumbered the military Buffaloes, and both carried guns.[25] A diarist complained about the rogue men in other counties, mainly Chowan and Gates, men of Union sentiment, who plundered, robbed, and destroyed. "They are poor ignorant wretches who cannot resist a fine uniform and the choice of horses . . . & liberty to help themselves without check to their rich neighbors . . ."[26]

Approximately two hundred men from Bertie County and fifty-six men from Hatteras joined the Union regiment of the First and Second North Carolina.[27] "The Union army in North Carolina drew white volunteers from all but twelve of the state's 86 counties."[28] Several captured Southern sailors joined the Union side instead of being paroled to go home. The Federal Army occupied Plymouth in May 1862. Once Plymouth became occupied by the enemy, Bertie men who had joined the U.S. Army moved their families to the protection of the town.[29]

In June 1862, Tyrrell, Martin, Bertie, Hertford, Gates, Chowan, Perquimans, Pasquotank, and Camden counties formed organizations for self-protection against rebel guerillas. Unionists around Albemarle Sound proposed to appropriate all the property belonging to rebel families within these counties to support this armed (Union) force. These yeomen farmers and laborers organized a "mutual aid society." Historian Druill has suggested, "Its members pledged to support each other in the event of a 'draft for the war.'" They also pledged to oppose "any arrest that may be made" and to compensate members for "damages sustained by reason of their opinions or conduct." They formed a secret militia, possibly the Heroes of America.[30]

Soon, Confederate soldiers canvassed through Washington County and arrested about forty men with treasonable ideas. They were first taken to Williamston, then transferred to Salisbury Prison.[31] Those who sought to be peaceful and refused to fight, whether Quaker or not, were looked upon as being disloyal. Two hundred records of dissenters were located by author Mark Neely Jr.[*][32]

Confederate forces harassed the Buffalo civilians. In Carteret County, Southern forces demolished the home and business of James Roberts and his brothers. The violence continued, "soldiers evacuating Elizabeth City set fire to the home of William Lister, a small

---

[*]   Neely was unable to find records for the piedmont and mountain counties at this time.

local manufacturer, and shot him to death when he came to the window for air." Mr. Lister frequently spoke out against the Confederacy. Pro-Southrons taunted their Union neighbors with real threats.[33]

"Thad Cox, a Pasquotank native serving as a lieutenant in the Federal army, when moving his family from the country to Elizabeth City, had been ambushed from an unfinished church by persons believed to be Confederate guerillas. Cox, his wife, and two of three children were killed. When the bodies of Thad Cox, his four-year-old daughter, and his mortally wounded wife were brought into Elizabeth City, there was great excitement among the people, both civil and military, who urged something be done to avenge [the murders], if possible, or at least to set an example to prevent the committing of such brutal outrages."[34] Perhaps they may have been murdered by Captain Caraway or a certain guerilla named O'Conner, who was known to execute his prisoners.[35] John Giles, leader of a local unionist group in Washington County, was murdered in January of 1863 by his Confederate neighbors.[36]

Captain C. C. Bower's Georgia cavalrymen patrolled Bertie County, assisting Southern sympathizers but taunting Union Tories. To further inflame them, he posted armed guards at the polls on November 4, 1863. He tried to force Union men to sign "an oath that they had not visited Plymouth since its occupation by Federal forces." Some men declined and protested. They refused to vote. Bower's tactics were certainly illegal; so the Justice of the Peace, Lewis Bond, went to the courthouse at Windsor to investigate. The three poll takers told Bond that they were required by Captain Bower to ask each man for an oath before voting. Justice Bond was making a list of those men who refused to take the oath when Captain Bower's cavalrymen stormed the building with loaded pistols aimed at officials, who were then arrested. This incident was reported to Vance, but he told state authorities he did not have the power to remove Captain Bower.[37]

The situation was so appalling in Bertie County that Vance wrote President Davis to "suspend the draft in the counties bordering Albemarle Sound." Davis did not. Governor Vance then asked the state legislature for a cavalry unit for Bertie, but their resolution did not pass. Instead, Vance ordered the militia enlarged. These included men over forty-five and teens eighteen years old.[38] In January 1864, Vance sought from President Davis a resolution to suspend the writ of habeas corpus in North Carolina. He felt that the Conscription Act contributed to the upheaval in both the eastern and western counties. Vance's idea was to keep the conscript officers out of the state. This proved to be another conflict between him and Jeff Davis.[39] The following address to the state's General Assembly goes into detail about it:

> *The Honorable, the General Assembly*
> *of North-Carolina:*
>
> Since your last adjournment, various and important changes in the situation of our affairs have occurred, and many of them require legislative action at your hands
>
> Among the acts of Congress referred to, that which has suspended the privilege of *habeas corpus* has most thoroughly aroused public attention. Neither the losses incurred by the radical and sudden changes in the currency, nor the conscription of the principals of substitutes, nor the extension of it to such an age, and upon such terms as to place the industrial pursuits of the country at the feet of the President, nor the heavy burdens of taxation—none of these, nor all of them together, have so awakened the public feeling as the withdrawal of this time-honored and blood-bought guard of personal freedom, from the people in times when it is most needed for their protection. It is true that our forefathers assumed . . . that in cases of rebellion and invasion, the public safety may sometimes require its suspension; and, therefore, we have conferred on the Congress the power of suspension in such cases, when the

public safety may require it. Nor can it be doubted that the power authorized to suspend is the sole power entitled to judge of the necessity for the act, and if the late statute had merely prohibited out and out the use of the writ for the time specified, there could be no complaint against its constitutionality, however ill-timed and unnecessary may have been the exercise of a rigor so great. But I have been as unable to see, in the times, any necessity for denying the writ, as I am to recognize in the law the constitutional exercise of the favor that is granted. Concurring in the doctrine that the protection against the abuse of the Constitution of the Confederate States, either by usurpation of powers or oppressive use of such as are granted, is "to be found in the responsibility of Congress to the people, ensured by their short tenure of office, and in the reserved right of each State to resume the powers delegated to the Confederate government, whenever in her judgment they are perverted to the injury or oppression of the people," I deem a duty devolved on the State . . . to make known to that government her complaints and to insist upon a redress of her grievances. Under this idea of duty, and in a spirit of regard for the government of our adoption, I deem it incumbent to present my objections against the late act.

It is declared in the preamble that "the President has asked for the suspension, and informed Congress of conditions of public danger which render a suspension of the writ a measure proper for the public defence against invasion and insur-rection." Thereupon it is exacted that the writ shall be suspended as to "the cases of persons arrested or detained by order of the President, Secretary of War, or the General Officer commanding the Trans-Mississippi military department."

The statute proceeds to classify under thirteen heads a very great number of acts, of which, if a man be accused, he shall be deprived of the benefit of the writ; and among them the act of attempting to "avoid military service." To prevent the outrage which may be perpetrated on an innocent man not subject to military service for merely attempting "to avoid military service," unlawfully demanded, it is provided that "in case of palpable wrong and oppression by any subordinate officer upon any party who does not legally owe military service, his superior officer shall grant prompt relief to the oppressed party, and the subordinate shall be dismissed from office."

And as a general protection of the citizens against abuses, under the act, it is provided, that "the President shall cause proper officers to investigate the cases of all persons so arrested or detained, in order that they may be discharged if improperly detained, unless they can be speedily tried in due course of law."

And, finally it is enacted that "no military or other officer shall be compelled in answer to any writ of *habeas corpus* to appear in person or to return the body of any person detained by the authority of the President, Secretary of War," &c.; "but upon the certificate, under oath, of the officer having charge of any one so detained, that such person is detained by him for any of the causes specified in the act under said authority, further proceedings under the writ shall immediately cease."

In order to ascertain whether the enactment is within the powers delegated, it is proper to keep in mind what are the privileges of the writ of *habeas corpus,* and we shall be sure to know what can be affected constitutionally, by suspension of it. This writ is the offspring of the love of liberty, and has been in use for ages by our ancestors and ourselves, as the hand-maid of fredem [*sic*] use is to have inquiry made according to the rules of law of the causes why persons are restrained of their civil freedom. If upon enquiry by the proper authority, there be no cause detention, the person is set at liberty. If there be cause he is remanded for further detention or allowed to go at large upon bail.—Now, these are all the privileges of the writ of *habeas corpus.* The writ finds no place for action until after the person is arrested. So that if there be any privileges or securities to the person attending the mode of arrest, these are not the privileges of the writ of *habeas corpus,* but exist independently of them. And it is therefore clear that a power to suspend the privileges of the writ is not a power to suspend the privileges secured in forms attending the mode of arrest.—They are too distinct to be confounded by any species of sophistry; and this distinction is plainly and notably observed in the bill to suspend the writ, passed through the Senate in January, 1807, which suspends it only when the person may have been "charged on oath," and arrested by virtue of "a warrant." The writ was as effectually suspended by that bill as by this act, and the Constitutional securities attending the mode of arrest, were left untouched and unimpaired. It may be then regarded as settled truth, that the suspension of the writ is no suspension of the constitutional forms prescribed for arrest, and that Congress has no power, express or implied, to suspend any other guaranty of civil liberty provided in the Constitution besides those secured by the writ alone. Notwithstanding this, the late act has strode over some of the most important guards of civil liberty, as if an express power had been conferred on Congress to suspend them likewise. Thus, while by paragraph 3, section 9, it is allowed Congress to suspend the privileges of the writ of *habeas corpus* in the emergencies mentioned, it is by the same section, paragraph 15, in the most emphatic terms, declared that "No warrant shall issue but upon probable cause, supported by oath or affirmation, and particularly describing the person to be seized." And by paragraph 16, that "no person shall be deprived of his liberty without due process of law"—that is, "law in its regular course of administration, through courts of justice," (1 Kent's Com. sec. 24, paragraphs 13-14.) The beginning of this due process is first the charge on oath, and the next step is the warrant describing the person to be seized. The third is the arrest, and until this takes place the *habeas corpus* has no status, and cannot possibly have any. At this point the writ springs into being, if not denied, and as here only its aid can be sought for the first time, so here for the first time can its privilege be denied. Yet the act involves with its suspension a suspension of the distinct and independent provisions which guard the citizen against a false charge and the dangers of a general warrant.

In my judgment Congress had the same power to suspend every other guard of civil liberty to be found in the Constitution—the same to deprive the citizen of the guaranty that he should not be held to answer for a capital crime, unless on presentment or indictment of a grand jury—that he should not be compelled to be a witness against himself—that he should have the right to a speedy and public trial by an impartial jury, and a trial in the district in which the crime shall have been committed.

The writ of *habeas corpus* is peculiar to the English people and ourselves. And a complete illustration of the operation of a suspension of its privileges will be seen by supposing that it had no existence here. In such case no provision would have been found for its suspension. But the clause requiring charge of crime to be made on oath and warrant to describe the person to be seized, would have been not only very proper, but the more necessary to be inserted. These could not have been legally disturbed by Congress, and any legislation dispensing with them had been mere usurpation and void.

Such is the general view I have taken of the act as it is supposed to relate to *crimes.* But the statute is construed to reach cases involving no offence whatever, legal or moral; and though there is some difference of opinion upon the question whether paragraph 5 of section 1, embraces the case of a citizen not liable military duty, who neithes [sic] flies nor resists, but simply appeals or tries to appeal to the constitutional repositors of the law for a decision upon his rights, yet there is too much reason to believe that the language is susceptible of the interpretation that it does include such persons; and such is the interpretation put upon it by the military authorities. And as the suspension was asked by the President, it is but just to infer that it was drawn to suit him, and his exposition carries the intended meaning of the paragraph.

I am unable to see any reason consistent with the principles of a free and civilized government, provided with a judiciary as a great and independent branch of its composition, for suspending the *habeas corpus* in cases which involve no evasion or attempt to evade military service that is due, but which merely ask when honest opinions differ to have the point settled by those tribunals which settle all matters of controversy between citizen and citizen, and a citizen and his government. If a citizen owe not any military service to the government, he has as much right to refuse to render it, when wrongfully claimed of him, as he has to refuse to pay a debt to the government wrongfully claimed of him; and if in both cases he stands fairly up and submits to an investigation of the question before those tribunals learned in such matters and appointed because of their fitness and skill, it would be just as reasonable to suspend the writ in the alleged debt of money as in the case of the alleged debt of service. This course might, and likely would, hasten the payment of a debt just or unjust, and so it may serve to put men in the army exempt by the laws of the land.

There is no instance of a suspension at any time of the writ, or the privilege of the writ, if there be any difference between them, for any other cause, either in England or America. Many suspensions of the privileges of the writ occurred in England between the passage of the *habeas corpus* act and the Revolution, running through a period of almost a century, and they all empowered the King either to "*apprehend and detain, or to secure and detain without bail, such persons as are suspected of conspiracy against the King and his government . . . .*"

The suspension during Shay's rebellion extended to crime or suspected crime. The attempted suspension in 1807 was confined to persons charged "with treason or other high crime or misdemeanor, endangering the peace, safety or neutrality of the United States." The idea cannot be entertained for a moment that the power of suspending the writ was granted for any such purpose as that of depriving a citizen of the privilege of a legal enquiry into his obligation to perform military service, in order to fill the army with soldiers. If such a power exist, the sovereignty of the States is at the mercy of the Confederate government. Where lies the relief against the conscription of the entire body of State officers? By this act it is deposited with the President alone! His officers alone can give the discharge—Confederate officers chosen without even the consent of the Senate, and removed at will. The appropriate tribunals are entirely over-looked: the State Judges are thrust aside without ceremony, and even the Confederate Judge, who holds his office during good behaviour [sic], is ignored, and in their room is placed an officer who lives on the breath of the Confederate Executive. If the State officers are not put into the army under such power in the Executive, it is because the incumbent does not will it; and when the rights of the State shall exist by such a courtesy, they will cease to have any existence at all. It is hard to divine a sufficient reason for displacing the civil tribunals already established, and substituting others so dependent upon the Executive for their existence.—

The assurance of public men, that the power will not be abused, can never remove the fears of freemen, who rely only upon written Constitutions to protect their liberties.—History is too full of wrong to allow them to forget for a moment that *eternal vigilance is the price of freedom.*

It is manifest that the act contemplates that the *military* shall be invested with full powers to arrest any person, who may be suspected of any of the vague and ill defined charges mentioned; and such is the interpretation put on it by the general orders of Adjutant General Cooper, thus suspending the civil authorities throughout the land, and it is equally clear that it also contemplates that the order of the President for arresting or detaining citizens, shall be a general order to arrest and detain all such as may come within the category of suspected persons—without naming or describing the individual—and each military officer who may be deputed for that purpose will be invested with a perfect discretion over the liberty of every citizen in the land. In substance and effect the President is intended to be empowered with authority to fill the land with military deputies, who may seize any citizen without warrant or oath of probable cause, under a general warrant from the President to arrest all suspected persons. Such a warrant is without precedent in England for the last hundred years, and during the entire century past has been forbidden, denounced and declared void.

In my judgment, the President is vested by the Confederate Constitution, with no part of the judicial authority, except in cases arising in the land and naval forces, or in the militia, when in actual service under his orders. If he is vested with a particle of civil judicial jurisdiction, where is the grant of it and how far does it extend? If he has the power to issue a warrant for the arrest of a civilian suspected of violating a law of the Confederate States, he may make it returnable and examinable before himself, and order a discharge or require bail. It is certain that the mere suspension of the writ of *habeas corpus* does not invest the President with the powers of a civil judicial magistrate, and if it could have that effect it could not give him an authority while discharging his judicial jurisdiction to lay aside the restraints imposed on all other judges.

The course adopted by the administration, of allowing the writ of *habeas corpus* to issue, and of forthwith checking the action of the judge and suspending his farther proceedings *ad libitum,* to await the reports of military officers having custody of the petitioner to their superiors, and finally subjecting the case to the decision of the war department in derogation of civil authority, is humiliating to the independent character of the judiciary and tends to the great danger of liberty, to familiarize the people with military supremacy.

It must be remembered, however, that these are merely my opinions. The Supreme Court, which alone has the power to decide upon the constitutionality of the law, has not yet spoken. When it does speak we must give heed to its voice, so long as the law remains on our statute books. But whether for constitutional reasons, or reasons of mere policy, the people have a right to demand the repeal of any obnoxious law. On both grounds I recommend that you urge Congress to repeal the act suspending the privilege of *habeas corpus;* or, should you concur in the judgment of Congress that a suspension is required by the exigencies of the times, that it should at least be modified and stripped of its unconstitutional or (at least) obnoxious features.

My opinion on this subject is well known. In the first message I had the honor to send to your body, in 1862, speaking of the then existing act authorizing a suspension of the writ, I used the following language: "I have not seen an official copy of the act, but learn from the newspapers that Congress has conferred upon the President the power to suspend the writ of *habeas corpus* in all cases of arrests made by Confederate authority. If this be once admitted, no man is safe from the power of one individual. He could at pleasure seize any citizen of the State, with or without excuse, throw him into prison and permit him to languish there without relief—a power that I am unwilling to see entrusted to any living man. To submit to its exercise would, in my opinion, be establishing a precedent dangerous and pernicious in the extreme." &c.

There is nothing of this I am desirous of taking away or adding to. My earnest remonstrance against the passage of the present act is herewith transmitted, together with divers other letters to the Confederate authorities, in relation to the execution of the civil laws, rights of the people, &c., and which will convince you, I trust, that I have been equally zealous to guard against the inner as well as the outer dangers which threaten us.

Many recurring dangers of serious conflict with the Confederate government, especially in relation to the seizure of principals of substitutes after discharge by a judge, have been upon me since your last session. They were fortunately avoided however; but their solution would have been easy could I but have had the assistance of the Supreme Court. I greatly regret that you did not see proper to comply with my recommendation, when you were last in session, to authorize some one to convene that body in cases of great importance, and which admit of no delay. I can but repeat it now, for many obvious reasons.

In addition to the many brilliant victories which have crowned our arms this spring in all parts of the Confederacy, I have the sincere pleasure to congratulate you upon the very splendid success of the opening of the campaign in our State, resulting in the re-capture of the towns of Plymouth and Washington, and the rescue of a considerable portion of our territory from the enemy. This is the more gratifying because it was accomplished by troops under the command of two distinguished sons of North-Carolina, Brigadier, now Major General Hoke commanding the land forces, and Commander Cooke, with the steam-ram Albemarle. I doubt not but that you will see the propriety of rendering suitable thanks to these galiant [sic] officers and the brave officers and men under their command for the conspicuous heroism which has been rewarded by such splendid results. We cordially and gladly welcome back our fellow-citizens of that region, thus rescued from the enemy, to the embraces of their mother State, and thank them for their steadfast adherence to our cause under the tyranny and oppression of our foe. Indeed, it is gratifying to observe the very great loyalty and patriotism of that whole portion of our State within or contiguous to the enemy's lines, which has been alike subjected to his blandishments and his ravages. May the day speedily come when our jurisdiction shall again extend to the sands of the Atlantic.

Several other matters which I deem it unnecessary to specify, will thrust themselves upon your attention . . . In regard to financial matters, the interesting report of the Public Treasurer is so full and complete that I am content merely to refer you to it, confident that I could not improve upon any of his suggestions, which I, in the main, endorse.

The poor, especially the indigent families of our soldiers, still demand our care. It is justly conceded that when they are not able to support themselves the State should support them in the absence of their natural protectors. I cannot, however, make any specific recommendation for their further relief, but should any plan occur to your superior wisdom, I doubt not but you will promptly act upon it. It will be very difficult for many of them to struggle through till harvest, especially in some of the counties of the west, which have been preyed upon alike by friend and foe.

Trusting that harmony will prevail in your councils, and that much good may, under God, result to the country therefrom, I close my message with an expression of readiness to co-operate with you—should it lie in my power—in the execution of the labors devolving upon you.   Z. B. Vance[40]

Depredations continued to occur in the coastal regions. Local men who had joined the United States troops raided homes in their own county. Two men in Hertford, a Mr. Cochrane and Timothy White, were killed by Buffaloes.[41] The next newspaper article speaks of atrocities committed by the lawless:

> For some time past outrages and depredations of the Buffaloes in Gates, Chowan, and Perquimans County, North Carolina have been unprecedented. But two or three weeks ago Mrs. Spivey residing in Gates, who is represented to have been a most estimable lady was robbed and then brutally murdered. Mr. M.H. Eure of the said county, has also been despoiled of much of his possessions by these soldiers; and others, whose names we now forget, have been similarly treated.
>
> Recently a party of gallant Confederates determined to break up the gang, and seeking a favorable opportunity, dashed in among them, killing and wounded several, and captured fourteen who were brought out. Ten of the scamps proved to be deserters from the Confederate army; and have been handed over to the proper authorities. The other four having participated in the foul robbery and murder of Mrs. S., were taken to the spot where the diabolical deed was committed, and there executed in retaliation. It is hoped that the vengeance which has a salutary effect in preventing others from engaging in such acts of crime and outlawry.[42]

U.S. Commodore Flusser referred to the eastern Union men as "our home guard thieves," meaning the Buffaloes.[43] Pro-Union men took to the swamps to avoid conscription. "Men were 'hunted down like foxes' and shot at by these [Southern] officers . . . ."[44] A Southern soldier, James K. P. Harrington, encamped near Kinston, sent a letter to his brother Archie: "The buffaloes are as thick as rabbits down here."[45] Because the Federals took a stance on recruiting black and white men to their side, Confederate guerillas sought these out to execute "with sanction of state officials."[46] David Haggard Jr., a Tory, ran to the swamps for protection, was caught, and killed.

On the morning of February 1, 1864, C.S. General Hoke forded the passage of Batchelder's Creek, nine miles from New Bern; the enemy abandoned their works and retreated upon the town. A large number of prisoners were captured. Among the captured prisoners, about fifty native North Carolinians dressed in Yankee uniforms, were recognized as men who had deserted the Southern Army. Fifteen of them belonged to Nethercutt's battalion and the Second North Carolina Volunteer Infantry (Union).

Many were deserters from North Carolina regiments guarding the railroad bridges locally. Others were partisan rangers similar to the Home Guard. They were tried at court, proven guilty, then hanged by order of C.S. General George Pickett.

"It became my duty to visit these men in prison before their execution, in a religious capacity," wrote Reverend Paris. "After their execution I thought it proper, for the benefit of the living, that I should deliver a discourse before our brigade, upon the death of these men, that the eyes of the living might be opened, to view the horrid and ruinous crime and the sin of desertion."[47]

A descendant of two of these unfortunate men, Jennifer Wisener, said "Mrs. Catherine Summerlin whose husband was hanged for desertion in 1864 in Kinston was asked by a fellow condemned soldier, William Haddock, to give his clothes to his mother." Author Patterson wrote that serviceable clothing was not wasted in a grave. Mrs. Summerlin had reason to be resentful because Confederate troops stole her horse, wagon, and provisions while she was visiting her husband in jail.[48] Mrs. Wisener related that Mrs. Catherine Dial Summerlin Weatherington was pregnant with her fourth or fifth child when Jesse was hung. She married Ruel Weatherington after the death of Jesse. Ruel had been branded with the letter *D* for desertion. William Hardy Daugherty with the Second Regiment NC USA Volunteers, another deserter, was hung at the same time.

Mixed in with all the unionists lived the Quakers. A small community of Quakers, though not as large as those of the piedmont, were active in Perquimans, Pasquotank, Wayne, Edgecombe, Halifax, Northhampton, Jones, Lenoir, Wilson, and the corner of Greene County. Rev. Thomas Kennedy—a Quaker, abolitionist, and slave owner—was tricked by Confederate soldiers dressed in Federal uniforms. They approached him and asked for food, which he gave to them. It was illegal to help the enemy; so he was promptly arrested, taken to jail in Goldsboro, and later removed to Salisbury Prison.[49] The story of his entrapment is described in a letter from Quaker Delphina Mendenhall to a friend:

> . . . on the last day of last year Isabella, wife of Thos. Kennedy entered our room on her return from a visit to him at Salisbury. He is there, charged with feeding a supposed Yankee, & showing him the way to a ford of the river. He is very calm & resigned—feeling no guilt on account of feeding the hungry & showing a man who pretended to be lost, the road that led to the ford he wished to cross. But he was entrapped into that act by a malicious neighbor, aided by Alabama soldiers. The whole affair was a wicked conspiracy . . .[50]

In November 1862, Thomas Crenshaw received another letter about Kennedy's imprisonment:

> . . . I saw his wife yesterday [.] she says she does not look for his release before the end of the war if he should live that long[.] I accompanied her to Salisbury to see Thomas . . . the old man seemed as cheerful aas[sic] though he had been about home [.] he has privilege of going anywhere at will in the enclosure. Brother Calvin is still there[.] he was brought to the gate of the garrison and I allowed to speak about ten words to him [.] we were then separated. I have been there three times during his nine months imprisonment and each time my interview has been equally as short as the last. Calvin had the promise of being exchanged some months ago but they refuse to carry out their promise.
>
> In the sixth mo last I served out a writ of Habeus [sic]Corpus in his favor. They confessed on trial that they had no charges against him yet the judge put off the trial for about ten days pretending they might find something against him. During this time the President declared martial law there [.] the judge said that put a stop to the case.
>
> Some three months ago the President was petitioned for his release [.] there was nothing found against him there [.] the Secretary of War ordered his release more than two months ago. The commandant of the prison requires a bond of $5,000.00 for his good behavior and take the oath of allegiance to the Southern Confederacy before he releases him [.] he says he will stay there until the end of the war before he would do either.
>
> Copied for W.H.S. Wood
>
> P.S. More than 140 Southern men in prison at Salisbury. Only two federals when I was there.*[51]

------

*   This note is written in another hand, probably N. T. Perkins's.

Mrs. Mendenhall went to the prison to visit Kennedy in February:

> I called on the Capt. of the prison . . . & showed him your letter & he gave
> me leave to see Mr. Kennedy . . . I delivered your letter & had a talk with him.
> The officers all sympathize with him. I have used & shall use all proper efforts
> to get him liberated, and am not without hope. If they were sure they had the
> power, there would be no difficulty, as they desire his release. Mr. Kennedy
> refuses to affirm allegiance to the Confederate Government & this is the only
> obstacle, for I offered to stand his surety for his fidelity & good behavior.
>
> He wishes to go to Wayne Court, so as to be there next Monday to attend
> to some Court business & I told the Officers, one & all, that I would stand his
> surety for his return. They have the matter under consideration & will allow
> it, if they can . . .[52]

In another letter written about a month later, Mrs. Mendenhall said that "Thomas
Kennedy was sent to the 'United States' some weeks ago, in conformity with the judgment
of the commissioner who was sent to Salisbury. He went in company with about 14 Federal
prisoners."[53] After he was exchanged, the reverend left the state and settled in Indiana,
where he died in 1864 due to hardships suffered while in prison.[54]

Other North Carolinians imprisoned for their Union ties were Amariah B. Allen, Jesse
W. Davis, and Edward B. Hopkins. Hopkins told authorities he had to take the oath to the
United States or starve. Authorities believed his story and released him. Most of these type
people arrested were of the poorer class. From Chowan County, Jeptha A. Ward became
an inmate when he said he did not believe in conscription or emancipating the Negro.
Quaker Calvin G. Perkins of Kinston made salt in New Bern. When under occupation by the
enemy, he claimed neutrality. Later, he was arrested by Southern men. Other religious men
in prison were Ison Wood and James Sinclair. Political prisoners included W. C. Loftin of
Craven County and Michael Tighlman and John Medlin Sr. of Union County. Medlin owned
fifty slaves but was sent to prison for harboring his son, a Confederate deserter. Down in
Beaufort, Eli Swanner voiced his anti-Southern views and was arrested twice.[55]

PIEDMONT

The disloyal in Davidson County burned two railroad bridges soon after the war began.[56]
No bridge was considered safe. Early in 1861, a High Point native was arrested for continued
anti-secession disturbances. John Hilton claimed he had a force of about five hundred who
would bring down the planters.[57] The same thing was taking place in Franklinville. Mr. J. P.
Aldridge told the governor that the men there had no jurisdiction to stop the abolitionists.
They had threatened to cause trouble once the volunteers left for camp. Local citizens
wanted the power to apprehend the hooligans.[58]

A man said that the Austin Whitsitt family were strong unionists. The news of dissention
quickly flew around the state. A correspondent wrote on March 7, 1862:

> I hear bad accounts from No. Ca. Disloyalty has boldly shown itself in
> Randolph, Chatham, and some adjoining Counties—and they openly declare
> they will not submit to a draft . . .[59]

Imagine the plight that a citizen confronted when his name was published in a
newspaper that told of his views. The *Raleigh Standard* did just that:

> We learn . . . that Alexander Russell and Joseph, worthy Union citizens,
> residing in Alamance co were treated very cruelly by a portion of the 6th NC
> cavalry, on account of their union sentiments . . . Arms will soon be placed in

the hands of local police and it will then be the right and duty of true men of the country to rid society of all desperation.[60]

This left the family exposed to other depredations by neighbors. It was difficult to keep your sympathies a secret. Neighbors knew which ones leaned to the loyal side. Elle Andrews said her neighbors Dr. James G. Ramsey, Absalom K. Simonton, A. B. F. Gaither, and L. Q. Sharpe were strong unionists.[61] Joshua Moon from the Albright Township helped Union sympathizers escape the county. People desiring to flee traveled at night. Those leaving in the day lay hidden in his wagon. His young son rode with him to stave off suspicion.[62]

Historian Auman voiced that "militant Unionists refers to southerners who, after the initiation of hostilities, either covertly or overtly remained loyal to the United States, actively supported the overthrow of the Confederate States, and hoped and worked for the return of their state and the South to the Union."[63] A person had to be careful how they showed their loyalty or disloyalty. "I am not a Tory, but I do wish this war would end," stated Julia Conrad Jones. Julia had two sons already in the war when another son, age seventeen, wanted to join. She wrote, "I cannot give you up." He was attending military school in Hillsborough.[64] Whether for the Union or not, Dr. Beeman became so upset over the plight of women and children that he spoke his mind in a moment of passion, "Jeff Davis and Secession ought to be in Hell, where Secession originated." He was sent to Fort Holmes as a prisoner for uttering that statement. He said upon arrival there was no shelter, the food was awful, and he waited days for his trial. Beeman walked home after being released.[65]

Citizens accused one another with taking the wrong side. The *Raleigh Standard* printed on January 29, 1862:

> We pronounce the charge that citizens of Salem are in correspondence with the Lincoln government, and that "at the proper time some sort of demonstration will be made to further the interests of the enemy," as a base and malicious calumny, without any foundation in truth.

Salem residents had mixed feelings about the war. Some attended church where the minister had pro-Southern feelings while others filled the church where the minister had Union sympathies. At Friedberg, Pastor Christian L. Rights said, "Praying for the Southern Confederacy is not popular here." Pastors were kept busy ministering to families mourning and to soldiers who were home on sick furlough. Salem resembled a resort town with people coming from Wilmington, Charleston, etc., to refuge. There were also many out-of-state students boarding at the girls' college.[66] In Salem, two newspapers opposed each other: the *Western Sentinel* was pro-states rights and the *People's Press*, anti-secession.

By the 1830s, the Moravians joined the North Carolina Militia voluntarily. They were becoming "Americanized"—owning guns, believing in state's rights, and some members of the church owning slaves. They did not oppose slavery but relaxed the rules regarding the ownership. You were not to have a personal slave within city limits, but certain Moravians circumvented the rule by placing a house outside the city limits for their bondsmen. The church could own slaves and did.[67]

In 1861, the Moravians felt that Lincoln had betrayed his promise of invading the South, so many Quaker men volunteered to fight for North Carolina with the blessing of the church.[68] Because of patriotic fervor in the beginning, Quaker Micajah Wright's four sons joined the Southern Army. Another Quaker, Bryant Scott, joined in protest over his abolitionist father. Harriet Howell's husband was against secession but went with the draft because he did not want to "lie out in the woods and disgrace his family."[69] Hinshaw women whose husbands had been captured and released after Gettysburg, along with their four children, left the Holly Springs area of Forsyth on September 1, 1864, in a covered wagon with tools and provisions furnished by church members. The women were determined to go to their husbands in Indiana. The church wrote them a letter of introduction and a letter of recommendation for the provost guard on the borders. The courageous women arrived after seven weeks on the trail—a distance of about six hundred miles. Thomas and Mary Hinshaw left Indiana in the same wagon, to return home about mid-April 1865.[70]

In New Garden, Guilford College open during the war, and "many Quaker boys had to flee through the lines to escape conscription at Greensboro. Baskets of food hung in the log barn behind the school farmhouse for passing Unionists, secessionists, or bushwhackers, all alike hungry men to the Quakers."[71] Sheriff Mathias Masten of Forsyth held Union sympathies and didn't care who knew it. He was threatened with imprisonment for his views. In 1865, when bushwhackers rode through Kernersville, they took the sheriff's son, John, as a prisoner. Sheriff Masten immediately rode toward them, threatened the gang, and got his son back.[72]

Lawless men combed the state. The public was growing accustomed to the ferocity of retaliation. "Even elite figures began to think of individual violence as a substitute for the legal process of the state," noted author Escott. "To shoot [robbers] in the act . . . is perfectly justifiable . . . ," so said Jonathan Worth.[73] As the war progressed, it grew more difficult for these Union men to stay in hiding. Friends and family helped, along with black people, free and bonded. Some hid in dugout caves and came out at night to get food. The brave ones showed their faces in the daytime on the farm. Their children or wife would give some prearranged signal when someone approached. Other signals may be the use of countersigns, horn blowing, quilt placement, or animal calls much like the type that runaway slaves used.

Elsewhere in the piedmont, crimes and atrocities continued to occur. Wesleyan ministers who leaned toward the Quaker side were blamed by some citizens of causing disloyalty in their area. Mrs. Davis commented that "it does provoke me to see so many who are doing nothing for the good of the country, and all the time trying to discourage those who are doing every thing and suffering every thing."[74] In the fall of 1864, Judge Thomas Settle wrote Vance about the wife of Bill Owens, leader of a gang of Confederate deserters. Upon investigation into the conflict, C.S. Colonel Alfred Pike said, "She cursed and abused us. She took her baby in her arms and said she would not go with them . . . . the men then tied her hands behind her back and hung her up by her thumbs from a tree until she agreed to tell them where her husband was hiding." The judge informed Vance that the Home Guard misunderstood his orders. Judge Settle said that about fifty women, five in advanced pregnancy, from Davidson, Chatham, and Randolph Counties "were dragged from their homes and put under guard and they were left for some weeks. Some were frightened into aborting their babies." Settle continued, "The officers boldly avow their conduct and say that they understand your orders to be a full justification."[75]

Soldier J. E. Yancey Albright wrote to his parents in Randolph City. A brother "tells us bad news about outlyers [.] I wish every one of them could be caught and dealt with according to the nature of their offense [.] They deserve the end of the law [.] They are not fit for soldiers and should be got rid of some way so they could not disturb the peace of loyal citizens [.] They are worse than the Yankees."[76]

In Randolph County, six attempts were made by the state to settle discord against deserters and unionists. When Tories began rioting the first summer, Governor Henry Clark sent troops to Randolph and Davidson Counties. Unionists rioted again in March 1862, requiring three hundred soldiers to quell tumultuous behavior. Outraged women sent letters to authorities over the atrocities committed. A good example is found in Phebe Crook's letter to the governor:

Davidson County . . . Mr. Vance Dear Sir

I unbrace this opertunity of writing you a few lines in order to inform you of the conduct of our officers and leading men of this county as you are appinted govenor of the state and I beleave that you are willing to do all that you can in trying to protect the civil laws and writs of our country. Whereas I believe you are a Man of high [*illegible*] and one that is willing to Do your Duty in every respect. I will now inform you of some of the conduct of our militia officers and Magistrates of this county. Thir imployment is hunting deserters they say and the way they manage to find them is taking up poore old grey headed fathers who has faught in the old War . . . some of them has done thir Duty in trying to support both the army and thir family and these men that has remained at home ever since the War [*illegible*] are taking them up the women and keeping tham under gard and Boxing thir jaws and nocking them a bout as if they ware bruts and keeping them from thir little children that they hav almost wore out thir lifes in trying to make surport for them. And some of this women is in no fix to leav homes and others have little suckling infants not More than 2 months old and they also hav taking up little children and hang them until they turn Black in the face trying to make them tell whear there fathers is, When the little children knows nothing atall about ther fathers. Thir plea is they hav orders from the Governor to do this and they say that they hav orders from the govner to Burn up this barn and houses and Destroy all that they hav got to live on because they hav a poor wore out son of [or] husband that has served in the army. Some of them for 2 or 3 yers and is almost wore out and starved to death and has come home to try to take a little rest and are doing no Body eny harm and are eating thir own Rations and these men that has remained at home ever since the war commenced will take thir guns and go out in the woods and shoot them down without Halting them as if the war [were] Bruts or murders and thise men will also pilfer and plunder and steel on thir creadits. As for my self I am a young lady that has Neather Husband, son, father, no brother in the woods But I always like to [see] peple hav jestis and I think if this Most powerful fighting men that has always remained at home would go and fight the enemy and let this poore wore out soldiers remain at [home] a little while and take a little rest that we would hav better times. But they say that if they are called to go they will lie in the woods until they Rot before they will go to the war. And now why should this men hav the power to punish men for a crime that they would be guilty of the same. So I will close by requesting and answer amediatly. Yours truly Phebe Crook

    Direct to Phebe Crook, Salem church p.o.   Randolph county, NC[77]

In Harnett County, disloyalty caused Confederate troops to take action against families hiding deserters, causing W. W. Holden, editor of the *Weekly Standard*, to write an editorial titled "Outrages by the Military." It goes as follows:

We published in our last the resolutions introduced by Mr. McKay, of Harnett, denouncing the conduct of a squad of Confederate troops in burning a house in that County, and requesting the Governor to call out any portion of the military force of the State to prevent such wanton and lawless destruction of property. These resolutions passed the Commons by a vote of 72 to 21. It seems that this squad of soldiers required the wife of a deserter to tell where her husband was, and because she refused to do so, or, not knowing, could not tell, they set fire to her house and burnt it to the ground. We learn that Gov. Vance has very promptly and properly had these soldiers arrested, and we suppose they will be held to answer for their conduct. In the course of the debate on the subject Dr. McCormick, of Harnett, said that the proof of this wanton destruction of property was ample, and he urged the house to take prompt action, so as to warn evil doers against such conduct. He said he was determined to insist at all hazards on the rights guaranteed to his constituents by the Bill of Rights, and to see to it, so far as his action was concerned, that those rights were not trampled on with impunity. He said he had it from good authority that preparations had been made to burn the house of another citizen of this county, thus showing a disposition to make these outrages more general.

Dr. McCormick and Mr. McKay deserve the thanks of their constituents for the firm and determined manner in which they have asserted their rights.

No citizen is disposed to obstruct or embarrass the military authorities in their efforts to arrest deserters. But nothing will justify the destruction of property, whether belonging to the innocent or the guilty. It is the business of the officers who command our troops to protect, not to harass and oppress the people. No deserter, unless in the act of resisting, should be shot without a trial; and the families of deserters ought not to be punished on account of the guilt of the deserters. But we have heard, and fear it is true, that horses have been taken from the plow, provisions seized and carried away, and even the fathers and mothers of deserters roped around the neck and hung up until life was in jeopardy, because they could not or would not tell where the deserter was. We have heard also that these cruelties, together with the arrest of citizens on the charge of disloyalty because they had attended public meetings, have depressed and alarmed the people in many localities in the western part of this State, insomuch that they were deterred from going to the polls and exercising the right of suffrage at the late elections; while the *domestic detectives*-certain Destructives-who are regarded by certain officers as the only *true* men, and who are swift to give false information against their Conservative neighbors, went to the polls with their heads up, and voted. We repeat, deserters must be arrested and sent to their regiments, and all proper steps to this end should be sanctioned and commended; but no military officer has a right to order the destruction of property, or the personal punishment of a citizen, or even the arrest of a citizen without civil process, or the death of a deserter without trial, unless the deserter is in a state of resistance or rebellion. *This is a government of Christian people, upheld by reason and based on LAW;* and every wanton, cruel, illegal, unconstitutional act by the military, tends to array our people against the government.

It is the interest as well as the duty of military officers to act in such a way as to make the people love, not hate the government. If they love it, they will die for it if necessary; but if they hate it, it will perish, and with it our independence.[78]

The beginning of 1865 became especially bad for the secessionists. Confederate women pleaded with Governor Vance for help. General Lee sent veteran troops to squelch the dissenters at this time. Soon, the war was to end; but the feuds didn't stop, continuing for months afterwards. "Six military operations were mounted against the deserters, draft-dodgers, and militant Unionists . . . Records indicate that at least 68 were killed, 16 wounded, and 5 mortally wounded (pro-and anti-confederate casualties combined), but the actual number must have been much higher." This number was for Randolph County alone.[79] An outlaw gang from Person County terrorized the locals. A woman from Person County told her son about "John Whitt, Tom Whitt, Jim Roswell, three Buchanons, & Moses Chambers is the ring leaders of this outlaw party . . . Mrs Whitt is very much destroyed . . ." Colonel Johns was the local Home Guard officer.[80]

MOUNTAIN COUNTIES

The following is a poem by a Union woman from Taylorsville sent to Governor Vance:

> Then Chiear up you uion ladies bold
> For of your courage must be told
> How youv withstood abuses
> When your property theyd take

> The witty ancers you would make
> That would vanish their rude forces.[81]

Before the state seceded, mountain citizens ran into conflict. James Gentry owned a hotel and store. He said on May 6, 1861, that "a man is in great danger to express northern preferences here now."[82] Two Wilkes County men in a letter to Governor Ellis related that "various illegal activities such as violence, plundering . . . , and breaking into residences, and theft of money . . ." was occurring near Lovelace one month after North Carolina seceded. Some people had been killed. They asked him for permission to form a Home Guard.[83] An Ashe County resident with leanings for the old Union wrote, "No one's life and property were safe if it was known he was in sympathy with the Union."[84] People could not express their sentiment publicly lest they get into trouble. Keeping silent on political issues was thought the best solution. "Men die very suddenly here and they would probably be dead and buried before you hear they are sick," observed Levi Gentry in Ashe County.[85] Yet "fighting for the right to be left alone was a cause mountaineers could rally around," said author Paludan.[86] Some Union men had fathers and grandfathers who were Tories in the Revolutionary War. Bill and Triphena Williams of Cherokee County had sons on both sides of the conflict—George, Bart, Marion, and William joined the Twenty-ninth NCT.

Howard's Gap was an important thoroughfare through the mountains to South Carolina and Tennessee. It was an old stock driven road—one branch going to Tennessee, the other to South Carolina, and the final one to Georgia. Men with Union alliances used the road to go into Tennessee thence Kentucky to join the Federal Army. "The mountain passes were underground highways all through the war, the two chief routes being (1) from Salisbury following the Yadkin River to Wilkes County (called "Old United States") and across the Blue Ridge to Banner Elk and to Union Lines in Tennessee, and (2) from Columbia to Saluda Gap, through Flat Rock, Hendersonville and then by guides through Buncombe County to Tennessee." The roads through the mountain passes were extremely narrow with dangerous precipices. At times, groups would lose a mule over the side of the trail. Author Lenoir Ray spoke of "loyal citizens [that] built fires along the road . . . at dangerous places, and also at difficult fords over the mountain streams" to guide runaways.[87] Lewis and Martin Banner near Banner Elk helped Union people and escaped Federal prisoners defect across the mountains.[88] While being transferred from Salisbury Prison to Danville Prison, Major Lawrence Duchesney escaped and fled for the mountains. Mr. Banner and the major traveled over hidden paths until they reached the safety of the other side. Jesse Leverett was known as a guide for disloyal men trekking through the passes near Hendersonville on their way into Kentucky. Some accused him of lawlessness too. Joseph V. Franklin, of Burke County, led men through the mountains to the Union side. David Ellis cooked rations for their trek.[89]

The stagecoach traveling through Howard's Gap in Polk County was "held up and its passengers robbed . . ." many times by bushwhackers and deserters.[90] The outliers in the mountains stole from wealthy secesh families much like the Lowrie gang of Robeson County. "The typical Unionist came from a poor, nonslaving tenant or small landowning household located away from the county's main commerce and political centers," wrote a historian. Some yeomen families were resentful of the economic success of their pro-Confederate neighbors.[91] "North Carolina's Alexander Jones accused his state's disunionists of being slavocrats who 'look upon a white man who has to labor for an honest living as no better than one of their negroes' . . . . these bombastic, high falutin, aristocratic fools have been in the habit of driving negroes and poor helpless white people until they think they can control the world of mankind."[92] New York journalist Sidney Andrews described the mountain people on his trip immediately after the war: "It was not so much an uprising for the [Federal] government as against a certain ruling class . . . . it was a rebellion against the little tyranny of local politicians [mainly the militiamen, conscription, etc.]."[93]

Pockets of Union lovers were found in Edneyville, Henderson County; Crab Creek, Transylvania County; Traphill and Mulberry, Wilkes County; North Fork, Ashe County; and Marshall and Laurel Mountains, Madison County. One researcher has suggested that Wilkes

County had the most people with unionist persuasion,[94] while another claimed Madison County as the worst county, with 50 percent loyalists. Jesse Price, two sons, and a nephew notably of Union sentiment were hanged in the spring of 1863. Southern militiamen and neighbors accused the group of depredations.[95] Goldman Bryson of Cherokee County was found at home by Cherokee Indian trackers of Thomas's Legion and shot because he favored the loyal side, but mostly because he had committed havoc to the opposite side.[96] Bryson, considered an outlaw by most mountain citizens who favored secession, roamed the Unaka Range with "Kirk's raiders" as an independent company. One Indian put on Bryson's bloody coat and wore it around town.[97]

One woman without either a Northern or Southern sentiment helped hide and fed her brother for eighteen months. He was a Confederate deserter. An inmate of Salisbury Prison said that at one time, the penitentiary held a respectable woman from the state who had been guilty of feeding a rebel deserter.[98] A Confederate woman was asked about her feelings of the war by Union scout Daniel Ellis. She replied, "I have no sympathy for them [Tories] whatever. I believe it is perfectly right to kill them whenever they are caught. I have a husband and two brothers in the Southern army, and every man who is unwilling to fight for the Confederacy, who may be caught in the act of running off to Kentucky, ought to be hung or shot."[99] In a letter to her uncle, a woman said the women were as bad as the men when it came to their beliefs:

> I am sorry to tell you of the Union sentiment existing in this county, among women as well as the men . . . . Tom had five sides of leather stolen [from] his tan trough the other night. William Hudson who lives between Tom and me had his house robbed lately by armed men.[100]

A master wood craftsman and musician, Joseph Wilbur Lewis and his wife, Jane, lived on Little Horse Creek in Ashe County. Lewis was stationed at the saltworks in Saltville, Virginia, when captured. He was sent to the military prison in Cincinnati, Ohio, before being paroled to work for a farmer in Covington, Kentucky. He did not try to break his parole because he did not favor the war. While he was in Kentucky, a guerilla band went to Jane's home in Ashe County and stole her cow. Her father-in-law accosted the alleged perpetrator and was killed. When Joseph Lewis learned this, he vowed revenge. The killer fled to the mountains of Kentucky. When the war ended, Joseph walked home, paying his expenses by fiddling for dances along the way. As the years passed, Lewis went back to Kentucky to find Charlie Mitchell, the murderer of his father. Rumors flew that Lewis had come looking for him, causing Mitchell to flee back to the North Carolina mountains.[101]

Louisa Stiles of Cherokee County lost her husband, two sons, and two brothers in the conflict. Her sons had joined the Federal Army. Southern troops killed them and attacked her as well. She was delivered of her worldly possessions too. After gracefully entertaining and feeding six men of a questionable character, Andrew Johnstone was shot dead in his own home in Flat Rock. His young son grabbed a pistol and killed two of the Tories before the rest escaped.[102] A similar instance happened to Phillip Sitton of Hendersonville, who lost his life.

Research has shown that Confederate troops and the Home Guard, along with other hotheaded secessionists, created violence against Tory/unionists families. Deserters or those who fled to the caves and crevices to avoid conscription brought havoc to families of Southern persuasion. It was a lawless land similar to circumstances occurring on the Missouri/Kansas border at the time. "The wives and families of known Unionists suffered far harsher displacement experiences," related author Crawford.[103] The ungovernable persons in this section could be divided into three groups: those who committed criminal acts, those who defied the government, and those who fought conscription. People, whether pulling for the Blue or the Gray, would fit into some of these categories.

Twelve loyal women and children from Henderson County fled the mountains for Knoxville, Tennessee, to escape persecution from their secessionist neighbors.[104] Other pro-unionist women decided to leave the area after constant threats to burn their homes. One North Carolina woman, to escape bushwhackers, took her family consisting of a mother, two sisters, and eight children across Transylvania County. She said she wanted to give up but could not. Sheriff (?) Hamilton of Morganton and his wife helped Union men escape to Tennessee.[105] Author Crawford wrote, "In 1862 Marion Goss's mother, Rachael, was arrested for trading with one of David Worth's slaves." Worth had a substitute, then took the job of salt commissioner, and he also was a postmaster at the North Fork in Ashe County. Goss joined the Federal Army. James G. Wiseman, of Mitchell County, claimed he was persecuted for his political beliefs. He said the Confederate soldiers destroyed his personal property and forced him to join the Home Guard. To avoid military duty, he became a tax assessor. In preparing his request for amnesty postwar, his lawyer wrote,

> So averse was he to entering service of the so-called confederate states that he prepared himself to escape from the Country & go North in the event that he could not avoid the military service in any other way.[106]

Starvation was more of a reality than harassment by neighbors or gangs. By 1862, the mountain people felt shortages acutely. Unfortunately, which side a woman was loyal to determined whether she and her family would receive handouts from their affluent neighbors or military agents. Calvin J. Cowles, a loyalist from Wilkesboro, wrote to his father-in-law, W. W. Holden, that Tory women in some places were near starvation, having been denied sustenance from officials. Another person said, "One old helpless bedridden mother with three sons in the army [Confederate] and three sons in the bushes has been despoiled of her property."[107]

One way to catch the deserters and unionists was by tricking the families of these men. The Southern soldiers, dressed as runaway soldiers in tattered clothing, approached the suspect's house, begged for food, and asked for a guide through Confederate lines. Suspicious in nature, the residents finally relented. The outliers were called from their hiding place to lead the way. Immediately, Confederate troops appeared, and the disloyal were arrested.[108] In early 1863, the unionist women of the Laurel section of Madison County were "coerced by beatings and threatened with ropes placed around their necks in preparation for hanging," writer McKinney said, "to make them reveal where their men were hidden."[109] The Laurel Valley was known locally as a hideout for outlaws.

When Confederate troops caught deserters in the mountains, they would sometimes shoot without first halting the runaways; other times, the miscreants saw jail time.[110] This did not guarantee a long sentence for the jailbirds. People took the law unto themselves. "A gang of local citizens forced open the jail and lynched them. At least six separate Federal attacks between September 1863 and April, 1865, thoroughly disrupted life in number of mountain counties." These Federal soldiers previously had been North Carolina Union sympathizers who at times had grudges with the residents.[111] A few mountaineers saw the war as an opportunity to avenge old feuds. Betrayal seemed the norm.[112]

A lady in Murphy gave an excellent description of the turmoil in a letter to her brother:

> I write you to let you know the condition of our county [.]we are almost in a state of insurrection, the deserters & Union men or rather Tories have collected in large numbers in the mountains, a great many are well armed & plenty of ammunition [.]they have threatened to kill several Suthern men, they shot an officer while he was hoeing his corn patch by his house, they have threatened Murphy in force they say they will burn the place. I cannot say what they will do kill burn or steal; on the 8th of this month their was 7 of them came too town well armed [.]they traded a little, in the evening they started off & went to the lower end of town to a Tory house & counciled a while then came back seemingly mad [,] commenced cursing the sitizens & shouting for Lincoln

& the United States they then went down street & commenced shooting two or three times in the air. then shot up the street at the crowd [,] came very near hiting several persons what few men were in town got their guns & went to fighting [.] after fireing on them while they left, there was no person killed one of them had a finger shot off [.] they shot a boy in the foot standing in our door. There was two lurking about McCombs last night [.] there is the greatest excitement prevailing, we have been guarding Murphy for weeks [.] we have over 60 men in town to night but not all armed.

We sold our property all lands & town property for $16-000 got $3-000 down [.] we intend going to Brasstown until pease is made then leave the country, if the crops was gathered [.] I would rather leave none owing to the condition of the country for we live in constant danger as people are two parts tories.

We are all well at this time [.] the crops are good that is wheat & rye, corn is [l]ingering for want of work owing to the wet weather [.] the children sends their love to all the friends [.] write soon give my love to all & accept of the same

.   Your affectionate sister—Ann[113]

Talking postwar, old-time residents claimed the cause of the violence and killings was due to arguments before the conflict; however, some historians disagree. Author Paludan voiced his opinion: "The positive evidence for prewar feuding is obscure. Cratis Williams, Rupert Vance, C.C. Colby, and L.C. Glenn all speak of neighborhood quarrels as helping to generate allegiances to the Union or the Confederacy."[114] A feud between the democratic sheriff of Madison County and a unionist voter took place the day of the polls to decide if North Carolina should send delegates to secede the state from the Union. Having an open bar on that day didn't help. A gunfight ensued. In the end, the sheriff was killed. Nance "Granny" Franklin of Shelton Laurel District, a Tory widow with four sons, saw troops shoot three of her boys. A bullet was fired at her and cut a lock of hair from her head. The shooter said years later: "Usually I can knock a squirrel out of a tree at 75 yards but I took aim at that woman, almost enough to touch her and all I did was shoot off a piece of her hair."[115]

The Nortons and Sheltons were feuding before the war. Shelton Laurel was seven miles from the Marshall jail and two days from Asheville. A massacre took place in the thickets of Shelton Laurel, vividly remembered by descendants today. The story is often retold. In Madison County, Bill Shelton, a Southern sympathizer, allowed the soldiers to camp on his land. Roderick Shelton was the type of person "whose loyalties were . . . with whomever offered him the most money." Local officials there would withhold salt from unionists to punish them, "forcing them to come in and give themselves up to avoid starvation." Citizens resorted to stealing when they couldn't get their supply of salt. When it became time to kill hogs in 1862, only those loyal to the South received salt in the area.[116]

In 1863, wintertime in Marshall found about fifty local men on a raid in town for salt, which had been denied their families. Felt they were due more, the raiders stole blankets and clothing as well. A portion claimed to be deserters from the Sixty-fourth North Carolina Regiment.[117] Other research found women to be a part of this raid:

Bill Kirk, from Greene Co, E. Tn, took a few men, went over the mountain into Madison Co, N.C. in the Laurel Mountains of Madison, where lawlessness reigned supreme, and all claimed to be Union men. By his flattery he soon added a hundred men to his list and several low women.[118]

When Captain John Peek, who was on furlough, confronted the looters, they shot him in the arm. Colonel Kirk's men killed sixteen-year-old Jim Ray of the Sixteenth Regiment also at home. It was told that these raiders killed and scalped Major Holcomb and James Arrington, who was home on leave. They wounded seventy-year-old James Garrett. If the thieves had then fled instead of going to Colonel Lawrence Allen's home, the killings may not have happened. Two of Mrs. Allen's children were sick with scarlet fever. Her six-year-old son died. The raiders destroyed her furniture, stole everything "toteable" on the place, and even took the children's clothing and blankets despite a deep snow on the ground. When they left her house, they continued pillaging the neighborhood.

After the Marshall raid, the governor instructed Confederate troops under General W. G. M. Davis to capture the perpetrators and deliver them to the proper authorities for trial. General Davis's troops searched for the raiders of the Shelton Laurel incident and rounded up thirty-six of the Tories—twelve were killed, and twenty became prisoners. The majority of those killed were deserters.[119]

C.S. Colonel Lawrence Allen and Colonel James A. Keith, cousins, were in the Sixty-fourth North Carolina Troops. They took their force to hunt down the Madison County unionist thieves. Near the home of Bill Shelton, they clashed, and eight Union sympathizers died. Colonel Allen went home to check on his children after he received a report of the death of his son. Within minutes of his arrival, his four-year-old daughter succumbed. Meanwhile, Colonel Keith continued to pursue the marauders. David Shelton was killed. Fifteen men of the raid were caught and promised a fair trial. Some were sent to jail in Asheville. All fifteen were related.[*] Of the fifteen prisoners, three boys were under the age of fourteen, and three were over forty. These men were held prisoner in Bill Shelton's house to be transported to Knoxville, Tennessee, the next morning. One person escaped. Johnny Morton, age twelve, hid under the bed as the prisoners were leaving. Colonel Keith marched the others down the valley, out of sight of the public. He halted the march, told five men to kneel, then ordered his men to shoot them. Soldiers of the Sixty-fourth Regiment refused to shoot the prisoners. Colonel Keith told them they could take the prisoners' place if they didn't obey orders. Fourteen condemned men were shot. The Sixty-fourth buried them in a mass grave.[120] The following day, as the families searched for the grave, they discovered that a wild hog had found it before them and ravished the corpses.

Secessionists around Marshall and the county felt that justice had been served against the loyalist guerrillas captured or killed at Shelton Laurel. Vance asked the secretary of war for an investigation of the incident. After two months' time had elapsed, Vance wrote again.[121] Colonel Keith was court-martialed. In May of 1863, he left the army and went into hiding. The former colonel hid out in the rough terrain and was not caught until the end of the war. For a more detailed study, see "The Killings on the Shelton Laurel" by Jim Taylor in the August/September 1989 issue of *Company Front* or *Victims* by Paludan.

When the war ended, unionist William W. Holden was elected governor. He left more information about Colonel Keith:

> In December 1862 occurred the famous or rather infamous execution of loyal men in the Laurel Valley . . . . Mr. Augustus S. Merrimon then Solicitor in the mountain district reported the facts to Governor Vance. I called at his office to get the facts. Governor Vance was very indignant . . . . he said, "This was done by Colonel Keith of the 64th N.C. and I will write to Mr. Seddon, Secretary of War at Richmond, to have him court-martialed, and I will follow him (Keith) to the gates of hell or hang him." The facts were, that a body of men and boys, eight or ten, had made a raid from Laurel Valley to Salisbury to get, as they said, their share of salt, and going and returning committed outrages by taking property, etc. on their route. For this Lt. Colonel Keith, commanding the 64th regiment in that locality, arrested them—men and boys and some women—and shot them and buried them on the spot in trenches.

---

[*]   Victims: Elison King, Joe Woods, Will Shelton (age twenty), Halen Moore (age twenty-five to thirty), Wade Moore (age twenty to twenty-five), Old Jim Shelton (age fifty-six), James Shelton Jr. (age seventeen), James Metcalf (age forty), Stob Rod Shelton, Joseph Cleandren (age fifteen), Aronnata Shelton (age fourteen), Jasper Chandler (age fifteen to sixteen), and David Shelton (age thirteen).[122]

The women, with ropes around their necks, were whipped. One of the boys, about fifteen years old, was shot and not killed. His arm, badly shot, hung by his side. His mother begged for his life and Colonel Keith killed him by shooting him in the head with a pistol. Mr. Seddon . . . had Colonel Keith court-martialed at Governor Vance's request, and Colonel Keith on the trial justified himself by showing that he had acted in the matter by the authority of General Harry Heth. Afterwards at the close of the war, Colonel Keith was arrested and lodged in a Raleigh jail. He thus strangely enough fell into my hands to be sent to Madison County for trial for his crime. The Sheriff of Madison County with the deputy called on me for him. I told him (the Sheriff) that I had heard that Keith's life would be in danger at the hands of the friends of the murdered people, if he was carried through Buncombe and Madison to the jail in the latter county, and that he must promise me as the condition of the delivery of Keith to him, that he would take him by way of the East Tennessee railway, to a point west of Madison County, and deliver him from that point to jail . . . . He promised to do this, and Keith was thus delivered safely . . . to be held for trial for this outrage, but he escaped from the jail and fled the State, and I, as governor offered a reward of $500 for his apprehension and detention, and this is the last I have heard from Keith. It is thought he escaped to California. He may be alive yet. And thus the blood of these people is still unavenged.[123]

Soldier N. G. Phillips requested help for his family to move to a safer place if one could be found:

Valley Town, NC
Dec 24 1863
    Col Cathey sir the condition of this county renders it untenable the yankies and bushwhackers have Ruined it, & I will have to move my family out & as I will soon have to Return to the army I want to move them in to your county & my Father is a good miller & if you have a good mill he will take it, & he can bring as good a Recommendation as you may desire. I want a house & 8 or ten acres of land for my family & father & mother want to ____ go with me [.] I hope you will try to help me [.] I have been in the Service nearly three years & my family has not got provisions to Do them a month & the frost & the Bushwhackers & Yankies has Ruined this County so it is impossible for them to stay here [.] Let me hear from you by the first mail as what I do I must do promptly [.] Direct your letters to Valley Town North Carolina

Yours Best   NG Phillips[124]

A mountain native wrote her soldier husband that neighbors had changed their sympathies, and many were getting out:

    The people is all turning to Union here since the Yankees has got Vicksburg. I want you to come home as soon as you can after you git this letter. The folks is leaving here, and going north as fast as they can.[125]

After Knoxville, Tennessee, fell to Federal occupation in 1863, Tories in the mountains became more active. They attacked Confederate soldiers and the Home Guard.[126] Secession soldiers were out gathering new horses. When there were no males in the household, it made it much easier for the Confederates to take their horses. Towards the end of the war, it was not unusual for outlaw bands to kill innocent women and male citizens. It didn't make any difference if the women were pregnant, ill, or whatever; they were treated badly. Martha White, mentally retarded, was roughed up and tied to a tree. So were Sarah and Mary Shelton.[127] In Madison County, a woman was killed, then scalped. In Rutherford County, guerrillas shot a young girl in bed, then beat and robbed her father. Mrs. Joe Bryson was killed in Buncombe County, and her two daughters were wounded.[128]

The *Weekly Progress* printed:

> Though living in an obscure region, and as many thought in the commencement of the war a safe and secure locality, no people in the Confederacy have suffered more from the ravages of the struggle than some of our citizens living beyond the Blue Ridge. We have a letter before us from Madison county, which exhibits that country in a most deplorable condition, and without protection from some quarter of all law and order will soon disappear and anarchy will reign supreme.
>
> Our correspondent says:
>
> "There is a small band of the worst men on earth who mostly stay upon Laurel, slipping over occasionally killing men and robbing the people. On the last Tuesday morning about 14 men and 3 [or 8, blurred] women came over the mountain on the head of the West Fork, in this county, and killed one man and beat another nearly to death, and then robbed several citizens. On their return they were pursued by some of our local forces and overtaken and fired upon at Mars College, but all made their escape except one man and one woman who was captured. The women were armed with revolvers and took a hand in the murder and robbery. The women were all from Buncombe county. The prisoners taken belong to the 29th Regiment North Carolina troops."[129]

From Wilkes County, James Eller, aged thirty-three, left his wife, Mary, and five children to enlist in the army. Found unfit for duty, he was discharged. His brothers in North Carolina supported the South, but his brothers in the Midwest were Union sympathizers. Correspondence within the Eller family described the circumstances surrounding the Fort Hamby skirmish. Fort Hamby "was a two story log house on a high hill overlooking the Yadkin River valley, near Holman's Ford in Wilkes County." It was on the north side of the river. The wooden fort was owned by a disreputable woman named Sallie Hamby who was "of questionable character."[130] "That gang was said to have contained eighty-five deserters from Wilkes, Iredell, Alexander, and adjoining counties," said Eller descendants. A U.S. deserter named Colonel Wade led the men, along with another Northern deserter named Lockwood. Men would meet there, then go out and pillage the residents of Alexander, Caldwell, and Wilkes Counties. During their last battle with the Home Guard, four bandits were killed, including the man named Lockwood. After two days, the rogues' ammunition gave out; one set fire to the kitchen, and Colonel Wade made his escape. Wade jumped in the river and hid underwater, breathing through a reed. The rest surrendered, and it was over. At trial, the men were found guilty and sentenced to be executed by a firing squad. Before they were executed, a minister named Powell was summoned to say the eulogy in their behalf. He refused, saying, "I cannot pray for such wicked men." Another preacher came, Reverend Steele, who prayed "for mercy on their souls, if God could have any mercy on them after much-deserved punishment." Conditions around the countryside improved after their capture.[131]

Eller descendants wrote that about forty local men, commanded by Colonel Sharpe of the Home Guard, were the ones involved in the skirmish and that when it was over, his crew found many items the gang had stolen and stockpiled, such as ladies' things, saddles, leather goods, and decorative objects. These items were removed, and the entire building was set afire.

Another gang operating out of Fort Hamby involved Confederate deserters led by G. W. Hayes of Purlear in Wilkes County.* Mr. Hayes' outlaws had more members than the Wade gang. Mr. Hayes "made his headquarters at his own home."[132] In the fall of 1864, a third bunch of outlaws, led by Harrison Church, also swept the area. He was wounded and taken prisoner whereby his cohorts disbanded.

The Ellers continued:

> James Eller was a local agent for the Commissary Dept. and when the Wilkes County soldiers were reported as deserters, it was his duty to cut off supplies of salt and meat that he had been distributing to the needy families of Confederate soldiers. As a result, James Eller became a marked man. The bushwhackers began by plundering his home. They finally determined to kill him. They raided his farm many times. Mrs. Eller said these men were "of little property. Some of them had worked for us and knew where to find things. They broke every glass in the windows and smashed most of the things they did not carry away. Besides driving off the livestock and chickens, they stole firearms, meat and flour." The situation became so desperate Mrs. Eller encouraged her husband to leave and he fled to friends in Grayson County, Virginia. When the outlaws returned and found him gone, they took their revenge out on the women. Cursing and threatening them, they stole pistols, a hidden ham, female clothing, quilts and pillows. During another raid, they threatened to kill an eighteen year old slave named Bill Carlton if he did not reveal the hiding place of Mr. Eller. Since he didn't know, he told the truth, but the ruffians didn't believe him, so used him as target practice. They failed to break him down so let him go. They killed the dog and chickens, then left. At another time, bushwhackers killed her cousin named Billie McNeill who was in the Home Guard.[133]

————————————

On July 25, 1863, Julia P. Gwyn wrote to her uncle:

> I am sorry to tell you of the Union sentiment existing in this county, among the women as well as the men . . . . they have a regular union company up at trap hill! March under an old dirty United States flag! &c. Some of the people about here actually rejoiced at the death of genl Jackson! It makes me so mad to think about that I just want to fight.[134]
> Tom had five sides of leather stolen [from] his tan trough the other night. William Hudson who lives between Tom and me had his house robbed lately by armed men.[135]

With all the different roving marauders, the populace got little rest. Brothers writing to each other said that he (Rufus) "never go to bed without thinking they may come before morning." People had many sleepless nights, or they never went to bed at all (speaking of all raiders).[136] Another gang operating near the Tennessee line in Watauga County was the Blalocks. "Many times the Blalock band swooped down on the rebels families' farms only to find that the confederate cavalry had ransacked the sites first." The Blalocks set fire to secesh families' homes.[137] Keith Blalock, first a Lincolnite, joined the Southern Army under pressure, with the idea he would escape to the Union forces as soon as he was able. His wife joined him in male disguise as his brother "Sam" shortly afterwards. Both were members of the Twenty-sixth Regiment, serving for only a few months' time. With a medical discharge, Keith left, thereby causing his wife to reveal her gender to officers.[138]

————————————

*   This is the same gang that terrorized the locals in Cherokee County.

L. McKesson Blalock was nicknamed Kesse or Keith. He and Malinda fled up Grandfather Mountain and lived in a primitive hut and survived on wild game after he got discharged from the army. Some draft dodgers joined them as they formed a gang to make war on Confederate sympathizers. When they were hunted up, a skirmish ensued, and Keith was wounded. For a time after this, the couple crossed the mountains into Tennessee and joined up with the notorious Colonel Kirk. James Monroe, who lived near the Globe community, accused the Blalocks of being traitors and deserters. Keith's band attacked Moore. A member of the Moore family happened to be wounded; then Malinda was shot in the shoulder. This only fueled the fire. In the third battle with these neighbors, Keith came out worse, having lost an eye.[139] Not gratified with this type of activity, the band hunted up Confederate officers at home and murdered them. Malinda and gang were seen in Union uniforms. In addition to their marauding activities, the two helped Tories escape through to Tennessee and Kentucky. A Haywood County woman led a rebel detachment to a Yankee ambush.[140]

Elkanah Williard, a Union man, found himself in jail for his antiwar views. He was a brother to the Williards in the Bond School shoot-out. In Yadkin County, a group of deserters from the Southern Army, Quakers, and Union sympathizers hid out in the school. Militiamen headed by Captain James West approached the school and demanded their surrender. West immediately died at the door from a gunshot to the head. Others were wounded. Part of the hideouts escaped and fled over the mountains to join the Federal Army. Catherine Dobbins rushed to the schoolhouse after the skirmish to look for her husband, Jesse. She was told he had escaped unhurt. Some conscripts were arrested and charged with murder while others joined the Southern Army. A sister of the Williard brothers went to the jail in Winston to visit them. She passed along an auger and a chisel hidden beneath her skirt to her brother, which they used to escape.[141]

The Bond School incident occurred in 1863, but another skirmish took place nearby in the summer of 1864 when a mob of thirty-three men overtook the jail in Yadkinville. Three men—William Williard, Harrison "Horace" Allgood, and Mr. Reed—found themselves incarcerated for murder. They also stole guns and ammo from the Home Guards. Two other locals, Dr. M. L. Cranfill and Alex Johnson, aided and abetted the criminals to escape.[142]

Milton Williard, his wife, Polly, and their daughter, Nancy, owned land in Yadkin County. Most in their area felt the state should remain in the Union. About sixty of his neighbors called a meeting to discuss their Union sentiments once conscription was enforced. It was told that several of these men wanted to remain neutral during the conflict. They decided to try to cross the mountains to the nearest Federal base. The men were hoping to join up, then fulfill their term of service and quit. They wanted to get jobs and return home after the war. The sixty men started across the mountains as one group. Stories handed down in the family relate that the men made good progress until they reached to within four miles at the Tennessee line. There the group skirmished with Confederate troops and scattered. All sixty reached the Federal camp except for Milton Williard. He became a prisoner and was sent to Petersburg for sentencing in July 1864. The Confederate Army at this time was experiencing a shortage of men due to different reasons. Desertion was rife, and conscription was thought to be against the right of liberty. Morale fell to its lowest. Officials decided that Williard was to be made an example to keep other men from resisting conscription.

Mr. Williard made his escape from Petersburg but was recaptured. It is believed that this may have caused authorities to be so harsh against him. He left a short diary but wrote some passages in his testament, so this part is documented:

September 25, 1864
Dear Wife: I have found out my doom and it is death I suppose. This is the last Sabbath I am ever to see on this earth, but I hope I am going where the Sabbath will never end and I hope you and my dear children may meet me never more to part.

Dear Wife, I don't want you to take on about me. I want to be remembered by you and all my friends and tell them that I was killed for nothing and for trying to get home to see you and help to raise my children. I want to see you all mighty bad, but I never will without God delivers me out of my enemy's hands. My time is but short.[143]

Harvey Dinkins, reporter of the story, stated, "Another letter, which was probably intended to be the last he should send home, was more lengthy and was written on pages of his diary which he had left beyond the date of his execution." At first were written the words "All the days of my troubles in this world, 400 days, beginning April 30, 1863, ending: September 30, 1864." Then started the letter that related experiences of his imprisonment:

Dear Wife: I hope by and through the blessings of God, you may live and raise your children in fear of the Lord. Teach them in the Quaker church for if I could be allowed to live I would join them, for they are the best of all saints. I want you to keep everything—[*illegible*] . . . Don't have a sale and sell off your things. Keep everything you want to keep and sell everything you don't need. Get something to live on.

I have not heard a thing from you since I left home. But I heard that a letter came to camp, but I never saw it. Jonathan Brown, Eli Brown, the three of us left the camp near Petersburg 16th of August and got in about 18 miles of Farmville, Va. Was Taken up by the Georgia cavalrymen and sent back to the guardhouse. Have been here ever since. A mighty miserable place it is. We get about half enough to eat and not a peach nor apple can be had here without money and I have had none of that. We get nothing here but meat and bread, sometimes a mess of peas or rice, but mighty seldom. Eli Brown came here. We have to lie on the ground and not a thing over us. And our hands are tied fast together. We are lousy as a hound, and cannot scratch ourselves. I tell you we have seen sights for the last three months if anybody ever did. The nights are very cold here. I lay very cold every night. But my trials last in this world are short and I hope I may find rest in heaven for my soul. I have been under guard about a month and was waiting to know my doom before I wrote you a letter.

"I tell you that here is no place for a poor man! [The following sentence was censored but could be made out.] Tell brother William never to come to this wicked war." I know nothing of brother Granville, but if you ever see him, tell him and every one of my friends to try to meet me in Heaven. Tell Dayton Shugart and William Adams and George Adams to never come here where they shoot North Carolinians for nothing. Dayton, I tell you to keep dark, if you want to live. Tell my poor mother farewell and try to meet me in heaven. So nothing more at present. Only your affectionate—[*illegible*]—until death.

The testament that he sent home with the letters, bore on the flyleaf a letter written to his daughter Nancy, the oldest:

Nancy Williard: I want you to keep this book. Learn it and be a good child to your mother. I don't want you to forget me, my little girl and boys. I want you to remember me and think I was killed for trying to get home to see you. Nathan and John, I want you to be good boys. So farewell. September 22, 1864, Milton F. Williard.

The author of the newspaper article said, "The letter of an officer in charge, written three days after the execution tells the little that remains to be told of the final chapter in the unfortunate man's life. This letter was written to a communication sent by Miss Claresy Williard, the condemned man's sister:"

> Petersburg, Virginia October 15, 1864
>   Miss Claresy Williard, I received your letter bearing date of October 2nd requesting of me to try to do something for your brother, Milton, if he wasn't slain. I am sorry to say that he is shot. He was shot the twelfth of this month. If I could a done anything for him I would. I was mighty sorry to see him shot for he looked mighty cut down. But he said he was prepared to die. You requested of me to put a board to his head so if you was to come after him so you would know him. Of course I will do so with pleasure, if it is any accommodation to you. And if you come after him while I stay here, I will go with you any way, although you are a stranger to me. Times is hard here and they are shooting lots of men.
>   I hope this unmerciful war will soon stop. I will close my remarks. Yours respectfully, Hoarce Eddleman to Clarsey Williard.[144]

Author Dinkins continued his article. Nancy Williard cared for her widowed mother afterwards as her mother was an invalid for forty years before she died. Circumstances had not embittered her attitude towards the world.

———————————

A mountain woman recalled this story:

> During the last year of the war deserters from both armies, who generally were thieves and murders, banded themselves together, and were called bushwhackers. About this time three men were murdered twelve miles from Valleytown, near Andrews, and this band of lawless men swore revenge on the best five men in this valley, Mr. William Walker was warned of his danger, but said he was an innocent man, and had fed out nearly everything he had, and he would not desert his family. He was sick at the time, and friends pleaded in vain. "On October 6, 1864, there came to my house at 11 a.m., twenty-seven drunken men. They had stopped at a still house and were nearly swearing drunk. Dinner was just set on the table, but they did not eat, as they were afraid they would be poisoned, but they broke dishes from the table, and went to my cupboards, and smashed my china and glassware. At the time Mr. Walker was warned, I took his papers and hid them, but he was so sure he would not be molested, that he made me put them back in his desk, but they were all taken." In spite of her tears and his pleadings he was taken from her. She followed with her sister the next day on horseback for fifteen miles, beyond which her sister was afraid to go; but Mrs. Walker went on six miles further, alone, where friends persuaded her to return home, which she did after one of them had gone to Long Ridge to ascertain if there were any tidings from her husband there. Nothing was found, however, and she has never had any satisfactory word of him since. She had searches made by the government, the Masons, the war department, and others, but discovered nothing. When she got back home she found that these thieves and thugs had stolen nearly all her bedding, and had even taken her dead baby's clothing, leaving not even a pin, needle or knitting needle, and tramping her fifteen feather beds full of mud. Still, neighbors contributed to her assistance; but it was three years after the war closed before she could buy even a calico dress for herself. Coley Campbell, a Methodist preacher and a tailor, taught her to cut and make men's clothing . . . .
>   My husband told a woman, Mrs. McDaniel, where he stayed all night after his capture, that he only worried that I might not live to raise the boys; but that if I did, he knew they would be raised right.[145]

Guerrillas and bushwhackers could be called the same thing. They hid out on both sides of the North Carolina highlands. These lawless men traveled back and forth over the craggy mountains to commit ferocious acts on innocent civilians in East Tennessee and North Carolina. Regular military soldiers from both states tracked these insurgents continually, but the rogues could not always be found. Members of the Seventh NC Cavalry rode to Tennessee's border counties to capture numerous North Carolina bushwhackers. Apparently, someone had tipped off the bandits, and they fled. By the end of the month, the group, much disappointed, had only captured about thirty.[146]

Briefly mentioned earlier, the Price family made the newspaper:

Bushwhackers Hung

For many months past the mountains along the border of East Tennessee and North Carolina, in the counties of Johnson and Ashe, have been infested by a band of Bushwhackers, led and controlled by one Jesse Price and his sons, who have committed many acts, both of murder and robbery. This man Price lived upon Big Rye Cove ridge, Ashe county, N. C. The Abingdon Virginian says:

"The militia of that county having been called out for his detection and [apprehension], he had kept close about home on the lookout for a week or two Whilst thus watching in the direction of Jefferson a company from Grayson, Va., came in upon him from the rear last week and nabbed him and four of his sons.

They were taken to Jefferson, and on Friday last the old man and three of his sons — Hiram, James and Moses — were hung, without judge or jury, or benefit of clergy. The fourth son in consideration of his youth, and the promise that he would discover the hiding places of others of the band, was, after the rope had been tied around his neck, permitted to live. Price and his sons were dangerous men, and a great terror to all the loyal men of the whole country-side."

More than a year ago they had escaped to Kentucky, were apprehended and taken to Knoxville, and, after taking the oath of allegiance to the Southern Confederacy were released.[147]

Other stories of lawlessness in the mountains are given: "In the fall of 1864 Levi Guy, an old and offensive white man who had allowed his sons to shelter at his home when being hunted for their robberies in the neighborhood of Watauga Falls, was hanged by Confederates from a chestnut tree . . . . The names of those who committed this act are still known, and all those who have not died violent deaths [,] have never prospered."[148]

The outrage continued: "Gen. B.M. Edney, a brave man, was shot down in his own room after making a desperate resistance. Capt. Allen, son-in-law of Mr. Alexander Robinson, a man of wealth and high social position, and a gallant soldier, after the armies had surrendered, while working at a mill near his home trying to earn bread for his wife and child, was murdered in cold blood, and his body stripped of coat and boots and left on the roadside."[149]

The headquarters of the Home Guard at Burnsville, located at Mars Hill College, was raided in April 1864 by seventy-five lawless men led by Montrevail Ray. These rogues stole arms and ammunition. What the thieves could not carry off they destroyed. Other nearby buildings were plundered. Fifty Yancey County females looted government warehouses. "One group of western Carolina females raided Confederate farms."[150]

UNWARRANTED DEATHS

An accidental death occurred in Transylvania County when a man, William Deaver, opened his door one night to a stranger. Mr. Deaver's son happened to be a Confederate officer who rounded up deserters in the area. Some people chose to take revenge on these men doing their duty. When the robber called at the Deaver home, he was expecting to murder the son, but the old man got shot instead. Lawless men knocked on the door of Philip Sitton, invited themselves in to partake of his evening meal, then shot him as they departed. Sitton recovered from his wound. Roaming robber bands murdered Robert Thomas of the same county.

Throughout the war, rebellion thrived in the mountain counties. Alleghany County appealed to Surry County for relief of the continuous robberies and violent acts. One hundred men left Surry County in 1863 to help the Home Guard. On one expedition, four riders left camp to get some cornmeal for the troops. Outlaws kidnapped one of the party, a Mr. Jeff Galyen, who was later found dead. Tom Pollard admitted to this shooting. The group from Surry rounded up a man by the name of Levi Fender and hung him for the murder. "It was decided by the officers to send General Pierce with his soldiers into this section. These soldiers scoured the country, captured a number of the robbers and carried them to Laurel Springs, where a number of them were hung. Among those hung were Lewis Wolfe and Morgan Phipps." Near Sparta, the Home Guard clashed with bushwhackers, whereas several members of the guard were killed—specifically Jesse Reeves, Martin Crouse, Wiley Maxwell, and Felix Reeves. Other deaths on the mountain trails were Manson Wells of Buncombe, Mitchell Caldwell, two men named Groomes, Henry Barnes, Levi Shelton, and Ellsworth Caldwell.[151] Mrs. Cynthia Parks heard the skirmish near Sparta and went to see if she could assist the wounded. She learned that the mail carrier had been fired upon, and he left the trail without his precious mail. She gathered it up and took it to the post office in town.[152] John Kirkland, known as Turkey-Trot John, and his kinsman called Bushwhacker Kirkland joined the Confederate army but broke out on their own, committing havoc in the mountains upon Tories known as Union sympathizers. U.S. Captain Lyon, a rogue from his unit, made a raid through the gap to Robbinsville on a killing spree. Laid dead were Jesse Kirkland, brother to the aforementioned, a Cherokee Indian, and two men named Hamilton and Mashburn.

Dave Black wrote:

> I suppose that you are aware of the Home Guards being called in camp in Allegany for several weeks and perhaps will remain for several weeks more. I expect that we will keep a guard out all the time. I have seen several men hung Dead since we were called out and others have been hung two as we went down the Blue Ridge and Vaugh's men enlisted one of our men proven to be robbers. Times had got so a man could scarely pas the Mulberry road without being robbed. Numerous houses have been plundered. A few of the bushwhackers have been shot in Alleghany . . . I must tell you a little about our fight with the bushwhackers in Wilkes but I supposed that David Pugh has given you a full history as he was one that participated.[153]

Black goes on to tell that he was carrying the ammo, so he did not fire. "The Alleghany boys fought like heroes." None from their group was hurt. Jack Potter was murdered by guerillas while Silver Arnold escaped with only wounds. Lizzie Stout, wife of unionist Thomas Stout, became the lookout for the Potter family. Neighborhood women through the highlands took part in the war in this way.[154]

Near the end of the conflict (September 11, 1864), William S. Gentry and sons John N. and Stephen M. were "taken prisoner by rebel soldiers at their farm on Hanging Dog Creek. They were taken to the Tomotla community, tied to a mulberry tree and shot to death." The family was against slavery. The widow Nancy Gentry raised twelve-year-old William Alexander and his sister Phoebe Caroline with the help of her older son, Christopher, who was home from the war at the time of the incident.[155] It is impossible to count the number of murders that occurred during the war years in North Carolina. The reader has learned of these few, but the total number may never be known.

THE SECRET ORGANIZATION OF THE HEROES OF AMERICA

The Heroes "was a secret order of southern 'militant Unionists' dedicated to the overthrow of the Confederacy. Its activities included espionage and sabotage; aiding deserters, draft-dodgers, and escaped Federal prisoners of war, operating underground railroad routes to the Federal lines; and the mutual protection of its members from the Home Guards, the militia, Confederate troops, and loyal Confederate citizens." Sometimes these anti-secessionist used guerilla-type warfare while others used the softer touch by having "peace movements" and distributing political tracts. "Militant Unionists were southerners who remained loyal to the US in 1861 . . ."[156] Most Heroes of America were unionists, but not all unionists were members of the secret group. Some HOA were Masons, but not all Masons believed in the peace movement.[157] The HOA tried to get Confederate soldiers to desert and become outliers. "The HOA were doing all in their power to extend that spirit [peace] in the army by writing letters to the soldiers, urging them to come home, and promising them protection when they arrived."[158]

The order recruited perhaps ten thousand poor white unionists, both yeomen farmers and landless laborers.[159] Chief among the adversaries was Bryon Tyson—a Quaker descendant in Randolph County, an anti-abolitionist, anti-secessionist, anti-Republican, and owner of four slaves. He believed that you should educate your slaves first before setting them free if they wanted to leave. To help disperse his sentiment, Tyson published a pamphlet against the South. His thin booklet, *A Ray of Light*, he distributed while on a train in the state and also in Virginia. Tyson would pass a note to certain individuals, which read:

Mr. ____,
    I Send you in today's mail a circular to a book . . . . Consider well what is set forth . . . and see if you can't do something to save our country from inevitable ruin . . .[160]

He was promptly arrested and imprisoned in the Moore County Jail. "With the help of influential friends . . . he gained an exemption from military service on the ground that he would be more valuable . . . as a manufacturer of agricultural implements . . ." Governor Vance told him that his book would have done better if it was distributed *before* the war started.[161]

Tyson went North to Washington City and secured a job as a clerk in the Treasury Department. He continued to print inflammatory tracts suggesting that the Northern people eject the abolitionist element in Lincoln's Congress, which he claimed would strengthen Southern unionists "in their struggle against the Confederacy." Tyson cited "the Emancipation Proclamation, the dismissal of General McClellan, a Democrat, and the selection of General Benjamin F. Butler, who was hated in the South . . . to take charge of the Union Army Department of North Carolina . . . at the time of the peace movement," as the cause of trouble. Tyson claimed that had the war been prosecuted strictly on constitutional principles, it would have ended long before in favor of the Union with the saving of thousands of lives. He declared that the "deluded, fanatical, and suicidal" Lincoln administration—which had made war on Southern unionists—was "nothing but a John Brown raid upon a large scale" and should be "hurled from power." Upon Lincoln's reelection, Tyson left his treasury job to help relocated Southrons find a place in the North.[162]

Authors Troxler and Vincent's research show that the Heroes of America was founded by a Lexington physician who moved to Forsyth County.[163] Dr. J. L. Johnson, a Moravian, was the chief organizer of this secret society in North Carolina during the war.[164] Johnson traveled to Washington City in 1863 describing the HOA to head officials.[165] Johnson's wife was imprisoned in Castle Thunder, Richmond, because of Johnson's raid to permit fascist Confederate soldiers to desert and go into the Union lines.[166] E. B. Petrie, also of Forsyth, professed to be a member. Rev. Orin Churchill of Caswell County and Bartholomew F. Moore, a Raleigh lawyer and Mason, were unionists. Some civilians reported these men joined the HOA to protect their family and farms from the enemy. They said they didn't know they were supposed to give information about the Confederates in exchange for protection. Many resigned when this was learned. "They had been told that the organization would furnish them certain info useful to them and their families in case the Federals overran that section." In one peace movement in mid-1863, over one thousand attended. Abraham Clapp, a unionist, was accused of organizing the HOA in the Alamance/Guilford area. Other members of the HOA include Thomas Settle and Chesley Faucett from the piedmont.[167] Ben Hedrick of the piedmont was forced to leave his position at the University of North Carolina due to his antisecession views. He joined the HOA.[168]

Lieutenant John R. Welborn, before he became an inmate in the Salisbury Penitentiary, helped those with anti-Southern views escape to the North. He carried provisions and books to the prisoners. A. R. Richardson, a Northern prisoner there, said that Welborn was a member of the Sons of America, which was probably the same as the Heroes. Welborn helped Richardson and others escape from the prison.[169]

Order participants were active in Ashe and Buncombe Counties. Linville Price claimed to be a member. General William Whiting, commander of Fort Fisher, reported to Governor Vance that "2/3 of the conscripts at the State Salt Works belong to the treasonable organization called the HEROES OF AMERICA." The historian Scarboro said that "many employees at the saltworks were simply disaffected within the Confederacy."[170] Black men also joined the HOA in Davidson County.[171]

A euphemism for the Heroes of America included the term Hiding Out of the Army.[172] Synonymous with the HOA were the Red Strings as they were called—men who wore red ribbons on their lapels to identify one another. The HOA had secret passwords, grips, and signs as did the Masons. A few people associated the HOA and Masons as one organization. This outraged the Masons. Members of the society voiced a secret salutation: "These are gloomy times. What are you looking for?" The answer: a red-and-white cord.[173] Other members placed symbolic red strings on top of their doors or windows, the gesture known only to other members or runaway slaves.[174]

Author Don Markle has said that another clandestine group, the Order of the Heroes, was formed in 1864 and was the same as the HOA. The Order of the Heroes had these rules: "To anyone who joined the Society, the Union guaranteed the following: Exemption from military service; protection for your family from union harm when territory was occupied; and after the war, during the Reconstruction period, first choice of captured real estate."[175]

In Raleigh, during the sweltering months of July 1863, the Red Strings had two meetings. Holden reported the meeting in the Standard that over sixty meetings that summer united men in thirty counties. When caught, members weltered in prison, though some got off such as B. F. Moore, an attorney, by the use of the writ of habeas corpus. Several members were tried for treason. "There seems to be no record that any of them were punished."[176] A prison term would be punishment. Salisbury Prison was known as having the most dissenters in the Confederacy.

PEACE MOVEMENT

The war took its toll on North Carolina's citizens. Historian Gordon McKinney found that "civil society disintegrated under the constant pressure applied by four years of war. Common yeomen lost . . . faith in their leadership. They questioned . . . authority and decisions." Due to shortages, constant destruction of property by guerillas, and loss of loved ones, those left at home desired peace—no matter the price.[177] By midsummer of 1863, citizens had grown very tired of war and began to hold meetings around the state. "More than 100 peace meetings were held within two months in North Carolina after the battle of Gettysburg . . . in order to promote negotiations for re-union."[178] Peace was discussed quietly behind doors lest the party would be arrested; however, staunch unionists chose to display their loyalty in different ways. Peace and Union meetings held the same meaning. The peace movement in North Carolina dwarfed all the other Southern states.

In the mountains, Calvin J. Cowles claimed, in his letter to the president postwar when he requested amnesty, that "in 1863 the U.S. flag was given to the breeze and followed by about 200 persons through the Streets and [I] was thrown into the Guard House on a charge of complicity therein and . . . . looked upon by the insurgents as disloyal and have suffered on account of my principles."[179]

Governor Vance reminded congressmen of his views on peace in a session on May 17, 1864:

> . . . I, amid all the embarrassments and perplexities of the situation, [have] been unmindful of the great object of all our blood and suffering—peace, or neglectful of all proper and honorable efforts to obtain it—knowing the great desire of our people to save the precious blood of their children. If by any possibility an opening might be found for the statesman to supercede the soldier, I approached the President on the first opportunity presented by the cessation of hostilities last winter, and urged him to appoint commissioners and try what might be done by negotiations. I had little hope, indeed, of those commissioners being received by the government of our enemy, but I thought it our duty, for humanity's sake, to make the effort, and to convince our own suffering people that their government was tender of their lives and property and happiness.

Vance continued: My letter to the President last December and his reply are sent herewith for your information:

> I respectfully recommend that you, as the representatives of the people of North-Carolina, should lay down what you would consider a fair basis of peace, and call upon our representatives in Congress, and those to whom is committed the power of making treaties, by the Constitution, to neglect no fitting opportunity of offering such to the enemy. These terms, in my judgment, should be nothing less than the independence of those States, whose destinies have been fairly united with the Confederacy by the voice of their people, and the privilege of a free choice to those which have been considered doubtful.

> I presume that no honorable man or patriot could think of any thing less than independence. Less would be subjugation, ruinous and dishonorable. Nobody at the North thinks of reconstruction, simply because it is impossible. With a Constitution torn into shreds, with slavery abolished, with our property confiscated and ourselves and our children reduced to beggary, our slaves put in possession of our lands, and invested with equal rights, social and political, and a great gulf yawning between the North and South, filled with the blood of our murdered sons, and its waves laden with the *debris* of our ruined homes, how can there be any reconstruction with the authors of these evils, or how can it be desirable if it were possible? Lincoln himself says it is not possible; so does Mr. Fillmore, a man whom we once respected, and so do nine-tenths of their orators and presses. The only terms ever offered us contained in Mr. Lincoln's infamous proclamation, were alike degrading in matter and insulting in manner, being addressed not to the authorities, Confederate or State, of the South, but to individuals, who by the very act of accepting its terms would have proven themselves the vilest of mankind.

I cannot too earnestly warn you, gentlemen, and the country, against the great danger of these insidious attempts of the enemy to seduce our people into treating with him for peace, individually or by the formation of spurious States or parts of States. Indeed, I might add that I look upon any attempt to treat for peace, other than through the regular channels provided by our constitution, so long as our government is maintained, as almost equally dangerous. It is the real peril of the hour. The long continuance and bloody character of the war have so exhausted the patience of our suffering people, that many of them are in a condition to listen eagerly to terms of peace, without duly considering what the results would be or how they are to be acquired. An example of this great danger is to be found in the attempt of the British ministry, in 1778, to seduce the loyalty of our forefathers from the cause of independence, by sending peace commissioners to the colonies, with the propositions contained in Lord North's "conciliating bills."

Strange as it may seem, these "specious allurements of peace," described and denounced by Gen. Washington, have not been presented by the enemy. We are trying to delude ourselves. So great is the hostility and so furious the fanaticism of the dominant party at the North, that they have not even offered us terms that could be regarded by the most timid and wavering as "alluring." Lincoln's proclamation is so grossly outrageous and so repugnant to our every idea of liberty, property and honor, as to ensure the rejection of the terms it holds out, while it adds weight and gives a tone of authority to the oft-repeated assertions of their public men and presses, that they want no compromise but will only be content with our subjugation. If our enemy were really willing, under any circumstances, to compromise with us upon any terms short of our absolute submission, they would certainly say so, and that to those whom they know to be authorized to entertain their propositions. The insidious attempts to invoke separate, individual and State action, proves this conclusively, and can have no other intention than to plunge us into civil war and to subjugate us beyond redemption. How strange then to think, as some our people honestly do, that the very plan proposed by the enemy for our destruction, is the best way to secure a speedy and honorable peace! I respectfully submit that my plan, based on the wisdom and patriotism of Washington, and the universal teaching of history—to strengthen and sustain the army, and negotiate through the proper channels—is the safer and the better one.

It seems to me that the safe, true and conservative path through all our troubles, lies in guarding alike against the destruction of law and liberty on the one hand, and the impatience of the people under the burdens of war on the other, while with both hands, and with all our strength and hearts and souls we uphold and maintain those who, even as I write, are battling and bleeding for the rights and independence of their country. I confess I am not of those who seem to think *the greatest* danger to our rights and liberties is from our own people and our own government. While struggling to resist the inevitable tendencies of revolution to destroy civil freedom at home, I cannot forget that the danger from without threatens the destruction of *everything*—that there comes from the North a rank and bloody despotism, fierce and fanatical, gory with our people's blood and blackened by the smoke of their burning homes, with hordes of armed slaves thirsting to complete the demoniac work of wasting and destroying, and panting to sow salt in the furrows of the plowshare of desolation, as it runs over our razed cities, and in whose march forms of law, constitutions, free governments, life, home, property, all, all go down to rise no more till God shall implant in the bosoms of a new generation the principles of liberty and love of peace, which this, in its madness, has cast off.[180]

Constant raids by the Buffaloes Down East probably influenced folks to consider a peace movement. They too had enough and felt that Confederate troops could not protect them. Society began to lose their patriotism. At Mulberry Grove, Dr. G. C. Moore wrote his feelings to his relative:

8 Feb 1865

> Our people are dispirited and not animated by the same determined spirit of resistance as they have been before. And these peace men among the politicians, poisoning mind of the Confederacy and unlettered masses by their violations and harangues, have done much to bring about the present condition of things. They have taught the masses to believe that the Confed. Gov't. is a despotism, having no sympathy with the people, regardless of every other feeling save its own promotion and attainment of its own desires, absorbing gradually the liberties no enjoyed by the people and establishing a military despotism. I think myself if one half of these liberty shriekers were thrown into prison at Salisbury with their dear friends the Yankees, our chance of ultimate success would be greatly increased. I feel confident, we had better stand by our army, and prepare to make effectual resistance if need be than trust the peaceful intention of the Yankees. They will subjugate us if possible, and will only relax their efforts when compelled under the force of our resistance or outside pressure.[181]

News of peace meetings began to trickle back to military camps located out of state. Soldiers would write their spouses, asking questions and discussing the situation. Many blamed W. W. Holden and his newspaper, the *Raleigh Standard*, for creating more dissention. Holden, they said, was akin to editor Parson Brownlow of East Tennessee, another agitator with Tory views. North Carolina's military men demanded that Vance do something about the peace meetings, whereas he "issued a proclamation of warning to the people to desist."[182] Lieutenant Ruffin Barnes with the Forty-third NCT corresponded with his wife, Mary, about rumors circulating in camp of peace meetings back home:

> I fear Such mad meetings as they are holding in North Carolina will make it. [It] is bound to stop before long. We are all feeling Depressed now.[183]

Also with the Forty-third, Cary Whitaker informed his brother:

> It is almost impossible for a soldier to go home on furlow without coming back somewhat demoralized and despondent for the gloom that seems to pervade the people at home . . . and their insane desire for peace on any terms which seems to have taken possession of many of them . . .[184]

One man at home with his friend in the army wrote:

> I wish this infernal war was over for if the Yankees don't whip pretty soon it appears that our own men will so we are whipped any how. you thought it was tight times when you was hear but I assure you it is worse now and no prospect of them getting any better at all that I can see.[185]

One month later, he said this about his feelings:

> I dont see much more Prospects of Peace now than I did two years ago But the war cant last much longer the way they are carrying it on now for we will all Perish to death if it keeps on much longer.[186]

Two months later, still the same opinion:

> There is now a great few people through this country for peace [.] I had rather see it than to hear of it. I think the commissioners are sent partly to quiet the people at home and the army throughout the confederates States though I should be extremely glad if we could have a speedy peace for it is badly needed and wished for by all people but if there is any that hear [?] it, you will hear it by the time we do up here.[187]

Another soldier wrote his father about the peace meetings:

> I see, from the papers, that a peace meeting was broken up in Greensboro; glad to hear of it and sincerely hope all attempts of the kind may share the same fate, and the leaders meet their just reward, which in my opinion, would be the gallows. It grieves me to hear of so many persons in Salem who by their actions almost make us ashamed to acknowledge that it is our home; who while we are not living the most pleasant and comfortable of lives, are at home making large fortunes, and enjoying themselves in every possible manner, and in their hearts wishing the war might continue, so long as their purses are being filled, unless I am much mistaken, there will be a fearful day of reckoning, when the small remnant of the men that have left all at home, and gone forth in defence of their country, return and hear the tales of misery and pity that their starving families will relate, and are told of the extortion of former friends, who when the volunteers left made numerous promises that no family should suffer as long as they had a mouthful to spare; then I think there will be such a rattling amongst the dry bones as has never yet been heard, and the speculators will have to do more dodging, than they do now to keep clear of the enrolling officer.[188]

The talk of armistice in the last year of warfare is mentioned in letters to soldiers on active military duty. Nancy Davis wrote to her son, Burwell, on February 18, 1865:

> This war is a terrible thing and I hardly know what to do or say about it, only that we all should try and be prepared for what ever fate awaits us, whether it be to live or to die.[189]

Men in C.S. General Hoke's brigade proposed harm should come to Holden for printing treasonous information in his newspaper. "Petitions were being sent to Richmond demanding that Holden be hung for treason." Governor Vance had to intercept the actions. Holden's inflammatory published rantings so incensed the military that some took action against his newspaper office. Enough was enough. Instead of North Carolina's soldiers, it was a group of Georgia troops traveling through Raleigh who burned Holden's office.[190] Not to be outdone, Holden's supporters retaliated and ransacked the *State Journal* printing equipment.

W. W. Holden with his unionist cronies were responsible for the peace movement in July 1863. The first peace meeting was held on January 6, 1864, although smaller clandestine meetings occurred earlier. "These meetings were directed toward pressuring the state government to call a convention, with the possibility of secession from the Confederacy and a separate peace with the U.S. Holden warned the people of North Carolina that if the Confederacy was subjugated by the North, a certainty if the war continued much longer, slavery would be destroyed forever; only a negotiated peace could save southerners from military defeat and a social revolution in race relations. Furthermore, Holden proclaimed, the only way to gain a negotiated peace was through a state convention because Confederate authorities under Davis's leadership were too stubborn to admit the inevitability of defeat and to negotiate a peace themselves."[191]

A historian has suggested, "Support for deserters, draft resisters, food rioters, and bandits became so substantial among the lower classes that some local leaders feared a loss of control." In many instances, "popular sympathy with war resisters was blocking the enforcement of the laws."[192] Former Senator Kenneth Rayner joined Holden's peace movement. Railroad conductor Nimrod Bell told of hauling soldiers back and forth for the war. He said at first he rallied for the South and the Confederate army, but as the war dragged on, "I prayed for the close of the war any way—just so as to stop it, and that we might have peace once more in our country."[193]

The peace movement was felt strongest in the western counties, although Randolph County should be included. Editor Holden was accused of being "a member, which he denied." He said he "would accept no peace movement that did not come with Confederate independence" while he was campaigning for governor.[194] In Greensboro, an official warned the central government about the Red Strings:

> The truth must be already known to you that disaffection has always existed to some extent in this part of the State, and I regret to say it is now largely on the increase. We are, I fear, on the verge of a state of things that the mind recoils from depicting. There are loyal people here, and many of them, and yet even these must acknowledge the force and justice of the complaints urged by disloyal men among us.[195]

The peace movement in 1863–1864 was mainly an interaction between Governor Vance and Holden. The two men were similar to each other: both were conservatives, both were unionists at the beginning, and both were "critical to Confederate policies." One difference between Vance and Holden was that Vance—while he jousted with Jefferson Davis about such matters as conscription, impressments, the suspension of habeas corpus, and infringements on state rights—was willing and determined to uphold North Carolina's honor on the battlefield. Holden, in contrast to the governor, openly attacked the Confederate government through articles in his newspaper and boldly cried for peace.[196]

Jonathan Worth, former Quaker and state treasurer, wrote to his unionist friends requesting them to push for peace. He drew up a petition, which basically endorsed a proposition written by Bryon Tyson, that North Carolina should secede from the Confederacy and rejoin the Union. Tyson was a unionist who moved to Washington City at the beginning of the conflict.[197] The petition read:

> To his excellency, Z. B. Vance, Govr. Of North Carolina,
> We the citizens of . . . County, think that "all, save those who owe their riches to their country's ruin, suffer by the war," and that it is manifest that the authorities of the United States and of the Confederate States, authorized by the power of the government to make peace, will not appoint commissioners to open negotiations for this purpose. We wish to know whether peace can be obtained on honorable terms;—and as this cannot be ascertained through regular channels of the government, we respectfully petition your Excellency to convoke the Genl. Assemby without delay, to the end that they authorize a vote of the people upon the question whether a convention ought not to be called in this state; and to authorize the election of delegates at the same time, (such election to be valid only in case majority of the people shall vote for a convention) with power to put on foot measures looking to a general peace, and with all the powers with which the people can invest it, with the limitations only that the power of such convention shall cease within two years

after the election of the delegates;—and that any action of said convention, agreeing on a final treaty of peace; or altering the constitution of the state shall not be valid until ratified by a vote of the people, at such time and under such regulations as said convention may prescribe.

We also pray your Excellency to lay this, our petition, before the Genl. Assembly. February 1864.[198]

Governor Vance didn't feel like a convention was the best way to start the peace movement, and he "refused to call the legislature into session."

During the political campaign for governor of 1864, W. W. Holden, the Peace candidate, and Governor Vance clashed. Holden was able to use his newspaper to push his views on readers. He called for unionists to rise up and demand peace. Vance shot off a letter to President Davis to "re-open negotiations. The effort to obtain peace is the principal matter."[199] "In July 1864 Davis had stated clearly to Union peace emissaries that southern independence—not the preservation of slavery—was his chief goal in continuing the war. 'We are fighting for Independence, and that, or extermination, we will have.'"[200]

Holden only carried Randolph and Johnston counties in the election for governor. Members of the HOA were urged to vote for Holden. "Without question, voting for Holden subjected one to violent unpopularity."[201] Vance carried the majority of the military. The election took place on August 4, 1864, with Vance being reelected.

Another editor printing dissenting remarks against the Confederacy was J. L. Pennington with the *Daily Progress*, a friend of W. W. Holden. Notable men around North Carolina were concerned of Holden's influence upon the peace movement. He was accused of influencing soldiers to desert. Other editors decried him a traitor.

After a visit to Wilmington mid-war, a man wrote his friend about Jeff Davis:

> The President has been in our mist, and made a very favorable impression. He has given great encouragement at the hopes of our immediate community by assuring them, that if it becomes necessary, efficient aid shall be given us to contest evy [every] inch of ground before the Yankee invaders. The Vandals have been playing sad work with the blockade runners *The Cornubia, Ella & Annie, Margaret & Jesse,* and it is feared the *Robert E. Lee* have fallen into their hands. Large auction sales frequently occur and goods bring ruinous prices. Confederate money steadily depreciates, and congress will have to act firmly and wisely to sustain its character. Your family are well—all—as far as I know. Write to me as often as you can for it affords a great pleasure to.
> Your friend & obt. servt. Will Geo Thomas[202]

Davis made another campaign-style trip. "Hillsborough enjoyed a lift in mood one night in January 1863 when Confederate President Jefferson Davis, traveling from Virginia to Greensboro, North Carolina, got off the train at the station, was greeted by former governor Graham as master of ceremonies, and made heartening speech to the assembled people, telling them he saw peace ahead. All assumed he meant peace through victory. Such expectations had faded, however, by the last year of war, and almost everyone longed peace at any price."[203]

A group of men met in January 1865 in Asheville to draw up resolutions for a peace conference to restore the state back into the Union. The paper was sent to the Union commander in Knoxville, Tennessee. It was believed that the paper may have influenced the invading army when they came across the border to raid in western North Carolina that April 1865.[204]

In January of 1865, Peace Commissioners A. H. Stephens, J. A. Campbell, and R.M.T. Hunter, appointed by President Davis, traveled through the lines to meet with President

Lincoln at Hampton Roads.[*] It failed because of "Lincoln's insistence that restoration of Federal authority precede any discussion of peace . . ."[205] Many historians believe that Davis agreed to peace meetings because he wanted to quiet the Southern peace movement. Others disagree. They felt Davis really wanted to end the war. W. W. Holden in his newspaper urged other Southern states to follow North Carolina's example to hold multiple peace movements.

Francis P. Blair Jr., a distinguished Northern man, went to Richmond on different occasions and talked with both Davis and Stephens on separate days after the New Year holiday of 1865. He carried messages to Davis from Lincoln and back again. The two presidents could not agree on negotiations at this time.[206]

The *Asheville News* summed up for its readers in February 1865 that the civilians were ready for "peace under any conditions." Just before the capitulation of Fort Fisher, five hundred women signed a petition for peace, which was sent to Governor Vance.[207] By March of 1865, officials in the western counties met in Marshall secretly to discuss forming a new state out of western North Carolina and East Tennessee.[208] "In April[1865], even before the surrender of all Confederate troops, Governor Vance appointed [Bedford] Brown with former governor Graham and John Gilmer, to go to Washington to confer with authorities on the policy to be pursued in regard to North Carolina." The trip was unsuccessful.[209] As much as the Southrons wanted peace, people in the North did also. Northern Democrats believed in "states rights. The Democrats constantly urged congress and the president to seek compromise with the Confederacy and to restore the Union through negotiation . . ." They also "strongly opposed Lincoln's Emancipation Proclamation . . ."[210]

The story of North Carolina's civilians continues with Chapter 12 in Volume II. Read about soldiers' letters (many unpublished), blockade-running, combative women, Sherman's march, slavery, black Confederate soldiers, the end of the war, and parolees.

---

[*]   A. H. Stephens, vice president; R. M. T. Hunter, president pro-tem of the senate; J. A. Campbell, former judge of the Supreme Court.

APPENDIX

This chapter will reveal several different items, including cipher codes used by the military, and recipes for various foodstuffs as well as how to waterproof cloth and tan hides. There are names of the donors (usually women) who helped with the war effort. Another lists the names of indigent soldiers' wives who received food and salt from authorities. Also included in this chapter are lists of goods sold by merchants. Of interest to genealogists is a list of free black men petitioning the government for exemptions from the military. There is a partial roster of slaves who worked in the hospitals in Raleigh. Some music and poetry is listed, including two poems by George Moses Horton, the "Black Bard." A couple of popular songs are arranged.

Chapter 1, #A

> "Oh tarnish not now her fame and her glory,
> Your fathers to save her their swords bravely wielded,
> And she never yet has to tyranny yielded,
> Defend the Old North State forever.
>
> The national eagle above us now floating,
> Will soon on the revels of loved ones be gloating,
> His talons will tear thee and his beak will devour,
> O spurn ye his way and delay not an hour,
> Defend, defend the old North State forever.
>
> The star spangled banner dishonored is streaming,
> O'r bands of fanatics their swords are now gleaning.
> They thirst for their live blood of those you most cherish,
> With brave hearts and true then arose or they perish,
> Defend, defend the old North State forever."

The song "A North Carolina Call to Arms" was found in two versions with a few of the words changed, different capitalization, and the addition of another verse. In one version only the last line is omitted. Below is the missing verse in fourth place:

> "The babe in its sweetness, the child in its beauty,
> Unconsciously urge you to action and duty!
> By all that is scared, by all to you tender,
> Your country adjures, arise and defend her!
> Defend, defend the old North State forever,
> Defend, defend the good old North State."[1]

CHAPTER 1, #B Remainder of the anonymous song to the "Locust Hill Home Guards:"

CHORUS

"We have no ships, we have no navies
But mighty faith in great Jeff Davis
Fight away, etc.
Due honor, too, we will award
To gallant Bragg and Beauregard

Fight away, etc.

CHORUS

The southern states were only seven
But now we've got up to eleven
Fight away, etc.

From the land of flowers hot and sandy
From the Delaware Bay to the Rio Grande
Fight away, etc.

CHORUS

Hold up your head indulge no fears
For Dixie swarms with volunteers
Fight away, etc.
The Old Dominion still shows plucky
The storm is bursting on Kentucky
Fight away, etc.

CHORUS

You hear the notes of this same ditty
In the streets of every southern city
Fight away, etc.
Abe's proclamation in a twinkle
Stirred up the blood of "Old Rip Van Winkle."
Fight away, etc.

CHORUS

Oh! Here's a story I like to have forgot
It's all about old Winfield Scott
Fight away, etc.
From his home and honor parted
Fight away, etc

CHORUS

Oh! I am glad "He" ain't in Dixie, etc.
We ladies cheer with heart and hand
Fight away, etc
The stars and bars are waving o'er us
Fight away, etc."[2]

Chapter 1, #C

Poem from a sweetheart to a departing soldier:

"To My Darling"

When the grass shall cover me
Head to foot where I am lying;
When not any wind that blows,
Summer blooms nor winter snows,
Shall wake me to your sighing
Close above me as you pass,
You will say 'How kind she was,'
You will say 'How true she was.'
When the grass grows over me.

When the grass shall cover me,
Holden close to earth's warm bosom,
While I laugh or weep or sing
Never more for anything
You will find in blade and blossom

Sweet small voices, odorous,
Tender pleaders in my cause,
That will speak me as I was
When the grass grows over me.

When the grass shall cover me!
Ah Beloved! In my sorrow
Very patient I can wait;
Knowing that soon or late
There will dawn a clearer morrow,
When your heart will moan, 'Alas!
Now I know how true she was,
Now I know how dear she was'—
When the grass grows over me."[3]

Chapter 1, #D
PRECEDURE TO GAIN PASSES IN BOTH DIRECTIONS:

"War Dept, Washington, June 8, 1863
Ladies desiring passes to go or return from the rebel States can receive permits under the following regulations:

1. All applications for passes to go South must be made in writing and verified by oath, addressed to Maj. L. C. Turner, judge-advocate:

> I,_____applicant for a pass to go to City Point, Va., and now residing at_____, do solemnly swear that if said pass be granted I will not take any property excepting my wearing apparel, and that all the articles to be taken with me are contained in the trunk or package delivered or to be delivered to the quartermaster on the transport steamer on which I am to go to City Point; that I have not been in any insurgent State nor beyond the military lines of the United States within thirty days last past; that I will not return within the military lines of the United States during the present war, and that I have not in my trunk nor on my person any papers or writings whatsoever, nor any contraband articles.
>
> No person will be allowed to take more than one trunk or package of female wearing apparel weighing not over 100 pounds and subject to inspection, and if anything contraband be found . . . the property will be forfeited and the pass revoked.

2. A Passenger boat will leave Annapolis, Md., on the 1st day of July next to deliver those permitted to go South at City Point, and the baggage of each applicant must be delivered to the quartermaster on said boat at least twenty-four hours previous to the day of departure for inspection.

3. Children will be allowed to accompany their mothers and relatives and take their usual wearing apparel, but the name and age of each child must be given in the application.

4. Ladies and children desiring to come North will be received on the boat at City Point and taken to Annapolis, and every adult person coming North will be required to take and subscribe the oath of allegiance to the Government of the United States before the boat leaves Fortress Monroe. L.C. Turner, Judge-Advocate."[4]

CHAPTER 2, #A
FLAG PRESENTATION SPEECH by Miss Julia Durham, age 15, from Shelby, to Captain A.W. Burton:

> "We in the name of the ladies of Shelby present you this flag. It is to assure you of the deep interest we feel in this coming crisis. Regardless of northern scoffing and Southern terrorism you have at last faced your destiny and may the god of battle assist you to maintain the honor of the Old North State and defend those rights maintained by our forefathers on the 20th of May, 1775. We have adopted the flag of the Confederate States, whose interests are inseparable from our own, and for the purpose of expressing our heartfelt sympathy for, and co-operate with our noble brothers of the Sunny South. These hands shall unfurl this banner to the breezes and it shall never be lowered at the command of the hired minions of Lincoln. Our cause is just and God will be with us. May you who have sacrificed your greatest interests to come forward and seek eagerly to defend your country at every hazard, return back to your homes and kindred uninjured. We bid you God speed."[5]

CHAPTER 2, #B

This long flowery flag presentation by Miss Martha J. Hall and the ladies of Wilkesboro to the Western Carolina Stars, was copied from *Raleigh Register*, January 4, 1862, after presentation to Captain Barbers' Company of Volunteers:

ADDRESS BY MISS MARTHA J. HALL

To the Western Carolina Stars, the ladies of Wilkes present this flag, as a token of the sincere regard of which their gallant defenders are most worthy. From your happy homes, you go to join your brothers in defence of our common country, and to form a part of that illustrious army, to which are committed the hopes of a nation. In every frank, beaming countenance, there is visible the spirit of that dauntless valor which characterizes the chivalrous sons of our noble state, and we believe that in every heart, there is the fixed determination and resolute will, to do and to dare whatever our imperiled rights and liberties demand.

The tocsin of war, responding though valley and over the hill has roused your latent strength, and our bravest and best are rallying forth to strike for the freedom bequeathed to them by their sires, and they have sworn by their holy graves, and by all they hold most dear, to resist to the death this treacherous invasion. And right nobly have our Mountain Boys responded to the call. With motives pure as the dreams which gush from their rocky sources, and firm as their native hills, fearlessly they rush to the struggle. With the names of the valiant dead as their noblest battle cry, and the loved ones, at home to urge them onward, they will acquit themselves as 'men who know their rights, and knowing, dare maintain them.'

Carolinians were of the first in the strife, and worthy are they of their mother, as Great Bethel and Manassas do attest. No fraction's voice nor proud ambition was their incentive, but only the consecrated love of home, which, when it wakes in all its greatness, is the deepest feeling that sways the soul.

Your own friends who have fallen in the combat, speak in silent but impressive language—Wilkes herself has lured laid upon our country's altar some noble sacrifices, and the cry of revenge is echoing far and wide. Go, then, right these wrongs, and break the chains with which a tyrant would bind you. A brilliant course may be yours. You ask no need of fame, but you are erecting in the heart of every countryman a monument which cannot decay.

With your own blue sky above you, and your own sunny land around you, we are confident that you will never falter. Our national flag IS FLOAT UPON THE BREEZE, a peerless constellation just risen above the horizon, and which is destined to brighten till it has reached the zenith of power. The stars and stripes, which we once loved, are darkened by fanaticism and crime, and we adjure you, brave men, to trail in the dust the hated emblem of an usurpers rule whenever it may fall into your hands. Should your courage ever waver, or, should an hour of darkness come, look to your own flag, and there behold the brightest star in all our Southern galaxy. North Carolina, ah! Well may every eye flash with patriotic fire at the mention of that loved name. Basely misrepresented though she be, yet no other land can boast of truer, and more honest hearts, than are found among those who are willing to offer their lives and their fortunes, rather than suffer a ruthless foe to tread her sacred soil.

We bid you retrieve her tarnished fame, and when peace and security shall once more visit our borders, most joyfully will we hail your return. Our last wish for you is, that in weal or woe, the Lord of Battles will be your guide, and tis our earnest hope that the name of the Western Stars and the gallant leader shall be emblazoned on the most glorious page of history of our Southern Republic.

'Take your banner—may it wave
Proudly o'er the good and brave;
When the battle's distant wail
Breaks the stillness of our vale,—
When the clarions music thrills
To the hearts of these lone hills;
When the spear in conflict shakes,
And the strong lance quivering breaks.

Take your banner—and beneath
The war-clouds encircling wreath,
Guard it—till your homes are free;
Guard it, then, where'er you be.
In the dark and trying hour,
In the breaking forth of power,
In the rush of steeds and men,
God's right hand will shield you then.'

CHAPTER 2, #C
FLAG PRESENTATION AND ACCEPTANCE, YADKIN COUNTY:

From the *People's Press*, Salem
"Gentlemen of the Yadkin Gray Eagles:

As representatives of the ladies of our county, we have come to present you this banner—an offering fresh from our hands, and one that will be accompanied by many heartfelt wishes for your success—you who go forth to battle for the maintenance of our rights. Our enemies have threatened to take from us our liberty that we hold dearer than life itself, and subject us to their hateful control. And even now they have invaded our soil—and are preparing to execute their threat. Who then can hesitate, when such may be our country's fate? Your mothers, wives, and sisters all bid you go, trusting to the God of Liberty and your own brave deeds to bring you off conquerors in the conflict. And may you return to your homes and firesides and enjoy once more the blessings of that freedom for which you have fought.

Then take this, Capt. Conelly, and remember that wherever you may be, through whatever scenes you may pass, we will look to you as our defenders, and our prayers will be for success and protection for you and all those engaged in this glorious Cause. We give it to you pure and spotless, but when the war is over and you return home, how much more beautiful it will be when faded and worn from use in such work.

The first in our midst to respond to your country's call, we feel secure that whenever the post of danger is, there our flag will wave o'er a brave and true band, who

Scorning the sordid lust of pelf

Will serve their country for herself."

The captain replied: "When this cruel war is over, Miss Lou, this flag untarnished shall be returned to you."

CHAPTER 3, # A

The ladies of New Bern forwarded to Mr. Isaac Walker, Chairman of the Committee on Collections, $79 and a bag of sage for the army.

CHAPTER 3, #B

The Methodist Soldiers' Relief Society of Raleigh gave Sheriff High: 77 shirts and 25 pairs of socks for needy soldiers at Kinston. Kemp Battle gave his paycheck of $140 (for being a member of the State Convention last session) to buy clothing for Colonel Vance's troops at Kinston.

CHAPTER 3, #C

Sheriff High acknowledges the receipt of the following articles for the soldiers: "Among these is a new article which we have seen, designed by Mrs. R.W. Marriott, and to which she has given the name of cotton protectors for the lungs. This article is made of layers of cotton bats [sic] on cotton cloth, and has strings for fastening to the chest. It cannot fail to be highly useful in protecting the chest against cold."

Mrs. O.D. Lipscomb . . . four pair of drawers, four pair of socks and four blankets.

Mrs. H.L. Evans . . . two blankets and two pair of socks.

Mrs. L. Marling . . . one flannel shirt, six pair of socks and soap.

Miss E. Marks Upchurch . . . four pair of socks.

Mrs. Sarah L. Hogg . . . two dozen pair of socks and two blankets.

CHAPTER 3, #D

Fayetteville Observer, November 4, 1861:

"The military Committee for the county of Robeson acknowledges the following donations since our last publication, for soldiers of Robeson:

Mrs. Daniel D. French . . blanket, 10 chest protectors, 14 pr. socks .

Mrs. Dr. Malcolm E. McNeill . . . 3 blankets, 2 pr. socks.

Col. John W. Powell . . . $50, (pledged) .

Mrs. F.R. McNeill . . . 4 blankets, 6 pr. socks .

Mrs. L.C. Ray . . . 2 blankets, socks.

Mrs. Stephen Smith . . . blanket.

Miss Susan T. Salmon . . . blanket and 3 pr. socks.

Miss Nancy Hill . . . 2 blankets.

Mrs. Julia Mitchell . . . blanket.

Mrs. Sarah Pitman . . . blanket.

Mrs. Mary C. Inman . . . blanket .

Mrs. Ann Bullock . . . blanket .

Mrs. Susan Inman . . . blanket.

Mrs. Sarah Ann Faulk . . . blanket.

Mrs. Nancy Bullock . . . blanket.

Mrs. Capt. Eliza Spivey . . . blanket and pr. socks.

Mrs. Malinda Rowland . . . blanket.

Mrs. Ann Jane Inman . . . blanket, pillows, 2 towels, bag of sage.

Mrs. Frances Bullock . . . blanket.

Mrs. F. P. Watson . . . mattress and comfort, pr. gloves, 2 pr. socks.

Miss Fannie E. Watson . . . 4 pr. socks, 2 pr. drawers, bag of sage.

Miss Kittle Watson . . . 2 pr. socks, towel, package of red peppers.

Miss Julia E. Watson . . . 2 pr. socks.

Miss Hettie Watson . . . 2 pillows, 3 pr. socks, drawers.

Miss Smith Watson . . . 3 pr. socks, towel.

Mrs. Nancy Bond . . . 2 pr. socks."

CHAPTER 3, #E

"A package for the Robeson Rifle Guards has also been sent from Mrs. Dr. Neill McNair, President of the Ladies Aid Society at Centre Church; but as no list of articles or donors' names was received, I am not able to publish them.

I must take the opportunity of returning my most sincere thanks to the Ladies of Robeson, for their noble and patriotic efforts to render our soldiers comfortable as possible. Their valuable services in the cause of our southern Confederacy deserve our profound gratitude and will save many, of our brave soldiers from suffering while defending our homes. May God bless and defend them. Tho. A. Norment, Ch'n"

CHAPTER 3, #F

"*Fayetteville Observer, November* 4, 1861 BLANKETS AND SOCKS FOR THE SOLDIERS

Mrs. Catherine McArthur, Rockfish . . . 2 blankets.
Mrs. Daniel McNatt, 71st district . . . 3 blankets, 2 pr. drawers. 8 towels, 8 shirts, 12 pr. socks. Mrs. Margaret McInnis, ditto, 1 shirt.
Miss Mary McGill, ditto, 2 blankets.
Mr. Daniel Shaw, ditto, 5 pr. socks.
Mr. M. C. Lamont, ditto, 2 pr. shoes.
Mrs. William J. Kelly, ditto, 3 blankets, 2 pillows and cases, bible, 2 pr. socks.
Mrs. Alex'r Darroch . . . blanket.
Mrs. Margaret Ray, Little River . . . 2 blankets, 8 testaments, 3 pr. socks.
Mrs. J. D. Gaddie . . . 2 blankets.
Miss Celia M. Monroe . . . 2 blankets 2 bibles, testament.
Mrs. McPhail . . . blanket, testament, lot of red pepper and sage, 3 pr. socks.
Mrs. Jno Ray . . . 2 blankets, 2 pr .sock; Mr. Duncan Ray, 2 blankets.
Mrs. J. W. Evans, Fayetteville . . . 2 pr. socks.
Mrs. Mex. Elliot, Carver's Creek . . . 6 dyed blankets, 12 pr. socks.
Mr. John Jackson . . . shoes.
Mrs. and the Misses Deming . . . 14 pr. socks, 4 shirts, 8 sheets, lot of extra hard soap, lot of pepper and sage, bottle of balsam apple in French Brandy."

CHAPTER 3, #G

BOXES FOR THE SOLDIERS:

"In the care of Capt. M. A. Bledsoe, Raleigh . . . 123 blankets, 296 pr. socks, 13 woolen neck comforts. 10 shirts, 3 pr. drawers, 3 pr. pants, and 5 pr. shoes to be divided between the Plough Boys, Capt. Blocker; Ellis Guards, Capt. Sinclair; Cumberland Minute Men, Capt. Mallett.
Also 1 box for the General Hospital, containing 7 quilts, 1 bed tick, 10 pillow cases, 10 towels, 18 sheets, 6 pillows, lot of bandages, large lot of wild cherry bark, red pepper, and &c. 1 lot of extra hard soap, 1 bottle balsam apple in fine French brandy. R.W. Hardie"

Same newspaper and date: "There are now about forty patients under medical treatment in the North Carolina Hospital [Virginia] on Perry Street, the condition of whom, individually and collectively, is highly favorable."

CHAPTER 3, #H

Fayetteville Observer November 4, 1861: "Beaumont, Chatham County, Messrs. E. J. Hale & Sons: Below is a list from a portion of the Rowe District, received by me as one of the committee:

Miss Sallie Harris . . . 5 pr. socks.

Mrs. Henry Harris . . . 5 pr. of socks, 2 blankets, *2* pillows and cases, 1 lot of sage, 1 bag of pepper, 1 towel, 14 lbs. of soap, 1 cake mutton suet, flax thread, 1 bundle bandage linen.

Mrs. Jno M. Green . . . 1 blanket, 1 coverlet and 2 pr. socks.

Mrs. J. F. Rives . . . 1 blanket, 1 pr. pillow cases, 2 pr. socks, 4 cakes soap, 1 lot of dried apples.

Mrs. Thomas Beal . . . blanket.

Mrs. Thomas Dowdy . . . quilt.

Mrs. A. J. Stone . . . pr. socks.

Mrs. John Fields . . . quilt.

Mrs. John A. Pugh . . . quilt.

Mrs. Mary Willet . . . blanket.

Mrs. Asa Beal . . . quilt.

Mrs. Thomas Moody . . . quilt.

Miss Lucy Rives . . . blanket, 2 pr. socks.

Mrs. Ed Harris . . . blanket, quilt, 7 pr. of socks."

CHAPTER 3, #I
LIST OF ARTICLES RECEIVED AT THE DEPOSITORY OF THE SOLDIERS' AID SOCIETY 1861:

"Mrs. S. Wilson . . . blanket; May M. Marlin . . . socks; Mrs. A. Martin . . . blanket; Mrs. A. Hart . . . ½ bushel of onions; Mrs. McKnight . . . ½ bushel dried peaches; J. Turner . . . bushel Irish potatoes; Mrs. Gales . . . ½ bushel dried apples; Mr. E. Correll . . . socks; Miss M. Gray . . . shirt; Miss J. Gray . . . drawers; Miss E. Gray . . . 2 pr. socks; Mrs. S. Culberton . . . socks; Mrs. E. A. Marlin . . . socks; Mrs. Purrine . . . ½ bushel dried apples; Mrs. S. Correll . . . ½ bushel dried apples; Mr. Tobias File . . . cash $4.50; Mr. Jacob Correll . . . cash $20, one bushel potatoes sold, 75cents; Mrs. Sophia Eagle . . . . socks, blanket; Catherine Bostian . . . 2 pr. socks, quilt; Moses Bostian . . . bushel Irish potatoes, 2 bushels sweet potatoes; Mrs. Charles Miller . . . pr. socks and bushel of sweet potatoes; John Lippaid . . . blanket, socks and 1 pr. drawers; Solomon Kluits . . . socks, bushel of sweet potatoes and ½ bushel of beans; M. A. Greaber . . . 2 pr. socks; Mrs. Lawson Brown . . . blanket, 2 pr. socks; Miss Mary D. Pinkston . . . 3 pr. socks."

CHAPTER 3, #J
BOXES FOR SOLDIERS *Weekly Catawba Journal,* January 10, 1865:

"The surgeon general of this state is doing our soldiers and their family's great service by forwarding all boxes, packages, and by special messenger the first of each month. On the first of December 800 boxes were sent, for the soldiers. For the soldiers' Christmas dinner 400 were forwarded, and we saw on yesterday some 200 to be sent on the last of January. This number will be highly increased before the messenger leaves."

CHAPTER 3, #K

September 4, 1861 *Spirit of the Age:* "We are pleased to learn that every body has sent, or is preparing to send socks, blankets, and other articles of clothing to our brave soldiers. Our ladies will not allow our . . . men . . . to suffer for such things as long as they can knit and sew too—they can send socks, and make shirts as well as their mothers, and they will be glad to do it. The men will buy the cloth for jackets, pants, shirts, & etc., and the women and girls will make them."

"FOR THE SOLDIERS—Mrs. Wilson W. Whitaker, of Wake . . . 6 blankets; Mrs. James T. Marriott, of Raleigh . . . 4 pairs of woolen socks and one cotton; Mrs. Elizabeth Fort . . . . 3 pairs of cotton socks; Miss Eliza Hill . . . . 2 blankets and 2 pairs of yarn socks; Mrs. Rufus Page . . . . 2 blankets; Mrs. William J. Brown, of Wake . . . 2 blankets, and 2 pairs of socks; Mrs. William H. High . . . . 2 blankets and 6 pairs of woolen socks; Mrs. Kenneth Rayner . . . 4 blankets; Mrs. John H. Bryan, Raleigh . . . . 6 blankets; Mrs. Mary Shepard, of Raleigh . . . 2 blankets, and 4 pairs of socks, flannel vest, pair drawers; Miss Emma Hunter . . . 3 blankets and 3 pr. socks."

CHAPTER 3, #L

Spirit of the Age September, '61, Wake County: "Sheriff High acknowledges the receipt of the following—he requests us to urge every lady in Wake to send at least one pair of socks. Others, more able, can send shirts, drawers, pants, coats, towels, blankets—anything in short to make our brave volunteers comfortable—Cakes of homemade soap would be acceptable:

Mrs. John Whitaker . . . 3 blankets and a pair of socks; Mrs. George W. Mordecai . . . 6 blankets; Mrs. Kline . . . 2 blankets; Mrs. Rosin Dowell . . . 4 pr. woolen socks; Mrs. T.D. Sledge . . . 2 blankets and 3 pr. socks; Mrs. Carter B. Harrison . . . 6 blankets; Mrs. James Murray . . . . 2 blankets; Mrs. E. Hall . . . 4 blankets and 2 pr. of yarn socks; Mrs. L.O.B. Branch . . . 4 blankets and 10 pr. woolen socks; Mrs. Thomas Bailey . . . blanket and pr. socks; Mrs. A.M. Gorman . . . 3 pr. woolen socks and 2 blankets; Mrs. Wilson W. Whitaker . . . 6 blankets; Mrs. James T. Marriott . . . 4 pair of woolen socks and one cotton; Mrs. Elizabeth Fort . . . 3 pair of cotton socks; Miss Eliza Hill . . . one pair of blankets and 2 pair of yarn socks; Mrs. Rufus Page . . . one pair blankets; Mrs. William J. Brown, a pair of blankets, and 2 pair of socks; Mrs. William H. High . . . two blankets and 6 pair of woolen socks; Mrs. Kenneth Rayner . . . 4 blankets; Mrs. John H. Bryan . . . 6 blankets; Mrs. Mary Shepard . . . two blankets, and 4 pair of socks, flannel vest, pair of drawers; and Miss Emma Hunter . . . 3 blankets and 3 pr. socks."

CHAPTER 3, #M

The Wake Female Aid Society donated 12 shirts and 9 pair of drawers, given to Sheriff High since November, 1861 for Col. Clark's regiment. Other ladies who gave: Mary & Fannie Whitaker . . . 24 pr. socks; Mrs. George Little . . . 4 blankets and 12 pr. socks; Mrs. Ruffin Tucker . . . . one blanket and 6 pr. socks; Mrs. C.W.D. Hutchins . . . 14 pr. Socks; Mrs. E.J. Newlin . . . 1 pr. socks; Mrs. E.H. Newlin . . . 1 pr. socks; Miss V.C. Royster . . . 1 pr. socks; Mrs. Charlotte Gorman . . . 6 pr. socks; Miss Maggie Haywood . . . 6 pr. socks; Miss E. Hinton . . . 14 pr. socks; Miss Leonora Fleming . . . 6 pr. socks; Master Alfred Haywood . . . 4 pr. socks; Master Burke Haywood . . . . 3 pr. socks; Gertrude Haywood . . . . 6 pr. socks; Mr. Simon Turner . . . . 2 blankets; Mrs. Hustead . . . . 12 pr. socks and 40 lbs soap.

CHAPTER 3, #N

"Col. Vance's men are destitute of socks & underclothing. P.F. Pescud calls for the ladies of Raleigh and surrounding counties to help. The clothing was lost in a retreat from New Bern."

CHAPTER 3, #O

"Furnished for Capt. Rand's Co, of Col. Vance's Regt:

Mrs. DeBank . . . 1 mattress, 5 pillows, 3 pantaloons, 2 towels, 2 shirts, 1 coat, 7 pr. socks, & 1 quilt; Mrs. Polly Stevens . . . 1 quilt and pr. socks; Mrs. Alred Rowland . . . 2 pr. socks, soap and lot of necessities for sick and wounded; Mrs. Alfred Myatt . . . 3 blankets; Mrs. Penelope Jones . . . 6 shirts, 3 towels, 2 drawers, 1 pr. socks, 2 bottles wine, 1 jar butter, soap, and other things necessary; Little Bettie Jones . . . 1 pr. socks; Mrs. Susan Banks . . . 3 shirts, 3 pr. drawers, 1 pillow, 1 pr. Pantaloons; Linn Banks . . . 1 blanket, 1 vest; Mrs. Edmund Stevens . . . 1 mattress, 1 bolster, 1 comfort, 2 pillows, feather and other necessaries; Mrs. Eliz. Young . . . 2 pr socks; Mrs. Nancy Stevens . . . 6 pr. socks; Mrs. Harrison Rend . . . 1 pr. socks, 1 pillow slip, & eatables for sick & wounded; Miss Amanda and Fanny Jewel . . . 2 pr. socks; Miss Martha Jewell . . . 2 pr. socks; Miss Comfort Jewell . . . 1 shirt; Mr. Simeon Williams . . . 2 sheets, 2 shirts, 1 pr. drawers, & 1 towel; Mrs. Lucy Rand . . . 10 pr. socks and other necessities; Miss Julia Ann Jewell . . . 2 pr. socks; Mr. Geo. Atkinson . . . 1 pr. socks, drawers, and a shirt; Mr. F. Medlin . . . 1 shirt & other necess."

CHAPTER 3, #P

Fayetteville Observer November 4, 1861
A list of articles of clothing contributed by the patriotic citizens of Pekin, Montgomery County, and its vicinity, for the volunteers:

Mrs. Dudley Baldwin	2 pr. socks, and 2 blankets
Miss Frances Benton	2 pr. socks
Mrs. Frances Bethune	1 pr. socks
Mrs. A. W. Chambers	1 quilt, 2 pillows and slips, 1 pr. sheets, 1 towel, 2 pr. socks, 2 neck comforts, 1 package of bandages, 5 lbs. red pepper, 4 lbs. sage, and 1 bottle of mustard
Phillis (servant of Mr. Chambers)	1 pr. socks
Mrs. Judy T. Chambers	1 blanket
Mrs. Robert Chambers	1 pr. pillow slips, 1 pr. sheets, and 1 comfort
Miss Amy Clark	2 blankets, 1 pr. socks, 1 towel, and 1 pr. pantaloons
Mrs. John Ewing	1 blanket and 2 pillow slips
Mrs. Jos Ewing	1 quilt, 1 pr. sheets, and 2 pr. socks
Miss Minerva Ewing	2 pr. socks
Mrs. Patience Harris	1 quilt and 2 pr. socks
Miss Mary Harris	1 quilt and 2 pr. socks
Miss Nancy Harris	2 pr. socks
Miss Mary Jenkins	2 pr. socks and 2 neck comforts
Mrs. Alex'r McKay	2 pillows and slips, 1 pr. sheets, and 1 pr. socks
Mrs. J. Luther	2 pr. sheets, 2 towels, 1 sheet and bundle of linen for bandages, 1 comfort, 2 blankets, bundle of mustard, sage pepper, 2 pr. socks, 1 pr. pillows and slips
Mrs. Alexander McDonald	1 pillow and slip, 1 towel, 1 tablecloth, 1 pr. socks, 1 bundle of bandages, and bundle of pepper

Miss Nancy McDonald	1 blanket, 1 sheet, 1 towel, 3 pr. socks, and a bundle of sage
Mrs. Margaret McLenan	1 blanket, 3 pr. socks, and 1 package of bandages
Mrs. Mary McLenan	1 blanket and 1 pr. socks
Miss Sarah McLenan	1 flannel shirt and 1 pr. socks
Mrs. Sarah McLenan	1 pr. socks
Mrs. Hector McKenzie	1 counterpane
Mrs. John McKenzie	1 counterpane
Mrs. A. F. Rush	1 comfort, 2 pr. socks, and 1 towel
Mrs. Calvin H. Rush	1 comfort, 2 pr. socks, and 1 towel
Mrs. Zebedee Rush	2 pr. socks
Mrs. James Skinner	1 comfort, 2 pillows and slips, 1 towel, 2 pr. drawers, 1 package of bandages, 1 lb. of red pepper, and 1 lb. sage
Mrs. Robert J. Steele	1 pr. socks
Mrs. Thomas Steele	2 pillows and slips, 1 yarn coverlet, 1 pr. sheets, 1 counterpane, 1 towel, 1 flannel shirt, bundle of bandages, and 3 pr. socks
Mrs. Green D. Tyson	1 blanket, 1 quilt, 2 counterpanes, 2 pillows and slips, 1 pr. sheets, and 1 pr. socks
Mrs. Samuel Usher Jr.	2 pr. socks
Mrs. Samuel Usher	1 pr. socks and bundle of sage
Miss Miranda Usher	1 blanket and 1 pr. socks
Mrs. Martha Wooley	1 quilt, 2 pillows and slips, 1 sheet, 1 towel, 1 package of bandages, 1 lb. sage, 1 lb. mustard, and 2 pr. socks

"I need not say for the Ladies of Montgomery county, that their hearts are with those noble and brave sons of the South who have left their homes and bid their friends adieu and have laid their lives upon the altar of their country, to sympathize with them; and their hands shall not be slack in furnishing them with all the comforts of life when they know that they are in need. This is, however, the first public contribution, but much has been done privately. Their whole duty will be performed. So Old Abe will learn that he not only has the men to contend with, but the Ladies also.

A Citizen"

CHAPTER 3, #Q

Fayetteville Observer October 2, 1861
"SUPPLY OF BLANKETS AND SOCKS
Messrs. E. J. Hale & Sons: Will you allow me through the *Observer*, to acknowledge the receipt of 3 blankets and 3 pr. socks from Mrs. W. C. Troy, Fayetteville; 6 blankets from Mrs. J. G. Shepard, Fayetteville; 4 blankets and 6 pr. socks from Mrs. James Jenkins, Rockfish; 2 blankets and 2 quilts from Mrs. Sally Arnett, Rockfish; 10 blankets from Mrs. E. J. Hale, Fayetteville; 1 blanket from Mrs. M. M. Wiley, Fayetteville; 2 blankets from Mr. John Shaw, Fayetteville; 4 blankets from Mrs. M. A. Fuller, Fayetteville. James G. Cook and A. M. Campbell will, in addition to the persons already named, receive contributions. Hector McNeill, Sheriff."

CHAPTER 3, #R

BLANKETS AND SOCKS FOR THE SOLDIERS Contributed by: Miss Jennet Ray . . . blanket; Miss Sarah Ray . . . quilt; Miss Sarah A. Colburn . . . 5 pr. wool socks; Miss Polina A. Godwin (aged 7 years & 7 months) . . . 1 pair of wool socks **knit by herself**; Mrs. Neil Priest, Jr . . . 1 blanket; Mrs. Margaret Priest . . . 1 blanket, 2 pr. socks; Miss Flora Priest . . . 2 pr. socks; Miss Catherine McArthur . . . 8 pr. socks; Mrs. Daniel McNatt . . . 8 blankets, 3 sheets, 2 pr. drawers, 3 towels, and 12 pr. socks.

Hector McNeill, Sheriff.

CHAPTER 3, #S

BLANKETS AND SOCKS FOR SOLDIERS

"In addition those acknowledged in the last Observer, the following have been received: From Mrs. E. J. Lilly . . . 8 blankets, 4 pr. socks; Mrs. J.D. Starr . . . 3 blankets; Miss Hattie Starr . . . 25 pr. socks; Mrs. M. Flack . . . 2 quilts lined with blankets, and 1 pillow and pillow case; Mrs. J. H. Cook . . . 2 blankets; Mrs. A. W. Steel . . . 2 counterpanes; Mrs. E. Glover . . . 2 blankets; Mrs. A. P. Hurt . . . 2 blankets; Mrs. French Strange . . . 2 blankets; Miss Marion Sandford . . . 2 blankets. H. McNeill, Sh'ff"

CHAPTER 3, #T

CENTRE RELIEF SOCIETY, FLORAL COLLEGE, ROBESON COUNTY "Messrs Editors:—The Ladies of Centre Church and vicinity have not been unmindful of the wants of our brave soldiers now in Virginia. A large box was got up and dispatched to the hospital in Virginia some weeks ago; but they organized themselves formally for the war, to do what they may be able, on the 10th Sept. by the election of the following officers: Mrs. Dr. N. McNair, President; Mrs. E. Lilly, Vice; Mrs. A. M. Nash, Sec; Miss Mary Morrison, Tres.

They have contributed and secured from others the following articles, which will be promptly forwarded to Richmond:

Mrs. Dr. McNair . . . 2 blankets, 1 quilt, 1 comfort, 1 spread, 2 sheets, 4 towels, 4 pillows and cases, 4 pr. Drawers, 2 under-shirts, 2 hospital shirts, 1 pr. socks, package of old linen, sage; Mrs. E. Lilly . . . 4 blankets, 4 pr. socks, 1 pillow and 2 cases, 1 pr. drawers, 8 teaspoons, package of old linen, sage, starch; Mrs. Archie Patterson . . . 2 blankets; Mrs. E. M. Johnson . . . 1 pillow and 2 cases; Mrs. D. H. McLean, H. McArn and E. Lilly . . . 24 towels; Miss Sarah Shaw . . . 1 comfort, pillow and case; Miss May McLeod . . . 2 pillows and cases, 1 towel, and 2 sheets; Miss Naomi McDiarmid . . . 1 blanket; Mrs. Harriet Malloy, 4 pillows and 10 cases, 12 towels, 3 blankets, 3 pillow ticks, 1 blanket, bottle of honey, old linen, sage, hops, mustard seed; Mrs. Murphy McNair . . . 1 pr. socks, 2 pillows and cases; Mrs. Jennet McNair . . . pr. socks; Mrs. M. McAlister . . . 2 pillows with cases and 2 towels; Miss Fannie Watson . . . . pillow with case; Miss Nancy Smith . . . pillow with case and 2 blankets; Mrs. William McKay . . . 2 sheets, 2 pillows with cases; Mrs. Robert McNair . . . blanket, quilt, pillow with case, and 2 pr. socks; Mrs. Duncan McNair . . . 2 pr. drawers, 3 shirts, 2 undershirts; Mrs. Archie Smith . . . 2 sheets, 2 pillows with cases; Miss Janet McNair . . . pair socks, pillow with case, one blanket; Miss Sarah McNair blanket, pillow and case, 2 towels, bundle of lint; Miss Jane Wilkerson . . . 2 pillows and cases, towel; the Misses Patterson . . . 2 blankets, 2 pillows and cases; Mrs. June Leitch . . . 2 pillows, sheet, pr. socks; Mrs. Eliza McLauchlin . . . socks; Mrs. Mary McLauchlin . . . socks; Mrs. E. McKay . . . . pillow and 2 cases, one sheet, 2 blankets; Mrs. Mary Jane Smith . . . 2 sheets; Mrs. James McLean . . . pillow and 2 cases; Mrs. Malcolm Purcel . . . quilt, 2 sheets, 2 pillows, 6 cases, bandages, lot of old linen, benne [seeds], sage; Mrs. Catherine Morrison . . . 2 blankets; Mrs. Watt McGrit . . . quilt; Mrs. Hugh Leach . . . . blanket.

A list of articles—8 drawers, 15 pr. hospital drawers, 14 hospital shirts, 14 undershirts were made by the following ladies: Mrs. D. N. McNair, Mrs. E. Lilly, Mrs. E. McLauchlin, Mrs. Duncan McNair, Mrs. M. McAlister, Mrs. Murphy McNair, Mrs. Julia Sellars, Mrs. William McKay, Mrs. P. A. McEachin, Mrs. Henry Alford, Miss Mary McLean, Miss Effie McLean, Miss Carrie McLean, Miss Fanny Watson, Miss Amanda Bethea, Miss Ariella McKay, Miss Mary McLauchlin, Miss May Watson, Miss Mary McWatson, Miss Fannie Purcel, Miss E. Gulick, Miss Maggie Nash, Miss Margaret J. Currie. Miss Mary Morrison, Miss Mary C. Smith, Miss Harriet Sellars, Miss E. Dixon, Miss Mary A. Sutherland, and Miss Sarah Shaw.

R. N. McNair, Pres't, Mrs. A.M. Nash, Sec'y

PS The Ladies of Robeson County, who have not connected themselves with other societies, are invited to co-operate with us."

CHAPTER 3, #U

Lumber Bridge Ladies' Aid Society . . . . . From the *North Carolina Presbyterian* (no date)—"At a meeting of the LAS of Lumber Bridge, Robeson County, for the purpose of contributing clothing and other articles for the 14th regiment of NC Volunteers now in Western Virginia:

The following articles were contributed to wit:

Mrs. M. Ausley	2 blankets, 7 pr. socks, 1 vest, 2 shirts, 2 pr. leggings, 2 pr. drawers, and 1 sheet
Miss S. E. Ausley	3 neck comforts
Misses Brown	1 blanket, 3 pr. socks, 1 overcoat, 1 pr. pants, 3 neck comforts, 1 shirt, and 1 towel
Mrs. Peter Brown	2 blankets, 1 quilt, 2 blankets, and 1 package envelopes
Mrs. Col. Cobb	2 pr. socks, 4 neck comforts, one bundle sage, pepper, mustard seed, and ginger
Miss Charlotte Cobb	1 comfort
Miss E. A. Cobb	1 pr. socks and 1 neck comfort
Miss H. C. Cobb	2 pr. socks and 1 neck comfort
Mrs. G. E. Cobb	2 blankets, 5 pr. socks, 1 shirt, 2 neck comforts, 1 cake suet, 6 candles, 1 pr. pillows and cases
Mrs. J. H. Cobb	1 blanket, 1 quilt, 2 pr. socks, 2 pr. drawers, 2 flannel shirts, 1 vest, 1 pr. pants, 1 pillow, 1 pr. cases, 1 pr. gloves, comfort, 1 bundle sage, pepper, and benne seeds
Mrs. James Conoly	2 blankets, 7 pr. socks, 1 pr. pants, 1 vest, 2 towels, 2 pr. pillow cases, 1 pr. sheets, package of paper and envelopes, 1 bundle cherry bark, and 1 bundle pepper
Mrs. Mary Currie	1 blanket and 3 pr. socks
Mrs. Nancy Currie	1 blanket, 1 bed cover, 1 vest, 2 pr. socks, 2 flannel shirts, 1 pr. drawers, 6 candles, 1 pillow and case
Mr. T. J. Crawley	2 pr. socks
Mrs. E. Davis	1 pr. pants, 1 vest, 1 pr. drawers, 1 flannel shirt, 1 cotton shirt, 1 pr. socks, and 1 towel
Mrs. Elizabeth Graham	2 pr. socks, 2 pr. drawers, and 1 neck comfort
Miss Nancy Galbreth	3 pr. socks
Mrs. Catherine Galbreth	3 pr. socks
Miss Graham	9 pr. socks, 1 towel, and 1 sheet

Mrs. William Graham	1 shirt, 1 pr. socks, 1 neck comfort, and 1 bundle of pepper
Mrs. T. Jones	1 bed comfort, 1 sheet, 1 pr. socks, 1 neck comfort, 1 bundle sage, 1 pr. gloves, 1 bundle dogwood bark, and life everlasting
Mrs. Alex Johnson	2 pr. socks, 1 bundle sage, 2 towels, and 1 bundle of linen
Miss Mag A. Johnson	1 quilt and 3 pr. socks
Mrs. Alex Little	1 blanket, 5 pr. socks, and 1 sheet
Mrs. Capt. Little	3 pr. socks, 1 quilt, and 4 towels
Mrs. D. Malloy	2 blankets, 6 pr. socks, 2 neck comforts, 2 pr. pants, 2 vests, 2 flannel shirts, 2 towels, 2 pr. drawers, 2 pr. gloves, and 1 package paper
Mrs. Mary A. McAlpin	1 blanket, 1 pr. socks, 1 neck comfort, 1 bundle of balm, sage, mustard seed, and 1 cake of suet
Mrs. A. McDonald	1 blanket and 2 pr. socks
Miss Sally A. McDonald	2 blankets and 2 pr. socks
Mrs. Mary McEachin	2 blankets, 6 pr. socks, 1 pr. pants, 1 vest, 2 pr. drawers, flannel, 2 neck comforts, one bundle sage, pepper, and dried fruit
Mrs. D. McGugan Sr.	1 blanket, 1 bed cover, 4 pr. socks, 2 pr. pants, 2 neck comforts, 2 pr. gloves, 2 towels, 1 pillow and case, 1 vest, 1 pr. leggings, 1 box soap, 1 bundle of sage, pepper, and 1 bottle of honey
Mr. D. B. McGugan	1 dressed sheep skin
Mrs. D. B. McGugan	1 blanket, 2 pr. socks, 1 shirt, 1 pillow, and case
Miss Isabella McGugan	1 blanket and 1 pr. socks
Mrs. John McGugan	1 blanket, 1 flannel shirt, 1 bundle sage, mustard seed, balm, burdock, and horehound
Miss Mag J. McGugan	2 pr. flannel drawers
Miss Mary Ann McGugan	2 flannel shirts and 1 cotton shirt
Mr. Arch McKinnon	1 pr. pants, 1 vest, 1 pr. drawers, 1 cotton shirt, 1 flannel shirt, 2 pr. socks, 1 pr. gloves, and 1 bottle ink
Mrs. D. J. McLeod	1 pr. socks, 1 package paper and envelopes
Miss Sarah McMillian	2 blankets, 1 pillow and case, 1 neck comfort, 1 towel, package of paper and quills, 2 spoons, 1 plate, and 1 bottle of camphor
Mrs. Elizabeth McNair	1 blanket, 1 pr. drawers, 1 shirt, and 2 pr. socks
Mrs. Caty F. McNeill	4 neck comforts and 1 pr. gloves
Mrs. D. C. McNeill	2 blankets, 4 pr. socks, 3 shirts, 3 flannel shirts, 4 pr. drawers, 2 sheets, 1 pr. pants, 1 pr. pillows and cases, 4 pr. gloves, 2 pr. leggings, 1 package paper and envelopes, 1 keg soap, 6 bars soap, 1 bundle linen, 1 bundle sage, balm, mustard seed, rose oil, and 1 overcoat
Mrs. W. C. McNeill	2 blankets, 1 bed cover, 4 pr. socks, 3 pr. pants, 2 flannel shirts, 2 pr. gloves, package of paper and envelopes, and bundle of linen for hospital purposes

Beck, a servant of D. J. McNeill	1 pr. gloves, also her 86 year old mother knit 1 pr. gloves without spectacles
Mrs. Flora Monroe	1 blanket and 1 pr. socks
Mrs. Cath Morrison	2 pr. socks and 1 towel
Miss Catherine Shaw	rockfish and 1 blanket
Mrs. Dr. Smith	2 pr. socks, 1 neck comfort, 1 bundle sage, mustard seed, and pepper
Miss Flora Smith	5 pr. socks
Miss Nelly Wilkerson	2 blankets, 1 pillow and case, 2 pr. socks, and 1 towel

Mrs. W. C. McNeill, Pres."

CHAPTER 3, #V

Fayetteville Observer November 4, 1861

Beaumont, Chatham County, Messrs. E. J. Hale & Sons, Below is a list of donations from a portion of the Rowe District, received by me as one of the committee:

Mrs. Asa Beal	1 quilt
Mrs. Thomas Beal	1 blanket
Mrs. Thomas Dowdy	1 quilt, 2 blankets, 2 pillows and cases, 1 lot of sage, 1 bag of pepper, 1 towel, 14 lbs. of soap, 1 cake mutton suet, flax thread, 1 bundle bandage linen, and 2 pr. socks
Mrs. John Fields	1 quilt
Mrs. John M. Green	1 blanket and 1 coverlet
Mrs. Ed Harris	1 blanket, 1 quilt, and 7 pr. socks
Mrs. Henry Harris	5 pr. socks
Miss Sallie Harris	5 pr. socks
Mrs. Thomas Moody	1 quilt
Mrs. John A. Pugh	1 quilt
Mrs. J. F. Rives	1 blanket, 1 pr. pillow cases, 2 pr. socks, 4 cakes of soap, and 1 lot of dried apples
Miss Lucy Rives	2 pr. socks
Mrs. A. J. Stone	1 pr. socks
Mrs. Mary Willet	1 blanket

CHAPTER 3, #W

Sheriff High has received the following contributions since November 19, 1861 for Colonel W.J. Clark's regiment

Miss Leonora Fleming	6 pr. socks
Mrs. Charlotte A. Gorman	6 pr. socks
Gertrude Haywood	6 pr. socks
Master Alfred Haywood	4 pr. socks

Master Burke Haywood	8 pr. socks
Miss E. Hinton	14 pr. socks
Mrs. Husted	12 pr. socks and 40 lbs. soap
Mrs. C. W. D. Hutchins	14 pr. socks
Miss Maggie U. Haywood	6 pr. socks
Mrs. B. W. Justice	6 pr. socks
Mrs. George Little	4 blankets and 12 pr. socks
Miss E. F. Newlin	1 pr. socks
Miss E. J. Newlin	1 pr socks
Mrs. Mahala Ross	6 pr. socks
Miss V. C. Royster	1 pr. socks
Mrs. Rufus Tucker	1 homemade blanket and 6 pr. socks
Mr. Simon Turner	2 blankets
Wake Female Aid Society	12 shirts and 9 pr. drawers
Misses Mary and Fannie Whitaker	24 pr. socks

October 2, 1861

The following is list of articles received by Kenneth Worthy, Sheriff of Moore County, on November 19, 1861 as donations to the volunteers of said county, to wit:

Mrs. Alex Black	1 blanket
Miss Catherine Black	1 pr. socks
Miss Jane Black	1 pr. socks
Mrs. Mary Black	1 blanket
Miss Penny A Blackman	1 pr. socks
A. M. Blue	$2.00
Mrs. A. M. Blue	2 pr. socks, 1 towel, and sage
Miss Sarah A. Blue	1 shirt and 1 pr. socks
Mrs. Malcom M. Blue	1 blanket
Miss Margaret J. Blue	1 pr. socks and 2 towels
Mrs. Daniel S. Blue	1 blanket and 1 pr. socks
Susannah Brewer	1 blanket
Miss Eleanor Brown	2 pr. socks
Miss Margaret Brown	2 pr. socks
Miss Nancy Brown	1 blanket and 1 pr. socks
Mrs. Arch'd Buchan	1 blanket
Miss Buchan	1 pr. socks
Miss Mary J. Buchan	1 quilt
Mrs. Martha Cagle	1 quilt, 1 pillow, 1 sheet, and lot of sage, balm, pepper, soap, hops, and mustard seed
Mary A. Campbell	1 pr. socks
Miss J. E. Campbell	1 pr. socks
Miss Mary A. Campbell	1 pr. socks

Mrs. John Campbell and daughter	8 pr. socks, 6 yards jeans cloth, and 1 blanket
Mrs. C. A. Clark	1 pr. socks
Mrs. B. Coffin	1 blanket and 5 pr. socks
John Cole Sr.	10 pr. socks
Nancy Craven	1 blanket and 1 pr. socks
Daniel B. Currie, Esq.	23 pr. socks
Mrs. Duncan B. Currie	2 blankets and 2 pr. socks
Mrs. Daniel B. Currie	1 blanket
Mrs. Arch'd B. Currie	1 blanket
Mrs. M. B. Currie	1 blanket
Mrs. J. R. Currie	2 blankets and 2 pr. socks
Lydia Davis	1 blanket and 1 pr. socks
Mrs. J. E. Everett	1 blanket and 1 pr. socks
Mrs. John Fry	1 blanket
Mrs. W. B. Fry	1 blanket and 1 pr. socks
Mrs. R. W. Goldston	1 coverlet
Mrs. W. W. Graham	2 blankets and 2 pr. socks
Mrs. O.S. Hanner	1 coverlet and 4 pr. socks
Miss Ann L. Hanner (9 years old)	2 pr. socks and 3 vials
Miss Eugenia Harrington	1 blanket and 2 pr. socks
Miss Caroline Husey	1 blanket
Miss Fanny Jordan	1 blanket
Mrs. K. B. Kelly	4 pr. socks
Mrs. Arch'd Kelly	2 blankets
Mrs. D. M. Kennedy	1 blanket
Mrs. Hugh M. Leach	2 blankets and 4 pr. socks
Mrs. Sarah Maness	2 pr. socks
Miss Christian Matheson	1 blanket and 2 pr. socks
Miss Isabella Mattheson	1 pr. socks
Miss Flora McCallum	1 blanket and 2 pr. socks
Miss Catherine McCasill	1 blanket
Mrs. Kenneth McCaskill	1 quilt
Mrs. Allen McDonald	2 blankets
Christian McDonald	1 pr. socks
Mary McDonald	2 blankets
Mrs. Neill McDonald	2 pr. socks
Mrs. S. McDonald	1 blanket
Mrs. John McInnis	1 blanket
Misses Catherine and Jane McKinnon	3 blankets
Mrs. Nancy McKenzie	1 quilt
Miss Margaret McKenzie	2 blankets
Mrs. Margaret McKenzie	1 blanket
Miss Mary McKinnon	1 blanket

Miss Nancy McLauchlin	1 blanket
Mrs. Neill McLauchlin and Mrs. Kenneth Ray	2 blankets
Miss Sarah McLauchlin	3 pr. socks
Miss Catherine McLean	1 blanket
Mrs. Malcom McLean	1 blanket, 1 pr. socks, and 1 pr. pants
Flora McLeod	2 pr. socks
Miss Harriet McLeod	1 blanket
Miss Sarah McLeod	1 pr. socks
Miss Ann McNair	1 blanket
Malcom McNeill	1 blanket and 1 pr. socks
Mrs. Malcom McNeill	1 blanket and 1 pr. socks
Martha Miller	1 blanket
Martha K. Miller	1 pr. socks
Mrs. Caroline Moffit	2 blankets
Miss Eliza J. Monroe	1 pr. socks
Miss Flora M. Monroe	1 pr. socks
Mrs. Frances Monroe	2 pr. socks
Mrs. John Monroe	1 blanket and 4 pr. socks
Mary B. Owen	2 blankets and 2 pr. socks
Mrs. Edward Patterson	1 blanket
Miss Frances A. V. Patterson	2 pr. socks, 4 pillowslips, 1 pillow, 4 towels, 1 testament and lot of pepper and sage
Miss Emeline M. Patterson	1 pr. socks
Mrs. W.A. Phillips	1 pr. socks
Mrs. Ann Ray	1 neck comfort
Arch'd Ray	1 shirt, 1 pillow, and 1 towel
Mrs. Arch'd Ray	1 pillow, 1 shirt, and 1 towel
Mrs. Archy Ray	1 blanket, 2 shirts, 1 pr. socks, and 1 dozen candles
Miss Catherine A. Ray	1 quilt, 61 towels, 1 pr. socks, and sage
Miss Martha A. Ray	1 blanket
Miss Mary A. Ray	1 blanket
Miss Mary L. Ray	1 towel
Mrs. Patrick Ray	1 blanket
Miss Patrick Ray	sage
Mrs. Sarah E. Ray	1 blanket and 1 pr. socks
Mrs. J. Rouse	2 pr. socks
Mrs. D. R. Shaw	1 comfort, 1 shirt, and 1 pr. socks
Miss Mary Sinclair	1 quilt
Miss Silva J. Sinclair	1 pr. socks
Mrs. W. P. Smith	2 pr. socks
Mrs. L. T. Sowell	1 pr. socks
Miss Martha J. Stuart	1 blanket and 1 pr. socks

Mrs. A. R. Wadsworth	1 blanket and 2 pr. socks
Mrs. Flora A. Wadsworth	1 pr. socks
Mrs. William Wadsworth	1 blanket
Mrs. Harden Warner	1 blanket
Miss Margaret Warner	2 pr. socks
Miss Piety T. Warner	2 pr. socks
Miss Sue F. Warner	2 pr. socks
Miss Darcus Williams	1 blanket and 3 pr. socks
Elizabeth Williams	8 blankets
Miss Judia Williams	1 blanket and 1 pr. socks
Miss Sarah Williams	8 pr. socks and 1 blanket
Mrs. K. H. Worthy	2 blankets and 6 pr. socks
Miss Elizabeth Wright	2 blankets
Miss Elizabeth B. You	1 blanket
Nancy C. You	1 blanket and 1 pr. socks
Miss Martha You	1 blanket

CHAPTER 3, #X

Raleigh Register February 12, 1862: "The Military Committee for the company of Robeson acknowledge the following donations for the Robeson troops:

Mrs. Judge French . . . cash of $10; Willie R. French . . . $10; Beverly Tucker French . . . $10; Miss Molly J. French . . . $5; Miss Berta S. French . . . $5; total cash, $40; Mrs. Captain Condary Goden . . . 100 pr. of socks; Mrs. Berry Goden . . . 100 pr. socks; Mrs. Thomas A. Norment . . . 6 pr. socks and 2 blankets.

Thomas A Norment, Chm'n, Presbyterian Military Committee"

CHAPTER 3, #Y

Raleigh Register, January 22, 1862, donations received:

"Mrs. E. G. Keith . . . 1 lb. of wool rolls and lot of butter, eggs, and potatoes; Mrs. E. A. Davis . . . 2 pr. socks and a lot of eggs; Mrs. Charity B. Davis . . . one bed quilt, 2 shirts, 4 pr. socks, pr. gloves; Mrs. Lydia Davis . . . a lot of butter, eggs, and turnips for a Christmas dinner for the soldiers and $2."

CHAPTER 3, #Z

Raleigh Standard, January 22, 1862: "Capt. C.L. Cook acknowledges the receipt of the following articles for Company B, 38th regt. of N.C. Volunteers, from their friends in Yadkin Co., collected by Jesse Couch, Esq., and forwarded to J. Cowles, Esq., per the hands of Messrs. Harris and Williams, and begs to return the thanks of the company to the donors:

Mrs. Susan Dennis . . . 2 quilts; Mrs. Lucy Windsor . . . 1 quilt; Mrs. Elizabeth Couch . . . 1 quilt, 1 towel, 1 blanket; Mrs. Mary Crater . . . 1 quilt; Mrs. Leah Robbins . . . 1 quilt; Mrs. Nancy P. Burgiss . . . 1 quilt; Mrs. Lovicy Mahaffee . . . 1 quilt; Miss Catherine Burgiss . . . 1 quilt.

The following was also collected and paid over for the soldiers' families: James Howard . . . $5; Jesse Couch . . . $5; Bennet Windsor . . . $3; Albert Aldred . . . $2; James Windsor . . . $1."

CHAPTER 3, #AA

During the war there were many illustrations of generosity and support of Confederate soldiers. One of the best documented, and most symbolic, was a group in the Little's Mill area of the county who called themselves the *"LADIES' AID SOCIETY."* A listing of items collected and contributed to the Confederate cause, along with the actual names of contributors, has survived for their February, 1862, effort:

Mrs. M. E. Austin . . . gloves, socks, shirt, red pepper.
Family of N. T. Bowden . . . $4, bed comforter, pr. drawers, shirt, pants, and quilt.
Miss Cornelia Bowden . . . gloves, pillow slips, socks.
Reddick Bowden . . . $3.
Master Thomas O. Bowden . . . one lot of slippery elm bark.
Family of W. F. Brookshire . . . socks, shirt, drawers, & $5.
Mrs. John F. Ledbetter . . . quilt, pillow & slip, socks.
Homer LeGrand . . . $4.
Mrs. William LeGrand . . . socks.
Family of John P. Little . . . wool pants, other clothing, & $10.
Miss Lizzie Little . . . socks.
Miss Sallie Little . . . socks.
Mrs. E. Little . . . socks.
Family of B. F. Little . . . cotton mattress, pillow slips, towels, bandages, [knit?] jackets, 6 pr. merino gloves, one gross buttons, 4 testaments, one cake mutton suet, ½ gal. honey, one lot slippery elm bark, $6 worth of woolen cloth, and $23.
Mrs. M. B. McRae . . . socks, drawers, red pepper, cotton mattress.
Miss Julia A. McRae . . . wool gloves.
Mrs. C. A. Patterson . . . linen blanket, shirts, wool pants, pr. wool gloves, pillow, 4 pr. socks, dressing gown, bandages and old linen, one paper of sage, one lb. candles.
Fanny, a servant of Mrs. C. A. Patterson . . . one lot of sage.
Mrs. L. S. Powell . . . linen blanket, pillows and cases, towels, pr. sheets, one bundle linen, lot of sage and mustard, one dozen phials.
R. J. Powell . . . $2
Miss Julia Powell . . . socks, neck comfort.
Hattie, a servant of Mrs. L. S. Powell . . . linen blanket, a roll of bandages, pr. gloves.
Mrs. E.J. Robison . . . linen blankets, shirt, pillows, 2 pillow cases, towel, 4 pr. socks, soap, red pepper, sage, pr. drawers, bundle of old linen, 2 lung protectors, mattress tick, pr. gloves.
Mrs. E. & Mrs. P. N. Stanback . . . cotton mattress, 8 sheets, 6 pillows, 5 pillow slips, linen blanket, drawers, 8 Confederate jackets, 8 pr. pants, 2 towels, 13 pr. socks, 2 pr. gloves, comfort, overcoat, shirt, 2½ yds. of sheeting, bottle & box of mustard, corn starch, bottle & box of boiled flour, bottle of blackberry wine, and honey.
William P. Stanback . . . $1."

The Little's Mill Society was not the only organized effort of this nature. Other groups were formed to give support, such as the Laurel Hill Soldiers' Aid Society, Laurinburg Soldiers' Aid Society, and the Rockingham Ladies' Society[6].

CHAPTER 3, #BB:

Iredell Express, January 9, 1862, from Brier Creek Soldiers' Aid Society—items donated:

Mrs. Fanny Carmichael	6 flannel shirts, 2 pr. pants, pillow, and 2 pillow cases
Henry Chambers	25 cents and boneset
S.C. Davis	2 pr. woolen gloves
E. M. Feltz	2 pr. socks
Miss Catherine Foster	2 pr. drawers
Miss Ann Foster	socks, sage, and balm
Miss Bettie Gray	$1
Miss Zilpha Henderson	sage
D. A. Hunt	1 blanket, 1 pr. socks, neck comforter, and 44 cabbages
Miss Ella Hunt	1 blanket, 1 neck comfort, 2 towels, and 2 pr. socks
Miss Sue Hunt	1 blanket, neck comfort, and 2 pr. socks
Mrs. Ladd	1 blanket
Miss Ella Martin	socks
Mrs. Elvira Martin	blanket, 3 pr. socks, 12 candles, towel, bottle of cordial, mustard seed, 10 cabbages, sage, and pepper
Mrs. Leland Martin	blanket, neck comfort, socks, gloves, and soap
Miss Mary Martin	socks
Miss Virginia Martin	2 pr. socks
Miss Dianah McBride	bed comfort, shirt, and drawers
Mrs. Malinda Pardew	1 bed comfort
Mrs. Lizzie Partiet	socks, sage, dittany [a form of mint]
Mrs. John Redding	sage and pepper
Mrs. Amelia Sale	1 quilt
Miss Augusta Sale	quilt and neck comfort
Mrs. Fannie Sale	2 pr. socks
John Sale Sr.	$5
Mrs. Judith Sale	blanket, drawers, shirt, and sage
Mrs. Susan Sale	1 blanket and 1 pr. socks
Mrs. Susan Walker	quilt, drawers, and socks

CHAPTER 3, #CC

Raleigh Register, January 29, 1862
Items donated by the Soldiers Relief Society of Strickland's District, Johnston County included socks, gloves, blankets, flannel shirts and drawers and money:

"James H. Raiford	$.50	Mrs. Polly Jones	$1.10
Mrs. Jas. H. Railford	$2.50	Troy Jones	.50
Mrs. Misey Ganus	.70	Jesse Thompson	1.00
Miss Isabella Ganus	.95	Miss N. E. Thompson	.80

Miss Penny Ganus	.55	Mrs. J. Thompson	2.15
Mrs. Cherry Ganus	.15	J. W. Thompson	.25
Mrs. Hepsey Ganus	1.65	Mrs. Eli Creech	.90
Mrs. P. Amons	.15	Miss E. J. Creech	.20
Mrs. J. Jourgan	1.00	Joshua Creech	.20
Miss Abi Tiner	2.80	Mrs. J. Creech	6.60
Mrs. W. A. Smith	7.80	Levi Creech	.50
Mrs. Sarah Langly	1.50	Joseph Overby	.50
Miss Nancy Langly	.50	Mrs. P. Creech	6.60
Mrs. W. Robbins	.30	Mrs. Overby	3.45
Mrs. N. Thompson	.30	William Brown	7.60
Miss S. A. Thompson	.30	Mrs. W. Brown	24.00
Mrs. Linsey Tiner	.15	Mrs. E. Thompson	.20
Mrs. Joel Smith	.50	Miss S. A. Thompson	.50
Miss Bettie Smith	1.00	George Daughtry	.25
Mrs. J. M. Whitley	1.70	Mrs. G. Daughtry	.20
Miss S. E. Whitley	1.45	Mrs. B. Daughtry	.40
Miss Eliza Whitley	.25	Miss N. Daughtry	.15
Mrs. S. J. Whitley	5.50	Mrs. H. Creech	.45
Mrs. Devero Talton	2.25	Mrs. M. Davis	.25
Mrs. B. B. Alford	2.10	Dixon Davis	.50
Miss K. Alford	.75	Mrs. J. Mathews	.55
Miss A Alford	.20	Miss R. Mathews	.40
Jacob H. Barnes	2.00	Miss Sallie Edwards	.55
Mrs. J. H. Barnes	1.50	Miss S. Edwards	.55
Dempsey Grant	2.25	John I. Massey	2.25
Mrs. D. Grant	1.30	Miss M. Gurly	.30
Josiah Strickland	1.00	Miss Mary Gurly	.15
Mrs. J. Strickland	.30	Mrs. Berry Price	.40
Soloman Daughtry	.25	Berry Price	.90
Mrs. S. Daughtry	.60	Mrs. Moses Hill	.55
John Creech	1.25	Mrs. Jno Hamilton	.55
Mrs. J. Creech	.60	Mrs. Polly Hamilton	.40
Miss M. Creech	.80	Mrs. Harry Lane	4.45
Mrs. Turner Jones	1.10	B. W. Johnson	1.00
Mrs. John Worley	.30	J. W. Watson	17.00
Mrs. N. Morgan	.30	Mrs. J. W. Barrow	1.00
Simon Godwin	7.00	A. J. Heath	16.25

CHAPTER 3, #DD

Fayetteville Observer, September 9, 1861: "Ladies Hospital Association—At a meeting of the Executive Committee . . . the name of the Association was changed to the 'Cumberland Hospital Association.' Mrs. John C. Smith was appointed vice-president. She contributed fifty dollars donated by neighbors and 'through her [,] fifty pairs of socks were ordered at twenty-five cents a pair, from the wives of soldiers who wish to dispose of them.' It was decided to send fifty dollars each to our companies at Ship Point, for hospital expenses, to expend thirty dollars for chloride of lime and medicines desired by Dr. Graham." The ladies agreed that they would also send money to other companies from Cumberland and Harnett Counties. The women decided to meet once a week and make soldiers' clothing. Following is a list of donators of cash subscriptions:

Mr. J. M. Beasley	$1.00
Miss Fanny Blake	$2.00
Mrs. Buxton	$5.00
Mrs. Ralph P. Buxton	$5.00
Mr. Calais	$1.00
Mr. Carver	$1.00
Mrs. Alexander Elliot	$5.00
Mr. J. J. Gilchrest	$2.00
Mr. J. T. Houston	$2.00
Mrs. James Jenkins	$5.00
Miss Sophia Mallett	$5.00
Mr. Thompson McDaniel	$5.00
Mr. John McDaniel	$3.00
Mrs. W. Mcl. McKay	$5.00
Miss M. Murphy	$2.00
Miss Mary E. Murphy	$1.00
Mrs. E. L. Pemberton	$2.00
Mrs. John A. Pemberton	$2.00
Mrs. M. H. Pierce	$1.00
Mrs. M. C. Rand	$3.00
Mrs. A. R. Smith	$2.00
Miss E. B. Smith	$0.50
Mrs. Isabella Smith	$5.00
Mrs. J. C. Smith	$4.00
Miss Kate Smith	$1.00
Miss Lena Smith	$0.60
Miss Lou Smith	$1.00
Mrs. Mary Smith	$3.00
Miss Sarah E. Smith	$1.00
Miss Maria Vann	$2.00
Mr. J. H. Williams	$3.00
Mrs. Doc J. Williams	$4.00
Mrs. Whitehead	$2.00

Other names were illegible. Total collected—$99 for hospital supplies.

CHAPTER 3, #EE

"PRESENT OF SOCKS TO THE IREDELL BLUES—We learn that the ladies of South Iredell (God Bless them!) have donated 100 pairs woolen socks to the Iredell Blues, Capt. Simonton, presented through T.S. Byers, Esq.

It is hoped this example will be emulated all over the country, for the soldiers generally. Like others, the ladies of Statesville have done much for the soldiers, but they are ready and willing to do more." *Iredell Express*

CHAPTER 3, #FF

THYATIRA SOLDIER'S AID SOCIETY
"The ladies of Thyatira and vicinity wishing to aid in providing clothing and other necessaries for the comfort of our soldiers, who are now engaged in the defense of our country, met . . . and organized themselves into a society by selecting the following officers: President—Mrs. J. C. McConnaughey; Vice President—Miss S. J. Sloan, Miss H. Houck, and J. Lowrance; Secretary—Mrs. J. K. Graham; Treasurer—Miss Lydia Lowrance.

The following articles have been contributed and forwarded: 3 mattresses, 19 pillows, 13 sheets, 19 blankets, 4 comforts, 1 counterpane, 1 woolen coverlet, 24 pillow cases, 54 towels, 61 cotton shirts, 32 flannel shirts, 8 pr. flannel drawers, 3 pr. cotton drawers, 1 pr. woolen pants, 16 pr. woolen gloves, 156 pr. woolen socks, 3 boxes lint, 60 bandages, 1 double wrapper, 2 jars of apple jelly, 3 gal. blackberry wine, 3 gal. brandy, 2 sacks dried fruit, 120 lbs. soap, sage, hops, red pepper, &c., 6 boxes provisions, 4 bibles, 7 testaments, 2 prayer books, tracts and other small books. Money contributed $62."
[*Carolina Watchman* Salisbury December 23, '61]

CHAPTER 3, #GG

From the Ladies Association at Dunn's Rock Hotel came 16 pr. socks, 2 pr. drawers, and 2 shirts:

Sam Allison, Esq . . . coat, vest, pr. of gloves.
D. B. Allison, Esq . . . 2 pr. socks, 2 pr. gloves, 2 shirts, 2 pr. drawers.
Mrs. M. A. Clayton . . . shirt, drawers, and gloves.
Mrs. Barton . . . 2 pr. socks, gloves, and blanket.
Mrs. Cox . . . 2 pr. socks, 2 pr. gloves.
T. Crumpton . . . 2 pr. gloves.
Miss. M. J. Deaver . . . 2 pr. socks.
Mrs. Deaver . . . 4 wool shirts, 4 pr. wool drawers, 3 pr. socks, 1 pr. shoes, pr. gloves, one kit of butter.
E. England . . . 2 blankets, 2 undershirts, 6 pr. socks, 2 pr. drawers, 2 pr. gloves, 2 bottles honey.
Alex England . . . 3 pr. pants, 2 pr. socks, 2 pr. gloves.
Mrs. Nelson Fortune . . . gloves and socks.
Mrs. Graves . . . blanket.
G. W. Galloway . . . 3 pr. socks.
Robert Hamilton . . . . blanket, shirt, drawers, 3 pr. socks, gloves.
Alex Holensworth . . . 2 pr. socks, gloves.
Mrs. Adam Hayes . . . 2 pr socks, gloves, neck comforter.
Mrs. W. P. Hogshead . . . . 2 shirts, drawers, 2 pr. socks, gloves, suspenders.
Mrs. D. P. Johnstone . . . 2 shirts.
Miss S. Kenemore . . . blanket.
A. D. Kenemore . . . coverlid.
Miss B. Lance . . . . socks and gloves.
Mrs. Lockaby . . . socks.
Miss M. E. Killian . . . 2 pr. socks.
Miss M. J. Lyons . . . . socks.
Mrs. George Orr . . . 13 pr. socks.
Mrs. N. Murray . . . pants, 2 shirts, 2 pr. socks.
Mrs. H. H. McKee . . . 2 pr. socks.
Miss Julia McKee . . . 2 pr socks.

Mrs. C. C. Raxter . . . 2 pr. gloves, 2 shirts, 2 pr. socks, 2 pr. drawers.
Mrs. William Wilson Sr . . . 2 pr. drawers, shirt, socks, neck comfort.
Mrs. W. A. Wilson . . . 3 pr. socks, coverlid.
Mrs. M. M. Wilson . . . 2 pr. socks, gloves.
Mrs. Marien Whitmire . . . blanket.
Mrs. Jane G. Wilson . . . 5 pr. socks, blue blanket.
Mrs. J. Shipman . . . . 2 pr. socks.
N. Thompson . . . 4 pr. socks, 3 pr. drawers, 2 pr. gloves, 3 shirts, 2 vests, 2 caps, neck comfort, 3 overcoats, 2 blankets.
J. S. Thompson . . . blanket, ½ gal. honey.
Phebe Tucker . . . 2 pr. socks, gloves.
Mrs. Ann Witsel . . . . shirt, socks, vest, cotton hanky.
Esther Wilson . . . . 2 pr. drawers, comfort, neck comfort.
From Messrs England and Thompson . . . . 8 bushels of apples."

CHAPTER 3, #HH

[*Semi-Weekly Raleigh Register*, October 9, '61] "Acknowledgment of Contributions, Surgeon General's Office, Raleigh, October 7th, 1861:
Mrs. W. H. Jones . . . 1 doz. shirts, 10 pair of drawers, 9 pair of pillow slips, 6 feather pillows, 4 pair sheets.
A gentleman . . . cloth, 1 pair of old sheets, 4 pair of woolen socks, 4 pair of cotton socks, 2 flannel shirts, 2 pair of flannel drawers, 5 lbs. toilet soap, 4 bottles mustard, 1 lb. tea, 1 qrt. camphor, 1 bag sage, 1 bag red pepper, 1 bottle cologne, 1 comfort, 3 packages corn starch.
Miss M. Hunt . . . 1 bundle of yellow root.
Mrs. Clara J. Ray . . . 3 cotton shirts, 2 bags sage, 1 bag red pepper.
Mrs. E. L. Harding . . . 1 doz. shirts, 4 pair drawers, 2 sheets, 2 pillow slips, 2½ lbs. toilet and castile soap, 1 package red pepper, 1 package sage.
Miss Kate Boylan . . . 4 pair flannel drawers, 4 pair woolen socks, 6 pair cotton socks.

Ladies Soldiers' Aid Society of Greensboro and vicinity . . . 19 comforts, 18 sheets, 8 quilts, 6 blankets, 20 feather pillows, 9 pillow cases to fill with paper or straw, 14 colored shirts, 48 white shirts, 34 pair drawers, 13 towels, 21 pair woolen socks, bandages, linen lint (carded), blackberry wine, blackberry cordial, blackberry vinegar, peach cordial, strawberry wine, preserves and jellies, brandy peaches, honey, Jamaica ginger, pickles, tomatoes in cans, sugar, tea and coffee, rice, sage, red pepper, capsicum, butter beans, dried fruits, black pepper, spices, vanilla, mustard, mutton suet, cherry and elm bark, gum arabic, corn starch, soaps, gelatine, cologne, bay rum.
Mr. George W. Mordecai . . . fifty dollars, and fifty from a gentleman who declines giving his name to the public.
Capt. Regan . . . three dollars.
Mr. W. J. W. Crowder . . . ten dollars.
Mr. John Spelman . . . ten dollars.
I have received the above articles and sums of money in the last few days.
Chas. E. Johnson, Surgeon General, N. C."

CHAPTER 3, #II

For the *Raleigh Register*:

"Messrs. Editor:—At the suggestion of the undersigned, Superintendent of Tar River Circuit, the congregation worshipping at 'The Temple,' in Edgecombe county, met at the Church and organized a society, the 23rd Sept., to be known as 'the Temple Soldiers Aid Society.' Fifty seven names were handed in as members. The officers appointed are:

Mrs. Dr. French Garrett, Pres't.; T. T. Thorne, Treas.; Jas. C. Knight, Sec'y.

Mrs. Sally Knight, Miss Betty Wheelus, Miss Sally Cutchin, Miss Martha Mayo and Dr. Jo. J. Garrett, together with the officers, were constituted a Board of Solicitors to procure material for manufacture; also, money and other articles for Hospital Stores.

There are two features in the organization of this Society differing from any I have seen. First, the Society is a mixed one, instead of being composed exclusively of females. To obviate any delicacy the ladies might have, provision is made that meetings may be held by the female members *alone* at any time desired; whereas the meeting of *the Society* are to be stated or adjourned.

Its second feature is, that it contemplates a two-fold object: 1st. To furnish the Hospital to be established under the general control of the Gov. of North Carolina, and to which attention has been recently called by Dr. Johnston, Surgeon General of the State, in your paper.

This will claim the first and immediate attention of the Society. When accomplished, then, 2nd To prepare clothing for the use of the efficient Soldiers in service from this State. The articles thus furnished are to go through the hands of the Sheriff of the county.

I am now on a visit to the 1st Regt. N. C. Volunteers. Many are absent on furlough; some are being discharged on account of sickness; but I am gratified in saying that the health of the Regiment is greatly improved. There is much regret expressed because of the withdrawal of Gen. Hill from this post by the Government. He is certainly held in high esteem by those who, until recently, were under his control. I hope the new post to which he may be assigned will appreciate his efficient services.

Respectfully,

Will H. Wills.

Camp Fayetteville, Va., 1st Oct., 1861."

CHAPTER 3, #JJ

[*Raleigh Register,* May 21, '62] "**GUNBOAT FUND** on the appeal of Mrs. Sally R. Collins—contributions flowed in for the building of an iron-clad steamer 'The Old North State.' Miss Elizabeth Hyman of Williamston, Martin County, took it upon herself the collection of funds, and collected $145 in 3-4 days. It was sent to General Martin."

Miss E. Bagley	$5	Miss M. Lavier	$3
Miss L. Biggs	$5	Miss S.E. Pender	$0.25
Miss M.L. Biggs	$5	Miss S.E. Pope	$1
Miss M.E. Carstarphen	$5	Mrs. M.E.C. Rhodes	$2
Miss A.E. Harrell	$0.50	Mrs. E. Rives	$3
Miss M.E. Harrell	$0.50	Miss S. Robertson	$5
Miss M.M. Hassell	$5	Miss S.. Robertson	$0.50
Miss M.B.Hopkins	$5	Miss M. Rogers	$10

Miss E. Hyman	$3.25	Miss H.B. Slade	$50
Miss F. Jordan	$0.50	Miss P. Slade	$10
Miss L. Knight	$2	Mrs. S.F. Spruill	$10
Mrs. Eliza Lamb	$1	Mrs. M. Tamon	$0.50
Miss M.E. Lamb	$1	Mrs. S.A. Williams	$1
Mrs. L.D. Latham	$5	Miss M.A. Williams	$2
Miss S.F. Latham	$3		

CHAPTER 3, #KK

[*Raleigh Register* May 14, '62] Letter from Adjutant General James Martin:

"Receipt of contributions of the North Carolina **Gunboat Fund**, in addition to $142 raised by a concert at Chapel Hill:

Mrs. Lucy D. Rives	$10	Mrs. R.A. Marriott	$10
Mrs. Jno P. Tillery	$ 3	Mrs. G.L. Gordon	$ 5
Mrs. Jas H. Chapman	$ 2	Miss M.R. Goodloe	$5
Miss G.W. Hammond	$1	Mrs. W. Hodges	$1
Mrs. M.D. Gray	$10	Miss Abby Burnett	$10
Miss Fanny Gordon	.10	Mrs. M.A. Howell	$1
Mrs. Price	.50	Mrs. P. Turner Westry	$10
Mrs. Kenelin H. Lewis	$20	Mrs. Jas J. Phillips	$50
Mrs. Francis Ann Ricks	$1	Mrs. R. Laughtery	$1
Mrs. Wm S. Battle	$50	Mrs. T.W. Battle	$25
Mrs. James P. Battle	$10	Mrs. J.E. Lindsay	$10
Mrs. Virginia Thorp	$10	Miss Hetty Battle	$1
Master Jacob and Joseph Battle	$4		
Master Armstead C. Gordon	$.10		
$250.70 total"			

CHAPTER 3, #LL

Raleigh Register January 22, '62

Mrs. Charity B. Davis	1 quilt, 2 shirts, 4 pr. socks and 1 pr. gloves
Mrs. E. A. Davis	2 pr. socks and a lot of eggs
Mrs. Lydia Davis	A lot of butter, eggs, turnips for a Christmas dinner for the soldiers, and $2
Mrs. E.G. Keith	1 lb. of wool rolls and lot of butter, eggs, and potatoes

CHAPTER 3, #MM

[*Raleigh Standard* January 22, '62] Captain C. L. Cook acknowledges the receipt of the following articles for Company B, 38th regiment of NC Volunteers The following was collected and **paid over for the soldiers' families:**

Albert Aldred	$2
Jesse Couch	$5

James Howard	$5
Bennet Windsor	$3
James Windsor	$1

CHAPTER 3, #NN

[*Hillsborough Recorder* January 20, '63]

"MR HEARTT: Dear Sir.—1 beg leave to return my sincere thanks, through the Recorder, to my neighbors, ladies and friends of the vicinity of Hillsborough, for the valuable and timely gifts they have bestowed on my exposed and needy men. Such noble acts of kindness fill our hearts with gratitude, and fire our zeal for the cause we have espoused. May the Prompter of these acts give strength to our arm in the day of battle, and speedily return us to our loved ones at home.

Miss Lucy Barracks	$0.25
Mrs. John Berry	1 comfort, 4 pr. socks, and sage
Mrs. A. M. Douglass	6 pr. socks
Mrs. Doc. Freeland	1 comfort, 3 pr. socks, 1 pr. drawers, 1 shirt, and pepper
Mrs. Harriet Freeland	1 comfort
Mrs. Julia Freeland	2 cotton shirt, 1 flannel shirt, and 1 pr. drawers
Mrs. Mary Ann Holden	2 lbs. wool
Mrs. William H. Holden	1 blanket and pepper
Mr. Benjamin Kinnion	$81.00
Mr. Laurence Kinnion	$0.50
Mrs. Latta and Walker	1 blanket and 11 pr. socks
Mr. John C. Latter	$31.00
Mrs. John C. Latter	3 pr. socks
Mrs. John McKerall	1 overcoat, 1 pr. pants, 1 hat, 1 pr. boots, and 1 pr. socks
Miss Mary McKerall	2 flannel shirts
Miss Sarah McKerall	1 pr. socks and 1 pr. gloves
Mr. John Redding	3 yrds. shirting
Mr. Robert Redding	$81.00
Mr. John Riley	$0.90
Mrs. John Riley	1 pr. socks
Miss Margaret Riley	1 pr. socks
Miss Mary Roberts	1 pr. pants and 2 pr. socks
Mrs. Sally Tinnen	1 pr. socks
Mrs. Louisa Turner	2 pr. socks and 2 lbs. wool
Mr. John Tuner	$84.00
Miss Annie Whirled	3 pr. socks
Miss Betty Whirled	2 blankets, 12 pr. socks, 1 pr. pants, 1 vest, and 1 comfort
Mrs. Hazelwood Wilkerson	knitting 6 pr. socks
Mrs. Mary Wilkinson	3 pr. socks
Miss Jane Williams	4 pr. socks
Miss Harriet Woods	1 lb. wool

3 pr. pants and 3 pr. gloves, bought with the cash given. I am respectfully, William J. Freeland, Capt."

CHAPTER 3, #OO

People's Press, October 24, 1862: "The Friends of the 26th Regiment Band will be pleased to learn that the series of concerts recently given by them, 'assisted by Gus Rich' in his inimitable deceptive feats, were very successful." They performed in Raleigh, Wilmington, Goldsboro, and Petersburg, Virginia. A donation of $253.35 was collected, a portion of the proceeds were donated to the North Carolina Hospital at Petersburg.

Chapter 3, #PP

Sampson County, Little Coharie District officers:
Mrs. T.N. Culbreth, President; Mrs. M. White and Mrs. B. Parker, Vice; Miss Maggie A. Owen, Secretay; and Miss Sallie Williams, Treasurer. The president appointed the following committee for their contributions to the Society, viz: Mrs. John W. Matthews, Mrs. John Culbreth, Mrs. W. F. Culbreth, Mrs. John R. Fisher, Mrs. F. Cooper, Mrs. John T. Fort; Mrs. W. G. Fowler, Mrs. T. Sessoms, Miss Virginia A. Owen, Miss Mary J. Owen, Miss Martha L. Culbreth.

The official members of the Burke County, Mountain Grove Church Society are as follows: Miss Lizzie M. Parks, Pres't; Miss Laura J. Avery, Sec'y; Miss Susan A. Moore, Assistant.

Franklin County's Ladies' Aid Society voted for vice president, Mrs. Parthenia Barnes; for secretary, Mrs. Minerva Overton; for treasurer, Mrs. Elizabeth O'Brien. The following ladies were elected to the Executive Committee, Miss Promelia Gill, Miss Martha Best, Miss Pattie E. Huller, Miss Fannie Hays, Miss Mariah Ellington, Miss Angelia Stone, Miss Bettie Smith, and Mrs. Lucy Hight.

Chapter 3, #QQ

"The General Tract Agency of this city is publishing from 20,000 to 50,000 copies of each of the following excellent tracts, approved by all the pastors here: 'A Mother's Parting Words to Her Soldier Boy,' 'Christ In You,' 'Are you ready?,' 'The Life Preserver,' 'Why Will Ye Die?,' 'Lovest Thou Me,' and so forth. We are striving to supply our whole army with the gospel truths. Each dollar given will send out 1,000 pages, which will be carried, through the great kindness of the Express Company, to the soldiers without charge. We can print 30,000 tracks a day. Yours truly, W.J.W. Crowder, agent"

CHAPTER 3, #RR

[*Raleigh Register,* December 10, '62]
"The Hillsborough Soldiers' Aid Society acknowledges the receipt of the following contributions during the month of November:

Misses Nash & Kollock . . . 3 carpets; Mrs. F. B. Hill . . . 2 carpets; Mrs. Col. Jones . . . 2 carpets; Mrs. Littlejohn . . . carpet; Mrs. P.B. Ruffin . . . 3 carpet blankets; Mrs. Dr. Cain . . .

carpet and ten dollars; Mrs. Curtis . . . carpet; Mr. Phillips . . . paper of carpet needles; Mrs. James Webb . . . 5 carpet blankets; Mrs. Strowd . . . 2 carpet blankets; Mrs. John Norwood . . . 4 carpet blankets, and two white ditto; Mrs. H. K. Nash . . . 8 carpet blankets; Mrs. Col. Meares . . . 2 carpet blankets; Mrs. Col. Tew . . . 2 white blankets; Mrs. deRoulhac . . . 4 blankets; Mrs. P. C. Cameron . . . 4 blankets and 20 hanks of yarn; Mrs. Pride Jones . . . 2 blankets, excellent size and quality; Mrs. Newborn of Lenoir . . . 8 carpet blankets and 10 pr. socks made by Mrs. Levi Newborn, Misses Rachael and Annie Newborn, Miss P. F. Moore & Barbary—a **slave**; Mrs. Evans . . . pr. cotton socks; Mrs. Collins, Sr . . . 2 pr. socks; Mrs. Rosco Hooker . . . pr. socks; Mrs. Martha Holeman . . . 3 pr. socks; Mrs. Thompson . . . 10 cuts cotton with the spinning of 20 cuts of wool and cotton; Mrs. Judge Nash . . . 4 pr. socks; Mr. John Webb . . . 250 pounds of cotton yard and 6 hams; Mrs. Stanley . . . 3 pr. socks; Mrs. Dr. Hill of Fredericksburg . . . $10; Mr. Wright of Georgia . . . $5; Mrs. Fred Jones . . . $5 and 2 pr. socks; Mr. Strowd . . . $10; Mr. Walter Cameron . . . $.25; a **servant girl** . . . $.05; Mrs. Phillips . . . $5; Mrs. Curtis, Kennedy, and Miss DeRosset . . . $15; Mr. Clark of Fairfield . . . $2; Mrs. General Walker . . . $5. This was sent to the Orange County soldiers under the care of Lt. Graham for the Orange Guards."

Chapter 4, #A

Sequestration Act: Amos Johnson and Amos T. Johnson's inventory of their store: suspenders, wrapping paper, fabric, dress patterns, thread, belts, hair brushes and combs, jewelry, looking glass, buttons, shears, fiddle strings, thimbles, needles and holders, axe handles, envelopes, blank books, pocket knives, gloves, handkerchiefs, knives, mittens, wool, flax thread, velvet braid, homespun fabric, snuff, iron pots, pants, socks, soap, brass rings, box starch, glue, harness, balances, hooks and eyes, stockings, indigo, shirts, and fish hooks.[7]

CHAPTER 4, #B

Equipping the troops—this ledger is specific as to the cost and items bought. "Report of Capt. J.M. Odell of the Randolph Hornets:

July 1861, an account with the Cedar Falls Manufacturing Co.

To paying J.M. Odell's Bill no. 1	$410.02
" "	Lyndsay & Campbell's Bill no. 2	136.30
" "	Seborn Perry's Bill no. 3	25.30
" "	Sarah C. Julian's Bill no. 4	66.00
" "	E.S. Crowson's bill no. 5	7.41
Paid	A. Creech for Pants goods	136.43
Paid	F. Fries " " "	300.50
Paid	498 ¾ yds. Osnaburg @ 10	40.87
"	495 ½ yds. Osnaburg 2 11	54.51
"	23 yds. Plain Lins(e)y @ 25	5.75
"	24 yds. Plain Linsy 2 16 ⅔	4.00
"	111 ½ yds Plain Linsy @ 25	27.87
"	Cotton Thread and Twine	2.44
Paid	27 ½ yds Plain Linsy @ 27 ½	$9.35
"	70 dozen buttons @ 4	2.85
"	¾ yd. Statian cloth [satinett]	33
"	11 pair of shoes @ 1.65	17.71
"	23 pr. Shoes @ 1.50	34.50
"	3 pr. Shoes @ 1.85	5.55
"	7 pr. Shoes @ 1.60	11.20

" 1 pr shoes @ 1.35 .... 1.35
" 9 ½ lb. Flax Thread @ 1.25 .... 11.87
" 18 ½ lb. Pieces Shirting @ 16.⅔ 3.13
" 26 lb. Coffee @ 25 .... 5.50
" 47 lb. Sugar 2 12 ½. 5.87
" 4 lb. 6 oz. Butter @ 69 and 4 lb. 11 oz ditto 1.39
" 383 lb. Bacon @ 15 .... 57.45
" 5 sacks flour @ 3.75 .... 21.75
" 4 sacks do. @ 3.50 .... 14.00
" 192 lb. Wool @ 2 .... 3.84
" 50 dz. Buckles 2 5 .... 2.65

$1,340.56

2nd. Page brought over: $1340.56
July, 1861: to Paying   1 Hand Axe .... $.75
"   "   1 Do. [ditto] .... .88
"   "   1 Do 1.00
"   "   1 ¼ yd. Jeanes [cloth] .... .75
"   "   ¼ yd. Do .... .20
"   "   9 yds. Salem Geans [Jean]@85 .... 7.65
"   "   6 yds. Salem Geans @ 1.00 .... 6.00
"   "   1 ¼ yd. Salem Geans @ 75 94
"   "   4 pr. Socks @ 30 .... 1.20
"   "   2 pr. Do. @ 75 50
"   "   9 Bonnet Braids 44
"   "   24 yds. Cambric @ 10 .... 2.40
"   "   4 pounds Powder @ 1.00 .... 4.00
"   "   4 lb. Shot @ 12 ½ 50
"   "   11 ¾ worsted twine(?) @ 52 .... 5.88
"   "   12 ½ lb. Nails @ 7 86
"   "   12 lbs. soap @ 4 48
"   "   87 ½ lb. Rope @ 28 .... 22.78
"   "   1 cake beeswax @ 30/lb 69
"   "   3 sets knives & Forks @ 75 .... 2.25
"   "   1 set   "   "   @1.50 .... 1.50
"   "   1 set   "   "   @ 1.75 .... 1.75
"   "   91 yds. Sheeting 2 10 .... 9.10
"   "   2 sets plates @ 35 70
July, 1861, cont.
To Paying   2 lbs. Candles @ 30 .... $.60
"   "   1 candle stick 15
"   "   38 Skeins Silk 1.90
Paid   Glasgow for cutting 55 pr. Pants @ 20 .... 11.00
"   "   "   extra work on same 64
"   18 yds. Velvet trimming @ 12 ½ 2.25
"   3 yds. Silk Twist @ 15 45
"   1 plug tobacco @ 15 15
"   6 yds. Stripes @ 12 ½ 75
"   Pattern (?) Ribbon 38
"   3 Pans @ 35 .... 1.05
"   4 do. @ 40 .... 1.60
"   1 pr. Blankets 3.50

"   6 ¾ yds. Satinett [cloth] @ 1.00 .... 6.75
"   16 Padlocks 2.80
"   Steel Pens 25
"   Paper.. 20
"   Envelopes.. 20
"   6 sacks @ 12 ½.. 75
"   6 tea Kettles @ 60.. 3.60
"   3 Coffee Pots @ 50 .... 1.50
"   6 Shovels @ 1.25 .... 7.50
"   7 buckets @ 50 .... 3.50
"   Teaming Lumber [paid to drivers]....................... 40

$1,465.13"

The next page has no date but is listed with the same pages in the file:

"RANDOLPH HORNETS
1st ....there was no donations in the account.
2nd. List of Equipment for soldiers:

80 pair of Pants of Salem Jeans @ 3.15...................................... $172.00 [sic]
80   "   "   "   " @ 2.40.................................... 192.00
80 Fatigue Shirts (Plain Linsey)@ 1.05.................................... 84.00
80 Fatigue Jackets (Salem Jeans)@ 2.85.............................. 228.00
80 Cloth caps @ 75... 60.00
80 pair Shoes (average)@ 1.75.. 140.00
80 Canteens & Straps @ 55 .... 44.00
80 Knapsacks & Straps @ 1.50 .... 120.00
80 leather belts (average) @20 .... 16.00
15 tents (of Osnaburg) @ 87 ½ & Rope   [no totals for the rest of supplies]
11 Chopping Axes   14 Coffee pots
7 hatchets   17 Camp & Mess Chests
12 Spades   14 sets knives & forks
6 Mattocks   80 Pint Tins
12 frying Pans   80 plates "
12 tea kettles   6 Camp Kettles
6 Skillets & 7 buckets   14 tin pans

Amount used by Commissioned Officers $56.00

I certify that the above is a true statement to the best of my knowledge.
                J.M. Odell, Capt. Co (M), Randolph Hornets"

"July 8th, 1861, Franklinsville, Capt. John M. Odell, Randolph Hornets
Bought of Cedar Falls Manufacturing Company:

17 ½ yds. Flax Cloth @ 25.. $4.37 ½
23 ¾ yds. Marlboro Checks @ 16 .... 3.80
1 Gallon Molasses... 50
2 lb. Coffee @ 25 50
1 ¼ yds Col'd Cambric [colored fabric]..................................... 12 ½
6 pr. Woolen Half hose 1.50
7 pr. Shoes @ 1.60... 11.20
12 pr. Shoes @ 1.75.. 21.00

1 Goat Skin 1.40
27 Tin Cups 1 pt.. 1.68
2 tin Pans @ 15.. 30
2 Bars soap 10
1 set Edged Plates.. 37 ½
8 lb. Coffee 2.00
½ bushel Salt... 62 ½
2 bu. Soda @ 15 30
156 ½ lb. Bacon @ 15 .... 23.47 ½
1 pr. Shoes 1.75
44 yds. Marlboro stripes @ 15 .... 6.60
4 hanks flax Thread... 70
2 tin Pans 6 Qt 1.00
3 Coffee Pots 4 Qt @ 50 .... 1.50
3 yds. Spotted flannel 1.20
2 lb. Coffee .... $.50
Paid for making 36 Fatigue jackets 5.40
    "   "   "   31 Towels .... 15 ½
    "   "   "   10 pr. Pants..................................... 2.50
    "   "   "   24 pr. Coats @ $.75 .... 18.00
    "   "   "   7 large boxes @ 2.25..................... 15.75
    "   " Teaming [hauling wages] bacon, flour &c.................. 1.00

$128.81"

"July 9, 1861 Cedar Falls, Randolph County, Account with J.M. Odell, Capt.
June 11, 1861 Paid expenses to J M Odell to Raleigh............$10.90
Amount paid for Coat buttons.. 14.50
    "   "   " 4 Hand Axes @ 1.00 .... 4.00
    "   "   " Freight on goods 1.00
    "   "   " Liquors.. 4.00
    "   "   " Oil Cloth 65.00
    "   "   " 11 Chopping Axes & 2 tea cans 12.95
June 15 Amount Paid . . . Expenses to Salem & Raleigh 16.50
        "   " for canteens and Camp Kettles 33.75
        "   "   "   freight 75
        "   "   "   73 belts of Kivett 12.41
        "   " Beef of L. Leonard 10.71
        "   " Potatoes... 3.15
July 1 Amount Paid Croson for goods & services.................... 38.00
    "   " 60 lb. Bacon @ 15.. 9.00
    "   " 15 lb. Butter @ 15 .... 2.25
July 6 Amount Paid J.R. Cole for services in drilling................. 28.00
    "   " Expenses in carting Drill Master to N.C.R.R 2.00
    "   " Onions, Potatoes, & Beans........................... 3.50
    "   " 20 pr. Shoes for sundry volunteers @ 1.75-35.00
    "   " 200 pr. Socks @25 .... 50.00
    "   " 6 Mattocks @ 1.00 .... 6.00
July 8 Amount Paid John Brower for drilling............................ 15.00
    "   " 50 tin cups @ 10... 5.00
    "   " 60 tin plates @ 12 ½.................................... 7.50
    "   " 4 spiders @ 1.25.. 5.00
    "   " 5 camp kettles @ 1.25................................. 6.25

"   " 8 Belts @ 30 .... 2.40
"   " 48 Pint tins @ 8 ½.. 4.08
                                                        ━━━━━━━━━
                                                        $410.02

.... Cr. by cash rec'd ....189.00 = $221.02"[8]

CHAPTER 4, #C

GUIDE FOR THE INSPECTION OF THE HOSPITALS AND FOR INSPECTOR'S REPORT . . .

Some of the questions the inspector needed to ask: "Construction of the building and adaptability to the purpose of a hospital in different seasons; light and ventilation by windows; supplied with water and gas fixtures; rooms in the building or continuous buildings for office, apothecary shop, laundry, kitchen, dining rooms, store rooms, bake houses, and privies; estimate of expense in fitting up and repairing building and out-houses; capacity of hospital, estimating fifty square feet floor surface for each patient with ordinary wound or disease, and in wards set apart for pyemia, hospital gangrene, erysipelas and typhoid fever [contagious diseases], 100 square feet; pitch of rooms and number of wards; number of hospital tents."

Another question: "Does he require the ward-masters to keep an account of the effects of patients, take proper care of them, and turn over the effects of deceased soldiers to the authorized receiver; to keep a record of hospital furniture, &c., and a weekly inventory of articles in use . . ."

Another question: "Does the surgeon in charge inspect each ward and every part of the hospital once daily?" "Does he visit daily, or as often as necessary, such cases as require his advice, consultation or active interference?"

More questions: Does he keep a list of the medical staff, their monthly pay, etc? "To what extent have female attendants been employed, (or volunteered their aid), especially the kitchen and pantry of the sick; in administering medicines and stimulants, and in supervision of the linen-room and laundry; has discipline and hygiene been promoted by their presence and their services?" "Is noise, profanity, intemperance and waste forbidden and punished; is there any library attached to your hospital or newspapers taken, any chaplain or religious observances?"

Additional questions: "Is there a dead-house; its condition; how are bodies identified and removed; are they promptly and decently interred? What is the condition of the hospital fund? Is there a diary or guard house? Do you have spittoon, bed-pans, and slop-pails? Are patients allowed to go into town and do they report back on time?"

These are only a *few* questions surgeons had to deal with. Government red-tape required duplicates of all the paperwork.[9]

CHAPTER 4, #D

SICK SOLDIERS' DIET:
Dr. William Little, assistant surgeon, N.C. Hospital, December 18, 1861, posted his diet for patients:

"LOW DIET (per meal)
Brekft . . . bread ¼ lb, 1 pint tea, ½ pt gruel
Dinner: 1 pt. Gruel, 1 pt milk
Supper: bread ¼ lb., 1 pt tea, ½ pt gruel

FULL DIET: (per meal)
bread 1 lb, 1 lb.beef or mutton, salt-1 oz,
tea ½ oz, coffee 1 oz, sugar 2 oz, 1 pint
soup, cornmeal 1 lb., milk for tea, 4 oz,
molasses 1 oz, potatoes or beans or rice 4 oz

Half diet:
Brkft: ⅓ lb. Bread, pint of tea, hominy and molasses
Dinner: beef or mutton ½ lb, ⅓ lb.bread, rice or beans or potato

Supper: ⅓ lb bread, tea 1 pint," . . . page torn . . . [10]

CHAPTER 4, #E

North Carolina furnished 120,000 men from the state as soldiers. Most served in the Army of Northern Virginia. The central government established hospitals for each state located around the Richmond/Petersburg area. North Carolina's Hospital is listed as General Hospital no. 24, located on Main and 26th St. in Richmond. It was established in July of 1864. Another building deemed Hospital no. 22, also called Howard's Factory Hospital or the North Carolina Hospital, housed 110 North Carolina men. It was open from 1862 through 1864. A third building used for North Carolina soldiers was Harwood Hospital, a former tobacco factory. This cared for 120 patients on the West end of Cary Street. To further confuse the reader, this last medical facility was also called Moore's Hospital and the 3rd, 4th, and 5th division of Winder Hospital. There was a hospital in Petersburg for troops from North Carolina as well.[11]

North Carolina General Hospitals:
Kittrell Springs .... no. 1
Wilson.................... no. 2
Greensboro............ nos. 3, 12
Wilmington............ nos. 4, 5
Fayetteville .... no. 6
Raleigh................... nos.7, 8, 13
Salisbury .... nos. 9, 10
Charlotte............... no. 11
Asheville .... the Sorrell Hospital

North Carolina Wayside Hospitals:
Weldon............. no. 1
Greensboro ...... no. 2
Salisbury........... no. 3
Goldsboro......... no. 4(?)
Wilmington....... no. 5
Charlotte .... no. 6
Tarboro............. no. 7
High Point

Total: 14 general and 7 wayside hospitals in N.C. according to research.[12]

A receipt says High Point was General Hospital no. 3; March 12, 1864, General Hospital no. 3 was listed as being in Goldsboro.[13]
General Hospital no. 8 was in Wilmington.
General Hospital no. 5 was in Greensboro.

CHAPTER 4, #F

"MEDICINE FOR THE ARMY—An experienced Army Surgeon in Virginia gives the following list of articles much needed by the sick and wounded. He says: Such persons as are inclined to do so, can contribute to the necessities of the sick . . . should we get into a battle, by making up a box of bandages, and furnishing any amount of almost any kind of medicines. A package of bandages might be made up as follows: Take a piece of coarse, unbleached sheeting from eight to ten yards long and tear in strips—

1 dozen needed	½ inch wide	
2 " "	2 inches wide	
3 " "	2 ½ inches wide	
4 " "	3 " "	
4 " "	4 " "	

These should be rolled tightly and the loose end pinned. Other articles needed:

Several pounds of tow; curved splints of all sorts; Oil cloths—20 dozen; Pillow cases—2 doz.; Pillow ticks—2 doz.; Sheets—4 doz.; Flannel, a bolt. All are needed.
Should any one take a notion to fit out a box of medicine and hospital stores, the annexed is a list of the articles most needed for a regiment:

Simple Ceraie......................10 pounds	Dover's Powder ....1 pounds
Basilicon Ointment ....5 pounds	Powd. Opium ....2 pounds
Chloroform ....2 pounds	Mustard ....12 pounds
Creosote ....6 ounces	Crushed Sugar ....25 pounds
Liquor Ammoniaie...............5 pounds	Spirits of Nitre ....½ gallon
Blue Mass ....1 pound	Brandy (good)....................24 bottles
Morphine............................5 drhms	Wine, Port, Madeira,
Spirits Turpentine ....5 gallons	Sherry ....24 bottles
Sugar of Lead......................2 pounds	Bourbon Whiskey ....24 bottles
Powd. Gum Arabic..............4 pounds	Opium Gum ....2 pounds
Cayenne Pepper ....½ pound	Sabaraque's Disinfectant ...3 bottles
Ipecac ....1 pounds	Chloride of Lime ....5 pounds

Seidlitz Powders
Laudanum, Paregoric, Es. Peppermint, Tinct. Capsicum, Liniments, and Cathartic Pills—any quantity.
The foregoing is an imperfect list, but may serve as a sort of guide for any person who may be moved by feelings of benevolence or duty to get up supplies for a regiment."[14]

CHAPTER 4, #G

LIST OF SUBSTITUTE MEDICINES MADE FROM HERBS
Red oak bark .... added to water is a disinfectant and astringent.
Inner red oak bark, blackberry or dewberry root, or red shank root .... A stronger astringent.
Bicarbonate of soda .... disinfectant in suppurative stages.
Slippery elm and wahoo root bark .... when emollients indicated.
Common salt .... when emollients indicated.
Poppy heads, nightshade, stramonium .... for excess pain relief.
Boneset tea .... for intermittent fever, use to induce vomiting.
Butterfly root or pleurisy root tea .... a quinine substitute.
Mandrake tea .... for remittent or bilious fever.
Virginia snake-root, yellow root, or Sampson's snake root .... as above.
Mayapple root, peach-tree leaves as tea .... moves the bowels.
Beef's feet tea, hog's feet oil, lard with syrup .... moves the bowels for children.
Mustard seed or leaves, stramonium leaves, hickory leaves, pepper, butterfly-root and sanguinaria .... use until nausea comes for pneumonia, pleurisy, or for catarrhal fevers. This takes the place of Dover's powders or quinine.
Black haw, squaw weed, partridge berry .... female complaints.
Black haw root tea .... to halt abortion, dysmenorrheal especially when combined with squaw-weed, partridge berry or red shank.
Poke either berries or roots .... chronic rheumatism, neuralgia, syphilis, scrofula, enlarged glands .... combined with alcohol or whiskey and combined with sarsaparilla root, alder, prickly ash, and sassafras.
Raspberry leaves, whortleberry leaves .... diarrhea.
Peach leaves steeped in water .... nausea or sick stomach.
Agrimony tea, the nut gall along with copperas .... use on warts, syphilitic sores, corns, ringworm, and old ulcers. Weakened properly, it is good in obstinate bowel diseases and can be used as an injection in gonorrhea and gleet.
Silk weed root in whiskey and drunk along with pills of rosin from the pine tree and blue vitrol will cure gonorrhea.
Poke root, onions, garlic, celery, pepper, parsley, sage, thyme, rue, as a poultices good for glandular enlargements.
Lobelia and turpentine .... useful in coughs, croup, asthma.

White sumac, red elm, prickly ash, poke used with black wash .... syphilis and chronic rheumatism.
Peach tree leaves, Sampson's snake root .... dyspepsia.
Honey and sage .... gargle for sore throat and tonsillitis.
Calamus, catnip, and soot teas are better than soothing syrups with opiates for infants.
Fennel seed tea .... used in place of paregoric for infants.
Red oak bark and alum .... used for a rash.
Goose grease and sorghum, or honey .... croup.
Turpentine with brown sugar .... croup.
Horsemint tea and tea from roots of the broom sage .... adult colds
Spice-wood tea .... eruptions and impure blood.
Rose geranium leaves .... tea for diarrhea.
Mutton suet, sweetgum, buds of the Gilead .... salve for cuts and sores
Balsam cucumber .... for burns and a tonic.
Black haw root .... hemorrhages.
Wood anemone .... as a vesicatory to remove corns.
Pond lily poultices .... ulcers.
Button snakeroot or globe flower .... expectorant and diuretic.
Aralia spinosa .... toothache or rattlesnake bite
Side-saddle or fly-catcher .... dyspepsia.
Epsom salts, with bicarbonate of soda and laudanum in water .... diarrhea.
Red pepper and pine rosin .... diarrhea.
Seeds of watermelon and gourds .... diuretic.
Red maple .... an astringent wash.
Violet leaves .... emollient application.
Buckeye lotion .... gangrenous ulcers, toothache.
Cotton seed decoction .... inflammation in mucous passages.
Roots of the cotton plant .... asthma
Bark of the root of China berry tree .... anthelmintic and to prevent "botts" in horses, and used to pack dried fruits to deter insects.
Ox-eyed daisy .... insecticide.
Fresh elderberry leaves .... lay on pillow of sick person to deter flies.
Roots and leaves of cockleburr .... use in passive hemorrhages, diarrhea, gonorrhea, liver disease.
Sweet shrub .... anti-spasmodic in the ague.
Verbena and leaves from the stone root used on poison ivy.
Rhus glabra .... used as a gargle for cleansing the mouth in putrid fevers, also for gonorrhea and gleet.
Black oak .... leucorrhea, amenorrhea, chronic hysteria, diarrhea, rheumatism, asthma, tonsillitis. Mixed with lard .... use on hemorrhoids.
Pyrethrum .... destroys insects, lice, on plants and animals.
Elder bush leaves and flowers .... pour boiling water over them. Use as a wash for wounds to keep flies away.
Sea myrtle .... colds and consumption.
Hound's tongue .... a mucilaginous drink. Roots made into poultice for bruises, sprains.
Gravel root .... emetic.
Virginian silk .... diuretic decoction in gonorrhea.
Long leaved pine, inside bark and buds .... coughs and colds, diuretic.
Catweed .... diseases of the chest and bowels.
Ragweed used in whiskey .... substitute for quinine.
Mountain laurel .... rheumatism, gout, enlarged glands.
Black alder .... a wash for cutaneous troubles.
Holly leaves .... emetic.
Woodbine .... asthma, a decoction of flowers given to calm pain of colic following childbirth.

IMPORTED ARTICLES	SUBSTITUTE
Columbo, Quassia	yellow root, Spanish fly, potato bugs, powdered leaves of Butternut.
Jalap	Wild Jalap, Mulberry bark, butternut, dock, wild potato Vine, American columbo.
Quinine and Peruvian Bark	tulip tree bark, dogwood, cotton seed tea, chestnut root and bark, thoroughwort, Spanish oak bark, knob grass, willow bark.
Digitalis	blood root, wild cherry, pipsissiwa, bugle weed, jasmine.
Conium	American hemlock.
Opium	American hemlock, mother-wort.
Sarsaparilla	wild sarsaparilla, soapwort, yellow parilla, china briar, Queen's delight.
Chamomile	dogwood.
Flaxseed	Watermelon seed.
Gum Arabic	low mallows, apple, pear and quince gum, balm, water-melon seed.
Ergot	Cotton root.
Guaiacum	boxwood, poke, prickly ash.
Ipecac	wild Jalap, Carolina hipps.
Mezereon	prickly ash.
Kino and Catechu	cranesbill.
Senna	wild senna.
Colocynth	alum root.
Tannin	smooth sumac.
Olive oil	peanut oil, beech-nuts oil, cotton seed oil.
Laudanum	hops, mother-wort.
Acacia	slippery elm bark, sassafras pith.
Bougies	slippery elm bark.
Corks	black gum roots, tupelo wood, corn-cobs.
Allspice	spice bush.
Pink root	cardinal flowers.
Assafoetida	wild chamomile.
Calomel	dandelion, pleurisy root, butterfly weed.
Belladonna and hyoscyamus	Jamestown weed.
Valerian	lady's slipper.
Colchicum	Indian poke.[15]

CHAPTER 4, #H

LIST OF MEDICINE AND SUPPLIES NEEDED FOR ONE YEAR FOR ONE THOUSAND TROOPS AT THE HOSPITALS:

Acetic acid .... 5 lbs	arsenic 5ozs	muriatic acid 8lbs
Sulphuric acid .... 8 lbs	tartaric acid ... 16lbs	sulphuric ether 16lbs
Alcohol .... 192 pints	ammonia 5lbs	nitrate of silver ...... 8 oz
Assafoetida .... 32 ozs	chloroform 8lbs	copaiba 40lbs
Catechu 5lbs	creosote .... 16 ozs	adhesive plaster ..... 40 yds
Extract belladonna 16oz	fluidi buchu ... 8lbs	gentian 8lbs
Glycyrrhiza 48lbs	hyoscyani 16oz	rhei 8lbs
Sarsaparilla 16lbs	valerian 64ozs	senna 8lbs
Mercuric chloride 5oz	iodine 16ozs	magnesia 5lbs
Ammonia 32lbs	ether .... 5 lbs	sulphate morphia .. 16drs

Myrrh.........................5lbs	aloes..............32 ozs	opium 5lbs	
Jalap 32ozs	cantharides ...16oz	sulphate quinine....80-160oz	
Sugar.........................160lbs	strychnia........8drs	digitalis 32ozs	
Unguenti hydrarg.......8lbs.[16]			

CHAPTER 4, #I

"**Roots, Herbs, and Barks Wanted**: The Medical Purveyor's Department, Charlotte, is in need of the following articles for the use of the Army, for which the annexed prices will be paid:

ITEM	AMOUNT PAID	ITEM	AMOUNT PAID	
Seneka Snake root	per lb. 60 cts	Dogwood bark	25	cts.
White Oak bark	per lb. 20 cts.	Butternut inner bark of root	50	"
Blood Root	40 "	Fever root	20	"
Meadow Sweet	25 "	Henbane leaves and seed	75	"
Wild Cherry bark	30 "	American Hellebore root	20	"
American Colombo root	50 "	Barberry leaves	50	"
Indian Turnip	20 "	Peppermint leaves	25	"
Willow Bark	20 "	Fleabane	25	"
American Ipecac root	$1.00	Skunk Cabbage-root	20	"
Tulip tree bark or		Scotch Broom-tops of stems	50	"
white popular	20 "	Jamestown weed,		
Blooming Spurge root	50 "	seed & leaves	20	"
Persimmon bark from root	20 "	Pink root	50	"
Indian Physic-root	25 "	Hemlock leaves	20	"
Century herb	20 "	Worm	25	"
Indian Tobacco	25 "	Hemlock seed	50	"
Boneset	20 "	Calamus	25	"
Black Snake root	50 "	Wintergreen or		
Butterfly Weed or		Partridge berry	50	"
Pleurisy root	30 "	Wild Ginger or		
Poke root	20 "	Canada snake root	50	"
Dandelion root	30 "	Horsemint	20	"
Cranesbill	20 "	Queen's root	50	"
Hops	$1.00	Sassafras-bark of root	20	"
Blackberry root	2 "	Slippery Elm	30	"
Wild Senna	50 "	Sassafras pith	$5.00	
American Gentian	20 "	Red Pepper	$1.00	
May Apple or Mandrake	75 "			

To be delivered in any quantity at the N.C. Military Institute, or to Drs. Duffy and Arendall, Medical Purveyor's Agents, who will visit the various towns in this State.

    July 16, 1862   M. Howard, Surgeon and Medical Purveyor, Charlotte."[17]

CHAPTER 4, #J

[*The Daily Dispatch*: July 4, '64] A List of North Carolina Sick and Wounded Soldiers, in the Hospitals at Richmond, on the 20th June, 1864: [not complete]

Names.	Rank	Regiment	Company	Hospital	Division
Gross W	Priv	28	B	Winder	No. 5
Gibson G W	Priv	4	B	Winder	5
Guffy J F	Priv	5	H	Winder	5
Gardner G A	Priv	32	H	Winder	5
Grant E	Priv	4	D	Winder	5
Garbode Lewis	Priv	48	K	Winder	5
Gardner H H	Priv	2 cv	G	Winder	5
Griffey J H	Priv	43	B	Winder	5
Green K P	Priv	6	E	Winder	5
Gilliam J	Priv	32	B	Winder	5
Goodson W M	Fergt	24	F	Winder	5
Gordon W H	Priv	44	A	Winder	5
Goulding J H	Priv	P	its's bat	Winder	5
Griffith A A	Priv	14	G	Winder	5
Guthrie C C	Priv	23	K	Winder	5
Griffin W A	Priv	53	I	Winder	No. 6
Gibbins A	Priv	16	G	Winder	6
Gameson W F	Sergt	48	H	Winder	6
Genes J W	Corpl	18	B	Winder	6
	Priv	4	H	Winder	6
H	Priv	13	F	Winder	6
Garner W B	Priv	13	B	Winder	6
Glover W W	Sergt	31	A	Winder	No. 7
Goodwin H	Priv	31	D	Winder	7
Galley L B	Priv	46	A	Winder	7
Gibbs J S	Priv	34	B	Winder	7
Gough G H	Priv	3	H	Winder	7
Golding C	Priv	61	E	Winder	7
Gordon R M	Priv	32	E	Winder	7
Gadd J	Priv	44	H	Winder	7
Gates T L	Priv	43	I	Winder	7
Gay J W	Priv	33	K	Winder	7
Goodman G	Priv	46	K	Winder	7
Gaddy A H	Priv	43	I	Winder	7
Gooch Wm	Priv	14	K	Winder	No. 2
Gay B	Priv	13	K	Winder	2
Goodman A M	Priv	57	C	Winder	2
Glenn R S	Priv	25	B	Winder	2
Gillaspie W L	Priv	1 cv	G	Winder	No. 4
Gothrie J R	Corpl	48	G	Winder	4
Grubbs W H	Priv	59	B	Winder	No. 6

Gilmore S M	Priv	21	M	Winder	6
Glasgow W H	Priv	12	G	Jackson	No. 1
Grimsley J M	Lieut	37	K	Jackson	1
Gortney F F	Lieut	37	B	Jackson	1
Gray W H	Lieut	33	F	Jackson	1
Gardiner W J	Lieut	Manly's	Bat	Jackson	1
Grimsley L	Lieut	26	A	Jackson	1
Gordon G T	Lt Col	34		No. 4	
Gideney J M	Capt	12	E	No. 24	
Griffin W J	Priv	31	F	H Grove	
Gould A J	Priv	15	A	H Grove	
Griffin Wm	Priv	47	D	Chimb'o	No. 3
Gardner J A	Priv	17	A	Chimb'o	3
Gillespie J B	Corpl	28	H	Chimb'o	3
Gains C W	Sergt	16	I	Chimb'o	No. 4
Gregery M	Priv	51	E	Chimb'o	4
Green J E	Priv	43	C	Chimb'o	4
Gillespie W G	Priv	6	C	Chimb'o	4
Hicks C	Priv	7	K	Winder	No. 1
Hall D F	Corpl	53	G	Winder	1
Hendricks W	Priv	12	C	Winder	1
Horton R T	Priv	4	F	Winder	1
Hicks S M	Priv	8	F	Winder	1
Harrell J C	Priv	6	H	Winder	1
Hanley W D	Priv	20	H	Winder	1
Hutton Geo	Priv	1 cv	H	Winder	1
Hardy J A	Priv	50	D	Winder	1
Harmon J	Priv	28	C	Winder	1
Halcombe J	Priv	66	K	Winder	1
Holder W H	Priv	57	C	Winder	No. 2
Harrold J F	Priv	57	D	Winder	2
Honeysuckler Wm	Priv	38	I	Winder	2
Hudson L	Priv	1	K	Winder	2
Harrald L	Priv	54	F	Winder	2
Happer T J	Priv	25	B	Winder	2
Hazell M C	Priv	1 cv	A	Winder	2
Hay G R	Priv	55	K	Winder	2
Harris W O	Priv	26	B	Winder	2
Hall R T	Capt	43	I	Winder	2
Harris T	Priv	21	L	Winder	2
Horton O C	Priv	17	B	Winder	2
Harkey J J	Priv	49	F	Winder	2

Huddiestine W	Priv	46	E	Winder	2
Hokes J P	Priv	21	A	Winder	2
Hargis R S	Priv	54	K	Winder	2
Holland Jno	Priv	54	F	Winder	2
Hooser E J	Priv	21	F	Winder	2
Hickman H	Priv	18	C	Winder	2
Heims L R	Priv	7	H	Winder	2
Holland W T	Priv	1	C	Winder	2
Hall Tho	Priv	32	G	Winder	2
Hunter W J	Priv	3 cv	I	Winder	2
Highfield W F	Priv	5 cv	I	Winder	2
Highsmith R S	Priv	3 cv	D	Winder	No. 3
Henderson S W	Priv	16	H	Winder	3
Horne S L	Priv	34	K	Winder	3
Hill M	Priv	23	H	Winder	3
Hopkins S A	Priv	38	H	Winder	3
Holton J M	Priv	54	H	Winder	3
Hunnicutt H	Priv	46	I	Winder	3
Hessin J W	Priv	55	B	Winder	3
Hodges J R	Priv	61	H	Winder	3
Huffsteden J H	Priv	12	G	Winder	3
Helms H	Priv	48	A	Winder	3
Hooks J	Priv	42	D	Winder	3
Hipp J	Priv	31	G	Winder	3
Helton W	Priv	54	B	Winder	3
Harrison P M	Priv	66	H	Winder	3
Holbrook W	Priv	7	K	Winder	3
Harvill J	Priv	52	G	Winder	3
Hall W J	Priv	47	C	Winder	3
Hall T W	Priv	23	C	Winder	3
Harrison J	Priv	17	A	Winder	3
Hayes L	Priv	47	G	Winder	3
Holmes O	Corpl	46	I	Winder	3
Hamilton J T	Priv	13	D	Winder	3
Hegler P	Priv	48	I	Winder	3
Holt D A	Priv	5	E	Winder	No. 4
Haynes R	Priv	11	I	Winder	4
Hynseiman J S	Priv	5	G	Winder	4
Harrison H	Priv	51	E	Winder	4
Holland J	Priv	43	I	Winder	4
Hoffer Jno	Priv	32	B	Winder	4
Hughes J	Priv	48	F	Winder	4

Herrin J	Priv	66	C	Winder	4
Hawkine J S	Priv	22	K	Winder	4
Hawkins A F	Priv	22	K	Winder	4
Haggin J F	Priv	52	G	Winder	4
Harrell G	Priv	52	C	Winder	4
Henry B G	Priv	11	H	Winder	4
Harris W H	Priv	2 cv	L	Winder	4
Harris J A	Priv	66	G	Winder	4
Hedgepath A	Priv	27	G	Winder	4
Hill Wm	Priv	48	I	Winder	4
Hagian J M	Priv	48	I	Winder	4
Hall N C	Priv	11	H	Winder	4
Holder J W	Priv	46	G	Winder	No. 5
Hoover J M	Priv	46	F	Winder	5
Hup W H	Priv	15	F	Winder	5
Hooker J W	Priv	2 bat	A	Winder	5
Hamrick E	Priv	12	E	Winder	5
Harvey R	Priv	45	K	Winder	5
Hoyt M	Priv	30	H	Winder	5
Huffins H	Priv	53	A	Winder	5
Henley A	Priv	6	H	Winder	5
Howard B	Priv	2	K	Winder	5
Hicks L	Priv	21	F	Winder	5
Harman W H	Priv	37	E	Winder	5
Holder A	Priv	5	A	Winder	5
Halterman J A	Priv	33	A	Winder	5
Hinsen J	Priv	20	K	Winder	5
Hager R T	Priv	23	K	Winder	5
Hatley N	Priv	27	F	Winder	5
Hooks W H	Priv	15	I	Winder	5
Hill J	Priv	27	G	Winder	5
Halloway J A	Priv	22	F	Winder	5
Herrings J	Priv	66	C	Winder	5
Haynes B	Priv	2	D	Winder	5
Haws E	Priv	20	G	Winder	5
Hales H	Priv	32	K	Winder	5
Hollingsworth	Priv	45	A	Winder	5
Harris J J	Priv	43	G	Winder	5
Hasper W H	Corpl	35	D	Winder	5
Hursh W	Prv	38	A	Winder	No. 6
Hanes S N	Prv	38	G	Winder	6
Hines J B	Prv	28	B	Winder	6

Haries G	Prv	26	H	Winder	6
Heless T H	Prv	1 cv	C	Winder	6
Hubbard J	Prv	43	K	Winder	6
Honycutt J	Prv	42	H	Winder	6
Hampton R F	Prv	27	B	Winder	6
Harris W O	Prv	11	A	Winder	6
Hicks G	Prv	33	H	Winder	6
Hennis P B	Corpl	22	H	Winder	6
Helms A C	Prv	37	D	Winder	6
Harding A	Prv	26	C	Winder	6
Horne N C	Prv	43	H	Winder	6
Hays S W	Sergt	5	B	Winder	6
Hopkins E	Sergt	43	F	Winder	No. 7
Holston A	Prv	63	A	Winder	7
Henry J A	Prv	14	C	Winder	7
Harrington C T	Prv	51	F	Winder	7
Hebner B	Prv	23	A	Winder	7
Holden H F	Prv	55	I	Winder	7
Hagger D L	Prv	16	C	Winder	7
Haynes L A	Prv	51	H	Winder	7
Hall H W	Prv	20	I	Winder	7
Hudson W	Prv	53	D	Winder	7
Harris G W	Prv	38	B	Winder	7
Huggins B F	Prv	61	K	Winder	7
Horton R R	Prv	17	C	Winder	7
Harris E K	Prv	14	G	Winder	7
Haines J F	Prv	28	I	Winder	7
Hudson S	Prv	46	I	Winder	7
Hill L	Prv	46	G	Winder	7
Hollemon C B	Prv	6	I	Winder	7
Hall N C	Prv	11	H	Winder	7
Henry B G	Prv	11	H	Winder	7
Hawkins W P	Prv	27	H	Winder	No. 1
Hall W D	Prv	28	F	Winder	No. 2
Harrison J H	Prv	45	E	Winder	2
Harrison Wm	Prv	21	F	Winder	2
Hurbert J	Prv	12	G	Winder	No. 6
Halen D	Prv	35	C	Winder	6
Harris M A	Prv	7	A	Jackson	No. 1
Hix W	Prv	53	D	Jackson	No. 2
Henry L J L	Corpl	63	E	Jackson	No. 3
Hunter H S	Priv	23	K	Jackson	No. 4

Holmes E H	Priv	2	C	No. 13	
Hicks J H	Lieut	48	B	No. 4	
Hand P H	Lieut	45	D	No. 24	
Hoke Asst Surg G M Hoke's Staff				24	
Hardista A S	Sergt	38	A	No. 24	
Hillsworth H	Priv	14	H	24	
Higgins F G	Priv	61	K	24	
Hall B F	Sergt	43	A	24	
Henderson D J	Priv	35	A	24	
Hobbe Wm H	Sergt	31	H	24	
Hedgepath J T	Priv	31	A	Ho Grove	
Hardy T W	Priv	30	B	Stuart	
Hanser H	Priv	11	I	Stuart	
Holder H H	Priv	2	F	Stuart	
Howard J M	Priv	49	F	Chimbo	No. 1
Horaback H	Priv	43	K	Chimbo	No. 3
Hood W L	Priv	30	K	Chimbo	3
Hudgins W J	Priv	51	H	Chimbo	No. 4
Hunter W	Priv	18	D	Chimbo	4
Hopkins P	Priv	1 cv	C	Chimbo	4
Hudson J	Priv	61	I	Chimbo	4
Hufts M N	Priv	65	H	Chimbo	4
Hicks A	Priv	35	B	Chimbo	4
Hicks J D	Priv	43	G	Chimbo	No. 5
Hasaw Z T	Priv	25	I	Chimbo	5

18

CHAPTER 4, #K

List of political prisoners at Salisbury:

NAME	RESIDENCE	OCCUPATION	ARRESTED	CHARGES
Ange, Samuel	N.C.	farmer	Nov. 9, 1862	disloyalty
Ange, J. B.	"	"	"	"
Allen, A.	"	"	"	"
Buck, B. T.	"	"	"	"
Buck, John	"	"	"	"
Bell, Solomon	VA	shoemaker	Apr. 10, '62	northern man, strong unionist
Bailey, A.	Richmond, VA	law student	Dec. 1, '61	English spy
Barnes, Edward	Pocahontas Co..., VA	—o—	Nov. 20, '61	no charges preferred
Butler, J. W.	Leesburg, VA	physician	May 21	—o—
Brown, J. L.	Cumberland Co..., TN	distiller	Nov. 5	endeavoring to get to the enemy

Name	Location	Occupation	Date	Charge
Batty, Geo.	Fentress Co.., TN	farmer	Apr. 1, '62	disloyalty
Billingsly, Geo. M.	Claiborne Co..., TN	blacksmith	Aug. 14	aiding & supplying stock to the enemy
Baxley, H.	"	farmer	Aug. 13	trading with the enemy
Bryant, Charles	Cock Co..., TN	"	Sept. 13	aiding & feeding the stampeders to Kentucky
Beard, L. M.	Campbell Co.., TN	"	Nov. 1	disloyalty
Bateman, J. W.	Washington Co.., NC	"	"	"
Bowman, Wm.	Claiborne Co..., TN	"	"	"
Beals, J. H.	Green Co.., TN	"	Mar. 22, '62	One of Fry's bridge burners in East Tennessee
Cox, W.C.	Jones Co.., NC	fisherman	Mar. 16	a Union man
Cheerers, Peter	Kinston	shoemaker	July 27	suspicious character, avowed Unionist
Curtis, John	Beaufort, NC	farmer	Nov. 9	disloyalty
Craddock, A.	Washington Co.., NC	tailor	Nov. 9	"
Collins, C. A. J.	City Point, VA		July 8	Spy, giving info to enemy where pickets were.
Carter, W. F.	Hancock Co.., TN	farmer	Feb. 19	disloyalty
Cox, David	Green Co.., TN	"	Mar. 22	One of Fry's bridge burners
Cogburn, N. J.	"	carpenter	"	"
Crabtree, C.	"	"	"	"
Caton, Thomas	Cock Co..., TN	blacksmith	Mar. 13	aiding with stampeders to get to the enemy
Cox, Eziekel	Lee Co.., VA	farmer	Aug. 25	anxious to show the Federals our position.
Clifton, Wm	Bledsoe Co.., TN	"	Nov. 1	disloyalty
Delancy, John	KY	"	Dec. 27, '61	no charges preferred
Davis, J. W.	Washington Co.., NC	"	Nov. 9, '62	disloyalty
Davenport, A.	"	"	"	"
Darling, R. B.	Green Co..., TN	clock repairer	Mar. 22	"
Elliott, R. B.	Tarborough	overseer	Sept. 16	Spy, trading with the enemy
Elder, W. R.	Green Co..., TN	farmer	Mar. 22	One of Fry's bridge burners
Fortner, Elija	Claiborne Co..., TN	"	Aug. 12	disloyalty
Fortner, Solomon	"	"	"	"
Fellows, Otty	Fayette Co.., VA	"	Aug. 4, '61	avowed unionist
Gahagan, N. B.	Madison Co., TN	"	Mar. 22, '62	One of Fry's bridge burners

Name	Location	Occupation	Date	Charge
Hazzard, Samuel	NY	sailor	Feb. 6, '62	Capt of schooner "Jenny Hunter" trying to get vessel & cargo to enemy.
Hatmaker, A.	Campbell Co..,TN	farmer	Oct. 1	disloyalty
Hair, A.	Washington Co., NC	"	Nov. 9	"
Jackson, J. E.	"	"	"	"
Jones, J.	Hancock Co., TN	carpenter	Mar. 21	One of Fry's bridge burners
Jones, C.	Green Co., TN	farmer	Mar. 22	disloyalty
Johnson, Andrew J.	"	carpenter	Nov. 16	"
Kennedy, Thomas	Kinston	farmer	Dec. 20	"
Kelly, D. H.	Green Co., TN	"	Mar. 22	One of Fry's bridge burners
Kelly, A. W.	"	"	"	"
Keller, Wm.	"	"	"	"
Lathinghouse, Wm.	Craven Co..	"	Apr. 6, '62	Avowed union man
Leonard, Allen	Philadelphia, PA	engraver	Jan. 2	Suspected of going to the enemy, a union man.
Lamb, W.W.	Washington Co., NC	farmer	Nov. 9	disloyalty
Leary, E.	Martin Co.	laborer	"	"
Luper, Wm.	Scott Co., TN	farmer	Apr. 1	"
Ledger, D.	Grainger Co., TN	"	Aug. 19	Associated with a band of marauders & renegades.
Loftin, W. C.	Craven Co.	farmer	Dec. 24	disloyalty
Mercer, John	Jones Co.	"	Apr. 1	a union man
Mercer, Louis	"	"	Apr. 7	"
Mercer, W. P.	Jones Co.	farmer	June 25,	avowed unionist
Marnex, B. F.	Williamsburg, VA	carpenter	Nov. 1, '61	"
McCelland, John	Richmond VA	sailor	June 2, '62	drunkenness, continually in jail, dangerous.
McGaha, A.	Loudon Co., VA	blacksmith	Dec. 15, '61	avowed unionist
McDonald, T. C.	NY		Sept. 2, '62	no charges preferred
Mason, Z. A.	Washington Co., NC	farmer	Nov. 9	disloyalty
McNair, John	Washington Co., NC	"	Nov. 9	disloyalty
Maxwell, Witley	western VA	"	Feb. 28	avowed unionist
McGee, Lemuel	Green Co., TN	"	Mar. 22	One of Fry's bridge burners
Miller, David	"	"	July 14	Going to KY, taken within enemy lines
Miller, R. B.	Lee Co., VA	"	Aug. 13	disloyalty
Malicote, Calvin	Campbell Co., TN	farmer	Oct. 11	"
Morrell, B. F.	"	"	"	"
Miller, Jordan	"	"	"	"
Monneham, James	"	"	"	"
Mealing, John Sr.	Union Co., NC	"	Feb. 6	aiding, abetting, harboring deserters
Nobles, Kinsey	Jones Co., NC	"	Mar. 16	avowed unionist
Perkins, C. G.	Goldsborough	merchant	Apr. 10	union man
Pancost, S. A.	Hamilton Co., VA	farmer	Nov. 10, '61	disloyalty

Payne, David	Blount Co., TN	farmer	July 5	disloyalty
Poor, Edward	Knox Co., TN	trader	July 16	giving info to the enemy
Perkins, Richard	Whitley Co., TN	farmer	Oct. 15	disloyalty
Rich, J. W.	Penn.	Engineer	June 20, '61	deserted the Confederate army
Ryan, Geo. W	Wytheville, VA	blacksmith	Mar. 1, '62	"
Ryder, S. H.	NY	tailor	Oct. 11	trading with Yankees & inducing the Negroes to go to Washington, DC.
Rogers, N. R.	Blount Co., TN	farmer	Sept. 10	a bushwhacker/ renegade
Rogers, W. P.	"	"	"	"
Rowe, Alfred	Campbell Co., TN	"	Nov. 1	disloyalty
Rush, Wm.	Hawkins Co., TN	"	"	"
Seeds, J. M.	KY Mississippi	river boat pilot	Nov. 6	a dangerous man
Sammons, J. R.	Craven Co.	farmer	Apr. 7	avowed unionist
Smith, H. H.	NY	printer	Aug. 1, '61	a dangerous union man
Smith, Samuel	"	farmer	May 3, '62	disloyalty
Scully, Daniel	Pendleton Co., VA	laborer	Oct. 11, '61	union man
Smith, W. M.	Loudon Co., VA	farmer	Dec. 10, '61	"
Sheets, C. C.	Winston Co., ALA	law student	Oct. 6, '62	suspicioned of treasonable conduct.
Swanner, Eli	Beaufort Co.	farmer	Nov. 9	disloyalty
Smith, James	Washington Co., NC	"	"	"
Spruel, A. A.	"	"	"	"
Stepp, John	Fentress Co., TN	"	Apr. 1	"
Smith, Joseph	Cumberland Co., TN	farmer	Sept. 8	"
Spears, W. M.	Hawkins Co., TN	"	July. 17	"
Swain, J. W.	Jefferson Co., TN	"	Oct. 18	"
Smith, Wm.	Loudon Co., VA	"	Dec. 18	avowed unionist
Smith, Thomas	Campbell Co., TN	"	Nov. 1	disloyalty
Tailor, F.	Craven Co.	fisherman	Apr. 20	avowed unionist
Thacher, Charles A.	Green Co., VA	physician	Mar. 28	"
Thornhill, Alex	Jefferson Co., TN	farmer	Apr. 17	disloyalty
Tripplet, Wm.	Green Co., TN	"	Mar. 22	One of Fry's bridge burners
Trail, James.	Fentress Co., TN	"	Apr. 1	disloyalty
Tompkins, E. A.	Overton Co., TN	"	"	professes to be a Federal soldier; no evidence to the fact.
Tillman, Michael	Lenoir Co., NC	"	Dec. 26	disloyalty
Taylor, Moses	Jones Co., NC	"	July 26	avowed unionist
Wesson, Wilson	Beaufort Co.	"	Apr. 2	"
Williams, Ed	Craven Co.	"	"	"
Winne, J. W.	Washington Co., NC	school teacher	Nov. 9	disloyalty
White, Baker	Edenton	waterman	Apr. 4	Spy & traitor

Wood, Isam	Davidson Co., NC	itinerant preacher	Apr. 4	treasonable conduct & practice, exciting slaves to insurrection.
Workman, Wm.	Boone Co., VA	farmer	Jan. 11	avowed unionist
Wilhight, E.	Hardy Co., VA	"	Sept. 30, '61	"
Watson, G. H.	Washington Co., NC	laborer	Nov. 9, '62	disloyalty
Woolsey, G.	Green Co., TN	carpenter	Mar. 22, '62	One of Fry's bridge burners
Walker, Horry	Hawkins Co., TN	farmer	Apr. 19	disloyalty
Winningham, R. A.	Fentress Co., TN	"	"	professes to be a federal soldier, no evidence of fact.
Wright, Mitchell	"	"	Nov. 1	disloyalty
Walker, Emmet	Hawkins Co., TN	"	Apr 19	"
Wiseman, C. W.	Marion Co., TN	printer	Apr. 7	"
Yount, Ephram	Campbell Co., TN	farmer	July 14	going to Ky, taken within enemy lines.

19

CHAPTER 5, #A:

A list of provisions provided to 1,800 white refugees in New Bern during the war for a three month period:

Flour .... 76.5 barrels
Beef .... 116 "
Hominy .... 4.25 "
Coffee .... 20.5 "
Sugar............. 24.5 "
Pork .... 29.5 "
Bacon............ 38 "
Rice .... 37 "
Candles......... 379 lbs
Tea .... 105 "

[Corn] Meal .... 432 lbs.
Fresh Beef .... 169 "
Peas........................... 549 "
Salt .... 219 "
Hard Bread .... 107 bxs
Molasses .... 43 gal
Vinegar .... 6 "
Soap .... 39 lbs
Beans....................... 7.5 "

Provisions for 7,500 black people New Bern area, for three months:

Flour .... 19 barrels
Sugar............. 7 "
Coffee .... 5 "
Rice .... 8 "
Beef .... 4.5 "
Pork .... 16.5 "
Candles......... 27.5 lbs.
Tea .... 4 lbs.
Meal .... 433 "

Hominy.................... 237 lbs
Beans....................... 369 "
Peas........................... 308 "
Hard Bread .... 3262 "
Vinegar .... 5 qts.
Soap .... 805 lbs
Salt .... 44 "
Fresh Beef .... 19 lbs.
Molasses .... 31 gal.[20]

CHAPTER 7, #A:

List of smuggled goods hidden by Emeline Pigott at one time:

1 pair of fine boots; 2 pair of pants; 1 shirt; 1 naval cap; 1 dozen linen pocket handkerchiefs; 1 dozen linen collars; 50 skeins of sewing silk; a lot of spool cotton and needles; tooth brushes; hair combs; 2 pocket knives; one razor; 4-5 pounds of assorted candy; dressing pins; several pairs gloves; also several letters addressed to rebels denouncing the federals . . . and giving information about supposed movement of federal troops.

CHAPTER 8, #A:

TAXES: SCHEDULE OF PRICES FOR NORTH CAROLINA: We the undersigned, Commissioners of Appraisement for the State of North Carolina, do herby declare the following to be the uniform prices for property impressed for the use of the Government for the next two months, subject to alteration should circumstances, meanwhile, occur to make it advisable: [these prices are rounded off]

December 26, 1863	1864
Apples, dried, peeled, per bushel of 28 lbs . . . $3,	$5.00
unpeeled apples per bush. 28 lbs..$2	3.00
Axes with handles . . . $5	12.50
without handles . . . $4	12.00
Bacon, sides per lb . . . $1.50	3.00
Beans, white or cornfield per bushel of 60 lbs. . . . $3	$7.50
Brandy, apple per gal . . . $10	$10.00
Brandy, peach . . . $12	10.00
Beef, fresh per lb . . . . $.45	1.00
Salted beef per lb . . . $.70	1.50
Corn beef per lb . . . $.75	
Brown Stuff per bushel, 28 lbs . . . $.90	
Candles, tallow per lb . . . $1	3.00
Candles, Adamantine candles per lb . . . $3	8.75
Chains, trace, per pair . . . $4	11.00
Cloth, woolen for soldiers' clothes ¾ yard wide, 10 oz to yard,	
and pro rata as to greater or less weight or width, per yard $4.50	6
Raw cotton per lb . . . $l	
Coffee, rye, per lb . . . $l; Rio coffee per lb . . . $3.50	4.50
Corn, unshelled per bushel, 70lbs . . . $5	5.00
Corn, shelled per bu, 56 lbs . . . $5	
Cornmeal per bu of 50 lbs . . . $5	5.20
Cotton drill, 7/8 yd wide, 3 yards, to pound, per yd . . . $.80	$.80
Flour, extra family, per bbl 196 lbs . . . $36	45.00
superfine flour, per bbl, 196 lbs . . . $34	41.25
fine, per bbl, 196 lb . . . $32	38.75
Fodder, baled per 100 lbs . . . $3.50	4.00
unbaled fodder . . . $3	3.50
Hats, wool . . . $3	5.00
Hay, baled per 100 lbs . . . $3.50	4.00
unbaled hay . . . $3.50	3.50
Hides, dry, per lb . . . $ 2.50	3.00
green hides . . . $1	1.50
Horses, first class artillery horses each . . . $500	1600.00
second class horses . . . $400	800.00
House rent, per room per month . . . $20	
Pig iron #1 per ton of 2240 lbs . . . $110	$350 (2000lbs)

Iron, square or round per ton . . . $350	#2 . . . $314
" hoop per ton . . . $440	#3 . . . $270
" flat or band per ton . . . $32 0	bloom per ton $710
" boiler plate per ton . . . $500	Smith's square/round . . . $1030
" serviceable railroad iron, per ton . . . $175	400.00
Jeans, wool per yd . . . $6	10.00
Kettles, camp, iron each . . . $5	per pound . . . $.30
Lumber per 1000 ft . . . $50	50.00
Lard per lb . . . $1.50	$2.75
Leather, sole, per lb . . . $5	$6.00
upper leather . . . $6	7.00
harness per lb . . . $7	
Molasses, cane per gal . . . $10	5.00
sorghum molasses . . . $5	10.00
Mules, first class per head . . . $500	1000.00
second class mules . . . $400	800.00
third class . . . $300	500
Nails, per keg . . . $100	
Oats, baled sheaf oats per 100 lb . . . $3.50	5.25
Unbaled . . . $3	4.50
shelled oats per bushel . . . $4	
Osnaburg, cotton, ¾ yd. wide, 7 ounces per yd . . . $.80	1.50
⅞ yd wide, 8 ounces . . . $.85	1.75
Onions per bu . . . $8	
Oxen, 1st quality per yoke . . . $1000	
second quality . . . $600	
Peas, cow, 60 lb bushel . . . $5	7.50
Potatoes, Irish, 60 lb bushel . . . $4	4.00
Potatoes, Sweet, 60 lb bushel . . . $3	4.00
Peaches, dried, peeled, 38 lb bushel . . . $8	8.50
Unpeeled . . . $5	5.00
Pork, fresh per lb . . . $.75	2.00
Salted . . . $1	2.25
gross pork . . . $1.40	
Pasturage per head near town per month . . . $8	
in the country . . . $4	
Quinine, ounce . . . $56	56.00
Rice, new, per lb . . . $.25	.50
old rice . . . $.20	.40
Rye, per 56 lb bushel $3.50	5.00
Sacks, osnaburg, holds 2 bu . . . $1.60	3.00
Shirting, cotton, ¾ yd wide, 4.5 yds to pound per yd 60	1.30
⅞ yd wide, 3.75 yds to pound . . . $.70	1.10
Cotton stripes per yd, 3 yds per pound . . . $.80	1.75
Salt, coastal salt 50 lb bushel . . . $15	20.00
Liverpool salt . . . $30	35.00
Virginia salt . . . $20	25.00
Steel, cast, per lb . . . $8	
Shoes, army shoes pr . . . $19	15.00
Shoe thread, flax, per lb . . . $10	10.00
Socks, soldiers' wool, pr . . . $1.25	2.00
Sheep, per head . . . $25	35.00
Sugar, brown, per lb . . . $1	3.00
Soap, hard, per lb . . . $.40	$1.00

soft soap . . . $.25	$.75
Shorts, per bu, 22 lbs . . . $.70	.75
Shucks, baled per 100 lbs . . . $3	4.00
Tea, black, per lb . . . $5	5.00
green tea . . . $8	8.00
Tent cloth, cotton, 10 oz per yard . . . $1	1.50
Tobacco, #1 extra . . . $3	
#2 . . . . $2.50	
#3 . . . $1.75	
Plugs of tobacco . . . $1.75	
Tallow; clean, per lb . . . $1	2.50
Vinegar, cider, per gal . . . $2	2.50
Manufactured, per gal . . . $1 unmanfactured . . . $1.00	
Whiskey, good, per gal . . . $12	10.00
Wheat, good white, 60 lb bushel . . . $6	7.50
fair . . . $5.75	
Wheat, bran, per bu 17 lbs . . . $.50	
Wheat straw, baled per 100 lbs . . . $1	1.50
Unbaled . . . $.75	1.00
Wool, washed, per lb . . . $4	8.00
unwashed wool . . . $3	$6
Wagon, wood axle, new, four horse . . . $360	$350
two horse wagon . . . $200	250
Wagon, iron axle, 4 horse, new . . . $350	
two horse . . . $250	
Yarn, cotton, per bunch of 5 lbs . . . $8	$8

The cost of hiring labor and equipment rose with inflation. The same two dates in the *Daily Journal* are compared here:

HIRE OF LABOR, TEAMS, WAGONS, AND HORSES

1863	1864
Bailing long forage per 100 pounds . . . $25.00	$75.00
Shelling and bagging corn, sacks furnished by gov., per bu . . . $.10	.25
Hire of 2 horse team, wagon, driver , rations	
furnished by government per day $10.00	$12.00
Hire of 2 horse teams, wagon, driver, rations	
furnished by owner, per day $5.00	$7.00
Hire of 4 horse teams, wagon, driver, rations	
furnished by government, per day $15.00	$20.00
Hire of same with owner furnished rations . . . $7.50	$10.50
Hire of 6 horse teams, wagon, driver, rations	
furnished by government, per day $9.00	$13.00
Hire of same, rations furnished by owner . . . $18.00	$26.00
Hire of laborer, rations furnished by owner per day . . . $.25	$4.00
Hire of laborer, rations furnished by government, per day . . . $1.25	$2.50
Hire of laborer, rations furnished by government, per month . . . $45.00	
Hire of laborers, rations furnished by owner,	
per month . . . $30.00 to $60.00	$90.00
Hire of horses per day . . . $1.25	$2.00

[Wilmington *Daily Journal* December 26, '64]

CHAPTER 8, #B:

1864 SCHEDULE OF PRICES FOR NORTH CAROLINA: "The period for the publication of the schedule of prices to govern agents of the government, for the next sixty days, having arrived, the commissioners of the state of North Carolina adopt the last schedule with the exception of the few changes shown below. The illness of Mr. Mordecai, depriving us of his services, we have called in Mr. Wm. H. Jones of this city, who has kindly given us the benefit of his judgment as umpire on the present occasion.

The commissioners respectfully suggest that if it be found practicable, the producer should be allowed to retain a fourth part of their surplus, to be sold at market rates, to pay for their necessary plantation supplies which they have to purchase at high market prices. They earnestly call upon the farmers to bring forward their corn now so necessary to the support of the army in the immediate front, and which alone will prevent the loss to the enemy, of all their crops, stock, Negroes, & etc. The commissioners would also recommend that the impressments should be universal and uniform, leaving out no one.

For the information of all persons concerned, we publish the following instructions, with the hope that they will be strictly obeyed.

No officer, or agent, shall impress the necessary supplies which any person may have for the consumption of himself, his family, employees, slaves, or to carry on his ordinary mechanical, manufacturing or agricultural employments." [*Daily Journal* December 26, '64]

CHAPTER 8, #C:

Members of the Poor House, Orange County, September, 1862:

Alcey Flint, Hannah Ray, Reuben Carden, Alfred Collins, S. Elli, Wm Baldsome, Betsy Ashley with one child, John Tyler Hellum, Hiram Riley, Wesley Forrester, Mary Bush with one child, Phillis Woods, Louvena Glenn with one child, Rebecca Baldwin, Mary Dennis, Nancy Jordan, Mary Durham, Ibby Kell with two children, and Betsy Baldwin.[21]

CHAPTER 8, #D:

Woman's letter to Governor Vance:

"Sir, it is with an aching heart and tremulous hand that I sit myself this morning to inform you of my condition. My only dear son volunteered and enlisted to fight for his country May the second, 1862. He rented my farm to Mr. Shearer and left myself and a sister in his care. He died last April. I could not get any person to tend my farm. My daughters are of a delicate constitution. My friends are all in the army and most of them dead. My son-in-law went with the recruits in March and died from the fatigue of the battles around Richmond. Our farms joined. He left six children. His name was Edson. He lost his life for his country. My dear son lives as far as I know. I received a letter from him last week. He was in the valleys in Va. near Strausburg, Gen. Lee's army and headed NC troops, co. H, care of Capt. Osborne. He is a soldier in that company. He is as fine a soldier as ever lived. He fought through the battles around Richmond and in Maryland and a great many more. The God of battle has spared his life. He is a true son as a Mother ever raised. He owed fifty old dollars when he enlisted for which security for my land is now advertised for sale for that debt. He has been trying to pay that debt ever since he left. It has taken all he could get for my support and to ameliorate his own sufferings. The cost and interest on that debt now amounts to ninety dollars. Please be so considerate as to bear with my weak position as necessity compels me to apply. I have made all exertions during this awful war to do all I could towards clothing the soldiers though it is hard to get much done at that. The speculators will prove too hard for us as we have every thing to buy and so little to buy with some times. I am almost ready to give up the struggle as there is not any to pity or hand to assist[?]. I live in a poor neighborhood. Those that can assist the needy will not do so. They all have excuses. Some say I could of kept my son from going. Others say their's would not have gone if it had not been for him.. I had one side of bacon from the government the summer after my son left, [that] is all I have had. I am 72 years old. My husband served 6 months in the last war. He has been dead 10 years and I was left [with] my son [who] had aged enough to take care of this awful war [and it] had oppressed me so I am forced to apply to you. My condition is unknown to my son. I do not know what he would do if he knew it. Please excuse this bad spelling and writing and help me if you please. I cannot see well. I'm old and nervous. Jamima A. Thomas"[22]

CHAPTER 8, #E

Rations issued in January, 1864 in Chatham County:

" . . . a list of amounts furnished to destitute families of servicemen . . . a woman and three children . . . $3.21 and to one person, an amount of 20c to $1.66. A mother and one child received $11.15 in the form of flour, $30 worth of beef which turned out to be 20 lbs, and $20 worth of corn (one bushel) this was December, 1964 In January, 1865 one mother and child received 11 lbs of Flour ($13.25), 3 gal of molasses at $36.00, and 1 ½ bu of corn which had gone up to $30.00"[23]

Chapter 8, #F

Rations issued March and April, 1864, by G.W. Collier to soldiers families of Dudley District, Wayne County:

Name	# of children	rations	meat	total meat
Mary J. Thompson	3	4	40 lbs	160 lbs
Betty Moore	4	5	50	200
Lidia Parker	4	5	50	200
R.A. Huler?	2	3	30	120
Sally Lewis	2	3	30	20
Dicey Fields?	1	2	20	80
Margaret B. Smith	3	4	40	160
Ann Miller	3	4	40	160
Mary Jernigan		1	10	40
Betsy Law	2	3	30	120
Edna Sanderson	2	3	30	120
Winy Grundy	1	2	20	80
Lucy Hines		1	10	40
Alice Hines		1	10	40
Edith Jones		1	10	40
Evaline Lossen	3	4	40	160
Harriet Lane	4	5	50	200

Mary J. or T. Benton		1	10	40
Charity Howell	2	3	30	120
Jane Thompson	4	5	50	200
Mary Creech		1	10	40
Elizabeth Dixon	2	3	30	120
Charisy Dail	4	5	50	200
Susan Dail	3	4	40	160
Balsey Norris	2	3	30	120
Catherine Thompson	5	6	60	240
Sarah Price	2	3	30	120
Charlotte Edwards		1	10	40
Martha Casey	1	2	20	80
Mary A. Price	2	3	30	120
Julia Grant	2	3	30	120
Winy Harrel	1	2	20	80
Nancy Hines	1	2	20	80
Anna Bass	1	2	20	80
Ressy Pearsall	2	3	30	120
Elizabeth Temegan	2	3	30	120
Sarah Bradley	1	2	20	80
Martha Benton	2	3	30	120
Elizabeth Brock	3	4	40	160[24]

CHAPTER 8, #G

Receipt for merchandise from W.A. Weathersbee to M. Staton, May 9, '61: 11½ yds of bleached domestic, $2.42; hoop skirt and a box of soap . . . $3.15; 2 pr. Shoes . . . $6.75; 14 lbs. sugar . . . $16.06.
June 30 1861: paid $9.10 for two pr. cotton cards.
July, '61: Louisa bought 17 pr. brogans for $23.80 and 40 lbs. salt for $8.
Adrian Staton bought from John Watts, 1861-62, a hair brooch for 75c; knife . . . 60c; 2 plugs tobacco . . . 50c; axe . . . $2; pants . . . $5; women's gaiters . . . $2.
James Staton bought from W.G. Carstarphen, May 1861: 1 pr. Boots . . . $3.75; 4 silk neck ties . . . $2.65; fiddle bow . . . 50c; vest . . . $4; silk vest . . . $6; paddocks and umbrella . . . $3.80; Violin strings . . . 40c; pr. Pants . . . $2.75; bag of shot . . . $2.50; plug tobacco . . . 40c; ready made coat . . . $1.50; black hat . . . $4.
March 22, '62: James bought from Mr. Lanier : 10 lbs. tobacco for the Negroes . . . $3.33.
Susan E. Staton bought from Mr. C.B. Hassel, January 3, '62: book bag and slate . . . $1.60; February 7, '62 she got India rubbers, gloves and shoes for $2.45. March 18, '62 7 ¼ yd French satin with 1 pr. soes and a hair brush . . . $8.97.

Louisa paid $280.30 to Thomas Pugh to pay expenses and secure a place for her Negroes at Danbury, May 17, '62. On the 23rd she paid $100 to Jesse Rell to carry the Negroes from Williamston to Danbury. In November, '62 three men from Nashville hired some of her Negroes of both sexes and these persons promised to get them back to her on January 1, '64[25]

Flour was selling for $500 a barrel in 1865. Wheat was $50.

Chapter 8, #H

From *Salt That Necessary Article*: 1/4lb of salt would be processed from one gallon of water. The State Salt Works near present day Wrightsville Beach used 120 cords of wood a day to distill 800 bushels of salt from seawater. Dr. Ebenezer Emmons, State Geologist, had the newspapers to print how to extract salt and brine from fish and meat barrels:

"The solid salt, if there is any in the barrels, should be scooped out and drained, and the drainings returned to the brine. Boil this brine down to a solid. This, together with the salt already removed from the brine, must be heated to a dull red heat; or sufficient to char the organic material contained in it; if it cakes in burning, it should be stirred to bring all parts in contact with the heat. Then dissolve in clean water, using no more water than is necessary for the purpose. This impure solution must be carefully strained through a fine cloth—a bag of Canton flannel is best. If it does not come through clean at first, run it through a second or third time, without washing the strainer. The strained brine must be boiled down again. As the evaporation progresses, salt will be formed at the bottom of the pan or kettle, and as this retards the evaporation, it can be ladled out and drained, the drainings returned to the kettle, and the salt spread out on clean vessels to dry, while the boiling must be continued until the water is nearly evaporated, when the salt may be removed and dried. In this way, salt equal to the finest table salt may be made from the most impure brine. A saturated solution of salt contains about one-fourth, by weight, of salt; consequently a gallon of brine should yield one and a half or two pounds of salt . . . . Earth from smokehouses may be leached and treated in the same manner."

Raleigh Register . . . We publish this letter from Prof. Emmons to Gov. Clark:

"Raleigh April 11, 1862

To His Excellency
Henry T. Clark
Gov of NC

Sir: The inquiry which you made yesterday respecting the value of brine which has been employed for preserving meat is important at this time. Old brine will contain a large portion of the salt used, and may be recovered by boiling it. Let the brine be poured into an iron kettle, and stir in, while cold the white of several eggs. Boil the brine & skim off the dirt from the top as long as it rises. Now strain the liquid, while hot, in order to free it from a stringy sediment. Boil and skim again, if necessary, reducing the quality of brine by evaporation until a pellicle of fine salt forms upon the surface. It may now be set aside to cool while crystals of nearly pure salt will be formed. The brine should never be boiled til a dry mass is formed, as in that case, it will be impure and dark colored. By repeating the evaporation, the salt may be obtained as pure & white as table salt.

Most truly your servant
E. Emmons, state geologist
PS If the brine is stirred while cooling, fine salt will be formed. If it is allowed to cool at rest, a coarse salt will be deposited."

Chapter 8, #I

NEWSPAPER REPORTS OF HOW TO ECONOMIZE:

"Economy in Boots: How to make three pair of boots last as long as six, and longer. The following extract is from Colonel Macerone's Seasonable Hints, which appeared in the Mechanic's Magazine, dated Feb 3rd, 1843. After stating the quality of sheepskin clothing, for persons whose employment renders it necessary that they should be much outdoors, etc., he says: I treat them in the following manner—I put a pound of tallow and a half a pound of rosin into a pot on the fire, and when melted and mixed, I warm the boots and apply the hot stuff with a painter's brush until neither the sole or the upper leather will suck in any more. If it is desirable that the boots should take polish, dissolve an ounce of beeswax with an ounce of turpentine, to which add a teaspoon of lamp-black, A day or two after the boots have been treated with the tallow and resin, rub over them the wax and the turpentine, but not before the fire. Tallow or any other grease becomes rancid and rots the stitching as well as the leather, but the rosin gives it an antiseptic quality which preserves the whole. Boots or shoes should be so large to admit of wearing in them cork soles—cork is a bad conductor of heat." [*Raleigh Register,* January 22, '62]

CHAPTER 9, #A

[*Greensborough Patriot,* April 16, '63]
WOMEN RAIDS
"We feel it to be a disagreeable duty to notice a little affair which took place in the streets of Greensborough on Wednesday of last week. Our first impulse was, to let the subject pass unnoticed, and if possible be forgotten; but as the 'thing' has 'got into the papers' elsewhere, perhaps it is best for us to make a statement of facts as they occurred, and thus prevent misrepresentation and exaggeration.

Early in the morning it was reported that some thirty or forty women were three or four miles west of town, on their way to Greensborough, to break into the stores here and help themselves to whatever their fancy might suggest. Some of our staid citizens immediately went out to meet them, to reason with them, and if possible to ascertain their designs, and particularly their necessities, so that if they were really suffering for the necessaries of life, that proper means might be taken to relieve their necessities. But before the return of the messengers sent West, some twenty women, armed with axes, hatchets, pistols, bowie knives, and sword canes, made their appearance from the East, and soon commenced battering down Mr. Williard's store door. At this juncture a Magistrate present ordered them arrested and disarmed. But little resistance was made by those women; one, however, presented her pistol at a soldier present, but did not understand pulling the trigger, and the soldier's life was thus saved.

These women were taken inside the jail lot enclosure, and replaced in the passage of the jail, though not locked up, and there guarded until it was ascertained that the company from the West had turned back, when they were released.

This affair has deeply mortified the friends of the soldiers and their families, and the fear is, that it will have a tendency to depress the efforts that are constantly being made in all parts of the county to prevent suffering among the poor and indigent of the county. We hope such may not be its effect. It has been ascertained that it was not bread and meat these women were after, but other articles. We would fondly hope that this will be the last frolic of the kind that will be attempted; for we can assure all concerned that there is a determination by the substantial citizens and Magistrates of at least Guilford county, to put down all such proceedings at all hazards. The civil laws of the land must be respected and observed; otherwise society would soon fall into disgrace and anarchy—a most dangerous state of affairs for any community.

Every possible effort has been made in Guilford county to afford the necessary support to the destitute families of the soldier. The county has been divided into eighteen districts, and two or more of the most reliable citizens of each District appointed to attend to the wants of the poor of the District, and from time to time, as may be required, draw on the Chairman of the County Court, for funds to meet all necessary expenses. And we know that many, and believe that all of these District Committee-men have devoted themselves to this work of benevolent and humanity, and have endeavored faithfully to relieve the wants of all, so far as possible, and we would most earnestly entreat them to continue their efforts in this way, as long as there is a necessity for it.

That there are men in the county who are withholding their provisions from market, refusing to sell at the present prices, with the hope that before harvest prices will rise still higher, we have no doubt; nor have any doubt that there are speculators watching and trying to buy up what provisions can be purchased, and thus secure a monopoly of the trade and secure whatever price they please . . . we are also satisfied that there are scattered all through the country persons who have a surplus of provisions, who, our hearing that these speculators and extortioners will pay a little more than the current price for provisions, forthwith sell the surplus to them, although their neighbors may be suffering for something to live upon. All this is wrong—heinously wrong; and all such persons should receive equally the scorn and contempt of the generous and humane. For all such acts, we have nothing but condemnation. Such conduct has been one of the main cause of the present *mania* for female raids."

CHAPTER 10, #A

LIST OF NAMES OF FREE NEGRO MEN PETITIONING FOR EXEMPTION:

Lieutenant Holt wrote: "The principle feature in white persons making application for free Negroes is that they can rent their lands and get one third of the produce [.] it makes them eager to have their free negroes around them." Lt. E.R. Holt, Lexington District, July, 1864

Oliver Mose, a free Negro wants exemption . . . denied.
Julius Belfour . . . denied
D. Phillips . . . denied. "He has a wife and five children. The boys are old enough to plow."
Joseph Chavice . . . denied
Alaxender Scott . . . denied
John Cranford . . . denied
Felix Belfour . . . denied
Jesse, Sandy and William Lytle
Jesse Potter
Thomas Potter works for Mrs. Rebecca Lowe . . . denied
Thomas Calicott . . . denied
Nathan Lineberry works for Sarah Uliss . . . denied
John Calvin . . . denied
Harrison Ward works for Mrs. Nancy Robbins . . . denied. Lt. Holt says he "is a very refractory disobedient fellow. Not at all safe to be left with a soldier's wife."
John Bell works for Bethany Vuncannon . . . denied
Robert Chavis works for Anna Vuncannon . . . denied
Wilson Carter . . . denied
Calvin Munn . . . denied
Ben and John Tuck . . . denied
Ellis Hicks . . . denied
William Tuck . . . denied
William Thigpen . . . denied
Green Fort . . . denied
Wiatt Roberson . . . denied
David Ownes . . . denied
George Bell . . . denied
Nathan and Edward Phillips . . . denied
Emsley Hill . . . denied
John Munroe . . . denied
Elias Potter . . . denied

Clement Locklin . . . denied
Reuben Phillips works for Sarah Hall . . . denied
John Hall works for Sarah Luther . . . denied
Whitley Hagan . . . denied
James Wilson . . . denied
Alfred Stuart works for Sarah Womble . . . denied

LIST OF FREE BLACK MEN <u>APPROVED</u> FOR EXEMPTION, same date:

Carney Walden
Edward Walder petitioned by Chatham County citizens. Asheboro, September 21, 1864
    to Major General Whiting. "He is a good worker."
Augustus Hill, a cooper, " . . . makes government barrels, he also makes syrup barrels for
    the neighborhood. He has had military service and is incapacitated by disease."
P. B. Spikes, a shoemaker, also works for Sarah Koonts.
John Oxandine
Enoch Brown works for Mrs. Jane Williams.
Joseph Nooe
Haywood Walden, works for Jane Brown.
Eli Brown works for Jane Luther who has five children and helpless in-laws depending
    on her.
Ben Stith
Henry Stith, petitioned by B. F. Stead, a wounded soldier at home . . . approved.
Martin Woodle, works for Larkey Medley, a poor woman.
William Newly
Joe Rush
William Jones
B. Goines, he has a family of five children, a wife; all would become dependant on the
    county. There are now 300 on the county roll [poor house].
John Gaines, a miller and cooper works for Stephen Hendly, a Quaker, who runs a flour
    mill and he also runs a carding machine.
Reuben Winslow, works for a family who would be destitute if he left.
Isreal Hanna
Thomas Gaines, a mechanic.
Wilson Williams, married to a white woman, has many children. If conscripted he
    would leave them to charity.
Madison Chavis, works for Lettie Rush, a soldier's wife, also children.
John Brown
Calvin Hill, works for Demercus Cranford, widow of a soldier. He also takes care of her
    family and his own.
Franklin Walker
Noah Rush
Joseph Bookshire, has nine children and helps a white family.

LIST OF PETITIONERS from Chatham County requesting Exemptions for Free Black men:

"Lizzie P. Merritt, Mary Holder, Elizar Holder, Sarah E. Stone, Martha A. Stone, Sallie
A. Hackney, Quintina Stone, Betty L. Johnson, Lina Jinkins, De Jinkins, Marina Jinkins, R. T.
Jinkins, Nancy Herndon, Caroline Herndon, Virginia Herndon, Malissa Herndon, Nancy E.
Carson, Cleary Upchurch, Partheney Yates, Clargy Upchurch, Matilda? Upchurch, Quinettar
Laseter, Cloyalet? Barbee, Martha Barbee, Sarah Barbee, Tempa Barbee, Sally Barbee, Dolly
Bell, Bettie Bell, Sally Luter, Chatiny? Luter, Pesperarm? Luter, Arline ?, Elizabeth Herndon,
Sarah A. Herndon, Malinda Williams, Carrie H. and Mary M. Williams, Dollie Williams, G. R.T.

Williams, M. A. Williams, Caroline Johnson, Annie Cole, Eliza Jinkins, Helan Jinkins, Artelia Jinkins, Levenia H. Sears, Lucetie Council, Penny Williams, Delia Upchurch, Delphia Williams, Susan M. Baldwin, Lizzie F. Bell, and Eliza A. Bell."[26]

CHAPTER 10, #B

Deserter's letter:
"Oct the 26/62
camp hanes Mr vanes I am abecesente for mi commande a voute lef ande I am sorey thate I done soe hite is the fiste defence I evr was gilte of and ef you will parden me and sende me to mi commande I nevr will doo so no more I com hom to see mi famley I didente come to gate shete of the war I com to per vide for mi famley and I am her under garde at this time I didente lieowte in the wodes to excape from bin taken upe I will wate for your Dispatches yours re spectfull [.] Jas Rhodes, Benegeman Lovless, Drewey gren, Alberte toney, Gilferde ones, calvin ones, Th camel, Henrey ramsey."[27]

Chapter 11, #A

OATH OF ALLEGIANCE TO THE STATE

_____1861
Having been appointed a .... I do hereby accept the same and certify that I am .... years of age, that I was born in ....
.... and that my residence when appointed was ....
.... , the nearest post office being ....

I do swear that I will be faithful and bear true allegiance to the State of North Carolina, and to the Constitutional powers and authorities which are or may be established for the government thereof, and maintain and defend the Constitution of the said State. So help me God.
Subscribed and sworn to before me   .... J.P.
This .... day of .... 1861[28]

ENDNOTES

CHAPTER ONE ENDNOTES

1. North Carolina, a History; p. 128.
2. Mountain Masters, Slavery, and the Sectional Crisis in Western North Carolina; p. 213; hereafter cited as Mountain Masters.
3. Powell, Eleanor. "Tensions Ran High in Goldsboro at the Outbreak of the Civil War." *History of Wayne County, N.C., a Collection of Historical Stories Created by the Heritage Committee.* ECU digital series; hereafter cited as History of Wayne County.
4. Caroline E. Clitherall Papers. Wilson Library, Southern Historical Collection, UNC.
5. "The Hospital at Danville." *Our Women in the War, the Lives They Lived, the Deaths They Died.* Attributed to Miss Hattie Kilgore, The Charleston Weekly News & Courier 1885; p. 219; hereafter cited as Our Women in the War.
6. Pictorial History of New Hanover County. NCC, UNC-CH.
7. Chronicles of the Cape Fear River 1660-1916; p. 271; hereafter cited as Chronicles of the Cape Fear.
8. IBID; p. 295, 276.
9. Richmond Daily Dispatch, January 4, `61.
10. Chronicles of the Cape Fear River; p. 272.
11. The War of Northern Aggression in Western North Carolina in 1861; p. 185-191.
12. Shuttle and Plow, a History of Alamance County, North Carolina. p. 263.
13. Mary Jeffreys Bethell Diary. Southern Historical Collection, UNC-CH.
14. Journal of a Secesh Lady, the Diary of a Catherine Ann Devereux Edmondston; p. 37; hereafter cited as Journal of a Secesh Lady.
15. Lenoir Family Papers. Southern Historical Collection, Wilson Library, UNC-CH.
16. Mountain Masters, Slavery, and the Sectional Crisis in Western North Carolina; p. 230; hereafter cited as Mountain Masters.
17. Raleigh Register, 1861.
18. Asa Biggs. Documenting the American South. UNC-CH.
19. North Carolina Quakers. p. 152.
20. History of Wayne County.
21. Diary of Elizabeth Wiggins. Private Papers.
22. Journal of A Secesh Lady; p. 42.
23. Asa Biggs, Documenting the American South, UNC-CH.
24. Divided Allegiances, Bertie County in the Civil War; p. 9; hereafter cited as Divided Allegiances.
25. Person Family Papers. Perkins Library, Duke University.
26. Port Town at War, Wilmington, N.C., 1861-1865. a dissertation by Robert B. Wood.
27. Harris, William C. "Lincoln and Wartime Reconstruction in North Carolina, 1861-1863." *North Carolina Historical Review.* Volume 63, #2, April, 1986; p. 149.
28. Journal of a Secesh Lady; p. 50.
29. Expedition to Kinston, Whitehall, and Goldsborough, December, 1862; p. 45-46.
30. Diary of Elizabeth Ellis Robeson. Bladen County Historical Society.
31. William H. Wills Papers. Southern Historical Collection, Wilson Library, UNC-CH.
32. The War of Northern Aggression; p. 3.
33. North Carolina in 1861; p. 207.
34. The War of Northern Aggression; p. 6.
35. Edgecombe County, a Brief History; p. 174.
36. The Anson Guards; p. 174.
37. Lenoir Family Papers. Documenting the American South, UNC-CH.
38. Person Family Papers. Perkins Library, Duke University
39. Papers of John Willis Ellis, Volume II, 1860-1861; p. 737.
40. History of Wayne County.

41. IBID
42. Letters of Joshua B. Hill April 29, '61 from his mother; courtesy of Thomas Schroder.
43. Papers of John Willis Ellis. p 733.
44. IBID; p. 854.
45. "Legal Aspects of Conscription and Exemptions in N.C., 1861-1865." *The James Sprunt Studies in History and Political Science,* Volume 47; p. 4; hereafter cited as Legal Aspects.
46. "How the Arsenal was Taken." *Our Women in the War, the Lives They Lived. The Charleston Weekly News & Courier;* p. 22; hereafter cited as Our Women in the War.
47. Edgecombe County, a Brief History; p. 38.
48. Rockingham County, a Brief History; p. 51.
49. North Carolina in 1861; p. 25.
50. Shuttle and Plow, a History of Alamance County, North Carolina; p. 264.
51. Dear Ones at Home; p. 33.
52. "The Hospital at Danville." *Our Women and the War;* p. 219-230.
53. Sallie Southall Cotton; p. 11.
54. The Civil War in North Carolina, Volume I; p. 21.
55. The Heritage: The Education of Women at St. Mary's College, Raleigh, North Carolina; p. 57; hereafter cited as Women of St. Mary's.
56. Ladies in the Making; *p.* 24.
57. Before the Rebel Flag Fell; page "I."
58. The Old South Illustrated; p. 169.
59. Asa Biggs. Documenting the American South, UNC-CH.
60. Forgotten Confederates, an Anthology About Black Southerners; p. 8.
61. The Papers of John Willis Ellis; p.785.
62. Forgotten Confederates, an Anthology About Black Southerners; p. 9.
63. Mountain Masters; p. 63.
64. Asa Biggs. Documenting the American South, UNC-CH.
65. Garrison, Randall, editor; Louis Leon. "Diary of a Tar Heel Confederate Soldier." *Company Front.* August, 1998; p. 5.
66. Rebel Boast: First at Bethel—Last at Appomattox; p. 261; letter April 25, '61.
67. Chronicles of the Cape Fear River; p. 356.
68. Strikeleather, J.A. "Recollections of the Civil War in the United States." *Company Front.* October, 1993; p. 10; hereafter cited as "J.A. Strikeleather." [Iredell Blues].
69. Lilly Hoffman Notebook; courtesy of Jodie Gee.
70. Carolina and the Southern Cross. Volume 1, #10, 1914.
71. Memories of an Old Time Tar Heel; p. 169.
72. David Brainerd Whiting Papers. North Carolina Department of Archives & History.
73. Rebel Gibraltar; p. 19.
74. John Motley Morehead and the Development of North Carolina, 1796-1866; p. 388.
75. Beavers Brothers Letters. Perkins Library, Duke University.
76. My Dearest Friend, the Civil War Correspondence of Cornelia McGimsey and Lewis Warlick.; p.18, June 5, '61; hereafter cited as My Dearest Friend.
77. The Papers of Willie Mangum; p. 387.
78. Before the Rebel Flag Fell; page "M."
79. Lenoir Family Papers. Documenting the American South, UNC-CH.
80. Melinda Ray Diary. North Carolina Department of Archives & History. October 9, '61.
81. Tillinghast Family Papers. Perkins Library, Duke University.
82. M.A. Cavin Papers. North Carolina Department of Archives & History.
83. Ashe County's Civil War: Community and Society in the Appalachian South; p. 78.
84. IBID (lost page).
85. Mansfield, C.E. "Letters of J.B. Mansfield, Part I." *Company Front,* September/October 1995; Letter from Ann to J.B.M., February, 1862.
86. Making of a Confederate; p. 69.

87. The Heart of Confederate Appalachia: Western North Carolina in the Civil War; p. 79; hereafter cited as Heart of Confederate Appalachia.

88. A Civil War Tragedy, the Lipe Family; p. 14.

89. Raleigh Register, April 20, `61.

90. Interview with Jennifer Wisener, descendant, 2005; ancestor in Co. K 2nd NC.

91. Rebel Boast; p. 82; George Wills to his sister, Maggie.

92. My Dearest Friend; p. 3.

93. Spirit of the Age, June 6, `61.

94. Trial Separation: Murfreesboro, North Carolina and the Civil War; p. 29; hereafter cited as Trial Separation.

95. Journal of a Secesh Lady; p. 65.

96. The Papers of John Willis Ellis; p. 731.

97. North Carolina in 1861; p. 33.

98. Ashe County's Civil War; p. 78.

99. When the Past Refused to Die; p. 185-187.

100. War of Northern Aggression; p. 7.

101. Guilford Under the Stars and Bars; p. 391.

102. Mothers of Invention; p. 57.

103. MacRae Letters. St. Mary's School. Box 80 #775; to John MacRae, Fayetteville.

104. Page Descendants Interview 2004.

105. Flashes of Duplin County; p. 218.

106. Trial Separation; p. 29.

107. Before the Rebel Flag Fell; page # N.

108. Trial Separation; p. 6.

109. "Battle of Shallowford," by Dr. P.F. Laugenour, Yadkin County Historical Journal, Volume 14, #3, July 1995; p. 14.

110. Person Family Papers. Perkins Library, Duke University.

111. Richmond County Record; p. 185.

112. My Dearest Friend; p. 11.

113. Beavers Brothers Letters. Perkins Library, Duke University; I.S. Upchurch letter November 16, `61.

114. Confederate Courage on Other Fields; p. 61.

115. John Sutton letter; courtesy of Betty Monteith, Jackson Co. He was KIA Gettysburg.

116. Doctor to the Front; page xv, preface.

117. Francis Pollock letter; courtesy Allen Cochran.

118. Beavers Brothers Letters; Perkins Library, Duke University; letter-July 2, `61.

119. IBID; August 24, `61.

120. Swindell letter, October 14, `61; courtesy of Merlin Berry.

121. Bright and Gloomy Days: the Civil War Correspondence of Captain Charles F. Bahnson, a Confederate Moravian; page xxxv; hereafter cited as Bright and Gloomy.

122. County of Warren; p. 139.

123. The Papers of Willie Mangum; p. 392, 388, 394.

124. Mountain Masters; p. 261.

125. Diary of Elizabeth Wiggins, private donor use.

126. Before the Rebel Flag Fell; page 'M."

127. Mountain Masters; p. 43.

128. Honey, Michael, "The War Within the Confederacy: White Unionists in North Carolina. Prologue, Summer, 1986; p. 84.

129. Southern Rights; p. 146.

130. The Papers of John W. Ellis; p. 867.

131. Southern Rights; p. 129.

132. The History of Warren County, North Carolina 1586-1976; p. 135.

133. The Civil War in Appalachia; p. 58.

134. Trial Separation; p. 29.

135. Southern Rights; p. 164.

136. Many Excelle.nt People: Power and Privilege in North Carolina 1850-1900; p. 74.

137. Southern Families at War; p. 198.

138. The Heart of Confederate Appalachia; p. 76.
139. Journal of a Secesh Lady; p. 54.
140. Tillinghast Family Papers. Perkins Library, Duke University.
141. Diary of Melinda Ray. North Carolina Department of Archives & History; August 21, `61
142. Southern Rights; p. 87-88.
143. IBID; p. 130-133.
144. "An Ordinance to Define and Punish Sedition." Documenting the American South. UNC-CH.
145. Jonathan Worth, a Bibliography; p. 126.
146. The Papers of Willie Mangum; p. 388.
147. The Thirty-seventh North Carolina Troops; p. 110, November 19, `62.
148. A Brief Historical Sketch of Mt. Carmel Baptist Church in Northampton County Near Seaboard, North Carolina. ECU digital series.
149. Bright and Gloomy Days; p. xxxii.
150. The Merging of the Gael; p. 110-111.
151. Orange County Presbyterian Minutes—microfilm.
152. Ashe County, a History; p. 140 .
153. A Brief History of the Episcopal Church Parish, Elizabeth City, North Carolina; p. 246; ECU digital series.
154. Brock Townsend descendants papers.
155. Scarborough Family Papers. Perkins Library, Duke University; letter to F. Scarborough.
156. Lenoir Family Papers. Documenting the American South, UNC-CH.
157. Mary Ann Buie Papers. Perkins Library, Duke University; letter May 4, `61.
158. Wake, Capital County; p. 470.
159. Schroeder, Greg. "Dear Burwell," *Awakenings: Writings and Recollections of Eastern North Carolina Women;* p. 14; hereafter cited as Dear Burwell.
160. Strikeleather, J.A. "Recollections of the Civil War in the U.S.," *Company Front.* October 1993; p. 12.
161. Mercer Family Papers. Southern Historical Collection. Wilson Library, UNC-CH.
162. "Changing Relationships," typed manuscript; courtesy of David McGee.
163. The Thirty-seventh North Carolina Troops; p. 28.
164. Rebel Boast; p. 287, April, 10, `64.
165. The Civil War on the Outer Banks; p. 31.
166. The History of Brunswick County; p. 153.
167. Day, William. "Personal History of the 49th, a History of Company I," *Company Front.* July, 1996; p. 5.
168. The Natural Bent; p. 37.
169. Diary of Elizabeth Wiggins.
170. R.P. Crawford at Nichols Sound on the Sea, letter November 29, `61; Hunter Library, WCU.
171. Leftwich, Rodney. "Four Letters of Thomas M. Garrison," *Company Front.* 1989; Company K, 25[th NCT].
172. Spirit of the Age, September, `61
173. The Civil War Life of John Muse as Told to Jennie Muse, edited by Charles Muse 1991; courtesy of Charles Muse.
174. Diary of John Young. North Carolina Department of Archives & History; no date but believe to be 1861.
175. Diary of Elizabeth Wiggins.
176. Bright and Gloomy Days; p. xxx; letter by Charles Bahnson in Philadelphia to his father, April 17, `61.
177. IBID; p. 17.
178. IBID; p. 38.
179. St Mary's School Letters, Box 88, #811; "Reminiscences of Margaret Weber."
180. William Wills Papers. Southern Historical Collection, Wilson Library, UNC-CH.
181. St. Mary's School Letters, Box 80, #770—this article appeared in *the Southern Studies,* Volume XXV, 1986 under "Disillusioned with Paradise: a Southern Woman's Impression of the Rural North in 1862," by John Hall.
182. Mast, Greg, editor. " The Letters of Joseph J. White, 1861." *Company Front.,* April, 1993.
183. A Civil War Tragedy—the Lipe Family; p.22.
184. Francis Marion Parker Papers. Southern Historical Collection, UNC-CH.
185. "The Joseph White Letters," *Company Front*
186. Lenoir Family Papers. Documenting the American South, UNC-CH.
187. Confederate Courage on Other Fields; p. 65, October 4, `61.
188. Raleigh Register, November 23, `61.

[189.] www.sallysfamilyplace.com/Wheeler/Page52a.html
[190.] Diary of Melinda Ray. North Carolina Department of Archives & History; Box 78, #32.
[191.] North Carolina Yeoman; p. 230.
[192.] Alonso E. Bell Diary. North Carolina Department of Archives & History.
[193.] Rebel Boast; p. 278. Louis Leon at Goldsboro. December, 25, `62.
[194.] Bright and Gloomy Days; p.44.
[195.] IBID; p. 103, 94.
[196.] Brown, Frank. "These Toils and Hardships." *Company Front*, Part I-II, Volume 2, 2003; *and* Barbara Breece Roesch.
[197.] Scarborough Papers. Perkins Library, Duke University; letter from S.E. Scarborough, Mt. Gilead, January 30, `64 to Millie Williams.
[198.] Hillsborough Recorder, December 25, `61.

CHAPTER TWO ENDNOTES

[1.] Carolina and the Southern Cross, Volume I-II, 1913; p.10.
[2.] North Carolina Booklet, Volume 16.
[3.] History of Anson County, North Carolina, 1750-1976; p. 104-105.
[4.] North Carolina Booklet, Volume 16.
[5.] Carolina and the Southern Cross, Volume I-II, 1913; p. 15.
[6.] A Researcher's Journal: Beaufort, North Carolina and the Civil War; p. 11, 68.
[7.] The Civil War in North Carolina.; p. 6.
[8.] Carolina and the Southern Cross, Volume I-II, 1912-1914, September; p. 3.
[9.] Raleigh Standard, June 21, `61.
[10.] The Natural Bent; p. 34.
[11.] The Thirty-seventh North Carolina Troops; p. 15.
[12.] Tar Heel Women; p. 124.
[13.] Historical Sketches of Franklin County; p. 60.
[14.] The County of Warren, North Carolina 1586-1976; p. 134 footnote.
[15.] Interview with researcher Greg Biggs, 2004.
[16.] History of Wayne County; p.184.
[17.] Wake, Capitol County; p. 471.
[18.] IBID; p. 473.
[19.] Raleigh Standard, April 29, `61.
[20.] North Carolina Women of the Confederacy; p. 115.
[21.] Spirit of the Age, June 12, `62.
[22.] Journal of A Secesh Lady; p. 11-12.
[23.] The Story of Henderson County; p.125.
[24.] The Heart of Confederate Appalachia, Western North Carolina and the Civil War; p. 71.
[25.] North Carolina Women of the Confederacy; p. 111; *and* History of Western N.C.; p. 602.
[26.] IBID; p. 111.
[27.] An illustrated History of Yadkin County 1850-1980; p. 97.
[28.] Page Family Descendants Papers, Morrisville.
[29.] North Carolina Women of the Confederacy; p. 111.
[30.] Bright and Gloomy Days; page xxxiii.
[31.] Blair, Marian H. "The Letters of Henry W. Barrows to John W. Fries," *North Carolina Historical Review,* January 1957; p. 72.
[32.] IBID, p. 72, footnote #11.
[33.] Rebels in Blue; p. 30.
[34.] Anna Cureton Stevens, South Carolina Women of the Confederacy; courtesy of Alexander Street Press, Civil War Letters and Diaries.
[35.] North Carolina Women of the Confederacy; p. 110.
[36.] Guilford Under the Stars and Bars; p. 390.
[37.] Article courtesy of Roy Parker, Fayetteville Observer, January, 2004.

38. History of Anson County; p. 107.
39. The Civil War Letters of John A. Muse as Told to Jennie Muse (typed manuscript).
40. North Carolina Women of the Confederacy; p. 109.
41. IBID; p. 113.
42. Live Your Own Life; p. 43.
43. Wake, Capitol County; p. 459.
44. My Dearest Friend; p. 146.
45. North Carolina Women of the Confederacy; p. 114.

CHAPTER THREE ENDNOTES

1. Miscellaneous Military Collection. North Carolina Department of Archives & History. Letter attributed to Mrs. Estelle Murray. Box 76, file #1.
2. Wake—Capitol County; p. 465.
3. North Carolina Women of the Confederacy; p. 32.
4. The Richmond Dispatch, May 1, `61.
5. The Papers of John W. Ellis; p. 637.
6. Divided Allegiances; p. 17.
7. Sketches of Polk County; p. 39.
8. Fayetteville Observer, September 2, `61.
9. Greensboro Patriot, May 7, `61.
10. The Morning Post, Special Supplement. "Historical Incidents;" August 17, 1905.
11. North Carolina Women of the Confederacy; p. 24.
12. The Last Ninety Days of the War; p. 133.
13. Journal of a Secesh Lady; p. 88.
14. Hayes Redbook, Volume 128. "The South, the Confederacy, Yankees, and Negroes."
15. Carolina and the Southern Cross. October 1913; p. 18.
16. Hoke, Colonel W.J. "What Lincoln County Did in the War." *Our Living and Our Dead,* Volume I; p. 430.
17. Raleigh Standard, April 29, `61.
18. Bright and Gloomy: The Civil War Correspondence of Captain Charles H. Bahnson, a Moravian Confederate; page xxxvi; hereafter cited as Bright/Gloomy.
19. Raleigh Standard, April 1861.
20. Diary of Laura Norwood. Courtesy of Jeff Stepp.
21. Journal of a Secesh Lady; p. 60.
22. Raleigh Register, April 27, `61.
23. The Heritage: the Education of Women at St. Mary's College, Raleigh, North Carolina, 1842-1982; p. 60, 62.
24. Wake—Capitol County; p. 465.
25. Stinson, Eliza "How the Arsenal was Taken." *Our Women in the War, the Lives They Lived, the Deaths They Died;* p.22-30.
26. North Carolina Women of the Confederacy; p. 31.
27. Bright/Gloomy; page xxxvii.
28. Raleigh Standard, war years.
29. Rights, D.L. "Salem and the War Between the States." *North Carolina Historical Review.* July 1950, Volume XXVII, #3; p. 282.
30. Raleigh Standard, war years.
31. Bright/Gloomy; page xxxiv-v.
32. Journal of a Secesh Lady; p. 87-88.
33. Alfred W. Bell Papers. Perkins Library, Duke University. At Camp Martin, letter to his wife, February 17, `62.
34. Spirit of the Age, August 7, `61.
35. North Carolina Women of the 1860s; p. 3.
36. Johns, Annie. "The Hospitals at Danville." *Our Women in the War, the Lives They Lived, the Deaths They Died;* p. 219.
37. Raleigh Register, April 20, `61.
38. Lower Cape fear Historical Society, Inc. Bulletin, Volume V, #1.

39. Chronicles of the Cape fear River 1660-1916; p. 292.

40. IBID; p. 414.

41. Guilford Under the Stars and Bars; p. lost.

42. Sallie Southall Cotton; p. 17.

43. Women of the South in War Times; p. 230.

44. Journal of a Secesh Lady; p, 112.

45. The Morning Post, August 17, 1905.

46. Jacob Mordecai Papers. Perkins Library, Duke University.

47. North Carolina in 1861; p. 202.

48. Ladies in the Making; p. 19.

49. Silk Flags and Cold Steel; p. 131.

50. North Carolina Women of the Confederacy; p. 29, 31.

51. Southern Illustrated News, December 27, `62.

52. Mothers of Invention; p. 96.

53. Sallie Southall Cotton; p. 17.

54. Wake—Capitol County; p. 464.

55. Spirit of the Age, November 22, `61.

56. Spirit of the Age, 1861.

57. Iredell Express, July 1861.

58. Fayetteville Observer, July 15, `61.

59. Fayetteville observer, October 9, `61.

60. Farley/McIver/Robeson Papers. Southern Historical Collection, Wilson Library, UNC-CH.

61. Bivouac Banner. Summer, 2004. Article by Charles Anspake.

62. Hillsborough Recorder, January 8, `62.

63. The Thirty-seventh NCT; p. 111, letter November, 1862.

64. The Papers of Zebulon Baird Vance, Volume I; p. 265.

65. IBID; p. 286, letter October 31, `62.

66. My Dearest Friend: the Civil War Correspondence of Cornelia McGimsey and Lewis Warlick; p. 67-68, letter October 4, `61; hereafter cited as My Dearest Friend.

67. Spirit of the Age, January, 1862.

68. IBID; July 14, `62.

69. IBID; March, 1862.

70. Spirit of the Age, January 3, `62; and Asheville News Weekly, January 9, `62; and Carolina Watchman, November 18, `61.

71. Charlotte Daily Bulletin, December 8, `62; and Asheville News Weekly, May 15, `62; and The Civil War in Yadkin County; p. 37; and John Chesson Papers, North Carolina Department of Archives & History; and Spirit of the Age, July 14, `62.

72. Ellie's Book; and Raleigh Register, February 12, `62.

73. Raleigh Register, January 29, `62.

74. Carolina Watchman, December 23, `61.

75. Journal of a Secesh Lady; p. 57, 44.

76. Nancy A. Jarrett Papers. Southern Historical Collection, Wilson Library, UNC-CH.

77. Tillinghast Family Papers. Perkins Library, Duke University.

78. Lenoir Family Papers. Documenting the American South. UNC-CH.

79. My Dearest Friend; p. 69.

80. The Thirty-seventh NCT; p. 215.

81. The Wilmington Daily Journal, November 30, `64.

82. Encyclopedia of Religion in the U.S; p. 6-7; and Flat River Church Minutes [microfilm].

83. Spirit of the Age, August 21, `61 and September 28, `61.

84. North Carolina Baptist State Convention. [microfilm]

85. Postmarks; p. 51.

86. The Chowan Baptist Association Church Minutes of the 56th Annual Session. [microfilm].

87. The Episcopal Church in North Carolina 1701-1959; p. 248.

88. Spirit of the Age, September, 1861.

89. Raleigh Register, February 19, `62.
90. The Episcopal Church in North Carolina 1701-1959; p. 251.
91. Raleigh Register, war years.
92. The Papers of Walter Clark, Volume I; p. 99.
93. Merging of the Gaels; p. 115.
94. Baptist State Convention Reports. [microfilm]
95. Merging of the Gaels; p. 114.
96. The Daily Confederate, June 3, `64.
97. Diary of Melinda Ray. North Carolina Department of Archives & History.
98. The Religious and Historical Commemoration Two Hundred Years of St. Paul's Parrish, Edenton, North Carolina; p. 23.
99. North Carolina Women of the Confederacy; p. 29.
100. The History of Tyrrell County; p. 51.
101. North Carolina Civil War Trails Newsletter.
102. North Carolina Women of the Confederacy; p. 30.
103. Raleigh Register, May 28, `62.
104. IBID; January 4, `62.
105. IBID
106. The Women's War in the South; p. 318.
107. Samuel F. Patterson Papers. Perkins Library, Duke University.
108. Raleigh Register, May 21, `62.
109. IBID
110. The Papers of Zebulon Baird Vance, Volume I; p. 285. Goldsboro, October 31, `62.
111. Asheville News Weekly, April 1861.
112. Time, Talent, Tradition; p. 46.
113. Storm in the Land; p. 14.
114. A Record of North Carolina's Thalian Hall From 1861-1865 as Reflected in the Wilmington Daily Journal. A typed thesis by Nancie Allen, 1972. UNC-CH
115. Lenoir Family Papers. Documenting the American South. UNC-CH.
116. Piedmont Soldiers' and Their Families; p. 81.
117. Gary Hunt Interview 2005.
118. IBID
119. Spirit of the Age, January and June, 1862.
120. Parramore, Tom. "Old Frank Johnson and the Day the Music Died." The State. April, 1989.
121. Singing the New nation; p. 231-232.
122. Tillinghast Family Papers. Perkins Library, Duke University. Letter May 23, `62 from ERT to Robina Tillinghast.
123. www.twainquotes.com/archangels.html
124. Pioneer Women; p. 145.
125. Daily Journal, October 20, `63.
126. A North Carolina newspaper, December 1864.
127. Confederate Guns Were Stacked; p. 10.
128. History of Anson County; page lost.
129. The Daily Conservative, March 27, `65.
130. Fayetteville Observer, Septembetr 9, `61.
131. Weekly Catawba Journal, March 24, `64; IBID
132. IBID
133. Mary Margaret McNeil Papers. Perkins Library, Duke University.
134. North Carolina in 1861; p. 202-203.
135. Piedmont Plantation; p. 116.
136. Diary of Elizabeth Wiggins, private papers.
137. The Papers of Walter Clark, Volume I; p. 100.
138. Journal of a Secesh Lady; p. 310.
139. Read McIntosh Papers. North Carolina Department of Archives & History.
140. Rockingham County, a Brief History; p. 55.

141. Forsyth, a History of a County on the March; p. 135.

142. Society of Women and the Civil War Conference, 2007.

143. Caswell County 1777-1877; p. 93, 96.

144. Scarboro, David. "North Carolina and the Confederacy: the Weakness of States' Rights During the Civil War." *North Carolina Historical Review*. April 1979, Volume LVI, #2; p. 469.

145. We Were There; p. 155.

146. Many Excellent People: Power and Privilege in North Carolina 1850-1900; p. 55.

147. Women of the Confederacy; p. 121-123.

148. The Commonwealth of Onslow County; p. 68.

149. Escott, Paul D. "Poverty and Governmental Aid for the Poor in Confederate North Carolina." *North Carolina Historical Review*. October 1984, Volume LXI, #4; p. 467.

150. General Order #9. NCC Vault #VC970.74N87a1862.

151. The Papers of Zebulon Baird Vance, Volume I; p. 309, letter from W.A. Houck, Salisbury. November 6, `62.

152. IBID; p. 333.

153. General Order #9. NCC Vault #VC970.74N87a1862.

154. Ashe County's Civil War; p. 105.

155. The History of North Carolina Since 1860; p. 50.

156. Chronicles of the Cape Fear River 1660-1916; p. 486.

157. Spirit of the Age, October 2, `61.

158. IBID

159. Spirit of the Age, September 1861.

160. North Carolina Women of the 1860's; p. 5.

161. The Daily Conservative, March 1, `65.

162. Wake—Capitol County; p. 485.

163. North Carolina Women of the Confederacy; p. 23.

164. The Weekly Conservative, May 18, `64.

165. Person County Court Minutes, May 21, `64. [microfilm]

166. Raleigh Register, January 8, `62.

167. www.csa-dixie.com/Liverpool_Dixie/bazaar.htm

168. The Daily Conservative, May 18, `64.

169. Journal of Samuel Hoey Walkup. Perkins Library, Duke University.

170. North Carolina Through Four Centuries; p. 355.

171. The Last Ninety Days of the War; p. 133.

172. Storm Over the Land; p. 12.

173. State Journal, April 10, `62.

174. North Carolina Women of the Confederacy; p. 135.

175. The Republican Advocate, a New York Newspaper, December 22, `63. transcribed by Linda Schmidt. Courtesy of Denna Larsen.

176. Journal of a Secesh Lady; p. 154.

CHAPTER FOUR ENDNOTES

1. Letters from the North Carolina Adjutant Generals' Letter Book [State Militia Letter Book] #AG-44; North Carolina Department of Archives and History; hereafter cited as Adjutant General Records.

2. North Carolina in 1861; p. 30-31.

3. IBID; p. 176.

4. New York Herald, April 20, 1861.

5. Master of the Shoals; p. 12.

6. Scientific America, Volume V, #11. September, 14, `61, Library of Congress.

7. Guns for Cotton; p. 7.

8. Donnelly, Ralph. "The N.C. Navy Bows Out." *The State*. January, 1989; p. 16; hereafter cited as the Navy Bows Out.

9. Civil War Pharmacy; p. 192.

10. Portraits of the Past, the Civil War on Hatteras Island, North Carolina; p. 24.

11. Frank Leslie's Illustrated Newspaper, May,18, '61.
12. New York Herald, May, 20, '61.
13. Frank Leslie's Illustrated Newspaper, as above.
14. IBID
15. The State; the Navy Bows Out.
16. Justice in Grey; p. 195.
17. Rebel Gibraltar; p. 29.
18. Rendezvous at Hatteras; p124.
19. Rebel Gibraltar; p. 28.
20. Justice in Grey; p. 193.
21. IBID; p. 196.
22. Confederate Court Records, Eastern Division, Pamlico District; Southern Historical Papers; microfilm.
23. IBID
24. Memories of an Octogenarian; p. 9; ECU digital books.
25. Hillsborough Recorder, January, 22, '62.
26. North Carolina in 1861; p. 36.
27. The Lost Light; p. 71.
28. The Outer Banks Reader; p. 118. (1958 version)
29. Adjutant General's Court Records. North Carolina Department of Archives & History.
30. The Papers of John W. Ellis; p. 785.
31. IBID; p. 870.
32. Raleigh Register, February,19, '62.
33. Scheroder, Greg. "Dear Burwell." *Awakenings, Writing and Recollections of Eastern North Carolina Women*, Brett, Everatt, Kinlaw, and Peek, eds.; p. 34, June, 25, '64.
34. Journal of a Secesh Lady; p. 133, 304.
35. Letters to the Home Circle; p. 36.
36. Our Heritage—Robeson County; p. 13.
37. Away Down Home, a History of Robeson County, North Carolina; p. 149.
38. Wilmington Daily Journal, September, 7, '63.
39. Two Centuries at Sycamore Springs Plantation; p. 155.
40. Diary of Elizabeth E. Robeson. Bladen County Historical Society.
41. Forgotten Confederates, an Anthology About Black Southerners; p. 8.
42. www.historync.org
43. General D.H. Hill's Address. Documenting the American South, UNC-CH; p16.
44. Carolina and the Southern Cross, June 1914, Volume III.
45. Long Rifles of North Carolina; p. 228.
46. North Carolina Works Progress Administration Guide to the Old North State; p. 429; hereafter cited as the NC WPA.
47. Silk Flags and Cold Steel; p. 167.
48. Western North Carolina, a History. 1730-1913; p. lost.
49. N.C. WPA Guide; p.392.
50. They Passed This Way; p. 69.
51. Raleigh Standard, January, 22, '62.
52. Raleigh Register, January,8, '62.
53. Confederate Conscript Department, Volume I-II, Box 2, #170. Southern Historical Collection, Wilson Library, UNC-CH.
54. Neither Lady Nor Slave; p. 305.
55. Battle of Plymouth; p. 79.
56. Fear in North Carolina; p. 74.
57. Milton Chronicle, April 4, '62.
58. Story of the Cape Fear and Deep River Navigation Company 1849-1873; page lost.
59. The Great Dismal Swamp; p. 46.
60. Old South Illustrated; p. 142.
61. Islands, Capes, & Sounds; p. 70.

62. Old South Illustrated; p. 143,145.
63. The Great Dismal Swamp; p. 49.
64. IBID, p. 107, 49.
65. w.historync.org/industry "N.C. Business Hall"
66. Lerner, Eugene. "Money, Prices, & Wages in the Confederacy." *Economic Impact of the American Civil War*; p. 27; hereafter cited as "Money, Prices, & Wages."
67. Long Rifles of North Carolina; p. 181.
68. The Civil War in Appalachia; p. 237.
69. IBID; p. 234, 236.
70. IBID; p. 235.
71. Long Rifles in North Carolina; p. 231.
72. IBID; p. 183.
73. Tom Belton's master thesis citation of Lucy Anderson article in Confederate Veteran Magazine, #36, June, 1958.
74. Peebles, Paul. "A Fair Rifle." *Company Front*, 2003, Issue 3; p.22.
75. Scrapbook of Fayetteville and Cumberland County. NCC UNC-CH; p. 102.
76. IBID; p.77.
77. Wake, Capitol County; p. 468.
78. Long Rifles of North Carolina; p. 182.
79. Shuttle and Plow, a History of Alamance County 1704-1910; p. 282.
80. Long Rifles of North Carolina; p. 182.
81. IBID; p. 181.
82. The Papers of Zebulon Baird Vance, Volume I ; p. 341 footnote.
83. Long Rifles of North Carolina; p. 182.
84. IBID; p. 183.
85. Norris, David. "The Yankees have Been Here." *North Carolina Historical Review*, January 1996, Volume LXXIII; p. 12.
86. A Sense of Place; p. 42.
87. G. W. Collier Papers [27th Militia]. North Carolina Department of Archives & History.
88. Raleigh Standard, January, 22,'62.
89. Milton Chronicle, April 4, '62.
90. Wake, Capitol County; p. 468.
91. N.C. WPA; p. 475.
92. Silk Flags and Cold Steel; p. 32.
93. Wake, Capitol County; p.469.
94. Weekly News, Volume 5, #12. June 3, `63. [a handwritten newspaper]. Perkins Library, Duke University.
95. The Battle for Saltville; p. 14.
96. Courtesy of Internet research by Leon H. Sikes.
97. Wake, Capitol County; p. 468.
98. Annuals of Progress, the Story of Lenoir County and Kinston, North Carolina; p. 43.
99. Carolina and the Southern Cross, November 1913, p. 8.
100. Edgecombe County, a Brief History; p. 67.
101. Fite, Emerson. "The Agriculture Development of the West during the Civil War." *Economic Impact*; p.50.
102. Running the Blockade; p. VIII.
103. Guns for Cotton, England Arms the Confederacy; p. 2-3.
104. From the Cotton Field to the Cotton Mill, a Study; p. 50.
105. N.C. WPA; p. 71.
106. Early Cotton Factories in North Carolina and Alexander County; p. 8.
107. Islands, Capes, and Sounds; p. 230.
108. www.historync.org/industry
109. The Textile Industry in North Carolina; p. 22.
110. Rebel Gibraltar; p. 112.
111. Shuttle and Plow; p. 280.
112. Richmond Whig, June 18, '64.
113. The Textile Industry in North Carolina; p. 21.

114. Claiborne Grey Personal Papers. Southern Historical Collection. Wilson Library, UNC.

115. Behind the Lines in the Southern Confederacy; p. 48.

116. The 8th United States Manufacturers Census; p. 424.

117. Courtesy of Gary Hunt.

118. Bright and Gloomy Days; p. 42.

119. Cedar Falls Manufacturing Company Ledger. North Carolina Department of Archives & History.

120. Confederate Supply; p. 15.

121. Rocky Mount Mills, a Careful History of Industrial Development, 1818-1943, printed by the RMM, North Carolina, 1943. n.a.; hereafter cited as Rocky Mount Mills.

122. Fear in North Carolina; p. 196.

123. Rocky Mount Mills.

124. Piedmont Soldiers and Their Families; p. 24.

125. Blair, Marian. "Civil War Letters of Henry W. Barrows to John W. Fries." *North Carolina Historical Review*. January, 1957; p. 69.

126. Piedmont Soldiers and Their Families; p. 25.

127. Economic Impact of the American Civil War; p.25.

128. Claiborne Grey Papers. Southern Historical Collection. Wilson Library, UNC. December 8, `61.

129. "Re-discovering the Confederate Treasury," by Tony Crumbly.

130. R.C. G. Love, a Builder of the New South, p. 21-22.

131. Early Cotton Factories; p. 32-37.

132. www.nchistory.org/industry

133. Webb, E.Y. "Cotton Manufacturing in North Carolina, 1861-'65." *North Carolina Historical Review*. April 1932. Volume IX, #2; p. 128; hereafter cited as "Cotton Manufacturing."

134. Portraits of Conflict; p. 42.

135. North Carolina Booklet, Volume IXX; p. 61.

136. Richmond Daily Dispatch, December 30, '61, taken from the Washington Star of the 23rd ; *and* The Richmond Whig, January 13, '64.

137. Rockingham County History, a Brief History; p. 42.

138. Here Will I Dwell; p. 121.

139. Women of Guilford; p. 51.

140. Lenoir Family Papers. Documenting the American South. UNC-CH. April 24, '63, letter from J. Gwynn to Rufus Lenoir.

141. Ashe County Heritage, Volume I; p. 47.

142. Confederate Court Records, Eastern Division, Box 76, File 39; North Carolina Department of Archives & History.

143. NCHR, "Cotton Manufacturing." p. 126.

144. The Papers of Zebulon Baird Vance, Volume I; p. 259, footnote #314.

145. NCHR, "Cotton Manufacturing." p. 126.

146. North Carolina Confederate Militia Officers Roster, as Contained in the Adjutant-General's Roster, Volume I; p. 47.

147. Silk Flags and Cold Steel; p. 85.

148. Claiborne Grey Personal Papers. Southern Historical Collection. Wilson Library, UNC-CH.

149. The Papers of Zebulon Baird Vance, Volume I; p. 127, March 17, '62.

150. IBID; p. 127, footnote #500.

151. IBID; p 258; S.H. Walkup, October 11, `62 letter to ZBV.

152. Scarboro, David. "The Weakness of States' Rights." *North Carolina Historical Review*. April 1979, Volume LVI, #2; p. 140; hereafter known as "Weakness."

153. Interview with Tom Belton, Curator, N.C. Museum of History, 2008.

154. Bright and Gloomy Days: the Civil War Correspondence of Captain Charles Frederic Bahnson, a Moravian Quaker; page xl. hereafter cited as Bright and Gloomy.

155. The Papers of Zebulon Baird Vance, Volume I; p. 279. Pleasant Hill, Guilford Co, October 25, '62.

156. Semi-Weekly Raleigh Register, January 30, 1861.

157. Interview with Tom Belton.

158. A New Geography in North Carolina; p. 646.

159. Rebel Gibraltar; p. 162.

160. Guns for Cotton; p. 66.

161. North Carolina History, as Told by Contemporaries; p. 304.
162. Richmond Whig, January 21, '64.
163. Fear in North Carolina; p. 234.
164. Cunningham, H.H. "Edmund Burke Haywood and Raleigh's Confederate Hospitals." *North Carolina Historical Review.* April 1958; p.153; hereafter cited as "Hospitals."
165. Doctors in Gray; p. 54.
166. Medicine in North Carolina; p. 293.
167. IBID; p. 299.
168. The Papers of John W. Ellis; p. 877.
169. The Papers of Zebulon Baird Vance, Volume I; p. 257.
170. Doctors in Gray; p. 287.
171. NCHR, "Hospitals." p. 160.
172. Ernest Haywood Collection of Haywood Family Papers. Southern Historical Collection, UNC-CH.
173. Carolina and the Southern Cross, Nov. 1913, p.21.
174. Journal of Thomas F. Wood; UNC-Wilmington. digital library.
175. E.B. Haywood Papers [date torn but after January, 1865] UNC-CH.
176. IBID; "Dr. Leach's Register for the General military Hospital, January, 1862.
177. Diary of John Young. North Carolina Department of Archives & Hisstory.
178. Letter from Charity Swindell, October 14, '61; courtesy of Merlin Berry.
179. Fear in North Carolina; p. 123 and 94.
180. "The Civil War Letters of John A. Muse as Told to Jennie Muse." a typed manuscript by Charles Muse.
181. Bright and Gloomy Days; p. 222.
182. The Lee Family. "Forget me Not." March 5, `62; Documenting the American South, UNC.
183. Southern Soldier Boy; p. 12.
184. Silk Flags and Cold Steel; p. 93.
185. The Papers of Walter Clark; p 84.
186. IBID; p.65.
187. History of North Carolina Since 1860; p. 197-198.
188. NCHR, "Hospitals." p. 153.
189. Loehr, Walter. "Civil War Medicine." *Medical Journal of North Carolina*, Volume 43, #2.
190. Raleigh Register, January, 29, 1862.
191. Mary H. Kennedy Papers, Documenting the American South. UNC-CH, August 18, '62.
192. Daily Conservative, May 18, '64.
193. The Heritage: The Education of Women at St. Mary's College, Raleigh, N.C. 1842-1982; p. 61; hereafter cited as Heritage of St. Mary's.
194. Confederate Courage on Other Fields; p. 141.
195. Women of the Confederacy; p. 96.
196. History of Wayne County; p. 108.
197. North Carolina Women of the 1860's; p. 11.
198. Through the Eyes of Soldiers, the Battle of Wyse Fork; p. 134.
199. North Carolina Women of the Confederacy; p. 41.
200. Tillinghast Papers. Perkins Library, Duke University.
201. Bright and Gloomy Days; page xliv.
202. Fear in North Carolina; p. 173; November 14, `63.
203. Spirit of the Age, July 1862.
204. Mast, Greg. "Some Experiences of Dr. V.W. Cooper in the Confederate Army," *Company Front.* July 1990; p. 37.
205. The First Hundred Years of Historic Guilford County, 1771-12871; p. 157.
206. Blackburn, Charles, Jr. "Turrets and Towers." *Our State*, May 2006; p. 40.
207. "Regulations of the Medical Department of the Confederate Army, 1862." Documenting the American South, UNC-CH; p. 10.
208. Daily Journal, September 7, `63.
209. Civil War Pharmacy; p. 189.
210. E. Burke Haywood Papers. Southern Historical Collection, Wilson Library, UNC-CH. "March 1864 ledger."
211. IBID, August, 1862.

212. To Bind Up the Wounds; p. 78.
213. E. Burke Haywood Papers. Perkins Library, Duke University. Letter October 8, `63 from Gen. Hospital #7 to S.P. Moore.
214. www.mdgorman.com; "Resources of the Confederate Medical Department, February, 1865" by S.P. Moore, MD from SHSP #2; p. 125-128.
215. E. Burke Haywood Papers. Perkins Library, Duke University.
216. Official Records, Series I—Volume XLVII, Part II; p 1148.
217. Magazine of Albemarle County History, volume XXII; p. 132-136; 1st letter October 31, `61; November 17 and 19, 1861.
218. Bright and Gloomy Days; p. 185.
219. The Making of a Confederate; p. 93, 95, 99.
220. Cochrane, Marion. "To the Front by Thousands." Company Front, 2003, #1.
221. Courtesy of Guy Potts, Wayne County.
222. Jacobs, Joseph. "Some Drug Conditions During the War Between the States 1861-1865." Southern Historical Society Papers,1905, #33; p. 5; hereafter cited as SHSP.
223. Civil War Pharmacy; p. 193..
224. www.mdgorman.com; same as #213.
225. Civil War Pharmacy; p. 182.
226. Doctors in Grey; p. 152.
227. IBID
228. Civil War Pharmacy; p. 183.
229. www.mdgorman.com ; same as #213
230. The Papers of Zebulon Baird Vance, Volume I; p. 244, footnote #202-203.
231. IBID; p. 183, footnote #75.
232. IBID; p. 383.
233. Civil War Pharmacy; p. 184.
234. Doctor to the Front; p. 130.
235. Civil War Pharmacy; p. 206.
236. SHSP, Jacobs, as above; p. 10.
237. Chimborazo; p. 95.
238. Tennessee Baptist, October 19, 1861; courtesy of Vicki Betts.
239. Raleigh Register, August 1862.
240. SHSP, p. 15, article by Jacobs.
241. Chimborazo; p. 98.
242. IBID; p. 128.
243. NCHR, "Hospitals." p. 163.
244. Moore, S.P. "Standard Supply Table of the Indigenous Remedies . . ." Documenting the American South, UNC-CH; March 1, `63.
245. Raleigh Register, December 10, `62.
246. Civil War Pharmacy; p. 174 footnote.
247. Raleigh Register, July 23, `62.
248. IBID, November 19, `62.
249. Weekly Catawba Journal, March 24, `64.
250. Loehr, Walter. "Civil War Medicine in N.C." N.C. Medical Journal, Volume 43, #2.
251. Civil War Pharmacy; p. 172.
252. Ashe County Heritage, Volume I; p. 64.
253. History of Brunswick County, North Carolina; p. 150.
254. John McNeill Papers. Perkins Library, Duke University. July 6, `62.
255. IBID, letter May 26, `63 to S.C. Fiemster.
256. Memories of an Old-Time Tar Heel; p. 181.
257. Ernest Haywood Collection of Haywood Family Papers. Southern Historical Collection, Wilson Library, UNC-CH; letter November 11, `64.
258. My Dearest Friend, the Civil War Correspondence of Cornelia McGimsey and Lewis Warlick; p. 153.
259. Ernest Haywood Collection of Haywood Family Papers; letter November 14, `64.

260. William A. Holt Papers. Southern Historical Collection, Wilson Library, UNC-CH; letter December 12, `64 and December 5, `64.

261. E. B. Haywood Papers; letter June 28, `64 from P.E. Hines to Capt. S.B. Waters, Provost Marshal, Raleigh.

262. The Papers of Zebulon Baird Vance, Volume I; p. 328, letter from Dr. Satchwell, November 10, `62, General Hospital, Wilson.

263. E. Burke Haywood Papers; letter March 17, `64 to Colonel Evans.

264. SHSP, p. 764, 1st Congress, 2nd Session.

265. Pictorial New Hanover County; page lost.

266. E. Burke Haywood Papers.

267. Thomas F. Wood Letters, 1765-1924. Perkins Library, Duke University. Letter November 11, `63, Wilmington, to TFW.

268. Richmond Enquirer, October 27, `62; courtesy of Mike Gorman.

269. Civil War Pharmacy; p. 173.

270. E. Burke Haywood Papers. Southern Historical Collection, Wilson Library, UNC-CH.

271. Daily Confederate, June 3, `64.

272. Jonathan Worth, a Biography of a Southern Unionist; p. 129-130.

273. Battle for Saltville; p. 14.

274. Bright and Gloomy Days; p. 131.

275. Reminiscences of Wilmington and Smithville—Southport 1848-1900; p. 29.

276. Scarboro, David. "Weakness;" NCHR; p. 140.

277. Corpening Papers. Perkins Library, Duke University.

278. Land of Wilkes; p. 100.

279. Garrison, Randall, ed. "The White Letters." *Company Front.* April, 1993; p. 16, November 23, `61.

280. North Carolina History Since 1860; p. 49.

281. The Papers of Zebulon Baird Vance, Volume I; p. 438 letter from J.A. Reeves. December 15, `62.

282. Milton Chronicle, November 24, `62.

283. Salt That Necessary Article; p. 93.

284. Land of Wilkes; p. 100; Johnson J. Haywood, Wilkes County Historical Society. 1962, Wilkesboro.

285. History of Brunswick County; p.164.

286. Jonathan Worth, a Biography of a Southern Unionist; p. 131.

287. History of Brunswick County; p. 154.

288. Salt That Necessary Article; p. 40.

289. Bright and Gloomy Days; p. 131.

290. Salt That Necessary Article; p. 27-30, 71, 109.

291. Awakenings; p. 31, June 6, `64.

292. n.a. "Excerpts from Letters Written in the Lower Cape Fear Area, 1861-1865." Lower Cape Fear Historical Society, Inc. Bulletin, Volume X, #2. June, 1967; letter December 1861.

293. Salt That Necessary Article; p. 135, 72, 124.

294. Rebel Gibraltar; p. 208.

295. Bright and Gloomy Days; p. 131.

296. Rebel Gibraltar; p. 208, 210.

297. Salt That Necessary Article; p. 130.

298. NCHR; "Weakness." p. 140.

299. Salt That Necessary Article; p. 143.

300. IBID; p. 145.

301. Corpening Papers. Perkins Library, Duke University.

302. www.carolinastamps.com/ncrail.html article by Gregory Field.

303. Paul Barringer Papers. North Carolina Division of Archives & History.

304. Amnesty Application Papers, # ID177, Berea College.

305. Sketches of Pitt County; p. 39.

306. The Heart of Confederate Appalachia, Western North Carolina in the Civil War; p. 191.

307. Port Town at War; p. 140. a dissertation by Robert A. Wood.

308. "Postal Operations in North Carolina," Gregory Field, internet as above.

309. Interview with John Humphrey, 2004.

310. Doctor to the Front; p. 129.
311. Here Will I Dwell; p. 135.
312. "The Confederate Postal Operations Adding Order to a time of Chaos and Disorder." Courtesy of Tony Crumbley.
313. Confederate Post Office; p. 11,15, 21.
314. IBID; p. 27.
315. Daily Republican Advocate, transcribed by L.Schmidt/DonLinda. February, 14, 2007.
316. Illustrated Civil War News and Magazine (electronic); courtesy of Alexander Street Press. notice August 13, `63.
317. This Was Home; p. 114.
318. Brown, Louis. "The Correspondence of David Olando McRaven and Amanda Nantz McRaven-1864-1865." *North Carolina Historical Review*. January 1949, Volume XXVI; p. 52 footnote; hereafter cited as McRaven Letters.
319. IBID
320. Hillsborough Recorder, December 25, `61.
321. The Secret Service, The Field, the Dungeon, and the Escape; hereafter cited as the Field/Dungeon; p. 400.
322. NCHR, McRaven Letters; p. 52 footnote.
323. IBID; p. 63, B.F. Booth, footnote.
324. Salisbury Prison; p. 92.
325. Rebel Gibraltar; p. 86.
326. The Field/Dungeon; p. 405, 412.
327. "The Fifth Massachusetts Voluntary Infantry in its Three Tours of Duty." Joyner Library, ECU.
328. Salisbury Prison; p. 92,120, 50.
329. This Was Home; p. 116.
330. North Carolina Argus, August 11, `64, copied from the Salisbury Watchman.
331. Salisbury Prison, p. 30.
332. IBID; p. 120, 129.
333. IBID; p. 106,127.
334. IBID; p. 51.
335. IBID p. 120, 110
336. NCHR, McRaven Letters; p. 53.
337. IBID; p. 81.
338. Last Days of Salisbury Prison by Gregory Fields (electronic).
339. Salisbury Prison; p. 143-144.
340. Honey, Michael. "War Within the Confederacy—White Unionists of North Carolina." *Prologue Journal of the National Archives*; p. 92 footnote.
341. Silk Flags and Cold Steel; p. 176.
342. NCHR, McRaven letters; p. 55 footnote.
343. Justice in Grey; p. 416.
344. Charles C. Gray Papers. Southern Historical Collection, UNC-CH.
345. Escape from Dixie; p. 21.
346. IBID; p. 80-86.
347. NCHR, McRaven Letters; p. 92.
348. Hover, Prvt. Charles. "From The Ranks to Prison," *Bivouac,* Spring 2006. Company K, 128th NY.
349. S.S. Boggs, 21st Illinois Infantry; p. 66,70,18.
350. Crossley, William J. "Extracts From my Diary and From my Experiences While Boarding with Jeff Davis in Three of his Notorious Hotels in Richmond, Virginia, Tuscaloosa, Alabama, and Salisbury, North Carolina From July 1861 to June 1862." American Civil War Letters and Diaries, Alexander Street Press.
351. They Went into the Fight Cheering; p. 216.
352. "The History of Agricultural Development of the West During the War," by Emerson Fite; p. 50.
353. Economic Impact; page IX.
354. Economic Impact, "Did the War Retard Industrialization," by Thomas Cochran; p. 151.
355. Guns for Cotton; p. 2-3.
356. The South, Old and New; p. 147.
357. Jonathan Worth, a Biography of a Southern Unionist; p. 139-140.
358. North Carolina in 1861; p. 37.
359. Nelson, B.H. "Some Aspects of Negro Life," *North Carolina Historical Review*. April 1948, Volume XXV, #2; p. 159.

[360] Land of Wilkes; p. 100.

[361] Jonathan Worth, a Biography of a Southern Unionist; p. 128.

[362] Guns for Cotton; p. 4.

[363] Raleigh Register, January 8, `62.

[364] Economic Impact, "Money, Prices, & Wages in the Confederacy, 1861-1865;" p. 11.

[365] Jonathan Worth; p. 140,144.

[366] IBID

[367] IBID; p. 145.

[368] IBID; p. 148.

[369] IBID; p. 14.

[370] National Tribune, December 29, 1891, Letter by Adjutant S.H.M. Byers to his brother [5th Iowa]; courtesy of Mike Gorman.

[371] Jonathan Worth; p. 156.

[372] "Money, Prices, & Wages;" p. 15.

[373] "Confederate Department Treasury Letter." Documenting the American South. UNC. March 14, `64; open letter to the Banks Concerning the Act of Congress to Reduce the Currency, Richmond, 1864.

[374] No Soap, No Pay, Diarrhea, Dysentery and Desertion; p. 39.

[375] "Money, Prices, & Wages; p. 22.

[376] A. W. Bell Papers. Perkins Library, Duke University. Letter to his wife, Mary, February 25, `64.

[377] "Money Prices, & Wages," p. 28.

[378] Sellers, James L. "The Economic Incidence of the Civil War in the South." *Economic Impact*; p. 85

[379] Daily Journal, August 30, `62.

[380] Blockade Runners of the Confederacy; p. 251.

[381] Economic Impact. "Money, Prices, Wages."

[382] Chatham County 1771-1971; p. 139.

[383] Scarborough Family Papers. Perkins Library, Duke University. Letter to Mary Scarborough from Susan McLeod.

[384] Economic Impact; p. 9,32.

[385] Norris, David. "Cash Crop." *Our State*, September, 2005; p. 104.

[386] Wudarczyk, James. "Crisis in the Confederate Currency." *Bivouac Banner*.

[387] Richmond Daily Dispatch, January 13, `65.

[388] Scientific America, New Series. Volume 4, # 3. June 8, `61; p. 357.

[389] Bivouac Banner article, "Crisis."

[390] Beavers Brothers Letters. Perkins Library, Duke University.

[391] Scientific America. Volume 10, #10. March 5, `64; p. 151.

[392] Brady Exchange Folder, Wilmington. NCC, UNC-CH.

[393] Southern Rights; p. 59.

[394] Miscellaneous Letters, Box 76, File 39. North Carolina Department of Archives & History. "Supplying the Troops During the War."

[395] Branch, Paul. "Ft. Macon as a Shelter for Buffaloes." *Ramparts*. Spring, 1997.

[396] The Lost Light; p. 83, 108, 121.

[397] New Geography of North Carolina; p. 606.

[398] The Lost Light; p. 3.

[399] Guns for Cotton; p. 11; *and* "Running the Blockade." *Classics of Naval Literature*, p. 26.

[400] Guns for Cotton; p. 12, 21.

[401] The Lost Light; p. 3-5.

[402] Guns for Cotton; p. 56, 53.

[403] IBID; p. 51, 56-61.

[404] Classics of Naval Literature; p. 27, 11.

[405] Guns for Cotton; p. 58-59, 62.

[406] Classics of Naval Literature; p. 90, 59 footnote.

[407] Guns for Cotton; p. 61-63.

[408] Behind the Lines; p. 80-81.

[409] Governor Vance Address to the General Assembly, May 17, 1864. Documenting the American South. UNC-CH.

[410] Annals of Progress; p. 50.

411. The South, Old and New; p. 153.
412. www.carolinastamps.com/ncrail.html; Gregory Field article.
413. Railroads of the Confederacy; *page lost; and* www.nchistory.org/industry
414. Chronicles of the Cape Fear; p. 414.
415. Classics of Naval Literature; p. 141.
416. Journal of a Secesh Lady; p. 48.
417. Gregory Fields article; p. 148.
418. North Carolina Railroads 1849-1871; p. 39, 159.
419. Experiences of a Confederate Chaplain; p. 23.
420. North Carolina Railroads 1849-1871; p. 168.
421. The Thirty-seventh NCT; p. 54.
422. My Dearest Friend; p. 122.
423. Mast, Greg. "The Setser Letters, Part II." *Company Front.* June/July 1989.
424. North Carolina Railroads 1849-1871; p. 166, 168, 429.
425. Raleigh Register, November 5, `62.
426. Melinda Ray Diary. North Carolina Department of Archives & History.
427. The Papers of Zebulon Baird Vance, Volume I; p. 448; December 26, `62.
428. Thomas Fanning Wood's Journal. UNC-Wilmington Digital Library.
429. Price, Charles. "The U.S. Military Railroads in North Carolina, 1862-1865." *North Carolina Historical Review.* July 1976. Volume LIII, #3; p. 244.
430. North Carolina Railroads 1849-1871; p. 162.
431. Women of the Confederacy; p. 119.
432. North Carolina Railroads 1849-1871; p. 165, 172.
433. Richmond Whig, July 19, `64.
434. Paul Barringer Papers. North Carolina Department of Archives & History.
435. Southern Rights; p. 2 introduction.
436. North Carolina Railroads; p. 177, 175.
437. The Making of a Confederate; p. 63.
438. A Confederate Nurse-Diary of Ada Bacot; p. 161, 168.
439. Southern Illustrated News, #30. May 4, `63.

CHAPTER FIVE ENDNOTES

1. Personal Narratives of Events in the War of the Rebellion, Being Papers Read Before the Rhode Island Soldiers & Sailors Historical Society. 4th Series, #9.
2. Waterman's Song; p. 61-62.
3. Letters to the Home Circle; p. 22.
4. Carolina and the Southern Cross, 1912-1914. Volume #1; p. 17.
5. The Long Roll; p. 81.
6. The Outer Banks Reader, 1584-1958; p. 120.
7. Rebel Gibraltar; p. 41.
8. Roe, Alfred S. *The Fifth Massachusetts Volunteer Infantry in its Three Tours of Duty;* p. 136; hereafter cited as the 5th MVI.
9. The Lost Light; p. 48.
10. Islands, Capes, and Sounds—the North Carolina Coasts; p. 43.
11. Portraits of the Past; p. 100, 114.
12. Letter by Arthur Palmer, courtesy of Scott Troutman
13. Traver, Lorenzo, MD. "Battles of the Roanoke Island and Elizabeth City." Second Series, #5.
14. The Lost Light; p. 49.
15. Burke, Kenneth , "The History of Portsmouth." *North Carolina Historical Review.* January 1994, Volume LXXI, #1; p. 45.
16. Dix, Mary S. editor. "And Three Rousing Cheers for the Privates." *North Carolina Historical Review.* June 1994, Volume LXXI, #1; p. 1994; hereafter cited as "Three Cheers."
17. Carolina and the Southern Cross. March 1913; p. 16.

18. Divided Allegiances; p. 146.
19. Raleigh Register, January 26, '62.
20. Justice or Atrocity; p. 79.
21. Spies and Spymasters of the Civil War; p. 5.
22. Carolina and the Southern Cross, March 1913; p. 16.
23. Traver, Lorenzo, MD. "Battles of Roanoke Island and Elizabeth City." Second Series, #5.
24. Carolina and the Southern Cross, March 1913; letter to Gen. John Wool, commander Dept. of Va., Fort Monroe, September 7, '61.
25. Courtesy of Scott Troutman.
26. The Lost Light; p. 59.
27. Before the Rebel Flag Fell; p. 8; October 7, '61.
28. Barfield, Rodney, "The Chicamacomico Races." State Magazine. May, 1992.
29. Islands, Capes and Sounds; p. 43.
30. www.sallysfamilyplace.com
31. Burke, Kenneth. "The History of Portsmouth, North Carolina." North Carolina Historical Review. January, 1994, Volume LXXL, #1; p. 45.
32. The Civil War on the Outer Banks; p. 45.
33. Duyckinck, Evert. "The Chicamacomico Races." The Outer Banks Reader; p. 132.
34. Spirit of the Age, September 1861.
35. The Lost Light; p. 72.
36. Journal of a Secesh Lady; p. 118.
37. The Great Dismal Swamp; p. 107.
38. Wood, John E. Brief Sketches of Pasquotank County; p. 11.
39. Creezy, Richard B. "The Bombing of Elizabeth City." Pasquotank Yearbook. www.elizcity.com/history/civilwar/civil-war-bombardment.shtml
40. IBID; courtesy of Jerome Flora.
41. Raleigh Register, February 19, '62.
42. http://files.usgwarchives.org/nc/files.htm "Aunt Mamie Civil War Early Memories."
43. Brief Sketches of Pasquotank County; p. 11.
44. Carolina and the Southern Cross, March 1913; p. 17; Gen. Wool's letter.
45. Divided Allegiances; p. 28.
46. Mothers of Invention; p. 28.
47. Sherman, Joan R. "The Black Bard of North Carolina: George Moses Horton and His Poetry." North Carolina Historical Review. July 1997, Volume LXXIV, #3.
48. Capehart Family Papers. Southern Historical Collection, Wilson Library, UNC-CH.
49. Journal of a Secesh Lady; p. 120.
50. The Papers of Zebulon Baird Vance, Volume I; p. 198.
51. Courtesy of Thomas Schroeder (rootsweb, Hyde Co.); letter from George Hill to Joshua A. Hill; March 16, '62.
52. Williams, Max R. "The Johnson Will Case: a Clash of Titans." North Carolina Historical Review. April 1990, Volume LXVII, #2; p. 200.
53. Journal of a Secesh Lady; p. 117.
54. A Researcher's Journal: Beaufort, North Carolina & the Civil War; p. 190; hereafter cited as a Researcher's Journal.
55. Refugee Life in the Confederacy; p. 64, 228, 230, 234.
56. Windsor, Adjutant Gershorn. "As I Saw It." The History of the Forty-fifth Regiment Massachusetts Volunteer Militia; p. 276; hereafter cited as the 45th MVM.
57. Henry T. Clark Scrapbook 1860-1920. North Carolina Department of Archives & History.
58. The Hard Hand of War; p. 58-60.
59. Journal of a Secesh Lady; p. 117.
60. www.albemarle-nc.com/Camden/history/civilwar "Battle of South Mills."
61. The Civil War on the Outer Banks; p. 132.
62. Dix, Mary S. "And Three Rousing Cheers;" p. 76.
63. Mary French Scott Papers. Perkins Library, Duke University.

64. Colyer, Vincent. "Report of Services Rendered by the Freed People to the United States Army in North Carolina in the Spring of 1862, After the Battle of Newbern." East Carolina University digital series; p. 16-17; hereafter cited as "Report of the Freed People."

65. Mary F. Scott papers. Perkins Library, Duke University. Letter from Mary F.E., Etheridgeville, March 13, '64.

66. Sallie Southall Cotton; p. 13.

67. Trial Separation: Murfreesboro, North Carolina and the Civil War; p. 40, 42.

68. The Papers of William Alexander Graham, Volume VI; p. 14; letter March 13, '64.

69. A New Geography of North Carolina, Volume II; p. 577.

70. Diary of Eugene Goodwin, 99th NYI. May 3, '64. Courtesy of Louise Goodwin McKlveen.

71. A New Geography of North Carolina, Volume II; p. 577, 589.

72. The Papers of Walter Clark, Volume I 1857-1901; p. 97. Letter from Clark's mother, November 20, '62.

73. IBID; p. 126. From Clark at Ft. Branch to his mother, November 5, '64.

74. Carolina and the Southern Cross, March 1913; p. 15-17.

75. Bryan, Mary Norcutt. "A Grandmother's Recollection of Dixie." Documenting the American South. Wilson Library, UNC-CH; p. 15.

76. Journal of a Secesh lady; p. 119.

77. To Bear Arms; p. 154. Letter from AF Harrington to his brother, John. April 22, '62.

78. Spirit of the Age, September 21, '61.

79. Raleigh Register, May 21, '62.

80. "A Grandmother's Recollection of Dixie."

81. Live Your Own Life; p. 158 and Anson County, North Carolina Abstract of Wills 1750-1880; p. 118.

82. The Heritage of Lenoir County; p. 29.

83. Elle's Book; p. 56.

84. The Last Ninety Days of the War; p. 264.

85. Many Excellent People: Power and Privilege in North Carolina 1850-1900; p. 32.

86. Ironclads and Columbiads; p. 17.

87. Rendezvous at Hatteras; p. 123-124.

88. Day, David. My Diary of Rambles With the Twenty-fifth Massachusetts Volunteer Infantry; courtesy of Alexander Street Press, Civil War Letters and Diaries; hereafter cited as the 25th MVI.

89. Outer Banks Reader; p. 155.

90. Divided Allegiances; p. 45.

91. Islands, Capes, and Sounds; p. 67.

92. Sigmon, Mark, "A Personal History of the 49th N.C. Regiment—Part II." Company Front, July 1996.

93. The Civil War on the Outer Banks; p. 130.

94. Perquimans County; p. 82.

95. www.sallysfamilyplace.com/Yankees.htm letter to Turner Westry, Rocky Mount.

96. Perquimans County; p. 80-82.

97. Portraits of the Past: the Civil War on Hatteras Island, North Carolina; p. 70.

98. Outer Banks Reader; p. 159, 161.

99. Wren, James. From New Bern to Fredericksburg, Captain J. Wren's Diary: B Company, 48th Pennsylvania Volunteers; May 28, '62.

100. Letters to the Home Circle; p. 184.

101. Biography of Edward Stanly; p. 370, 375.

102. "Report of the Freed people." ECU digital series.

103. Free at Last; p. 97. January 20, '63.

104. Biography of Edward Stanly; p. 217, 206, 375.

105. Letters to the Home Circle; p. 184.

106. Courtesy of Thomas McGowan (rootsweb, Hyde County) letter November 18, '62, Sylvester McGowan.

107. IBID.

108. Harris, William C. "Lincoln and Wartime Reconstruction in North Carolina 1861-1863." North Carolina Historical Review. April 1986, Volume LXIII, #2; p. 166.

109. Biography of Edward Stanly; p. 243.

110. Two Centuries at Sycamore Springs Plantation; p. 188. ECU digital series.

111. Free at Last; p. 34.

524   Blood and War at my Doorstep

112. Outer Banks Reader; p. 161.

113. "Report of the Freed People." ECU digital series.

114. Mann, Albert, "The Enlistment of Colored Troops." 45th MVM; p. 301.

115. IBID.

116. Outer Banks Reader; p. 264.

117. Free at Last; p. 175.

118. Captain J. Wren's Diary; p. 23. April 9, '62.

119. Spraggins, Linsley. "The Mobilization of Negro Labor for the Department of Virginia and North Carolina." *North Carolina Historical Review.* April 1947; p. 187-188.

120. Shapleigh, Sam. "The Mud March: the Expedition to Jonesville, Pollocksville, and Trenton." 45th MVM; p. 211 hereafter known as the "Mud March."

121. Free at last; p. 176-177.

122. National Archives. Letters Received, Department of North Carolina Records Group 393, part 1, series 3238, box 2.

123. The Congregationalist; September 18, '63. Letter from Chaplain James; p. 149. ECU-dig.

124. Report of the Freed People—ECU digital series.

125. IBID.

126. IBID.

127. Time Full of Trial; p. 137.

128. The Waterman's Song; p. 171.

129. Journal of a Secesh Lady; p. 193.

130. Report of the Freed people—ECU digital series.

131. Free at last; p. 200.

132. Time Full of Trial; p. 130.

133. Free at Last; p. 223.

134. IBID; p. 208.

135. IBID; p. 222-226.

136. Outer Banks Reader; p. 164.

137. Divided Allegiances; p. 50.

138. Journal of a Secesh Lady; p. 242.

139. Homelands and Waterways: the American Journey of the Bond Family, 1846-1926; p. 73.

140. The 5th MVI; p. 138.

141. "A Personal History of the 49thNCT," *Company Front.* July 1996 p. 6.

142. Journal of a Secesh Lady; p. 311.

143. Confederate Heroines; p. 143.

144. Courtesy of Thomas McGowan.

145. Parramore, Thomas C. "The Burning of Winton in 1862." *North Carolina Historical Review.* Winter 1962; p. 28, 35.

146. Courtesy of Thomas Schroeder (rootsweb Hyde Co.) Joshua B. Hill letter March 19, '62.

147. Carolina and the Southern Cross, 1912—May 1913, Volume I; p. 10.

148. "Miss Carroll Poem." *The 25th MVI.* August 12, '62; Courtesy of Alexander Street Press.

149. True tales of the South at War; p. 84. Letter to wife from Col. LL Polk, May 9, '63.

150. A Researcher's Journal; p. 15.

151. Portraits of the Past; p. 94.

152. An anonymous N.J. soldier. February, 1865.

153. Captain James Wren's Diary; p. 7, March 9, '62.

154. Homelands and Waterways; p. 73-75.

155. Old Port Town of Beaufort; p. 11.

156. To Bind up the Wounds; p. 73, 90, 136.

157. Homelands and Waterways; p. 77.

158. A Researcher's Journal; p. 27, 29, 23.

159. Waterman's Song; p. 163.

160. A Researcher's Journal; p. 30.

161. Homelands and Waterways; p. 74.

162. Dear Ones At Home; p. 148.

163. Forgotten Confederates; p. 12.

164. Carraway, Gertrude. *Years of Light: History of St. John's Lodge*. ECU digital series.

165. Courtesy of Thomas Schroeder (rootsweb, Hyde Co.) Joshua B. Hill letter.

166. Free at Last; p. 35.

167. The 5th Massachusetts; p. 135.

168. Mann, Albert. "Camp Armory on the Trent." A History of the 45th MVM; p. 78.

169. Derby, William. *Bearing Arms in the 27th Massachusetts Regiment of Volunteer Infantry During the Civil War*; p. 162. ECU digital series.

170. IBID, "Provost Duty in New Bern by Company A;" p. 213-216.

171. The Episcopal Church in North Carolina; p. 246.

172. "Camp Armory on the Trent;" p. 83-84.

173. North Carolina Women of the Confederacy; p. 19.

174. Carolina and the Southern Cross, August 1914, Volume I, #4; p. 6.

175. Journal of a Secesh Lady; p. 194.

176. Union soldier letter "H.A.C.;" source lost.

177. Courtesy of espdesigns—John Proctor and Henry Brown. Letter June 10, '62 from Private Henry Brown with the 21st Massachusetts.

178. Waterman's Song; p. 166.

179. Douglas, W.M. "The Relief of Washington, North Carolina." *The Fifth Rhode Island Volunteers*; p. 8; ECU digital series.

180. The Civil War on the Outer banks; p. 120.

181. Anonymous Union soldier's comments.

182. Carolina and the Southern Cross, 1912-1914, Volume I; p. 11.

183. Winsor, Gershorn. "As I Saw It." The 45th MVM; p. 284.

184. Captain James Wren's Diary, March 13, '62.

185. Black, WW. "The Civil War Letters of E.N. Boots." *North Carolina Historical Review*. April 1959, Volume 36, #2; p. 213; letter to his mother April 28, '63.

186. Leonard, Charles H. "Provost Duty in New Berne." The 45th MVM; p. 219.

187. The 25th MVI; letter May 4, '63; courtesy of Mike Kendra.

188. The 45th MVM; p. 219-220.

189. The 45th MVM; p. 345.

190. The 27th MVI; p. 503; March 28, '62.

191. Captain James wren's Diary (White Mane edition); p. 28.

192. The 27th MVI; p. 436.

193. "Prison Life Among the Rebels: Recollections of a Union Chaplain." Courtesy of Alexander Street Press, Civil War Letters and Diaries.

194. The 45th MVM; p. 222.

195. The 27th MVI; p. 440 *and* Carolina and the Southern Cross, April 1914, Volume II, #1; p. 96 *and* The Great Epidemic; p. 37 *and* A History of the 15th Connecticut; p. 234-235.

196. Collection of Charlie Harsell, grandson of Charlie Hatsell, copied by Mary Warsaw, Beaufort.

197. Courtesy of Scott Troutman.

198. IBID.

199. THE 45TH MVM; p. 301.

200. THE 27TH MVI; p. 442.

201. Terns, Sgt. Ephraim S. "Four Months at Ft. Macon, from Early December, 1862 to April, 1863." *The 45th MVM*; p. 201-202.

202. Branch, Paul. "Fort Macon as a Shelter for the Buffaloes." *Ramparts*. Spring, 1997.

203. Journal of a Secesh Lady; p. 442.

204. History of Edgecombe County; p. 186.

205. The 45th MVM, "the Mud March."

206. "The Burnside Expedition and the Engagement of R.I." *Personal Narratives of Events in the War of the Rebellion Being Papers Read Before the Rhode Island Soldiers' and Sailors' Historical Society*. 4th series, #9.

207. The Papers of Zebulon Baird Vance, Volume II; December 29, '63; p. 357.

208. Shuttle and Plow, a History of Alamance County, North Carolina; p. 305.

209. Richmond Daily Dispatch, December 25, '63.

210. Report by Samuel Tolles, Commander US, South Mills. History of the 15th Connecticut Volunteers in the War for the Union; p. 226.

211. The 44th Massachusetts letters; December 22, '62, Newbern.

212. The Papers of Zebulon Baird Vance, Volume I; p. 264. Letter from Annie Terry, October 13, '62.

213. Mary French Scott Papers. Perkins Library, Duke University. November 22, '62.

214. IBID. From Sarah Murrill of Catherine Lake, Upper Plum Hill. January 1, '63.

215. IBID. From M.L. McLean, January 28, '63.

216. The 45th MVM; p. 55.

217. Howe, W.W. "The Expedition to Kinston, Whitehall and Goldsboro, North Carolina, December 1862;" p. 45-46.

218. Frank Leslie's Illustrated Newspaper, July 25, '63.

219. Flashes of Duplin's History and Government; p. 235. ECU digital series.

220. Mann, Albert. "Hyde County Raid, March 1-6, 1863 by the #rd New York Cavalry and the 1st Regiment North Carolina Union Volunteers." *The 45th MVM;* p.219-220.

221. *www.sallysfamilyplace.com* and courtesy of Chuck Viet, Official Records, December 5, '64.

222. A Researcher's Journal; p. 499-500.

223. Journal of a Secesh Lady; p. 509, 518.

224. Parramore, Thomas. "The Burning of Winton;" p. 20, 23-24.

225. IBID; p. 26-28.

226. Spirit of the Age, July 14, '62.

227. Bearing Arms in the 25th Massachusetts; p. 120-121.

228. Journal of a Secesh Lady; p. 211.

229. Hubbard, Corp. Charles E. Company A. "The Official Reports of the March to Kinston and the Battle of Kinston." *The 5th MVI.*

230. *Journal of a Secesh Lady; p. 216.*

231. IBID; p. 293.

232. IBID; p. 293.

233. James B. Morgan Letters, VMI Archives. Letter to his son, Patrick, January 28, '63.

234. IBID; February 13, '63 letter.

235. IBID; May 16, '64.

236. IBID; October, 1864.

237. Norris, David A. "The Yankees Have Been Here: Story of Brig. General Edward Potter's Raid on Greenville, Tarboro, and Rocky Mount, July 19, 1863." *North Carolina Historical Review.* January 1996, Volume LXXIII, #1; hereafter cited as "The Yankees."

238. IBID; p. 6-10 *and* The Petersburg Express, July 24, '63.

239. IBID, "The Yankees."

240. IBID; p. 15-25.

241. Mead, C.N.D. "The Great Cavalry Raid in N. Carolina." *Republican Advocate,* July 29, '63; courtesy of Denna Larson.

242. "The Yankees."

243. Sketches of Pitt County, a Brief History of a County 1704-1910; p. 132, 136.

244. IBID; p. 140, 144.

245. Courtesy of Vicki Betts. July 28, '63.

246. The Cry is War, War, War; p. 53.

247. IBID; p. 56. Letter January 22, '62, GT Huntley to his family.

248. IBID; p. 59-60.

249. IBID; p. 65. Letter March 6, '62.

250. "Heroic Deeds," *The 45 MVM;* p. 108.

251. Carolina and the Southern Cross, October 1913. Volume I, #8.

252. Annuals of Progress, the Story of Lenoir County and Kinston; p. 43.

253. "Heroic Deeds;" p. 108.

254. Prison Life Among the Rebels by Chaplain Henry White. Letter #4, November 8, '64. Courtesy of Alexander Street Press; hereafter cited as "Prison Life."

255. IBID; letter #5, November 10, '64.

256. Annuals of Progress; p. 43.

257. Howe, W.W. Expedition to Kinston, Whitehall and Goldsboro, North Carolina, December 1862; p. 73.

258. Leaves From a Diary While Serving in Company E, 44th Massachusetts, Department of North Carolina; p. 57-58.

259. IBID; p. 56-57.

260. "Heroic Deeds;" p. 107.

261. The 5th Massachusetts; p. 163.

262. "Heroic Deeds;" p. 108.

263. Hubbard, Charles, "Official Report of the March to Kinston." *Harper's Weekly;* p. 122.

264. IBID.

265. The 15th Connecticut; p. 121.

266. The 5th Massachusetts; p. 184 *and* "Heroic Deeds."

267. "Prison Life."

268. The 45th MVM, "Heroic Deeds;" p. 108.

269. Letter #16 from a Union soldier "George" (no last name)at New Bern to his aunt Maria. January 8, '63; courtesy of Martha Marble *and* ECU, Joyner Library.

270. Diary of a Tar Heel Soldier—Louis Leon. Documenting the American South. UNC.

271. New haven Journal & Courier, August 25, 1892; p. 248-255.

272. The 15th Connecticut; p. 148, 247, 255.

273. The 45th MVM, "Heroic Deeds;" p. 112.

274. To Bear Arms; p. 154. Letter from AF Harrington to his brother John. April 22, '62.

275. "A Personal History of the 49th NCT—Part II."

276. The New York Times, January 9, '64. Article by Tewsbury.

277. IBID.

278. Courtesy of Thomas Schroeder. Letter from Joshua Hill to his father, George.

279. Beaufort—Two Centuries of History; p. 185. ECU digital series.

280. The 5th Massachusetts; p. 230.

281. IBID.

282. IBID; p. 225.

283. The Hard Hand of War; p. 58.

284. Bearing Arms With the Twenty-seventh Massachusetts; p. 186.

285. Richmond Whig, January 30, '64.

286. Sparrow, Annie. "Recollections of the Civil War." Grimes-Bryan Papers. Joyner Library ECU. A typed manuscript; hereafter cited as "Recollections."

287. Carolina and the Southern Cross, October 1913; p. 1-2.

288. Beaufort—Two Centuries of History; p. 190.

289. The 27th Massachusetts; p. 176.

290. War of Another Kind; p. 91.

291. The Battle of Plymouth; p. 37.

292. Goss, Warren. "A Soldier's Story of His Capture." *The 2nd Massachusetts* Heavy *Artillery;* hereafter cited as the 2nd MHA.

293. The Battle of Plymouth; p. 37.

294. The 5th Massachusetts Volunteers; p. 149.

295. IBID.

296. Black, W.W. "The Civil War Letters of E.N. Boots." *North Carolina Historical Review.* April 1959, Volume 36, #2; p. 220.

297. Journal of a Secesh lady; p. 316.

298. The Battle of Plymouth; p. 203, 206.

299. The 5th Massachusetts Volunteers; p. 149.

300. A Family of Women; p. 156.

301. IBID; p. 155.

302. The Battle of Plymouth; p. 174-170.

303. IBID; p. 41.

304. Josiah Collins Papers. North Carolina Department of Archives & History.

305. IBID.

306. The Century [magazine], July 1888, Volume 36, #3; p. 420-422.

307. The 2nd MHA.
308. The Battle of Plymouth; p. 55.
309. Life and Death in Rebel Prisons; p. 36-37.
310. The Battle of Plymouth; p. 174, 176.
311. Life and Death in Rebel Prisons; p. 64, 42-44.

CHAPTER SIX ENDNOTES

1. Franklin County, 1779-1970; p.68.
2. IBID.
3. A Walk Through History; p. 13.
4. North Carolina Women of the 1860's; p. 12.
5. Pearce, TH, "Aunt Abby," *The State*; October 1972; p. 8-9.
6. IBID; p. 9, 24.
7. The Civil War Letters of Ben Freeman; p.24.
8. IBID; p. 53.
9. Historical Sketches of Franklin County; p.234-235 .
10. Whitakers Reminiscences, Incidents, and Anecdotes, NCC, UNC-CH.
11. The State, October, 1972, part I, p. 24.
12. Historical Sketches of Franklin County; p.238.
13. Scoundrels, Rogues, and Heroes of the Old North State; p. 88.
14. Tar Heels Track the Century; p. 49.
15. Wilmington Daily Journal, September 21, 1`62.
16. McEachern and Williams, "Miss Buie, Soldiers' Friend," *Lower Cape Fear Historical Society, Inc. Bulletin,* October 1974, Volume 18, #1; hereafter cited as the LCFHSIB.
17. Daily Dispatch, February 10, 1866.
18. Gov. Vance Papers, microfilm reel 18,#1069, correspondence in the Daily Journal.
19. LCFHSIB, October 1974, "Miss Buie, the Soldiers' Friends."
20. IBID.
21. The Daily Journal war years.
22. The Daily Journal war years.
23. IBID.
24. Port Town At War, Wilmington, North Carolina 1860-1865. A dissertation by Richard Wood, p 136.
25. The Civil War in North Carolina; p. 260-261.
26. Daily Journal war years.
27. LCFHSIB, October 1974, article by McEachern and Williams as above.
28. Columbia: History of a Southern Capitol; p. 88.
29. The Daily Journal, December 25, `64.
30. Daily Conservative; January 17, `65.
31. The Papers of Zebulon Baird Vance, Volume 1; p. liii.
32. Daily Conservative, January 26, `65.
33. Amnesty Papers from Berea College, courtesy of Gordon McKinney.
34. Piedmont Soldiers and Their Families; p. 95.
35. Bright and Gloomy Days; page xxxviii.
36. The Papers of Zebulon Baird Vance, Volume I; p. 285, October 13, `62.
37. Sutherland, Daniel E., "C.F. Deems and the Watchman," *North Carolina Historical Review,* Autumn 1980;p. 411-412.
38. Memoir of Rev. JL Prichard, Late Pastor of the First Baptist Church, Wilmington; ECU digital series; p. 122.
39. IBID; p. 134.
40. Women of Guilford; p. 50, 52.
41. Augusta Daily Constitutionist, June 21, `61.
42. Piedmont Soldiers and their Families, p. 24.
43. Pictorial History of New Hanover County; p. 79.
44. Elle's Book; p. 48, September 14.

45. Port Town at War, a dissertation; p. 100.
46. Piedmont Soldiers and their Families; p. 20.
47. E. Burke Haywood Papers, Southern Historical Collection, Wilson Library, UNC-CH.
48. Mary B. Hinshaw, Quaker; p. 78.
49. Piedmont Plantations; p. 116.
50. The Papers of Willie Mangum; p. 389.
51. IBID; p. 406.
52. Excerpts from Dr. Thomas Fanning Wood's Journal, UNC Wilmington Digital collections.
53. Richmond Daily Dispatch, March 30, `65.
54. Journal of a Secesh Lady; p.100.
55. IBID; p. 205.
56. IBID; p. 271.
57. IBID
58. Fayetteville Observer, November 4, `61.
59. Raleigh Standard; November 12, `62.
60. Jonathan Worth, a Biography of A Southern Unionist; p. 134-135.
61. To Die Game; p. 42.   .
62. North Carolina Women of the Confederacy; p. 65.
63. John Graham Young Papers, North Carolina Department of Archives and History.
64. Raleigh Register, September 4, `61.
65. Bright and Gloomy Days; page xxxi.
66. From the Cotton Field to the Cotton Mill; p 57.
67. Bennett Place Quarterly, "North Carolina Chinese Confederates," by Kent McCoury.
68. Flashes of Duplin County; p. 218.
69. Doctor to the Front; p. 59.
70. Chronicles of the Cape Fear River 1660-1916; p. 339.
71. IBID; p. 656.
72. Memoirs of an Octogenarian; ECU digital series; p. 7.
73. Diary of Mary Jeffreys Bethell: January 1 1861-December 1865; Documenting the American South, UNC-CH; July 29, `63.
74. A Civil War Tragedy; p. 31.
75. Two Centuries at Sycamore Springs Plantation; p. 165.
76. North Carolina Women of the Confederacy; p. 66.
77. Schroeder, Greg, "Dear Burwell," *Awakenings: Writings and Recollections of Eastern North Carolina Women*, edited by Sally Brent, Everatt, KinLaw, and Peek; p. 21.
78. Confederate Courage on Other Fields; p. 141.
79. Morning Post, "Our Women in the War Supplement," August 17, 1905.
80. IBID.
81. Two Centuries at Sycamore Springs Plantation; p. 165.
82. Raleigh Register; January 29, `62.
83. Last Stand in the Carolinas; p. 106-107.
84. North Carolina Argus; March 5, `63.
85. Milton Chronicle, November 9, `63.
86. IBID, November 4, `64.
87. Milton Sidelights, p. 58.
88. Caswell County History 1777-1977; p. 216.
89. Raleigh Standard, April, 1863.
90. IBID, March 25, `63.
91. Spirit of the Age, March 31, `62.
92. Rebel Gibraltar, p 18.
93. Carolina and the Southern Cross, April 1914, Volume II, #1, p. 19.
94. Weekly Catawba Journal, March 24, `64.
95. Silk Flags and Cold Steel; p. 177.
96. North Carolina Women of the 1860's; p. 13.

[97.] Arthur, Billie, "Acts of Defiance," *The State*, June 1991.

[98.] Garrison, Randal, editor. "The White Letters," *Company Front,* April 1993; p. 29.

[99.] Carolina and the Southern Cross, Volume 2, #3, June, 1914.

[100.] Centennial History of Alamance County 1849-1949; p. 116.

[101.] Columbus County North Carolina Recollections & Records; p.232.

[102.] Burch, Sergeant John, "A Few Incidents Occurring During the Civil War," *Company Front.* Sept/October 1990; p. 10.

[103.] North Carolina Women of the Confederacy; p. 125.

[104.] Confederate Women; p. 155.

[105.] Carolina and the Southern Cross, Volume I, #10, January, 1914.

[106.] North Carolina Women of the Confederacy; p. 60.

[107.] Western North Carolina, a History 1730-1913; p 208.

[108.] North Carolina Women of the Confederacy; p. 25.

[109.] Southern Stories, Slaveholders in Peace and War; p, 135.

[110.] Our Heritage; p. 354.

[111.] Reflections of Cataloochee Valley and its Vanished People in the Great Smoky Mountains; p. 77.

[112.] The South's Last Boys in Gray; p. 107.

[113.] North Carolina Women of the Confederacy; p. 34.

[114.] IBID; p. 29.

[115.] Dr. D.H. Hill Address at the Unveiling of the Women's Statue, Memorial Address, 1914; Documenting the American South, UNC.-CH.

[116.] Southern Stories, Slaveholders in Peace and War; p. 135.

[117.] North Carolina Women of the Confederacy; p. 34.

[118.] Southern Families at War; p. 89.

[119.] Ashe County's Civil War: Community and Society in the Appalachian South; p. 152.

[120.] Confederate Women; p. 155.

[121.] North Carolina Women of the Confederacy; p. 52.

CHAPTER SEVEN ENDNOTES

[1.] Fallen Angels; p.169.

[2.] Schroeder, Greg, "Dear Burwell," by Rebecca Davis. *Awakenings: Writing and Recollections of Eastern North Carolina Women* by Sally Brett, Everatt, Kinlaw, and Peek; p. 10.

[3.] The Plantation Mistress; p. 112-113.

[4.] The Lee Girls; p. 183.

[5.] Fallen Angels; p 22.

[6.] Within the Plantation Household; p 81.

[7.] IBID; p. 110, 225, 228, 238.

[8.] IBID; p. 228.

[9.] IBID; p. 230.

[10.] Fallen Angels; p. 171.

[11.] The South As It Is, 1865-1866; p. 116-121.

[12.] Within the Plantation Household; p. 232, 235.

[13.] IBID; p. 213, 215.

[14.] Spirit of the Age, May 7, `61.

[15.] The Papers of John W. Ellis; p. 731.

[16.] IBID; p. 731.

[17.] North Carolina in 1861; p. 191.

[18.] Anspake, Charles, "Letters from the Front: Portrait of a Soldier," Bivouac Banner (electronic), Summer, 2004.

[19.] Wilmington Daily Journal, May 28, `61.

[20.] Southern Historical Society Papers, Volume XLIII and XLIX; "Confederate First Congress, Second Session;" p. 237.

[21.] IBID.

[22.] Excerpts from Thomas Fanning Wood's Journal, UNC—Wilmington, digital collections.

[23.] Spirit of the Age, September 25, `61.

24. History of Tyrrell County; p. 56.
25. Blair, Marion, editor, "The Civil War Letters of Henry W. Barrow." *North Carolina Historical Review.* January, 1957; p. 76.
26. Raleigh Register, July 4, `61.
27. Weekly Catawba Journal, March 24, `64.
28. Women of the Confederacy; p. 89.
29. State Troops and Volunteers; p. 196.
30. North Carolina Women of the Confederacy; p. 18-19.
31. Charleston Daily Courier; September 26, `64.
32. North Carolina Women of the Confederacy; p. 17.
33. IBID; p. 32.
34. Courtesy of Guy Potts [Wayne County's genweb page], Claude Moore article from Mt. Olive Tribune.
35. When Sherman Came; p. 270.
36. IBID; p. 275.
37. History of Nursing in North Carolina; p. 20.
38. Medicine in North Carolina; p. 298.
39. Women of Guilford; p. 52-53.
40. Confederate Guns Were Stacked; p. 4.
41. Raleigh Register, September 28, `61.
42. Women of Guilford, p. 55.
43. Forsyth, History of a County on the March; p. 135.
44. Confederate Courage on Other Fields; p. 141 *and* North Carolina Women of the Confederacy; p. 45.
45. Ashe County's Civil War; p. 153.
46. Piedmont Soldiers and their Families; p. 52, July 1864.
47. Carolina and the Southern Cross, November 1913; p. 6.
48. Confederate Courage on Other Fields; p. 141.
49. Carolina and the Southern Cross; November 1913, p. 6.
50. Mast, Greg, "Some Experiences of Dr. V.W. Cooper in the Confederate Army." *Company Front.* July, 1990; p. 39.
51. My Dearest Friend; p. 153.
52. Wake—Capitol County; p. 491.
53. United Daughters of the Confederacy Magazine, Volume LXIII, #9, October, 2000.
54. Morning Post, Our Women in the War Supplement, August 17, 1905.
55. Johns, Annie E., "The Hospital at Danville." *Our Women in the War: the Lives They Lived, the Deaths They Died* attributed to Miss Hattie Kilgore from the Charleston Weekly News & Courier 1885 [bound]; p. 219-230.
56. They Passed This Way; p. 99n.
57. Joab Lee Family Papers, Johnston County, private papers.
58. Spirit of the Age, September, 1862.
59. A Grandmother's Recollections of Dixie. Documenting the American South, UNC-CH, p. 18.
60. Carolina and the Southern Cross, May 1913, Volume I, #1, p. 10.
61. Ernest Haywood Collection of Haywood Family Papers. Southern Historical Collection, Wilson Library, UNC-CH.
62. Civil War Pharmacy; p. 71.
63. Dear Ones at Home, "Northern Soldiers in Eastern North Carolina." p. 18.
64. The Fifth Massachusetts Volunteer Infantry in its Three Tours of Duty; p. 166.
65. Spies and Spymasters of the Civil War; p. 85-86.
66. War Between the Spies; p. 151.
67. North Carolina Women of the Confederacy; p. 18.
68. A Researcher's Journal; p. 178.
69. IBID; p. 181.
70. Old Port Town of Beaufort, North Carolina, p. 78.
71. A Researcher's Journal: Beaufort, North Carolina & the Civil War; p. 57-59.
72. Typed manuscript, "The Sacrifice or Daring of a Southern Woman During the WBTS," by Mildred Wallace found in the Benjamin F. Royal Papers. Southern Historical Collection, Wilson Library, UNC-CH.
73. Anonymous Union soldier.
74. Benjamin F. Royal Papers, as above; found unsigned but believe to be in Ms Pigott's handwriting.

75. Old Port Town of Beaufort, North Carolina.; p. 12

76. "A North Carolina Heroine," *Our Living and Our Dead,* Volume IV.

77. Carolina and the Southern Cross, Volume 2, #1, April 1914, p. 121.

78. IBID; April 1913, p. 18.

79. North Carolina Women of the Confederacy; p. 18.

80. IBID; p. 62.

81. IBID; p. 17.

82. Carolina and the Southern Cross, April 1914, Volume 2, #1; p. 6.

83. "Subtlety and Subterfuge," by Paul Branch; Ramparts (Magazine), #1footnote.

84. The Civil War on the Outer Banks; p. 133.

85. North Carolina Women of the Confederacy; p. 18.

86. North Carolina Women of the 1860's; p. 8.

87. North Carolina WPA Guidebook to the Old North State; p. 494.

88. Chronicles of the Cape Fear River, 1660-1916; p. 486.

89. Ramparts, article by Paul Branch as before.

90. Carolina and the Southern Cross, May 1913; p. 9.

91. IBID; p. 10.

92. Moore, Sally "How We Blew Out the Light," *The State,* July 1969; *and* A Researcher's Journal; p. 44, 47, 201.

93. Valor and Lace; p. 116.

94. Hall, James O. "The Veiled Lady: Saga of Sarah Slater," *North/South Magazine,* August 2000, Volume 3; p. 36-44.

95. IBID; p. 43.

96. Secret Missions of the Civil War; p. 319.

97. Spies and Spymasters; p. 164-165.

98. Raleigh Register, November 13, `61.

99. Sally Hawthorne's Memories. North Carolina Department of Archives & History.

100. The Secret War for the Union; p. 5.

101. Spies and Spymasters of the Civil War; p. 4.

102. North Carolina Women of the Confederacy; p. 55.

103. Women of the Confederacy; p. 80.

104. Blockade Runners, True Tales of Running the Blockade of the Confederate Coast; p.155.

105. Here Will I Dwell; p. 136.

106. Portraits of a Conflict, a Photographic History of North Carolina in the Civil War; p. 73.

107. Piedmont Soldiers and Their Families; p. 82; *and* Rebels in Blue; p. 27.

108. Kirk's Raiders; p. 65.

109. History of the 26th Regiment North Carolina Troops; page lost.

110. McKinney, Gordon, "Women's Role in Civil War North Carolina." *North Carolina Historical Review.* January, 1992; p. 42.

111. Patriots in Disguise; p. 100-101; *and* Company Front, June 2001, "Unusual Story of Private William R. Thompson Co B., the Bladen Light Infantry 18th Regiment NCT" by Jeff Stepp.

112. Richmond Sentinel, March 4, `65.

113. Richmond Daily Dispatch, February 20, `65.

114. Heart of Confederate Appalachia, Western North Carolina and the Civil War; p. 189.

115. Richmond Whig, October 3, `64.

116. North Carolina Whig, March 13, `63.

117. Spirit of the Age, September 25, `61.

118. Raleigh Register, January 22, `62.

119. Diary of a Tar Heel Confederate Soldier; p. 66 June 8, `64.

120. Trial Separation: Murfreesboro, North Carolina and the Civil War; p. 29.

121. Monroe, Haskell, editor. "The Road to Gettysburg," *North Carolina Historical Review.* October, 1959.

122. Spirit of the Age, June 22, `61.

123. The Papers of Walter Clark; p. 134.

124. Trial Separation; p. 63.

125. www.nchistoricsites.com/somerset/union-somerset.htm

126. http://hometown.aol.com/cwrapes/index.htm

127. Last Four Weeks of the War; p. 80.
128. Magazine of Albemarle County History, Volume XXII; p. 54.
129. Trial Separation: Murfreesboro, North Carolina and the Civil War; p. 63.
130. IBID
131. Official Records, Series II, Volume V, page 389-390; March 24, `63; letter from General Hill to Union General Foster.
132. War Time Reminiscences, the Coming of the Yankees, by J.M. Hollowell; Joyner Library, East Carolina University digital series.
133. Unruly Women; p. 117.
134. Jay B. Hubbell Papers. Perkins Library Duke University.
135. Greensboro Patriot, June 7, `61.
136. Official Records, Series I, volume XLIX, Part II; and http://hometown.aol.com/cwrapes/index.htm
137. The Heart of Confederate Appalachia, Western North Carolina and the Civil War; p. 196.
138. No Soap, No Pay, Diarrhea, Dysentery & Desertion; p. 106.
139. Thomas P. Lowery Lecture, Society of Women & the Civil War, 1998.
140. Thomas Settle Jr. Papers, North Carolina Division of Archives & History.
141. Fear in North Carolina; p. 62.
142. IBID; p. 288 June 4, `65; letter to W.L. Henry from Cornelia Henry.
143. National Archives, RG 153, MM3937.
144. The Story the Soldiers Wouldn't Tell; p. 128.
145. Official Records, Series I, Vol. XLVII, Part 3, p. 79.
146. IBID
147. Magazine of Albemarle County History, Volume XXII; p. 54.
148. Official Records, Series I, Volume XXVII, Part 2; p.983.
149. Public Women and the Confederacy; p. 16.
150. Salisbury Prison; p. 54.
151. Brown, Louis A., editor, "Correspondence of David Olando McRaven and Amanda Nantz McRaven, 1864-1865." North Carolina Historical Review. January 1949, Volume 26; p. 93.
152. IBID; p. 65; letter to her husband stationed as a prison guard, November 29, `64.
153. New Hanover Criminal Court Records. (microfilm)
154. They Went into the Fight Cheering; p. 48.
155. Encyclopedia of the Confederacy; p. 1277.
156. IBID; p. 1276-1277.
157. To Bear Arms, February 24, `63; p. 198-200; and December 27, `63.
158. Swamp Doctor; p. 179-182.
159. IBID; p. 161.
160. The Heritage of Lenoir County; p. 34.
161. Tennessee Baptist [a newspaper], January 11, `62.
162. Grimes-Bryan Papers. Annie Sparrow, "Recollections of the Civil War." Joyner Library, East Carolina University.
163. Drury Lacy Papers. Southern Historical Collection, Wilson Library, UNC-CH.
164. Curtis, W.A. "A Journal of Reminiscences of the War." Our Living and Our Dead. Volume II.
165. Women of the Confederacy; p. 124.
166. Fear in North Carolina; p. 99, 235.
167. Anonymous northern soldier diary.
168. From Newbern to Fredericksburg: Captain James Wren's Diary: B Co, 48th Pennsylvania Volunteers February 20 1862-December 17, 1862.
169. Divided Houses, Gender and the Civil War; p. 237-238.
170. The Story the Soldiers Wouldn't Tell; p. 143.
171. n.a. "The Richard P. Paddison Papers," Lower Cape Fear Historical Society,Inc. Bulletin, March 1968, Volume XI, #2; p. 41.
172. Mary French Scott Papers. Perkins Library, Duke University.
173. WPA North Carolina Slave Narratives, LOC.
174. IBID
175. The Heart of Confederate Appalachia, Western North Carolina and the Civil War; p. 119.

176. Thomas Merrill Papers, North Carolina Department of Archives & History.
177. Richmond Dispatch, May 13, `62.
178. The Heart of Confederate Appalachia: Western North Carolina in the Civil War; p. 121.
179. Diary of a Tar Heel Confederate Soldier; p. 25. Documenting the American South, UNC.
180. A Johnny Reb Band From Salem; p. 78.

CHAPTER EIGHT ENDNOTES

1. Escott, Paul D. "Poverty and Governmental Aid for the Poor in Confederate North Carolina." *North Carolina Historical Review.* October 1984, Volume LXI, #4; p. 465; hereafter cited as "Poverty."

2. Scarboro, David D. "North Carolina and the Confederacy: The Weakness of States' Rights During the Civil War." *North Carolina Historical Review.* April 1979, Volume LVI, #2; p. 145-146; hereafter cited as "Weakness."

3. Ashe County's Civil War; p. 85.

4. NCHR, "Poverty;" p. 472.

5. North Carolina Booklet #6.

6. Sketches of Pitt County, a Brief History of the County 1704-1910; p. 135.

7. Away Down Home a History of Robeson County, North Carolina; p. 116.

8. Telephone interview with Jean Newell, Person County historian, August 15, 2005.

9. Richmond Daily Dispatch, December 11, `64.

10. Brown, Louis A., editor. "The Correspondence of David Olando McRaven and Amanda Nantz McRaven, 1864-1865, Part I." *North Carolina Historical Review.* January 1949. Volume XXVI; p. 45; hereafter cited as McRaven letters.

11. Jones, H.G. "Bedford Brown: States' Rights Unionist-Part II." *North Carolina Historical Review.* July 1955, Volume XXXII, #3; p. 563.

12. A Bill to Regulate the Price of All Articles Produced, Manufactured, or Sold in This State. Senate Bill #2. Documenting the American South, UNC-CH.

13. NCHR, "Poverty;" p. 470.

14. Land of Wilkes; p. 100.

15. Corpening Papers. Perkins Library, Duke University.

16. The Letters of Walter Clark; p. 95; November 15, `62.

17. Carolina and the Southern Cross, October 1913; p. 4.

18. Journal of A Secesh Lady, The Diary of Catherine Ann Devereux Edmondston 1860-1866; p. 116; hereafter cited as Journal of a Secesh Lady.

19. IBID; p. 133.

20. IBID; p. 233.

21. IBID; p. 304.

22. Milton Chronicle, April 4, `62.

23. IBID.

24. Winston-Salem, a History; p. 99.

25. Fear in North Carolina; p. 175.

26. NCHR, "Poverty;" p. 472.

27. History of North Carolina Since 1860; p. 52.

28. NCHR, "Weakness;" p. 471.

29. NCHR, "Poverty;" p. 475.

30. Person County Court Records, reel: #30005. December 21, `63.

31. The North Carolina Experience; p. 277. November 16, `63.

32. Person County Court Minutes, microfilm. May 2, `64.

33. J.M. Sneed to A.M. Gray November 23, `64 (anonymous citation).

34. IBID; November 30, `64.

35. North Carolina, Volume II; p. 195.

36. The Papers of Zebulon Baird Vance, Volume I; p. 404.

37. IBID; p. 405.

38. Person County Court Minutes, microfilm.

39. The Papers of Zebulon Baird Vance, Volume I; p. 429-430.

40. Governor's Message to the General Assembly, May 17, 1864. Documenting the American South, UNC-CH.

41. Milton Chronicle, war years.
42. "Notice: Confederate Tax, August 11, 1864;" Documenting the American South, UNC-CH.
43. The Papers of William Alexander Graham Volume VI 1864-1865; p. 104, April 11, `64.
44. Bright and Gloomy Days, the Civil War Correspondence of Captain Charles F. Bahnson, a Moravian Confederate; p. 145; hereafter cited as Bright and Gloomy.
45. J. Isaac Brown Papers. North Carolina Department of Archives & History.
46. Letter by Charles Phillips, November 23, `64; Documenting the American South, UNC-CH.
47. NCHR; "Poverty," p. 475-477.
48. IBID; p. 465, 477.
49. NCHR; "Weakness," p. 144.
50. Lenoir Family Papers. Documenting the American South, Wilson Library, UNC; January 15, `64. W.W. Lenoir to his mother.
51. Company Front, July, 1996; "The Letters of John Frazier, Sr." J.M. Frazier, Carolina Co., Va. to his wife, February 14, `64; p. 30.
52. Mary French Scott Papers. Perkins Library, Duke University.
53. Schroeder, Greg, "Dear Burwell." Awakenings: Writings and Recollections of Eastern North Carolina Women; p. 20; hereafter cited as Dear Burwell.
54. IBID; June 25, `64.
55. Letters of George Washington Walker, 1864.
56. Daily Journal, December 26, `64.
57. IBID; S.V. Reid, Chief Confederate Forces, Wilmington.
58. NCHR; "Weakness;" p. 145.
59. The Papers of Walter Clark, Volume I, 1857-1901; p. 129, November 19, `64.
60. Southern Families at War; p. 11.
61. Unruly Women; p. 127.
62. Women of the Confederacy; p. 231; Stanley County, February 7, `64.
63. Confederate Women; p. 176.
64. Southern Stories, Slaveholders in Peace and War; p. 136.
65. Confederate Women; p. 177.
66. Women of the Confederacy; p. 121-123.
67. Bright and Gloomy Days; p. 165.
68. IBID; p. 174, 176.
69. The Papers of Zebulon Baird Vance, Volume 2; p. 3.
70. Ashe County's Civil War; p. 85.
71. Many Excellent People: Power and Privilege in North Carolina 1850-1900; p. 53; hereafter cited as Many Excellent People.
72. NCHR; "Poverty," p. 479-480.
73. Victims: a True Story of the Civil War; p. 80.
74. Historical Sketches of Person County; p. 113.
75. Ashe County's Civil War; p. 85.
76. Confederate Women; p. 147.
77. Rebels in Blue; p. 27.
78. Lifeline of the Confederacy; p. 27.
79. Nancy A. Jarrett Papers. Southern Historical Collection, Wilson Library, UNC; letter July 14, `61.
80. Storm in the Land; p. 14.
81. The Two Williams; p. 75.
82. NCHR; "Poverty," p. 464.
83. Hillsborough Recorder, December 10, `61.
84. Ersatz of the Confederacy; p. 49.
85. NCHR; "Poverty," p. 463, 470.
86. IBID; p. 144, 468.
87. Raleigh Register, April 29, `62.
88. Journal of a Secesh Lady; p. 140.
89. The Commonwealth of Onslow County, a History; p. 68.

90. Tillinghast Family Papers. Perkins Library, Duke University; letter from Sarah to Robina N. Tillinghast, care of W.J. Bingham at the Oaks. June 9, `63.

91. Divided Allegiances; p. 61.

92. Victims: a True Story of the Civil War; p. 80.

93. Our Heritage; p. 232.

94. NCHR; "Poverty," p. 478.

95. Chatham County 1771-1971; p. 140-141.

96. No Soap, No Pay, Diarrhea, Dysentery and Desertion; p. 84.

97. Corpening Papers. Perkins Library, Duke University.

98. Morning Post, August 17, 1905.

99. Orange County Court Records, Wardens of the Poor Proceedings-1856-1879.

100. NCHR; "Poverty," p. 477.

101. Morning Post, August 17, 1905.

102. A Family of Women; p. 176.

103. Cathey Family Papers. Hunter Library, Western Carolina University; letter from Nathaniel Phillips, Valley Town to Colonel Cathey; December 24, `63.

104. NCHR; "Poverty," p. 467.

105. The Heart of Confederate Appalachia, Western North Carolina in the Civil War; p. 181; hereafter cited as Heart of Confederate Appalachia.

106. Lyman Sheppard Letters. North Carolina Department of Archives & History; letter to J.A. Bracy, October 14, `64.

107. Cathey Family Letters. Hunter Library, Western Carolina University.

108. The Papers of William Alexander Graham, Volume VI; p. 100.

109. The Twelfth New York Cavalry, by Giles Ward; courtesy of Ken Wooster.

110. Southern Railroad Man; p. 31.

111. Mary B. Hinshaw, Quaker; p. VIII.

112. Dear Burwell; p. 29; May 27, `64.

113. The County of Warren, North Carolina 1586-1976; p. 146.

114. Southern Families at War; p. 11.

115. Many Excellent People; p. 54.

116. McKinney, Gordon B. "Women's Role in Civil War Western North Carolina." North Carolina Historical Review. January 1992, Volume LXIX, #1; p. 47; hereafter cited as "Women's Role."

117. History of Anson County, North Carolina, 1750-1976; p. 123.

118. Journal of a Secesh Lady; p. 302, 330.

119. J. Isaac Brown Papers. North Carolina Department of Archives & History; letter Hillsboro, August 15, `64.

120. Sallie Southall Cotton; p. 22.

121. Salisbury Prison; p. 106.

122. Many Excellent People; p. 57.

123. Encyclopedia of the Confederacy, Volume III; p. 1245.

124. Many Excellent People; p. 39, 55.

125. NCHR; "Poverty," p. 463.

126. Morning Post, August 17, 1905.

127. Women of the Confederacy; p. 126.

128. Daily Conservative, January 26, `65.

129. Fisher, Clyde. "Relief of Soldiers' Families." South Atlantic Quarterly. June 1917, Volume XVI; p. 67.

130. Our Women in the War: The Lives They Lived, The Deaths They Died; "How the Arsenal Was Taken," by Eliza T. Stinson; The Weekly News & Courier, Charleston, bound copy; p. 27.

131. IBID; "The Way We Lived," p. 427.

132. Hayes, Francis B. "The South, the Confederacy, Yankees, and Negroes." Hayes Redbook, Volume 128.

133. Read McIntosh Papers. North Carolina Department of Archives & History; November 4, `64.

134. Elle's Book; p. 120, 124.

135. Diary of Elizabeth Ellis Robeson; January 23, `63 and September 8, `63.

136. Mary French Scott Papers. Perkins Library, Duke University.

137. Person Family Papers. Perkins Library, Duke University; Sallie E. Blount to aunt.

138. North Carolina Department of Archives & History, Civil War Correspondence Miscellaneous Letters; box 76, file 38, Mrs. Boles letter.

139. Diary of Elizabeth Ellis Robeson. January 18, '65.

140. Shuttle and Plow, a History of Alamance County, North Carolina; p. 287; hereafter cited as Shuttle and Plow.

141. Poor Whites of the Antebellum South; p. 38-39.

142. NCHR; McKinney, "Women's Role," p. 54.

143. Tillinghast Family Papers. Perkins Library, Duke University; October 5, '63, W.N. Tillinghast to his brother.

144. Port Town at War, Wilmington North Carolina 1860-1865; p. 140; a dissertation by Richard B. Wood.

145. Amnesty Papers #132 for Mrs. D A Hunt. Digital Appalachia, Berea College; October 1, '65, Wilkes County.

146. Poor Whites of the Antebellum South; p. 38-39.

147. Daily Confederate, June 3, '64.

148. Live Your Own Life; p. 74.

149. Carolina and the Southern Cross, September 1914; p.14.

150. North Carolina Women of the Confederacy; p. 102, 86.

151. Raleigh Register, 1861.

152. Fear in North Carolina; p. 37, October 3, '61.

153. Forget-Me-Not: a Romance Containing Reminiscences and Original letters of Two Confederate Soldiers; p. 50, 155; Documenting the American South, UNC-CH.

154. Morning Post, August 17, 1905.

155. Frances M. Manning Papers. Joyner Library, East Carolina University; (Miss Lloyd).

156. Behind the Lines; p. 49; Mary C. Moore to Z.B. Vance, no date.

157. Beaufort County—Two Centuries of its History; p. 183; ECU digital collection.

158. The Papers of Zebulon Baird Vance, Volume I; p. 410-411; November 9, '62, from Jamima A. Thomas.

159. Corpening Papers, Perkins Library, Duke University; October 1, '63 from Golson Smith to James Corpening.

160. Elle's Book; p. 108.

161. Spirit of the Age, August 21, '61.

162. War of Another Kind; p. 163.

163. NCHR; "Poverty," p. 180.

164. The Papers of William Alexander Graham, Volume VI 1864-1865; p. 21; Adam B. Davison of Rural Hall to W.A. Graham, January 30, '64.

165. Courtesy of John Humphrey. Daniel McPhail letter to his brother, May 24, '63.

166. After many months of searching, I cannot find the reference. Sorry.

167. Monroe, Haskell, editor. "The Road to Gettysburg, the Diary and Letters of Leonidas Torrence of the Gaston Guards." North Carolina Historical Review. October 1959; p. 481, 489.

168. Within the Plantation Household; p. 108.

169. NCHR; "Weakness," p. 144.

170. No Soap, No Pay, Diarrhea, Dysentery and Desertion; p. 106.

171. Two Centuries at Sycamore Springs Plantation; p. 147.

172. North Carolina History as Told by Contemporaries; p. 292-3, February 5, '63.

173. Justice or Atrocity; p. 70.

174. Two Centuries at Sycamore Springs Plantation; p. 164.

175. Anna Fuller's Journal 1856-1890; April 17, '64.

176. Anonymous citation of letter. J.M. Sneed to A.M. Gray, March 19-20, '65.

177. Anonymous citation of letter Mary Gray to A.M. Gray, February 18, '65.

178. Mary French Scott Papers. Perkins Library, Duke University; Mary F.E., Etheridgeville, to Mary F. Scott. September 13, '63.

179. Daily Conservative, January 17, '65.

180. Person County Court Minutes. September Term, 1864, microfilm.

181. Dear Burwell; p. 22.

182. Lenoir Family Papers. Documenting the American South, UNC-CH; August 17, '63.

183. Kimberly Family Papers. Documenting the American South, UNC-CH; June 8, '62 from Chapel Hill.

184. The Correspondence of Jonathan Worth, Volume I; letter from Wyatt Jordan to Jonathan Worth; courtesy of Alexander Street Press, American Civil War Letters & Diaries.

185. Blockade Runners of the Confederacy; p. 48.

[186.] Lifeline of the Confederacy; p. 145.

[187.] Confederate Guns Were Stacked; p. 39; poem from North Carolina Christian Advocate, 1958.

[188.] Anonymous citation of letter. J.M. Sneed to A.M. Gray, December 28, '64.

[189.] Many Excellent People; p. 54.

[190.] The Letters of George Washington Walker.

[191.] Awakenings; p. 35, November 1, '64.

[192.] J. Isaac Brown Papers. North Carolina Department of Archives& History; August 15, '64.

[193.] True Tales of the South at War; p. 59.

[194.] Holland Papers. Gaston Museum Collection; Hanna Holland to M.L. Holland; no date but believed to be 1862 or 3.

[195.] Journal of a Secesh Lady; p. 376.

[196.] Tillinghast Family Papers. Perkins Library, Duke University; W.N. Tillinghast to his sister Robina, July 27, '63.

[197.] Lenoir Family Papers. Documenting the American South, UNC; March 15, '64.

[198.] IBID; letter from cousin Lily Norwood to Emily Tillinghast, November 26, '62.

[199.] The Civil War in North Carolina; p. 168; Davidson County, May 29, '64.

[200.] Scarborough Family Papers. Perkins Library, Duke University; letter May 10, '63 from cousin S.E. Scarborough of Mt. Gilead to Mittie Williams.

[201.] Chronicles of the Cape Fear River 1660-1916; p. 288.

[202.] Blockade Runners of the Confederacy; p. 186.

[203.] This Was Home; p. 113.

[204.] Hillsborough Recorder, December 20, '62.

[205.] A Grandmother's Recollections of Dixie; p.17.

[206.] Tillinghast Family Papers. Perkins Library, Duke University; July 21, '63 from Emily Tillinghast to her sister.

[207.] War of Another Kind; p. 154.

[208.] Courtesy of Dr. Ann Hertizer.

[209.] Raleigh Register, September 28, '61.

[210.] IBID; January 8, '62.

[211.] Lenoir Family Papers. Documenting the American South, UNC; W.W. Lenoir to his mother, January 5, '64.

[212.] Chronicles of the Cape Fear River 1660-1916; p. 413.

[213.] The Heritage of Lenoir County; p. 35.

[214.] Drury Lacy Papers. Southern Historical Collection, Wilson Library, UNC; March 3, '64.

[215.] Recollection From My Slavery Days; chapter 8.

[216.] Journal of a Secesh Lady; p. 368, March, 1863.

[217.] Garrison, Randall editor. "The White Letters." Company Front, April 1993; letter to Joseph J. White from his parents, November 3, '61; hereafter cited as "White Letters."

[218.] www.mdgorman.com February 9, '65; letter from Dr. S.P. Moore, Richmond.

[219.] Spirit of the Age, January, 1862.

[220.] Raleigh Standard, war years.

[221.] IBID

[222.] Southern Rights; p. 36.

[223.] Raleigh Register, February 12, '62.

[224.] Southern Rights; p. 41.

[225.] John McLean Harrington Papers. Perkins Library, Duke University; letter from D.O. Harrington to his brother Sion; May 31, no year listed.

[226.] Asheville Weekly News, March 27, '62.

[227.] Southern Rights; p. 34.

[228.] New Hanover County Criminal Court Records, microfilm.

[229.] Raleigh Register, March 26, '62.

[230.] Daily Chronicle & Sentinel, March 18, '62.

[231.] Southern Rights; p. 41.

[232.] Excerpts from Thomas F. Wood's Journal. Randal Library, UNC-W digital library

[233.] North Carolina Postal Society; courtesy Scott Troutman, September 22, '61.

[234.] The Heart of Confederate Appalachia; p 17.

[235.] Last Stand in the Carolinas; p. 403.

[236.] Ladies in the Making; p. 18.

237. Winston-Salem, a History; p. 105.
238. Piedmont Soldiers and Their Families; p. 13.
239. The Heritage: the Education of Women at St. Mary's College, Raleigh, North Carolina/History of St. Mary's; p. 62.
240. Record of the Moravians in North Carolina, Volume XI; p. 6066-6068.
241. IBID; p. 6068.
242. The Heritage: the Education of Women at St. Mary's College; p. 62-70.
243. North Carolina Baptist State Convention Papers; Orange Co. Library, microfilm.
244. Here Will I Dwell; p. 115.
245. No Soap, No Pay, Diarrhea, Dysentery, and Desertion; p. 362.
246. The County of Moore 1847-1947; p. 65.
247. Sketches of Pitt County: a Brief History of the County 1704-1910; p. 162.
248. NCHR; "Women's Role," p. 47.
249. Battle for Saltville; p. 14.
250. The Papers of Zebulon Baird Vance, Volume II; p. 228.
251. Watson Family Letters. Hunter Library, Western Carolina University.
252. Scarborough Family Papers. Perkins Library, Duke University; October 25, `61.
253. Sandhill Families: Early Reminiscences of the Fort Bragg Area; p. 36.
254. Company Front, April, 1993; "White letters."
255. History of Alleghany County; p. 254-255.
256. Fear in North Carolina; p. 117, November 27, `62.
257. Journal of a Secesh Lady; p. 182.
258. Mary Hunter Kennedy Papers. Southern Historical Collection, Wilson Library, UNC-CH.
259. Tillinghast Family Papers. Perkins Library, Duke University.
260. John M. Morehead and the Development of North Carolina 1796-1866; p. 403; letter to General Bragg, November 22, `64.
261. The Heritage of Ashe County; p. 27; (contributed by Stella Faw) letter from Robert Francis to his sister, Mrs. Faw.
262. The Heritage of Lenoir County; p. 35.
263. Fear in North Carolina; p. 83, 86.
264. Raleigh Register, January 4, `62.
265. The Papers of Zebulon Baird Vance, Volume I; p. 418.
266. IBID; p. 425-426.
267. Storm in the Land; p. 32.
268. Here Will I Dwell; p. 135.
269. Raleigh Register, November 26, `62.
270. Historical Sketches of Franklin County; p. 198.
271. A.W. Bell Letters. Perkins Library, Duke University; letter July 24, `64 written from LaFayettte, GA. to Mary Bell.
272. North Carolina Women of the 1860's; p. 3.
273. A Grandmother's Recollection of Dixie; p. 15.
274. Fear in North Carolina; p. 79, 107-108, 115, 125-126.
275. Frances M. Manning Papers. Joyner Library, ECU; letter December 3, `62.
276. Journal of a Secesh Lady; p. 249, 298, 310.
277. Dix, Mary S. "And Three Rousing Cheers for the Privates; A Diary of the Roanoke Island Expedition." *North Carolina Historical Review*. January 1994, Volume LXXI, #1; p. 78.
278. Morning Post, August 17, 1905.
279. Bright and Gloomy Days; p. 66.
280. Courtesy of Derrick Hartsoe [rootsweb, Catawba County]; May 24, `62.
281. Drury Lacy Papers. Southern Historical Collection, Wilson Library, UNC-CH.
282. Lenoir Family Papers. Documenting the American South, UNC; November 15, `64.
283. The Thirty-seventh North Carolina Troops; p. 111; letter November, 1862.
284. Bright and Gloomy Days; p. 89; letter November 9, `63 from Camp Palmyra Church, Va.
285. They Went into the Fight Cheering; p. 160.
286. Within the Plantation Household; p. 121.
287. Mary French Scott Papers. Perkins Library, Duke University.
288. Anna Fuller Journal's 1856-1890; p. 25, May, 1863.

289. The Civil War Collection of Lucy Strickland. Granville County Library; Henry Turner.

290. Dear Burwell; p. 37.

291. From the Cotton Field to Cotton Mill; p. 56.

292. North Carolina, Volume II; p. 224.

293. A.W. Bell Papers. Perkins Library, Duke University; letter to Mary, January 18, `62.

294. Journal of a Secesh Lady; p. 249.

295. Milton Chronicle, May 1, `62.

296. Tillinghast Family Papers. Perkins Library, Duke University; from Sarah to Robina.

297. Journal of a Secesh Lady; p. 374.

298. IBID; June 18, `63.

299. Dear Burwell; November 1, `64.

300. Frances M. Manning Papers. Joyner Library, East Carolina University.

301. Hillsborough Recorder, August 5, `62.

302. The Papers of Zebulon Baird Vance, Volume I; p. 44, February 4, `63.

303. Southern Watchman, Athens Georgia; October 22, `62; courtesy of Vicki Betts.

304. Rebel Gibraltar; p. 112.

305. Milton Chronicle, October, 1864.

306. The North Carolinian, a Fayetteville newspaper, May 17, `64.

307. Mary French Scott Papers. Perkins Library, Duke University.

308. Misc. Civil War Records, North Carolina Department of Archives & History, #111.31.

309. Read McIntosh Papers. North Carolina Department of Archives & History; 1st letter November 6, 1864; 2nd letter January 22, 1865; 3rd letter January 15, 1865; 4th letter March 5, 1865; 5th letter April 8, 1865.

310. The Papers of Walter Clark; p. 110 November 24, `63.

311. Fear in North Carolina; p. 47, 192.

312. Women of the Confederacy; p. 150, March 20, `62.

313. IBID.

314. Lenoir Family Papers. Documenting the American South, UNC-CH; July 25, `63.

315. Scarborough Family Papers. Perkins Library, Duke University.

316. A.W. Bell Letters. Perkins Library, Duke University; February 11. `62 letter at Mt. Zonah from Sally, a sister to Mary Bell.

317. The Papers of Walter Clark; p. 110, November 24, `63.

318. Fear in North Carolina; p. 136, April 19, `63.

319. Elle's Book; p. 82.

320. Lenoir Family Papers. Documenting the American South, UNC-CH, January 15, `64.

321. Frances M. Manning Papers. Joyner Library, East Carolina University.

322. Journal of a Secesh Lady; p. 268.

323. Diary of Elizabeth Ellis Robeson.

324. Fear in North Carolina; p. 193-194, 296.

325. North Carolina Department of Archives & History, Civil War Miscellaneous Collection; Box 76, File 39.

326. William Howard Hooker Papers. Joyner Library, ECU; from Clara Young, a friend to Mattie, February 5, `64.

327. "The Last Flag of Truce," by Dallas Ward. Documenting the American South, UNC-CH.

328. Frances M. Manning Papers. Joyner Library, ECU; ledger from the Staton Family.

329. Diary of Elizabeth Wiggins. April, 1861; copy given to me.

330. Raleigh Register, April 2, `62.

331. Courtesy of Merlin Bell, rootsweb Hyde County; Charity Swindell Letter, October 14, `61.

332. Tillinghast Family Papers. Perkins Library, Duke University; letter June 6, `63, Sarah Ann Tillinghast to Robie.

333. The Textile Industry in North Carolina; p. 21.

334. Anna Fuller's Journal, 1856-1890; p. 39.

335. Journal of a Secesh Lady; p.385.

336. The Heritage: the Education of Women at St. Mary's College Raleigh, North Carolina 1842-1982; p. 73.

337. The Lee Girls; p. 95.

338. Carolina and the Southern Cross, Volume 12, 1914.

339. Raleigh Register, January 8, `62.

340. Elle's Book; December 1864.

341. Hayes Redbook, Volume 128; N&O article 1940 by Sadie Robards.
342. Drury Lacy Papers. Southern Historical Collection, Wilson Library, UNC-CH.
343. Hartung, Bruce. "War Comes to Qualla." *The State*. May 1983.
344. Journal of a Secesh Lady; p. 268, 378.
345. North Carolina Women of the 1860's; p. 3.
346. North Carolina Booklet; "Conditions During the War;" p. 216.
347. Daily Constitutionist, December 11, `61.
348. General D.H. Hill's Address at the Unveiling of the Memorial to the North Carolina Women of the Confederacy; p. 17; East Carolina University digital collection.
349. Winston-Salem, a History; p. 101.
350. Fear in North Carolina; p. 80.
351. Morning Post, August 17, 1905 "Our Women in the War Supplement."
352. IBID
353. North Carolina Department of Archives & History, Civil War Miscellaneous Letters, Box 76, File 24; letter from Mrs. Julia Rankin Forbis, 1914.
354. Fear in North Carolina; p. 47-48, 94, 140, 243, 228, 36, 55.
355. Our Women in the War: The Lives They Lived—The Deaths They Died; p. 427; Charleston News& Courier [bound], 1885.
356. Diary of Elizabeth Wiggins. Copy given to me by descendants.
357. Journal of a Secesh Lady; p. 349, 287, 276.
358. Dear Burwell; p. 31, June 6, `64.
359. Journal of a Secesh Lady; p. 298.
360. Tillinghast Family Papers. Perkins Library, Duke University; letter June 9, `63 from Sarah Tillinghast to her sister Robina; IBID; letter from W.N. Tillinghast to Robina, September 8, `63.
361. Plantation Memories of the Cape Fear River County; p. 15.
362. Milton Sidelights of History; May 16, `62.
363. Daily Progress, September 4, `64.
364. Confederate Conscript Department Letters, 7th District. Southern Historical Collection, Wilson Library, University of North Carolina at Chapel Hill.
365. Diary of Melinda Ray. North Carolina Department of Archives & History, Civil War Miscellaneous Letters.
366. Journal of a Secesh Lady; p. 385.
367. County of Moore, 1847-1947; p. 48.
368. North Carolina Department of Archives & History, Civil War Miscellaneous Letters, Box 76, file 24; Mrs. Julia R. Forbis, 1914.
369. Carolina and the Southern Cross, Volume 12, 1914.
370. Daily Journal, October 20, `63.
371. Daily Conservative, January 26, `65.
372. Turners and Burners; p. 334, 133, 267.
373. Our Women in the War: The Lives They Lived-The Deaths They Died; "The Way We Lived Then," by Rose Fry; The Charleston Weekly News & Courier [bound]; p. 427-429.
374. Fear in North Carolina; p. 236.
375. Winston-Salem, a History; p. 153, People's Press, 1863.
376. Unruly Women; p. 127
377. History of Alleghany County, "Civil War Stories & Battles," letter from L.D. Andress to James M. Andress, October 25, `62.
378. Western North Carolina, a History; p. 618.
379. Salisbury Prison; p. 106.
380. Raleigh Register, February 12, `62.
381. Weekly Catawba Journal, March 24, `62.
382. Daily Progress, September 14, `64.
383. The Confederate Post Office Department, April 4, `63; p. 40.
384. The Wagg Family of Ashe County; p. 48; letter May, `64.
385. Diary of Elizabeth Ellis Robeson, February 8, `64.
386. Drury Lacy Papers. Southern Historical Collection, Wilson Library, UNC; July 3, `63.

387. Journal of Samuel H. Walkup. Perkins Library, Duke University.
388. County of Warren, North Carolina 1586-1976; p. 33.
389. Morning Post, August 17, 1905.
390. NCHR; "Women's Role," p. 50.
391. Storm in the Mountains; p. 23.
392. Winston-Salem, a History; p. 22.
393. Forsyth, History of a County on the March; p. 136.
394. Record of the Moravians in North Carolina, Volume XI; p. 6070, 6077.
395. Daily Progress, September 19, `64.
396. The Eight Agricultural Census of the United States.
397. Tillinghast Family Papers. Perkins Library, Duke University; letter from Eliza Tillinghast to her sister Emily, December 31, `62.
398. Elle's Book; p. 67.
399. IBID; p. 106, 123.
400. A Woman's Life; p. 18.
401. The Lee Girls; p. 71.
402. Scarborough Family Papers. Perkins Library, Duke University. Letter from S.E. Scarborough to Millie Williams, January 30, `64.
403. Carolina and the Southern Cross, Volume 2, June 1914, p. 17; and This was Home; p. 125.
404. Women of Guilford; p. 58.
405. Elle's Book; p. 73.
406. IBID; p. 82, 102, 108, 111.
407. Anna Fuller's Journal, May 16, `65.
408. Jacobs, Joseph. "Some of the Drug Conditions During the War Between the States, 1861-1865." Southern Historical Society Papers, Volume 3; p. 20, 23, 25.
409. North Carolina, Volume II; p. 194.
410. Daily Progress, September 19, `64.
411. J. Isaac Brown Papers. North Carolina Department of Archives & History; January 27, 1865.
412. Sandhill Families; p. 36.
413. Gass, W. Conrad. "A Felicitous Life: Lucy Martin Battle, 1805-1874." North Carolina Historical Review. October 1975, Volume LII, #4; p. 391.
414. Daily Chronicle & Sentinel [Augusta, GA], November 10, `61.
415. From Newbern to Fredericksburg: Captain James Wren's Diary March 9, 1862; p. 6.
416. Paul Barringer Papers. North Carolina Department of Archives & History.
417. Raleigh Weekly, June 24, `64.
418. Mercer Family Papers. Southern Historical Collection, Wilson Library, UNC-CH.
419. North Carolina Women of the 1860's; page lost.
420. Spirit of the Age, August 7, `61.
421. North Carolina Department of Archives & History; Civil War Miscellaneous Letters, Box 76, File 38, Mrs. Boles of Wilmington.
422. Gunn's Domestic Medicine, April 4, `61; p. 350.
423. Weekly Catawba Journal, June 30, `62.
424. Fayetteville Observer, October 28, `61.
425. Raleigh Register, January 15, `62.
426. North Carolina Argus, February 19, `63; courtesy of Julie H. Ganis.
427. Raleigh Register, April 11, `62.
428. Spirit of the Age, October, 1862.
429. Raleigh Register, January 22, `62.
430. Weekly Catawba Journal, August 30, `64.
431. Fayetteville Observer, November 11, `61.
432. Raleigh Register, June 8, `61.
433. Footprints of Northampton County; no page listed.
434. The Carolina Quaker Experience; p. 108.

CHAPTER NINE ENDNOTES

1. Doctor to the Front; p. 9.
2. Burke County, a History of a North Carolina County 1777-1920; p. 151.
3. Here Will I Dwell; p. 127.
4. Journal of a Secesh Lady; p. 63.
5. North Carolina in 1861; p. 45.
6. Journal of a Secesh Lady; p. 141.
7. Spirit of the Age, September, 1862, F.S., Henderson County.
8. The Papers of Zebulon Baird Vance, Volume I; p. 308, footnote.
9. North Carolina Booklet; p. 215.
10. The Civil War in North Carolina; p. 77.
11. The Papers of Zebulon Baird Vance, Volume I; p. 371; November 18, '62 letter.
12. IBID; p. 323; November 9, '62.
13. IBID; p. 230; September 26, '62.
14. IBID; p. 404.
15. IBID; p. 321.
16. IBID; p. 313.
17. IBID; p. 341.
18. IBID; p. 305 November 4, '62.
19. IBID; p. 427 December 8, '62.
20. IBID; p. 367.
21. IBID; p. 347.
22. Silk Flags and Cold Steel; p. 87.
23. Salisbury Prison; p. 38.
24. The Papers of Zebulon Baird Vance, Volume I; p. 437.
25. Alfred W. Bell Letters. Perkins Library, Duke University.
26. The Papers of Zebulon Baird Vance, Volume I; p. 304.
27. Raleigh Register, April 29, '62; and Carolina Watchman, September 29, '62.
28. Raleigh Standard, January 22, '62.
29. IBID; November 5, '62.
30. Southern Illustrated News; November 27, '62; courtesy Alexander Street Press, Illustrated Civil War Newspapers and Magazines.
31. Shuttle and Plow, a History of Alamance County, North Carolina; p. 288.
32. Asa Biggs Autobiography. Documenting the American South, UNC-CH.
33. The Fifth Massachusetts Volunteer in its Three Tours of Duty; story of James R. Gist, p. 140.
34. Mary S.M. Buie Letters. Perkins Library, Duke University; February 1, '64 to cousin.
35. Schroeder, Greg. "Dear Burwell," by Rebecca Davis. Awakenings: Writings and Recollections of Eastern North Carolina Women, by Sally Brett, Everatt, Kinlaw, and Peek; p. 19.
36. Swamp Doctor; p. 148; April 17, '63.
37. Blockade Runners of the Confederacy; p. 47.
38. Daily Journal, December 26, '64.
39. The Papers of Zebulon Baird Vance, Volume I; p. 425.
40. Tillinghast Family Papers, Perkins Library, Duke University; letter April 14, '63.
41. IBID; October 5, '63.
42. J.B. Crenshaw Papers & Letters, Friends Historical Collection. Hege Library, Guilford College; letter #B5 January 19, '63.
43. Scarborough Family Papers. Perkins Library, Duke University; letter February 7, '64, M.A. Scarborough in Mt. Gilead to brother Franklin.
44. IBID; September 29, '62.
45. Milton Chronicle, exact date lost but 1861-1865.
46. Frances M. Manning Papers. Joyner Library, East Carolina University; Mrs. Stanton in Hamilton.
47. Caswell County 1777-1977; p. 217.
48. J. Isaac Brown Papers. Perkins Library, Duke University.

49. Weekly Catawba Journal, August 30, `64.

50. The Papers of Walter Clark; March 30, `65, letter from his father.

51. Courtesy of John Humphrey. letter to Angus McPhail of Philadelphus, April 23, `63.

52. Women of the Confederacy; p. 126.

53. "Dear Burwell," Awakenings: Writings and Recollections; p. 26.

54. Southern Stories and Slaveholders; p. 138.

55. Salisbury Prison; p. 38.

56. The Papers of Zebulon Baird Vance, Volume 2; p. 92-93.

57. Silk Flags and Cold Steel; p. 168.

58. Unruly Women; p. 55, April 9, `63.

59. IBID; p. 146.

60. Fear in North Carolina; p. 140.

61. Unruly Women; p. 128, 146.

62. IBID; p. 146, 133-134.

63. IBID; p. 125, 129.

64. McKinney, Gordon B. "Women's Role in Civil War Western North Carolina" *North Carolina Historical Review;* January 1992, Volume LXIX, #1; p. 47.

65. The North Carolina Experience; p. 277; April 22, `64.

66. Sallie Southall Cotton; p. 19.

67. Unruly Women; p. 128.

68. Heritage of Lenoir County; p. 35.

69. Many Excellent People: Power and Privilege in North Carolina 1850-1900; p. 65, 67.

70. Courtesy of Ken Wooster. The 12th New York Cavalry, Giles Ward letter May 10, `63.

71. Company Front, 2002, #1; "Kiss my Little Boys and Think of Me, the Letters of Private Benjamin Franklin Gatton." Compliments of the Bentonville Chapter UDC.

72. The Papers of Zebulon Baird Vance, Volume I; p. 438 Jesse Reeves.

73. Weekly Catawba Journal, March 1864.

74. Many Excellent People; p. 67.

75. Making of a Confederate; p. 136.

76. Van Noppen, Ina W. "The Significance of Stoneman's Last Raid," *North Carolina Historical Review.* January-October 1961, Volume XXXVIII, #1-4; p. 500-526.

77. Greensborough Post, April 16, `63.

78. Confederate Guns Were Stacked; p. 77-78.

79. Guilford County, a Brief History; p. 19.

80. Confederate Guns Were Stacked; p. 78.

CHAPTER TEN ENDNOTES

1. The James Sprunt Studies in History and Political Science, Volume 47, Legal Aspects of Conscription and Exemptions in North Carolina 1861-1865; p. 51, 61, 9; hereafter cited as Legal Aspects.

2. IBID; p. 16-17.

3. Confederate States of America Bureau of Conscription, 7th North Carolina Congressional District. Southern Historical Collection, Wilson Library, UNC-CH.

4. They Went into Fight Cheering; p. 106.

5. IBID; p. 99, 91, 93.

6. Milton Sidelights; p. 59.

7. Changing Relationships Between Confederate Soldiers and Their Families and Communities During the Civil War, a case study; courtesy of David McGee. 1998.

8. Read McIntosh Papers, Department of Archives & History. February 18, `62.

9. Scarborough Family Papers, Perkins Library, Duke University. October 12, `62.

10. Lyman Sheppard Papers, North Carolina Department of Archives & History. May 5, `63.

11. Papers of William Graham, Volume VI; p. 21; to William Graham from Adam B Davidson, January 30, `64.

12. Mary Hunter Kennedy Papers, Southern Historical Collection, Wilson Library, UNC. December 12

13. Victims; p. 81.

14. Scarboro, David, "North Carolina and the Confederacy: the Weakness of States' Rights," *North Carolina Historical Review*. April 1979, Volume LVI, #2; p. 134; hereafter cited as "Weakness."

15. Confederate States Bureau of Conscription. Southern Historical Collection, Wilson Library, UNC-CH, 7th District. Oct/Nov/December 1863.

16. Ashe County's Civil War; p. 87.

17. The Papers of Zebulon Baird Vance, Volume I; p. 424.

18. Ashe County's Civil War; p. 105.

19. Chatham County, 1771-1971; p. 122.

20. Scarborough Family Papers. Perkins Library, Duke University.

21. The Heart of Confederate Appalachia: Western North Carolina in the Civil War; p. 99.

22. Amnesty Papers of B.F. Atkins, Berea College Digital Appalachia; courtesy Gordon McKinney.

23. The Thirty-seventh North Carolina Troops; p. 38.

24. History of Allegany County; letter from Martha Choate to her husband William, January 13, `63.

25. Ernest Haywood Collection of Haywood Family Papers. Southern Historical Collection, Wilson Library, UNC-CH.

26. Courtesy of John Humphrey. Letter from HH Ellis to Angus McPhail, April 23, `63.

27. McKinney, Gordon. "Women's Role in Civil War North Carolina," *North Carolina Historical Review*; p. 53; hereafter cited as "Women's Role."

28. Legal Aspects; p. 18.

29. The Papers of Zebulon Baird Vance, Volume I; p. 374-375. November 18, `62.

30. Legal Aspects; p. 12.

31. Raleigh Register, April 30, `62.

32. Legal Aspects; p. 35.

33. Railroads of the Confederacy; page lost.

34. Confederate States Bureau of Conscription. Southern Historical Collection, UNC-CH, 7th District, Volume I-II, February, 1864; Southern Historical Collection, Wilson Library, UNC-CH.

35. Justice in Gray; p. 133.

36. Weekly Progress, April 17, `62.

37. Lerner, Eugene "Money, Prices, and Wages in the Confederacy," *The Economic Impact of the American Civil War*; p. 27.

38. Internet site of Sarah Rutledge, "Capt. Goldman Bryson, Union Volunteers of 1863."

39. The Papers of Zebulon Baird Vance, Volume I; p. 267, letter to John G. Reagan.

40. Jonathan Worth, a Biography of a Southern Unionist; p. 73, 125.

41. The Carolina Quaker Experience; p. 154-155.

42. The First One Hundred Years of Historic Guilford County 1771-1871; p. 148.

43. North Carolina Confederate Militia and Home Guard Records; Henry L. Street, 63rd NC Militia, Asheboro, January 12, `63; p. 60.

44. Letter from Jonathan Worth to Wm A. Graham, June 8, `64; Courtesy of Alexander Street Press, Civil War Letters and Diaries.

45. Bright and Gloomy Days: the Civil War Correspondence of Captain Charles F. Bahnson, a Moravian Confederate; p. 174-176; hereafter cited as Bright and Gloomy Days.

46. Southern Rights; p. 89.

47. IBID; p. 92.

48. Jonathan Worth, a Biography of a Southern Unionist; p. 174-177.

49. NCHR, April 1979, "Weakness;" p. 142.

50. Bright and Gloomy Days; p. 172.

51. Jonathan Worth; p. 172.

52. The Carolina Quaker Experience; p. 155-156.

53. Mary Baker Hinshaw: Quaker; p. VIII.

54. IBID; p. 63.

55. IBID; p. 63.

56. IBID; p. 68.

57. Vestal Letters, #J32; Friends Historical Collection, Hege Library, Guilford College.

58. Honey, Dr. Michael, "War Within the Confederacy: White Unionists in North Carolina," *Prologue*, Summer 1989; p. 81; hereafter cited as "War Within."

59. An Illustrated History of Yadkin County 1850-1980; p. 96.

60. The Haydock's Testimony, Joyner Library ECU digital series; p. 96, 100-101, 109, 113.

61. John B. Crenshaw Papers, Letter #A2; Friends Historical Collection, Hege Library, Guilford College; April 19, `62.

62. IBID; letter # B9 to JBC from Westminister March 13, `63.

63. IBID; Letter # B18 April 15, `63.

64. IBID; letter # A14 to JBC.

65. IBID; letter # B12 from Delphina Mendenhall.

66. IBID; letter # B17.

67. IBID; letter # J17.

68. Courtesy of Scott Mingus.

69. John B. Crenshaw Letters, Friends Historical Collection, Hege Library, Guilford College, Letter # J9; JBC to Tilghman Vestal.

70. Tilghman Vestal Letters; letter # J3; Friends Historical Collection, Hege Library, Guilford College.

71. IBID; letter # J11.

72. IBID; letter # J12, Judith Mendenhall to Crenshaw October 20, `63.

73. IBID; letter # J 17.

74. IBID.

75. IBID; letter # J18 March 1, `64.

76. Mary Hinshaw, Quaker; p. 84.

77. IBID; p. 93.

78. IBID; p. 78, 168.

79. IBID; p. 66.

80. Prologue Magazine, "War Within;" p. 81.

81. The Carolina Quaker Experience; p. 156.

82. John B. Crenshaw Papers, letter # A5; Friends Historical Collection. Hege Library, Guilford College; letter from Delphina Mendenhall, September 29, `62.

83. Escott, Paul, "Poverty and Governmental Aid for the Poor in Confederate North Carolina.," *North Carolina Historical Review*; October, 1984, Volume LXI, #4; p. 456; hereafter cited as "Poverty."

84. Carolina Watchman, March 7, `64.

85. Southern Stories: Slaveholders in Peace and War; p. 135.

86. John B. Crenshaw Papers, letter # A6; Friends Historical Collection. Hege Library, Guilford College.

87. The Papers of Zebulon Baird Vance, Volume I; p. 312.

88. IBID; p. 299.

89. IBID; p. 308.

90. IBID; p. 389.

91. IBID; p. 424.

92. The Papers of Walter Clark; p. 131.

93. Southern Families at War; p. 89, June 27, `62.

94. IBID; p. 88-89.

95. IBID; p. 89.

96. Shuttle and Plow, a History of Alamance County, North Carolina; p. 282.

97. Confederate States Conscription Department, 7th District; March 24, `63.

98. IBID; February, 1864.

99. The Papers of William Alexander Graham, Volume 6; p. 64-65.

100. Mary French Scott Papers, Perkins Library, Duke University.

101. Confederate States Bureau of Conscription. Southern Historical Collection, UNC-CH, 7th District Book, Volume I-II, July 1864, Box 2.

102. IBID October/November/December 1863.

103. IBID

104. IBID

105. Southern Stories, Slaveholders in Peace and War; p. 135.

106. Women of the Confederacy; p. 231 .

107. The Civil War in North Carolina; p. 84, November 29, `62.

108. Mary French Scott Papers. Perkins Library, Duke University.

109. Original letter owned by author.
110. The North Carolina Experience; p. 275, February 27, `63.
111. NCHR "Poverty;" p. 465.
112. Steelman, Lala Carr. "The Life-Style of an Eastern NC Planter: Elias Carr of Bracebridge Hall," *North Carolina Historical Review*. January 1980, Volume 57; p.24.
113. Confederate States Bureau of Conscription. 7th District. Southern Historical Collection, UNC-CH; filed October, November, and December 1863; From Greensboro, Innis? or James Sloan? [difficult to read] October 15, `63.
114. IBID; October 28, `63, Exemption Office, Pittsboro.
115. IBID; October 14, `63, Lt. Reuchs to Capt Little.
116. Confederate States Bureau of Conscription, 7th District. Southern Historical Collection, UNC-CH. Volume I-I, Box 2.
117. IBID
118. The Haydock's Testimony; p. 89.
119. Confederate Guns Were Stacked; p. 103.
120. Bivouac Banner, Summer 2004. article courtesy of Clarence Anspake.
121. Confederate States Bureau of Conscription, 7th District. Southern Historical Collection, UNC-CH; March 25, 1863; p. 74.
122. Shuttle and Plow, a History of Alamance County, North Carolina; p. 285.
123. Confederate States Bureau of Conscription, 7th District. Southern Historical Collection, UNC-CH, Volume I-II July 1864, Box 2; Wilson Library, UNC-CH.
124. IBID
125. IBID
126. They Went Into the Fight Cheering; p. 137.
127. IBID; p. 157.
128. IBID; p. 166.
129. IBID; p. 179.
130. IBID; p. 105.
131. IBID; p. 210-211.
132. Berea College Confederate Amnesty Letters, #181, August 10, `65.
133. Salisbury Prison; p. 92.
134. Southern Railroad Man; p. 30-31.
135. Anna Fuller's Journal, August 10, `64; p. 32.
136. Legal Aspects; p. 88.
137. Historical Sketches of Person County; p. 113.
138. IBID
139. They Went Into the Fight Cheering; p. 41.
140. They Passed This Way; p. 69.
141. Milton Chronicle, April 10, `63.
142. Legal Aspects; p. 19.
143. Turner May Papers. Joyner Library, East Carolina University; May 7, `63.
144. Silas Stepp Letters. Ramsey Library, UNC-Asheville.
145. Confederate Courage on Other Fields; p. 70.
146. Courtesy of John Humphrey; letter May 24, `63.
147. IBID.
148. Confederate States Bureau of Conscription, 7th District. Southern Historical Collection, Wilson Library, UNC; October, November, December, 1863.
149. To Bear Arms; p. 132.
150. Excerpts from Dr. Thomas Fanning Wood's Journal, 1st book; Randall Library, UNC—Wilmington digital collection.
151. They Passed This Way; p. 73.
152. Interview with John Humphrey, 2003.
153. Justice in Gray; p.78, 82.
154. Southern Rights; p. 64-65.
155. Justice in Gray; p. 209.
156. Legal Aspects; p. 83.
157. IBID; p. 88.

158. Justice in Gray; p. 120.
159. Legal Aspects; p. 3, 91.
160. Southern Rights; p. 56.
161. Adjutant General State Reports. North Carolina Department of Archives & History, June 16, '63.
162. IBID; June 16, 63, Brig. Gen. G.A. McCraw, 18th Brigade NCM, Mt. Airy.
163. An Illustrated History of Yadkin County; p. 82.
164. Southern Rights; p. 75-76.
165. The Papers of Zebulon Baird Vance, Volume 2; p. 191.
166. The North Carolina Experience; p. 276.
167. Mary French Scott Papers. Perkins Library, Duke University. March 12, '63.
168. Confederate States of America Bureau of Conscription, 7th NC Congressional District, Southern Historical Collection, UNC-CH; hereafter cited as CSA Conscript Letters.
169. The Civil War in North Carolina; p. 73, September 27, '62.
170. The Papers of Zebulon Baird Vance, Volume I; p. 441-442.
171. Prologue Magazine, "War Within"; p. 82.
172. CSA Conscript Letters, October, November, December, 1863.
173. Civil War Pharmacy; p. 172.
174. Prologue Magazine, "War Within;" p. 82.
175. Brief Historical Sketches of Mt. Carmel Baptist Church in Northampton County near Seaboard, N.C.; East Carolina University digital collection.
176. Adjutant General's Book; p. 53 letter from Col. JC Mullis, 119th NCM, Walkersville.
177. IBID; p. 38 from Colonel John E. Parker 25th Rgt. NCM, Clinton, October, 1862.
178. Weekly Standard December 31, '62.
179. Daily Journal, September 7, '62.
180. Brown, Louis A., editor. "The Correspondence of David Olando McRaven and Amanda Nantz McRaven, 1864-1865," North Carolina Historical Review. January 1949, Volume XXVI; p. 5 footnote.
181. No Soap, No Pay, Diarrhea, Dysentery, and Desertion; p. 33.
182. Salt That Necessary Item; p. 146.
183. Winston-Salem, a History; p. 102.
184. Many Excellent People; p. 78.
185. The Papers of Zebulon Baird Vance, Volume I; p. 280-281.
186. Rebels in Blue; p. 113.
187. Jay B. Hubbell Papers. Perkins Library, Duke University; Eller Family Letters & Papers.
188. Doctor to the Front; p.147.
189. Rebel Boast; p. 227; Whitaker—43rd NCT.
190. Courtesy of John Humphrey; letter to Angus McPhail from Daniel McPhail.
191. Lenoir Family Papers; Documenting the American South, Wilson Library, UNC-CH; July 25, '63.
192. Cart, Doran L. "A Soldier's Conscience, the Letters of Thomas F. Price," Camp Chase Gazette, July/August 1987.
193. Courtesy of Scott Troutman, North Carolina Postal Historical Society newsletter, "Sinful Doings in Stokes County." p. 13.
194. McGee, David, editor, "The TL Morrison Letters, Part II," Company Front. January/February 1990.
195. Tragedy at Montpelier, the Untold Story of Ten Confederate Deserters from North Carolina;" p.122, July 31, '63.
196. Tillinghast Family Papers. Perkins Library, Duke University.
197. Tragedy at Montpelier; p. 66.
198. IBID; p. 64 May, 1863.
199. IBID; p. 73-74.
200. No Soap, No Pay, Diarrhea, Dysentery and Desertion; p. 18.
201. Tragedy at Montpelier; p. 79.
202. IBID; p. 83-90 September 5, '63.
203. Making of a Confederate; p. 130.
204. Many Excellent People: Power and Privilege in North Carolina 1850-1900; p. 83.
205. Tillinghast Family Papers. Perkins Library, Duke University; August 22, '63, Rutherford, from Sarah A. Tillinghast.
206. Many Excellent People; p. 83.
207. Southern Stories; p. 137.

208. Jay B. Hubbell, Perkins Library. Duke University; Eller Family Letters & Papers.
209. History of Brunswick County; p. 158.
210. Ashe County's Civil War; p. 153.
211. The Civil War in North Carolina; p. 186.
212. Eberhart, James W. "Diary of Salisbury Prison." *Western Pennsylvania Historical Magazine*, July 1973. Florence McLaughlin, ed.; p. 38.
213. Prologue Magazine, "War Within;" p. 83.
214. NCHR, "Women's Role;" p. 55.
215. North Carolina Argus, March 26, `63.
216. IBID; November 29, `64.
217. IBID; July 21, `64.
218. Ashe County's Civil War; p. 153.
219. IBID; p. 145.
220. Rebels in Blue; p. 57.
221. Victims, a True Story of the Civil War; p. 67.
222. The Story of Henderson County; p. 128.
223. North Carolina Experience; p. 276, April 23, `63.
224. Rebels in Blue; p. 57.
225. The History of Alleghany County; p. 252, letter to Alax Black from Dave Black, December 25, `64.
226. They Went into the Fight Cheering; p. 145.
227. Fear in North Carolina; p. 160, September 20, `63.
228. Rebels in Blue; p. 100.
229. NCHR, "Women's Role," p. 45.
230. Making of a Confederate; p. 101.
231. Lenoir Family Papers. Documenting the American South, Wilson Library, UNC-CH; Joseph Norwood to Walter Lenoir, August 13, `63.
232. IBID
233. Postmarks; p. 294.
234. The Papers of Zebulon Baird Vance, Volume 2; p. 188, July 10, `63.
235. Shuttle and Plow, a History of Alamance County; p. 280.
236. Richmond County and the Civil War; p. 436.
237. Greensborough Patriot, May 14, `63.
238. Raleigh Register, August 5, `62.
239. The Civil War on the Outer Banks; p. 121.
240. The Heart of Confederate Appalachia, Western North Carolina in the Civil War; p. 128.
241. Portraits of Conflict, a Photographic History of North Carolina in the Civil War; p. 44.
242. Official Records, Series L, Volume XLVII; p. 1354; hereafter known as O.R.
243. Sigmon, Mark, transcriber. "A Personal History of the 49th NC Regiment, Part II, A Reminiscence," *Company Front*, July, 1996; p. 6.
244. Last Ninety Days of the War; p. 243.
245. Interview with descendent Peter Edwards, 2004.
246. Mary S.M. Buie Papers. Perkins Library, Duke University; letter to a cousin February 1, 1864.
247. Courtesy of Myrtle Bridges [Weekly Standard, November 25, `63].
248. Two Centuries at Sycamore Springs Plantation; p. 170.
249. Letters of Jonathan Worth; courtesy of Alexander Street Press, Civil War Letters and .Diaries; letter from his overseer in Chatham County to Jonathan Worth, December 12, `62
250. Davie County, a Brief History; p. 78.
251. Weekly News, Volume 4, #5; July 30, `62.
252. Anonymous citation; Letter from J.M. Sneed to A.M. Gray; March 20, `65.
253. Many Excellent People: Power and Privilege in North Carolina 1850-1900; p. 76-77.
254. To Die Game; p. 39.
255. IBID; p. 44.
256. IBID; p. 45, 47, 54, 59, 57.
257. The Cruel Side of War; May 30, `62.

258. Barrett, John, "General Sherman's March Through North Carolina," *North Carolina Historical Review*, Spring, 1965; p. 195.

259. O.R. Series I, Part II, Volume XLVII, p. 1312.

260. old period newspaper.

261. Confederate States Bureau of Conscription, 7th District. Wilson Library, UNC-CH.

262. Beaufort County, Two Centuries of its History; p. 175.

CHAPTER ELEVEN ENDNOTES

1. Southern Rights; p. 146, 133.

2. Disloyalty in the Confederacy; p. 8.

3. Southern Rights; p. 87-88.

4. Auman, William, "Neighbor Against Neighbor: The Inner Civil War in the Randolph County Area of Confederate North Carolina," *North Carolina Historical Review*. January, 1984, Volume LXI, #1; p. 59; hereafter cited as "Neighbor."

5. Mary Hunter Kennedy Papers. Southern Historical Collection, Wilson Library, UNC-CH.

6. Many Excellent People: Power And Privilege in North Carolina 1850-1900; p. 83; hereafter cited as Many Excellent People.

7. Making of a Confederate; p. 56-57.

8. IBID; p. 56, 30-31.

9. Disloyalty in the Confederacy; p. 3.

10. A Family of Women; p. 155.

11. Unruly Women; p. 133.

12. Dix, Mary S., editor, "And Three Rousing Cheers for the Privates: a Diary of the 1862 Roanoke Island Expedition." [Diary Henry W. Gangewer, 51st PA] *North Carolina Historical Review*, January 1994, Volume LXXXI, #1; p. 76 and February 27, `62 entry.

13. Thomas Merrill Papers. North Carolina Department of Archives & History.

14. Justice or Atrocity; p. 69.

15. New Hanover Criminal Court Records, microfilm.

16. North Carolina in 1861; p. 96.

17. Harris, William C. "Lincoln and Wartime Reconstruction in North Carolina., 1861-1863." *North Carolina Historical Review*. April 1986, Volume LXIII, #2; p. 152; hereafter cited as "Lincoln and Wartime."

18. Henry T. Clark Papers. North Carolina Department of Archives & History. [his scrapbook]

19. Biographical History of North Carolina, Volume 5; p. 370.

20. NCHR, "Lincoln and Wartime," p. 152.

21. Journal of a Secesh Lady; p. 596.

22. The North Carolina Experience. "Diary of Thomas Bragg;" p. 274.

23. War of Another Kind; p. 216.

24. Williams, Max R. "The Johnston Will Case: a Clash of Titans." *North Carolina Historical Review*, April 1990; p. 201; hereafter cited as "The Johnson Will Case."

25. The Civil War on the Outer Banks; p. 118, 130.

26. Journal of a Secesh Lady; p. 242.

27. Divided Allegiances; page XII.

28. Prologue Magazine, "War Within the Confederacy: White Unionists in Confederate North Carolina." by Michael Honey; p. 86; hereafter cited as "War Within."

29. Divided Allegiances; p. 38, 107.

30. War of Another Kind; p. 108, 44.

31. IBID; p. 124.

32. Southern Rights; p. 128.

33. "War Within," p. 83.

34. NCHR, "The Johnston Will Case;" p. 202.

35. History of the 15th Connecticut Volunteers in the War for the Defense of the Union; p. 142.

36. War of Another Kind; p. 166.

37. Divided Allegiances; p. 105.

38. IBID; p. 69.
39. War of Another Kind; p. 186.
40. Governor's Vance's Speech, May 17, 1864, Documenting the American South, UNC-CH.
41. Corpening Papers. Perkins Library, Duke University.
42. Daily Conservative, January 26, `65.
43. The Heritage of Chowan County, Volume I; p. 74.
44. Divided Allegiances; page XIV.
45. To Bear Arms; p. 214.
46. War of Another Kind; p. 169.
47. "A Sermon: Preached Before Brig-Gen. Hoke's Brigade at Kinston, North Carolina, on the 28th of February, 1864, by Reverend John Paris, Chaplain Fifty-Fourth Regiment North Carolina Troops, Upon the Death of Twenty-Two Men Who Had Been Executed in the Presence of the Brigade For the Crime of Desertion." Documenting the American South, UNC-CH.
48. Justice or Atrocity; p. 104.
49. Wayne County Heritage; p. 18.
50. John B. Crenshaw Letters #B4. Friends Historical Collection, Hege Library, Guilford College; Delphina Mendenhall to J.B. Crenshaw, January 10, `63.
51. IBID; Letter #A10; from N.Y. Perkins to J.B. Crenshaw, November 11, `62.
52. IBID; Letter #B7; D.E. Mendenhall to J.B. Crenshaw, February 11, `63.
53. IBID, Letter B10; D.E. Mendenhall to J.B. Crenshaw, March 31, `63.
54. Wayne County Heritage; p. 18.
55. Southern Rights; p. 130-131, 164.
56. Shuttle and Plow, a History of Alamance County, North Carolina; p. 295; hereafter cited as Shuttle and Plow.
57. Silk Flags and Cold Steel; p. 183; hereafter cited as "Silk Flags."
58. North Carolina in 1861; p. 35.
59. The North Carolina Experience: an Interpretive and Documentary History; p. 274.
60. Raleigh Standard copied from the Daily Progress, April 24, `65.
61. Elle's Book; p. 21.
62. Chatham County 1771-1971; p. 138.
63. NCHR, "Neighbor," p. 61.
64. Winston-Salem, a History; p. 100.
65. Anson County, North Carolina Abstract of Wills 1750-1880; p. 144.
66. Right, D.L. "Salem in the War," North Carolina Historical Review, July 1950, Volume XXVII, #3; p. 16
67. "A Storm in the Land." Moravian Conference, November 5, 2005 in Old Salem, North Carolina.
68. IBID
69. Prologue Magazine, "War Within" — article #28.
70. Mary Baker Hinshaw: Quaker; p. 102-116.
71. North Carolina Works Progress Administration Guide to the Old North Sate; p. 486.
72. Piedmont Soldiers and their Families; p. 22.
73. Many Excellent People: Power and Privilege in North Carolina 1850-1900; p. 75.
74. Schroder, Greg, "Dear Burwell," Awakenings: Writings and Reminiscences of Eastern North Carolina Women; p. 35.
75. The North Carolina Experience; p. 274, Diary of Thomas Bragg.
76. Company Front, December, 1996; "Letters from the Front," n.a.; Letter from J.E. Yancey Albright at Drewy's Bluff to his parents. November 14, `62.
77. Professor Victoria Bynum's Lecture, Raleigh, 1999. Letter from Phebe Crook, a Unionist, to Governor Vance, September 16, `64; or Unruly Women; p. 143.
78. Courtesy of Myrtle Bridges, www.rootsweb.com/~ncharnett. Weekly Standard, November 25, `63.
79. NCHR, "Neighbors;" p. 92.
80. The Civil War in North Carolina, Volume I; letter from Mary Satterfield, Roxboro, to her son, William in the 55th NCT, March 4, `65; p. 198.
81. The Heart of Confederate Appalachia; p. 193
82. Crawford, Martin, "Dynamics of Mountain Unionism," The Civil War in Appalachia; p. 58; hereafter cited as "Dynamics."

83. North Carolina in 1861; p. 35.

84. McKinney, Gordon, "Women's Role in Civil War Western North Carolina." *North Carolina Historical Review.* January 1992, Volume LXIX, #1; p. 86; hereafter cited as "Women's Role."

85. Ashe County's Civil War: Community and Society in the Appalachian South; p. 100; hereafter cited as "Ashe County's."

86. Victims, a True Story of the Civil War; p. 69.

87. Postmarks; p. 263-264.

88. Rebels in Blue; p. 65.

89. Western North Carolina, a History 1730-1913; p. 614-615.

90. Sketches of Polk County History; p. 41.

91. Ashe County's Civil War; p. 132.

92. Victims, a True Story of the Civil War; p. 61.

93. The Heart of Confederate Appalachia; p. 91.

94. NCHR, "Women's Role;" p. 91, 68.

95. Rebels in Blue; p. 102.

96. The Heart of Confederate Appalachia; p. 123.

97. Storm in the Mountains; p. 51.

98. The Field, the Dungeon, and the Escape; p. 422.

99. Rebels in Blue; p. 130.

100. Lenoir Family Papers. Documenting the American South, UNC-CH.

101. Courtesy of descendant Lila Ford.

102. The Heart of Confederate Appalachia; p. 191, 129.

103. IBID; p. 197.

104. IBID; p. 201.

105. NCHR, "Women's Role;" p. 91.

106. Amnesty Letter #256, roll 43, July 15, 1865; Berea College, Digital Appalachia.

107. The Heart of Confederate Appalachia; p. 197, 171.

108. Victims, a True Story of the Civil War; p. 76.

109. NCHR, "Women's Role;" p. 43.

110. Taylor, James, "The Killings of Shelton Laurel," *Company Front,* August/September 1989; p. 6; hereafter cited as "The Killings."

111. NCHR, "Women's Role," p. 46.

112. Victims, a True Story of the Civil War; p. 77.

113. Corpening Papers. Perkins Library, Duke University; letter July 19, `63, most likely from Ann Ramseur to her brother, Joseph.

114. Victims, a True Story of the Civil War; p. 21-footnote.

115. IBID; p. 57, 21.

116. Company Front, "The Killings;" p. 6-7.

117. Victims, a True Story of the Civil War; p. 85.

118. Partisan Campaigns of Col. Lawrence M. Allen, Commanding the 64th Regiment, North Carolina State Troops During the Late Civil War; p. 9.

119. Victims, a True Story of the Civil War; p. 85, 89.

120. Company Front, "The Killings;" p. 8.

121. OR, Series II, Volume V; p. 836, 838-839.

122. The Heart of Confederate Appalachia; p. 100, 104.

123. Memoirs of W.W. Holden; p.27-29. Documenting the American South, UNC-CH.

124. Cathey Family Papers. Hunter Library, Western Carolina University.

125. Disloyalty in the Confederacy; p. 123; Martha Revis, Madison County, 1863.

126. The Heart of Confederate Appalachia; p. 101.

127. Victims, a True Story of the Civil War; p. 96.

128. The Heart of Confederate Appalachia; p. 238-240.

129. Weekly Progress, May 17, `64.

130. Eller Family Letters contained in the Jay Hubbell Family Papers. Perkins Library, Duke University.

131. IBID; Eller Family, letter from my mother, Ruth Eller Hubbell to her grandchildren, August 15, 1931 *and* letter from Harvey A. Eller, Bina, NC, to Adolphus H. Eller, September 21, 1931.
132. IBID H.A. Eller to his brother A.H. Eller.
133. IBID
134. Lenoir Family Papers. Documenting the American South, UNC-CH.
135. IBID
136. Making of a Confederate; p. 134.
137. Rebels in Blue; p. 112 .
138. IBID; p. 86.
139. Here Will I Dwell; p. 136.
140. http://scholars.lib.vt.edu/faculty-archives/mountain-slavery/civilwar.htm
141. The Civil War in Yadkin County; p. 79, 151.
142. IBID; p. 79.
143. Greensboro Daily News, October 4, 1925; "Aunt Nancy Willard, Yadkin County, Recalls Troubled Days of the Civil War," by Harvey Dinkins. Courtesy of Thad Wiseman.
144. IBID
145. Western North Carolina, a History; "A Spartan Mother," p. 611.
146. War at Every Door; p. 76.
147. Richmond Daily Dispatch, April 20, `63.
148. Western North Carolina, a History, "An Old Man, My Lord;" p. 612.
149. IBID
150. http://scholars.lib.vt.edu/faculty-archives/mountain-slavery/civilwar.htm
151. Western North Carolina, a History; p. 614-616.
152. IBID, "A Civil War Joan of Arc;" p. 616.
153. The History of Alleghany County; p. 252-253; letter from Dave Black to Alax Black, December 25, `64.
154. Crawford, Martin, "The Dynamics of Mountain Unionism," *The Civil War in Appalachia;* p. 69.
155. Courtesy of William A. and Mary M. Burgess Gentry, descendants, Cherokee County.
156. NCHR, "Neighbors," p. 64.
157. Shuttle and Plow; p. 296.
158. O.R., Series I, Volume 25, Part II; p. 746-747.
159. War of Another Kind; p. 186-187.
160. Auman, William T. "Bryan Tyson: Southern Unionist and American Patriot." *North Carolina Historical Review.* July 1985. *Volume LXII, #3;* p. 264; hereafter cited as "Byran Tyson."
161. IBID; p. 261, 263.
162. Dictionary of North Carolina. Biography, Volume 6; p. 71-72.
163. Shuttle and Plow; p. 296.
164. NCHR, "Neighbors;" p. 61.
165. Disloyalty in the Confederacy; p. 134, 130.
166. Auman, William T., "The Heroes of America in Civil War North Carolina." *North Carolina Historical Review.* Autumn 1981, Volume LVIII, #4; p. 341; hereafter cited as "HOAs."
167. Shuttle and Plow; p. 298-299.
168. NCHR, "Bryan Tyson;" p. 257.
169. The Field, the Dungeon, the Escape; p. 429, 438.
170. Scarboro, David D. "N.C. and the Confederacy: The Weakness of States' Rights during the Civil War." *North Carolina Historical Review.* April 1979, Volume LVI, #2; p. 141-142; hereafter cited as "Weakness."
171. Prologue Magazine, "War Within;" p. 86.
172. NCHR, "HOAs;" p. 352.
173. Disloyalty in the Confederacy; p. 134, 33.
174. Silk Flags; p. 182.
175. Spies and Spymasters in the Civil War; p. 27.
176. Disloyalty in the Confederacy; p. 120, 133.
177. NCHR, "Women' Role;" p. 38.
178. North Carolina in 1861; p. 129.
179. Amnesty Letter #65, roll 38 July 29, `65; Berea College, Digital Appalachia.

180. Z.B. Vance's Speech, May 17, `64. Documenting the American South, UNC-CH.
181. Letter to Turner Westry at Rocky Mount, from his brother-in-law. Courtesy of Sally Koestler. www.sallysfamilyplace.co/yankies.htm
182. History of North Carolina Since 1860; p. 43.
183. Johnston, Hugh B. "The Civil War Letters of Ruffin Barnes," *North Carolina Historical Review*. January 1954, Volume XXXI, #4; letter September 8, `64; p. 84.
184. Rebel Boast; p. 227.
185. Letter from J.M. Sneed to A.M. Gray, November 23, `64; anonymous citation.
186. IBID; letter December 28, `64.
187. IBID; letter February 2, `65.
188. Bright and Gloomy Days; p. 108, February 8, `64.
189. "Dear Burwell;" p. 38.
190. Bright and Gloomy Days; p. 218.
191. NCHR, "Bryan Tyson;" p. 280.
192. Many Excellent People; p. 76.
193. Southern Railroad Man; p. 33.
194. The Heart of Confederate Appalachia; p. 162.
195. Shuttle and Plow; p. 299.
196. Bright and Gloomy Days; p. 177.
197. IBID; p. 181.
198. Jonathan Worth, a Biography of a Southern Unionist; p. 180.
199. The Confederate States of America, 1861-1865; p. 234, December 30, `63.
200. Sanders, Charles W. Jr. "Jefferson Davis and the Hampton Roads Peace Conference: to secure peace to the two centuries." *Journal of Southern History*. November 1997, Volume LXIII, #4; p. 825; hereafter cited as "Jeff Davis and Hampton Roads."
201. Disloyalty in the Confederacy; p. 133.
202. Thomas F. Wood Papers. Perkins Library, Duke University; letter November 11, `63 from Will George Thomas to Dr. T.F. Wood.
203. Kirkland's of Ayr Mount; p. 165; *and* the Smithfield Herald, February 23, 1954.
204. Western North Carolina, a History, "A Peaceful Overture;" p. 639-640.
205. "Jefferson Davis and Hampton Roads;" p. 820, 804-805.
206. IBID; p. 810.
207. Yates, Richard, "Governor Vance and the End of the War in N.C." *North Carolina Historical Review*. October 1941, Volume XVIII, #4; p. 319.
208. The Heart of Confederate Appalachia; p. 164.
209. Jones, Houston G. "Bedford Brown: States Rights Unionist-Part II." *North Carolina Historical Review*. August 1955, Volume XXXII; p.503.
210. NCHR, Byran Tyson; p. 266.

APPENDIX END NOTES

1. Ch. 1, #A: "Luola" in Miles A. Cavin Papers. North Carolina Department of Archives & History. Credited to M. A. Brown.
2. Ch. 1, #B: When the Past Refused to Die; p. 185.
3. Ch. 1, #C: The Story of Lenoir County and Kinston, North Carolina; p. 45; from the Wait & Leone Hines Collection, NCADH.
4. Ch. 1, #D: Procedure to Gain Passes in Both Directions.
5. Ch. 2, #A: North Carolina Women of the Confederacy; p. 111.
6. Ch. 3, #AA: Richmond County & the Civil War; p. 36-37.
7. Ch. 4, #A: Confederate Court Records, Pamlico County, Eastern District. North Carolina Department of Archives & History, microfilm.
8. Ch. 4, #B: Courtesy of Roger Johnson.
9. Ch. 4, #C: Guide for the Inspection of the Hospitals & for the Inspector's Report. Documenting the American South, UNC.

10. Ch. 4, #D: E. Burke Haywood Papers. Southern Historical Collection, Wilson Library. UNC-CH.

11. Ch. 4, #E: Civil War Richmond. Courtesy of Mike Gorman.

12. Ch. 4: Doctors in Gray; p. 54 and History of North Carolina since 1860; p. 287.

13. Ch. 4: William A. Holt Papers. Southern Historical Collection, Wilson Library. UNC-CH.

14. Ch. 4, #F: Augusta Daily Chronicle & Sentential, August 29, `62; courtesy of Vicki Betts.

15. Ch. 4, #G: Jacobs, Joseph, "Some of the Drug Conditions During the War Between the States." Southern Historical Society Papers. Volume 33; p. 161-187.

16. Ch. 4, #H: IBID; p. 14.

17. Ch. 4, #I: a Charlotte newspaper, war years.

18. Ch. 4, #J: Richmond Daily Dispatch, July 4, `64.

19. Ch. 4, #K: List of political prisoners in Salisbury. Documenting the American South. UNC. #1278conf.c.2

20. Ch. 5, #A: Report of the Freed People by Vincent Colyer.

21. Ch. 8, #C: Orange County Records, microfilm.

22. Ch. 8, #D: The Papers of Zebulon Baird Vance, Volume I; p. 410-411.

23. Ch. 8, #E: Chatham County 1771-1971; p. 140.

24. Ch. 8, #F: Corpening Papers. Perkins Library, Duke University.

25. Ch. 8, #G: Frances M. Manning Papers. Joyner Library, ECU.

26. Ch. 10, #A: E. Burke Haywood papers. Southern Historical Collection, Wilson Library. UNC-CH.

27. Ch. 10, #B: The Papers of Zebulon Baird Vance, Volume I; p. 280-281.

28. Ch. 11, #A: Oath of Allegiance. Documenting the American South. UNC, #970 74N87al.

LIST OF ABBREVIATIONS

Names or sources used repeatedly are abbreviated:

C.O.I . . . . Camp of Instruction
CS . . . . Confederate
CSA . . . Confederate States of America
ECU . . . . East Carolina University
MOC . . . Museum of the Confederacy, Richmond
N.C.O . . . . Non-commissioned Officers
NCT . . . . .North Carolina Troops
NCC . . . . .North Carolina Collection, UNC-CH
NCDAH . . . . North Carolina Department of Archives and History
NCHR . . . . .North Carolina Historical Review
P.A.C . . . . a Moravian/Quaker term meaning Provinzial Aeltesten Conferenz
POW . . . . Prisoners of War
SHSP . . . . Southern Historical Society Papers
UDC . . . . United Daughters of the Confederacy
UNC . . . University of North Carolina at Chapel Hill
US . . . . United States
VMI . . . . Virginia Military Institute
WCU . . . Western Carolina University
WFU . . . . Wake Forest University

"Cards" . . . . not the playing kind, but wool/cotton combs for breaking down the fibers in preparation for spinning
Flying . . . . usually running around, sparking, or dating
"Janes" or "jeans" . . . . jeans cloth . . . the strong wool/cotton weave cloth, not like today's blue jeans
"Press" . . . means to impress items, to commandeer them for military purposes
Outlyers, outliers . . . . men hiding from Confederate authorities
The cars . . . railroad cars, the train
Tories . . . . usually referred to as persons loyal to the U.S.

BIBLIOGRAPHY

Abel, E. Lawrence. *Singing the New Nation.* Stackpole Books. 2000.

Abbott, John S.C. "Heroic Deeds of Heroic Men—The Expedition to Goldsboro." *Harper's New Monthly Magazine.* May-Dec. 1864.

Absher, W O. *The Heritage of Wilkes County.* Winston-Salem, NC, Wilkes County Genealogical Society in co-operation with Hunter Publishing Co. 1982.

Address at the Unveiling of the Memorial to the North Carolina Women of the Confederacy . . . ECU digital library

Agnew, Dr. C.R.. "Extracts from a Letter of Dr. CR Agnew, of the U.S. Sanitary Commission," *United States Sanitary Commission Bulletin,* No.35. Philadelphia, April 1, 1865.

Albemarle County Historical Society, editors. *The Magazine of Albemarle County History, Volume XXII.* The Mitchie Company, printers. 1964.

Alexander, Adele L. *Homelands and Waterways, The American Journey of the Bond Family, 1846-1926.* New York, Pantheon Books. 1999.

Alexander, Nancy. *Here Will I Dwell; the Story of Caldwell County.* Salisbury, Rowan Printing Co. 1956.

Anderson, Jean B. *Piedmont Plantation.* Durham, Printed by the Historical Preservation of Durham. 1985

Anderson, Jean Bradley. *The Kirklands of Ayr Mount.* Chapel Hill, U.N.C. Press. 1991.

Anderson, Lucy "Last Days of the Confederacy in North Carolina," *Confederate Veteran,* Volume XXXVII. 1931.

Anderson, Lucy. *North Carolina Women of the 1860's.* n. p. n.d.

Anderson, Lucy. *North Carolina Women of the Confederacy.* Self-published. Cumberland Printing Co. 1926.

Anderson, Lucy. *Scrapbook of Fayetteville and Cumberland County.* n.p., n.d.

Andreano, Ralph. *The Economic Impact of the American Civil War.* Cambridge, Schenkman Publishing Co., Inc. 1962.

Andrews, Matthew P. *Women of the South in War Times.* Baltimore, the Norman, Remington Co., 1920.

Angley, Wilson. *A History of Fort Johnson on the Lower Cape Fear.* Published by the Southport Historical Society in Association with the Division of Archives and History. Broadfoot Publishing Co. 1996.

Aragon, Lorraine V. *Sandhills Families: Early Reminiscences of the Fort Bragg Area.* Cultural Resources Management Program, Environmental and Natural Resources Division, Fort Bragg, N.C. 2004.

Archbell, Lillie V., editor. *Carolina and the Southern Cross.* Volume I-II, 1912-1914. Volume I, Number I .

Arnett, Ethel S. *Confederate Guns Were Stacked.* Greensboro, N.C., Piedmont Press. 1965.

Arnett, Ethel S. *O. Henry of Polecat Creek.* Greensboro, Piedmont Press. 1963.

Arnett, Ethel Stephens. *Greensboro, North Carolina.* U.N.C. Press. 1955.

Arnold, Robert. *The Dismal Swamp and Lake Drummond—Early Recollection,—Vivid Portrayal of Amusing Scenes.* Norfolk, Green, Burke & Gregory, Printers. 1888.

Arthur, John Preston. *Western North Carolina, A History (1730-1913).* Published by the Buncombe Chapter of the Daughters of the American Revolution of Asheville, North Carolina. Edwards & Broughton Printing Company. 1914.

Ashe, Samuel and Charles Van Hoppen . *Biographical History of North Carolina.* Volume V, MCMVI. Greensboro, Charles L. Van Hoppen, Publisher. 1902.

Auman, William T., "Neighbor Against Neighbor: The Inner Civil War in Randolph County Area of Confederate North Carolina." *North Carolina Historical Review.* Volume LXI, #1, January. 1984.

Auman, William. "Bryan Tyson: Southern Unionist and American Patriot." *North Carolina Historical Review.* Volume LXII, #3, July, 1985.

Auman, William. "The Heroes of America in the Civil War, North Carolina," *North Carolina Historical Review.* Volume LVIII, #4. Autumn, 1981.

Avery, William B. *The Marine Artillery With the Burnside Expedition and the Battle of Camden, North Carolina.* 1st Regiment Marine Artillery. Providence, R.I., Soldiers and Sailor's Historical Society of Rhode Island, #4, 2nd Series. Bangs Williams & Co. 1880.

Avirett, James Battle. *How We Lived in the Great House and Cabin Before the War.* New York, N.Y., F. Tennyson Neely Company. 1901.

Axelrod, Alan. *The War Between the Spies.* New York, Atlantic Monthly Press. 1992.

Bailey, Anthony. *The Outer Banks.* Michael diCapua Books. New York, Farrar, Straus, & Giroux Publishing. 1989.

Ball, John. *Escape From Dixie.* Williamsville, N.Y., Goldstar Enterprises. 1996.

Barden, John R., Editor. *Letters to the Home Circle.* Raleigh, Division of Archives and History, N.C. Department of Cultural Resources.1998.

Barfield, Rodney. "The Chicamacomico Races." *The State,* May, 1992.

Barney, William L. *The Making of a Confederate.* Oxford University Press, 2009.

Barrett, John G. *American Civil War Battleground 1861-1865.* Division of Archives & History, N.C. Department of Cultural Resources. 1980.

Barrett, John G. *Sherman's March Through the Carolinas.* U.N.C. Press. 1956.

Barrett, John G. "General Sherman's March Through North Carolina" *North Carolina Historical Review,* Spring, 1965.

Barringer, Dr. Paul B. *The Natural Bent.* U.N.C. Press. 1949.

Barrow, Charles, and J.H. Segars, and R.B. Rosenburg. "Forgotten Confederates, An Anthology About Black Southerners." *Journal of Confederate History Series..* Volume XIV, Southern Heritage Press. 1995.

Barry, Sgt. Royal. "The Sergeant's Story," *History of the Forty-fifth Regiment Massachusetts Volunteer Militia: "the Cadet Regiment."* Jamaica Plains, Mass. Brookside Printing. 1908.

Battle, Kemp P. *Memories of an Old-Time Tar-heel.* U.N.C. Press. 1945.

Belew, Kenneth. *Cavalry Clash in the Sandhills: the Battle of Monroe's Crossroads North Carolina.* Published by Dept. of the Interior, NPS. Midwest Archeological Center. 1997.

Bellamy, Ellen. *Back With the Tide.* n.p. 1941.

Bellamy, John D. *Memories of an Octogenarian.* Charlotte, Observer Printing House. 1942. ECU digital series.

Benjamin, W.S. *The Great Epidemic in New Berne and Vicinity.* New Berne, N.C. Published by George Mills Joy. 1865.

Berlin, I., B. Fields, S. Miller, J. Reidy, and L. Rowland. *Free At Last.* New York, The New Press. 1992.

Berlin, Jean V. Editor. *A Confederate Nurse: The Diary of Ada W. Bacot.* University of South Carolina Press. 1994.

Betts, Rev. Alex D. *Experiences of a Confederate Chaplain.* Published by his son, Rev. W.A. Betts, n.d.

Biggs, Greg and Karen. "Uncovering the Business of the Confederacy," *Citizens' Companion.* Volume X, #5, Susan L. Hughes, editor.

Bishir, Catherine W. *The Bellamy Mansion.* Published by the Bellamy Mansion Museum of History and Design Arts. 2003.

Bivans, John Jr. *Long Rifles of North Carolina.* Published by George Shumway. 1968.

Black, Robert. *Railroads of the Confederacy.* Chapel Hill, U.N.C. Press. 1998.

Black, W.W. "The Civil War Letters of E.N. Boots," *North Carolina Historical Review.* Volume XXXVI, #2, April, 1959.

Blackmun, Ora. *Western North Carolina: Its Mountains and its People to 1880.* Appalachian Consortium Press. 1977.

Blair, Jayne. *Tragedy at Montpelier, the Untold Story of Ten Confederate Deserters from North Carolina.* Heritage Books, Inc. 2003.

Blair, Marian H., editor. "Civil War Letters of Henry W. Barrow to John W. Fries" *North Carolina Historical Review.* January, 1957.

Blanton, DeAnne and Lauren M. Cook. *They Fought Like Demons.* L.S.U. Press. 2002.

Boaz, Thomas. *Guns for Cotton, England Arms the Confederacy.* Burd Street Press. 1996.

Boggs, S.S. *Eighteen Months a Prisoner Under the Rebel Flag.* Self-published in Lovington, Illinois. 1887.

Bolton, Charles C. *Poor Whites of the Antebellum South.* Durham, Duke University Press. 1994.

Boykin, James H. *North Carolina in 1861.* New Haven, Conn. Bookman Assoc., N.Y., United Printing Services, Inc. 1961.

Boyd, William K. "Conditions During the Civil War." *North Carolina Booklet.*

Boyko, Beverly A. and William H. Kern, editors. *Cemeteries of Fort Bragg, Camp MacKall and Pope Air Force Base North Carolina.* United States Army. October, 2005.

Bradley, George S. *The Star Corps: or, Notes of an Army Chaplain, During Sherman's Famous march to the Sea.* Milwaukee, WI: Jermain & Brightman Printers. 1865.

Bradley, Mark. *Last Stand in the Carolinas.* Savas Publishing Co., 1996.

Bradley, Mark. *This Outstanding Close . . . The Road to the Bennett Place.* Chapel Hill, N.C., UNC Press. 2000.

Bradley, Dr. Stephen, Jr. *North Carolina Confederate Home Guard Exams 1863-1864.* Keysville, VA. Self-published. 1993.

Bradley, Stephen E. *North Carolina Confederate Militia Officers Roster, as Contained in the Adjutant-general's Officer Roster, Volume 1.* Wilmington, N.C., Broadfoot Publishing Co. 1992.

Bremmer, Robert H. *The Public Good: Philanthropy & Welfare in the Civil War Era.* New York, Alfred A. Knopf. 1980.

Brett, Sally; Everatt; Kinlaw, and Peek. *Awakenings: Writing and Recollections of Eastern North Carolina Women.* "Dear Burwell," by Greg Schroder. N.P. Printed by Schroder, Stephenson, and Sutherland. 1978.

Brockett, Linus P. and Mary C. Vaughan. *Woman's Work in the Civil War: A Record of Heroism, Patriotism & Patience.* King & Baird Printers. 1867.

Brooks, Aubrey and Hugh Lefler, editors. *The Papers of Walter Clark.* Volume I, 1857-1901. Chapel Hill, U.N.C. Press. 1948.

Brotherton, Ken. *A Civil War Tragedy: the Lipe Family.* Davidson, N.C. Howard and Broughton Printers. n.d.

Brown, Alonzo L. *History of the 4th Regiment Minnesota Infantry Volunteers During the Rebellion.* St. Paul, Minnesota. Pioneer Press. 1892.

Brown, Joseph P. *The Commonwealth of Onslow County, A History.* O.G.Dunn, Publisher. 1960.

Brown, Louis A. *The Salisbury Prison.* Wendell, Avera Press, Broadfoot's Bookmark. 1980.

Brown, Louis A., editor. "The Correspondence of David Olando McRaven and Amanda Nantz McRaven, 1864-1865," *North Carolina Historical Review.* Volume 26, January, 1949.

Brown, Mary. *A Call To Arms.* Raleigh, Thompson & Company, Printers. 1861.

Brown, Norman D. *Edward Stanley: Whiggery's Tarheel "Conqueror."* University of Alabama Press. 1974.

Brown, Susan W. *The Wagg Family of Ashe County.* n.p. 1995.

Brown, Frank. *North Carolina Folklore.* Duke University Press. 1952.

Brown, T. Frank. "These Toils and Hardships," *Company Front, Part I-II, Volume 2, 2002 and Volume I, 2003.* Published by the 26th N.C.T. Re-activated.

Brownlee, Fambrough L. *Winston-Salem, a Pictorial History.* Norfolk, Donning Company Publishers. 1977.

Browning, Judkin. "Removing the Mask of Nationality: Unionism, Racism, and Federal Military Occupation in North Carolina 1862-1865." *Journal of Southern History,* Volume LXXI, #3, August 2005. Published by the Southern Historical Associates.

Bruney, Sandra. "Yankees in Anson County," *State Magazine.* October, 1992.

Bryan, Mary Norcott. *A Grandmother's Recollection of Dixie.* New Bern, N.C., Owen Dunn Printer, n.d.

Budington, W.I. *A Memorial of Giles F. Ward, Late First Lieutenant Twelfth New York Cavalry.* Published by Anson D.F. Randolph in N.Y. 1866.

Bullard, E.M. "The Civil War Comes to Sampson Co" *Huckleberry Historian,* Volume 30, #111 July, 2008.

Bumgarner, Matthew. *Kirk's Raiders.* Hickory, N.C., Tarheel Press, LLC Publishers. 2000.

Bumgarner, Matthew. *My Face to the Enemy.* Hickory, Tarheel Press. Printed by Westmoreland Printers. 2001.

Bunch, Jack . *A Roster of the Courts Martial in the Confederate States.* Shippensburg, Pa., White Mane Books. 2001.

Burke, Kenneth. "The History of Portsmouth, North Carolina." *North Carolina Historical Review,* Volume LXXI, #1. January, 1994.

Butler, Lindley S. and Alan D. Watson. *The North Carolina Experience: An Interpretive and Documentary History.* Chapel Hill, N.C., U.N.C. Press. 1984.

Butler, Lindley S. *Rockingham County: A Brief History.* Raleigh, North Carolina Department of Archives and History. 1982.

Bynum, Victoria. *Unruly Women.* Chapel Hill, U.N.C. Press. 1992.

Byrd, William L. III. *North Carolina Slaves & Free Persons of Color, Chowan County.* Volume I. Heritage Books. 2003.

Cain, Elizabeth Frost. "When the Yankees Came Through, As Told to Annie Laurie Etchison." A Transcription. Davie County Library. 1936.

Carpenter, Reva N. compiler. *Anson County, North Carolina; Abstract of Wills 1750-1880.* San Diego, California. Grasshopper Press. 1976.

Carr, Dawson. *Gray Phantoms of the Cape Fear.* Winston-Salem, John Blair Publishing Co. 1998.

Carroll, Karen A. "Sterling, Campbell, and Albright: Textbook Publishers, 1861-1865." *North Carolina Historical Review,* Volume LXIII, Number 2, April, 1986.

Cart, Doren "A Soldier's Conscience, the Letters of Thomas F. Price" *Camp Chase Gazette.* July/August, 1987.

Cashin, Joan E. *First Lady of the Confederacy.* Cambridge, Mass. The Belknap Press of Harvard University Press. 2006.

Casey, Cindy H. *Piedmont Soldiers and Their Families, North Carolina.* Arcadia Publishing Co. 2000.

Casstevens, Frances H. *The Civil War and Yadkin County, North Carolina.* McFarland and Co, Publishers. 1997.

Cecelski, David S. *The Waterman's Song.* Chapel Hill, U.N.C. Press. 2001.

Chamberlain, Hope Summerell. *This Was Home.* Chapel Hill, U.N.C. Press. 1938.

Chapman, Sarah Bahnson, editor. *Bright and Gloomy: The Civil War Correspondence of Captain Charles F. Bahnson, a Moravian Confederate.* University of Tennessee Press, 2003.

Cheshire, Joseph B., DD. *Bishop Atkinson and the Church in the Confederacy.* Raleigh, Edwards & Broughton Publishers. 1909.

Cisco, Walter B. *War Crimes Against Southern Civilians.* Gretna, Pelican Publishing Co. 2007.

Clark, Walter. "The Raising, Organizing, and Equipment of the North Carolina Troops During the Civil War." *North Carolina Booklet,* Volume 19, # 1.

Clark, Walter. *Histories of the Several Regiments and Battalions from North Carolina.* Wendell, N.C. Reprinted by Broadfoot's Bookmark. 1982

Click, Patricia C. *Time Full of Trial.* Chapel Hill and London, U.N.C. Press. 2001.

Clinard, Karen and Richard Russell. *Fear in North Carolina.* Asheville, Reminiscing Books. 2008.

Clinton, Catherine. *Public Women and the Confederacy.* Marquette University Press. 1999.

Clinton, Catherine. *The Plantation Mistress.* New York, Pantheon Books. 1982.

Clinton, Catherine, editor. *Southern Families at War.* Oxford Press. 2000.

Clinton, Catherine & Nina Silber. *Divided Houses—Gender and the Civil War.* New York, Oxford Press. 1992.

Cobb, Harriet. *For My Children.* Typed manuscript in the Sheppard Memorial Libray, Greenville.

Cochran, G.W. "To the Front by Thousands," *Company Front.* Volume II, 2003.

Cochran, Hamilton. *Blockade Runners of the Confederacy.* The Bobbs-Merrill Co, Inc. 1958.

Cochran, Thomas C., "Did the Civil War Retard Industrialization?" *The Economic Impact of the American Civil War,* by Ralph Andreano. Cambridge, Schenkman Publishing Co, Inc. 1962.

Confederate Scrapbook. Published for the benefit of the Memorial Bazaar held in Richmond April 11, 1893. Richmond, J.L. Hill Printing Co. 1893.

Conner, R.D.W. *North Carolina, Volume II.* Chicago & New York. Published by the American Historical Society, Inc. 1929.

Conner, Sallie and Mrs. Thomas Taylor, editors. *South Carolina Women in the Confederacy, Volume I;* Published by the UDC, Columbia SC State Company. 1903.

Cook, Gerald W. *The Last Tarheel Militia 1861-1865.* Privately printed in Winston Salem. 1987.

Cotton, Sallie S. *A Woman's Life in North Carolina.* Greensboro, William Stephenson, Pamlico Press. 1987.

Coulling, Mary. *The Lee Girls.* Winston-Salem, J.F. Blair Publishing Co. 1987.

Coulter, E. Merton. *The Confederate States of America, 1861-1865.* L.S.U. Press. 1950.

Council, Mrs. C.T. Newspaper article, "Nerve" Puts Up with Hospital Sheets," Julian S. Carr Chapter U.D.C. Scrapbook. 1938, Durham Public Library.

Covell, Elizabeth Greene. *The Two Williams.* Cambridge, Mass., University Press. 1954.

Colyer, Vincent. *Report of the Services Rendered by the Freed People to the United States, in North Carolina.* Self-published. 1864.

Crabtree, Beth and James Patton, editors. *Journal of a Secesh Lady, The Diary of Catherine Ann Devereux Edmondston.* Raleigh, Division of Archives & History, Department of Cultural Resources. 1979.

Crawford, Mark J. *Confederate Courage on Other Fields.* Jefferson, North Carolina & London, McFarland & Co., Inc. 2000.

Crawford, Martin. *Ashe County's Civil War: Community and Society in the Appalachian South.* Charlottesville, Va., University of Virginia Press. 2001.

Crawford, Martin. "The Dynamics of Mountain Unionism." *The Civil War in Appalachia.* edited by Noe and Wilson. University of Tennessee Press. 1997.

Crittenden, Mrs. S.A. *"South Carolina Women of the Confederacy, Volume I."* Edited by Mrs. Thomas Taylor and Sallie E. Conner. Printed by the UDC, South Carolina Division, Columbia, South Carolina State Comp. 1903.

Creecy, Richard B. "The Bombardment of Elizabeth City." *Pasquotank Historical Yearbook.* Vol. #1. 1954-55.

Crews, Daniel C. *Neither Slave Nor Free.* Moravian Archives. 1998.

Crews, Daniel C. *A Storm in the Land.* Moravian Archives Publishing, n.d.

Crews, Daniel. *Faith and Tears.* Winston-Salem, Moravian Archives Publishing. n.d.

Crossley, William J. *Extracts From My Diary and From My Experiences.* Providence, R.I. Stone and Farnham Printers. 1903; courtesy of Alexander Street Press, Civil War Letters & Diaries.

Crouch, John. *Historical Sketches of Wilkes County.* Self-published. Wilkesboro. 1902.

Crow, Terrell and Mary Barden, editors. *Live Your Own Life.* University of South Carolina Press. 2003.

Crow, Vernon. *Storm in the Mountains.* Cherokee, N.C., Press of the Museum of the Cherokee Indians. 1982.

Cunningham, H.H. "Edmund Burke Haywood and Raleigh's Confederate Hospitals." *North Carolina Historical Review.* Volume XXXV, #2, April 1958.

Cunningham, H.H. *Doctors in Gray.* Glouchester, Mass. L.S.U. Press. 1958.

Current, Richard N. and Simon & Schuster, *Encyclopedia of the Confederacy.* Vol. III. Prentice Hall Publishers. 1995.

Curtis, Dr. W.G. *Reminiscences of Wilmington and Smithville—Southport 1848-1900.* Southport, Printed by Herald Job Office. 1905.

Dannett, Sylvia & Katherine M. Jones. *Our Women of the 60's.* Published in Washington, D.C. by the Centennial Commission. 1963.

Davenport, Winston, Whitfield. *A History of the Towns and Schools of Franklinton, North Carolina.* Hawkins Printers. 1998.

Davis, Burke. *Sherman's March.* New York, Vintage Books.1988.

Davis, David E. *History of Tyrrell County.* Norfolk, James Christopher Printing. 1963.

Davis, Edward H. *Historical Sketches of Franklin County.* Raleigh, Edwards & Broughton Publishers. 1948.

Davis, Hattie Caldwell. *Reflections of Cataloochee Valley and Its Vanished People in the Great Smoky Mountains.* Published by the author. Printed in Waynesville. 1999.

Day, D. L. *"My Diary of Rambles With the 25th Massachusetts Volunteer Infantry.* Milford, M.A. King & Billings Printers. 1884.

Dedmondt, Glenn *The Flags of Civil War North Carolina.* Gretna, Louisiana, The Pelican Publishing Co. 2003.

Delfine, Susanna and Michele Gillespie. *Neither Lady Nor Slave, Working Women of the Old South.* Chapel Hill, U.N.C. Press. 2002.

Derby, William P. *Bearing Arms in the Twenty-Seventh Massachusetts Regiment of Volunteer Infantry.* Boston, Wright & Potter Printing Co. 1883.

deRosset, William L., editor. *Pictorial and Historical New Hanover County and Wilmington, 1723-1938.* Self-published. 1938.

Devereux, Margaret. *Plantations Sketches.* Privately printed at the Riverside Press, Cambridge. 1906.

Dietz, August. *The Confederate Post-Office Department.* Richmond, The Dietz Press. Published by Crown Rights Book Co. 1948.

Dimity, Adelaine Stuart. *War-Time Sketches, Historical and Otherwise.* New Orleans, La. Printing Company Press. 1911.

Dix, Mary S., editor, "And Three Rousing Cheers for the Privates: A Diary of the 1862 Roanoke Island Expedition." *North Carolina Historical Review.* Volume LXXXI, #1, January, 1994.

Douglas, William M. *Relief of Washington, North Carolina, by the 1st Rhode Island Volunteers.* Providence, printed by the Soldiers and Sailors Historical Society. 1886.

Duffus, Kevin P. *The Lost Light.* Raleigh, Looking Glass Productions, Inc. 2003

Dunbar, Aaron, *History of the Ninety-third Regiment Illinois Volunteer Infantry: From Organization to Muster Out—Statistics.* Revised and edited by Harvey Trimble, Adjutant. The Blakely Printing Compnay. 1898.

Durrill, Wayne K. *War of Another Kind.* Oxford University Press. 1990.

Duyckinck, Evert A. "The Chicamacomico Races." *The Outer Banks Reader,* selected and edited by David Stick. U.N.C. Press. 1998.

Eby, Cecil Jr., editor. *The Old South Illustrated.* U.N.C. Press. 1959.

Edmunds, Mary L. Rucker. *Recollections of Greensboro.* Self published by the author, Greensboro. 1933.

Edmunds, Pocahontas W. *Tar Heels Tract the Century.* Raleigh, Edwards & Broughton Company. 1966.

Edwards, Tom J. and William H. Rowland. *Through the Eyes of Soldiers: The Battle of Wyse Fork.* n. p. Owned by the Lenoir County Historical Assoc.

Elliott, Gilbert, "Albemarle—the Career of the Confederate Ram. 1. Her Construction and Service. By her Builder," *The Century.* July 1888, Volume 36, #3. New York, the Century Company.

Elliott, James C. *The Southern Soldier Boy*. Edwards & Broughton Printing Co. 1907.

Ellison, Deborah and Jearlean Woody, editors. *North Carolina Century Farms: One Hundred Years of Continuous Agricultural Heritage.* Published by the Department of Agriculture, Raleigh. 1989.

Escott, Paul. *Many Excellent People: Power and Privilege in North Carolina 1850-1900.* Chapel Hill and London, U.N.C. Press. 1985.

Escott, Paul D. Editor. *North Carolina Yeoman.* University of Georgia Press. 1996.

Escott, Paul D. "Poverty and Governmental Aid for the Poor in Confederate North Carolina." *North Carolina Historical Review*. Volume LXI, #4. October, 1984.

Evans, W. McKee. *Ballots and Fence Rails: Reconstruction of the Lower Cape Fear.* New York, W.W. Norton and Co., Inc., 1966 [U.N.C. Press 1967]

Evans, W. McKee. *To Die Game*. Baton Rouge, L.S.U. Press. 1971.

Faust, Drew Gilpin. *Mothers of Invention*. Chapel Hill and London, U.N.C. Press. 1996.

Faust, Drew Gilpin. *Southern Stories, Slaveholders in Peace and War.* Columbia and London, University of Missouri Press. 1992.

Fenn, Elizabeth A. "A Perfect Equality Seemed to Reign: Slave Society and Jonkonnu," *North Carolina Historical Review*. Volume LXV, Number 2. April, 1988.

Ferebee, L.R. *A Brief History of the Slave Life of Reverend L.R. Ferebee, Written from Memory.* Raleigh, Edwards, Broughton & Co. 1882.

Fisher, Clyde. "Relief of Soldiers' Families in North Carolina," *South Atlantic Quarterly.* Volume XVI. June, 1917.

Fisher, Noel C. *War at Every Door.* Chapel Hill, U.N.C. Press.1997.

Fite, Emerson, "The Agricultural Development of the West During the War" *The Economic Impact of the American Civil War,* by Ralph Andreano. Cambridge, Schenkman Publishing Co, Inc. 1962.

Fleming, Monika S. *Echoes of Edgecombe County 1860-1940.* Arcadia Printing. 1996.

Fletcher, Arthur L. *Ashe County, A History.* Jefferson, N.C., Ashe County Research Associates. 1963.

Fletcher, J.F. *A History of Ashe County, North Carolina: and New River, Virginia Baptist Association.* Raleigh, Commercial Printing Co. 1935.

Fonville Chris E. *The Wilmington Campaign: Last Rays of Departing Hope.* Savas Publishing Co. 1997.

Ford, Arthur Peronneau and M.I. Ford. *Life in the Confederate Army, Being Personal Experiences of a Private Soldier in the Confederate Army.* New York, the Neale Publishing Company. 1905.

Forkner, Ben and Patrick Samway, editors. *New Reader of the Old South.* Atlanta, Peachtree Publishers, Ltd. 1991.

Fowler, Malcolm. *They Passed This Way.* Published by the Harnett County Centennial, Inc. 1955.

Fox-Genovese, Elizabeth. *Within the Plantation Household, Black and White Women of the Old South.* U.N.C. Press. 1988.

Franklin, J. H. and Loren Schweninger. *Runaway Slaves.* Oxford University Press. 1999.

Franklin, John H. *The Free Negro in North Carolina,1790-1860.* Chapel Hill, N.C., University of N.C. Press. 1995.

Freel, Margaret Walker. *Our Heritage.* Asheville, Miller Publishing Co. 1956.

Freeman, D.S. *Confederate Calendar—a Calendar of Confederate Papers.* Kraus Reprint Company. 1969.

Freeman, Ozell. *North Carolina, the Goodliest Land..* Charlotte, Delmar Co. 1973.

Freemantle, Sir Arthur. *Three Months in Southern Sates . . . Sir Arthur J.L. Freemantle . . . Englishman . . . Visiting the South.* Published in Mobile, by S.H. Goetzel. 1864.

Fries, Adelaide L. and Stuart T. Wright and J. Edwin Hendricks. *Forsyth: The History of a County on the March.* U.N.C. Press, 1976.

Fries, Adelaide L. *The Road To Salem.* U.N.C. Press. 1944.

Gaddy, David. "William Norris and the Confederate Signal and Secret Service." *Maryland History Magazine.* Volume 70, #2. 1975.

Gallagher, Gary W. *Stephen Dotson Ramseur, Lee's Gallant General.* Chapel Hill, U.N.C. Press. 1985.

Garrison, Randall, editor. "The White Letters" *Company Front,* April,1993

Garrison, Randall, editor. "Daniel Liles Letters" *Company Front,* May, 1994.

Garrison, Randall, editor. "For the War, The Letters of David and Peter Mull" *Company Front,* February, 1994.

Gass, W. Conrad. "A Felicitous Life: Lucy Martin Battle, 1805-1874." *North Carolina Historical Review,* Volume LII, Number 4. October, 1975.

Gaston, A.P. *Partisan Campaigns of Col. Lawrence M. Allen, commanding the 64th Regiment, North Carolina State Troops during the Late Civil War: Valiant Deeds of Heroic Patriotism."* Raleigh, Edwards & Broughton, Printers. 1894.

Gibson, John M., *Those 163 Days.* Bramhall House Publishers. 1961.

Gill, Mattie Taylor. *An Appreciation of Grandfather: John Mercer and Grandmother Anna Jane.* [typescript, Southern Historical Collection, Wilson Library, UNC]

Glass, Brent, *The Textile Industry in North Carolina.* Jefferson, N.C., McFarland & Co. 1992.

Goff, Richard D. *Confederate Supply.* Duke University Press. 1969.

Goss, Bernard and Ruth W. Shepard. *The Heritage of Ashe County.* Ashe County Heritage Book Commission in co-operation with the History Division of Hunter Publishing Co. 1984.

Goss, Sgt. Warren L. *The Soldier's Story of His Capture at Andersonville, Bell Isle, and Other Rebel Prisons.* Boston, Lee & Shepard Publishers. 1866.

Gragg, Rod. *Confederate Goliath.* Harper Collins Publisher, 1991.

Gragg, Ron. *Covered With Glory.* Perennial Publishing. 2000.

Green, Carol C. *Chimborazo.* Knoxville, the University of Tennessee Press. 2004.

Green, Wharton J. *Recollections and Reflections.* Raleigh, Edwards and Broughton Publishers. 1906.

Greenberg, Kenneth S. *Honor & Slavery.* Princeton, New Jersey. Princeton University Press. 1996.

Grimsley, Mark. *The Hard Hand of War, Union Military Policy Toward Southern Civilians 1861-1865.* Cambridge University Press. 1997.

Gunn, John C. *Gunn's Domestic Medicine.* Privately printed. 1830.

Hackett, Roger C. "Civil War Diary of Sergeant James Louis Matthews." *Indiana Magazine of History,* Volume 24, #4 December, 1928.

Hadden, Lee. "Recollections of the Civil War in the United States by J.A. Strikeleather," *Company Front.* October, 1993.

Hadley, Jr., Wade H. *The Story of the Cape Fear and Deep River Navigation Company, 1849-1873.* The Chatham County Historical Society. Siler City, N.C., printed by Beane and Efird.1980.

Hadley, Wade H. and Doris G. Horton and Nell C. Stroud. *Chatham County,* 1771-1971. Moore Publishing Co. 1976.

Hall, Harry H. *A Johnny Reb Band from Salem.* Raleigh, North Carolina Confederate Centennial Commission. 1963.

Hall, James O. "The Veiled Lady, the Saga of Sarah Slater." *North/South Magazine,* Volume 3. August, 2000.

Hall, Lewis Philip. *Land of the Golden River.* Wilmington Printing Company. 1980.

Hall, Susan E. *She Was All Love.* Published by James Sprunt. 1961 [about
Jane D. Sprunt, 1823-1892.]

Hamilton, J.G. deRoulhac. *History of North Carolina Since 1860.* Volume 3. Spartanburg, S.C., The Reprint Co. 1973.

Hamilton, J.G. deRoulhac. *Heroes of America.* Publication of the Southern Historical Association #1. 1907.

Hamilton, J.G. deRoulhac. *The Correspondence of Jonathan Worth, Volume I.* Raleigh, Edwards & Broughton Publishing. 1909.

Hamilton, Kenneth G., editor. *Records of the Moravians in North Carolina.* Volume XI, 1852-1879. Raleigh, State Dept. of Archives & History. 1969.

Hanson, Kathleen S., *Turn Backwards O Time.* Edinborough Press. 2006.

Hardy, Michael C. *The Thirty-seventh North Carolina Troops.* Jefferson, N.C., McFarland & Company, Inc. 2003.

Harmon, George D., "The Military Experiences of James A. Peifer 1861-1865," *North Carolina Historical Review.* October, 1955.

Harper, C.W. "House Servants and Field Hands: Fragmentation in the Antebellum Slave Community." *North Carolina Historical Review,* Volume LV, Number 1. January, 1978.

Harrington, Zeb D. and Martha. *To Bear Arms.* Self-published. 1984.

Harris, George Washington. *High Times and Hard Times, Sketches and Tales.* Edited by M. Thomas Inge. Kingsport, Tenn., Vanderbilt University Press. 1967.

Harris, William C. "Lincoln and Wartime Reconstruction in North Carolina, 1861-1863." *North Carolina Historical Review,* Volume LXIII, Number 2. April, 1986.

Harrison, Malcolm. "The Cape Fear," *Chronological Bibliography of Rivers of America Series by Joel Samuels.* New York: Chicago: San Francisco, Holt, Rinehart, and Winston. 1965.

Hartung, A. Bruce. "War Comes To Qualla," *State Magazine.* May, 1983.

Hassell, Clarence Biggs. *History of the Church of God, from Creation to AD 1885: including especially the History of the Kehukee Primitive Baptist Association.* Revised by Elder Syl. Hassell. Middletown, NY, Gilbert Beeb's Sons. 1886.

Hatcher, Edmund N. *The Last Four Weeks of the War.* Columbus, Ohio, the Co-Operative Publishing Co. 1892.

Hatley, Joe M. and Linda Hoffman, editors. *Letters of William F. Wagner, Confederate Soldier.* Broadfoot's Bookmark, Publisher. 1983.

Havens, Jonathan. *The Pamlico Section of North Carolina.* Newbern, Richardson & Son, Practical Book & Job Printers. 1886.   ·

Hawkins, Rev. William G. *Lunsford Lane.* New York, Negro University Press. Reprint 1969.

Hays, Francis B. "The South, the Confederacy, Yankees, and Negroes." *Redbook by Hayes.* Volume 128. n.p. 1980.

Hays, Johnson J. *Land of Wilkes.* Wilkesboro, N.C., Wilkes County Historical Soc. 1962

Haywood, Martha H. *North Carolina Booklet.* Published by the North Carolina Society, Daughters of the American Revolution. Raleigh, Capital Printing Company. 1901-1926.

Henderson, Dwight, editor. *Private Journal of Gholson Walker 1863-1865 With Sections from Post War Years 1865-1876."* Tuscaloosa, AL. Confederate Publishing Co. 1963.

Henry, Phillip N. and Carol M. Speas. *The Heritage of Blacks in North Carolina,* Volume I. Published by the N.C. African-American Heritage Foundation in cooperation with the Delmar Company, Charlotte. 1990.

Herran, Kathy N. *They Married Confederate Officers.* Davidson, North Carolina, Warren Publishing. 1997.

Hertzler, Dr. Ann. "Civil War Heroines Wilmington Soldiers' Aid Society," *Lower Cape Fear Historical Society Bulletin.* Volume L, #3, October, 2006.

Higham, Charles. *Murdering Mr. Lincoln.* New Millennium Press. 2004.

Hilderman III, Walter C. *They Went into the Fight Cheering.* Boone, N.C., Parkway Publishers, Inc. 2005.

Hill, George F. *A Brief History of Christ Episcopal Church Parish, Elizabeth City, North Carolina.* n.p. June, 1948. Joyner Library, ECU digital series.

Hill, Samuel S. and Charles H. Lippy and Charles R. Wilson. *Encyclopedia of Religion in the South.* Macon, GA, Mercer University Press. 2005.

Hinshaw, Seth and Mary. *Quaker Women of North Carolina.* published by the North Carolina United Society of Friends Women. 1994.

Hinshaw, Seth B. *Mary Baker Hinshaw: Quaker.* Friends United Press, N.C. Yearly Meeting. N.C. Friends Historical Society. 1982.

Hinton, Mary Hilliard, editor. *North Carolina Booklet.* Volume 16 and 19, #1-2. Published by the North Carolina Society, Daughters of the American Revolution. Printed by the Commercial Printing Company, Raleigh. 1919.

Hoar, Jay S. *The South's Last Boys in Gray.* Bowling Green, Ohio. Bowling Green State University Popular Press. 1986.

Hollar, Cheryl F., editor. *A Walk Through History.* Louisburg, Cypress Creek Publishers. 1992.

Hollowell, James Monroe. *War-Time Reminiscences & Other Stories.* 1939. Joyner Library, ECU digital series.

Honey, Michael. "The War Within the Confederacy, White Unionists of North Carolina." *Prologue Magazine.* Volume 18, #2, Summer, 1986.

Horan, James D. *Confederate Agent.* New York, Crown Publishers. 1954.

Horner, Dave. *The Blockade Runners, True Tales of Running the Yankee Blockade of the Confederate Coast.* Mead-Dodd Publishing. 1968.

Houck, Peter W. *Medical Department Letters Sent and Received Medical Director's Office Richmond, Va. 1862-1863. Chapter VI, Volume 416.* Lynchburg, Va., Warwick House Publishing. n.d.

Hover, Private Charles H. "From the Ranks to Prison." Published in the Spring 2006 electronic edition of the *Bivouac Banner.*

Howe, W.W. *Expedition to Kinston, Whitehall and Goldsboro, North Carolina December 1862.* New York, Howe Publishing. 1890.

Hubbard, Charles E. "The Official Reports of the March to Kinston and Battle of Kinston," *Harper's Weekly.* May-December, 1864.

Hufham. James D. *Memoir of Reverend J.L. Prichard, Late Pastor of the First Baptist Church, Wilmington, North Carolina.* Raleigh, Hufham & Hughes, publishers. 1867.

Hunt, Gary. "*Gus Rich, the Wizard of the Blue Ridge.*" Private papers.

Hunter, Robert, editor. *Sketches of War History, 1861-1865,Papers Prepared for the Ohio Commandrey of the Military Order for the Loyal Legion of the U.S. 1888-1900.* Published by the Commandrey, Volume III. Cincinnati: Robert Clarke & Co. 1890.

Hurmence, Belinda. *My Folks Don't Want Me to Talk About Slavery.* Winston-Salem. John T. Blair, Publishers. 1984.

Inge, M. Thomas, editor. *High Times and Hard Times,* Sketches and Tales by George Washington Harris. Vanderbilt University Press. 1967.

Inscoe, John C. and McKinney, Gordon B. *The Heart of Confederate Appalachia. Western North Carolina in the Civil War.* Chapel Hill and London, U.N.C. Press. 2000.

Inscoe, John C. *Mountain Masters, Slavery, and the Sectional Crisis in Western North Carolina.* Knoxville, University of Tennessee Press. 1989.

Jackson, Blyden. "George Moses Horton, North Carolina." *North Carolina Historical Review.* Volume LIII, No 2, April, 1976.

Jacobs, Joseph. "Some of the Drug Conditions During the War Between the States, 1861-5" *Southern Historical Society Papers.* #33. 1935.

James, Joshua Stuart. *Two Centuries at Sycamore Springs Plantation.* n.p. 1990.

Jervey, Edward, editor. *Prison life Among the Rebels: Recollections of a Union Chaplain.* Kent State University Press. 1990.

Johansson, M. Jane, editor. *Widows by the Thousand.* Fayetteville, University of Arkansas Press. 2000.

Johns, Annie E. "The Hospital at Danville," *Our Women in the War: The Lives They Lived, the Deaths They Died.* Compiled by Ms. Hattie Kilgore. The Charleston News & Courier. 1885.

Johnson, Charles F. *The Long Roll.* New York, Roycrofters Printing. Reprint. 1986.

Johnson, Clint. *Pursuit: the Chase, Capture, Persecution, and surprising Release of Confederate President Jefferson Davis.* Citadel Press, Kensington Publishing Co. 2008.

Johnson, Talmage C. and Charles R. Holloman. *The Story of Kinston and Lenoir County.* Raleigh, Edwards and Broughton Publishers. 1954.

Johnston, Frontis W. *The Papers of Zebulon Baird Vance,* Volume I, 1843-1862. Published by the N.C. Department of Archives & History. 1963.

Johnston, Hugh B. "Vinson Confederate Letters," *North Carolina Historical Review.* Volume XXV, #1. January, 1948.

Johnston, Hugh B., Jr. editor. "The Confederate Letters of Ruffin Barnes," *North Carolina Historical Review,* Volume XXXI, #1. January, 1954.

Johnstone, M. D. *Wayne County Heritage.* Wayne County History Association, Inc. and Old Dobbs County Genealogy Society in cooperation with the Hunter Publishing Co., Winston-Salem. 1982.

Jolly, Ellen Ryan LL.D. *Nuns of the Battlefield.* Providence, R.I., the Providence Visitor Press. 1927.

Jones, HG. "Bedford Brown; States Rights Unionists, Part II." *North Carolina Historical Review.* Volume XXXII, Number 3. July, 1955.

Jones, Katherine M. *When Sherman Came: Southern Women and the "Great March."* Indianapolis, the Bobbs-Merrill Company, Inc. 1964.

Jones, K. Randell and Catlin D. Jones, editors of Dr. H.G. Jones. *Scoundrels, Rogues and Heroes of the Old North State.* Charleston, History Press. 2004.

Jones, Nellie Rowe. *Guilford Under the Stars and Bars.* n.p. n.d.

Jordan, Paula S. and Kathy W. Manning. *Women of Guilford County, North Carolina.* Published by the Women of Guilford, a non-profit corporation, 1979.

Joslyn, Mauriel, editor. *Valor and Lace: The Roles of Confederate Women, 1861-1865.* Heritage Press. 1996.

Kane, Harnett T. *The Southern Christmas Book.* New York, David McKay Company, Inc. 1958.

Kane, Sharyn and Richard Keeton. *Fiery Dawn—The Battle of Monroe's Crossroads.* Southeast Archeological Center. 1999.

Kell, Jean B. *The Old Port Town Beaufort, North Carolina.* n.p. 1989.

Kellogg, Robert H. *Life and Death in Rebel Prisons.* Hartford, Conn. L. Stebbins Publisher. 1867.

Kendall, Katherine K. *Caswell County 1777-1877 Historical Abstracts of Minutes of Caswell County North Carolina.* Wendell, N.C. Reprinted by Broadfoot's Bookmark. 1977.

Kennedy, Joseph. *Agricultural Census of the United States in 1860 complied from the Original Return of the Eighth Census Under the Direction of the Secretary of the Interior.* Washington: Government Printing Office. 1864.

Kent, Scotti. *More Than Petticoats.* Falcon Publishers, Inc. 2000.

Killian, Ron V. *A History Of The Third Mounted Infantry Volunteers, USA.* Heritage Books, Inc. 2000.

King, Henry T. *Sketches of Pitt County: A Brief History of the County, 1704-1910.* Edwards and Broughton. 1911.

King, Myrtle C. *Anna Long Fuller's Journal 1856-1890.* Alpharetta, Anson County. 1999

Konkle, Burton A. *John Motley Morehead and the Development of North Carolina 1796-1866.* Spartanburg, S.C. reprint 1971 from a 1922 edition—the Reprint Co.

Koonce, Donald B., editor. *Doctor To The Front.* University of Tennessee Press. 2000.

Lamont, Daniel S. *The War of the Rebellion, a Compilation of the Official Records.* Series I. Volume XLVII, part II. Government Printing Office. 1895.

Lassiter, Thomas and Wingate. *Johnston County 1746-1996.* Self-published. 1996.

Lawing, Mike and Carolyn, editors. *My Dearest Friend, The Civil War Correspondence of Cornelia McGimsey and Lewis Warlick.* Durham, Carolina Academic Press. 2000

Lee, Lawrence. *History of Brunswick County, North Carolina.* n.p. 1980.

Lefler, Hugh T. *North Carolina History, as Told by Contemporaries.* Chapel Hill, U.N.C. Press. 1934.

Lerner, Eugene. "Money Prices, and Wages in the Confederacy 1861-1865," *The Economic Impact of the American Civil War* . [internet site]

Leftwich, Rodney, compiler. "Four Letters of Thomas M. Garrison, Co. K, 25th Regt. NCT." *Company Front*, June, 1989.

Leon, Louis. *Diary of a Tar Heel Confederate Soldier.* Charlotte, Stone Publishing Company. 1913.

Levine, Bruce C. *Confederate Emancipation: Southern Plans to Free & Arm Slaves During the Civil War."* Oxford University Press. 2006.

Lessoff, Howard. *The Civil War With "Punch."* Broadfoot Publishing Co. 1984.

Libera, Joanne Johnson. *Letters of George Washington Walker.* n.p. 1993.

Little, Ann C.W.. *Columbus County North Carolina Recollections & Records.* Published by the Columbus County Commission and Columbus Co. Library. 1980.

Loehr, Walter, M.D. "Civil War Medicine in N.C." *North Carolina Medical Journal*, Volume 43, #2.

London, Lawrence F. and Sarah M. Lemmon. *The Episcopal Church in North Carolina, 1701-1950* . Published by the Episcopal Diocese of North Carolina. 1987.

Long, Dorothy, editor. *Medicine in North Carolina, Volumes I-II.* Raleigh, the North Carolina Medical Society. 1972.

Long, Mary A. *High Time to Tell It . . . Reminisces.* Duke University Press. 1950.

Long, Spurgeon and Audrey. *A Brief Historical Sketch of Mt. Carmel Baptist Church in Northampton County near Seaboard, North Carolina.* n.p. 1947.

Love, James Lee. *R.C.G. Love, a Builder of the New South.* U.N.C. Press. 1949.
Lowery, Dr. Thomas P. *Swamp Doctor.* Stackpole Books. 2001.
Lowery, Dr. Thomas P. *Confederate Heroines.* Baton Rouge, L.S.U. Press. 2006.
Lowery, Dr. Thomas. *The Story the Soldiers Wouldn't Tell.* Stackpole Books. 1994.
Loy, Ursula F. & Pauline M. Worthy. *Washington and the Pamlico.* Published by the Washington-Beaufort County Bicentennial Committee. 1976.
MacBryde, Ann C. *Elle's Book: The Journal Kept By Ellie M. Andrews From January 1862Thru May 1865.* Davidson, N.C., Briarpatch Press. 1984.
Maher, Sister Mary Denis. *To Bind Up the Wounds.* Baton-Rouge, Louisiana State University Press. 1989.
Mallison, Fred M. *The Civil War on the Outer Banks.* Jefferson, N.C., McFarland Publishing Co. 1998.
Mann, Albert. "Camp Armory on the Trent." *History of the Forty-fifth Regiment Massachusetts Volunteer Militia: "the Cadet Regiment."* Jamaica Plains, Mass. Brookside Printing. 1908.
Mann, Albert. "The Enlistment of Colored Troops." *History of the Forty-fifth Regiment Massachusetts Volunteer Militia. As above.*
Markle, Donald E. *Spies and Spymasters of the Civil War.* New York City, Hippocrene Books Publishers. 1994.
Martell, Joanne. *Mille-Christine, Fearfully and Wonderfully Made.* Winston-Salem, John Blair Publishers. 2000.
Marten, James. *The Children's Civil War.* Chapel Hill, U. N. C. Press. 1998 .
Marvel, William. *The Battle For Saltville.* Schroeder Publishing Co. 1992.
Massey, Mary E. "Southern Refugee Life During the Civil War," *North Carolina Historical Review,* April, 1943.
Massey, Mary E. *Ersatz of the Confederacy.* Columbia, S.C., U.S.C. Press. 1952.
Massey, Mary Elizabeth. *Bonnet Brigade.* New York, Alfred Knopf Publishers. 1966.
Massey, Mary Elizabeth. *Refugee Life in the Confederacy.* L.S.U. Press. 1964.
Mast, Greg. *State Troops and Volunteers, Vol. 1.* Raleigh, N.C. Dept. of Cultural Resources. 1995.
Mast, Greg, editor. "War Reminiscences of Mrs. Charlotte E. Grimes." *Company Front.* 1992.
Mast, Greg, editor. "A Yankee at Bentonville" *Company Front* April/May, 1989.
Mast, Greg, editor "The Setser Letters, Part III" *Company Front* August/September, 1989.
Mast, Greg, editor "War Record from 1862-1865," by Sergeant Henry C. Clegg. *Company Front* January/February 1990.
Mast, Greg, editor. "The Adventures of a Conscript", Part II, by W.H. Younce *Company Front* September/October 1990.
Mast, Greg, editor. "Reminiscences of Roanoke Minute Men" *Company Front,* July/August 1990.
Mast, Greg and Randall Garrison, editors. *Company Front,* a quarterly publication.
Matthews, James L. edited by Roger C. Hackett. "The Civil War Diary of James Louis Matthews." *Indiana Magazine of History.* 24, #4. December, 1928.
McCaslin, Richard B. *Portraits in Conflict, a Photographic History of North Carolina in the Civil War.* Fayetteville, Arkansas, University of Arkansas Press. 1997.
McCoury, Ken. "Eng and Chang." *Bennett Place Quarterly.* 2004.
McDaniel, Jo Anna. *Civil War Documents, Granville County, North Carolina.* Published by Granville County Historical Soc., Inc. n.d.
McEachern, Leora and Isabel M. Williams. "Miss Buie, the Soldier's Friend." *Lower Cape Fear Historical Society, Inc. Bulletin.* Volume LXIX, No. 1, January, 1992.
McEachern, Leora and Isabel M. Williams. *Salt—that Necessary Article.* n.p. Wilmington. 1973.
McEachern, Leora and Isabel M. Williams. "The Prevailing Epidemic—1862." *Lower Cape Fear Historical Society Bulletin.* Volume XI, #1, November, 1967.
McGee, David. *"Changing Relationships Between Confederate Soldiers and Their Families and Communities During the Civil War: A Case Study.* 1998. [private papers]
McGee, David, editor. "The Morrison Letters, Part II" *Company Front April/May, 1990.*

McGee, David, editor. "History of the Twenty-Sixth North Carolina" *Company Front* April, 1993.

McGowen, Faison W. and Pearl C., editors. *Flashes of Duplin's History and Government.* 1971 ECU digital services.

McKinney, Gordon B. "Women's Role in Civil War Western North Carolina." *North Carolina Historical Review,* Volume LXIX, Number 1, January, 1992

McLaughlin, Florence C., editor. "Diary of Salisbury Prison, by James W. Eberhart," *Western Pennsylvania Historical Magazine.* July, 1973.

McLaurin, Joe. *Richmond County Record.* Salem, Mass., Higginson Book Co. 1999.

McLean, Eddie. "Sweet Old Days in Dixie." Raleigh, Edwards & Broughton Printing Company. 1907.

McNeil, Jim. *Masters of the Shoals.* Da Capo Press. 2003.

Medley, Mary L. *History of Anson County, North Carolina,* 1750-1976. Published by the Anson County Historical Society. 1976.

Menius, III, Arthur C. "James Bennitt: Portrait of an Antebellum Yeoman," *North Carolina Historical Review.* Volume LVIII, #4. Autumn, 1981.

Miles, Jim. *To The Sea.* Rutledge Hill Press. 1989.

Mitchell, Memory F. *The James Sprunt Studies in History and Political Science, Volume 47, Legal Aspects of Conscription and Exemptions in North Carolina 1861-1865.* Chapel Hill, U.N.C. Press. 1965.

Mitchell, Sally. *The Fallen Angel.* Bowling Green University. Popular Press. 1981.

Mobley, Joe A. *James City: a Black Community in North Carolina 1863-1900.* Raleigh, Division of Archives & History, Department of Cultural Resources. 1981.

Mobley, Joe A. editor. *The Papers of Zebulon Baird Vance, Volume 2*— 1863. Raleigh, Division of Archives and History. 1995.

Monroe, Haskell, editor. "The Road to Gettysburg, The Diary and Letters of Leonidas Torrence of the Gaston Guards." *North Carolina Historical Review.* October, 1959.

Montgomery, Lizzie W. *Sketches of Old Warrenton, North Carolina.* Spartanburg, S.C., The Reprint Company. 1984.

Montgomery, Lizzie W. *The Saint Mary's of Olden Days.* Raleigh, Bynum Printing Co. 1932.

Moore, Frank. *Rebellion Record—a Diary of American Events.* New York, G.P. Putnam, Van Nostrand. n.d.

Moore, Jeanelle C. and Grace R. Hamrick. *The First Ladies of North Carolina.* Charlotte, Heritage Printers, Inc. 1981.

Moore, Mark A. *The Wilmington Campaign and the Battle for Fort Fisher.* Maron City, Iowa, Savas Publishers. 1999.

Morel, Anne V., Editor. *Gleanings From Long Ago by Ellen Mordecai.* Savannah, Ga., Braid and Hutton, Inc., Printers. 1933.

Morgan, James M. *Recollections of a Rebel Reefer.* Houghton Mifflin Company. 1917.

Morton, Chris, editor. "The Battle for Asheville" *Company Front* June/July, 1989

Moss, Juanita P. *The Battle of Plymouth.* Willow Bend Books, Publisher. 2003.

Motley, Charles B. *Milton North Carolina Sidelights of History.* n.p. 1976.

Murray, Elizabeth Reid. *Wake—Capital County.* Raleigh, Capital County Publishing Co. 1983.

Murray, Paul and Stephen R. Barlett, Jr., editors. "Letters of S.C. Barlett," *North Carolina Historical Review.* Volume XXXIII, #1. January, 1956.

Muse, Charles, editor. *The Civil War Life of John A. Muse As Told to Jennie Muse. [typewritten pages given to me 1991]*

Muse, Amy. *The Story of the Methodists in the Port of Beaufort.* Newbern, Owen G. Dunn & Co, printers. 1941. Joyner Library, ECU digital series.

n.a. *Born in Slavery—Slave Narratives Federal Writers Project 1936-1938.* LOC

n.a. *Born in Slavery: Slave Narratives from the Federal Writer's Project* 1936-1938. The Library of Congress. Division of Manuscripts and Prints.

n.a. *Cape Fear Region, Minute Book Confederate District Court, Pamlico.* Prepared by the National Archives, microfilm.

n.a. *200 Years of Progress, A Report of the History* & Achievements *of the People of Lenoir County.* Published by the Lenoir County Board of Commissioners and the Johnston-Lenoir County Bicentennial Committee. 1976.

n.a. *Confederate Scrapbook.* Published for the benefit of the Memorial Bazaar held in Richmond April 11, 1893. Richmond, J.L. Hill Printing Co. 1893.

n.a. *Footprints in Northampton.* Published by Northampton Bicentennial Committee, 1976.

n.a. *Heritage of Lenoir County.* Published by Lenoir County Historical Association. Winston-Salem, Hunter Publishing Company. 1981.

n.a. *History of Allegany County, 1859-1976.* Sparta, NC; n.d. or n.p.

n.a. *History of Butler County, Pennsylvania—1883.* Chicago: Waterman, Watkins, & Co.

n.a. *History of Wayne County.* Created by the Heritage Committee of the Bicentennial Commission. 1979.

n.a. *Journal of Confederate History Series,* Volume XIV. Southern Heritage Press, Atlanta. 1995.

n.a. *Magazine of Albemarle County History.* Published by the Albemarle County Historical Society. Volume 22, 1963-1964. Printed by the Michie Company. 1964.

n.a. *North Carolina Biographical Dictionary.* Volume I. Somerset Publishing, Inc. 1999.

n.a. *North Carolina, the WPA Guide to the Old North State.* Compiled by the Federal Writers' Project of the Federal Work's Agency, Work Project Administration, Univ South Carolina Press, 1939.

n.a. *Manufactures of the United States in 1860 Complied from the Original Returns of the Eight Census.* Washington, Government Printing Office. 1865.

n.a. *North Carolina, the WPA Guide to the Old North State.* Compiled by the Federal Writers' Project of the Federal Work's Agency, Work Progress Administration, University of South Carolina Press. 1939.

n.a. *Personal Narratives of Events in the War of the Rebellion, Being Papers Read Before the Rhode Island Soldiers & Sailors Historical Society* 4th Series, #9. Providence Press: Snow & Franham Printers. 1890.

n.a. *Our Heritage—Robeson County, North Carolina 1748-2002.* Sam West, Chairman of the Robeson County Heritage Book Committee. Printed by the Wadsworth Publishing Company. 2003.

n.a. *Preliminary Report of the Operations of the U.S. Sanitary Commission in N.C., March 1865.* Report #87. New York, Sanford Harroun & Company. 1865.

n.a. *Randolph County 1779-1979.* Edited by the Randolph County Historical Society and the Randolph Arts Guild. Winston-Salem, Hunter Publishing Company. 1980.

n.a. *Record of the Service of the Forty-fourth Massachusetts Volunteer Militia in North Carolina, August 1862-May 1863.* Boston, Privately printed. 1887.

n.a. *Richmond County and the Civil War.* Compiled by the Richmond County Heritage Book Committee. Wadsworth Publishing Company. 1995.

n.a. *Rocky Mount Mills, A Case History of Industrial Development, 1818-1943.* Printed by the Rocky Mount Mills, North Carolina. 1943; Joyner Library, ECU digital series.

n.a. *Some Pioneer Women Teachers of North Carolina.* Compiled by The Delta Kappa Gamma Society of NC State Organization. 1955.

n.a. *Scientific America.* New Series, Volume 4, Issue 3, June 8, 1861. New York, Scientific America, Inc.

n.a. *Southern Historical Society Papers.* [title in cursive] Volumes XLIII and XLIX. January 29 through May 1, 1863. Milwood, New York. Kraus Reprint. 1980. n.a. *War of the Rebellion: a Compilation of the Official Records, Series II, Volume V.* Washington, Government Printing Office. 1899.

n.a. *Southern Historical Society Papers.* Volumes XLIII and XLIX. January 29 through May 1, 1863. Millwood, New York, Kraus Reprint. 1980.

n.a. *The Sanitary Commission Bulletin.* No. 35. Philadelphia. April 1, 1865

n.a. *University Magazine.* Old Series, Volume 40, #1.

n.a. *War Days in Fayetteville, North Carolina, 1861-1865*. Compiled by the JEB Stuart Chapter UDC, May 1910. Fourth Printing by Williams Printing Co. 1990.

n.a. *Wilmington Directory 1865-66*. Published by P. Heinsberger. 1865.

Nash, Ann Strudwich. *Ladies in the Making*. Durham, Seeman Printing Co. 1964.

Nelson, B.H. "Some Aspects of Negro Life in North Carolina During the Civil War." *North Carolina Historical Review*. Volume XXV, #2. April, 1948.

Neely, Jr. Mark E. *Southern Rights*. Charlottesville, University of Virginia Press. 1999.

Newman, Laura S. "Grandma Ramsay's Account of Stoneman's Raid." Typed manuscript given to me. 1995.

Noble, Tolbert. *The Papers of John W. Ellis*. Raleigh, Edwards & Broughton Publishers. 1909.

Noe, Kenneth and Shannon Wilson, editors. *The Civil War in Appalachia*. Knoxville, University of Tennessee Press. 1997.

Norment, Mary C. *The Lowrie History*. Lumbee Publishing Company. 1909

Norris, David. "For the Benefit of Our Gallant Volunteers." *North Carolina Historical Review*. July, 1998.

Norris, David A. "The Yankees have Been Here!: The Story of Brig. Gen. Edward Potter's Raid on Greenville, Tarboro, and Rocky Mount, July 19-23, 1863." *North Carolina Historical Review*. Volume LXXIII, #1. January, 1996.

North Carolina Dept of Agriculture. *North Carolina Century Farms: 100 Years of Continuous Agricultural Heritage*. Raleigh, the Department of Agriculture. 1989.

O'Brien, Sean Michael. *Mountain Partisans: Guerilla Warfare in the Southern Appalachians 1861-1865*. Westport, Conn. Praeger Publishers. 1999.

Osborn, Thomas W. "Fiery Trial—a Union Officer's Account of Sherman's last Campaign." *A Complete History of the 12th Indiana Volunteer Infantry*.

Padgett, Mary. "The Woodfield Wonders" *State Magazine*. September, 1992.

Paludan, Phillip S. *Victims, a True Story of the Civil War*. Knoxville, University of Tennessee Press. 1981.

Paris, Reverend John A. *A Sermon Preached before Brig-Gen. Hoke's Brigade at Kinston, North Carolina on the 26th of February, 1864, by Rev. John Parish, Chaplin 54 Regiment*. Documenting the American South, Wilson Library, UNC-CH.

Parker, Allen. *Recollections of My Slavery Days*. Raleigh, Department of Archives and History, N.C. Dept. of Cultural Resources. 1999.

Parker, C.W. "Slaveholding in Western North Carolina," *North Carolina Historical Review*, Volume LXI, #2. April, 1984.

Parramore, Thomas and F. Roy Johnson and E. Frank Stephenson, Jr. *Before the Rebel Flag Fell*. Murfreesboro, Johnson Publishing Co. 1965.

Parramore, Dr. Thomas. *Trial Separation: Murfreesboro, North Carolina and the Civil War*. Pierce Printing Co., Inc., 1998.

Parramore, Thomas C. "The Burning of Winton" *North Carolina Historical Review,* Winter Edition, 1962.

Parramore, Thomas. "The Bartons of Bartonsville," *North Carolina Historical Review*. Volume LI, #1. January, 1974.

Paschal, George W. "Baptist Academies in North Carolina," *North Carolina Historical Review*. January, 1951.

Patterson, Gerard A. *Justice Or Atrocity*. Gettysburg, Pa., Thomas Publications. 1998.

Patton, Sadie Smathers. *The Story of Henderson County*. Asheville, North Carolina, The Miller Printing Company. 1947.

Patton, Sadie S. *Sketches of Polk County History*. Spartanburg, S.C., the Reprint Co., 1976.

Pearce, T.H. "Aunt Abby," *The State*. October 1 and 15, 1972.

Pearce, T.H. *Franklin County, 1779-1970*. Freeman, S.D., Pine Hill Press. 1979.

Pease, William and Jane. *A Family of Women*. U.N.C. Press, 1999.

Phelps, Loretta. *Cooking Great-grandma's Style*. n.p., n. d.

Phifer, Edward William. *Burke, The History of a North Carolina County, 1777-1920 With a Glimpse Beyond.*. Privately printed by author in Morganton. 1977.

Philyaw, Margaret D.D. *Some Things Mother Endured During the War 1861-1865.* n.p., n.d. North Carolina Collection, Wilson Library, UNC-CH.

Poe, Clarence, editor. *True Tales of the South at War.* Chapel Hill, U.N.C. Press. 1961.

Pool, S.D., editor, "A North Carolina Heroine." *Our Living and Our Dead. Volume IV.* Raleigh. n.p. and n.d.

Powell, Eleanor. "Tensions Ran High in Goldsboro at the Outbreak of Civil War." *A History of Wayne County North Carolina, A Collection of Historical Stories.* Created by the Heritage Committee of the Bicentennial Commission. Republished by the Wayne County Historical Assoc., Goldsboro, N.C. 1979. Joyner Library, ECU digital series.

Powell, William S. *Annals of Progress, the Story of Lenoir County and Kinston, North Carolina.* Raleigh, State Department of Archives and History. 1963.

Powell, William S. *Caswell County History 1777-1977.* Durham, Moore Publishing Company. 1977.

Powell, William S. *Dictionary of North Carolina Biography. Volume II.* Chapel Hill and London, U.N.C. Press. 1994.

Powell, William S. *North Carolina Through Four Centuries.* U.N.C. Press. 1989.

Powell, William S. *North Carolina, A History.* U.N.C. Press, 1977.

Powell, William S. *When The Past Refused to Die, a History of Caswell County 1777-1977.* Yanceyville, Caswell County Historical Assoc., Inc. 1977.

Price, Charles L., "The United States Military Railroads in North Carolina, 1862-1865." *North Carolina Historical Review.* Volume LIII, #3. July, 1976.

Priest, John M. *Captain James Wren's Civil War Diary : From New Bern to Fredericksburg.* Shippenburg, PA, White Mane Publishing Co, Inc.1990.

Pugh, Jesse F. *300 Years Along the Pasquotank: a Biographical History of Camden County.* Durham, Seeman Printery, Inc. 1957.

Pullen, Drew. *Portraits of the Past: The Civil War on Hatteras Island North Carolina.* New Jersey, Published by Aerial Perspective. 2001.

Putnam, A.A., editor. *The Old Flag.* Volume I, #1. Plymouth, North Carolina. May 19, 1865.

Rable, George. *The Civil War—Women and the Crisis of Southern Nationalism.* University of Illinois Press. 1989.

Ramsdell, Charles W. *Behind the Lines in the Southern Confederacy.* New York, Greenwood Press, Publishers. 1969.

Rankin, Emma. *Stoneman's Raid, A North Carolina Woman's Experience.* Typescript, courtesy of Davie County Library.

Ravi, Jennifer. *Notable North Carolina Women.* Winston-Salem, Bandit Books. 1992.

Ray, Lenoir. *Postmarks.* Adams Press. 1970.

Reed, Colonel C. Wingate. *Beaufort County—Two Centuries of Its History.* Self published. 1962.

Reid, Richard. "A Test Case of the 'Crying Evil': Desertion among North Carolina Troops during the Civil War." *North Carolina Historical Review,* Volume LVIII, Number 3. July, 1981.

Renard, Laura F. *The May, Lang, Joyner, Williams Family of North Carolina.* n.p. 1975.

Richardson, James D. Editor. *The Messages and Papers of Jefferson Davis and the Confederacy, Volume I* New York, Chelsea House-Robert Hector Publisher. 1966.

Rights, Douglas L. "Salem in the War Between the States." *North Carolina Historical Review,* Volume XXVII, #3, July 1950.

Rives, Mrs. M.V. "Contraband Conscience," *Our Women In the War: The Lives They Lived, the Deaths They Died* arranged by Miss Hattie Kilgore. Charleston News & Courier. 1885.

Robinson, William M., Jr. "The Rendezvous at Hatteras, 1861" *The Outer Banks Reader.* Selected and edited by David Stick. UNC Press. 1998.

Robinson, William M., Jr. *Justice in Gray.* New York, Russell and Russell. 1968.

Roe, Alfred S. *The Fifth Regiment Massachusetts Volunteer Infantry in its Three Tours of Duty.* Boston, Mass. Published by the Fifth Regiment Veteran Assoc. 1911.

Rogers, Lou. *Tar Heel Women.* Raleigh, Warren Publishing Co. 1949.

Ross, Malcolm. *The Cape Fear, Rivers of America.* New York, Holt, Rinehart, and Winston Publishers. 1965.

Russell, Lucy Phillips. *A Rare Pattern.* Chapel Hill, U.N.C. Press. 1957.

Rutledge, William E. and Welborn, Max O. *History Of Yadkin County 1850-1965.* Published in Yadkinville, 1965.

Rutledge, William E. Jr. *An Illustrated History of Yadkin County, 1850-1980.* Self-published in Yadkinville. 1981.

Salsi, Lynn Sims and Margaret Sims. *Columbia: History of a Southern Capital, South Carolina.* Arcadia Publishing. 2003.

Scarboro, David D. "The Heroes of America in Civil War, North Carolina." *North Carolina Historical Review.* Volume LVIII, #4. Autumn, 1981.

Scarboro, David D., "North Carolina and the Confederacy: The Weakness of States' Rights during the Civil War." *North Carolina Historical Review.* Volume LVI, #2. April, 1979.

Schoenbaum, Thomas J. *Islands, Capes, and Sounds—The North Carolina Coast.* . Winston-Salem, John F. Blair. 1982.

Schultz, Jane E. *Women at the Front.* Chapel Hill and London, U.N.C. Press. 2004.

Seapher, Janet. *Time, Talent, Tradition.* Wilmington, Cape Fear Museum Publications. 1995.

Seawekk, Joseph L. *Law Tales For Laymen.* Raleigh, Alfred Williams & Co. 1925.

Segars, J.H. and Charles K.Barrow. *Black Southerners in Confederate Armies.* Atlanta, Ga, Southern Lion Books, Inc. 2001.

Sellers, James L. "The Economic Incidence of the Civil War in the South." *The Economic Impact of the American Civil War,* by Ralph Andreano; Cambridge, Schenkman Publishing Co, Inc. 1962.

Shanks, Henry T., editor. *The Papers of Willie Person Mangum.* Volume V, 1847-1894. Durham, N.C., Christian Printing Co. 1956.

Sharp, Bill. *A New Geography of North Carolina, Vol. II.* Published by Sharpe Publishing Co., Raleigh. 1958.

Sherman, Joan R. "The Black Bard of North Carolina—George Moses Horton and His Poetry." *North Carolina Historical Review*, July 1997, Volume LXXIV, #3.

Shephard, Ruth W. *Ashe County Heritage, North Carolina.* Volume I. 1984.

Sherrill, Miles. *A Soldier's Story, Prison Life and Other Incidents in the War of 1861-1865.* Documenting the American South, Wilson Library, UNC-CH.

Shipman, Derrick and Jim Howell. *The War of Northern Aggression in Western North Carolina.* Greatunpublihed.com. 2003.

Sider, Gerald M. *Lumbee Indian Histories.* Cambridge University Press. 1993.

Sikes, Leon, H. *Duplin County Places, Past and Present.* Baltimore, Gateway Press. 1985.

Simpkins, Francis B. and Patton, James W. *The Women Of the Confederacy.* Richmond and N.Y., Garrett and Massie, Inc. Publishers. 1936.

Simpkins, Francis B. *The South Old and New, A History, 1820-1947.* New York, Alfred A. Knopf. 1947.

Simpson, Bland. *The Great Dismal Swamp.* UNC Press. 1990.

Singleton, W.H., Introduction and Annotations by Katherine Charron and David Cecelski, *Recollections of My Slavery Days.* Raleigh, Division of Archives and History. 1999.

Swint, Henry Lee, editor. *"Dear Ones From Home, Letters From Contraband Camp.* Vanderbilt University Press. 1966.

Smith, Dr. Claiborne T. *Smith of Scotland Neck: Plantations on the Roanoke.* Baltimore, Gateway Press. 1976.

Smith, Drew F. *Mothers of Invention.* Chapel Hill & London, UNC Press. 1996.

Smith, Drew F. *Southern Stories, Slaveholders in Peace and War.* University of Missouri Press. 1992.

Smith, Janie. *"Where Home Used To Be."* Letter in the Averasboro Battlefield Museum, courtesy Walt Smith, descendant.

Smith, Major W. A. *The Anson Guards.* Charlotte, Stone Publishing Co., 1914.

Smith, Mary K. Watson. *Women of Greensboro, 1861-1865*. Little Rock, Arkansas. Published by the Democrat P&L, Company. 1919.

Snipes, D. Brewer. "Cherokees in Gray." *Our State*. February 1980.

Spraggins, Linsley L. "The Mobilization of Negro Labor for the Department of Virginia and North Carolina." *North Carolina Historical Review*. April, 1947.

Sprunt, James. "Christmas in Dixie During the War Between the States." *Chronicles of the Cape Fear River 1860-1916*. Raleigh, 2nd edition, Edwards & Broughton Printing. 1916.

Sprunt, James. *Chronicles of the Cape Fear 1660-1916*. Wilmington, Dram Tree Books. Reprinted 2005.

Sprunt, James. *Tales and Traditions of the Lower Cape Fear, 1661-1896*. LeGwin Brothers Printing. 1896.

Starnes, Richard. "The Stirring Strains of Dixie: the Civil War and Southern Identity in Haywood County, N.C." *North Carolina Historical Review*. Volume LXXIV, #3. July 1997.

Steelman, Lala C. "The Life-Style of an Eastern North Carolina Planter: Elias Carr of Bracebridge Hall." *North Carolina Historical Review*. Volume LVII. January, 1980.

Stern, Phillip Van Doren. *Secret Missions of the Civil War*. Wings Books, Publishing. 1959.

Stevens, Peter. *Rebels in Blue*. Dallas, Texas. Taylor Publishing Co. 2000.

Stevenson, William. *Sallie Southall Cotton*. Greenville, N.C., Pamlico Press. 1987.

Stick, David. *An Outer Banks Reader*. U.N.C. Press. 1998.

Stick, David. *The Outer Banks, 1584-1958*. Chapel Hill, U.N.C. Press. 1958.

Stinson, Eliza B. "How the Arsenal Was Taken," *Our Women in the War: The Lives They Lived, the Deaths They Died,* arranged by Miss Hattie Kilgore. Charleston News & Courier. 1885.

Stoeson, Alex. *Guilford County, A Brief History*. Raleigh, the North Carolina Department of Archives and History, Cultural Resources. 1993.

Stoops, Martha. *The Heritage: The Education of Women at St. Mary's College, Raleigh, North Carolina, 1842-1982*. n.p. 1984.

Sutherland, Daniel E. "C.F. Deems and the Watchman." *North Carolina Historical Review,* Autumn 1980.

Swayze, J.C. *Hill & Swayzes Confederate Rail-Road & Steam-Boat Guide*. Griffen, Georgia, Hill & Swayze Publishers. 1862. Documenting the American South, UNC-CH.

Swint, Henry L., editor. *Dear Ones At Home, Letters From Contraband Camp*. Vanderbilt University Press. 1966.

Tatum, Georgia Lee. *Disloyalty in the Confederacy*. University of Nebraska Press. 2000.

Taylor, Michael W. *The Cry Is War, War, War*. Morningside House Press, Inc. 1994.

Taylor, Jim. "The Killings on the Shelton Laurel" *Company Front,* August/September, 1989.

Taylor, Thomas E. "Running the Blockade," *Classics of Naval Literature*. Annapolis, Maryland, Naval Institute Press. Reprinted 1995.

T., M.R. "The Last Place Captured," *Our Women in the War: The Lives They Lived, the Deaths They Died,* arranged by Miss Hattie Kilgore. Charleston News & Courier. 1885.

Terrell, Bob *Historic Asheville*. Ralph Roberts Publisher. 1997.

Tessier, Mitzi *Asheville: a Pictorial History*. Norfolk, Donning Co. Publ., n. d.

The Diary of Elizabeth Ellis Robeson, from 1847-1866. Copied by Bladen County Historical Society. n.p. and n.d.

Tew, Jerome. *Ten Days in Hell*. Self-published. n.d.

The Magazine of Albemarle County History. Volume XXII, edited by the Albemarle County Historical Society. The Michie Co. Printers. 1964.

Thompson, Holland. *From the Cotton Field to the Cotton Mill*. MacMillian and Company. 1906.

Thomas, Cornelius, editor. *Letters from the Colonel's Lady: Correspondence of Mrs. (Col.) William Lamb Written from Fort Fisher, N.C., C.S.A*. Winnabow, N.C., published by Charles Towne Preservation Trust. 1965.

Thomas, Gerald W. *Divided Allegiances*. Raleigh, Division of Archives and History, N.C. Department of Cultural Resources. 1996.

Thomas, Maude. *Away Down Home, A History of Robinson County, North Carolina.* Lumberton. 1982.

Thornton, Mary L., editor. "The Prison Diary of Adjutant Francis Atherton Boyle, C.S.A." *North Carolina Historical Review.* Winter, 1962.

Tise, Larry. "The Issue of Slavery." *North Carolina Experience: an Interpretive and Documentary History* by Lindley S. Butler and Alan D. Watson. Chapel Hill, NC. UNC Press. 1984.

Toalson, Jeff. *"No Soap, No Pay, Diarrhea, Dysentery, & Desertion.* New York, iUniverse, Inc. 2006.

Towle, Lisa H. *A Heritage of Healing* Birmingham, Association Publishing Co. 2003.

Travor, Lorenzo. *Battles of Roanoke Island and Elizabeth City.* #5, 2nd Series. Printed by EL Freeman and Company. 1880.

Trelease, Allen W. *North Carolina Railroad, 1849-1871.* U.N.C. Press. 1991.

Trivette, Ruth Jane. *The Merging of the Gaels: A History of Fayetteville Presbytery 1813-1983.* Published by The Pilot, Inc. 1887.

Trotter, William. *Bushwhackers.* Greensboro, Signal Research, Inc., 1988.

Trotter, William. *Ironclads and Columbiads.* Winston-Salem, John F. Blair, Publisher. 1989.

Trotter, William. *Silk Flags and Cold Steel.* Winston-Salem, John Blair Publishing Co. 1988.

Troxler, Carole W. and William M. Vincent. *Shuttle & Plow, A History of Alamance County, North Carolina.* Published by the Alamance County Historical Assoc., Inc. 1999.

Turner, J. Kelly and John L. Bridgers, Jr. *The History of Edgecombe County, North Carolina.* Raleigh, Edward Broughton & Company. 1920.

Tursi, Frank. *Winston-Salem: A History.* Winston-Salem, J.F. Blair, Publisher. 1994.

Vandiver, Frank. E. "The Capture of a Confederate Blockade Runner; Extracts from the Journal of a Confederate Naval Officer." *North Carolina Historical Review.* Volume XXI, #2, April, 1944.

Van Noppen, Ida W. 'The Significance of Stoneman's Last Raid." North Carolina Historical Review [in CURSIVE] January-October, 1961, Volume XXXVIII, #1-4.

Waddell, Alfred M. *Some Memories of My Life.* Raleigh, Ed. Broughton and Company. 1908.

Walker, James L., Jr. *Rebel Gibraltar.* Wilmington, N.C., Dram Tree Books. 2005.

Wall, James W. *Davie County, a Brief History.* Raleigh, N.C. Department of Cultural Resources, Division of Archives and History. 1976.

Wallace, Mildred. "The Sacrifice or Daring of a Southern Woman During the War Between the Sates." *Benjamin F. Royal Papers.* Typescript, Wilson Library, UNC.

Ward, James A., editor. *Southern Railroad Man, Conductor N.J. Bell's Recollection of the Civil War.* DeKalb, Ill., Northern Illinois University Press. 1994.

Warren, Lindsay C. *Beaufort County's Contribution to a Notable Era of North Carolina's History: a Series of Articles.* Washington, U.S. Government Printing Office. 1930.

Watford, Christopher M., editor. *The Civil War In North Carolina.* Volume I. Piedmont Press, McFarland & Co, Inc. 2003.

Watson, Alan D. *Edgecombe County—A Brief History.* N.C. Dept. of Cultural Resources, Division of Archives and History. 1979.

Watson, Alan. *Perquimans' County, a Brief History.* Raleigh—Division of Archives and History, N.C. Dept. of Cultural Resources. 1987.

Watson, Bishop Alfred A. *The Religious and Historic Commemoration of the Two Hundred years of St. Paul's Parrish, Edenton, North Carolina.* Goldsboro, Nash Brothers Book & Job Printers. 1901.

Watt, W.N. *Early Cotton Factories in North Carolina and Alexander County.* n.p., n.d.

Watters, Fanny C. *Plantation Memories of the Cape Fear River Country.* Asheville, Stephens Press. 1944. Joyner Library, ECU digital series.

Waugh, Charles G. and Martin H. Greenburg. *The Women's War in the South.* Nashville, Tennessee., Cumberland House Publishing, Inc. 1999.

Weatherly, A. Earl. *The First Hundred Years of Historic Guilford 1771-1871.* Greensboro Printing Co. 1972.

Webb, Elizabeth Yates. "Cotton Manufacturing and State Regulations in North Carolina." *North Carolina Historical Review*. Volume IX, #2. April 1932.

Welch, William L. ""Personal Narrative of Events in the War of the Rebellion, Being Papers Read Before the Rhode Island Soldiers & Sailors Historical Society." *The Burnside Expedition and the Engagement of Roanoke Island*. 4th Series, #9. Providence Press: Snowden-Franham Printers. 1890.

Wellman, Manly Wade. *Rebel Boast: First at Bethel—Last at Appomattox*. New York, Henry Hold and Company. 1956.

Wellman, Manly W. *The County of Moore 1847-1947*. Greensboro, Published by the Moore County Historical Assoc. 1962.

Wellman, Manly W. *The County of Warren, North Carolina. 1586-1976*. North Carolina Press. 1959.

Wertheimer, Barbara M. *We Were There*. Pantheon Books. 1977.

Wharton, Don. *Smithfield As Seen by Sherman's Soldiers*. Smithfield Herald Publishing Co. 1977.

Wharton, H.M., D.D., *War Songs and Poems of the Southern Confederacy 1861-1865*. John C. Winston Company. 1904.

Wheeler, Richard. *Sherman's March*. New York, Thomas Crowell Publisher. 1978.

Whitaker, Reverend R. H. *Whitaker's Reminisces, Incidents and Anecdotes*. Edward and Broughton Publishers. 1905.

Whitaker, Walter. *Centennial History of Alamance County, 1849-1949*. Charlotte, Dowd Press. 1949

White, Henry S. *Prison Life Among the Rebels: Recollections of as Union Chaplin*. Kent State University Press. 1990.

Wiley, Bell I., *Confederate Women*. Westport, Conn. Greenwood Press, 1975.

Williams, Isabel and Leora McEachern. "River Excursions 1864." *Lower Cape fear Historical Society, Inc. Bulletin*. Volume XXI, No. 3, May, 1978.

Williams, Max R. *The Papers of William Alexander Graham*. Volume VI, 1864-1865. Raleigh, N.C. Department of Cultural Resources, Division of Archives and History. 1976

Williams, Max R., "The Johnston Will Case: A Clash of Titans." *North Carolina Historical Review*. Volume LXVII, #2. April 1990.

Wilson, Mamr'e M.. *A Researcher's Journal: Beaufort, North Carolina & the Civil War*. Griffin and Tilghman Printers, Inc. 1999.

Wimmer, Nadia and Johnston, Elizabeth Roten. "Jacob Roten; A Reminiscence" *Company Front* March, 1996.

Windler, Penny Nichols. *Placid*. Sponsored by the Hampton Chapter U.D.C. Warwick, Virginia, Published by High-Iron Publishers. 1961.

Winsor, Adjutant Gershom. "As I Saw It." *History of the 45th Regiment Massachusetts Volunteer Militia the Cadet Regiment,* by Albert Mann. Jamaica Plains , Mass. Brookside Printing. 1908.

Wise, Stephen R. *Lifeline of the Confederacy*. University of South Carolina Press. 1988.

Wood, John E. *Brief Sketches of Pasquotank County*. Printed by the Elizabeth City Chamber of Commerce. 1963.

Wood, L.C. *The Haydock's Testimony*. Camden, N.J., Milliette Press. 1890.

Wood, Richard B. *Port Town at War, Wilmington, North Carolina 1860-1865*. Ann Arbor, Mich., UMI Dissertation Services. 1976.

Wren, James. *From New Bern to Fredericksburg: Captain James Wren's Diary: B Company 48th Pennsylvania Volunteers February 20, 1862-December 17, 1862*. Shippenburg, PA, White Mane Publishing Company. 1990.

Wright, Annette C. "The Grown-up Daughter: The Case of Cornelia Phillips Spencer," *North Carolina Historical Review*. Volume 74, #3. July, 1997.

Wright, Marilyn. *A Sense of Place, Part II*. Wadsworth Publishing Co. 1996.

Wright, Stuart T. *The Confederate Letters of Benjamin H. Freeman*. Hicksville, NY, Exposition Press. 1974.

Wright, Stuart Thurman. *Historical Sketches of Person County.* Danville, the Womack Press. 1974.

Wyche, Mary L. *The History of Nursing in North Carolina.* Chapel Hill, U.N.C. Press. 1938.

Yates, Richard. "Governor Vance and the End of the War in North Carolina," *North Carolina Historical Review.* Volume XVIII, #4. October, 1941.

Yeatman, Ted, editor. "Fear in North Carolina 'What an Awful and Grand Spectacle it is!'" *Civil War Times.* March 1999.

Young, Perry D. *Our Young Family, the Descendants of Thomas and Naomi Hyatt Young.* Overmountain Press. 2003.

Zuber, Richard L. *Jonathan Worth, A Biography of a Southern Unionist.* Chapel Hill, U.N.C. Press. 1965.

Zug, Charles G. III. *Turners and Burners.* U.N.C. Press. 1986.

PRIMARY SOURCES

East Carolina University, Special Collections, Joyner Library

Agnes Foy Papers
Barnhardt Family Papers
Foster's Goldsboro Expedition, #816
Frances M. Manning Papers
Grimes—Bryan Papers
Kate Wheeler Cooper Papers
Ronald C. Caldwell Letters
Thomas Sparrow Papers
Turner May Papers
William Howard Hooker Papers

East Carolina University, Special Collections, Digital Library

East Tennessee State University Archives

Findley P. Curtis Diary
James McKee Collection of Letters
R.A. Spainhour Diary Extracts

Duke University, Rare Books and Manuscripts, Perkins Library

Aurelia Hooper Papers
A.W. Bell Papers
Beavers Brothers Letters
Corpening Papers
Cronly Papers
David Murphy Papers 1856-1865
Eliza J. McEwen Papers
John McLean Harrington Papers
John H. McNeil Papers
John Haywood and E. Burke Haywood Letter to Surgeon Moore
Jay B. Hubbell Papers with the Eller Family Papers
Jacob Mordecai Papers
Lenoir Family Letters
Jane Fisher Papers
Journal of Sam Hoey Walkup
Lunsford R. Cherry Papers
Major John Johnson Papers
Mary S.M. Buie Letters
Mary French Scott Papers
Mary Margaret McNeil Papers
Person Family Papers with Sallie E. Blount Letters
Samuel F. Patterson Papers
Scarborough Family Papers
Theophulis Hunter Holmes Papers
Tillinghast Family Papers
Thomas F. Wood Papers
V.V. Anderson Papers
William Schaum Diary

Gaston County Museum and Library
M.L. Holland Letters

Guilford College, Friends Historical Collection, Hege Library
John B. Crenshaw Letters
Sarah L. Smiley's Journal

Museum of the Confederacy, Richmond, Eleanor S. Brockenbrough Library
Edward H. Armstrong Letters 1861-1864
Alexander Stone/ John Henry Stone Letters
William Baughn Family Letters

North Carolina Division of Archives and History, Raleigh
Adjunct General State Records
Aleda Fales Papers
Cedar Falls Manufacturing Ledger
Civil War Miscellaneous Military Collection Letter Box
David Brainerd Whiting Papers
Diary of Melinda Ray
G.W. Collier Papers
Henry T. Clark Papers
J.G.M. Ramsey Papers
John Washington Calton Letters
John Chesson, Jr. Papers
John Augustus Young Diary, 1861-1888
John Graham Young Papers 1861-1864
J. Isaac Brown Papers
Julia R. Forbes Papers
Letters from the North Carolina Adjutant Generals' Letter Book (State Militia Letter Book)
Letters of Col. Collett Leventhorpe
Lyman Wilson Sheppard Collection
Miles A. Cavin Papers
Miscellaneous Civil War Collection, Correspondences
Nash County Superior Court Records
Paul Barringer Papers
Read McIntosh Papers
R.H. Bacot Letters
R.H. Hutspeth Letters
Sally Hawthorne Reminiscences
Superior Court Minutes—New Hanover County
State Convention Records, November, 1861
Thomas Merrill Papers
Thomas Settle, Jr. Papers
Williams/Dameron Papers

St. Mary's School, Kenan Library, Raleigh
Bessie Cain's Letters
Josie MacRae Letter
Lizzie Wilson Montgomery Reminiscences
Margaret Walker Weber's Reminiscences
Mildred Lee's Scrapbook
Nannie Broadnax Letter
Susan Becton Letters

University of North Carolina, Rare Books and Manuscripts, Southern Historical Collection, Wilson Library

Benjamin Franklin Royal Papers
Capehart Family Papers
Caroline Eliza B. Clitherall Diaries
Carrie H. Clack Papers
Charles Carroll Gray Diary
Claiborne Gray personal papers
Confederate States of America Bureau of Conscription, 7th NC Congressional District
Drury Lacy Papers
Ernest Haywood Collection of Haywood Family Papers
Farley, McIver, and Roberson Family Papers
Federal Soldiers' Letters Unit 49
Francis Marion Parker Papers
George Washington Baker Papers
Kimberly Family Papers
Lenoir Family Papers
Mary Hunter Kennedy Papers
Matthew Cary Whitaker Papers and Diary
Mercer Family Papers with Mattie Taylor Gill Papers
Nancy Avaline Jarrett Papers
William A. Holt Papers
William Henry Wills Papers
Williamston Night Watch Reports
Young Allen Papers

University of North Carolina at Chapel Hill, Documenting the American South:

The Southern Homefront 1861-1865 Digital Series:

Anderson, Lucy.	*Scrapbook of Fayetteville and Cumberland County*
" "	*Last Days of the Confederacy in North Carolina*
" "	*North Carolina Women of the 1860's*
Bellamy, Ellen.	*Back With the Tide*
Brotherton, Ken.	*A Civil War Tragedy*
DeRosset, William.	*Pictorial and Historical New Hanover County and Wilmington*
Gaddy, David.	*William Norris and the Confederate Signal & Secret Service*
Greene, Wharton.	*Recollections & Reflections*
n.a.	*Wilmington Directory 1865-66*
Cheshire, Rev. Rt. Jospeh Blount	*Bishop Atkinson and the Church in the Confederacy*
"	*University Magazine Volume 40*
"	*General Order #9, Adjutant General Office, October 25, 1862*
Philyaw, Margaret.	*Some Things Mother Endured*
Whitaker, Rev. R.H.	*Whitaker's Reminisces, Incidents, and Anecdotes.*

Arthur P. Ford Papers
Dallas Ward. The Last Flag of Truce
George Moses Horton [his life and poetical works]
Gill, Mattie. An Appreciation of Grandfather.
Hinshaw, Seth. Mary Baker Hinshaw: Quaker
L.R. Ferebee. A Biographical History of Slave Life.
Laura L. Battle Papers
MacBryde, A.C. Ellie's Book

Mary Jeffery Bethall Diary
Mary Norcutt Bryan Papers
Memories of W.W. Holden
Miles Sherrill. A Soldier's Story
Vance, Gov Z.B. To the People of North Carolina, a printed proclamation.

University of North Carolina at Asheville, Rare Manuscripts, D.H. Ramsey Library
Silas Stepp Letters
Carpenter Genealogy Records

University of North Carolina at Wilmington, Randall Library, Digital Department
Extracts From the Journal of Thomas Fanning Wood
Nicholas W. Schenck Diary

University of Georgia, Rare Books
Cornelius C. Platter Civil War Diary, 1864-1865

Virginia Military Institute Archives
William H. McDowell Letters
James Radcliffe and Martha Choate Family Letters
J.N. Morrison Letters
James B. Morgan Family Letters

Wake Forest University, Z. Smith Reynolds Library
Herbert Valentine Collection

Western Carolina University, Special Collections, Hunter Library
Elizabeth and James Watson Letters
Emma Shoolbred Letters
George J. Huntly Letters
James Watson Family Letters
Parris Family Letters
N.G. Phillips Letters
W.L. Love Letter
Estes Family Letters
Carden Family Letter

PERIODICALS AND MAGAZINES

American Civil War Magazine
Appalachia Quarterly
Bennett Place Quarterly
Camp Chase Gazette
Carolin a and the Southern Cross
Citizens' Companion
Civil War Times
Company Front
Confederate Veteran
DeBow's Review
Harper's New Monthly Magazine
Huckleberry Historian
Indiana Magazine of History
Journal of Burke County Genealogical Society
Journal of Confederate History Series
Journal of Southern History
Lower Cape Fear Historical Society, Inc. Bulletin
Magazine of Albemarle County History
Maryland History Magazine
North and South Magazine

North Carolina Booklet
North Carolina Historical Review
North Carolina Medical Journal
Our Living and Our Dead
Our State
Prologue Magazine of the National Archives
Ramparts (Friends of Fort Macon)
Scientific America
South Atlantic Quarterly
Southern Historical Society Papers
The Century
The Journal of Southern History
The State
Trinity Alumni Register
UDC Magazine
University Magazine
U.S. Sanitary Commission Bulletin
Western Pennsylvania Historical Magazine
Yadkin County Historical and Genealogical
Society Journal

UNPUBLISHED PRIVATE PAPERS AND LETTERS:

Allen Cochran Collection of Civil War N.C. Letters
Donald Humphrey Family Letters
Elihu Gant Letters . . . descendant Robert Eades
Elizabeth S. Wiggins Diary . . . from descendants
Emma Sommerville Family Letters
Eugene Goodwin Letters . . . descendant Louise Goodwin McKlveen
F.Y. Hicks Letters . . . descendant Tommy Smith
Gary Hunt , *Gus Rich, the Wizard of the Blue Ridge."* Private Papers
George Allen Family Letters
Greg and Linda Humphries Letters
J.A. Benbury Letters from descendants
Jeff Stepp, Laura Norwood Diary
John A. Handy Letter
John Humphrey Family Papers
M.R. Holeman Family Papers
Page Family Papers . . . from descendants
Peter Edwards Family Letters
Scott Troutman Collection of Civil War N.C. Letters
Steven Schaufler Collection of Civil War N.C. Letters
William E. Benbury Letters . . . from descendants
William Newlin Letters . . . from descendants

19TH CENTURY NEWSPAPERS

Asheville Citizens Times
Carolina Watchman (Salisbury)
Charleston Mercury
Charleston News and Courier
Charlotte Daily Bulletin
Charlotte Daily Courier
Christian Advocate
Daily Confederate (Raleigh)
Daily Conservative (Raleigh)
Daily Chronicle & Sentinel (Augusta, GA.)
Daily Journal (Wilmington)
Daily Progress (Raleigh)
Fayetteville Observer
Frank Leslie's Illustrated Newspaper
Greensboro Patriot
Harper's Weekly
Herald For the Union, Wilmington-1865
Hillsborough Plain Dealer
Hillsborough Recorder
Illustrated London News
Iredell Express
Lewisburg Chronicle (PA)
Milton Chronicle
Nashville Daily Union (TN)
New York Sunday Times
North Carolina Argus
North Carolina Presbyterian
North Carolina Whig (Charlotte)
People's Press
Raleigh Conservative
Raleigh Register
Raleigh Standard
Richmond Daily Dispatch
Richmond Enquirer
Richmond Examiner
Richmond Sentinel
Richmond Whig
Southern Field and Fireside
Southern Illustrated News
Southern Watchman
Spirit of the Age
Tarboro Mercury
The National Tribune
The Old Guard
The Republican Advocate (N.Y.)
The Tennessee Baptist
Weekly Catawba Journal
Weekly News [hand-written, Harnett County]
Weekly Asheville News
Western Democrat

MODERN NEWSPAPERS

1. Catawba News—Enterprise
2. Charlotte Observer
3. Courier-Times Crossville Chronicle (TN)
4. Durham News Herald
5. Fayetteville Observer
6. Franklin Times
7. Goldsboro Herald
8. Morning Post
9. Raleigh News & Observer
10. Salisbury Post
11. Wilmington Star

INTERNET SOURCES

www.csastamps.com
www.elizcity.com/history/civilwar/aunt-mamie-war-memory.shtml
www.marywarshaw.com
www.albemarle-nc.com/camden/history/cvlwar01.htm
www.russcott.com/~rscott/12thwis/dimihaw.htm
www.CSA-Dixie.com/Liverpool_Dixie.bazaar.htm
www.twainquotes.com/archangels.html
www.ls.net/~newriver/nc/ashe/1861.html
http://members.aol.com/sholmes54/hist16ct.html
www.carolinastamps.com/ncrail.html
http://dig.galileo.usg.edu/hargrett/platter/platter
www.wachoviatract.org
www.historync.org
http://web.cortland.edu/woosterk/gf_ward.html
www.northcarolinasouth@yahoo.com
www.berea.edu/ApCenter
http://ehardingwbtsancestors.homestead.com/Index.html
www.geocities.com/Heartland/Prari/7305/polk.htm?200818
www.tonycrumbley.com
www.elizcity.com/history/civilwar/burn-elizabeth-city.shtml
www.USGENNET.org/USA/NC/county/Wayne/bio
www.rootsweb.com/~nchyde/LETTER15.HTM
www.rootsweb.com/~nchyde/SYLVESTE.HTM
www.illinoiscivilwar.org/cu93-hist-ch10c.html
www.ftp.rootsweb.com/pub/usgenweb/nc/wayne/collections/robinson/robnson37.txt
www.sallysfamilyplace.com
www.mdgorman.com
http://hometown.aol.com/cwrapes/index.htm
www.rootsweb.com/~ncharnett
http://scholars.lib.vt.edu/faculktu-arcives/mountain-slavery/civilwar.htm
www.ncgenweb.us/anson/people/ratliff.htm
www.pipow.com.Pilgrimage2008.htm
www.bivouacbooks.com
http://files.usgwarchive.org/nc/files.htm

Alexander Street Press.com Civil War Letters and Diaries
Internet sources from ECU, UNC-Documenting the American South, UNC-A, UNC-W, and NCDAH.

OTHER SOURCES

Thesis:
Allen, Nancie W. *A Record of Thalian Hall From 1861-1865: As Reflected in the Wilmington Daily Journal.* Thesis at UNC, 1972 [NCC]
Wood, Richard B. *Port Town At War, Wilmington, North Carolina 1860-1865.* Ann Arbor, Mich., UMI Dissertation Services. 1976
McGee, David. *"Changing Relationships Between Confederate Soldiers and Their Families and Communities During the Civil War:* A Case Study. 1998

Bennett Place Chapter of the United Daughters of the Confederacy Scrapbook
Francis Hayes Scrapbook, Granville County Library— Hayes, Francis B. *Redbook By Hayes:* "The South, The Confederacy, Yankees, and Negroes." Vol. 128. N.P. 1980 [Hays 1867-1959, former Clerk of Granville Co. had 150 volumes made from his scrapbooks and manuscripts]

Conferences with private persons and Civil War themed conferences attended over the years.

Microfilm from various universities and county libraries.

INDEX

AUTHOR'S BIOGRAPHY

Brenda Chambers McKean has been an independent researcher and collector of ante-bellum and Civil War history for twenty-five years. This book is a compilation of ten years work. Ms. McKean is a retired nurse anesthetist, a graduate of Duke University. Presently she lives in Timberlake, North Carolina with her grandson.

Edwards Brothers Malloy
Thorofare, NJ USA
June 13, 2012